THE COLLEGEVILLE BIBLE COMMENTARY

THE
COLLEGEVILLE BIBLE COMMENTARY

BASED ON THE NEW AMERICAN BIBLE

Old Testament

General Editor

DIANNE BERGANT, C.S.A.

THE LITURGICAL PRESS
COLLEGEVILLE, MINNESOTA

NIHIL OBSTAT: Robert C. Harren, J.C.L.
Censor Deputatus

IMPRIMATUR: ✛ Jerome Hanus, O.S.B.
Bishop of St. Cloud
October 19, 1988

Photos: Front and back covers, *Richard T. Nowitz*. Spine: Mount Sinai, *Roger Kasprick, O.S.B.*

Printed in the United States of America.

92 93 94 95 96   8 7 6 5 4 3 2 1

Library of Congress Cataloging-in-Publication Data

The Collegeville Bible commentary : based on the New American Bible.
    p.   cm.
   Contents: [1] Old Testament / general editor, Dianne Bergant —
[2] New Testament / general editor, Robert J. Karris.
   ISBN 0-8146-2210-0 (Old Testament). — ISBN 0-8146-2211-9 (New
Testament)
   1. Bible—Commentaries. I. Bergant, Dianne. II. Karris, Robert
J.
[BS491.2.C66 1992]
220.7'7—dc20   92-23578
                                                                    CIP

CONTENTS

CONTENTS

PREFACE

Today we are witnessing an increased interest in the Bible. Women and men from all walks of life are enrolling in classes, attending workshops, and organizing study groups. Guided reflection on the biblical tradition is a fundamental component of evangelization programs such as the Rite of Christian Initiation of Adults (RCIA) and RENEW. Prayer groups look for leaders who can guide them beyond private interpretation into the spiritual depths of the tradition. People are searching for new insights and are turning to biblical scholars to provide them. Non-specialists are no longer satisfied with a merely devotional understanding of the Bible. They are asking literary, historical, and theological questions that require learned answers.

In an effort to address this need, The Liturgical Press commissioned thirty-four respected scholars to provide individual booklets that together would interpret the entire Roman Catholic canon. Utilizing the most recent critical methods and incorporating the fruits of contemporary scholarship, they brought to completion in 1986 the *Collegeville Bible Commentary*, a series of thirty-six booklets, each including questions for review and discussion. The wide selection of authors resulted in a variety of theological positions and methodological approaches, which contributed to the richness of the enterprise. There was a consistent attempt throughout to be sensitive to contemporary concerns. This project was completed in a little over five years, thus ensuring the up-to-date character of the interpretation. In 1988 the authors of the New Testament commentaries redid their works in the light of the revised edition of the New Testament of the New American Bible.

These two volumes bring together the commentaries of all thirty-six booklets. Their comprehensiveness make them invaluable resources, enabling the reader to refer easily to the interpretation of any or all of the biblical books. Besides being used for Bible study, they can also serve as references for liturgy planning, homily preparation, and biblical prayer services. These volumes are an admirable response to the injunction of the Second Vatican Council: "Access to sacred Scripture ought to be wide open to the Christian faithful" (*Dei Verbum*, no. 22).

DIANNE BERGANT, C.S.A.
General Editor, Old Testament Commentary

ROBERT J. KARRIS, O.F.M.
General Editor, New Testament Commentary

ABBREVIATIONS

OLD TESTAMENT

Gen	Genesis	Prov	Proverbs
Exod	Exodus	Eccl	Ecclesiastes
Lev	Leviticus	Song	Song of Songs
Num	Numbers	Wis	Wisdom
Deut	Deuteronomy	Sir	Sirach
Josh	Joshua	Isa	Isaiah
Judg	Judges	Jer	Jeremiah
Ruth	Ruth	Lam	Lamentations
1 Sam	1 Samuel	Bar	Baruch
2 Sam	2 Samuel	Ezek	Ezekiel
1 Kgs	1 Kings	Dan	Daniel
2 Kgs	2 Kings	Hos	Hosea
1 Chr	1 Chronicles	Joel	Joel
2 Chr	2 Chronicles	Amos	Amos
Ezra	Ezra	Obad	Obadiah
Neh	Nehemiah	Jonah	Jonah
Tob	Tobit	Mic	Micah
Jdt	Judith	Nah	Nahum
Esth	Esther	Hab	Habakkuk
1 Macc	1 Maccabees	Zeph	Zephaniah
2 Macc	2 Maccabees	Hag	Haggai
Job	Job	Zech	Zechariah
Ps(s)	Psalm(s)	Mal	Malachi

NEW TESTAMENT

Matt	Matthew	1 Tim	1 Timothy
Mark	Mark	2 Tim	2 Timothy
Luke	Luke	Titus	Titus
John	John	Phlm	Philemon
Acts	Acts	Heb	Hebrews
Rom	Romans	Jas	James
1 Cor	1 Corinthians	1 Pet	1 Peter
2 Cor	2 Corinthians	2 Pet	2 Peter
Gal	Galatians	1 John	1 John
Eph	Ephesians	2 John	2 John
Phil	Philippians	3 John	3 John
Col	Colossians	Jude	Jude
1 Thess	1 Thessalonians	Rev	Revelation
2 Thess	2 Thessalonians		

OTHER ABBREVIATIONS

NAB	New American Bible	RSV	Revised Standard Version
NEB	New English Bible		

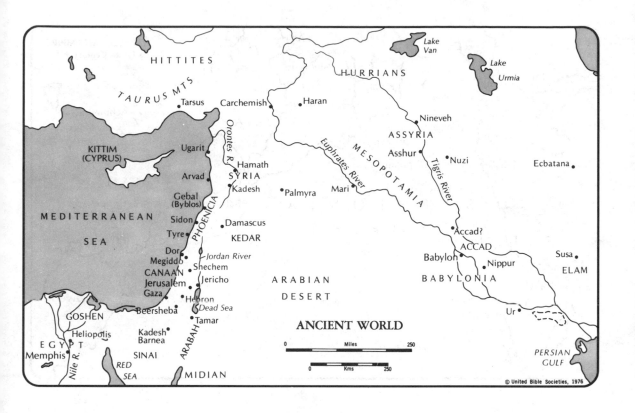

ANCIENT WORLD

HITTITES
TAURUS MTS
HURRIANS
Lake Van
Lake Urmia
Tarsus
Carchemish
Haran
Nineveh
ASSYRIA
KITTIM (CYPRUS)
Ugarit
Orontes R.
MESOPOTAMIA
Asshur
Nuzi
Ecbatana
Hamath
Arvad
SYRIA
Kadesh
Palmyra
Mari
Euphrates River
Gebal (Byblos)
PHOENICIA
Sidon
Damascus
Tyre
KEDAR
Accad?
ACCAD
Dor
Jordan River
Babylon
Nippur
Susa
Megiddo
Shechem
BABYLONIA
ELAM
CANAAN
Jericho
MEDITERRANEAN SEA
Jerusalem
Gaza
Hebron
ARABIAN DESERT
Beersheba
Dead Sea
Tamar
GOSHEN
Heliopolis
Kadesh Barnea
EGYPT
Memphis
Nile R.
SINAI
RED SEA
ARABAH
MIDIAN
Ur
PERSIAN GULF

Miles 0 250
Kms 0 250

© United Bible Societies, 1976

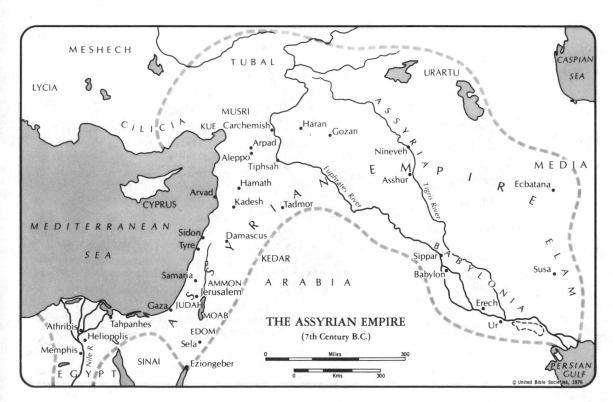

THE ASSYRIAN EMPIRE
(7th Century B.C.)

MESHECH
TUBAL
CASPIAN SEA
LYCIA
CILICIA
URARTU
MUSRI
KUE
Carchemish
Haran
Gozan
ASSYRIAN EMPIRE
Arpad
Nineveh
MEDIA
Aleppo
Tiphsah
Asshur
Ecbatana
Hamath
Euphrates River
Tigris River
Arvad
Kadesh
Tadmor
CYPRUS
MEDITERRANEAN SEA
Sidon
Tyre
Damascus
KEDAR
Sippar
BABYLONIA
Susa
ELAM
Samaria
AMMON
ARABIA
Babylon
Gaza
JUDAH
Jerusalem
Athribis
Tahpanhes
MOAB
Heliopolis
EDOM
Erech
Memphis
Nile R.
Sela
Ur
SINAI
Eziongeber
EGYPT
PERSIAN GULF

Miles 0 300
Kms 0 300

© United Bible Societies, 1976

BABYLONIAN EMPIRE
Early 6th Century B.C.

M E D I A N   E M P I R E

Tarsus

Carchemish
Haran
Nineveh
Calah
Asshur
A S S Y R I A
Achmetha

Hamath
Dura-Europos

Arvad
Gebal
Tadmor

Great
Sea
Damascus
B A B Y L O N I A N
E M P I R E
Babylon
Nippur
Larsa

E L A M
Susa

Tyre
Samaria
Jerusalem
Ashdod
Ur

E G Y P T
Dumah
Lower
Sea

Elath

Tema
A R A B I A

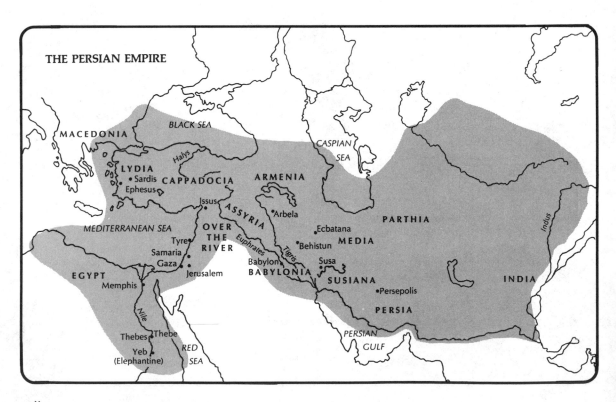

THE PERSIAN EMPIRE

MACEDONIA
BLACK SEA
CASPIAN
SEA

LYDIA
Sardis
Ephesus
CAPPADOCIA
Halys
ARMENIA

Issus
ASSYRIA
Arbela
PARTHIA

MEDITERRANEAN SEA
OVER
THE
RIVER
Euphrates
Ecbatana
Behistun
MEDIA
Indus

Tyre
Samaria
Gaza
Jerusalem
Babylon
BABYLONIA
Susa
INDIA

EGYPT
Memphis
SUSIANA
Persepolis

Nile
PERSIA

Thebes Thebe
Yeb
(Elephantine)
RED
SEA
PERSIAN
GULF

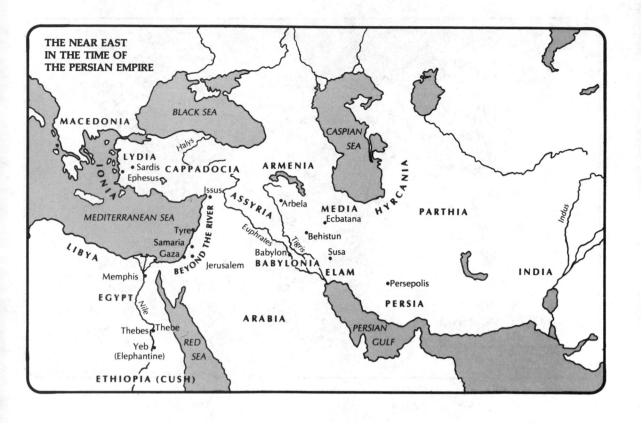

THE NEAR EAST
IN THE TIME OF
THE PERSIAN EMPIRE

MACEDONIA

BLACK SEA

CASPIAN
SEA

LYDIA

•Sardis
Ephesus

CAPPADOCIA

Halys

ARMENIA

MEDITERRANEAN SEA

Issus

ASSYRIA

•Arbela

MEDIA
•Ecbatana

HYRCANIA

PARTHIA

Indus

Euphrates

Tigris

•Behistun

LIBYA

Tyre•

Samaria

Gaza•

BEYOND THE RIVER

•Jerusalem

Babylon•

BABYLONIA

•Susa

ELAM

INDIA

•Persepolis

Memphis•

EGYPT

Nile

ARABIA

PERSIA

PERSIAN
GULF

Thebes

•Thebe

Yeb
(Elephantine)

RED
SEA

ETHIOPIA (CUSH)

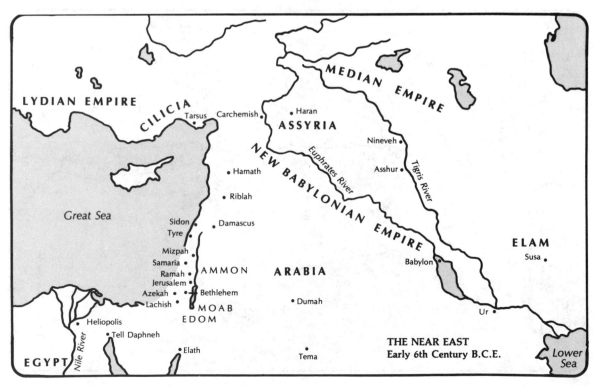

LYDIAN EMPIRE

CILICIA

•Tarsus

•Carchemish

MEDIAN EMPIRE

•Haran

ASSYRIA

•Nineveh

Euphrates River

•Asshur

Tigris River

•Hamath

NEW BABYLONIAN EMPIRE

ELAM

Great Sea

•Riblah

Sidon•
Tyre•

•Damascus

•Susa

Mizpah•

Samaria•
Ramah•
Jerusalem•

AMMON

ARABIA

Babylon•

Azekah•

•Bethlehem

MOAB

Lachish•

EDOM

•Dumah

Heliopolis•

Ur•

•Tell Daphneh

Nile River

EGYPT

•Elath

•Tema

THE NEAR EAST
Early 6th Century B.C.E.

Lower
Sea

xiii

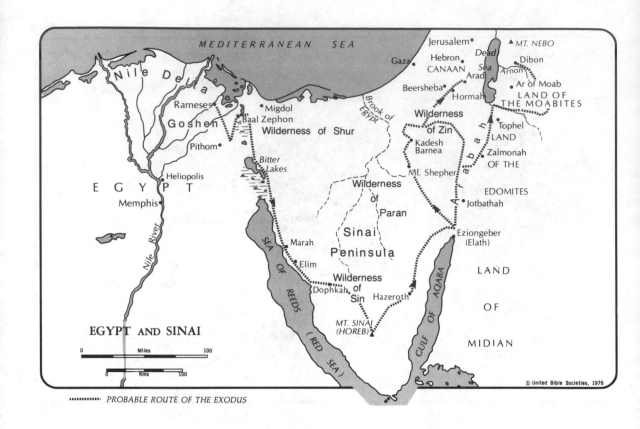

EGYPT AND SINAI

MEDITERRANEAN SEA

Nile Delta

Rameses
Goshen
Baal Zephon
Pithom
Migdol
Wilderness of Shur

EGYPT

Heliopolis
Memphis

Bitter Lakes

Nile River

SEA OF REEDS (RED SEA)

Marah
Elim
Dophkah
Wilderness of Sin
Hazeroth
MT. SINAI (HOREB)

Wilderness of Paran

Sinai Peninsula

Brook of Egypt

Gaza
Jerusalem
Hebron
CANAAN
Beersheba
Hormah
Arad
Wilderness of Zin
Kadesh Barnea
Mt. Shepher

Dead Sea
MT. NEBO
Dibon
Arnon
Ar of Moab
LAND OF THE MOABITES
Tophel
LAND OF THE EDOMITES
Zalmonah
Jotbathah

Arabah

Eziongeber (Elath)

GULF OF AQABA

LAND OF MIDIAN

Miles 0 100
Kms 0 100

© United Bible Societies, 1976

············· PROBABLE ROUTE OF THE EXODUS

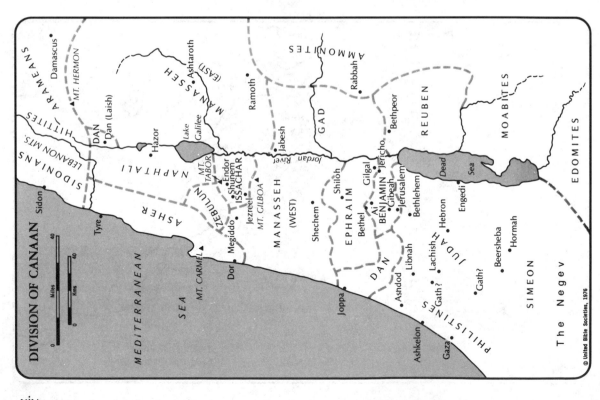

DIVISION OF CANAAN

Miles 0 40
Kms 0 40

MEDITERRANEAN SEA

Sidon
Tyre
Dor
Megiddo
MT. CARMEL
Joppa
Ashdod
Ashkelon
Gath?
Gaza

SIDONIANS
ARAMEANS
Damascus
MT. HERMON
LEBANON MTS.
HITTITES
DAN
Dan (Laish)
Hazor
NAPHTALI
Lake Galilee
MT. TABOR
ZEBULUN
Endor
Shunem
ISSACHAR
MT. GILBOA
Jezreel
ASHER
MANASSEH (EAST)
Ashtaroth
Ramoth
Jabesh
Jordan River
GAD
Rabbah
AMMONITES
Bethpeor
REUBEN
Dead Sea
Engedi
MOABITES
EDOMITES
Jericho
Gilgal
Bethel
Ai
BENJAMIN
Gibeah
Jerusalem
Bethlehem
Hebron
Lachish
Libnah
JUDAH
Beersheba
Hormah
SIMEON
The Negev
PHILISTINES
DAN
Shechem
EPHRAIM
Shiloh
MANASSEH (WEST)

© United Bible Societies, 1976

xiv

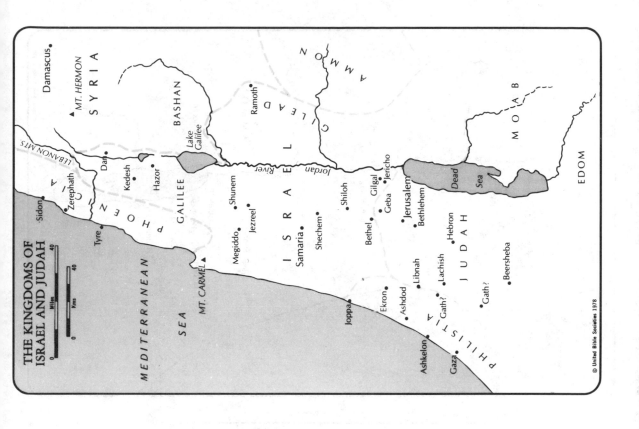

THE KINGDOMS OF ISRAEL AND JUDAH

Damascus

MT. HERMON

S Y R I A

LEBANON MTS.

Sidon
Zerephath
Tyre

P H O E N I C I A

BASHAN

Dan
Kedesh
Hazor

Lake Galilee

G I L E A D

G A L I L E E

A M M O N

Ramoth

MEDITERRANEAN

SEA

MT. CARMEL ▲

Megiddo

Shunem
Jezreel

Samaria
Shechem

I S R A E L

Jordan River

Shiloh
Gilgal
Geba
Jericho
Jerusalem
Bethlehem

Joppa

Ekron
Ashdod

P H I L I S T I A

Libnah
Gath?
Lachish
Hebron

J U D A H

Beersheba

Gath?

Ashkelon

Gaza

M O A B

Dead Sea

E D O M

Miles 0 40
Kms 0 40

© United Bible Societies 1978

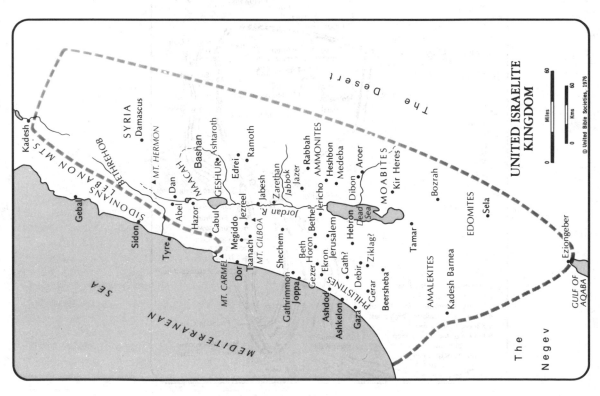

UNITED ISRAELITE KINGDOM

Kadesh

LEBANON MTS.

SIDONIANS

BETHREHOB

S Y R I A

Damascus

MT. HERMON ▲

Dan
Abel
Hazor

MAACAH

GESHUR

Bashan
Ashtaroth
Edrei
Ramoth

Sidon
Gebal

Tyre

SEA

MEDITERRANEAN

MT. CARMEL ▲
Dor
Megiddo
Taanach
MT. GILBOA ▲
Jezreel
Cabul

Jabesh

Zarethan
Jabbok
Jazer

Rabbah
AMMONITES
Heshbon
Medeba

Shechem

Beth Horon
Bethel
Jericho
Jerusalem
Hebron

Dibon
Aroer

MOABITES
Kir Heres

Gathrimmon
Joppa
Gezer
Ashdod
Ekron
Ashkelon
Gaza

PHILISTINES

Debir
Gerar
Ziklag?
Gath?
Beersheba

Tamar

Bozrah

AMALEKITES
Kadesh Barnea

EDOMITES
Sela

GULF OF AQABA
Eziongeber

The Desert

Dead Sea

The Negev

Miles 0 60
Kms 0 60

© United Bible Societies 1976

xv

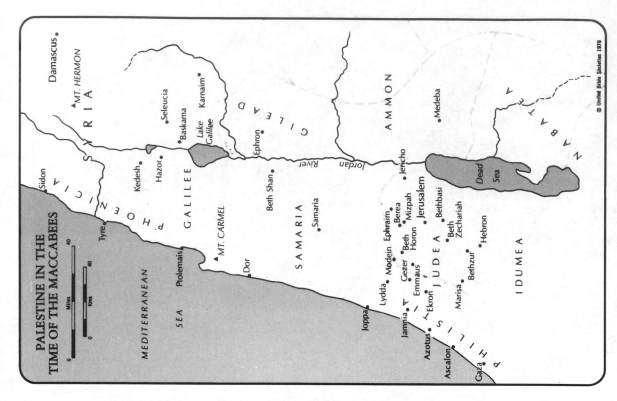

PALESTINE IN THE
TIME OF THE MACCABEES

© United Bible Societies 1978

Damascus

SYRIA

MT. HERMON

Seleucia
Baskama
Karnaim
Lake Galilee
Hazor
Kedesh

GILEAD

Ephron

Jordan River

AMMON

Medeba

Jericho
Jerusalem
Mizpah
Berea
Beth Horon
Ephraim
Modein
Gezer
Emmaus
Lydda
Jamnia
Ekron
Azotus

Bethbasi
Beth Zechariah
Hebron
Bethzur
Marisa

JUDEA

IDUMEA

NABATEA

Dead Sea

Bethsaia

PHOENICIA

Sidon
Tyre
Ptolemais
Dor

GALILEE

MT. CARMEL

Beth Shan

SAMARIA

Samaria

MEDITERRANEAN SEA

Joppa

Ascalon
Gaza

PHILISTIA

Miles 40
Kims 40

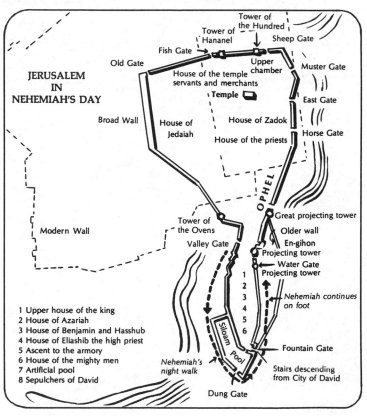

JERUSALEM
IN
NEHEMIAH'S DAY

Tower of the Hundred

Tower of Hananel

Sheep Gate

Fish Gate

Old Gate

House of the temple servants and merchants

Upper chamber

Muster Gate

Temple

East Gate

Broad Wall

House of Jedaiah

House of Zadok

House of the priests

Horse Gate

OPHEL

Great projecting tower

Modern Wall

Tower of the Ovens

Valley Gate

Older wall

En-gihon

Projecting tower

Water Gate

Projecting tower

1
2
3
4
5
6

Nehemiah continues on foot

Fountain Gate

Siloam Pool

Stairs descending from City of David

Nehemiah's night walk

Dung Gate

1 Upper house of the king
2 House of Azariah
3 House of Benjamin and Hasshub
4 House of Eliashib the high priest
5 Ascent to the armory
6 House of the mighty men
7 Artificial pool
8 Sepulchers of David

THE
OLD TESTAMENT

INTRODUCTION TO THE BIBLE

Dianne Bergant, C.S.A.

An introduction to the Bible is not merely a preface to the entire work, something elementary or preliminary, leading up to the major part. It is primarily a theological discipline in its own right and normally examines the origin of the individual books of the Bible, the history of the canon, and the history of the textual tradition. This article, though not an introduction in this strict sense, does treat some of the issues that fall within the range of an introduction.

Since the introductions to the books of the Bible in this volume address questions pertaining to the origin of particular books, such information can be found within the respective commentary. In this article attention is given to the origin, growth, and development of the biblical traditions in general—traditions that ultimately comprise the canon of Sacred Scripture. Next, a sketch of the history of the canon is offered, followed by a survey of the textual witness. The tradition formation, the development of the canon, and the textual witness are topics that seem to follow one another logically. Since the Bible claims divine authorship, the role of God's activity in this process of composition is also discussed. Finally, the interpretative tools necessary for understanding the Bible are described.

At first glance the material treated in this article may appear to be esoteric and of interest only to the professional student of Scripture. Upon closer examination, however, it should become clear that many of the basic questions that the average person asks about the Bible are answered within these pages—questions such as: What books belong to the Bible? Why do some churches have more books than others? Which is the best version? What does the Bible really mean? The sections have been arranged in such a way as to answer some of these questions as they may arise.

Perhaps one of the first questions asked by the beginning student of Scripture is: What books belong to the Bible? Close on its heels is: Why do some churches have more books than others? These are questions that pertain to the CANON of the Bible, and they are addressed in the first section. Rather than merely provide the factual information about the canon and explain the role that authority played and continues to play in this area, the first section attempts to describe the growth of the Scriptures from their very beginnings up to the time of the later decisions to "close the canon." Our knowledge of the development of the traditions, be they religious, social, political, or literary, has aided us in our investigation of this process of growth and development. Our knowledge of the socio-political and religious histories of both ancient Israel and early Christianity has also made significant contributions in this area. It seems that the process of tradition formation was dynamic rather than static, a communal venture rather than an individual accomplishment, that is, it was the work of a historical community rather than of a single author.

In this same section attention is given to the question of biblical authority. What is it? Who has it? How did they get it? The importance of historical movements and particular events has been highlighted. Thus, the Bible is seen as growing as the people grow, changing as the people change, and becoming standardized as the people seek stability. Viewing the Scriptures from this perspective should help the reader appreciate the description of the Bible as "the word of God in human words."

Even a detailed look at the human dimension of the composition of the Bible cannot adequately answer the fundamental question about its nature as Sacred Scripture. How is it the word of God? How did God speak this word in the first place? How does God speak this word today? These questions touch on the topic of INSPIRATION, the focus of the second section. This section is quite a bit shorter because it presumes the description of tradition formation outlined in the preceding one. It presents an understanding of inspiration that regards it as dynamic and operative within ordinary human events and situations. Such a view in no way detracts from the authoritative claims of the Bible; rather, it expands the scope of divine activity and places the exercise of authority squarely within the context of the believing community.

The claim that the Bible is inspired influences how its truthfulness is perceived. Human comprehension is limited and human judgment is subject to error, but surely the word of God is trustworthy. Several attempts at solving the dilemma of dual (divine and human) authorship, and the strengths and weaknesses of each solution, have been advanced over the years. Some of them are discussed in this section.

Even the beginning student of the Bible is soon aware that a variety of editions of the Bible are available. Unless every member of a Bible study group is consulting the same edition, confusion could result. This confusion may result from different translations or from the use of different sources used in constructing a text. The third section offers a brief summary of the history of the TEXTS AND VERSIONS which have survived the ravages of time and which form the basis of present-day Bibles.

The meaning of the text is ultimately the most important question. To know how the traditions developed, to believe that they were inspired by God, to be able to recover early versions of them are of very little significance if they remain unintelligible. HERMENEUTICS provides tools and methods for interpretation. These tools and methods are described in the last section. As more and more people become involved in serious study of the Bible, easy explanations of the Scriptures are being questioned and sometimes even rejected. Bewilderment over conflicting interpretations still remains. In addition, the use of biblical passages to strengthen one's point of view has become very popular in the broader society, even when a contradictory interpretation is advanced by another. All this points to the need to understand ways of interpretation in order to judge the validity and the appropriateness of the use to which the Bible is being put.

In no way does this final section claim to cover all the interpretative approaches. Its intention is to explain the basic methods used in contemporary scholarship. The authors of the commentaries in this volume frequently identify the methods they have employed in their research. The definitions found in this section might throw some light on that research and thus on the findings offered by the respective authors.

As with any other work, another author might perceive the material under discussion in another way. One of the primary goals of the COLLEGEVILLE BIBLE COMMENTARY is to bring the findings of contemporary scholarship to the beginning students of Scripture. These findings may be very new to some, not so new to others. Because of the wide selection of authors, these commentaries offer a variety of theological positions and methodological approaches. There has been a consistent attempt to be sensitive to contemporary concerns. Although efforts have been made to refrain from referring to God in gender-specific language, the lack of consensus in this area is reflected in the different styles of the authors. The work undertaken here is offered as a part of the ongoing process of biblical interpretation.

THE CANON

CANON AND AUTHORITY

Even before opening the Bible to begin a study of its contents, the serious inquirer is faced with several basic questions. What is the Bible? How did the Bible acquire its present form? Who is responsible for the contents of the Bible? Why has the Bible endured over the centuries? Is the Bible relevant to the contemporary world? While well-known answers to these questions may come immediately to mind, one very important common denominator is frequently overlooked: each answer presumes some dimension of *authority*.

What is the Bible? It is a collection of religious traditions that are revered as sacred because they are inspired by God. The believing community's official recognition of the inspired character of these traditions has accorded them "canonical" status. This means that they enjoy an authoritative status possessed by no other traditions of the community.

How did the Bible acquire its present form? The history of its origin and development is long and complicated and will be treated later. Here it is enough to say that the traditions that have been incorporated into the Bible and the shape that they have taken were dependent upon choices made within the community, choices made by persons and groups having the authority to so choose.

Who is responsible for the contents of the Bible? Prominent lawgivers, prophets, and teachers whose names are mentioned in the texts themselves were not the only ones responsible for the biblical material; there were also editors and compilers who refined and selected material from the community's vast literary and theological treasury. They preserved what they thought were religious norms, and thereby they exercised a significant amount of authority within the community.

Why has the Bible endured over the centuries? Acknowledging that it contains material stemming from times of the distant past and from cultures so different from our own, one can only marvel at its perdurability. The reason lies in the fact that believers throughout the ages have continued to be convinced of its authoritative character. They, too, have regarded its contents as normative and have tried to fashion their lives in accord with it.

Is the Bible relevant to the contemporary world? This question is at the heart of most of the biblical debate of our time. One does not merely ask, *How* can the Bible speak to the modern world? but, *Can* the Bible speak to the modern world? The first query raises the question of interpretation; the second, the issue of authority. Does the Bible still have normative value for women and men today? It is not enough to say that it is inspiring. The point is: Is it inspired, and therefore authoritative?

When addressing the authoritative character of the Bible, one must deal with some quite distinct but interrelated questions: (1) Why did these traditions emerge and not others? (2) Who had the right to decide about them? (3) Is the Bible relevant and still normative?

Why these traditions?

This study must begin with a brief working description of "biblical tradition." Put quite simply, a biblical tradition is at root a statement about the self-understanding of ancient Israel and/or the early Christian community. It not only specifically defined them as they perceived themselves, but it directed the further development of their self-understanding.

The expression "God's people" can serve as an example. Our religious ancestors believed that they were "God's people," and this concept not only identified them but shaped the way they developed through history, and it kept explaining for them why they continued to survive. For them, being "God's people" meant that God had called them and was leading and protecting them. They believed that they were recipients of divine revelation, and their traditions were testimonies to this revelation. Such traditions can be called authoritative to the extent that they authentically express the basic self-understanding of the people.

Slightly differing and sometimes even quite different traditions could and did arise. Examples of such diversity include the two accounts of creation (Gen 1:1–2:4a and Gen 2:4b-25) and the several accounts of Paul's conversion (Gal 1:13-17; Acts 9:1-9; 22:6-11; 26:12-18). Different traditions did not necessarily cause undue tension within the community as long as the self-identity of the people was not threatened. However, when there was a crisis of identity, the survival of the group demanded that some kind of agreement be reached. This crisis of identity frequently ushered in a crisis of authority as well. Which of the various statements of self-understanding was authentic? Which traditions could draw together the dissipated forces within the community? These were the ones that would subsequently function as the normative version of the community's self-identity. They would serve as a kind of "canon," a kind of authority within the community. They would continue as such as long as they expressed the identity of the group.

Scholars agree that not all the sacred traditions of ancient Israel and/or of early Christianity have survived. Among those that have survived, not all enjoy the same degree of authoritativeness. This brief description of the dynamic process known as tradition formation explains why such is the case. As their experience of life and the events of history forced the people to search for meaning, they came to understand themselves and their relationship with God in terms of that history. Thus, traditions arose, developed, and often had to be refashioned as the circumstances of life demanded.

The ultimate explanation for the endurance of a tradition seems to have been its ability to remain fundamentally unchanged and yet applicable to new situations. If it could not be refashioned or retraditioned, it would cease to be authoritative and its revelatory value would be questionable. In a very real sense, biblical authority has always resided in the interaction between an authentic tradition and the living community.

Who decides?

To acknowledge the authoritative character of the process known as tradition formation is not to deny the role played by significant people within the community. Some people had to make very important decisions for the rest of the group. However, these significant people did not simply create religious understandings or teachings independently of the community. Some may have had unique creative insights, but whatever they brought forth had to be recognized and endorsed by the others as a valid interpretation of the communal faith. That explains why some of the proclamations of the prophets, for example, were not accepted immediately. The majority of the people may not have regarded their proclamations as authentic. In such instances it was often the disciples of the prophets who preserved the teachings. Only at a later date was the authoritative character of the pronouncements broadly recognized.

According to this view, a variety of forces were at work shaping and reshaping the religious consciousness and self-understanding of the people. This means that there was no single locus of authority. Some individuals and groups originated the traditions; others contributed to their development and reshaping; others were involved in determining their place and significance in the communal self-understanding. Those in leadership positions within the community may have authenticated the traditions, but it was the people who had to confirm this decision.

Is the Bible relevant and still normative?

This question can be asked by believer and nonbeliever alike. In either case, it will proceed from a particular understanding of the nature of the material and will elicit a different answer. Anyone can be profoundly moved by the inspirational quality of literature, religious or nonreligious. A believer, however, accepts the traditions of the faith-community as somehow binding. They are regarded as not only explaining the faith but as forming the members within that faith. They are the norms and standards that direct the lives of the believers. They exercise a type of authority over these people. *That* they do this is a matter of the obedient faith of the believing community. *Why* they do this is a question of inspiration. *How* they speak to a new situation is a concern of interpretation.

The canon, then, has to do with reference to authority. It is a statement from the past that continues to be operative in the present. As literature, it is a collection of the constitutive religious writings of the community. Believers hold that these writings had their origins in revelation and that as historical memory they continue to be a source of revelation today.

THE GROWTH OF TRADITION

The study of biblical tradition is a very complicated undertaking. It includes not only an analysis of the final or "canonical" testimony of the community but also a probing into the long and labyrinthian process that brought that testimony into being. It is not enough to view tradition as a completed statement. One should also appreciate the traditioning process that created and refined that articulation. A brief examination of this process will throw light on what might otherwise be very confusing.

One of the major characteristics of this transmission process was the community's constant interpretation and application of older traditions. Tradition growth was not merely the handing down of static formulations; it also included the repeated process of actualizing earlier material within new contexts. Changes in the political, social, or religious worlds necessitated new expressions of fundamental faith as well as the articulation of new insights. The interaction between historical events and forces within the community determined the shape of the tradition, a shape that might change at another time or in another place. This process might have continued to the present day had not several significant events compelled the community to endorse certain statements over others and to confer authority on them. The destruction of the Solomonic temple at the time of the Babylonian Exile (587–538 B.C.E.—Before the Common Era) was one such event. A second historical watershed was the destruction of the Herodian temple at the time of the emergence of early Christianity (70 C.E.—Common Era). Each of these catastrophes played a major role in the choice of which traditional materials were to be preserved, the specific arrangement of what was transmitted, and their subsequent interpretation as normative theology.

Everyone is familiar with the designation "the tribes of Israel." While scholars differ in their understanding of the history of the tribal origins, most agree that the earliest organization of the people was that of a loosely united federation of clans and tribes, each retaining its unique traditions and each fiercely loyal to its own chieftains and military leaders. The traditions that grew out of their experiences were probably preserved in poetic forms, while the stability of their social structures was safeguarded by their laws. These early traditions were embedded in sagas and other narratives, the details of which readily could and did change with retelling, while the core traditions remained intact.

This was a period of great fluidity (ca. 1200–1040 B.C.E.). Groups of people changed location and shifted social and political allegiance quite frequently. As diverse peoples amalgamated, their traditions were brought together into a common story. Although this common story now flows quite smoothly, the process of assimilation never completely erased characteristics that might identify one group from another. These characteristics can be detected upon careful study of the text.

The socio-political move from a federation of tribes to a nation under the administration of a king (ca. tenth century B.C.E.) called for a review of the relationship of the people with their God. The people were forced to scrutinize their religious traditions, restating some while reshaping others. Earlier tribal narratives were retold with a bias in favor of the monarchy. Since the contemporary situation influenced the way the past was understood, inevitably these new interpretations became part of the original narrative in such a way that details from different periods now comprised one story. This interpretative process explains why the tradition known as the Yahwist (J) is both a narrative epic of early Israelite history and a justification of the Davidic monarchy.

At still another time and from another perspective, the tradition now known as the Elohist (E) took shape. This was a retelling of basically the same story as that told by the Yahwist, but the concerns were not the same and so the focus was different. During this period prophets such as Amos and Hosea in the north and Isaiah in the south were also calling for a reevaluation of the current beliefs and practices of the people. Although some of this theology had probably already established itself with some degree of authority, much of it was still in flux.

When the northern kingdom fell to the Assyrians (722 B.C.E.), the traditions that had originated there were incorporated with those of the south. Thus, different portraits of the tribal ancestors were woven together into one; legal customs that operated within one community became part of the law of another. The selection, codification, and crystallization of these various traditions resulted in a rich and sometimes contradictory testimony to the action of God in the history of the nation. This testimony became the official story, the authoritative self-understanding, of the people. The messages of early prophets were probably proclaimed again and again as long as they could be adapted to the needs of the people. More than likely they were preserved by followers of the prophets, and these disciples were the ones who made the necessary yet appropriate adaptations.

The demise of the northern kingdom had its theological repercussions in the south as well. It became a catalyst for the retelling of the stories of the initial settlement of the land, stories that not only pointed to the reasons for the fall but also served as a warning to the south. There was a renewed attention to the Law and a resurgence of prophetic critique. These concerns and the subsequent reshaping of earlier traditions set the stage for both the Deuteronomistic (D) and Priestly (P) theologies.

As stated earlier, the destruction of the temple, the downfall of the monarchy, and the deportation of the people all played a part in the fashioning of traditions. This critical period of captivity probably forged the two major biblical portions known as the Law and the Prophets. Early historical, prophetic, and legal traditions were given the shape that has, for the most part, been handed down to the present time. The precise text of the primary history of Israel, including the Law, was then fixed and was not to undergo any further significant reinterpretation. References to the existence of a version of the Law and its importance in the postexilic community are found in Ezra 7:14 and Neh 8:1. The prophetic books such as Jeremiah and Ezekiel would still be somewhat expanded and revised as new material was added, but once this expansion and revision had ceased, the prophetic corpus was also accorded a kind of authoritative status. There is a second-century mention of this status in 2 Macc 15:9. The believing community now revered these traditions as normative for them. What the institutions of monarchy, priesthood, and prophecy had done in shaping the self-identity of the pre-exilic community, the authoritative traditions that emerged from the crucible of the Exile did for the self-identity of later Judaism.

These literary and theological books of material told the story of the people's beginnings, but they ended the story with the people on the threshold of the land of promise, thus proclaiming a message of hope for a nation looking to the future for a land of its own. The national history now described prosperity as contingent upon fidelity to covenantal commitment, thus explaining the nation's present plight as both a judgment for past failures and an incentive to future repentance. The prophetic material established the credibility of the major prophets as spokespersons for God. Their teachings were to be heeded. In this way the newly forged exilic community reactualized its normative traditions, preserving them for the future.

The needs of the postexilic community called for new and different religious traditions. Theological interpretations of events, prophetic pronouncements, sapiential reflections on life, didactic stories, hymns, and other cultic songs emerged as part of the religious treasury of the second temple period. The significance of these traditions was a focus of dispute within the community.

The Samaritans appear to have dissociated themselves from the returned community sometime around 300 B.C.E., and to this day those who remain faithful to the Samaritan tradition consider only the Torah, or Pentateuch, as inspired. The Sadducees of the early Christian era were descendants of this same point of view. Not until well into the Christian period did official Judaism decide upon the authoritativeness of the third section of the Scriptures, known as the Writings. By that time there were several collections of inspired material, each claiming a position of privilege within the community.

The spread of Hellenistic thought and language prompted the translation of the traditions into Greek. This version came to be known as the Septuagint (LXX) or Alexandrian version. The former name comes from a tradition which claimed that seventy (LXX) translators, working independently of one another, produced the same translation. The latter designation stems from the name of the city of its origin. This version contains some books not found in the Hebrew Bible. It seems that both the Hebrew and the Greek versions enjoyed the same prestige, each within different communities.

A third collection that has survived from this period belonged to a sectarian group known as the Essenes. Portions of their library have been found in the caves at Qumran, a settlement in the Judean desert. They appear to have included more books in their Scripture than did either the Septuagint or the more traditional Hebrew Scriptures of the time. The existence of these different "canons" is evidence of what was stated above about the diversity of religious traditions within the believing community. This diversity resulted from different life perspectives as well as different hermeneutical or interpretative ways of understanding the material.

The "event of Christ" constituted an impact not unlike that of other revelatory events in the history of "God's people" in that it forced the believers to seriously reexamine their beliefs. It was radically different, however, in several significant ways. It was not merely another revelation of God—believers insist that it was *the* revelation of God. For that reason earlier traditions may now be seen in an entirely new light. By this time Judaism was a religion of "the Book"; Christianity, on the other hand, is a religion of "the living Christ." The Gospels portray Jesus as claiming authority in his own right. He did not seem to place himself within the stream of traditional authority but called directly upon divine authority. Further, he explained the traditions of Israel in terms of himself. Clearly, Jesus, not the Bible, is the focus of authority here. Hence the ultimate question inevitably arises: What relevance does the Hebrew Bible have for the Christian experience and for Christian theology? This is a question that confronted the very earliest Christians and has confronted every generation of Christians since their time.

The first Christians, like Jesus himself, had been formed within the ancient biblical traditions. Thus, they accepted or rejected him in the light of those traditions. The Scriptures became the basis of their faith in him as Lord, and he became the focus through which they understood the Scriptures. A new religious group was born out of this faith in Jesus and this reinterpretation of the traditions. The new phenomenon was the source of conflict within the original community. Jesus' radical perspective was challenged by the religious authorities of his day. The Gospels have preserved recollections of this new interpretation (see Matt 5:17-48). His followers faced the same opposition. Stephen was stoned for this reason (see Acts 7), and Paul himself suffered for his preaching (see Acts 14:4f. and 19).

This new teaching of Jesus and its furtherance by his followers gave rise to a new tradition that soon enjoyed a prominence parallel to the Scriptures (see 2 Pet 3:2). This did not happen without internal strife, however. There were those within the Christian community who felt that the Law was not only irrelevant but was actually a hindrance. This attitude appeared most frequently in the Gentile churches established by Paul (see Gal 3:23–4:7). Others clung tenaciously to observance of the Law as necessary for themselves as well as for new converts. The Judeo-Christian communities, notably the church in Jerusalem and a group known as the Ebionites, represented this position (see Acts 15:1-4). Once again, the issue was the relationship of earlier traditions to a new revelation.

Various forces were at work during this period. The Christian community was expanding and assuming several different and flexible shapes. Within the Jewish community, of which many Christians were a part, the biblical traditions were moving toward a final shape. Books that were somehow associated with the great figures of the Hebrew past were given a prominence not accorded to other writings. All the criteria for making these decisions are not known to modern scholarship, and therefore much about the closing of the canon remains unclear. One thing can be said: Neither the collection of the Septuagint nor that of the Qumran became the official canon of the Jewish community. That is interesting, since studies have shown that the version most popularly used at this time was the Septuagint, especially among Christians. When they quoted from the older traditions, they usually cited the Greek version.

While the Jewish community may have made some decisions about its authoritative list, the Christian community, which drew on the same sources, certainly did not. Although there are references to "the law and the prophets" (Matt 5:17) and to "the law of Moses and the prophets and the psalms" (Luke 24:44), significant controversy continued well into the fourth century. It was not so much conflict with forces outside the community as it was internal strife that brought the question of canon to the fore again and again. Groups like the Gnostics and teachers like Marcion, who were later condemned as heretics because of their views of Christianity, had used their biblical interpretations, especially their rejection of the Hebrew Scriptures, as fuel for their theological arguments. Thus, both the Jewish and the emerging Christian Scriptures became the weapons in the fight over Christian orthodoxy.

The great second-century apologist Justin Martyr was one of the first to witness to the practice of reading Christian writings in conjunction with the Jewish Scriptures at liturgical services. Defense of the Scriptures was at the heart of his teaching. The early champions of the faith such as Irenaeus, Clement of Alexandria, Tertullian, Origen, and Eusebius all preserved canonical lists of Christian writings. Some of them agreed with each other, others did not. In the fourth century both the church in the West and the church in the East accepted a Christian list of twenty-seven books but did not adopt a standard for the Jewish Scriptures. That would have to wait for the Reformation and the Council of Trent's response to it.

THE SHAPE OF THE CANON

The long process of tradition formation and development that has been described here was finally brought to a close. This closure resulted in a normative version of the tradition which, as the recognized testimony to divine revelation, could henceforth enable the believing community to organize its life and verify its hope. A canon or standard was thus established in this normative version. The word "canon," it should be noted, has a long and complicated history. Originally meaning "reed," it came to signify something that acted as a norm, a measuring stick. In Christian usage it refers to a model or rule.

The final canonical forms of the biblical traditions attest to God's presence and revelation in the past experiences of the people. These forms became the rule or standard for determining revelation within the believing community in the present and in the future. They also provided a means of achieving unity within the faith. Born of the community, they were instrumental in the rebirth of that community generation after generation.

There are three major Jewish theories concerning the closing of the canon. Since most of the Hebrew Scriptures were in existence at the time of Ezra in the fifth century B.C.E., Ezra himself was credited with the completion of the collection. This tradition is legendary and enjoys little prominence today. A second theory holds that a group of leaders of the postexilic community, forerunners of what came to be known as the Great Synagogue, worked under the impetus of Ezra and established the canon. However, there is no evidence that a body resembling the Great Synagogue existed before the Middle Ages, and so this theory is also usually discounted. The third position, the one generally held today, suggests that it was not until the Christian era that the Palestinian Jewish community closed its canon. The town of Jamnia (also known as Jabneh) appears to have been the center of Pharisaic Judaism. Here the leaders of the community that had survived the fall of Jerusalem and the destruction of the temple built by Herod decided upon the list of inspired books.

Just as it was a particular interpretation of God's presence and revelation that had shaped the tradition, so it was another particular interpretation that eventually considered the canon closed. There is no certainty about the exact criteria followed in making these decisions. Knowledge of the sociopolitical and religious forces at work at that particular time may throw some light on this question, but much necessary information has been lost to history. However, some criteria can be assumed.

If the Scriptures do testify to divine revelation, then obviously the prophetic tradition, that bearer of revelation *par excellence*, played a significant role in the canonization of these Scriptures. Only those books that were believed to have originated before the termination of genuine prophecy were considered uniquely inspired. Liturgical usage was a second criterion. Books that gained prominence because of their cultic or liturgical function were also accorded canonical status. Adherence to these criteria yielded the tripartite Bible: the Torah, or Law (the first five books); the Prophets (the Former Prophets, or Historical Books; and the Latter or Writing Prophets); and the Writings (Psalms, Wisdom writings, the five liturgical scrolls, Daniel, and the postexilic history). These were the sacred books of Israel that "soiled the hands." This curious phrase indicates that after handling the above-mentioned scrolls, the reader's hands were to be washed in a ritual acknowledgment of the holiness of the traditions and the unworthiness of the reader.

As stated earlier, the Greek version that originated in Alexandria was probably the one in popular use at this time (ca. 90 c.e.). However, it was the older Hebrew version that was adopted by the Jewish community at Jamnia. Some believe that this choice was due to the rivalry that had developed between the Jewish and the Christian interpretations of some of the traditions as well as to the Christian practice of adding Christian writings to the collections. Other scholars hold that disputes within the Jewish community itself influenced the decision about the canon. At this time the Pharisees were in conflict with some of the more apocalyptically minded Jewish sects, and they took a stand in favor of a more conservative interpretation. (Apocalyptic was a very imaginative and symbolic way of interpreting the events of history. It frequently included a description of the future.) The time of Ezra, the time after the destruction of the first temple, was recalled at this, the time of the destruction of the second temple. At the time of Ezra apocalyptic and messianic speculation was eliminated, and the collection of books that came out of the Exile became the normative version. So the same selection occurred at the time of Jamnia.

The apocalyptic and messianic speculation did, however, serve the Christian need to come to grips with "the event of Christ." That was probably one of the reasons for the continued use by Christians of writings that were part of the Greek version. Whether Jesus and the disciples used the Hebrew or the Greek version is not clear. What is clear, however, is that the communities from which the Christian Scriptures were born quoted from the Greek, for the vast majority of the Christians of the first century were Greek-speaking Gentile converts. Since they did not believe that revelation had ended with the death of the last prophet but continued in Christ, they continued to use the more extensive Greek version.

It was not until the second and third centuries that the debates within Judaism precipitated a move by Christians to close their list of Jewish sacred books. By the fourth century the Western churches had accepted the decision of the North African councils and had adopted the Greek Bible. The Eastern churches, on the other hand, appear to have preferred the list drawn up by the Jews. These decisions were made by local or regional churches. It was the Council of Trent that finally decided upon the canon for the churches in union with Rome.

Since the Reformers rejected the authority of the papacy and its use of Scripture to authenticate some of its teachings, they looked to the Scriptures themselves as the norms for interpreting tradition and chose the shorter Jewish canon as their official list. The Roman church, in accepting the wider Greek canon, has preserved an authentic early church tradition and is consistent with that community's usage of certain books rejected by the Jewish community. The Protestant churches, in their retention of the shorter canon, have preserved a more ancient version. These ecclesiastical decisions have resulted in the lists given on the next page.

The story of the growth and development of the Jewish canon provides solid reasons for the threefold division of Law, Prophets, and Writings. But one can only conjecture about the reasons for the order of the Alexandrian canon: Pentateuch, History, Poetry, Prophets. Perhaps it can be traced to the fact that Hellenistic Jews were trained in Greek schools of rhetoric, where literature was studied according to literary types. Finally, there is an interesting theological feature in the differing orientations with which each collection concludes. In the Jewish canon the reader is left with an exhortation to go up to Jerusalem and to rebuild the temple (2 Chr 36:23), a message dear to every Jewish heart. The Alexandrian order, reflecting a messianic concern, ends with the promise to send Elijah the prophet at the inauguration of the day of the Lord's coming (Mal 4:5). Christians could easily see this as an appropriate transition to their own sacred traditions.

Those seven books about which canonicity was disputed (Judith, Tobit, 1 and 2 Maccabees, Wisdom, Sirach, and Baruch) are called "deuterocanonical" by Roman Catholics and "apocryphal" by Protestants, who frequently include them in a separate section at the end of their Bibles. The term "deuterocanonical" does not suggest a separate canonizing process so much as a deliberate canonical recognition deemed necessary because of controversy within the community. Initially "apocrypha" meant "hidden," implying that

JEWISH CANON	ALEXANDRIAN CANON
TORAH (LAW)	PENTATEUCH
Genesis	Genesis
Exodus	Exodus
Leviticus	Leviticus
Numbers	Numbers
Deuteronomy	Deuteronomy
PROPHETS	HISTORY
(Former)	Joshua
Joshua	Judges
Judges	Ruth
1-2 Samuel	1-2 Samuel
1-2 Kings	1-2 Kings
	1-2 Chronicles
(Latter)	Ezra-Nehemiah
Isaiah	Esther
Jeremiah	Judith
Ezekiel	Tobit
(12 minor)	1-2 Maccabees
Hosea	
Joel	POETRY
Amos	Psalms
Obadiah	Proverbs
Jonah	Ecclesiastes
Micah	Song of Songs
Nahum	Job
Habakkuk	Wisdom of Solomon
Zephaniah	Sirach
Haggai	
Zechariah	PROPHETS
Malachi	(Major)
	Isaiah
WRITINGS	Jeremiah
Psalms	Baruch
Job	Lamentations
Proverbs	Ezekiel
Ruth	Daniel
Song of Songs	
Qoheleth	(Minor)
Lamentations	Hosea
Esther	Amos
Daniel	Micah
Ezra-Nehemiah	Joel
1-2 Chronicles	Obadiah
	Jonah
	Nahum
	Habakkuk
	Zephaniah
	Haggai
	Zechariah
	Malachi

the message of these books was hidden from the majority of the community and understood only by the truly wise. Gradually the term took on a negative meaning because the orthodoxy of the books was suspect. Today the word "apocryphal" merely refers to writings that may be profoundly religious and inspirational but not canonical. Though absent from the Hebrew canon, the deuterocanonical or apocryphal material was considered part of the Jewish (and therefore also the Protestant) religious literature and was frequently used in liturgical settings.

There is another group of religious writings that, although not considered canonical by either Jewish or Christian communities, greatly influenced both. In them can be found the background for such themes as the kingdom of God, the Son of Man, the resurrection of the dead, the teachings about angels and demons. These intertestamental works (writings from the period between the times of the Old and the New Testaments), frequently apocalyptic in character, were in a rather fluid state between 200 B.C.E. and 100 C.E., and sometimes enjoyed the same respect as did some of the "Writings" that eventually became canonical.

A large number of manuscripts from this group of writings have been discovered at Qumran, a Jewish community that shared many of the same apocalyptic and messianic hopes as did the early Christians. The intensity of these widespread hopes explains the popularity of this kind of literature, which include such works as the Book of Enoch, the Book of Jubilees, the Testaments of the Twelve Patriarchs, the Sibylline Oracles, the Assumption of Moses, to name but a few. Because their proclaimed authorship is questionable, these works have often been referred to by Protestants as "pseudepigrapha"; because of their somewhat esoteric nature, Catholics call them "apocrypha." Actually, neither term is really satisfactory, but, because of traditional usage, the designations stand.

The rise of Christian writings to the status of Scripture is easier to trace than that of the Jewish writings because witnesses to their influence can be found in the writings of the "apostolic teachers" of the early Christian centuries. Their authority rested not so much on the fact that they were the traditions of the earliest Christians as on the fact that they preserved the authentic "Jesus tradition." It was the words of Jesus that were authoritative. Paul called upon this authority when teaching about the final coming (1 Thess 4:15) and the institution of the Lord's Supper (1 Cor 11:23ff.). Although the oral tradition may have been preferred, the need for Christian writings soon became obvious. With the founding of Christian communities at great distances both from Jerusalem and from one another, written communication became necessary. As the apostles became dispersed and the eyewitnesses to Jesus began to die, the need for authoritative written testimonies increased. These testimonies became the building blocks of the Christian Scriptures.

These Scriptures themselves existed as individual works long before they were collected into fixed groups. The earliest known writings were the letters of Paul. They might have been lost to history had not someone collected them and circulated this collection throughout the church. Scholars have suggested that the compiler was the author of Ephesians, who wrote that letter under Paul's name and sent it as a general introduction to the entire collection. Whatever the case may be, even before the end of the first century an early Christian writer called Paul's letters "true inspiration" (1 Clement 47:3) similar to the Hebrew Scriptures (see 2 Pet 3:15-16). The great teachers of the second and third centuries—Ignatius, Polycarp, Tertullian, and Origen—all knew of Paul's letters and acknowledged their authority. Even Marcion, a Gnostic who repudiated the entire Jewish tradition, considered Paul as prominent. He devised a canon that consisted only of ten Pauline letters and the Gospel of Luke.

The first reference to a "Gospel tradition" appears toward the middle of the second century; a short time later Justin Martyr mentions a Gospel reading as part of Sunday worship. While there may have been earlier hints that the "Jesus tradition" was enjoying the same authority as the Hebrew tradition, this is the first clear evidence of a new canon growing up beside the traditional one.

One cannot but ask: Why four Gospels? Why not just one, as Marcion had suggested? And if more than one, why only four out of the many that were composed in the first centuries of the Christian period? Even Luke tells us that "many have undertaken to compile a narrative . . ." (1:1). Modern scholarship claims that this variety of Gospels reflects the diversity and pluralism within early Christianity and the adaptation of the Gospel tradition to new and different Christian communities.

A careful study of the apocryphal Gospels may explain why the church rejected most of them, but it does not answer the question about the fourfold Gospel tradition. Different answers have been put forward, all somewhat hypothetical. Some say that since apostolic origin was a criterion for canonization and all four Gospels could claim such origin (Matthew and John were among the Twelve; Mark was associated with Peter, and Luke with Paul), all four had to be accepted. Irenaeus thought that since there were four world regions, four major winds, four covenants in the Hebrew tradition, there should be four Gospel witnesses as pillars of the church. Others suggest that Marcion's rejection of every Gospel but Luke's played a part in the decision in favor of a fourfold Gospel tradition. Whatever the reason, by the end of the second century the collection of four Gospels was accepted everywhere but Syria, where a harmonized account known as the Diatessaron of Tatian continued as authoritative until the fifth century.

By the end of the second century a new two-part canon was taking shape. It consisted of a fourfold Gospel canon and a collection of apostolic writings. The status of several of the apostolic writings was the subject of controversy down through the fifth century. Although the early church citations and lists were the two main criteria for determining the authoritativeness of the Christian Scriptures, it is clear that there was not yet universal agreement. These diverse early church lists may reflect nothing more than the custom of each author's local church. If this was the case, the extent of the agreement that one finds is quite significant.

The earliest official or ecclesiastical list still in existence is called the Muratorian Fragment and is thought to be representative of late second-century Roman usage. The fact that Irenaeus, Polycarp, Clement, and Tertullian were all in basic agreement with it points to its catholicity. Twenty-two of the twenty-seven books of our canon were included in this listing.

At the beginning of the third century, Origen further classified the books then in use. Having traveled widely, he was able to compare the lists of various churches in different regions, categorizing them as: (1) "acknowledged"—four Gospels, thirteen Pauline letters, Acts, two other non-Pauline epistles (later called "catholic," because they are more like encyclicals intended for the whole church rather than for individual communities as the Pauline letters were); (2) "disputed"; (3) "false."

In the fourth century Eusebius categorized the writings in a similar fashion. However, it was Athanasius whose list included all and only those books that comprise our canonical Christian testament. In addition to the canonical books, he listed some of the writings that had been included in several earlier lists and suggested that they would be good for reading. The Latin church was influenced by this Greek decision, and, subsequently, several North African councils sanctioned the same list of twenty-seven books. Although there was general agreement throughout both the Greek and the Latin churches, it came about as the result of decisions made by provincial synods, not by an ecumenical council. The canon grew out of the common usage of the Christian communities.

While the West had canonized four Gospels, the Syrian church clung to the Diatessaron until the fifth century. It never completely accepted all the catholic epistles or the Apocalypse. The Ethiopic church, on the other hand, enlarged its canon. Thus, the church in the East continued to revere a different Christian Bible.

As already mentioned, several other early Christian works were often considered canonical well into the fifth century. These were: 1 and 2 Clement, the Epistle of Barnabas, the Didache, and the Shepherd of Hermas. It is still not clear in every instance why they were not included in the final listing.

Certain factors seem to have been gradually accepted for determining which books should be considered canonical and which books should not. First among these factors was apostolic origin. The work had to be associated with an apostle or with someone from the apostolic age. Second, there had to be a catholic or universal dimension to the message. This requirement did not deny that some of the writings were originally intended for individual communities, but it demanded that the message speak to all. Third, the teaching had to be in accord with the basic rule of faith and not propose some esoteric message. There is no direct evidence that these were the criteria used to determine canonicity; however, books seem to have been rejected because they deviated seriously from just this kind of criteria.

The church now had a twofold canon which, it believed, was inspired by God and which attested to God's presence and revelation in the past experiences of the people. Further, it cherished this twofold canon as the rule or standard for determining revelation within the believing community in the present and in the future.

INSPIRATION

INSPIRATION AND AUTHORITY

The Bible has been defined as a collection of religious traditions that are revered as sacred because they are inspired by God. In the preceding section we examined the process of tradition growth and development, showing how the ebb and flow of Israel's history significantly influenced it as it reshaped and reinterpreted the tradition, and how decisions about canonicity brought an end to this creative process.

Up to this point the focus of this study has been on human authorship. The communities first of ancient Israel and then of early Christianity, believed that God had been revealed in their midst through the events of their history. The Bible is a collection of those traditions that were cherished as authentic and enduring testimonies of God's revelation. By canonizing these testimonies, the community declared that, while God may be revealed in many ways, there is a unique relationship between revelation and these sacred Scriptures. This relationship is spoken of in terms of inspiration and divine authorship. Those who in any way contributed to the writing of the Bible were inspired by God. Thus, the Bible boasts both human and divine authorship.

The present consideration of biblical inspiration begins with a passage from the Bible itself: "All scripture is inspired of God and is useful for teaching—for reproof, correction, and training in holiness" (2 Tim 3:16). Here the word "inspired" can mean either "breathes" God or "is breathed of" God. While the community does indeed believe that the Scriptures continue to communicate God's word to us today (breathes God), it is the passive sense of the verb that is traditionally preferred: the Scriptures have been "breathed of" God. This idea recalls the familiar prophetic theme of the breath or spirit of God, that dynamic manifestation of God's action in the world.

It is no wonder, then, that biblical inspiration has often been understood as akin to prophetic inspiration or prophetic possession. However, if one uses the prophetic model of inspiration to understand biblical inspiration—as many people have done in the past and some continue to do in the present—one may tend to assume that each individual book can be traced back to one author who was inspired or whose words were inspired. The process of tradition formation that has been discussed in these pages rejects such a notion of authorship and finds the model inadequate and misleading.

Besides presuming single authorship, the prophetic model frequently minimizes the role played by human reflection and creativity. At times God is depicted as taking possession of the imagination and thought of the individual, and sometimes even as dictating the ideas and the very words. There can be little doubt about the difficulty in balancing the roles of the human and the divine in this kind of joint undertaking. But it is better that a difficulty stand unresolved than that the contribution of either partner in this venture be underestimated.

Without denying the unique role played by certain individual members of the community, the present study has suggested that it was really the community itself that gave birth to the sacred traditions. If this is the case, and if these traditions are indeed inspired by God, then it is within the community, and not merely in select members of that community, that inspiration is operative. Those who first recognized the action of God within their history and then developed a tradition to testify to that action, those who later reshaped that tradition in order that it speak to a new community at a new time, and those who set the

tradition down in its final form were all communities inspired by God. From this perspective, the biblical text itself is not seen as the initial expression of inspiration; rather, this text is the written form that has since become normative. The Bible represents one point in the long process of divine inspiration. It was preceded by the inspired growth and development of religious traditions, and it frequently has been followed by the inspired reinterpretation of those traditions.

Before proceeding to a discussion of the process of inspiration, we must pose a crucial question: Just *what* is inspired? Is it the author? And how is this last question answered if one thinks that the community rather than select individuals authored the Bible? Are the words inspired? But then, *which* words? Would it be the ones used in the first expression of the traditions, words that probably have been lost in history? Or the words of the final text, in the original languages? And what about translations? And further, which versions of the translations? These are all very important questions and will not be neglected, but a more fundamental question has to do with the way inspiration operates within the community. The other questions will be addressed within that context.

Our earlier discussion about the formation of tradition will serve as the framework for this discussion of inspiration. Not every event left a lasting mark on the consciousness of the community. Only those events that helped to shape and refine their fundamental faith became central to the tradition. A particular event itself may have been either momentous or outwardly insignificant. It was the religious meaning of the event that was cherished and handed down from generation to generation. Those who had the actual experience saw it as contributing to their identity and to their life. By transmitting this formative tradition to others, they were inviting these others to be formed by the tradition just as they had been. Thus, there was a dimension to the tradition that was continually formative.

Now, if it was the dynamic power of God that fashioned a people in the first place, what but the same dynamic power could continue this process of formation? It must be noted here that a mutual formation was taking place: As the community formulated the tradition, so the tradition formed, that is, influenced, the self-identity of the community. The dynamic force operative in the development of the people was God's self-disclosure. The dynamic force operative in the development of the tradition was God's inspiration. Thus, it should become apparent that to limit inspiration to but one moment in this development is to confine God's activity to that moment.

Difficult as it may be, it is possible to trace the development of a tradition. The same cannot be said about tracing the movement of inspiration. The former is a verifiable human endeavor; the latter is by definition a divine activity and calls for, and is accessible only by means of, faith. A community of faith believes that God is revealed in its midst and communicates with the people through their religious traditions. These traditions will be revered as inspired as long as God is perceived as speaking through them. Since the dynamic faith of the community claims that God is not bound to the past but brings the power of the past into the newness of the present with an openness to the future, then, correspondingly, God's inspiration must be seen as ongoing. To the extent that a tradition continues to be open to God's communication, it can be said to be inspired. Traditions that originated in the past must continue to speak to the active presence of God in the ongoing life of the community. The Bible *was* inspired, for during its growth and development it continually formed a believing community. The Bible *is* inspired, for it has not ceased to perform this same wonder, giving witness even to this day to the community's origin and continually awakening it to its purpose.

INSPIRATION AND TRUTH

When one claims that God is the author of the Bible, one is thereby making a statement about its truthfulness. Surely the word of God is trustworthy. God would not deceive the community, nor would God allow the community to be led astray by either the ignorance or the limited perspectives of the human authors. In following this train of thought, many people have insisted that the Bible is inerrant, or free from all error. Such a claim raises several difficult questions.

How does one explain differing and even contradictory traditions? (Human beings were created after the plants and animals appeared—Gen 1:12, 21, 25, 27. Human beings were created while the earth was still uninhabited—Gen 2:5, 9.) Must one adhere to a perception of the universe that is contrary to scientific findings? (Light itself was created before the heavenly bodies that give off light—Gen 1:3, 16.) Can one reconcile conflicting chronology in the Gospel story? (Jesus cleansed the temple at the beginning of his ministry during one of his several visits to Jerusalem—John 2:13-17. The cleansing occurred during his only visit, which took place just before his death—Matt 21:12-17; Mark 11:15-19; Luke 19:45-48.)

Efforts to explain the inconsistencies found within the Bible have resulted in various methods of interpretation. Those who have opted for fundamentalist interpretations have frequently spurned historical and scientific evidence and have adopted the literal sense of the text, claiming that there are no real inconsistencies, for God can do even the impossible if need be.

Another approach attempts to reconcile the theory of inerrancy with the discrepancies present within the text. The Scriptures are taken quite literally until one comes upon a difficult passage. Then, believing that God's revelation can be neither illogical nor inaccurate, the interpreter concludes that what appears to be an inconsistency is really meant to be interpreted allegorically. Thus, what could otherwise be seen as discordant is harmonized.

A third way of resolving the dilemma is to make a decision about the kind of truth the Bible is intended to reveal. Biblical scholars have done just that, distinguishing between historical and/or scientific truth and religious truth—not an easy decision to make. Historical, scientific, and religious references are found to be intertwined. It is not always clear why the authors expressed ideas as they did. If their historical and scientific references are not to be understood as accurate expressions of theological truth, were they merely the best literary and figurative constructions available? Or is the very human, very limited understanding of reality simply the platform from which they launched their profound theological search for God and upon which the drama of God's loving involvement unfolded? However these questions are answered, one must decide which guidelines are to be followed when making the distinctions mentioned. Attempting to focus on what in the text is truly theological, critical biblical scholarship has taken great pains to be as honest as possible in applying literary and historical methods of research. In this way it has thrown new light on the question of the truthfulness of the Bible.

At this juncture something should be said about what is meant by "truth." Is it to be understood as something akin to honesty, integrity, the antithesis of deception? Or does it also imply precision, accuracy of fact, freedom from mistake?

Contemporary scholarship insists that the Bible is indeed inspired by God, but inspired through the natural process of the growth and development of tradition. Since the Bible is not merely the record of God's word but also of the human response to that word, the character of human authorship cannot be disregarded. Obvious discrepancies and apparent contradictions may be attributed to human error, but they may also result from those interpretations and reinterpretations produced by the living community over generations of tradition development. Both the needs of a specific community of faith and the particular insights it had into its religious tradition may also have influenced the quality or limitation of theological expression that emerged from the transmission of tradition. One would certainly not reject as either inadequate or in error the theology of Isaiah or Jeremiah simply because the prophets did not refer to or believe in the Trinity or in life after death.

The biblical traditions have been described as testimonies. The focus of the last section was on the very human composition of those testimonies. The issue in this section is the relationship between the testimonies and the revelation of God to which they testify. This relationship has been understood in significantly different ways, depending upon how one has come to understand inspiration. Those who hold that the words are inspired are more likely to revere the Bible itself as revelation. Others who believe that God is revealed primarily in the events of history are more inclined to regard the Bible as the interpreted testimony to those events. According to this latter view, the Bible is a witness to

revelation. The basic difference between these two views, in essence, is the difference between what is said and what is meant. While both perspectives are indeed aspects of the same reality, they most certainly are not identical. Knowing what the Bible says is not the same as knowing what the Bible means.

A study of tradition development indicates that what the community cherished was not primarily some specific expression of the tradition but rather the fundamental meaning of it. Were this not the case, the community consistently would have resisted any attempt at reformulation.

As stated earlier, the dynamic force operative in the development of the people was God's self-disclosure. The dynamic force operative in the development of the tradition was God's inspiration. The Bible claims to be not only a testimony to God's self-disclosure and to the community's transformation in the past, but also a unique occasion for a comparable disclosure and transformation in the present. To the extent that this claim is verified again and again, the truthfulness of the Bible can be affirmed. It is not so much the accuracy of the words but rather the power of the message that bears witness to its truthfulness. The same Spirit that was operative in the formation of the Scriptures continues to bear witness to its truthfulness and to convince us of its inspired nature. Therein lies the authority of the Bible.

TEXTS AND VERSIONS

Anyone beginning the study of the Bible is quickly aware of the number of versions that are available. Why are there so many? Which one is the best? Questions such as these touch upon another very complicated but fundamental issue of biblical investigation—that of textual criticism. This particular aspect of biblical scholarship will be examined in some detail in the section on interpretation, or hermeneutics. Here attention will be given to the various texts themselves rather than to the method of examining them.

There are several reasons for the variety of biblical versions. The most obvious one is a difference in translations. One language does not easily lend itself to a literal translation in another, and translators have to make decisions about the choice of words and phrases used. Some translators made one choice, others make another; hence different translations result. This issue will be addressed at greater length below.

Another reason for some of the differences is scribal error. We all know how easy it is to make mistakes when transcribing something. If we add to this very human, very common occurrence the fact that scribes had to work long hours with manuscripts written in languages seldom their own, then the repetitions, omissions, and mistranslations are understandable. Only by pursuing the meticulous task of comparing various texts (and this is a task of textual criticism) can one correct some of these errors. As more of the ancient texts are found, more corrections can be made.

These two explanations presume that there was one common biblical version, and from this came different translations, some of which had suffered from occasional scribal error. A third reason given for the variety of translations has implications that reach deeper into the tradition. Scholars believe that even though there may have been lists indicating which books were included in the canon of inspired writings, in many cases there was not one fixed, standard text. Rather, several very similar but still different versions of the tradition were in existence. This explanation would account for some of the real discrepancies found in the modern versions.

Until recent times the earliest available complete editions of the Hebrew version of the Old Testament could be traced back no further than the fifteenth century. We know now that these editions were based on a very limited selection of manuscripts, some of which are no longer available to us for study. The earliest Greek versions containing both Testaments date from the fourth century; some fragments of books are even older. Archaeological discoveries of the twentieth century have brought the number of these manuscripts or fragments of manuscripts to the thousands. They have been classified on the basis of both material used (papyrus or parchment) and the style of writing (block-lettered uncials or cursive minuscules).

Papyrus came from a tall, reed-like plant that grows abundantly along the Nile River. It was the customary stationery of the Medi-terranean world. The stem was cut lengthwise and the strips laid side by side to form a layer. The layers were then laid at right angles and pressed together to form a sheet. After being dried, they were glued together to form a scroll, which was then rolled around a stick. Scrolls averaged about thirty-five feet in length. At some time during the second century the church began to use a new format. Sheets of papyrus were sown rather than glued together, thus producing a kind of book that has come to be referred to as a "codex." While it was relatively inexpensive, papyrus became brittle with age. Hence a new, costlier, but more durable material gradually came into use. The skins of sheep and goats, once they were scraped and dried, were found to provide a smooth surface for writing. This parchment, or vellum, as it is called, soon became the most commonly used material.

Most of the early texts that have been preserved were written in large blocklike letters. This is true not only of the Hebrew, whose script was relatively square, but of the Greek as well. The influence of ancient Greek inscriptions that used only capital letters (uncials) is recognized in early Greek manuscripts. For this reason, these manuscripts have come to be known by the same name—uncials. This form of block-writing was prominent until the ninth century, when cursive script came into popular use. This script enabled the scribes to copy manuscripts much more quickly and thus to make more copies available. These more numerous copies, however, were not necessarily easier to read. Cursive script, like its uncial counterpart, gave its name to a manuscript form—minuscule.

TRANSMISSION OF OLD TESTAMENT TEXTS

The first edition of the Old Testament that can in any way be called critical did not appear until the sixteenth century. Along with the complete text, it included a system of markings that represented vowel sounds (Hebrew is a consonantal language), an Aramaic paraphrase of the Hebrew text (Targum), and some of the traditional medieval Jewish commentary. This edition was a marked improvement over those that preceded it. They were based on earlier manuscripts which, as contemporary critical scholarship has shown, were quite limited in comprehension and inferior in legibility and accuracy. The sixteenth-century edition became the norm for most of the Hebrew Bibles until 1929, when members of a German Bible Society published a very sophisticated critical edition. This work, which has undergone periodic revision, continues to enjoy a place of prominence in some circles today. This German edition includes mention of variant readings as well as citations from the Septuagint.

Two discoveries in Egypt at the turn of the century offered the scholarly world a preview of things to come. It was customary in many medieval synagogues to store copies of the sacred texts in a specially designated room, since these texts were not to be destroyed, even when they ceased to be useful. In a Cairo synagogue one such room, or *geniza*, was found to contain a treasury of eleventh- and twelfth-century manuscripts, including several biblical variants. In addition to the biblical and liturgical content of the manuscripts, the material revealed a primitive system for facilitating pronunciation. Studying these findings, scholars have been able to trace the development of vowel pointing, a procedure originally intended to aid public proclamation, which eventually became part of the Hebrew language.

The second discovery was a papyrus manuscript dating from about 150 B.C.E. and containing the Ten Commandments and a liturgical passage from the sixth chapter of Deuteronomy. These findings would have to await the revelation of the Dead Sea Scrolls before their value could be properly assessed and appreciated.

The year 1947 proved to be a milestone in the world of text criticism. In that year ancient scrolls were discovered in caves in the vicinity of the Dead Sea. The first finds occurred at a place known as Qumran. Manuscripts dating as far back as 250–175 B.C.E. were uncovered. Other fragments were found up and down the region of the Dead Sea well into 1964. About 190 manuscripts or fragments have been discovered in sites that date back to the first and second centuries of the Common Era. A comparison of the variant texts shows that the Jewish communities of this time had not yet standardized their traditions. They may have reached some agreement about which books were inspired, but

they also tolerated a great diversity of textual expression.

This extensive material has not yet been completely translated and evaluated. Nonetheless, any critical edition of the Hebrew Scriptures must take into account the knowledge gleaned from these findings if it is to be considered a fully reliable version of the Old Testament.

The history of the Greek version of the Old Testament is no less complicated. As mentioned earlier, the tradition about the seventy scholars working independently yet producing identical translations is now considered legendary. Comparisons of early Hebrew manuscripts with Aramaic Targums and Greek versions have provided invaluable insights. At the same time, such comparisons have left scholars with many new questions. One of the first questions to be addressed is: Was the Greek translation made from the particular Hebrew version that eventually became the standard version known as the Masoretic Text? According to the study of the transmission of the text summarized above, the answer is no. The Masoretic Text, though a careful reconstruction from early manuscripts, does not claim to originate before the Common Era. In addition, the standardization of the Hebrew version apparently did not take place before the second century of that era. The Greek or Alexandrian version, on the other hand, claims a third-century B.C.E. origin. Most likely there was no unified Hebrew tradition used by the translators.

The translation itself shows textual inconsistencies. Most scholars agree that the books of the Pentateuch probably achieved comparative standardization during the postexilic period. That might be true not only of the content but also of the textual form. This standardization could explain why the translation of this material appears to be quite consistent with and faithful to a Hebrew text very similar to the one behind the Masoretic Text. The same is not true of the translation of the other books of the Old Testament; this process probably developed over a period of two hundred years. Since there was no standardization of the Hebrew, there would be no uniformity in the Greek.

One is led to ask a second question: From what was the Greek translated if not from a standardized Hebrew text? There were probably many sources. The first to be considered is the variety of Hebrew renderings which existed along with those that ultimately became the standard texts but which were not themselves included in that group. Translation of the Greek back into Hebrew and a comparison of that Hebrew with the Masoretic Text have led scholars to believe that some of the Hebrew tradition behind the Septuagint is older than that behind the Masoretic Text.

A second source came from the liturgical texts of the community. As Greek became the language of the people and knowledge of Hebrew became less and less common, the people devised a way of translating the Hebrew sounds into Aramaic. In this way they could still pray the Hebrew while reading it in Aramaic. These transliterations were known as Targums. They, too, provided biblical material that could be used in a Greek translation.

Finally, the New Testament itself has thrown some light on this question. As noted earlier, most of the citations from the Old Testament that are found in the New Testament were taken from the Greek version. Retranslating them back into Hebrew has, in some cases, uncovered a version more in line with the Samaritan Pentateuch than with any other extant Hebrew source.

These three examples suggest that when the biblical traditions were being translated into Greek, whatever Hebrew versions were in use at that time and in that place by that community were the ones that were translated. Because the Hebrew tradition was rather fluid, the Greek version would be no less variant.

The second century saw the Christians and the Jews in heated controversy. The Christians frequently used the Septuagint in their arguments, and this led the Jews to reject that version and to produce new translations of their own. Three of those translations played a role in text criticism that their authors and proponents could never have imagined. The third-century Christian writer Origen produced a sixfold version of the Old Testament called the Hexapla. He arranged his material in six parallel columns in this order: (1) the Hebrew consonantal text that was standard in the second century; (2) a Greek transliteration of the Hebrew; (3) Aquila's Greek version (one of the Jewish translations); (4) Symmachus'

Greek version (another Jewish translation); (5) the Septuagint; (6) Theodotion's Greek version (the third Jewish translation). This monumental work has survived in fragments as well as in citations of it made by various early Christian writers.

Of all of the versions of the Old Testament, it was the Septuagint that served as the basis for the major manuscripts. These major manuscripts are the uncial codices that have come down from the fourth to the tenth centuries.

TRANSMISSION OF NEW TESTAMENT TEXTS

Within the last century archaeological findings have unearthed papyrus fragments of New Testament manuscripts that date as early as the second century. Prior to that time the oldest available copies of the New Testament were the great uncial codices mentioned above. There are four major witnesses and several less important works in this category: (1) Codex B or Vaticanus, so named because it has been preserved in the Vatican Library, is probably the oldest, dating from the fourth century. Though it must have once included the entire Greek Bible, it is missing certain sections today. (2) Codex א or Sinaiticus is the only version containing the entire New Testament. Although it, too, dates to the fourth century, it was relatively unknown until the nineteenth century, when it was found at the Monastery of Saint Catherine on Mount Sinai—hence the name. (3) Codex A or Alexandrinus is a fifth-century work. Like the other manuscripts, it is now incomplete. It may have received its name from the city Alexandria, renowned for its school of biblical interpretation. (4) Codex D or Bezae dates from the fifth or sixth century. It lacks an Old Testament as well as some New Testament material. It is a polyglot Bible, that is, it is written in more than one language. The Greek and the Latin are given on facing pages. The work is named after Theodore Beza, the successor of John Calvin.

One other codex might be of interest. It is Codex C or Ephraemi Rescriptus. The very name tells us that rewriting (rescriptus) has occurred. The earlier writing, probably a fifth-century Bible, was scraped off, and the skin was reused in the twelfth century to preserve some of the writings of Ephraem. Such was the fate of many biblical manuscripts. This codex is a famous example of reused manuscripts, called "palimpsests."

As mentioned earlier, the ninth century saw a kind of revolution in writing. Cursive (running hand) began to replace uncial (block) writing. This resulted in a new and quite extensive category of biblical manuscripts that date from the ninth on into the eighteenth century.

In addition to the uncial and minuscule manuscripts, another source of information about the New Testament tradition is evidence from early theological works. Early church writers, such as Eusebius and Clement, cited the Scriptures in their writings. Examination of these citations has been invaluable for text criticism.

Not until the sands of Egypt yielded their papyrus treasures in the late nineteenth century were scholars able to reconstruct a New Testament text that dated earlier than the fourth century. Some of the fragments that have been recently found can be traced to the second century, only a century or less away from the original composition. Although only fragments have been found, they show that at least in second-century Egypt there was no dominant type of New Testament text.

Finally, the importance of ancient liturgical texts is beginning to be appreciated. Since worship played such an important role in forming believers in the biblical tradition, these texts should be very enlightening. Because the study of lectionaries is only in its initial stage, no definite statement can be made at this time about their contribution to the study of the text.

With all the various text sources—uncials, minuscules, citations from early church writers, lectionary readings—how is one to decide on a single text? Certainly the reconstruction of a complete New Testament is more than a subjective selection from various manuscripts. One of the most famous responses to that question is a version known as the Textus Receptus (TR), or "Received Text." The phenomenon of printing perhaps more than the excellence of scholarship brought this work of a printer-editor to the public. Until recently, versions that grew out of this edition remained prominent for many Protestant Christians. However, current scholarship has furnished us with more manuscript evidence, and therefore a truer reconstruction of the text is possible.

One way this has been accomplished is by a process of classifying all the data into categories of families of texts. The quality of the Greek used, the literary style employed, and the content are all evaluated in this process. Once this has been done, editors can confine themselves to manuscripts with similar characteristics as they attempt to reconstruct the text. In the late nineteenth century the New Testament texts were classified into four main groups:

1) Neutral texts were thought to be the earliest and purest forms. They were free from emendations and deliberate reinterpretation, and were considered the common tradition of the entire Eastern church.

2) Alexandrian texts were named for the literary center in Egypt. These texts had considerable style and polish.

3) Western texts were preferred by the Western Christian writers and were clearly edited and interpolated to reflect that bias.

4) Syrian texts were marked by a combination of readings from the other groups. They showed great similarity to the Byzantine tradition.

New archaeological discoveries and diligent reexamination of these categories have resulted in refinements in the classifications. Collation and evaluation of the material have not yet been completed, and so scholars do not yet have all the information necessary to arrive at a consensus regarding the groupings. The present study does not require more detailed information about this field. It is enough to know that steps have been taken to enable scholars to work with a particular textual tradition and thus arrive at as good a text as possible.

This brief summary of the history of the transmission of texts and of the discovery of new evidence is intended to provide some initial explanation for the many versions of the Bible. If contemporary editions appear to be saying quite different things, the reason may be that they have originated from different textual sources. One edition might base its translation on evidence derived from an uncial manuscript, while another judges the Qumran reading as superior. A good critical edition will identify its sources so that the en-

21

lightened reader will know from which text tradition the reading has come.

ANCIENT VERSIONS

As both the Jewish and the Christian religious traditions spread into new areas, the need to translate the original languages became obvious. We have already seen that it was this need that prompted the creation of the Septuagint and other Greek versions. It also led to the formation of Aramaic paraphrases known as Targums. Gradually the original Hebrew and Greek manuscripts of both Testaments, as well as the Septuagint and the Targum versions, were translated into other ancient languages. Chief among these were Syriac, Latin, Coptic, and Ethiopic. Some of these ancient versions continue to play significant roles in the study of the early Bible.

We all know from a study of ancient history that after Alexander the Great conquered the world in the fourth century, Greek culture and the Greek language began to dominate the ancient world. What we may have overlooked is that since about the fifth century B.C.E., Aramaic remained the international language of the Fertile Crescent. This situation endured well into the Common Era. Targums began to appear in the last centuries B.C.E. and on into the medieval period. They continue to be a source of Jewish study today.

In addition to the Samaritan Pentateuch, the Targums, and the Masoretic Text, the *Syriac* writings also stem from the Hebrew version rather than from the Septuagint. Two works from this tradition will be noted. Mention has already been made of Tatian's Diatessaron, the harmonization of the four Gospel accounts into one narrative. This document was the official Syrian Gospel until the fifth century. That same century saw the wide acceptance of a Syriac version of the Old and New Testaments. This Bible is really a blending of several sources. The Old Testament was probably based on the Hebrew version, but with Targumic and Septuagint influences. The New Testament shows several Syrian characteristics. This Bible is known as the Peshitta, the "simple" version.

The most widely known *Latin* version is Jerome's Vulgate, which was the authoritative text of the Roman Catholic Bible from the time of the Council of Trent until recently. Although Jerome was undoubtedly influenced by the Septuagint and some Latin versions stemming from it, the Old Testament section of the Vulgate is a translation from the Hebrew. The New Testament, however, does come from Old Latin versions. Some scholars think that Jerome revised only the Gospels, leaving the rest of the rendition for someone else to complete.

Coptic is an Egyptian language written in the Greek alphabet. This fact would render translation from the Greek much easier than from the Hebrew version of the Old Testament. The Coptic Bible itself does not derive from one tradition but from several recensions, or editorial revisions. This makes the quality of the work rather uneven. As is often the case, the New Testament is more consistent than the Old, probably because fewer New Testament sources were used, and those that were employed were more standardized.

The language of Ethiopia, like Hebrew and Aramaic, is a Semitic language. However, the Old Testament of the *Ethiopic* Bible derives from the Greek version, not the Hebrew. In fact, it is one of the most reliable witnesses to the unrevised Septuagint. The New Testament is the section that shows the most revision and is consequently discounted as a reliable version.

MODERN ENGLISH VERSIONS

The past few decades have seen a proliferation of new English versions of the Bible. A noteworthy development of the ecumenical period in which we live is the interconfessional character of the committees working on the translating and editing of such projects.

One of the most memorable facets of Martin Luther's revolt was the priority he placed on biblical interpretation and the accusations he hurled at the Catholic church for its use (or, according to him, its misuse) of the Scriptures. From that time until the recent past, the Bible has been seen as a kind of measuring stick for one's orthodoxy, each side of the dispute deciding upon the criteria of measurement. While the Protestants encouraged personal reading of the Scriptures and accepted a certain amount of private interpretation, the Catholic church discouraged and even forbade the practice.

It was with great caution that the first English version of the Bible appeared in print. The New Testament appeared at Rheims in 1582, followed by the Old Testament at Douay in 1609. These were the works of English Roman Catholic scholars who had been exiled or fled from their homeland because of religious persecution and settled in France. This version, the Douay-Rheims retained exclusive authoritative status in the Catholic church until 1943, when Pope Pius XII issued the encyclical *Divino Afflante Spiritu*, encouraging Catholic scholars to return to manuscripts written in the original languages in an effort to produce new translations. The Douay-Rheims version of Latin Vulgate manuscripts was in accord with the Council of Trent's designation of that version as authoritative. About 150 years after its appearance, it was revised to bring the English in line with the development that the language had undergone. With the exception of that one revision, the Douay-Rheims remained standard until recent times.

Although the first English Bibles produced by Protestants appeared sometime in the fourteenth century, the one that enjoyed the greatest prominence for the longest time was the King James Version (KJV). It was commissioned by King James I of England and completed in 1611. A careful study of the text reveals that the committee relied heavily on several existing translations, the Rheims New Testament included. Because the Vulgate version was superior to many of the Greek codices available at that time, and because the King James Version was based on editions that relied on the inferior Textus Receptus, which utilized those Greek manuscripts, we can easily see why the King James Version underwent a major revision. The original edition was called the Authorized Version (AV), and the revision, which appeared about 250 years later, came to be known as the Revised Version (RV). The King James Version is renowned for its eloquence and lyrical quality. Quotations from this work have been woven into much of the music and literature of the English-speaking world. The beauty and artistry with which this has been done contribute to the difficulty many people have experienced in accepting a new revision of the text.

Since most of the manuscript discoveries occurred well after the appearance of the King James Version and its Revised Version, a new and even more comprehensive revision seemed in order. Some claim that the Revised Standard Version (RSV), which appeared in 1946, is in fact a new translation because the committee that produced it used all of the new text evidence that was available. Others contend that because the committee was instructed to stay as close to the King James tradition as possible, it must rightly be called a revision. Whatever the case may be, despite initial fundamentalist reaction against relinquishing the King James Version, the Revised Standard Version finally established itself as one of the best English versions of the time. Although the work was done under Protestant auspices, the Revised Standard Version received Catholic ecclesiastical approval in 1966 and has continued to be used by Catholics in educational as well as liturgical settings.

Another edition that has been quite popular in recent years is the Jerusalem Bible (JB), which appeared in 1954. Most of the translation was done from the original languages, yet it was carried out under the direct influence of the French version, *La Bible de Jérusalem*, thus producing what some have called a translation of a translation. This edition is replete with introductions, explanatory notes, and cross references, making it a helpful tool for study.

In 1970 several denominations of the British Isles published the New English Bible (NEB). The project was not bound to any prior biblical version or tradition. It was free to avoid unfamiliar non-English idioms in favor of modern expressions. Evidence from the latest archaeological finds was used, and variant readings are often cited in footnotes. Some of the English is more British than American, but this is to be expected from a British work that attempts to bring the best biblical witness to a contemporary audience.

Finally, the major American Catholic effort at translation has been the New American Bible (NAB). What was begun in 1941 as the Confraternity of Christian Doctrine (CCD) Version was eventually published in 1970 under the new title. Going directly to the best manuscripts in the original languages, the translating committee, which included Protestant scholars, left behind the strictures placed upon Catholic biblical scholarship by the Council of Trent.

All the versions reviewed here have strengths and weaknesses. Some are especially concerned with refinement of translation, and when critical choices have to be made, they tend to sacrifice points of fluency in favor of fidelity to the original. Others opt for a smooth-flowing rendition, forfeiting precision of translation. Still other readings are quite colloquial, a feature which might be beneficial for certain communities but which also limits the version to those groups.

A final point should be made. The Revised Standard Version and the New American Bible are being replaced by new translations. These new versions will be new translations, not revisions of the respective versions. Thus, new and ever more accurate readings of the biblical texts are being produced in order to bring the word of God closer to the people of God.

HERMENEUTICS

INTERPRETATION

One of the most exciting and challenging issues in contemporary biblical study is that of interpretation, or hermeneutics. Not only has it captured the imagination of scholarship, but it has also caused considerable confusion for the general public. Just what precisely *does* the Bible mean? Among the many conflicting interpretations, which one is right? Which school of interpretation or which particular scholar is one to follow? A closer look at this complex and controversial issue, while it certainly will not answer all these questions with satisfaction, may throw some light on the sources of some of the confusion about the meaning of the biblical text.

We must remember that the Bible, as a basic literary reality, is a form of communication comprised of three principal components: a sender or author; a message or text; and a receiver or audience. Historically, as long as the communication recorded in the biblical texts remained within the community of its origin, the audience required very little interpretation. Most of the audience belonged to the same world of meaning as did the author. It was only when a particular biblical message was carried into another world of meaning that extensive efforts of interpreta-

tion became necessary. Inevitably, different understandings resulted, depending primarily upon whether the major interpretative focus was principally on the sender, the message, or the receiver.

The message

It seems that throughout the earliest centuries of Christianity the primary focus of most interpretations was on the message. Hence, the interpretative task was to translate this message into the new world or worlds of meaning. By the Middle Ages four distinct types of interpretation of the message had been developed. They have survived the march of time and continue to influence the way many people today understand the Bible. They are: the literal, the allegorical, the moral, and the eschatological. Since these specific designations may be unfamiliar to the reader, a brief look at each will provide some understanding.

The *literal* sense of a text usually refers to a meaning that the words themselves convey. In this case the text is accepted at face value. Such an understanding implies that the audience immediately grasps all the nuances of the language in the very manner intended by the author. This understanding may be readily available whenever both author and audience share the same world view. However, an audience that holds a very different world view will not so easily grasp the author's intention. The elusiveness of the literal sense becomes obvious when we reflect, for example, on how quickly the meaning of words changes. Parents of teenagers frequently stand dumbfounded as they listen to their children speak an English that has absolutely no meaning for them. Basically, the two worlds of meanings—that of the parents and that of their teenagers—simply do not coincide completely; thus they cannot understand one another fully.

Rigidly literal or fundamentalistic interpretations of biblical texts often fail to take into account the undeniable change and development of language. Biblical fundamentalists seem reluctant to recognize that the world of meaning, the world view of the biblical texts, is not the same as the contemporary one. Add to this the fact that the Bible is the product of a different culture and a different time, and the need for interpretation is magnified. The literal sense of the Bible, then, while it may seem the most reasonable and likely one, is not always arrived at with the ease that some claim.

The *allegorical* sense of Scripture, especially prominent in the early centuries of the Christian era as well as in the Middle Ages, opens the Bible to a myriad of interpretations. According to this approach, the text really intends to say something other than that which its literal wording suggests. The contention is that deeper mystical meanings lie hidden beneath the words. Actually, these alleged deeper meanings usually originate from outside the biblical text itself and are brought to it by interpreters who read meanings into the images and actions of the text from their own world view. For example, the story of Mary of Bethany listening to Jesus while Martha prepares a meal was allegorically interpreted to mean that the contemplative life symbolized by Mary is a higher call than the active life symbolized by Martha. Yet, this was hardly a concern of the original author. Thus, there can be as many allegorical interpretations of one text as there are interpreters with their various points of view. Hence, while a text may yield a rich breadth of meanings, these may seem arbitrary, subjective, and remote from the more immediately apparent message of the text.

In the *moral* sense, the text is understood primarily in terms of the spiritual life of every individual believer. For example, anyone and everyone is Abraham called into a new relationship with God. The political liberation of ancient Israel is understood as really describing the personal freedom that salvation brings to the soul of the individual believer. Although this method of interpretation has frequently been employed by spiritual writers to nourish the interior lives of religious persons, it has serious deficiencies. The Bible's communal sense is frequently lost, and social responsibilities are often overlooked. The historical references are minimized in importance, and the text sometimes seems to be forced to fit an interpreter's predetermined format.

The fourth approach is called *eschatological.* It refers to the spiritual meaning of the text as this pertains to the future heavenly or eschatological realities. According to this sense, the "promised land" is neither historical Israel, as a literal interpretation would indicate, nor the church of Christ, as an allegorical sense might suggest, nor the soul of the redeemed Christian, as the moral sense would assert. It is the future kingdom of heaven. This kind of interpretation, which was so common in the later Middle Ages and well into the modern era, tended to minimize the importance of life in this world. Everything was focused on the next life. Like the moral sense, this manner of understanding principally served the devotional lives of the people. Whether it did justice to the biblical text is an altogether different question.

As stated earlier, these four senses of Scripture continue to influence the way many people today understand the Bible. Some of the current confusion may stem from the diverse perspectives employed in the individual approaches as well as from any mixture of the four. Traces of all these approaches frequently surface in contemporary preaching and are prominent in certain contemporary devotional literature.

The sender

One outgrowth of the Reformation was a persistent attempt to avoid any trace of dogmatic or theological bias in the interpretation of the Bible. Many of the Reformers were particularly critical of the manner in which (they alleged) the Roman church was dealing with the Bible. They insisted that the Bible was being misused to bolster official doctrine not at all rooted in the Bible, and demanded that the original meaning of the text rather than a subjective or denominational interpretation be sought.

This concern brought a halt to the allegorizing tendencies of much of biblical scholarship. While this style of interpretation persisted among Roman Catholics, most Protestant scholars and communities began to stress the historical background of the Bible. Thus began the historical-critical movement, that is, a broad enterprise among predominantly Protestant biblical scholars to seek for the meaning of a biblical text by pursuing a careful investigation and analysis of its historical background. It was not until very recently that this movement gained prominence in

Catholic circles. It had been encouraged since the time of Pope Pius XII (1943) and was given broad endorsement at the Second Vatican Council (Dogmatic Constitution on Divine Revelation).

The focus had now shifted from the multiple meanings of the message or text to the "real" meaning intended by the author. Thus, the biblical scholar now had to be as informed as possible about the circumstances surrounding the origins of the writings. Their historical, cultural, and religious settings took on new importance. The sources employed in their composition, the audiences for which they were intended, and the purposes they were to serve became the subjects that occupied the attention of interpreters.

The results of this shift in method were numerous. The Scriptures, while always recognized as inspired, began to be appreciated as human expressions of the faith of a people. From this human perspective, contemporary women and men could now see their ancient counterparts as being engaged in the very same struggles of life as they themselves were and are. They began to read the biblical narratives with renewed enthusiasm. Biblical theology came to occupy a significant place in their lives. They sought to respond to God's presence in their own history, as their ancestors of biblical times had done. The biblical revival ushered in by the historical-critical movement undoubtedly brought new life to the church.

The study of Scripture quickly became a very sophisticated undertaking. Those untrained in the method frequently grew discouraged with both its demands and some of its first fruits. Some felt that the very foundation of their faith was now being shattered by findings that did not square with their own devotional, allegorical, moral, or eschatological interpretations. Those who did acquire some facility in the approach and could appreciate its value, however, soon had to acknowledge its inadequacies. They could see that it was not enough to know the theology of the past. The questions they were grappling with had to do with the applicability of the biblical message to the present: Does biblical theology have any relevance for our day? If so, how is one to translate into the present a theological message of another era, another culture, another world view?

These questions led scholars to look beyond historical criticism and to turn to the issue of hermeneutics, or interpretation. But even this turn did not seem to be enough. More radical and more comprehensive questions were surfacing. Did revelation only occur thousands of years ago? Are we merely to reenact in our lives the saving events of the past? A second significant interpretative shift was about to take place.

The receiver

Attention is now being focused on the receiver, or the audience. This means that the contemporary interpreter and the act of interpreting have now become the objects of the analysis. The historical-critical method assumes that an objective understanding of the original meaning is possible. Such a position ignores the fact that the interpreter comes to the text with historical and religious biases. The new methods of interpretation admit that the way the text is understood depends to a large extent upon the socio-political and religious perspectives of the interpreter. Thus, for example, people from a situation of political, economic, or religious oppression will view the Bible quite differently than will those from a secure and comfortable vantage point.

This new approach is only in its infancy and therefore cannot yet be adequately evaluated. However, some very exciting and challenging results have already been achieved. Women and men are beginning to appreciate their own lives as the stage wherein revelation, as authentic as that revelation described in the biblical texts, is taking place. Biblical spirituality is no longer concerned exclusively with the individual. It has reclaimed its communal dimension.

CONTEMPORARY HERMENEUTICS

Another way to approach the question of interpretation is to distinguish between what the Bible *means* and what the Bible *meant*. As mentioned earlier, this is no problem when the authors and the audiences share the same worlds of meaning. It becomes an issue when cross-cultural and/or cross-generational communication no longer guarantee a common understanding. The professional scholars engaged in contemporary hermeneutics span a wide spectrum of positions regarding the major focus of these two poles. Some hold that the *real* meaning is that intended by the original author (what the Bible *meant*). Others contend that once a piece of literature leaves the hands of the author, it enjoys a life of its own, independent of authorial intention (what the Bible *means*). Most contemporary hermeneutical approaches can be found somewhere between these two poles, bridging the gap between the authorial intention and a present-day context.

Scholars today refer to authorial intention (what the Bible *meant*) as the literal sense. It is important to be clear as to the precise meaning of this designation. This way of understanding takes the words at face value, but it takes them as they were intended by the original author(s) or editor(s), not primarily as they have come to be understood today. A fundamentalist reading of Scripture understands the words in a literal sense too, but it ascribes contemporary meaning to them. The presupposition operative in this approach, though often unconsciously, is that today's world of meaning is identical with that of the ancient writers. A fundamentalist position claims to be able to arrive at the literal meaning merely by reading the text. Critical scholars, on the other hand, insist that extensive, precise historical analysis is required if the authors' world of meaning is to be unlocked. This critical analysis encompasses a large number of distinct but related methodologies. The principal ones will be discussed below.

Concentration on what the Bible *means* has led many scholars into studies that are less historical and more literary in character. Various literary theories have been examined and employed in biblical interpretation. This trend has led to further analysis of literary forms, study of the meaning of symbols, and probing into the very nature of language itself as a means of communication. Unlike historical studies, which strive to learn more about the world of the author in order to discover the original meaning, literary studies inevitably open the text to a plurality of meanings.

Without denying the importance and validity of each of these two approaches, many scholars believe that neither one is sufficient in itself. They insist that the Scriptures are more than literary works—they are also inspired tradition of an ongoing believing community. Thus, the literal sense plays a norma-

tive role in helping the present-day community come to an understanding of its identity and to an appreciation of the kind of lifestyles that should flow from that identity. If this is true, however, then different historical and/or cultural contexts will reinterpret and restate these biblical traditions in various ways. The result will be a plurality of valid meanings. The challenge of contemporary hermeneutics is to devise a method that will take both of these approaches into consideration. Such a method will be equipped to faithfully transmit the inspired tradition. Thus, a particular valid expression of the meaning of the text will function as the word of God, forming a new people into a community of believers.

HISTORICAL-CRITICAL APPROACHES

The phrase "historical-critical method" or "historical criticism" has been used so loosely and erroneously that the designation has become ambiguous and the usefulness of the interpretative approach has been questioned. As understood here, it is an approach that employs every available historical tool in an attempt to reconstruct history and to understand the documents which that history produced. Its goal is historical, and it works toward that goal critically and systematically. It seeks to understand and to interpret but not to judge the findings.

The nineteenth century saw a broadscale revolution in historical consciousness and the birth of a new historical theory. This led to the development of critical tools for studying the past. Sacred texts could not escape the critical eye of this kind of investigation. Soon believing communities were torn between the excitement of new discoveries, new interpretations, and new challenges to faith and the fear that what was exciting was also a potential threat to that faith. What had been cherished as "truth" was now questioned as "myth." Longstanding practices were viewed as irrelevant and lacking historical foundations.

Although there are still people who reject this critical approach as "faithless," it has come to be generally accepted. However, this acceptance does not imply that the historical methods have answered all the questions of interpretation. As a matter of fact, scholars now are becoming more and more convinced of their inadequacy. They are beginning to realize that more was expected of these methodologies than they could offer. The approach may succeed at addressing the historical issues, but it certainly is not adequate to uncover the theological issues. Realizing this, scholars continue to employ these historical methods, but not in a manner exclusive of other critical approaches.

Both biblical research and biblical spirituality are indebted to the historical approach. It has provided the believing community with critical editions of the Bible that far outstrip earlier editions in textual reconstruction and translation. It has thrown light on the life and history of both ancient Israel and early Christianity. It has brought the people of those times into sharper focus, enabling the reader to see them as real people whose concerns and dreams can be understood. It has revealed the depth of faith and the complexity and power of the religion of the believing communities.

Textual criticism

The function of textual criticism is twofold: (1) to reconstruct the original wording of a biblical text; (2) to trace the transmission of that text down through the centuries. The first goal is an impossible one. Since the autograph, or original copy, of every book of the Bible has been lost, the best that scholars can do is to reconstruct the text from manuscripts that are available. This task guarantees no historical certainty because of the inconsistency that exists in the manuscript material. It is by comparing manuscripts that scholars develop what is called a "critical text." This is a hypothetical reconstruction, usually accompanied by extensive footnotes (called critical apparatus) that indicate the manuscript sources of the passages as well as alternative readings. Modern translations are based on just such critical texts.

The second goal is also achieved by a comparison of texts, but with a different end in view. Reconstruction is a move backward toward one reading; the history of textual transmission is a search forward for variant readings that will enable the scholar to trace the change and development that took place. Origen's sixfold work called the Hexapla may well be the earliest attempt at such a textual criticism. It provides evidence of the changes that occurred as the text developed.

Since no manuscript contains the original text, all are more or less corrupt. The question is not which reading is reliable but in which way it is reliable. Every text reflects the period of history and the specific community from which it originated and within which it survived. Critical examination of the text and comparison with the variant texts tell us something about that period of history and that particular community. The translations reviewed in the previous chapter perform that same function. They reveal the particular stage of critical scholarship at which the community has arrived, the current stage of the language into which the text has been translated, and frequently some theological issues that the community must address.

This particular discipline requires expertise not only in the original languages but in related languages as well. Literature from cultures other than the biblical communities is studied in order to understand these biblical communities in the broader context of their respective worlds. While few people may devote themselves to this kind of research, the findings that derive therefrom must be considered by both translator and interpreter. Before any other interpretative step can be taken, the best possible rendition of the text must be established.

Much of the history of textual criticism, as well as explanations of the major manuscript sources and traditions, has been discussed in the previous section and need not be treated here.

Literary criticism

The term "literary criticism" is understood in at least three different ways. (1) In the classical sense it is the critical approach to the study of the literature. The structure, form, and language are analyzed. Such critique was brought to bear on biblical material, and as early as the time of Origen it led scholars to question the supposed authorship of some of the biblical books. (2) With the rise of historical consciousness in the nineteenth century, historical questions were being asked about literary differences, and the discipline came to be called "source criticism" by some. (3) Recently scholars have again been asking questions of a more literary nature, questions dealing with the relationship of content to form and with the philosophy of language.

Literary criticism in the traditional biblical sense actually grew out of a textual study. After noticing the use of different names for God in the Book of Genesis, an eighteenth-century scholar discovered literary patterns in that book. He concluded that the book had been composed of various preexisting sources. Eventually the explanation for the composition of the Pentateuch came to be known as the "Documentary Hypothesis" (four sources were "discovered": the Yahwist, the Elohist, the Deuteronomic, and the Priestly). Similarly, the explanation for the differences in the gospel tradition was called the "Two-Source Hypothesis" (it maintained that the Gospel of Mark and a collection of sayings known as Q were used by both Matthew and Luke). Once scholars believed that there were various sources for the biblical texts, they began to ask questions about their origins, their life settings, and the reason for their composition. Literary criticism thereby became a historical discipline.

With all the questions that were answered, literary criticism also raised some new ones that it seemed unable to address. The door was open to a new discipline that would address those questions. (New literary criticism will be explained later.)

Form criticism

The function of form criticism is to get behind the sources identified by literary criticism and to discover the life situations out of which they grew. Literary or source criticism may well be interested in authorship, but it still identifies this author in the singular. Form criticism, on the other hand, is interested in the original settings in the life of the community. It discovers these settings by identifying and analyzing the typical forms of expression found within the existing literature. Although it begins as a literary approach, its intent is to discover the historical setting and the historical function of the forms in order to understand their pre-literary (oral) stage.

Ancient Israel was probably not a highly literate culture. Thus, its oral forms of communication were most likely quite conventional. This would mean that before they attained literary form, these forms achieved a quite consistent oral expression. Such expressions were very much a part of the ordinary life of the community. Recognizing and interpreting these forms is the first step in gaining insight into that life.

In order to accomplish their task, form critics first examine the structure of the text so as to isolate the individual units of which it is composed. These units are then classified according to genre, or literary type. This classification leads directly to conclusions about the setting. Setting here does not refer to geographic location or to specific dating; rather, it refers to sociocultural situations that may or may not include a particular social or religious structure. For example, a study of the psalms of lament can tell us much, while at the same time leaving many things unanswered. A lament points to a human situation that may or may not be identified. These psalms frequently speak of social corruption and oppression or national calamity, although they also complain of personal misfortune. We know that psalms were part of the temple liturgy, but their use was not restricted to that site or to official liturgy. Thus, a lament reflects human suffering, but it is not always specific about that suffering. It suggests liturgical practice, but it was not limited to formal ritual. It was associated with the temple, but its use was not restricted to that religious institution.

The final step in the analysis of a particular form is to determine just what the genre was meant to accomplish within the community. Was the lament intended to inspire confidence in God? To offer a legitimate avenue for complaint? To serve as an admission of guilt and an acknowledgment of repentance?

Form criticism may appear to some to be a negative process, breaking down the biblical story. In fact, its goal is positive: to reconstruct the oral tradition behind the literary narrative. The forms are seen as the remnants of the early tradition. Hence, matching the fabrics, blending the colors, and discovering the designs enable scholars to detect something of the original piece.

As literary criticism grew out of textual study, so form criticism addresses questions that literary or source criticism could not answer—questions about origins and settings and reasons behind composition. But, like its predecessor, this discipline also had its limitations. It may have been able to identify the forms of the literary work, but it could not explain how they became part of the whole. Form criticism could take the text apart but could not put it back together. It would take tradition criticism to do that.

Tradition criticism

Tradition criticism, or tradition history, as it is sometimes called, is an analysis of the history of the transmission process of the traditions. It is that discipline which traces the growth and development of traditions as this process was described in the first section of this article. While form criticism locates the life-settings of the units, tradition criticism attempts to describe what happened within those settings. It is interested in what shaped the tradition as it was preserved and handed down, and it seeks to trace this development. Hence the name tradition *history*. Although it is really concerned with the process of transmission, it does examine the tradition that is being transmitted, primarily the oral stage of that tradition. (Redaction criticism examines the literary stages of this development. Some scholars treat redaction as a step in the tradition-history approach.)

The recurrence of similar motifs or forms makes tradition criticism possible. Various examples are analyzed in order to detect significant differences. (This process differs from form criticism, which highlights similarities.) Having uncovered the differences, the next step is to ascertain whether or not these differences are the result of development and, if so, to hypothesize as to the cause of that development. It is difficult enough to reconstruct literary history. When one is exploring the oral stages of a tradition, there is even less solid evidence available, and scholars must be on their guard lest their reconstructions be far afield of what the text actually says.

As scholars discover why the believing community preserved the traditions in the forms that it did and why these traditions went through the changes that occurred, they are able to reconstruct the tradition history of the community. In addition to this, their study also uncovers information that can be called historical, in the strict sense of that term. Streams of tradition have been found to be associated with one or another community or group, for example, the prophets or the Lukan community. Examining these streams of tradition brings one into contact with that group, with its preferences, its strategies, and its influence. Frequently traditions are also associated with specific locations. Jerusalem is a case in point. The more one knows about the site, the better one is able to reconstruct the traditioning process that took place there. All of this can aid in the discovery of the socio-political as well as the religious dynamics at work in the growth and development of the traditions.

The fruits of tradition criticism can perhaps be more directly appreciated by the average believer than can the findings of other disciplines that have so far been described. They tell us how ancient Israel understood its history. (Because the traditioning process that resulted in the New Testament took place in a considerably shorter span of time, it is usually studied under the heading of redaction criticism. Tradition criticism has become primarily an Old Testament discipline.) It also shows how significant events in that history have become types for understanding other experiences; for example, Exodus typology is often used to describe the Exile. Finally, tradition criticism shows how Israel understood the revelation of God. It was within the very process of tradition formation that Israel discerned the activity of God. As the community struggled to retain the validity of its inspired traditions within new situations and at new times, it recognized the active and directive involvement of God.

Redaction criticism

Redaction criticism is devoted to the study of how written sources were used by an editor or redactor and what this interpretative editing says about the theological interests of the redactor. This discipline is like tradition criticism, for both are concerned to show how stages of development gave new shapes to the tradition. Redaction criticism, however, is concerned with the literary rather than the oral stages. As tradition criticism is primarily an Old Testament discipline, redaction criticism developed in conjunction with New Testament study. Its principal focus is on the final literary form, the form that has come down to us.

It has been in Gospel studies that redaction criticism has provided the greatest insights. By comparing episodes from one synoptic Gospel with parallels that appear in the other two Gospels, redaction critics are able to discern the theological point of view of the evangelist. In this way they have contributed to our knowledge of the theological history of early Christianity.

NEW CRITICAL APPROACHES

Over the years the critical methods summarized above underwent constant development and refinement. Within recent years, however, new areas of interest have been probed, new analyses have been employed, and new information has been gathered. This is true with regard to both the historical approach and the more strictly literary analysis.

Sociological approaches

Sociology has come to be understood in two distinct but related ways. In the broad sense, it is the study of society. This would include the social sciences, such as sociology itself, anthropology, economics, political science, etc. In the narrow sense, sociology is concerned with the origin, development, and patterns of social behavior.

Traditional historical criticism produced detailed studies of the social realities of ancient Israel and of early Christianity (sociology in the broad sense). Scholars focused on the structures of social life and used available research methods to gather the data. Archaeology was invaluable in this approach, providing artifacts, literature, and official documents that were scrutinized, classified, and interpreted. The unearthed findings were compared with similar material belonging to other ancient cultures. Although some comparative studies proved valuable, the material analyzed had been lifted from its unique social context and was presumed to have in its own context the meaning and importance of similar material in another context. In addition, the social theories of the day determined the framework of interpretation. Prominent among these theories was the evolutionary perspective that frequently equated change and development with growth and improvement. Thus, sociological investigations were focused on the development of religion and religious structures and not on the dynamic at play.

The turn of the century saw scholars asking sociological questions and developing sociological methods to answer them. The social sciences had come of age, and sociology in the narrow sense (the sense in which it will be meant henceforth) began to make its impact not only in scholarly circles but in the world at large. This new study encouraged biblical scholars to employ sociological approaches in their investigation of the Scriptures.

Sociological study of the Scriptures is still in its early stages, and so it is difficult to evaluate its contributions. However, significant insights have already come to light. An understanding of the social and political structures of ancient Israel have underscored the role that prophets played in critiquing that society and have furthered an appreciation of the prophetic message. Studies of first-century Roman society have shown the Christian church as a unique and challenging community of equals.

One of the branches of anthropology, a second sociological field, has had a profound impact on the literary study of the Scriptures. That branch is linguistics, or the study of the structure of language. Out of it has developed structural exegesis, or structuralism. Unlike the historical-critical methods, which investigate the historical process and seek to discover the original meaning of the text, structural methods search for the meaning within the language itself rather than within the historical event beyond the language. In this way they share the same focus as does the new literary criticism.

Perhaps one of the most important insights that sociological approaches have brought to biblical studies is the realization that not only does the text have a special social context or contexts out of which it grew, but the interpreters also operate with social biases. All contexts have assumptions and pre-understandings that must be admitted if there is to be any cross-cultural and/or cross-generational communication. Just as one cannot presume that language has the same meaning in every context, one cannot expect that social structures or dynamics always play the same roles.

Canonical criticism

A second new development in biblical study, known as canonical or canon criticism, is only a little more than a decade old. Its interest is the biblical text in its canonical or final form and the role which that form plays in the faith of the community. It seeks to trace the development of the canon from the beginnings of tradition formation through the stages of interpretation, the selection and organization of material in the formation of a biblical book, and the final decisions that determine canonicity. It differs from tradition criticism (which is interested in the same development) in that it is not concerned with the historical dynamics that shaped the tradition but with the hermeneutical methods that were employed in the shaping. This does not make canonical criticism just another historical method, for its goal is not historical but theological.

Since it was interpretation that brought earlier traditions alive in a new setting, a study of the principles of interpretation should uncover how this was done. Proponents of this approach believe that the methods employed in the formation of the Bible might well be used by contemporary believers as they seek to do the same thing that was done by their ancestors, namely, to bring earlier traditions alive in new settings. Thus, the Bible can be read not merely as literature but also as the Sacred Scripture that it is.

Although scholars acknowledge that interpretative principles were employed by the different communities throughout the stages of tradition growth and development, they do not have a clear record of them. Only by applying the methods of historical and literary criticism, the very methods that have been described here, can scholars hope to bring these principles to light. The more that is known about each stage of development, the easier it will be to discern the process of development and the principles that guided that process.

It is clear that context, whether sociopolitical or religious, plays a major role in this approach. One must attend to the context when analyzing the meanings of the past as well as when arriving at meanings for the present. When a tradition of the past encountered new concerns or a new context, it was reinterpreted according to some theological perspective. In a similar manner, if that tradition is to be shaped anew in an authentic and meaningful way, it behooves the interpreter to accurately comprehend the contemporary situation. One's view of reality will influence, if not determine, the shape that the tradition will take. For example, the covenant theme might be used to assure a comfortable society that its security is a sign of God's good pleasure and it has every right to cling to it. On the other hand, it might challenge that society to assume its responsibilities to the less fortunate and to redistribute its resources in the name of social justice. The deepest needs of the community (assurance or challenge) must be recognized.

Although still in its initial stages, this approach to interpretation has generated quite a bit of excitement. Many hope that it will be a way of bridging the gap between what the Bible *meant* and what the Bible *means* today.

New literary criticism

New literary criticism seeks to understand the Bible strictly as literature. The historical issues that relate the material to its origin are ignored. The world that interests this critic is not some world of the past but the imaginative world created by the literary piece itself. To understand this world, one does not consult archaeology, sociology, or source criticism but rather the language and forms used, the structures created, and the literary movements developed within the work. To say that the world of a literary piece is imaginative does not mean that it is unreal. Rather, it means that the work does not claim to describe reality as it is; it imitates reality. Its integrity is not determined by its historical accuracy but by its internal harmony.

If the imaginative world of literature is an imitation of the historical world of reality, then the components of which the world is fashioned are not historically real but stand for historical reality. They are all basically metaphorical, analogous to something else. Clues to what they represent are not found outside the work but within it. The interpretation of these clues is to be sought within the scope of the genre or literary form to which the piece belongs. Because a genre is not so much a set of meanings as it is a set of relationships, every literary piece is open to a plurality of interpretations. There is little if any external control over the interpretation, and so one must hold strictly to the patterns set by the genre. Although a literary work may allow for several different renderings, this does not mean that its analysis can be done in a haphazard manner or that it can mean anything the interpreter wants it to mean. For example, a play can have different interpretations, but its internal relationships set certain limits. The same is true for sonnets, limericks, parables, miracle stories.

This kind of literary criticism has itself undergone stages of development. At first texts were characterized as windows through which the interpreter could look to the meaning beyond. Later other critics saw them more as mirrors within which meaning was to be found. Contemporary critics choose to see the text functioning as both window and mirror. Its meaning is to be found within itself, but not in such a way as to confine the reader to it. Good literature takes the reader beyond itself. This interpretative approach enables the critic to discover what the text *means*, but with no regard for what it *meant*.

TOWARD DEVELOPING A WAY OF INTERPRETATION

Clearly, interpretation is more than just the gathering of information about a text (narrow historical criticism). It is an explanation of the meaning of that text. And when the text in question is revered as the sacred tradition of a believing community, a tradition that is somehow rooted in the self-identity of that community, some kind of historical continuity with that ongoing community seems essential for correct interpretation. The following is an example of how both historical and literary approaches can contribute toward developing a way of interpreting the biblical text as Scripture (sacred tradition) and not merely as literature.

Returning to the model of communication described at the beginning of this section, one can focus on the sender, the message, or the audience. Another way of understanding this triad is to speak of three worlds: the world out of which the text grew; the world created by the text itself; and the world of the reader. Each world is independent of the others. However, the world of the text is indebted to the world out of which it grew for its structure and for the fundamental meaning which that structure projects. This does not mean that the text is restricted to the original meaning and cannot generate a plurality of legitimate meanings. The new literary criticism has shown that this can be done. "Indebtedness to the world out of which it grew," as used here, means that the scope of the possible interpretations was broadly set by the original context. That world intended to articulate a message (the original meaning), and it fashioned the text in such a way as to communicate that message. For example, the prophets chastised the nation through the use of an oracle of judgment. That literary form (the oracle of judgment) limits the number of ways in which the literary piece can be interpreted.

Interpretation can be defined as the meeting of the world of the reader with the world of the text in a way that the meaning of the text takes hold of the reader. This meaning may or may not be the original meaning of the text—that will depend upon whether or not the interpreter used historical or literary approaches. According to the new literary criticism, with the exception of the choice of form and all the internal relationships that are intrinsic to that form, the world out of which the text grew need play no part in the interpretation. However—and this is a most important point—the Bible is a unique kind of literature. It is the inspired word of God. No believer will deny that it is revelatory, but is its revelatory character in any way dependent upon the original meaning? In other words, is the original meaning normative? And if it is normative, in what way? The present study contends that the original meaning is indeed normative, and it explains this normative quality in the following way.

Just as during its growth and development the tradition contributed to the shaping of a believing community, it has not ceased to perform that same wonder down through the centuries. That is, it has given witness to the community's identity and has continually awakened that community to its purpose. This took place in the process of the community's reshaping of the tradition as that tradition had been handed down to it. The interpretation or understanding of the tradition that the community received may not have been identical with the tradition's original meaning (fidelity to the covenant might call for different responses in different circumstances). However, the meaning received was the meaning that had been preserved for it and transmitted to it, and it was the meaning that the community considered the correct expression of its understanding of its own identity. It appears that throughout the process of tradition formation, the believing community exercised a good deal of creative freedom. This freedom was restricted, however, by the concept of self-identity that it inherited from the preceding generation. Although different generations may have understood and expressed this identity in various ways, they safeguarded its essence. Each generation had to grasp this essence and then restate it in ways that were expressive of its time. From this point of view, the original meaning can be understood to be normative, while subsequent meanings can also enjoy validity.

A point that must be kept in mind is the role played by the believing community in determining the validity or appropriateness of various meanings. The *community* is the carrier of the tradition. The *community* is the agent of creative reinterpretation. Thus, while the interpretation of the Bible as literature might be done by any critic, only the believing community can interpret it as revelatory Scripture, because the refashioning of tradition takes place within a believing community.

Interpretation has been defined as the meeting of the world of the reader with the world of the text. The reader brings a particular perspective or understanding of life to the text; the text articulates the community's received tradition. The meaning of that tradition is shaped by the reader's perspective and in turn takes hold of the reader. In this way the tradition gives witness to the community's identity and is itself reshaped in the process.

GENESIS

Pauline A. Viviano

INTRODUCTION

The Book of Genesis often confronts us as an antiquated work of literature containing stories of questionable value for our sophisticated civilized world. And yet, because it forms a part of the Bible, we feel that it should say something to us, something about God that transcends time and place. Part of the problem in finding meaning in the Book of Genesis is the vast distance between the world that produced Genesis—a pre-scientific, Eastern world—and our own world, characterized by a scientific, Western approach to reality. To understand the Book of Genesis, we must enter its world, determine what it meant in its time, and only then can we venture to say what it means now for our world.

In this commentary we will interpret the Book of Genesis against its historical background. To do so, we will draw upon the discoveries of archaeology and the critical tools of literary analysis. Before turning to the biblical text itself, however, we want to discuss how the Book of Genesis came to be written and the forms in which it is written.

The formation of the Book of Genesis

The Book of Genesis is the story of the prehistory of Israel. Israel became a nation only when it came to occupy and rule the land of Canaan. This nation came to identify itself as a federation of tribes in covenant with a God who had brought their ancestors out of Egypt and led them to the Promised Land. The Exodus was interpreted as the moment of birth for this nation. But as these tribes consolidated

their traditions that spoke of the actions of God in their past, they began to realize that even before the time of the Exodus, God was at work leading them to that moment. The Exodus came to be viewed as the culmination of a process that started when God first called Abraham and promised to make him a great nation.

Eventually Israel began to view its own history in the context of world history, and joined to the story of its origins the story of the beginnings of the universe and the history of humanity in the primeval period. It is important to recognize that this process took centuries. Stories were told and retold, adapted and reinterpreted. They were given a new context and acquired new meaning. These stories grew and developed beyond their original telling until they found their way into the larger story of Israel's relationship to God. The Book of Genesis bears the imprint of this long process of growth.

Scholars began to pay close attention to the formation of the Pentateuch (the first five books of the Bible) when it was recognized that there were two different Hebrew names given to the Deity in the Book of Genesis, namely, Yahweh, the personal name of Israel's God, and Elohim, translated simply God. The presence of these different names in various stories coincided with differences in style and vocabulary in the stories in which they appeared. Contradictions within stories (for example, compare Gen 6:19 with 7:2), which had long puzzled scholars, were resolved when these stories were divided, on the basis of the use of the divine name, into what were originally two independent traditions or sources. Further support for this theory about two or more separate traditions is evident in the occurrence of two, and sometimes three, versions of the same story (Gen 12:10-20/ Gen 20/Gen 26:1-11).

By careful analysis of the data, scholars were led to conclude that there were at least four different authors who contributed to the formation of the Pentateuch. These are identified as the Yahwist (J), Elohist (E), Priestly (P), and Deuteronomic (D) authors, also referred to as "sources" or "traditions." Of these four authors, only the Yahwist, Elohist, and Priestly are to be found in the Book of Genesis; thus we will omit from our discussion the Deuteronomic source.

The YAHWIST source (J) is so called because it uses the name Yahweh (spelled *Jahweh* in German, hence the abbreviation J) for the Deity. The Yahwist is the earliest of the sources, originating in the tenth century B.C.E., the age of David and Solomon. The stories of the Yahwist tradition are characterized by a vivid folk-tale style and a colorful portrayal of characters, setting the Yahwist apart as an author of great skill. The author allows the actions of the characters to speak for themselves and rarely passes moral judgment on their behavior. The anthropomorphic presentation of God in the Yahwist tradition gives a very personal character to the Deity. For the Yahwist, God is actively involved in the history of humanity and, in particular, in Israel's history. The Yahwist begins the story with creation (Gen 2:4b-31), presenting the history of humanity as the background against which Yahweh calls Abraham and extends to him a promise that is fully realized only by the Exodus and the conquest of Canaan. The theme of promise and fulfillment is dominant in the Yahwist's presentation of patriarchal history.

The ELOHIST (E) uses the name Elohim for Israel's God until Exod 3:14, where the name Yahweh is revealed to Moses. This source is generally dated in the ninth century B.C.E. and is believed to have originated in the northern kingdom. The Elohist source has been so intertwined with the Yahwist that it is difficult to separate the two sources in all instances. Since the Elohist source has been subordinated to the Yahwist, what remains of the Elohist narrative is often incomplete. Where we do find a complete story, for example Gen 22, the Elohist is seen to be an author of some skill. The Elohist resorts to dreams and angels as means of divine communication rather than allowing direct contact with the Deity, as does the Yahwist. The Elohist is most noted for his moral sensitivity, which is evident in his attempts to justify, explain, or gloss over the misdeeds of Israel's ancestors. The Elohist begins his story in the patriarchal period, and can be found for the first time in Gen 20, though perhaps in fragmentary form as early as Gen 15.

The PRIESTLY author (P) also prefers the name Elohim for the Deity until the time of Moses (Exod 6). Though the actual writing of the Priestly work is to be dated during the period of the Babylonian Exile (ca. 550 B.C.E.), the sources used by this author come from a much earlier period. The Priestly style tends to be repetitive, and his stories are rigidly structured, giving a very solemn tone to his work. The Priestly author preserves the transcendent character of God by avoiding anthropomorphisms in his portrayal of the Deity. The Book of Genesis opens with the Priestly account of creation. This author is responsible for the genealogies that form the framework of the Book of Genesis. The chronological format imposed on the Pentateuch also derives from the Priestly author.

It is generally held that the Priestly author is responsible for the final editing of the Book of Genesis. It has been theorized that the Priestly tradition incorporates the earlier Yahwist and Elohist narratives. However, there is some evidence to suggest that a later redactor, or editor, actually combined the Yahwist, Elohist, and Priestly writings. This commentary will accept the presence of these three sources in the Book of Genesis and will often refer to the final form or context of a story. Whether that final form or context comes from the Priestly author or a later redactor will be left an open question.

Forms in the Book of Genesis

In interpreting the Book of Genesis, we cannot ignore the forms in which it is written. Interpretation rests upon form. If we hear a story that begins "Once upon a time . . . ," we have no difficulty in recognizing that the story is a fairy tale; we would never mistake it for history, because we know its form. But the forms of the Book of Genesis are no longer common knowledge. Scholars in this past century have delineated and identified the forms in the Book of Genesis. Since this commentary is built upon their work, it is important to "rediscover" the forms in the Book of Genesis.

Narrative is the primary literary classification that we find in the Book of Genesis. A narrative is simply a story. To refer to the form of the Book of Genesis as story is not to devalue the book nor to minimize in any way its theological significance. Indeed, Israel's most distinctive way of speaking of the Deity is to tell the story of God's acts in its life as a nation.

The dominant form of narrative in the Book of Genesis is the saga. Sagas are stories that have a basis in fact, but as the stories are transmitted, they are expanded and enhanced by non-factual elements. Sagas originate at an oral level combining tradition and imagination. It is not unusual to find reported in a saga the direct intervention of God in human affairs. In a saga the incredible is simply part of the flow of events. Sagas may explain why something is the way it is (etiological sagas), why something or someone has a particular name (etymological sagas), why tribes relate as they do (ethnological sagas), why certain places or actions are considered holy (cult sagas), or why a particular locale has unique characteristics (geological sagas). All of these types of sagas are evident in the Book of Genesis.

In the patriarchal sagas of Genesis, the world is seen in terms of families. Jacob is no longer Jacob, he is Israel; Esau is the father of the Edomites. The history of the relationship between these tribes becomes the story of the relationship between these brothers. The patriarchs are characters larger than life. They no longer represent historical persons but become the embodiment of the characteristics of their tribes.

Many individual sagas have been joined together to form the story of the patriarchs. These stories have become a part of a larger context, and so their original meaning is changed. As we work our way through the stories, we will pay particular attention to the levels of meaning acquired by a story as it became a part of the Book of Genesis.

Scholars continue to debate about the presence of myth in the Book of Genesis. Whether or not they find myth in Genesis depends upon their definition of myth. The common definition of myth as a story about gods and goddesses excludes myth from the Bible, because Israel accepts only Yahweh as its God. But myth need not be so narrowly defined. Myth is a way of thinking about reality. What distinguishes myth is that it speaks of reality symbolically in terms of interacting divine powers in the primal era. These powers continue to affect our world through the cult.

The dominant form of expression among Israel's neighbors was myth. It was inevitable that Israel would appropriate the mythological motifs of the ancient Near East. However, Israel did not simply absorb the mythology of the nations that surrounded it; their mythology was changed and adapted to suit Israel's distinctive view of God and the world. We will find, particularly in Gen 1–11, mythological motifs that Israel borrowed but transformed. There are other forms in the Book of Genesis, but we will attend to these in context in the commentary itself.

COMMENTARY

THE PRIMEVAL HISTORY

Gen 1:1–11:27

The first eleven chapters of the Book of Genesis are designated "primeval history" because they treat of the history of humanity, and not specifically of the history of Israel. The universalist perspective of the Yahwist is seen in the placement of Israel's history within the larger context of human history, beginning with creation. The Yahwist narrative is now introduced and supplemented by the traditions of the Priestly author, but the overriding theme is still that of the Yahwist: humanity, because of sin, moves further and further from its God.

THE PRIESTLY CREATION ACCOUNT

Gen 1:1–2:4a

The Book of Genesis opens with a highly structured, hymnlike account of creation by the Priestly author. Though there are similarities between this account and the Babylonian creation account, the *Enuma Elish*, the Priestly author has reinterpreted and rewritten the ancient myth to reflect Israel's distinctive theology. In contrast to the *Enuma Elish*, creation does not result from conflict. There is no war between the gods, there is nothing that opposes God. Instead, we are informed, in a carefully ordered sequence, that God creates the world solely by the power of the divine word.

1:1-25 The creation of the world. The opening verse identifies God as the main actor, and creation as the result of God's action. In addition, the opening verse tells us that prior to God's creative act the world was a formless mass, existing as a watery chaos. This description of the world is in agreement with the mythology of the ancient Near East. Notice that darkness exists—it is not created by God. The origin of darkness, which symbolized evil and terror in the ancient world, is left in mystery. The abyss was the primordial ocean, which had to be "harnessed" for creation to occur. Upon this watery chaos the wind of God begins to act. The Hebrew text literally reads "wind of God," not "mighty wind" as in the New American Bible (v. 2). While the translation "mighty wind" captures some of the sense of the original, it fails to take account of the fact that God is the source of this wind.

The Priestly account of creation is characterized by repetition. By using a framework that remains more or less constant for each day of creation, the author achieves a maximum of repetition, with enough variation to keep the account moving forward at a rhythmic pace. This rhythm gives the account its hymnlike quality. A tone of solemnity pervades the entire creation account. The repeated framework is as follows:

1. *Announcement:* "And God said . . ."
2. *Command:* "Let there be . . ."
3. *Report:* "And it was so . . ."
4. *Evaluation:* "And God saw that it was good . . ."
5. *Temporal framework:* "It was evening, it was morning . . ."

In addition to this structural pattern, the author correlates the acts of creation of the last three days with those of the first three days.

Day 1	Light
Day 2	Sky, separating the upper and lower waters
Day 3	Earth and vegetation
Day 4	Heavenly lights
Day 5	Birds and fish
Day 6	Land animals and humanity

The creation of light on the first day is correlated with what gives light on the fourth day. Correspondingly, the sky, which separates the upper waters from the lower waters, becomes the habitat of the birds, whereas the lower waters are filled with fish. Animals and humanity dwell on the earth and eat its vegetation. This highly schematized picture accentuates the orderliness of creation. Nothing is left to chance or whim, but all is well organized and proceeds as planned by the Creator.

The first act of creation is light, even though that which gives light, the sun and the moon, are not created until the fourth day. The author is not concerned with scientific fact but with an ordered universe, and light is necessary in order to see. The author may also be forced to put light first because in the *Enuma Elish* it is a property of the gods, emanating from them, and is mentioned first in that creation account. For our author, light is no longer a property of the gods but an element of the created world. God names the light "day," and the darkness "night" (v. 5). In ancient Israel, naming signified one's power over that which was named. God names the day and night because God above has authority over them. Likewise, God will name the sky and the earth and the sea. The light is seen as good, as is the entire created universe. A strong affirmation of the goodness of the created world pervades this account. The section concludes with the temporal framework, in which evening is mentioned first, then morning. This reflects ancient Israel's manner of keeping time—the day began at sunset.

God then creates the sky (vv. 6-8), which separates the waters above the heavens from the waters below. The cosmology envisioned by the author is one that he shared with the rest of the ancient Near Eastern world. Water surrounded the entire world and was held back only by the heavens above and the earth below. It threatened to overwhelm the earth, especially when storms and floods enveloped the earth. The sky was pictured as a bowl set upside down to keep the upper waters in place. This bowl had windows, allowing the rain, snow, or hail to reach the earth. The waters below appeared on earth as streams, lakes, and springs.

God puts limits on the expanse of water so that earth can appear. From the earth God calls forth vegetation that is able to reproduce itself ("with its seed in it," v. 11). Fruitfulness is not something dependent on the gods of fertility, but God has put the power of reproduction in vegetation itself. Here again the author shows a world that is not under the control of pagan deities.

Next God creates the lights and places them in the heavens. The author carefully avoids the terms "sun" and "moon," but uses instead the terms "greater light" and "lesser light" (v. 16). The sun and moon were considered deities in the ancient pagan world. By avoiding the use of these terms, the author is in effect saying, "See what other nations consider deities! They are nothing but a 'big light' and a 'little light' in the heavens." The sun and the moon are simply elements of the created universe, not gods to be worshiped.

The sky separating the waters above from the waters below is filled with birds, and the waters below with fish. On the sixth day animals and humanity are created to inhabit the earth, which was created on the third day.

1:26-31 The creation of humanity. The whole creation account has been leading up to the creation of humanity. A habitat has been created in which humanity will dwell; time has been created as a measure by which humanity will govern its life. And finally when all is ready, man and woman are created. Since the Priestly author describes the creation of humanity in more detail than the previous creative acts, and since this act is the last in the series, the author is indicating that humanity is the high point of all creation. The special character of this creation is underscored by the fact that only humanity is described as being created in the "image and likeness" of God (v. 26).

There are three problematic expressions in this section that often cause confusion and misunderstanding. Who are the "us" in Gen 1:26? What does it mean to be created in the "image" of God? What kind of creature is this "man" created both male and female?

The "us" in Gen 1:26 is not easily explained. Several theories have been advanced, but none is entirely satisfactory. Some scholars argue that the "us" is to be explained as an example of the "plural of majesty." The plural of majesty accounts for the fact that in Hebrew the word for God (*Elohim*) is in the plural but is found with a singular verb, indicating that it is meant to be taken as a singular noun. It is supposed that because God is so great and powerful, the ancient Hebrews spoke of their Deity in the plural. For these scholars, the "us" in Gen 1:26 is an instance of this plural of majesty.

Since there is no other language that uses a plural of majesty, other scholars prefer to find in the use of "us" a remnant of pagan mythology. In ancient Near Eastern myths the high god creates humanity in consultation with the heavenly council. The heavenly council is composed of the lesser gods who surround the high god and act as advisors. This may well be in the background, but since the author has avoided other pagan overtones, one wonders why less care would be taken here.

More recently it has been argued that the "us" of Gen 1:26 is to be understood as a rhetorical device without much significance. It is something like saying "Let's do it" after one has debated with oneself over a course of action. Possibly the problem of the "us" in Gen 1:26 will never be solved, but each of these theories is at least plausible, if not entirely satisfactory.

In order to determine what kind of creature the human being is, it is essential that we understand what is meant by the term "image." Often this has been taken to mean that humanity is endowed with a soul, and that the soul is in the image of God. This could not be further from the intent of the author of Gen 1. The view that the human person is composed of a body and a soul is a distinctly Greek idea; in fact, the Hebrew language does not even have a word for "soul." In what way, then, does humanity "image" God? In the ancient world, "image" was used to refer to a statue of the king that was sent to the distant corners of the kingdom where the king could not be present in person. This "image" was to be the representative of the king in that area. If we apply this to Genesis, to be created in the image of God is to be God's representative on earth. This is underscored in the very next sentence of verse 26, in which humanity is given dominion over the earth. As God is ruler of the heavenly realm, so humanity, as God's representative, is ruler of the earthly realm. This is a very exalted view of humanity.

The final problem in these verses arises more from the limitations of the English language than from the original Hebrew text. In Hebrew, 'adam generally means "humanity." To refer to an individual male, Hebrew used another term. In Gen 1:26 the term is 'adam, and so the text can be translated, "God created humanity in his image; . . . male and female he created them." Humanity is not created as some kind of androgynous being, but rather humanity consists of the male and the female. Together man and woman constitute humanity.

2:1-4a The hallowing of the sabbath. Sabbath rest is associated with the rest of God on the seventh day. In six days there have been eight separate acts of creation. The author has varied the framework noted above by placing two acts of creation on the third and sixth day, and is then able to maintain a six-day structure in spite of the fact that there are eight acts of creation. This is done to underscore the significance of the sabbath. The sabbath rest mandated in the commandments in the Book of Exodus (20:8) is here bound up with the very beginnings of the world; it is tied to the created order.

CONCLUSION

The Priestly account of creation is a theological reflection on the world that the author has experienced. It is a world wherein God is seen as a powerful Being, able to create by merely speaking a word. God is seen as standing outside the universe that is called into being. The Deity transcends the created order. Humanity is seen as the high point of creation. The world in which humanity lives has been organized by God, but as God's representative on earth, humanity is to be sovereign over the world.

THE YAHWIST ACCOUNT OF CREATION AND SIN, AND THE PRIESTLY GENEALOGY OF ADAM

Gen 2:4b–5:32

Though the Yahwist account of creation follows upon the Priestly account, it is actually the earlier of the two accounts. It is written in the style of a folk tale, without the repetition and carefully delineated structure that characterizes the Priestly account. Creation is *formed* by Yahweh, not called into existence by the power of the divine word. The focus in this story is not on the creation of the world as such, but on the relationship of man and woman to each other and to the world.

2:4b-9 The creation of "the Human." In this creation account, what exists prior to God's creative act is not watery chaos, as in Gen 1, but rather desert. The earth is viewed as barren for two reasons: there is no water, and there is no one to till the soil. The background of this creation story is clearly the experience of the farmer, for whom water and the tilling of the soil are necessary in order to bring forth vegetation from the earth. Water aids creation, whereas in Gen 1 water had to be confined for creation to proceed.

The first thing formed by Yahweh is "the Human." This is not to be understood as an individual named Adam; rather, "the Human" is the whole of humanity. That the author views this original creature as a representative of undifferentiated humanity and not as an individual is clear from the use of the definite article "the" before "humanity" in the Hebrew text.

The human creature is made from the ground. In Hebrew, "human" and "ground" are similar-sounding words ('adam, 'adamah), and so bear a special relationship to each other. This play on words is characteristic of the Yahwist author. By using two similar-sounding words, the author is able to focus the attention of the reader on the relationship between the two words. The relationship between humanity and the ground is thus underscored. The human creature comes from the ground and so depends upon it for life.

Yahweh breathes life into "the Human" and it becomes a "living being" (v. 7). In the past this has been interpreted as the creation of the soul, but, as indicated above, the Hebrew language did not have a word for "soul." "The Human" becomes a living being. Humanity lives because Yahweh's breath is in it; when Yahweh's breath leaves, it dies. Every breath of every person depends directly upon Yahweh. It should be noted that the animals are also living beings (2:19). Humanity and animals are living, breathing creatures. Humanity and animals are to be distinguished from each other by the fact that Yahweh speaks to the human creature but not to the animals. In addition, the human creature names the animals, thus signifying humanity's control over the animal world.

Once the human creature is formed, Yahweh proceeds to create a place in which humanity will dwell. This is unlike Gen 1, where the habitat was created first, and only later were people created to live in it. Here Yahweh creates a garden (v. 8), which resembles a park with trees, not a garden of plants and flowers. These park-like gardens were cultivated by great kings in the ancient Near East. They were a source of shade from the sun, the kind of place where a king could relax. This is Yahweh's garden, and Yahweh uses it in the cool of the evening to "relax."

The author mentions two trees that will function significantly in Gen 3, the tree of life and the tree of the knowledge of good and evil. The tree of life appears again only at the end of Gen 3, and thus it can be seen to play a marginal role in the story. The tree of life was a symbol of immortality in ancient Near Eastern mythology; it plays the same role in this story. As long as the first couple are in the garden and have access to this tree, their life is not threatened. Once they are expelled from the garden, they become subject to death. The tree of the knowledge of good and evil, by contrast, plays an integral role in the story that follows, and we will consider its symbolism in the context of that story.

2:10-14 The four rivers. It is commonly recognized that these verses interrupt the story of the Yahwist. They contribute nothing to the action of the story. Verse 15 seems to be the continuation of verse 9, not of verses 10-14. Moreover, this insertion contradicts what was said earlier in the text about the location of Eden (v. 8). According to this passage, Eden is located in the north, and the four great rivers that surround the world flow from it. Only two of the rivers can be identified—the Tigris and the Euphrates. The Pishon and the Gihon cannot be identified with certainty, but they probably refer to rivers in the same general area as the Tigris and Euphrates. The purpose of this insertion seems to be to link the garden of Eden with a specific geographical area in an attempt to historicize the story.

2:15-17 The command. The human creature is placed in the garden and given the task of cultivating and taking care of it. This echoes ancient Near Eastern mythology, in which humanity is created to do the work of the gods. A command not to eat from the tree of the knowledge of good and evil is given, without any explanation for this prohibition. It is simply stated that Yahweh has created humanity and has placed certain limits upon human activity.

2:18-24 The creation of woman. The motive given by Yahweh for the creation of woman is that "It is not good for the human to be alone." While this aspect of the story has often been interpreted as a reference to the social nature of humanity, what is really intended by the author is to account for the marriage relationship, as the concluding verse of the story indicates (v. 24). We must bear in mind that in presenting that relationship the author is writing from the perspective of the tenth century B.C.E. and presents the woman from that viewpoint. A woman's position was one of support to her husband. She is, in the literal translation of the Hebrew text, a "helper fit for him." In the Old Testament, "helper" means one who gives support or strength, one who enables others to fulfill their destiny. Frequently in the Old Testament, it is actually God who is called "helper" (Deut 33:7; Ps 33:20; 70:6; etc.). No one would argue that God is subservient to anyone. The story is not about the essence of woman, but about her dignity in the institution of marriage. Woman is intended to be one in whom man finds support and strength.

In contrast to the Priestly account, creation does not appear as an organized, step-by-step process. Rather, one thing is made, then another, until God is satisfied with the results. Like the human creature, the animals are formed from the ground and become "living beings" (2:19—the phrase "living beings" is curiously omitted in the NAB). The human creature and the animals share a common origin. They are distinguished from each other by the fact that the human creature names the animals, signifying authority over them. Moreover, as previously stated, Yahweh speaks to the human creature but does not address the animals.

Even though the human creatures and the animals are both living beings, the animals do not prove to be suitable as a "helper." A second time Yahweh attempts to form a suitable helper, and this time forms a woman from one of the ribs of "the Human," who is put into a "deep sleep" lest the act of creation be witnessed. The act of creation remains a divine mystery.

One of the most puzzling aspects of this passage is the fact that Yahweh forms the woman from a rib (v. 22). We have no parallels in ancient Near Eastern mythology, and what a rib may symbolize in the text is simply unknown. We do know that in the Sumerian language "rib" and "life" are the same word. The goddess of life is at the same time the "Lady of the Rib." It is interesting to note that at the conclusion of chapter 3 the man calls his wife "Eve," a form of the Hebrew word for "life," and recognizes that she will be the "mother of all the living" (3:20). The

association of life and rib with woman may indicate that in the background of the story is something akin to the Sumerian wordplay.

When the woman is brought to the man (v. 23), he exclaims in poetic form that at last a suitable helper has been found. No longer is he alone. There is a wordplay between the terms "man" and "woman" in Hebrew (*'ish, 'ishshah*) that highlights the special relationship between man and woman. Woman comes from man and so depends upon him. This is consistent with the position of woman in ancient Near Eastern society in the tenth century B.C.E. This passage has often been used to substantiate the view that woman is inferior to man and subservient to him. This is certainly not the intent of the author. It is clear that woman is not inferior to man. Her mysterious creation by God from human substance underscores the common nature she shares with man and the bond that unites them. That she is his "helper" does not indicate subservience.

Verse 24 is clearly the conclusion of chapter 2 and shows that our story is an etiology, a story about the past that explains a present reality. This story tells us why men and women are drawn to each other sexually and marry. The terms "leave" and "cleave" are covenant terms and suggest that marriage is here viewed as a covenantal relationship.

CONCLUSION

The Yahwist account of creation is much more local in scope than the Priestly account; it is concerned with the human relationship to the soil and the relationship between man and woman, not with the creation of a universe. Clearly drawn from an agricultural milieu, the story presents humanity as coming from the ground, and dependent upon the ground for life. In death humanity will return to the ground from which it came. Woman is the only suitable helper for man, since she is formed from human flesh. The attraction of the sexes and the institution of marriage are described as the natural destiny of man and woman, flowing from the way they were created. Yahweh, in turn, is not distant from creation but is directly involved in the act of creation and concerned about all creatures.

2:25–3:7 The sin of Adam and Eve. The final verse of chapter 2 is transitional and serves more to introduce the next story than to conclude the previous one. That man and woman are naked and yet feel no shame is more than a mere observation of their being undressed. As will be obvious later, their nakedness becomes a symbol of their relationship to God. At this time in the story, that relationship to God is still intact; thus nakedness does not cause shame. Only with the disruption of that relationship is their nakedness an embarrassment.

A new character is now introduced into the story—the serpent. This creature is characterized as being "cunning." This term carries connotations of craftiness and cleverness, and contrasts with the naiveté of the woman. In Hebrew, "cunning" ('arum) forms a wordplay with "naked" ('arummim). This wordplay underscores the fact that man and woman become aware of their nakedness because of the cunning of the serpent. It should be noted that nowhere in this text is the serpent identified as the devil; this identification does not come about until the first century B.C.E. (Wis 2:24; Enoch 69:6).

What, then, does the serpent represent? In Canaan the serpent was associated with the fertility cults. We know that these cults were a constant source of temptation to Israel, and, as indicated in the Old Testament, Israel often succumbed to such temptation. The choice of a serpent to represent the tempter of humanity is the author's way of saying, "Don't get involved with serpents (that is, the fertility cults); they will only cause trouble, as they did for the first man and woman." It becomes a way of warning Israel to stay away from fertility cults.

The story of Gen 3 says nothing about the serpent's motives in tempting the man and the woman. Indeed, the source of evil itself is left a mystery in Gen 3. What the story does tell us is that the presence of evil in the world is due to humanity's decision to oppose God's command.

Many scholars have attempted to explain why the serpent engages the woman in conversation and not the man. Their answers range from interpreting woman as inherently weak, incurably curious, to viewing her as much stronger than man. If she can be made to sin, man will automatically follow. The text supports none of these views. It is clear that the author portrays both man and woman as

listening to the serpent. She eats the fruit and gives it to the man "who is with her" (v. 6). The fact that woman is presented first can be explained as simply a literary device that keeps the story moving. The serpent is introduced first, then the woman, then the man. When God comes to the garden, the man is addressed first, then the woman, then the serpent. When God punishes them, the serpent is punished first, then the woman, then the man. This movement from serpent-woman-man, man-woman-serpent, serpent-woman-man maintains an even flow to the story and has no great significance beyond this fact. It is clear that the woman is included in God's command even though she is never the explicit recipient of that command (2:11, 17). And it is clear, as indicated above, that the man is with the woman during the whole temptation scene.

The temptation scene has all the characteristics of a universal picture of temptation. This is the way every human being is tempted. The serpent, with an opening question, insinuates that God has some ulterior motive for the command, that God is keeping something from humanity. The woman jumps to God's defense, but the serpent has succeeded in attracting her attention and proceeds with three half-truths: (1) "you will not die"; (2) "your eyes will be opened"; (3) "you will be like God, knowing good and evil" (vv. 4-5). It is true that when the man and the woman eat, they do not die, yet they become subject to death and will eventually die. It is true that their eyes are opened, but not in the way they anticipated. They are now aware, as they were not before, of a whole new area of human experience—the experience of guilt and shame. They know that they are naked. And finally, they become like God, knowing good and evil, but not in the way they had expected. To determine what it means to be "like God, knowing good and evil," we must attempt to explain the meaning of the symbol of the tree of the knowledge of good and evil.

There are many theories as to the meaning of the tree of the knowledge of good and evil in Gen 3. While some of these theories are attractive, they are generally based upon present philosophical positions that bear little relationship to what is actually at issue in the Genesis account. The question to which we must attend in dealing with this symbol is:

What does the expression "knowing good and evil" mean in this story? What kind of knowledge does God forbid?

To determine the meaning of this symbol is very difficult, for we have no comparable symbol in any other literature of the ancient Near East. Nor is the symbol, as such, treated elsewhere in the Old Testament. However, we do find the expression "to know good and evil" in the Old Testament. If we can discover what it means in other contexts, and then test that meaning in the Genesis context, it may be possible to find a plausible meaning of the tree of the knowledge of good and evil.

In Deut 1:39 and Isa 7:15, 16, the phrase "knowing good and evil" refers to a kind of knowledge not possessed by children. They are too young to "know good and evil." In 2 Sam 19:35, Barzillai refuses the king's offer that he return with him to Jerusalem by saying, "I am now eighty years old. Can I know good and evil?" The implication is that Barzillai as an old man is beginning to lose his faculties and so cannot be of service to the king. In 1 Kgs 3:9 and 2 Sam 14:17, the phrase "good and evil" is used (though not with the verb "to know") in the context of making wise judgments by the king on behalf of his people. In summary, we can say that to know good and evil entails the kind of knowledge required in order to make adult decisions on one's own behalf.

Does this definition make sense in the Genesis story? God places a limit on humanity. Humanity can know many things, but who is to decide what is best for humanity—the God who created humanity or the creature who was created? Chapter 3 of Genesis says that God wished to retain the knowledge of what was best for human creation. The problem is that humanity overstepped the limit imposed by God and appropriated that knowledge. Now humanity exists in the position of deciding for itself what is best. It defines itself in rebellion against its Creator.

Humanity does "become like God" in the sense that now it makes its own decisions as to what is best for itself, but it makes these decisions as creature, without the wisdom and vision of the Creator. Who knows what is best for the creature—the One who created it or the creature itself? Humanity makes its own

decisions, but its decisions lack the breadth and depth of God's wisdom.

The most immediate consequence of the sin of the man and the woman is the consciousness of their nakedness, which they seek to remedy by sewing loincloths of fig leaves (v. 7). We see almost at once the futility of this gesture. In the ensuing dialogue between Yahweh and the man, we note that the man, rather than answering Yahweh's question "Where are you?," gives the reason why he hid—"because I was naked." The reason is appropriate, in spite of the fact that it appears to be untrue. He is not naked, he is clothed with fig leaves. However, in relationship to Yahweh, he is naked, that is, his relationship to Yahweh has been disrupted and remains so. Humanity cannot "cover up" its own guilt and shame and restore its relationship to Yahweh. It is Yahweh alone who can remove humanity's guilt and shame. This is symbolized at the end of the story (v. 21), when Yahweh makes garments for the man and the woman.

3:8-24 The consequences. The purpose of the interrogation of the man and the woman is to bring them to an admission of their sin. It is interesting to note the all too human response of the man as he blames the woman and indirectly even God ("the woman you put here," v. 12). The woman, in turn, blames the serpent.

The punishments that follow are expressed in poetic form and are thought to be older than the story in which they are now found. The story is seen, then, as an etiology explaining such things as the reasons why serpents crawl, why there is pain in childbirth, and why farming is so difficult. These punishments are drawn from the world in which the author lives. They reflect the environmental and social conditions found in ancient Palestine.

The ongoing struggle of humanity to survive against the attacks of venomous serpents is highlighted in the first curse (vv. 14-15). The pain associated with childbirth, incongruous with the great joy that surrounds the gift of life, is attributed to woman's participation in sin. That her husband would rule over her reflects the position of woman in ancient society (v. 16). The curse under which man works (vv. 17-19) testifies to the rocky soil and desert-like conditions of Palestine, which make farming so difficult in that region. But the story does not end on a negative note. The woman receives her name, Eve, and she will become the mother of all the living. In spite of sin and its consequences, life will go on. Yahweh makes garments for the man and the woman, thus "covering up" their guilt and shame. Yahweh's care of humanity does not cease because of sin, but continues in spite of sin. On Yahweh's initiative the relationship disrupted by sin is restored.

At the end of chapter 3 the tree of life assumes importance. It has not yet functioned as an integral part of the story, but now, because of sin, humanity is denied access to this tree and is expelled from the garden. Humanity is not able to seize the Deity's prerogative of immortality. This is ensured by stationing the cherubim at the gate. They function as guardians of the tree of life and prevent humanity from re-entering the garden. These cherubim are to be identified with the winged animals that stood as guardians at the entrances of palaces and temples in Assyria and Babylon. The fiery revolving sword represents lightning, which is often a symbol of God's wrath.

4:1-16 The first murder. The story of Cain and Abel follows upon the story of the sin of humanity and represents humanity's further alienation from Yahweh. The opening verses are transitional. They once formed the introduction to the genealogy that begins in verse 17, but now they serve to introduce the main characters of our story. Cain, whose name means "I have produced," is Eve's first-born. The etymology of Abel's name is not given, but the Hebrew root of the name means "emptiness," and may refer to the very brief life of Abel. The separateness of these brothers is brought out only by the terse sentence that contrasts their professions: Cain is a farmer; Abel, a shepherd.

As the story unfolds, it moves quickly to the actual murder of Abel and Yahweh's judgment on Cain. Many details that would interest the modern reader are simply ignored. We do not know why Cain's sacrifice was not acceptable, nor how Cain discovers that his sacrifice did not please God. The story focuses on Cain's reaction, the subsequent murder of his brother, and God's judgment on Cain. Verse 7 suggests that Cain could have con-

trolled his anger. Sin is presented figuratively as "lurking at the door" to take possession of him, yet Cain could still overcome sin by "doing well." He does not, and so bears full responsibility for his sin.

When interrogated by Yahweh, Cain lies and then addresses a sarcastic question to Yahweh (v. 9). He is worse than the first sinners, who sought merely to shift the blame. Cain's sin cannot be ignored. The blood of his murdered brother cries out to Yahweh. In ancient Israel it was believed that blood and life are inextricably bound. As life belongs to God, so too does blood.

The punishment of Cain is more severe than that of the first parents. He is banished from the soil, cursed to be a wanderer. As in chapter 3, the punishment of the sinner is not the final word. When Cain cries out against the severity of his punishment and states his fear that others may seek vengeance against him, Yahweh places a mark on Cain to protect him. Though Cain leaves the presence of Yahweh (v. 16), he is mysteriously under God's protection.

The story of Cain and Abel is only loosely connected with the preceding story of the fall in chapter 3. This story presupposes the existence of other people (v. 14) and an organized society in which there are distinct professions and in which a sacrificial cult has been developed. The story bears all the marks of having been reduced to the bare necessities. The concern of the passage rests entirely on Cain's sin and his subsequent punishment, leaving many unanswered questions. It seems likely that we are dealing with a story that once existed independently but has been adapted by the Yahwist to suit his particular purpose.

It has been suggested that the concern of the original story was the animosity between peoples of different backgrounds and vocations, specifically farmers and shepherds. In the story the pastoral way of life wins out over that of the farmer, as can be evidenced by Yahweh's acceptance of Abel's sacrifice. If this was the concern of the original story, it is no longer the primary concern of the Genesis story. Another way of accounting for the origin of the story is to see it as an account of the origin (etiology) of the Kenites. The Kenites were a tribe that worshiped Yahweh and yet never became a member of Israel.

They were smiths and metalworkers, and continued to live as a wandering tribe long after many nomadic tribes had settled. It is believed that the members of this tribe wore a sign or tattoo on their foreheads, setting them apart from other tribes. This story suggests that Cain is the founding father of this tribe, and the story is told to account for the distinguishing characteristics of the Kenite tribe.

Though certain elements of the story may help us to better ascertain its original intention, they no longer fully explain the Yahwist's use of it. It is this level of the story that is most important to the reader. For the Yahwist, the story illustrates humanity's inclination to sin. From the first sin in the garden onward, humanity continues to move away from Yahweh, becoming so hardened in sin that Yahweh regrets ever having created the human race (6:6). According to the Yahwist, it is against the backdrop of the increasing sinfulness of humanity that a people is eventually chosen through whom all of humanity will be reconciled to God (12:1ff.). Left to itself, humanity moves toward sin. Hope is found in Yahweh's ever-present mercy and in Yahweh's will to save.

4:17-26 The Cainite genealogy. While most of the genealogies in Genesis are attributed to the Priestly author, this Cainite genealogy is the work of the Yahwist. That this piece is a separate tradition not originally linked to the Cain and Abel story is evident in the surprising appearance of Cain's wife. Since no other people are mentioned, where did the woman come from? In the previous story Cain is cursed to be a wanderer (vv. 12, 16), but in this genealogy he is the builder of a city (v. 17) and the father of civilization. Similarly, whereas Abel was described as a shepherd (v. 2), in this genealogy Jabal is the father of shepherds (v. 20). This genealogy is introduced in order to account for the origin of cities and the development of civilization with its attendant professions. Its inclusion fills the gap in the story between the account of creation and that of the flood.

There are points of contact between this genealogy and the Priestly genealogy in Gen 5. Some of the same names are repeated (Enoch, Lamech), and some names are simply variations of names appearing in the Yahwist genealogy (Mehujael/Mahalalel; Methusael/Methuselah). It appears that both genealogies

come from a common source that has undergone a long period of transmission. This would account for the differences in the spelling and sequence of names. Behind both genealogies stands the tradition of an antediluvian (pre-flood) list of the kings of Mesopotamia. The points of contact between these traditions and the Genesis genealogies will be noted in the commentary on Gen 5.

Inserted into the Cainite genealogy is a "boasting song" of Lamech (vv. 23-24). It is distinct from the genealogy both in form and content. It is probably included because Cain is mentioned in the last line. The song reflects the pride and arrogance of unbridled revenge, and it is used by the Yahwist as another example of humanity's sinfulness. The disobedience of the first parents has led to an ever-increasing rebellion of humanity against God—first murder, and now wanton vengeance. As civilization advances, so does humanity's rebellion.

A Sethite fragment is appended to the Cainite genealogy. Verse 25 is similar to verse 17, and with it we return to Adam. There is, as is typical of the Yahwist, a play on words: the word for "granted" sounds like "Seth." In contrast to the Cainite genealogy, which ended with the rebellion of humanity against God, this fragment states that now humanity began to call upon Yahweh. Consistent with Yahwist theology, the section ends on a positive note.

Much scholarly debate has centered on the fact that whereas Gen 4:26 states that humanity called upon the name of Yahweh from the time of Seth, the Priestly and Elohist traditions do not introduce the name until the time of Moses (Exod 6:2; 3:14). Since we are unable to reconstruct with any certainty the pre-history of Israel's traditions, it is impossible to reconcile these two traditions. It may be that the name Yahweh was known to a small group or tribe and only later became known to the whole people, but this is highly speculative.

5:1-32 The genealogy of Adam. The first two verses of this section recall the creation of humanity in the Priestly account (1:26ff.) and serve as a transition to the genealogy of Adam drawn from that source. The relationship of this genealogy to the Cainite genealogy was noted above and can be clearly seen in the following comparison. The order of names in the Yahwist genealogy has been changed to highlight the similarity between the two lists. The numbers to the left indicate the order of appearance in the text.

Gen 4:17-26(J)	Gen 5:1-32(P)
1. Adam	1. Adam
8. [Seth]	2. Seth
9. [Enosh]	3. Enosh
2. Cain	4. Kenan
5. Mehujael	5. Mahalalel
4. Irad	6. Jared
3. Enoch	7. Enoch
6. Methusael	8. Methuselah
7. Lamech	9. Lamech
10. [Noah]	10. Noah

These are essentially the same genealogies. The Yahwist's reference to Noah is found in Gen 5:39. The change in the order of names reveals the fluid nature of genealogical traditions; they could be rearranged to suit the purposes of the author.

There is no doubt that the genealogy in chapter 5 bears some relationship to the antediluvian list of the kings of Mesopotamia. In both lists the seventh position is of special significance. In the Mesopotamian list the name of the seventh king, Enmeduranna, is the same as the capital city that served as the center of worship of the sun god. This may explain why it is that Enoch, the seventh in the Priestly list, lives precisely 365 years, the same number as that of the days in a solar year. It was believed that the seventh king was taken into the company of the gods. This could explain the rather cryptic reference to Enoch's fate (v. 24). The last king in the Mesopotamian list, like Noah, who is the last person mentioned in the Priestly genealogy, has an important role in the story of the flood. There is no direct relationship between any of the names in the two lists, nor are any of the numbers the same. Indeed, in contrast to the considerable length of reign in the Mesopotamian list (18,600–64,800 years), the life span of the biblical patriarchs is remarkably short. Nonetheless, there are striking similarities.

The genealogy in Gen 5 is introduced by the phrase "This is the record of the descendants . . ." (in literal translation: "This is the book of the generations . . ."). Since succeeding Priestly genealogies begin with a similar formula, it is commonly believed that the

Priestly author took the lists from a collection of genealogical tables called by scholars the "Book of Generations."

Consistent with the Priestly style seen in Gen 1:1–2:4a, the genealogy follows a strict pattern. It is composed of the following elements: (1) the age of X when his first son is born; (2) the number of years X lived after that birth; (3) the statement that X had other sons and daughters; (4) the age of X when he died.

As with the Yahwist genealogy, the purpose of this genealogy is to fill the gap between the accounts of creation and that of the flood. But in addition to this, some distinctly Priestly concerns are evident. The blessing and command to multiply given by God in Gen 1:28 are now realized. The image of God in which the first couple were created is passed on from generation to generation, so that all humanity is created in the image of God (v. 3). Enoch's fellowship with God (v. 10) will save him from the flood. The name Noah literally means "rest," but in verse 29 it suggests comfort or relief, anticipating Noah's future role.

THE STORY OF THE FLOOD

Gen 6:1–9:29

The Genesis story of the flood is remarkably similar to Mesopotamian flood accounts, especially the Babylonian version of the Gilgamesh Epic. Gilgamesh, the hero of that story, embarks upon a search for immortality that brings him to an ancient ancestor named Utnapishtim, who is immortal. As Utnapishtim recounts how he became immortal, we readily recognize parallels to the Genesis flood story. The story is as follows. The council of the gods decides to destroy humanity. Ea, the god of wisdom, appears to Utnapishtim in a dream and warns him of the coming disaster. He instructs Utnapishtim to build a boat to save himself and his family. Utnapishtim brings his family, wild and tame animals, and artisans with him aboard the boat. The gods unleash a storm that quickly gets out of control, and the gods themselves cower in fear in the upper spheres of heaven. When the storm ends, the boat rests on a mountain and Utnapishtim sends birds from the boat to determine the extent to which the waters have receded. Upon leaving the boat, the survivors of the storm offer a sacrifice pleasing to the gods, who in turn bless Utnapishtim and his family with immortality.

It is clear that the Genesis version is essentially the same story, but there are some significant differences. In the Genesis account there is no hint of polytheism. God, and only God, is in control throughout; the storm never gets out of control. The flood is not the result of whim but is sent as punishment for sin. Noah does not gain immortality but rather enters into covenant with God.

Unlike Gen 1–5, where the Yahwist and Priestly traditions are for the most part separate, in Gen 6–9 the two versions are extensively interwoven. This is evident in the duplications and contradictions in the story in its present form. The duplications are as follows: God observes the sinfulness of humanity (6:5/6:12); God decides to destroy humanity (6:7/6:13); God announces the flood (7:4/6:17); Noah is ordered to enter the ark (7:1-3/6:18-20); Noah obeys (7:5/6:22); Noah enters the ark (7:1-3/7:18ff.); all living creatures on earth die (7:22/7:21); the waters recede (8:1/8:3a); God promises never again to destroy creation by a flood (8:21/9:11). The contradictions in the text include: the number of animals taken into the ark (7:2/6:19-20; 7:15-16); the cause of the flood (7:4, 12; 8:2b/7:11; 8:2); the flood's duration (7:24; 8:2a, 3b; 8:13/7:4, 10, 12; 8:8-12). The differences in the two versions will become clear in the commentary that follows.

6:1-4 (J) The intermarriage of the divine and the human. This is no doubt one of the strangest stories in the Old Testament. It appears to be a shortened myth taken over by the Yahwist and rewritten to serve as an introduction to the account of the flood. The "sons of heaven" (literally, "sons of the gods" or "sons of God") are certainly gods and not angels, as is often assumed. In ancient mythology the sons of God were considered members of the heavenly council, lesser deities that were of service to the high god.

What seems to be at issue here is not licentious behavior but the intermarriage between gods and human beings. If we were to eliminate verse 3, the story could be seen simply as an etiology explaining a race of giants or superhuman heroes of old. Verse 3 leads us to interpret the action described in verse 2 as

a great sin. The Yahwist uses the myth to illustrate the extent of sin; it even violates the boundaries between the heavenly and earthly realms. Interestingly, the punishment is directed against humanity, whose lifespan is shortened, and not against the gods, who initiated the action. This can be explained by recognizing that the Yahwist uses the story to introduce his version of the flood, the means by which humanity is punished for its wickedness.

6:5-8 (J) Yahweh's decision to destroy all living creatures. In this section the Yahwist calls further attention to the extent of sin. It is universal. Everything conceived in the human heart is evil. In Hebrew anthropology the heart is not primarily the center of the emotions but the source of intellect and will. All human thoughts and actions are evil. Yahweh's regret over creation gives a very human touch to the Yahwist's portrayal of God. Yahweh's resolution to destroy what has been created is in response to humanity's behavior, and as such is not an arbitrary decision. The flood is Yahweh's judgment upon humanity, but this judgment is balanced by Yahweh's will to save, which is signified in the preservation of Noah and his family. Yahweh's choice of Noah remains a mystery in the Yahwist version of the flood story.

6:9-22 (P) God's decision to send the flood, and instructions on building the ark. The formula "These are the descendants of . . ." indicates that we have returned to the Priestly author. Noah's righteousness is immediately noted; because of it he is preserved from the flood. God's choice is not a mystery, as is the case in the Yahwist story. It is not simply humanity that is corrupted but the earth itself. As in the Yahwist account, God's will to destroy is in response to sin. Typical of the Priestly author, we find great attention given to details, such as the construction of the ark and the dating of the flood. Noah is to take his family and male and female members of every species of animal into the ark, as well as enough food to feed them all for the duration of the flood.

7:1-5, 7-10, 12, 16b, 17b, 22-23 (J) Instructions to Noah and the coming of the flood. Omitted from the Yahwist version of the flood is the command to build the ark. It was probably deleted in favor of the Priestly version. In view of the statement in 7:1 that

Noah alone was found to be just, it is possible that the building of the ark serves as a test for him. He is instructed to bring seven pairs of clean animals and one pair of unclean animals into the ark, at obvious variance with Gen 6:19. For the Priestly author, the distinction between ritually acceptable and unacceptable (clean and unclean) animals cannot be made until ritual laws are introduced by Moses in the Sinai narrative. The Yahwist has no problem presenting sacrificial worship as part of humanity's earliest history (4:3-4; 8:20-22). The anthropomorphic style (depicting God in human terms) of the Yahwist author is evident in the depiction of Yahweh shutting the door of the ark (7:16b). Here the flood is the result of forty days and nights of rain. The Priestly account offers another explanation.

7:6, 11, 13-16a, 17a, 18-21, 24 (P) A reversion to primeval chaos. In the Priestly account the flood is not caused by rain but by the waters above the heavens joining the waters below the earth. In other words, the world returns to the watery chaos that existed before creation (1:2). The extent of the flood is far greater in the Priestly account, for it entails the destruction of the entire cosmos and a reversion to primeval chaos.

8:2b, 3a, 6, 8-12, 13b, 20-22 (J) The receding of the waters, Noah's sacrifice, Yahweh's promise. The waters remain on the earth a total of sixty-one days. Noah sends out birds to determine if the waters have receded sufficiently so that he can disembark. The use of birds by sailors for navigational purposes was not unknown in the ancient world. The Yahwist, in good storytelling style, builds the bird-sending motif to a climax by having Noah send out three birds, the last of which is successful. As in the Babylonian myth, a pleasing sacrifice is offered to God upon leaving the ark. The mythological overtones of the phrase "the Lord smelled the sweet odor" (v. 21) cannot be overlooked. The expression is drawn from a primitive notion that food offered to the gods was actually eaten by them. This idea was later rejected by Israel. In our story this detail serves to show that the sacrifice was accepted by Yahweh, and thus reconciliation with humanity was effected. As the Yahwist's story opened with Yahweh's reflection upon humanity (6:5-8), so it now closes with comparable reflections. Humanity is the same, "evil from the start"

(v. 21), but humanity's wickedness will never again become the basis for Yahweh's destruction of the earth. The order of creation is assured by Yahweh.

8:1-2a, 3b, 4-5, 7, 13a, 15-19; 9:1-17, 28-29 (P) God remembers Noah. In the Priestly account the flood lasts a full year and ten days, and restoration entails a re-creation. The "wind of God" that begins to move over the waters echoes the "wind of God" that functioned similarly in Gen 1. The turning point in the story is God's remembrance of Noah. It is God's "remembering" that sets in motion this new act of creation. The bird-sending motif is not as successfully integrated into the Priestly story as it is in the Yahwist version. Indeed, it is God who tells Noah to leave the ark; Noah does not rely on information gained from sending out the bird.

God's first words to Noah and his sons are a reiteration of the blessing given at creation: "Be fertile and multiply." In the postdiluvian (post-flood) world, the blessing of procreation continues in effect. What is altered is humanity's relationship to the animals. Recognizing humanity's violent nature, God permits animals to be killed and eaten, but the blood, because of its association with life, which belongs to God alone, must not be eaten. The prohibition against the taking of human life continues in effect; interestingly, the reason given is that humanity is created in the "image of God." If God's law against murder is transgressed, it is humanity, not God, that bears the responsibility of punishing the crime. The ancient legal formula in verse 6 was probably originally intended to set limits to blood revenge.

The divine promise never to destroy the earth again by flood takes the form of a covenant in the Priestly conclusion to the story. A covenant was a way of regulating the relationships between individuals and groups in ancient society. This covenant is introduced by the Priestly author as an anticipation of the future covenant between God and Israel. The initiation of the covenant and the responsibility to keep it rests entirely with God. The rainbow is a sign of that covenant. It is a reminder to God of the pledge to preserve the world; it is a reminder to humanity of God's faithfulness and mercy.

The story concludes in 9:28-29. These verses reveal the Priestly author's concern with chronology. Verse 29 recalls the genealogy of chapter 5, which was interrupted by the story of the flood, and in turn provides a transition to the Table of the Nations in chapter 10.

9:18-27 (J) The curse of Canaan. Again we find the Yahwist adapting a story that originally served another purpose. The original story functioned as an etiology explaining the origin of viniculture and the discovery of the intoxicating effects of wine. As such, there is no moral judgment on Noah's condition; it is simply stated that he became drunk. The interest of the Yahwist is not in Noah's drunkenness but in the curse on Canaan and in the blessings on Shem and Japheth that resulted from their behavior toward their father during his drunken stupor. Exactly what Ham did to Noah is not clear, but certainly it involved more than merely looking upon his father's nakedness (see 9:24). Nor is it clear why Canaan is cursed when, according to the story, Ham is the guilty party. The phrase "Ham was the father of Canaan" (v. 18) is certainly intended to bring the curse into harmony with the story, but this does not really remove the difficulty.

The curse of Canaan and the blessings of Shem and Japheth seek to account for the relationships between the peoples who descended from these three ancestors. The Canaanites did become the slaves of the Israelites (descendants of Shem). The identification of the descendants of Japheth is not certain. Perhaps they are the Philistines, who did "dwell among the tents of Shem," or the Hittites, who disappeared from the land shortly after the arrival of Israel. In any case, they are presented as sharing in the overlordship of Israel in the land of Canaan.

THE NATIONS OF THE WORLD

Gen 10:1–11:27

10:1-32 Table of the Nations. The genealogy of Gen 10 is actually an extensive tabulation of the nations of the ancient Near East. It is basically the work of the Priestly author, as signaled by the generation formula, but it now contains some fragments drawn from the Yahwist. The principle of division among the nations is not race or language, but geographic boundaries and political affiliations.

The order in which the sons of Noah are listed—Shem, Ham, Japheth—is reversed in the genealogy that follows, in order to present the ancestors of the Israelites in a climactic final position.

The descendants of Japheth inhabit the region north of the Fertile Crescent to the coastlands west of Palestine. Many of the peoples mentioned are Indo-Europeans, but it is not possible to identify them all with certainty. Among those whose identification is certain are the following: the Madai are the Medes, the Javan are the Greeks, the Kittim are the people of the island of Rhodes.

The descendants of Ham include African and Arabic tribes that inhabited the region surrounding the Red Sea, northeastern Africa, and the land of Canaan. Ethiopia (Cush), Libya (Put), and Egypt are well known among the nations mentioned. It is surprising to find the Canaanites, who were Semites, identified as descendants of Ham, but this probably reflects the fact that Egypt controlled the region prior to Israel's claim on the land. The inhabitants of the Asiatic side of the Red Sea are also listed. Many of these names are familiar as peoples displaced by Israel's conquest of Canaan.

The descendants of Shem are the peoples occupying the region of the Fertile Crescent and the Arabian Peninsula. The known nations include Elam, Assyria, and Aram.

A later editor inserted Yahwistic materials into this Priestly genealogy (vv. 1b, 8-19, 21, 24-30). These insertions are clearly separate from their surrounding material in form and content. The Nimrod insertion (vv. 8-12) takes the form of a story rather than a genealogy. The identification of Nimrod with any known hero of the past is difficult. He is credited with the founding of several great cities, which has led scholars to identify Nimrod with Tukulti-Ninurta I (thirteenth century B.C.E.), the Assyrian king who conquered Babylon. Most of the names in verses 21, 24-30 are intended by the Yahwist to be names of individuals, unlike the Priestly author's names, which stand for peoples. Eber is the eponymous ancestor of the Hebrews, that is, the one from whom they took their name. The origin and meaning of the wordplay on the name Peleg (v. 25) is lost.

Though there is much uncertainty about this Table of the Nations, its theological significance is clear. It shows the fulfillment of God's command to increase and multiply found in Gen 1:28 and reiterated to Noah in Gen 9:1. It also shows us that Israel is one among many nations. The choice of Israel by Yahweh does not rest on any special achievement or quality that Israel possessed, but only on God's gracious intervention in its history.

11:1-9 The tower of Babel. The Yahwist tells in story form what the Priestly author has presented in genealogical form in chapter 10. The story may have once been an etiology explaining the diversity of languages and nations. The Yahwist, however, uses it not only as an example of humanity's ongoing sin, but also as a counterpoint to the call of Abraham in Gen 12:1ff. The background of the story is Babylonian. Shinar is an ancient name for Babylon (Babel). The method of brickmaking is characteristic of Mesopotamia, not Palestine, which used stone for building. In spite of the Babylonian milieu of this story, we have not as yet found an actual parallel to this story in any ancient Near Eastern mythology.

The narrative can be divided into three parts: verses 1-4, verses 5-8, verse 9. The first part is a report in which humans are the actors; the second part is discourse in which Yahweh is the chief actor. The final verse is an explanatory supplement that includes a popular etymology of the name Babel and concludes the story. It leads us back to the beginning by reversal: the people were united and their language was one, now they are not.

The people build a city with a tower, and Yahweh punishes them. It is not clear exactly why they are punished. What did they do to force Yahweh's hand? The sin can be inferred from the motive given for building the city: "to make a name for ourselves, lest we be scattered" (v. 4). There is a double motivation. On the one hand, they wish to make a name for themselves on their own initiative, in obvious independence from Yahweh. On the other hand, they seek to avoid being "scattered," which was commanded by God when they were told to "fill the earth" (1:28; 9:1). In this story the people do just the opposite: they come together in one place, a city.

Commentators often focus on the "tower with its top in the sky" (v. 4) as a sign of the sin of pride and rebellion against God, but there is no reason to separate the tower from the city. Most ancient cities were built with watchtowers. "With its top in the sky" simply means that it was a very tall tower. There is no need to identify the tower as a Babylonian temple (ziggurat), as is commonly done. Even if the tower was at one time associated with one of these ancient worship sites, in our story no religious significance is given to the tower.

As is characteristic of the Yahwist stories, this one presents Yahweh very anthropomorphically and contains wordplays. Yahweh "comes down" to see what the people are doing, appearing almost jealous or afraid of the people's growing skills. It is presumed that the "us" whom Yahweh addresses (v.7) are members of the heavenly council (compare Gen 1:26; 6:2). There are wordplays between the Hebrew for "Babel" and "confusion," for "name" and "place." The people sought to make their "name" great, but "from that place," from "Babel," "confusion" arose.

Against the background of the Babel story the Yahwist presents the call of Abraham. The people sought to make their name great, but it is Yahweh who will make Abraham's name great (12:2). They are scattered across the face of the earth; Yahweh will choose one nation, and through that nation all nations on earth will be blessed. Left to themselves they pursue sin; now Yahweh will intervene, not in punishment as in the flood, but in saving love, using Israel to call them back.

11:10-27, 31-32 The genealogy of Abraham. This genealogy of the Priestly author is patterned on the one found in chapter 5, but the lifespans given are considerably shorter. There is an insertion from the Yahwist tradition in verses 28-30. These verses really introduce the Abraham narratives and so will be treated with the call of Abraham (12:1ff.). Some of the names mentioned are actually cities of northwestern Mesopotamia (Serug, Nahor, Terah, Haran), but it was not unusual in the ancient Near East to borrow a name from a place.

In both the Priestly (v. 31) and Yahwist (v. 28) traditions, the birthplace of Terah, Abraham's father, is Ur of the Chaldeans. The identification of Ur as the city of the Chaldeans is anachronistic—the Chaldeans had entered the Mesopotamian region only after the city had reached its peak, and consequently it could not have been connected with the Chaldeans at the time of Abraham's migration. Abraham's migration begins from Haran (11:31; 12:5), and the cultural background assumed in the patriarchal narratives is that of the northwestern Mesopotamian region, not the southern Tigris-Euphrates valley, where Ur was located. Both cities, Ur and Haran, worshiped the moon god, Sin, and there was regular travel between these two cities. The Ur insertions into the text probably reflect the ancient associations between the two cities.

CONCLUSION

The primeval history in Gen 1–11 is a blend of traditions that relates a history of sin that marred the goodness of God's creation. The superiority of humanity over the rest of creation is indicated both by the statement that man and woman are created in the "image of God" and by God's command that they are to have dominion over the world. But because of its continued disobedience against God, humanity is bound to the very earth from which it was formed. Left to itself, it becomes ever more deeply caught in sin. God's forbearance is shown when each divine chastisement is tempered by care, protection, and restoration. The first eleven chapters of Genesis are the background against which the history of salvation moves forward with God's call of Abraham.

THE PATRIARCHAL NARRATIVES

Gen 11:28–36:43

From the story that ended with the whole of humanity scattered across the earth, the Yahwist now narrows the focus to one individual and his descendants. In this complex of sagas the connecting link is the theme of the promise and its fulfillment. The earliest form of the promise may have been only the promise of a son, but as the tradition developed it was expanded to include many descendants, land, greatness as a nation, and blessing. The concern for a descendant occupies most of the Abraham cycle.

It is legitimate to ask historical questions of the patriarchal narratives, but we are cautioned against an oversimplified reconstruction of the lives and historical period of the patriarchs by the nature of the narratives as

saga. Nevertheless, the field of archaeology has contributed to our knowledge of the history of the ancient Near East, and there is general agreement that in view of the lifestyle and customs reflected in the patriarchal narratives, the patriarchs are to be situated in the region of the Fertile Crescent in the second millennium B.C.E.

THE ABRAHAM CYCLE

Gen 11:28–25:18

11:28-29; 12:1-9 The call and response of Abram. There is little preparation given for the call of Abram. (Abram and Abraham are variants of the same name, as are Sarai and Sarah. The changes in their names occur in 17:5 and 15 to indicate their new relationship to God as a result of the covenant.) Only the briefest mention is made of the migrations of Terah and his family. It is interesting that Milcah's father is remembered, but not the more important Sarai. Sarai's barrenness is mentioned in anticipation of later narratives and makes all the more paradoxical Yahweh's promise of many descendants in 12:2.

The promise to Abram represents a new phase in the Yahwist narrative. Previously we moved within the realm of primeval history, the history of all humanity; now we center on an individual, soon to become a family, and finally a nation. The choice of Abram remains a mystery in the Yahwist story, resting solely on God's initiative. The promise is dominated by the term "bless" (five times). What Yahweh offers to Abram will prove to be a sign of divine favor and a source of happiness to Abram himself. To be a great nation, Abram will need descendants and land. Both these aspects of blessing are spelled out in more detail in the following narratives. Abram's fame will come as a result of his trust in Yahweh's actions, not, as in the case of the Babel story, by means of making a name for himself. The final element in God's promise, the promise that all communities of the earth will find blessing in Abram, probably meant that Abram would be taken as the exemplar of divine blessing (Gen 48:20). Eventually, it came to be understood that Israel would actually be the mediator or agent of God's blessing to the world (Sir 44:21).

The Yahwist gives us no information about Abram's reaction to Yahweh's promise nor any indication of Abram's motives in obeying God's command. It is simply stated that "Abram went as the Lord directed" (v. 4). We can infer Abram's unquestioning faith and obedience from his response. The subject of the faith will come up again and again in the Abraham cycle of stories.

The narrator deliberately records that Shechem was Abram's first stop, because this ancient Canaanite city became an early center of Israelite cult (Josh 24:1; 1 Kgs 12:1). The patriarchs Abraham and Jacob are frequently presented as establishing altars and worshiping God in ancient Canaanite cities in response to some experience of the holy in these cities. This is a way of explaining why these originally pagan cities became worship centers in Israel. The terebinth of Moreh (v. 6) was a sacred tree, indicating that an ancient cult already existed at Shechem prior to Abram's visit. Old Testament events of great significance often occur near sacred trees, which were believed to be special places for receiving divine communication. It is here that Yahweh promises to give Abram the land of Canaan. Beyond being a statement of fact, the phrase "the Canaanites were then in the land" (v. 6) points to the unusual character of the promise given to Abram. The land will be possessed and the promise fulfilled by his descendants, not during Abram's own lifetime.

As Abram continues to journey south, he stops between Bethel and Ai, other ancient Canaanite cities that become important in Israel. Again he builds an altar to Yahweh, though we are not told why. Abram's travels bring him to the Negeb region, which is especially associated with him.

12:10-20 The ancestress in danger. Soon after the promise of land (12:7), we find Abram traveling to Egypt because of a famine. It was not unusual for Semitic peoples to go to Egypt in search of food, as is evidenced in Egyptian records of the period. But in light of the promise of land, it does not put Abram in the best light. What is even more striking about the story is that the patriarch, in order to ensure his own safety, knowingly compromises his wife's honor. He fears that his wife's beauty will come to the attention of Pharaoh and that Pharaoh will kill him in order to take Sarai into the royal harem. He persuades Sarai to lie by saying that she is his sister so that his life will not be in danger. As Abram had predicted, Sarai's beauty comes to the attention of the Egyptians, and Pharaoh, assuming that Abram is her brother, bestows gifts upon Abram and takes Sarai into his harem. Yahweh intervenes by sending a plague on Pharaoh's house but does not punish Abram. Pharaoh reprimands Abram and sends him away under military escort.

The wife-sister motif in this story may reflect an ancient Hurrian practice in northern Mesopotamia by which a husband adopted his wife as his sister. This gave the husband greater control over the wife, but it also gave the wife protection and privileges beyond those given to the ordinary wife. Such a practice eventually died out, and the narrator of the story does not seem to be aware of it.

Essentially the same story is also found in Gen 20:1-18 (E) and Gen 26:6-11 (J), but with some variations in characters and incidents. The alterations in subsequent versions indicate a greater sensitivity to the moral overtones of the story. Abraham no longer lies, since Sarah is said to be his half-sister, and God intervenes before her honor is compromised. The narrator of Gen 12 does not seek to excuse Abram's behavior, but rather seems to take delight in his shrewdness. The story also shows that in spite of what Abram and Sarai do, they are under God's protection, and God will intervene to secure the future realization of the promise when it is placed in jeopardy.

The story and the context in which it is found presents some difficulties. How does Pharaoh know that the plague is sent because of Sarai? How does he learn that Sarai is Abram's wife? These questions are never answered. The mention of camels in verse 16 is certainly anachronistic, for camels were not domesticated until the thirteenth century B.C.E. Is one to suppose that Sarai is actually sixty-five years old in the story (see Gen 12:4b; 17:17)? These inconsistencies were not of importance to the narrator, though they bother contemporary readers. The narrator's interest is in God's intervention that redeems the situation.

13:1-18 Separation of Lot and Abram. Abram's journey, first to the Negeb and then, by stages, north to Bethel, was typical of nomads in search of pastures for their flocks. Their movements were governed by the need for grazing land, and they were often found moving about near cities. Both Abram and Lot are described as having large flocks, and they agree to separate to forestall future arguments between them over rights to pastureland. Their herdsmen have already begun to quarrel. Abram, though older and by rights the one who could choose first, very magnanimously defers to Lot. Lot picks the land that looked lush and fertile, the Jordan Plain, and settles near Sodom. Lot's choice is ironic, for this is a territory that will be destroyed by Yahweh. The events of Gen 19 are here anticipated by the narrator.

Verses 14-17 may not have been part of the original story, but they now serve as its climax. The promise of land parallels the promise given in Gen 12:2-3, 7; the promise of innumerable descendants is added. Abram's walking the length and breadth of the land is a symbolic act indicating that he is taking legal possession of it, even though it is not his (13:7). Abram finally settles near the terebinth of Mamre.

14:1-24 Abram and Melchizedek. There is universal agreement that Gen 14 is one of the most difficult chapters in the Book of Genesis. It is very different from the rest of the patriarchal narratives. It begins like a report from an ancient chronicle and is replete with historical and geographical details. Abram is pictured, not as a peaceful nomad, but as a commander of forces involved in a war. The sequence of events that flows from chapter 13 to chapter 15 is interrupted by chapter 14. It is impossible to determine the source of this chapter. Consequently, scholars speak of it as an insertion into the patriarchal narratives, independent of any of the sources (J, E, P).

There is considerable debate about the historical reliability of the chapter. Are the cities and kings that are named evidence of the antiquity and historical reliability of the passage, or is the author of this insertion merely imitating historical style? Can we identify with certainty the kings and cities mentioned in chapter 14? The answers to these questions are very complex and, while of interest, are beyond the scope of this commentary. Our concern in chapter 14 will center mainly on Abram and his meeting with Melchizedek.

Chapter 14 is composed of two distinct parts: verses 1-16, 21-24, and verses 17-21. It seems that Abram has been introduced into the first part of the chapter precisely because of his encounter with Melchizedek, which serves as the conclusion and climax of the chapter. The name Melchizedek means "Zedek [a god] is my king." The city of Salem is to be identified with the city of Jerusalem (Ps 76:2). That Melchizedek is both a king and a priest is not unusual—that was often the case in the ancient Near East. The god he worships, "God Most High, the creator of heaven and earth" (v. 19), was the head of the Canaanite pantheon and supreme over the other gods and the world. Melchizedek offers Abram bread and wine, which may simply have been refreshment but could have had some ritual significance; he also blesses Abram. Abram, for his part, identifies Yahweh with God Most High (v. 22) and accepts Melchizedek's blessing. There is some question regarding who pays tribute to whom (v. 20). The subject of the sentence in the Hebrew text is simply "he" and not Abram, as supplied in our text. The context would seem to indicate that it is Melchizedek who not only blesses Abram but also pays him tribute.

Many scholars see in this passage an argument in support of the reign of the Davidic dynasty and its assimilation of priestly duties. It is true that Melchizedek was seen as a prototype of the ideal Davidic king (Ps 110:4), but it goes beyond the text to say that Abram's acceptance of Melchizedek's blessing suggests that Abram's descendants will accept the Davidic dynasty. The inclusion of the passage probably reflects the author's interest in linking Abram with Jerusalem and its priest-king, and in the identification of Yahweh with the God in whose name Abram is blessed.

15:1-21 The covenant with Abram. A source analysis of chapter 15 is difficult. Some scholars have argued for the presence of the Elohist source in 15:1-6, but the consensus is that the entire chapter was composed by the Yahwist, in spite of several inconsistencies that point to a combination of sources. It is likely that the Yahwist author is drawing from several traditions and harmonizes them with only partial success.

The problems in the text are obvious. The covenant ceremony takes place at sunset in verses 12 and 17, yet in verse 5 it is already night. In verse 8 Abram expresses doubt, whereas his faith is emphasized in verse 6. Yahweh's name is revealed in verse 7 but is already known by Abram in verse 2. These inconsistencies are removed if we separate verses 1-6, 13-16, which are concerned with the issue of descendants, from verses 7-12, 17-21, which focus on a covenant ritual surrounding the promise of the land. Thus we have at least two separate traditions that make up this chapter, though they are interrelated in a carefully constructed passage.

The first six verses show elements drawn both from prophetic traditions and from the cultic sphere. The opening phrase, "this word of the Lord came to Abram," is recognized as a prophetic formula (compare Isa 1:1; Ezek 1:1; Amos 1:1) and suggests that the author sees in God's summons to Abram a call similar to that of a prophet. The cultic background of the passage is clear, for its structure is patterned after the format of cultic celebrations: God's self-manifestation (v. 1) is followed by a salvation oracle (vv. 4, 5) and a declaration of righteousness (v. 6). Yahweh's admonition against fear is not unusual, for in the ancient world an encounter with the Deity was understood as a terror-filled event. "Fear not" is often found in the Old Testament accompanying a manifestation of God (see Judg 6:23; Isa 41:10). The title "shield" is frequently used of God as protector and deliverer (see Pss 3:3; 18:2; 28:7, etc.). It is a title drawn from the cult, and this is its only occurrence in the patriarchal narratives. The reward that Yahweh promises to Abram is certainly to be read against chapter 14, where Abram returned home with no recompense.

Difficulties in the original Hebrew text make the translation of verse 2 uncertain. However, verse 3 is clear and parallels the content of verse 2: Abram is concerned that a servant born in his household will become his heir. The practice of a slave becoming the heir of a childless couple accords with the customs of Mesopotamia in the fifteenth century B.C.E., as confirmed by the discovery of legal texts from Nuzi. Yahweh's answer to Abram is not a mere reiteration of the promise of innumerable descendants, but specifically assures Abram that his own issue will be his heir. Abram's response is faith in Yahweh. He trusts Yahweh completely and sets aside his doubts and anxiety. His righteousness is af-

firmed on the basis of this response. His total reliance upon Yahweh puts him in right relationship to Yahweh.

Verse 7 begins with a second self-introduction of the Deity in language and form drawn from the cult. The promise now focuses on land, not descendants. The confirmation of Yahweh's promise of the land is secured in the covenant ceremony described in verses 9-11, 17-20. This primitive ritual and its significance are mentioned in Jer 34:18, and discoveries within the past century have shown that this manner of making covenants was widespread in the ancient Near East. Cutting the animal in two and walking between the separate pieces bound the parties in covenant. If they failed to keep the terms of the covenant, they were cursed to share a fate like that of the split animal. The birds of prey that swoop down upon the carcasses are probably to be interpreted as omens of evil, but the exact meaning of the portent is not clear. Abram falls into a deep sleep, a state of suspended activity, in which he can receive a divine revelation. The covenant ceremony concludes when a fire pot and a flaming torch pass between the severed parts of the animal (v. 17). Fire is often a sign of the presence of God, and this is certainly what it represents in this passage. Yahweh initiates the covenant and agrees to be bound to it. The final verses (vv. 18-21) specify the extent of the promised land, which corresponds to the extent of the Davidic empire under Solomon.

Verses 13-16 interrupt the description of the covenant ceremony. They explain why it is not Abram himself but his descendants who will possess the land. Yahweh is not lacking in power; rather, the Amorites are allotted a measure of time before they are judged by God. These verses show a theology of history in which Yahweh rules over history and brings about the fulfillment of the divine promise to Abram in that history.

Chapter 15 confirms God's covenant with Abram: he will have a son, he will have many descendants, and one day they will possess the land.

16:1-16 The birth of Ishmael. The story of the birth of Ishmael is primarily the work of the Yahwist. Only in verses 3 and 15-16 do we find insertions from the Priestly author. The Priestly insertions give the essentials of the story but lack the lively, dramatic character of the Yahwist story. Through the eyes of the Yahwist we glimpse the frustration and jealousy of Sarai, the arrogance of Hagar, and the passivity of Abram.

Actually the elements that make up the story are not as scandalous as they may appear to the modern reader. Sarai's proposal that Abraham impregnate her servant, Hagar (v. 2), was in conformity with the legal customs of Mesopotamia. A barren wife could give her servant to her husband so that children could be fathered. The children of the concubine were considered the legal offspring of the wife, just as Sarai states: "perhaps I shall have sons through her" (v. 2). It is certainly understandable that a servant who now shares the master's bed may assume a certain equality to, or even superiority over, the barren wife. The law provided for servants who "forgot their place," however, by specifying that they be returned to their former status of servant. This is precisely what happens in the story (vv. 4-6). Abram is following the law when he returns Hagar to Sarai's control. Nonetheless, Sarai's severity with Hagar exceeds the law and does not enhance her character.

Hagar, an Egyptian, flees south because of Sarai's harsh treatment. She is apparently on her way back to Egypt when she is met by the messenger of Yahweh (v. 7). There is no clear distinction between Yahweh and the messenger of Yahweh (v. 13); it is simply a way of indicating that a message comes from Yahweh and at the same time preserves Yahweh's transcendence over the created world. The messenger's words of assurance echo the promise given to Abram: Hagar will be the mother of many descendants (v. 10). The name Ishmael is explained by popular etymology as meaning "God hears." Yahweh has heard Hagar's cry and has come to her aid. The description of Ishmael that follows (v. 12) is etiological in character. Ishmael, the son of a proud and rebellious mother, becomes the ancestor of the desert tribes, known for their wild, free spirit and warlike nature. Israel does not forget that it is closely related to these peoples; they are offspring of the same father.

The final verses (vv. 13-16) are not entirely clear, but it seems that some connection is drawn between the name given to a well, "Well of living sight" (?), and the name given to Yahweh by Hagar, "God of Vision." In an-

cient times there may have been a sanctuary to this God at this place. "God of Vision" was the name of a deity worshiped in Canaan.

The interest of the Yahwist does not center on the etiologies in the story; rather, the episode is intended to show that the fulfillment of God's promise depends upon God alone, not on human inventiveness. By situating this incident between the promise and its fulfillment, the story delays the realization of the promise and thus heightens the suspense. The reader is drawn into the story: When will Yahweh fulfill the promise?

17:1-14 The covenant with Abram. The covenant with Abram, recounted by the Yahwist in chapter 15, is told here by the Priestly author. This account consists primarily of an address by Yahweh and lacks the human-interest quality so characteristic of the Yahwist. It is more theological in tone, telling us very little about Abram's personal reactions. The chronological details, the theological orientation, and the concern with circumcision are all typical of the Priestly author.

Like the Yahwist version, the passage opens with God's self-introduction. The name "God Almighty" (El Shaddai) has special significance for the Priestly author, who limits the use of this name for God to the patriarchal narratives; it thus becomes the distinctive name of God associated with this period (28:3; 35:11; 48:3). In the primeval history God was called Elohim; in the future God will be known to Israel as Yahweh (Exod 6:3f.). The meaning of the name El Shaddai is uncertain, but there is some evidence to support the view that it means "mountain god."

The covenant is portrayed, not as an oath taken by God, as in the Yahwist version, but as a contract. God will give Abram many descendants; Abram, for his part, is commanded to walk in God's presence, to be blameless, and to practice circumcision as a sign of the covenant between them. The change in Abram's name (v. 5) signals his new relationship to God and the new life granted by the covenant. The new name, Abraham, is said to mean "father of a multitude of nations," but actually the name is simply a variation of the name Abram, which means "my father [the god] is exalted."

Some new elements introduced into the Priestly account are to be noted. The covenant is made not simply with Abraham but also with his descendants, and it will be an everlasting covenant (v. 7). In addition, a new relationship with God forms part of the covenant: this God who makes covenant with Abraham will be his God and the God of his descendants. This anticipates the relationship between Yahweh and Israel that will be established at Sinai.

Circumcision only became an important sign of the covenant during the Babylonian Exile (586–538 B.C.E.); it is doubtful that it always had this significance for Israel. Circumcision was practiced in ancient Egypt and by the Semitic peoples that lived in Canaan. It was not practiced in Mesopotamia nor by the Philistines, whom Israel referred to as the "uncircumcised" (2 Sam 1:20). It is not clear why the practice of infant circumcision developed, since circumcision was associated with puberty rites in other cultures. Circumcision may originally have had some religious significance now lost to us, or it may have been done simply for hygienic reasons. The exiles living in Babylon took circumcision to be a sign of their religious identity over against the Babylonians, who did not practice the ritual. For the Priestly author, whose writing originated in the exilic community, circumcision becomes the sign of inclusion in the community that worships Yahweh. Circumcision is so important for this source that if one is not circumcised, he is not considered a member of the covenanted people (v. 14).

17:15-27 The birth of Isaac. The announcement of the birth of Isaac interrupts the account of the command to circumcise and its eventual enactment related in verses 23-27. In all three sources—the Yahwist, Elohist, and Priestly—Isaac is the child of promise, and the unexpectedness of his birth points to God's great power in making the impossible a reality. As Abram's name is changed to signal his new role, so too Sarai's new role as mother is accompanied by the change of her name (v. 15), even though Sarah is really only a dialectical variant of the name Sarai.

Abraham's reaction to the announcement of Isaac's birth to Sarah, who is well beyond childbearing age (ninety years old), is an understandable mixture of respect and disbelief; he shows reverence to God by paying homage, but he cannot help but laugh. The laughter motif is also found in the Yahwist and Elohist traditions. It explains Isaac's name, which means "laughter" in Hebrew. Abraham thinks of Sarah's advanced age and directs God's attention to Ishmael. God seems to have forgotten how old Sarah is, and Abraham offers God a way out, but God is not to be diverted. The promise will be fulfilled in Sarah's descendants, not Hagar's. Ishmael will not be forgotten. He too will become a great nation, but the covenant is to be with Isaac's descendants.

18:1-15 The announcement of the birth of Isaac. This is one of the Yahwist author's most delightful stories. The Yahwist draws upon a common folk-tale motif—a story in which strangers who have been treated hospitably turn out to be divine guests. They, in turn, reward those who have been gracious to them. With this motif, developed against the background of the custom of desert hospitality, the Yahwist interweaves the announcement of the birth of Isaac, and the story moves one step closer to the fulfillment of the promise.

The only real problem in the narrative is the relationship between Yahweh and the three strangers. The text states that Yahweh appeared to Abraham, and then, suddenly, Abraham sees three strangers. The shift back and forth between Yahweh and the three visitors continues throughout the story. It is difficult to determine what the author means. Is Yahweh one of the three, or do all three stand for Yahweh? Perhaps the author is drawing upon a tradition that was originally polytheistic and feels constrained to leave it unchanged. The Yahwist may have kept the ambiguity in the story to suggest the mystery that surrounds God's presence in the world.

It must be remembered throughout this story that Abraham is an old man and Sarah is an old woman. Though the exact ages of ninety-nine years for Abraham and ninety years for Sarah come from the later Priestly source, even the Yahwist considers both Abraham and Sarah to be advanced in years (v. 12). The setting of the story is the terebinths of Mamre, a holy place very appropriate for this divine visitation. Abraham is sitting in the entrance of the tent in the heat of the day, which is the only place to be in midafternoon when the desert sun scorches the earth, especially if you are an old, old man. The three visitors suddenly appear at this unusual time. Who would be out walking in the heat? Equally strange is the detail that says that this old man runs and bows profusely to the ground. All of Abraham's actions are in excess, suggesting that he suspects the divine character of his guests and hopes that by displaying his great hospitality he may exact a favor from them.

Abraham becomes extremely verbose, in contrast to his later behavior (v. 9). His offer of a morsel of bread ("little food" in our text) and a little water ("some water" in our text) is an understatement in the extreme, for he has Sarah bake nearly a bushel's worth of flour into bread, he has prepared the best steer from his herd, and, in addition, he serves curds and milk with the meal. This is not a drop of water and a crumb of bread but a banquet befitting a king. As a good host, Abraham serves his guests and, as was the custom, Sarah is not present, since women did not eat with the men. She is nearby in the tent, however, as is evident later in the story.

After the meal the strangers ask a question that could only have caused great shock to the storyteller's audience (v. 9). According to desert hospitality, a guest was given anything that was requested. This included taking his pleasure with the wife of the host. It was certainly rude to ask for the host's wife, but a guest could not be denied. The abruptness of Abraham's answer indicates his shock at their request. Sarah, who is listening near the entrance of the tent, finds the exchange quite humorous. She may have been a beauty in the past (12:10ff.), but now she is old.

The shocking request is not what it seemed at first, however, but serves to introduce the announcement of the birth of Abraham's long-awaited descendant. That the guests are aware of Sarah's laughter and inner thoughts must certainly have unnerved her, for she hastens to deny that she laughed. But the guests do not allow her denial to stand, and the final word of the story, "You laughed," would have reminded a Hebrew audience of the name of the promised child, Isaac, meaning "laughter."

18:16-33 Abraham's intercession for Sodom. This section was evidently not drawn from ancient traditions but was freely composed by the Yahwist. In it we find a rather developed theology presented in two short conversations. In the first (vv. 17-18), in terms reminiscent of the promise (12:2-3), Yahweh decides to tell Abraham of the judgment made upon Sodom. God's intentionality and actions, previously hidden, are now revealed to the chosen one, Abraham, in order that he might be able to teach his descendants about God's justice. Thus the destruction of Sodom takes on a special admonitory significance for future generations.

The second conversation is between Abraham and Yahweh. It is a rather entertaining example of Oriental bargaining at its best, but its underlying concerns are quite serious. The question of justice is at stake: Is it just to destroy the innocent, few as they may be, along with the vast majority who are guilty? Are the innocent important enough to forestall the punishment of the wicked? Tension in the encounter is created by Abraham, who, though deferential toward Yahweh, dares to enter into debate and continues to press Yahweh at each step of the exchange by boldly attempting to reduce the minimum number of innocent needed to save the city. Not only is Yahweh's patience revealed in the dialogue, but also Yahweh's great willingness to set aside punishment for the sake of the innocent few.

19:1-29 The destruction of Sodom. The story of the destruction of Sodom, though once an independent saga, is now well integrated into the Abraham cycle. The two messengers, who separated from Yahweh in 18:22, arrive in Sodom. The purpose of their visit is to determine whether the outcry against Sodom (18:20) is justified. Lot is found at the city gate, which was the usual gathering place for townsmen. Unlike chapter 13, where Lot was pictured as a herder and a nomad, he is now a city-dweller. He persuades the strangers to spend the night at his home. In the course of the evening, Lot's fellow townsmen come and demand that his guests be sent out to them so that they may take pleasure with them. It is clear that for the Yahwist, inhospitality, so serious in a nomadic society, and sexual perversion, against which there is a strong Old Testament bias, are the sins for which the city is condemned.

We are shocked by Lot's attempt to placate the townsmen by offering to give them his two virgin daughters for their pleasure, but it is unlikely that an ancient audience would have been as horrified. They would have seen in Lot's offer a noble attempt, even if extreme, to fulfill the demands of hospitality. Lot is unsuccessful, and he himself is rescued by the two guests, who strike the townsmen blind. The wickedness of Sodom is confirmed and its destruction is imminent. Lot and his family must flee to save themselves from the destruction. The weak and vacillating character of Lot is revealed in his hesitation to leave; he must be led out of the city (v. 16).

There are etiological motifs tied to the story. Lot refuses to flee to the mountains but wants to escape to a "small" city, Zoar (v. 20). The name Zoar means "little" or "insignificant." He is granted this favor, and Zoar is spared from judgment. Lot's wife becomes a pillar of salt when she turns to see the destruction, for they had been commanded not to look back. There are many salt formations surrounding the southern end of the Dead Sea; the story explains their presence and shows the consequences of disobedience.

The destruction of Sodom may be based on some actual violent natural disaster in the distant past, but this is impossible to verify. The concern of the Yahwist is to explain the destruction of the region as God's judgment upon sin. The final verse (v. 29) is a summation of the story and is attributed to the Priestly author.

19:30-38 The ancestry of the Moabites and Ammonites. This story deals with the ancestry of the Israelites' neighbors, with whom they recognized a certain kinship but who nevertheless were their enemies and were barred from ever becoming members of the covenant community (Deut 23:4). The story was probably originally told in praise of the actions of the ancestresses, who take extreme measures to ensure the continuance of the family line. They are certainly not ashamed of their actions, since their children proudly bear names that tell of their deeds: Moab ("From my father") and Ammon ("The son of my kin"). The Yahwist includes the story in order to disparage the ancestry of Israel's traditional enemies.

20:1-18 Endangering the ancestress a second time. This story is immediately recognized as a doublet of the Yahwist story in 12:10-20. There is universal agreement that it is to be identified as the product of the Elohist. In addition to the use of the Hebrew Elohim for the divine name, the Elohist's authorship is indicated by the use of dreams as a means of divine communication. The distinctive concerns of the Elohist are all the more apparent when contrasted with the earlier version. Whereas the Yahwist presented at some length Abraham's motives for passing off Sarah as his sister and explained how she came to be in Pharaoh's harem, these concerns are largely ignored by the Elohist, who focuses rather on Abimelech's guilt and deliverance. In spite of the fact that Abimelech acted in ignorance and consequently did not intend to do wrong, he is considered guilty. He has sinned by taking another man's wife into his harem, even if he acted unknowingly, and that act cannot go without some form of punishment. In this case it is Abraham, whose own guilt is overlooked, who will be able to intercede on Abimelech's behalf. Abraham, who has special access to God in virtue of his call, is depicted in the role of mediator and prophet.

There are other differences between the two accounts. It is not clear in the Yahwist's version whether Pharaoh actually had relations with Sarah, but the Elohist leaves no doubt that God intervened before Abimelech even touched her. Here Abimelech's gifts to Abraham stand as testimony to the honorableness of Abraham and Sarah. In the Yahwist's version gifts are given when Sarah is first taken into Pharaoh's harem. The Elohist's moral sensitivity is indicated by his attempt to justify Abraham's action, stating that Sarah was indeed Abraham's half-sister. Whereas the Yahwist allows the patriarch's behavior to speak for itself, the Elohist explains Abraham's actions in order to present a more honorable picture of his ancestor.

21:1-21 The birth of Isaac and the expulsion of Hagar and Ishmael. All three sources are found in this account of the birth of Isaac. The Yahwist version (21:1, 6b, 7) simply presents the birth of Isaac in Sarah's old age as the fulfillment of Yahweh's promise (18:10). Laughter is connected with Isaac's name because it is the response Sarah expects from her neighbors when they hear that she has given birth in her old age. In the Priestly version (21:2-5), Isaac's birth is also said to be the fulfillment of God's promise (17:21), but this author adds that Abraham named and circumcised the child according to God's command (17:19, 12). Regarding the Elohist version (21:6a), only the motif of laughter associated with the name Isaac is retained.

The child is called Isaac because of Sarah's joy (laughter) at his birth.

The Elohist narrative of Isaac's birth (vv. 8-21) is a duplicate of the story of the expulsion of Hagar and Ishmael found in the Yahwist version in chapter 16. But as one might expect, there are significant differences in this version. It is Sarah's jealousy, not Hagar's arrogance, that leads her to demand that Abraham expel the two. She fears that Isaac's future inheritance is threatened by Ishmael's presence in the home. Here Abraham reacts more strongly to Sarah's demand than in the Yahwist version, where he remained passive. He gives in to her demand only when God tells him to do so and when God assures him that Ishmael will be the father of a great nation.

The Elohist paints a very poignant picture of Hagar's departure and of her subsequent despair when lack of water threatens her life and that of the child. God intervenes through a messenger, and Hagar is assured of Ishmael's future and, by means of God's assistance, she finds water. Ishmael becomes the father of camel nomads (Ishmaelites), who lived in the wilderness between Palestine and Egypt. They lived by hunting and plundering, as indicated by the phrase "he became an expert bowman" (v. 21).

The Elohist story suppresses the etiological interests of the Yahwist version. It ennobles the figure of Abraham, and even Hagar is presented in a better light than in chapter 16. God directs the action by ensuring the future of both the child of promise and the child of Hagar.

21:22-34 Abraham and Abimelech at Beer-sheba. The passage contains two separate agreements between Abraham and Abimelech, and thus the question of separate sources arises. Some scholars attempt to find evidence in this passage of both the Yahwist and the Elohist; others suppose that one author, the Elohist, drew upon two separate traditions in the composition of the passage.

The first agreement (vv. 22-24, 27, 31, 32b, 34) is initiated by Abimelech and presupposes the events of chapter 20. Abimelech wants to be assured of Abraham's friendship and suggests a covenant as a guarantee of Abraham's loyalty. Abraham agrees. The covenant oath is sworn at Beer-sheba, a name meaning "well of the oath."

The nature of the second agreement (vv. 25-26, 28-30, 32a, 33) is quite different. Abraham initiates the covenant in response to a dispute over a well. The seven lambs accepted by Abimelech indicate that he recognizes Abraham's claim to the well. The place was called Beer-sheba, "well of the seven," because of Abraham's gift. The purpose of this account is to show that the well at Beer-sheba, a sacred place for Israel, originated with Abraham. Its cultic significance is suggested in verse 33. At Beer-sheba, Abraham calls upon "God the Eternal" (El Olam), a divine name used by the Canaanites and eventually given to Yahweh by Israel (see Ps 102:25, 28).

22:1-19 The sacrifice of Isaac. The story of the sacrifice of Isaac, generally attributed to the Elohist, is one of the great masterpieces of narrative art in the Bible. We are drawn into the action of the story from the very start and are held in suspense until the climax. We know, as readers, that what is recounted is a test for Abraham; thus we focus on Abraham's response and not on the horror of God's command. We are left to imagine Abraham's inner thoughts while the narrator tells us only what he does. We follow Abraham each step of the way as he complies with the divine command. We feel the silence as father and son walk together, coming closer with each step, to that moment of ultimate decision. We smile at Isaac's innocent question and sympathize with Abraham in his tender but evasive answer. We watch as each detail of that final moment unfolds, from the building of the altar to Abraham's poised knife, ready to claim his son's life. We wait expectantly until the angel intervenes, and finally we rejoice at the turn of events. Abraham has withstood the test, and Isaac still lives.

It is clear that the story is concerned with Abraham's great faith, which is expressed in his willingness to sacrifice his son, the child of promise, in accord with God's command. A connection between this story and human sacrifice is often made. Human sacrifice was commonly practiced among Israel's neighbors, and on a few occasions even in Israel, though it was forbidden (see 1 Kgs 16:34; 2 Kgs 3:27; 23:10). It may be that the story originally centered on a repudiation of the practice of human sacrifice. However, any earlier significance is now superseded by the motif of the testing of Abraham's faith.

The original conclusion of the story was verse 14, but a supplement was added (vv. 15-19) to link the story with the theme of promise, the dominant theme of the patriarchal narratives.

22:20-23 The genealogy of Nahor. This genealogy is attributed to the Yahwist. It lists the twelve sons of Nahor, who are Semitic (Aramean) relatives of Israel. The purpose of its inclusion is to prepare the way for the appearance of Rebekah (v. 23) in chapter 24.

23:1-19 Abraham's purchase of Machpelah. It is often argued that the Priestly author is responsible for this story, though the vividness of presentation reminds one of the Yahwist. The passage tells how Abraham bought a piece of land in Canaan as a place to bury his wife. In doing so, it provides us with another delightful glimpse at the art of Oriental bargaining.

Abraham is a sojourner in the land, and as such has only limited rights; he cannot own property legally. For Abraham to acquire property, the matter must be decided by the elders of the city. The Hittites with whom Abraham negotiates would not have been Anatolian Hittites, who were powerful in the sixteenth/fifteenth centuries B.C.E. but one of the many groups living in pre-Israelite Canaan. In the exchange each party attempts to outdo the other in courtesy. The Hittites are hesitant to sell land to a sojourner but will allow Abraham to bury Sarah in any of their burial sites. This is not what Abraham wants, and he purposely ignores their suggestion and indicates the precise piece of land he wants to buy. Ephron, the owner of the land, magnanimously offers to "give" Abraham not only the cave he wants but also the field where the cave is located. Abraham graciously refuses to take the land as a gift but insists that he will pay for it.

This exchange is entirely within the bounds of the convention of bartering. While Abraham could have continued bartering for a lesser price, he accepts Ephron's first offer. It is difficult to determine whether the four hundred shekels paid by Abraham was considered exorbitant, because the value of the shekel varied. The fact that it was Ephron's first offer, when he certainly expected Abraham to make a counteroffer, suggests that the price was high. By comparison, David pays only fifty shekels for a threshing floor and oxen (2 Sam 24:24). In verses 16-20 we find a formal contract of sale. Abraham achieves his objective—he now owns property in Canaan for Sarah's burial.

Though this chapter correctly reflects the legal and social customs of the ancient Near East, its purpose is not simply to record an event in the life of Abraham. Rather, Abraham's possession of a portion of the land stands as a pledge of the future possession of the land in its entirety.

24:1-67 Finding a wife for Isaac. This charming story is another instance of the superior storytelling art of the Yahwist. There is some evidence of compilation, but it does not affect the unity of the story. The repetition, which the modern reader finds tiresome, is typical of biblical narrative and does not really detract from the story. The theme of promise remains in the background. In the forefront is God's guidance, but this guidance is directed through the heart. God does not intervene directly.

Abraham, according to custom, must arrange for the marriage of his son. Since he is old and near death, he entrusts the task of finding a wife for Isaac to a servant, who functions more like a trusted steward than a mere servant. Abraham binds the servant by oath to carry out this mission, underscoring its supreme importance. The "thigh" of verse 2 is a euphemism for the genitalia, which were viewed as sacred because they were understood to be the source of life. The servant is not to let Isaac marry a Canaanite woman. This prohibition is meant to exclude the possibility of intermingling religions; it does not reflect a racial bias as such. Under no circumstances is Isaac to be allowed to return to Abraham's country (v. 6). Such a journey apparently was viewed as a turning back on God's promise of the land. The assurance is given that God will guide the entire enterprise and bring it to successful conclusion.

The story barely mentions the servant's lengthy journey to Haran but moves immediately to the search for a suitable wife. At a well outside the city, the servant places the success of his mission in God's hands and suggests a sign by which he will recognize God's choice. The sign of drawing water, not only for the servant but also for ten thirsty camels, is meant to reveal the character of the woman; only a generous and industrious woman would willingly draw the many gallons of water needed. Rebekah arrives (v. 15) and, unknowingly, carries out the requirements of the sign. For this she is showered with gifts, which are probably meant to be part of the bride price. The servant is even more certain of God's guidance when he discovers that Rebekah is the grand-niece of Abraham and she invites him to her mother's home. It seems clear from this reference to her mother's home and from the fact that all subsequent negotiations take place with Laban, her brother, that Rebekah's father is deceased.

Laban's character is revealed in his haste to invite this wealthy stranger to his home after seeing the expensive gifts Rebekah has been given. His greed will become even more apparent in the Jacob-Laban stories that follow. The servant is treated with all due courtesy, but the urgency of his mission compels him to relate his story before eating. This section repeats Abraham's speech in the opening scene, with one significant omission: the servant does not allude to Abraham's refusal to allow Isaac to go to his homeland, for this would probably offend Rebekah's family. Laban admits that God has directed the servant and agrees to the marriage. Appropriately, more gifts are given to seal the agreement (v. 53).

Custom demanded a period of celebration, but the servant wants to be on his way and suggests that he leave immediately with Rebekah. The family understandably objects, but the servant reminds Laban that Yahweh has been directing the mission and so there is no need for delay. Rebekah's feelings in the matter are now solicited, in accordance with ancient customs, which held that a woman's consent was necessary when her brother arranged the marriage or when that marriage meant that she would have to leave her homeland. In this instance both stipulations are operative. Rebekah agrees and is given an ancient blessing promising fertility and power over enemies in the future (v. 60).

The final scene shifts to the Negeb as the caravan is returning. The text is untranslatable, so we can only guess what Isaac was doing as he saw his future bride approaching. Rebekah veils herself, according to custom—the groom was not to see the bride until after the wedding. The passage ends with their marriage and subsequent love. The order of marriage first and love second reflects what was often the case with arranged marriages.

25:1-18 Abraham's death. This section combines genealogies of the Yahwist (vv. 1-6, 11b) and Priestly (vv. 12-18) sources with an account of Abraham's death (vv. 7-11a, P). It is hard to fit the opening verses, which tell of Abraham's marriage, with the previous story, wherein Abraham is old and certainly dies before Rebekah marries Isaac (see 24:65: Isaac is now the servant's master). This discrepancy is probably to be explained by the juxtaposition of Yahwist and Priestly stories that do not follow the same chronologies. Keturah, Abraham's second wife, becomes the mother of the Arabian tribes that inhabited southern Palestine and northwestern Arabia. The gifts given to these children by Abraham testify to his generosity but also safeguard the inheritance for Isaac.

Abraham dies after a full life. It is not surprising to find Ishmael present at his father's funeral (v. 9), for the Priestly author does not provide an account of Hagar's expulsion. Abraham is laid to rest in the family tomb (see ch. 23). The chapter concludes with the Priestly genealogy of Ishmael, who becomes the father of twelve tribes that occupy the northwestern Arabian wilderness. The promise given to Abraham about Ishmael (21:13, E) is seen as fulfilled.

THE JACOB CYCLE

Gen 25:19–36:43

The Jacob cycle of stories differs from the Abraham cycle in the inner coherence of the cycle. Only the thread of promise united the Abraham cycle; each segment remained a separate unit. In the Jacob cycle, in addition to the theme of promise that continues to run through these stories, we find the theme of the quarrel between brothers integrating these stories at a deeper level. Even the Laban cycle of stories, which may once have circulated apart from the Jacob-Esau stories, is now also related to this theme.

25:19-26 The birth of Esau and Jacob. With the Priestly genealogy (vv. 19-20) that introduces this passage, we move into a new phase in patriarchal history—the period of Isaac and Jacob. What starts as a genealogy of Isaac is interrupted by a story about the birth of Jacob and Esau, usually attributed to the Yahwist (vv. 21-26a). The story may seem out of place in view of what precedes and follows, but it is clearly presupposed in chapter 27.

The barrenness of Rebekah echoes the barrenness of Sarah, but its resolution is almost immediate, and the motif does not become a major theme of the Isaac-Rebekah traditions, as it did with the Abraham-Sarah traditions. As with Sarah, God intervenes and Rebekah becomes pregnant. Only a remnant of the cultic background of the passage is retained in the use of the words "entreat," "heard this entreaty," "went to consult," and "answered." The joy of Rebekah at her pregnancy quickly turns to despair at the struggle going on in her womb. The oracle (v. 23), which is certainly the focus of the entire passage, is both a reassurance and a cause for concern. That Rebekah is to be the mother of two nations is indeed a blessing; that one will surpass the other is not unusual. What causes trepidation is that they will be divided and that, quite apart from the ordinary course of events, the elder will serve the younger, which means a painful struggle between the two. This oracle becomes programmatic as the story of Jacob and Esau continues.

By a series of implied and explicit wordplays the narrator underscores characteristics of Jacob and Esau that form a part of the future behavior and relationship of these two brothers. Esau is "reddish" ('admoni) and "hairy" (se'ar); he later becomes the father of the Edomites, who live in the region of Seir. The statement that Jacob is gripping Esau's "heel" functions as a wordplay on Jacob's name as well as a sign pointing to his grasping nature and the fact that he will supplant his brother. The name Jacob is actually a shortened form of a name similar to Jacobel, which means "may God protect."

25:27-34 Esau sells his birthright. The tension between the two brothers is exemplified in their different vocations. Esau is a hunter, a man of the field, and, by implication, wild and crude; Jacob is a shepherd, a tent-dweller, and therefore more civilized. The difference between the two brothers is further accentuated by Isaac's preferential love for Esau, and Rebekah's for Jacob.

The unfolding story shows Esau so concerned with immediate gratification that he loses all sense of proportion. For a mere pot of "red stuff" (v. 30) he sells his birthright, which was a double portion of the family inheritance. The narrator comments at the end that "Esau cared little for his birthright" (v. 34), which is certainly shown by his actions. There is no explicit criticism of Jacob's outright manipulation of his brother. Jacob clearly takes advantage of his brother by pushing him not only to sell his birthright for a bowl of lentils, but to make the deal irrevocable by forcing Esau to swear to it.

The character of Jacob is one of the most carefully developed in the patriarchal narratives. While the narrator refrains from making explicit moral judgments, he does show that Jacob's actions will lead him away from home, penniless, and at the mercy of Laban. God's choice of Jacob remains a mystery, but from the moment God appears to Jacob (28:10ff.) his character begins to improve.

26:1-35 Fragments about Isaac. There is little to unify this chapter except the presence of Isaac. Indeed, this is the only chapter devoted to Isaac, but most of its contents are duplications or echoes of stories about Abraham. With the exception of verses 34-35, which are from the Priestly source, the chapter is the work of the Yahwist.

The story found in verses 1-11 is another version of the story of the ancestress in danger (12:10ff.; ch. 20). This narrative is the least offensive of the versions and the least intriguing. For a second time famine is given as the reason for moving into a new territory, but this famine is clearly distinguished from the famine of Abraham's day. There is never any real threat to Isaac or to Rebekah. That she has been taken into Abimelech's harem may be surmised from the other versions but is never mentioned in this version. God is surprisingly absent. Abimelech sees Isaac "fondling" Rebekah (v. 8) and realizes their relationship is not that of brother and sister. Once again Isaac's name is the basis for a pun, since "fondling" and "laughter" are derived from the same Hebrew root. No gifts are given at the conclusion of the episode, but Isaac and Rebekah are guaranteed protection.

Isaac is twice the recipient of a divine appearance (vv. 2-5, 24) in which the promise given to Abraham is reiterated in nearly the same terms. Verse 5 is certainly an insertion from a later hand, for it speaks of Abraham's obedience in Deuteronomistic language. Like Abraham, Isaac built an altar at the site of God's appearance (v. 25).

God's blessing on Isaac is immediately realized in the abundance of the harvest and his growing wealth. The dispute over wells (vv. 15-25) was already found in the Abraham stories, and this seems to be a variant tradition of the same event, just as the covenant between Abimelech and Isaac (vv. 26-33) is a variant of the Abraham story (21:22ff.). Here we find yet another etymology of the name Beer-sheba (v. 33).

The Priestly addition (vv. 34-35) prepares for the events of 27:46–28:9. The conflict between Esau and Jacob is curiously missing from the Priestly tradition. What becomes a matter of contention in the household is Esau's foreign wives.

27:1-46 The blessing. The story of Jacob's deception, by means of which he receives the blessing intended for Esau, is a masterful blend of the Yahwist and Elohist sources, but it it impossible to separate the sources in this carefully structured and dramatic story. The scene opens with Isaac and his favorite son, Esau, then shifts to Rebekah and her favorite, Jacob. Following Jacob's deception, Isaac is again with Esau, and Rebekah with Jacob. Only in the central scene, the important scene in which the blessing is transferred, is the parent not with his or her favorite son.

In the opening scene Isaac, who is old and blind, wishes to bless Esau before he dies. In the ancient world, deathbed blessings were believed to be particularly effective, and the meal that was prepared and eaten prior to the bestowal of the blessing had a sacral character. Rebekah has overheard Isaac's words to Esau and devises a plan to have Jacob receive the blessing intended for Esau. Rebekah's scheme seems incapable of success, which only heightens the suspense in the following scene. Jacob's only fear is what will happen if he is caught in the deceit. Rebekah draws upon herself any curse that might be directed against Jacob, and he makes no further objection. In the central scene of the chapter, the suspense is heightened by each of Isaac's statements: "Which of my sons are you?"; "How did you succeed . . . ?"; "Come closer that I may feel you"; "Are you really my son Esau?" Only when Isaac finally smells his son

does he become convinced of the lie and proceed with the blessing.

No sooner does Jacob depart than Esau enters (v. 30). The revelation of Jacob's deception greatly affects both Isaac and Esau, who respond in shock and grief. It was believed in the ancient world that a blessing or a curse, once spoken, had a life of its own and thus could not be recalled. The blessing given to Jacob is irrevocable; there is nothing Isaac can do to call it back. Esau recognizes the correctness of Jacob's name, for he has "supplanted" (another wordplay on the name Jacob) him twice—first in bartering for the birthright, and now in gaining the blessing. Esau begs for some kind of blessing, and though Isaac attempts to comply, his words sound more like a curse. Understandably, Esau bears a murderous grudge against Jacob, compelling Rebekah to send Jacob away for his own safety. Neither realizes that they will never see each other again.

The blessing given to Jacob assures him of future fertility of the land and lordship over his brothers. Esau's "blessing" is its opposite, but his subjugation to his brother is to be only temporary. Both of these oracles reflect upon the brothers as representatives of their respective nations, Israel and Edom. Edom became a nation before Israel but was later conquered by David and became a vassal of Israel. The Edomites frequently rebelled against Israel and eventually regained their independence.

Interestingly, the narrator refrains from making an outright moral judgment on the deception carried out by Rebekah and Jacob. The narrator cannot condemn Jacob, for he knows him to be the inheritor of the promise. The oracle has been spoken: the elder will serve the younger (25:23). Is Rebekah to be condemned for assisting in the fulfillment of the divine word? Is Isaac not going against God's word by wanting to secure the blessing for his elder son? The narrator leaves these questions unanswered; he only tells the story. Yet, in the very telling of that story, the narrator directs our sympathies to Esau as the innocent and aggrieved victim. Surely he gives us a hint of disapproval as he portrays the shattering effects of this deceit. The family is torn apart by it. It will be twenty years before Jacob returns home. He has not only grasped his brother's heel but has replaced his brother, at a tremendous cost.

27:46–28:9 Jacob leaves to find a wife.
This passage of the Priestly author continues
the story about Rebekah's dissatisfaction with
Esau's marriages, a theme begun in 26:34-35.
The motive for Jacob's departure in this tradition is quite different from that of the previous story. Jacob is not fleeing from Esau's
wrath; rather, he leaves with his father's blessing to go in search of a suitable wife. The enmity between Esau and Jacob has disappeared.
Indeed, Esau tries to imitate Jacob's good example and obtains a wife from his father's
family. The issue of intermarriage between
Jews and non-Jews was especially acute during the period of restoration (after 538 B.C.E.),
when Israel was concerned with the integrity
of its religious practices and purity of race.

28:10-22 Jacob's dream at Bethel. The
story of the origin of Bethel as a sacred shrine
serves as a link between Jacob's previous life
in the land of Canaan and his future life in
Haran. It is a combination of the Yahwist and
Elohist sources, and continues the narrative
of 27:42-45. In both versions of the story,
Jacob has a profound religious experience at
Bethel, which testifies to the holiness of the
place.

The Elohist version (vv. 11-12, 17-18,
20-22) dominates the passage. Jacob, having
fled from Esau's wrath, finds himself at a
shrine, where he rests for the night, using a
stone for a pillow. Characteristic of the Elohist tradition, the divine revelation comes in
a dream. Jacob sees a stairway going from
earth to the heavens and identifies it as the
"gateway to heaven" (v. 17). It was believed
in the ancient world that there were certain
places on earth where the divine and earthly
realms met. One such place was Bethel. Jacob
recognizes the sacredness of the place; the
stone itself he calls Bethel, that is, "house of
God" (v. 22; our text has "God's abode").
Jacob consecrates the stone and sets it up as
a memorial stone. Such memorial stones were
Canaanite cult symbols of fertility and have
been found at major cultic centers. When Israel conquered the land, it inherited Canaanite
cultic sites with these stones but associated the
cultic sites with events in the lives of the patriarchs, thereby eliminating the pagan religious
significance of the stones, and used them
simply as memorials.

The Yahwist version (vv. 10, 13-16, 19)
uses the appearance of Yahweh as an opportunity to extend the promise of Abraham to
Jacob (12:1-3). Yahweh is identified as the
God of Abraham and Isaac, and assures Jacob
of the divine presence and protection on his
way. Yahweh is revealed as the God of the
ancestors, that is, committed to a family or
clan, not bound to a specific place or land.

The association of both Abraham (12:8;
13:3-4) and Jacob with Bethel shows Israel's
preoccupation with this city. Bethel became
an extremely important cultic center in ancient
Israel (see Amos 5:5, 7:10-13; Hos 10:5). It
dominated Israel's cultic life in the north from
the time of the divided kingdom (1 Kgs
12:28-29) until it was destroyed during the period of Deuteronomic reform (2 Kgs 23:15).

29:1-14 Jacob's arrival in Haran. The
Yahwist source dominates in this story of
Jacob's arrival in Haran. He comes upon a
well, presumably the same well where Abraham's servant found a wife for Isaac. Jacob,
who has previously contributed little in the
way of conversation, becomes quite loqua-
cious in this passage. The author vividly portrays an eager young Jacob trying to engage
the local, rather taciturn shepherds in conversation. The dialogue focuses on the shepherds'
inactivity, which is explained by the fact that
they are waiting to water their flocks, and
cannot do so until the large stone covering the
well is removed. Apparently the stone was
meant to guarantee equal access to the limited supply of water in the well; only when
all the shepherds were gathered could the
stone be removed.

The conversation includes inquiries by
Jacob about his uncle (vv. 5-6). In answer, the
shepherds point to Rachel, Laban's daughter,
who is approaching. When Rachel arrives,
Jacob removes the stone from the well and
waters Laban's sheep. This is a reverse of
chapter 24, where Rebekah watered the servant's camels. Rolling back the stone, Jacob
reveals his great strength, which impresses
Laban when he hears about it. Jacob is overcome with joy upon meeting Rachel.

After Rachel relays the news of Jacob's arrival, Laban goes out to greet him. Laban's
response, "You are indeed my flesh and
blood" (v. 14), is ambiguous. It may express
his pleasure at meeting Jacob, but it could also
betray his disappointment at meeting this
poor relative. Jacob comes to him, not with
the wealth that accompanied Abraham's ser-

vant, but penniless. What can Laban do but offer Jacob his home? After all, he is family. In view of Laban's later treatment of Jacob, it is more likely that the expression is an indication of his disappointment.

29:15-30 The marriages. Motifs are introduced in verses 15-30 that become dominant in the stories that follow. These motifs are developed around the words "service" and "wages"—Jacob's service and the wages paid by Laban.

The question "Should you serve me for nothing just because you are a relative of mine?" (v. 15) begins the crafty and devious dealings that will characterize the relationship between Laban and Jacob. It sounds as if Laban is being magnanimous in offering to pay Jacob for his services, but in fact he is declaring the bond of family relationship (uncle-nephew) null and void. It is replaced by a lord-servant relationship.

Jacob suggests seven years of labor for the hand of Rachel in marriage; his labor would serve as the bride price. This custom of paying a bride price recognized a woman's usefulness and was meant to compensate the family for the loss of her labor through marriage. Laban's answer to Jacob is ambiguous. He never says that he will give Rachel to Jacob in marriage; rather, he says that he "prefers" to give "her" to Jacob than to an outsider (v. 19). The reason for his lack of clarity becomes obvious as the story unfolds.

For Jacob, who is in love with Rachel, the seven years pass quickly. When the time for payment comes, Laban gives the older daughter, Leah, to Jacob. A modern reader is often puzzled by Jacob's apparent "blindness" in failing to notice that his bride is not Rachel, but it was possible for such a thing to have happened in view of the marriage customs of that age. The bride was heavily veiled, and in the course of the wedding feast she was escorted in the darkness of the night to her husband's home. We can only assume that the darkness, the veil, and probably a dullness of the senses induced by the celebration prevent Jacob from realizing that the woman he has married is not Rachel. Jacob, who deceived a blind man (ch. 27), is himself treated by Laban as if he were blind. He is made to look even more foolish than Isaac, for he has sight and yet was easily deceived by Laban.

Jacob's indignation when he discovers his uncle's deception is dismissed by Laban. Laban says that it is against their custom "to give the younger before the first-born" (v. 26, in literal translation). This has to be meant as a direct affront to Jacob, who, though younger, had usurped the position of first-born in gaining his brother's birthright and blessing. Without giving Jacob time to respond, Laban suggests that when the week-long marriage festivities end, Jacob can marry Rachel, on the condition that he will continue to work for Laban another seven years. Jacob, destined to be a ruler (27:20), remains a servant in his uncle's home. Laban has used Jacob's love for Rachel against him, without giving thought to the position in which he has placed Leah. She not only becomes the unloved wife but is a constant reminder to Jacob of his uncle's deception.

29:31–30:24 The birth and naming of Jacob's children. A number of smaller units of the Yahwist and Elohist sources are joined together to form an integrated account of the birth and naming of Jacob's children. Popular etymology is freely used to draw out the relationship between the names of the children and the bitter struggle between Leah and Rachel for love and recognition in the home. Laban has created a situation in which Jacob finds himself married to two women, only one of whom he loves. Ultimately, God controls the course of events by making Leah fruitful and Rachel barren, but at the human level the story revolves around the jealousies of Leah and Rachel. Jacob's role in the story is largely confined to fathering children.

The paradox of the story centers on the position of the two women. Leah, as first-born, first wife, and first mother, should have the love and recognition of her husband, but Jacob loves the younger, Rachel. Rachel, though loved, is barren and fears the loss of Jacob's love because of her inability to give him offspring. With each son that Leah bears, Rachel becomes more and more desperate, even to the point of demanding children from Jacob. He reminds her that it is God who gives children. Consequently, Rachel's struggle is not only for love but also for the favor of God. Rachel, like Sarah before her (ch. 16), finally becomes a mother through her maid. Likewise, Leah gives her maid to Jacob when she has ceased to bear children for a time. This was according to custom (see ch. 16).

The story of the mandrakes (v. 14) reveals how much the domestic situation has deteriorated. Leah is denied access to her husband by a jealous Rachel. Leah barters for her rights and "hires" her husband for the evening. Jacob, who had become a "servant" of Laban for "wages," now becomes a "servant" to Leah for "wages" paid to Rachel. The wages are mandrakes, herbs believed to have magical powers and used as an aphrodisiac and as an aid to fertility. In this story, however, it is because of God's intercession that Rachel becomes pregnant. It is interesting to note that God remembers Rachel only after she has granted Leah access to Jacob's bed.

Of Jacob's daughters, only Dinah is mentioned, but no etymological association is given for her name, as in the case of the name of each son. The reference to Dinah may be an insertion meant to anticipate her story in chapter 34. The birth of Benjamin is not included here but is postponed until 35:17ff., possibly because Rachel dies in childbirth and her death would be out of context in chapter 30.

30:25-43 Jacob acquires great wealth. Though there is some evidence of multiple sources in this text, it is primarily the work of the Yahwist. The motifs of "service" and "wages," previously dominant, come to the fore once again. In chapter 29 Laban deceived Jacob and was able to get fourteen years of "service" in exchange for wives, his "wages." But Jacob learned his lesson well, and now he attempts to outwit the wily old Laban.

The conversation between the two is another example of the art of Oriental bargaining. Reminding Laban of his years of service, Jacob requests permission to leave. Laban, who wants Jacob to continue working for him, ignores Jacob's request. But he admits that he has benefited from Jacob's service and asks what wages Jacob wants. Jacob, in turn, ignores Laban's question and asserts his intention to provide for his own household. He even says that Laban does not have to pay, which is certainly an overstatement, since he immediately sets the wages for his continued service. Laban is taken in by Jacob's meager request. As payment, Jacob will take the dark sheep and speckled goats, which would have been very few animals, for sheep were generally all white and goats black. Laban agrees but seeks to undercut any loss by removing all abnormally colored animals from the flock and pasturing them a distance of three days' journey from the herd in Jacob's care. The distance works against Laban, for it gives Jacob a chance to carry out his plan unobserved.

Jacob's breeding practices are based on the ancient belief that what a mother experiences while pregnant is transmitted to the fetus. Jacob sets up tree branches that he has cut in order to expose their white center. The black goats look upon these branches while mating, and the white from the inner core of the branch is transferred to their offspring and so they produce speckled offspring. He makes the white sheep look at the dark goats in order to achieve the same results. He purposely uses only the best of the flock for his selective breeding, leaving Laban with a flock of weak and inferior animals.

Throughout the account of Jacob's breeding practices, there is a series of wordplays. The "poplar," the "white stripes," and the "white core" are words that in Hebrew sound like and relate to the name Laban and its meaning, "white." In a sense, Jacob is using his knowledge of Laban's nature (white) against him. Jacob, the one deceived (ch. 29), becomes the deceiver once again.

31:1-16 Jacob prepares to leave Laban. The most important differences between the Elohist version in chapter 31 and that of the Yahwist in the previous chapter concern the role of God and of Jacob. In this version it is Yahweh who initiates the action and not Jacob himself (vv. 12-13). God has protected Jacob from Laban's double-dealing, has caused Jacob to succeed in gaining wealth, and now commands him to return home. Jacob's meeting with his wives allows him to justify himself and to see whether his wives are in agreement. Throughout the story it is implied that Jacob is not free to leave his father-in-law with his wives and children, but it is not clear why this is the case. It may indicate that Jacob's marriage was an adoption-marriage, a custom in the ancient Near East. If this were so, Jacob would be considered an adopted son of Laban, and his wives and children would be considered Laban's property. Jacob's flight with his wives and children would then have been illegal.

Yahwist insertions into the text (vv. 1, 3) indicate that the attitude of Laban's sons caused Jacob to decide to leave. The Priestly author's contribution to the story is minimal. Indeed, there is only the brief notice that Jacob left to return home (v. 18).

31:17-35 Jacob's flight. The Elohist version continues to dominate the story, though the hand of the Yahwist appears now and then. Jacob's flight takes place while Laban is occupied with the annual sheep-shearing. Jacob is able to "deceive" Laban ("hoodwink," v. 20). When the Hebrew text is translated literally, it reads, "Jacob stole Laban's heart." (The heart in Hebrew anthropology was not the seat of the emotions but the intellect.) Jacob's action is paralleled by Rachel's theft in verse 19: "Rachel stole her father's household gods." Rachel's motives are not clear. The household gods, at least in Nuzi documents, represented the credentials of the true heir. Rachel may be attempting to secure a future claim to the inheritance, or she may simply be hoping to derive prosperity and blessing from them.

Before Laban overtakes Jacob, God appears to him in a dream and warns him not to harm Jacob (v. 24). This puts Laban in a very awkward position. He has arrived ready to do battle but can only fuss and fume. He can do nothing about Jacob's departure, but the theft of the household gods cannot be ignored. Jacob denies any knowledge of the theft and unwittingly pronounces the death sentence on his beloved Rachel. The suspense that builds up during Laban's search is dissipated the moment the reader discovers that the menstruating Rachel is sitting on the household gods (v. 34). There is something ironic about the "gods," revered as sacred, being protected by the ancient taboo of "unclean" associated with blood. Whatever the original significance of these gods, there can be no doubt that the author, for whom idols are nothing but wood and stone, is ridiculing the pagan belief in, and worship of, idols.

31:36–32:3 Jacob's covenant with Laban. Jacob gains an advantage when Laban fails to find his gods. He proceeds to detail his loyal service over against Laban's shabby treatment. Laban seems unimpressed by Jacob's speech, for he continues to assert his ownership of Jacob's wives and children and flocks, but he can do nothing because of God's warning.

The present form of the agreement that Laban and Jacob eventually reach is a combination of two separate covenants, one from the Yahwist source and the other from the Elohist. The covenant in the Yahwist version is a non-aggression pact between Aram and Israel. The sign of the covenant is a mound of stones, and the covenant is sealed by a meal. The Elohist version is drawn from a boundary agreement between Aram and Israel. The covenant is marked by a memorial stone and ratified by a sacrifice and a meal. In both covenants there are wordplays associated with the name of the place where the covenant was ratified. In the Yahwist story, Gilead is a play on the Hebrew word for "mound of stones"; in the Elohist version, Mizpah is so named because it sounds like the Hebrew for "memorial stone."

The episode concludes with Laban returning home and Jacob continuing his journey (32:1-2). Jacob immediately encounters God's messengers. This experience provides the name of the place, Mahanaim ("two camps"). The reason for including this fragment certainly must exceed the meaning of the word, but it is not clear what that purpose is. Does the encounter with God's messengers give Jacob the idea of sending "messengers" to Esau? Of dividing his family into two camps? Does it prepare for the mysterious being Jacob encounters in 32:23-33?

32:4-21 Jacob prepares to meet Esau. We continue to find a blend of the Yahwist and Elohist sources as the narrative moves toward Jacob's meeting with his brother Esau. In the Yahwist story (vv. 4, 14a), Jacob sends messengers to Esau, hoping to gain his favor. When the messengers report that Esau is coming with four hundred men, Jacob is understandably alarmed and divides the camp in order to avoid total disaster. Having taken practical measures, Jacob finally turns to God in prayer. His prayer reveals his state of anxiety as he appeals for God's help by reminding God of the promise.

In the Elohist's account (vv. 14b-22), Jacob seeks to appease his brother with many gifts. The Hebrew for "gifts" and for "camp" recalls the previous wordplay of verse 3 (Mahanaim); the frequent use of the word "face" anticipates the Peniel ("face of God," v. 31) episode that follows.

32:22-33 Jacob wrestles with God. This story, which delays Jacob's encounter with Esau, is generally attributed to the Yahwist.

Jacob, left alone after sending his wives, children, and possessions across the river, is attacked by a "man," with whom he struggles until dawn. Exactly who wins remains ambiguous. The "man" cannot prevail (v. 22) and resorts to wounding Jacob by magic, yet in verse 27 the "man" asks to be released, as if he cannot best Jacob. Jacob demands a blessing but is given a new name. When he asks his mysterious contender for his name, his request is brushed aside. Verse 29 suggests that Jacob won, but in verse 31 Jacob is surprised to have seen God and still be alive. Perhaps the ambiguity is maintained to avoid stating explicitly that Jacob won, for in this story the nocturnal attacker is eventually identified as God (v. 31).

The story incorporates elements drawn from very ancient sources. The theme that one must appease a river-god in some way in order to be allowed to cross a river is often found in ancient folklore. There is also the notion from ancient folklore that the power of certain supernatural beings is limited to nighttime; they must leave or be overpowered when dawn breaks. These ancient elements explain only one level of the story. They leave unanswered questions about the relationship of this story to the larger Jacob cycle.

There is no doubt that the story, in addition to preserving ancient folkloric elements, was given a distinctly Israelite bias. Jacob's struggle is remembered by means of his new name, Israel, which is explained by popular etymology as "one who contends with God." The city of Peniel also receives its name following upon Jacob's struggle, and again popular etymology becomes the vehicle of explanation (v. 31). Finally, the story accounts for the dietary rule that prohibited Israelites from eating the sciatic nerve in memory of Jacob's wounded thigh, but this law is not recorded elsewhere in the Old Testament and Israel did not observe it.

The Yahwist's interest in the story goes beyond any of the concerns mentioned thus far. The Yahwist shows that Jacob, the contender with Esau and Laban, is brought to contend with God's very self and henceforth will never be the same. The character of Jacob is profoundly altered by this experience. From this moment until his death, he is a person of honor and integrity. In addition, Jacob (now Israel) reveals in his life Israel's own struggle with God in living as the people of covenant.

33:1-20 The meeting of Jacob and Esau. It is generally assumed that the Yahwist source is responsible for this final scene in the narrative of Jacob's return to Canaan, though traces of the Elohist can still be discerned. The actual meeting of the brothers turns out to be rather anticlimactic. Jacob's extensive preparations and subservient gestures prove to be effective. Esau no longer wishes to kill him and even expresses great joy at Jacob's return (v. 4). Jacob, for his part, compares his meeting with Esau to his encounter with God (v. 10).

Jacob's subsequent conversation with Esau suggests, however, that neither really trusts the other. Jacob will not allow Esau or Esau's men to accompany him, but persuades Esau to go on without him. Then, rather than follow Esau, Jacob turns in another direction and proceeds to Succoth. Eventually Jacob moves on to Shechem. According to the Elohist insertion in verses 19-20, Jacob buys land in Shechem and sets up a memorial stone to El, the God of Israel. Shechem was a very ancient city, important from the earliest days of Israel's occupation of the land.

34:1-31 The rape of Dinah. This story is basically from the Yahwist but has been supplemented by Elohist fragments. Dinah is raped by Shechem, but he comes to love her and wants to marry her. Hamor, Shechem's father, speaking on his son's behalf, recommends to Jacob and his sons expanded intermarriage and commerce between the Shechemites and the Israelites. Jacob's sons agree to this, on the condition that the Shechemites first be circumcised. Hamor brings the matter before the Shechemites, convincing them that they would benefit economically through intermarriage with the Israelites. The Shechemites agree to submit to circumcision, and while they are recuperating from the operation, Simeon and Levi attack Shechem and kill all the men of the city. Jacob reprimands his sons, but he is motivated more by a fear of reprisal from the neighboring inhabitants than from any moral objection to his sons' method of revenge. Simeon and Levi show no remorse but justify their behavior in avenging the injustice done to Dinah.

The narrative may preserve in story form an actual attack on the city of Shechem by the tribes of Simeon and Levi. In addition, the story may serve to explain the eventual decline of the tribes of Simeon and Levi.

35:1-29 The end of the Jacob cycle. This chapter includes two stories from the Elohist: the story of Jacob's fulfillment of his vow to build an altar at Bethel (vv. 1-8) and the story of the birth of Benjamin (vv. 16-20). The summarization of the life of Jacob (vv. 9-15), the list of Jacob's sons, and the death of Isaac come from the Priestly source. The Yahwist's only contribution is the brief notice about Reuben in verse 22a.

According to the Elohist, Jacob returns to Bethel because of a direct command from God to fulfill the vow he took on his first visit to that city (28:10ff.). The preparations for the trip indicate that Jacob's journey is to be a pilgrimage and may reflect the actual practices later associated with pilgrimages in Israel. The ritual purification before leaving on a pilgrimage includes a formal renunciation of foreign gods and anything associated with pagan cult, such as earrings, which were cultic symbols, or amulets. Changing one's clothes is a common religious symbol of renewal. The "terror from God" (v. 5) that protects Jacob's family is a kind of inexplicable paralysis or panic that renders the enemy incapable of attack (1 Sam 14:15; Exod 23:27; Josh 10:10; etc.). Arriving in Luz, Jacob builds the altar in fulfillment of his vow and renames the place Bethel.

The birth of Benjamin (v. 17) is the fulfillment of Rachel's prayer when Joseph was born (30:24). She would have named the child "Son of my sorrow" (Benoni) because of her pain in bearing him, but Jacob renames the child "Son of my right hand" (Benjamin). In the ancient world it was thought that there was a mysterious relationship between a name and its bearer; a name could determine the destiny of its bearer. Rather than mark the life of the child by the sorrow surrounding his birth, Jacob wisely gives the child a name that suggests an honorable and successful future. The name Benjamin means "southerners" and probably refers to the original geographical location of the tribe. The site of Rachel's tomb is unknown. According to 1 Sam 10:2 and Jer 31:15, it is located in the territory of Benjamin, north of Jerusalem. Thus Ephrath cannot be Bethlehem (v. 19), which is in the territory of the tribe of Judah and south of Jerusalem.

The Priestly author's contribution to the traditions surrounding the patriarch Jacob are limited. They consist of little more than summaries of the earlier traditions found in the narratives of the Yahwist and the Elohist. The Priestly author mentions only what is considered theologically important, making note on the change of Jacob's name to Israel (v. 10) and reiterating the promise given to Abraham (vv. 11-12). The list of names of the sons of Jacob given by the Priestly author (vv. 22b-29) is similar to that found elsewhere in the Old Testament (49:1ff.; Num 26:5ff.; Deut 27:12ff.; 33:2ff.; etc.), but it conflicts with the story of the birth of Benjamin in verses 16-20. For this author, the birth of Benjamin takes place, not in Canaan, but in Mesopotamia, while Jacob is still living with Laban. The Priestly author, who recorded the death and burial of Abraham, now recounts the death and burial of Isaac. Both Jacob and Esau are present at their father's burial (as were Isaac and Ishmael at their father's), for in the Priestly account there has been no break in the relationship between Jacob and Esau.

The reference to the incest of Reuben (v. 22) is but a fragment of an account that must have included Jacob's reaction to Reuben's offensive behavior. It is alluded to again in 49:4, but without any further elaboration that might give us a more complete picture of the event.

36:1-43 The genealogy of Esau. At the conclusion of the Jacob cycle of stories a genealogy of Esau is inserted. This genealogy is actually composed of six distinct lists: (1) verses 1-8; (2) verses 9-14; (3) verses 15-19; (4) verses 20-30; (5) verses 31-39; (6) verses 40-43. The first and second lists are parallel and differ only at the beginning and end. The second list includes grandchildren whose names are repeated again in the third list. The fourth list names the descendants of the original clans that settled in the territory of Seir, later inhabited by the Edomites. These people are called Horites, the biblical designation for the Hurrians. But there is no archaeological evidence that the Hurrians occupied Edomite territory, and the names of the list are clearly Semitic; thus the identity of these ancestors is difficult to determine. The fifth list contains the names of the kings of Edom who reigned prior to the establishment of monarchy in Israel. The sixth list, the clans of Esau, duplicates some of the names of the second list.

It is difficult to determine the historical reliability of any of these lists. The Edomites came east in the thirteenth century B.C.E. with the Ammonites and Moabites. They became a nation before Israel but were conquered and made vassals of Israel by David in the tenth century B.C.E.

The patriarchal sagas begin with a call to venture forth to a strange land with nothing more than a promise. Israel saw in Abraham's journeys its own call to go forth trusting in God. Israel saw in the story of Abraham's faith a testimony to its own faith. Even in the questionable behavior of Jacob, Israel saw its own history. But more important, Israel recognized in these stories God's activity. It saw a gracious God who chose to intervene in our world through a people called to be a special people. This God did not choose a perfect people, but one that, for all its faults, was willing to listen and to follow, and was open to the intervention of the Deity in their lives.

THE JOSEPH STORY

Gen 37:1–50:26

The Joseph story is set apart from the other narratives in the Book of Genesis by its distinctive literary form. It is often referred to as a "novelette" because the narrative is a unified organic whole. From beginning to end, each segment of the story is integrated into the entire narrative. It has its own distinctive theme—peace in the family—but it is also brought into the larger complex of stories. We must be attentive to its unique character, and yet also see it in the context of the entire Book of Genesis.

There is general agreement that the Joseph story has been influenced by the wisdom tradition of Israel. One of the concerns of the wisdom tradition was the success of the individual in life. Success was achieved by diligence and self-discipline. It was important to learn appropriate behavior, self-control, and propriety in speech. In Israel, fear of God was also a necessary factor in attaining wisdom. Joseph embodies all of these characteristics and thus is presented throughout the narrative as a model of wisdom.

37:1-36 Joseph is sold into slavery in Egypt. The Priestly author's contribution to

this chapter (vv. 1-2), as in the entire Joseph story, is minimal. Verse 1 is the Priestly author's conclusion to the Jacob story, and verse 2 begins the Joseph story. The Jacob stories began under the caption "These are the generations of Isaac . . ."; likewise, the Joseph story begins with a reference to the generations of Jacob. The Yahwist and Elohist sources, separate at first (vv. 3-4, J; vv. 5-11, E) have been combined to form the climax of the chapter (vv. 12-36, JE).

Each of the three sources gives its own reason for the hostility of the brothers against Joseph. In the Priestly tradition (vv. 1-2), Joseph brings "bad reports" of his brothers to Jacob. The content of the reports is not specified, but the statement reveals the tension existing between Joseph and his brothers. Jacob's partiality for Joseph is the cause of the dissension in the Yahwist tradition (vv. 3-4). The "long tunic" given to Joseph is a sign of Jacob's favoritism and further arouses the jealousy of Joseph's brothers. This garment was a special coat distinguished by its length and its sleeves, not its color. The older translation "coat of many colors" was based on the Greek text of the Old Testament, not on the Hebrew.

The Elohist (vv. 5-11) introduces into the Joseph story a dream motif that is found again in chapters 40 and 41. In the dreams there is no direct address; rather, the dream itself communicates its message when interpreted. The science of dream interpretation developed to assist in deciphering a dream. The ancients held that in some dreams there was a foreshadowing of the future, and this is the sense in which these dreams are to be understood. The obvious import of the dreams—that Joseph would rule over his brothers—further alienates Joseph from them.

Once the characters have been introduced and the situation delineated, the story is set in motion when Joseph is sent on an errand by Jacob to his brothers, who are pasturing their flocks at some distance from Jacob's settlement. The contradictions in the episode are traced to the presence of the two different sources, the Yahwist and the Elohist. In the Yahwist tradition the brothers plot to kill Joseph, but Judah intercedes and the brothers decide to sell Joseph to the Ishmaelites (v. 27). It is Reuben, in the Elohist narrative, who persuades his brothers not to kill Joseph but to place him in a cistern (vv. 21-22). He hopes to return later to save Joseph, but Midianite traders find Joseph and bring him to Egypt.

It is ironic that the brothers relay the news of Joseph's death by using the now blood-stained tunic of Joseph. It once signaled Joseph's privileged status; now it announces his death. Jacob's great grief is vividly portrayed, but rather than end on this tragic note, the scene shifts to Egypt and the sale of Joseph to Potiphar, an official of Pharaoh's court.

38:1-30 Judah and Tamar. Given the importance of the tribe of Judah in Israel's history, it is not surprising to find a story specifically about its founder. The problem with the story is its present location, for it interrupts the Joseph story. But as we shall see, there are some connections between this story and the context in which it is now found.

The story is attributed to the Yahwist, who telescopes an entire generation in a few verses. Judah separates from his brothers, marries a Canaanite woman, and sires three sons who reach marital age rather quickly. The eldest son, Er, marries a Canaanite woman, Tamar. For an unspecified reason he displeases Yahweh and dies. In the ancient world an unexpected death in the prime of life was believed to be caused by sin. According to the levirate law (Deut 25:5-10), Er's brother must marry his widow because Er died without fathering a child. The first son of this union would be legally recognized as the heir of the deceased brother. Judah, therefore, gives his second son, Onan, to Tamar. But Onan is unwilling to raise up a son for his brother and fails to complete the sexual act. Onan dies because he refused to fulfill his obligation to his brother; no moral judgment is passed on his sexual behavior (vv. 9-10). Judah, after losing two sons, is hesitant to give his third son to Tamar. Judah's failure to carry out his duty sets the stage for the next act, in which Tamar has the dominant role.

After his wife dies, Judah journeys to Timnah for the shearing of his sheep (v. 12). Tamar takes advantage of the situation, disguises herself as a prostitute, and seduces Judah. She insists on taking his seal and cord and staff as pledge of payment. The seal functioned as an ancient means of identification. A seal was incised with the special design of its owner and was worn around the neck by means of an attached cord. When Judah sends his servant with the payment, Tamar cannot be found.

Rather than embarrass himself further by searching for the woman, Judah drops the matter.

Tamar, as expected, conceives a child by Judah (v. 18). Tamar's pregnancy is made known to Judah, who has jurisdiction in this case because Tamar is betrothed to his third son. He sentences her to death, the punishment for adultery, but at the crucial moment she produces his seal and staff, which identify him as the father of the child. Judah exonerates Tamar and admits that he is at fault for his failure to fulfill the levirate law.

The struggle in Tamar's womb (v. 29), like that of Rebekah (25:21-26), anticipates the future conflict between tribes as one child seeks dominance over the other. The name of each child is associated with the manner of his birth. Perez "pushes" ("breach" in the NAB) his brother out of the way in order to be the first-born; Zerah gets his name from the "crimson" thread tied about his wrist by the midwife. Through Tamar's bold act, Judah's line is saved from extinction; from that line will come the greatest of the kings of Israel, David.

Few scholars find any connection between the story of Judah and Tamar and the Joseph story. It does appear to be an intrusion into a narrative otherwise concerned with Joseph and his fate. Nevertheless, there are points of contact that should be noted. The same formula ("please verify . . . he recognized") spoken by Jacob's sons to hide their guilt (37:32-33) is used by Tamar to uncover Judah's guilt (38:25-26). The payment of a kid (38:20) by the deceived Judah recalls the goat in whose blood Joseph's garment was dipped (37:31) to deceive his father, Jacob. Finally, Judah's exposure results from his sexual incontinence, whereas Joseph's continence in chapter 39 brings him through seeming defeat to ultimate triumph. The story permits the narrator to contrast the lives of Judah and Joseph; at the same time, it gives Joseph time to journey to Egypt.

39:1-23 The rise and fall of Joseph. The Yahwist narrative of the Joseph story continues by referring the reader back to the moment when Joseph was sold to the Ishmaelites (37:26-27, 28b). Upon arrival in Egypt, Joseph is sold as a slave to an Egyptian (identified as Potiphar in the Elohist tradition). Joseph soon rises to a position of trust, and the Egyptian is blessed with prosperity because of him. In the Yahwist's view, Joseph's success is due entirely to Yahweh. Yahweh's behind-the-scenes presence is felt throughout the Joseph story and gives it its distinctive theological character.

Verses 1-6 set the scene for the attempted seduction of Joseph by Potiphar's wife. The successful and handsome Joseph is noticed by Potiphar's wife. Joseph refuses her sexual advances, for the act of adultery would be a sin against the trust his master has placed in him and a sin against God. The woman is persistent in her demands, so much so that she seizes hold of Joseph one day, and he eludes her only by leaving behind his garment (v. 12). The garment is then used as evidence against him when she falsely accuses him of trying to seduce her. The punishment for adultery is death. Joseph is in the same position that he was in in chapter 37—facing a life-and-death situation. In chapter 37, instead of being put to death he was sold into slavery; in chapter 39, instead of being put to death he is sent to prison. As Joseph had become a trusted slave, so too in jail he rises to prominence and a position of trust. The advance, as before, is attributed to the presence of Yahweh in his life.

The motif dominant in this chapter, that of an indiscreet woman incriminating a man who refuses her advances, is common in world literature. It is interesting to note that one of the closest parallels to this story is an Egyptian version entitled "A Tale of Two Brothers." This story, except for its ending, is similar to the one in Genesis. This is not to suggest, however, that there is direct relationship between the two stories; rather, both find their origin in widely distributed folklore.

40:1-23 Joseph interprets the prisoners' dreams. A return to the Elohist tradition is signaled by the difference in Joseph's position in jail and the presence, once again, of dreams. In chapter 39 Joseph was put in charge of all the prisoners, but in chapter 40 he is depicted as a slave of two noble prisoners, the royal cupbearer and the baker. The cupbearer was the official keeper and taster of Pharaoh's wine, an important position held by the most loyal and trusted of officials. Likewise, the royal baker occupied a prominent position in Pharaoh's court.

As Joseph serves the two officials, he notices their distress and discovers that it stems from the fact that they cannot get anyone to interpret their dreams (v. 8). Dream interpretation was done by professionals in Egypt. In prison these two officials do not have access to dream interpreters. Joseph dismisses their problem by maintaining that dream interpretation belongs to God. After hearing the dreams, Joseph proceeds to interpret them. Both the cupbearer and the baker will have their heads "lifted up" (vv. 13, 19); for the cupbearer this means reinstatement in Pharaoh's court, but for the baker it means death. Within three days the dreams come true. Though Joseph has asked the cupbearer to bring his case before Pharaoh, the cupbearer forgets about Joseph until Pharaoh himself dreams. Thus Joseph remains in prison for two more years.

41:1-57 Joseph interprets Pharaoh's dreams. The Elohist source continues in this chapter until Joseph comes to power in Egypt, at which point the Yahwist version is intertwined with that of the Elohist. Joseph is brought to Pharaoh to interpret his dreams after "all the magicians and sages of Egypt" (v. 8) have failed. Pharaoh tells his dreams to Joseph, not merely repeating verbatim the account found in verses 1-7 but expanding and enhancing the retelling with added detail (vv. 17-24). Joseph, for his part, repeats that dream interpretation comes from God and then proceeds with his interpretation, which is shown to come true by the end of the chapter (vv. 53-57). The symbolism of the dreams fits in well with the Egyptian background of the story. Seven good years, represented by fat cows and healthy ears of grain, will be followed by seven devastating years of famine, depicted as gaunt, ugly cows and shriveled ears of grain. Joseph follows his interpretation with practical advice, which Pharaoh immediately accepts.

In the Elohist tradition Joseph is installed as master of the palace, which puts him in charge of Egypt's finances. According to the Yahwist, Joseph is appointed vizier of Egypt, an even higher office. Joseph is placed in charge of the administration of the land. The ceremony of installation authentically reflects the political and social customs of Egypt. The signet ring was the royal seal kept by the vizier, and the gold chain was probably a ceremonial emblem of office (v. 42). The robes of fine linen and the chariots indicate Joseph's noble status, as do the criers who run before his chariot.

Joseph is completely drawn into the Egyptian royal court. He is given an Egyptian name, Zaphenath-paneah ("God speaks and lives"), and an Egyptian wife. His new name and the fact that he marries the daughter of an Egyptian priest apparently cause no problems for the Yahwist, who simply records it as part of Joseph's new position in Egypt. During the time of prosperity two sons are born to Joseph and are given names that relate to his new life. His previous suffering is "forgotten," so his first child receives the name Manasseh; his present state of prosperity is echoed in the name of the second child, Ephraim, "God has made me fruitful" (vv. 51-52).

The Priestly author's only contribution (v. 46a) tells of Joseph's age. Thirteen years have elapsed since Joseph's entry into Egypt and his rise to power.

42:1-38 Joseph tests his brothers. This chapter is dominated by the Elohist source but is supplemented by a few fragments of the Yahwist (for example, vv. 27-28). The narrative returns to the theme of the relationship between Joseph and his brothers after depicting his rise to power in Egypt. The famine has spread to Palestine, causing Jacob to send his sons to Egypt, for he has heard that food is available there. He does not send Benjamin, Rachel's other son, who presumably has replaced Joseph in his father's affection.

Joseph's dreams (37:5-10) are fulfilled when his brothers bow before him (v. 6). He recognizes them, but they do not recognize him. He begins to play a game with them, the import of which becomes clear only as the story continues. Joseph accuses his brothers of being spies. In their eagerness to defend themselves, they reveal to Joseph what he wants to know about his family. He insists that they bring Benjamin to him to prove the truth of their claim that they are not spies. By this means Joseph can determine whether or not his brothers have changed. Do they bear the same jealous hatred against Benjamin that they once directed against him? They had subjected Joseph to an unknown fate; now he does the same to them.

At first Joseph insists that all the brothers must stay in prison while one of them returns to fetch Benjamin, but finally he keeps only Simeon in prison as a guarantee that the other brothers will return (v. 24). He returns their money to their bags; they will not discover it until later. The conflation of sources is revealed by the contradiction between verses 27 and 35. According to the Yahwist (v. 27), the money is found on the first day of the journey home, but in verse 35 it is found only when the brothers arrive at their destination. The chapter ends on the same note as chapter 37, the lament of Jacob for his favorite son.

43:1-34 The brothers return to Egypt. The tension begun in chapter 42 intensifies in chapters 43–44 until it is resolved in chapter 45. In the narrative of chapters 43–44, we return to the Yahwist source, which accounts for some of the irregularities in the story as it continues. Simeon, imprisoned in Egypt, seems to have been completely forgotten in the opening scene. It also appears that Jacob is only now informed of the condition of their return to Egypt. Only the hopelessness of their situation, coupled with Judah's vow to assure Benjamin's safety, convinces Jacob to allow Benjamin to accompany his other sons to Egypt. Jacob sends gifts with them, hoping to placate the Egyptian official who has so falsely accused his sons.

When the brothers arrive in Egypt (v. 16), everything seems to go well for them. The Egyptian official has provided a banquet for them. Simeon has been returned. Gradually their hesitancy is overcome. Their attempt to return the money found in their bags is brushed off. The money is mysteriously spoken of as a gift from God (v. 23). Though they approach the banquet with a certain wariness, it disappears when they see how Joseph treats Benjamin. Finally they begin to relax and enjoy the festivities. Upon seeing Benjamin, Joseph is overcome with emotion and must leave the room to regain control, yet he still does not reveal himself to his brothers.

44:1-34 Joseph's final test of his brothers. The seriousness of the game Joseph is playing is seen in the final test of his brothers. He instructs his steward to return the money of his brothers and to place his own silver cup in Benjamin's bag. One wonders why the money is returned, for it is never mentioned again in the story; the cup alone serves as incriminating evidence. This cup was a sacred object used for divination. Exactly how it was used is not certain. One possible way was to drop objects into the cup filled with liquid and decipher the resultant rippling of the liquid. Another possibility was to mix oil and water in the cup and examine the patterns created to find their meaning. That Joseph used such a cup does not seem to have bothered the narrator, but divination practices were forbidden in Israel (Lev 19:31; Deut 18:10-11).

The brothers have gone but a short distance when they are overtaken by Joseph's steward (v. 6). They are genuinely shocked when accused of theft. Proclaiming their innocence, they vow death to the thief and slavery for the rest of them if the cup is found in their possession. These extreme punishments are rejected by the steward and later by Joseph himself. The punishment will be slavery, not death, for the thief, and the rest of them will go free. By isolating Benjamin from his brothers, Joseph wants to see whether or not they will allow Benjamin to become a slave and seize the opportunity to go free themselves.

As expected, the cup is found in Benjamin's bag, and the brothers return to Egypt. After a harsh reprimand from Joseph, Judah issues an impassioned speech. We may be surprised that he admits their guilt (v. 16) so soon after maintaining their innocence, but Judah sees in their present situation God's judgment upon them for what they had done to Joseph. They are indeed guilty, but until now they have escaped detection and punishment. Judah's stress on his father's grief at the loss of Joseph and his great fear that Benjamin would not return home become the basis for his request that he take Benjamin's place. Through Judah's speech Joseph learns that his brothers have changed. The murderous hatred that caused them to get rid of him has been replaced by a self-sacrificial concern for Benjamin. Brothers who once were indifferent to their father's grief display great solicitude and will do what they can to spare him further sorrow.

45:1-28 Joseph reveals himself to his brothers. In this chapter the Elohist source is again intertwined with the Yahwist story, giving rise to doublets (vv. 3a/4b) and discrepancies (45:16ff./46:31ff.). But rather than distracting from the chapter, the blending of sources actually adds to the chapter's inner credibility.

With Judah's speech the game has gone as far as it can go. The climax has come—Joseph must act. He is overcome by emotion upon hearing Judah's appeal and decides to reveal his identity at last. His brothers' bewilderment opens the way for Joseph's second disclosure: "do not reproach yourselves . . . . God has sent me here ahead of you" (v. 5). The underlying theology of the Joseph story is made explicit. God has directed and guided the course of events. What the brothers meant as evil, God has redeemed. God is the one who sent Joseph to Egypt to preserve a remnant and to deliver Jacob's family. The terms "remnant" and "deliverance" (v. 7) become important Old Testament terms expressing Israel's conviction that God intervenes in its history and preserves it from total destruction.

Joseph acquits his brothers and they are reconciled (vv. 14-15). The brothers are "able to talk with him" (v. 15), showing how completely the situation of chapter 37 has been reversed (see 37:4). The tension that has been building since chapter 42 is finally resolved. The denouement will include telling Jacob the news that Joseph lives, Jacob's relocation in Egypt, and the meeting between Joseph and his father.

When the brothers reveal to their father that Joseph lives and holds a position of honor in Egypt, Jacob is understandably dumbfounded. But gradually he is convinced of the truth of their claim and decides to go to Egypt. No mention is made of the brothers' guilty deed, for it has been superseded by God's saving intervention.

46:1–47:12, 27-28 Jacob travels to Egypt and settles there. The Yahwist source dominates in the final scenes of the Joseph story, but the Elohist and Priestly authors also contribute to its conclusion. According to the Yahwist, Jacob decides to go to Egypt (45:28; 46:1a), but for the Elohist this trip is taken in response to God's command (46:2-4). This Elohist insertion is different in style and form from the Joseph story. It shifts the focus of the Joseph story from that of the relationship between brothers to Jacob's descent into Egypt, and incorporates the Joseph story into the larger picture of Israel's history as a preparation for the Exodus.

The genealogical insertion of the Priestly author (vv. 6-27) certainly existed independently of its present context. Benjamin, who was a child in the Joseph story, now has ten sons! The list appears to be a summary of the genealogy found in Num 26. The number "seventy" for the descendants of Jacob (v. 27) is arrived at only by including Jacob himself and Dinah among Jacob's descendants. The original purpose of this genealogy cannot be determined, nor is it clear what purpose it serves in the present context. The Priestly conclusion to this genealogy (47:27-28) has been displaced by the conclusion of the Joseph story.

Verse 28 resumes the story interrupted by the Priestly genealogy. The long-awaited meeting between Joseph and his father presents a moving picture. Jacob's joy is complete in being reunited with this son whom he believed to be dead (46:30).

The final scene of the Joseph story takes up the practical consideration of where in Egypt Jacob and his family are to settle. Joseph's diplomatic skills are shown in his instructions to his father and brothers in preparing them for the meeting with Pharaoh (vv. 33-34). The territory of Goshen would have offered suitable grazing land for Jacob's flocks, but would Pharaoh agree to settle these foreigners in an unsupervised border province? Joseph's insistence that the family represent themselves as shepherds is meant to assure Pharaoh of their peaceful intentions as well as to indicate that Goshen would be suitable pastureland away from the city. There is no extrabiblical support for the statement that "shepherds are abhorrent to the Egyptians" (v. 34), but the attitude of distrust between settled peoples and nomads is well attested.

The meeting between Pharaoh and Joseph's family goes better than anticipated. Not only does Pharaoh give them Goshen as the place to settle, but he also suggests that they be appointed superintendents of the royal herds (v. 5a).

The final scene, with Jacob before Pharaoh (vv. 5b-11), comes from the Priestly source. In a polite exchange between Pharaoh and Jacob, the patriarch describes his 130 years of life as "few and hard" (v. 9) in comparison with the 175 years of Abraham's life and the 180 years of Isaac's life. He refers to his life as that of a "wayfarer." The term is often used in the patriarchal narratives (17:8; 28:4; 36:7; 37:1) to describe the lifestyle of the patriarchs, for whom the possession of the land is given only in promise, a promise not fulfilled for generations.

47:13-26 Joseph's land policy. There is no logical connection between verses 13-26 (from the Yahwist) and the previous section; the passage would be more appropriately located following the account of Joseph's rise to power in chapter 41. The passage relates how Joseph's economic policies during the period of famine enabled the Egyptians to survive only by selling their land to Pharaoh and becoming serfs. Only the temple lands were exempt. The situation presented describes accurately the decline of the free peasantry in Egypt. However, the story is remembered, not for its historical interest, but for the picture of Joseph that it presents. He is a wise and capable administrator, able to deal effectively with each new crisis.

47:29–48:22 The blessing of Ephraim and Manasseh. The tradition of Jacob's last days is found in all three sources. In the Yahwist version (47:29-31), Jacob's dying request is that he be buried with his ancestors in Canaan. Jacob's insistence that Joseph take an oath (compare 24:2) that he will do as asked indicates the importance of this request. Burial in the family tomb was not simply a fitting end to one's life but signified a bond with one's ancestors. In addition, for Jacob, burial in Canaan represents a claim to the land and anticipates the day of his descendants' return from Egypt.

In the Elohist tradition (48:1-2, 7), Joseph is called to his father's bedside, repeating essentially the scene found in 47:29. The reference to Rachel's grave in 48:7 is certainly incomplete. Perhaps in the Elohist tradition Jacob requests to be buried with Rachel, unlike the Priestly tradition, in which Jacob is buried in the cave of Machpelah.

In 48:3-6 the Priestly author depicts Jacob's adoption of Joseph's sons, Ephraim and Manasseh, in terms reminiscent of the promise given to Jacob at Bethel (35:6, 9-12). The tribe of Joseph, early in its history (Judg 5; Num 26:5-51) split into two separate tribes, the tribes of Ephraim and Manasseh. They settled in the Samaritan mountains and became powerful tribes of the northern kingdom. The adoption scene is meant to show how Ephraim and Manasseh became tribal leaders even though they were not the natural sons of Jacob. By adoption Jacob makes his grandsons full members of the family (Israel) and equal to the other tribes.

A second version of the blessing and adoption of Manasseh and Ephraim is ascribed to the Yahwist (vv. 8-12). Manasseh and Ephraim are not simply adopted as sons, but the future position of the two tribes is indicated in the manner in which Jacob blesses them. Joseph seeks to place the elder under Jacob's right hand, the place of honor, but Jacob crosses his hands, so that the younger is given precedence over the elder. This is a common motif found in the Yahwist (Abel over Cain, ch. 4; Isaac over Ishmael, 17:19-21; Jacob himself over Esau, ch. 27; Perez over Zerah, 38:27-30), and reflects the future destiny of the two tribes, for the tribe of Ephraim will soon surpass the tribe of Manasseh and become the most powerful tribe in the northern kingdom.

The blessing itself is found in two forms: verses 15-16 and verse 20. Both forms use traditional blessing formulas. In verses 15-16 Jacob invokes God as the God of Abraham and Isaac, thus establishing a link between the God worshiped by his ancestors and the God he himself worships. He addresses God as "shepherd," a frequent Old Testament title that suggests God's concern for the people. The third title, "Angel," refers to Jacob's own experience of the Deity as deliverer. The blessing ensures numerous descendants and a glorious future for the tribes represented by Joseph's sons. The blessing of verse 20 is reminiscent of the promise to Abraham (12:3b).

The final verse of chapter 48 is not clear. It appears that Jacob gives a part of the land of Canaan to Joseph. The term translated as "Shechem," referring to the city, also means "shoulder" or "mountain slope." It is not clear which Jacob means, but the city itself is later associated with the tribes of Ephraim and Manasseh. If the city is meant, then the final phrase presents a problem, for according to chapter 34 Jacob condemned the violence of Simeon and Levi in Shechem. Perhaps a variant tradition of the conquest of Shechem forms the background of this verse.

49:1-27 The blessing of Jacob. In chapter 49, under the fiction of Jacob's deathbed blessing of his sons, we find a rather haphazard collection of sayings about the characteristics and future destiny of the twelve tribes.

Some of the sayings are certainly ancient, but the poem itself cannot predate the tenth century B.C.E., for it speaks of the rule of the tribe of Judah, which occurred at that time. The text is corrupt and parts of the poem are untranslatable, compounding the problems of interpretation.

The tribe of Reuben disappeared early as an independent tribe. The saying of verses 3-4 explains its fall from prominence as retribution for Reuben's incestuous crime (35:22). Behind the curses of Simeon and Levi (vv. 5-7) stand the events recorded in chapter 34; the violence of their revenge against Shechem for the rape of Dinah is condemned. The text about Judah (vv. 8-12) is in part obscure. What is clear is the allusion to the future rule of Israel through the tribe of Judah (v. 10). Of the tribe of Zebulun, it is said only that it dwelt by the sea (v. 13). The tribe of Issachar is derided for allowing itself to be lured by the fertile plain, only to become slaves of the Canaanites (vv. 14-15). By a play on words (Dan comes from a Hebrew root meaning "to judge"), the tribe of Dan is praised for establishing justice in its own territory (v. 16). The serpent image in verse 17 is not meant to be derogatory but calls to mind the small tribe's victories over mighty enemies. The tribe of Gad is characterized as successfully defending itself against raiding bands of nomads (v. 19). The tribe of Asher occupied the fertile region north of Mount Carmel, which was noted for its rich produce (v. 20). The saying about Naphtali is obscure (v. 21). The blessing on Joseph (vv. 22-27) stands apart from the rest of the poem because of its distinctive form. It is the only blessing properly so-called, and it appears to be derived from a very ancient fertility blessing. In verses 25b-26a there are direct parallels to Canaanite blessings. The tribe of Benjamin is praised for its might (v. 28).

49:28–50:14 The death and burial of Jacob. The Priestly account of Jacob's deathbed scene (49:1a), interrupted by the "blessing" of chapter 49, is now resumed. It parallels the Yahwist's version of Jacob's request to be buried with his ancestors (47:29-31). The conclusion of the Priestly author (50:12-13) shows Jacob's sons carrying out his last request. According to this tradition, Jacob is buried in the cave of Machpelah, the burial site of Abraham and Sarah.

The death and burial of Jacob from the Yahwist source are found in 50:1-11, 14. The embalming of Jacob's body does not seem to have religious significance but is done simply to preserve the body for the long trip to Canaan. The long mourning period (v. 3b) and the presence of high Egyptian officials in the funeral procession (vv. 7-9) suggest that Jacob was given a kingly funeral. According to the Yahwist, Jacob was buried in the Transjordan (50:10-11).

50:15-21 Joseph assures his brothers. Joseph's brothers fear that he will take revenge upon them now that their father is dead. This scene gives the Elohist the opportunity before closing his story to reiterate the theology that underlies the story of Joseph. What they meant for evil, God meant for good. Joseph insists that what they did to him has been overshadowed and redeemed by God's saving will. They were but instruments in God's plan for the salvation of Israel.

50:22-26 Joseph's death. In the epilogue Joseph's last days are reviewed by the Elohist. Joseph's adoption of Machir's children provides a basis for this tribe's later standing within the Israelite confederacy (Num 32:39-40; Judg 5:14). Joseph's final words about the land of promise are significant. They indicate that though this story ends in a foreign land, the promise given by God to Abraham, Isaac, and Jacob will be fulfilled. The end of Genesis points to the destiny of Israel: they are to become the liberated people of Yahweh.

CONCLUSION

In the Book of Genesis we have moved from the moment of creation through a history of sin to the call of Abraham, of Isaac, of Jacob, and finally to Joseph and the tribes in Egypt. In these stories we have learned of God's relationship to the world and to Israel. We have learned of God as creator, as judge, as redeemer. We have met a God who accepts the weakness of humanity and continues to love, a God who guides and directs, a God who is able to bring good out of evil. Genesis is only the beginning of the story, the beginning of the acts of God. The story continues not only throughout the Old and New Testaments but in our own lives and our world.

EXODUS

John F. Craghan

INTRODUCTION

The significance of the Exodus

The Exodus or the going out from Egypt lies at the very heart of Israel's faith experience. The God who acted on her behalf was not an insignificant deity of the ancient Near East cut off from reality and relegated to the realm of mythical time. Rather, Israel's God dramatically entered the arena of real time and real people. As the introduction to the Decalogue puts it, "I, the Lord, am your God, who brought you out of the land of Egypt, that place of slavery" (Exod 20:2). To mention the name Yahweh means to conjure up the image of a totally involved deity. To utter that name is to provide an identity. Yahweh without the Exodus is no Yahweh at all!

The Exodus identifies not only Yahweh but also Israel. Israel emerges as God's people precisely in the Exodus. That event implies that the former Egyptian slaves were different from all their contemporaries. The Exodus with its covenant experience at Sinai distinguishes them as Yahweh's people. The going out, therefore, was a selection process. The author of Exodus 3:7 succinctly expresses that process in these words: "I will take you as my own people, and you shall have me as your God."

The biblical book that captures this twofold identity is the Book of Exodus. It is the biblical document par excellence for exposing Israel's roots. Israel realized that those roots lay outside the Promised Land. However, it is the glory of Israel's writers that her origins could be presented in such a powerful yet intimate way. The Book of Exodus is not simply the record of Israel's itineraries. It is her identity papers, the record of human interaction and divine grace, of human success and failure, and of divine assistance and forgiveness.

The experience captured in the Book of Exodus was never subject to a generation gap. By providing identity, this unique book did not stifle growth. Thus Israel could apply the memory of the first going out to varied but nonetheless precarious situations in her history. In the sixth century B.C.E. Second Isaiah could recount the return from Babylon to Jerusalem as a second Exodus: "In the desert prepare the way of the Lord! Make straight in the wasteland a highway for our God!" (Isa 40:3). In the second century B.C.E. the author of Judith described the overthrow of another threat to Israel's faith (Hellenism in the guise of Holofernes and his troops). Among other things he fittingly depicted his heroine after the manner of Israel at the Reed Sea: "For the Lord is God; he crushes warfare, and sets his encampment among his people; he snatched me from the hands of my persecutors" (Jdt 16:2). In the first century B.C.E. the author of the Book of Wisdom sought to resolve the problem of retribution for the just and the wicked in metropolitan Egypt. He adapted the Exodus experience and concluded: "For by the things through which their foes [the Egyptians] were punished they [the Israelites] in their need were benefited" (Wis 11:5).

No historical account

The Egyptian records are as silent as the Sphinx regarding this key event in Israel's faith experience. And this is hardly surprising. The Egyptian texts envision the greater honor and glory of Pharaoh. Moses' dealings with the handicapped leader of Egypt in the plagues would hardly contribute to the thrust of Egyptian historiography. Moreover, according to a widely accepted view, those involved in the Exodus were a typical phenomenon in the ancient Near East.

The Egyptian records speak of Apiru while those written in Akkadian (an eastern Semitic language) refer to Habiru. These 'Apiru/Habiru are often described as displaced people, disturbers of the peace, malcontents who harassed the ancient Near East during the second and third millennia. Not infrequently these 'Apiru/Habiru hired themselves out as mercenaries. It is also known that these Bedouin also provided a work force for Egyptian building campaigns.

The word "Hebrew" derives from "Habiru." However, one must bear in mind that "Habiru" is originally a sociological, not an ethnic, term. It is significant that "Hebrew" occurs in the Book of Exodus especially when the sojourn in Egypt and the Egyptian oppression are concerned (see 2:11). It is likely that a process of assimilation took place: ancestors of the Israelites who had freely gone down to Egypt later became assimilated to other 'Apiru/Habiru. Since such ancestors were seminomadic herders, they would obviously have resented a change in their lifestyle whereby they were reduced to a slave labor force.

Not only were there several entries into Egypt over the centuries but there were also several departures. The text itself reflects an awareness of several different routes. However, from the vantage point of Israel's faith experience there is only *the* Exodus. This is the going out led by Moses that also included the theophany at Sinai. It is likely that this group was relatively small. As this event was recited in worship and pondered by Israel's theologians, it gradually took on epic proportions. The small band grew in both size and importance. At the same time it was not simply a question of arithmetic enlargement. It was also a matter of faith perception. All Israel saw herself represented in the small yet expanding group that had managed to break free of Pharaoh's brickyards.

Setting of the Exodus

Although the biblical account provides no historical report in the modern sense of the term, there are some indications of the setting. Most authorities place the Exodus in the thirteenth century B.C.E. According to these authorities the Pharaoh who oppressed the Israelites was Ramses II, the great builder of the New Kingdom who reigned from 1290 to 1224 B.C.E. One reason for this view is the testimony of Exod 1:11 that refers to the supply city of Raamses. It is known that Ramses II set up his capital in the northeast corner of the Nile Delta and that the term "city of Raamses" was not used after 1100 B.C.E.

Although some would distinguish Ramses II, the oppressor of the Israelites, from his successor, the Pharaoh of the Exodus, on the basis of Exod 2:23, reliable authors still identify Ramses II as both the oppressor and the Pharaoh of the Exodus. According to this view the Exodus would have occurred around 1250 B.C.E. in an area northeast of present-day Cairo and west of the Suez Canal. At the same time one must frankly note the ongoing study of the Exodus and Conquest date. One recent study, for example, suggests dating these events in the fifteenth century B.C.E.

The type of literature

The Book of Exodus is popular literature. As mentioned above, it is not a sober scientific historical treatise. In the other direction it is the blending of different literary types to correspond to Israel's basic perceptions and attitudes. In the plagues there is clear evidence of legendary embellishment. In the crossing of the Reed Sea there is all the dramatization of an epic account. In the rubrics for Passover the effects of liturgy are obvious. In the Covenant Code (20:22–23:19) and the Priestly legislation (chs. 25–31, 35–40) the legal hand is at work. In 15:1b-18 the songwriter is present. The variety of literary types in this popular literature witnesses to the variety of human efforts to capture a central experience. Israel did it her way and the reader must be willing to accept this fact and thus be enriched in the process.

Given the centrality of the Exodus for Israel's faith, one should not be surprised to find a number of theologians at work. Exegetes usually point to at least three theologians in the composition of this work. The first is the Yahwist (= J) who writes in the tenth century B.C.E. during the heady days of the Davidic-Solomonic kingdom. The second is the Elohist (= E) who reflects a period of religious turmoil and syncretism in the eighth or ninth century B.C.E. The third is the Priestly Writer (= P) who struggles to offer a picture of hope during the debacle of the Exile in the sixth century B.C.E. It would be wrong for the reader to attempt to harmonize their sometimes conflicting views. Rather, the reader must allow such theologians the requisite freedom to interpret. Such a stance recognizes that these writers judged the past in the light of their present and with a view to the future needs of Israel. As the commentary will show, such writers had their prejudices—inspiration does not neutralize the human tendency to impose one's view. Ultimately one must be as open as the Bible itself. It canonized not one party line but indeed a variety of party lines.

New exoduses—new liberations

The Exodus story continues to have an impact today, especially in Latin America, the locus of liberation theology. For liberation theologians the chief task is to reread the text in a new light, that is, against the background of exploitation that has characterized so much of Latin American history. In their view the ancient story of Israel's bondage and subsequent deliverance is as timely as ever. It shows that liberation is a process, not an acquired result. It is an ongoing human concern to uncover the manipulation of fellow humans and to proffer the means of genuine human transformation.

The Exodus story also underlines the need for the emergence of ever new prophets after the manner of Moses. It points up the task of such prophets to make people aware of the real malaise from which they suffer. Such prophets, therefore, must articulate the absence of genuine freedom that modern society so heartily encourages. There are ever new Pharaohs whose claims to divinity must be unmasked. At the same time these prophets are bidden to speak a word of hope. They are called upon not only to transport their people from the brickyards but also to energize them to the radical possibility of a genuine existence where misery is known as evil and hope is recognized as attainable. Moses thus transcends the limitations of the thirteenth century B.C.E. to let God's Word have an ever new impact.

COMMENTARY

PART I: THE EXODUS FROM EGYPT

Exod 1:1–15:21

The first part of Exodus provides both the background for the departure and the actual start of the going out. The final editor of the book (perhaps writing around 400 B.C.E.) has pulled together the work of his principal sources (JEP) as well as some independent traditions. In a spirit of fidelity to these sources and traditions this final editor has chosen not to even out various repetitions and inconsistencies. Nevertheless he has attained a certain unity so that, despite these variations, there is a certain flow to his narrative.

In this first part of his work the final editor seeks to provide answers to the following questions: What brought about the misery experienced by the Israelites in Egypt? What are the credentials of the leader? How did this leader respond to God's call? In what ways did the leader attempt to deal with Pharaoh? What was the final catalyst that provoked the going out? How should Israel continue to celebrate this going out? What happened as Israel journeyed to the Reed Sea? How did God intervene at the Reed Sea?

1:1-7 Israel's growth. The background of this introduction is Gen 46:1-4. This passage sums up the past by referring to the patriarchs (Isaac and Jacob/Israel). It also anticipates the future: namely, Israel will become a great nation in Egypt and God himself will lead them out. At the same time this passage creates tension and raises a problem. What will happen to God's people when they do leave Egypt? But, more fundamentally, how can such a small group become a great nation?

P is the author of 1:1-7. Genealogies and lists are a favorite device of this writer (see Gen 5:1; 6:9). Moreover, the language of verse 7 reflects P's vocabulary ("fruitful," "numerous," "filled"). It is the fulfillment of the command in Gen 1:28: "Be fertile and multiply; fill the earth . . . ." Against the background of Exile this passage is intended by P to offer hope and encouragement to God's despondent people. Their temptation is to disparage the Promised Land and not return from Exile (see Num 14:1-3, 5-10, 26-38). In its present position this passage explains how the small group developed into such a significant number.

1:8-14 The oppression of God's people. This section consists of J (vv. 8-11) and P (vv. 13-14). P states in a rather straightforward manner the results of Israel's fertility, that is, their reduction to the slave labor of building. While this policy was only logical for the Egyptian autocratic state (compare Gen 47:13-26), it was totally opposed to Israel's tradition of freedom. J, however, is not content to register Egypt's usual attitude. He accentuates the threat that Israel posed and the opposite results of Egyptian oppression.

J notes the new policy of the Egyptian government. With the emergence of a new king (whom the tradition chooses to leave nameless) there is a new manner of dealing with the prolific Israelites. Thus the oppression is directly related to the political threat that such numbers imply. One can legitimately ask whether the imposition of slave labor is really calculated to achieve the reduction of the Israelite population. With a certain irony, however, J wryly observes that the Egyptian plan was counterproductive. Instead of limiting the population, the policy only succeeded in encouraging its growth.

1:15-22 The suppression of God's people. E is generally considered the author of this doublet, that is, the repetition of substantially the same account in a somewhat different form. (Here the author prefers "God" [*elohîm*] to J's "Lord" [*Yahweh*]; he also designates the political ruler "the king of Egypt" whereas J opts for "Pharaoh."). Here the manner of defeating God's people is not by oppression—the slave labor of building—but

by suppression—the killing of all the baby boys. While suppression would appear to be more apt than oppression for the purposes of population control, it flies in the face of political expediency. Rulers are not likely to deplete their labor force and thus endanger their building programs by killing off the supply of workers. However, in this popular literature it does provide a marvelous setting for resolving the dire situation. The final editor will link E's account with J's birth of the hero in the following chapter.

There are other indications of this popular literature. Although the birth rate is enormous, only two midwives are required to care for the deliveries. Although the Egyptians thought the king was divine and therefore remained secluded from the masses of the people, here two Hebrew midwives have direct access to divine Pharaoh. Moreover, their devious explanation of the increasing population (v. 19) and hence their ability to outwit the sagacious Egyptian monarch are also in keeping with the character of popular literature.

The episode reflects what many critics regard as a motif of the E author, the fear of God (see Gen 20:11; Exod 20:20). It is this emphasis on fear of God (v. 17) that leads to civil disobedience. But the civil disobedience in such a righteous cause is not without its reward. Not only does the nation continue to increase and multiply (v. 20) but so do the offspring of the two midwives (v. 21). Nevertheless, the chapter closes on an ominous note that sets the stage for the birth of the hero.

2:1-10 The birth of the hero. There is a natural propensity to know something about the birth and youth of the hero (compare the theologically oriented infancy narratives of Jesus in Matt 1–2 and Luke 1–2). Humans seek to find extraordinary signs that stamp the person as superhuman right from the moment of birth. For example, Hercules strangles a snake in his cradle. Here J accedes to the needs of his own audience.

The ancient Near East provides certain analogues. Sargon, the great Semitic king who reigned in the twenty-fourth century B.C.E., is described in a legend as follows. His mother placed him in a basket of rushes which she sealed with bitumen. She then cast him into the river upon which he floated until drawn out. There is also an adoption account in which a child is found and then given to a nurse who is paid to keep him for three years. Afterwards the child is adopted and trained as a scribe. It is not unlikely that J's account is also inspired by this adoption story.

The final editor has wisely chosen to connect this passage with E's account of the suppression and thus set the stage for Moses' legend. This arrangement results in having the villain, Pharaoh, caught in his own trap. It is not simply anyone who rescues the baby boy—it is the Pharaoh's own daughter!

Moses is an Egyptian name meaning "is born." In keeping with Israelite sensitivities the name of the Egyptian god is omitted. (Compare Thutmose, that is "the god Thut is born.") This form of Egyptian name was given to children born on the god's anniversary. There is further evidence of Moses' Egyptian background in the Egyptian names borne by members of his family (see 6:16 for Merari and 6:25 for Phinehas). It is also noteworthy that Reuel's daughters in 2:19 refer to the hero as "an Egyptian." However, apart from these notices there is no further information about Moses' background. To be sure, the interest of the Israelite audience lay elsewhere.

2:11-22 The flight to Midian. J, the author responsible for this episode, endeavors to show Moses as a person interested in his own people. He is bent upon foreshadowing or anticipating a problem that will appear later. This problem is the question posed by the Hebrew in verse 14: "Who has appointed *you* ruler and judge over us?" It is precisely this question of credentials that Moses will have to face shortly. Moses' flight to Midian also foreshadows or anticipates other happenings. Just as Moses has to flee to the desert, so too the people of Israel will head for the desert. Just as Moses encounters God at the mountain (3:1), so too the people of Israel will experience God at the mountain (19:18).

The land of Midian, Moses' home for the time being, is a desert area in the Sinai peninsula. In later traditions (see Num 25:6-9; Judg 6:1–7:25) these desert-dwelling Midianites will become the implacable enemies of Israel. In the present tradition, however, the Midianites and those associated with Moses are related tribes. (Reuel is a tribal name, not a personal name.) Chapter 18 will show how Moses learned many practical things from these Midianites.

J presents Moses as a man with a checkered background. Although J likes stories of wells, for example, Rebecca (Gen 24:15) and Rachel (29:10), he must introduce this lady at the well, Zipporah, as a non-Israelite. Thus Moses is an Israelite of the tribe of Levi (2:1) who is brought up as an Egyptian but who must then flee his Egyptian home only to meet non-Israelites, one of whom he marries. These are hardly the best credentials. Hence the lingering question: With such credentials, will Moses be able to offset the oppression/suppression in Egypt?

2:23-25 The Exodus as lament liturgy. This description is not merely a passing note in the overall story. The final editor has combined the long period of time (v. 23a—probably from E) with the miserable state of the people (vv. 23b-25—a P passage). This state is presented in lament language ("groaned and cried out"). (Note the repetition of this language in 3:7, 9; 6:5.) The verb "to cry out" is the typical expression of the poor and disenfranchised; it is a cry that God cannot ignore. Lament is linked to covenant (v. 25). In covenant theology the people's problem necessarily becomes God's problem; the people's frustration necessarily becomes God's frustration. Liberation always begins by recognizing the plight of the poor.

3:1-6 The burning bush. This scene is a combination of J and E, though mostly J. (E is present in parts of verse 1, for example, "Horeb, the mountain of God," and verse 4b.) This combination of sources is significant theologically, since it indicates the diversity and richness of Israelite tradition. No one tradition could claim an exclusive right to tell the whole story. (This combination of sources will be very evident in the rest of chapter 3.) One should also note that here (v. 1) Moses' father-in-law is Jethro, whereas in 2:18 it is Reuel. Unlike Reuel, Jethro is a personal name. (For further complications see Judg 1:16; 4:11.)

J probably chose the term "bush" (in Hebrew s^eneh) in order to connect this scene with Yahweh's mountain (in Hebrew $sînai$). The burning of the bush is thus linked to the fire of the theophany of Sinai (see 19:18). Hence there is a close association of the Exodus and Sinai right from the very start. What emerges from this scene for J is the twofold dimension of awe and historical continuity. Awe is expressed in Moses' gesture of removing his sandals because of the intrinsic holiness of the encounter with Yahweh—Yahweh's presence sanctifies the ground. Consequently, Moses hides his face. Historical continuity is articulated in verse 6. The God who speaks to Moses has been active over the centuries in his concern for this people. The God of Moses is also the God of the patriarchs (see also 3:16).

3:7-15 The commissioning of Moses. This scene is intimately bound up with the divine revelation at the burning bush. The experience of God is thus related to Moses' function in Israel. Israel's theologians reflected the tradition that regarded Moses as a prophet. He was, therefore, one who spoke on God's behalf to the people of Israel—he was God's spokesperson (see Deut 18:15-20). Faithful to the perception of Moses' prophetic office, both J and E employ the literary genre of call narrative. (See Judg 6:11-21; Isa 6:1-13.) This is not intended to be a blow-by-blow account of what transpired in Midian. Rather, it attempts to communicate the meaning of God's choice for a given audience without excluding some type of original experience. The call narrative builds upon the human need for signs and reassurances.

Both J and E offer somewhat different versions of Moses' call. However, the basic structure is the same: (a) divine response to prayer that presupposes a given difficulty: 3:7 (J), 3:9 (E); (b) God's promise to save: 3:8 (J), 3:10 (E); (c) the commission: 3:16-17 (J), 3:9 (E); (d) Moses' objection: 4:1 (J), 3:11 (E); (e) overcoming the objection by a sign: 4:1-9 (J), 3:12 (E); (f) second objection: 4:10 (J), 3:13 (E); (g) God's final or quasi-final answer: 4:13-16 (J), 3:14-15 (E), 4:17 (E?).

Both J (3:7) and E (3:9) begin by noting the plight of the people in lamentation language ("cry"). In developing the divine promise to save, J and E stress different dimensions of Moses' office. In 3:8 (J) Yahweh is the one who intends to deliver the Israelites, while Moses in 3:16 (J) is dispatched to speak to the people. In 3:10 (E) Moses is sent specifically to bring the Israelites out of Egypt. Although the verb "to send" (vv. 10, 12, 13) designates the prophet as an envoy (see Jer 1:7; 26:12, 15), E appears to allot a much more substantial role to Moses.

J emphasizes not only Israel's deliverance from the Egyptians but also the goal of that

intervention: entrance into the Promised Land. That land flows with milk and honey (v. 8). This expression is borrowed from mythology, depicting the land as a veritable earthly paradise. The reference to the Canaanites, Hittites, and others (vv. 8, 17) is to the pre-Israelite inhabitants of the land (for a seven-people enumeration see Gen 15:20-21; Deut 7:1). The Exodus, therefore, is not only a going out—it is also a going up, namely, into the land formerly inhabited by these nations.

The proofs demanded by Moses in the E tradition are significant. In verse 12 the sign to provide credentials for Moses before Pharaoh and Israel is that the people will later meet to worship God on this very mountain. This is an anomaly in the call narrative, since signs occur immediately, not at some point in the future. Perhaps the compactness of the E tradition is the reason for this anomaly.

Moses still needs further proof in approaching the Israelites (v. 13). In the E tradition this proof is the disclosure of the divine name (vv. 14-15). It should be pointed out that for J this disclosure of the name Yahweh (consistently translated "the Lord" in the NAB) demanded no special scene. From the very beginning of his narrative (Gen 2:4b) J uses the personal name Yahweh and in Gen 4:26 onwards presumes that this name is known by humans. Up to this scene in chapter 3, E has simply employed the general word "God" (*elohim* in Hebrew—hence the distinction of divine names early became a key criterion in separating the J and E sources). As one might suspect, this scene is theologically central in E's scheme of things. (For P's use of divine names see 6:2.)

For Israel as well as for the ancient Near East, names implied real existence. Something was a reality when one knew its name. The name implied a dimension of intimacy. By knowing someone's name, one was on personal terms with that person. When one comes to the personal name of the God of Israel, however, there are two distinct issues.

The first issue is the etymology of Yahweh (actually the Hebrew text supplies just four consonants [YHWH]—the addition of the vowels a and e is already an attempt at interpretation). The solutions to this etymological problem are legion and no one suggestion commands the field. A popular view is that the divine name is really a causative form of the verb "to be." Hence "he causes to be" = "he creates." The second issue is the meaning that the author of the passage (E) intended. Here one stands on firmer ground, the context itself.

Verse 15 ("The Lord . . . has sent . . .") is the real answer to verse 13, since it provides the name that Moses asked for. Verse 14a ("I am who am") explains the name in terms of being: Yahweh's being means active participation and involvement. According to verse 10 the name means leading the people out of Egypt; according to verse 12 it means assisting Moses. Verse 14b ("I AM sent me to you") links verse 13 ("The God of your fathers has sent me") to verse 15 ("The Lord . . . has sent me"). Yahweh is committed to act on behalf of the people.

3:16-22 Expansion of the commission. In this section from J, Moses is first commissioned to assemble the elders (v. 16) and then to communicate the divine displeasure with the oppression of the Israelites. This commission is then expanded in verses 18-22. Not only Moses but also the elders are to approach Pharaoh (v. 18). This expansion is not a useless appendage. The author is preparing the reader for a twofold exodus: an exodus-flight and an exodus-expulsion. In verse 19 Pharaoh will not permit the people to go unless he is constrained; hence the people will be forced to flee. In verses 21-22 Yahweh will make the Egyptians well disposed toward the Israelites. Indeed, the Israelite women will even receive gifts of jewelry and clothing. Yahweh will so arrange matters that the Israelites finally will be expelled (see 12:35-36).

4:1-9 Moses' objection and subsequent signs. Like E in 3:11-12, J has his tradition of objection (v. 1) and signs (vv. 2-9). In order that Moses may authenticate himself to his people and thus substantiate his claims, there is the need of signs. The signs provided are a staff or type of magic wand (vv. 2-4) and a leprous sleight of hand (vv. 6-8). It is interesting to note that P will later use the J rod-turned-serpent tradition in a different context (7:9-12). In any event, the signs mentioned here are subsequently successful (4:31) and establish Moses' right to speak on behalf of Yahweh.

4:10-17 More objections, replies, and signs. J heightens the enormity of the task given Moses by formulating a second objection. Moses now maintains that he does not possess the wherewithal for public relations because he really cannot communicate (v. 10). Yahweh's reply focuses on divine omnipotence (v. 11). Yahweh promises to provide two things: (a) help in oral delivery and (b) assistance in content (v. 12). These concessions notwithstanding, J's call narrative continues with a final effort on Moses' part to evade his vocation and with a final reassurance on Yahweh's part to support the wavering candidate. There is a certain audacity here but an audacity consonant with the human penchant for escaping responsibility and passing it on to someone else (v. 13). Yahweh's reaction is anger, but, surprisingly, the anger is quickly suppressed, so that Aaron becomes Moses' prophet (vv. 14-15). Thus Moses is to function after the manner of Yahweh, and Aaron will be the divine spokesperson (v. 16; see Deut 18:18; Jer 1:9).

Concerning the staff (v. 17), one is naturally disposed to think of the J tradition in verses 2-4 where the staff is *a* sign given to Moses to authenticate his mission and dispose the people to accept him. Here, however, the staff is linked to *signs*. Perhaps this was originally part of the E tradition where here and now signs are lacking (see 3:12).

4:18-23 Moses' return to Egypt. With the exception of verses 18 and 20b this passage is from J. According to E, Moses made the return trip to Egypt by himself (v. 18; see 18:5), but according to J, Moses made this journey in the company of his wife and children (v. 20a). (The presence of Moses' wife and children will be important for the circumcision rite in verses 24-27.) In view of Pharaoh's reluctance to let Israel go (the exodus-flight tradition), J has Moses exercise the office of prophet in verses 22-23: (a) commission ("So shall you say to Pharaoh"); (b) messenger formulary ("Thus says the Lord"); (c) message ("Israel is my son, my first-born"). Pharaoh's refusal to heed the prophetic word anticipates the death of the first-born in the tenth plague (see 11:5).

4:24-26 The circumcision. The J scene, where Yahweh tries to kill Moses, seems linked to the J story of Gen 32:24-32, where Jacob wrestles with Yahweh. In both cases Yahweh suddenly appears in the night as a threatening demonic power. Jacob is on his way to the land of promise, but he must first confront his hostile brother Esau. Moses, too, has received a promise, but he must first confront the hostile Pharaoh.

The Egyptians did not practice circumcision, whereas the Hebrews apparently did. Although some see this scene as an apotropaic act on the occasion of a marriage—that is, designed to ward off all dangers on such an occasion—it is at least conceivable that Moses' lack of circumcision caused an infection. Zipporah's action would then have saved his life and have given rise to the expression "a spouse of blood." In any event, J has Zipporah circumcise her husband because, given the Israelite practice, it was not fitting for the great leader to be uncircumcised.

4:27-31 Meeting between Moses and Aaron. Aaron is a somewhat enigmatic character, yet this early tradition (J) seems constrained to associate him with Moses. In verse 30 it is Aaron who performs the signs, but according to the J tradition in 4:2-9, it is Moses who is to perform them. Nonetheless, the outcome is positive. In verse 31 the people are convinced and, rejoicing, they bow down and worship. J, however, feels compelled to express their fickleness or lack of real faith, for in the following scene the people will grumble. For J, the people genuinely believe in Yahweh and his servant Moses only in the aftermath of the Reed Sea event (see 14:31).

5:1-6:1 First audience with Pharaoh. Now that the Israelites have heard and accepted Yahweh's message as presented by Moses and Aaron, it is time to have the leaders approach Pharaoh with a view to negotiating their release from Egypt. This well-constructed J story consists of six scenes, five of them opening with a verb of action.

The first scene (5:1-5) begins with the report that "Moses and Aaron *went*." Verse 2 poses a question that the rest of the story will develop: Who is Yahweh? The three-day journey into the desert is probably connected with the exodus-flight tradition. According to the tradition preserved in chapters 15–19, there are only three days or camps between Egypt and Sinai (15:27; 16:1; 17:1; 19:2). This scene provides a realistic attitude toward a labor force, namely, not to allow the slaves to get away and so keep them at their work. Such an attitude rejects E's view of a suppression in 1:15-22.

The second scene (5:6-9) has Pharaoh speaking to the Egyptian taskmasters and the Hebrew foremen. (This deployment of foreign labor, whereby the taskmasters are Egyptian and the foremen members of the subject people, is historically accurate.) Unlike the rest of the scenes, here there is no verb of action, since one cannot expect the divine Pharaoh to go out to his underlings. The bricks in question are adobe—unburnt bricks dried in the sun.

The third scene (5:10-14) begins with a verb of action ("So the taskmasters . . . *went out*") and brings together the taskmasters, the foremen, and the people. The people are forced to look for straw while the foremen are flogged because the people cannot produce.

The fourth scene (5:15-19) has the Hebrew foremen before Pharaoh. Popular literature permits, indeed demands at times, the interaction of the divine Pharaoh with such underlings, in this case the depressed foremen. Once again the scene opens with a verb of action ("Then the Israelite foremen *came*"). However, the outcome of the meeting is less than what the foremen hoped for. The quota must remain the same but still no straw!

The fifth scene (5:20-21) focuses on the foremen and Moses and Aaron. Once again there is a verb of action whereby the foremen bump into the two leaders ("they . . . *came upon* . . . ."). The less than accidental encounter does not augur well for the two leaders. They are the recipients of nothing less than a curse: "The Lord look upon you and judge!" The start of Moses' grandiose plan is hardly optimistic, and the future looks dismal indeed.

The sixth scene (5:22–6:1) has Moses appealing to Yahweh. The verb of action in verse 22 (in Hebrew "and he *returned*") is expressed by the English adverb "again." The scene depicts a discouraged Moses, indeed a typical Moses, who will not cease to badger Yahweh with his complaints. One is hardly surprised, therefore, that he was hesitant about accepting his office. In any case, Moses learns that Yahweh will intervene dramatically. The reader is naturally set for the first plague. However, P chooses to review the call of Moses.

6:2-13 P's commissioning of Moses. Although P knew of J and E traditions of Moses' call in chapters 3–4, he opts to provide his own version of that call. In response to the people's lament in 2:23b-25 and in light of the setbacks in 5:1–6:1, the call of the prophet is the guarantee of support for God's chosen one and, at the same time, the overcoming of oppression/depression for God's chosen people.

For P it is a question of both continuity and discontinuity. The God who speaks to Moses is the same God who appeared to the patriarchs. However, there is a difference; that God did not reveal his personal name Yahweh to them. Instead, he employed "El Shaddai" (translated "God the Almighty," "God of the mountain," "God of the steppe," or "God of the breasts"). Unlike 3:14-15, this passage (see vv. 6-8) does not entail a personal honor for Moses that provides credentials. It is a special communication that looks to alleviating Israel's pain. For P there is only one covenant in question, the one made with Abraham in Gen 17. This scene, therefore, creates tension: the ancient promise and the present lack of fulfillment. That lack will now be addressed.

In commissioning Moses, P adopts the same basic call narrative as J and E: (a) divine response to prayer (v. 5); (b) God's promise to save (vv. 6-8); (c) the commission (vv. 9-11) (the commission to the people is only alluded to); (d) Moses' objection (v. 12, repeated in verse 30); (e) overcoming the objection (7:1-5).

Verses 6-8 are an oracle of salvation, a literary genre at home especially in the prophetic literature of the sixth century B.C.E. Against the background of P's setting of the Exile, such an oracle provides hope and lays a new foundation for Israel's faith. It shows that the God who judges is also the God who delivers. More important, this bestowal of grace is not bound up with the success of institutions in the past. Paradoxically, Israel's lack of success cannot defeat God.

The expression "I am Yahweh" is typical of P. This is royal style, such as is used at the beginning of royal inscriptions. It was taken over and used as a self-introduction in liturgy (see 20:2). It suggests that "I am here, present and acting." It is a formula that calls for responsive action on Israel's part. (See the Holiness Code in Lev 17–26, for example, 19:4.) For P as well as for the priestly school of theologians, God's interventions on behalf of Israel are clear clues to the identity of this God (see Ezek 20).

6:14-30 Genealogy of Moses and Aaron. P has interrupted the account of Moses' commissioning to insert this genealogy. (An indication of the insertion is the repetition of the last line before the insertion [see vv. 13 and 26-27].) Although some tend to find genealogies rather boring and hence skip over them, one should observe their usefulness. They represent a form of survival—the tribe, for example, takes care of all its members. They provide identity—they tell a person who he or she is. They indicate status—for example, they inform the king as to his lineage. They structure history—they are the parameters of human and/or divine activity.

Here it is clear that P is really interested in the tribe of Levi. He rushes past Reuben and Simeon to get to Levi (vv. 14-15—all three were Leah tribes [see Gen 29:31-34]). Both Moses and Aaron are sons of Amram (v. 20) and ultimately descendants of Levi. Although P makes Miriam the sister of both Aaron and Moses (v. 20), Exod 15:20 makes her the sister of only Aaron. (Note also the opposition of Aaron and Miriam to Moses in Exod 32 and Num 12.)

Originally "Levite" was a secular name, meaning "member of the tribe of Levi." Only at the end of a long process was it changed into a designation for a somewhat lowly person who performed menial cultic tasks (see 28:1-43). By emphasizing Aaron, P intends to establish a claim for the legitimacy of the group of priests that ultimately controlled the temple in Jerusalem. (P has passed over other ancient priestly families such as the Mushites mentioned in verse 19.) For P, therefore, this genealogy has served to provide identity and undergird the status of Aaron's descendants.

7:1-7 Reassurance and compliance. In answer to Moses' objection about his speaking abilities (6:13, 30), P has Yahweh reassure Moses that he will have a quasi-divine function (the Hebrew 'elohim can mean someone other than God—see Ps 45:7 vis-à-vis the prophet Aaron). The outcome of divine intervention will be that Yahweh will actually lead Israel out of Egypt (vv. 4-5). However, this intervention will also provoke Egyptian recognition of Yahweh's real identity: "so that the Egyptians may learn that I am the Lord . . ." (v. 5).

The literal translation of the beginning of verse 3 is "But I will harden Pharaoh's heart."

For the biblical writers the heart was the organ of thinking and willing (see Isa 6:10; 29:13) that focused on the person as the thinking and willing subject. It should be noted that Exodus employs three different ways of expressing the hardening of Pharaoh's heart: (a) Pharaoh's heart was hardened (7:13, 14, 22; 8:15; 9:7, 35); (b) Pharaoh hardened his (own) heart (8:11, 28); (c) Yahweh hardened Pharaoh's heart (7:3; 9:12; 10:1, 20, 27). Exodus, therefore, admits both human freedom and divine omnipotence. Like the rest of the Bible, Exodus attempts no explanation of that admission.

Besides noting the compliance of Moses and Aaron in verse 6, P goes on to record the ages of the two leaders. This fits in with his overall chronological interests. After the forty-year wandering, P later mentions that Moses died at the age of one hundred and twenty (see Deut 34:7).

7:8-13 Introduction to the plagues. In this scene P mentions the first demonstration of Yahweh's power before Pharaoh, since for him this is the first meeting between Pharaoh and Yahweh's emissaries (for J see 5:1–6:1). As noted earlier, P has changed Moses' staff from an authenticating instrument before the people (see J in 4:2-4) to a permission-seeking device before Pharaoh. Not surprisingly, Aaron has a key role to play. As Yahweh foretold (see 7:4), Pharaoh refuses to comply, despite Aaron's serpent-consuming staff.

This introductory scene should serve as a guide of sorts in approaching the plagues. A staff turned into a serpent and a river changed to blood are indications of the world of folklore, not of scientific explanations. Nonetheless, interpreters have sought a so-called natural explanation of the phenomena. According to the *cosmic* interpretation, a comet made contact with the earth, bringing in its wake red dust, small meteorites, earthquakes, etc. According to the *geological* explanation, a violent eruption of a volcano in the fifteenth century B.C.E. caused a tidal wave the aftereffects of which brought about the plagues. According to a *third* view, there was a natural succession of catastrophes beginning with an exceptionally large flooding of the Nile in July and August and culminating with a sirocco in March or April that killed off the remaining first fruits, not the first-born.

Ultimately, however, one must conclude that the biblical writers had only an imperfect knowledge of Egyptian matters. For example, locusts (the eighth plague) are known both in Egypt and Israel. However, the red Nile (the first plague) and frogs (the second plague) are known only in Egypt, while hail (the seventh plague) is exceptional in Egypt but not in Israel.

The biblical account itself contains doublets and inconsistencies, thus precluding a scientific exposition and suggesting a popular-literature approach. Thus the fourth plague (the flies) is a doublet of the third plague (the gnats). Similarly, the sixth plague (the boils, an epidemic affecting livestock and humans) is a doublet of the fifth plague (the pestilence, that is, the livestock epidemic). With regard to consistency, one may raise some questions. If all the livestock were killed in the fifth plague (9:6), then how could they have been affected by boils in the sixth plague (9:10), hail in the seventh plague (9:25), and death of the first-born in the tenth plague (12:29)? If frogs already covered the land of Egypt (8:2), how could the magicians repeat the feat (8:3)?

Before moving on to the question of the literary arrangement of the plagues, one should note that the presence of E is doubtful in these accounts. Hence one speaks more cautiously of JE, a combination of the Pentateuch's earliest written sources, rather than further distinguishing them as J or E. As for distribution, the final editor has taken five plagues from JE alone (the fourth, fifth, seventh, eighth, and ninth), two from P alone (the third and sixth), and three from a combination of JE and P (the first, second, and tenth).

The differences between JE and P touch on several points. With regard to roles, JE has Moses appear simply as a prophet, whereas P has Aaron play the principal part, so that Moses is upstaged. Concerning formulae, JE has Moses employ the messenger formula, while P has Yahweh speaking to Moses, who then speaks to Aaron. Finally, in terms of character, for JE the plagues are genuine afflictions to chastise Pharaoh for refusing to let the people go. For P, however, they are signs and wonders that legitimate Moses and Aaron as representatives of Yahweh, not scourges as such. (Compare the plague of gnats [8:12-15—P] with that of flies [8:16-28—JE].)

The presence of the different biblical traditions raises some further questions: How did the final editor put everything together? Did he hope to attain something concrete? If so, what indications are there?

In seeking to answer these questions, one must keep two points in mind. First, the plague account really begins in 7:8-13 because this scene contains the same outlook and vocabulary as the plagues themselves. Second, the tenth plague (the death of the firstborn) is excluded here, since its make-up and literary characteristics are different. The result is that there are ten episodes: the introduction in 7:8-13 and the nine plagues (7:14–10:29). Moreover, they are arranged concentrically so that the introduction, the first plague, etc., have counterparts of approximately the same length and with the same formula in the ninth plague, the eighth plague, etc. (Compare 8:12-15 with 9:8-12.) This concentric arrangement is not haphazard. It is intentionally designed to indicate definite progress as one reads the remainder of the story.

The plague account is not so much a series of devastations as it is a series of disputes between Pharaoh and Moses linked to the question in 5:2: "Who is the Lord that I should heed his plea to let Israel go?" The failure of Moses and Aaron in these dealings with Pharaoh is not decisive, since the story continues in the Reed Sea account. These plagues look to an even greater wonder at the sea.

7:14-25 First plague: water turned into blood. The final editor has combined JE (vv. 14-18, 20b-21a, 23-25) and P (vv. 19-20, 21b-22). According to JE it is the Nile, *the* river, that will be affected. Moreover, JE makes reference to the general death of the fish and the subsequent pollution. According to P, however, the waters of all Egypt are affected (v. 19), not just the Nile.

In terms of progress, one must note that the Egyptian magicians are able to match the feat performed by God's emissaries (v. 22). With regard to Pharaoh, the recognition demanded of him is relatively simple: "This is how you shall know that I am the Lord" (v. 17). As the plague account continues, there will be significant differences on both scores.

7:26–8:11 Second plague: the frogs. Both JE (7:26-29; 8:4-9a) and P (8:1-3, 11b) are unmistakably present in this account. As with

the first plague, this episode reveals that the Egyptian magicians are still able to match the feats performed by Moses and Aaron (8:3). However, there are other differences. Now Pharaoh actively seeks out the intercession of Moses (8:15), although he remains adamant in the end (8:11). Besides, the recognition now demanded of Pharaoh is more embracing than 7:17: "That you may learn that there is none like the Lord, our God" (8:6).

8:12-15 Third plague: the gnats. In this account, which is solely from P, there is clear evidence of progress. Unlike the first two plagues, this plague is one which the Egyptian magicians are incapable of reproducing. In the magicians' report to Pharaoh there is the further observation: "This is the finger of God" (v. 15). However, as Yahweh had predicted, Pharaoh chooses not to let Israel go.

8:16-28 Fourth plague: the flies. This passage from JE seems to presuppose that the Egyptians are not very remote from the Israelites, since the former would be able to view the sacrifices offered by the latter (v. 22). This note is somewhat surprising, since the author claims a distinction for the Israelites, namely, that the plague will not affect the land of Goshen (v. 18). Hence the Egyptians and the Israelites do not live side by side. In any event, the animal sacrifices of the Israelites would upset the religious sensitivities of the Egyptians. Perhaps this is because animals had a conspicuous place in Egyptian religion or because the sacrifice of whole animals was not the usual practice among them. What is significant here is, first of all, the acknowledgment by Pharaoh "that I am the Lord in the midst of the earth" (v. 18). Thus Pharaoh is to admit that Yahweh is present in Egypt. Second, the permission for the three-day trip is for a point in the desert that is not too far away (v. 24). Once again Moses is to pray on behalf of the mighty ruler of Egypt. Clearly there is development in Pharaoh's character.

9:1-7 Fifth plague: the pestilence. In this JE account one must note that there is no negotiation between Pharaoh and Moses after the start of the plague, as in 8:21. However, in keeping with the preceding plague, there is the distinction between the Egyptians and the Israelites. The pestilence will strike Egyptian, not Israelite, livestock. One can see that in this account Pharaoh takes pains to be assured that this distinction is really so (see vv. 6b-7a).

9:8-12 Sixth plague: the boils. In this P account it is somewhat astonishing that Aaron plays a relatively minor role, that of Moses' assistant. In terms of development, what emerges is the downward spiral of the magicians. Although they were able to match the first two plagues, they were unsuccessful in the third and were forced to admit the work as God's doing. Here the final editor has so arranged matters that the magicians are singled out for their lack of uniqueness. They too suffer from the skin disease and are unable to stand in Moses' presence (v. 11).

9:13-35 Seventh plague: the hail. In this JE account there is an explanation given for the failure of the previous plagues to induce Pharaoh to relent. Yahweh has acted this way to show his power and to make his name resound throughout the earth (v. 16). One almost expects Yahweh's final and decisive act here and now. While even this plague does not bring Pharaoh to grant the necessary permission to leave, it does contribute to the unfolding character of the divine ruler of Egypt.

There is the notice in verse 14 that Pharaoh (as well as his subjects) is to confess that there is no one like Yahweh anywhere on the earth. This is followed in verse 27 by the *mea culpa* of Pharaoh: "I have sinned again! The Lord is just; it is I and my subjects who are at fault." This is truly a remarkable confession. Finally there is the statement that the plague of hail will induce an even greater confession, namely, that the earth is Yahweh's (v. 29). The God of Israel is receiving a more fitting recognition from the mighty Egyptian god, Pharaoh himself.

10:1-20 Eighth plague: the locusts. This JE account opens with an explanation of the hardness of heart of Pharaoh and his servants. This obduracy is calculated to demonstrate Yahweh's might and to provide an ongoing tradition of those exploits in the Israelite community (vv. 1-2). The author makes special mention of Moses' actual going to Pharaoh and dwells upon Yahweh's vexation: "How long will you refuse to submit to me?" (v. 3b). For the first time one learns that Pharaoh's servants are becoming exasperated to the point of urging their king to exercise restraint and so be reasonable (v. 7). The result of this intervention is that Moses and Aaron are recalled to Pharaoh's court (v. 8). In this scene, the author points out Pharaoh's suspicion that a conspiracy of sorts is underway, since Moses petitions for the whole Israelite community to take part in the desert worship (vv. 10-11).

The progress in depicting Pharaoh's change of character is found in vv. 16-17. After the speedy summons there is the clear protestation of sin: "I have sinned against the Lord, your God, and against you." Thus Pharaoh has advanced in his awareness of Yahweh's presence and power from the time of the first plague. After the customary request for forgiveness and the successful outcome of that request, there is nonetheless the concluding remark that Pharaoh remains adamant and so the people remain in Egypt.

10:21-29 Ninth plague: the darkness. Many connect this darkness with a typical Near Eastern phenomenon, the *khamsin*. This is a hot wind that blows off the desert in March and April, bringing darkness and a very oppressive atmosphere in its wake. In the biblical account such darkness takes on a more foreboding character inasmuch as it suggests the evil powers of chaos. Such a character matches the thrust of this JE account. There is exasperation leading to the breaking off of any further negotiations (v. 28). Pharaoh is now willing to let all Israel leave for purposes of worship (contrast 10:11), but not the livestock (v. 24). Moses reacts to such permission rather ironically. He points out that animal sacrifices are a part of their worship and hence required. However, since the sacrificial animals can be determined only upon arrival at the place of worship, it is, therefore, necessary to bring all the livestock along. Pharaoh's response to Moses' ironic request is the cessation of all further negotiations. An impasse has been reached, one which will result in Moses' death if he should attempt to appear once again before Pharaoh. To be sure, a new way must be found to force Pharaoh's hand.

11:1-10 Tenth plague: the death of the first-born. Given Moses' seemingly final appearance before Pharaoh, the reader expects a quick dash to the sea and then the trek in the desert. In other words, the writers up to this point have created suspense, and the reader naturally anticipates release of tension and denouement. To the contrary, there is another (and final) plague that is totally out of character with the previous nine. (Actually the scene at the Reed Sea does not presuppose the tenth plague.) The reader now becomes bogged down, not in a Sea of Reeds, but in a whirlpool of rubrics. There is the sudden command to prepare for liturgy, not the expected bolt for freedom. Presumably the biblical writers had a reason for the temporary demise of narrative and the exaltation of liturgy.

The death of the first-born does not come as a total surprise. In 4:23 Yahweh addressed Pharaoh through Moses in these terms: "If you refuse to let him (Israel, Yahweh's first-born) go, I warn you, I will kill your son, your first-born." Neither does the plundering of the Egyptians come as a complete surprise. In 3:21-22 the Israelites were assured that they would not leave Egypt empty-handed. However, 11:1-3 (either J or E), belonging to the exodus-expulsion tradition, assumes that this tenth plague is really the one and only plague. How else could the Israelites get silver and gold ornaments and clothing from the Egyptians? How else can one explain Moses' prestige with Pharaoh's servants and Egypt as a whole?

The literary arrangement of verses 4-8 (from J; verses 9-10 from P) suggests that this plague is not linked to the previous nine. J usually informs the reader that Moses is to speak to Pharaoh, but in verse 4 it is not clear to whom Moses delivers the divine message. Up to verse 6 the recipient seems to be Israel, but in verses 7-8 Pharaoh is addressed. At the end of verse 8 Moses leaves Pharaoh's presence in a rage. But according to 10:29 (JE) he was never again to appear before Pharaoh. Although some posit a historical link—an epidemic that struck the Egyptians and hence facilitated the departure of the Israelites—it is not unreasonable to conclude that the tenth plague has been contrived to connect with the feast of the Passover.

12:1-20 The Passover ritual. In this rubrical section P provides details for a feast that was already old among seminomadic shepherds of the ancient Near East. It was an offering by such shepherds for the welfare of their flocks when the tribe set out to search for new pasture grounds. This was in the spring and indeed at a very critical time in the life of the flock. This was the time when the young of the sheep and the goats would be born. Indications of the antiquity of the feast are the fol-

lowing: no priests, no sanctuaries, no altars.

Other details fit in with this pastoral background. The animal is roasted, not boiled (v. 9), since cooking utensils are at a minimum. Perhaps this explains why the bones are not broken (vv. 9, 46). The time is the twilight of the first full spring moon (v. 6). This coincides with the return of the shepherds to the camp on the brightest night of the month. The unleavened bread (v. 8) is the ordinary bread eaten by such shepherds, and the bitter herbs (v. 8) are the desert plants used by these shepherds for spices. The clothing and attire suit this background: "with your loins girt, sandals on your feet and your staff in hand, . . ." (v. 11). The blood rite (v. 7) is apotropaic in purpose, that is, the smearing of the blood on the tent poles is intended to ward off all danger to the members of the tribe and especially to the young about to be born. This danger is personified in "the destroyer" (v. 23). The blood, therefore, prevents him from striking humans and animals.

It is the blood rite that establishes the link between the tenth plague and the Passover. "The destroyer" is now subject to a new interpretation arising from Israel's history. Yahweh will go through the land of Egypt, striking down the first-born of both humans and beasts (v. 12). But when Yahweh sees the blood on the houses, "the destroyer" will not be permitted to strike. Rather Yahweh will "pass over" (v. 13).

While the etymology of "passover" is far from clear, the meaning of the term for Israel is abundantly clear. "To pass over" means "to spare, protect, deliver." What Israel did, therefore, was to interpret the ancient feast of seminomadic shepherds in terms of her own relationship with Yahweh. It was no longer the quest for a temporary pasture but for the final pasture, the Promised Land itself. The ancient feast with its focus on change lent itself admirably to interpreting the change in Israel's destiny. The shepherds were now a people in flight (v. 11). (For the unleavened bread in verses 14-20 see 13:3-10.)

12:21-28 Promulgation of the Passover. In this J passage (with the exception of P in verse 28) Moses approaches the elders, those leaders responsible for carrying out Yahweh's command. Here the emphasis is principally on the blood rite. Hand in hand with the sprinkling is the prohibition to go outdoors until morning (v. 22) because of the nocturnal devastation.

The rubrics in verses 24-27a are significant for Israel's abhorrence of any and every form of generation gap. Those taking part in the original Exodus and all subsequent Israelite communities are linked together in this pivotal experience. The question asked by the children in verse 26 is not one of mere historical interest. It is a contrived question designed to interpret the past in view of the present. To be sure, Yahweh spared the Israelites but crushed the Egyptians. But the happenings of the thirteenth century B.C.E. affect the present community: "When he struck down the Egyptians, he spared *our* houses" (v. 27a). To celebrate the Passover means to span generations and coalesce in an experience explaining and unifying the entire people.

12:29-39 Death of the first-born and departure. J, the author of these verses, follows up the exodus-expulsion tradition of 11:1-3. The death of the first-born has been so grave that Pharaoh summons Moses and Aaron at night (v. 31). There is no longer the hesitancy to keep the livestock from going along (v. 32; see 10:24). Indeed the devastation has been so severe that the Egyptians urge the Israelites to advance their timetable. The haste in this departure is reflected in the condition of the bread. The Israelites were so rushed that their dough was not leavened (v. 34), and, consequently, they had to be satisfied with unleavened loaves (v. 39). (P in verse 15 gave no reason why the people would eat such bread for seven days.) Finally, in keeping with the exodus-expulsion tradition, the Israelites asked the Egyptians for silver and gold articles as well as clothing. However, the despoiling went far beyond such limitations. The Israelites ended up by getting from the Egyptians whatever they wanted (v. 36).

J mentions the first destination and the number of people involved. Succoth lies thirty-two miles southeast of Raamses and is approximately in the middle of the isthmus between the Mediterranean Sea and the Gulf of Suez. J sets down the number as "about six hundred thousand men on foot, not counting the children" (v. 37). This would imply a population of some three million men, women, and children. While it is probable that the Hebrew word for "thousand" originally meant a subsection of a tribe and hence

a total number of five thousand or six thousand, the epic nature of this popular literature emphasizes the larger number. "A crowd of mixed ancestry" (v. 38) suggests that non-Israelite elements of the slave labor force also departed Egypt in the company of Moses.

12:40-51 Chronology and further Passover regulations. In verses 40-41 P reveals his penchant for chronology. He calculates the sojourn of the Israelites in Egypt as a period of 430 years (see Gen 15:13). The complexity of the biblical data, however, demands greater precision. In view of such data this sojourn was not necessarily continuous, made by the same group, and comprising the entire people. From a theological viewpoint P reveals a God absorbed in the real life of his people. Yahweh acted at a precise moment in time. Consequently, Yahweh's keeping vigil at the moment must be reflected in Israel's keeping vigil on this occasion each year.

P also provides additional Passover regulations, relating chiefly to admission to the Passover celebration. (Such regulations presuppose a setting where Israel is already leading an agricultural existence in the Promised Land.) Transient aliens (v. 45) and hired servants (v. 45) are excluded; their existence in the land was not so firmly rooted. Resident aliens (v. 48) and permanent slaves (v. 44) may take part in the celebration, provided they have been circumcised (see Gen 17:13). The celebration is further depicted as a domestic one (v. 46) which "the whole community of Israel" (v. 47) is to keep. This is a favorite P expression stressing the organization of Israel, especially in the desert, and underlining those responsible within this organization.

13:3-10 Feast of Unleavened Bread. 13:1-16 has been judged to reflect the language of the Book of Deuteronomy. However, its language is more proto-Deuteronomic, that is, an incipient style that would eventually culminate in the more developed language found in Deuteronomy. In its present context, this tradition deals with two matters: (a) the redemption of the first-born (vv. 1-2, 11-16); (b) the feast of Unleavened Bread (vv. 3-10).

Unlike Passover, which required no sanctuary and was celebrated at home, Unleavened Bread was a pilgrimage feast that required the attendance of the adult male at the sanctuary (see 23:15). Whereas Passover was the feast of seminomadic shepherds, Unleavened Bread was the feast of farmers. The feast expressed newness, noting the beginning of the barley harvest (the first crop to be gathered). For the first seven days of this harvest, one had to eat bread made from the new grain. Such bread was unleavened or unfermented because it contained nothing of the previous year's harvest. Since this feast presupposes an agricultural environment, it was adopted by the Israelites (possibly from the Canaanites) only after their desert experience.

It was only later that the feasts of Passover and Unleavened Bread were joined together. This was probably around the time of King Josiah (the second half of the seventh century B.C.E.—2 Chr 35:17). Since both feasts occurred around the same time of the year and since both likewise made use of unleavened bread (but for different reasons—see 12:8), they were eventually combined.

Whereas J in 12:34 connects the unleavened bread to the haste of the Exodus, the author of 13:8 attaches a more personal note: "This is because of what the Lord did to *me* when *I* came out of Egypt." This flows from the concept of remembrance expressed in verse 3. To remember means to relive, to make actual/meaningful now. Hence the feast is not the static recalling of the past but the dynamic reliving of the past because of its repercussions on the present.

13:1-2, 11-16 Redemption of the first-born. It is interesting to observe that this tradition is not attached to the Passover account itself but to the deaths of the first-born of the Egyptians. Similarly, other texts (for example, 22:28-29) do not link the redemption of the first-born to the Exodus experience (v. 15).

The practice of "buying back" the first-born reveals Israel's concern for human life and her special treatment of the first-born. Although Israel was aware of the sacrifice of the first-born among her Canaanite neighbors, she revolted against such a practice (see Gen 22:1-19). Rather, she viewed the first-born both of humans and of animals as God's exclusive property. Consequently, they had to be bought back (see Luke 2:23).

After hearing that the Israelite must buy back his first-born, one tends to think that God's act of redemption is merely that—a buying back. One is prone, as a result, to limit

God's redemptive action in Jesus as another instance of such buying back. However, this passage (and several others in Exodus) provides examples of the depth and the variety of biblical thought.

According to verse 3 Israel "came out." This verb is a legal term which Israel's storytellers have borrowed (see 21:2) to interpret the Exodus experience. In both verses 3 and 8 it is a going out of Egypt, and verse 3 adds "that house of slavery." Redemption for the Israelite is thus the acquisition of freedom, something particularly important to a seminomad.

Another term is the verb "to dismiss, let go." Against its legal background it means "to set free" (a favorite verb of J). For example, in 21:26-27 a master who mistreats his slave must set that slave free. The author of the present passage uses this verb in verse 15 and thus implies that Pharaoh is a slaveholder who refuses to emancipate his slaves. Redemption for the Israelites means being removed from the caprice of Pharaoh and thus regaining their integrity.

Another term is the verb "to bring out." Since Pharaoh has refused to set Israel free, Yahweh decides to bring them out. In the present context the verb is used four times (vv. 3, 9, 14, 16), three times with the phrase "with a strong hand." This conveys the powerful, miraculous way in which Yahweh liberates his people. (Most likely the phrase derived from the very graphic way in which Yahweh delivered Israel at the Reed Sea.) Redemption means, not merely a juridical act, but a dramatic intervention that results in victory for the oppressed and defeat for the oppressors.

Another term is the verb "to cause to go up." This verb is not concerned with slavery and setting free but looks to the future (see 3:8). It means going up to the land of Canaan and so it is the precise opposite of the going down into Egypt (see Gen 46:3-4). Although those taking part in the Exodus knew it as a going out, later generations saw it in terms of entering a new land, a going up. Redemption means that the Israelite has a home, a future.

Another term is the verb "to save." (The noun usually translated "salvation" is found in 14:13; 15:2.) The word is from the language of the courtroom, whereby the savior is always on the side of justice as an advocate or witness for the defense. In the prophet Second Isaiah, who sings of a second Exodus, Yahweh is a savior since he gets back his rightful property, Israel (see Isa 43:3). Redemption also means that Yahweh takes up the cause of those treated unjustly.

A final term is "to be a redeemer" (see 15:13). A redeemer is the family member responsible for the integrity of the family. For example, if family property is in danger of going to an outsider, the redeemer sees to it that the property remains in the family (see Ruth 4; Jer 32). The redeemer thus intervenes at crucial moments of family life. Redemption also means that God is identified as a member of the family interested in other members of the family. Redemption is much more than simply buying back.

13:17-22 Israel on the march. This section, consisting of E in verses 17-19 and J in verses 20-22, brings up the problem of the route of the Exodus. While the question must remain open, it is possible to offer a hypothesis, an effort to explain a number of the data contained in the biblical traditions. This hypothesis allows for two different routes by two different groups.

Although the New American Bible consistently refers to the Red Sea, the probable translation of the body of water connected with the Exodus is the Reed Sea or the Sea of Reeds. The reed in question is a papyrus plant that is known to grow in the marshes at the north of the Delta (not in the Gulf of Suez or the Gulf of Aqabah). Although this name suggests a comparatively small body of water, its localization is doubtful and not overly significant in dealing with the problem of the route of the Exodus. (The term "Red Sea" derives from the Greek translators of the Hebrew Scriptures. The term, however, includes even the Persian Gulf.)

The first route is the *northern* route. According to this itinerary, when the Israelites came out of Egypt, they would have gone directly east, that is, across the northern part of the Sinai peninsula to Kadesh Barnea. However, the E tradition in verse 17 notes that the Israelites did not take the way of the Philistines, that is, the way along the Mediterranean Sea connected with the northern route. Still, the mention of Raamses (1:11), Succoth (12:37), Etham (13:20), and Pi-hahiroth in connection with Migdol and Baal-

zephon (14:2, 9—all from J with the exception of the last two) tends to support this northern route.

The second route is the *southern* route. According to this route the Israelites on leaving Egypt would have headed to the south or southeast to the lower part of the Sinai peninsula where they would have experienced the covenant making at Sinai. This would be the way of the desert mentioned by E in verse 18.

It is likely that these two traditions recall two different exodus experiences. Elements of the tribes of Reuben, Simeon, Levi, and Judah (the Leah tribes) were possibly the first to leave Egypt, taking the northern route. It is further likely that they are the group connected with the exodus-expulsion tradition that invaded the land of Canaan from the south (see the J tradition in Num 13:22-23; 14:24). Elements of the tribes of Benjamin, Ephraim, and Manasseh (the Rachel tribes) possibly left Egypt later under the leadership of Moses by means of the southern route. This group would have wandered in the desert, experienced Yahweh at Sinai, and invaded the land of Canaan from the east (the Jordan River). Furthermore, this group would be connected with the exodus-flight tradition. When the different entries into Canaan were combined in the final narrative, these different exodus experiences were united as well.

In verses 21-22 J distinguishes between a column of cloud by day and a column of fire by night. However, in 14:24 J has one column of cloud and fire. Despite this variation, what is clear is the experience of God's presence. The cloud/fire is Israel's perception of her God's participation in the key events of the Exodus and desert wandering. This cloud/fire manifestation is not unlike Yahweh's "angelic" presence (compare 3:2 with 3:4a).

14:1-10 Egypt's pursuit of Israel. The liturgical connection of Passover (and Unleavened Bread) with the Exodus by way of the tenth plague and the liturgical suture between the redemption of the first-born and the tenth plague have now come to a close. The narrative resumes the action of the nine plagues in chapters 7-10 and, after the exodus-expulsion interlude (see 11:1-3; 12:33-36), resumes the exodus-flight tradition (v. 5). The action now switches to the miracle at the sea, a military undertaking that does not presuppose the death of the first-born.

This section contains both P (vv. 1-4, 8-10) and J or JE (vv. 5-7) traditions. For example, according to P Israel is trapped in the wilderness but, more accurately, it is Pharaoh who is trapped into thinking thus. The reason P gives is that Pharaoh's absolute determination to pursue Israel will result in Yahweh's definitive reception of glory through Pharaoh and his army. In the JE tradition Pharaoh has changed his mind, realizing full well the loss of such an invaluable labor force.

What is common to both traditions is that they have interpreted the crossing of the sea in terms of a holy war. A holy war was not merely the encounter between two opposing forces; it was a religious undertaking. For Israel this meant that Yahweh fought for Israel, not Israel for Yahweh. (This view persisted until the time of David's "secular" army in the tenth century B.C.E.) A holy war has five elements: (a) sacrifices and oracles to consult Yahweh (by reason of the pillar of cloud/fire Yahweh already marched with Israel); (b) absolute confidence in Yahweh (see 14:31); (c) ritual purifications (see 19:14-15); (d) fear put into the enemy by Yahweh (see 14:24-25); (e) total destruction of the enemy (see 14:28, 30). What Israel's writers clearly understood was that their commander-in-chief was none less than Yahweh himself.

14:11-18 The conquest of fear. In verses 11-14 J takes up the all-too-human reaction to the pursuit of the Egyptians. It is the reality of fear that threatens to undermine the whole purpose of the Exodus. The people are tempted to prefer the resumption of slavery in Egypt to death in the desert. This murmuring motif is one that will reappear in Israel's wandering experience. Arguing from faith, Moses replies that such an either-or is invalid. Pressing the holy war theology, he makes a demand for renewed commitment (v. 13) and concludes with the assurance of victory. "The Lord himself will fight for you; you have only to keep still" (v. 14).

In verses 15-18 P responds to Israel's cry of frustration. Yahweh's action consists of giving directions that will ensure the safe passage of the Israelites through the sea. Thus Moses is to lift his staff, stretch out his hand, and divide the sea in favor of Israel. As predicted in verse 4, the obstinate Egyptians will pursue Israel into the sea. Their corpses will then become mute yet eloquent witnesses to Yah-weh's power. The Divine Warrior will thus be duly acknowledged.

14:19-31 Two traditions for the crossing of the sea. The biblical traditions are unable to present a blow-by-blow account of what actually transpired at the Reed Sea because the required sources are wanting. However, Israel has chosen to interpret that event by dwelling on Yahweh's military prowess. Holy war theology enables the traditions in this section to unfold the picture of a God who thinks resolutely on behalf of the fleeing Israelites. Liberation means, not to be free *from* the ennui of Israel's laments, but to be free *for* the bewildered and beleaguered people.

According to J Yahweh manifests himself in two ways: (a) the angel of God (v. 19a) and (b) the column of cloud (v. 19b). Yahweh in the form of a divine messenger and in the form of a cloud now takes up a position between the Israelites and the Egyptians (v. 20). This position implies protection for Israel. Moreover, during the night Yahweh drives back the sea with a strong easterly wind (v. 21b), thus making possible a passage on dry land. Just before dawn Yahweh, present in the column of cloud and fire, startles the Egyptians with a glance that results in the loss of military discipline (v. 24). Yahweh's panic-creating glance is now followed by the clogging of the Egyptian chariot wheels, a gesture that leads to the sounding of retreat (v. 25). However, at dawn the sea resumes its normal depth. At this juncture Yahweh hurls the retreating Egyptians into its midst (v. 27b). The outcome is that Israel acknowledges Yahweh's intervention to the point of believing in Yahweh and his servant Moses (vv. 30-31).

According to P Moses stretches out his hand over the sea (v. 21a). The result is a very special miracle. Dry land appears for the safe passage of the Israelites with the water forming something resembling walls to their right and left (v. 22). At this point the Egyptian forces pursue the Israelites on the dry land (v. 23). At Yahweh's command Moses once again stretches out his hand over the sea (vv. 26-27a). The returning waters then engulf the entire Egyptian army (v. 28). P finally notes much more dramatically than J the Israelite passage on the dry land with the contained waters to the right and left (v. 29). In P Moses' gesture has replaced Yahweh's strong easterly wind.

15:1-21 The Song of the Sea. The earliest tradition about the crossing is found in this section (vv. 1-18, 21) that, unlike the J and P traditions, is in poetry, not prose. It is generally regarded as an independent tradition that has been fitted into its present position by means of vv. 19-20. On the basis of several criteria the poem may be dated around 1100 B.C.E.

This poem is based on an earlier (around 1400 B.C.E.) Canaanite poem that describes the battle between Baal, god of fertility, and Yamm, god of the sea. The outcome of the battle is that Yamm is overcome by Baal who in the next episode receives his temple/palace. In this biblical account Yahweh overcomes the Egyptians by creating a storm at sea that in turn capsizes their boats and leads to their death by drowning (vv. 8-10). (J's easterly wind [14:21b] has apparently been adapted from the poem's reference to Yahweh's strong wind in verse 10.) It is interesting to note that the poem focuses on the destruction of the enemy with only an allusion to the passage of the Israelites. However, the poem goes beyond the exploits at the Reed Sea to mention the effects of such destructive power on Israel's neighbors (vv. 14-16). Finally, the poem concludes by speaking of Yahweh's kingly possession of his sanctuary (v. 17). (This need not be limited to Jerusalem. It is a general formula to denote Yahweh's dwelling place in the wake of the successful battle.)

This crossing of the Reed Sea is obviously related to the ritual crossing of the Jordan in Josh 3-4. It is perhaps due to the influence of the Jordan crossing that the Reed Sea crossing shifted focus from Yahweh's military exploits over the Egyptians to the march of his people into the Promised Land (v. 13).

PART II: ISRAEL IN THE DESERT

Exod 15:22-18:27

These chapters offer a summary of Israel's desert experience. For example, they deal with Yahweh's protection in terms of providing food and drink (15:22-17:7), the defeat of Israel's enemies (17:8-16), the organization of the people (18:13-27). At the same time, these chapters foreshadow events that the Book of Numbers will exploit. Hence the reader is not taken by surprise when the entire desert generation with the exception of Caleb and Joshua is forbidden to enter the Promised Land, but condemned to wander in the desert.

These chapters also deal with the human symbol of wandering. This symbol reflects life as a search for meaning both on the level of individuals and community (see also *The Aeneid, Moby Dick, The Divine Comedy)*. One is thus reminded of the Lukan Jesus who resolutely determines to make the journey to Jerusalem (Luke 9:51) and so capture the meaning of his own life and his community's by experiencing passion, death, and resurrection. In their present setting these chapters are the prelude to Israel's experience of covenant making at Sinai.

In the prophetic literature there are two different traditions of this period in Israel's history. First, there is the tradition of God's graciousness and Israel's generous response to that graciousness: "I remember the devotion of your youth, how you loved me as a bride, following me in the desert, in a land unknown" (Jer 2:2; see also Hos 2:17). Second, there is the tradition of Israel's rebellion against Yahweh that is captured in the murmuring motif so prevalent in the confrontation between Yahweh and Israel: "But the house of Israel rebelled against me in the desert. They did not observe my statutes, and they despised my ordinances that bring life to those who keep them" (Ezek 20:13). In Exodus and usually in Numbers the first tradition, God's graciousness, is primary while the second tradition, Israel's rebellion, is secondary. Israel's theologians were free to adapt the wilderness experience in order to explain later theological crises.

15:22-27 Grumbling at Marah. This episode consists of three traditions: P (vv. 22a, 27), J (vv. 23-25), and Deuteronomistic (v. 26). P provides information after the manner of an itinerary—departure and arrival from stopping place to stopping place. Thus Moses leads the people from the Reed Sea through the desert of Shur to Elim. Verse 26 applies the basic theology of the book of Deuteronomy to this incident at Marah. Obedience to Yahweh's will as expressed in his commandments and precepts will prevent disastrous consequences, such as the diseases inflicted by Yahweh on the Egyptians.

The J tradition emphasizes God's generosity in meeting the needs of the desert community. After three days of travel the community comes upon water at Marah which, however, because of its bitterness is not drinkable. The people's predicament leads to Moses' cry to Yahweh that, in turn, leads to Yahweh's remedy for sweetening the water. Although J speaks of the people grumbling against Moses (v. 24), there is no indication at all that the people are in rebellion. Moreover, the content of the people's complaint is far from clear. According to verse 25 it is Yahweh who puts Israel to the test, not vice versa (see 17:2). Thus, given a concrete need, Yahweh generously responds.

This scene together with 16:1–17:7 underlines the femininity of Yahweh. In the sociology of that day it was the task of the mother and wife to provide food and drink. Mother Yahweh, therefore, senses the needs of her children in their plight and takes the necessary steps to alleviate the situation. The Divine Warrior who overcame the mighty Egyptians at the Reed Sea is also the tender mother who quickly responds to family problems.

16:1-36 The quail and the manna. This account focuses on two realities of the Sinai peninsula. The manna is the secretion of two insects that live on the tamarisk tree. The substance drops from the tamarisk to the ground where it hardens somewhat in the night air. This delicacy of central Sinai is prized by the Bedouin for its sweetness. The quail migrate to Europe in the spring and return in the fall. When they land exhausted on the northwest coast of the Sinai peninsula, they can be easily captured. (For the quail as a replacement for the manna see Num 11:5-6, 31-33.)

P, who is the principal author in this account (J is probably to be found in verses 4-5, 29-32), chooses to elaborate certain "spiritual" dimensions. Thus in verses 17-21 there is just enough manna whether one gathers a large amount or a small amount. Moreover, any quantity kept over for the next day is summarily wormy and rotten. Similarly in verses 22-26 there is the link between the manna and the sabbath. Consequently, on the sixth day one may gather twice as much in order to observe the complete rest required on the seventh. Whatever is left over from the sixth day is then used for the seventh. Indeed, those who venture out on the sabbath to find manna are in violation of that sacred day—besides,

nothing is to be found then (v. 27).

The original tradition in this episode was God's gracious care of the people in the desert. Given the grumbling mentioned in verses 2 and 7, one would expect that the sudden arrival of Yahweh's glory (v. 11) would involve a punishment of sorts for the rebels. Instead, in verse 12 Yahweh assures the people through Moses that their food needs will be met. If the people had rebelled against Yahweh, it would be rather surprising for Yahweh to accede to the demands of the rebels. The simplest explanation, therefore, is the invocation of the graciousness tradition: the people were hungry and Yahweh answered their petitions for bread and meat by supplying the manna and the quail (see Ps 105:40).

In view of the Exile and hence an explanation of that debacle as the rebellion of the desert generation, P has introduced the murmuring motif. This is expressed in the form of a death wish in verse 3: "Would that we had died at the Lord's hand in the land of Egypt, as we sat by our fleshpots and ate our fill of bread!" This death wish, however, contains the element of rejection of God's saving plan. By opting for an earlier death in Egypt, they are thereby rejecting the events that led to the present impasse, the Exodus. It is not hunger pangs but the theological despair that commands center stage on this level of the tradition. The reply of Moses and Aaron in verse 6 sustains this interpretation of their rebellion. It is a question of the God who brought them out of Egypt. The tradition of God's graciousness has thus been converted into the tradition of refusing to acknowledge that the God of Israel can indeed accomplish what he sets out to do.

17:1-7 Grumbling at Massah and Meribah. This is a J narrative that is introduced by P's itinerary in verse 1a. Like the J story at Marah, this episode has the primary tradition of Yahweh's graciousness to his needy people. Unlike the Marah tradition, this episode also contains the secondary tradition of Israel's contention with Yahweh over the matter of the Exodus.

If one omits the people's attack on Yahweh at the end of verse 2, the rest of that verse may be understood simply as a quarrel with Moses and a demand that he meet the needs of the people. Moses' cry to Yahweh in verse 4 is not unlike his demand in 14:15 (P) that results in a positive answer from Yahweh. Here the favorable reply is found in verse 5 where Moses is commanded to strike the rock with his staff. (Contrast the different interpretation in Num 20:11-13.) The outcome is that Yahweh once again meets the needs of his people—in this case the need for water. One should also observe that in verse 5 there is no indication of any punishment.

Verse 3 contains the secondary tradition of rebellion in this account. It is not really the thirst that is central. Rather, the thirst serves as a backdrop for impugning the value of the Exodus: "Why did you ever make us leave Egypt?" As in chapter 16, the Exodus is the object of attack because of the lack of water. On this level of the tradition there is the rejection of the divine plan.

One view of the origin of the J murmuring motif is that it is a polemic directed against the northern kingdom of Israel, specifically against the cult of Jeroboam I (931–910 B.C.E.) in Dan and Bethel (see 1 Kgs 12:26-33). This fresh orientation of the desert experience is intended to explain how the northern kingdom lost its rights to divine election and why the southern kingdom retained them (see Ps 78:67-72). Through the rebellion of the desert generation the north forfeited its election while the south preserved its status through the Davidic king in Jerusalem.

17:8-16 Battle with the Amalekites. It is refreshing to come upon a narrative extolling a great human accomplishment in the midst of the awesome display of divine power. This J narrative is a legend, a narrative whose purpose is to edify, in this instance to reflect upon the heroic stature of Moses. While salvation always involves the interplay of divine grace and human cooperation, it is reassuring to note a story where the limelight falls on the human protagonist.

Apart from the notices in verses 14-15 explaining Israel's implacable hatred of the Amalekites and the origin of a particular altar (such explanations are called etiologies), the entire movement centers upon Moses, not Yahweh. In verse 9 Moses commissions Joshua to make the battle preparations and adds that he (Moses) will take up his position on a nearby hill. While no details of the battle are given, there is an abundant description of Moses' contributions to the successful outcome. It is Moses' tenacity and steadfastness

that win the day for Israel. The stamina displayed in keeping his hands raised, albeit with the support of Aaron and Hur (v. 12), is precisely what one would expect of such a giant. These heroic dimensions are captured by the expression "steady hands" in verse 12. The steadiness described in the account is the faithfulness shown in fulfilling an official task (see 2 Kgs 12:16; 22:7). It is the courage of this one man that turns the tide of battle. For all his failings Moses retains his image as hero and superman (see Deut 34:7, 10-12).

The Amalekites who controlled the caravan routes between Egypt and Arabia lived in the Negeb, the southernmost section of Israel (see 1 Sam 15:7). Since they are linked to the tribe of Judah and are quite likely associated with the exodus-expulsion tradition, the story is out of place here. However, as a portrait of the heroic qualities of Moses, it is indeed most apropos in its present position.

18:1-27 Meeting between Moses and Jethro. This chapter, the work of E, contains two scenes: (a) the meeting between Moses and his father-in-law that culminates in a covenant meal (vv. 1-12); (b) the decentralization of judicial authority in Israel that results in the appointments of "minor" judges (vv. 13-27). It is in the desert near the mountain of God (v. 5). Unlike the mountain of God in chapter 19, this mountain is not the scene of a theophany but of a meeting.

Jethro is hardly a new character in the story. In 2:11-22 J narrated Moses' marriage to his daughter. What is striking in the present account is E's concentration on Jethro. Although the latter does indeed bring his daughter and two grandsons to meet Moses (in 2:22 Moses has only one son, but see 4:20), the woman and the two sons play a rather unimportant role. In verse 7 Moses all but ignores his wife and family. Clearly Moses and Jethro are the central figures.

The meeting revolves around Moses' story of Yahweh's exploits (v. 8), Jethro's joy-filled reaction to the story (vv. 9-11), and a covenant meal with Jethro, on the one hand, and Aaron and the elders, on the other hand (v. 12). Although some see Jethro's declaration as an indication of his conversion to Yahwism (v. 11; see 2 Kgs 5:15), it is also likely that Jethro merely recognized that Moses' god, Yahweh, was more powerful than all other gods (see Josh 2:9-11). Although Jethro is called a priest (v. 1) and hence exercised a cultic office, there is really no firm basis for suggesting that he was a priest of Yahweh or that he shared his Yahwistic faith with Moses. In verse 12, as a matter of fact, Moses is conspicuous by his absence. Here Jethro accepts (rather than "brought" as in the NAB translation) the sacrificial offerings, thereby indicating his acceptance of a mutual relationship with the Israelites. Given the subsequent enmity between Midianites and Israelites, this tradition reflects an early friendlier association between the two groups.

Verses 13-27 presuppose a situation that developed after the desert experience, in a time when the population was large and sedentary. The distinction between the more important and less important cases (v. 22) indicates a decentralization of legal authority. According to some authorities it may suggest the judicial appointments during the time of King Jehoshaphat (871–848 B.C.E.—see 2 Chr 19:5-11). In any event, a subsequent situation has been read back into the desert experience and thus the later solution has been attributed to Moses. At the same time, however, the story provides another occasion for E to emphasize his fear of God motif (see 1:17, 21). Hence Moses is instructed by his father-in-law to select God-fearing men (v. 21). This basic orientation of fear of God will ensure the common good, especially by the avoidance of bribes (see Deut 16:19).

PART III: THE MAKING OF
THE COVENANT

Exod 19:1–24:11

Covenants are part and parcel of human social life. Since humans are drawn into relationships with other humans, the terms of those relationships must first of all be clarified and then accepted. A covenant, therefore, is a relationship in which the moral bond between the parties involved is defined and then accepted. For example, in Gen 31:43–32:3 Jacob and Laban make a covenant. A significant element in that relationship is the sworn oath by both parties not to attack each other (31:52-53). Moreover, a pile of stones serves as a witness to the covenant (31:45-48). A ritual meal, finally, is also central to the relationship: "He [Jacob] then offered a sacrifice

on the mountain and invited his kinsmen to share in the meal" (31:54).

An obvious difference between the Jacob-Laban covenant and the Sinai covenant is the position of Yahweh. Yahweh is not an equal partner to the covenant. Rather, Yahweh is the superior and Israel the inferior. Consequently, Yahweh is the one who commands, while Israel is the one who is expected to obey. Israel's pledged word to abide by the terms of the relationship is, therefore, essential to her existence as Yahweh's chosen people. Covenant life is by definition the constant challenge to ongoing fidelity.

Since the covenant on Sinai was *the* experience whereby this people became God's people, it is only natural to assume that the scene at the mountain would be the logical meeting place for a variety of interpretations of this relationship. The variety of traditions reflects Israel's unrelenting efforts to fathom her unique position with Yahweh. Hence Yahweh and Israel could be perceived in various ways. At the same time, these chapters witness to a certain conservatism. Israel was not content to employ one tradition and then discard it. Instead, Israel chose to retain different traditions because each of them preserved a distinct value.

In the midst of the distinctiveness of Israel's covenant traditions there is also a certain basic outline for most of them. First of all, there is the encounter with Yahweh who overawes his people. Second, there is the expression of Yahweh's will for this people. Moses is here the recipient of the terms of covenant existence. Third, Moses reports to the people the will of Yahweh as he received it. This basic outline is also a testimony to Moses' unique position as the covenant mediator.

19:1-2 The setting. P continues his itinerary (see 16:1; 17:1), this time noting that the Israelites have arrived at Sinai. P's next tradition will come only in 24:15b, so there is no tradition of covenant making on Sinai comparable to J and E. For P there is only the one covenant made with Abraham that still perdures (see Gen 17:13). Nonetheless Sinai will become P's ideal place for many of Israel's cultic traditions.

The exact location of Sinai is not known. For those who follow the southern route of the exodus-flight tradition the mountain in question is often identified as Jebel Musa (Mount Moses). The size of the mountain (7,647 feet) is often thought to be imposing enough for the importance of the traditions associated with the biblical narrative. At the base of this mountain in the Sinai desert, the Greek Orthodox monastery of St. Catherine's now stands.

19:3-8 Attitude toward the covenant. The tradition embedded in verses 3b-8 is an independent tradition drawn from the liturgy that is now introduced by verse 3a. Its purpose is to foster the proper attitude that should guide God's people. While it is clearly a proclamation, it is not a proclamation that provides precise rules of conduct. Rather, it is one which underlines the notion of word (verse 5: "if you hearken to my voice"). Israel is bidden to listen and thus act upon Yahweh's word. The use of direct address ("I" and "you") adds both solemnity and power. Indeed, Israel is to learn from God's mighty deeds against the Egyptians (v. 4) the nature of Yahweh and the serious responsibility to heed his word.

There are other dimensions too. There is emphasis on intimacy. Yahweh brings the people, not just to a given destination in the desert but to himself (v. 4). The covenant is specifically Yahweh's (verse 5: "my covenant"), and the people are uniquely his own. The Hebrew word translated "special possession" (v. 5) conjures up the notion of the personal private property of a king (see Deut 7:6; 14:2; 26:18). There is also a stress on Israel's holiness (v. 6), a characteristic by which she is removed from the realm of the profane. The expression "kingdom of priests" does not imply that every Israelite is a priest. Quite likely the totality of Israel is intended: a royalty of priests and a holy nation. Finally, there is the accent on liberty. Israel is not coerced to accept this relationship (verse 5: "Therefore, *if* you hearken to my voice"). In Israel, Yahweh is never a puppeteer who capriciously pulls the strings to control human behavior. Only a free response is a fitting response.

This liturgical tradition suggests an approach whereby Yahweh can be considered the overlord and Israel the vassal. There are hints of such a conception here, hints that would come to fruition in the Book of Deuteronomy where the model of covenant is that of a treaty, in which Yahweh is the overlord

and Israel is the vassal. Israel could thus use political models to great advantage.

19:9-20 Two theophany traditions. This section contains the J and E traditions of the Sinai theophany—God's manifestation on the mountain. (Verse 9 is a gloss that ties together the previous tradition with J and E.) For J (vv. 10-11a, 12-13a, 14-16a, 18, 20) the theophany is that of a volcanic eruption. It is a literary depiction that does not demand that one search for a now extinct volcano somewhere in Arabia. For E (vv. 11b, 13b, 16b-17, 19) the theophany is that of a fear-producing storm.

In the J account it is Yahweh who selects Moses to hear the revelation and then share it with the people (v. 10). Moses is to prepare the people for a ceremony on the third day (vv. 11a, 15a—see also Hos 6:1-3 and 1 Cor 15:4 for the use of the third day in a covenant setting). The ceremony involves washing their clothing and continence (vv. 14b, 15b). While the mention of readiness (vv. 11a, 15a) is also part of holy war preparations, the accent is more on holy and less on war (see 7:14; 38:7). What is expected of the people is that they will respect the limits of the mountain (v. 12) since Yahweh will occupy it (v. 20). The power and majesty of this God are evident in the fire, smoke, and shaking of the mountain. It is the presence of this God that brings about the covenant. (The precise stipulations of this relationship are now found in chapter 34.)

In the E account it is the people who select Moses to be their spokesperson (20:19). It is the fear caused by the storm (v. 16b) that provokes their decision. It is also this fear that makes them willing to receive the will of the storm god. Unlike the J account, the E tradition has Moses organize a liturgical procession but one that will place the people at the bottom of the mountain (vv. 13b, 17b). The tradition also alludes to meeting this God in the setting of a holy war. The camp in verse 17 need not be limited to a nomadic camp; it is also a military camp. While the trumpet is a liturgical instrument (see Ps 47:6), it is also a military instrument used for purposes of warfare (see Judg 7:20; also Josh 6 where the ram's horn mentioned here in verse 13b is both liturgical and military). The Hebrew verb used in verse 17 ("they stationed themselves") also means to line up in battle array (see Judg 20:2). Israel at Sinai is thus God's militia, ready to accede to the will of this commander whose presence is also marked by the cloud over the mountain.

19:21-25 The holiness of the mountain. In this passage J continues the theme of the holiness of the mountain first mentioned in verses 12-13a. Realizing that the people will be tempted to see Yahweh, J has Moses urge the people to observe a reverent distance. Not only are the people in general to sanctify themselves (v. 10) but also the priests (v. 22). Although Aaron is allowed to accompany Moses in his ascent to Yahweh, the priests and the people are expressly forbidden (v. 24). Yahweh's turf must be respected.

20:1-17 The Ten Commandments. While the basic outline calls for the expression of the divine will following the encounter with Yahweh, the condition of the biblical text is still somewhat disconcerting. In the J text of 19:25 Moses goes down the mountain to speak to the people. Next, in 20:1 God communicates the Ten Commandments rather abruptly. This is, in turn, followed by the remark in the E text of 20:19 that God's direct speaking to them will result in death. Finally, in 20:22 Yahweh speaks directly to Moses.

Both the Ten Commandments and the Covenant Code (20:22–23:19) have been associated with the E tradition. Most likely they are not E's personal work but independent traditions inserted by E at this point. At a first stage, the fear experienced by the people (see E in 20:18) was the direct result of the storm theophany in chapter 19. Moses was consequently deputed to hear the entire revelation. At a second stage, because of the importance of the Ten Commandments, the people listened to this fundamental law. This listening led to their fear that, in turn, led to Moses' receiving the rest of the legislation (the Covenant Code). This second stage clearly enhanced the stature of the Ten Commandments since, unlike the Covenant Code, God communicated them directly to the people.

The form of the Ten Commandments is significant. It is a series of apodictic laws, that is, laws that impose a command directly on a person, obliging that person to perform (or refrain from performing) some action that the legislator judges to be desirable (or harmful). Apodictic laws admit two formulations: (a) third person, as in Deut 17:6—"No one shall be put to death on the testimony of only one witness"; (b) second person, as in Lev 18:8—"You shall not have intercourse with your father's wife." Although these apodictic laws are found rather exceptionally in the ancient Near East, they are characteristic of Israel. Moreover, second person formulations, insofar as they express the fundamental religious orientation of an entire people, are unique to Israel. There is, therefore, a dimension of intimacy, especially in these second person singular formulations, since Yahweh speaks directly to the individual Israelite. Such laws are grounded in a person, not an impersonal legislative system (note Gen 2:17). Although murder and adultery were already forbidden in the ancient Near East, the fifth and the sixth commandments are new laws.

With the exception of the first three commandments, the Ten Commandments are originally a form of tribal wisdom. Before being united in their present form, they circulated in different series of commands that the young of a tribe were expected to learn from their elders (see Lev 18; Tob 4; Jer 35). These tribal elders sought to provide for the common good, and their position lent authority to the sayings.

As is clear from verse 1, Yahweh is the person behind this legislation. He is, however, more than a tribal elder. He identifies himself as one who has acted on behalf of the community. Using the liturgical introductory formula ("I am"), the text insists on the centrality of Yahweh's role in Exodus. Israel is bound to these commandments, not only because they are for the common good but also because this God has intervened decisively in her life. (Note how Deut 5:15 uses the Exodus tradition as motivation for the sabbath observance rather than the creation tradition used here in verses 9-11.)

20:18-21 Moses' appointment as mediator. The fear originally attributed to the theophany (19:16b) is now related to the divine proclamation in the Ten Commandments. (The smoking mountain in verse 18 harmonizes the traditions of J and E.) In this E passage Moses is deputed to hear the rest of the revelation (v. 19). Not surprisingly, E accentuates the fear of God motif in verse 20; such fear will be a help in avoiding sin. E concludes here by mentioning Moses' ascent in verse 21, an ascent that he will expand in 24:12-15a.

20:22-26 Introduction to the Covenant Code. The legislation that Moses now hears by himself begins in 20:22 and concludes in 23:19. It is called the Covenant Code or the Book of the Covenant because in 24:3 the people agree to accept God's will, which is then specifically labeled in 24:7, "the book of the covenant." As with the Ten Commandments, E has borrowed an independent collection or independent collections which he inserts at this point in the Sinai theophany. While this section of Exodus may strike some readers as being overly legal and perhaps legalistic and hence dry, one should nonetheless search for the values that Israel perceived here. One such value is Israel's regard for the human person, a value that stands out when viewed against other ancient Near Eastern legal codes. Such an attitude stems from her religious convictions.

These opening verses continue the apodictic form of the Ten Commandments (verse 23 is in the plural, however, and verse 25 is a mixed form). Unlike the J and E traditions that associate God's presence in one form or another with the mountain, this independent tradition has God speak from heaven (v. 24). The prohibition against images stems from the fact that Yahweh could not be seen and hence could not be represented. The law of the altar (vv. 24-26) presupposes Israel's early life in the land. More than one sanctuary is permitted—in fact, as many as there were places where God's presence was recognized. An elevated altar is forbidden, since it may involve immodesty on the part of the sacrificer (see the precautions taken in 28:40-42).

21:1-11 The law for slaves. Verse 2 introduces the casuistic or case law section of the Covenant Code. (This section continues to 22:16.) This form of law was the typical law of the ancient Near East. By its nature casuistic law is pragmatic; it does not depend directly on any ethical principle. The subject is simply reminded of the unpleasant consequences that will follow a violation of the law. In terms of obligation, case law binds the judge or judges who act for the legislator. The very core of these laws is the solution: if such and such has occurred, then such and such is the outcome. Although these laws have a personalistic overtone because of their setting at Sinai, they are, apart from that important note, practical human lay laws written, for the most part, in the third person. (For an example of second person casuistic law, see 21:2.) Their background indicates a time in Israel shortly after the occupation of the land.

This section on slaves clearly distinguishes between slaves and slaveowners, although there are certain limitations on the slaveowners' rights. The word "Hebrew" in verse 2 originally meant "Habiru"—those displaced people and malcontents who harassed the ancient Near East. In its present usage, however, the term means "Israelite." The situation described in verse 4 implies that women are the master's possessions. Ideally (see Jer 34:8-22), the enslavement of Israelites is only temporary: six years for Israelite men (v. 2). (Deut 21:10-14 applies the same to Israelite women.) Verses 8-11 contain special legislation when there is a question of giving the female slave in marriage. In that case she enjoys certain rights as a wife.

21:12-17 Offenses punishable by death. Although this section contains a mixture of legal forms, what makes it a unity is its subject—attacks on human life that involve the death penalty. While verse 12 establishes a general principle, verses 13 and 14 make distinctions. In the case of unpremeditated homicide or accidental manslaughter ("an act of God"), asylum is provided in a sanctuary. In the case of willful murder, not even the sanctuary will avail. In reverence due to parents (vv. 15, 17), Israelite legislation is more demanding than that of the ancient Near East in general.

21:18-31 Laws regarding bodily injuries. Masters cannot dispose of their slaves at their mere whim. The cases mentioned in verses 20-21 and 26-27 indicate limitations on the masters' rights. Verses 23-25 enunciate the law of talion. This law intends to curb unbridled revenge by insisting on proportionate compensation. Slaves, however, do not enjoy this right because they receive only their freedom in compensation for the injury inflicted on them (vv. 26-27). Verse 32 is another indication of the plight of the slave. In the goring death of a slave, the culpably negligent owner is obliged to pay the master the current price for a slave.

21:33–22:14 Laws regarding property damages. Israel never exacted the death penalty for crimes against property, something that the more progressive western states did not acknowledge until the beginning of the last century. The general principle exemplified in this section is that an individual who has been wronged in his property is to be compensated. The compensation is penal in character and usually greater than the damage caused. Thus a man who steals an ox or a sheep and then slaughters or sells it must pay fivefold for an ox and fourfold for a sheep (21:37). A thief who cannot make full restitution for his crime is to be sold into slavery (22:2).

Verses 6-10 have to do with divine adjudication. According to verses 7 and 8, justice is administered before God, that is, in a holy place or a sanctuary. In the legal disputes expressed in these verses, the manner of adjudication is best explained by verse 10. The party or parties involved must swear by Yahweh. This procedure reflects the sacredness of the divine name; to disparage the name is to disparage the person.

22:15–23:9 Social laws. (Although verses 15-16 belong to the casuistic section of the Covenant Code, they are grouped here because of their content.) The legislation in 22:17–23:19 constitutes the apodictic section of the Covenant Code. What is noteworthy about many laws here is the ethical sensitivity to the demands of charity toward one's fellow Israelite. By insisting so often on the obligation of love, it transcends the Ten Commandments, which concern only the demands of justice.

The deflowering of an unbetrothed virgin implies serious financial problems for a father because it would be difficult for her to obtain a suitor. (For a father's worry over a daughter see Sir 42:9-14.) The law in 22:15 states that the seducer must marry her or, in the event of the father's unwillingness to give her, pay the customary marriage price for virgins. In Israel a certain double standard exists. It is the status of the woman that determines adultery, not the status of the man. If the woman is either betrothed or married, and therefore the property of another man, it is adultery. If the woman is neither betrothed nor married, it is not adultery, even if the man in question is married.

Both sorcery (22:17) and bestiality (22:18) involve the death penalty. Sacrifice to false gods (22:19), while a capital offense, is nuanced differently. Such a person is to be doomed—totally destroyed. Some think this destruction applies to his belongings as well.

The laws in 22:20-23 and 23:9 concern those who are legally helpless. Aliens (see 12:48) are foreigners who live in the midst of Israel and enjoy certain rights. Since they do not enjoy full civic rights on a par with Israelites, they are often victims of oppression. Verse 20 exhibits a peculiarity of Israelite jurisprudence, namely, exhortation. Israel not only states the law but often provides reasons for its observance. In this instance Israel is to recall her own precarious existence in Egypt and thus treat the alien appropriately. Since the economy depends on the male heads of the household, widows and fatherless (such is the meaning of orphan in this sociological context) are exposed to the greatest dangers. To counteract these dangers, the legislation in verses 22-23 insists on divine involvement. Yahweh will listen to the laments and take punitive action against the guilty. Israel's conviction is that a truly strong society provides for its weakest members.

Exhortation is also prominent in verses 24-26. A cloak taken in pledge must be returned before sunset because this cloak also serves as bedding. The cry of such a cloakless Israelite merits prompt action from Yahweh.

The material in 23:1-3, 6-8 looks to legal procedures. Those who compose Israel's popular courts are urged not to bear false testimony (v. 1), not to follow the majority view to the detriment of justice (v. 2), and not to accept bribes (v. 8). On the positive side, they are to acquit the innocent and condemn the guilty (v. 8). Since it is unlikely that one would tend to favor the poor in court action, some emend verse 3 to read: "You shall not favor a wealthy man in his lawsuit." In any event, verse 6 clearly advocates due concern for the needy in litigation. Unfortunately, Israel's prophets had to decry the manipulation of the poor in the administration of justice (see Isa 1:23; 10:2; Ezek 22:29; Amos 5:10).

The provisions of 23:4-5 focus on one's personal enemy (some would identify this enemy in terms of an actual or imminent legal dispute). Allegiance to the covenant Lord takes precedence over personal antipathies. Or better, such allegiance demands seeing one's enemy from a new perspective. In any event, straying oxen or asses are to be returned to the proper owner and an overburdened ass is to be helped up.

23:10-19 Religious laws. Verses 10-12 refer to the sabbatical year and the sabbath itself. According to verses 10-11 the fields, vineyards, and olive groves are to lie fallow every seven years. The poor are envisioned as the primary beneficiaries of this institution (see also Lev 25:2-7; Deut 15:1-3). The mention of the sabbath in verse 12 suggests that the sabbatical year is to take place at a fixed date. However, there is little positive evidence to document its actual observance. With regard to the sabbath, the law in verse 13 declares that slaves, aliens, and even beasts are to benefit from the day of rest. (The word "sabbath" in Hebrew suggests "to halt, stop." It is a day marked by rest when everyday activities stop.)

After mentioning the exclusive worship of God's name (and hence person) in verse 13, the Covenant Code considers the pilgrimage feasts to be observed in Israel, that is, feasts requiring male attendance at local sanctuaries. The feast of Azymes or Unleavened Bread celebrates the beginning of the barley harvest (see 13:3-10). It is here linked to the time when Israel came out of Egypt (v. 15). The feast of the grain harvest or Weeks that takes place about fifty days after Unleavened Bread (Pentecost) marks the end of the wheat harvest. Finally, the feast at the end of the year, also called Tents or Tabernacles, celebrates the ingathering of all the produce of the field. Since these three pilgrimage feasts are agricultural, they were celebrated only after the desert experience.

The Covenant Code concludes with several sacrificial injunctions. Since leavened bread implies a change, it may have been deemed unfitting for use in sacrifice (v. 18a). Since the fat of an animal is considered the choicest part (see Lev 3:17), its being kept overnight would result in spoiling (v. 18b). Because Yahweh is Israel's God, he is worthy of receiving the first fruits of the soil at the local sanctuary (v. 19a). The prohibition against boiling a kid in its mother's milk (v. 19b), once thought to be a cultic practice among the Canaanites, is not clear. It seems to be a pagan practice whose specifics are not yet known.

23:20-33 Behavior in the Promised Land. Some see this passage after the manner of Lev 26 and Deut 28—a list of blessings that flow from obedience to the terms of the code. Others regard it as a departure speech that is rather loosely linked to the code. Since these blessings are not closely joined to the preceding stipulations, the second view is to be preferred. (The source of the tradition is not clear, however.)

The passage is a departure speech that aims at encouraging the people during the early monarchy in the tenth century B.C.E. (see the boundaries of the Davidic-Solomonic kingdom in verse 31). It is thus a time when Israel is threatened by Canaanite ways, since she is now living side by side with Canaanites as members of the one people of Israel. God is present through his messenger (vv. 20, 23). Such presence will mean protection, even against overwhelming odds. However, God's military action will be only gradual (vv. 30-31). During this entire time allegiance to Yahweh and his covenant must be uppermost (vv. 21-22, 24, 32-33). Although they are to live with Canaanites, they are not to adopt their ways. It is obedience of this caliber that will bring about the blessings of abundance of food and drink, health, fertility, and a long life (vv. 25-26).

24:1-2, 9-11 Covenant making and the ceremonial meal. In the wake of the J and E traditions of the theophany and the subsequent legislation in chapters 20–23, there now come two more traditions of covenant making: (a) verses 1-2, 9-11 and (b) verses 3-8. Most likely they are independent traditions. In the form of ritual actions they provide yet two more views of response to God's initiative. Although 24:1 is rather clumsily appended to the J and E traditions, and although 24:3 breaks up the initial tradition, still they preserve great values in terms of covenant making, values that Israel took great pains to preserve.

In 24:1-2, 9-11 there is the celebration of a meal in God's presence. This very simple but profound scene is a very ancient tradition stemming from Israel's perception of Yahweh as tribal chief. By means of the meal, Yahweh takes the whole community, represented by the clan elders, into his family. The meal is the assurance and support given by the superior, Yahweh, to the inferior, Israel. What is striking is that the clan elders do not accept any particular stipulations. What they do accept is the protection afforded them by the tribal chief. Israel's specific response to that gesture would be developed in subsequent traditions.

24:3-8 Covenant making and the blood rite. Sacrifices (here communion sacrifices) effect covenant. In response to the people's willingness to accept Yahweh's will (v. 3; see also v. 7), Moses writes down the stipulations (v. 4). After reading "the book of the covenant," he sprinkles the people with half of the blood of the slaughtered animals. For Israel, blood is life. The sprinkled blood joins them to the blood splashed on the altar, which symbolizes God. A union has been created from this blood relationship. However, the terms for preserving that relationship are also spelled out. By living up to those terms, Israel is assured of her ongoing union with Yahweh. Unlike the ancient ceremonial meal, this manner of covenant making lays greater stress on the demands of the covenant God.

PART IV: INSTRUCTIONS FOR THE BUILDING OF THE SANCTUARY

Exod 24:12–31:18

After the final traditions of covenant making (24:1-11), Moses ascends the mountain with Joshua to receive the tablets. This departure will set the stage for the Golden Calf story in chapter 32. Sandwiched in between these two texts is P's account of Moses' receiving divine instructions for the construction of the desert sanctuary. While P clearly rejects any covenant at Sinai, he nonetheless finds this setting the ideal place for developing his cultic interests. Hence this section as well as chapters 35–40 may rightly be termed P's political document.

Recalling Israel's infidelity that provoked the sack of Jerusalem and subsequent exile in 586 B.C.E., P aims at underlining the nature of the restored community, a holy people. Concretely, holiness entails such institutions as priesthood, sacrifices, etc. But the institutions are designed to achieve one purpose— God's presence. While Sinai is not, for P, the place of covenant making, it is the place par excellence for Yahweh's manifestation.

While P makes the desert sanctuary a portable replica of the Jerusalem temple, it is wrong to regard all his cultic elaborations as a retrojection of that temple into the desert experience. As a matter of fact, P also employs older traditions, many of which are at home in ancient Canaanite religion. While P appropriates such Canaanite institutions, he also confronts them, imposing upon them a theology of God's presence consonant with Israelite faith.

24:12-15a Moses' ascent. This E passage expands the rather laconic statement of Moses' ascent in 20:21. Although it now introduces the P material, it originally served to position Moses on the mountain to receive the divine revelation (see 20:18-20). This revelation is linked to the tablets that Yahweh will write. (In P the tablets are written by God's finger [31:18], whereas in J Moses writes them down [34:28].) It is interesting to observe that in the ancient Near East only Israel pictured her God as drafting or dictating legislation. For E the cloud is also significant as marking God's presence (see 19:16b; 20:21). Finally, the notion of additional judges in verse 14 is in keeping with E's "minor" judges in 18:21-26.

24:15b-18 P's theophany. For P this brief scene is not only an introduction to chapters 25–31; it is also a profound theological statement of the significance of Sinai. Here he links the divine manifestation on Sinai with the construction of the sanctuary (40:17, 33b) and the execution of the first sacrifice (Lev 9:1, 23-24). Just as the cloud covers the mountain and Yahweh's glory settles there (vv. 15b-16a), so too the cloud covers the tent of meeting, and Yahweh's glory fills the sanctuary (40:34). In verse 16b Yahweh calls Moses on the seventh day, and in Lev 9:1 Moses summons Aaron, his sons, and the elders of Israel on the eighth day. According to verse 17 Yahweh's glory is viewed as a consuming fire, and according to Lev 9:24a fire comes from Yahweh's presence and consumes the sacrifice. There is thus a clear parallelism between the manifestation on Sinai and the first act of worship after that manifestation. Hence Sinai becomes the model for worship.

25:1-9 Collection of materials. P's concept of Yahweh's earthly dwelling borrows yet reinterprets ancient Canaanite traditions. In that religion El, the head of the pantheon, had a tent on a mountain where he issued authoritative decrees or oracles (see 33:7-11). In verse 9 Moses is instructed to make a copy of the tent on the mountain. There is thus a similarity of form between the deity's earthly dwelling and its heavenly model. P employs two names for Yahweh's place: (a) the more traditional "tent of meeting" (for example, 40:34) and (b) his own special archaic "the dwelling" (always capitalized in the New American Bible). By using the latter term, P understands the transcendent God of Israel who will meet with that people (see 29:42-43; 30:36). For P, Yahweh will take up a permanent abode in the midst of his people (compare 33:7-11).

Unlike J and E, P provides directions for setting up the sanctuary and furnishing it (see also 36:8-38). Despite P's elaborations, modeled after the Jerusalem temple, the basic reality is that of a portable sanctuary, a tent similar to Israel's own tents during the time of the desert. This is similar to the practice of ancient Bedouin tribes that carried a small sacred tent made of red leather. During their journeys such tribes could experience the presence of their gods, owing to the stone idols carried in the tent. In human experience the presence of one's god is judged to be imperative.

25:10-22 Plan of the ark. After the manner of the practice mentioned above, Israel can meet with her God because of the ark that was most likely housed by the tent. The ark is a rectangular wooden cabinet about four feet long, two and a half feet wide, and two and a half feet high that contains the stone tablets given to Moses by Yahweh (vv. 16, 21)—hence the name "ark of the covenant" or "ark of the testimony." (In the ancient Near East it was a common practice to deposit treaties in a sacred place with a view to reading them at stipulated times.)

Although J and E do not associate the ark with the tent, P goes on to add that the ark has a propitiatory flanked by two cherubim. The propitiatory is the gold plate on top of the ark that is associated with divine forgiveness. From above the propitiatory Yahweh can speak to Moses and thus to the Israelites. (For the role of the propitiatory on the Day of Atonement see Lev 16:15-16; note Rom 3:25.) It is likely that this propitiatory was a substitute for the ark, that is, the seat of God's presence or mercy after the ark itself was destroyed (see Jer 3:16). The original ark probably functioned as a support or a pedestal for Israel's invisible God (see Num 10:35-36).

Once the ark reached the Promised Land, it served as Yahweh's throne or footstool (see 1 Sam 4:4). The two golden cherubim, lesser deities borrowed from Israel's neighbors, provided protection for the throne and thus suggested the presence of Israel's God.

25:23-40 The table and lampstand. The table contains the showbread (v. 30) that consists of twelve loaves of unleavened bread (see Lev 24:5-9), replenished every sabbath and reserved to the priests. This bread serves as a reminder of God's covenant with the twelve tribes of Israel. The lampstand or "menorah," although elaborately described, is somewhat baffling to scholars. In any event it is a candelabrum that holds seven lamps. Today the term "menorah" is used for one of the best-known symbols of Judaism, the seven-branched candelabrum. (For the ten lampstands in Solomon's temple see 1 Kgs 7:49.)

26:1-37 Instructions for making the desert sanctuary. In P's conception the desert sanctuary is a collapsible temple that is exactly one half the size of Solomon's temple (see 1 Kgs 6:2, 16-17). First of all, wooden frames form a rectangular building that is approximately forty-five feet long, fifteen feet wide, fifteen feet high, and open on the east (vv. 15-29). Second, sheets of finely woven materials are sewn together to make two large sheets. These sheets are joined together by means of loops and clasps and have the cherubim embroidered on them (vv. 1-6). Third, sheets woven of goat hair are stretched like a tent over the sanctuary. These sheets are slightly longer than those in verses 1-6 and are left hanging down on both sides (vv. 7-13). Finally, ram skins dyed red cover the whole building, and tahash skins (light leather hides), cover the ram skins (v. 14).

This passage also mentions two veils. There is a veil over the entrance to the sanctuary (vv. 36-37) and one between the Holy of Holies and the Holy Place (vv. 31-32). The latter veil is more costly than the former. Behind the veil in the Holy of Holies (the most holy or most sacred area) there stands the ark with the propitiatory (vv. 33-34). This is the area reserved to Yahweh. In the Holy Place are the lampstand and the table of showbread (v. 35).

27:1-8 The altar of holocausts. This altar is basically a hollow wooden box, about seven and a half feet long, seven and a half feet wide, and four and a half feet high that was plated with bronze. It is difficult to understand how it operated, since the heat from these whole-burnt offerings would destroy the altar. To resolve this problem, some suggest that stones are placed on top of the altar for burning (see 29:18). The four corners of the altar are provided with horns. These were significant for seeking asylum in the temple (see 1 Kgs 1:50; 2:28).

27:9-19 Court of the sanctuary. P now describes the rather elaborate courtyard for the desert sanctuary, approximately one hundred and fifty feet long, seventy-five feet wide, and seven and a half feet high (v. 18). A barrier of bronze columns and silver curtain rods (that hold linen curtains) sets off the court from all other areas. One is naturally reminded of Ezekiel's vision that pictured the temple surrounded by a wall "to separate the sacred from the profane" (Ezek 42:20).

27:20-21 Oil for the lamps. The pure olive oil is to come from the people but it is to be handled by the priests. The sanctuary light is obviously intended to be a perpetual reminder of Yahweh's presence in the desert sanctuary (see Lev 24:2-4).

28:1-43 The priestly vestments. Some knowledge of the history of the priesthood in Israel is useful, if not necessary, to appreciate P's political document. Priesthood properly so called did not appear until there was considerable development of the social makeup of the community. (Note the lack of priests for the Passover in 12:1-20.) With the rise of the monarchy two phenomena occurred: (a) rival sanctuaries and (b) increased centralization at the Jerusalem temple (see 1 Sam 2:27-36; 2 Sam 15:24-29). With Deuteronomy's doctrine of only one sanctuary, Jerusalem, the priests serving the country sanctuaries were put out of work (see Deut 12:4-14). These country priests, many of whom were descendants of Levi, became second-class citizens in the Jerusalem temple and were often the objects of charity, along with the widow, the fatherless, and the alien (see Deut 26:12). The only legitimate priests were the Jerusalem Zadokites—those descended from Zadok (see 1 Kgs 2:26-27; 4:2) who were not descendants of Levi. In order to fulfill the Deuteronomic ideal that all priests, regardless of lineage, should be descendants of Levi (see Deut 17:9), the origi-

nally non-Levitical Zadokites claimed to be a special group of Levites, namely, the Aaronites or those descended from Aaron. The outcome was that the Levites now became synonymous with inferior cultic employees who were subordinate to the sons of Zadok (see Ezek 44:10-31). In Exodus, P reflects the claim of the Zadokites to be Aaronites.

This chapter endorses the claims of the Zadokites (v. 1). It focuses on Aaron, allotting only verses 41-43 to the sons of Aaron. Here it is worth noting that there was no ordination of priests as such in the Old Testament. The word translated "ordain" in verse 41 is, literally, "to fill the hand," a phrase whose original sense is not evident. In any event, priests were made holy or sacred by reason of their work.

Of the vestments mentioned here the most interesting are the ephod and the breastpiece. Originally the ephod was a garment worn by the priests and attached to the breastpiece of decision (v. 15). This breastpiece of the same material as the ephod was a bag containing the sacred lots known as Urim and Thummim (v. 30). These lots provide "yes" or "no" answers for those seeking oracles from the priests (see 1 Sam 14:36-37; 28:6). With the ascendancy of prophetism, priests were no longer sought out to give oracles. In keeping with that development the Urim and Thummim, unlike the other priestly items, are merely mentioned and not elaborated. In the P description these originally oracular devices now contain stones engraved with the names of the twelve tribes (vv. 12, 29).

29:1-9 Investiture of the priests. This investiture involves three steps: purification, clothing, and anointing (see also Lev 8:1-38). As a result of the purification or washing, the priest is enabled to enter the realm of the holy (see 30:17-21). The rite of anointing the high priest (v. 7) probably arose only after the Exile when the high priest assumed a political position and consequently received the mark of royalty. (According to 28:41 and other texts all priests are anointed.) This passage concludes by unequivocally stating the Aaronite claims of the Jerusalem Zadokite priests (see also v. 44).

29:10-37 The sacrifices of priestly consecration. There are three different types of sacrifice in this elaborate description. First, there is the sin offering, the bullock (vv.

10-14). Since the offering is for the sins of the priests, they do not share in the victim. Second, there is the holocaust, the first ram (vv. 15-18). Third, there is the communion sacrifice, the second ram (vv. 19-26, 31-37). In verse 20 Moses consecrates the priests by rubbing the animal's blood on the extremities of the body of Aaron and his sons. In verses 24-25 Moses then puts parts of the victims in their hands, has them perform the office of waving them before Yahweh, and receives them back. As a result of this ritual gesture, Aaron and his sons are invested with priestly power. (Verses 27-30 interrupt the ceremony. They determine the offering due the priests and make provision for handing down the priestly vestments.) Next, the priests boil the flesh of this second ram and share it in a sacred meal. Since this meal is a holy meal in connection with their priestly consecration, lay persons may not join them (vv. 31-35). This section concludes by noting the length of the ceremony. The exceptional holiness of the altar (Yahweh's meeting place—see verses 43-44) is underlined in the rubric of a daily sacrifice of a bullock for this seven-day period (vv. 35-37).

29:38-46 Daily sacrifices. The daily sacrifice of two yearling lambs (vv. 38-42) leads into a profound theological statement by P (vv. 43-46). The consecration of the altar, the sanctuary, and the priests looks to God's ongoing presence in the midst of Israel. Specifically, this God who dwells among them is none other than Yahweh, who brought the Israelites out of Egypt. Israel's cultic institutions are thus rooted in the Exodus and in Sinai.

30:1-38 Further cultic ordinances. The altar of the incense (called the golden altar in 1 Kgs 7:48) is perhaps a later priestly insertion, since it should be logically mentioned in 26:33-37 and is not included in the incense-related episodes in the desert (see Num 16:6-7, 17-18; 17:11-12). Each morning and each evening (vv. 7-8) a priest removes pieces of coal with a shovel from the altar of holocausts, sprinkles powder on the coals, and places them on the altar of incense (see Luke 1:8-9). Verses 34-38 provide the mixture for this absolutely sacred perfume. On the Day of Atonement (v. 10) the high priest takes this life-saving smoke screen into the Holy of Holies and rubs the blood of the sacrificial ani-

mal on the horns of the altar of incense itself (see Lev 16:12-13, 18).

Census taking is construed as a dangerous undertaking (see 32:30-35; 2 Sam 24). Everyone, therefore, of twenty years of age or over, who seeks to be enrolled and wishes to avoid the census plague must make a contribution to the sanctuary of a half-shekel (vv. 11-16; see Neh 10:33-35). Such a religious precaution is a fitting offering to the upkeep of Yahweh's dwelling place.

Verses 17-33 enact further requirements for cultic personnel and objects. According to verses 17-21 the priests must employ the laver (see 2 Chr 4:6) for washing their hands and feet prior to entering the sanctuary and when officiating at the altar (all Moslems observe this rite before prayer in the mosque). Since there is no mention of the laver in 38:29-31 and since it logically belongs with the altar of holocausts in 27:1-7, it is very likely a later priestly insertion. In addition to the washing, the priests (v. 30) and all the sacred furniture (vv. 26-28) are to be anointed with a very special holy oil (vv. 23-25). These rubrics indicate the unique character of cultic personnel and objects. They must be removed from everything that smacks of the profane (vv. 32-33). For P, however, the holiness of the sanctuary with its personnel is intended to have a sanctifying effect on the entire people of Yahweh.

31:1-11 Choice of artisans. The construction of a god's temple is not a haphazard decision. In ancient Canaanite literature the construction of Baal's temple falls to a special craftsman god. Against this background P has Yahweh single out Bezalel and, as his assistant, Oholiab. P emphasizes that Bezalel's talent results from a divine spirit (v. 3; see also 35:31). This detail is central to P's plan of divine presence whereby the creation of the world, the construction of the desert sanctuary, and the erection of the sanctuary are interrelated. Thus God's spirit in Gen 1:2 is linked to the spirit-filled architect of the desert construction (v. 3), who is, in turn, linked to the spirit-filled leader of the occupation forces, Joshua (see Num 27:18; Deut 34:9).

A key structural element in P is the execution of a command given directly or indirectly by God (see 7:6; 12:28). As noted in 25:1-9, it is eminently important to have exact correspondence between God's plan and its execution. Thus the divine command communicated through Moses to the artisans (vv. 6, 11) will be carried out exactly. In chapter 39 that execution will be noted in a context that also links the construction of the sanctuary to the creation of the world.

31:12-18 The significance of the sabbath. Although P earlier connected sabbath observance with the manna (16:23-30), he now develops the meaning of that institution for Israel. As in the other traditions of the sabbath in Exodus, there is the mention of cessation of work (see 20:9; 23:12; 34:21) and of the link to creation (see 20:11). In this passage, however, P underlines the sign value (vv. 13, 17) and the covenant thrust (v. 16) of the sabbath. Since Yahweh sanctified the sabbath (Gen 2:3) and rested (Gen 2:2) in the aftermath of creation (here in verse 17 Yahweh refreshes himself), Israel acknowledges through its observance the Holy One in her midst. Israel thereby enters into the whole rhythm of creation, celebrating anew her bond with the creator God and the created world. Israel is sacred and given over to Yahweh (v. 13), just as the sabbath is sacred and given over to Yahweh (vv. 14, 15). Later (39:43) P will connect Yahweh's action of blessing on the seventh day with Moses' blessing of the artisans.

PART V: ISRAEL'S APOSTASY AND THE RENEWAL OF THE COVENANT

Exod 32:1–34:35

This section of Exodus bristles with enormous difficulties. The source division of chapters 32–33 is far from clear. The original event behind the story of the Golden Calf is not really apparent. Nevertheless, despair should not control the general interpretation of the final text. Though the history of the traditions in these chapters continues to be elusive, what does emerge with clarity is Israel's ultimate understanding of herself as a covenanted people. The multiplicity of traditions, moreover, points to the centrality of this episode for her self-understanding.

Not a few scholars are convinced that a real event stands behind the story of the Golden Calf and that it occurred during the wilderness experience. There may have been a group that opposed Moses and his ark of the covenant symbol. Such a group under the leadership of Aaron may have broken away from allegiance to Moses and insisted on a bull figure as their symbol of the divine presence. However, to be more specific is to go beyond the evidence.

It should be noted that the Golden Calf does not violate the prescription of the Ten Commandments regarding false images (20:4-5). That prohibition concerns the person of Yahweh, whereas the Golden Calf (actually a young bull) looks to an attribute of Yahweh—strength. Such bulls could serve as supports for Yahweh's throne (see the cherubim in 25:10-22). Israel's history, however, shows that the people did not always distinguish between the deity and the deity's attribute and so identified the young bull with Yahweh (see Hos 13:2).

Jeroboam I (931–910 B.C.E.), the first king of the northern kingdom, set up such a young bull image in the cities of Dan and Bethel (see 1 Kgs 12:26-32) as a cultic move against Solomon's temple. Jeroboam's use of these images suggests that they were already an old tradition. Hence Exod 32 need not be construed as directly condemning this king's cultic changes. However, it is likely that this chapter is an indirect condemnation of Jeroboam's cultic reforms.

In their present setting chapters 32–34 reflect a theology of covenant renewal. The elements in this theological construct are: (a) sin, which is generally apostasy; (b) punishment; (c) repentance; (d) restoration (see Num 13–14; Judg 3:7-11). This pattern is theologically significant. It implies that Yahweh chooses to reveal himself, not only through a people (which is indeed a plus) but also through a sinful people. In this respect Israel considers herself a refuge of sinners.

32:1-6 Making of the Golden Calf. The sin in this covenant renewal pattern is the desire of the people to get rid of Moses and so obtain a new leader (vv. 1, 4). This tradition is certainly non-priestly. In such traditions Aaron is never identified as a priest or an ancestor of priests; indeed, as here, he even opposes Yahweh's chosen leader (see Num 12:1-8). Aaron readily accedes to the wishes of the people, constructs the young bull image, and calls for a celebration involving holocausts and communion sacrifices (vv. 2-5). It is not really clear that the reveling in verse 6 is some form of debauchery. Israel's sin of apostasy consists in rejecting Moses as leader and hence in rejecting Yahweh.

32:7-14 Yahweh's wrath and Moses' mediation. Moses appears as a covenant mediator, one who intercedes for the people, here in the context of winning forgiveness that ultimately leads to covenant renewal. Israel, therefore, envisioned a special role of intercession whereby the relationship of the people to Yahweh was bound up with the relationship of certain endowed individuals to Yahweh. It is also interesting to observe that Moses is able to oppose the God of Israel and still not be labeled unloyal.

Yahweh's violent reaction is precisely the reverse of that envisioned by the young bull devotees. Yahweh plans to wipe this people out and begin anew (vv. 7-10). Moses begins his mediatory role by pursuing the argument of continuity in history. To have the people die in the desert would only provoke ridicule from Yahweh's enemies in Egypt. The action begun in Egypt should be carried on to completion. To abandon Israel now would be to renege on the promises to the patriarchs (vv. 11-13). In the end Yahweh allows the persuasive Moses to win the argument (v. 14).

32:15-24 Twofold destruction. The tablets play a significant part in this story. In verses 15-16 these tablets are unique. Although the custom was to have such inscriptions on only one side, these are on both sides. E's tradition is hinted at. (Joshua's presence in verse 17 has already been explained by E in 24:12.) The divine revelation which Moses was to have communicated to the people is now recast to tell the account of Israel's infidelity and so necessitate Moses' return to the mountain where he will receive new tablets. Although J has Moses inscribe the tablets (34:28), this tradition insists that God himself actually did the engraving (see also P in 31:18). The tradition, therefore, went beyond the ancient Near Eastern understanding of divine writing whereby a deity did not produce the document physically. Yahweh's writing, as a result, stresses their value and authority. In the other direction, the breaking of the tablets is the breaking of the covenant relationship between Yahweh and Israel. The action of the people in the construction of the young bull image results in the destruction of the covenant bond.

The destruction of the tablets is followed by the account of the construction and subsequent destruction of the Golden Calf. Although verses 21-24 make a feeble attempt to exculpate Aaron's role in verses 2-5, they are interesting from the standpoint of the making of cultic objects. In ancient Canaanite literature, for example, cultic objects acquired their desired form by themselves. The palace of Baal is completed after a fire has worked on the silver and the gold for six days. Aaron's reply in verse 24 that the image emerged by itself is thus readily intelligible. The destruction is even more interesting. According to verse 20 Moses employs mutually exclusive acts in undoing the image: burning and grinding. In ancient Canaanite literature Mot, the god of death, is undone in the same way. Anat, Baal's consort, burns, grinds, and scatters Mot. The final act of making the Israelites drink the image-polluted water (see also Deut 9:21) is similar to Anat's scattering of Mot's remains in the open fields where birds consume them. In Exodus the Golden Calf, like Mot, is utterly destroyed and made totally irretrievable.

32:25-29 The zeal of the Levites. There are two traditions for the punishment of the people. According to verse 35 Yahweh smites the people for their sinful action. According to verses 25-29 members of the tribe of Levi rally to Moses' call to arms and execute the Israelites who sacrificed to the Golden Calf, including their own relatives. This loyalty wins for them their priestly prerogatives (see Deut 33:9). This tradition does not condemn Aaron as the ancestor of the Aaronites. It expresses the reaction of the covenant-committed Levites who rejected the cult established by Jeroboam I at Bethel, one of the cities where this king erected a young bull image. This episode also condemns the action of the king in making priests from among the people who were not Levites (see 1 Kgs 12:31).

32:30-35 The atonement. This tradition stresses Moses' identity with the people. If Yahweh is unrelenting, then the mediator wishes to share the fate of the people. The concept of God's book was known in the ancient Near East and is at home in the notion of military conscription where the lives of those enrolled in the book were fraught with danger. In this section Israel adapts the tradition—an Israel that considers herself

God's army. At the time of a census (see 30:11-16) there was a rite of expiation (see "atonement" in verse 30) and the names of the Israelites were inscribed on tablets. Those so inscribed enjoyed the rights of a member of God's militia, for example, possession of the land and worship in the sanctuary. Anyone removed from the tablets was placed among the dead, that is, separated from the community.

33:1-6 Orders for the departure. This section pursues the thrust of 32:33-34, the continuation of the journey to the Promised Land with the aid of an angel. However, the angel in 32:34 merely affirmed Moses' leadership role. The basic issue here is the personal presence of Yahweh with Moses and the Israelites (vv. 2-3). An angel is not the same as Yahweh. This bad news is reiterated in verses 4-6 and is marked by a sign of Israel's repentance, the removal of all ornaments. The people now stand under God's judgment. One naturally wonders about the efficacy of Moses' mediation.

33:7-11 Moses and the Tent of Meeting. This tradition, which is generally ascribed to E, takes up the question of divine presence already broached in verses 1-6. However, the text itself is not a unity. According to verse 7 any Israelite can visit the tent. However, according to verse 8 only Moses visits the tent while the people remain at their own tents in awe. According to verse 11b an official resides permanently in the tent. Yet verse 11a presumes that the intimate dialogue between God and Moses precludes the presence of a third person. Verses 8 and 10 presume that the tent is placed in the middle of the camp (see P in 25:1-9). But verse 7 states that the tent is outside the camp and indeed at some distance from the camp.

It seems that E has introduced changes into an older tent tradition from Israel's desert experience in order to demonstrate that the tent theophany is a miniature reproduction of the revelation of Sinai. Both the mountain and the tent are outside the camp (v. 7; 19:17). In both cases the people remain at a distance (v. 8; 20:18). (In Hebrew the same verb is used for the people stationing themselves [v. 8; 19:17].) In both cases a cloud indicates the divine presence (vv. 9-10; 19:16ab). In both cases Joshua assists Moses (v. 11b; 24:13). Finally, in both cases Moses appears as God's intimate. Israel's relationship to Yahweh hinges in no small measure on this unique mediator.

33:12-17 Moses' intercession. This section is linked to Moses' position vis-à-vis Yahweh (v. 11a) and his order to lead the people on (v. 1a). According to verse 12 the implication is that an angel simply will not do. Appealing to his status as divine intimate, Moses argues on behalf of the people (v. 13). If the leader's status is genuine, the divine conclusion must be to provide for the people. Verse 14 shows that the appeal is successful. However, it is directed only at Moses. Still dissatisfied, Moses presses his case by demonstrating that divine intimacy is real only if the people are included (vv. 15-16). The community-directed argument of Moses finally obtains divine approval (v. 17). The significance of this argumentation should not be overlooked. It implies that the welfare of the covenant people (here their renewal as God's people) is grounded in the love and trust between the covenant God and the covenant mediator.

33:18-23 Preparations for theophany. With no little audacity Moses seeks further surety for his people, since the pronouncing of the divine name is the guarantee of presence and hence of compassion (for this compassion see 34:6-7). Divine name goes hand in hand with covenant. Because of the dangers connected with the direct display of God's glory, Moses is to be set in the hollow of a rock and covered by God's hand (vv. 21-22). The viewing of God's back (but not his face) is both the limit and the proof of Moses' intimacy, but of intimacy as related to the well-being of the people. (For Elijah's similar theophany see 1 Kgs 19:9, 11-13.)

34:1-9 The theophany. Most of this section is from J (vv. 1a, 2-4, 6a, 8). Indeed, together with most of the remaining material in chapter 34, this scene is the natural sequel of Moses' ascent of the mountain in 19:20 (J). In keeping with the basic outline of the covenant proceedings, an expression of God's will is expected in J's account. This expression has been removed from its natural place—after 19:20—because of Israel's infidelity in the Golden Calf incident. In other words, the expression of God's will in the initial encounter on the mountain in J has become the expression of God's will in the second encounter of covenant renewal. According to the pattern of covenant renewal, restoration is now in order. The making of new tablets symbolizes the making of a new covenant. (References to the former broken tablets in verse 1b and to the cloud in verse 5 are editorial touches to make the J account fit its new setting.)

J's theophany has, first of all, Moses cutting the tablets and ascending the mountain alone (vv. 1a, 2-4). Next, Yahweh passes before Moses (v. 6a). Finally, in deference to the divine presence, Moses bows down to worship (v. 8).

Verses 6-7 and 9 are the conclusion of Moses' mediatorial role begun in 33:12-23. The theophany announced in 33:19 now takes place. The cultic saying in verses 6-7 (see also 20:5-6) in its present position is a statement about divine forgiveness and divine punishment. The word translated "merciful" in verse 6 (also the verb "to grant mercy" in 33:19) derives from the Hebrew word for "womb." Thus Mother Yahweh demonstrates that compassion for Israel which a mother is expected to show the child of her womb. At the same time, Yahweh will not let the guilty escape (v. 7). Ultimately the request for forgiveness (v. 9) is grounded once again in the relationship that Moses enjoys with Yahweh. The covenant renewal can now proceed because Moses has identified with Israel.

34:10-26 The Dodecalogue. There is no mention of Israel's explicit response to Yahweh's overtures in this covenant renewal. Moses' intercession and the people's repentance seem adequate (see also 1 Sam 12:16-25). The opening verses (vv. 10-11) transcend the immediate setting by focusing on the dangers that will confront Israel in the Promised Land (note also 23:20-33). Sinai appears, therefore, as the apt place for anticipating those dangers by reason of the covenant bond that will distinguish Israel from her neighbors.

Although verse 28 speaks of the Decalogue or Ten Commandments, this series of laws is actually a Dodecalogue or Twelve Commandments. (The expression "ten commandments" in verse 28 is a later development.) The Dodecalogue is often labeled cultic or ritual in contradistinction to the ethical Decalogue (see the injunction for the pilgrimage feasts in verse 23 and the law of redemption in verses 19-20). However, the prohibitions of images (v. 17) and intermarriage with the Canaanites (v. 16) are patently ethical. Moreover, most of these commandments are second person

singular formulations (see 20:1-17). For J, this collection creates a healthy tension in his theological approach. According to Gen 12:1-3, Israel is to mediate blessings to the conquered nations. But a pagan environment can pose problems in mediating those blessings. This Dodecalogue, therefore, is J's form of insistence on fidelity to the covenant God in a pagan setting (vv. 12-15). It is rightly called by some Yahweh's privilege law—a statement of Yahweh's prerogatives grounded in his character as the Jealous One (v. 15). The distinctiveness of Israel flows from the distinctiveness of her God.

34:27-35 The impact of theophany. J mentions the divine command to write down the terms of the covenant and the subsequent execution of that command on the mountain for a period comprising forty days and forty nights (vv. 27-28; see Deut 9:9,18; Matt 4:2). J then narrates Moses' gathering of the people and his enjoining on them all that Yahweh commanded on the mountain (vv. 31-32).

The tradition contained in verses 29-30, 33-35 deals with Moses' shining face. It is linked to Moses' mediatorial position already noted in chapters 33 and 34. According to the tradition, Moses must veil his face when he is not performing his official duties (vv. 33-34). Whatever the background of the veil itself, what is central to the biblical account is the radiant face of Moses insofar as it derives from God and is the symbol of his authority before God. The man who was rejected by the people (32:1, 4) is the man who restored them in covenant and who now fittingly wears the symbol of his divine office. (See Paul's application of this tradition in 2 Cor 3:7–4:6.)

PART VI: THE EXECUTION OF THE INSTRUCTIONS FOR THE BUILDING OF THE SANCTUARY

Exod 35:1–40:38

P now recounts the execution of the instructions given to Moses in chapters 25–31. It is tempting to construe chapters 35–40, together with chapter 34, as a type of restoration. Thus chapters 25–31 are a creation and chapters 32–33 a fall. In any event, P utilizes the Sinai setting to develop his theology of divine presence.

35:1–36:7 The start of construction and Israel's generosity. P's basic structure here is the execution of commands given directly or indirectly by God. Thus there are divine commands for: (a) the observance of the sabbath (35:1, including the prohibition against lighting fires, in verse 3); (b) the collection of materials (35:4); (c) the call for artisans (35:10); (d) the start of work on the project (36:1). P goes on to note that the Israelites generously respond to Yahweh's command (35:20-29). In fact, they are overzealous. Moses has to make a special appeal to stop the flow of contributions (36:2-6). The outcome is nonetheless an abundance of materials to complete the work (36:7). The spirit-endowed Bezalel and Oholiab (see 31:1-11) as well as the other artisans are also portrayed as responding to the divine command to execute all the work. It is rather interesting to compare this wholehearted response in P's ideal account with the reluctance to rebuild the temple after the Exile (see the prophets Haggai and Zechariah). The biblical record does not hesitate to register both the ideal and the real.

36:8–39:31 Execution of the divine instructions. With the exception of 38:21-31 this section details how the divine instructions communicated to Moses in chapters 25–31 were in fact carried out. There is a difference, however, in the sequence. While the ark with the table and the lampstand (25:10-39) heads the list of instructions because of their greater importance, the tent (26:1-37) comes first in the order of execution. In this way there is progress from the outside inward. In general, this section basically duplicates chapters 25–31, belaboring the point that the final product corresponds to the initial directions. For the tent cloth, coverings, wooden frames, and veils (36:8-38) see 26:1-29, 31-37. For the ark with the propitiatory, table, and lampstand (37:1-24) see 25:10-39. For the altar of incense (37:25-28) as well as the anointing oil and fragrant incense (37:29) see 30:1-6, 23-25, 34-36. For the altar of holocausts and the court (38:1-7, 9-20) see 27:1-19. For the priestly and other vestments (39:1-31) see 28:1-43.

In 38:8 P notes that the bronze laver (30:18-21) was made from the mirrors of the women who served at the entrance of the sanctuary. These women reappear in a gloss of 1 Sam 2:22. Just what function they performed is not clear. There is no evidence to suggest that they exercised an office in public worship.

The passage dealing with the amount of metal used (38:21-31) is a later insertion into the text. The sanctuary tax in verse 26 that draws on the first census of Israel (to be mentioned later in Num 1:45-46) apparently ignores the tradition of 35:21 and 36:3. According to this tradition Israel generously contributes on a voluntary basis. Verse 21 notes the position of Ithamar, son of Aaron, as head of the Levites. However, the Levites (see 28:1-43) are not instituted until Num 3:5-10 and Ithamar assumes his role as head only in Num 4:33.

39:32-43 Presentation of the work to Moses. Besides enumerating the finished cultic materials that are presented to Moses, this section is especially significant for P's theology of God's ongoing presence. By a subtle use of structures, P interconnects the creation of the world, the construction/erection of the desert sanctuary, and the establishment of that sanctuary in the Promised Land (for this last point see 40:1-33). Despite Israel's infidelity, God's plan will not be thwarted. The God who created in the beginning will continue to create in Israel's ongoing history. Cult, therefore, is the principal means by which the creative presence will be manifest among the Israelites.

P not only reintroduces his execution-of-command structure (see 35:1–36:7) but here he also embellishes it with a more solemn formulation. Verse 32b may be translated literally: "And the sons of Israel did [it] according to everything that Yahweh had commanded Moses. Thus they did [it]." Similarly verse 42: "According to everything that Yahweh had commanded Moses, thus the sons of Israel did all the work." P also brings in a second structure, successful completion of work (v. 32a). In addition P has Moses make a judgment on the people's work. Verse 43a may be translated literally: "And Moses saw all the work, and behold, they had done it." Right after this judgment, P has Moses bless the people (v. 43b).

The parallels with P's creation account are evident. In Gen 1:31 God looks at everything he has made and labels it very good. Gen 2:1 observes that the heavens and the earth and all their array are finished. After concluding the six days of creation, God blesses the seventh day (Gen 2:3). Since God cannot issue a command to God, the creation account does not allow for the execution-of-command structure. As mentioned earlier (31:1-11), the spirit at work in creation (Gen 1:2) is also operative in Bezalel, the chief engineer of the sanctuary construction.

40:1-33 The erection of the sanctuary. Here P minutely relates how Moses carries out Yahweh's instructions in setting up the desert sanctuary. Besides pinpointing the time (vv. 2, 17) and accentuating the privileges of the Aaronites (vv. 13-15), P takes pains to highlight the significance of the event by means of his structures. The execution-of-command structure is mentioned no less than eight times (vv. 16, 19, 21, 23, 25, 27, 29, 32). Indeed, verse 16 has the more solemn form of the structure, which may be translated literally: "And Moses did according to everything that Yahweh had commanded him, thus he did [it]." The structure of successful completion of work is also in evidence. According to verse 33 Moses finishes everything.

P links not only creation and the erection of the sanctuary but also the setting up of that sanctuary in the apportioned Promised Land. In Num 27:18 and Deut 34:9, P describes Joshua as the spirit-filled leader and the architect of Israel's plan of occupation. In Josh 14:5, when narrating the division of the land, P employs the more solemn form of the execution-of-command structure. It may be translated literally: "As Yahweh had commanded Moses, thus the sons of Israel did [it] and they divided the land." In the same book, P also uses the successful completion-of-work structure in narrating the final apportionment: (literally) "And they finished dividing the land." This final act, moreover, takes place in front of the tent at Shiloh. In keeping with the divine command to subdue the earth (Gen 1:28), P states in Josh 18:1 that the earth was indeed subdued. In the same text he notes that the community of Israel gathered around the tent which was set up in Shiloh. For P, therefore, the event at Shiloh looks back to Sinai, which in turn looks back to the first creation. God's abiding presence in the land is the sacrament of hope for P's despairing exiles. In the final analysis, the dull rubrics are charged with life.

40:34-38 The abiding presence. For P, Sinai is the model of worship. According to 24:15b-16a the cloud covers the mountain and settles there. Here, too, the cloud covers the sanctuary and Yahweh's glory fills it (v. 34). For P, therefore, the desert sanctuary captures the experience on Sinai and perpetuates it.

This tradition of the cloud's covering and settling is also the seal of approval on and legitimation of everything that Moses and the Israelites have done. Yahweh here takes possession of his sanctuary. This is also Israel's experience when Yahweh's glory fills Solomon's temple and the priests are unable to minister because of the cloud (see 1 Kgs 8:10-11). P's cloud theophany also anticipates Israel's ongoing trek through the wilderness. P's cloud, which now does duty for the tradition of the pillar of cloud and the pillar of fire (see 13:21-22; 14:19-20), also serves as a signal. It will indicate when and how long Israel will set up camp and when Israel is to strike camp (see Num 9:15-23).

In these concluding chapters, P reveals himself to be a truly pastoral theologian. For a people that experienced God's absence in the fall of Jerusalem and subsequent exile, P now proclaims the good news of God's presence. Aware that Israel is deprived of temple worship because she dwells in a foreign land, P announces that Israel will be restored to the land and indeed that the land will be sanctified by God's presence in the sanctuary. (For the conditions of return see Lev 26.) One thus returns to the gospel of creation. By careful and proper attention to cult, the Israelite is empowered to move from chaos to cosmos.

LEVITICUS

Wayne A. Turner

INTRODUCTION

This is a book about holiness. Known also as the third book of Moses, the Book of Leviticus is one volume in the five-volume work called the Pentateuch. The term Torah, which usually means law, but more exactly is teaching, instruction, or direction, refers to the message of this book. Even though we customarily refer to Leviticus as a book, it is better to call it one chapter in the whole story of the Torah. This chapter is about a holy God and a people called to be holy.

1. Holiness means wholeness

To understand this chapter in the Torah story we need to consider "wholeness" as one meaning of holiness. This is more than a play on words and is necessary to understand the Book of Leviticus. Wholeness, in a sense, describes the life of God. More precisely, wholeness describes our lives when they reflect the life of God.

The biblical meaning of holiness includes not only the mystery of God but also the creature's response to that mystery. "Be holy, for I, the Lord, your God, am holy" (11:44-45; 19:2; 20:7, 26). The root of the word holy means "to cut off, separate," referring to the separation of the holy from the profane (unholy). "Holy" refers to persons, places, or things approached or touched only under certain conditions of ritual purity.

"Wholeness" describes particularly the response of the people to the command "Be holy, for I, the Lord, am holy." For, while there is a certain wholeness to the idea of oneness, God alone resides in absolute oneness. There is also a certain oneness about wholeness, which can reflect what Genesis calls the "image and likeness of God" (1:26).

Wholeness, unlike oneness, has parts or components. It is in the proper ordering of the parts of life that wholeness comes about and serves the cause of holiness. For example, a jigsaw puzzle must be put together in a particular order. If even one piece is left over, the puzzle lacks wholeness and oneness.

As we read the Book of Leviticus, we must keep in mind that everything fits together in a proper order. This serves the wholeness that reflects the oneness of God who called the people to be holy. The simple order of obedience, ritual purity, and holiness is as valid today as when first presented by the Priestly writers. True obedience plants the seed of an authentic ritual that purifies and prepares for the life of holiness. Once this simple lesson-plan was recognized, the Levitical material took its shape. Then this book acted as the key piece for the Pentateuch and became the third book of Moses. The five books formed one complete account of divine-human relationship, with Leviticus as the very heart of the Torah.

2. The titles tell the story

The Hebrew titles of the five books of Moses spell out a theme that is repeated again and again in the Bible and in life itself—God

115

creates, identifies, and calls people from the wilderness of this life into the one, complete (holy) life that is God's. These books act as the "entrance" to the whole Bible.

In the Hebrew Bible the first significant word of each book is the title for that book. In the Pentateuch the Hebrew titles make a logical statement of the divine-human experience. *In the beginning* (Genesis) God created; these are the *names* (Exodus), *and he called* (Leviticus) Moses *in the wilderness* (Numbers) to speak these *words* (Deuteronomy). Note the place of Leviticus; the *names* (Exodus) of those led out of slavery needed direction to follow their calling as a "kingdom of priests and a holy nation" (19:6), especially *in the wilderness* (Numbers).

When reading Leviticus keep in mind the "guideline character" of this chapter in the one story that makes up the Pentateuch.

3. The title

The title in Hebrew is one word meaning "and he called." Today the common title is the Latinized Greek name *Leviticus*, which describes activities of the Levites (priests) from the tribe of Levi. The Hebrew title points to a vocation-call in the instruction of the Torah. So when using *Leviticus*, it is well to keep in mind the Hebrew overtone of "calling" or "vocation."

This central theme of a call to holiness is found in the Code of Holiness (17–26). It possibly formed an original "manual of holiness" around which the final editors of the book gathered other priestly (Levitical) material.

4. Three codes of law (instruction) in the Pentateuch

Three such Codes of Law have been identified in the Pentateuch: the Sinai or Covenant Code, which is the oldest and found in the Book of Exodus (19–24); the Levitical Code of Holiness (Lev 17–26); and an updating of the Torah in the Deuteronomy Code (Deut 12–26). Even though these three are considered the Codes of Law, many other passages in the Pentateuch speak of legal regulations. In fact, the Levitical regulations are not only in the Book of Leviticus but also in the second and the fourth books of Moses, Exodus and Numbers. Actually, there is more mention of the Levites elsewhere in the Pentateuch than in the Book of Leviticus. Here we concentrate on the "call to holiness."

5. Leviticus—heart of the Torah

Leviticus not only teaches holiness; the book itself is an example of holiness. The orderly arrangement is our first evidence of the presence of holiness. A simple arrangement of the material can be an important witness to holiness. Note that the matter of sacrifices (chs. 1–7) leads naturally into the subject of those who offer them (chs. 8–10) with their dispositions of legal purity (chs. 11–16) and legal holiness (chs. 17–27)—such a simple arrangement and yet filled with importance and authority calling the people to follow the Torah.

The book is something like the simple but decisive presence of the heart in the human organism. Even when its presence and precision of function are taken for granted, it continues to beat for the good of the whole organism. The material assigned to Leviticus seems to have a similar relation to the whole Torah. Leviticus is the heart of the Torah, and the beat of this heart is called the Code of Holiness (chs. 17–26).

The depth and elegance of the simple arrangement of Leviticus is revealed, first in the pulsating rhythm of the repeated "And the Lord spoke to Moses." After the vocational call of Moses in chapter 1, almost every chapter begins with this same refrain. The repetition is also a reminder of the form of a legal document with its repetition of formal phrases, details, and directions. In fact, roughly corresponding to the above four areas of arrangement, some legal-minded commentators point to underlying detailed arrangements. Some find seven sets of decalogues in each section. They say that they are patterned after the Decalogue (Ten Commandments) given on Mount Sinai. Thus, Leviticus, as the heart of the Torah, reflects the fine design of a heart and the simplicity of one of its single life-giving beats.

The commandments were now to come alive in the lives of the newly-formed people. The heart of the new priestly nation must now begin to beat and carry out the instruction to be holy (19:2). This holiness is at work in the Torah and throughout the whole Bible. "Holy" and "sacred" and other related forms are used over a thousand times, with nearly one quarter of such references in Leviticus.

St. Jerome in a letter to the cleric Paulinus affirms the holiness of the book: "In the Book of Leviticus it is easy to see that every sacrifice, yes, almost every syllable and both the garments of Aaron and the whole order of Leviticus breathe heavenly mysteries." Years later another Scripture writer, Peter, encourages the vocational call of Leviticus: "So gird the loins of your understanding, live soberly, set all your hope on the gift to be conferred on you when Jesus Christ appears. As obedient sons, do not yield to the desires that once shaped you in your ignorance. Rather, become holy yourselves in every aspect of your conduct, after the likeness of the Holy One who called you; remember Scripture says, 'You shall be holy, for I am holy'" (1 Pet 1:13-16 quoting Lev 19:2). This same pulsating beat of holiness endures today in the vocational call of everyone.

6. The shape of Leviticus—date and authorship

Today we usually think of a book as having one or two authors and written over just a few years. However, the Bible is the history of the people of God written by many authors and editors over two thousand years. Just as we can expect many changes in the history of a people, we can expect changes in the documents that record that history. Scholars sometimes speak of a particular manuscript family when referring to various manuscripts.

We now recognize that some final editors were not just compilers, but were true authors. Editors also reshaped or added material along the way. In Leviticus the form of the material is *historical* and *legal,* dealing with the call to holiness. Much of the material, especially in the first chapters, is "liturgical," having been written and edited by Levites or priests and given the name "Priestly" (P).

The Book of Leviticus has a unique shape and fits into a larger unit of the Pentateuch. This larger unit extends from Exod 25 through Leviticus to Num 10. Every book of the Pentateuch has some sections written by P. The emphasis given by these writers and final editors focuses on the underlying need to be holy.

One gets the impression that Leviticus, though edited, was substantially preserved, rather than abbreviated, to form a synthesis of worship regulations. This might explain why the Bible reader often bypasses Leviticus with the expression "Oh, it's just a bunch of laws and regulations." This is a valid first impression, but the editors used this material to fill a need for guidance and completeness. The final editors intentionally gave a wilderness setting to Exodus, Leviticus, and Numbers. What could be more needed in the wilderness than a book on law (direction) and order?

Just as we recognize schools of writers, so we find today schools of scholars presenting various answers to dating, text, and authorship questions. For some, Moses is the author, while others hold that the book is postexilic (late fifth century B.C.E.). Yet another group stands a near-middle ground and gives a date around the eighth century B.C.E. Further, it may be that the final shape was not decided at any one of these times. Such theories should help the reader understand the final form of a biblical book.

It is in the final editing that the whole message is conveyed. The shape of the book at the time it is born into the holy life of the Bible is the time when its divine source of life (i.e., divine inspiration) is affirmed. All the oral and written traditions, development of thought and practice, writing, editing and reediting come together in the Bible to serve the one, holy God. Leviticus witnesses this presence of God.

In considering the wilderness setting of the Book of Leviticus, somewhere a prejudice against temple worship could have influenced the shaping of the material. This prejudice could have occurred more than once. Also, the dispersion of population and distance of travel affect ritual practice. It is further possible that there were those who were convinced that Yahweh should be a pilgrim God, not having a fixed abode in this world except in the Holy of Holies of the Tabernacle, an abode that could travel with them wherever they would go, even into exile.

This commentary seeks to affirm the Book of Leviticus as it is in the Pentateuch, since this is the result of the final editing. The ancient editors presented a particular coherence for the ingathering of all the materials and traditions. Sometimes that ancient part of Leviticus, the Code of Holiness (17–26), is attributed to an author called H who is earlier than any of the Priestly writers.

117

7. Levitical themes

A. *Read the directions.* One regulation in everyday life simply says, "Read the directions." Sometimes it is touched with irony when someone says, "When everything else fails, read the directions!" Reading the directions is, no doubt, the first thing to do when beginning a new project. This advice could act as a meditation for reading the Book of Leviticus. In a way Leviticus serves as the directions for the whole Torah.

Leviticus gives a simple direction for life. The direction is as important and enduring as the beat and pulse of the heart is to the body. It is found in the lesson plan of obedience, purity, and holiness. The order is important. We begin with an obedience that brings about purification. This combination, in turn, conditions one for the life of holiness. So the direction for living a holy life is in Leviticus, centered around the simple directive of chapter 19, "Be holy, for I, the Lord, your God, am holy."

The Holy One of Israel (Isa 1:4) is God and God's name is Holy (Lev 22:32). The people, too, are to be holy. This is the regulation of life: "Sanctify yourselves, then, and be holy. . . . Be careful, therefore, to observe what I, the Lord, who make you holy, have prescribed" (20:7-8; *see also* 22:31-33).

B. *Israel's responsibility to its neighbors.* To understand the Book of Leviticus, we must respect the neighborhood in which Israel lived and moved. We proceed with caution from what we know to search out the unknown. Sometimes we expect a greater responsibility (ability-to-respond) on the part of Israel than we should. This is often done by including all the people of the then known world into the circle of Israel's response to life. This approach tends to become a smothering, rather than a drawing-out experience. We need to know more about the people of that time before we transfer the biblical narrative into real life experiences and judge historical events.

The relationship of Israel with the Canaanite and other peoples into whose land they sojourned or moved is of prime importance. The discoveries at Ras Shamra (on the Mediterranean, dating from 1400 B.C.E.) and Ebla (75 miles northeast, dating from 2300 B.C.E.) shed some light on the neighbors of the people of the Bible (*see*, for example, Exod 23). However, much material is still in the stage of critical analysis and publication. The translations themselves take many years. Ras Shamra (Ugarit) was first excavated in 1929, and some parallels to Israel's language and literature both there and at Ebla (1968-1974) have been recognized.

C. *My holy name.* A more exact translation of "my holy name" is "the name of my holiness." In Hebrew "holiness" refers to a concrete reality for which the emphasis is intended. Another example, "my good day," is really "the day of my goodness." Hebrew places the emphasis where it belongs.

Another important difference is using the superlative to preserve a certain dignified identity. For "holiest," the Hebrew says "the Holy of Holies."

A third difference not to be overlooked when reading the Bible is that certain realities in Hebrew thought are not considered separate entities as they are in our Western thought. Ideas such as body and soul, blood and life, thought and action, are almost always considered the same reality. In Hebrew thought, for instance, there is no word for body. "Flesh" is used instead. Thus, "all flesh" is really every created living thing and is equivalent to "every living soul." Because blood and life are intimately associated, it is the blood of Abel that cries out to God from the soil (Gen 4:10). Nor are understanding and good apart from life itself, "Give me understanding (discernment), that I may live" (Ps 119:144). The expression "Adam knew Eve and she conceived Cain" means that they had intercourse (since there is no separation of body and soul, the action can be called a knowledge). It is sharing one's life with another in the action that truthfully (knowingly) expresses the oneness of God reflected in the man-woman creation.

Biblical thought does not really contain what we are accustomed to think of as a code of ethics. Thus, in speaking of the Torah we should avoid the Western term law. The Torah is not a system of laws. The Torah comes from God, to teach, regulate, instruct and distinguish. "Law," in our Western thought, makes it a mere code of ethics. The Bible says, "Oh how I love your Torah, it is my meditation all the day" (see Ps 119).

D. *A common language of cult activity in the ancient Near East.* Over the centuries various reasons have been given for ritual and dietary regulations. The historian Philo and the philosopher Maimonides believed that God gave some of the commands and regulations in order to serve as a self-discipline of the appetites. Philo says that Moses forbade pork, since it is the most delicious of all meats and that self-denial would curb one's self-indulgence. He forbade flesh-eating animals and birds in order to teach one to be gentle and kind. Sometimes analogies were made between physical and spiritual. Thus, the cud-chewing animals are permitted, since they help one grow in wisdom (by chewing over and over what one has learned). And the cloven-footed animals, because they have a divided hoof, help one know how to decide between ideas.

Regarding the prohibitions concerning food, we suspect that most ancient peoples used the trial-and-error method based on taste. What tasted good and did not make one sick was clean or good. What we call taboo was probably a scare tactic to keep people from being poisoned. The "good sign" encouraged people to eat properly. What were practical considerations for one people became directives based on religious beliefs for another and were handed on as traditions to succeeding generations. Much of what we call ancient myth was simply the stirrings of humans in seeking the source of life and how to survive in life. Nomadic, agricultural and, eventually, urban living, would inevitably bring change in outlook, custom, and religious practice. Just the natural change of the seasons and the struggle for food, which we sometimes refer to as acts of nature, influenced the shaping of desire, understanding, planning, and celebration of life.

We recognize a certain kind of common language used throughout the Near East in regard to religious belief and practice. Israel used this language also, but with a particular meaning and emphasis directed to the One Holy Yahweh.

When people began to settle in the land with an agrarian lifestyle and with food assured, the need to preserve a certain stability became dominant. Priests, prophets, kings, and queens established order to survive, not only as individuals, tribes, or small family groups but as nations. Thus the Bible is a two thousand-year-old record of a people establishing their identity in relation to their God and their neighbors.

We really do not know a great deal about the early development of cult and religious practice. Exegesis, which applies critical methods of study to Scripture with the help of other sciences, especially archaeology, has helped our understanding in some measure. We know very little about the actual ritual of the sacrifice and practically nothing about the prayers or the commentary accompanying the ritual action and the dietary laws. The Book of Leviticus is a listing of ritual regulations, rather than a detailed description of actual performance. We do not have records of what was prayed, said, or sung during the discharge of the regulations.

It is in service of the Holy One then that we live our life of holiness, and our first regulation is to re-establish the order of God's creation in oneself and community. "Be holy" is the core meaning of "Seder" ("everything in proper order") in the Passover celebration that continues to this day in Jewish-Christian religious practice. The heart of the Torah still beats in the Book of Leviticus. The repeated call of Moses and the people to holiness in the pulse of the Code of Holiness is heard and answered at the Passover meal.

COMMENTARY

PART I: RITUAL OF SACRIFICES

Lev 1–7

It is helpful to begin reading the Book of Leviticus at Part IV, Code of Legal Holiness (chs. 17–26).

The first seven chapters of the book speak of ritual regulations for offering sacrifices and seem to take for granted that the reader has already been introduced to basic ideas of Israelite holiness. Chapters 1, 2, and 3 deal with burnt offerings (holocausts); chapters 4 and 5 generally speak of atonement sacrifices, while chapters 6 and 7 give special regulations for the priests.

Now that the presence of God finds a place in the midst of the people, in the tabernacle constructed by Moses (Exod 26–40), Moses is called by God to tell the people how to recognize the presence of the holy. If we read the first three chapters together, we can see that the same order runs throughout and that the emphasis is on obedience, which is the beginning of holiness.

1:1 Moses is still the mediator. Verses 1 and 2 are connecting links to the second and fourth books of Moses (Exodus and Numbers). Throughout Exodus, Yahweh tells Moses, "Speak to the Israelites." This phrase follows through Leviticus and on into Numbers. It acts as an introductory phrase to various regulations of worship and as an assertion of Israelite solidarity. A dispersed people needs to rally around their one leader and mediator Moses to celebrate their unity and solidarity.

The Hebrew title of this book, translated "and he called," is the first word of chapter 1. The "and" keeps us in contact with the call of Moses to build the Dwelling (Exod 24:16). Now that the Dwelling is complete, Moses is to act as the mediator of the worship action (Exod 40:32 and Lev 1:2). God calls Moses to speak the rules of worship for the people to obey. Moses is the one mediator, and we are reminded again and again of the Torah instruction for the unity of the people under Moses.

1:3-9 To give oneself entirely to God. At first glance it seems that we are presented with just a number of ritual regulations. Our first impulse is to set them aside, turning away from the blood of the killing, the cutting-up and burning of animals. The stench of slaughter, squealing animals, and the choking smoke of carcasses in holocaust are repulsive to our Western atmosphere of liturgical banquet. We must consider, however, that this is the record of the people of God, a people who at this time in their history carried the painful memory of slavery in their very bones. And in view of the first law of the Sinai Covenant they needed to be weaned from the other gods to the one God Yahweh.

The incident of the worship of the molten calf along with the call to holiness on the part of the mediator Moses could have evoked some of the ritual response of the first chapters of Leviticus. Rituals attending animal sacrifice were not something new for their world. Their attempt, then, would be to return everything to Yahweh. The first command for the people is to divest the community of any alien allegiance and invest in the life of the one, holy God. The natural response would be to use the ritual practices already developed until a covenant relationship would dictate otherwise.

Disciplinary action because of infidelity seems also to have played a part in some of the ritual behavior. Whatever the history or initial reasons for some of the practices that seem so strange to us, the main purpose for including this material is to teach a lesson in obedience. The lesser member of a covenant relationship needs to learn this lesson first and witness to its exercise within the community in order to preserve the tradition. The accent is on an enduring obedience, since ritual expression can change its mode of expression. Without obedience there can be no life of holiness for the people.

One meaning of holiness is "wholeness." To be free from slavery and return to the Lord is to restore wholeness to life. Every corner of life needs to be continually examined and affirmed in the light of the call to wholeness. When this vocation is set to writing in the Hebrew way of thinking, it is no wonder that the song of Israel reaches our ears in a very concrete way, in what we might call fleshy terms (Exod 3:9; Lev 23; Deut 12:7). Just as it was the blood of Abel that cried out to God from the soil, so now the heart and flesh of this people cry out for the living God (Ps 84:3). Even the inner organs of the sacrificial animal are arranged in a special way and brought back in offering to the Lord of creation (Lev 1:8, 9, 13).

1:10-17 The sacrifice that goes up to the Lord. The three sacrifices of the bull (v. 5), the sheep or goat (v. 10), and the bird (v. 14) are described as holocausts (burnt offerings). The Hebrew verb simply means "to go up"; so the primary meaning of these offerings is to affirm the Lord as giver of the gift of life. The sacrifice is burnt up to the Lord. The smoke of the burning, along with the smoke of the sacred incense "going up" and covering up the smell of the slaughter, presents a sweet-smelling oblation to the Lord (Exod 30; Lev 1-8).

1:9, 13, 17 A sweet-smelling oblation. In Gen 8:21 the Lord smelled the sweet odor of Noah's offering and promised never again to doom the earth. In the Pentateuch God is spoken of in human terms, and for God to smell the sweet-smelling odor is like saying that God is pleased with the sacrifice. This idea of the "sweet odor" is often repeated in the Pentateuch: in Exod 29 the ram, the unleavened food, and the lamb become sweet-smelling oblations (see also Lev 1-8, 23, 26 and Num 15, 18, 28, 29). Also in the flood story of Mesopotamia "the gods are smelling the savor of the sacrifices." This show of approval was probably used in Canaanite cult and taken over by the Israelites from the time when it was believed that the gods received nourishment from the smelling or inhaling of the burning food. Even the accounts of cereal and peace offerings conclude in this same way, "a sweet-smelling oblation to the Lord" (Lev 2 and 3).

When the offering was wholly burned by the priest, a certain completeness, a holiness of the return of creation to the Lord, was expressed and experienced. It meant the same going-up or giving-up of self to God as a sweet-smelling oblation (1:4). Now the people had found a way to be wholly involved.

Note that usually the offerer performed the slaughter. The sprinkling, spilling, or splashing of the blood on the altar was reserved to the priests. The people brought the sacrificial victim to the entrance of the meeting tent where the whole community was included in the sacrifice action. There they were to accommodate and make holy the customs of the Canaanite people with whom they lived.

The Law given on Mount Sinai demanded complete obedience over the use of herd, flock, and grain (1-3). All creatures are included in "when any one of you." Even the poor, who otherwise might not be able to take part, can take from the turtledoves or pigeons plentiful in the area. Thus, Exod 19:6, "You shall be to me a kingdom of priests, a holy nation," could become a reality. By faithfully obeying these decrees, they would identify with the offerings and find favor as sweet-smelling oblations to the Lord.

Throughout Exodus, Leviticus, and Numbers, the Dwelling of the Lord is in the meeting tent. It is the place from which the call comes and it is the place of the sacrifice. In the offering the people and the priests are made holy by coming in contact with the presence of the Lord. The real and concrete thinking of the Hebrew mind speaks of the Lord calling from the meeting tent and of the people coming to the entrance of the tent in obedience (Lev 1:1-4). This action prepares for contact with holiness, and the sacrifice is not complete (holy) unless this condition is fulfilled (1:3; 3:8; 4:4).

2:11 Leaven or honey not to be burned. The offerings to be burned were already dead, but the action of yeast and the fermentation of the fruit syrup (included in the term honey) suggest something is still alive and, as such, could not be burned on the altar (2:11). In the Passover tradition (23) leaven was forbidden (Exod 12:15) and the people were to eat unleavened bread (*matzah*) for seven days (some say, in memory of the first seven days of the Exodus). One should also note that to carry unleavened bread is certainly a practical and secure way to keep wheat, barley, and oats when on a journey. It is also stated that they had to leave Egypt in a hurry and had no time for the leavening action (Exod 12:33, 34). To eat unleavened bread would be a reminder of the hurried departure. This custom was kept in the feast of Unleavened Bread (Exod 12:17).

This latter feast was joined with the Passover feast, wherein a lamb was sacrificed and the blood was put on the doorposts as a sign for the Lord to pass over these houses. People on the move need to take along something to eat. Thus, both feasts came together quite naturally. Today, however, just the bread celebration remains. The Passover victim for the Jew is remembered only in the shankbone of the lamb and the order (*seder*) of the celebration. Both memorials are fused into one, called the Passover Seder (Lev 23). Within the Code of Holiness of the Book of Leviticus, these pilgrim feasts have their own particular emphasis.

We have cautioned not to read into the text more than can be seen at present. We should not, however, overlook a call to holiness that is conveyed by the sacred writer. To err in either regard would do an injustice to the living Word of God. So, in the Hebrew way of thinking, everything had to be brought to the Lord. Every slaughter, even killing for food, needed to be holy. It had to be in some way interpreted as a sacrifice, a making holy, since the blood shed had to return to the source of its life, the Creator. Life is in the blood (17:14; 19:26). For the people of God and those with whom they lived or who lived with them, every mark of living had to fall into the circle of the Holy (Exod 23).

This people struggled to respond to their call to holiness (wholeness). Such a struggle is the drive and desire of life itself to which the desire to survive is related. The duty now was to cooperate in a covenant with the Holy One present in their midst (Exod 19) and to bring about a certain completeness to their life and language (Exod 23). A covenant arrangement necessarily includes the condition of obedience for the one party and a recounting for the other of the blessings and curses that will follow upon obedience or disobedience to the covenant (Lev 26).

2:13 The salt of the covenant. Salt was a symbol of the lasting covenant, since salt kept food from spoiling. In ancient times partaking of salt together was a sign of friendship and alliance. There may also be a Hebrew wordplay on the word for salt which is related to the word for king. It is to God and God alone that the first obedience belongs, and this is the meaning of covenant obedience.

3:3, 16 "All the fat belongs to the Lord." References to food for the Lord may be for the Israelites honest attempts to gather in the practices of their neighbors and to return everything, including health, property, and the general well-being of the whole community, to the one, holy Lord.

There is a sharing of food (2:10; 3:9-11, 14-16), and thus, the custom of eating with the gods is now included (accommodated, sanctified) in the expression of the relation between the one God and the people, brought on by the covenant obedience. Even today we cement relationships by inviting one to share in a meal. Here is an outward expression in the act of obedience. In Hebrew belief and practice the presence of a neighbor affirmed the presence of God in their midst.

Burning the fat on the altar may have played a role in determining that the fatty portion belongs to the Lord. On hot fire grease will flare up and produce a cloud of smoke, perhaps reminiscent of the column of fire during the night and the column of cloud during the day (Exod 13). The Hebrews may have taken this graphic reminder as divine indication that this part of the victim belonged to the Lord.

Thus the fatty portion on the altar would cause great excitement. In the cloud (Exod 13:21; 16:10; 19:9; 24:16; 40:34; Lev 16:2, 13; Num 12:5) and in the column of fire (Exod 13:21, 22; 40:38), the Lord revealed the divine presence. God came to speak to Moses and through him to the people. (See Matt 17:5; Acts 1:9; 2 Pet 1:17; Rev 14:14—in these New Testament references and in the Old Testament references cited above, both the Hebrew and the Greek words for cloud and splendor are wrapped up in the idea of appearance-revelation.)

A concluding comment to chapters 1, 2, 3. The orderly arrangement of the material in these first three chapters may have also served as a memory aid, the key words being holocaust, cereal, and peace. The order has a certain holiness (completeness) in presenting the account of the sacrifices.

Chapters 4 and 5 exhibit an order that revolves not so much around the object of the sacrifice as around the disposition of the offerer. Sin and guilt are the subject matter, along with atonement for sin committed out of ignorance (4:1-35), out of omission (5:1-13), or by commission (5:14-26). These situations seem to cover the possible dispositions of the sinner and the offerings that are needed to atone for the situations in the covenant relationship.

Chapters 4 and 5, sin and guilt offerings.
In chapters 1, 2, and 3, sacrifices were brought out of obedience (because of the covenant), but willingly. In chapters 4 and 5 offerings of obligation are treated for those who are guilty of either unintentional (4:1-31) or intentional (5:1, 21-26) sins. In this covenant relation, since every action is in a relationship with God, every action is also related with everyone else involved in the same covenant. God is the source of life and the covenant is in a sense the return to life (Gen 2:7 and 6:17, 18). (The material is also summarized in Num 15:22-31.) The first person considered here is the priest who sins. The people are thereby also made guilty (Lev 4:3). Just as the priest offers on behalf of and along with the people, so the community is affected by other actions of the priest's life.

4:2 Inadvertent sin. All cases of ritual uncleanness which are unavoidable (for example, burying the dead) are included here. Note in Lev 4:1-12 that in the purification rite for a priest, the whole victim is disposed of outside the camp. Not even the hide is kept, to be given to the priest, as was the usual case (7:8). Now even the sanctuary is unclean, since the one who would usually receive the impurity of the people is himself unclean. There are other cases of inadvertent sin that affect the whole community (see Num 15:26, 27).

4:5-7 The blood rite. The angel of death passed over the houses on whose doorposts the blood of the Passover lamb was smeared (Exod 12:23). Here and in Lev 14:7 the blood is sprinkled before the Lord seven times. Some of the blood is put on the horns of the altar (Exod 29:12; Lev 8:15; 9:9). The sprinkling is a reminder of the blood of the covenant and its renewal (Exod 24:8). The smearing on the horns would remind one of every blood smearing: on the tent post in the field camp, the doorposts in the city, and on the altar at the foot of Mount Sinai. The basic idea was to ward off death and be attached to the source of life. In this case the intention is to be freed from the slavery of uncleanness, which divides the membership of the covenant, and to be restored as a full member of the human-divine community. The life that is in the blood is now returned to the Lord by actual contact with the altar. By this returning of life to the source of life, the in-

dividual, and thus the community, regains purity and the freedom to live again.

The whole community is affected by the impurity, even though it was committed by an individual. The reference to inadvertence is the attempt to cover every possible situation.

4:6 The blood is sprinkled seven times. Here and elsewhere (4:17; 14:7, 16, 27; 16:19; Num 19:4) the blood is sprinkled seven times. The number seven in ancient times was a sign of wholeness and completeness (holiness). Seven admits of a grouping of one flanked by two groups of three. Note the design of the menorah lampstand: a single center stem with two groups of three stems flanking the center. The menorah is the symbol of the perfect (holy) life. Many other examples could be cited in the use of seven as a sacred number. A primary example is the holy work of creation. God created the world in six days and then blessed the seventh day and made it holy (Gen 2:3). In Exod 31:15, the seventh day is a day of complete rest, sacred to the Lord.

5:1-26 Special cases. Here we sense the editors' insistence to include every possible situation of guilt and punishment, in reference not only to those asked to testify about a particular case but even to those who know anything at all about another's sin (impurity), but refuse to testify. These latter also have a community responsibility to speak up. Note that the Hebrew word for guilt contains not only the conscious aspect of guilt from acting contrary to law (Torah) or the omission of a particular regulation but even self-accusation and the acceptance of the penalty.

6:1–7:38 Answers to questions. Chapters 6 and 7 provide regulations that seemed to have developed from questions that came up while carrying out the basic ritual described in the first five chapters. For example, Where should this be done? What is the priest to wear? How should ashes be disposed of? What if the animal were wild and/or killed by a wild animal? As these questions were answered, they formed other regulations which eventually found their way into the Book of Leviticus. Additional regulations do not seem in any way to disturb the simple order of the first chapters. Note, however, the order that is preserved here. Chapter 6 deals with the material of chapters 1, 2, and 3 while chapter 7 gives some additions for chapters 4 and 5.

But we must stress that everyone and everything must be included in the covenant. Nothing can be omitted in the gathering-in of even the slightest ritual regulations; every possible life-situation must be ordered as construction material for purity and the eventual life of holiness.

In chapter 7 we first meet the punishment of being "cut off from the people" (7:20, 21, 25, 27; 17:4, 9, 10, 14; 18:29; 19:8; 20:3, 5, 17, 18 and on into the Book of Numbers). Lev 17:10 and 20:6 make it clear that God, rather than the priest or people, will measure out this punishment. Some commentators interpret this penalty to be a premature death. It seems that this penalty is simply a statement of fact of what happens when one party violates the covenant. The Hebrew phrase for making a covenant is "to cut a covenant." So, in the violation of a covenant, one cuts oneself off from the other. Besides the Hebrew wordplay, there is a good scare tactic in stating a fact. In eating the blood (17:10) and the wanton ways of the mediums (some may have been involved in neighboring blood rites, *see* 20:6), it would follow that this punishment would come from God, since the life is in the blood and God is the source of life. God would then be the immediate source of the punishment for the direct violation of life.

To avoid being cut off, in whatever way it could happen, is of special concern, for being excommunicated would not reflect the presence of the Holy One in the midst of the people. Later, in chapter 20, we see the necessity of preserving the unity of the family and a proper order to the whole of one's life in order to preserve the community as a unit. In the community, the oneness of God is reflected. Therefore, one must avoid ever being cut off. In fact, everything concerning one's own life (and thus the community's life) must in some way move in relation to the Holy One. Belief is practice.

The order of belief and practice is obedience (chs. 1–27), then purification through ritual (chs. 11–27) and finally, sanctification (chs. 17–27). It seems as simple as the example of one who takes a prescription, finds healing, and then enjoys good health. The secret is in the "order" of making holy. And one experience does not end where the other begins. Obedience is at work in purity, both obedience and purity are at work in sanctifica-

tion, and all three are fully alive in the life of holiness. However, if we concentrate on just one or try to escape from one into another, we find our life to be only an endless request of obedience. This could explain why the Book of Leviticus is often neglected or even avoided (*see also* Introduction, no. 5, p. 116).

The overall arrangement in the book is very simple, but it is possible for the reader to become entangled in the many regulations and traditions. We need only witness the volumes upon volumes of legal transactions in our own court system with their varying decisions and changing regulations. Add to this the ease that oral traditions have of growing and changing of themselves. Then, even a long period of time may elapse before the oral traditions are written down. Finally we need to consider the time lapse of gathering the materials and the countless things that can happen between the gathering and the final editing. In the Book of Leviticus, the final editing seems to point to the very simple progression for living the life of holiness—obedience, purity, holiness.

PART II: CEREMONY OF ORDINATION

Lev 8–10

Chapters 8, 9, and 10 are a fitting place to introduce the dedication of the tabernacle and the ordination of the priest into the arrangement of the material for the Book of Leviticus. P, the Priestly writing, will continue later with the regulations for purity (chs. 11–16) and regulations for holiness (chs. 17–27). Even though the ordination ceremony and the dedication of the tabernacle have already been explained in Exod 29, they are introduced again to keep the proper order of the holiness theme.

At the same time, we can almost hear the rhythmic beat and repetition of the life flow of the people: the arrival at and covenant on Sinai (Exod 19–24); the revelation of God (Exod 19); the tabernacle construction and ceremony (Exod 25–28); the consecration of priests and altar (Exod 29); the sabbath law (Exod 31); the sin (Exod 32); Moses the mediator (Exod 33); the renewal of the covenant (Exod 34) and the giving of the sabbath law, with regulations for the construction of the tabernacle (Exod 35–40); the ceremony (Lev

1-7); the ordination of priests (Lev 8-10); the cleansing of the sanctuary, priests, and people (Lev 11-16); a new covenant life (Lev 17-27); and the revelation of God. This rhythmic beat is not just a meaningless repetition. Each time the statement of life is given in the heartbeat of the people.

Signs of life, maturing, and new insights are evident. The placing of chapters 1-7 where they are points out the necessity of obedience to the ritual of sacrifice. This ritual expresses both the desire for holiness and the conditioning element for purification. All this is antecedent to the life and practice of holiness (chs. 17-26).

8:1-36 The ordination ceremony. Moses is the mediator even of the priesthood (vv. 1-4). A more detailed description of the vestments and ceremonies has already been given in Exod 28-29. In keeping with the theme of Leviticus, the *order* to be followed in the ordination ceremony (vv. 5-33) is affirmed. Stress is put upon atonement for the altar and for the ones being ordained (vv. 15, 34), identifying them with the victim of sacrifice (vv. 22-31), rather than stressing their appointment by God through Moses (v. 35).

9:1-7 The octave (eighth day) sacrifice. The sacrifice completes the consecration of the priest. It consists of a combination of a calf-sin offering, a ram-holocaust (on the part of a high priest), and a he-goat sin offering. A calf and lamb for a holocaust, and an ox and ram for a peace offering, along with a cereal offering mixed with oil, are also offered on the eighth day. What a tremendous celebration that includes virtually all the sacrifices at which the priest later assists. The celebration is magnificent, for on that day, the "glory of the Lord was revealed to all the people" (v. 23; *see also* vv. 4, 6).

The writer or writers seem to convey two essential marks of the priesthood. First, as for the intercessory duty of the priest, every sacrifice needed to be brought forth to stand before the Lord. The priests were to intercede regarding decisions already made and ones for which understanding was needed. This is what making holy was all about—to be present to the presence of the Lord (9:5). The priest is to "keep in touch" with the Lord. The community had to present itself at the entrance of the tent and then come to the altar in the person of the priest (v. 7). The divine power

could then be at work in the midst of the people, through the priest in touch with the presence of God. The second essential which the writers seem to be intent on was Moses as the mediator. He was the prophet to Pharaoh. He acted as the king in leading the people out of Egypt. He is now the high priest in the sacrifice and the ordination of those who will assist in sacrifice.

10:1-5 Death of Nadab and Abihu. Some have suggested that Aaron's sons Nadab and Abihu had filled their containers with fire that was not holy, that is, taken from a place other than the altar. Others say that their incense was not the clean mixture it should have been. Thus, they were punished with death by fire, a holy fire from the altar. Lightning could have struck them dead. Since they were at the altar at the time, the people would certainly interpret any happening as coming from the Lord.

10:9-10 Ability to distinguish. Whatever happened, the main point is brought out in verses 9 and 10, where Moses says that no wine or strong drink is to be taken before priestly duty at the meeting tent. "You must be able to distinguish between the sacred and profane." So, in the seven-day celebration, it could be that Aaron and his sons might have imbibed too much wine. Even though Nadab and Abihu could have been struck by lightning, it is possible that they put the wrong mixture on the fire, resulting in a flare-up and consequent asphyxiation (since verse 5 says they were buried in their tunics).

In view of other references in Exod 24 and Num 3, and aside from the Moses injunction to avoid on-the-job drinking of wine or other strong drink (10:9), we would do well to look further. The moment is very sacred: "Through those who approach me I will manifest my sacredness; in the sight of all the people, I will reveal my glory" (10:3). Abihu ("He is my father") and Nadab ("Na is generous") might also represent an earlier priesthood now replaced by the Aaronic and Levitical priesthood. The incident, then, is used here to introduce, in a literary but nonetheless real way, the new order (or at least the demise of the old). It is now through Aaron and his sons that both the new and the old are represented at the ordination ceremony (10:3). Other sacrifices of fire are forbidden. Recall in chapter 9, after the seven-day ordination ceremony, that on the eighth day the people saw the glory of the Lord coming forth in the form of fire from the Lord's presence. If lightning occurred, it would have given occasion for an explanation.

10:11 The priests are to teach the Torah. There is an interesting and added responsibility for the priest in regard to preparation for and maturing in holiness. He is to be a teacher of the Torah, "all the laws that the Lord has given through Moses" (v. 11—once again, an insistence on Moses as the mediator). The Hebrew word means both "to teach," and "to direct." The priest is to learn the proper direction (order) and then teach others. In English we have the fuller meaning in basically the same word, which now has the meaning of "disciple" and "discipline."

PART III:
LAWS REGARDING LEGAL PURITY

Lev 11–16

The insertion here of the chapters on the priesthood is natural. Otherwise, obedience might be practiced for obedience's sake. Obedience has now become a response to the covenant relation through the mediation of the priesthood and continues to be alive in the purification-preparation (chs. 11–16) for holiness (chs. 17–27).

Now legal purity (chs. 11–15) will be explained and emphasized as a condition, along with obedience, for legal holiness that comes later (chs. 17–27). (Chapter 16 is a bridge-chapter for chapters 11–15 and 17–27.)

Recalling what has been said about Hebrew thought patterns, we can respect these regulations as alive, not simply as directions for life. They all point to and are part of the life of holiness or completeness—to be fully alive is to respect the power of the Creator of life. It seems that the final editors laid a very simple pathway to holiness. They realized that now was the time, in the whole body of the Torah, to mention this Levitical regulation. Without it, the Torah would be without a heart and its beat. The beat should be an evident sign of the presence of the Holy and the expression of the fullness of life, the Code of Holiness in 17–26 (chapter 27 is another bridge-chapter). Since the Book of Leviticus is the heart of the Torah, we refer to the Code of Holiness as the beat of that heart.

For those who are to become holy, the Lord says, "Speak to the whole Israelite community and tell them, 'Be holy, for I, the Lord, your God, am holy'" (Lev 20:7; Exod 31:13; and Lev 11:44). Obedience comes first (chs. 1–7); then the Lord manifests his glory to the people through the holy priesthood-group of the community (chs. 8–10). But before one can experience holiness, one must be clean (pure) (chs. 11–16). And since "cleanliness is next to Godliness," so purity which results from obedience to the law comes next to holiness. This is the material treated next on the way to holiness. Obedience, purity, and holiness cannot be separated any more than can body, blood, and soul. (In Hebrew thinking, these latter three are included in the one word "being.") It is important to consider this way of thinking if we are to understand the way the Levitical material conveys the meaning of holiness. Obedience is included in the understanding and experience of purity. The regulations now become more exacting. Purity conditions one for the Code of Holiness.

Since purity can come only from God, the presence of God must be in the midst of the people, above the ark (16:2). This is the place of atonement in which is contained the forgiveness and reconciliation which result in purity.

Chapters 11–16 tell how the condition of purity is established. The materials brought together in these regulations present a fit (pure) receptacle, "for-giving" of holiness. This last sentence contains the ideas of forgiveness and the condition needed for holiness. It is one thing to be forgiven, but it is another to live a life of holiness. The state of purity resulting from the forgiveness of God is the receptacle for the life of holiness; it is not the state of holiness. This is why, once a year, even to this day, atonement is made for all the sins on the feast of Yom Kippur, the Day of Atonement.

This explains the placement of the Code of Holiness (chs. 17–27) in the Book of Leviticus; there is an orderly progression to the fullness of life, the life of holiness (19:1-7). It also explains the placement of the bridge-chapter 16 with the Day of Atonement, the ongoing condition for the life of holiness. Later we will see how chapter 27 also becomes a bridge-chapter, following the presentation of the material on holiness.

Chapters 11–16 concern the clean and the unclean. Chapters 11 and 12 consider what is taken internally: clean and unclean food and the uncleanness of childbirth resulting in loss of blood (the seed was taken internally). What shows up externally on the skin or garments is the subject of chapters 13 and 14. Chapter 15 deals with what flows from within a person. The well-known chapter 16, giving the account of the Day of Atonement, is the important bridge-chapter connecting the clean (pure) and the holy.

11:1-23 Clean and unclean food: the dietary laws. Animals that may and may not be eaten are listed here: those of the land (vv. 1-8), of the sea (vv. 9-12), and of the air (vv. 13-19), and finally, those found in all three areas—insects and swarming creatures (vv. 20-23).

The dead bodies of the unclean must not be touched or else one becomes unclean (vv. 24-32). For the most part these regulations are repeated in Deut 14:3-20. Both in Leviticus and Deuteronomy the people are warned to make themselves holy and to keep themselves holy by simply avoiding certain foods (Lev 11 and Deut 14:3-21). However, a straightforward reason why certain foods cause uncleanness or defilement is not known. Simple obedience seems to be a good reason in view of Gen 2:16 wherein God initially said, "You are free to eat . . . except . . . ." Even today, there are certain foods permitted by Jewish dietary regulation, called *kosher*, which means "proper" to eat.

Sometimes assumptions are made concerning Israelite relationship with the cult practice of their neighbors. Even though some literary references have emerged, we need to be cautious and apply studied research for further evidence of real life associations. There seems to have been a common cult language used in the Near East. From this base every tribe or nation took what would best express their relationship with the presence of the Holy in the whole of creation (*see also* Introduction, 7. D).

The simple and clear thrust of this material in Leviticus seems to be that everyone and everything must be brought into the order and dominion of the one, holy God. The whole of creation had already been joined to God's

order and dominion in the creation stories of Genesis; now the worship-life of the people is directed to that God. The Tabernacle had just been erected (Exod 40), and now the time had come for the "Levitical material" to go through the Holy Place in preparation for entry into the Holy of Holies. The experience of the divine-human relationship could be lived out even in the written record of this people. As St. Jerome remarked, "There is an odor of holiness about the book of Leviticus."

11:36 A spring or cistern remains pure. The purity of water was necessary, not only because drinking water was scarce but also because this water had not yet been drawn out by human hands. The water is holy because its present source is the ground (spring) or heaven (rain in the cistern).

12:1-8 Uncleanness of childbirth. The reason for this defilement is found in verse 7: "Thus, she will be clean again after her flow of blood." It is the flow of blood that defiles. (The life is in the blood and because the flow is recurrent, proper control cannot be maintained. Lev 15:32-33 mentions that men and women are treated alike.) They could only come to the entrance of the tent or, in another time, they were barred from the temple mound.

Today there is still a great deal of mystery and pain connected with menstruation and childbirth. We have unraveled some of the mystery, but the pain remains (Gen 3:16). At that time fear and taboo also played a part in the experience. The afterbirth might tend to make one think that some kind of punishment was being put upon a person. And, of course, there were the stories and taboos of neighbors. The rate of miscarriage may also have been high. This would accentuate the need to explain the disorder and call for a regulation concerning defilement and the need for purification.

The offering is made only after the flow stops (Lev 15:13-14, 28-29), so there is no question of practicing magic—a ritual performed in order to bring about some change.

12:2, 5 The doubling of purification time for females. This may have something to do with menstrual flow. Remember, the life is in the blood and every precaution must be taken to recognize God as the source of life.

13:4 Seven-day quarantine. This is probably a practical precaution in the case of skin disorder. Any change in the skin should take place by then so that the priest can decide about the purity of the person. The waiting is made holy by choosing seven days.

13:46 Living outside the camp. In some cases this means living alone. To live outside the camp came to be expressed as "outside the walls of the city," or sometimes in the case of temple regulations, "outside the temple mound," or in the wilderness, "outside the tabernacle community." One could come only to the entrance of the tent, as seen in chapters 12 and 15.

In view of the extensive treatment of skin disease in chapters 13 and 14, it seems that at the time there may have been an epidemic of unknown skin disorders. We do know without a doubt the importance of the blood as containing the life of every living body (17:11, 14). Today, the importance of a blood analysis is well-known as an indication of a person's general health. Likewise in Leviticus the slightest discoloration or bruise would need to be analyzed so that proper care would be taken to affirm the power of God in any flow of blood.

If we cut a finger, we know how easy it is to bring it to our mouth. The Hebrew word in the prohibition is "not to eat" (Lev 7:26; 17:10). Even though the prohibition may have had reference to some practice in the rituals of other peoples, its primary meaning should be considered as respect for life in recognition of the creator of life.

14:3 The priest goes outside the camp. The unclean person is not a part of the living community, but the priest can go to that person. However, to avoid defilement of the community, the priest must go outside to make his analysis. "Leprosy" here stands for any number of skin disorders.

14:4 The rite of purification. A vessel of fresh water is perhaps drawn from a spring or cistern by dipping clean pottery into the water. Fresh water is taken because the cleansing was outside the camp and its pure community. The blood from the one slain bird drips into the fresh water and receives proper care by contact with the water. The water can then be poured onto the ground and the vessel cleansed. The cedar wood (type used in the construction of the temple roof), scarlet yarn (blood color), and hyssop make a sprinkler. The hyssop is probably tied onto the cedar

wood with the yarn. Everything is touched with the blood of the clean bird, for the life is in the blood. One of the birds stands for Israel (the afflicted person) about to reenter into the covenant relationship. The bird mediates the purification, since much of its life is spent flying between heaven and earth.

14:7 Purification through sevenfold sprinkling. Some references to sprinkling of the blood are found in Exod 12:22; 24:8; 29:21; Lev 4:6; 5:9, and reminds one of the Sinai Covenant. In fact, in Exod 24 the blood that is sprinkled on the altar and the people is called "the blood of the covenant." So now, at the renewal of the covenant, the blood is sprinkled. It is also a reminder of the Passover blood which freed the people from slavery. The slavery now is the skin disease, holding a person captive outside the camp.

In the ancient world, seven was a sacred number and considered a complete (holy) number. There were seven planets (five plus the sun and the moon) that had movement of their own among the fixed stars. Seven is one flanked by two groups of three; three was also a perfect number since it has a beginning, a middle, and an end (1-1-1). The sprinkling towards the Lord must be perfect, complete, holy; the sprinkling in atonement for the afflicted must also be complete (holy), since the skin infection is hardly ever in just one spot but in a number of different areas on the body. The purification must extend to the entire body of the leper; leaving one spot untouched would make the person unclean and further purification would be needed.

14:7 The second bird is set free. The bird is like the scapegoat, taking the leprosy away to a place of no return. Note the important ritual directive: one shall let the living bird fly away. First, the priest sprinkles the afflicted one. Then, as the purification takes place, one is handed the other bird. The purified one releases the (scape)bird. Thus the purification is completed. One can imagine the person feeling a real cleansing receiving the remaining bird from the priest and then releasing the infection along with the bird (a real carrier pigeon!) in the direction of the atoning God. Covenant life, wholeness, is restored for the individual with God and community. There is no question of magic, since the person is already healed when the rite of purification is performed (14:3). A parallel is the present-day rite of reconciliation, which deals with the leprosy of sin. The penitent approaches the rite of reconciliation, even though the sin is forgiven by an act of contrition. The priest mediates the sacramental (holy moment-um) ritual that affirms the forgiving and healing power of God present in the community and reconciles the person to the covenant-community relationship.

14:8 The one purified remains outside. One is inside the camp now, but outside the tent. This could mean outside the tabernacle or temple, since it was only on the eighth day that one was allowed to bring sacrifice into the temple.

14:9 The afflicted shaves again on the seventh day. The root ends of the hair have grown out and the ends of the defilement are cut off. The hair is cleansed and again washed. The reason may be more practical than symbolic, since by then a good decision can be made about the disorder.

14:10 The eighth-day offering. The ritual takes place in the temple. The ephah was about half a bushel, and a log was about two-thirds of a pint. The only type of offering not mentioned is the peace offering, since peace offerings were usually voluntary. The guilt offering would be required (see 5:14-26). Also, the one cleansed may have had to bring the guilt offering to make up for the absenteeism from temple ritual during the time of being cut off.

14:12-13 The wave offering. This action might better be described as a "lifting up" rather than a wave offering. Perhaps this is the lifting up of one's hands in the manner of the priest today at the offering of the bread and wine. It could refer to praying with hands lifted up. In any case the Hebrew word is related to the English "height." Verse 13 refers to the guilt offering as "most sacred," since the wholeness of every member of the covenant is affirmed.

14:14 Blood put on the tip of one's ear, thumb, and big toe. The ancients believed that access to one's life by spirits was made through these extremities—as in the case of unclean (5:2) or sacred (6:11). Blood was used to cleanse and to ward off the unclean or evil. Later we shall see the anointing over the blood with oil. This anointing would seemingly prepare for the purification and entrance of the good spirit. Today, during baptism, the tip

of the ear and the mouth are touched in preparation for receiving and speaking the word of God.

In the ordination rite of the priest, the blood of the ordination ram is splashed on the altar (Exod 29:19-25 and Lev 8–9). The priest is consecrated to the Lord. The altar splashing is not mentioned here, since it is the guilt offering of lamb's blood that is sprinkled seven times before the Lord. A change in the direction of the ritual action, or the omission of a particular rite where one might expect it to be repeated, may indicate a meaning of the present ritual. Thus, every area of life can be covered with positive regulation. However, the precision of the Levitical regulation seems to make some readers shy away from these Torah instructions. But to others this precision offers an exciting treasure hunt.

14:17 Oil over the blood of the guilt offering. Putting the oil over the blood signifies the complete return to covenant life. The oil represents God at work in the individual and community life of the people. God gives life to the blood relationship. For a priest needing such purification, this ritual acts as a mini-reconsecration rite (see also 8:10). The covenant is renewed and all are ready for the life of holiness with its enduring and maturing obedience, purification, and holy conduct.

14:21 A poor leper's sacrifice. The reduced requirement of turtledoves rather than lambs makes the purification ritual easier on the poor. The emphasis is on the recognition of the covenant, not on the requirement of the offering. However, the requirement of the guilt offering seems to have remained the same for all, since the affirmation of both God and neighbor is involved. The same requirement for everyone openly expresses this involvement, even though the guilty party acted unwillingly or inadvertently (5:14-26).

14:33-57 Cleansing the houses. Like the individual in need of cleansing and purification, so the dwelling place of the individual. Recall that even the dwelling place of the Lord was in need of purification from time to time. On the Day of Atonement there was purification of every possible defilement that could have occurred throughout the previous year (16:16-19).

14:37 "Infection on the walls . . ." This seems to be mold and rust, but in view of verse 34 and in the opinion of some rabbis, it was considered a defilement sent in punishment for one's lack of faith. Mold and rust assured that some type of life must be present. Therefore, a regulation had to ensure proper recognition of the source of life and respect for the life itself.

Some types of defilement are unavoidable or accidental, and some occur even in the normal course of events (recurrent body flows and sickness). Some can happen while performing commendable acts (Lev 16:21-28; Num 19:7, 8, 10). The rabbis call these "defilements of the body."

The rabbis thought that sin occurs when the unclean and the holy, or the clean and the profane, are brought together in a spirit of disobedience—for example, the entry into the Holy Place by one forbidden to do so or eating clean food while one is in an unclean state. Obedience is still the key in a covenant relationship. God is the only one who can say, "I am the Lord."

Obedience is the key to purification and holiness. It may seem that the Book of Leviticus speaks only of *ritual* obedience, but the Code of Holiness points to the necessity of obedience in the *whole* of life. Lev 1–7 concern obedience. Chapters 11–15 express the purification that results from obedience. Then, and only then, will one begin to live a holy life.

15:13 One is to bathe in fresh water. Cleanliness contains a twofold idea: first, to be healed of a disease or purified from uncleanness (see 14:48, 49), and second, washed (in some cases, bathing in a stream or freshwater lake, or whatever assigned regulation) to establish the purification. The process is a mini-freedom from Egypt leading into the Promised Land.

16:1-34 The Day of Atonement. This chapter has a unique place in Leviticus because it acts as a bridge connecting the rite of purification and the life of holiness (chs. 17–26). It is the Lord who initiates the atonement. The Lord does this by demanding the purification of the Holy of Holies, which has been defiled by the deaths of Nadab and Abihu.

Then the rite of sanctuary purification is joined with the confession and removal of the sins of both priests and people (16:33). This latter purification takes place in what is called the scapegoat ritual. This joint celebration,

along with the mortification of fasting (vv. 29-31), begins the life of holiness. On the Day of Atonement, the sanctuary and the nation celebrate the atonement feast.

16:1 Purification after the death of Nadab and Abihu. This is the place to refer again to chapter 10, since it sets the stage for sanctuary purification. Here is a known defilement of the sanctuary. Their corpses made the Holy of Holies unclean and in need of purification. Perhaps they had gotten too close to the propitiatory (seat of mercy) on the ark. There were certain regulations for making a proper entry into the Holy of Holies. Note how the first span of the bridge to holiness is constructed from some leftover material of chapters 11–15 and reaching back into chapter 10. This first span is set in place. God and nation are ready to obey the order of purification.

16:2-5 The propitiatory on the ark. This is the mercy seat of the Lord. The place of at-one-ment must be at the mercy seat of the Lord. It is the cover over the ark containing the Ten Commandments. The cleansing of the sanctuary with its consequent purification is now able to take place here. In Hebrew the very word for *cover* is related to the word for *atonement.* It means that the guilt is covered over or that atonement is payment for being reinstated.

16:3-21 The rite of purification. The gold and white vestments are interchanged, signifying the presence of God and the people at work together. Mutually they take part in the atonement action that removes all the defilement of the past year, even that which may have happened inadvertently. Together in the life of holiness a new year is begun for God and people (chs. 17–27).

So, this atonement chapter acts as the bridge where the two members of the covenant (God and the people) come together to celebrate the at-one-ness to be experienced in the Code of Holiness.

16:20-28 The scapegoat ritual: means of atonement. There are actually two goats and a ram for a holocaust. One goat is offered as a sin offering. By the laying on of hands, the other receives the sins of the community and is sent to carry them off to a place of no return. Azazel (perhaps "power of El") seems to be a wordplay on the subduing of a foreign god (demon).

One goat represents the action of the purification of the sanctuary (v. 20). The other represents the atonement of the people in what has come to be known as a scapegoat ritual. The goat is driven into the desert, the place of no return and also the place of "just desert." This latter wordplay on desert alters the entire meaning of the word.

With the additional span of removal and punishment complete, the bridge-chapter furthers its construction towards covenant renewal.

During the ritual Aaron changes from gold to white, back to gold, and to white again. Before and after each change there are ritual bathings. God and people are represented in the vestments. Ritual directs the priest to dress up in different costumes to portray different characters. The simple white lines were also a sign of humility and honest contrition flowing between the two members of the covenant. Actions like the vestment changing (16:4, 23, 24, 32) pave the way for the atonement that is in progress.

Today Yom Kippur or the Day of Atonement is celebrated with great faith in the at-one-ment of God and people. It is a very important day for the Jew who seeks reconciliation with other members of the community and then receives atonement from God (see also Matt 5:24). One of the readings of the Jewish atonement celebration today is Isa 57:14–58:14, which speaks of a real inner, moral renewal by fasting (Lev 16:29-31). Fasting is made genuine by going out to others, especially the poor and the unfortunate, and by concentrating on a change of life for all (vv. 29, 30). In Leviticus all are now ready for the change to a life of holiness.

PART IV: CODE OF LEGAL HOLINESS

Lev 17–26

This section in Leviticus emphasizes life more than ritual, but obedience to the command of God is still at work. The covenant arrangement is still to be preserved (17:2). God is to be recognized first (v. 4). If this is not carried out, one is to be cut off from those who wish to keep this life-covenant arrangement (v. 4). It is a whole new way of life (vv. 5-7). What is presented in the Code of Holiness (17-26) is for everyone (v. 8). We need

to be in touch with regulations that have gone before, but we cannot forget the practice of obedience, and the bridge (Lev 16) must be kept intact (17:2, 4, 9). Obedience is still at work now, with emphasis on principle rather than regulation. It is this change that seems to encourage more people to read this section of Leviticus rather than chapters 1–16, which stress ritual obedience. Ritual conformity, practiced only for the sake of obedience, becomes a very heavy burden in time. However, obedience, along with purification, is required in order to be fully alive in the life of holiness. Now the obedience is to a life-style embodied in the Code of Holiness.

The difference between "sacrifice" and "sanctification" should be noted. Sacrifice is the "making holy" and sanctification can be the "living holy" of life. One's living-out of purification (chs. 11–16) through obedience (chs. 1–7) opens the way to sanctification (chs. 17–27).

We now come to the very beat of the heart in the Code of Holiness (chs. 17–27). "Be holy, for I, the Lord, your God, am holy." Even the flow of the accent in this English quotation of the central theme (19:2) has a pulsating rhythm.

These chapters offer directives for living a life of holiness. They were guidelines for the people of old as they are for the people of today.

We accept, then, the real life situation of our ancestors and rejoice in their liturgical activity, whatever the expression. We can imagine the closeness they had with life and death; their struggle with the animals being dragged to the entrance of the meeting tent or temple; the shame, exposure, inconvenience, and humiliation of being people who had to keep at a distance at a time when community care and support was so needed and who were obliged to call out, "Unclean, Unclean!" (13:45). What a variety of offertory processions to the Holy One! Then came the slaughter, with the spurting, sprinkling and smearing of blood, and the smell covered over by incense. Like a grand finale, the cloud suggested that the sounds of sin and death were then transformed into a chorus of praise of the presence of God in the midst of the people (26:11-13). One can almost hear the ram's horn (shofar) and the soothing sound of the lute that are now silent. There may be a certain "away from home" feeling in the hearts of all people today, but the holy message of Leviticus is alive and pulsating, in the expectation and excitement of the Holy One, the Messiah-Redeemer, who is to establish the everlasting dwelling place (Ps 43:3).

Here we are given laws, directives, morals, and morale that beat and pulsate to real life situations. Lev 26 will put the finishing touches on the covenant arrangement by detailing the rewards of obedience and the punishments of disobedience—specifics usually included in a covenant treaty. They were both an incentive and a scare tactic to assert the dominion of the king over the subject and to encourage the subject to follow the commands of the king.

Chapter 17. Scholars have discussed whether or not this chapter is a part of the Code of Holiness. Some think that chapter 17 acts as a bridge over all the material *preceding* the Code of Holiness, since there is mention of the offerings of Lev 1–3 as a prelude to Lev 18:5. There God is recognized as the source of the command to be fully alive.

The people were commanded to bring everything to the entrance of the meeting tent to be offered to the Lord (Lev 1:3, 2:2, 3:2, and corresponding to these commands are 17:4, 5, and 6). The priesthood (chs. 8–10) and purification (chs. 11–16) also parallel chapter 17. Because of these features, chapter 17 seems to assume a fitting role as the introduction to the Code of Holiness. The chapter could even have been an addition to the original little "Manual of Holiness." But we see more reason to accept chapter 17 as the original first chapter of the Manual of Holiness. The preceding chapters 1–16 could be expanded ideas, practices, and traditions of the original Code of Holiness.

In Lev 1–7 the emphasis was on obedience, simply because God commanded obedience. Chapter 17 gives reason why a person is to obey, and the command to obey assumes fuller import in the covenant relationship.

17:3, 8, 13, 15 The sacredness of blood. Everyone is commanded to recognize the source of life in the one, holy God. By respecting the life that is in the blood and acting out this respect through the ritual of putting the blood on the altar (17:11), the atonement (at-one-ment) of the people's lives is effected. The text says that the blood, as the seat of life,

makes the atonement. This is interesting and understandable, since the presence of the Lord is believed to reside over the seat of mercy that covers the ark in the Holy of Holies. God, the source of life, is hidden in the blood, and the sin of the people is now hidden or covered by the atoning presence of God (16:13).

The Code of Holiness will be issued in chapter 18. It is an invitation to the human-divine marriage (18:5)—to partake of the fruit of the tree of life, to eat of it, and live forever the life of holiness. The final chapter of Leviticus will hint at the everlasting character of this life.

First, we have a final comment concerning the respect and use of blood. Many regulations concerning the blood were wrapped in the fate of the lifeblood of the bleeding animal. While Western thought tends to spiritualize life and reality (in the sense of constructing an ideal world) and to speak of death as disturbing proper order, for the biblical people everything was concrete. Blood was life, and the pouring out of blood was death, and death acted as a thief stealing life.

To be able to think as did the writers of Sacred Scriptures is crucial to understanding the Bible. The biblical people thought and expressed themselves in concrete terms. Since God chose to use this medium for the Divine Word to enter into the world, we need to be aware of this way of thinking.

For the Hebrew mind the Word of God was real, spoken as real as the greeting exchanged between neighbors ("The Lord spoke to Moses . . . , and from the meeting tent gave him this message . . ."). The life of the ancient Hebrews was lived in the presence of God. The language of Scripture reflects a people who thought, lived, and moved in a real world, and their God was very much a part of the real world. Their expression of what God had to say was also real. Truth, justice, and peace were not ideas, but living things. For the Hebrew, "Kindness and truth shall meet; justice and peace shall kiss. Truth shall spring out of the earth, and justice shall look down from heaven" (Ps 85:11-12).

Also, every slaughter of an animal, even if just for food, had to be a sacrifice (a making holy) or a sanctification (a living holy), since the animal victim enabled the offerer to continue living. God, the source of life, had to be recognized in some way. Thus when people were no longer in proximity to the altar, the first regulation of putting the blood on the altar was modified (Deut 12:24). It was to be poured out on the ground like water and could then return to the Lord.

17:13 The blood of the clean animal. In the case of a clean animal killed while hunting, the blood was to be buried. Similarly, a scribe who erred in copying the Sacred Scripture did not crumple the page and start over. Rather, he carefully extracted the infected portion of the scroll (as in a surgical procedure), encased it in a little casket, and buried it (as in a funeral). As the life is in the blood (v. 14), so the Spirit of Holiness is in the Holy Word.

Even though the putting of the blood on the altar was later modified in Deuteronomy and is not possible today (the temple was destroyed by the Romans in A.D. 70), the prohibition of eating blood has remained in Jewish practice to this day. The regulation could be changed only if God, the source of life, would invite people to eat the blood. So, the command would then be, "Eat my blood," which, in Hebrew thought would be, "Become one with my life."

18:1-30 The sanctity of sex. It follows from the affirmation of the source of life that any control over that life would need to follow the order (command) of the source of life. Covenant relation concerning life demands that the lesser partner (creature) takes direction (life and order) from the greater or source-partner (creator). Holiness in the control of life (sex) is to be found in the ordering which accords with God's plan. Not only does one have life (18:5) but one can also share in the control of life (18:3). This is the reason for the constant reminder that God is the source of life, "I am the Lord." The only authentic plan of living (Code of Holiness) is the plan of the "God who is" (Yahweh). Thus, the writer begins chapter 18 with the Lord saying to Moses, "Speak to the Israelites and tell them: I, the Lord, am your God" (v. 2). One can hear this beat of the heart of the Torah in 18:2-6, 21, 30; 19:2, 4, 10, 11, 13, 15, and elsewhere. Life is found by following God's plan (v. 5).

18:18 A bridge-verse. In the language of regulation the word sex stands for both male and female, even though each has a unique sharing in the control of the one life of God.

Verse 18 is a bridge-verse. It connects a list of incest prohibitions with a list of other "out-of-order" sexual relations. Lev 18:6-17 lists the disorderly acts of incest; then verse 18 says, "While your wife is still living, you shall not marry her sister as her rival; for thus you would disgrace your first wife." The second part of the verse refers to the disorder created in the life plan of God (in the Hebrew, Yah-God is mentioned as joined to the very life of the wife). This part also acts as a bridge to all the other disorders or immoral relations that are prohibited (vv. 19–23). The disorder implied in the first part of verse 18 results because a man already united to a woman violates the covenant arrangement, marries his sister-in-law, and creates a polygamous relationship. This disorder relates to incest and affects the community in which all, including the sister, should live the same holy life. The first part of the verse connects as a bridge to prohibitions of incest; the "disgrace" connects with other community disorders.

One should notice, for the sake of completeness, that the incest of father and daughter should not even have to be mentioned, but it is included in verse 6 and is accorded one of the pulsating phrases, "I am the Lord." In verse 22 the disorder is called an abomination, which in Hebrew means trying to make holy a union that cannot be completed in the real sense of the action. This is the reason why it is usually referred to as making a sacrifice to a strange god. The ordering of the source of life and the orderly plan of God within the covenant is cut off.

When the marriage invitation in chapter 18 is accepted by both parties of the covenant, the holy life takes on the renewed dimension of oneness along with completeness. To be at one in the Lord is the goal of the divine-human covenant.

In chapter 19 we need to be careful not to read into the text more or less than the writer or editors intended.

In chapters 17–26, the Code of Holiness (H), some material has vocabulary and unity of its own and is recognized by scholars as having a very early date. It, too, centers around the call of Israel to be holy. This Code may have been the core around which the final editors gathered other Priestly material. For these reasons this section is often referred to by the letter H. Ritual regulations are absent, and the text begins to talk in terms of principle and conduct. The tone is more ethical than ritual. The reader may feel more at home in this section of Leviticus. Here we have directives for living a holy life. Echoes of Genesis and Exodus commands are heard in the regulations of the Code of Holiness. For Adam and Eve in Gen 1:28, for Noah and family after the flood in Gen 8:17 and 9:7, and for all the people in Exod 20, "Eat and multiply," is the directive, "but do not divide by defilement for I, the Lord, am your God."

19:1-37 Various rules of conduct. The two basic rules of the divine-human relationship are found here—love of God and love of neighbor. That this twofold directive is alive and breathing today is witness enough to its enduring validity. Verses 2 and 18 give the commands "Be holy, for I, the Lord, your God, am holy" and "You shall love your neighbor as yourself."

In 20:1-8 and 20:9-21, the respective penalties are given for disobeying these commands. The remaining verses of chapter 20 spell out, in no uncertain terms, what will happen to the disobedient. In other words, ethically as well as ritually, the covenant relationship is still founded on obedience. This is a basic tenet of the covenant agreement and points to a proper order. Obedience to the order of covenant relations is the basis of accepting the rules of the life of holiness. The important question is not "Who's on first?" but "Who comes first?" Often we may think that holiness is achieved by giving up some part of life or by depriving one member of the covenant. However, to submit to the superior member of the covenant is the basic meaning of a covenant treaty.

The negative directives of chapter 18 were issued because at various times the people had taken direction contrary to the plan of holiness. Often, in assessing guilt, it is not the good or evil of the action that needs to be considered, but rather the order or manner of its performance. Examples abound in chapter 18. Intercourse is not forbidden in itself. What is forbidden are the disorderly situations that are contrary to the Code of Holiness and the life-giving power of the Creator.

What seems to be given as a penalty—the "vomiting of the people out of the land"—is simply a stated result of disorderly conduct similar to what happens in the case of a social stomach disorder. In chapter 26 we find

that God, as the source of life, uses time itself to retrieve the divine order from the disorder caused by the human member of the covenant. This is an aspect of the everlasting covenant—God still gives us time to live and sustains us in life even when we choose to make fools of ourselves or even when we cut ourselves off from the covenant.

19:2 "Be holy, for I, the Lord, your God, am holy." This is the first rule of conduct in the life of holiness—to recognize God as the source of life. If we wish to live we must keep God's order. Holiness is of primary importance because God is first of all holy. In God, holiness (wholeness) and oneness are the same. We speak of the one, holy God. The secret to a full (holy) life is found in the Code of Holiness. The order is so simple that we are apt to overlook the meaning of command.

The order in God is perfect, since there is only one God. The oneness of God is a mystery, and in oneness there is no room for disorder. This monotheistic conception of life and the source of life in the world and in the history of the Israelite people is traced to the revelation to Moses in Exod 3:14: "I am who am." The divine drawing out of one leader (Moses) and one people (Israel) reflects a new monotheistic way of thinking. God is drawing out of the people the life of God present in their midst, in their very living. As the people were held in slavery, so the life of God in the people was held captive. The command to be holy completes the circle by drawing out and returning life to the source of life. "I am who am" is God's way of saying "I am the source of life."

Order is heaven's first law. The proper order comes first. The "One" comes first. God is the only One who can say "I am who am." So God comes first and the Book of Leviticus records the proper order. To be holy because God is holy is to accept God as the source of life.

In Lev 19:3 the next command in order is reverence for parents, since through them we come into covenant contact with God, the source of life. This is why reverence for parents and keeping the sabbath are joined together in the text. Filial reverence recognizes parents as the contact point with the reality of life and the Creator of the whole of life.

Both parents and sabbath are joined for another reason. God rested on the seventh day and made it holy (Gen 2:3). The sabbath is, then, a holy day for the whole family. Celebration of the prime source of life will, in proper order, include the secondary source (parents). The order cannot be reversed. There is a proper order to living the Lord's day. The regulation of the sabbath is, in its final analysis, the regulation of the tithe, which puts God first. The portion, one day in seven (the holy unity), is the tithe commanded by God (Lev 27:30).

19:4 "Do not turn aside to idols or make molten gods for yourselves." Note that the making of images is not forbidden, but to turn to molten gods or images used as objects of worship is forbidden. In fact, it is the Spirit of God who continues to move today in the creative talent of artists who try, in a particular ordering of creation, to express the image and likeness of God as the source of all life. In the Hebrew rendering of this rule of conduct (v. 4), there is a wordplay on "El," the name of the god of neighboring people (18:3). The same root word is used to express "dumb idols."

19:5-8 An acceptable peace offering. Peace is the tranquility of order. If order is kept, peace results. The peace offering should be eaten on the day it is offered or on the next day, but not on the third day for then it becomes refuse (unclean). One living the life of holiness profanes oneself by eating the three-day-old offering. The obvious reason, besides spoilage, is that order is not followed. It was directed that on the third day the remaining part was to be burned, not eaten. Recall that those peace offerings are better called welfare or well-being offerings. Thus the recognition of the source of life and the insurance of the well-being of the people are brought about by following the order. The very reason for the peace offering is to recognize the continuing presence of the divine as the source of life for the well-being of the people. To partake of unclean food profanes the sacred presence of the One who is the vital part of the community.

19:9 Sharing the harvest. Next in the life-order are those lives threatened by a lack of food. Those who have food and are able to acknowledge the source of life through the peace offering (thanksgiving for well-being) are really unable to give authentic witness to a life in holiness (completeness of the community) as long as there are those in that community who are poor. The regulation in verse 9 was established to give the poor the chance to live. This allows God as the source of all life to be at work in the whole community. Completeness and wholeness are what the life of holiness is all about.

The same rule is true in regard to the vines. The people are commanded to leave the grapes that have fallen (v. 10). This is God's way of giving them to the poor and the stranger. But they are not to leave anything for the fertility gods in payment for the crop, as was the custom of the land. "I am the source of all life; I, the Lord, am your God."

This latter exclamation is repeated several times in chapters 18 and 19. It appears that these chapters are a unit; perhaps they are the very first gathering of the materials into a manual of holiness. The exclamation "I, the Lord, am your God" is a clear reference to the first commandment of the Sinai Covenant Code and draws attention to the one God as the source of life. This recognition comes first in order (Exod 20:2-6; Lev 26:45). The repetition of the exclamation could have been used as a memory aid for the original manual. It could also mean that there were neighboring unacceptable practices (Lev 18:3; 20:23) well known to them at the time, and the frequent pauses in the text would make room for a litany-like response of short oaths of allegiance. The exclamation is the beginning of the first commandment. The community would continue, then, to publicly acclaim God, the Holy One, as the source of life.

19:16 "You shall not stand by idly when your neighbor's life is at stake." This regulation is joined to the command to avoid slander. No wonder, since the phrase used for slander means "to cut someone down by the spoken word." One can either stand in the way, stand by idly, or stand up to support the life at stake in one's neighbor. A witness to the truth can be an assertion of God as the source of life. In every circumstance we are obliged to weigh properly the life of our neighbor in the scale of justice. Therefore, if we accept the life of holiness we cannot stand by idly when falsehood is parading in the guise of truth for the destruction of life.

19:17, 18 "You shall love your neighbor as yourself." This and 19:2, "Be holy, for I, the LORD your God, am holy," are the most quoted verses of Leviticus. Later Jesus will join these two together in answering "Which commandment of the Torah is the greatest?" His answer will be "You shall love the Lord, your God with your *whole* heart, with your *whole* soul and with *all* your mind" (Matt 22:37 quoting Deut 6:5). "The second is like to it, You shall love your neighbor as yourself" (Matt 22:39 quoting Lev 19:18). If one is living the life of holiness, which is described by the use of *whole* and *all*, then, everyone is neighbor to each other in this life. However, there is a holy sequence. Love of God comes first and includes love of neighbor, but love of neighbor does not, of necessity, lead immediately to love of the Holy One.

In verse 19 certain mixtures are prohibited. In the attempt to reflect the oneness of God in the wholeness of community life, the Priestly writers list some disorderly arrangements: crossbreeding, sowing two different seeds (one atop the other), and the tension of incompatible threads. The result of crossbreeding can be monstrous; different seeds vie for the same ground and moisture; the purity of the fabric is lost and the unity of the weaving is gone.

19:20-22 Atonement for relations with a female slave. The affirmation of the one source of life and the reflection of this oneness in the community is of prime importance. Thus the seriousness of sexual disorder or disorder in the control of life (v. 20) is shown by the requirement of a ram guilt offering in reparation. The importance of recognizing and affirming the source of life is deeper than meets the eye. For example, the slave girl does not have a life of her own since she is not free. Supposedly she would win her freedom if she were put to death (the creature's relationship with God goes beyond life and death), and the justice of Yahweh would be satisfied. The question at hand is not only that justice be done but also that the holiness of life be preserved. The man in this disorderly sexual relation also has a life of his own. Thus through the guilt offering he is forgiven his sin (v. 22). She then keeps her "non-status," death is not affirmed, and the man is purified for life in holiness. The proper order of recognition of God as the source of life is not disturbed. The sanctuary is also involved (v. 21), since the text is talking about sex as the sacred control of life. The ultimate support of life-control (sex) must be a proper orientation

(order in worship) to God, the source of life.

The sex act of humans outside marriage is out of order. There is an order to the use of sex. The coming together of two people in the act of sex forms one body (Gen 2:24). It is the two that choose to act as one. This new oneness can result in the affirmation of existing life and creation of life. When God blesses man and woman in Gen 1:28 with the command "Be fertile and multiply," God is inviting them to a deeper share in the divine oneness, a share in the very power of the one source of life to create new life. It is this added dimension of oneness that must be affirmed before the couple engage in sexual union—a oneness that in turn can become a source of life here on earth. This new affirmation of God as the one source of life also affirms the true role of the couple in the covenant relationship. This affirmation is what the marriage covenant is all about.

In the case of the slave girl, it must be remembered that she is already living with a man (Lev 19:20). This could mean that the oneness of the Source of Life is already recognized and affirmed. The man who now has sexual union with her is definitely acting out of order. Sexual union among humans, then, has to do with the proper ordering or control of life. First, the oneness of God as the one source of life is affirmed, and then the oneness of the couple as a secondary source of life follows.

19:23-25 Uncircumcised fruit. Fruit trees take time to mature and first fruits cannot be given to the Lord until the fourth year. Then the first fruits can be given to the Lord for that year's harvest as a thanksgiving offering. As the rite of circumcision brought a Jewish male into life-relationship with the covenant, so the fruit had to be looked upon as uncircumcised (v. 23) until the fourth year, when it was brought into the covenant. Only in the fifth year could the fruit be eaten.

19:32 Respect for the elderly. The verse states that to stand up in the presence of the aged is a way to show respect. The length of life is a gift of the Lord; respect for the length of life is reverence for the God of life. In other words, we are not looking at the person as such. The criterion for respect is not the wealth the person has accumulated nor fame attained, but simply the length of years. The time that the life-power of the Creator has been at work in the world, in the individual, and in the community must be respected in the life of holiness.

20:1-21 Penalties for various sins. There are two groups of penalties here, corresponding to the twofold commandment of love of God and love of neighbor. In verses 1-8 violation of the holy name (the name of holiness) is treated. In verses 9-21 love of neighbor, starting with one's parents, is considered. The penalty for transgression is, of course, real or symbolic death. To be cut off and to be put to death seem to come together in the meaning and the extent of the penalty. The Code puts the recognition of God as the source of life at the head of the list. It follows that one who acts contrary to the recognition is cut off from the whole of life; this is the meaning of death. To be holy means to be fully alive.

20:2 Capital punishment. Israel allowed capital punishment by stoning. It was carried out by the whole community. One who refused to recognize God as the source of life was cut off from the community and put to death by stoning. There is a reference here to Molech. The word is akin to the Hebrew word for king and may be a graphic way of explaining that God comes first. The sanctuary becomes defiled when the palace becomes the place of worship. If the king is put first, then the king becomes one's source of life. One is cut off from the life of the Holy One and is dead to life in holiness. If the king is called upon, Yahweh is not acknowledged as the source of life. God alone can say, "I am who am" (meaning of Yahweh). No wonder the Jews were disturbed when Jesus said, "I solemnly declare it: before Abraham came to be, I AM," and they picked up rocks to stone him (John 8:58, 59). The holy name is blasphemed in Lev 24:16, and the consequent punishment is stoning by the community. No longer is that person allowed to be a member of the community of people who are living the life of holiness.

20:9 Cursing one's parents. These penalties concern the regulations of chapters 17, 18, and 19. The sacredness of the parental relation heads the list. The other penalties concern the disorder of control of life (sexuality) and of relationships of family and neighbor. Cursing is making light of something. To not only refuse proper crediting but even to discredit the proper order is what convicts a per-

son. One who curses his or her parents, forfeits life (v. 9). This, in turn, leaves little room for recognition of God as the direct source of life. Such a state results in death. One cannot cut off the source of life without experiencing death.

20:22-27 Land ownership. Identity is fixed when people have a place to call their own. God has set the land apart for the people, who are to set themselves apart from the customs of the neighbor (vv. 24, 26). They must recognize this order and actually bring it about by setting themselves apart, the clean from the unclean (20:25). Thus they assert the commanding position of Yahweh.

20:24 A land flowing with milk and honey. Exod 3:8 is referred to here. The secondary source of the milk is the cow, sheep, goat, or camel, but God is the primary source of the milk and of honey from bees (see Sir 39:26). Because of the scarcity of clean water, milk was their most important drink. The land of Canaan is *fat* or wealthy (one of the meanings of the Hebrew word for milk). It is truly a "land flowing with milk and honey." Bees were plentiful, and deposited honey in the crevices of rocks or in hollow trees, even in the wilderness. In verse 24 God is affirmed as the source of these life-sustaining foods.

In verses 1-21 the penalties for not recognizing relation with God and neighbor are listed. In verses 22-27 the proper order of obedience is identified. Through obedience both God and people maintain an identity which is founded on covenant faith, not on fortune-telling (20:27).

Chs. 21–22 Mediators, sacrificial banquets, and sacrificial victims. The identities of God and people have been established. For God the identity is in the ordering. For the people their identity is in the obedient response. It is appropriate to consider now the mediators of these covenant relations: Moses who directs the priesthood (21:1-24) and the victim of the sacrifice (22:17-33). The irregularities concerning priest and victim find a certain balanced presentation in the text. Many regulations required for the state of purification are restated in relation to the priest and the victim. These considerations act as an introduction for what is to come in chapter 23. Moses is still the mediator. His role might best be described as the lawgiver-high priest. He is the one to direct and guide Aaron's sons, the priests (21:1).

The irregularities of chapters 21:2–22:33, especially those of 21:16ff., may seem strange to us, but we must remember that today we know a great deal more about many of these maladies than did the biblical people. At that time, some irregularities were simply considered punishment from God. Judgments of impurity and profanation were often based on the person's inability to perform a particular action, as in the case of blind, crippled, and disfigured individuals.

Chapter 23 has a beauty all its own. It describes the life of holiness in terms of the feasts of Israel. The list begins with the sabbath rest (23:3). By keeping a day of complete rest God is recognized as the source of the life of holiness (Gen 2:3). The list continues with mention of Passover, Pentecost, New Year's day, the Day of Atonement, and finally the third pilgrim feast, the feast of Booths. The order in which these are presented is significant. The purpose of Leviticus is not to give a detailed instruction for festival observance but to draw attention to the need for these celebrations in order to give recognition to God's plan of life. "I am the Lord, your God," must be repeated every six days. The holy number was seven; thus the seventh day became the Lord's day. The seventh day represents the tithe of time that belongs to God.

23:1-44 Holy days. Throughout the Pentateuch there are calendars of holy days (Exod 23:14-18; 34:18-25; Lev 23; Deut 16:1-16). In Leviticus the three pilgrim feasts are mentioned: Passover-Unleavened Bread (23:4-14); the feast of Weeks or Pentecost (23:15-22); and the feast of Booths (23:33-44). New Year's day (vv. 23-25) and the Day of Atonement (vv. 26-32) are added. The sabbath heads the list (v. 3). God made the sabbath holy (Gen 2:3; see Exod 20:8-11 and Heb 4:4, 9). The listing is merely an announcement on the part of Moses (Lev 23:44). As long as one is a covenant member, every day is holy. Certain days, however, are designated by God, through Moses, to be celebrated with a holy assembly (23:1-3).

In ancient stories of other peoples, the sacred assembly took place among the gods. With Israel the Holy One initiates the gathering of the people (Lev 23:4; Exod 12:16). By

gathering the major feasts into one place (in the Levitical material of the Pentateuch), the Priestly writers affirm the mediatorship of Moses in the celebrations of the people.

The order in which the list appears gives the reader a mosaic of the life of holiness in the world—the Holy One living in the midst of the people. The feast of Passover-Unleavened Bread celebrates freedom from slavery. Fifty days later, the end of the harvest and the offering of the first fruits begins with the celebration of Weeks (Pentecost). Then, there is one final look back at the wilderness with the feast of Booths, which commemorates the booth made from branches and the tent dwelling of the wanderings in the wilderness. It was also called the feast of Tabernacles, and since it was celebrated at the end of harvest time it received the name of Ingathering. Throughout this description of life, the beginning of each year is announced at a celebration, and every year the whole of life rejoices in the Day of Atonement.

The feast of Booths is mentioned at the end of the list. Its many names and its accent on dwelling show a development in its significance. No wonder that later Peter will want permission to erect three booths, one for Moses the lawgiver, one for Elijah the prophet, and one for Jesus the life-giver.

Chapters 23–25 should probably be read as a unit, since they speak of holy days, holy places and holy land. The days are holy (23:1-44) and the sanctuary lamp (24:1-4) and showbread (24:5-9) point to the holy meeting place. The sabbatical year (25:1-7) and the jubilee year (25:8-22) with redemption of property (25:23-55) deal with the holy land (25:1-22), property rights (25:23-38), and freedom (25:39-55). Chapter 23 describes the life of holiness with emphasis on the presence of the Holy One living in the midst of the people, whereas the sabbatical and jubilee celebrations of chapter 25, with their note of perfection in the holy number seven, seem to be looking beyond this life to the life of perfect holiness in God (the eternal Holy of Holies). Every seven years the whole land has a complete rest as a sabbath for the Lord (25:2-4). Then, in the jubilee life of perfection (seven times seven weeks of years), all shall return to their property (25:10, 13). But the Lord does not have a role in redemption of the land as the sanctuary had a role in purification (ch. 16) because God is the source of life and the owner of the land (25:23). Recall that God actually dwelt only in the cloud above the propitiatory seat of mercy in 16:2.

24:1-4 The sanctuary lamp. This repeats the regulations in Exod 27:20, 21. Exodus closes with Moses putting the lampstand in the meeting tent and arranging the bread on the table before the Lord (40:22-40). So now, at the close of Leviticus, the lamp and the table of display are arranged in the proper Levitical order. Here, however, the emphasis is not on the pure oil as in Exod 27, but on the presence of the Holy. (This is much like the symbolism of the tabernacle light in churches today.) When there is a light in the window, there is somebody home. So, the Holy One and the people who are to be holy are at home in the one covenant. The showbread, or the bread of display, represents the people (Lev 24:5-9), with six loaves in each of two piles on a small table. The piles are a reminder of the twelve tribes, like the two onyx memorial stones with the engraved tribal names as part of the priest's vestments (Exod 28:9-12). Thus, the Holy One and the people are present to each other by real signs of life. The oil is replenished (Lev 24:2) and the bread is kept fresh (24:8). For a life of holiness it is necessary to have an ongoing experience of the presence of each other—of the Holy One and the people who are to be holy.

24:10-23 Punishment for blasphemy and murder. What is holy can become profaned (the light is snuffed out when it should be burning) or the people can become defiled (the bread becomes unclean, stale). However, means will be given to affirm both the holy and the people or to redeem them from profanity or defilement (see ch. 25). In this life of holiness there is no atonement/redemption that can be made for the blasphemer (24:16) or for the murderer (Num 35:31). The reasoning is thus: the Hebrew word for blasphemy suggests a piercing, in some way, of the name of the Holy One. Piercing could bring about the flow of the lifeblood of the victim as in the case of murder. The life of God is in the Holy Name and the life of the human is in the blood, so by blasphemy and by murder, both God and human are pierced. The blasphemer and the murderer must be put to death.

There is also a wordplay in the text on the name Shelomith (24:10), a name similar to that of a neighboring goddess who was considered complete, holy. Such a substitution for the Holy One of Israel would be a blasphemy. The punishment for this violation would be stoning and consequent cutting off such an offender from the covenant of the life of holiness.

It is important to note that the text maintains the covenant arrangement (24:23). Moses is asked what to do about the blasphemer, but God is the Holy One who gives the command for the blasphemer to be cut off from the life of holiness (v. 14). Those who heard the blasphemy must join in, since they received the profanation through their ears. They are joined together in the life of the Holy One. By the laying on of their hands, they return the blasphemy to the offender and by stoning send it to death, a place of no return (24:14).

In chapter 25 the focus is on atonement, not in the sense of forgiveness but in the sense of at-one-ment, union resulting from full acceptance of the covenant relationship. The orderly arrangement of the Priestly material continues in these final chapters.

We can now see the atonement (ch. 16) effected in and reflected by the life of holiness (chs. 17–26). The celebration of the holy days (ch. 23) brings atonement for a more complete living (ch. 25) with the rewards and punishments attached to obedience or disobedience to the Code of Holiness (ch. 26). The two members of the covenant are reidentified and reaffirmed (ch. 24). Chapter 27 becomes another bridge-chapter but, unlike chapter 16, this bridge is only partially constructed.

25:1-22 Sabbatical and jubilee years. During the seventh year the land shall have a complete rest (25:4), a sabbath for the Lord. Even the land is holy and, as the Lord set aside the seventh day, so the land is affirmed as holy in the seventh year. In the seventh month of the forty-ninth year and continuing into the fiftieth year, the celebration is called jubilee, "the year of the ram's horn." We think of jubilation. On this Atonement Day the horn is blown to call the sacred assembly. The word for horn also has the meaning of removing the veil to see the beauty of the woman or to see the clear blue sky when the cloud is gone. Chapter 25:10 says, "You shall make sacred this fiftieth year, by proclaiming liberty in the land for all its inhabitants. It shall be a jubilee for you."

The people are free and return to their families (25:10). There is no more sowing or reaping (v. 11). If they obey, their dwelling is secure (not movable as in the wilderness, v. 18). The land will yield its fruit. They will have food in abundance so that they may live without worry (v. 19). There will be crops for three years, and even in the ninth year they will eat from the old planting because the eternal covenant in the life of holiness has begun.

In 24:17-21 we saw the legal aspect of the Code of Holiness in what is usually referred to as the law of retaliation or recompense—an eye for an eye, a tooth for a tooth, a life for a life, etc. Each of three Codes in the Torah mentions this human balance of justice (Exod 21:24; Lev 24:17-21, and Deut 19:21). As we continue in the Code, we begin to experience the justice of God at one with an unconditional love. A certain holiness begins to enter into real-life situations, given unconditionally by God. A certain stability and wholeness of every life relationship comes to those who, in obedience, recognize the one, holy God as the source of life and live according to the Code.

We are not dealing here with just memories or vain hopes. These are moral directives that give beat and pulse to real living. They are life-support dynamics of the celebration of the wholeness (holiness) of life. They are the vertebrae of the divine-human covenant. Slavery and exile are still the human condition of unfaithful covenant partners, but the enduring and sustaining presence of the Holy One is at work in the midst of the people (Lev 26:44, 45).

This is as far as the Book of Leviticus takes us in the Torah of the Holy One.

Some commentators refer to these later sections as a portrayal of an ideal life. This is true but the life of holiness was never meant to remain just an ideal. When the Torah was given, with Leviticus as its heart, the world received the plan of living a holy life.

The final form of the holiness begins to take shape. The remaining pieces will fall readily into place. This chapter in the five-volume work of the Law is about to complete its message.

Before we consider the partially constructed bridge (ch. 27), we need to look at a final note about the redemption of property in chapter 25 and the material in chapter 26, which was the standard way of closing a covenant treaty.

25:23-55 Redemption of property. The perfect (holy) calendar is presented in the first part of chapter 25, followed by the sacred activity of the holy jubilation year (vv. 23-55). The intended results of the Code were to be: Yahweh recognized as king (vv. 23, 55); wealth redistributed every jubilee (vv. 6, 7); families (v. 10), the land (vv. 2-4), and everyone enjoying liberty (vv. 10, 54); the land bearing fruit (v. 19) of itself (v. 11); all debts canceled (vv. 36, 37); the poor lifted up (vv. 25, 35, 39, 47, 48)—everyone and everything whole in the life of holiness. Note that the land remains the possession of the Holy One. "The land shall not be sold in perpetuity; for the land is mine, and you are but aliens who have become my tenants." (Later you may become my children but, for now you are my renters.) "Therefore, in every part of the country you occupy, you must permit the land to be redeemed" (vv. 23, 24). That is, if they live in the life of holiness, they must acknowledge Yahweh as the original owner, the source of life.

Yahweh had already ordered and taken part in the cleansing and purification of the sanctuary, the meeting tent and the altar, as well as the priests and all the people of the community (16:20, 33). Now a further order is given. Unlike the negative order in Gen 2:17 (see also Gen 3:22), "From that tree you shall not eat," there is the positive command to share in the life of holiness: "Be holy."

While we cannot with certainty sort out the various traditions woven together in Leviticus, we can see changing conditions in the story and can come to some conclusions as to its message at the time of the final editing. For example, walled cities and open-air villages are provided for here, and throughout Leviticus the traveling tabernacle is given emphasis. Such references suggest different chronological times in Israel's development. Yet, behind these observations and the ordered structure of the regulations and directives we see the truth of Lev 25:23: God is the owner of land and property; the people are but aliens who have become tenants.

25:25 Redemption of property. After recognizing that Yahweh owns the land and the property, the poor come first and this for the good of the family (vv. 23-28). As we read verses 23-55, it is as though the owner is preparing to buy back the dwelling in the midst of the people in the wilderness. Chapter 27 will expand this idea of the plan of redemption. Chapter 26 seems to say, "Take your choice, but there is only one correct choice if you want to live the life of holiness. If you choose obedience or disobedience, here are the respective consequences!"

26:3-13 "Live in accord with my precepts." If one gives obedience to these precepts of the life of holiness and the commandments (actually the Code of Holiness in chapter 19 includes the commandments of the Sinai Code in Exod 20), then all kinds of life-giving experiences will happen (vv. 3-13). "If you obey, I will set my Dwelling among you, and will not disdain you" (vv. 11-13).

26:14-46 Punishment for disobedience. If the community members are unfaithful, terrible things will happen (vv. 16, 17). If they still disobey, terrible things will happen to the world in which they live (vv. 19, 20). If they become defiant, things will get worse by seven times (each time in vv. 18, 21, 24, and 28 punishment is increased seven times over), until they will be forced to eat their own children (v. 29). This dire situation could happen in order to survive the siege of walled cities. In their defiant struggle to survive, they themselves would revoke the results (children) of their covenant with the Source of Life. A complete breakdown in the relations of God and people with the whole of life being overturned in death and exile (vv. 30-33) would occur.

26:34 The land shall retrieve its lost sabbaths. This is the built-in payment plan put there by God. While the people are in exile, the land rests. Everything comes to a standstill. The sabbaths must be kept and the precepts followed by the people, even though unwillingly. Sabbath payments are made to God and the people can do nothing about it. Verse 36 returns to the threat of verse 17. Finally, when "their uncircumcised hearts are humbled and they make amends" (v. 41), God will start over with the people. God is holy and remembers the covenant made with their ancestors (v. 42). Exile actually gives the land and the people time to rest (v. 43). The land became defiled when the people defiled themselves by their disobedience. Now both lie desolate, in reprieve for the land and in punishment for the people (v. 43), until time has elapsed equal to the sabbaths defiled. The land is holy because it also belongs to the Lord (25:23). Whenever the land is defiled (polluted), it lies desolate.

God's love is unconditional, since the Holy One does not allow the covenant to be voided, even though God is the only faithful one remaining (vv. 44, 45). This unconditional love is under, behind, and all around the Torah Law. The Book of Leviticus has now become the heart inserted into the Torah and, with its lively beat of the Code of Holiness, the People of God find themselves invited again to share in the life of the Holy One.

Throughout the reading of Leviticus, this simple outline has been stressed: obedience (chs. 1–27), purification (chs. 8–27) and holiness-sanctification (chs. 17–27). Obedience endures as a requirement. Obedience of the human partner of the covenant is requested by and made possible by God. The purification of the relationship reaches its anticlimax in the atonement chapter (Lev 16). Here the covenant partners meet and prepare for the climax of the covenant relationship in the life of holiness (Lev 27). Chapter 27 describes only the beginning of the perfect life, and for this reason is "an open-ended bridge-chapter." The perfect life of holiness is begun in the acceptance and practice of the Code of Holiness.

PART V:
REDEMPTION OF VOTIVE OFFERINGS

Lev 27

It is understandable why many commentators treat this final chapter as an appendix to Leviticus. It gives the impression of an afterthought, added later because of its importance. The meaning of Lev 27 is so simple that it can be easily overlooked: It affirms God and people as faithful covenant partners. Its open-ended character suggests that the divine-human covenant is still in the stage of promise.

Some might be tempted to read into the text the fact that the Messiah-Redeemer had not as yet come as reason for the open-ended treatment. This would be an assumption beyond what is contained in Leviticus. The concentration is still upon God as creator of life and Moses as lawgiver-mediator presenting the rules of conduct of the Sinai Covenant. Leviticus has reaffirmed the Sinai Covenant in adding the new dimension of holiness in the sense of completeness. The people are now to become fully alive (holy).

The secret in understanding chapter 27 lies in the meaning of the vow and the tithe. It begins by vowing all of creation to God: persons (vv. 2-8); livestock (vv. 9-13); dwelling (vv. 14, 15); hereditary land (vv. 16-24). The chapter ends by returning everything to God in the tithe (vv. 26-34).

In the preceding chapter the divine partner of the covenant spelled out the results, good and bad, of the obedience or disobedience of the junior member. Here the Holy One respects the free will of the human partner and points the way of respect for the divine partner.

The practice of making a vow to a deity in order to receive a favor or cure is very ancient. However, we are dealing with a more basic idea: the holiness of life. The vow and its redemption, along with the practice of tithing, make possible the holy life. As a free-will offering, the vow affirms human life. The tithe affirms divine life.

In chapter 27 God affirms human free will and gives conditions whereby the votive offering can be redeemed. Everyone and everything in creation is considered. The meaning of vow goes to the very root of life. In a way every vow to God is a promise to live a holy life. God wills the creature to be fully alive, that is, holy. In Gen 1:26, 27 the creature is created in the image and likeness of God, able to assert its own freedom. The buying back of life in all of creation must be done according to God's terms. The priest sets the price, but the terms are according to the rules of the jubilee, God's life-giving celebration (vv. 17, 18, 21, 23, 24). God, then, remains the source of life and holiness.

Certain offerings cannot be redeemed: the first-born and, at the other end of life, those doomed to die (vv. 26-29). They affirm God as the ultimate source of life. There is a refinement here of the dedication of Exod 13. Every first-born that opens the womb among the Israelites, both of humans and beasts, belongs to the Lord. It cannot be the object of a vow (dependent on human free will). It still acts

as a reminder of the death of the first-born of the Egyptians, who would not recognize Yahweh as the source of life (Exod 13:14-16). Death is still the human condition (Gen 3:19), but now the emphasis is on dedication and redemption.

27:28-29 "All human beings that are doomed." The Hebrew word for "doomed" in verse 28 also has the meaning of "dedicated," that is, "set aside for the Lord." God alone has control over the human being, animal, or land that has become most sacred (dedicated). In modern-day parallel, people on death row are doomed to die, but appeal can be made to the highest authority. Another meaning of the word is "people dedicated by solemn vow to God." In the order of holiness they are on "life's row." It is the will of the divine covenant member that all live. Life, not death, is the will of God. Death came into the world because of the *human* covenant member (Gen 3), and death is still present to the community of the human covenant members. However, the divine partner could play the role of the lesser member and then restore life to the human condition.

27:30-33 The sacredness of tithes. The above explanation is only partial. In an unfinished bridge-chapter we expect some partial answers. As in Gen 28, the vow and the tithe are now brought together in chapter 27 to affirm and ensure the continued presence of God. The tithe becomes the span of the bridge that we set in place, even though constructed of material belonging to the Lord.

We need to rethink our definition of tithe. We are not speaking of one-tenth as of multiples of ten. In the creation of the world, the tithe was the seventh day. Each of the six days of creation is made up of the created things of the previous day plus its own works. The seventh day was made holy (Gen 1:3). The seventh day in the creation blueprint became a miniature world, holy and complete, a fitting expression of the creator's gift of the world. The Lord's day is a holy day. It is the original form of the tithe. "Seventh" and "complete rest" are from the same Hebrew root. The seventh day is the day of completion.

Deut 14:22-29 puts the finishing touches on the understanding of tithing. "Each year you shall tithe all . . . then in the place which the Lord, your God, chooses as the dwelling place of his name you shall eat in his presence your tithe . . . . that you may learn always to fear [respect the source of life] the Lord, your God" (14:22-23). In verse 26, after making provision for everyone, Deuteronomy directs all to partake of the tithe and make merry with their families.

Deuteronomy continues the regulation "at the end of every third year, you shall bring all the tithes . . . for that year and deposit them in community stores, that the Levite . . . the alien, the orphan and the widow . . . may come and eat their fill" (14:28-29). Let everyone enjoy fully the life of holiness.

The payment of the tithe is in the eating of the meal together (the Holy One and the ones called to be holy) with the feeding of the poor so that all may have life to the full. This is the life of holiness, a life that is being lived today in the Eucharist-Passover, the celebration of the redemption of the First-born. Gathered with the writers of the Book of Leviticus on the partially constructed bridge to the Dwelling of the Holy Name, we begin to hear the song of celebration: "Holy, holy, holy is the Lord of hosts! All the earth is filled with God's glory!"

NUMBERS

Helen Kenik Mainelli

INTRODUCTION

The Book of Numbers, the fourth book of the Pentateuch, is so named because it contains two censuses of the Israelite tribes (1:20-46 and 26:5-51) and of the Levites (3:14-51 and 26:57-62). It also includes lists of various kinds, some with numbers: a list of the princes who assist with the census (1:5-15); a list of gifts brought for the dedication of the altar (7:10-83); a list of the scouts sent to explore the land (13:4-15); lists of offerings to be brought for feast days and festivals (28:1–29:38); and a list of the booty taken from the Midianites (31:32-52). While the name "Numbers" fits some of the content, it does not accurately suggest the story told in the book.

The story in Numbers begins in the desert of Sinai just after the covenant event and ends forty years later with the people waiting on the plains of Moab to enter the Promised Land. It is the story of the people of God as they journey through the wilderness for almost forty years under the leadership of Moses and Aaron.

The central issue is the presence of Yahweh with the people as they journey through the wilderness: God walks with them and directs their lives. The people, for their part, often grumble and rebel; they provoke divine judgment and seek forgiveness.

The Book of Numbers is the last part of the story that begins in the Book of Genesis with creation and continues in the Book of Exodus with the liberation and election of God's people. As we read the Book of Numbers, we will continually be reminded that this is but one piece of a continuous story identified as the primary history.

The organization of the primary history

The primary history is divided into eras: the ages of Adam, Noah, and the ancestors of Israel (Genesis); the era of Israel's movement from Egypt to Sinai (Exodus); and the era of Israel's movement from Sinai to the threshold of the Promised Land (Exodus to Numbers).

The Sinai event stands at the center. What begins in the Book of Exodus with Sinai continues in the Book of Numbers. All the directives in Num 1–10, for example, are communicated to Moses at Sinai.

Likewise, from Sinai there is a look backward to creation. The law of the sabbath, given at Sinai (Exod 31:12-17), links with the creation event (Gen 2:2-3).

The Priestly authors and their audiences

The primary history was put into final form in the sixth century B.C.E. by priests intent on the restoration of the temple cult. The work is therefore called "Priestly," or "P" for short. The authors were from the family of priests, the sons of Zadok, who secured leadership among the displaced people of the Exile (sixth century B.C.E.) and motivated this people to center its life on the worship of Yahweh. They wrote the history specifically to give the exiled Israelites hope and comfort based on memory of God's actions. They challenged the exiles to recall the events of old, especially the ways in which God was present among the people, led them, and provided for them in their formative years.

The priests wrote the story of *God with Israel* for people whose identity and faith, like ours, were questioned in the face of dramatic political, cultural, social, and religious upheaval. They stirred people to reach behind the collapsed institutions to that early time of God's love-relationship in covenant to discover again the benefits of dependence and obedience. The priests detailed the ways of God's presence in that early time so that people might rediscover God in their midst in new ways in a new age. The priests provided a word of hope and encouragement for all of us in our wilderness experiences that we might know that others have walked before us under the protection and guidance of Yahweh.

The priests handed down traditions from Israel's past. They were not authors who made up stories nor historians whose intention was to report past events. Rather, they were writers who collected ancient documents, lists, reports, and stories, which they edited and arranged into an account of *God with the people* that at once told the story of the past and addressed the needs of contemporary generations. They were writers who *remembered* the past and *handed down* essentials from tradition to provide a basis for the reidentification of God's people.

The Priestly theology

The selection and organization of traditional material in the narrative were determined by covenant theology. The priests traced the covenants from the beginning of Israelite history, and in so doing they emphasized the perpetuity of the relationship between God and the people. Yahweh's covenant is eternal. The covenant with Noah (Gen 9:1-17) and the covenant with Abraham (Gen 17:1-27) prepared the way for God's ultimate self-disclosure to Israel at Sinai, the covenant that endured to the Exile and beyond.

At Sinai the covenant issued in one benefit—the presence of Yahweh in Israel's midst. The glory of the Lord settled upon Mount Sinai and remained present with the people in covenant (Exod 24:16; 25:8). The Priestly writer chose his words very carefully. Here the verb translated "settled upon" means literally "to tent" or "to walk about among."

This was not a presence in the static sense of nearness in a shrine. The priests remembered the days when Yahweh, present on the ark and in the tent, moved with the people. By linking together the idea of Yahweh's "tenting" or "moving among" with various covenant formularies, they make the theological point that is central to the whole narrative:

> I will *dwell in the midst* of the Israelites and will be their God. They shall know that I, the Lord, am their God who brought them out of the land of Egypt, so I, the Lord, their God, might *dwell among them* (Exod 29:45-46; see Lev 26:11-13 and John 1:14).

Special vocabulary used in the Priestly edition

Glory of the Lord is the distinctive designation for the God-self revealed in majesty and power. The Priestly source uses the term "glory of the Lord" whenever it speaks about God being actually present and manifest (see Num 16:19; 17:7).

Dwelling is the key word of Priestly theology. Derived from the verb "to tent" or "to walk among as a tent-dweller," this idea implies mobility and nearness as well as holiness and transcendence. It is the word chosen by the Priestly author to indicate the place of Yahweh's covenant presence and carries the idea that Yahweh is always present with the people (see Num 1:50-53). This special word encompasses all of the other designations for Yahweh's presence: the tent, ark, holy place, etc.

Meeting tent refers to the traditional place of divine-human meeting. This is the place where Yahweh meets and speaks with the people through Moses (Exod 29:42; Num 1:1; 2:2; 3:7-8, etc.). The Priestly tradition sometimes uses "meeting tent" as a metaphor for the Dwelling, the place where the glory of the Lord is revealed (see 16:19).

Ark is identified by the Priestly writer as the "ark of the covenant" (Num 10:33) and as the "ark of the commandments" (Num 4:5; 7:89). In early tradition the ark was the seat upon which Yahweh was believed to be invisibly present. This instrument of Yahweh's presence was reinterpreted by the priests as the container for keeping the covenant document. In the Priestly tradition the covenant is the Decalogue, or the tablets of the law (see Exod 25:16, 21, 22).

Sanctuary is used to talk about the most sacred place, the location of the ark and the meeting tent, where Yahweh dwells among the people. It is a general term for "holy place" and is used interchangeably with "Dwelling."

Community refers to the people of the covenant and the whole family of the people of God. The priests think of Israel as a congregation, in the sense of a people at worship. This community, which participates in cult and worship, will gain the blessings inherent in the eternal covenant (see Num 1:2, 16, 18; 3:7, etc.).

"I am Yahweh" is a recognition formula that identifies God as the liberator of the people from slavery in Egypt, and therefore as the God who has chosen Israel for a special relationship:

I am Yahweh.
I will free you from the forced labor of the
  Egyptians . . . .
I will take you as my own people, and you shall
  have me as your God (Exod 6:6a, 7a).

The Priestly writer uses this recognition formula throughout the narrative to lead the people to recognize that the God Yahweh who acted in the past continues to be present and active on behalf of the covenant people (see Num 3:13, 45; 35:34).

Stylistic features in the Priestly edition

The priests present their material in such patterned ways that it will be helpful for the reader to be able to recognize some of the literary peculiarities. We divide this commentary into chapters, for example, on the basis of the Priestly writers' use of the journey formula. The content in the book is set into the various segments of the journey schema.

Journey formula. The march through the wilderness begins at Sinai and ends at Moab in a sequence of stages. At precise moments the Priestly author inserts the formula "they moved on from _____ and came to rest in _____" to indicate the movement from place to place. After the events in the wilderness of Sinai (Num 1:1–10:10), the people move from Sinai to the desert of Paran (10:12); from the desert of Paran to the desert of Zin at Kadesh (20:1); from Kadesh to Mount Hor (20:22); from Mount Hor to the desert east of Moab (21:10-11); and finally they move on to the plains of Moab (22:1), where they remain at the end of the book.

The journey from Sinai to Moab takes place in six stages. The journey from Egypt to Sinai also takes place in six stages. The journey formula occurs at Exod 12:37a; 13:20; 14:1-2; 15:22a; 16:1 and 17:1a. These twelve stages correspond to an ancient tradition about the journey which the Priestly writer preserves in Num 33:5-49.

God's word spoken and obeyed. Moses is presented in the Book of Numbers as an illustration of a leader who faithfully carries out God's word. It is helpful to notice the typical formulation: "The Lord said to Moses: 'Do such and such.' Moses, therefore, did such and such in accordance with the command the Lord had given him" (see Num 1:1, 18-19; 3:14-15, 40-42, etc.).

Cycle of rebellion, punishment, forgiveness. One of the Priestly writer's intentions is to illustrate the history of Israel's infidelity. To do this, he borrows traditions of unfaithfulness and sets the incidents into a predictable story pattern. Each story has these elements: (1) the people complain; (2) God becomes angry and punishes; (3) the people cry out for help; (4) Moses intercedes on behalf of the people; (5) Yahweh responds by giving relief from the punishment. This pattern occurs in the stories in Num 11:1-3; 12:2; 9-16; 17:6-15; 21:4-9.

OUTLINE OF THE BOOK

1:1–10:10
In the desert of Sinai: Preparations for the journey

10:11–22:1
On the journey from Sinai to Moab
  Events in the desert of Paran (10:11–19:22)
  Last stops along the way (20:1–22:1)

22:2–36:13
On the plains of Moab: Preparation for life in the land

COMMENTARY

IN THE DESERT OF SINAI: PREPARATIONS FOR THE JOURNEY

Num 1:1–10:10

These beginning chapters of the Book of Numbers describe events that take place while the people are camped at Sinai. They are being readied for the great march into the Promised Land. First, a census is taken (ch. 1), and the people are organized around the Dwelling, the presence of Yahweh among them (ch. 2). Next, there is a numbering of the Levites, whose principal duty is the care of the Dwelling (ch. 3), and a description of their duties (chs. 4 and 8). There follows a series of regulations that ensure the sanctity of the camp (chs. 5 and 6). There is then a listing of the offerings by the princes/leaders to serve the Dwelling in transport (ch. 7), with final preparations for the movement out of the camp: the lights are lighted in the Dwelling (8:1-4), and guidance is provided for the trek through the wilderness (9:15-23). The second Passover is celebrated to remember that a year has passed since the deliverance from Egypt (ch. 9), and the silver trumpets are blown to signal the march (10:10).

These chapters were set down by priests in the exilic period, when the community needed instructions regarding its present circumstance. It viewed itself as being once again in the wilderness and preparing for a return to the homeland. The vision of a community organized about the Dwelling encompasses at once that early first entry into the land of promise and this new time of waiting for the return to the land.

These first ten chapters contain remembrances about life in the wilderness. The traditions are ancient ones preserved by members of the Priestly school to construct ideally that early experience. More important to the priests is the message of hope contained in the memory of the past. The account presents the exilic community with a model that has Yahweh at the center and the people as a community at worship, organized around the Dwelling. The regulations given clarify responsibilities for priests, leaders, and people that they might be holy within the organization of the new community of faith.

1:1-3 The census. The scene is the wilderness at the foot of Mount Sinai, where Yahweh and Israel celebrated the unique relationship of covenant. There, according to Yahweh's command, Moses erected the Dwelling and placed the ark in the meeting tent on the first day of the *first* month in the second year after the Israelites came out of the land of Egypt (Exod 40:2, 17-19; see 19:1).

Yahweh speaks with Moses in this tent one month later, on the first day of the *second* month of this second year after the Exodus (v. 1), commanding him to take a census of the people. The command specifically states that the sons of Israel are to be registered individually, as well as according to their clan in the father's line (v. 2). Only males twenty years or older are to be counted. Twenty years is the age at which a male person becomes an adult, and therefore subject to the full range of religious duties, including participation in military service (v. 3).

The census marks the initial preparation for the great pilgrimage to the Promised Land. Yahweh has appointed Moses as leader of the grand march. Moses is to be the people's representative before God and the one through whom God speaks with the people. The formula "The Lord said to Moses" (v. 1) is repeated over eighty times in the book. The importance of Moses cannot be emphasized enough. In continuity with the Exodus tradition (Exod 24 and 32), Moses will be assisted in his leadership role by his brother Aaron: "You and Aaron shall enroll . . ." (v. 3). The dominant role of Aaron will unfold in the course of the book.

1:4-19a Moses' assistants: Twelve princes of Israel. To assist Moses and Aaron with the census, a man holding a position of authority in each tribal unit is designated to conduct the count in his clan (v. 4). These individuals hold authority that extends to all dimensions of life. They are "councilors," or representatives in the worshiping community, "princes" within the family, and "chiefs" over the military forces (v. 16). As representatives within the worshiping community, these leaders present offerings for the dedication of the altar (7:10-88). As princes in their respective families, they are responsible for order in the camp (2:3-31). As chiefs of the military forces, they lead the people as they embark on the journey from the wilderness of Sinai (11:13-28).

It is uncertain whether the names of the leaders of the tribes have survived from an early time or whether they are names of leaders from the period after the Exile. Since some of the names appear in 1 and 2 Chronicles (see 1 Chr 6:12; 7:26; 12:3, 10; 15:24; 24:6; 2 Chr 11:18; 17:8; 35:9, etc.), which come from the time when the temple was rebuilt, we assume that these men were actual leaders known to the priests and not a recollection of leaders from the time of the wilderness sojourn.

The list of the twelve tribes found in verses 5-15 is one of the important genealogies of the people and reflects the rules of protocol in tribal hierarchy. This list follows the sequence of names first recorded in Gen 35:22b-26 in the narration of the birth of Jacob's sons, with variations that reflect the needs of the later period. According to protocol, the sons of the legitimate wives always take precedence over the sons of the maids. The lists are as follows:

	Gen 35:22b-26	Num 1:5-15	
Jacob's sons by Leah:	Reuben	Reuben	Because in Numbers, the tribe
	Simeon	Simeon	of Levi is enrolled separately (see
	Levi		1:47-54), Levi is omitted from
	Judah	Judah	the list.
	Issachar	Issachar	
	Zebulun	Zebulun	
by Rachel:	Joseph	Ephraim	To retain the count of twelve,
	Benjamin	Manasseh	the tribe of Joseph is divided
		Benjamin	into the two sons (see Gen 48:1).
by Bilhah, Rachel's maid:	Dan	Dan	
	Naphtali	Asher	
by Zilpah, Leah's maid:	Gad	Gad	In all lists where the sons of
	Asher	Naphtali	Joseph are listed separately, the
			names Naphtali and Asher reverse order for a reason unknown (see 13:4-15).

There is another pattern for the listing of the tribes that we will discuss when we comment on the arrangement of tribes in the camp and on the march (see ch. 2).

On the very day on which the Lord instructs Moses and Aaron to take the census, that is, on the first day of the second month (v. 18; compare v. 1), the assistants are named and the census begins. Every adult male is registered according to the Lord's command (vv. 18b-19; compare vv. 2-3). Thus the census takes place, with Moses, Aaron, and the tribal leaders responding obediently to God's word.

1:19b-46 Count of the twelve tribes. Rigid structure and formulaic expression characterize the Priestly narrative. The record of the census count is typical of the patterned language. Each of the twelve tribes, with its count of male members, is set forth in stylistic rhetoric that is nicely captured in our translation. Notice that the schematized recital has an introduction, "This is their census"

(v. 19b), and a conclusion (vv. 44-45) that reiterates the formulas to indicate that God's command has been carried out exactly. The stylized presentation serves two functions: (1) it puts emphasis on the group included in the census—male adults capable of military service, registered in their individual tribes in their father's line; (2) it points up the names of the individual tribes and the size of each group.

The order in which the tribes are presented falls into the pattern we have described above. The only variation from the list given in verses 5-15 is the substitution of Gad for the tribe of Levi. The repetition of the precise pattern gives us a sense of the priests' reliance on traditional information in recounting the memory of that early time in the wilderness in order to sustain the faith of the people in their current passage from an exilic wilderness.

The total 603,550 in verse 46, as well as

the numbers given for the individual tribes, can hardly be historically accurate. What was remembered of that idyllic period in the wilderness was the multitude of ancestors who populated the land and the pride in national history that had its beginning in the Exodus-wilderness experiences. Memory of that glorious past, however idealized and exaggerated, nurtures a people for whom the hope for a future is built on memory of the past.

1:47-54 The Levites. Because the Levites are assigned the care of the sanctuary, they are not included in the census of those who are capable of military service (v. 47). Their duties are to carry the Dwelling, to care for it, and to camp around it (v. 50). They alone are allowed to take it down and set it up again as the people move from site to site. Death is the punishment for any non-Levite who approaches the Dwelling (v. 51). When the tribes are encamped around the Dwelling, the Levites form a kind of shield to insulate the people from the divine presence (vv. 52-53).

The Dwelling is the place where Yahweh is present with the people, a presence rooted in the covenant. The phrase "Dwelling of the commandments" (v. 50) points to the Dwelling as the place where the ark with the commandments is located. There is here a merging of the various traditions of God's presence in order to emphasize what has always been true: God resides in the midst of the people. This Dwelling, given to the care of the Levites, represents Yahweh's presence not concretely but by covenant relationship.

The task assigned to the Levites is the *service* of the Dwelling. In verse 53 the phrase "shall have charge" is from the verb meaning "to serve," which is used most frequently in contexts of worship. It means to do worthy service, to honor and care for that which is sacred. The Levites' task is a kind of continuous performance of worship.

2:1-34 Camp around the meeting tent. Now that the census has been completed, the focus changes to the arrangement of the tribes around the meeting tent. According to tradition, the meeting tent was that place where God communicated with the people through the mediatorship of Moses (see Exod 33:7-11). The meeting tent could be moved along with the people. Wherever the people moved, Yahweh's voice could always come to Moses. In the introductory address Moses' name pre-cedes that of Aaron because Moses is traditionally the mediator at the tent as well as the designated leader of the people on the way to the land.

The word of the Lord comes to Moses and Aaron (v. 1) with the command that the people should encircle the meeting tent, leaving some distance between themselves and the tent, and should group themselves according to the clan and family divisions of the census (v. 2). The tribes are to be arranged in a precise formation, three on each side, around the meeting tent (see next page). The Levites are situated in the center to shield the Israelites from the tent of Yahweh's presence (v. 17a; see also 3:24, 29, 35, 38).

The east side of the camp is the most prominent, since it faces the rising sun in front of the tent. As we move clockwise from the east, we discover the relative status of the tribes. Priority is given to the tribe of Judah, and the least position is given to three tribes that trace their birth to the maids of Jacob's wives (see Gen 35:25-26).

The order of the tribes differs slightly from the lists of the census in 1:5-15 and 20-43. It begins with Judah rather than Reuben.

1:20-43	*2:3-31*
Reuben	Judah
Simeon	Issachar
Gad	Zebulun
Judah	Reuben
Issachar	Simeon
Zebulun	Gad
Ephraim	Ephraim
Manasseh	Manasseh
Benjamin	Benjamin
Dan	Dan
Asher	Asher
Naphtali	Naphtali

By grouping the tribes in triads, we can see that the Judah group is positioned ahead of the Reuben group in order of status. The variation is important because the tradition of the preeminence of Judah in the arrangement of the camp carries over into the order of worship (7:12-83) and into the order of march (10:14-28). With this order the Priestly author is reflecting an actual situation of his own day. The exiles originally came from the territory of Judah, and they return there to reestablish Jerusalem as the religious center for the

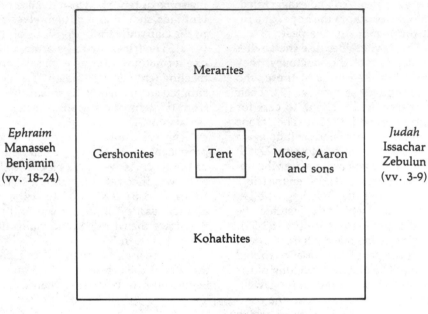

Dan
Asher and Naphtali
(vv. 25-31)

Ephraim
Manasseh
Benjamin
(vv. 18-24)

Judah
Issachar
Zebulun
(vv. 3-9)

Reuben
Simeon and Gad
(vv. 10-16)

ARRANGEMENT OF THE TRIBES
AROUND THE MEETING TENT

people. The prominence of Judah thus suggests the importance of the southern region as the place where the people will establish themselves as well as the new temple for Yahweh's presence.

When the tribes move, they will move in precisely the designated order (v. 17b)—the Judah triad first (v. 9), the Reuben triad second (v. 16), the Ephraim triad third (v. 24), and the Dan triad last (v. 31). Each group consists of the males who have been numbered (v. 32), and each moves under the banner of the clan (v. 2). All this was done "just as the Lord had commanded Moses" (v. 34).

3:1-4 Priests distinct from Levites. This chapter opens with a genealogical formulary distinctive of the style of the Priestly writer:

"The following were the descendants of so and so." This heading is typically used by the Priestly writer to mark off major periods in the history of God's people. From creation to the ancestors of Abraham, the formulary occurs five times to indicate major junctures (Gen 2:4a; 5:1; 6:9; 10:1; 11:10), and from the ancestors of Abraham to Jacob five more times (Gen 11:27; 25:12, 19; 36:1; 37:2). After the account of Israel's ancestors, the formulary is not used again until this place in Numbers, where we find the genealogy of the sons of Aaron, to whom the priests trace their ancestry. Thus, there is a conscious link from the priests back to the ancestors and, before them, to creation.

The name of Aaron comes before that of

Moses (compare 2:1) because here the Priestly writer is talking specifically about the descendants of Aaron, who exercise the duties of the priesthood. From this point on in Numbers, a distinction is made between the priests who are descended from Aaron and the Levites who identify with Moses. The appointment of the sons of Aaron to the duties of the priesthood is everywhere emphasized (see especially 17; 25:10-13; 27:12-23).

We note that the events recorded in Numbers are always linked back to the Sinai event. So, too, is the designation of the sons of Aaron linked to "the time that the Lord spoke to Moses on Mount Sinai" (v. 1b; compare Exod 24:1-2). Aaron had four sons: Nadab, Abihu, Eleazar, and Ithamar (v. 2; see also Exod 6:23), who were "anointed" and "ordained" to the priesthood (v. 3). Priests were anointed by the pouring of oil on their heads (Exod 29:7), the act by which they were dedicated to God (Lev 21:12). Ordaining means literally to "fill one's hand," that is, to give some task or responsibility in trust into someone's hands. The priests are entrusted with the good of the people who come to the presence of God. They are in charge of the liturgy, sacrifices, and feasts, the activities through which God's gifts of healing and life flow to the people. By being anointed and ordained, the priest is consecrated to carry out these responsibilities (see Exod 28:41).

Of Aaron's four sons, Nadab and Abihu died tragically in the wilderness of Sinai, leaving no descendants (v. 4a). This story can be read in Lev 10:1-5. The ancestry of Aaron was thereafter carried on by Eleazar and Ithamar (v. 4b). These two branches of the family can be traced through the time of David: Zadok from Eleazar, and Ahimelech from Ithamar (see 2 Sam 8:17; 1 Chr 18:16; 24:1-4). Eventually the line of Zadok rose to a position of prominence (see 2 Sam 15:24-29; 1 Kgs 2:35; Ezek 44:15-16). The designation of the sons of Aaron as a group assigned the special duties of the priesthood reflects, therefore, the actual practice from the tenth century on. The distinction between the priests and the Levites persisted into the time when the people returned from exile and after (see Ezra 2:36, 40; Neh 7:39, 43).

3:5-13 Levi's sons: assistants to the priests. In the remainder of this chapter, the Lord speaks to Moses alone (vv. 5, 11, 14, 40, 44). The concern is the Levites as distinct from the priests, and specifically as assistants to the priests (v. 6).

The Levites are traditionally identified as followers of Moses (see Exod 32:25-29), though actual descent from Moses is unclear. What is clear is the traditional status of the Levites as ministers to the priests and to the community. Only the sons of Aaron may function as priests (v. 10). The Levites are given to the priests as individuals "set apart" from the people Israel; they are "given" for Yahweh (v. 9; see 8:16; 18:6). They are to "discharge" the duties of Aaron and the community (v. 7) and to "have custody" of the furnishings of the meeting tent (v. 8). In both cases, the verb is "to serve," which more accurately means "to honor and care for something sacred." The Levites, then, would see that both priests and the community properly worship the divine presence (v. 7) by caring for the furnishings and overseeing the functions of the people at worship (v. 8).

The Levites are understood to be the property of Yahweh in place of the first-born of Israel (vv. 12-13). To commemorate Yahweh's claim on Israel, demonstrated with the death of the first-born of the Egyptians (v. 13a; Exod 11:4-8), the first-born of Israel belonged to Yahweh from that time on (v. 13b; Exod 13:2-16; 34:19-20). The Levites, as Yahweh's possession, act as substitutes for what is Yahweh's true right—the first-born of the other tribes. Yahweh has chosen the Levites, and they are given to Yahweh in place of the first-born (v. 12). The idea of being ransom for the first-born is discussed again in our commentary on 3:40-51 and 8:5-26.

3:14-39 Levi's sons: census and duties. We are once again invited to remember that these events are taking place in the wilderness of Sinai in accord with Yahweh's command (v. 14). The sons of Levi were excluded from being counted among the people of Israel in the census (see 1:47-48). As a sign that they are dedicated for service, a special census is taken of their numbers (v. 15). In their case, it is not males of twenty years or more, fit for military service that are counted (compare 1:3, 18, 45), but the entire male population from one month of age (v. 15b). This means that the Levites are "given" to Yahweh from birth, in the sense that they belong to Yahweh from the beginning of their existence. The

151

indication of "one month" means that the infant has withstood the critical period of infancy and therefore has the potential for a full life. The Levites actually fulfill the duties assigned them only between the ages of thirty and fifty (see 4:3). Like all the Israelites, the Levites are registered by clans in their father's line (vv. 15a and 20b).

The listing of the names of the sons of Levi is intended to parallel that of the sons of Aaron in 3:2, though here the genealogical formulary is lacking. Obviously, the Priestly writer intends that the emphasis be on the priests, who are linked by the genealogical introduction to the ancestors and creation. The status of the Levites is secondary to that of the priests.

There are three sons of Levi, each of whom is named together with his descendants: Gershon, with his descendants Libni and Shimei; Kohath, with his descendants Amram, Izhar, Hebron, and Uzziel; and Merari, with his descendants Mahli and Mushi. This list of names in verses 17-20 corresponds to the data given in sections in verses 21, 27, and 33. While information about the descendants is scant, it is probable that they reflect persons as well as places. What the Priestly author has done is to put the traditional material about the Levites into a pattern of relationships that has a correspondence to the other Israelite tribes.

The information about the clans in each of the sections is presented in a patterned sequence. After the names in verses 21, 27 and 33, the count of each clan is given: Gershon numbers 7,500 (v. 22); Kohath numbers 8,300 (v. 28); and Merari numbers 6,200 (v. 34). The total of 22,000 is given in verse 39. These numbers have no purpose except to highlight the disparity in size between the Levites and the other tribes (1:20-43). If we remember that all Levites from one month old were counted, in contrast with the count of adult males only from the other tribes, the disparity is even more pronounced. The priests want the reader to be aware of the comparatively small number of Levites.

Next in each section, the Levitical clans are assigned to one of the compass points between the sanctuary and the tribes of Israel. They camp immediately around the Dwelling and thus function to protect and to atone in a mediatory capacity (see 8:19). The Ger-

shonites are located on the west (v. 23); the Kohathites on the south (v. 29); and the Merarites on the north (v. 35b). The assignment to a specific compass point appears to be arbitrary. The favored eastern side, however, is reserved for Moses, Aaron, and the sons of Aaron (v. 38a). See the model on p. 150.

Each of the groups has specific duties in regard to the holy place. The sons of Aaron alone carry out the service at the sanctuary (v. 38b). The Levites attend to the appointments of the sanctuary. According to verses 25-26, the Gershonites tend to the tent itself, with all its curtains, hangings, coverings, and ropes. (Compare the description of the wilderness sanctuary in Exod 26; 27:9-16; 36:8-19, 35-38.) The Kohathites, according to verses 28b and 31, are charged with the care of the sacred contents of the wilderness sanctuary: the ark, table, lampstand, altars, utensils, and sanctuary veil. (These appointments are described in Exod 25; 27; 30:1-10; 37; 38.) According to verses 36-37, the Merarites attend to the frames, bases, poles, that is, those parts that secure the physical structure. (Read the elaborate descriptions of these physical features in Exod 26:15-37; 27:9-19; 36:20-34; 39:40.) Together with this division of assignments, we ought to recall the description of the Levitical duties given in 1:50-51, especially the Levites' role when the camp is broken and reestablished as the people move from place to place in the wilderness.

In each section there is also the name of a "prince" from each of the Levitical clans (vv. 24, 30 and 35a) to correspond to the listing of leaders from each of the Israelite tribes in 1:5b-15. Because these individuals are not mentioned again, their leadership function remains obscure. What is certain is the leadership of Eleazar, son of Aaron, who is identified as chief prince of the Levites (v. 32). It is to the priest Eleazar, the eventual successor to Aaron, that the Levites are accountable in the execution of their various duties (compare 3:6, 9a).

3:40-51 First-born of the Israelites. This section takes up again the matter introduced in 3:11-13—the Levites as substitutes for the first-born. Here the working out of the ransom is described in detail.

The presentation falls into the pattern of Yahweh's word (vv. 40 and 44), followed by the execution of that word (vv. 42 and 49-50).

Moses does exactly as the Lord directs him. He takes a census of the first-born males, those one month of age and over. These number 22,273 (v. 43). He then assigns the Levites as ransom for the first-born of Israel, and the cattle of the Levites as substitutes for the first-born cattle (vv. 41 and 45).

The number of the first-born males of Israel matches that of the Levites, with a difference of 273 (v. 46). The surplus can be ransomed by a sum of money given to the priests (v. 48). A price of five shekels, measured by the value of the temple shekel instead of the merchant shekel, provides a ransom for those remaining among the first-born (v. 49).

Such attention to detail points to the significance of the first-born, who were spared on that night when the first-born of Egypt died (see Exod 12:29). The first-born of every Israelite family in every succeeding generation remembers this event and therefore is himself spared. On account of this event, the first-born belongs to Yahweh (Exod 13:2, 12-25; 34:19-20).

The rationale for the Levites belonging to Yahweh is rooted in this tradition of the first-born belonging to Yahweh. By memory of this event, the people come to know Yahweh their God. The recognition formula "I am Yahweh" appears here: ". . . that the Levites may belong to me. I am the Lord" (v. 45b; see 13b). The connection between the delivery from Egyptian bondage and the dedication of the first-born provokes the realization that Israel is Yahweh's own, called into a unique relationship that endures forever. The dedication of the Levites witnesses to the nature of Israel's God as one who continues to act on Israel's behalf and who also demands dedication and service. (See p. 146 for a brief discussion of the recognition formula.)

4:1-33 Levitical duties defined. The word of the Lord is again addressed to Moses and Aaron, in that order (vv. 1, 17; see also 34 and 46). The command is to take a census of the subgroups of the Levites (vv. 2, 22, 29), those falling into the age bracket of thirty to fifty years old (vv. 3a, 23a, 30a).

The descriptions of the duties of each of the Levitical groups are set within the frame of the census command. Males of the designated age are assigned specific tasks in transporting the meeting tent. In each case the formulary "to undertake obligatory tasks"

(vv. 3b, 23b, 30b) introduces the particular responsibilities. The verbs in this formulary emphasize *service*, in the sense of an army prepared to engage in battle together with the idea of *service* in worship. In their choice of words, the author underscores the seriousness of the Levitical duties. The specific tasks correspond to those assigned to the Levitical groups in 3:25-26, 31, 36-37. Here the emphasis is on the dismantling and transport of the tent and the sacred objects (compare 1:50-51).

The duties of the Kohathites are given first because theirs is the care of the most sacred objects (v. 4); presumably this gives them special status. Theirs is an unassuming task, however, for they may not touch the sacred objects nor even look upon them (vv. 15b, 18-20). Only after the priests have properly covered the objects (vv. 5-14), put the carrying poles in place (vv. 6b, 8b, 14b), or set the objects on litters (vv. 10b, 12b) are the Kohathites permitted to lift them (v. 15).

In this section, attention is diverted from the Kohathites to the priests, who alone may touch the sacred objects. First they cover the "ark of the commandments" with three layers: with the temple veil, skins, and an elaborate outer cloth (vv. 5-6). Only the ark, which contains the document of covenant with Yahweh, has a colored outer covering, making it stand out among the objects in transport. The other objects are each covered with a precious cloth and an outer skin covering (vv. 7-14). The Kohathites are not permitted, under pain of death, to touch anything but the handles of the carriers. It is the holiness and transcendence of God that are being emphasized in this reverential treatment of those objects that have a direct use in worship.

The priests and the Levites each have specific functions in regard to the sanctuary. The division of duties is uppermost in the mind of the author, who represents priestly families and who is writing this account at a time when the priests are dominant in the governance of the religious life of the people. The sons of Aaron alone have charge of the holy place, and Eleazar, in particular, has charge of the Dwelling (v. 16; compare 2:32 and 3:1-4).

The duties of the Gershonites and Merarites correspond to those assigned to them in 3:25-26 and 3:36-37, respectively. Here again the emphasis is on the transport of the holy place on the journey about to be undertaken. The Gershonites will carry all the cloths, coverings, skins, ropes, etc., that are part of the physical structure and its adornment (vv. 25-26). The Merarites will carry the boards, columns, pegs, etc., the wooden and metal parts that give the place shape or are used to secure it (vv. 31b-32a). As in the case of the Kohathites, these Levitical groups come under the direction of the priests (v. 27), and specifically under the supervision of Ithamar, the other son of Aaron (vv. 28 and 33; see 3:1-4).

The reader today cannot help but sense the reverence the Israelites had for the holy place and its appointments. Only the most precious cloths and the rarest of skins were suitable for covering the sacred objects (vv. 5-14). It is this regard for the place of worship and for the position of the priests in relation to the holy place that has influenced religious practice throughout history. Without minimizing the word of God, it is important to remember that this document comes from one period in history and reflects ancient practice. The truth contained here about the *presence of God* with the people for all time and in all places is sometimes lost in reading the detailed regulations. It is important for the reader to remember that the delimitation of duties and the distinction of roles point to the sacredness of the Presence among the people. This Dwelling of God in the midst of people cannot be limited to one mode, nor is it dependent on particular institutions. The whole point of this dramatic account is that *God is present* and continually reveals the God-self in ways that are meaningful in each new era of history.

4:34-49 Census completed. The results of the census commanded above (vv. 2-3, 22-23, 29-30) are summarized in this concluding section. Composed of repetitious formularies so characteristic of the Priestly writer, it states that Moses, together with Aaron, took the census of each of the Levitical groups (vv. 34, 38, 42), as the Lord had commanded (vv. 17, 41, 45). The males, registered by clans in their father's line, were those falling within the age limit for mandatory service—thirty to fifty years of age. (Contrast this census with that of all Levites in 3:15 and 40.) The total number of Levites designated for service in the transport of the meeting tent is correspondingly less than the total of all Levites who were registered (v. 48; compare 3:43).

Thus, the Levites, set apart for special service, are assigned tasks directly related to the sanctuary. As the people prepare to embark upon the journey through the wilderness toward the Promised Land, the Levites have the important duty of dismantling and carrying the physical structure of the Dwelling. All this elaborate preparation and designation of duties stresses the fact that the divine presence remains with the people and, indeed, accompanies them on their journey.

There is a pause in the preparations at this point as attention is focused on life within the camp. Because God dwells in the midst of the people, there is no place for anything unworthy of the all-holy God. At this juncture, therefore, the Israelites are given a series of laws pertaining to ritual and ethical purity (ch. 5) and laws concerning the nazirites, who dedicate themselves completely to the Lord (ch. 6).

5:1-4 Expulsion of the unclean. The laws given here are to ensure the cleanliness of the place where Yahweh dwells in the midst of the people (v. 3b; see Lev 15:31). These were laws that actually governed life in the land of Canaan, and they were especially important for the life of the postexilic worshiping community as mirrored in the organization and order of the wilderness camp. This place of the Lord's presence is a holy place. Everything unclean must be expelled; such things are incompatible with the holy place as long as they remain unclean (vv. 3-4).

According to customary law, the unclean were those with skin disease, those emitting a discharge from the genitals, and those who came into contact with a corpse (v. 2). These particular laws governed all the people but were especially rigid in regard to the priests (see Lev 22:4).

The skin disease, identified as leprosy, could be any variety of problems that are common in tropical climates. The distinctive factor is sores that are open and running. It is the discharge from the open sore that makes the diseased person ritually unclean. The laws that govern such disease are found in full in Lev 13-14. There we learn that several periods of seven days of quarantine, that is, exclusion from the camp, may be required before being declared clean (see Lev 13:4-6, 26-27, 31-34, 50-51; 14:8-9). Every disease, insofar as it is visible, is a contamination and therefore excludes the individual from the cultic community where Yahweh dwells (v. 3b).

The discharge refers to fluids from the sexual organs of both males (see Lev 15:1-17; Deut 23:10-15) and females (see Lev 15:19-30), whether such discharge is normal or linked with affliction. There is no provision for exclusion from the community in the Levitical laws; only in Numbers is such exclusion indicated. Exclusion from the community does not imply a negative attitude toward sex. It is rather the idea that all bodily discharges are defiling. They are incompatible with physical perfection and therefore unworthy of the holiness of God who dwells among the people (v. 3b). The prescribed purificatory rites for males and females were exactly the same, as was the required offering (see Lev 15:5-10, 19-24; 15:13-15, 25-30). Especially in this matter do the priests demonstrate a consciousness of the equality of the male and female person (v. 3a; see Lev 15:32-33).

The connection between death and evil was a strong one in antiquity, as it often still is today. It was believed that evil issued from a corpse, making anyone who came into contact with it unclean and therefore unworthy of the presence of God (v. 3b). According to the law, a person who touched a dead body was banned for the stipulated period of seven days (see Num 19:11).

5:5-10 Restitution for wrongdoing. This sets up a situation of wrongdoing in very broad terms. It specifies both the man and woman as possible offenders (v. 6a) and describes the offense as any transgression of human beings, that is, wrongs done to one another (v. 6b). This is a restatement of the law of restitution given in Lev 5:20-26.

In biblical teaching there is a direct connection between evils done within the human community and relationship with God (v. 6c). Love for God and love for neighbor are inextricably bound together. We have only to read the Decalogue (Exod 20:1-17 and Deut 5:6-21), the rules given for conduct within the community (Lev 19:1-37), prophetic speeches (Hos 4:1-3; Amos 5:21-24; Isa 1:12-16), or the New Testament (1 John 4:20-21; Matt 5:23-24; 23:34-40; 25:31-46) to be made aware that regard for the community's well-being is a direct expression of reverence for God.

According to the law, an individual who transgresses against another shall not only confess the wrong and compensate for the wrong done or the character defamed, but shall also make restitution in the value of one-fifth over and above the due amount (v. 7). Compensation plus one-fifth of that value is the standard restitution demanded in all cases (see Lev 5:16, 24; 22:14; 27:13, 27, 31). So sacred is the person in the community that any harm to an individual causes harm to the whole body. And so sacred is the community that any violation of its well-being demands restitution. God's presence within this community requires that nothing violate or disrupt the integrity of the common good, and when such occurs, restoration as well as restitution is required.

If this restitution cannot be paid to the one offended, it is to be paid to the next of kin (v. 8a). If there is no next of kin, the restitution belongs to the priests, who accept it as given to the Lord (v. 8b). This restitution is over and above the offering of a ram that is required as an expiation offering in atonement for sin (v. 8c; see Lev 5:14-26).

The place given to the next of kin tells us something about the solidarity of the community of God's people. The next of kin is the nearest male blood relative on the father's side of the family. Being the next of kin carries grave responsibilities to ensure the life of the immediate and extended family. If a woman becomes a widow and is childless, the next of kin has to marry her in order that the family line might flourish (Ruth 4). If there is threat of losing property that belongs to the family, the next of kin is required to buy it so that it remains in the family (Lev 25:25). If a family member becomes enslaved, the next of kin is responsible for securing that person's freedom (Lev 25:47-52). Just as the next of kin provides when life or property is threatened, so the next of kin becomes the recipient of goods when restitution cannot be made to a wronged party. That which was taken from a particular family is thus restored and compensated, and thereby the community is made whole within itself and with God.

Appended to this law governing restitution is a general statement about the "sacred contributions" or holy gifts that belong to the priests (vv. 9-10). This sacred contribution can be a reserved portion of the offering that the priest moves up and down in ritual action, or it can be the whole offering that an Israelite presents to Yahweh by lifting it up. In either case, the sacred contribution is that which is lifted up, and it belongs to the individual officiating priest.

5:11-31 Ritual for judgment. Another circumstance inappropriate to the place of God's presence is mistrust between husband and wife, described as jealousy (vv. 14, 30a). The case presents a husband who suspects that his wife has committed adultery (vv. 12-13, 29) and might therefore bear him a child that is not his own, but who has no concrete evidence and so cannot institute normal legal proceedings through the courts. The husband may resort to a trial by ordeal when there are no witnesses or other proof.

This is the only instance in the biblical literature where a ritual of ordeal is described in detail. The ordeal seems to have been used when the question of guilt or innocence could not be ascertained by the normal methods of making judgment. The accused person submits to some practice, such as drinking a potion or walking on fire. If he or she is unhurt, innocence is proven. Adultery was the offense for which the ordeal was most often invoked, as is suggested by the detailed description in this text. Deut 17:8-13, however, states that cases involving homicide, disputes over ownership rights, and personal assault may be settled by ordeal.

The case presented here is decidedly one-sided in that the man may accuse the woman, who then must bear the burden of the charge, while the man remains without guilt even when the accusation is groundless (v. 31). To be decided is the serious matter of paternity. The rite is designed to determine the legitimacy of the man's children.

The husband brings his wife before the priest with an offering of barley that has neither oil nor frankincense over it because "it is a cereal offering of jealousy" (v. 15). The dry grain signifies that the offering is an atonement for sin (see Lev 5:11-13). Oil and frankincense on the coarse grain would produce a sweet-smelling oblation, suggesting joy and bounty (Lev 2:1-2; 6:8).

The ritual for judgment follows. Essentially the woman stands before the Lord (vv. 16, 30b), a posture that brings God into the process of legal investigation. Her head is uncovered, a sign of disgrace and uncleanness, and she holds the cereal offering in her hands (v. 18). The priest meanwhile prepares the water by placing dust from the floor of the Dwelling into it (v. 17). This water is called "holy" because it is kept in the sanctuary. The addition of the dust increases the sacredness of the drink and its danger to the woman who will drink it. It is the drinking of this water, called "bitter," that decides innocence or guilt (v. 18c). Notice that reference is made to this water throughout verses 19, 22, 24, and 27.

The priest then puts the woman under oath to speak the truth (vv. 19a, 21a). The words pronounced by the priest cause the bitter water to be effective in confirming innocence (v. 19b) or guilt (vv. 20-22). The woman responds with "Amen, Amen," thereby agreeing with the effectiveness of the ordeal procedure. The curse itself is a euphemism for miscarriage or possibly sterility. "Thigh" is often used to mean the sexual organs. It is characteristic in accounts of judgment that the punishment is a reversal of the sin. If the woman has sinned by illicit intercourse, her punishment is the termination of the pregnancy (v. 27) or the inability to bear children. The opposite situation, described in verse 28, would be the ability to bear children.

Before the woman drinks, the words of the curse are written on, then washed off, the parchment into the water (v. 23) so that the words of the curse will be effective in themselves (v. 24). Last of all, the priest burns a handful of the cereal offering on the altar; the remainder of the cereal belongs to the priest (see Lev 2:2-3). Once the woman drinks the water, there are two possible outcomes (vv. 27-28): she is either proclaimed guilty and therefore unclean, or innocent and therefore clean.

6:1-21 Dedication of nazirites. In the context of preparation for the journey toward the land, where there will be the ideal community that has God dwelling among the people, we have noted the emphasis on the holiness and purity required of the believing community. The Priestly writer includes at this point a text about the consecration of individuals, both male and female (v. 2), underlining the sacredness and nobility of total dedication to the Lord. Such an individual is called a "nazirite," a term derived from the verb meaning "to set apart" or "to consecrate." A nazirite makes a vow of dedication to the Lord (v. 21) for a set period of time (vv. 4, 5, 6, 8, 12, 13).

The tradition of the nazirite was of long standing among the people of God. Samson (Judg 13:5) and Samuel (1 Sam 1:11) are thought to have been consecrated for life. The practice continued into the time of John the Baptist (Luke 1:15) and Paul the Apostle (Acts 18:18; 21:23-26).

Our text consists of three independent sections within the framework of verses 1-2 and 21. Verses 3-8 describe the conditions and laws that govern an individual who chooses to make a vow for a set period of time. Verses 9-12 outline the required purification if a person inadvertently becomes unclean. Verses 13-21 introduce the ceremonies to be observed when the period of the vow is fulfilled.

The nazirite assumes three restrictions when taking the vow of dedication. The obligations cover the matter of drinking and eating (vv. 3-4), the cutting of the hair (v. 5), and contact with the dead (vv. 6-7).

The nazirite is forbidden to consume the grape in any form—no drinking of wine, vinegar, or even grape juice (v. 3a), nor eating of grapes, raisins, the seeds or skins of the grape, or any part of the vine (vv. 3b-4). The abstention is from the grape, not from alcoholic drink as such. The grapevine represents urban culture, settled life, comfort, and high living—pleasures in opposition to faithful allegiance to Yahweh (see Amos 4:1b; 6:6).

Second, the nazirite does not put the razor to the hair of the head (v. 6). The growth of hair is a visible sign of consecration. Symbolic of integrity and dignity, the long hair dramatically distinguishes the individual as one who serves God in a special way (v. 7b).

Third, the nazirite never approaches the dead, not even the corpses of family members (vv. 6-7a). (On the uncleanness associated with contact with the dead, see the commentary on 5:1-3 and 9:11-22.) This law is stricter than in the case of the ordinary priest, who is exempted in the case of family (Lev 21:1-3); it is, however, comparable to the restrictions imposed on the high priest (Lev 21:11).

These practices set the nazirite apart as a continual reminder to the community of what total dedication of Yahweh should be. Apparently, in Amos' day the witness of the nazirites was so disturbing that the people tried to get them to break the vow (Amos 2:11-12).

The second section of the text addresses a situation in which the nazirite might accidentally become unclean by contact with a corpse (vv. 9-12). The hair, the sign of consecration, has thereby become polluted and must be shaved off (v. 9), and the period of dedication, now invalid, must be begun anew (v. 12). The period of purification, according to law, lasts seven days (v. 9b; see Num 19:11, 14, 16). Afterward the nazirite brings the simple offering of two birds, the offering required of the poor (v. 10; see Lev 5:7; 12:8; 14:22; 15:13-15). The priest offers one bird as a sin offering to restore the relationship with a holy God that has been interrupted by contact with that which makes one unclean; the other is offered as a holocaust, the sacrifice required of everyone coming before the Lord, and therefore must be completely consumed (v. 11). After the atonement has been made, the head of the nazirite is once again consecrated (v. 11b), and a guilt offering of a year-old lamb is made. This last is a kind of punitive fine paid to God for the loss of what is due. With the nullification of the vow, something that had properly belonged to Yahweh on the basis of the vow was lost. (See Deut 23:22-24 for the laws governing anyone who chooses to make a vow, and note the restrictions imposed on women in Num 30:4-16.)

The third section prescribes the ritual to be observed at the completion of the period of consecration (vv. 13-20). The instructions are addressed to the priest who will carry out the particulars of the ceremony. The individual comes forward to the meeting tent with specified offerings (vv. 13-15). After the priest has offered the sacrifice, the nazirite's head is shaved and the hair burned in the fire of the peace offering (vv. 16-18). The priest takes his share of the sacrificial gifts (vv. 19-20), and only then is the nazirite permitted to drink wine (v. 20c).

The full range of sacrifices indicates the solemnity of the occasion (vv. 14-15). The holocaust is offered by everyone who approaches the Lord; the sin offering is given in atonement for all violations committed, however unintentional. The peace offering is presented in thanksgiving together with cereal and drink offerings. This last suggests a banquet and signifies communion between God and the participant (vv. 16-17). The hair that has been cut is burned in the fire of the peace offering, signifying the destruction of that

157

which had been consecrated to the Lord once it has served its purpose (vv. 18-19a).

In carrying out the sacrifice, the priest puts a share of the sacrifice into the hands of the one consecrated so that the portion may be formally presented to the priest (v. 19b) in a gesture of waving (v. 20a). This motion seems to represent the act of giving back to God from the bounty God has given. This share is part of the special gift presented to the priest. The usual gift due to the priest from every offering is the breast and the leg (v. 20b; see Lev 7:34 and Num 18:8-11). The nazirite is required to make the offerings prescribed, but other offerings may also be presented in accord with the individual's means (v. 21a).

With the completion of this ritual, the nazirite has fulfilled the period of vow and wine may be taken (v. 20c). The individual then resumes an ordinary life.

6:22-27 The priestly blessing. As a kind of interlude, unconnected with what precedes or follows, the Priestly author inserts a benediction formulary that is one of the oldest pieces of poetry in the Scriptures. Perhaps the blessing is placed here to show God's blessing on the people who live the holy life in accord with the regulations set forth in chapters 5–6.

The prayer itself (vv. 24-26) is positioned within a framework that begins with the typical "The Lord said to Moses." That the priests bless the people is seen as the Lord's will communicated through Moses (see Deut 10:8; 21:5). The specific reference to the Aaronic priesthood (v. 23a) reflects the postexilic time, when the principal duty of the priests in the sanctuary was to mediate the blessing, the wellspring of life that derives from Yahweh, the source of all life (see Pss 115:12-15; 118:26; 129:8; 134:3). At the installation of the priest, his first act was to raise his hand in blessing (Lev 9:1-24, esp. vv. 22-24). This strength for life that is mediated through the priests keeps alive the promise that through this people God's blessings flow to the world.

In the blessing, the name Yahweh is repeated three times and is the implied subject three more times. Pronouncing this name is itself an effectual blessing. Thus, the conclusion states that the priests "invoke my name upon the Israelites" (v. 27a). The Hebrew rendering is an unusual expression that literally states that they "put the name on" the people,

rather than the expected "call on the name." This specific idiom would seem to imply a close relationship, an indication of God's ownership and protection. The Israelites are proclaimed to be Yahweh's property through the putting of Yahweh's name on them by the priests. The concluding statement "and I will bless them" (v. 27b) means, then, that when the priests put the divine name on the Israelites, Yahweh will indeed bless them.

The blessing itself is one of the finest pieces of ancient poetry. It is written in three lines, each with two parts, and in a complex metrical pattern that increases progressively in the number of words (three in the first line, five in the second line, and seven in the third line) and in metrical counts (ten, twelve, and fourteen, respectively). The blessing is addressed to "you" in the singular, meaning the whole of Israel as a corporate entity as well as each individual. This "you" is expressed three times as a direct object (vv. 24ab, 25b) and three times as the object of a preposition (vv. 25a, 26ab).

The first half of each line invokes Yahweh's personal act upon the people: "bless" (v. 24a), "let [your] face shine upon" (v. 25a), and "look kindly upon" (v. 26a).

To "bless" means to pour forth the continual and sustaining power of life that manifests itself as growth, increase, success, fertility, and prosperity (see Gen 24:34-36). Blessing derives from the essential divine being out of which arise the promises: "I will bless you; I will make your name great" (Gen 12:2); "I will be with you and bless you" (Gen 26:3).

To "let [Yahweh's] face shine upon" means to look with pleasure or favor. Clearly an anthropomorphism used metaphorically, reference to "face" implies the totality of divine goodness directed to the recipient of the blessing (see Ps 67:2). When Yahweh is gracious toward the people, they see Yahweh's face (Pss 31:17; 80:4, 8, 20). On the other hand, to express displeasure with the people, Yahweh declares, "I hide my face" (Ezek 39:23; see Isa 57:17).

To "look kindly upon" suggests the bestowal of divine love in gestures of favor and help. Yahweh's attention is directed toward the one who is dependent and in need of help (see Pss 33:18; 34:16; 1 Kgs 8:29, 52).

Each of these acts of Yahweh is followed

by a consequence of the blessing invoked. Yahweh will "keep" (v. 24b), "be gracious" (v. 25b), and "give peace" (v. 26b).

To "keep" means that in consequence of the blessing, Yahweh will protect Israel from the misfortunes that bring about the opposite of life and prosperity, such as childlessness, crop failure, threat from enemies. To "be gracious" means to show undeserved favor. As a consequence of Yahweh's face shining upon Israel, this people experiences the goodness that derives from the divine nature (see Exod 33:19; 34:6; Num 14:18; Deut 5:9-10). Finally, Yahweh "gives peace" as the consequence of looking kindly. The concept of peace is the summation of the act of blessing: "May the Lord bless his people with peace" (Ps 29:11). It is a term that means much more than freedom from war or discord. Peace is the state of being whole, of completeness, of happiness and harmony, so that a person is capable of a full and free development of life. Peace means the salvation that belongs to those whose lives are totally in harmony with God's will (see Ps 34:15; Isa 32:17). The purpose of Jesus' life was to bring peace (John 14:27; 16:33; 20:19, 21, 26).

7:1-88 Offerings of the princes. Chapter 7 returns to the preparations for the departure from Sinai after the interlude of the regulations governing life in the camp and in the community. There has been no passage of time from the date of the census (1:1, 18), which occurred exactly one month after the completion, erection, and consecration of the Dwelling (v. 1; Exod 40:2, 17; see the commentary on 1:1-3). The elaborate description of gifts creates a scene of dedication to the Lord as the tension heightens in the last preparations for the march (chs. 7-9).

The chapter is divided into two unequal sections. In the first, verses 1-9, the princes give wagons with oxen. In the second, verses 10-88, there is an elaborate listing of the gifts presented by each of the leaders.

The princes, the heads of the ancestral houses, are the same leaders of the people who assisted Moses with the census (v. 2; see the commentary on 1:4-19a). These men contribute six wagons and twelve oxen for use in the transport of the sanctuary (v. 3). The vehicles and animals will carry the sacred objects on the long journey through the wilderness.

In the stylistic pattern of Yahweh's word

spoken and obeyed (vv. 4, 6), Moses is told to accept the offering and to assign the wagons to the Levites for use in carrying out their duties (v. 5). Moses gives two wagons with four oxen to the Gershonites (v. 7), whose responsibility is the tent itself and all the cloth hangings (3:25-26; 4:24-26); and four wagons with eight oxen to the Merarites (v. 8), who attend to the physical structure of the sanctuary (3:36-37; 4:31-32). Only the Kohathites, who take care of the most sacred objects, including the ark (3:28b, 31; 4:4-15), have to carry the carefully covered parcels on their shoulders (v. 9).

The remainder of the text (vv. 10-88) consists of Yahweh's command that the offerings brought by the princes for the dedication be presented on successive days (vv. 10-11); it gives a repetitive and detailed description of the gifts offered by each leader (vv. 12-83) and a final summary, with an accounting of the total number of gifts (vv. 84-88).

While the leaders are the same as those named as Moses' assistants in 1:5-15, their sequence corresponds to that of the tribes in the camp in 2:1-34 and again in the order of the march in 10:14-28 (see the commentary on 2:1-34). The privileged position of the Judah group reflects the importance of that tribe in the reestablishment of the religious center for the people who return from exile.

The gifts presented by each prince are identical in order and quantity. They are recounted in precise formulation, except for slight grammatical variation in verse 19. The only changes are in the names of the leaders and tribes. The princes bring gifts for all regular offerings—for the holocaust, the sin offering, and the peace offering. They also present silver plates and silver basins full of flour mixed with oil for the cereal offering, and a gold dish with incense. This exhaustively repetitive and detailed description of the offerings emphasizes the generosity of the leaders and has as its intention example and exhortation regarding provisions for the place of worship and its cultic celebrations. The text intentionally does not specify the offerings. The focus is not distracted from the liberality in giving.

The text concludes with a kind of accountant's report of the number of gifts presented on the occasion of the dedication of the altar (v. 84a). There is a precise listing of the numerous gifts (v. 84b), weights of the precious metals (vv. 85-86), and the number of each kind of animal offered (vv. 87-88) to reveal the extent of the princes' generosity in offering such gifts for the worship of God.

This display of gifts is a suitable conclusion to the preparation of the sanctuary and the worship therein. The Priestly writer's intention in re-creating this ideal scene in the wilderness is that it will be emulated in the postexilic community, where the people of Israel appropriately gather about the Presence among them, where everything unclean is purified, where total consecration is encouraged, and where the people tend to regular worship and contribute generously to the support of worship and the priests.

7:89 The voice. Appended to the description of the people of God gathered about the Dwelling in readiness for worship is a short piece that seems incomplete in itself but in reality concludes more than the particular chapter to which it is attached. The verse tells of Moses entering the meeting tent to communicate with the Lord (see Exod 33:7-11). Though Moses hears *the voice,* the message is lost to the reader. It is probable that the text is intended to convey the idea that the divine presence does indeed dwell in the holy place, and from there will speak to the people through Moses. The hearing of Yahweh's voice is the purpose of the entire preparation of the Dwelling.

At Sinai, where instructions for the construction of the Dwelling were communicated to Moses, the Lord promised that when the holy place was complete, "I will meet you . . . and from above the propitiatory, between the two cherubim on the ark of the commandments, I will tell you all the commands that I wish you to give the Israelites" (Exod 25:22). Our text is the direct fulfillment of Yahweh's promise.

The "propitiatory," sometimes called the "mercy seat," is a slab of gold set on top of the ark, where the covenant document is kept (see Exod 26:34). At either end of the propitiatory are facing cherubim, with wings extended in a kind of canopy over the ark. This is the highest place of atonement, where, on the Day of Atonement, the priest burns incense and sprinkles the blood of the sacrifice to cleanse the people from all their sins (Exod 25:17-22; 37:6-9). At this place the people turn again to

the covenant and the hearing of the voice that bonds them with Yahweh.

8:1-4 The lampstand. Activities continue in readying the camp as the place where Yahweh is present and worshiped. In accord with the Lord's word (vv. 1, 3), Aaron sets up the seven lamps. This event culminates what had been commanded at Sinai. Instructions for the material and design of the lampstand were presented in Exod 25:31-40. Verse 4 corresponds exactly with that description. A detailed account of the making of the lampstand is given in Exod 37:17-24. Finally, the lampstand is set up against the south curtain of the meeting tent, opposite the table at the north end (Exod 40:22-25).

Emphasis in our text is upon the direction of the light "toward the front of the lampstand" (vv. 2-3; see Exod 25:37). This positioning of the wicks in the lamps of oil is necessary to focus the light in one direction. As the only source of light in the meeting tent, the wicks are set to cast light upon the table on which the bread of the Presence is placed (Exod 40:23).

8:5-26 Purification of the Levites. Continuing emphasis on complete dedication to Yahweh focuses our attention on the ritual for the consecration of the Levites. The text first outlines the rites as well as the purposes for the Levites' dedication in the pattern of God's word given (vv. 5-19) and obeyed (vv. 20-22), then designates the limiting age for Levitical service (vv. 23-26).

Earlier, in chapters 3 and 4, we learned about the census and duties of the Levites. Here the emphasis is on the Levites as a special offering to Yahweh. They "belong to Yahweh" (vv. 14, 16, 18); they are "taken from among the Israelites" (vv. 6, 14, 16, 18) and "dedicated" (vv. 16, 19) for service as a special contribution (vv. 11, 13, 15, 21; see the discussion below on the wave offering).

When the Levite reaches the age of service, he submits to a rite of purification (v. 7). He is first sprinkled with the "water of remission," that is, water that effects the forgiveness of sins. He then shaves the hair from his entire body, thereby removing all imperfection and rendering future growth pure and clean. Last of all, he washes his clothes to make them clean, just as the Israelites did at Sinai to ready themselves for the divine presence (Exod 19:10, 14).

These Levites are clearly distinguished from the priest who is consecrated with oil (Exod 29:7; Lev 8:12) and adorned with completely new garments (Exod 28:40-43; 29:8-9; Lev 8:13). The Levites are men taken from among the people to represent the people. To dramatize this representation, the Levites come before the assembled community. The people "lay their hands" upon them (vv. 9-10). The dedication of the Levites substitutes for the consecration of the first-born of every Israelite family (vv. 16-18; see 3:11-13, 40-51). The Levites thus serve in the place and in the name of the community. Their service in the care of the sanctuary is a kind of protection so that no harm will come to anyone who might approach the sanctuary unworthily (v. 19).

For the sacrifice, the Levites bring offerings for a holocaust and a sin offering (vv. 8, 12). Each Levite lays his hands on the head of the animals to demonstrate his giving of himself totally to God. The one bull and the cereal, like a banquet meal, symbolize union between Yahweh and the Levite, and are therefore wholly consumed. The other bull is offered to atone for sin.

The priest participates by offering the Levite as a "wave offering" (vv. 11, 13; also vv. 15, 21). The ritual for other occasions would be for the priest to put a share of the sacrifice into the hands of the offerer, who would return it to the priest. The priest would receive this share as the portion for his own use. The motion of this giving back and forth and to Yahweh resembles a waving. On this day of dedication the priest receives the Levite himself, who is given as the share from all Israel for the use and service of the priest (vv. 13-14; see 3:5-10). The Levite enters the service of the sanctuary as a subordinate to the Aaronite priests (v. 19). He belongs to Yahweh and takes care of the place where Yahweh dwells among the people.

The Levites engage in this special service of the sanctuary only during their prime years. The age limits given are between twenty-five and fifty years old (vv. 24-25). Apparently the time for initiation into service varies according to need and numbers of men available. In chapter 4, the age given for beginning service is thirty years old (vv. 35, 39, 43, 47); in other texts, twenty is given as the entry age (1 Chr 23:24; 2 Chr 31:17; Ezra 3:8).

There are no variations for the age of retirement from service. Once the Levite has reached the age of fifty, he may assist the younger Levites in their work, but he may no longer be responsible for particular duties (v. 26).

9:1-14 The second Passover. A sense of excitement is created with a series of final preparations for departure from the wilderness of Sinai. It is the prescribed time for the celebration of Passover (vv. 1-5), which was first celebrated on the eve of deliverance from bondage in Egypt (see Exod 12–13). The legislation for keeping the feast is enjoined by Moses in the style of Yahweh's command (vv. 1-3), followed by obedient execution of the command (vv. 4-5). Moses commands the people to celebrate the feast when the same calendar date and time come around again, that is, at the beginning of the year in the month of Abib in the evening of the fourteenth day (vv. 2-3, 5; see Exod 12:2, 6, 18; 13:4; Lev 23:5).

The remainder of the text presents real-life situations that interfere with the observance of Passover. We find here an example of new instructions that become the precedent for subsequent practice. The people consult Moses regarding these problems, and Moses seeks direction from Yahweh to answer them (v. 8; see 15:34; 27:5; Lev 24:10-23 for other examples of seeking a decision from Yahweh).

The first situation is one of uncleanness. What should a person do who has become ritually unclean from contact with a corpse (v. 6; see 19:11-22) but who desires to participate in the feast (v. 7)? The instruction given in response includes another situation—that of a person who "is absent on a journey" (v. 10). While the case of uncleanness reflects the wilderness situation, this latter case suggests a later time when people traveled abroad and the practice of observing the feast in the central sanctuary prevailed (see Deut 16:2; Ezra 6:16-22).

The answer to these situations is the stipulation that a secondary feast might be celebrated one month later at the same time and in accord with all the laws for the feast (vv. 11-12; see Exod 12:8-10). According to this provision, one who is unclean might be purified, and one who is absent on a journey might be able to observe the feast on this later date. That this supplementary legislation was actually observed is evident in the case of Hezekiah. The Chronicler (2 Chr 30:1-5) records the occasion when Hezekiah invited the people from the northern tribes to Jerusalem for the feast. To accommodate the situation, the Passover feast was observed during the second month that year.

This provision must not be misconstrued, however, to exempt people from observance of the feast on the specified day for just any reason. From the tone of verse 13, only accidental circumstances or situations beyond one's control are legitimate exemptions. Those who excuse themselves from this community observance for reasons of neglect bring exclusion from the community upon themselves. The text says that they "shall be cut off from [their] people" (v. 13).

The second situation pertains to aliens or foreigners who wish to keep the feast. This is an issue that must have arisen time and again in the course of Israelite history. The problem is also addressed in Exod 12:43-49 in the regulations for the Passover feast. What we find in Numbers corresponds exactly. The stranger who has accepted circumcision, the one who "lives among you" (v. 14), meaning one who has accepted the God of the Israelites, may participate in the feast. There are no exceptions to the rules and regulations for these individuals, however. They will observe the feast in exactly the same manner as the natives.

9:15-23 The cloud and the Presence. The time has come for departure from the wilderness site. The great event at Sinai reaches its conclusion at this point. The Dwelling is now complete; it is filled with the "Glory of the Lord" and the "cloud settles down upon it" (Exod 40:34-35).

This cloud is the visible sign of the divine presence in the Dwelling. Where the cloud is visible, Yahweh is present. It manifests Yahweh "in the midst of this people" (Num 14:14). The cloud guided the people as they fled from Egypt (Exod 13:21-22), and it hid them from the approaching Egyptians (Exod 14:19, 24). When the cloud is visible over the meeting tent, Moses enters the tent to speak with the Lord (Exod 33:9-10; Num 12:5). This same cloud will determine Israel's movements on the long journey through the wilderness (Exod 40:36-38; Num 10:12). It hovers over the Dwelling by day, and at night it takes on the appearance of fire (vv. 15-16).

With the focus on Yahweh's presence in the midst of the people under the symbol of the cloud, the author stresses two points that are important for the generations of believers who will read or hear the story over and over again. The first is that the cloud determines the length of Israel's stay in a given place (vv. 19-22). Sometimes the stay is long; at times it is for a few days; sometimes it is only from evening to morning. The time of departure and the time for setting up camp are in no way self-determined. As the people embark on their journey, every phase of movement will be in response to the cloud.

Second, the point being made emphatically is that Yahweh speaks through the cloud. Two phrases emphasize that the Israelites obediently heed Yahweh's direction in the breaking and setting up of the camp. They move "at the bidding of the Lord" (vv. 18, 20, 23), an expression used seven times over; they "obey the Lord" (v. 19), and they "heed the charge of the Lord" (v. 23). Israel conforms totally to the will of God every step of the way on the long trek toward the land. The picture is of an ideal time when the people listen to the voice of God and comply willingly with God's instructions and commands.

10:1-10 Two silver trumpets. Our attention turns from the cloud as the Lord's guiding presence to the silver trumpets, the instruments used to assemble and move the community (v. 2). Known from the period of the postexilic community, the association of the trumpets with the wilderness generation reinforces the realization that the Priestly author intends to merge the ideal wilderness community gathered about the holy place with the worshiping community of the later period, when the people are being instructed in the ideals for living properly in the presence of a holy God.

These trumpets are blown in a sustained blast to give the signal for assembly. The specific verb "blown" is used in verses 3-4 and again in verses 7a, 8, 10 to indicate the type of signal. When both are blown, the entire community is being called to assembly (v. 3); when one trumpet is blown, only the leaders are being called (v. 4).

The signal for setting out, whether on a journey or into war, is a series of short, staccato-like notes. The silver trumpets are mentioned here because the people are ready to set out on the journey. The preparations that have been undertaken as described in the preceding chapters are now complete, and the people are ready to move forward under the guiding protection of Yahweh. When the first alarm is given, the Judah group on the east side of the camp marches out (v. 5); at the second alarm, the Reuben group, positioned south of the sanctuary, follows; then the Ephraim group from the west side of the camp; and finally the Dan group from the north side (v. 6; see ch. 2 for the arrangement of the tribes around the Dwelling). The tribes are readied to move out in an orderly manner and in the order of precedence.

The remainder of the text regulates the use of the trumpets once the people have come into "their own land" (v. 9a). It is the task of the priests to blow the trumpets (v. 8). This practice is frequently mentioned in the literature of the postexilic period (see 1 Chr 15:24; 16:6; 42; 2 Chr 7:6; Neh 12:35; 41). The trumpets are used to signal entry into battle (v. 9; see 2 Chr 13:12). They are blown most often to announce the observance of the various feasts, to summon the community to worship, and to express thanksgiving on joyous occasions (v. 10; see 2 Chr 5:12-13; 29:26-28; Ezra 3:10-11).

The text tells us that the reason the trumpet is blown is to cause God to "remember . . . and save" (v. 9b; see also v. 10b). The blowing of the trumpet is an act of prayer and dependence, a calling upon God to be present especially in situations of need and celebration.

This passage, and indeed the entire section in chapters 1–10, ends with the recognition formula, "I, the Lord, am your God" (v. 10c; see p. 146 for an explanation). It was Yahweh who invited Israel into the unique relationship that resulted in so many blessings. It is Yahweh who acts at this moment to be with the people, to lead them, protect them, and bring them safely to their own land.

ON THE JOURNEY FROM SINAI TO MOAB

Num 10:11–22:1

Up to this point the people have been encamped in the wilderness of Sinai. They now embark on a journey that will include a number of stops in the course of many years and will end on the plains of Moab, located across the Jordan River opposite the land of promise. This section begins with the departure from Sinai (10:12) and ends with the arrival at Moab (22:1). Throughout we will notice the journey formula and mention of various locations that make the reader aware of movement from site to site (10:12, 33; 11:35; 12:16; 20:1a, 22; 21:4, 10-20; 22:1). The Priestly writer uses a structure based on the tradition of the wilderness journey to support the record of events that happen along the way.

Many stories about the threat of danger, lack of food and water, tribal factions, and jealousies were passed down within the families who made the journey. These stories became the source from which our author gathered material to tell about the trials of the journey. The stories are found in chapters 11–14, 16–17, 20–21. Their narration is lively and very unlike the stylized language of the earlier chapters. These stories give the reader a glimpse of the very real struggles of people whom God had favored. They teach important lessons about the consequences for individuals and groups who turn from following God and the designated leaders. Directed at the community that is in passage from the wilderness of the Exile to their own land and in the process of resettlement and reorganization as a faith community, the stories provide lessons from history for future life.

Scattered throughout the narration of these chapters we find treasures of ancient poetry at 10:35-36; 12:6-8; 21:14-15, 17-18; 21:27b-30. These pieces survived from the time of the events they celebrate and allow the reader to hear what Israel itself sang, recited, and remembered.

As a kind of interruption to the dramatic action of these chapters, the author inserts some regulations in chapters 15, 18, 19. There is no apparent connection between the content of the narratives and these cultic regulations. They are directed to future generations, providing them with guidelines for living in a holy manner in the presence of a holy God.

Events in the Desert of Paran

(10:11–19:22)

10:11-28a Departure from Sinai. The departure from the wilderness is once again associated by date with the Exodus experience. After nearly a year's delay at Sinai—from the first day of the third month (Exod 19:1) to the twentieth day of the second month a year later (v. 11a)—and after final preparations that are telescoped to just nineteen days (compare Num 1:1), the signal is given for the beginning of the march.

The cloud covering the Dwelling rises from its place to signal movement from the camp (v. 11b; see the discussion on the cloud at 9:15-23). The cloud will guide the Israelites on the move until it settles in the desert of Paran, the first camping site on the continuing journey (v. 12). While the location is not certain, it is probable that this first stop was at Wadi Feiran, an oasis in the northern Sinai Peninsula south of the Negeb (see 13:17). The name Paran suggests that the author has the well-known Feiran oasis in mind.

The order of the march in verses 13-28 corresponds to the designated arrangement in the camp and the instructions for departure in 2:1-31, once again including mention of the leaders of the individual tribes. The Judah group from the east side of the Dwelling holds first place and leads the march (vv. 14-16). After them, the Levites, who transport the paraphernalia of the Dwelling, set out (v. 17; 2:17; see the duties of the Gershonites and Merarites in 4:21-33). Next come the three tribes headed by Reuben (vv. 18-20), followed by the sacred objects of the Dwelling carried by the Kohathites (v. 21; see 4:4-20). The sacred items are separated from the structure and coverings so that the tent might be readied at the new site in preparation for housing the ark, altar, table, and lampstand at the new campsite (v. 21b). The Ephraimite group follows the sacred objects (vv. 22-24), acting, no doubt, as a rear guard. Finally, as "rear guard for all the camps," the Dan group follows last of all (vv. 25-27).

10:28b-32 Moses' brother-in-law as guide. The very practical need for human wisdom on the journey through the wilderness balances the story that has focused exclusively on divine guidance. Moses asks his brother-in-law Hobab, a Midianite (v. 29a), to serve as "eyes" for the people, because he "knows where [they] can camp in the desert" (v. 31). The Midianites are nomads who live in the wilderness and know its routes and camping places. Hobab is from the clan of Zipporah,

Moses' wife, who was, according to one tradition, the daughter of Reuel (see Exod 2:15-22). Elsewhere Jethro is the name of Moses' father-in-law (see Exod 3:1; 4:18; 18). The traditions agree that the father-in-law was a priest of Midian (Exod 2:16; 18:1).

In his bidding, Moses promises Hobab a share in the prosperity that the Lord has promised in the land (vv. 29b, 32). The implication is that those who associate themselves with the people of Yahweh share in the benefits that come as a result of Yahweh's covenant promise.

Hobab at first declines the invitation because he prefers to return to his own people (v. 30). This passage does not report Hobab's final answer. We presume his positive response, since Moses' relatives are mentioned among those who enter the land (see Judg 1:16; 4:11; 1 Sam 15:6. The Kenites named in these texts are part of the Midianite group).

10:33-36 The ark leads into the desert. Attention once again turns to the Lord's continual presence with the people. In the camp the cloud rested upon the sanctuary (v. 11), and on the march the cloud moves with the "ark of the covenant of the Lord" (v. 33) to lead the people forward. The ark, which traditionally was the portable seat of Yahweh's invisible presence, is specifically mentioned to show that Yahweh indeed moves with the people and leads them.

Inserted here is an ancient ritual cry that was recited over many years whenever the people of Israel engaged in warfare (see Pss 68:2; 132:8). One hymn is sung when the ark sets out with the troops (v. 35), another when it returns with them to the camp (v. 36). The hymns carry the tradition that Yahweh, the God of the armies, marches ahead to defeat the enemy.

The language of the hymn is clear. When the ark is moved, Yahweh arises and goes before the people to scatter their enemies. When the ark rests, Yahweh returns and sits enthroned in the midst of the troops.

According to tradition, the ark led the people through the wilderness, and it led the people into the land (see Josh 3:1-8). The ark remains with the people in the camp when they complain and prove themselves to be faithless.

11:1-3 Discontent at Taberah. No sooner have the people moved from Sinai than they do what they will do over and over again—they "complain in the hearing of the Lord" (v. 1). This first account of the people's discontent functions as a summary introduction in that it sets forth a pattern of behavior that will recur often in the stories of events in the wilderness. There is a predictable cycle of actions: the people complain (v. 1a); Yahweh's anger provokes punishment (v. 1b); the people cry to Moses to obtain relief (v. 2a); Moses intercedes on behalf of the people (v. 2b); Yahweh hears Moses' prayer (v. 2c).

There are actually two separate themes stressed in these stories. One theme is that of rebellion and punishment as characteristic of Israel's relation to Yahweh in the wilderness (see also Exod 14:11-22; 15:23-25a; 16:2-15; 17:1-7, though the telling in Numbers is highly stylized in comparison). The other theme is that of Moses as the intercessor to whom Yahweh responds with forgiveness and deliverance. This latter theme is especially important. Moses' unique leadership position and his authority are issues of such concern that the controversies regarding him are the basis for the stories in chapters 11–12 and 16–17.

The incident at Taberah is told to introduce the two major themes. There is no explanation of why the people complain nor any particulars about the fire sent as punishment. The cycle of rebellion and forgiveness moves quickly to the explanation for the name of the place (v. 3). The name Taberah derives from the verb "burn" or "consume." Stories were often told to explain the names of places. This feature is, in fact, a characteristic of the older stories (see, for example, Gen 16:13-14; 19:20-23; 21:31; 28:19-22; Exod 15:23; 17:7).

11:4-35 Complaint at Kibroth-hattaavah. Another incident, more complex in its structure, also ends with the explanation of the name of the place. Kibroth-hattaavah means "graves of greed" (v. 34). The story is about the people's complaint that they do not have enough meat in the wilderness. As a result, the people are fed with quail (vv. 4-9, 10, 13, 18-24a), and they also are punished for their greed (vv. 31-33).

Intertwined with the account about the craving for meat is a story about the sharing of Moses' leadership (vv. 11-12, 14-17, 24b-30). We will look at each story separately and consider how they are combined.

The account of the quail contains the elements of a typical complaint story. Two separate groups of people—the foreign element and the Israelites—complain about the lack of meat (v. 4). They long for the days in Egypt, when they enjoyed an abundance of fish and vegetables (v. 5). They are dissatisfied that all they have to eat is the manna, out of which they daily make loaves that taste like cakes with oil (vv. 6-9; see Exod 16:13-14, 31).

The "Lord became very angry" at the Israelites' display of greed (v. 10). Moses and Yahweh will each respond to the complaint. Rather than responding with intercession, Moses feels sorry for himself. He grieves that he alone must provide for the great multitude, saying, "Where can *I* get meat to give to all this people? They are crying to *me*" (v. 13). Moses presumes that it is his responsibility to find meat but expresses his inability to do so. Rather than seeking Yahweh's help, he shows resentment at the position in which he has been placed.

Yahweh, however, ignores Moses' lament and speaks to him in his capacity as mediator (vv. 18a, 24a). Yahweh responds, not to Moses' expressed concern, but directly to what the people have said. Yahweh makes plain that the people are in reality wishing to return to Egypt (vv. 18, 20b), thereby rejecting the Lord's deliverance. Yahweh instructs Moses to tell the people to "sanctify" themselves (v. 18), for they will receive meat in such abundance that they will become sick from it (vv. 19-20). Moses interjects again with a doubt about Yahweh's ability to provide the amount of meat that would be required to satisfy so many people (vv. 21-23).

In the fulfillment of Yahweh's word (vv. 31-34), Moses is conspicuously absent. Yahweh sends quail from the sea in great abundance. The people gather it (vv. 31-32), but before they can begin to eat it, Yahweh sends a plague to punish the greedy for their complaint (v. 33). Thus, the place was called "graves of greed," because those who were greedy were buried there (v. 34).

If we compare the elements in this story with those outlined in the incident at Taberah (vv. 1-3), it is obvious that Moses' response to the situation makes the difference. When Moses intercedes for the people, Yahweh responds with forgiveness (v. 2). In the incident of the quail, Moses' intercession is lacking, and the result is Yahweh's anger. By placing these stories side by side, the author is deliberately highlighting the effectiveness of Moses' intercession.

The lament of Moses (vv. 11-15) provides the link for the inclusion of the second story concerning the sharing of Moses' leadership. The issue raised by this lament is that he is burdened with the sole leadership of a people who are not his (vv. 12,14). Moses sees this as a punishment (v. 11), and his distress is so great that death is preferable (v. 15). Moses does not ask for help in leadership; he requests only the ultimate end of the burden.

Yahweh ignores Moses' death wish and takes up the matter of Moses' being *alone*. Yahweh instructs Moses to choose seventy elders and to bring them to the meeting tent (v. 16; see Exod 18:13-26 for the tradition regarding the selection of judges to help Moses with the care of the people). Yahweh will "take some of the spirit that is on [Moses] and will bestow it on [the elders], that they may share the burden" (v. 17). Moses does exactly as Yahweh has instructed (vv. 24b-25a). However, in the execution, a new element is added. In the sharing of Moses' spirit, nothing is said about sharing the burden with him (v. 25b). Instead, when the spirit rests on the elders, they prophesy (v. 25c). This story also supports the uniqueness of Moses' position as leader. Others may prophesy, but they cannot share the burden of the responsibility assigned to Moses—to communicate Yahweh's word and to bring the people safely into the land of promise (v. 12).

The theme of prophecy is continued in yet another story (vv. 26-30). Eldad and Medad, though not called elders, are among those chosen by Moses. Instead of going to the meeting tent with the seventy, they remain in the camp, where the spirit comes upon them also so that they prophesy (v. 26). Joshua, Moses' young assistant (see Exod 33:11), for some reason objects to this and pleads with Moses to stop them (vv. 27-28). Moses instead voices the wish that the "Lord might bestow his spirit" on all the people that they might all be prophets (v. 29). It is not Moses' spirit but rather Yahweh's spirit that is upon them. Moses approves of the distribution of Yahweh's spirit and is not concerned that his own prestige might be lost: "Are you jealous for my sake?" (v. 29). What appears to be a diminishing of Moses' position in the sharing

of the spirit leads instead to a further delineation of Moses' uniqueness in chapter 12, a delineation that focuses the prophetic role.

Before the next story, there is a brief note about the people's move from Kibroth-hattaavah to Hazeroth (v. 35), the site of the next incident of rebellion.

12:1-16 Jealousy of Aaron and Miriam. Opposition to Moses comes from those closest to him. The tradition holds that Aaron and Miriam accompanied Moses from the time of the Exodus event (Exod 15:20-21; see Exod 6:20). Miriam and Aaron challenge Moses on two accounts: his marriage to a Cushite woman (v. 1) and his unique position as sole spokesman for Yahweh (v. 2). We have here another story that is told in the pattern of rebellion and eventual forgiveness through the intercession of Moses (see the discussion on 11:1-3).

The reason for the complaint that Moses has married a Cushite woman is obscure, since there is no evidence for a marriage other than with Zipporah, a Midianite (see Exod 2:15-22; 4:24-26; 18:2-3). If, however, the reference to Cush is actually a parallel to Midian, as in Hab 3:7, then the complaint is in opposition to Moses' marriage with a foreigner. There is, in fact, a tradition recorded in Num 25:6-18 that polemicizes marriage with Midianites, who are described as archenemies of Israel. This complaint reflects a strong anti-Moses bias because of his foreign wife.

In the second complaint Miriam and Aaron challenge Moses on the ground that they are prophets as well as he—"Does the Lord not speak through us also?" (v. 2). This opposition reveals resentment against Moses' exclusive role as mediator between God and the people. This issue was raised in the preceding story (11:26-30). If all people can be prophets, does Moses have a claim to uniqueness? The response and punishment are such that they both clarify (vv. 6-8) and affirm (vv. 13-14) the authority of Moses.

Moses makes no response to the complaints. The text states that he is the "meekest man on the face of the earth" (v. 3). This statement has been interpreted as a description of a person with personal honor and integrity of character. In spite of opposition, Moses will honorably stand by his responsibility as leader when he is called upon to intercede for Miriam (v. 13).

The response to the complaint comes directly from Yahweh in the form of an instruction (vv. 4-8) and a punishment (vv. 9-15). Overhearing the complaint, Yahweh summons Moses, Aaron, and Miriam to the meeting tent (v. 4), calls Aaron and Miriam aside (v. 5), and instructs them with a detailed account of the difference between Moses and a prophet (vv. 6-8). The words that Yahweh speaks express a tradition about Moses that survives in a piece of ancient poetry. The poem states that Yahweh communicates with the prophet in "visions" and "dreams" (v. 6), but with Moses, Yahweh speaks "face to face" and "plainly" (v. 8). Moses' relationship is more personal and intimate. He beholds the "presence of the Lord" (v. 8). He is thus set over all others as the peerless mediator of Yahweh's word. Aaron and Miriam stand rebuffed with the final question upholding the authority of Moses—"Did you not fear to speak against my servant Moses?" (v. 8b).

After this rebuke, Yahweh responds in anger (v. 9). Miriam is made snow-white with leprosy (v. 10). Aaron thereupon appeals to Moses for help and identifies with the punishment in his confession that both have sinned (v. 11). Moses prays for her healing and by his intercession wins Yahweh's forgiveness. Moses' authority receives legitimation and confirmation in the restoration of Miriam (vv. 14-16).

Miriam's leprosy is described as being "snow-white" (v. 9) and is compared to the appearance of a stillborn child (v. 12). She is fully restored after a period of seven days outside the camp (vv. 14-15a). To illuminate the situation, we look at the law pertaining to a leprous person in Lev 13:9-17. In summary, the law states that the leprous person is brought to the priest. If the leprosy covers the whole body and the body has turned white, the priest pronounces the leper clean. Miriam's whiteness and her confinement outside the camp for seven days point not to active but to burnt-out leprosy. Miriam was punished with a post-leprous condition. Her exclusion from the camp is for the period necessary to verify her cleanness.

During the period of Miriam's confinement, the people remain encamped at Hazeroth (v. 15b). Afterward they set out and settle in the desert of Paran (v. 16; see the discussion on 10:11-28).

Chapters 13-14 present the continuing drama of the people's rebellion, even when they are in sight of the Promised Land. These chapters are developed from a number of ancient traditions that the Priestly author weaves into one explanation for Israel's long sojourn in the wilderness. Though we have one story, we will approach the content in sections to facilitate reading.

13:1-24 Scouts enter Canaan. In accord with Yahweh's word (v. 1), Moses sends a delegation of scouts to explore the Promised Land (v. 2). The Israelites are encamped in the desert of Paran (v. 3a) at Kadesh (see v. 26), a well-known oasis located southwest of the southern tip of the Dead Sea. They are situated directly south of the Promised Land and in range of entrance. From this location Moses dispatches twelve leaders, one from each tribe, to look around (vv. 3b-16).

The names of the leaders are set in a tribal list that is a rather free arrangement of that in 1:5-15. The leaders are not the same as those appearing earlier (see also 7:12-83). And except for Caleb and Joshua, who play a major role in this story (13:30; 14:6, 24, 30), the leaders are not mentioned again by name. There is a special note that Moses has changed the name of Hoshea to Joshua (v. 16). Joshua, which means "Yahweh is salvation," is related to Hoshea, which means "salvation." Joshua receives his new name in preparation for his future role as successor to Moses (see 27:12-23). It is Joshua who will finally lead the next generation of Israelites into the land (14:30; see Deut 31:7-8; Josh 1:1-11).

The scouts are sent into the Negeb, a parched area south of Judah, to proceed into the highlands that run the length of central Canaan (v. 17). They reach Hebron, a city located about twenty miles south of Jerusalem, where three tribes are settled (v. 22; see Josh 15:14; Judg 1:20). The territory around Hebron has a reputation for its grapes, pomegranates, and figs. It is because of this that the place is called Wadi Eshcol, the "valley of the cluster," and the exaggerated story is told about two men required to carry the grapes (vv. 23-24).

One tradition says that the men scouted from the desert of Zin as far as Hamath (v. 21); that is, they went from the southern frontier to the northern limit of the land. The desert of Zin is part of the desert of Paran near

Kadesh (see 20:1; 27:14; 33:36), and Hamath, a pass near the Orontes, is located in Lebanon at the northern border of Israel's territory (see 34:8; Josh 13:5; Judg 3:3; 2 Kgs 14:25; Amos 6:14).

Moses instructed the scouts to secure information about the land and the people (v. 18), the towns and fortifications (v. 19), the terrain and the soil. He also told them to bring back some of the fruit of the land (v. 20).

13:25-33 Return of the scouts. After forty days, a stay of significant duration to adequately survey the situation (v. 25), the scouts return to Kadesh, where they report to Moses, Aaron, and the entire community and present them with the fruit (v. 26). They describe the land as flowing "with milk and honey" (v. 27), an expression that traditionally identifies the land as that promised by Yahweh (see Exod 3:8, 17; 13:5; 33:3, and frequently in Deuteronomy). But they quickly add that the inhabitants are powerful descendants of the Anakim, and the towns are well fortified (vv. 28, 31-33). A tradition prevailed that the Anakim were a numerous, tall, and strong people (see Deut 1:28; 2:21) who had to be defeated when Israel entered the land (Josh 11:21-22; 14:12, 15). That the population was mixed—Amalekites, Hittites, Jebusites, Amorites, and Canaanites (v. 29)—also accords with tradition regarding the inhabitants before the conquest. The Amalekites were encountered near Sinai (Exod 17:8-16); the Hittites were early inhabitants in Hebron (Gen 23:13-19); the Jebusites controlled Jerusalem (2 Sam 5:6-9). The Amorites were early inhabitants of Canaan who were later forced from the coastal plains and the Jordan valley to settle in the highlands. They were part of the indigenous Canaanite population. This latter group had settled in the fertile valleys and coastal region.

The scouts paint a fearful picture and recommend that the Israelites abort their attempt to enter the land because they will never survive the might of the inhabitants (vv. 31-33). The scouts thus challenge the guidance of Yahweh and the promise of the land to their ancestor Abraham. They, in fact, reject the land Yahweh is about to give them. Only Caleb encourages the people to proceed and expresses confidence in their success (v. 30). The interjection of Caleb at this point prepares

for his role, along with Joshua, as one of the leaders who trusts the God of Israel (14:6-9). In tradition, the descendants of Caleb controlled the bountiful territory of Hebron and its surroundings (Josh 15:13-14; Judg 1:20). This story in Numbers provides an explanation of why Caleb and his descendants were favored with such a possession.

With the report from the scouts, the stage is set for the rebellion of the people. In this sense, the whole of chapter 13 functions as an introduction to the cycle of rebellion and forgiveness that follows in chapter 14.

14:1-10 The people's complaint. The whole community grumbles against Moses and Aaron on account of the report from the scouts (vv. 1-2a). The people reject Yahweh when they wish that they had never left Egypt. They are fearful of the disaster that awaits their families and themselves (vv. 2b-3). They conclude that it would be better to return to the security of bondage in Egypt, and they even decide to choose a leader of their own mind (vv. 3b-4).

Moses and Aaron respond by falling to the ground in helplessness (v. 5). Caleb and Joshua tear their garments in grief (v. 6). They appeal to the people, reminding them that the land is good (v. 7), that the Lord promised the land and will bring them to it (v. 8). They exhort the people to trust Yahweh who is with them (see Exod 33). And they remind the people that they need not fear the inhabitants, because "their defense has left them" (v. 9). The term "defense" is actually the word "shadow," which means literally that the inhabitants are left exposed and vulnerable to the ferocity of the sun, and metaphorically that Yahweh has removed the protection of their local gods. The inhabitants who have no protection will be "food for us," that is, they will be easily consumed.

The words of Caleb and Joshua are not heeded. The people rebel and threaten to stone them (v. 10a) and would have succeeded if Yahweh had not intervened. The "glory of the Lord appeared at the meeting tent" (v. 10b). The phrase "glory of the Lord" is always used by the Priestly author to express the revelation of Yahweh in power and majesty.

14:11-19 Punishment and Moses' intercession. Yahweh, manifest to all Israel, laments to Moses about the contempt of the people and their refusal to believe in spite of all the signs (v. 11). Yahweh announces the obliteration of the whole people and promises to start anew by creating a greater and mightier nation from Moses (v. 12).

Moses intercedes at this point and persuades Yahweh to set aside this harsh judgment (vv. 13-19). Moses pleads boldly, using Yahweh's reputation among the other nations as his argument (vv. 13-16). He asserts that Yahweh is known as a God in the midst of the people, a God who accompanies them by day and night. Should this people be annihilated, the nations will have cause to say that Yahweh did not have the power to bring them into the land and therefore killed them in the desert. Moses advises that Yahweh's honor and standing among the gods are at stake.

Quoting a confessional formulary from Exod 34:6-7, Moses suggests that the Lord's power will be better shown, not by killing, but by patience, kindness, forgiveness, and by just punishment of sin (vv. 17-18). Moses summarizes his request by asking that Yahweh forgive the iniquity of this people according to the greatness of the covenant love, just as Yahweh has forgiven them many times from Egypt until now (v. 19). Moses is pleading with Yahweh to preserve the covenant relationship that was made when Yahweh brought the people from Egypt. He thus appeals to Yahweh's covenant faithfulness and at the same time recognizes Yahweh's utter freedom to maintain or break off relationship with the people. The forgiveness that Moses asks is the preservation of relationship between Yahweh and the people, and the decision not to disinherit the present community by creating a new nation from Moses or from anyone else. Because Israel's only existence is relationship with Yahweh, there is room for punishment that does not include dissolution of the covenant.

14:20-38 The sentence. Yahweh answers Moses' prayer by announcing forgiveness (v. 20), that is, the continuation of the fundamental covenant relationship that is the basis of Israel's existence. But there is punishment also. In the strong language of an oath (v. 21; see also vv. 28, 35), Yahweh asserts that those who rebelled will be denied entry into the land on account of their infidelity: "not one shall see the land which I promised on oath to their fathers" (vv. 22-23). Only Caleb, who trusted the Lord's promise, will

enter the land, and his descendants will inherit it (v. 24; see Josh 14:6-15). So also is Joshua spared the punishment (vv. 30b, 38; 32:12).

Yahweh continues with a description of precisely which members will be denied entry into the land: all those who "grumble against me" (v. 27) and those over twenty years old who were registered in the census (v. 29). Only the children, the next generation, will enter the land to enjoy it (v. 31). The Israelites are thus sentenced to remain in the wilderness for forty years, a year for each day of the scouting (v. 34). The children have to suffer the sin of their parents by languishing with them in the wilderness until the last of the generation has lived out a natural life (vv. 33, 35). While the community is being punished, Yahweh's covenant continues and endures.

There is a more immediate judgment on the scouts who instigated the grumbling by their discouraging report. They are struck with a plague and die (vv. 36-37).

This story of rebellion answers two questions. First, it gives the reason for Israel's prolonged stay in the wilderness, so that the whole generation that came from Egypt perished there. Because the Israelites rejected the land, they are rejected from entering the land. Second, it explains why Israel journeyed east to enter the land from the Transjordan rather than taking the more direct route from the south. The explanation given is that because the Amalekites and Canaanites live in the valleys, Israel must return south and travel the road that will take them around the Dead Sea (v. 25; see 20:14–22:1 for the details of the journey).

14:39-45 Unsuccessful invasion. Another story of rebellion arises from the issue of the route to be taken for entry into the land. It is an account of failure because of refusal to obey the word of God.

The people grieve when Moses tells them that they are to turn and head southward away from the Canaanites and Amalekites (v. 39; see vv. 25, 43a, 45). The people admit that they were wrong when earlier they listened to the report of the scouts (13:27-33; 14:1-4), and they resolve to head directly north into the foothills of Canaan (v. 40). Moses admonishes them that they are acting disobediently. He warns that failure is certain because the Lord is *not* in their midst (vv. 41-43). This head-strong people dare to set out without the presence of the ark, the leadership of Moses, and in opposition to the word of Yahweh (v. 44).

This is a story of failure. It demonstrates the consequences of acting apart from the word that is the basis for covenant relationship with Yahweh. Israel faces the enemy on its own counsel and is pursued as far as Hormah, a city located in the region of Beersheba (v. 45; the ultimate defeat of Hormah is reported in 21:1-3).

The long section in chapters 11–14 contains five stories of rebellion: the incident at Taberah, the greed for meat, the jealousy toward Moses, the rejection of the land, and the unsuccessful invasion. There follows an insertion of five ritual laws that have no apparent connection. All the instructions are intended for the guidance of the community when it has reached the land. The laws are thus future-oriented. They reflect modifications arising from everyday practice.

15:1-16 Secondary offerings. Every dimension of life belongs to Yahweh; therefore, all laws are directly attributed to Yahweh. Each directive is the Lord's explicit instruction (v. 1). Each focuses on the time when Israel will have entered the land (v. 2).

The first law outlines the quantities of grain, oil, and wine that are to accompany the "sweet-smelling oblation" given for the various sacrifices (v. 3). The phrase "sweet-smelling" means that the oblation is acceptable to the Lord. It is based on the idea that God smells and delights in the sacrifice presented on occasions of joy.

Each sacrifice, whether of a lamb (vv. 4-5), a ram (vv. 6-7), an ox (vv. 8-10), or goat (v. 11), should be presented with a proportional weight of cereal, oil, and wine. The quantities of cereal, oil, and wine increase with the size of the animal.

It is uncertain why a grain offering and a drink offering are to accompany each sacrifice. It could be the idea of providing a complete meal. It could also be the idea of giving from the natural resources of the land (see Deut 7:13). Whatever the meaning of the sacrifice, the text is concerned with giving God a full and acceptable offering.

There is an additional note which stresses that the instruction applies to the native and the alien alike (vv. 13-16). It states that the foreigner who has made a home among the Israelites has equal rights as well as the corresponding obligations. The detail of this note suggests that the presence of "resident aliens" is a matter of considerable concern. The principle of the law—"Before the Lord you and the alien are alike" (v. 15)—reflects a basic attitude of justice that witnesses to the authenticity of Israelite faith.

15:17-21 Offering from the first batch of dough. The second regulation belongs in the category of first things belonging to Yahweh (see Exod 13:11-16; Deut 26:1-2; Num 18:12-13). The text is focused on the future time in the land (vv. 18-19a) and applies to all future generations (v. 21a).

The regulation specifically identifies the cake made from the coarse grain taken from the threshing floor (v. 20). Since the whole harvest is a gift from God, the first dough made from the harvest grain belongs to God.

In the temple period, the cake made from the first dough was presented to the priest to eat. This offering symbolized the giving back to God from the abundance that was given. This offering was part of the priests' provisions (see 18:13; Lev 23:10-11).

15:22-31 Sin offerings. The third instruction is divided into two sections: the offerings for sin or violations that are "inadvertent" or unintentional (vv. 22-29), and punishment for willful sin (vv. 30-31).

In the case of the unintentional violation of instructions, separate provision is made for atonement when the community is involved (vv. 22-26) and when an individual is involved (vv. 27-29). Prescribed sacrifices (vv. 24, 27) are to be offered in atonement by the priest so that the sin committed unwittingly may be forgiven (vv. 25, 28). There is specific mention again that the regulation applies to the native and alien alike (vv. 26, 29).

When it is a case of deliberate sin, an "insult" to the Lord, no sacrifice can atone. The individual, native or alien, who has defiantly "despised the word" or "broken [the Lord's] commandment" has, in fact, chosen to be cut off from the community of God's people. The punishment for this person is separation from the community.

15:32-36 The sabbath-breaker. The fourth regulation is given as the solution to a specific behavior that is described. The people find a man gathering wood on the sabbath day (v. 32). They keep him in custody because there is "no clear decision as to what should be done with him" (v. 34). The case in point is an example of the way new regulations arose that would be normative for future similar situations (see the commentary on 9:6-13).

The law of the sabbath clearly states that work is forbidden (see Exod 20:8-11), and the death penalty is the prescribed punishment for breaking the law of the sabbath (see Exod 31:14-15; 35:2-3). What is unclear is the form of execution to be used in the case of deliberate violation of the law.

The answer given is that the man is to be stoned by the whole community outside the camp (v. 35). This person is thus excluded from the community symbolically by being led outside the camp as well as physically by the death sentence (v. 36). The strict observance of the sabbath took on greater importance after the Exile and continued into the time of Jesus (see John 9:16).

15:37-41 Tassels on the cloak. The fifth regulation makes the ancient practice of wearing tassels on the end of the outer garment a requirement with a specific meaning (see Deut 22:12). This practice survived into Judaism (Matt 9:20; 14:36; 23:5; Mark 6:56; Luke 8:44).

The tassels are attached with a violet cord (v. 38) and function to catch the eye. They thereby serve as a reminder of the Lord's presence and commands (v. 39). The external ornament is intended to continually remind the people that a holy God is among them and that to live in the presence of a holy God, they must observe the commandments by which covenant is preserved. Observance of the commandments is the mark of a holy people (v. 40).

The reason for observing the instruction is that Yahweh is present and will continue to be with a faithful people. The formulary "I, the Lord, am your God who . . . brought you out of Egypt that I, the Lord, *may be* your God" (v. 41) is a reminder of the very basis of Israel's existence. It concludes the last instruction as well as the series of five instructions. The people are invited to obedient response to demonstrate loyalty to covenant. If the covenant relationship is broken, it is because Israel has turned from observing the word that the Lord has given for their direction since Egypt.

The section 16:1–17:5 picks up the theme of rebellion once again. This is one continuous narrative made up of two separate stories of rebellion: Korah and company against Aaron (16:1a, 2-11, 16-24, 32b, 35; 17:1-5), and the two Reubenites, Dathan and Abiram, against Moses (16:1b, 12-15, 25-32a, 33-34). Each story reflects ancient struggles for power that broke out again and again in the course of history. The Priestly tradition is responsible for knitting the two incidents into a continuous narrative of simultaneous rebellion.

16:1-11 Rebellion of Korah. The report begins with a presentation of the lineage of Korah, son of Izhar, son of Kohath, son of Levi (v. 1a; see Exod 6:17-25, esp. vv. 18, 21, 24). Generally, the longer the list of names, the more significant the individual. It is noteworthy that Korah is a Levite and belongs to the family of Kohathites, to whom is assigned care of the most sacred items of the sanctuary (see 3:27-32; 4:1-20). In the execution of their service, however, they are always subservient to the priest (4:15, 20).

Korah's rebellion undoubtedly arises from a long struggle for greater authority. The Kohathites are allowed to come near the holy vessels, but if they touch them, they will die. They carry them in transport, but only after the sacred utensils have been covered by the priests. Korah, a leader among the Kohathites, leads the rebellion against the authority of the priests. The tension between these groups will come to the forefront again at the very time when the document is being written down by the Priestly writer. There was a struggle to secure the priesthood by the Zadokites, descendants of Eleazar (see 3:1-4, esp. v. 4b; 1 Chr 24; Ezek 44:10-31). The story in Numbers reflects the supremacy of Eleazar and the Zadokites (17:1-5). The Levitic Korahites had to be content to be doorkeepers (1 Chr 26:1) and temple singers (Pss 42–49, 84, 85, 87, 88).

The story of Korah itself reflects two major conflicts. In one, Korah and the two hundred fifty conspirators maintain that the tribe of Levi, which includes Moses, Aaron, and their descendants, is not more sacred than the other tribes (vv. 2-3). They argue that because Yahweh is in the midst of the community, Moses and Aaron have no right to claim holiness for themselves above the rest. Each member of the community is holy because of

Yahweh's presence. A second conflict represents Korah and his followers as Levites who oppose the authority of Aaron and attempt to take the power of the priesthood for themselves (vv. 8-11). The Levites are not content with the special status assigned them in the service of the sanctuary but desire the full authority of the priesthood. These two very ancient and very real struggles—recognition of the holiness of each person and conflict over the privileged status of the priesthood—merge into one story of rebellion to which Moses responds.

Moses falls prostrate (v. 4); he does not intercede. Instead, he lets Yahweh decide who is the holy one and whom God chooses to come near (v. 5). This rebellion against the leaders is recognized as a rebellion against Yahweh to be resolved by Yahweh (v. 11).

Moses instructs Korah and his followers to prepare censers with fire and incense (vv. 6-7), an action reserved to the priest. Moses is telling Korah to take the priesthood and then see whom Yahweh will choose.

16:12-15 Rebellion of Dathan and Abiram. The lineage of Dathan and Abiram appears at the head of the chapter in the merging of the two separate stories. They are descendants of Jacob's first-born son Reuben (v. 1b; 26:5-8; Gen 35:23). The tradition of their rebellion is an ancient one that is recounted elsewhere (Ps 106:16-18 and Deut 11:6).

Dathan and Abiram represent the political faction that refuses to acknowledge the leadership of Moses. When they say, "We will not go" (vv. 12b, 14c), we are inclined to think that they might be leaders who conspired with the scouts in refusing to enter the land (14:1-4). Their concerns identify them. They lament having been brought from Egypt, and they fear perishing in the wilderness (v. 13a). They complain that Moses has set himself up as prince (v. 13b; see Exod 2:14). They complain, further, that Moses has not fulfilled his promise to bring them into a land where they will acquire fields and vineyards (v. 14a). As the ultimate insult, the rebels claim that Moses is deceiving them when they ask, ". . . will you also gouge out our eyes?" (v. 14b). This is an idiom for leading astray with false promises (see 1 Sam 11:2; Prov 30:17).

Moses responds angrily. He does not defend himself against the accusations but rather confesses that he has not harmed anyone (v. 15). The statement "I have never taken a single ass from them" is used to defend oneself against the charge of abuse of position (see 1 Sam 12:3; 8:16).

16:16-24, 35 Punishment of Korah. The story of Korah is resumed here, continuing from verse 11. Moses tells Aaron, Korah, and his supporters to each prepare a censer and to take his stand at the entrance to the meeting tent (vv. 16-17). The preparation of the censers is described in detail to emphasize the action of assuming the priesthood (v. 18). This is done in anticipation of judgment.

At this moment the "glory of Yahweh" is manifest in power and majesty before the entire community (v. 19). Moses and Aaron are instructed to separate themselves from the group about to be punished because they are exempt from judgment (vv. 20-21). They respond by falling down and pleading that the whole people of God might not perish on account of the sin of one group (v. 22). They address Yahweh by the old title "El," which is simply God, the Creator of life. They ask that God not destroy the life that has been given (see also 27:16). Yahweh thus exempts the community from judgment. The people are told to move away from the place (vv. 23-24). No sooner have they done this than fire bursts out from the Lord and consumes the rebellious individuals (v. 35). There is a note in 26:11 which states that not all descendants of Korah died.

This story settles once and for all the question of priestly authority. The object of Korah's rebellion was the desire and ambition to be a priest, to take the censer, the fire, and the incense and stand before the Lord. The Kohathites had been warned that they should not touch any of the sacred objects under pain of death (4:15, 20). Death by fire was foreshadowed in the taking of fire from the altar (compare the story in 3:1-4 and Lev 10:1-2).

The mention of Dathan and Abiram alongside Korah in verses 24 and 35 reflects the intent to make the two stories one. Korah's punishment occurred near the meeting tent. Reference to the Dwelling in these verses comes from the story of Dathan and Abiram, who, according to the following account (vv. 25-34), are punished near their own tents.

16:25-34 Punishment of Dathan and Abiram. This is the conclusion to the story of rebellion against the leadership of Moses. It picks up directly from verse 15.

Moses and the elders approach the defiant Dathan and Abiram (v. 25). Moses speaks directly to the community, warning them to separate themselves from the rebellious Reubenites, lest they also suffer punishment (v. 26). Dathan, Abiram, their wives and children stand outside their tents in expectation (v. 27). The scene is set for an act of judgment.

The word of judgment comes directly from Moses in confirmation of his authority and in refutation of any suspicion that he is acting on his own (v. 28). The judgment will be recognizable by the fact that death, "the fate common to all mankind," will not be from natural causes (v. 29). The Lord will do "something entirely new," that is, Yahweh will do an act of creation, so that they will die in a way that has been unheard of until this time (v. 30a). The earth will literally open up and swallow them and all their possessions (v. 30b).

No sooner has Moses spoken the word of judgment than his authority is vindicated in the sight of all. The earth opens, and those who refused to *go up* (vv. 12, 14), ironically, face the fate of *going down* to the nether world with everything belonging to them (vv. 31-33). Those who accused Moses of bringing them out of Egypt "to make [them] perish in the desert" (v. 13) suffer the fulfillment of their accusation. Dathan and Abiram disappear from the face of the earth and there is no evidence or trace of them. Mention that Korah's men suffer the same fate is made in verse 32b to knit the two accounts.

Quite understandably, all the Israelites flee in fear that the same thing might happen to them (v. 34). The story is told so that Israel might know the uniqueness of Moses in his call to lead the people from Egypt and into the land of promise.

17:1-5 A sign for the Israelites. This piece offers an explanation for the layer of copper that covers the altar, and it also foreshadows the succession of Eleazar as priest after Aaron (see 20:22-29). The word comes to Moses (v. 1) that Eleazar is to gather the censers that have been consecrated, and, after scattering the fire, he is to hammer them into plates to overlay the altar (vv. 2-3). Eleazar does exactly as the Lord commands (vv. 4-5). Because the censers have been made sacred at the cost

of so many lives, they are to be protected from any abuse (see Exod 29:37; 30:29). The cover made from the consecrated censers would be a reminder that no person who is not a proper priest, a descendant of Aaron, should ever approach the altar. The cover stands as a warning of the consequences of any improper action.

17:6-15 The people grumble. Another story that contains the elements of the typical rebellion-forgiveness story (see commentary on 11:1-3) evolves out of the events of Korah's rebellion. The people grumble and blame Moses and Aaron for the death of so many of their compatriots (v. 6).

Yahweh appears in the usual manner and resolves to consume the entire community. Only Moses and Aaron are to be spared. Moses instructs Aaron to take his censer, fill it with fire from the altar, put incense on it, and make atonement for the people (v. 11). Aaron's intercessory action puts an end to the scourge, but not before a significant number of people have perished (vv. 12-15). Aaron the priest thus acts in the capacity of high priest, mediating healing and life from God. He stands "between the living and the dead" (v. 13); he makes intercession that effectively averts further destruction.

This story vindicates Aaron and his descendants and clarifies still further the role of the priest. The priest is consecrated for the good of the people. Through the priest the life-giving forces flow from God. For this mediatory task the priest is uniquely chosen. God's choice of the priestly family is based on the following legend.

17:16-26 Aaron's staff. The legend of the blooming of Aaron's staff is a delightful literary piece developed upon a wordplay. The Hebrew words for "staff" and "tribe" are exactly the same. The dead staff that bursts into life represents the tribe that God chooses and blesses for the service of the priesthood. The story is told to silence once and for all the "grumbling" (vv. 20, 25) against Aaron and his sons as the chosen of God.

The repetition of details in the word of God to Moses (vv. 16-20) carried out exactly (vv. 21-23) emphasizes the divine choice of the staff/tribe. In accord with Yahweh's direction, Moses requests that each prince representing one of the tribes bring a staff on which is written the prince's name. The name of Aaron is inscribed on the staff from the tribe of Levi (v. 18). The twelve staffs are then laid in the meeting tent in front of the commandments. Yahweh will signify the choice of tribe by a miracle.

The next day Moses enters the tent and finds that Aaron's staff has not only sprouted and sent out shoots but has blossomed and bears ripe almonds (v. 23). Moses brings all the staffs out for the people to see and returns each to its owner (v. 24). Aaron's staff, however, is returned to the meeting tent, where it will remain as a sign and a warning for future generations that the sons of Aaron are chosen to be the sole legitimate priests (v. 25).

17:27-28 Sacred objects. These verses are appropriately inserted as a transition between the preceding series of stories and the following clarification of priestly duties and rewards. The verses present the people crying out to Moses, as they have done so often when facing punishment (v. 27). In this instance they cry out in fear that all of them will surely die if they ever come near the Dwelling (v. 28). The concern expressed here reflects an actual question that caused disputes among the categories of priests. It is also a legitimate concern of the people who encamp about the Dwelling and know the punishment that befalls those who encroach upon the holy. The despair that resounds in the choice of verbs—"perishing," "lost," "die"—highlights the seriousness of the issue. The clarification of the duties of the priests and Levites that follows answers the concern.

18:1-7 Duties of the priests and the Levites. Only in this section is Yahweh's word addressed directly to Aaron (v. 1; see also vv. 8, 20). This is appropriate, since the instruction distinguishes the priests from the Levites and gives priority to the priests. The role of each is made clear. Aaron, his sons, and their descendants, as legitimate possessors of the priesthood, have sole responsibility for the sanctuary (v. 1). Only they may draw near the altar, perform the priestly functions, and touch that which pertains to the altar (vv. 1, 5, 7).

Death is the punishment for any layperson who comes near the altar (vv. 4b, 5b, 7b). The Levites, kin to the Aaronites, have been set apart in place of the first-born of Israel for the service of the sanctuary so that "no plague may strike among the Israelites should they come near the sanctuary" (see the commentary on 8:19). They are dedicated to the Lord and given as a gift to the priests (v. 6; see 3:5-4:49; 8:5-26). The Levites are to be assistants to the priests. Theirs will be the service of the priests and the holy place, but they may not touch the altar or the sacred objects (vv. 2-4).

The clear priority of the Aaronic priesthood over the Levites is defined in this text by the word "gift" (v. 6). The Levites are given as a *gift* to the priests, and the priesthood is given as a *gift* to Aaron and his sons. The ascendancy of the Aaronic priesthood was most pronounced in the period of the Exile and after.

18:8-20 Priests' share of the sacrifices. This is an elaborate description of the remuneration due to the priests and their families for their services on behalf of the people. The priests have no land or property; their sole possession is the God to whom they belong (v. 20; see Josh 13:14; 14:3-4). They therefore have a right to support from the people. What is offered to God in sacrifice belongs to the priests as their share (v. 8).

The priests have a share of all the most sacred offerings, be they cereal offerings, sin offerings, or guilt offerings. The only injunction is that their portion be treated as most sacred (vv. 9-10). They receive the breast and right leg from the wave offering (vv. 11, 18b). Also, the best of the oil, the new wine, and the grain presented as first fruits belong to the priests and may be consumed by members of their families (vv. 12-13). Theirs is whatever is "doomed," that is, whatever has been devoted to God and cannot be redeemed (v. 14). In early Israel, for example, everything taken in war belonged to God and had to be destroyed. In later years, what belongs to God is claimed by the priests, including all the first-born. The first-born sons and unclean animals are to be redeemed and the money presented to the priests. The first-born of the clean animals belong to the priests, except for the blood, which is splashed on the altar, and the fat, which is burned in the fire (vv. 15-18a).

The Lord promises all this to the priests and their families, both sons and daughters, as "an inviolable covenant to last forever" (v. 19). This very strong language reads literally "a covenant of salt." The phrase occurs again only in 2 Chr 13:5 in reference to the Davidic kingship. According to the priests responsible for both texts, only that which applies to the priests and to the family of David is guaranteed forever.

18:21-24 Tithes due the Levites. The Levites who attend the property of the sanctuary shield the people from danger (vv. 22-23a). They have no heritage of their own (vv. 23b, 24b) and therefore depend on the support of the people. The Lord designates that the tithes given as a contribution to the Lord be assigned to the Levites in return for their service (vv. 21, 24a). The tithe consists of one-tenth of the produce of the land, trees, and cattle (see Lev 27:30-33). The practice of presenting the tithe for the support of the Levites continued, with some variations, from early to postexilic times (see Deut 14:22-29; 12:17-19; 26:12; 2 Chr 31:4-6).

18:25-32 Tithes paid by the Levites. The tithes presented to the Levites for their support are to be looked upon as God's gift to them from the earth and the vineyard. The Levites, too, must tithe. Yahweh commands that they present a "tithe of the tithes" (v. 26) to the priests as their offering, as if from their own threshing floors and winepresses (vv. 27, 30). They are cautioned to offer the best part, so that they return to God the very best of that given to them (vv. 28-30, 32a). What remains can be eaten by themselves and their families—it is their remuneration for service. This food is sacred because it has been offered as a contribution to God. It must therefore be consumed, lest the Levite bring upon himself punishment for abuse of that which has been consecrated (vv. 31-32).

Besides distinguishing between the priest and the Levite, this chapter establishes the practice of providing support for those dedicated to God who carry out duties in service of the people.

Chapter 19 presents an ancient ritual that is entirely unrelated to the context other than the fact that it is carried out by a priest. The ritual has to do with cultic purity, specifically purification after contact with the dead.

19:1-10 Ashes of the red heifer. The animal to be used for the rite is a young red heifer which is without defect in the cultic sense and which has not been used for any other purpose (v. 2). It is to be given to Eleazar, taken outside the camp, and slaughtered in his pres-

ence (v. 3). The priest will take some of the blood on his finger and sprinkle it seven times in the direction of the meeting tent, presumably to signify total dedication (v. 4). The animal is then burned in its entirety before the priest, who adds to the fire some cedar wood, hyssop, and scarlet yarn (vv. 5-6). These items are understood to have a cleansing and purifying effect, and are used otherwise to purify lepers (see Lev 14:6-7). After the burning the priest and the one who has burned the animal are to wash their garments and bathe themselves. They remain unclean until evening, when they may reenter the camp (vv. 7-8).

Finally, a man who is clean from a cultic point of view gathers the ashes and stores them in a clean place outside the camp, so that they are available for use in the water of purification (v. 9a). The statement that the heifer is a sin offering (v. 9b) is strange, since the animal is not sacrificed or presented to God but is totally burnt and used to produce ashes for the purifying water sprinkled in rites of purification. The man who gathers the ashes also becomes unclean. He, too, must wash his garments and remain outside the camp until evening (v. 10). The ritual described here has no parallel. It carries magical overtones that suggest adaptation of a practice from the foreign environment.

19:11-22 Use of the ashes. The ashes are prepared specifically for use in the purification rites of those who have become unclean from contact with the dead. We saw earlier that contact with the dead is a means of defilement (5:2). The various regulations and rituals for cleansing this uncleanness are presented in this one place.

According to law, anyone who touches a corpse becomes unclean for a period of seven days. This individual must be banned from the camp lest the community be defiled. The unclean person is unworthy of the holy place where Yahweh dwells. To become clean, the person must be purified by being sprinkled with water on the third and seventh days (vv. 11-13).

There follows a listing of circumstances that bring about uncleanness (vv. 14-16). Anyone who enters a tent where there is a corpse, as well as those already in the tent at the time of the death, are unclean. So also is anything exposed to the dead, such as the contents of a jar that has been left open. A person does not have to touch the body. However, if anyone touches a corpse—even a part of it or the grave—that person is unclean. It does not matter whether the death was caused by natural or unnatural causes.

Instructions for purification are presented next (vv. 17-18). The unclean individuals are required to submit to a ritual of purification in which the ashes of the red heifer, mixed with fresh water, are sprinkled on them, their tents, and possessions. This is done by someone ritually clean, not necessarily a priest, on the third and seventh days. Those being cleansed then wash their garments, bathe themselves, and return to the camp in the evening of the day of purification. The person who sprinkles the water also becomes unclean and must therefore wash his garments and remain outside until evening.

An unclean person who does not submit to the purificatory rite remains unclean. Everything and everyone who comes in contact with this unclean person becomes unclean. This individual must be excluded from the community, being unworthy of the place where Yahweh dwells (vv. 20, 22).

It is probable that this reminder about ritual cleanness is added at this point to focus attention again on the community about to move forward on its journey to the land. This is a people among whom Yahweh dwells. Whether in the wilderness or in the land, only a ritually clean people is worthy of the presence of a holy God. Ritual cleanliness is, then, a sign of the people's fidelity to Yahweh.

Last Stops Along the Way (20:1–22:1)

20:1 Death of Miriam. After a long interval of struggles and rebellion, focus is again on the community encamped in the desert of Zin at Kadesh (v. la). This desert is part of the larger desert of Paran, from which the scouts were sent (see 10:12; 13:3, 21, 26). A sequence of events follows to mark the passage of time and the movement toward the land.

There is a brief note that Miriam died and was buried at Kadesh (v. lb; see ch. 12 and Exod 15:20-21). This is a reminder that because of the people's rebellion an entire generation will pass away before Israel moves on to the Promised Land.

20:2-13 Moses and Aaron punished. In a retelling of the Meribah incident (v. 13; see Exod 17:2-7), an explanation is offered of why Moses and Aaron are denied entry into the land. The reason develops from the event of contention over water. (Meribah means "contention" or "controversy.") The people quarrel with Moses and Aaron and accuse them of bringing the community from Egypt, where there was plenty of food, to the wilderness, where there is not even water to drink (vv. 2-5). All Moses and Aaron can do is turn to Yahweh, who at that moment is revealed to them at the entrance of the meeting tent and speaks to them (vv. 6-7). Yahweh instructs Moses and Aaron to take the staff, to assemble the people, and, in the presence of the community, to order the rock to give forth water for all to drink (v. 8).

There is a significant difference between the older story and the incident as told here by the Priestly writer. In Exod 17:5-6 Moses is told to strike the rock with the staff. Here Yahweh commands Moses and Aaron to "order" the rock, that by a miraculous occurrence in the presence of all, the "sanctity" (holiness) of Yahweh might be shown (vv. 12-13; see Isa 29:23). The Hebrew words for "sanctity" and for "Kadesh," the place of the present controversy, derive from the same root (see v. 1). It is to hint at this association that the point of Yahweh's sanctity is stressed.

However, the staff becomes the object of disobedience. It is identified with the staff of Aaron, which was placed before the Lord in the sanctuary (v. 9; 17:16-26). Rather than doing exactly as Yahweh has commanded, Moses asks the community a question that suggests doubt and lack of faith: "Are we to bring water for you out of this rock?" (v. 10). Using the staff, Moses subsequently strikes the rock not once but twice. The rock issues enough water for all to drink (v. 11), though Moses did not "order" the rock as Yahweh had directed.

Tradition holds that this infidelity is the reason for Yahweh's decision that neither Aaron nor Moses would enter the land (v. 12; see v. 24 and Ps 106:32-33). It is unclear, however, whether the infidelity is a lack of faith or an act of disobedience. Perhaps the lack of clarity is intentional so that the people will remember both. This story is told near the end of the journey to prepare for the designation of new leaders as well as to supply a reason for the need for new leaders. (See Deut 1:37; 3:26 and 4:21-22 for another explanation of why Moses is denied entry into the Promised Land.)

20:14-21 Edom's refusal. The easiest passage from Kadesh across the southern tip of the Dead Sea would be through Edom and Moab. To do this and to avoid conflict, Moses sends messengers to the king of Edom requesting permission to pass peacefully through his land (v. 14a). Moses appeals to the kinship between the two peoples (v. 14b), since Edom/Esau and Israel/Jacob are twin ancestors of the nations (Gen 25:21-26; 32:4; 33:1-17). Moses recounts the history of how Yahweh has led the people from Egypt to this place in the wilderness near the edge of Edomite territory (vv. 15-16). He promises that the people will not disturb their fields or vineyards nor drink any of their water. They will pass through the district on the royal road without deviating right or left (vv. 17, 19). The royal road, sometimes called the King's Highway, was an ancient, frequently traveled caravan route through Edom (see 21:22; Deut 2:27).

Edom refuses Moses' request twice and threatens attack if Israel attempts passage (vv. 18, 20; see Amos 1:11-12). Israel is then forced to travel southward as far as Elath on the Gulf of Aqaba to skirt the territory of Edom and to penetrate from the eastern desert. This story, rooted as it is in the tradition of dissension between the brothers, gives an explanation for embarking on such a circuitous route.

20:22-29 Death of Aaron. Before beginning the trek southward, the whole community moves to Mount Hor, which is located a short distance north of Kadesh on the border of Edom (vv. 22-23).

Yahweh's word spoken (vv. 23-26) and fulfilled (vv. 27-28a) once again indicates divine direction in the course of events. The word is very simple and clear. Aaron is about to die (v. 24; see 33:37-39), in fulfillment of the word given in 20:12. God commands that Moses install Aaron's son Eleazar as priest in succession to his father by transferring the robe from Aaron to his son (vv. 25-26, 27a, 28a; see Exod 39:1-31 and Lev 8:7-9 for a description of the robes and the installation ceremony). When this has been done, Aaron

dies on the mountain and the community mourns him for thirty days (v. 28b). Of the first generation, only Moses remains to lead the people toward the land. Later Moses will die on a mountain and will be mourned for a thirty-day period (see Deut 34:1, 5-8).

21:1-3 Victory over Arad. This story explains the name Hormah, which is related to a Hebrew word meaning "doomed" (v. 3b; see Judg 1:17). In an earlier report the Israelites had attempted to enter Canaan from the south on their own initiative. They were routed by the inhabitants and chased back to Hormah (see 14:39-45 and Deut 1:41-46). The successful attack by the Canaanite king is a detail continuing from this earlier story (v. 1). A change of events occurs, however, when the Israelites turn to the Lord with the vow to "doom their cities" if Yahweh will deliver the Canaanites into their hands (v. 2). Because of this vow, Israel destroys the defeated Canaanite cities and calls the place Hormah, the "doomed" place (v. 3).

This story seems out of place, for the Israelites, who are heading southward, must travel north to Hormah. In an old list there is allusion to the event after the death of Aaron (see 33:40). Because the Priestly writer used that list as the basis for the present narrative, the story of Hormah is told here regardless of the geographical problem created.

21:4-9 The bronze serpent. This is a very old story that explains why a bronze serpent stood in the temple of Jerusalem. This figure was destroyed in the time of Hezekiah because of the worship that grew up around it (see 2 Kgs 18:4). Because of its ability to regenerate itself the serpent symbolizes life and was used as a fertility symbol from ancient times.

As we have the story, it is told in the formalized pattern of rebellion-punishment-intercession-forgiveness that has been used a number of times (see 11:1-3; 12:2-16; 17:6-15; 21:4-9). Our attention is turned once again to a rebellious people. Though this is a new generation and though they are within range of entrance into the land, they complain against God and Moses (v. 5a). The people have no sooner set out from Mount Hor and upon the road south toward the Gulf of Aqaba than they lose patience (v. 4). The complaint once again centers on food and drink and a longing to return to Egypt (v. 5b).

Yahweh responds immediately with punishment by sending serpents that bite the people, resulting in a great number of deaths (v. 6). The people turn to Moses for help. They confess that they have sinned and ask Moses to pray that Yahweh will remove the serpents from them (v. 7). Moses intercedes for them and receives instructions for bringing about an end to the suffering. He does exactly as Yahweh commands. He makes a bronze serpent and raises it on a pole. Anyone who looks at the serpent recovers (vv. 8-9). The healing of the bites is linked to obedience and to faith. And, ironically, the healing comes from a source like that of the punishment.

For the last time in the wilderness, Israel rebels and is forgiven. As the new generation advances toward the land, they walk in the footsteps of their ancestors who perished on account of their rebellion.

21:10-20 Journey around Moab. A remarkable piece, made up of a series of place names interspersed with fragments of ancient poetry, hastens the journey toward the plains of Moab, where the next events will take place. The movement is from the Arabah, the region south of the Dead Sea, through the Jordan Valley. The people reach the Wadi Zered, the boundary between Edom and Moab (vv. 11-12). From there they push on to the Arnon, a river dividing the territory of Moab from that of the Amorites (v. 13). The Amorite kingdom lies between Moab and Ammon. It is this territory that Israel will have to traverse to reach the Jordan (see vv. 21-32). All the sites named in verses 16, 18b, 19-20, as far as is known, are on the east side of the Dead Sea. Nahaliel is a valley a short distance north of the Arnon, and Pisgah is one of the peaks overlooking the plain where the Jordan River enters the Dead Sea.

Within the travel schema, there are two pieces of poetry (vv. 14-15, 17-18). The first of these is said to be from the "Book of the Wars of the Lord" (v. 14). Though the book is unknown otherwise, it is probable that there once existed a collection of songs celebrating victories from the early days of the settlement. The poem is included because it mentions the Arnon and verifies that this river formed the border of Moab. The other poem is a traditional song celebrating the springing up of well-water when the well was first dug. It was added in this context because of the place name Beer, meaning "well," and because the gift of water at any site in the wilderness was celebrated as a gift from God (see v. 16).

21:21-32 Victory over Sihon. The Amorite kingdom, with its capital of Heshbon, is located between Moab and Ammon. Its ruler Sihon had warred against Moab and had taken the entire plateau of Moab between the Jabbok River on the north down to the Arnon River, and from the desert on the east to the Jordan River on the west (v. 26; see Judg 11:22). Possession of this territory would put Israel within reach of the Promised Land. The defeat of the Amorites is therefore the first of the conquest stories.

According to the text, Moses sends messengers ahead to request passage through the land on the royal road. The alert reader recognizes immediately that the request parallels exactly that made to the king of Edom (vv. 21-22; compare 20:14, 17). Scholars believe that the Heshbon tradition is the older and that the Edom text was modeled after it.

Sihon, king of the Amorites, denies the request and engages Israel in battle at Jahaz (Jahzah). Israel defeats the forces of Sihon and takes possession of the entire land between the Jabbok and Arnon Rivers up to the territory of the Ammonites (vv. 24-26, 31-32). So significant is this victory that gives Israel possession of Canaanite land that the tradition of it is recorded again in Deut 2:24-37 and Judg 11:19-22.

Linked with this victory narrative there is also an ancient poem in verses 27-30 celebrating the victory. What is interesting is that the poem is a non-Israelite composition of great antiquity. The reference to Chemosh (v. 29a), the god of the Moabites, and the statement that Moab and the people of Chemosh are taken captive by the Amorite king Sihon suggest that this is the poem originally sung in celebration of the Amorite victory over Moab. The poem was appropriated by the Israelites without alteration and included as a reminder that the conqueror is now the conquered. This poem is quoted once again in a prophetic word against Moab (see Jer 48:45).

21:33-22:1 Victory over Og. Because the names of the kings Sihon and Og are associated in the tradition (Pss 135:11; 136:19-20), the story of Og's defeat follows immediately upon that of Sihon's defeat.

Bashan is the Amorite territory north of the Jabbok River. A fuller description of the confrontation with Og, king of Bashan, is given in Deut 3:1-11. Verses 1-3 of the Deuteronomy speech of Moses form the substance of the Numbers narrative. It is told as a story of Yahweh's victory (v. 34; see Deut 3:2-3a). As a sign of total dedication to Yahweh, the population is destroyed and the land is inhabited by the Israelites (v. 35; compare Deut 3:3b-6). With this victory Israel has gained control of the entire region outside the limits of Ammon, Moab, and Edom. Israel is now in possession of the entire Canaanite land of the Transjordan, separated from Canaan proper only by the Jordan River.

An itinerary formula concludes the section to summarize the final movement to the plains of Moab (22:1; see the discussion on the journey formula on p. 146). All the remaining events in the book take place while the people remain encamped here. Moses will die and be buried here (Deut 34:1-8), and from here Joshua will lead the people forth (see 27:12-23 and Deut 34:9).

ON THE PLAINS OF MOAB: PREPARATIONS FOR LIFE IN THE LAND

Num 22:2-36:13

The long journey from Sinai has spanned an entire generation. The length of the sojourn in the wilderness and the denial of entry into the land to Moses and Aaron are understood to be the consequence of infidelity to Yahweh's word. The deaths of Miriam and Aaron mark the passage of time to a new generation of adults. The people who survived the wilderness finally arrive, under the leadership of Moses, on the plains of Moab. The whole of the third part of the Book of Numbers takes place in Moab and focuses on the future life in the land of promise.

The content of this section is a mixture of traditions collected by the Priestly school from a variety of sources spanning the history of the nation.

The story of Balaam (chs. 22-24), the account of the unfortunate incident at Shittim (ch. 25), and the Midianite polemic (ch. 31) are very old narratives incorporated by the Priestly author. These accounts retain their original lively narrative and poetic style and

therefore stand out against the formalized language of the legislation (27:1-11; chs. 28-30, 32, 35, 36) and lists (chs. 26 and 33).

The primary objective of this material is preparation for the future, when Israel will organize itself as a worshiping community of faith centered on Yahweh's presence in its midst. Questions about territorial possession and issues pertinent to inheritance of property are settled prior to entry into the Promised Land to forestall quarrels and divisions within the community. Laws for the observance of the major feasts guarantee an ordered religious life. Stress upon obedience to Yahweh's word reminds Israel that it alone can turn away from the covenant relationship. Observance of the law and the cult makes possible Yahweh's dwelling in the midst of this people forever.

When putting together this material, the Priestly author is reflecting upon Israel's history for the instruction of a people who are once again in a wilderness of exile and looking to the day when they can reenter the land of promise and reorganize themselves as a community of faith.

Chapters 22-24 contain a remarkable narrative complex, made up of a legend about a foreign prophet and told as the basis for a series of oracles that express Yahweh's blessing on the people of God. The setting for the narrative is the arrival of the Israelites on the plains of Moab. Frightened by the presence of the Israelites so near his borders, Balak, the king of Moab, seeks out the prophet Balaam to utter a curse on Israel. Balaam, however, presents himself as a prophet who speaks nothing else but Yahweh's word and therefore becomes a hero and model for all generations of Israelites.

Yahweh's word for Israel is one of blessing. Each of the oracles presents Israel as a people of election who have been wondrously blessed in the past and who will be victorious and prosperous in the future. The oracles are told at this juncture because of their content, which foreshadows what Israel will become in the land and provides an example of a truly obedient individual who is radically dependent on God's word.

22:2-14 Balaam summoned. The narrative begins with the introduction of one of the main characters, Balak, the king of Moab. He fears the Israelite forces encamped so near his borders. This is the army that defeated the Amorites, the people who had earlier defeated Moab (vv. 2-3; see 21:26). The Israelites are a numerous people who "cover the face of the earth" and who have demonstrated their strength (v. 6a).

Balak sends messengers from Moab and from Midian (vv. 4, 7) to hire Balaam to curse this enemy in order to make victory over them possible (v. 6a). The aim of the curse is to create a situation that will make defeat of the Israelites possible, that is, remove the protection of their God. To curse is to set one god against another and thereby unleash the destructive forces of the enemy God (see Jer 10:25; Pss 35:4-8; 79:6-7; 2 Sam 18:32).

Why the Midianites, neighbors from the desert south of Moab, are involved with Balak raises questions. Perhaps they are named here for the sake of continuity with the Peor and Midian incidents that follow, both of which are linked with Balaam in 31:8 and 16.

As the story goes, Balak involves Midian by pointing out the devastation of which Israel is capable, using the striking metaphor "as an ox devours the grass of the field" (v. 4). They seek out a foreigner, a reputed seer from the Euphrates valley in Mesopotamia, to utter a curse (v. 5a). This prophet, Balaam by name, is known to speak the word of God so effectively that Balak can be certain of the power of his word: "For I know that whoever you bless is blessed and whoever you curse is cursed" (v. 6b). Prophets such as Balaam were known in many of the countries of the ancient world from very early times. He can be compared to the earlier prophets of Israel, such as Samuel and Elijah, who were respected for their powerful word from God.

Following this introduction, there is a series of scenes that feature the prophet. In the first scene, verses 7-14, the messengers, with fee in hand, visit Balaam in his own territory (v. 7). From the perspective of those who solicit the prophet, Balaam is one of the diviners who deliver a message for pay. When a seer is paid for his services, as one would expect, he is more likely to utter words that the client wants to hear.

The response that the messengers receive for their offer, however, shows Balaam to be of a different disposition. He is a man who speaks only the word of Yahweh, regardless of the consequences and without reward. The messengers and the reader ought to take notice, for this Balaam, a foreigner from Mesopotamia, names Yahweh as the source of his word. Right from the start Balaam identifies himself as a prophet attentive to the God of the people upon whom Balak is seeking a curse. The stage is set for each of the scenes that follow.

Balaam invites the messengers to stay the night that he might inquire of Yahweh what to do (v. 8). The reader is privy to the conversation that takes place between God and Balaam. God asks Balaam to identify his visitors (v. 9). Obviously, these are individuals unknown to the God of Israel. Balaam answers by restating the request sent from Balak (vv. 10-11; compare vv. 5-6). God tells Balaam not to go with the messengers and not to curse the Israelites, because "they are blessed" (v. 12). This statement is the crux of the narrative. Because Yahweh has "blessed" this people, they are blessed; no word of curse will come upon them. The word "blessed" identifies Israel as a people to whom a unique identity has been given. The repetition of the phrase "out of Egypt" in this section (vv. 5, 11) points to the Exodus event as the foundation for Israel's life, the covenant relationship that unites Yahweh and Israel. Because of this unique relationship, Israel is blessed with greatness, prosperity, and the presence of Yahweh in their midst (vv. 3, 5, 11).

The telling point is that Balaam acts according to God's direction. His response to the invitation of the messengers is that Yahweh has refused to let him go (v. 13). He thus presents himself as a prophet who is faithful to the word spoken to him.

When the messengers report back to Balak, they do not mention that Balaam sought direction from Yahweh but say only that Balaam refused to come back with them (v. 14).

22:15-20 Second appeal to Balaam. Once again Balak sends messengers to Balaam. This time they are more numerous and more distinguished (v. 15). They entice Balaam with the promise of a handsome reward and anything he desires if he will come and put a curse on the Israelites (vv. 16-17).

Balaam's response indicates his total dependence on God's word in every instance. He says that regardless of what Balak will give him, "I could not do anything, small or great, contrary to the command of the Lord, my God" (v. 18). This warning given, Balaam inquires once again what Yahweh will command him (v. 19). That night, God comes to Balaam, gives him permission to accompany the messengers, and cautions him to do exactly as he is told (v. 20).

The focus of the narrative is Balaam's dependence at each step on word from Yahweh. God had earlier directed Balaam not to go; now Balaam is told that he may go. Earlier Yahweh had told Balaam not to curse this people; now Yahweh's word is simply "do exactly as I tell you" (v. 20).

22:21-35 The talking ass. An independent fable that is awkwardly fitted into the narrative follows. God has just told Balaam to go, but when Balaam goes off with the princes, God is angry at him for going (vv. 21-22a). At the end God again tells Balaam to go and to speak only what Yahweh tells him (v. 35). This is a return to the theme of the narrative. Within these literary parameters, a once independent fable about a talking ass is inserted to heighten the sense of the prophet's need to be attentive to Yahweh's direction.

According to the fable, Balaam travels from his home to an unnamed location. Because this journey is in opposition to what God has told him, an "angel of the Lord" blocks his way. Three times the ass sees the angel and responds appropriately; and three times Balaam beats the ass to force it to continue the journey (vv. 23-27). Only the ass sees what the seer does not see; it responds to the angel sent to prevent Balaam from continuing on a road that is contrary to God's intention.

In the next scene the animal and Balaam converse as if it were perfectly normal for them to be talking. The ass asks why Balaam has beaten it three times and points out that it has never before treated Balaam this way and would not this time had there not been a reason (vv. 28-30). The implication seems to be that Balaam ought to have trusted the perception of the animal against his own.

Then the seer sees what only the animal has previously seen. Balaam falls to his knees and bows to the ground before the angel of God (v. 31). The angel rebukes Balaam for his treatment of the animal and explains to him that the way is blocked because his journey

is contrary to Yahweh's designs (vv. 32-33; see the use of this in 2 Pet 2:15-16). Balaam confesses that he has sinned and resolves to return to his home (v. 34).

The fable shows a Balaam who tries to act contrary to Yahweh's word. Yahweh, however, intervenes to reverse the action. This negative tradition about Balaam was one often remembered and restated to demonstrate the action of God for good (see Deut 23:5b-6; Josh 24:9-10; Mic 6:5; Neh 13:2).

22:36-40 Balaam arrives. The third scene in the narrative reports the first direct meeting between King Balak and Balaam. When Balak hears that Balaam is coming, he goes to the Arnon, the river separating Moab from the Israelites, to meet the prophet (v. 36). His greeting is more of a chiding that Balaam did not come promptly when summoned. Balak reminds the prophet that the rewards would be great (v. 37).

As an apology for his initial refusal, Balaam explains that he can speak only what God puts in his mouth (v. 38). Balaam's answer picks up the theme of the legend and further clarifies the prophet's dependence on Yahweh. The king hears for himself what Balaam has said about the source of his word, but he does not understand the implication of Balaam's reliance on Yahweh, the God of the Israelites.

The scene concludes with the king's sacrifice of animals, portions of which are sent to Balaam and those with him. Each of the oracles about to be spoken is delivered at a different site where animals have been sacrificed. The change of sacrificial scene separates one oracle from another.

22:41-23:12 The first oracle. Balak and Balaam go to Bamoth-baal, the high places of Baal, from which they can see some of the clans of Israel (22:41). Balaam there orders Balak to prepare seven altars and to offer sacrifice on each (23:1-2), the usual way to implore a deity. The prophet leaves Balak beside the altar, however, and goes aside to seek Yahweh. He announces to the king that if Yahweh meets him, he will report whatever Yahweh lets him *see*. God does meet him, "puts an utterance in [his] mouth," and tells him to go back to Balak and to speak the word (vv. 3-6).

In prophetic tradition the words "see" and "hear" (23:3; 24:4, 16) are often interchanged to express the means by which Yahweh's word is received (see Isa 1:1; 2:1; 13:1; Amos 1:1; Mic 1:1). Some of the prophets were visionaries who spoke the word out of the visions given to them (see Isa 6:1-13; Amos 7:1-3, 4-6, 7-9; 8:1-3; 9:1-6; Ezek 1-3).

Balaam returns to the altar, where he had left Balak and the princes, (v. 6) and speaks the oracle Yahweh has put in his mouth (vv. 7-10). While the oracle does not contain an explicit word of blessing, Balaam does not curse Israel: "How can I curse whom God has not cursed?" (v. 8). The oracle stresses that Israel is a people that lives apart from the nations; they are a unique people because they are Yahweh's own (v. 9). They are a people so numerous that they cannot be counted; they are like "dust" or "wind-borne particles" (v. 10a). This greatness is a sign of the blessing promised to Israel (see Gen 13:16; 28:14). Balaam ends the oracle by invoking a blessing on himself, that he and his descendants may be given such increase as Israel has received under God's blessing (v. 10b).

Balak is understandably distressed by Balaam's oracle (v. 11). Balaam retorts with a reminder that he can repeat only what Yahweh has put into his mouth (v. 21). Thus, Balaam consistently presents himself as one who depends totally on Yahweh for each word he will speak.

23:13-26 The second oracle. Balak and Balaam move to another site, the top of Pisgah (see 21:20), from which some of the Israelites can be viewed. There they prepare seven altars and offer sacrifice in anticipation of the curse (vv. 13-14). The circumstances of this meeting are told in the same pattern as the previous attempt to secure a curse.

The prophet tells the king to remain by his sacrifice while he goes apart for a meeting (v. 15). Yahweh meets Balaam once again, puts an utterance in his mouth, and sends the prophet back to Balak to speak accordingly (v. 16). Upon his return to Balak and the princes standing near the sacrifice, it is the king who names Yahweh as the source of the prophet's word: "What did the Lord say?" (v. 17). In answer, Balaam delivers the oracle of blessing on Israel.

When seeking oracles, it was the practice to persist until a favorable word was received. Balak does this, because he does not appreciate Yahweh's relationship with Israel. The

Moabite king has no realization that Yahweh is a God who will never "change his mind" (v. 19). Yahweh has blessed Israel and the word given to Balaam to speak will always be a word of blessing (v. 20). No harm can come to Jacob/Israel because Yahweh-God, its King, is with it (v. 21). Israel's God has brought this people from Egypt, and the wonders that God will yet do on Israel's behalf cannot be imagined (vv. 22-23).

Two metaphors describe the nation of which Yahweh is an ally. Israel is called "a wild bull of towering might" (v. 22b), an animal with horns capable of goring the most powerful of enemies (compare Deut 33:17). And Israel has the strength of the "lioness" and the "lion," which do not rest until they have devoured their prey (v. 24; compare Gen 49:9; Mic 5:7). The oracle is a clear warning that Israel, supported by the power of Yahweh, can easily defeat Moab or any other nation.

After this oracle the king shows impatience with Balaam. He tells the prophet that if he cannot curse Israel, at least he should not bless it (v. 25). Rather than diminishing Israel's strength, Balaam has instead acclaimed the union between Israel and Yahweh, the source of its power and might.

Balaam's explanation shows once again why the narrative is told: Balaam is a man who "must do all that the Lord tells him" (v. 26). In this the prophet exemplifies a characteristic that is desirable for all Israel.

23:27–24:13 The third oracle. Though two attempts to secure a curse have been unsuccessful, Balak tries one more time. The pair move to the top of Peor and prepare a sacrifice on seven altars as before (23:27-30). This time, however, Balaam does not leave the king in order to inquire of Yahweh; he *sees* Yahweh's blessing on Israel immediately (24:1). Balaam stands forth, with the Israelite tribes in view, and the spirit of God comes upon him (v. 2). To say that the "spirit of God" comes upon someone is to ascribe to the recipient the onrush of power from God. Balaam is like other great figures through whom Yahweh acted for Israel, such as the judges (see Judg 3:10; 6:34; 14:6, 19); the prophets (see 1 Sam 10:10; Mic 3:8); and the kings (see 1 Sam 10:6, 10; 11:6; 2 Sam 23:2).

Balaam's oracle comes from one who sees the truth, because what the prophet sees and hears is Yahweh's word given to him (vv. 3-4).

The oracle emphasizes once again the strength and vitality of the Israelites. It speaks of the fullness of Israel's blessing and the power, prosperity, and life that flow from that blessing. So many and great are the tents of this nation that they are compared to the abundance of well-watered gardens and to the strength of the mighty cedars (vv. 5-6). There will be no end to their prosperity: their wells will flow with water; they will possess the lands all the way to the sea; and their king will dominate all others (vv. 6-7). Israel is described in its greatness, the result of the blessing promised to Abraham (Gen 12:2-3) and fulfilled in its becoming a nation (2 Sam 7–8).

On account of the covenant relationship rooted in the deliverance from Egypt (v. 8a), Israel has a vitality that can be compared to that of a wild bull that devours the nations like grass (v. 8b; compare 23:22) and to that of a lion and a lioness stalking their prey (v. 9a; compare 23:24). The message to Israel's neighbors is that this people is blessed because it is the people of Yahweh. For the nations to affirm the blessing would be to accept Yahweh as God and therefore come under the promise of blessing themselves. This would fulfill the promise "Blessed is he who blesses you, and cursed is he who curses you" (v. 9b; see Gen 12:3a). Because the king of Moab is intent on cursing Israel, the consequence for his nation is certain defeat.

Balak is extremely angry that Balaam has blessed Israel three times and dismisses him without reward and with the remark that the Lord is responsible for withholding the reward (v. 11), as if to ridicule Balaam because he obediently spoke God's word and did not try to earn a rich reward and honor by manipulating the word. To the end, Balaam is unmoved in his purpose. Remuneration does not matter, as he told the messengers earlier (v. 12; see 22:18). His sole motivation is to do what the Lord commands and to say what the Lord puts in his mouth (v. 13). Only one thing matters to him—not pleasing the host, not wealth nor honor, but only doing and saying what Yahweh commands.

24:14-25 The fourth oracle. Before going on his way, Balaam speaks an unsolicited word that announces Israel's ultimate victory over the peoples of the region. This is a most magnificent oracle spoken on the word of

Yahweh (vv. 15-16), the culmination of the series of oracles. It promises the future rise of the nation—a "star" and "staff" from Jacob/ Israel (v. 17a). These symbols for rulers and kings point to the Davidic monarchy (see Gen 49:10). The empire will include Moab and Edom, the peoples who denied Israel passage through their lands (vv. 17b-19; 20:14-21; 21:10-20; compare 2 Sam 8:11-12). The oracle proper ends at this point with the announcement of the defeat of the nations.

The oracle is expanded with a series of sayings that begin in the same way: "Upon seeing _____, Balaam gave voice" (vv. 20a, 21a, 23a). These sayings attack other nations that threatened Israel at various times throughout its history. "Amalek" (v. 20b) refers to the wandering tribes of the deserts of Sinai, who were traditionally the most hated of Israel's enemies. The Israelites faced the Amalekites when they first came from Egypt (Exod 17:8-13; Deut 25:17-19) and again as they sought to enter (14:43-45) and settle the land (Judg 3:12-13; 6:3, 33; 7:12; 10:12). The Amalekites were defeated under Saul (1 Sam 14:48; 15:2-9) and again under David (1 Sam 30:1-20; 2 Sam 8:12).

The reason why the Kenites are named among the enemy nations is not certain, for according to tradition the Kenites are ancestors of Moses (see Judg 1:16 and 4:11). The tradition also states that the Kenites lived among the Amalekites (see 1 Sam 15:6 and Judg 1:16). It is probable that because of their association with the worst of Israel's enemies, they face the defeat described in the oracle (v. 22). The first line of the oracle, verse 21b, obscure as it is in meaning, contains the words "smith" and "nest," both of which play on the sound of "Kenite" in the Hebrew. The poetic value carries more importance than the meaning.

Finally, the Ishmaelites, descendants of Abraham and the maidservant Hagar (Gen 16 and 21), are named among the enemies to be defeated (v. 23b; see Gen 16:12). The Ishmaelites, who dwelt in the wilderness of Paran (Gen 21:20-21), were scattered throughout the land from Egypt to Asshur (Gen 25:18), among the other neighboring foes (see Ps 83:7-8).

The victors in this case will not be the Israelites but rather the Kittim, who will also defeat Asshur (the Assyrians and Eber), the patronymic ancestor of the region that Abraham left for the land of promise (see Gen 10:21-25). "Kittim" is the name given to the people who settled the island of Cyprus (Isa 23:1, 12; Jer 2:10; Ezek 27:6). The Kittim were no doubt the Sea Peoples, the Philistines, who invaded lands along the Mediterranean Sea, including Canaan and that of other enemies of Israel. Reference here to the victories of the Philistines looks to their future role as provocateurs in the rise of the empire (see 1 Sam 4-6; 2 Sam 5:17-25) and their defeat by Israel: "He too shall perish forever" (v. 24b; Josh 13:2-3; 2 Sam 5:17-25; 8:12).

All the oracles, even those appended, are directed to the defeat of Israel's enemies and to the rise of Israel as a great nation. The oracles are fittingly recited at the moment of Israel's arrival on the plains of Moab to project from this place to the future possession of the land. The entire emphasis in the remainder of the book is on Israel's future life in the land. Even Balaam, as he is cast in this tradition, serves as a model for living faithfully by the word of God. As Balaam obeyed Yahweh's word, the result was blessing, and such is promised to an obedient Israel.

Chapter 25 contains two stories, verses 1-5 and 6-13, that have as their setting a place near the Promised Land. Both involve women, and both tell about Israelite infidelity and consequent punishment. These stories function as a foreshadowing of life as it will be when Israel enters the land (see Judg 2:10-23). They immediately follow the oracles of blessing to illustrate that the blessing is not automatic but rather is dependent on fidelity to the covenant relationship between Yahweh and Israel.

25:1-5 Worship of Baal of Peor. Ironically, what Balak was unable to do to Israel by curse, the people do themselves. Balak had hoped that the curse would effect vulnerability and destruction, the results of separation from God. This narrative recounts how the people turn from God and unleash upon themselves the anger of God and the punishment of death.

The incident takes place at Shittim (v. 1a; 33:49), the very place from which the Israelites would later depart to cross the Jordan into Canaan (see Josh 2:1; 3:1). The people have relations with the Moabite women, sacrifice

to their gods, and eat the sacrifices (vv. 1b-2). This description suggests that the people took part in the fertility rites of Canaanite religion. The fertility god Baal was appeased by sexual acts and sacrifice in an attempt to guarantee productivity of the soil and procreation. These practices proved especially tempting to Israel in the Promised Land (see Hos 2:10, 15; 4:14) and were expressive of Israel's rejection of Yahweh (see Judg 2:13; 3:7; Deut 6:12-14; 7:5; 8:19, etc.). There were high places for Baal worship throughout the land. The name Baal of Peor refers simply to one of these places at Peor (v. 3a).

To turn to another god is to reject Yahweh and to arouse the anger of Yahweh, who is a jealous God (see Deut 4:24; 5:9; 6:15; Exod 20:5; 34:14-15). Because the people have indeed turned from Yahweh, Moses is commanded to have the leaders execute the guilty ones in the sight of the whole community (vv. 4-5). The usual punishment for violation of covenant unity is public hanging with the breaking of the bones (see 2 Sam 21:6, 9, 13). The word used for this punishment means also to alienate one from another (Jer 6:8; Exod 23:17-18). Thus, the consequence of alienation between covenant partners is the alienation of the members in the body.

25:6-15 Zeal of Phinehas. The second story carries the theme of infidelity and punishment, but its primary point of interest is the legitimation of the Zadokite priesthood, which claims descent from Eleazar through Phinehas (see Exod 6:25; 1 Chr 24:3a; 2 Sam 8:17).

There is no connection with the event at Peor, and parts of the story seem to be missing. The people are weeping at the entrance of the meeting tent (v. 6b), and a slaughter of Israelites is in process (v. 8b). There is no explicit mention of a plague, the usual punishment for sin, though it is certainly implied. And the nature of the sin is unclear. The story fragment tells only that an Israelite has brought a Midianite woman into the camp (v. 6a) and that when Phinehas, the grandson of Aaron, sees this, he pierces the two of them with his sword, thereby appeasing God's wrath (v. 11). To put the deed of Phinehas in bold relief, the names of both the man and the woman appear in the text, along with their ancestry. Both individuals were of noble descent (vv. 14-15).

The action of Phinehas gains him a reputation for zealousness for God's honor (v. 11; see Sir 45:23-24), and succession to the priesthood. Yahweh's word to Moses is a pledge of friendship with Phinehas and his descendants that bestows on them special rights (vv. 12-13; see the story of the Levites in Exod 32:25-29).

The presence of the Phinehas story in Numbers reflects the struggles among the groups of priests for position and power after the Exile. Though the Zadokite priesthood, descended from Phinehas, dominated from the time of the early monarchy, its position needs to be secured once again as the community looks forward to reestablishing itself in the land.

25:16-18 Vengeance on the Midianites. An appendix to the stories serves to knit the two preceding incidents together by claiming that the Midianite woman was responsible for the infidelity at Peor and by linking her death and the slaughter of the Israelites with the infidelity at Peor (v. 18).

This is the work of the Priestly author, who has another purpose in mind—to explain why the Midianites have become such enemies (v. 16), though traditionally they were friends and even related to Moses' wife (see 10:29). The continuation of this piece and the execution of the curse on the Midianites will follow in 31:1-18.

26:1-51 The second census. The Priestly writer links the new census with the narrative by referring to the slaughter (25:18b and 25:8-9), though the census is not the result of that punishment. Because a whole generation of Israelites perished in the wilderness, so that not one of those named in the first census remained except Caleb and Joshua, Yahweh orders Moses and Eleazar, who has succeeded Aaron (20:22-29), to take a register of those about to enter the land. This census takes place while the people are camped along the Jordan on the plains of Moab, in anticipation of entry into the land (v. 2; see v. 63).

The heading of the listing, those "who came out of the land of Egypt" (v. 4b), can be misleading. It is intended to show that the second census parallels and replaces the first taken at Sinai (compare 1:1, 19a).

The criteria for those registered are the same as for the first census. The count includes the men of twenty years or more who are fit for military service; they are listed by their father's lineage (vv. 2, 4; see 1:2-3, 18). The order of the tribes is the same as in the first census (1:20-43), except for Manasseh, who is listed before Ephraim (v. 28; compare 1:32-35). In this second list the individual clans are also named to emphasize the tribal structure, size, and ancestry in the postexilic time. (There are other lists of clans in Gen 46:8-25 and 1 Chr 2 with variations that reflect fluctuations in structure at different times in history.)

The purpose of the census list, as it is given here, is to determine the proportionate size of each group in preparation for the land assignment that will follow (vv. 52-56). A comparison between the numbers in the two lists reveals that while the totals do not differ dramatically—601,730 in 26:51 and 603,550 in 1:46—there is a marked change in the strength of individual tribes. Five tribes—Reuben, Simeon, Gad, Ephraim, and Naphtali—have decreased in size; and Simeon, which was the third largest in the first census (1:23), is now the smallest (v. 14). The greatest increase is registered by Manasseh (v. 34; compare 1:35), a fact that accounts for the transposition in order between it and Ephraim (v. 28; compare 1:32, 34). Judah holds its position as the largest of the tribes in both lists (v. 22; compare 1:27).

The list is made more interesting by the commentary in verses 9-11. This elaboration is placed here to account for the loss of particular clans. Dathan and Abiram (v. 9) perished because of their rebellion, as did the sons of Korah (see ch. 16). The reminder that not all the descendants of Korah died (v. 11) reflects a later period when the sons of Korah were active as singers (see the headings to Pss 42, 44-49, 84, 85, 87). The mention in verse 19 of the death of Er and Onan, sons of Judah, has the same effect. The loss of these clans is called to memory because they failed to abide by God's law. That story is told in Gen 38:6-10.

An opposite problem, the possibility of the extinction of a clan, is the reason for the comment on Zelophehad in verse 33. It states that this individual, the head of a clan, has five daughters but no sons. The problem that arises when there are only female heirs is dealt with in 27:1-11 and chapter 36.

26:52-56 Allotment of the land. The census is taken in preparation for the distribution of the land. Two principles upon which the allocation will be based are stated in this legislation. The land will be apportioned in accord with the size of the tribe (vv. 53-54); and the land will be distributed by lot (v. 55). A summary legislation attempts to reconcile the two principles by combining the two methods (v. 56; 33:54). The summary combines the human element of tribal size and the divine element of lot.

26:57-62 Census of the Levites. A separate census is taken of the Levites, just as it was earlier (3:17-39). The criterion for their numbering, as in the first census, is the time of their birth (v. 62a; see the commentary on 3:14-39). However, they are numbered separately in the first census because of their consecration for the service of the sanctuary (1:47-54); here it is because they receive no land for a heritage (v. 62b). This census is taken in preparation for the assignment of cities and land where the Levites might dwell in the land given to the tribes as a heritage (see 35:1-8).

The groups of Levites named in verse 57 are the traditional three: Gershon, Kohath, and Merari. They are listed here as the heads of clans rather than simply as the sons of Levi (compare 3:17) to emphasize that it is their descendants who will live in the assigned cities. The clans named in verse 58 are only five from the list given in 3:17-20. We can only speculate that these five Levitic clans were more prominent at the time this was written.

The ancestry of Amram, a descendant of Kohath, is traced in detail because from this line came Moses, Aaron, and Miriam (vv. 59-60; see Exod 6:20). Only the family of Aaron (v. 60) is given further mention. Recollection of the death of Nadab and Abihu accounts the loss of these families to their infidelity (v. 61; see 3:4; Lev 10:1-5) and indirectly points to Eleazar and Ithamar as the sole successors in the priestly line.

26:63-65 Census completed. A summary statement announces the completion of the census on the plains of Moab, as if to bring the reader once again to an awareness that the people are in readiness on the threshold of the land (v. 63). Those who are registered are the new generation who grew up in the wilderness while waiting for the death of their parents. They, together with Caleb and Joshua, were spared the judgment (v. 65; see 14:28-35).

27:1-11 Inheritance by daughters. This passage contains a legal question for which there is no solution in existing legislation. The matter, therefore, must be brought before the leaders of the community (v. 2), who in turn seek direction from Yahweh (v. 5). We have come across other such cases in 9:6-14 and 15:32-36. Each provides an example of new instruction for a specific situation, becoming a precedent for subsequent practice.

The case in point concerns the five daughters of Zelophehad of the tribe of Manasseh (v. 1; see 26:33), who are the sole descendants of their father. In ordinary circumstances the family land passes to the sons, who alone have the right to retain it and the family name. The daughters argue that their father's name will be dropped from the tribe just because he has no sons. With no male members to inherit the land, there will be no land ownership in the family, and the family name will no longer exist in the community. The daughters ask that they might inherit the land and thus keep alive their father's heritage and name (v. 4). Their argument is persuasive. They stress that though their father died in the desert, his death was not related to the judgment on Korah (16:16-24, 35). He died "for his own sin," which is to say that he came under the general judgment on rebellious Israel (see 14:26-35). There is, therefore, no reason that their father's name should be blotted out.

Moses' decision first answers the request of the daughters and then gives new general legislation pertinent to inheritance. The case is decided in favor of the daughters: they receive their father's inheritance and a place within the family by virtue of their inheritance (v. 7). The general legislation that follows provides that the family heritage be retained within the family even though there are no children (vv. 8-11a). The property never passes to the wife. If there are no sons, the land passes to the daughters in the family (v. 8); if there are no daughters, it is given to the man's brothers (v. 9), uncles (v. 10), or the nearest surviving relative in the clan (v. 11a). The legal norm stipulates that the land be retained in the family in the father's line (v. 11b) to ensure that no property is lost to a particular tribe, thus unbalancing the tribal holdings.

This particular legislation is of significance at this place in the narrative because the land in question belongs to the half-tribe of Manasseh that will settle in the Transjordan (v. 1; compare 32:39-42). The issue of land inheritance by the daughters of Zelophehad settles a territorial claim to land that will be assigned prior to crossing over the Jordan.

27:12-22 Joshua to succeed Moses. The time of Moses' leadership is drawing to a close. The scene patterns that of the death of Aaron in 20:22-26. Moses is told to go into the Abarim Mountains (v. 12) to Nebo, the place of his death, to view the Promised Land (see Deut 32:48-52; 33:47; 34:1-6). Before his death Moses is reminded that he is deprived of the land because of his infidelity in the wilderness (v. 14a). Mention of "the water of Meribah of Kadesh" (v. 14b) is meant to trigger memory of the incident. It involved a "contention" (Meribah) over water during which Moses was instructed to manifest Yahweh's "sanctity" (Kadesh) by commanding the water to come forth (see 20:2-13).

Moses' last concern is to provide a capable successor to lead the people. Addressing Yahweh as "God of the spirits of all," a title for the Creator (see also 16:22), Moses asks Yahweh to preserve the life of the nation by choosing a new leader for it (v. 16). This leader will, literally, "go out and come in," "lead out and bring in" the people, as a shepherd leads the sheep (v. 17). The role of the leader, though in succession to Moses, will be a new one. That is why Moses calls upon the Creator to bring about a new thing. The phrases "go out and come in," "lead out and in" are technical language for political and military leadership (see 1 Sam 18:13, 16; 29:6; Josh 14:10b-11; 1 Kgs 3:7), as is the shepherd reference (1 Kgs 22:17; Ezek 34:5-6; Zech 10:2-3; 11:8; 13:7). The successor to Moses will lead the people in the conquest battles and in the settlement of the land.

The man chosen for this task is Joshua, son of Nun, a man of spirit who has already demonstrated his God-given abilities for leadership (see 11:28; 14:6, 30, 38; compare Deut 34:9).

The commissioning ceremony has the effect of distinguishing the role of priest from that of political leader. Joshua stands in the presence of Eleazar the priest and the whole community (vv. 19, 22), where Moses lays his hands on him (v. 18), a sign of passing his authority on to his successor (v. 20). Joshua,

however, is unlike Moses, who received instruction directly from the Lord (see 12:6-8). Joshua will seek direction through the priest, who will use the sacred lots, the Urim and Thummim, to obtain the Lord's decision (v. 21; see Deut 33:8; Exod 28:30).

In his commissioning, Joshua receives authority from Moses that the people might obey him (v. 20b); but in all other respects Joshua's role is different. The transition in leadership stresses the uniqueness of Moses' role in all of Israelite history; it also traces the distinction between the priestly and political powers to the time of Joshua. This last was a matter of particular concern in the time after the Exile (see Zech 6:12-13; 4:14; Ezek 45:17; 46:2).

Moses carries out the commissioning of Joshua exactly as Yahweh commanded him (vv. 22-23). The provision of a successor is complete and Moses' death is expected. The account of the death is separated, however, in the structure of the document so that Moses might complete the instruction of the people. All of the final legislation is thus attributed to Moses. The report of Moses' death is found in Deut 32:48-52 and 34:1-9.

Chapters 28–29 contain the regulations for public sacrificial worship to be carried out by the community in the land. The emphasis is on worship by the community as a whole and deals with daily, weekly, monthly, and yearly observances. These are regulations that the priests gathered in this one place and attributed to Moses. A comparable, though less detailed, list of observances is found in Lev 23.

28:1-2 General sacrifices. This introduction stipulates that at designated times food offerings will be presented to God. Burned upon the altar, they produce an odor pleasing to the Lord. The language speaks figuratively of God actually delighting in the aroma of the food presented. A "sweet-smelling oblation" is a metaphor for an acceptable sacrifice.

28:3-8 Each morning and evening. The morning and evening food offerings consist of two yearling lambs, one offered in the morning and one in the evening (vv. 3-4), along with a cereal offering (v. 5) and a drink offering (v. 7). The wine is poured out around the altar and the food is completely burned upon the altar as a sign of full dedication to the

Lord. This oblation is the required regular communal offering and the basic sacrifice to which all other offerings are added. As such, it was legislated at Sinai (see Exod 29:38-42). Reference to this Sinai tradition is made in verse 6.

28:9-10 On the sabbath. To set the sabbath day apart from all others, a food offering of lambs, cereal, and wine is presented in addition to the regular oblations. Thus, the sabbath offering is double that of a weekday.

28:11-15 At the feast of the New Moon. In the ancient calendar the day of the new moon marks a new beginning and is treated as a festival day. A sacrifice of greater quantity is required. In addition to the regular food offerings for each day (v. 15b), the sacrifice for this festive occasion consists of two bullocks, a ram, and seven lambs (v. 11), with proportionate amounts of cereal and wine for each of the animals (vv. 12-14; see the commentary on 5:1-16). In addition, a goat is sacrificed as a sin offering (v. 15). The offerings listed here are the usual oblations for all solemn occasions.

28:16-25 At the Passover. The feast of the Passover is celebrated on the fourteenth day of the first month of the year (v. 16; see 9:1-5 and Exod 12:2, 18); and the following day, called the feast of Unleavened Bread, is the beginning of the seven-day period during which only unleavened bread is eaten (v. 17). The first and seventh days of this week are sacred occasions for assembly when no work is done (vv. 18, 25). On each of the seven days the oblation appropriate for solemn festivals is offered (vv. 19-22; see vv. 11-15 above). This is in addition to the food offering required for each day (vv. 23-24).

28:26-31 At Pentecost. Seven weeks after the feast of Passover, the grain harvest is celebrated. Gifts of the harvested first fruits are brought to the temple as an offering (v. 26a; see Lev 23:9-22). This day is a sacred occasion on which no work may be done (v. 26b). The acceptable sacrifice for this solemn festival consists of the prescribed food offerings and sin offering for all such feasts (vv. 27-30; compare vv. 19-22, 11-15). These offerings are made in addition to the offerings required each day (v. 31).

29:1-6 On New Year's Day. The first day of the seventh month, also an occasion of the New Moon (see 28:11-15), marks the beginning of the New Year. This solemn feast is sometimes called the feast of Trumpets, because on it the trumpet is sounded (v. 1c; see the commentary on 10:1-10). No work is permitted on this sacred occasion (v. 1b), and the prescribed oblations for all such festivals are offered, except that only one bullock, rather than the usual two, is prescribed (vv. 2-5; see 28:11-15). That the offerings for the occasion are in addition to the oblations required for the monthly New Moon and for the daily offering (v. 6) accounts for the change in the number of animals required.

29:7-11 On the Day of Atonement. The tenth day in the same month as New Year's Day (v. 7a; compare v. 1) is the Day of Atonement, a day of fasting and self-denial. No work may be done on this day (v. 7b). The offering is the same as on New Year's Day, with one less animal (v. 8; compare v. 2) and the usual cereal (vv. 9-10) and sin offerings (v. 11a). The prescribed offerings for this day are in addition to that required for the atonement sin offering (v. 11b; see Lev 16 for the ritual of the scapegoat).

29:12-39 On the Feast of Booths. Exactly six months after Passover and the seven-day pilgrimage of Unleavened Bread, Israel celebrates another feast that lasts for eight days (v. 12; compare 28:16-17). The first and last days are sacred occasions on which no work is permitted (vv. 12, 35). This is a joyous celebration of the harvest, with pilgrimage and great sacrifices. On this day Israel remembers the time spent in the wilderness (see Lev 23:39-43).

The required food offerings for each day of the festival are listed in detail. On the first day thirteen bullocks, two rams, and fourteen yearling lambs are offered (v. 13). On each subsequent day the number of bulls decreases by one, while the number of other animals remain the same (vv. 17, 20, 23, 26, 29, 32). The proportionate offerings of cereal and drink accompany each animal sacrifice each day, and the sin offering is sacrificed each day in addition to the usual offerings required for every day (v. 16). On the eighth day (vv. 35-38) the prescribed sacrifice is the same as that required for the other festivals celebrated in the seventh month—New Year's (vv. 2-5) and the Day of Atonement (vv. 8-10).

The final comment in verse 39 concludes the whole of chapters 28–29. It is a reminder that the listing of offerings is the required sacrifice for each occasion. Individuals, however, may make offerings over and above these in accord with their own ability and desire.

30:1-17 Validity and annulment of vows. The total obedience of Moses is stressed with the comment in verse 1. It is placed here as a reminder that the regulations before and after must be obeyed by the faithful worshiping community.

This section deals only with the question of when vows or pledges made to God are binding. This legislation on vows clarifies a matter of authority and is, therefore, addressed to the heads of the tribes (v. 2).

A male person, having full authority, is always responsible for his own actions and must therefore fulfill the vow or pledge he makes (v. 3). A female person, on the other hand, has no authority of herself; she is dependent on her father before marriage and on her husband after marriage (see v. 17). Only a widow or a divorced woman, both of whom fall among the disenfranchised, retain responsibility for their own actions (v. 10). All other women come under the authority of men. The regulations in this chapter ensure that a woman will do nothing that might divest the family of property or progeny, the rights to which are retained by the male members. For example, a woman might vow a child to God (see 1 Sam 1:11), or make a pledge that would result in the loss of possessions.

The legislation is divided into three sections: laws governing the unmarried woman in her father's house (vv. 4-6); laws governing the woman who is under vow at the time of her marriage (vv. 7-9); and laws governing the married woman (vv. 11-13). In each case the situation for making a vow is the same. If her father or husband says nothing when he learns of the vow, the vow is valid and the woman must fulfill it (vv. 5, 8, 11-12). If, on the other hand, the father or husband disapproves of the vow, it is not binding. The voice of the man invalidates the vow and releases the woman from fulfilling it before the Lord (vv. 6, 9, 13).

The final section, verses 14-16, is meant to prevent a vow from becoming a matter of divisiveness in marriage. The husband's authority must be exercised upon hearing of the vow. The responsibility for failure to keep the vow falls upon the husband if he tries to invalidate it at a later time.

Chapter 31 reports a holy war against the Midianites as a prelude to the series of wars that Israel will fight to take possession of the land. In all instances a holy war ends in an ideal victory, because it is a war in which Yahweh participates.

The account of the war is followed by descriptions of the rites of purification and disposition of booty that have as their interest the ritual cleanliness and loyalty to God expected of a people who live with God in their midst. The actions following the battle are in compliance with regulations set forth in Numbers and witness to Israel's faith in Yahweh's covenant presence. This chapter is put together to illustrate the meaning of utter and uncompromising loyalty to Yahweh and to encourage those returning to the land from the Exile if they should run into difficulties in their attempt to reestablish themselves as a community of faith.

31:1-18 War against the Midianites. The narrator chooses as the context for the holy war the incident of the Midianite woman (25:6-15). Earlier this incident was linked with Peor (25:16-18), and here both the Peor and Midianite stories are linked with Balaam the prophet (vv. 8b, 16). Other points of contact are the priest Phinehas, who leads the battle against the Midianites (v. 6) and who, in the Midianite incident, demonstrated zeal for the Lord by thrusting his sword into the couple (25:7, 11-13); and mention of Zur, one of the five Midianite kings killed (v. 8a), who was also the father of the Midianite woman (25:15). The holy war is waged to fulfill the curse on Midian that followed from the affair with the Midianite woman (see 25:16-17).

The basis for a holy war is the understanding that an enemy of a people is an enemy of the god of that people. Thus the god would execute vengeance (v. 3b). In this context the technical word "vengeance" means the demonstration of power or use of force by legitimate authority against the enemy of that power and authority. For a reason that is unclear in the old story, the Midianites show themselves to be enemies of Israel and thus provoke a display of Yahweh's power. The ingredients of a holy war are the usual: a limited number of men take part in the battle (vv.

189

4-5): they rally behind the leader, who carries with him the sacred vessels and trumpets to sound battle (v. 6); and the victory is total (vv. 7-8). There is another description of a battle with the Midianites under the leadership of Gideon to which this account corresponds at many points (see Judg 6-8).

To signify complete possession by the victorious deity, all that is taken in battle belongs to Yahweh. For this reason the Israelites kill all the men (v. 7); they burn the towns and encampments (v. 10); and they present the women, children, livestock, and valuable items to Moses, the priest Eleazar, and the community (vv. 9, 11-12). But because of the circumstances that necessitated the war, Moses is angry that the lives of the women have been spared (vv. 13-16). He orders the death of all the male children and all the women except the virgins (vv. 17-18).

31:19-24 Purification after battle. Anyone and anything that comes into contact with a corpse is made unclean and must therefore submit to a ritual of purification (see ch. 19). Following the war with the Midianites, the combatants and everything with them must undergo the seven-day period of exclusion from camp and the ritual of sprinklings (v. 19). Perishable items, such as cloth, leather, goats' hair, and wood, are purified with them (v. 20). Materials that can withstand burning have to be cleansed in fire as well as in the purification water, whereas those materials that cannot withstand the fire are cleansed in the water alone (vv. 22-23).

On the seventh day, after washing their clothes, the soldiers are clean and may reenter the camp (v. 24).

31:25-42 Division of the booty. There remains the final disposition of all that is taken in battle. To signify its dedication to Yahweh, it is distributed proportionately in the community. Half is given to those who took part in the battle and half to the rest of the community, so that they, too, share in the glory and benefits of the victory (v. 27). From the distributed property, a portion is given to the priests and Levites as a contribution to the Lord (see ch. 18).

The amount assigned to the priests comes from the booty given to the combatants. They give one out of every five hundred of the people and livestock to the priest (vv. 28-29). The amount assigned to the Levites comes

from the community's half of the booty. They are taxed at the rate of one out of every fifty persons and animals given to them (v. 30). The tremendous amount of booty taken in the war—a sign of the significance of the battle—is spelled out in great detail in the text: the total numbers of the spoils taken (vv. 32-35); the numbers of the half given to the combatants as well as that levied for the priests (vv. 36-41); and the numbers of the half given to the community, with mention that one-fiftieth belongs to the Levites (vv. 42-47).

31:48-54 Gifts of the officers. A final offering is presented by the officers of the campaign in thanksgiving for the safety of all the Israelites who engaged in the battle (v. 49). They pledge that each will contribute a precious article from the items they picked up on their own in the course of the battle (v. 50). The gold that the priests receive from the commanders is of great value (vv. 51-52). It is placed in the meeting tent as a portion freely offered to God (v. 54). The comment in verse 53 that the soldiers are allowed to keep their loot points up the free will and generosity of the officers in giving from their treasure. Placed in the sanctuary, the gold is a reminder that as God has spared the lives of all the warriors (compare 17:5), so God will remember Israel in the future.

Chapter 32 deals with the assignment of the Transjordanian land, the territory that the Israelites seized from Sihon (21:21-32) and Og (21:33-35) as they journeyed to the plains of Moab. Decisions in regard to the land are made by Moses in dialogue with the requesting tribes. The expected phrase "the Lord said to Moses" is noticeably absent in the telling. The fact that Yahweh does not speak and that God does not give the land suggests that the division of the people on two sides of the Jordan remains an unresolved issue. So important is this matter that its conclusion is narrated in full in Josh 1:12-18; 4:12-13; 22:1-8.

32:1-5 Request of Gad and Reuben. The tribes of Reuben and Gad request of Moses, Eleazar, and the leaders of the community that they might be given the land east of the Jordan for their inheritance. They argue that the region would be ideal for their livestock. And to make the request legitimate, they remind the leaders that this is land "which the Lord has laid low before the community of Israel" (v. 4). They are referring to the region extending from the Jabbok River south to the Arnon, land that the Israelites had taken from the Amorites (see 21:24).

The problem caused by the request is summarized in the statement "Do not make us cross the Jordan" (v. 5b). From Sinai and through the wilderness, the picture has been of *one people* journeying to enter *one land*. The granting of the request would mean a divided people in a divided land.

32:6-15 Moses' angry response. Moses' response to the idea of division within the community is immediate and passionate. He sees the request as a threat to all of Israel. The other tribes will be discouraged from going into the land the Lord has given them (v. 7). Moses accuses the Gadites and Reubenites of being "a brood of sinners" responsible for diverting the Israelites from entering the land and thus bringing the anger of God on the nation once again (vv. 14-15).

Moses invokes the incident (told in chapters 13–14) of the Israelites' failure to enter the land from the south (vv. 8-13). He claims that the behavior of the two tribes is like that of the spies who earlier discouraged the people. Just as Yahweh's anger caused Israel to wander for forty years until a whole generation died out, Yahweh will punish again. The result will be the ruin of the whole nation (v. 15b).

32:16-19 Compromise. The tribes of Gad and Reuben offer a compromise. Moses does not object to possession of the Transjordanian land; his concern and anger center on the unwillingness of these groups to cross the Jordan. The tribes therefore promise that they will accompany the Israelites into the land as the vanguard, that they will not return until every one of the Israelites has taken possession of his heritage, and that they will not claim a heritage for themselves in the land of Canaan (vv. 17a, 18, 19a).

The Gadites and Reubenites, however, make provision for themselves before helping the rest of Israel. Their promise of help is contingent upon their receipt of a heritage in the Transjordan (v. 19b) and on securing their families and animals before departure (vv. 16, 17b).

32:20-32 Agreement reached. Moses accepts the compromise proposed by the Reubenites and Gadites. The negotiations are settled in a sequence of four speeches.

In his acceptance Moses proposes the opposite of that suggested by the two tribes (vv. 20-24). He provides first for the entry and settlement of the Israelites in the land of Canaan, and only afterward for the establishment of the tribes in the Transjordanian territory.

The Gadites and Reubenites reaffirm their commitment (vv. 25-27). They reply that they, leaving their families and livestock behind, will indeed go across the Jordan to fight the battle before the Lord. They still put their own interests ahead of those of the rest of the Israelites.

Moses then instructs Joshua, the priest, and the leaders about the carrying out of the agreement (vv. 28-30). The settlement depends upon the good faith of the two tribes. If they cross the Jordan as combat troops and when the victory is complete, Joshua will give them Gilead as their property. But if they do not keep their promise to accompany and fight with the Israelites, they will be given a heritage in Canaan with all of Israel. Moses' instruction points to a *future* resolution of the situation. The request will not be honored if the Gadites and Reubenites do not keep their part of the bargain.

The two groups readily reply that they will do what the Lord commands (vv. 31-32). They thus perceive that Yahweh wills their actions. They reaffirm that they will cross the Jordan into the land of Canaan as troops before the Lord and that they will retain the property in the Transjordan. Their response is enthusiastic and religiously motivated.

32:33-42 Moses gives the land. It would seem that Moses is responding to the evidence of faith in the two tribes, for, contrary to his instructions in verses 28-30, he proceeds to give the land to the Gadites and Reubenites as well as the half tribe of Manasseh. The land distributed is that taken from Sihon, king of the Amorites, and from Og, king of Bashan (vv. 33; see 21:21-35). The land is not assigned by lot nor by tribal size, as the instruction clearly stipulates (see 26:52-56). In this sense the land falls outside that legitimately assigned to the Israelites.

The Reubenites and Gadites are assigned the territory of Sihon, the region south of the Jabbok River (vv. 34-38). The half tribe of Manasseh is given the land north of the Jabbok taken from Og. This land of Gilead was assigned to the Machir and Jair clans of the Manasseh tribe, which had invaded and settled in it (vv. 39-42; compare 21:33-35). It is because of this territorial possession prior to entry into the land that the case of land inheritance by women of the Machir line of the Manasseh family became an issue (27:1-11).

With this assignment of land, provision is made for the settlement of part of Israel. Other issues pertinent to designation of boundaries will also be settled by Moses before his death (chs. 34–36). The history of this time is presented in such a way that the future is seen as the fulfillment of Moses' leadership under the authority of Yahweh.

33:1-49 Stages on the journey. To both summarize and conclude the account of the journey through the wilderness, the Priestly author adds a very old record that lists the stations from Egypt to the plains of Moab (vv. 5-49). This is the same list used as the structure for the narrative account of the wilderness journey.

The formal introductory words echo the stylized heading that is characteristic of the Priestly author. "The following are the stages . . ." (v. 1a) is patterned after the heading "These are the generations . . ." (see Gen 5:1; 6:9; 10:1; 11:10; 11:27; 25:12, 19; 36:1; 37:2). The bold introduction highlights the importance of the list of stations that follows. Its significance is also underlined by the fact that Yahweh commands that Moses record it (v. 2).

The journey began at Rameses in Egypt (Exod 1:11; 12:37) with the celebration of Passover (Exod 12-13) at the time when Yahweh slew every first-born in the land of Egypt (Exod 12:29-30). The memory of the beginning out of Egypt in verses 3-4 comes from a song composed to celebrate the occasion.

The list of stations in verses 5-49 is much more detailed than the sequence of stops mentioned in the narrative. No tradition about many of the places was preserved, so the Priestly author employs the list in broad outline only.

The first segment goes *from Rameses in Egypt to the desert of Sinai* (vv. 5-14). This is the part of the journey told in the Book of Exodus from 12:37 to 19:2. Most of the places in the list occur also as headings in Exodus (see Exod 12:37; 13:20; 14:1-2; 15:22-25a; 16:1;

17:1a; 19:2). The events that took place at Sinai are related by the Priestly writer in Num 1:1 to 10:10.

The second segment outlines the journey *from Sinai to Kadesh* (vv. 16-36). This leg of the journey is recounted in Num 10:11 to 19:22. The limits of the journey are mentioned in the journey formula at 10:12, though in this text Kadesh is replaced by the desert of Paran, the name for the locality that includes Kadesh (see Num 2:16; 13:3, 26). Kibroth-hattaavah (vv. 16b-17a) appears in the narrative in connection with the quail story (11:34-35a); and Hazeroth (vv. 17b-18a) is the place where Aaron and Miriam rebelled against Moses (11:35b; 12:16). In the narrative, the desert of Paran is meant to include the whole range of places in the list not explicitly cited (vv. 18b-36).

The third stretch of the march goes *from Kadesh in the desert of Zin to Mount Hor* (vv. 36-40), places named in journey formulae at Num 20:1a and 22. The events are told in the relatively brief section of 20:1 to 21:9. The list in verses 38-39 is expanded with mention of two specific incidents that are part of the narrative: the death of Aaron (vv. 38-39; see 20:23-29) and the confrontation with the king of Arad (v. 40; see 21:1-3 and 14:39-45).

Finally, the Israelites traveled *from Mount Hor to the plains of Moab* (vv. 41-49). These places are named in the journey formulae at Num 21:10-11 and 22:1, headings that encompass the narrative material from 21:10 to the end of the book. In the narrative, the locality called the "desert fronting Moab on the east" (21:11) is cited to include the whole range of places named in verses 42-48a.

33:50-56 Rules for the conquest and division of Canaan. The effect of the list of stations is to bring the reader back to an awareness that the people remain on the border of the land. At this place Yahweh gives Moses more instructions concerning the future (v. 50). The first one deals with the taking and distribution of the land across the Jordan (v. 51).

The task before the Israelites is to drive out the inhabitants of the land and to destroy all the vestiges of their religion (vv. 52, 55a; see Deut 12:2-3). The conquest must be absolute. There are to be no non-Israelites remaining nor anything uncharacteristic of Israel's God. This is a land that Yahweh has given to Israel as an inheritance. It is a sign of the covenant relationship between Yahweh and Israel (v. 53). This relationship demands total love and loyalty.

The command is followed by a warning expressed in the typical conditional curse (see Deut 30:16-17). If the inhabitants of the land are permitted to remain, they will be a constant source of irritation and trouble (vv. 55; see Josh 23:13); and ultimately the removal from the land intended for the inhabitants will befall the Israelites themselves (v. 56). This last statement has special meaning for the people in exile who have been removed from the land. At issue is radical and uncompromising loyalty. Yahweh's land, as a theological idea, is the place for the faithful followers of Yahweh only.

Wedged into the instruction concerning occupation of the land is a repetition of the procedure for division of the land (v. 54; compare 26:52-56). That the land will be assigned "by lot" is repeated intentionally so that Israel might know that *Yahweh will give* the land, emptied of its inhabitants, for the possession of the families of Israel.

34:1-49 The boundaries. Yahweh's instruction for the future in the land continues with a description of the boundaries of the territory that will be given to Israel (vv. 1-2). An ancient boundary list is used for this idealized territorial description. The description does not correspond with the actual boundaries during any period after the tenth century B.C.E; it does correspond with the limits of Egypt's possession in Canaan in the thirteenth century B.C.E. as those limits are defined in the peace treaty between Egypt and the Hittites. The Priestly writer borrows this specific description of the land of Canaan because it includes only territory actually possessed by Israel, and because the eastern limit borders on the Jordan. For the purpose of the narrative, the writer is not interested in the land beyond the Jordan at this time.

The description of the southern boundary (vv. 3-5) is very similar to that of the southern border of Judah as presented in Josh 15:1-4.

The western boundary at the Great Sea (v. 6) is reminiscent of the idealized description in the promise statements, such as Gen 15:18 and Exod 23:31.

The description of the northern boundary

(vv. 7-9) has only slight variations from the limits of the land as described in Ezek 47:15-17 and 48:1.

The eastern boundary, however, differs from the usual idealized extent of the land that would include territory on both sides of the Jordan (compare Ezek 47:18). The definition in verses 10-12 follows the line of the Jordan River and thus excludes the Transjordanian land.

The boundary at the Jordan is, of course, intentional, to indicate that the land in question is that to be divided among the "nine and one half tribes" (v. 13). The other two and one half tribes have already received their heritage on the eastern side of the Jordan (vv. 14-15; ch. 32). It is the land to be divided in the future that is highlighted.

To carry out the allotment of the land, Joshua and Eleazar are to be assisted by leaders from the individual tribes (vv. 17-18), in much the way that Moses and Aaron were assisted in the census (see 1:4-16). All the names of the leaders in verses 20-28 are new. Only Caleb (v. 19), who survived the wilderness period, has a place in tradition (see 14:6, 24, 30, 38).

The order of the tribes differs from any other, whether for the census or for the arrangement in the camp. Here the listing is governed by the geographical order in which each tribe holds land in Canaan, going from the south to the north (compare Josh 14–19). The nine and one half tribes that will occupy Canaan are grouped into the four southern tribes (vv. 19-22), the one and one half central tribes of the family of Joseph (vv. 23-24), and the four northern tribes (vv. 25-28).

35:1-8 Cities for the Levites. Because the Levites have no land for their inheritance, they are assigned cities in which to live and an expanse of land around the cities for their pastures (vv. 2-5). The cities and the land are to be appropriated from the tribes according to their size (v. 8). Forty-eight cities in all will be given to the Levites (v. 7).

We have here only the regulation for the assignment of cities and lands to the Levites. The apportionment that totals precisely forty-eight cities can be found in Josh 21:4-8. The land is to come from territory of all the tribes, including those in the Transjordan.

35:9-15 Cities of asylum. The cities of asylum are linked with the Levitical cities in verse 6. This verse states that of the forty-eight cities assigned to the Levites, six must be set aside as places where a person who takes a life unintentionally may find refuge (also v. 11). Three of these cities will be located in Canaan and three in the Transjordan (vv. 13-14). This regulation only specifies that such cities must be set aside; their names are given in Josh 20:1-9, especially vv. 7-8, and 21:21, 27, 32, 36, 38.

The cities are designated as places where all people, resident or alien (v. 15a), may seek refuge from revenge before they have had a chance to face trial (vv. 12, 15b) in cases where blood has been spilled. The law stipulates that a person who commits murder deserves death (Exod 21:12, 14). The death sentence is often carried out by the "avenger of blood" (v. 12), the nearest male relative of the deceased, before there is proof that the death was caused deliberately. The designation of cities of refuge represents a development in the law based on respect for human life. The legislation guarantees legal protection for an accused person.

35:16-34 Murder and manslaughter. The stipulations make clear which individuals have the right of asylum. The willful murderer is to be handed over to the avenger, the next of kin to the deceased, who is responsible for carrying out the death sentence (vv. 19, 21b). Willfulness is evidenced by a death-dealing weapon in hand (vv. 16-18) or when there is indication of hatred or enmity (vv. 20-21).

On the other hand, if death was caused accidentally (vv. 22-23), the community is required to protect the accused from the avenger (vv. 24-25a). After first determining that there was no intention to kill, the community will send the accused back to the city of asylum, where that person will stay safely until the death of the high priest (v. 25b). Loss of life is such a serious matter that, though it may have been caused accidentally, the person involved is nonetheless deprived of freedom. In fact, an accused person who leaves a city of asylum before the specified time can still be put to death by the avenger (vv. 26-28). Underlying this eagerness to take a life for a life is a keen sense of maintaining the balance of power in individual tribes. Intentional loss of life in one family calls for loss of life in the other.

Other norms govern the community when it is making decisions that justice might prevail and that both the accused and the community might be protected (v. 29). First, an accused person cannot be condemned to death except on the evidence of several witnesses (v. 30; see Deut 17:6; 19:15). Second, the condemned murderer may not substitute payment in place of suffering loss of life (v. 31); nor may a person relegated to a city of asylum buy release from the city (v. 32).

The demands seem very great. Israel is a society in which life is regarded as a precious gift from Yahweh. The shedding of blood desecrates the land—the very land in which Yahweh dwells in the midst of Israel, where Yahweh is present with the people in covenant. The land is not to be defiled for the simple reason that the God who is present with Israel is Yahweh, the God who brought Israel out of Egypt in order to dwell among them (v. 34; see Exod 29:45-46; Lev 26:11-13).

The chapter ends on a note that summarizes the theological focus of the Priestly work. All the preparations for entry into the land and all the legislation for living faithfully in the land have one motivation—to make Israel a holy place worthy of a holy God who is present in its midst.

36:1-12 Property of heiresses. The case brought to Moses for resolution in 27:1-11 created a problem that is presented here for consideration. The case has its immediate setting in the Machir clan of the tribe of Manasseh, which has already been assigned territory in the Transjordan. The leaders of that clan now come before Moses and Eleazar (v. 1) with the concern that the daughters of Zelophehad might marry into another Israelite family and thereby cause the loss of land to their father's tribe (vv. 2-3), for when a woman marries, all her possessions become the property of her husband. At issue is the diminishment of land allotted to the tribe under God's direction. The leaders add that the land would become the permanent possession of the husband's tribe in the jubilee year (v. 4; see Lev 25:8-34). The laws governing the jubilee year require that all land that has been sold be returned to its original possessor every fiftieth year. This law apparently does not affect land that has passed to another tribe as a result of marriage into the tribe.

The first ruling created a problem that requires modification. The new ruling does not negate the first decision, which gives women the right of inheritance when there are no male members. Moses offers the modification that Zelophehad's daughters may marry only into a clan within their own family so that no land will be lost to the family (vv. 5-7). The new legislation, then, becomes the precedent for all cases of inheritance by women so that each tribe might retain the inheritance allotted to it (vv. 8-9).

A final note is added with the announcement that the daughters of Zelophehad did marry within the clans of their father's family (vv. 10-12).

36:13 Conclusion. The Book of Numbers closes with a subscription to the rules and regulations gathered together in chapters 27–36. These were given while the people remained on the plains of Moab so that they might live faithfully when they enter the land Yahweh has given them and thus possess the land as a permanent inheritance.

DEUTERONOMY

Leslie J. Hoppe, O.F.M.

INTRODUCTION

Deuteronomy and the biblical tradition

The Book of Deuteronomy is certainly one of the most important and influential books in the Hebrew Scriptures. It provided the theological perspectives that dominated the Former Prophets (Joshua, Judges, Samuel, and Kings), now commonly known as the Deuteronomistic History of Israel. It exerted its influence over the final shape of a number of prophetic books, notably Hosea and Jeremiah. Indirectly it influenced the Chronicler's History of Israel (Chronicles, Ezra, and Nehemiah). The Temple Scroll of the Qumran community was basically an Essene reinterpretation of Deuteronomy. The New Testament cites or alludes to Deuteronomic texts almost two hundred times. Deuteronomy's reinterpretation of selected items of ancient Israelite law and history provided a model for the rabbis who produced the Mishnah and the Talmud. Finally, Deuteronomy's self-understanding as a written, authoritative document gave rise to the very concepts of Scripture and canon.

Deuteronomy stood at a pivotal point in the life of ancient Israel. Its pages preserved traditions that were ancient at the time of its own production. Some of the legal traditions handed on by the Deuteronomists had their origins in the pre-Israelite era of the ancient Near East. The Deuteronomists, however, were not antiquarians or even historians. Their purpose in preserving, transmitting, and reinterpreting ancient tradition was to provide Israel with some direction for its future at a time when that future was in great doubt. The

Deuteronomists did their work well, for the phenomenon we know today as early Judaism was shaped in large measure by the Book of Deuteronomy. Their work, then, stood as the bridge between the religion of ancient Israel and the faith of early Judaism.

The meaning of Deuteronomy

Because of its obvious importance, the Book of Deuteronomy has attracted much attention over the years. Interpreters of the book have described it as a covenantal document, an example of Levitical preaching, a charter for religious revival, a response to the culture shock of foreign domination, an attempt at humanizing ancient laws, a call for cultic purity, and the basis for cult centralization. It has been disparaged as being morally simplistic and praised for its call for Israel to love God (Deut 6:5). The Deuteronomists have been called harsh and unsympathetic teachers as well as some of the greatest liberal theologians of all time. The diversity of these comments on, and characterizations of, Deuteronomy show how difficult it is to find a simple description for this very complex and sophisticated theological work.

Despite the complications presented by interpreters of Deuteronomy, the aim of the book was really quite simple. The Deuteronomists wanted to make ancient tradition speak again in a time of great crisis for Israel in order to help Israel survive that crisis. They saw that the great institutions of ancient Israel were dead or dying. The monarchy, prophecy, temple, and priesthood had all failed to prevent the nation from arriving at the brink of destruction, which was being caused by both internal and external forces. Deuteronomy suggested that Israel relearn the lessons of its formative years in the wilderness under Moses: obedience to the law of the Lord was the only way for Israel to secure its future. The meaning of Deuteronomy, then, was Deuteronomy itself. The book presented itself to Israel as the last hope: obey and live, or disobey and die (Deut 30:15-20).

The origins of Deuteronomy

There is no universal agreement as to the specific crisis that prompted the production of Deuteronomy. One of the longest held positions of modern biblical studies dates from the early nineteenth century and identifies the Book of Deuteronomy with the "book of the law" found in the temple by the high priest Hilkiah during the reign of Josiah (2 Kgs 22:8ff.). While the book includes much material that can be dated to the late seventh century B.C.E. and earlier, it is clear that Deuteronomy, in the form it now has, dates from the Babylonian Exile (587–539 B.C.E.). It was during the Exile that the remnant of the nation stood on the edge of extinction. In this life-or-death situation, the Deuteronomists presented Israel with the challenge of obedience to a written, authoritative book of the law and called for the nation to choose life (Deut 30:19). This exilic date for Deuteronomy does not eliminate the possibility that earlier traditions were used in the production of the book. On the contrary, Deuteronomy was the result of a conscious reinterpretation of ancient legal traditions for the sake of providing Israel with hope for the future.

Who were the Deuteronomists? From what circles did they emerge? Again, there has been a variety of answers to that question. At first, the prophets were presented as responsible for Deuteronomy, because at one time anything in the Hebrew Scriptures of ethical or theological value was ascribed to prophetic circles. But Deuteronomy does not treat the prophets very well (see the comment on 18:9-22).

Other interpreters have suggested that Deuteronomy reflects the preaching of the Levites. However, there are no examples of Levitical preaching in the Bible, so it is impossible to say that Deuteronomy is the product of such activity. In addition, the book consistently portrays the Levites as objects of charity, hardly a flattering self-portrait.

The sages of Israel have even been credited with the production of Deuteronomy, but they never even appear in the book that they supposedly composed and presented to Israel as the pattern for its life.

The one group that remains a possibility is the elders of Israel. These were the leaders of the community who were the traditional administrators of the very laws preserved in Deuteronomy. They were the principal guardians of ancient Israel's legal traditions. Why should they not be credited with Deuteronomy, the depository of these traditions?

Deuteronomy was composed in order to provide a new pattern of life for Israel in its land. During the Exile, Israel found itself outside that land, hoping to take possession of it once again. Deuteronomy came to light during the Exile. It was created by the elders, who considered themselves to be the custodians of Israel's ancient legal traditions. They took those traditions, altered them, developed them, enlarged them, and drew theological conclusions from them—all for the sake of providing Israel with a new pattern of life. It was this vision for a new life that gave the elders the impetus to create the Book of Deuteronomy.

Form and structure

Any analysis of Deuteronomy's literary form must begin with the book's connections with ancient Near Eastern treaty traditions. In the ancient world, treaties between nations followed a particular pattern, which usually included the following five components: (1) a title that identified the king offering the treaty; (2) a historical prologue, in which the king offering the treaty listed his beneficent acts toward the people accepting the treaty; (3) stipulations or demands made by the king offering the treaty; (4) a list of witnesses to the treaty, and occasionally provisions for storing and periodic reading of the treaty; (5) curses and blessings that would follow upon violation and observance of the treaty. Even a superficial reading of Deuteronomy will make it clear that there is a connection between Deuteronomy and the international treaty form.

At the same time, it is important to note

that Deuteronomy is not presented as if it were a treaty. It makes use of literary forms from the treaty tradition, but it is presented as a series of addresses given to Israel by Moses just before his death. Deuteronomy is Moses' testament to Israel, which is to take possession of the land of Canaan in a short while. It is not the text of a treaty or covenant. While the book may contain elements of the treaty form, it also contains material that cannot be included among such forms (see Deut 32–34).

In its present form, Deuteronomy is composed of four addresses given to Israel by Moses. The tone of these addresses is exhortatory. The book is meant to encourage Israel to obey the law. Moses portrays Israel as specially chosen by God to take possession of Canaan. Israel will maintain its hold on that land as long as it is obedient. (This commentary will follow the structure evident in the book itself, which divides the material into four separate addresses, each introduced by a formulaic expression which asserts that what follows are the words of Moses: Deut 1:1; 4:44; 29:1; 33:1.)

The exhortation to obedience is the core of Deuteronomy, but, as Deut 29:1 indicates, this exhortation was transformed into the text of a treaty or covenant between God and Israel. The ancient customs and laws that regulated the mutual relationships of the people became the test of their loyalty to God. The quality of intersocietal relationships within Israel became the barometer of Israel's relationship with God. Accordingly, for Deuteronomy, to know and love God means to love one's neighbors and do them justice. This, of course, is affirmed in the New Testament in a number of places, for example, Mark 12:29-31 and 1 John 4:7-12, 20-21. Thus, the elements of the ancient Near Eastern treaty tradition were introduced into the Book of Deuteronomy in order to give new value and importance to obedience. The effect of this transformation was to make one's love of neighbor the standard and test of one's love of God.

COMMENTARY

MOSES' FIRST ADDRESS

Deut 1:1–4:43

The scene of Moses' address to Israel is the region known as the plains of Moab, immediately east of the Jordan River. The time is just before the tribes are to take possession of the land promised to their ancestors. The context of these final words of Moses is an exhortation to obedience. This "testament" of Moses is his advice to Israel to heed the lessons of the past if it wants to secure its future. The lesson is simple enough: God expects complete loyalty from Israel; nothing less is satisfactory. Israel's trek through the wilderness after its departure from Egypt has taught it over and over again that loyalty is rewarded and infidelity is punished. Moses will now spend his last energies in trying to move Israel to the kind of obedience, loyalty, and commitment that will secure Israel's future in the land it will soon come to possess.

1:1-5 The preface to the first address. These verses function as a preamble, introducing not only the first of Moses' four addresses but also the entire book as well. They specify the persons involved in the events of the book, the scene of the action, and the exact time and purpose of the work. Deuteronomy purports to be the words of Moses addressed to all Israel. Here the book underscores the unity of the people of God, all of whom are subject to the divine will.

While the location where the address is given is specified with precision (vv. 1b-2), the exact location of all the sites mentioned is not known, though it is clear that the scene of the action is on the east side of the Jordan River.

Moses begins his first address to the tribes just before Israel is to cross the Jordan to take possession of the land promised to its ancestors. It is now forty years since the Exodus. Preliminary victories have already been won, but Israel, poised on the plains of Moab, hears Moses deliver a final plea for obedience as he makes the Lord's will absolutely clear to all Israel. The purpose of this exposition is to move Israel to renewed commitment.

1:6-18 The move from Horeb. Moses' first address begins with a direct quotation of

God's words at Horeb (Mount Sinai) calling Israel to begin the journey that will end with acquisition of the land that is to be the scene of its subsequent history. The dimensions given for the land (v. 7) reflect the promise made to Abraham (Gen 15:18) rather than any set of historical borders. This promise is now fulfilled as the land is shown to Israel and thereby passes into its possession. All that remains is for Israel to take physical possession of its inheritance. That, however, will be no easy task.

Verses 9-18 interrupt the account of Israel's departure from Horeb, which is resumed in verse 19. After arriving at Horeb, Moses foresaw the difficulties ahead and suggested that the people select leaders to share the burdens of leadership with himself (v. 13). Though Moses had played an indispensable role in leading Israel from Egypt to the threshold of the Promised Land, Israel reached a point in its life when others were to first share, and then finally take over, the responsibilities which up to that point Moses had had to bear alone. It is significant that Israel was to choose its own leaders. Any breakdown in the morale or loyalty of the people would be due to the decisions of these leaders. God could not be blamed, since Moses simply confirmed those leaders whom the people themselves presented to him.

Among the leaders confirmed in office by Moses were judges, who were specifically charged to administer justice without regard to the social and economic differences between the people who had disputes before them (vv. 16-17). Justice among Israelites was based on the premise of the equality of all Israelites. In fact, the mantle of equality was even placed on the shoulders of aliens residing among the Israelites (v. 16).

This section closes with the parenthetical note that Israel was fully instructed regarding its responsibilities in its new relationship with God (v. 18). Israel could not plead ignorance if it failed in that relationship.

1:19-46 Israel's failure at Kadesh-barnea. The journey from Horeb ended at Kadesh-barnea, a site in the south of Canaan. Kadesh-barnea was to serve as a base of operations from which the Israelite tribes were to begin the process of acquiring the land promised to them. It should have been the scene of initial victories; instead, it was the scene of Israel's

first defeat. The nation was defeated because of its lack of confidence in God.

The people suggested that spies be sent to reconnoiter the land and its inhabitants (v. 22). The spies returned with glowing reports about the land, but with terrifying reports about the indigenous population of Canaan. The Israelites recoiled at the possibility of having to face the Canaanites in any type of armed conflict. Moses tried to encourage the people by reminding them of God's deliverance of Israel from Egypt and the guidance through the wilderness, but to no avail.

God's response was to allow the people just what they wanted—a safe haven outside the Promised Land. God would wait for the next generation to begin the settlement of Canaan. In addition, Moses was condemned to die outside the new land (v. 37). As the people's leader, he was most responsible for Israel's loss of faith. Only Caleb, Joshua, and the children of the rebellious generation would be spared the effects of the people's decision to remain outside Canaan.

After some time the people decided that they indeed wanted to take possession of Canaan, but it was too late. They were easily defeated by the Amorites. They had to live with the effects of their disobedience. Kadesh, not Canaan, was to be their home.

2:1-23 Peaceful transit through Edom, Moab and Ammon. In telling the story of Israel's experiences in Transjordan, the Deuteronomists assume that there was a peaceful transit through the areas that were not settled by the Israelite tribes. There was to be no conflict over these territories, since God had allotted them to their respective inhabitants at another time (vv. 5, 9, 19).

Other biblical traditions consider the populations of these territories to be related to the Israelites: in the case of the Moabites and Ammonites, through Lot, Abraham's nephew (Gen 19:36-38); and in the case of the Edomites, through Esau, the brother of Jacob (Gen 36:9).

Still other traditions preserve the memory of tensions that did exist between these people and the advancing Israelites. According to Num 20:14-21, Edom refused to permit the Israelites to traverse its territory, and Num 22–24 reports the attempt of Balak of Moab to obtain a curse upon Israel.

The most significant feature of the Deuteronomic tradition about Israel's relations with these peoples is the universalism which undergirds that tradition here. The God of Israel also gives the peoples of these Transjordanian countries the land they inhabit. Clearly, God's concern extends beyond the pale of Israel.

While Israel was spared conflict with these nations, according to Deuteronomy, Israel was locked in a conflict that took the lives of a whole generation of warriors. The enemy who caused Israel to suffer such a devastating defeat was none other than God (vv. 14-15). Israel's infidelity at Kadesh-barnea cost it dearly. Though God had fought for Israel against Pharaoh, God will just as easily turn against an unfaithful Israel. The Deuteronomists want to issue a warning: divine acts of deliverance in the past are no guarantee for the future! There is only one way Israel can look to the future with any hope, and that way is through obedience.

2:24–3:22 Conflicts with Sihon and Og. Though the historical presence of Israel on the east bank of the Jordan was short-lived, Deuteronomic tradition holds that the tribes of Reuben and Gad and two clans of Manasseh settled there. The tradition also assumes that the territory of these tribes was acquired in much the same way as were the lands west of the Jordan, where the other tribes settled— through armed confrontation with the indigenous population. The conflicts with the Amorites under Sihon and the people of Bashan under Og are presented as violent in the extreme (2:34; 3:6). Any conflict over the limited amount of arable land in the region had the potential for becoming very costly in terms of human lives, as are similar conflicts in the same region today. The intensity of these conflicts is not surprising, nor is the human tendency to attribute them to the divine will. The dark side of Israel's belief that it received the land as a gift from God was the practice of eliminating those who held a different belief.

Another theological issue raised by this text is the relation between the human and the divine wills. Sihon opposed Israel's entrance into his territory, but this came about because God hardened his heart (2:30). The victories that Israel won over Sihon and Og were the Lord's doing (2:33; 3:3), yet Israel's armies had to fight and defeat the forces of these two kings. The text seems to assert that both the divine and the human actions were necessary, but it does not deal at all with how the two were related.

Verse 11 is a parenthetical remark on the great size of Og's bed or sarcophagus, which was still to be seen in the Deuteronomists' day. In spite of Og's great power, his kingdom fell to an obedient Israel. Fidelity has a power that far outweighs military or political power.

The victories over Sihon and Og resulted in the distribution of their territories among the tribes of Reuben and Gad and among Machir and Jair, two clans of Manasseh. Since Sihon and Og defied the Lord (2:30; 3:1), they were defeated by the Lord's might. Their lands were now forfeit and passed to Israel. The allocation of the conquered territories was more than the settling of geographic boundaries. It was, first of all, a celebration of God's victory and a statement of belief in the divine origin of the territorial claims made by the tribes and clans named here. The same pattern— conquest followed by allocation of land— provides the basic outline of the Book of Joshua (conquest: Josh 1–12; allocation: Josh 13–21). The victories over Sihon and Og and the distribution of their land among the Israelite tribes were a harbinger of future victories on the other side of the Jordan.

The stipulations in 3:18-20 emphasize the unity of Israel, an important Deuteronomic theme. The militia of any tribe cannot rest until *all* the land of Canaan is acquired according to God's promise.

3:23-29 Joshua. Tradition locates Moses' grave outside the Promised Land (Deut 34:5). There then needs to be an explanation for this apparent injustice and for the eventual succession to Moses' position of leadership among the tribes. Regarding the former issue, the Deuteronomists opt for a solution that preserves Moses' integrity. Though he was personally innocent of any guilt, Moses was unfortunately caught up in the wake of infidelity that enveloped the whole generation of rebellion at Kadesh-barnea (1:26). This contrasts with the Priestly tradition, which accused Moses himself of a breach of faith that resulted in his exclusion from the Promised Land (Num 20:12). These two different explanations for the tradition about the grave of

Moses probably reflect the exilic debate between communal guilt and personal responsibility as an explanation for the presence of evil and suffering in Israel's life.

Another concern of the Deuteronomists is to demonstrate that the Mosaic office could continue beyond the death of Moses. Joshua was the first successor to Moses. There could then be others in the future who could do what Moses once did for Israel—transmit and interpret the divine will for Israel. If the law was to be the one guide for Israel's life in the land, Moses had to have legitimate successors who could provide Israel with access to the law and its interpretation (see Matt 23:2; *Pirke Aboth* 1:1).

4:1-40 The conclusion to the first address. Moses' first address concludes with a summary not simply of the foregoing material but of the entire Book of Deuteronomy. The material found here was incorporated into Deuteronomy during the Exile (587–539 B.C.E.), when circumstances forced Israel to reconsider the meaning of its relationship with God and to examine the status of that relationship.

The Book of Deuteronomy as a whole and this chapter in particular speak of the fundamental loyalty that is essential to Israel's unique relationship with God. Here the Exile is explained as one result of a serious lapse in that loyalty as manifested in Israel's disregard of the prohibition of images (vv. 25-27). The folly of serving other gods brought on the Exile (v. 28). Once Israel realizes what befalls those who are unfaithful, repentance is possible (vv. 29-30). Finally, the compassion of God does not allow Israel's infidelity to end the relationship that exists between God and Israel, since God remains faithful to the promise made to Israel's ancestors (v. 31). As disastrous as was Israel's disloyalty, it still did not mean the end of its relationship with God.

It is clear that obedience is the key to maintaining Israel's relationship with God, which is made tangible by its possession of the Promised Land. Five times this text speaks of the connection between obedience and possession of the land (vv. 1, 5-8, 14, 21-22, 40). The text uses the concrete example of the prohibition of images to show the results of disobedience (vv. 3-4, 15-26). When Israel disregarded God's commandments, disaster followed. Flouting the stipulations of the covenant (v. 13) resulted in Israel's exile from the land (vv. 26-27). The faith of the Deuteronomists leads them to expect that God will bring blessing from the curse of the Exile (v. 31) and restore Israel to an intimacy with God that is unparalleled (vv. 32-39).

Obedience, then, is the foundation of Israel's relationship with God, since it brings Israel closer to God than is thought humanly possible (v. 6). It is the uniqueness of Israel's God (v. 39) and of the covenant this God makes with Israel (v. 13) that makes Israel unlike any other people. To secure its future, Israel need only recognize what is so obvious and order its life according to the commandments. A life lived in obedience will bring not only renown (vv. 6-7) but also long life in the Promised Land (v. 40).

This text is a clear warning: disobedience arouses Israel's God, who does not tolerate infidelity. Disobedience will mean that God's power will be turned *against* Israel just as easily as it was once manifested *for* Israel (vv. 34-35). The key of Israel's future is the Book of Deuteronomy itself, since it is the collection of the "statutes and commandments" that Israel must obey to secure long life in the land (4:1, 40).

4:41-43 The cities of refuge. A complete presentation on the cities of refuge occurs in Deut 19, which makes no allusion to this passage. In Num 35:13-14 it is stated that three cities of refuge are to be set up on the east side of the Jordan. The three cities in question are named in Josh 20:8. Clearly, this text was added to its present context under the impression that these cities were established by Moses. This text probably would have fit better after Deut 3:12-17, in which Moses allots land to the tribes and clans that will remain in Transjordan. The exact location of these cities is unknown.

MOSES' SECOND ADDRESS

Deut 4:44–28:69

4:44-49 Introduction. Both the time and place of Moses' second address are specified. Moses gives this speech near Beth-peor (v. 46). This was the site of an infamous act of apostasy (Num 25). Here the Israelites had shown themselves ready to compromise the absolute fidelity that God expected of them. It was also within the borders of the new land that God had just given the tribes (Deut 2:24–3:17). Thus, Beth-peor is a reminder of God's graciousness, which overcame Israel's infidelity. The law that follows is to be the means of assuring that Israel will remain committed to the service of God alone. This speech is given by Moses after the initial victories of Israel over the Amorites (vv. 46-47). These latest demonstrations of God's graciousness should be a powerful stimulus to fidelity.

5:1–6:3 The Ten Commandments. With Israel standing in Transjordan, the promise made to the ancestors of the Israelite tribes is on the verge of fulfillment. The people who have been living by the promise now need to learn how to live with the fulfillment. The most dramatic shift in this transition is to learn that continued possession of the land is dependent upon fidelity to God. The initial acquisition of the land is the result of God's fidelity to the promises made to the ancestors of the Israelite tribes; now the Israelites need to respond to that fidelity if they wish to remain in their new land.

The Ten Commandments are to guide Israel in this transition from living by the promise to living with its fulfillment. The Decalogue provides Israel with a means to maintain a continuing relationship with God. These Ten Words, as Jewish tradition calls them, serve to pattern Israel's response to the God who brought it out of slavery in Egypt (5:6) and who is about to lead it into a new land. The commandments are restrictive in only one way: they call for Israel's uncompromising fidelity to the God who has fulfilled every promise made to Israel. They commit Israel to the exclusive service of God. This ensures that Israel will live and prosper in the land God is about to give it (5:33–6:3).

(*Note:* The numbering of the commandments here follows the Roman Catholic and Lutheran tradition. Other Christians and the Rabbis divide the prohibitions against false worship into two separate commandments [vv. 6-7 and 8-9] and unite the prohibitions of coveting into one [v. 21]. Another version of the Ten Commandments can be found in Exod 20:2-17.)

The first commandment (vv. 6-10) exemplifies God's passion for Israel's absolute fidelity. Once Israel settles in its land, there will be temptations to compromise the loyalty owed to God. The Israelites are looking forward to what will be a new experience for them—a life of freedom in their own land. What must not change for them is their commitment to God. Their whole life is to be determined by their relationship with the God who brought them out of Egypt. The prohibition of images (vv. 8-9) reminds Israel that its knowledge of God is to be gained from its experience of the reality of God that it encountered in the Exodus from Egypt and in the guidance in the wilderness.

The second commandment (v. 11) prohibits the attempt to harness with magic the power that the ancients believed was inherent in the divine name. In early Jewish tradition it became customary to avoid mentioning the divine name entirely. The God of Israel was beyond manipulation. God's name was not to be linked with any selfish human purpose. The commandment regarding the sabbath (vv. 12-15) imposes two obligations: to make the sabbath day holy (v. 12) and to cease work on that day (v. 13). The two obligations are related, since the day of rest provides the Israelites with the opportunity to remember their slavery in Egypt and their liberation by the power of God. The sabbath is to be a regular weekly reminder of Israel's dependence upon God.

The fourth commandment (v. 16) stands as a bridge between those that precede and those that follow it. The commandments deal with two kinds of relationships. The first three commandments focus on the relationship between God and Israel, while the last seven deal with the relationships that must exist within the Israelite community itself. Israel will be able to remain loyal to God as long as the people remain loyal to one another. The parent/child relationship is not only analogous to the divine/human relationship (1:31), but it is also the core relationship within the Israelite community.

This community will not be able to endure if human life can be taken for personal and illegitimate reasons, so murder is prohibited (v. 17). Murder ignores a person's status and worth as God's creature, and as such it is an attack on the Creator's prerogatives. Another threat to the life of the community is any threat to the binding commitment of faithfulness made by husband and wife. The sixth commandment (v. 18) aims to protect the marriage relationship. Infidelity is reprehensible to God, who is always faithful.

The seventh commandment (v. 19) is most probably concerned with crimes against persons rather than theft of property. Members of the Israelite community are not to turn against one another. For example, the slave trade is forbidden here. But in a wider sense, any action by which one human being takes control over the life of another is outlawed. Human beings are not to be manipulated but are to be given the freedom necessary to maintain a faithful relationship with God.

Another prerequisite for a healthy community is integrity and honesty in human relationships. The eighth commandment (v. 20) seeks to protect these values. The God who is faithful in every word and deed requires the same honesty in human relationships. Finally, the last two commandments (v. 21) prohibit coveting. Not only are actions disruptive to community life forbidden, but also proscribed are the desires that lead to such crimes. Self-interest must be kept in close check before it becomes the dominant force in a person's life. The position of the wife in the Deuteronomic form of this commandment differs from that of Exod 20:17, in which the wife is placed among the husband's property. Here the woman has a more favorable status.

The commandments come from God, but they are interpreted through Moses (vv. 22-33). Both the people and God choose Moses as the mediator of the law, which derives its authority from God and its applicability from Moses. Later, Deuteronomy will speak about the successors to the Mosaic office (18:15-19). But this text attests to the authenticity of Israel's encounter with God as mediated through a human being.

The section of the second address containing the Ten Commandments closes with a short exhortation that attempts to provide motives for obedience (6:1-3). The principal reason given is that obedience will lead to the fulfillment of the promises made to Israel's ancestors: a fruitful land and a numerous progeny. The Exile, which meant living outside the land and in numbers decimated by the war with Babylon, could be seen as nothing less than a course resulting from Israel's disobedience.

6:4-25 The love of God. The concern of this text is to promote obedience to a particular commandment: the prohibition of the worship of gods other than the Lord. The Israelites are preparing to enter a very prosperous land (vv. 10-11). Moses warns them against rashly concluding that the prosperity of the land is due to the beneficence of the gods worshiped by that land's indigenous population. Israel is never to forget what happened in Egypt (v. 12). The Lord's liberation of Israel from slavery in Egypt has forged a bond that must never be severed by Israel's service of deities worshiped by other peoples. Israel is not to divide its loyalties.

There are a variety of ways in which verse 4 can be translated (compare the rendering of the Revised Standard Version: "The Lord our God is one Lord"). Though each can be defended on linguistic and theological grounds, the New American Bible translation best fits this context, which emphasizes the exclusiveness of Israel's service of Yahweh. While this verse and its context underscore the loyalty that Israel owes to the Lord, this is not a statement of explicit monotheism. In fact, the possibility that other gods exist is implicit here. For Israel, however, there is only one God, and all of its energies are to be directed to the service of that one God.

Some may find it odd that verse 5 *commands* the love of God. The love envisioned here is the kind of deep loyalty and affection that Israel owes to the God who ended its cruel bondage in Egypt. Secondly, in Deuteronomy love is virtually synonymous with obedience. The image behind this injunction is the parent/child relationship, in which love and obedience are equivalent terms. The love that Israel owes God is all-encompassing. In fact, the entire Book of Deuteronomy is nothing else but a drawing out of the practical implications of verse 5. Jesus cited this verse when asked about the greatest commandment of the law (Matt 22:36-37; Mark 12:28-30).

The injunctions of verses 7-9 stress how total Israel's devotion to God's commands must be. Israel is to keep the commandments in mind at all times and under all circumstances. Early Judaism turned these metaphors into commands. Jews began the custom of wearing phylacteries (small leather containers holding tiny scrolls, on which were inscribed verses 4-9 as well as other biblical texts). Jesus' criticism of this custom assumes that obedience to this command was not always accompanied by the kind of total obedience envisioned by verse 5 (see Matt 23:5). Jews also began to attach a *mezuzah* (a small container holding a written biblical text) to the upper part of the right doorpost. Rather than establishing any specific customs, Deuteronomy is trying to insure that individual Israelites, their homes, and the entire community will be outstanding in their loyalty to God. The basis of this loyalty is God's liberation of Israel from slavery (v. 12) and God's insistence on fidelity (v. 14). There is no need to determine the strength of God's loyalty to Israel; that was tried once before, with disastrous results (v. 16; see Exod 17:1-7).

The last section of this passage (vv. 20-25) is simply a reprise of what has already been said. (Such repetitions are characteristic of Deuteronomy and lead some interpreters to locate the origins of the book in the situation of teaching and/or preaching.) At one time Israel was a slave of Pharaoh (v. 21). God freed Israel from slavery through a mighty display of power against Egypt (v. 22). The purpose of this gracious act was the fulfillment of the promises made to Israel's ancestors (v. 23). God now requires absolute loyalty from Israel, and this loyalty is Israel's only hope for the future (v. 24). Obedience, loyalty, and reverence are the keys to the kind of relationship with God that will preserve Israel's future (v. 25).

7:1-26 The nations. The Bible's pendulum swings back and forth with regard to the non-Israelite nations. At times the nations, too, will share in the blessings promised to Israel (Gen 12:1-3; Isa 42:1-4). They will be converted to the Lord (Isa 45:14-25; Jonah). At other times the nations are presented as Israel's implacable enemies, whose downfall is cause for rejoicing (Amos 1-3; Nahum).

This text is one of the harshest condemnations in the whole Bible, requiring Israel to annihilate the indigenous population of Canaan in the process of settling in the land promised to the ancestors of Israel (v. 2). Such a command is clearly abhorrent to the moral sensitivities of contemporary readers, but we should remember that this command was never carried out, nor was it ever intended to be. What, then, would have been the point of forbidding covenants and marriage with non-Israelite nations (vv. 2b-3)? This chapter represents a theological judgment on the nations, not a historical account of Israel's treatment of them.

While this theological judgment also is not very attractive to believers today, it reflects Israel's experience with the nations, especially Assyria and Babylon, which were serious threats to Israel's very existence at the time the Deuteronomic tradition was beginning to take shape. In these circumstances, Deuteronomy uses the strongest possible terms to mandate that Israel avoid any contact with the nations. The assumption behind such a prohibition is that cultural assimilation is just as great a threat to Israel's existence as is the political and military pressure being brought to bear upon Israel by the powerful nations warring against it.

7:1-5 Israel's enemies. Here the attitude toward the nations is unmistakably negative: every possible contact with them is to be avoided. No political agreements are to be made with them (v. 2b), for entering into such agreements would entail an explicit acknowledgment of the gods of the nations. While verse 3 may be directed at any type of intermarriage, the Deuteronomists more than likely have in mind marriages as political maneuvers (see 1 Kgs 11:1-8). These, too, inevitably involve explicit recognition of foreign deities. Finally, Israel is to destroy the appurtenances of the worship associated with these gods (v. 5). Adapting these to the worship of Yahweh, which apparently has been attempted (see 2 Kgs 18:4b), results in blurring the distinction between the God of Israel and the gods of the nations. Israel is to be committed to the service of Yahweh alone (Deut 6).

7:6-11 Holiness. The prohibitions regarding contact with the nations arose, not from any superiority on Israel's part, but because of Israel's election and the grave danger of Israel's failure to its responsibilities to God. Israel has been set apart from all other nations. The law was given to Israel in order to maintain that special relationship with God. The basis of this relationship is not Israel's inherent qualities but the divine love that focused its choice upon the least of all nations. People are to recognize Israel as God's choice because of Israel's love and obedience directed toward God. This fidelity will be rewarded, but quick retaliation will come to the unfaithful.

7:12-16 Blessing. God's fidelity is beyond question. The course of Israel's future, then, is largely dependent upon the quality of its adherence to the responsibilities that flow from its unique relationship with God. In a sense, the complete fulfillment of the promises made to Israel's ancestors depends upon Israel's obedience. Here Deuteronomy welds two covenantal traditions together. The unconditional promises made to Abraham, Isaac, and Jacob become bound to the conditional covenantal traditions related to Moses. The result of obedience is blessing, which is described here as abundance of life, prosperity, and well-being—a stark contrast to the conditions that afflicted those who experienced slavery in Egypt. But these blessings depend upon Israel's firm commitment to God and the preservation of its unique identity as the elect people of God.

7:17-26 Israel's victories. The nation of Israel ought to devote itself to obedience with reckless abandon. The metaphor used to illustrate this kind of obedience is Israel's armed conflicts with the population of Canaan. If Israel approaches these conflicts with absolute trust in God and total fearlessness in the face of human opposition, victory can be assured, for God will throw all Israel's opponents into a terrible panic, resulting in Israel's total victory. Verse 22 is an interesting bit of apologetic to explain why Israel's victories during the conquest were not complete. Judges 2:20-23 provides still another explanation: a few of Israel's enemies were allowed to survive in order to test Israel's faith.

8:1-20 A study in contrasts. Though Israel may eliminate external threats to the loyalty it owes to God, this does not mean that this loyalty is assured. There are also internal threats to Israel's commitment. These need to be identified. They may not appear to be as insidious as the worship of foreign gods, but in reality they are no less threatening to the allegiance that God expects of Israel. Moses now turns to these dangers from within and speaks of them by contrasting "remembering" and "forgetting," the desert and the arable land, human self-sufficiency and dependence upon God. These three contrasts are interwoven throughout this chapter, whose purpose is to keep Israel ever mindful of God.

Remembering the gracious acts of God in the Exodus from Egypt and in the guidance in the wilderness is basic to Israel's relationship with God, for such remembering is a stimulus to obedience. Remembering what God has done allows every generation to experience the reality and fidelity of God. Forgetting God leads inevitably to disobedience. The human will substitutes for the divine will. The claims of God are pushed to the sidelines of human awareness.

The contrast between the desert and the arable land does not intend to highlight the sterility of the former and the fertility of the latter; the contrast between the two lies in how the desert kept Israel from forgetting God, while the richness of the new land that Israel will possess can numb Israel to the divine presence. The wilderness was a place of testing as Israel learned to see its existence as totally dependent upon God. The harshness of life in the wilderness made it almost impossible to ignore divine nurture. To drive the point home even more dramatically, God cut off even the meager supply of food in the desert and had Israel live off manna, a miraculous source of nourishment. In the land of promise, Israel will have food in abundance, and then will come the inevitable temptation of believing that the abundance is the result of human efforts. In reality, divine providence supplies Israel's needs in both the wilderness and the new land.

God's purpose for Israel was achieved through human cooperation. Moses was the instrument God used to lead Israel out of Egypt and through the wilderness. The land of the promise is to be acquired through the leadership of Joshua and the efforts of the tribal militia. What begins with human cooperation can end with the pride of human self-sufficiency. Moses warns Israel that it can never afford to ignore the sustaining power of God, which may have been more evident in the wilderness but is just as much a reality in the arable land. Israel will be as dependent upon God in the new land as it was in the desert.

These three contrasts are intertwined with three commands calling for the fundamental, unswerving loyalty to God that is the hallmark of the Deuteronomic tradition (vv. 1, 11, 18). In each of these commands the word "today" emphasizes that every generation of Israel needs to remember God. Forgetfulness will lead to disaster.

The first command (v. 1) is the typical Deuteronomic call for obedience. It locates the motivation for obedience in the gifts of land and prosperity.

The second command (v. 11) is a more specific warning against ignoring the continuing role that God plays in Israel's life. Yahweh's sustenance of Israel is not limited to the wilderness period. Israel should broaden its horizons beyond that which is immediately known and experienced. Its prosperity in the land must not allow the reality of God to fade from its consciousness.

Finally, the third command (vv. 18-20) is a stern reminder of the consequences of "forgetting." It puts Israel on the same level as the nations that were not chosen to be God's own people. This, of course, would be the worst kind of disaster, for Israel is to remain a people with a unique relationship to God. But if Israel does not "remember" God, it will become easy to follow and serve the gods of the nations. Israel would then behave just as the nations it dispossessed behave. If Israel forgets God, it can look forward to being expelled from the land just as the nations were expelled.

9:1–10:11 Israel's stubbornness and God's grace. Another internal threat to Israel's relationship with God is Israel's belief in its own righteousness. Israel is, of course, totally dependent upon God's help in acquiring the land, but in order to reinforce the theme of Israel's unworthiness, Deuteronomy reminds Israel of its rebellion in the wilderness. Even as Moses was sealing the covenant between God and Israel, the people were worshiping an idol. The act of rebellion was enough to prompt God to destroy Israel. It was only through the intercession of Moses that Israel was saved from the full effects of God's anger so that the promises made to Israel's ancestors might be fulfilled.

9:1-6 The land as gift. Israel's victories over the Canaanites, represented by the Anakim (legendary giants), and their fortified cities will be due to God's power and fidelity. But because Israel itself will have to subdue the Canaanites (v. 3b), there will be the temptation to ignore God's help. In addition, the belief stated here (vv. 4-5) and in Gen 15:16 that the nations are being dispossessed because of their wickedness can easily be warped into a belief in Israel's righteousness.

The truth is that Israel is no better than the nations. Despite all that God had done for Israel, the people were rebellious and stubborn in their refusal to serve God alone. The only reason Israel is favored over the nations is the oath that God swore to Abraham, Isaac, and Jacob (v. 5).

9:7-14 Rebellion. While Moses was in communion with God at Horeb, Israel turned to idolatry. At the very moment the covenant was being sealed, it was being broken by Israel. The irony is bitter. There could not have been a more inappropriate time for Israel to rebel, yet rebel is just what Israel did even as it stood at the very foot of God's mountain.

In verse 6 Moses called Israel a "stiffnecked" people; in verse 13 it is Yahweh who voices this condemnation of the people, along with the clear intention to destroy them. The wickedness of the nations led God to dispossess them; Israel's rebellion was now turning God against it as well. God's words to Moses in verse 14, "Let me be," were not taken by him as a prohibition but rather as an invitation to intercession. It is Moses who was able to turn God's anger from Israel, but before he began his intercession, Moses came down from the mountain and confronted the people who forgot their God.

9:15-21 The covenant is broken. Whatever the reason for the construction of the golden calf, Deuteronomy understands it as a direct breach of the command of God prohibiting false worship and the use of images. Moses' action in breaking the two tablets was not the result of an angry fit; he destroyed the tablets, which symbolized the covenantal bond between God and Israel, because Israel chose to destroy that relationship. As symbols, the tablets were robbed of all their significance when Israel constructed the golden calf. By not hesitating to include Aaron among the guilty (v. 20), the Deuteronomists are ready to indict the priesthood for helping Israel choose the way of rebellion.

9:22-24 More rebellion. Israel rebelled more than once. These verses mention four other incidents of rebellion in order to attest to Israel's rebellious character. This fatal flaw showed itself more than once during the wilderness period. Israel survived because of Moses' intercession, but what will become of Israel when there is no one like Moses to make intercession?

9:25-29 Moses' prayer. This prayer is another contrast drawn by the Deuteronomists. When speaking to Israel, Moses recalled the past to remind the people of their wickedness and disobedience. When speaking to God, Moses reminded God about the promises made to Israel's ancestors (v. 27) and of the gracious acts of salvation in the Exodus from Egypt (v. 29). Moses reminded God about the identity of the people destined for destruction: they are *"your* people and *your* heritage" (v. 25). They are the people whom God liberated from the slavery of Egypt. Moses was hoping that he could elicit from God another act of divine liberation. Israel needed to be freed from the debilitating effects of its own rebelliousness.

10:1-5 The ark of the covenant. To symbolize a renewed covenant between God and a rebellious Israel, the Lord authorized the manufacture of two new tablets. Once these had been inscribed with the Ten Commandments, they were placed in an ark, a wooden container used to hold these memorials of the covenant. Originally the ark was a symbol of the Israelite tribes' resistance to the Philistines (see 1 Sam 4:1b; 7:2). Later it was housed in the temple and was considered to be the footstool of God's throne and therefore symbolic of the divine presence (see Exod 25:1-22). In Deuteronomy the ark is simply a container for the tablets of the law. It is obedience to that law which guarantees God's favor, not any supposed presence of God in the temple.

10:6-9 An insertion. This text intrudes upon the story of Moses' intercession for the rebellious Israelites. Verses 6-7 reflect a somewhat different tradition about Aaron's death than is found in Num 20 and 33. Verses 8-9 give information found elsewhere in Deuteronomy (see 31:9, 25-26). The Levites were the ones who transported the ark when necessary. Two other Levitical functions are mentioned: their responsibility to lead worship and to bless the people in God's name.

10:10-11 The answer to Moses' prayer. Israel was not to be destroyed; the covenant was to be re-established. All this was the result of God's mercy and love. Divine justice called for Israel's annihilation. The Lord's fidelity to the promises made to Israel's ancestors and the Lord's willingness to hear Moses' pleas made the continued existence of Israel possible.

10:12–11:32 The great commandment. Before the Deuteronomists get into the specifics of the law for Israel's life in the land (chs. 12–26), they restate the great commandment, which calls for Israel's wholehearted love for God (10:12–11:25). Then, as a bridge to the specific commands, a warning is given (11:26-32), stating that the law has the potential of bringing a great blessing or a terrible curse upon the people. The requirements God makes of the nation have consequences. Israel's experience has shown quite conclusively that God is capable of fulfilling every promise made. If Israel wishes to secure its future in the land, loyalty to God and obedience to the law provide the only way to do so. Infidelity to the Lord and disregard of the commandments will bring disaster.

10:12-22 Israel's allegiance. The command calling for total commitment to God begins this transition to the Deuteronomic Code (chs. 12–26). In a variety of ways a single message comes through: the love of God is the centerpiece of Israel's response to Yahweh. This God is none other than the Creator of the universe, who freely chose to single out Israel's ancestors for special love. Israel's response is to include observance of rituals which celebrate that choice. Among these rituals is circumcision. But these observances must go beyond ritualistic activity to transformation of the spirit. Israel's entire approach to God must be overhauled (v. 16).

One way the people can show how seriously they take their election as the people of God is to accept responsibility for those members of the community whose social and economic status does not ensure their survival. In choosing Israel, God singled out a weak and powerless people to be the object of a unique love (Deut 7:7). In responding to that love, Israel must love the same kind of people God loves. Such a pattern of behavior will bring the complete fulfillment of the promises made by God to Israel's ancestors. One of those promises has already been fulfilled by the phenomenal growth in Israel's numbers (v. 22; see Gen 15:5-6). Another part of the promise, the gift of the land (Gen 17:8), still remains to be fulfilled. Israel's obedience will lead to the total fulfillment of all God's promises.

11:1-25 Memories. Here commands alternate with stories from Israel's collective memory to encourage obedience. Verse 1 begins this pattern. Its formulation of the basic command underlying the entire book introduces three lessons from the past that ought to promote obedience: the Exodus (vv. 2b-4), the wilderness experience (v. 5), and the affair of Dathan and Abiram (v. 6; see Num 16). These references to Israel's past provide both positive and negative illustrations of how God's grace and judgment affect the lives of the obedient and the disobedient. Remembering these great and terrible experiences is an education into the ways of God.

Verse 8 once again urges the people to keep the commandments of the Lord. In verses 9-12 a comparison between Egypt and Canaan provides the motivation for obedience. The Promised Land that awaits Israel is blessed by an abundance that rests on the provision of God. Egypt, by way of contrast, yields harvests only because of an irrigation system that is the work of human ingenuity and labor. The providential care of God over the land of Canaan is another inducement to obedience.

The thought of the previous section is carried on by verse 13, which calls for obedience as the means to ensure provision and prosperity from God in the future. God will provide the rain which, at the proper time, will bring success to Israel's agricultural endeavors. If Israel succumbs to the lies which assert that the land's fertility is guaranteed by other gods, Israel will find it impossible to survive in the land. The people will then have to learn the truth the hard way.

The last few verses of this section (vv. 16-25) are a concluding summary of Moses' address thus far. The main emphasis here is the obligations that God places upon Israel. These verses are a pastiche of admonitions given by Moses previously (see Deut 1:7-8; 2:25; 4:9-10, 38, 40; 6:2, 8-9, 17; 7:23-24). The repetition of this message underscores its importance: Israel's very existence is dependent upon its willingness to respond in kind to God's love.

11:26-32 The alternatives. Moses wants Israel to decide its future. He states the alternatives very clearly. The people can choose to be blessed, or they can choose to be cursed. Blessing is, of course, contingent upon Israel's obedience to the law. The detailed stipulations of that law are about to be presented to the

people. Moses advises his audience that their acceptance of a life guided by the law is the only way they can expect the blessings promised to their ancestors. The law, then, is not simply a legal code to pattern Israel's behavior; it is the key to the fullness of life that awaits Israel on the other side of the Jordan River.

The last few verses (vv. 29-32) provide the outline of a ritual celebrating the relationship between God and Israel (a more detailed presentation of this ritual is given in Deut 27:1-26). The choice the people are called to make is really quite simple—it is a choice between Yahweh and other gods. Israel's choice is represented dramatically by a ritual celebrated near Shechem on the twin mountains Gerizim and Ebal. Israel knows that God has chosen it from all the nations of the world. Now it remains for Israel to choose Yahweh above all other gods. In reality, there is no real choice, but if Israel abandons Yahweh for what are really no gods, only misery and disaster will follow. If, however, Israel remains loyal to God, there is no limit to the expressions of God's love.

12:1–26:19 The Deuteronomic Code. Some of the laws found here are unique to Deuteronomy; most, however, are found in other codes, both Israelite and ancient Near Eastern. Deuteronomy's particular stamp may be recognized in its abiding concern for the poor, its humanization of older laws, and especially in its association of obedience with continued existence in the land. If the people wish to secure a future for themselves in the land God has provided, there is only one way—the way of obedience.

The term "code" is used rather loosely here. The Book of Deuteronomy is less a practical guide to legal matters than a recitation of traditional values and practices that the respected members of the community see as constitutive of the Israelite identity. There is no "logical" arrangement in this code, and, beginning with chapter 22, there is a succession of isolated laws that are not explained at any length; in fact, they seem to be unrelated to one another. This may confuse the contemporary reader.

Key words sometimes provide the connection between various laws, but sometimes this is not readily apparent in translation. In addition, the study of Hebrew rhetorical style is just beginning. Perhaps someday the "logic" of Deuteronomy's arrangement will become clear. Nonetheless, it is still important to remember that this book is not an exhaustive legal collection. It offers its readers a convenient summary of traditional practices and calls for their observance. The Deuteronomists are trying to inspire an attitude of submission and obedience. They are not necessarily concerned with providing the people with a complete code of law.

12:1-28 Centralization. The law requiring the centralization of Israel's sacrificial worship is unique to Deuteronomy and the literature dependent upon it. Previous legislation and practice envisioned such worship as taking place at any number of altars throughout the land (see Exod 20:24). Deuteronomy's departure from earlier usage is based on a concern for purity in Israel's cult and on the belief that a multiplicity of sanctuaries is incompatible with the worship of Israel's God. This concern for cultic purity and the desire for cultic unity are related, because both are founded on the recognition that Israel's God is not like the gods of the nations. The many local shrines that were once associated with the old Canaanite deities are unfit for Yahwistic worship. Those shrines have been replaced in favor of a single site chosen by the one God.

There are two other important dynamics in this passage that are characteristic of Deuteronomy: desacralization and humanization. Unlike the old gods of Canaan, the Lord is not a personified natural force; consequently, nothing in nature is sacred in itself. If a place becomes a medium of the divine presence, it is because of God's free choice rather than because of the site's inherent sacredness.

Second, this passage allows the slaughter of domestic animals for profane use (vv. 15, 20). Though blood is not to be consumed with the meat, it has no special sacred character and is therefore poured out like water (vv. 16, 24). The blood is to be offered to God (v. 27), probably as an acknowledgment of the divine sovereignty over life, which is symbolized by the blood.

Finally, Deuteronomy invests sacrifice with a twofold purpose. The first represents private religious concerns, such as the fulfillment of a vow (v. 7). A second purpose is more humanitarian in its orientation, provid-

ing the worshiper with an opportunity to share the blessing of the land, rejoice in the Lord, and offer help to the economically dependent (vv. 7, 12, 18).

In this passage there are repetitions, conflicting viewpoints, and differences in terminology, pointing to its complicated literary history. The original law regarding the central sanctuary can be found in verses 13-19. Later additions (vv. 2-7, 8-12 and 20-28) all agree to the restriction of worship to a single shrine, the choice of which is left to God alone.

12:1-7 Destruction of Canaanite sanctuaries. Centralization of worship is presented as the logical consequence of carrying out a previously given command to destroy Canaanite shrines and their appurtenances (v. 3; see Deut 7:5). Hills and shady trees were often chosen as sites for sanctuaries because they were associated with the divine by various Semitic peoples. The cultic activity that took place at these sites was unequivocally condemned as evil by the prophets (see Hos 4:3; Jer 2:20; Ezek 6:13).

The expression "designated as his dwelling" (v. 5) is a formula used by kings in the ancient Near East to indicate ownership. The Deuteronomistic History uses this same expression to refer to Jerusalem (1 Kgs 9:3; 11:36; 14:21; 2 Kgs 21:4, 7). Similarly, the expression "out of all your tribes" refers to Jerusalem in 1 Kgs 8:16; 11:32; 14:21; 2 Kgs 21:7. This implies that the place chosen by the Lord for the one sanctuary permitted is Jerusalem. Of course, Deuteronomy could not name the city, since Jerusalem was not incorporated into Israel until the time of David (see 2 Sam 5:6-12).

12:8-12 Centralization as the goal of Israel's pilgrimage. The Deuteronomists are very well aware that the requirement of a single sanctuary flies in the face of earlier, legitimate practices. This passage characterizes all those earlier usages as provisional. The "rest" that the Lord gives to Israel (see 1 Kgs 5:4; 8:36) inaugurates a new age marked by worship at one sanctuary chosen by God. Centralization of worship was apparently attempted by Hezekiah (2 Kgs 18:4) and Josiah (2 Kgs 23:8-9, 12-15, 20), but their attempts did not outlive them. Deuteronomy's goal of centralization of worship succeeded because the war with Babylon reduced the land under

Israelite control to Jerusalem and a few square miles surrounding it. Thus, the Deuteronomists made virtue out of necessity.

12:13-19 Some effects of centralization. The earliest of the laws about the central sanctuary is addressed to Israel in the second person singular, as is the case with most of the early Deuteronomic legislation. One consequence of this law is permission for profane slaughter of domestic animals. That becomes a practical necessity because ritual slaughter is to be limited to the central shrine. Even though the daily diet rarely includes meat, the slaughter of animals for food has to be disconnected from the cult. The Levites who minister at the shrines to be eliminated in favor of the one sanctuary are commended to the charity of the Israelites, as are other economically dependent groups (widows, orphans, and aliens: see Deut 12:12; 14:27-28; 16:11; 18:6-7; 26:11-12).

12:20-28 A limitation. The effect of verse 21 is to limit the rather broad permission of verse 25 regarding the non-cultic slaughter of animals for food. Such permission is restricted to sites whose distance from the central sanctuary makes ritual killing of the animals a practical impossibility. Verse 28 is a homiletical conclusion to the entire passage about the central shrine. Obedience is commended because it assures Israel of God's favor.

While the law of centralization is an important Deuteronomic innovation, the bulk of the book deals with legislation that neither requires nor even mentions centralization. Still, this innovation was a decisive moment in the life of ancient Israel. It offered a sense of unity and cohesion at a time when Israel's other institutions were dead or dying. Centralization of worship was indeed an innovation, but one that resulted from a fresh interpretation of the ancient cultic pattern of the wilderness. What was entirely feasible in Moses' day was never again realized by Israel until Deuteronomy. Under the influence of this book, centralization became the way to express the unique nature of Israel's God and Israel's unique relationship with the Divine.

12:29-13:18 The specter of infidelity. The unsympathetic treatment of the nations in Deuteronomy is not so much the result of a feeling of ethnic or cultural superiority by the Deuteronomists as it is the result of their fear that Israel is in very real danger of being lost forever in a sea of assimilation. If Israel is to have any future at all, it will be because of a clearly formulated self-definition manifested through distinctive cultural patterns that mark Israel as different from the nations. Certainly the most distinctive of those cultural patterns is Israel's religion, with its emphasis on loyalty to one, and only one, God. As a result of this concern, Deuteronomy is almost ruthless in its determination to ensure that Israel maintain its loyalty to Yahweh alone. This particular section deals with attempts at subverting Israel's allegiance and how these are to be handled.

12:29-31 Foreign religious rituals. Historians of religion are quite certain that much of Israel's cult was adopted from the religious rituals of Canaan, which were modified to conform with Yahwistic beliefs. For example, the agricultural festival of Passover took on a distinctively Yahwistic tone through its association with the Exodus (see Deut 16:1-6). In a similar fashion, the Israelite priesthood, sacrificial system, and even the Jerusalem temple derived from Canaanite patterns in use for a long time before Israel came into existence. But all this was lost in Israel's collective memory by the time Deuteronomy was written.

What the Deuteronomists have before their eyes is the temptation Israel faces: the desertion of Yahweh in favor of the gods of the conquered nations. To counteract this temptation, Deuteronomy recalls traditions associated with the settlement period (vv. 29-30) and reminds Israel of the disgusting nature of the religious rituals never adopted officially by Israel, such as child sacrifice (v. 31). The unremitting critique of non-Israelite religion is to overcome the impulse toward assimilation that threatens not only Israel's unique religious identity but also its very existence.

12:32–13:18 Internal threats. As severe as their critique of non-Israelite religions is, the Deuteronomists recognize that the most serious threats to the covenant come from within. The steps to be taken with regard to these threats show how seriously Deuteronomy takes the obligation of absolute loyalty to God.

Surprisingly enough, the first to come under scrutiny are the prophets (13:1-5). The enticement to apostasy can and has come from religious authorities such as the prophets. Deuteronomy betrays a real lack of confidence in those religious authorities by listing them as first among those who can lead Israel to compromise its allegiance to Yahweh. Of course, Deuteronomy presents itself as the authoritative word from God which, in effect, makes prophecy obsolete. The people can determine the divine will by consulting this written, authoritative document rather than by relying on human and fallible religious authorities who have the potential of leading them astray. Israel will never go astray by obeying the prescriptions found in Deuteronomy.

The loyalty Israel owes to God transcends every human bond, even that of the family (13:6-11). If a family member is an enticement to idolatry, Israelites loyal to God will not let familial love take precedence over the love they have for God. While this text makes use of legal language, its basic thrust is homiletical. It focuses on the value of allegiance to God rather than on the presentation of specific rules of conduct. It should be understood and interpreted as are similar passages in the New Testament, such as Matt 10:34-38 and its parallels.

A third internal threat can be an entire city that has gone over to the worship of other gods (13:12-18). From the perspective of the Exile, this is not simply a rhetorical exaggeration. The Assyrian and Babylonian conquests reduced Israel to a fraction of what it once was. All of Galilee and central Palestine was lost. From the perspectives of the Deuteronomists, those losses could be explained in only one way—Israel's disloyalty. If the remnant of Israel will not be engulfed by the nations, it will be because of a firm decision to foster absolute loyalty to the Lord.

According to Deuteronomy, Israel's continued existence is dependent upon maintaining its commitment to God. Any compromise is equivalent to communal suicide. The Deuteronomists make their point with shocking clarity and single-minded conviction. There is no room whatsoever for anyone within the community who fosters an attitude of apostasy. Israel's life and future hang in the balance. What choice does Israel have?

14:1-21 Holiness. At first glance the material of this chapter seems to have little to do with holiness. That is true if one defines holiness in terms of virtues to be acquired and vices to be avoided. From the Israelite perspective, holiness is a consequence of God's uniqueness. The God of Israel is not like the gods of the nation, and so those who serve this God cannot pattern their behavior according to the customs associated with the service of foreign gods. Israel is to be holy, that is, unique, as its God is holy.

Verses 1 and 2 prohibit the observance of mourning rites practiced in Canaanite religions. (Such rites apparently perdured throughout Israel's history, even into the exilic period—see Ezek 9:14-15.) Those mourning rituals are associated with the worship of the dying and rising god, reflecting the alternating agricultural cycles of infertility and fertility. For Israel, those cycles do not form an apt metaphor for Yahweh, whose rule over the cosmos is absolute. Israel is the Lord's own possession (v. 2). It is unthinkable, then, for the Lord's own people to observe foreign rituals.

The rest of this unit (vv. 3-21) deals with dietary laws. The origin of these observances is beyond recovery. Even the English translations of the names of some of the animals and birds listed here are no more than educated guesses. No matter what the origin of these laws may have been, their importance in the exilic and postexilic community cannot be overestimated.

Observance of these dietary laws helped early Judaism develop its identity. It effectively cut off socializing with non-Jews and thereby helped to fend off the impulse to assimilation. Gradually these dietary laws, as they were developed and enlarged in early Judaism, became so ingrained in the Jewish religious identity that the first Christians had a difficult time conceiving of the possibility of genuine religion without them (Acts 15:29; Col 2:21). The basic assumption behind these dietary laws is that the people of God cannot be like the people who worship foreign gods, and this distinction is to extend even to matters of diet.

Especially interesting is verse 21b, which prohibits the boiling of a kid in its mother's milk. (Later the rabbis extrapolated from this law the prohibition of eating dairy and meat products at the same meal.) This prohibition is unlike the others in this section, which deal with clean and unclean animals. There is some evidence that this law may be a conscious rejection of a particular Canaanite ritual, but the evidence is not sufficient to make a firm conclusion. In any case, all these laws remind Israel that its future depends on its willingness to keep away from anything that may be construed as compromising its commitment to God.

14:22–15:23 Israel's bounty. A basic Israelite belief was that though God gave the land to Israel, it really belonged to the Lord who gave it as a gift to Israel, in accordance with the promises made to Abraham, Isaac, and Jacob. An important consequence of this belief was a recognition of Israel's dependence upon God's bounty. The wealthy and the poor alike were to acknowledge God as the source of their sustenance. The legislation in this section describes some of the ways in which Israel chose to express this belief: the tithe, the year of release, the treatment of slaves, and the offering of firstlings.

Throughout this section Deuteronomy's particular regard for the poor is quite evident. In fact, Deut 15:4-5 claims that obedience could make poverty non-existent, but a more realistic assessment of Israel's potential for obedience recognizes the existence of poverty and the need for generosity on the part of the wealthy (15:11). This concern for the poor is one manifestation of a broader humanitarian bent within Deuteronomy. For example, Deut 14:22-27 implies that the purpose of tithing is to provide food especially for the poor. There is no mention of any sacral purpose for tithing, as an offering made for God's benefit. Even the use of the tithe as support for priests and Levites is ignored by Deuteronomy (compare Num 18:21-28). The Levites receive part of the tithe, not because of their priestly status, but because of their need as those without economic status (14:27, 29).

Finally, Deuteronomy makes practical accommodations in view of its expectation that there is to be only one sanctuary. Deut 14:25 speaks of turning the tithe into cash, which would obviate the necessity of transporting agricultural products over long distances to the central sanctuary. Similarly, while Exod 22:30 expects the sacrifice of the firstlings to take place eight days after birth, Deut 15:20 eliminates the necessity of frequent trips to the central sanctuary by stating that this sacrifice could take place anytime during the year.

The tithe (14:22-29) was an offering of a portion of agricultural produce originally intended for the support of sanctuaries and their personnel. It was a custom widely practiced in the ancient Near East. (Though the word "tithe" in Hebrew appears to be etymologically related to the word "ten," not all Hebrew philologists agree. They see "tithe" as related to the Ugaritic word for "libation, offering.") In the monarchic period, the king probably appropriated a portion of the tithe to support royal sanctuaries, such as the temple in Jerusalem. Deuteronomy ignores this use of the tithe. It simply provides the menu for a festal meal celebrated at the central sanctuary. Every three years the tithe is to be used locally for the welfare of the poor (14:28-29).

The law of release (15:1-11) reflects the Israelite practice of allowing the land to lie fallow at regular intervals (Exod 23:10-11). Obviously, the observance of such a practice would have been staggered throughout the land, but each time it was observed by an individual farmer, the fallow year made it difficult for those economically dependent upon agriculture. They would have found repaying their debts almost impossible. This law probably intended that debts not be called in during a farmer's fallow year, though later Jewish tradition required that the debt be forgiven rather than simply postponed. The "foreigner" spoken of in 15:3 is not the resident alien, who is somewhat integrated into the Israelite economic and agricultural system, but the traveling merchant or craftsman, who is not affected by the fallow year. The law makes it clear that no one is to take advantage of another's financial difficulties. The poor are to experience the generosity of their fellow Israelites (15:9-11).

One way to settle a debt is for debtors to work off their indebtedness. Verses 12-19 attempt to prevent abuses in this system. The service of the slave working off debts is to be limited. Male and female slaves have the same rights. When the service of slaves is completed, they are to be given financial support in order to ease their transition to freedom. To provide motivation for the observance of these humane regulations, Deuteronomy reminds its readers that they are descended from slaves. The Israelite who is working off a debt always remains an Israelite. The lender needs to remember the origin common to all (15:15).

The law regarding the offering of male firstlings (15:19-23) probably had its origin in rituals intended to ensure continued fertility by offering the firstlings to the gods. Deuteronomy upholds this practice adopted by Israel (see Exod 13:2), but once again the purpose of this action is not for the sake of supporting the sanctuary and its clergy; rather, it is to supply food for a festal meal.

Israel has experienced the wondrous power of the Lord to provide for all the people. Israel's response to this experience of God's abundance is to be a sharing through which both rich and poor can acknowledge their dependence upon God. Through their tithes the rich testify that God is the source of their abundance. By accepting the generosity of their fellow Israelites, the poor receive their support from God, who gives all Israel a share in the wealth of the land.

16:1-17 A calendar of feasts. This section deals with the pilgrimage feasts of Passover-Unleavened Bread, Weeks, and Booths. These feasts are known from other portions of the Pentateuch (Exod 23:14-17; 34:18-23; Lev 23; Num 28-29). Deuteronomy's particular stamp on the celebration of these festivals lies in transforming them into occasions of pilgrimage to the central sanctuary. For example, according to this text, the Passover meal must be eaten at the central sanctuary (vv. 5-6) rather than in the towns of the land, as was the previous custom (Lev 23:3).

The first feast, Passover-Unleavened Bread, is a combination of what were originally two separate observances. The Passover, marked by eating a lamb from the flock, probably originated among shepherds as they were changing pastures in the spring (Abib corresponds to March/April). The feast of Unleavened Bread probably originated among farmers as they renewed their supplies of leaven each year by first ridding themselves of the previous year's supply. These two feasts were joined already before the Deuteronomists began their work. Israelite tradition associated this feast with the Exodus from Egypt. Deuteronomy maintains this association but does not develop it in any significant way, except to insist upon its celebration at the central sanctuary.

The feast of Weeks derives its name from the way the time of its celebration is calculated. Since this feast is observed on the fifti-

eth day after Passover, the New Testament calls it Pentecost (Acts 2:1). It, too, originated as an agricultural festival, celebrating the grain harvest (see 15:9), which occurs in June. In rabbinic tradition this feast became associated with the giving of the law on Sinai, but no such association is made here. Verse 12 does remind the readers of Israel's slavery in Egypt in order to move them to obedience. Again, the principal concern of Deuteronomy is to encourage a pilgrimage to the central sanctuary for a festival of rejoicing for all to enjoy (v. 11).

The third feast is Booths, which is an autumnal agricultural feast celebrated at the conclusion of the harvest of dates, olives, grapes and other fruits. The name probably derives from the temporary dwellings that were erected in the orchards for the harvesters. Rabbinic tradition used this feast to commemorate Israel's time in the desert, when the people lived in temporary dwellings (tents). Again, this text makes no such allusion. The agricultural dimensions of this celebration are dominant here. In fact, there is no allusion at all to any element of the Exodus tradition. Deuteronomy simply describes the feast of Booths as the third pilgrimage feast to be celebrated at the central sanctuary.

The final two verses (15:16-17) summarize the obligation to make the three annual pilgrimages to the central sanctuary. Since these feasts celebrate the agricultural abundance of the land, it is appropriate that those making the pilgrimage come with offerings as a sign of thanksgiving for the bounty God has given them. This legislation as stated is quite impractical. It envisions the entire male population (at the very least) at the central sanctuary for each of these three festivals. The improbable scene becomes a bit more probable if this portion of Deuteronomic legislation is considered to have originated in the exilic or postexilic period, when Judah was reduced to Jerusalem and about twenty square miles surrounding it.

16:18-18:22 Israel's leaders. An important concern in Israel was the quality of its leadership. The Deuteronomists describe their expectations of those who are to hold specific offices: judge, king, priest, and prophet. What is most significant in Deuteronomy's presentation is the assumption that Israel's leaders, especially the king, are subject to the written, authoritative law found in the Book of Deuteronomy. The rule of the king is not absolute. All Israel's leaders are bound by the sacred traditions that find expression in Deuteronomy. This serves to limit the authority of the leadership class and makes it more responsible to the people as a whole. Deuteronomy clearly espouses belief in the value of limited government.

16:18–17:7 Judges and officers. Before the establishment of the monarchy, Israel's leaders were tribal elders for the most part. The elders were the leaders of important families and clans. They functioned in such a way as to prevent political power from being concentrated in the hands of a single person. With the rise of the monarchy, the influence of the elders waned, and their role in Israelite society was taken by officials appointed by the king. Verse 18 suggests official appointments made by some sort of centralized authority. It is difficult to be certain of all this because the Bible presents no theoretical account of Israel's social, political, and judicial institutions. In 2 Chr 19:5 there is mention of the judicial reforms of Jehoshaphat, who reigned in Judah during the ninth century B.C.E., so there is evidence for the appointment of judges by the central authority.

The role that the judges played in Israelite society was not confined to the judicial sphere. The judges were probably the equivalent of local governors responsible for the affairs of the district assigned to them. They exercised executive and legislative prerogatives as well as judicial ones. While the judges formulated policy, the officers were responsible for communicating and enforcing the decisions of the judges to whom they were responsible.

Deuteronomy is adamant about the integrity of the legal system, which was even more open to corruption in antiquity than is the case now. Judges supported themselves from their positions, and bribery was the easiest way to acquire a comfortable position. Verse 20 asserts that justice is the way to ensure prosperity for all. Harsh experience has taught Israel how destructive lapses in judicial authority can be.

At first glance the material in 16:18–17:7 seems to be intrusive in a context that deals with leadership. The concern of these verses is the purity of Israel's worship. What this section does, however, is to provide an example of how the judicial system operates (17:2-7) and samples of the matters that ought to concern the judiciary (16:21–7:1). Judges are to keep a keen eye on any attempts at introducing Canaanite religion practices into Yahwistic worship. Such attempts would be repulsive to God and destructive of Israelite society.

Second, the judges are to oversee sacrificial practices in order to ensure that Israel is taking this aspect of worship seriously. To offer inferior animals for sacrifice is nothing less than a mockery of the very purpose of such worship.

Finally, the judicial process demands integrity not only of those administering it but of all involved in it (17:6-7). No one can be convicted on the testimony of a lone witness. Witnesses have to be prepared to face the severest of penalties if their testimony proves false. All Israel is responsible for the integrity of the judicial system. The principal purpose of that system is to purge Israel of corrupting practices that threaten the very existence of the community.

17:8-13 The court at the central sanctuary. Deuteronomy makes provision for the handling of matters too involved for the local judiciary. The text does not make it clear who initiates the appeal, though Exod 18:13-23 suggests that appeals are made by local authorities. The central court is composed of priests and a judge. The inclusion of the former rests on the traditional expertise of priests in legal matters. The Deuteronomists probably introduce the judge as a way to break the exclusive control of the priests in such matters. The judgments of the central court are to resolve legal problems in a definitive way. Without such finality the judicial system would be too weak to be effective.

17:14-20 The king. The institution of the monarchy began as a response to the anarchy caused by the pressure brought to bear on the Israelite tribes by the Philistines (see 1 Sam 8–10). Because the beginnings of the monarchy were part of Israel's historical memory, this institution could not be mythologized, as it was in the other ancient Near Eastern cultures, as part of the divinely willed order of creation. Israel knew that the monarchy was established as a result of human initiative. This made Deuteronomy's approach to the monarchy possible.

Deuteronomy does not reject the monarchy as such. It is part of Israel's past and cannot be ignored; however, its role in Israel's future needs to be carefully understood. The king is not to imitate his counterparts in the ancient Near East by amassing a large standing army, by engaging in diplomacy through marriage, or by accumulating vast wealth. If Israel's God is unlike the gods of the nations, Israel's king has to be different as well.

For Deuteronomy, what makes Israel's monarchy unique is the subjection of the king to the law. Like every other Israelite, the king, too, is to order his life according to the Book of the Law. This is an important check on the monarchy's inherent tendency toward absolutism. Obedience to the law will lead to the maintenance of the king, while disobedience will surely lead to disaster. The king, like every other Israelite, is bound to the observance of the law. United in this observance, king and subjects are one people of God.

18:1-8 Priests and Levites. Priests and Levites as such are not discussed in Deuteronomy except when a layperson has some occasion to deal with them. The lone exception is this text. This is in marked contrast to the legislation of the Priestly writer. This passage tries to deal with the conflict over priestly rights—a conflict that raged between the priests of Jerusalem and the priests of the outlawed local shrines. The latter lost their source of income with the centralization of sacrificial worship mandated by Deuteronomy. The solution provided by verses 6-8 is completely impractical and was probably never put into practice (see 2 Kgs 23:8-9). Early in the post-exilic era an accommodation was worked out by which the Levites became a type of second-rank clergy in the temple, while the priests of Jerusalem retained their exclusive position as those responsible for the conduct of the sacrificial cult (see Ezek 44:9-31). The end of the feud between these two groups, however, was not the achievement of Deuteronomic circles.

Some interpreters suggest that Deuteronomy was the product of Levitical circles. In light of this text, such an alternative seems unlikely, since the presumed authors of a book such as Deuteronomy would settle any disputes to which they were a party in their own favor. At the very least, they should have presented a more workable suggestion than is given here. In a few of the other times the Levites are mentioned in Deuteronomy, they are presented as objects of charity whose economic situation is so perilous that they need the help of their fellow Israelites (14:28-29; 16:11-14; 26:12). This is not a very flattering self-portrait by the supposed authors of Deuteronomy.

18:9-22 Prophets. Before the Deuteronomists discuss the role of the prophet, they deal with some of the mantic techniques that were obviously very popular in ancient Israel. According to the biblical tradition, there are three legitimate methods of divine-human communication: dreams (Gen 40); the Urim and Thummim (see the comment on 33:8-11 below); and prophecy.

The ancient Near East in general, and Mesopotamia in particular, was renowned for the variety of techniques developed to determine the divine will. Verses 10-11 mention a few of these. Deuteronomy rejects all of them as being incompatible with Yahwism. The chief objection to these techniques probably is not their use for determining God's will but rather their use in various rituals designed to manipulate the deity. Once the divine will has been determined, the ones making the inquiry would be given advice as to how they might change any decisions of the deity that might affect them adversely. The child sacrifice cited in verse 10 is likely one of the more gruesome rituals used with divination. From Deuteronomy's perspective, the God of Israel is above such gross manipulation. Use of divinatory techniques is the grounds justifying the Canaanites' expulsion from the land (v. 14). This ought to be warning enough for Israel.

Deuteronomy's treatment of the prophet does not lead to unqualified confidence in this form of leadership. Verses 15-19 apparently presume the continuance of the prophetic office, but who can claim to be another Moses (v. 15)? The text does not assume that there will be many prophets able to make this claim. Some interpreters suggest that this text testifies to the existence of a succession of prophets to an office of "the prophet." There is no direct evidence of such an office anywhere in the Bible. Its existence is unlikely.

Prophets are mentioned only twice in Deuteronomy—here and in 13:1-6. In both instances the prophets are presented as potential threats to the loyalty that Israel owes God.

Prophets are to be monitored very carefully, for they can lead, and presumably have led, Israel away from undivided service and obedience to the Lord (see Jer 28). The test for true prophecy given in verse 22 is quite impractical and of no use to anyone who has to make a decision regarding a specific case with any immediacy.

Deuteronomy can afford to be so negative about prophecy because it effectively eliminates its usefulness. If people want to know the divine will, all they need to do is study the Book of the Law, that is, Deuteronomy itself. The book's treatment of prophecy makes it highly unlikely that Deuteronomy arose amid prophetic circles, as some interpreters claim. At one time any text reflecting moral sensitivity was attributed to prophetic circles. Deuteronomy shares with prophecy a passionate concern for the ethical dimension of Israel's life with God, but it presents a singularly unflattering portrait of the prophet.

19:1-13 The cities of refuge. Though Deuteronomy itself does not use the term "cities of refuge," as does Num 35, both texts envision the same institution. Its origins are not easy to determine. Because the cities of refuge presuppose a transtribal identity, they must have been established some time in the latter part of the settlement period. On the other hand, the monarchy probably provided some sort of centralized authority to deal with the judicial determination of any killing as accidental or criminal. The cities of refuge, then, were an intertribal institution that attempted to restrain acts of revenge. Deuteronomy provides the theological support for this institution by asserting that it prevents the shedding of innocent blood and the consequent guilt, one effect of which would be the loss of the land (compare Gen 4:8-14).

In its presentation of the cities of refuge, Deuteronomy discusses both their use (vv. 4-10) and their abuse (vv. 11-13). As unfortunate as an accidental killing may be, its terrible effects will be multiplied if people rush to judgment and punish people responsible for accidental deaths as if they were murderers. Such a reaction would set off another act of "justice" and could thereby begin an unremitting cycle of killings. The cities of refuge provide the opportunity for a calm determination of guilt or innocence.

Unfortunately, the wrong people may take advantage of the sanctuary provided by these cities. The elders, who were the premonarchic dispensers of justice, must be vigilant to prevent a murderer from escaping justice. Those guilty of murder are themselves to be killed, because their shedding of innocent blood threatens the continued existence of Israel in the land. According to the religious perspectives of the Deuteronomists, the effects of a sin such as murder touch not only the one responsible for it but all those who seemingly acquiesce to it. By punishing the guilty individual, the community demonstrates its revulsion for the crime and thereby escapes any guilt and punishment flowing from it. While the cities of refuge help prevent the shedding of innocent blood, they must never become a way for the guilty to escape the consequences of their crimes.

19:14 The landmark. This is the Deuteronomic version of an ancient, pre-Israelite law found in other ancient Near Eastern law codes. Without the legal safeguards of deeds recorded and maintained by civil authorities, respecting landmarks is essential in avoiding disputes over territory. Deuteronomy adds its own typical flavor to this ancient law: the land was given by the Lord to its present owners. Attempts at expropriating it are nothing less than acts of rebellion against the Lord.

19:15-21 Witnesses. The integrity of the judicial system depends on the truthfulness of witnesses. What was decreed with regard to accusations of idolatry (17:6-7) is extended to all cases. When the veracity of witnesses is in doubt, appeal is to be made to the court at the central shrine (v. 17). The text does not describe the procedures used by the court to decide the issue of perjury. The focus here is on the punishment due to those guilty of lying in the course of judicial proceedings. The punishment for perjury corresponds to the punishment for the crime of which the false witnesses accused their fellow Israelites. In the end, evil will overtake those who plan evil for others. Verse 21 underscores this principle. Those who endanger the lives of the innocent by their perjury will find that their own lives are forfeit.

20:1-20 Rules for warfare. Deuteronomy has already dealt with the topic of war (see 7:1-26). This chapter provides additional legislation, which will be augmented by Deut

21:10-14; 23:9-14; 24:5; 25:17-19. All this attention to war may be offensive to modern sensibilities, but one cannot deny that ancient Israel acquired the land of Canaan, in part, through violent means. In fact, some interpreters believe that war was a cultic institution in the early years of Israel's history. The term "holy war" was coined to describe this institution. "Holy war" is a particularly infelicitous expression. It occurs nowhere in the Bible. It is doubtful that any manner of waging war was ever a fixed cultic pattern in Israel's history. The theology of divinely willed and directed wars was an ancient Near Eastern commonplace. What we read here and elsewhere in Deuteronomistic literature is an interpretation of Israel's battlefield experiences and memories. It hardly describes actual strategy and tactics.

A basic conviction of this ideology of warfare is that the outcome is determined in the heavens, where the gods of the warring nations fight one another for power and domination in the heavenly sphere. What happens on earthly battlefields merely reflects what has already happened in the heavenly realms. That is why the priest is the first to exhort those entering battle (vv. 2-4). That is why Israel's strength does not depend on numerical superiority or formidable weaponry. Deuteronomy reminds Israel that God fought against and defeated Egypt, a powerful empire, when Israel itself was powerless.

This chapter deals with three specific concerns regarding the conduct of war: exemption from military service (vv. 5-9); the treatment of enemy cities (vv. 10-18); and the protection of natural resources in time of war (vv. 19-20).

The laws specifying circumstances allowing for various exemptions from military service find many parallels in the laws of other ancient Near Eastern countries. Originally these exemptions recognized that people in "transition" were in a particularly vulnerable situation. The ancients spoke of that vulnerability in terms of subjection to demonic powers. There was no need to expose the entire army to these dangers, so those experiencing transitions in their lives were simply exempted from military service. Deuteronomy demythologizes those practices and allows for the same exemptions on purely humanitarian grounds. In addition, Deuteronomy exempts

from battle all those whose faith is weak. In difficult circumstances their weakness could affect the whole army. It is better that they not be a part of the battle at all.

The treatment of enemy cities appears brutal, but what is described here (vv. 10-18) is not any more brutal than the practices of other nations in the ancient Near East. In interpreting these verses, it is important to remember that Deuteronomy is more ideological than realistic in its presentation of Israelite military policies. Israel is not in a position to conduct itself according to these prescriptions. Israel is more in danger of having its cities destroyed than its neighbors are.

No quarter is to be given to any Canaanite cities because of the dangers the Canaanites pose with regard to the absolute fidelity that Israel owes to God (vv. 16-18). That Israel's prophets consistently upbraided it for following the ways of the nations is proof enough that Israel did not engage in any full-scale extermination of the Canaanites. Though there were conflicts between the Israelites and the Canaanites, most of the latter gradually became assimilated among the Israelite population as Israel acquired hegemony over Canaan.

Finally, verses 19-20 indicate that Israel is not to implement a scorched-earth policy in its conflicts with other nations. Resources, especially those connected with food production, are to be preserved with care. Here Israel departs from the more common practice of the day, which witnessed the indiscriminate use of military destructiveness. Only that which threatens Israel's loyalty to God is to be treated without mercy; in other cases humanity and common sense ought to keep a rein on the destructive potential of war.

21:1–25:19 Miscellaneous laws. The next five chapters contain laws covering a wide variety of topics. They are not arranged in any particular order, but all serve to describe the pattern of Israel's life in the land. They all are supported by a single assumption: obedience to these laws will help Israel secure its future in the land.

21:1-9 The unsolved murder. This is another instance of Deuteronomy's adaptation of a practice that was probably pre-Israelite in origin. Ancient Near Eastern law codes held that the city nearest the site of an unsolved murder had to bear responsibility for the crime. The leaders of that community were required to perform a ritual that not only accepted responsibility for the crime but also deflected the guilt and punishment for the crime from the city. This practice reflects the strong ancient Near Eastern belief in group solidarity and the religious implications of a crime such as murder. Unless specific action was taken, the consequences of that crime had the potential of destroying innocent people.

The text describes a ritual that cannot be considered sacrificial, since Deuteronomy allows sacrifice only at the central shrine. The Levitical priests are simply mute witnesses rather than officiants. The ritual is conducted entirely by the elders of the city nearest the site of the unsolved murder. At the conclusion of the ritual, the elders pray that the guilt of the crime not be attached to their city nor to the nation as a whole. The words of this prayer transform the remnants of a magical rite into an act of obedience to the law and a petition for mercy. This Deuteronomic composition testifies to the belief that forgiveness is an act of God's grace, which cannot be manipulated by the performance of any ritual.

21:10-21 Family relationships. In the first two situations dealt with here (marriage with a female prisoner of war, vv. 10-14; and the inheritance rights of the first-born, vv. 15-17), the Deuteronomists assume the existence of polygamy. Though polygamy was practiced in ancient Israel, monogamy was far more common because of economic and social problems, such as those presented in this legislation. Later, for theological reasons, monogamy became the only form of marriage permitted in Judaism.

When an Israelite soldier wishes to marry a prisoner of war, he has to consider the woman's sensibilities and control his own impulses. First of all, the woman is to have time to deal with the shock of captivity, the separation from her family, and the integration into a new household. To allow for these transitions, the marriage is to be consummated only after one month. Once the former captive becomes the wife of an Israelite, she must be treated as his wife. In the case of divorce, she does not revert to her former status but is given the freedom due to any Israelite woman.

Laws of inheritance in the ancient world tended to favor the first-born. As a consequence, there developed the custom whereby a father selected his "first-born." This situation became especially complicated in a polygamous household. The Deuteronomists want to secure the rights of the actual first-born son, irrespective of the father's feelings toward him or his mother. No doubt conflicts like this one contributed to favoring the monogamous form of marriage.

Finally, the Deuteronomists deal with disputes that arise between parents and children (vv. 18-21). Because of the great respect due to the older generation in general, and parents in particular, rebellious young people put themselves into a precarious situation. The elders (v. 19) probably serve as mediators to calm the passions that might develop out of domestic squabbles. They prevent parents from becoming carried away by their anger with a recalcitrant son. The elders are permitted to let the full penalty of the law (v. 21) fall upon the "stubborn and rebellious" son only in cases where there are no other alternatives. The elders, then, serve as a societal safety-valve preventing family arguments from being blown all out of proportion.

21:22-23 Hanging. Hanging was not a form of capital punishment in ancient Israel. After some other form of execution, the criminal's body was put on public display as an object lesson to those who might threaten Israel's existence by their crimes. The Deuteronomists mercifully limit this gruesome spectacle by requiring burial on the same day as execution.

22:1-4 Respect for property. The principle behind this law is that a person's ownership of property does not cease when that property becomes lost. It is the duty of every Israelite to respect the property rights of all people. Another version of this law is found in Exod 23:4-5. Deuteronomy generalizes the beneficiary of the law from "your enemy" (Exod 23:4) to every Israelite, and the property concerned from livestock to every type of property. For Deuteronomy, these prescriptions do not arise from any abstract notion of property rights but from the conviction that Israel's future is dependent upon the ability of the people to remain united. Disputes over property can be nothing but divisive. Respect for others' property is one of the practical components of a genuinely effective communal spirit.

22:5 Transvestism. This law is more extensive than a simple prohibition of wearing the opposite sex's clothing. The Deuteronomists also have in mind ornaments, weapons, and other objects that pertain to one or the other sex. It is not possible to be certain whether this text forbids transvestism because of its association with homosexuality, which is proscribed by Lev 18:22, or because of possible links it may have with various Canaanite religious rituals. This prohibition also reflects a concern evident throughout the cultures of the ancient Near East to accept the distinctions that exist in nature. From the perspectives of antiquity, blurring these obvious distinctions is foolish, since they are present in nature for a good reason determined by the Creator.

22:6-7 Birds in the nest. Here the Deuteronomists show how ahead of the time they could be. This law, which is unique to Deuteronomy, accepts the possibility of raiding a bird's nest for food. While it allows the taking of eggs and the young, the text requires that the adult bird be freed. Such action precludes the possible extinction of a species in the quest for food. The adult bird is free to reproduce again, and thereby the survival of the species is ensured. Unrestricted hunting threatens the survival of the species.

22:8 The Deuteronomic building code. Roofs of homes in ancient Israel were part of the homes' living space. Roofs were used for entertaining, sleeping, and working. Here the Deuteronomists require the taking of simple safety precautions. Though the erecting of a parapet is an additional expense, it can prevent serious accidents and their consequences. In our culture these consequences would include lawsuits. In ancient Israel an accident resulting from negligence could set off a blood feud. Deuteronomy wants to prevent that.

22:9-11 Combinations. One of the recognized scholarly pursuits in the ancient world was the classification of natural phenomena. These verses probably reflect a concern to respect the differences in nature that these classification efforts brought to light. Elements that are separate in nature should not be combined by human efforts. Rabbinic Judaism took up and developed this Deuteronomic concern. An entire tractate of the Mishnah is devoted to the elaboration and application of the principle behind these verses.

22:12 Tassels. This is another bit of Deuteronomic legislation that became quite important in rabbinic Judaism. Matthew 23:5 testifies to the concern of Jesus' contemporaries over the observance of this law. It is still observed by modern orthodox Jews, who attach tassels to a special inner garment they wear. Again, the origin and purpose of this law are unknown. A similar law in Num 15:37-41 describes the tassels as reminders of the commandments that Israel is to obey. This is surely a later homiletic explanation of a custom whose original meaning was unknown even to the Priestly authors of Numbers.

22:13-29 Marriage and sexual relationships. The rest of this chapter is devoted to legislation regulating the expression of human sexuality. While the ancients were generally quite reticent about such matters, they did not regard human sexuality as an evil force that must be carefully controlled or suppressed. On the other hand, they were quite aware of how powerful a force human sexuality can be. What on the surface may be behavior between consenting adults can have important repercussions for the entire community. These matters must be handled prudently in order to maintain healthy relationships within the community.

The first case deals with the accusations against the virtue of a newly married woman by her disaffected husband (vv. 13-21). The case is spelled out in some detail, as compared with the others presented in this chapter. The values behind this law, as well as the law itself, do not immediately resonate with contemporary views regarding the role and status of women in society. In particular, the concern for the woman's virginity, without any concomitant concern for that of her husband, is inequitable. Second, the absence of any role for the woman in the forum where her future is being determined is unjust. This legislation underscores how different ancient Israelite society was from our own. While we may rightly reject some of the presuppositions behind this law, we ought to admire the concern it shows for the woman's rights in view of her husband's false accusations.

The cases envisioned by the rest of the chapter are not presented in as much detail as the previous case is. The value at stake in each of these cases is the prohibition of adultery (Deut 5:18). Because adultery involves a breach of the marriage relationship, the penalty is severe. (A betrothed woman is treated the same as a married woman, since both are committed to an exclusive relationship with a man.) The rape of a single woman (vv. 28-29) is treated differently because it does not involve the breach of any marriage relationship. This, of course, ignores the single woman's trauma resulting from a rape; it will not be any less severe than that of a married woman. The law does attempt to protect the raped woman's rights, but not in a way our culture finds acceptable.

The final law in this series (v. 30) forbids an incestuous relationship between a man and his father's wife. This law probably had in mind a man's stepmother, for it is doubtful that an explicit law would be needed to prohibit incest with one's natural mother.

23:1-9 Who is an Israelite? This legislation has a rather narrow view on full membership in the community of Israel. This attitude is understandable, given the situation in which Deuteronomy was written. It was a time when Israel's very existence was threatened by both internal and external forces. It is little wonder that the Deuteronomists were not in a very inclusivist mood as they dealt with the question of who should be admitted to full membership in the community.

While the Deuteronomists do not go so far as to withdraw the traditional protection accorded to the resident alien (see 1:16 and 10:18-19), still they draw the circle of full membership in the community very carefully—some might say too carefully. For example, the laws of verses 1-2 probably intend to bar people who are directly associated with the service of foreign deities. Verse 1 most likely envisions those who have had themselves castrated in order to participate in certain non-Yahwistic rituals. There also may be some cultic concerns behind the law of verse 2, which may refer to children conceived by a woman involved in Canaanite fertility rituals. Rabbinic tradition has understood this law as referring to children of incestuous relationships.

This interpretation may have been fostered by the permanent prohibition denying Moabites and Ammonites full membership in the Israelite community. Genesis preserves the tradition that both groups were offspring of the incestuous relationship between Lot and

his two daughters (Gen 19:30-38). Deuteronomy, however, justifies its prohibition by adverting to traditions associated with Israel's entrance into Canaan (see Deut 2 and Num 22-24). The Deuteronomists show a bit more openness toward the Egyptians and the third Transjordanian nation, the Edomites. Individuals from both groups may be admitted to the Israelite community because the Edomites are kin through Jacob, and the Egyptians provided hospitality to Jacob and his family during a time of famine (Gen 25:24-26; 36:1).

At a later time, elements within early Judaism attempted to break the strictures of these laws. The Isaianic school especially is noted for its more universalist approach. In particular, Isaiah 56 should be pointed out as a later and more open approach toward some of the same groups mentioned here.

23:10-15 A sense of shame. Shame was a more powerful force among the ancient Israelites than it is among people of contemporary Western culture. These laws specify certain actions as expressions of that sense of shame. In a positive light, one can say that Deuteronomy here reflects ancient Israel's concern for dignity and hygiene. Deuteronomy wants to maintain these standards. Later the community at Qumran will be marked by a strong solicitude regarding these same issues. The practices of that community show a further specification of the general laws found here.

23:16-17 Escaped slaves. This law deals with slaves who have run away from foreign masters (no provision is made for slaves who have fled their Israelite masters). Escaped slaves who seek asylum in Israel are to be given protection. Usually international treaties provided extradition for runaway slaves. Deuteronomy does not envision the possibility of such agreements, because an international treaty is at least an implicit acknowledgment of foreign deities. While this law provides help for escaped slaves, its real intent is to preserve the sanctity of Israel's covenant relationship with Yahweh.

23:18-19 Cult prostitution. Sexual activity cannot be mythologized into a quasi-sacral rite that ensures divine favor, especially regarding fertility. That is what Canaanite rituals of fertility are all about. Sexual activity is human activity. Acting as if it were anything else implies a lack of faith in God, who is the one source of the land's fertility. Since cult prostitution is forbidden as evil, any monetary profit made from it is tainted and cannot be offered to the Lord.

23:20-21 Interest. The loans envisioned here have no resemblance to the loaning practices that are central to a modern capitalist economy. In the situation addressed by Deuteronomy, loans are used only as a means to escape economic disaster. To take advantage of partners in the covenantal community when they are in financial distress is incompatible with Deuteronomy's view of community. Loans made to those outside the community are another matter. God will give adequate provision to all Israel if the community is faithful to the law. There should be no need to supplement God's gracious bounty with interest earned on loans to brothers and sisters in financial need.

23:22-24 Vows. The making of vows out of religious devotion is not a required but a permitted form of piety. Once people commit themselves to some form of action by a vow, it is important that they fulfill the vow. Unfulfilled vows create an atmosphere in which it becomes acceptable to countenance failures in Israel's relationship with God. From Deuteronomy's perspective, such an attitude is disastrous.

23:25-26 Sharing God's bounty. Deuteronomy looks upon the fertility of the land as a gift given by God to all Israel. Individuals should be willing to share God's bounty with their fellow Israelites. The Deuteronomists are practical enough to recognize that such an attitude can be abused. The one who sowed the wheat and planted the vineyard is the one who should reap their harvest. Others may help themselves in time of need, but this right is limited by the property rights of those who own the field and vineyard.

24:1-4 Remarriage after divorce. This text does not legislate regarding divorce but simply accepts it as a matter of custom. Its concern is to forbid a man from remarrying his former wife if she has remarried and been divorced by another man. The reasons for this prohibition are not immediately clear, but perhaps the Deuteronomists are concerned that unrestricted divorces and remarriages serve to make divorce a legal form of adultery.

24:5 Another exemption for the military. This is an addition to the exemptions granted in 20:5-8. Similar exemptions are found among other ancient Near Eastern peoples. The transition from the single state to the married state was considered by the ancients as a time when a man is particularly vulnerable to attacks from evil powers. It would not make any sense to have such people in the army. Deuteronomy offers its own humane rationale for this exemption.

24:6 Collateral. If a lender requires a borrower to hand over collateral for a loan, it should not be a millstone, which is an essential piece of equipment in the home. Without it, grain cannot be ground to prepare bread, the staple in the ancient Israelite diet. Demanding such collateral would involve a genuine hardship for any family.

24:7 Kidnapping. The kidnapping described here does not involve holding someone for ransom but the sale of a person into slavery. It is treated as a capital crime because the victims of this crime are cut off from their communities, which are the source of their lives. The law protects the person who does not enjoy the safety afforded by family and wealth, since the victim of kidnapping would typically be a social outcast. No one, however, should be cut off from the covenantal community, no matter what his or her social or economic position may be.

24:8-9 Leprosy. This passage offers no guidance on how leprosy is to be treated. That is a matter for the priests. Deuteronomy's readers are advised to respect the expertise of the priests in this matter. The text probably presumes the existence of the Priestly legislation of Num 13–14 and specifically refers to the tradition about Miriam (Num 12:9-16). This is good evidence that the origins of Deuteronomy are to be found among the laity and that the Priestly source antedates Deuteronomy by a few years at the very least.

24:10-13 More on collateral. It is difficult enough to ask for a loan without having to deal with the hounding of creditors. The treatment of the borrower is to be marked by understanding, compassion, and charity. There is no excuse for adding to the burdens of the poor.

24:14-15 The wages of the poor. Deuteronomy is marked by a special concern for those whose economic status is marginal. Here the Deuteronomists require that the wages of the poor be paid each day, for the little they make is the only hedge their families have against hunger and want. Failure to pay the poor their wages will cause them to turn to the Lord for help. Since God hears the cry of the poor (Ps 69:34), the Lord's anger will be directed against Israel for its failure to consider the welfare of those in need.

24:16 Individual responsibility. This text seems to be opposed to that of Deut 5:9. Both texts contain important insights into the reality of crime and punishment. This text states unequivocally that each person is to be treated as an individual when it is a question of criminal responsibility. This means that the guilty individual must accept the criminal penalty for any breach of the law. The text of Deut 5:9 states that the nature of the criminal act is such that its effects cannot be confined to a single individual. For example, a parent's actions will inevitably affect the entire family. Punishment of a crime may be directed at individuals, but its repercussions will touch many more people.

24:17-22 Gleaning the harvest. Once again Deuteronomy's concern for the poor comes to the foreground. This legislation addresses the prosperous landowners and asks for some form of studied inefficiency in harvesting. That will allow the poor to survive without requiring them to accept obvious charity. They will have to work for their own support. The Deuteronomists remind the wealthy that all Israel would have the status of slaves were it not for God's mercy. One response expected from those who have benefited from God's goodness is compassion for those who do not have a full share in the community's wealth.

25:1-3 Corporal punishment. The Deuteronomists accept corporal punishment as one way to deal with the guilty. At the same time, they require specific safeguards to protect the ones undergoing punishment, because, despite their crimes, they are still Israelites. Punishment is to follow a legal trial. It is to be administered under the supervision of a competent authority and is to be limited to a specified number of lashes. Rabbinic tradition limited any whipping to thirty-nine lashes to avoid any possibility of breaking the requirement of verse 3 (see 2 Cor 11:24).

25:4 Concern for the ox. This is another law that is unique to Deuteronomy and shows to what extent this tradition went in its concern that all share in the land's God-given bounty. Even the oxen are not to be denied their fair share. The New Testament cites this passage as a justification for the practice whereby ministers of the gospel gained their support from their ministry (1 Cor 9:9; 1 Tim 5:18).

25:5-10 Levirate marriage. The custom described here (*levir* is Latin for "brother-in-law") was practiced in some form throughout the ancient Near East. The presumed origin of this custom lay in the desire of the patriarchal social system to keep the wealth (dowry) and fertility of the widow in the same patriarchal line. With the rise of urbanization and the devolution of the patriarchal extended family in ancient Israel, this issue became less important, though levirate marriage apparently persisted into the first century of the Common Era (see Matt 22:23-28; Luke 20:27-33). The elders can use their moral authority to encourage compliance with this ancient custom, but they cannot compel it (v. 8).

25:11-12 Mutilation as a penalty. Though mutilation was a common penalty in the ancient Near East, this is the only instance of such a penalty in the Bible apart from the *lex talionis* (Deut 19:21). In fact, some interpreters consider this an extension of the *lex talionis*, which, in this case, cannot be applied literally. While the wife's intention to save her husband from injury may be a good one, there are limits to the kind of action she can take on his behalf.

25:13-16 Trade laws. What kind of society could have any cohesion if every commercial transaction were suspect? Trust is a basic component of community life. Here the Deuteronomists require that those involved in trade adhere to honest business practices.

25:17-19 The Amalekites. By the time Deuteronomy was written, the Amalekites had already disappeared into the pages of history. The Deuteronomists imply that this was due to people who were obedient to the Lord's command. An additional implication is that Israel is to remember all that the nations did to it. That memory should help Israel avoid the disaster of assimilation, so that those nations will not achieve by Israel's cooperation what they cannot achieve by force of arms.

26:1-15 Two liturgies of remembrance. Ancient Israel's ritual was one vehicle for acknowledging its debt of gratitude to God who gave Israel a bounteous land. In paying that debt of gratitude, Israel also chose to remember a prior act of God on its behalf that was even more important than the gift of the land. That was the Exodus, which transformed Israel from a nation of slaves into a people set free. The two rites described here fuse both traditions of thanksgiving: gratitude for freedom and for the land.

Verses 1-11 deal with the annual tithe of agricultural products made by the grateful Israelite. The portrait the Deuteronomists paint here is that of a highly successful farmer who comes to the central sanctuary to present his tithe. His party includes not only his family but also the economically dependent Levites and resident aliens. The whole community benefits from the bounty God gives to Israel, and so all Israel is to be involved in the ritual of thanksgiving.

The heart of this passage is the confession that the Israelite makes as the offering is set before the Lord (vv. 5-10). The worshipers acknowledge their origins as a people without land or freedom. They can now present their tithes only because God took the side of their ancestors against the Egyptians and because God gave them a bountiful land as their new home.

Following the ritual, the whole group assembled by the wealthy farmer celebrated with a festal meal the bounty given by God. This is in accord with the typically Deuteronomic view of the elements of a sacrifice being used for a meal to be shared by the participants in the ritual.

Verses 12-15 deal with the triennial tithe, which is not brought to the central shrine but is to be used in each locality for the support of the poor. Instead of a profession of faith in God's gracious activity for Israel, the farmer offering the tithe makes prayerful assurances that he has been obedient to all stipulations regarding the offering of the tithe. The prayer ends with a petition for God's continued benevolence toward Israel, which is completely dependent upon God for its sustenance.

This passage marks Israel as distinct from its Canaanite neighbors, who see fertility as the outcome of skillful manipulation of divine powers. For Israel, fertility is a gift that can only be gratefully received. Israel's freedom, bounty, and future belong to God alone. Israel rejoices because of the gifts God has freely chosen to give it.

26:16-19 Recommitment. The Deuteronomic Code, which began with chapter 12, concludes with a mutual declaration of commitment made by both God and Israel. The people proclaim their allegiance to God, and through Moses God assures the people of the blessings that come to the obedient. The triple occurrence of "today" (vv. 16, 17 and 18) reflects a liturgical assembly at which Israel once again accepts the law as constitutive of its relationship with God. One effect of this relationship is Israel's great renown among the nations. A national life lived in accord with the divine law cannot help but reflect divine glory (v. 19). The substance of this ritual of recommitment or covenant renewal serves as the conclusion to the Deuteronomic Code as well as a transition to what follows: Moses' serious warning regarding the dire consequences that will come to a disobedient Israel.

27:1–28:69 Blessings and curses. Now the Deuteronomists turn to the future. For the law to have its beneficial effect, every generation will have to remember the law and its stipulations and be prepared to commit itself to that law. This address describes efforts to make certain that Israel will never forget that law but remain firmly committed to it.

27:1-8 The written law. These verses consider Deuteronomy as the written, authoritative law for Israel's life in the land. It is fitting, then, that copies of this law be left at significant sites connected with Israel's entrance into the land. A set of stones inscribed with the law are to be erected at the very spot where Israel crosses the Jordan. A second set of stones are to be left on Mount Ebal, where a great ceremony of covenant renewal is to take place.

This text indirectly preserves the memory of two Israelite shrines at which the entrance into the land was remembered in ritual. The first was at Gilgal, just west of the Jordan; the second was at Shechem, the town at the foot of Mount Ebal. The rituals at both these shrines celebrated not only Israel's entrance into Canaan but also the giving of the law, which became operative at the moment the people began to enter their new land.

27:9-10 Moses and the priests speak. These two verses are very significant from a theological perspective, for they assert that obedience to the commandments is to be Israel's response to its election. Obedience was not the reason why Israel became the elect people of God; Israel's election was an act of grace. Deuteronomic theology is usually caricatured as a theology of retribution that infuses a mentality of bargaining with God. Here it is quite clear that Deuteronomy holds that the basis of the divine-human relationship is an unmerited act of divine grace. It is because the Israelites have been chosen as the people of God that they are to obey the commandments.

27:11-26 A ritual on Mounts Gerizim and Ebal. Like the rest of this chapter, these verses reflect some sort of rite connected with the renewal of the covenant between God and Israel. Unfortunately, it is not possible to reconstruct the shape of that rite simply on the basis of what remains here. The image created by this text has the worshipers divided into two groups, each assembled on one of the two mountains that overlook Shechem. These two groups are to recite the blessings and curses associated with Israel's covenant with Yahweh. This ritual is probably meant to demonstrate Israel's free acceptance of the consequences flowing from the relationship established with God through the law.

The twelve curses in verses 14-26 provide a summary list of actions that are incompatible with Israel's status as the people of God. This list is certainly not exhaustive; it simply serves to remind the people that obedience to the law is to characterize the life of the nation. The people's response to each curse indicates their understanding and acceptance of the consequences that come to the disobedient.

There does not seem to be any unifying theme to the content of the curses, though some interpreters see the secrecy of the proscribed acts as a common element. If this is correct, the Deuteronomists are probably trying to avoid a type of legalism that identifies guilt with discovery. Here they may be saying that any action which disregards the law is an offense against God, whether that offense comes to the light of day or not.

The last curse is all-inclusive. It brings under God's curse the apathy and inactivity of those who know what the law requires but make no effort to obey. The term "this law"

(v. 26) is another indication that this list of curses was composed at a time after Deuteronomy had been accepted as a written, authoritative document.

28:1-69 Blessings and curses. Many interpreters believe that the Deuteronomists consciously used covenant (international treaty) as a metaphor in presenting the relationship between God and Israel. While all the elements of the typical covenant form are not found in Deuteronomy, the three most important are. Chapters 5-11 are equivalent to the prologue of the covenant, which is an exhortation to fidelity based on what God has done for Israel. The stipulations of chapters 12-26 make up the core of the covenant, in which Israel's obligations to God are spelled out clearly. Finally, this chapter represents one of the concluding elements of the covenant, the blessings and curses. Here the consequences of fidelity and infidelity are stated with unmistakable clarity. As is the case with ancient Near Eastern treaties, the curses far outnumber the blessings. The covenant metaphor explains the relationship between God and Israel in a manner readily understandable to the ancient Israelites. In addition, it underscores the Deuteronomic presentation of the law as a loving response of Israel to the God who saved it from Egyptian slavery.

The sheer number of curses (vv. 15-68) as compared with the blessings (vv. 1-14) appears to belie the assertion that, for the Deuteronomists, obedience is a response of love. While some of these curses may have been introduced into this list after the Exile (for example, verses 36-68), the number of curses may simply be a rhetorical device to encourage Israel to obedience. For the Deuteronomists, many of these curses have already become a reality. They are trying to recommit the people to obedience, for their future depends upon faithful obedience.

In terms of form, verses 1-46 and 58-68 contain conditional blessings and curses. If Israel is obedient, it may expect God's favor; if Israel is disobedient, it may expect God's judgment. The election of Israel, though it was a matter of divine grace, does not exempt Israel from bearing the consequences of infidelity. Israel's relationship with God is dependent upon fidelity to the divine will as expressed in the law.

Verses 47-57 promise God's curses on a

disobedient Israel. There seems to be no question of "if Israel is disobedient." These verses presuppose the people's infidelity: "Since you would not serve the Lord, your God . . ." (v. 47a). This text apparently reflects the tragedy that befell Israel during the siege of Jerusalem and the other cities of Judah (597–587 B.C.E.). Verses 53-57 are particularly gruesome in their description of the horrors that accompany a lengthy siege. The consequences of disobedience are terrifying indeed.

One common thread running throughout the blessings and the curses is how these are related to the land. First and foremost, blessing means fertility of both the people and their land. The curses bring sickness, death, drought, disease, poor harvests, and a horrifying siege, followed by exile from the land and reenslavement in a foreign land. The land is God's great gift to a liberated Israel. Disobedience brings the reversal of all God's beneficent acts (vv. 60-68). As great as God's deeds for Israel were, they could be undone by an ungrateful people. This is the curse for disobedience, which is simply specified in verses 15-68.

Moses' second speech closes with a powerful call for Israel's fidelity. The intensity of language displayed in these curses shows how seriously Israel is to take its relationship with God. It is indeed a matter of life and death.

MOSES' THIRD ADDRESS

Deut 29:1–32:52

The major concern of this address is Israel's immediate future. Moses makes provisions for Joshua to assume the leadership of the tribes after his death. Equally important are the provisions made for storing the book of the law and for its periodic reading. The law is to be the guide in Israel's future existence in the land. Individual human leaders come and go, but the law endures as the most effective way to safeguard Israel's commitment to the Lord.

29:2-8 A call for fidelity. Moses' third address begins in a fashion that should be quite familiar by now—the recital of God's saving acts on Israel's behalf, from the defeat of Pharaoh (v. 2) to the defeat of Sihon and Og (v. 8). It continues in typical style with a plea for obedience, followed by a promise of prosperity in the new land (v. 8).

What makes this passage unique is the comment in verse 4 which asserts that Israel has not always been able to recognize God's presence in the events we consider "miraculous." This should be a reminder that God's saving deeds are not so unequivocal that they do not require faith on the part of those who experience them. If Israel is to recognize God's presence in its life, it will be because God supplies the kind of understanding and insight which can discern that presence.

29:9-14 Parties to the covenant. Here the Deuteronomists wish to include every generation of Israelites as partners in the covenant made with God. The obligation to fidelity falls not just on the people who experienced the Exodus and the guidance in the wilderness but on every generation. The covenant that Moses concludes between God and Israel involves not just those present at Horeb and Moab but those who are yet to be born and will likewise experience the benefits of God's goodness toward Israel.

29:15-20 A warning against false worship. The great commandment of the law is Israel's obligation to serve God alone. Moses repeats this central command here. Usually when Moses mentions Egypt, it is to remind Israel of its wondrous deliverance from slavery; here, however, Egypt serves as a model of the kind of false worship Israel is to avoid. The people will be tempted to abandon the service of God for that of foreign deities. If any of the people succumb to such a temptation, they may expect the severest of penalties. There can be no compromise whatever regarding the exclusive commitment God requires of Israel.

29:21-27 Consequences of disobedience. When people see the terrible effects of Israel's infidelity, they will have to be told the truth. Their first impulse may be to credit the gods of the nations who defeated Israel. They may conclude that a small nation such as Israel could not possibly withstand the onslaughts of powerful world empires. The real truth is that Israel's downfall was caused by its own failures to observe the stipulations of the Lord's covenant (v. 25). The consequences of these failures were defeat and exile. This constant emphasis on God's response to Israel's behavior emphasizes the personal nature of Israel's God. This was already revealed in the many acts of love that God has done for Israel's sake; it can also be revealed through the acts of judgment upon an unfaithful Israel.

29:28 A disclaimer. This verse is probably a gloss introduced into the text by a late editor. This, of course, does not affect its theological value in any way. Though there is no consensus on the meaning of the text, it may serve to acknowledge that Israel's God cannot be measured by the theological perspectives of the Deuteronomists, no matter how respected their views may be. What we have is a partial insight into the workings of the divine. While this insight is given for our sake, it should not serve to limit the prerogatives of God. This is as close as Deuteronomy gets to an acceptance of the relativity of human insight. The mystery of the divine always eludes our grasp.

30:1-14 Repentance. Human beings are not only limited in their ability to grasp fully the mystery of the divine, but the human will cannot make the kind of commitment that eliminates the possibility of unfaithfulness. This passage calls for Israel to return to the Lord after lapses. Repentance will bring restoration to the land from which Israel has been exiled (v. 4). Restoration will mean the complete reversal of the effects of infidelity. Not only will Israel be restored to its land, but it will enjoy a renewed prosperity. The only requirement is obedience—obedience that is the offshoot of Israel's love for God.

To prevent Israel from becoming discouraged by its failures, God will provide an inner source of commitment that was previously unavailable. Israel will no longer have to rely on its own strength but will receive a heart circumcised by God and fit for a renewed commitment (v. 6). Moses goes on to assure the people that obedience is not an impossible task. Israel's past performance may give rise to the view that the commandments are impossible to fulfill, but this text (vv. 11-14) presents obedience as a genuine possibility.

The law is designed as a guide to human life. It is not part of an inaccessible divine mystery (v. 12). To believe otherwise is nothing less than an attempt to evade responsibility. Second, the law is a practical guide to daily living. It is not some obtuse, rationalist system that is beyond most people (v. 13). The law is the way of life open to all.

30:15-20 The choice. The whole of Deuteronomy has been leading up to this dramatic choice that Moses sets before the people. These verses contain all the elements found in the rest of the book: commandments, blessing and curse, the appeal for obedience. After all has been said, the entire thrust of the book comes down to a choice that people need to make. Israel's future is dependent upon that choice. God's graciousness is not at issue. It is the response of Israel that causes its future to hang in the balance. Moses is not a neutral observer in the process; he is passionately concerned for Israel's future. That is why he virtually commands Israel to choose life (v. 19).

The life-and-death alternatives are broader than may be apparent to the contemporary reader. "Life" refers to that sphere of human activity under the protection of the divine; "death" refers to that sphere of human activity which is devoid of the divine presence. Death, then, is more than the cessation of physical life; it is existence outside the land, existence in the nether world of exile. Death is life without God. Life is *the* blessing, death *the* curse.

Good and evil here do not necessarily refer to moral choices. Good refers to the consequences of life with God: fertility, prosperity, and happiness. Evil refers to the consequences of life apart from God: exile, disease, and death. It is up to Israel to make one of two choices: (1) life with God, which brings blessing and good; or (2) life apart from God, which is nothing less than the curse of death. There are no other alternatives.

Moses calls upon the heavens and the earth to witness Israel's choice (v. 17). In ancient Near Eastern treaties, personified forces of nature were witnesses to the conclusion of a treaty, and it was presumed that they would deal with any partner to the treaty who proved unfaithful to its provisions. Israel, of course, demythologizes this aspect of covenant form, but it retains the idea of witnesses to the covenant by referring to the heavens and earth here.

Israel will find its true self by making a decision for life. The nation's very purpose is to love the Lord (v. 20). Every generation of Israel is to put itself in the place of those who were personally addressed by Moses, because all Israel needs to remember is that it has only two choices and that in making the right choice Israel will find "a long life" (v. 20).

31:1-8 Joshua, the successor of Moses. The Deuteronomists have already prepared their readers for the death of Moses and its significance for Israel's future (1:37-38 and 3:23-29). Though Moses was more than a heroic figure in the epic story of Israel's deliverance from Egypt and its guidance into the Promised Land, God, after all, was the actual liberator of and warrior for Israel (v. 3a). Moses is to die, but his death will not deprive Israel of the leadership it needs to settle the new land. Moses' role in Israel's life will be taken by Joshua. He is the one to lead Israel as it faces the crucial period of the settlement in Canaan.

31:9-13 Reading the law. While Moses' responsibility of providing leadership for the people is to be taken up by Joshua, there is to be a different arrangement regarding Moses' function as the people's teacher of the law. Moses has written the law and now gives it to the Levitical priests who carry the ark, which is the depository for the written document.

The written law is also given to the elders. The priests are given custody of the document, but the elders actually take up Moses' task of teaching the law. The elders were traditionally responsible for preserving the common life of the community through guiding its life and settling disputes in terms of traditional practices and values. The elders were the guardians of traditional legal lore not only in Israel but throughout the premonarchic societies of the ancient Near East. Here the elders are told to have the law read to the people periodically so that "they may hear it and learn it, and so fear the Lord . . ." (vv. 12, 13). This custom of public reading was the vehicle of covenant renewal.

There is no record of this command being fulfilled as prescribed here, though there was undoubtedly some ritual of recommitment. More important than the ritual itself is the expression of Deuteronomy's view that the Mosaic office is carried on in part by the elders, who handed down and administered the observance of ancient Israel's legal traditions.

31:14-32 Introduction to the Song of Moses. God's instructions to Moses concerning the song he is to compose and teach Israel (vv. 16-21) are framed by God's commissioning of Joshua. Again, provisions are being taken in view of Moses' imminent death (vv. 14, 16). Joshua is to provide Israel with the leadership it needs as it begins the settlement of Canaan. The song is to be a moral force touching Israel's conscience in the midst of the material blessing that the new land is to bring.

The determinism that marks verses 16-21 indicates their late introduction into this context. Israel's infidelity is not a possibility—it is inevitable. God's abandonment of the people in view of their infidelity is just as inevitable. These verses date from the Exile, when the full effects of Israel's rebellion and God's absence were being experienced by Israel. It is in the midst of this experience that the song will serve to remind Israel that what has happened to it is nothing but the curse that falls on the disobedient.

31:24-29 The book of the law. This is another attempt to deal with the loss of Moses. The law that he promulgated is to be preserved for future generations. Moses has written an account of the covenant that he has mediated between God and Israel. This written document, under the protection of the Levites, will be a perpetual reminder of the covenant. Moses calls the elders of the people and advises them of his own lack of faith in Israel's willingness to remain committed to God. Bitter experiences have shown the level of the nation's commitment. Again Moses calls upon the heavens and the earth to witness his final charge to Israel (v. 28). Moses' call for these witnesses is the link connecting this passage to the song that follows. The song begins with a similar invocation (32:1).

31:30–32:47 The Song of Moses. The Song of Moses is, in part, an indictment of Israel's infidelity to the covenant. It resembles the legal procedures used by an offended party in covenant to receive satisfaction from the offending party. The song begins with the summoning of witnesses (vv. 1-3). In this case it is the heavens and the earth that can testify that a covenant existed between God and Israel (see 30:19; 31:28). Next follows a statement of Israel's lack of commitment to the covenantal relationship (vv. 4-6). The prosecution begins with evidence of God's goodness toward Israel (vv. 7-14) and concludes with the evidence of Israel's apostasy (vv. 15-18). Finally, the people's guilt is declared and sentence is passed (vv. 19-25). Israel can expect total destruction in view of its total apostasy.

Following the trial, the song takes an abrupt turn in verses 26-27. God's enemies will misunderstand Israel's defeat. Those nations that cannot discern God's power at work in Israel's defeat will find themselves facing their own doom. The song encapsulates Israel's tragic history while affirming that the nation's defeat is not God's last word to Israel.

The song is a subtle corrective of a mechanistic application of Deuteronomic theology. From the perspective of the Exile, it is clear enough that Israel chose death rather than life. Here Deuteronomy makes a significant advance when it envisions blessing beyond the curse and proclaims a new life for Israel in spite of its infidelity. What begins with a sentence of death ends with a promise of new life.

32:48-52 The imminent death of Moses. These verses are an elaboration of Num 27:12-14, which come from the Priestly history of Israel. This is evident from the explanation that verse 51 offers for Moses' death outside the Promised Land. In Deut 1:32 Moses' fate is blamed on the people's sin and not on any personal failing of his own.

MOSES' FOURTH ADDRESS

Deut 33:1–34:12

The final component of Deuteronomy includes Moses' final testament to the tribes (ch. 33) and the account of his death (ch. 34). Moses' last words take the form of a blessing in which he foresees the fate of individual tribes (compare Gen 27 and 49). The final chapter does not come from the Deuteronomists, who wished to emphasize the continuity between the Mosaic era and every subsequent period in Israel's history. The thrust of the final chapter emphasizes a radical change that takes place with the death of Moses.

33:1-29 The blessing of Moses. The core of this text is the blessings Moses speaks upon individual tribes. These blessings are framed by a song of praise celebrating God's kingship and victories on Israel's behalf, as well as the gift of the land's prosperity (vv. 2-5, 26-29). It is through the conquest that Yahweh becomes the king of the Israelite tribes (v. 5). At this point the blessings begin.

The blessings name twelve tribes, though Simeon is missing (compare Gen 49 and Num 1:5-15). The number twelve is retained because the tribe of Joseph is divided into Ephraim and Manasseh. Apparently each tribal blessing existed independently, as evidenced by the diversity of their form and content. These independent sayings are brought together as a fitting climax to Deuteronomy. The last word spoken to the tribes is a word of blessing.

Of the particular blessings that call for specific comment, the blessing of Levi (vv. 8-11) stands out. The Thummim and Urim (v. 8) are lot oracles by means of which answers to yes-or-no questions can be ascertained. How these objects looked or how they were manipulated cannot be determined with certainty (see 1 Sam 14:18-19, 41-42; 23:9-12). Verse 10 shows that priests are more than cultic functionaries; they are also responsible for teaching traditional Israelite moral values.

34:1-8 The death of Moses. These final verses are an elaboration of what the Deuteronomists have written above in 3:27. The statement that Moses was buried "in the ravine opposite Beth-peor" might give the impression that a well-known grave site is indicated; however, the remark in verse 6b states that the exact spot of Moses' burial is unknown. Apparently by the time these words were written, the grave of Moses was no longer visited or even known, though the writers were aware of a tradition about the general area associated with Moses' death.

34:9-12 The conclusion. Here Moses is a unique, irreplaceable leader (compare Deut 18:18). In fact, verse 12 describes Moses in language usually reserved for God alone. Such a portrait could become oppressive. Though Moses is remembered as a great leader, others will have to take his place if Israel is to remain loyal to the covenant. Certainly the Deuteronomists consider themselves as continuing the role of Moses for their generation. Later, even Jesus will recognize the Pharisees' claim to the Mosaic office (see Matt 23:2). Jesus, too, believed that his mission was to fulfill "the law and the prophets" (Matt 5:17-18) and thereby bring Moses' task to completion. Thus, later generations that recognized Moses' special role in Israel's life also recognized that what Moses did for the first generation of Israelites, others must do for succeeding ones.

JOSHUA

John A. Grindel, C.M.

INTRODUCTION

The Book of Joshua is named after its chief actor, Joshua, the son of Nun. Joshua had been Moses' aide and succeeded him as the leader of the people. In Hebrew the name Joshua means "Yahweh saves" or "May Yahweh save."

The theme of the book is the occupation of the land west of the Jordan River. The book falls into three distinct sections: the conquest of Canaan (chs. 1–12); the division of the land (chs. 13–21); the return of the Transjordan tribes and the farewell of Joshua (chs. 22–24).

The Deuteronomistic History

In the Hebrew Bible the Book of Joshua is the first of what are termed the "former prophets," so called because of the importance of the prophetic word in the books. Today the book is usually seen as the first volume in what is known as the Deuteronomistic History. The Deuteronomistic History includes the Books of Joshua, Judges, Samuel, and Kings, and spans the period from the conquest of Canaan in the twelfth century B.C.E. down to the time of the Exile in the sixth century B.C.E. The Book of Deuteronomy is often considered the introduction to these books.

Our modern understanding of the larger Deuteronomistic History owes much to the work of a German scholar, Martin Noth. He was able to show that someone who shared the theological perspective, as well as literary style found in the Book of Deuteronomy, formed a continuous historical work by pulling together into a coherent whole many different units of material which were origi-nally independent and came from various periods of Israel's history. The author drew from numerous written and oral sources, such as annals, kings' lists, and stories of different kinds. Some of the units were of substantial size, such as Josh 2–11. The author's own additions established an interpretative framework that linked the disparate material together and provided judgments on the events in the story. The editor's additions are especially found in punctuating comments—sermons and speeches put into the mouths of important characters at periods of significant transition in the story (e.g., Josh 1 and 24; 1 Sam 12; 1 Kgs 8), bridge passages, and summaries. Scholars debate whether one person produced this work or a school of writers. Most presume that the present edition was composed soon after the last event reported in it, namely, the release of the last Judean king, Jehoiachin, from a Babylonian prison in 561 B.C.E. Though most believe the work to have been composed in Palestine, others think that it was written in Babylonia.

While Martin Noth thought that there was only one edition of the work, written around 550 B.C.E., it is more common today to speak of two editions. The earlier first edition was probably written during the reign of King Josiah (620–609 B.C.E.). The later second edition, which was quite thorough, would have been compiled during the Exile in the sixth century. This commentary will explain the book from the perspective of the second edition, that of the exilic editor.

The Deuteronomistic History was not written just to preserve a memory of the past;

rather, its purpose was to give a theological explanation of the loss of the two kingdoms of Israel and Judah, and to provide a theological basis for a hope in the future. To understand the work it is necessary to see it against the background of the times in which it was written.

In 721 B.C.E. the Assyrians destroyed the northern kingdom of Israel; and in 587 B.C.E., the Babylonians destroyed the southern kingdom of Judah. When Jerusalem fell in 587 B.C.E., the city, with its magnificent temple and palace, was leveled, and the leaders of the people were led off into exile in Babylonia.

The period of the Exile was a time of despair and deep questioning on the part of the people. Yahweh had promised to watch over the people, and to protect and guide them; but now all had been lost. Why had the Lord allowed this destruction and the loss of everything? The people especially wondered if they were still the people of God, and if there were any basis for a hope in the future. Would God remain true to the promises made in the past despite all that had happened since? It was in this context that the Deuteronomistic History was written.

The author's purpose is to explain that Israel had lost all because of her sinfulness. The Lord had called the people to fidelity to the covenant, and had warned them of the consequences of infidelity, but the people had sinned. Hence, in exile they were experiencing the divine judgment. Israel had not been faithful to Yahweh, and her long history of sin justified the punishment she was enduring.

The work is also an exhortation to the people to repent and turn back to the Lord and to trust that God will keep the ancient promises. The people are to believe that as God responded positively to repentant people in the past, so will God now hear their cries and forgive them once again. All the ancient promises are still in force, though temporarily suspended because of the sinfulness of the people. At the same time these promises can serve as a basis for the future if the people will only repent.

The purpose of the Book of Joshua

In the context of the Deuteronomistic History the specific purpose of the Book of Joshua, with its emphasis on the conquest and division of the land, is to show the fidelity of God to the promises made in the past to the patriarchs and Moses—particularly the promise of the land. One of the chief themes found in the Pentateuch is the promise of the land. That promise is fulfilled in the Book of Joshua so as to engender in the people a trust in God's promises. Now Israel, in the midst of the Exile, can trust in God's continuing care and presence, and trust especially that the promise of the land remains in force. At the same time, obedience to the Law is important lest, having been forgiven and brought back to the land, Israel again bring down upon her head such destruction as she is now experiencing.

Historical accuracy

A question that is often raised regarding the Book of Joshua is just how accurate is it from a historical perspective, especially in terms of its reporting on the conquest of the land in the twelfth century B.C.E. This is not an easy question to answer. There are inconsistencies and contradictions in the book itself (compare 4:3 and 4:9; 8:3 and 8:12). What are we to think of the conflicting reports of the conquest of the land found in Josh 1–12 and Judg 1:1–2:5? While the picture presented in Joshua is that of a violent and complete conquest of the land by a united Israel, the picture painted in Judges is that of individual tribes or clans slowly taking their own land and settling down next to the Canaanites in the country. This latter picture is probably closer to the reality.

The author uses different kinds of material in the book, ranging from factual documents to legends. It is also clear that the author, writing over five hundred years after the events being presented, has chosen material so that it would stress a theological viewpoint. In addition, the author has interspersed speeches created out of this theological perspective throughout the work.

Archaeological evidence also raises questions concerning the historical reliability of some of the material in the book, especially the traditions about the cities of Jericho and Ai. While the Book of Joshua gives extensive reports about the conquest of these two cities, archaeological evidence shows that they were not occupied after the fourteenth century B.C.E., and that Ai had been destroyed about a thousand years before the Israelites entered the land.

In conclusion, then, it is clear that the story, as we have it in the Book of Joshua, is simplified, schematic, incomplete, influenced by the theological views of the author, and the result of compiling very diverse material. We will make some judgments about the historical accuracy of the individual stories as we continue this commentary.

It is interesting to note that most of the material in chapters 1-12 dealing with the conquest of the land seems to be associated with the territory of Benjamin (see ch. 18:11-28) and the sanctuary of Gilgal. It would appear that the traditions in the first part of the book were gathered together and handed on at the sanctuary of Gilgal. The tribal lists in chapters 13-21, on the other hand, all date from the period of the monarchy. While some of the lists incorporated here may go back to the time of David and Solomon in the tenth century, others, such as those in chapters 20 and 21, come from the period of Josiah in the seventh century. One must be careful in accepting too quickly the biblical story of the conquest and the division of the land at face value. The reality was much more complex. We must keep in mind that the author was more interested in bringing out the meaning and significance of the events reported than in reporting exactly what happened. For it is in the meaning of events that one learns of God, oneself, and what God demands of us.

The person and work of Joshua

Against the above background on the historical reliability of the material in the Book of Joshua the person and work of Joshua also becomes a problem. If one accepts the view presented in the Deuteronomistic History that the conquest was the result of a united military action, then Joshua, as the supreme commander of the Israelite forces, plays an important role. But when we know the conquest to have been a century-long process of internal revolution, slow infiltration, and occupation by individual groups, then the figure of Joshua is difficult to explain. What adds to the problem is that while the traditions of the conquest preserved in the Book of Joshua are from the tribe of Benjamin, Joshua was from the tribe of Ephraim.

What all of this shows is that the very complicated history of the conquest has been reduced in the Book of Joshua to a small group of typical stories which are now attributed to all Israel, but which originally came primarily from the traditions of the tribe of Benjamin. These exploits have now been attributed to Joshua, a well-known person who had been active either militarily or in resolving conflicts in the central hill country of Palestine.

COMMENTARY

PART I: THE CONQUEST OF CANAAN

Josh 1:1–12:24

1:1–2:24 Preparations. The book begins with a report on the preparations for entrance into the land of Canaan. First, there is the Lord's commissioning of Joshua (1:1-9), which is followed by Joshua's orders to the people (1:10-18) and the sending of spies across the river to reconnoiter the land, especially Jericho (2:1-24).

1:1-9 The commissioning of Joshua. This passage, like all of chapter 1, comes from the hand of the Deuteronomistic Historian (henceforth D) and forms the transition from the death of Moses (see Deut 34) to the conquest of the land. The passage picks up on and develops the original commissioning of Joshua in Deut 31. In sermon style the passage follows the formula for the divine installation of a person into public office: a description of the task to be performed, an expression of encouragement, and an assurance of divine assistance. Joshua is presented as the successor to Moses with the command to complete his work.

The task that is given to Joshua is to lead the people into the land that the Lord will give to the Israelites. From the beginning (v. 2) it is made clear that the land is a gift of the Lord to the people; it is not something that they have earned. The granting of this gift is the fulfillment of the promise to Moses (v. 3). The description of the boundaries of the land in verse 4 is the most comprehensive description of the land found anywhere in the Bible. There are three fixed points in this description: the "desert," which refers to the Negeb in the south and the area east of the Jordan River; the "Euphrates," which describes the northeastern boundary; and the "Great Sea," which describes the Mediterranean on the west. As defined here the land included the area of Lebanon to the northwest and almost the whole of present-day and ancient Syria. However, these boundaries were never a reality. The only time Israel even began to have such extensive boundaries was in the time of David and Solomon in the tenth century. Joshua will be able to fulfill the promise because of the Lord's presence with him (v. 5).

Though the land is a gift of the Lord, verses 6-9 insist upon the necessity of Israel being "firm and steadfast," i.e., observing all that is written in the law in order to attain possession of the land. In other words, Israel's disobedience can frustrate the divine promises. All of this is an important message for the exiles, who can hear in this passage both the reason for the loss of the land (their disobedience) and the conditions for regaining the land (obedience to the law, trust in the Lord, and the Lord's promises of presence).

1:10-18 Joshua's orders to the people. Having received the Lord's instructions, Joshua now gives orders that the people are to be instructed to prepare provisions, because in three days they are to march in and take possession of the land that the Lord is giving them (vv. 10-11). Notice how the conquest is described as something peaceful, almost like a cultic procession. It is as if the Lord has already decreed that Israel will possess the land and now the people need only to carry it out.

In verses 12-15 Joshua reminds the tribes who have already settled in the area east of the Jordan River of the command of Moses (see Deut 3:12-20) that all the warriors from these tribes must help their kinspeople to settle in the land across the Jordan before they can return to their own land. The conquest must be seen as a unified undertaking by Israel.

Verses 16-18 present the response of the Transjordanian tribes. They will do all that Joshua commands as long as they are assured of the presence of the Lord with him (vv. 16-17). The main purpose of these verses is to show the acceptance of the transfer of leadership from Moses to Joshua.

2:1-24 Reconnaissance of Jericho. The attentive reader will notice immediately the tension between this chapter and the material in chapters 1 and 3. First of all, the location of the Israelite camp is now said to be at Shittim, which is probably the Abel-shittim mentioned in Num 33:49.

Secondly, the chronology of this chapter is incompatible with that of chapters 1 and 3. Chapter 1 speaks of three days as the interval between Joshua's orders to the people and the actual entrance into the land (see v. 11). However, the present story says that the spies spent three days in the hills before returning to the Israelite camp (2:22), not to mention the time spent going to Jericho and returning. Also, verses 1 and 2 of chapter 3 seem to flow directly after 1:18.

Finally, one encounters a different style in the present story from the style of the material in chapters 1 and 3. All of this means that this present story undoubtedly was a later insertion into the narrative. In fact there are indications that the story of Rahab is quite old and possibly goes back to the time before David. It appears that D has used the story as it was found, with the possible exception of Rahab's profession of faith in verses 9-11. This profession of faith reflects Deuteronomic themes (compare to Deut 26:5b-9 and Josh 24:2b-13).

In its original form the story of Rahab and the spies was probably an etiological tale, i.e., a narrative that explained something by giving the story of its origins. What the story explained was the survival of the Canaanite family of Rahab in the midst of the Israelites after the conquest. In its present context, however, the interest of the author is in Rahab's profession of faith. Through Rahab's profession D is emphasizing that it is the Lord who is responsible for all that is about to take place. The one who is God in heaven above and on earth below has given the land to Israel and with power will now lead them into the land. D is attempting to instill hope in the exiles by reminding them of who their God is. If the Lord could act like this in the past, then that same Lord can act with power on their behalf now.

3:1–5:12 The crossing of the Jordan. Having dealt with the preparations for entering the land, the author narrates the crossing of the Jordan. What is found in this section is a series of events that lack internal unity but are held together by their concern with the crossing and with the ark of the covenant. This is the only place where the ark is mentioned in the conquest narrative. The crossing falls into five scenes: preparations (3:1-13); the crossing (3:14-17); the setting up of memorial stones (4:1-9); the completion of the crossing (4:10-18); and the cultic encampment at Gilgal (4:19–5:12).

3:1-13 Preparations. This narrative, along with the narrative of the crossing, presents the event as a solemn liturgical procession. More than likely the story developed as a cultic

reenactment and memorial of the crossing of the Jordan. The author has taken this ancient liturgy and used it as an outline for the story, mainly to show that it was the living God, the Lord of the whole earth, who was responsible for bringing Israel into the land (vv. 10-11). Once again an important message is here for the Israelites, namely, that the Lord is powerful and can bring the exiles back to the land as the Lord once before had brought the people into the land.

The text in verses 1 and 2 follows more from 1:18 than from chapter 2. Verses 2-6 point out that it is Yahweh who leads the people. The ark is a sign of the Lord's presence. The distance that people are to keep from the ark emphasizes the respect that one must show the Lord. The call to holiness in verse 5 flows from the idea that the people are about to experience wonders performed by the Lord, i.e., extraordinary actions. Such a divine intervention requires adequate human preparation. Involved in this sanctification is a series of purification rites and abstinence from all sexual activity and certain foods (see Exod 19:10-15; Num 11:18; Josh 7:13).

Verse 7 presents the purpose of the action to follow: it is to exalt Joshua in the sight of all Israel and to confirm his role as the successor of Moses. What will happen will show the presence of the Lord with Joshua. Joshua's sermon in verses 10-13 states who is responsible for what is about to happen—the living God who is the Lord of the whole earth. It is this Lord who will bring the waters to a halt so that the people can cross over. Verse 10 lists the indigenous population of the land in standard form: the Canaanites are found in the coastal cities; the Hittites in small colonies here and there; the Hivites around Shechem and Gibeon; the Amorites inhabited the hill country; and the Jebusites lived in Jerusalem. It is not clear who the Perizzites and Girgashites were.

3:14-17 The crossing. Everything happens now as foretold. In solemn procession the people follow the priests carrying the ark of the covenant and, when the waters halt, the people cross. The crossing is consciously presented as a parallel to the crossing of the Red Sea, because the entrance into the Promised Land is, in a sense, the conclusion of the Lord's great act of deliverance that began with the Exodus. One sees here how the

Exodus becomes the prism through which all of God's great acts of deliverance are seen. The return from the Exile will also be seen as a new Exodus. To heighten the sense of the miraculous and the greatness of God's activity, it is made clear that it is late winter or early spring, when the Jordan overflows its banks because of melting snow from the mountains to the north. The river halts at "Adam," a city at the junction of the Jabbok and the Jordan Rivers, several miles north of Jericho. The Salt Sea refers to the Dead Sea, and the Arabah is the desert south of the Dead Sea. The people cross over opposite Jericho. There are several known times when the Jordan has been dammed up for a period of hours because its banks collapsed and formed a natural dam. Perhaps such an event stands behind this story.

4:1-9 The memorial stones. The present episode is a secondary insertion into the text. This is clear from the summary statement in 4:10, which refers back to the crossing in 3:14-17, and from the special interest in the twelve stones at Gilgal. Though the actual location of Gilgal is unknown, it is somewhere in the area of Jericho. From a very early period it was an Israelite national shrine. More than likely it was the natural presence of a group of stones at this sanctuary, later linked to the crossing of the Jordan, that gave rise to this episode. The stones were understood to be a physical reminder, a perpetual memorial (v. 7), of how "the waters of the Jordan ceased to flow before the ark of the covenant of the Lord when it crossed the Jordan." The episode, then, originated as an etiological tale, like the story of Rahab in chapter 2. In these verses two traditions are combined: one that explains the presence of the stones at Gilgal (vv. 1-8) and one that explains the presence of stones in the middle of the Jordan River (v. 9). It is unclear where the latter tradition came from and why it is included in verse 9.

In the present context these verses are meant to emphasize that it was the Lord who brought the Israelites across the Jordan. For the exiles this is a message of hope: this same Lord can bring the exiles back into the land. The explanation of the twelve stones in verse 17 is the midpoint of the whole block of material in 3:1–5:12. The inclusion of this episode may also be an attempt at a further assimilation of the crossing of the Jordan to the tradition of the Exodus-Sinai event (compare with the twelve stones for the twelve tribes of Israel commemorating the covenant at Sinai in Exod 24:4).

4:10-18 Completion of the crossing. Though these verses seem jumbled, there is a certain logic to them. The condition of the text here is the result of several editors dealing with various concerns. After the insertion of 4:1-9, verse 10 returns the reader to the main narrative by summarizing 3:14-17. Verse 11 is a summary in advance of the exit of the ark from the river. In this liturgical procession the people, having safely crossed the river, now line up to witness the ark being brought out of the river.

Verses 12-13 are an addition by D, who wishes to emphasize here, as in 1:12ff., that all the tribes of Israel were involved—even those that had been granted land east of the Jordan. The number forty thousand is certainly an exaggeration. Perhaps the solution is that the word that can be translated as "thousand" can also be used as a technical term to indicate a military unit of considerable size.

Verse 14 returns to 3:7 and stresses the major purpose of this miraculous crossing, namely, to exalt Joshua before all Israel. This purpose was accomplished by the great miracle; henceforth, the people respected Joshua as they had Moses. With all the goals of the miracle accomplished, the priests now come up from the river and, as soon as they hit dry ground, the Jordan resumes its course and once again overflows its banks.

4:19–5:12 Cultic encampment at Gilgal. With the crossing of the Jordan, one period in the life of Israel is about to end and another to begin. This section, with its emphasis on various cultic rites at Gilgal, forms the transition from the period of deliverance to the occupation of the land. The section is framed by two cultic events that explicitly refer back to the deliverance from Egypt: the actual setting up of the stones at Gilgal (4:20-24), and the celebration of the Passover (5:10-12). The narrative in 5:1 shows the impact of Israel's entrance into the land on the inhabitants of the area. The circumcision of all males, reported in 5:2-9, is to prepare for the celebration of the Passover.

The scene is set in 4:19. The date is the

tenth day of the first month, known as Nisan. This is the time of the harvest in March–April. The date is important in view of the celebration of the Passover, which is soon to follow. The place where the people camp after crossing the Jordan is explicitly identified for the first time; it is at Gilgal, here located on the eastern limits of Jericho.

In the story of the memorial stones (4:20-24), it is the explanation of the stones that is important. Notice the explicit comparison of the drying up of the waters of the Jordan to the drying up of the Red Sea (see Exod 14:21). The two events provide the beginning and ending points of the period of deliverance. With the entrance into the land, Israel has achieved the goal for which she was delivered from Egypt (see Exod 3:8). The purpose of the Lord's actions is explicit: that all the people of the earth might learn of the might of God, and that the Israelites might fear the Lord. This is an important message for the exiles: in the midst of their pain they must put hope in the power of their God, and give their full allegiance to the Lord who can deliver.

The point of 5:1 is to show that the Lord's purpose has been achieved among the kings in the land of Canaan. They have recognized the might of the Lord in the events of the crossing and have become "disheartened"; literally, "their hearts melted." See the same term used by Rahab (2:10-11) and in Exod 15:13-17, which narrates the results of the Exodus. Once again the author parallels the crossing of the Jordan and the crossing of the Red Sea.

The story of the circumcision in 5:2-9 is placed here more for theological reasons than for historical ones. Exod 12:48 explains that only the circumcised can take part in the celebration of the Passover. For whatever reason (the text gives none), however, the children who were born in the desert during the forty years of wandering since leaving Egypt had not been circumcised. Hence, for a proper celebration of the Passover, circumcision is now necessary. The reference to circumcision taking place for a "second time" (v. 2) intends to show the circumcision and celebration of the Passover at Gilgal as a repetition of the rites surrounding the Exodus (see Exod 12). The site of the ritual is called Gibeath-haaraloth, which means "Hill of the Foreskins," referring to a place near Gilgal where

the rite of circumcision was practiced. Notice D's need to explain the reason for the death of all the warriors who had come out of Egypt (see Num 14), probably to explain to the exiles why they had lost their land, namely, because of their disobedience. In verse 9 an attempt is made to explain the name Gilgal. The place is so named because here the Lord "removed," literally, "rolled away" the reproach of Israel. One of the meanings that the root of the word "gilgal" can have is "to roll away." It is not clear what is meant by the "reproach of Egypt."

The section concludes with the celebration of the Passover (vv. 10-12), the festival celebrating the Exodus. The fourteenth day of the first month was the proper date for this celebration (see Exod 12:1-6). As the Exodus began with the celebration of the Passover, so the entrance into the land, which brings this period of deliverance to an end, concludes with the same celebration. The next day the people eat of the produce of the land, and with this event the manna (see Exod 16 and Deut 8:3) ceases, since there is no longer a need for it. It is truly the end of an era.

5:13–12:24 The conquest. These chapters contain the narrative of the conquest: the conquest of the central part of the land (5:13–9:27); the conquest of the southern part (10:1-43); and the conquest of the northern part (11:1-15). The concluding verses (11:16–12:24) present a summary.

5:13–9:27 The conquest of the center of the land. These chapters narrate the capture of Jericho (5:13–6:27), the defeat and victory at Ai (7:1–8:29), the altar on Mount Ebal (8:30-35), and the Gibeonite alliance (9:1-27).

5:13–6:27 The capture of Jericho. The story begins with the apparition of a divine being that recalls Exod 3, the call of Moses. Joshua is to be understood as the new Moses. Though the material in 5:13-15 probably belonged originally to an independent epic, it now forms a unit with 6:1-5, which tells of the Lord's pronouncement of the fall of Jericho and instructions on how the city is to be taken. The presence of the captain of the host of the Lord shows the presence of the Lord in the conquest, right from the beginning. As 6:2 brings out, it is the Lord who is responsible for the fall of Jericho. The trumpets made of rams' horns (6:4) were commonly used in warfare and liturgies.

Archaeological evidence shows that Jericho was already in ruins when the Israelites entered into Canaan. Any habitation of the site of Tell es-Sultan, the site identified as Jericho, was sparse at the time of the conquest. What gave rise to the belief that it had been destroyed in the conquest was the fact that the site had lain in ruins in the period of the Judges and on into the period of the monarchy. Being close to the national sanctuary of Gilgal, the presupposition arose of its destruction under Joshua. Historically, it is not possible to say what lies behind the present narrative.

The narrative in chapter 6 is quite complicated and seems to have gone through various editions. In its final form the story has the characteristics of a religious ritual, a liturgy. D wants to stress to the exiles that it was Yahweh who was responsible for the conquest of the land and that same Yahweh can once again lead them to victory. This first success in Canaan takes on a symbolic value of the power of the Lord. The multiple use of the number seven, a sacred number in Israel, plays up the presence of the Lord in this narrative.

Having received instructions from the Lord on how to go about the conquest of Jericho, Joshua passes them on to the priests and people. These orders are executed and the city falls before the Israelites (6:12-21). The point of the "ban" in verses 17ff. is that since the Lord is the warrior and the victor, the enemy and booty belong to the Lord. Hence, they are sacred and taboo. To approach too close is to approach too close to God. To destroy such is an act of devotion to the Lord.

Verses 22-25, along with the reference to Rahab in verse 17, are probably an addition to help tie the story of the fall of Jericho to the story of Rahab in chapter 2. These verses conclude the etiology begun in chapter 2 that explains the presence of Rahab and her family in the midst of Israel. The mention of the treasury of the house of the Lord in verse 24 is often understood to refer to the temple of Jerusalem, which had not yet been built! More likely, it refers to the sanctuary at Gilgal.

The narrative of the fall of Jericho seems to recall memories of a military conquest on the basis of a ruse (6:1, 20, 21, 25). These may well be ancient memories of the original fall of the city. The curse, which is reported in

6:26, explains why the city was not rebuilt, and finds its fulfillment in 1 Kgs 16:34. (One of these texts depends upon the other, but it is not clear which way the dependency goes.)

7:1–8:29 Defeat and victory at Ai. The material in chapters 7 and 8 is composed of at least two narratives that were combined, probably before the time of D. The main story told of an original defeat of Israel at Ai. To this has been combined an ancient story of the crime and punishment of Achan in order to give an explanation of the defeat. The only difficulty with the combined narrative is that at the time of the Israelite conquest, Ai (today identified as et-Tell) was uninhabited. Archaeological evidence shows that the city was last inhabited at the end of the third millennium and not settled again until the eleventh century. Several theories have been advanced to explain the present narrative. One prominent theory says that the story originally described the fall of Bethel, which is only a couple of miles away, and was later connected with the ruins at et-Tell. The basis for this theory is the archaeological evidence, which shows that Bethel was destroyed toward the end of the thirteenth century. However, it is not clear that this destruction was due to the Israelites. Though the real source of the story is unknown, it is evident that both narratives are quite old. As we shall see, the major thrust of the combined narratives is to show to the exiles that a violation of the covenant leads to defeat and destruction, while faith and obedience lead to victory.

The author begins (v. 1) by explaining that the Lord was angry with Israel because Achan had violated the ban (see 6:18); hence, there should be no surprise at the defeat that is about to take place. Here is introduced the idea of corporate guilt, i.e., how the whole people could suffer because of the sin of one person.

Notice that nothing is said in verses 2-3 of the Lord's involvement. All is being done at the initiative of Israel. Hence, when Israel attacks she is defeated and the confidence of the people melts away (vv. 4-5). The word used here for "thousands" probably refers to a military contingent of some size.

Joshua with the elders now consults the Lord (vv. 6-9). Joshua's real concern is expressed in verse 9, namely, that when the other inhabitants of the land hear of the defeat, they will turn on Israel. The rites described in these verses pertain to the ritual of mourning (see Deut 9:26; Exod 32:11; 2 Sam 12:15-17). The passage recalls Israel's complaints against Moses and the Lord when they were in the desert (see Exod 16:2-8).

In the Lord's response (vv. 10-15) Joshua learns of the reason for the defeat, namely, that Israel has taken goods subject to the ban and so has violated the covenant. Israel is now under the ban and the Lord cannot and will not remain with Israel unless she removes from her midst the one who has incurred the ban. The legal procedure described (v. 14) is that of a trial by sacred lot, though we are given no details of the procedure. The verses express clearly the idea that the whole community can suffer for the sins of one.

Once Achan is identified as the culprit, he and all of his possessions are taken to the valley of Achor and stoned, and the Lord's anger toward Israel relents (vv. 16-26). The final verses present two etiologies as an explanation of the story of Achan. One of them explains a pile of stones in the valley of Achor (v. 26); the other, the name of the valley of Achor (vv. 24 and 26). This latter etiology is developed through a play on the words "Achor" and "Achan" and by the fact that the Hebrew root for "misery" and "afflicted" (see v. 25) is similar in sound to "Achor." More importantly, however, the purpose of the story is to explain to the exiles that the violation of the covenant leads to defeat.

Now that the Lord's anger against Israel has relented, the Lord tells Joshua to prepare to attack Ai. Notice that in contrast to chapter 7 victory is assured (8:1) because it is the Lord who leads Israel into battle. Hence, Israel is not to be afraid; she is only to be obedient and destroy Ai as she destroyed Jericho (v. 2). However, the Israelites are now allowed to take booty, and the Lord sets out the general lines of the conquest—it is to be through an ambush.

Joshua then gives instructions to the warriors who are to carry out the ambush (vv. 3-8), and they leave to take up their positions (v. 9). Notice again the emphasis that the Israelites will be able to take the city because the Lord has delivered it into their power (see 8:1).

Verses 10-23 describe the battle. As the main body of Israelites fled once again in seeming defeat before the king of Ai, all of the soldiers in Ai came out after the Israelites, leaving the city open and unprotected. When Joshua, at the Lord's command, stretches out his javelin towards Ai, the soldiers in ambush rise up and take the city, setting it on fire. By the time the soldiers of Ai realize what is happening, it is too late. They find themselves caught between the two parts of the Israelite army and are cut down to the last person. Only the king of Ai is spared, and he is taken alive and brought to Joshua. Joshua's stretching out of the javelin (v. 18 and v. 26) recalls the action of Moses during the war with Amalek (see Exod 17:8-13). This appears to be another incident in which the life of Joshua is paralleled to the life of Moses.

The story concludes (vv. 24-29) with the report of the slaying of all of the inhabitants of Ai (see Deut 20:16-18), the taking of booty, and the destruction of the city. These final verses contain another double etiology that explains how all was reduced to a mound of ruins, "as it remains today" (an explanation of the name of the city, "the ruin"), and how the pile of stones at the entrance of the city gate came into being—they were used to cover the body of the slain king of Ai.

In contrast to chapter 7, chapter 8 shows how Israel, when she fights under the leadership of the Lord and does the Lord's will, can be victorious. The message for the exiles is clear: while sin leads to disaster, obedience leads to victory.

8:30-35 The altar on Mount Ebal. These verses are an editorial addition, since they interrupt the flow of the story in 8:29 and 9:1. The verses report the fulfillment of the commands of Moses (see Deut 27:1-8, 11-13 and Deut 11:29) concerning what is to happen once the people have entered the land. Notice the often repeated reference to Moses in these verses. We shall see later that these verses are closely related to the material in chapter 24.

Mounts Ebal and Gerizim face one another across a deep ravine in north central Israel, about 20 miles north of Ai. Between them is the city of Shechem, an ancient cultic site. These two mountains flanked the important east-west pass through the central hill country of Israel.

9:1-27 The Gibeonite alliance. The two narratives in verses 1-2 and 3-27 show the possible responses of a people threatened with total destruction: to form a common alliance against the threat, or to enter into an alliance with the threatening party.

The reference (v. 1) to the mountain region, the foothills, and the coast of the Great Sea identifies the three regions (from east to west) of the land of Palestine.

The narrative about the Gibeonites in verses 3-27 reflects a complex literary history. Aside from D's later additions in verses 9-10, 24-25 and 27b, the figure of Joshua appears to have been a secondary insertion into the text, and verses 16-27 appear to be a secondary addition to the original story (one can jump from 9:15 to 10:1 without any sense of a gap). It is also not clear whether one city or four cities (see v. 17) entered into the alliance with Israel; nor is it always clear who was acting for Israel—the "men of Israel" or Joshua.

Like the story of Rahab (see ch. 2) this story is an etiology that has been preserved to explain the presence of the Gibeonites in the midst of Israel, despite the prohibitions of Deut 20:10-18, and their role as slaves (hewers of wood and drawers of water) at an Israelite sanctuary. The story also explains how Israel came into control of the central hill country and serves as background for chapter 10. For the exiles in the sixth century, the purpose of the story would have been to call them to faith in the power and promises of Yahweh (see vv. 9-10 and 24-25). There is little question about the historicity of an alliance between Israel and the Gibeonites (see 2 Sam 21:1-9).

The first part of the narrative (vv. 3-15) reports the deception of the Gibeonites and the conclusion of the alliance. Gibeon is identified with modern el-Jib, a site in the central hill country about seven miles northwest of Jerusalem and situated along an important east-west road from Jericho to the coastal plain. Seemingly, Gibeon belonged to a small four-village alliance (see v. 17). Whatever settlement existed at el-Jib in the time of Joshua, archaeological evidence shows that it was not a large settlement, although it later became an important city.

The Gibeonites come to Israel at Gilgal (v. 6), to which Israel has returned after the covenant ceremony reported in the preceding chapter. Israel's hesitancy regarding the proposed alliance (v. 7) flows from Deut 7:2 and 20:10-18. The alliance would have included peace between the two parties, as well as mutual defense (see 10:1-15). The reason given for seeking this alliance is the fame of the Lord, the God of Israel, and all that this God had done for Israel in Egypt and against Kings Sihon and Og (see Num 21:21-35). Israel, without seeking the advice of the Lord, agrees to the alliance and the parties partake of a covenant meal to seal it (vv. 14-15).

The second part of the narrative (vv. 16-27) reports the discovery of the ruse and Israel's response. The oath was so important that even the discovery of the trickery was not sufficient reason to release Israel from her obligations. However, the Gibeonites must be punished, so it is recommended that they be made "hewers of wood and drawers of water" (vv. 16-21), an expression referring to an inferior form of membership in the community (see Deut 29:10). Joshua confronts the Gibeonites and tells them that they are to carry out their tasks for "the house of my God" (v. 23). It is not clear if the reference here is to Gibeon or Gilgal. In their response (vv. 24-25) the Gibeonites seem to reflect a knowledge of Deut 20:10-18.

10:1-43 The conquest of the south. In a series of related incidents Joshua takes control of the southern part of Israel. The occasion for this conquest is the attack on Gibeon by the five kings from the south.

10:1-27 The Gibeon campaign. When Adonizedek, the king of Jerusalem, hears of how Joshua has dealt with Ai and Jericho and their kings, and that Gibeon has made a covenant with Israel, he becomes frightened and sends for four other kings from the neighborhood to help him attack Gibeon (vv. 1-4). The fear springs from the strength of Gibeon and because Gibeon has gone over to Israel, thus giving Israel an important bridgehead in the central hill country. Thus, the five kings put Gibeon under siege, as a way of stopping Israel's advance into the hill country, and as a punishment. The Gibeon in chapter 10, "large enough for a royal city" (v. 2), contrasts with the Gibeon in chapter 9, so weak that it sought an alliance with Israel. The picture presented in chapter 10 is also at odds with archaeological evidence. When the Gibeonites appeal to their protector, Joshua, he responds immediately and, after an all-night march, takes the five kings by surprise and inflicts a great slaughter on them (vv. 5-10). The march would have covered about eighteen miles along mountainous roads. Note that Joshua is victorious because the Lord has delivered the five kings into his power (v. 8). The hailstones mentioned in verse 11 were, no doubt, the result of an unusually severe midsummer storm that wreaked as much havoc as the army of Israel. Beth-horon was the name of an important pass that was a major point of entry from the west into the hill country.

Verses 12-14 should not be taken too literally. The compiler certainly understood them to be the description of a miraculous prolonging of the day so that Joshua would have enough sunlight to finish off the enemy. However, we should view these verses as a poetic description emphasizing that Yahweh fought for Israel and was responsible for the victory. Much of this story is reported in Judg 1:4-20, where three of the cities listed here are said to have been captured by the tribe of Judah.

Verses 16-27 describe the death of the five kings who had initiated the attack on Gibeon. Makkedah was west of Jerusalem. When the kings are discovered, Joshua does not want to waste time with them. He tells his men, after making sure that the kings cannot escape, to pursue the fleeing soldiers, and to kill them before they escape into their fortified cities (vv. 16-19). The later humiliation of the kings (v. 24) was meant to build up the confidence of Israel and to emphasize the power of the Lord in her midst. The story ends on an etiological note that explains the existence of a pile of stones at the mouth of a cave in Makkedah (v. 27). The point of the story, then, is to build up the confidence of the exiles in the power of their God to overcome their enemies (see vv. 8-14 and 25).

10:28-43 The conquest of the south concluded. Having defeated the coalition of five kings, Joshua follows up this victory with raids against six cities to the west and southwest of Jerusalem (vv. 28-39). The descriptions of these raids follow a definite pattern that reports how the city was captured and its inhabitants put to the sword with no survivors. In this way Joshua fulfilled the doom on each city according to the will of the Lord (Deut 20:10-18). Israel was successful because the Lord had delivered the cities into her power.

It is not possible to harmonize fully the description of the coalition in verses 1-5 with the account of the campaign against the south depicted in these verses. While there is some overlapping of cities, verses 28-39 seem to reflect a tradition different from the one in verses 1-5. What seems to lie behind these verses is a presupposition that Israel's enemies always followed the same route when advancing against Jerusalem at different points in history. It was the route of Sennacherib in 701 B.C.E. (see 2 Kgs 18:13) and of Nebuchadnezzar in 587 B.C.E. (see Jer 34:7) when they advanced on Jerusalem.

The concluding verses (40-43) summarize this part of the conquest. The author's purpose is to show that Israel had conquered all of the territory south of Gibeon under Joshua's leadership. The description is highly exaggerated, the author using the summary to emphasize how Joshua had followed the Lord's commands and had been successful because the Lord fought for Israel. Again, the message for the exiles is clear: they are to be obedient and trust in the power of the Lord.

11:1-15 The conquest of the north. The chapter begins abruptly with no clear connection to the preceding material except that the king of Hazor "learned of this." Originally, this material was probably an independent tradition that is now presented as the northern counterpart to the conquest of the south reported in chapter 10. This tradition may have belonged to one or more northern tribes and was later extended to all Israel. So too, the figure of Joshua has probably been introduced into the story secondarily. However, the tradition seems to rest upon a historical foundation. Notice that this chapter follows the same outline as chapter 10: one king forms a coalition to defeat the Israelites, but Joshua defeats the coalition through a surprise move, and attacks the cities involved.

The narrative begins with Jabin, the king of Hazor, calling together a coalition of northern kings. Notice how the description begins with specific details and then becomes more and more vague. All of the members of the coalition, with their troops, horses, and chariots, now gather together at the waters of Merom, a few miles southwest of Hazor, to launch an attack against Israel (vv. 1-5). The topography of these chapters covers the general area of Galilee, an area that was later as-

239

signed to the tribe of Naphtali. Archaeological excavations show that Hazor, located about eight miles north of the Sea of Galilee, was a very impressive city in the thirteenth century B.C.E. and could well have fit the descriptions of it in these verses. Excavations also show that it was destroyed in the mid-thirteenth century, which would coincide with the time of Joshua. The other three cities named here are located south of Hazor. The Arabah is the great rift that contains the Sea of Galilee (here called "Chinnereth"), the Jordan River, and the Dead Sea. The size of the opposing army is no doubt exaggerated here to magnify the victory.

Israel was successful against the coalition because the Lord had delivered the Canaanites into her power and because Joshua had obeyed the Lord by following the tactics laid out for him (vv. 6-9). Notice that nothing is said about where Joshua received the word of the Lord. From the context it would seem that he was still at Gilgal. The crippling of the horses prevented the Canaanites from using their chariots, which were subsequently burned. The Canaanites then had to flee on foot, allowing Israel to defeat them. Since Israel did not begin to use chariots until the time of David and Solomon, it is doubtful that they could have defeated a chariot-equipped army.

The reason for Joshua's actions against Hazor is that Hazor had been the chief of all those kingdoms (vv. 10-12). Behind the remark about Israel not burning any of the other cities "built on raised sites" (v. 13) is a reminder that Israel had neither the strength nor the technical knowledge to defeat the chariot armies of the Canaanites. The extent of the destruction described in these verses is, therefore, probably exaggerated.

This section concludes with a summary regarding the obedience of Joshua: he did all that the Lord had commanded Moses (v. 15). The message to the exiles is reiterated: the need for obedience to the Lord and trust in the power of the Lord. With such trust, victory is possible.

11:16–12:24 Summary of the conquest. The conquest is now summarized in an idealistic fashion by two separate texts. The editorial summary in 11:16-23 was the original summary and conclusion to the narrative. Chapter 12, with its list of conquered kings, was inserted later.

11:16-23 Editorial summary. These verses come from the original compiler of the conquest stories. The basic theme, set out in verses 16 and 23, is that Joshua "captured all this land." Therefore, the Lord has kept all the promises made to Moses (see Josh 1:1-9). The description of the conquered land (vv. 16-17) goes significantly beyond the description in the preceding chapters and also beyond the classical description of "from Dan to Beersheba." Mount Halak, which marks the southern boundary, is at the southern end of the Negeb desert, south of Judah. Baalgad, the northern boundary, refers to a site at the southern end of the Beka valley in Lebanon.

Verse 18 attempts to correct any notion that the conquest was swift. It is pointed out that Israel had to do battle with all these cities because it was the will of the Lord. The Lord had designed it so that all the cities, except Gibeon, would wage war against Israel and so give reason for their extermination (see Deut 20:10-20).

Verses 21-22 are a bit jarring in the context. The Anakim are described elsewhere as "giants" (Num 13:33). The editor wants to show that there were trouble spots where not all the indigenous population had been driven out.

Once more, the conclusion in verse 23 emphasizes that the Lord has kept the promises made to Moses. The same verse forms the transition to the apportioning of the land that begins in chapter 13. The insistence on the Lord's fidelity to the promises made to Moses was an important message for the people in exile.

12:1-24 List of conquered kings. This chapter falls into two parts: a listing of the kings conquered by the Israelites under Moses, east of the Jordan (vv. 1-6), and a listing of those kings whom Israel had conquered under Joshua, west of the Jordan (vv. 7-24). The chapter is an elaboration of 11:23, and is intended to emphasize that the whole country had been conquered by Israel.

The material in verses 1-6 has been developed from Deut 3:8-17 and Josh 13:9-32. Verse 1 points out the northern and southern boundaries of the territory conquered east of the Jordan, namely, Mount Hermon in the north and the River Arnon in the south. The southern half of this area from the River Arnon to the River Jabbok had belonged to Sihon, king of the Amorites, who had his capital in Heshbon (vv. 2-3). The area north of the Jabbok had been under the control of Og, king of Bashan (vv. 4-5). Num 21:21-35 (see Deut 2:26–3:11) recounts the defeat of Sihon and Og. Num 32 reports how Moses had assigned this land to the Reubenites, Gadites, and the half-tribe of Manasseh (v. 6). The Rephaim mentioned in verse 4 were a legendary people of great stature who had inhabited Syria and Palestine in ages past (see Deut 2:11, 3:11; Gen 14:5; 2 Sam 21:16-20).

The listing of the kings conquered west of the Jordan in verses 7-24 is a very important list because verses 13b-24 contain names of cities not previously mentioned. These latter verses are not simply a summary of the preceding stories but represent an independent tradition of the conquest that some scholars say is very ancient, dating from the time of Solomon. Verses 16b-24 are especially interesting, since they list cities found in the territories of Ephraim and Manasseh in central Palestine, where no previous conquests have been mentioned.

The impression given by these lists is that of a total conquest of the land; and that is almost certainly the intention of the author. The interest of the author in these chapters of the conquest (6–11) has not been to give an exact historical account, but rather to show God keeping past promises through great acts on behalf of Israel.

PART II: THE DIVISION OF THE LAND

Josh 13:1–22:34

13–22 The division of the land. These chapters contain elaborate geographical details about how the land was divided among the various tribes, and provide statistical information about persons, places, and tribes. Their purpose is to show how God has given the whole country to Israel as its heritage, just as the Lord had promised Moses (see 11:23). This was an important message for the original audience of this book, the exiles, who had recently lost the land. To these exiles the Book of Joshua is promising above all that the Lord is faithful to the ancient promises made to the patriarchs.

The data found in these chapters are the result of combining various sources. Martin

Noth claims that the section is the result of combining two documents: a list of towns of the kingdom of Judah, which dates from the time of King Josiah (d. 621), and a survey of boundaries dating from before the monarchy. Admittedly, the roots of some of this data are quite old, but the chapters reflect the impact of later events. This section may have been composed before the writing of Joshua, and may even be a later insertion into the original narrative of the conquest (compare 13:1b and 23:1b).

While the primary interest of these chapters is with the area west of the Jordan, the section begins with a survey of the allotments of the land east of the Jordan that Moses had made to the tribes of Reuben, Gad, and the half-tribe of Manasseh (13:8-33). It concludes with the narrative of the return of these tribes to their territory in order to take possession of it (22). Chapters 14–21 deal with the allotment to Judah and the Joseph tribes at Gilgal (14–17), the allotment at Shiloh to the remaining seven tribes (18–19), and the setting aside of the cities of asylum (20) and the Levitical cities (21).

In the material that follows, this commentary will not present a detailed analysis of the boundaries and lists of towns given in the biblical text. Readers interested in such detail are referred to the more technical commentaries and atlases. This commentary will limit itself to general remarks.

13:1-33 Introduction to the division of the land. With Joshua far advanced in years, the Lord orders him to apportion the land west of the Jordan among the nine tribes and the half-tribe of Manasseh that still do not have land. This chapter is a D composition in which the author points out that not all of the territory to be allotted had been conquered (v. 1), describes the lands that must still be conquered (vv. 2-6), reminds the reader that the tribes of Reuben, Gad, and the half-tribe of Manasseh had already been allotted territory east of the Jordan by Moses (v. 8), and gives a general (vv. 9-13) and a specific description (vv. 15-31) of this land. Two footnotes have been added to explain why the tribe of Levi had not received an allotment of a block of territory like all the other tribes (v. 14 and v. 33). While the author's purpose seems clear, a certain lack of logic and continuity in these verses is apparent (compare

v. 7 to vv. 1-6 and v. 14 to vv. 8-13). This tells us that there are several layers of material in these chapters.

Verses 1-7 identify the parts of Canaan that Israel had not been able to conquer. That verses 2-6 were added secondarily is apparent from the lack of connection between the description of the land to be conquered and the subsequent order to apportion the land among the nine and a half tribes (v. 7). The area envisioned by verses 2-6 is the area belonging to the empire of David and Solomon.

Verses 8-14 are another addition to the text to explain why Joshua was to apportion land only to nine and a half tribes (v. 8), and to give a general picture of this territory (vv. 9-13). These verses seem to be based on Deut 3.

Verses 15-31 describe the lands allotted to the tribes of Reuben and Gad and the half-tribe of Manasseh. The Reubenites receive the tableland stretching north of the Arnon River to Medeba and Heshbon; the Gadites receive the highlands north of Heshbon; and the half-tribe of Manasseh receives the area of Bashan and a portion of Gilead.

The chapter concludes with another reminder that Moses had apportioned these lands to these tribes when he was in the plains of Moab (v. 32).

14:1–21:42 Allotment of the land west of the Jordan. This is the core section of the second half of the Book of Joshua and falls into five sections: an introduction (14:1-5); the allotment to Judah and Joseph at Gilgal (14:6–17:18); the allotment at Shiloh to the remaining seven tribes (18:1–19:51); a list of the cities of asylum (20:1-9); and a listing of the Levitical cities (21:1-42).

14:1-5 Introduction. These verses present the specific introduction to the allotment of the land west of the Jordan. They stress that Eleazar the priest and Joshua and the heads of the families divided the land (v. 1), and that it was done by lot, in accordance with the instructions that the Lord had given through Moses (vv. 2 and 5; see Num 33:54; 34:13). It is also explained why the land was divided among twelve tribes, even though the tribe of Levi was not given a block of land, namely, because the descendants of Joseph formed two tribes (vv. 3-4).

In the later traditions in the Old Testament Eleazar the priest (v. 1) is presented as a son of Aaron (Exod 6:25; Lev 10:5; Num 3:2).

Though the use of the lot is referred to several times in the Old Testament it is not clear from the contexts what was involved. The reason for the need to explain why Joseph's descendants formed two tribes (vv. 3-4) flows from the tradition that Israel was composed of twelve tribes. Not all of the traditions agreed, however, on the identity of the twelve tribes; and some traditions did not even recognize the twelve tribe schema. For example, while one tradition spoke of Joseph as one tribe (17:14-18), another tradition spoke of Joseph's descendants as two tribes. Hence, the editor clarifies from the beginning that the descendants of Joseph formed two tribes: Ephraim and Manasseh.

14:6–15:63 Allotment to the tribe of Judah. This section is composed of four units: the portion given to Caleb (14:6-15); the list of the boundaries of Judah (15:1-12); the gift to Othniel (15:13-19); and the list of the cities of Judah (15:20-63).

14:6-15 Caleb's portion. The story tells how Caleb came into possession of the city of Hebron: it was a reward for his loyalty to the Lord when Moses had sent him to spy out the land many years earlier. Num 13–14 (see Deut 1:20-45) reports how all the spies, except Caleb and Joshua, advised against invasion. As a result God delayed the conquest until that whole generation, except Caleb and Joshua, had died. While a specific promise of land to Caleb is not found in Num 13–14, it is presupposed in Deut 1:36.

In several Old Testament passages, Caleb is identified as a Judahite (e.g., Num 13:6; 34:19), but elsewhere as a Kenizzite (e.g., Num 32:12). The Kenizzites were originally part of the Edomite people (Gen 36:11, 15, 42) who had settled in the southern hill country of Judah and were eventually assimilated into the tribe of Judah. Accordingly, Caleb is presumed to be part of the tribe of Judah. Note that in Judg 1:10 the region shown here as occupied by Caleb was conquered by Judah and Simeon, who defeated the three Anakim chiefs.

Because this passage, as well as 15:13-19, disrupts an otherwise carefully organized presentation of tribal allotments, some claim that they were inserted into the text secondarily. Some also argue that 14:6-15 originally followed 11:21-23 and that 15:13-19 has been drawn from Judg 1:10-20.

15:1-12 Boundaries of Judah. This first of the boundary lists is also the most detailed, indicating that the D editor had more complete records for Judah than for the other tribes. The list, though idealistic, is ancient, and may predate the period of the monarchy. It is certainly older than the list of cities in 15:21-62.

15:13-19 The gift to Othniel. This story, an almost verbatim duplicate of Judg 1:10-15, is an etiology to explain why the Othnielites, who also belonged to the Kenizzite group, had access to pools of water which should have belonged to the Calebites in Hebron. Notice that Caleb is said here to have taken by force the area given him as his heritage in 14:6-15.

15:20-63 Cities of Judah. This list of cities is based on a catalog of twelve provinces that composed the southern kingdom of Judah, probably drawn up for governmental administrative purposes sometime after David. Verse 63 has been added to explain why Jerusalem has not appeared in the city list, namely, because the Judahites could not drive out the Jebusites who lived in the city. It will be David who eventually captures the city (2 Sam 5:6-9).

16:1-17:18 Allotment to the Joseph tribes. This section is made up of four parts: a broad description of the area occupied by the Josephites, in which the Josephites are presented as one tribe (vv. 1-3); a list of the boundaries of the tribe of Ephraim (vv. 4-10); a list of the allotment made to the descendants of Manasseh, other than Machir, who had already obtained land east of the Jordan (17:1-13); and a story of how Joseph's descendants complained that they needed more land (17:14-18).

These lists are in obvious contrast to the detailed Judahite lists in the previous chapters. Fewer details are given and the material is often presented in a very confused way. Notice the concern to explain why Canaanites continued to live in the midst of these tribes (16:10; 17:12), though in both cases it is insisted that the Canaanites were eventually impressed as laborers, even if they were not driven out.

In verses 1-6 we find delineated, by means of a genealogical formulation, the members of the half-tribe of Manasseh, who settled in the area west of the Jordan (see Num 26:28-34). The clan of Machir (v. 1) made up

the half-tribe that settled east of the Jordan.

Verses 14-18 consist of two versions (14-15; 16-18) of the same tradition combined into one narrative. The theme of both is a request by Joseph's descendants for more territory, because the hill country they had been given was not large enough to accommodate all of them. In verses 16-18 they also complain that they had been unable to drive out the Canaanites because of their iron chariots. In both versions Joshua responds by telling the Josephites to make better use of their hill country by clearing out some of the forest. In the second version he also encourages them to overcome the Canaanites.

18:1-19:51 Allotment at Shiloh. Having presented the allotment of land to the major tribes of Judah and Joseph, the editor, after an introduction (18:1-10), describes the allotments to the seven remaining tribes: Benjamin (18:11-28); Simeon (19:1-9); Zebulun (19:10-16); Issachar (19:17-23); Asher (19:24-31); Naphtali (19:32-39).

The introduction (18:1-10) describes the procedure of allotting the land: after a representative body (three members from each tribe) surveys and prepares a description of it, the land is divided into seven parts. Joshua assigns the various parts to the seven tribes by casting lots, but it is highly unlikely that the tribes actually received their land in this way. In reality the process was a highly complex one of historical settlement over a period of time. Note that whereas the tribes of Judah and Joseph initiated the procedure for getting their allotment, Joshua is pictured here (v. 3) as admonishing the other seven tribes for not taking more initiative in possessing the subdued land. The reference to Shiloh is probably secondary, since the reference to Judah in the south and Joseph in the north (v. 5) does not make sense if the reference point is Shiloh, which was in the territory of Ephraim. The original tradition supposed Gilgal as the place for this allotment of land. Historically, Shiloh succeeded Gilgal as the national shrine. The reference to the meeting tent (v. 1) is curious, since references to the meeting tent are very rare in the Deuteronomistic sections of the Old Testament (see Deut 31:14-15; 1 Sam 2:22). This reference to the meeting tent is probably due to a later editing of the text.

In general the allotments given to the different tribes are described in terms of ancient boundary lists and city lists drawn up for administrative purposes. Notice that for Simeon (19:1-9) no tribal boundaries are given. The reason is that from a very early period the tribe of Simeon was absorbed into the tribe of Judah and had no territory of its own. Rather, Simeon occupied certain cities within the area belonging to Judah. D justifies this allotment to the Simeonites on the basis that Judah's portion was larger than it needed to be.

Seemingly, the original allotment to Dan was very small. However, the main reason the Danites were forced to migrate north (v. 47) was because they could not conquer the Canaanites in the coastal plain that was part of their original allotment (see Judg 17–18).

That Joshua was granted a specific city as his own is reported only here. Perhaps the passage (vv. 49-50) was added to justify the later statement that Joshua was buried within his own heritage (Josh 24:30; Judg 2:9).

The conclusion to this section is based on 14:1 and 18:1.

20:1-9 The cities of asylum. The right of sanctuary is an ancient tradition that is found in both classical and oriental antiquity and is normally associated with certain sanctuaries. This passage lists those cities where a person who has accidentally killed another could find refuge and asylum. Behind this passage is the fact that in ancient semitic society, in the case of murder, it was the responsibility of the victim's next of kin to avenge the death by taking the life of the murderer. This was true even in the case of an accidental killing. Hence, there was a need to protect a person who accidentally killed another. Cities of asylum have no parallel that we are aware of. The six cities that are listed here show up again in the list of Levitical cities in chapter 21, and Shechem and Hebron housed famous sanctuaries. That a sanctuary also existed at Kadesh (the name means "holy") is also probable. Therefore, it would seem that the right of asylum is connected with these cities because of the sanctuaries located in them.

A difficulty with the picture this chapter presents is that, aside from the laws concerning this custom of asylum in Num 35:9-15 and Deut 19:1-13, no biblical text provides a concrete example of its practice. So, serious questions may be raised about the historicity of what is presented here, and no sufficient evi-dence is available to give any satisfactory answers.

21:1-42 Levitical cities. D has pointed out several times that the tribe of Levi received no heritage, i.e., no block of territory (13:14, 33; 14:4; 18:7). The Levites received only cities to live in along with their pasture lands (14:4). This chapter lists those cities that were given to the Levites in fulfillment of the Lord's command to Moses (Num 35:1-8).

The major issue regarding the chapter is whether the institution of the Levitical cities is historically true. The list of cities as we have it is artificially arranged, as is apparent in the twelve-tribe scheme imposed upon it. Again, we see nowhere in the Old Testament any concrete example of how this institution functioned. It is not surprising, then, that some see the institution of Levitical cities, and hence this list, as purely theoretical and idealistic. However, there are scholars today who claim that there is a historical reality underlying the story. Specifically they say that the Levitical cities represent "colonies," i.e., places assigned to faithful groups like the Levites in order to bring stability to a given area. Others argue that the list represents an administrative arrangement established by David for governing the frontier areas of his new empire. It is true that Israel controlled the extensive territory presupposed by the list only in the time of David and Solomon, and the majority of the cities listed here are known to have been difficult frontier areas of the empire conquered by David. The Levites were not the only inhabitants of these cities, but they did have certain prerogatives and rights regarding these cities and their pasture lands.

The story of the origin of the Levites as descendants of the three sons of Levi (Kohath, Gershon and Merari) is both late (post-exilic) and an over-simplification of the reality. Notice that the Kohathites are divided into two groups: the descendants of Aaron (the priests) and the other Kohathites.

21:43–22:34 Conclusion. These verses conclude the narrative of the division of the land (21:43–22:9) and provide an appendix regarding the building of a great altar by the Transjordanian tribes on their return to their own lands (22:10-34).

21:43–22:9 Summary and dismissal of the eastern tribes. Verses 43-45 are a summary of the book up to this point. This summary, like the others noted in the book (9:1-2; 10:40-43), goes beyond what has actually been reported in the individual stories that precede it. Despite allusions to the contrary (13:1-6), the editor claims here that Israel has conquered all of the land. What is important, however, is the message that the editor wishes to convey here, namely, that the Lord has been faithful to all the promises made to the patriarchs. As a result Israel has taken possession of all the land and has found peace. As we have noted, this is the major theme of the Book of Joshua and an important message for the people in exile in the sixth century. The exiles can trust this God who is faithful to past promises and who has the power to fulfill them.

The material in 22:1-9 is closely linked to 21:43-45 because it is the "peace" described in 21:45 that permits the dismissal of the eastern tribes reported in 22:1-9. These verses frame the theme developed in 1:12-18. Joshua acknowledges the fidelity of the eastern tribes (vv. 1-3) and, because the tribes west of the Jordan are settled, he dismisses the eastern tribes so that they can return to their own lands (v. 4) with the admonition to remain faithful to the law of Moses (v. 5). He then sends them on their way with his blessing (v. 6). The editor gives special attention to the eastern tribes throughout the book in order to emphasize that the conquest of the land was the work of all Israel. The unity of all of the tribes was quite important to the editor.

22:10-34 Appendix: The construction of the great altar. This story constitutes an appendix to the narrative of the conquest and division of the land. On the surface it tells of how, on their way home, the eastern tribes construct a very large altar in the region of the Jordan River (v. 10). When the other tribes hear of this, they meet to declare war on the eastern tribes (vv. 11-12). The reason for such a strong reaction to the altar is found in the accusation of the delegation sent to get an explanation, namely, the altar is seen as an act of rebellion against the Lord (v. 16). The objecting tribes are fearful of the ramifications of this sin upon all of the tribes (vv. 17-20). What is presupposed here is the belief of the D editor that there can be only one place of worship. The western tribes are mollified when the eastern tribes assure them that the altar is not meant for sacrifices but for a

memorial—a reminder to all the tribes that the eastern tribes, though not living in the Promised Land, strictly speaking (see v. 19), did have a right to worship the Lord (vv. 21-29).

Behind the story stands an older narrative that probably dealt with some conflict between the eastern and western tribes over religious practices, and which provided an etiology to describe some great altar. The story has been so thoroughly reworked, that it is impossible to say anything about the original narrative. As it stands, it is a clear warning against illegitimate cultic places, and it stresses the unity of all the tribes. This latter point is found in the concept of corporate guilt expressed in verses 17-20, where the presumed treachery of the eastern tribes is understood to affect all of the tribes, and in the reason given by the eastern tribes for building the altar—as witness to the unity of the eastern and western tribes.

It is not clear from verses 10 and 11 if the altar was built on the western or eastern side of the Jordan. For the story of Peor, see Num 25:6-18. The thrust of the remark in verse 18 would seem to imply that Israel is still offering sacrifices to atone for that sin.

PART III:
JOSHUA'S FAREWELL AND DEATH

Josh 23:1–24:33

23–24 Joshua's farewell address. Though these two chapters have separate introductions, they go together in the final edition of the book as the last will and testament of Joshua. Joshua, realizing that his end is near, gathers the people together to remind them of all that has taken place and to encourage them to be faithful to the covenant. He also warns them of the dire consequences of rebellion against the Lord.

Both chapters must be seen against the background of ancient Near Eastern treaties. Scholars are aware of strong parallels between the way the covenant at Sinai is presented in the Old Testament and the form of ancient Near Eastern vassal treaties. These treaties usually contained the following elements: self-introduction by the sovereign; a recounting of history, i.e., what the sovereign has done for the vassal; stipulations that the vassal is to observe as a response to what the sovereign has done for him; blessings and curses for fidelity, or lack thereof, to the treaty; calling upon witnesses; and a demand that the treaty be read periodically before the people. These elements, in different ways, give shape to these two chapters.

23:1-16 Joshua's final plea. This chapter falls into the category of a farewell address. Joshua recalls the past, especially God's actions on behalf of the people, reminds the people of what the Lord asks of them, and of what must still be done. The address has been affected by the style of the Levitical sermon, in which there is much repetition and a mixture of history, stipulation, curses, and blessings. In these latter elements one sees the influence of the ancient vassal treaties.

The chapter is a total creation of the D author, and forms the conclusion to the narrative of the conquest. The purpose of the chapter is to explain to the exiles why they have lost the land, namely, because of their disloyalty to Yahweh, which has brought about the fulfillment of the Lord's threats of destruction. By emphasizing that the Lord has fulfilled all the promises made in the past (vv. 2-11), the author is telling the people that if they again turn to the Lord, they can have their land back; because the Lord is faithful to past promises. Through specific warnings in the text, the author is telling the exiles how they must act in their present situation.

After the Lord has given the Israelites rest from all their enemies, Joshua, in his old age, summons Israel for his farewell address (vv. 1-2). He recalls all that the Lord has done for the people (v. 3), points out that in accord with the promises that have been made, the Lord will drive out the nations before the Israelites from the regions allotted them (vv. 4-5), and calls the people to obedience to the law of Moses (vv. 6-8). The people are to avoid any activity that might even imply the existence of the gods of the foreigners (v. 7). Then the author once again recalls how the Lord drove out the nations before Israel (v. 9) out of fidelity to the promises made in the past (v. 10), and calls Israel to love the Lord (v. 11). Joshua threatens Israel: if she abandons Yahweh and in any way allies herself with the foreign nations (v. 12), then the Lord will no longer drive out the nations before her, but will abandon her to the nations (v. 13). Israel is to acknowledge that every promise

of the Lord has been fulfilled (v. 14). Joshua points out that as the Lord has fulfilled all the promises made in the past, so also will the Lord fulfill every threat, namely, to exterminate Israel from the land if she transgresses the covenant (vv. 15-16).

24:1-28 Renewal of the covenant. In contrast to chapter 23 this chapter is based on a tradition that contains authentic memories of ancient covenant renewal ceremonies. The dating of this covenant ceremony to the end of Joshua's life is provided only by the context—not by the report itself. These verses are closely related to the ceremony on Mount Ebal reported in 8:30-35 and, historically, would fit better into that context than at the end of Joshua's life.

While the text may be rooted in some past ceremony, such as a renewal of the Sinai covenant in which the Shechemites were invited to participate, the present text has been influenced by covenant renewal ceremonies that were celebrated periodically in Israel. These ceremonies in turn had been influenced by the form of the ancient Near Eastern vassal treaties.

Joshua gathers together all the tribes of Israel at Shechem in order to address them (v. 1). Shechem, an ancient cultic center, is near the present town of Nablus, about 30 miles north of Jerusalem. No information is available on how Israel came into control of the central hill country where Shechem is located. It was probably a peaceful occupation. Joshua now addresses the people (vv. 2-15). The major part of the address is a recitation of Israel's history from the time of the patriarchs to the period of the conquest (vv. 2-13). Joshua stresses that it was the Lord who was responsible for all that had taken place.

The river referred to in verses 2 and 3 is the Euphrates, and the mountain region of Seir (v. 4) refers to the area south of the Dead Sea. The land of the Amorites (v. 8) is the region east of the Jordan. On Balaam, see Num 22–24. Verse 14 contains the stipulation of the covenant: total commitment to Yahweh because of all that Yahweh had done for them. Verse 15 contains Joshua's challenge to the people: decide whom you will serve! The response of the people (vv. 16-18) is that they, as Joshua's household, will serve the Lord because of all that the Lord has done for them.

In response to the warning of Joshua about

the implications of disloyalty (vv. 19-20), the people reaffirm their commitment (v. 21). Following upon the declaration of witnesses (v. 22), the people solemnly profess their willingness to serve the Lord in response to Joshua's invitation (vv. 23-24). The covenant is then made, a large stone is set up to commemorate the event, and the people are dismissed (vv. 25-28). The function of the stone is not clear. It is possible that the terms of the covenant were written upon it.

In its present context the purpose of this chapter is clear. The author is calling the exiles to total loyalty to the Lord in response to all that the Lord has done for them. As the original Israelites had committed themselves to Yahweh, so now must the Israelites in exile choose whom they will serve. By reporting the renewal of the covenant the editor also makes it clear to the exiles that the covenant can be renewed again if Israel is willing to commit herself completely to Yahweh as her ancestors had done. The threat about the response of the Lord to Israel's infidelity (vv. 19-20) is meant to remind the Israelites once again that the reason they had lost their land was because of their disobedience.

24:29-31 The death of Joshua. After a long life Joshua dies and is buried at Timnath-serah, the Ephraimite town that had been given to him for his services (19:49-50). Verse 31 serves as a transition to the Book of Judges.

24:32-33 Burial traditions. Someone else has added these brief notes about the reburial of the bones of Joseph at Shechem (see Gen 50:25 and 33:19), and the burial of Eleazar, the contemporary of Joshua.

JUDGES

John A. Grindel, C.M.

INTRODUCTION

The Book of Judges tells the story of Israel between the death of Joshua and the rise of Samuel. The core of the book is a collection of stories about several heroes from Israel's past—the judges. Attached to the stories are various traditions concerning the period before the monarchy.

The book is in three sections: a prologue (1:1–2:5); stories of the judges (2:6–16:31); and an appendix dealing with the migration of the tribe of Dan and the civil war against Benjamin (17:1–21:25).

The judges

The book is named for its major protagonists, who are said to have "judged" Israel. The writer distinguishes between the "major" judges and the "minor" judges. The major judges are charismatic military leaders, the subjects of extended narratives. The minor judges are those about whom little information is given beyond their names and the length of their office.

The Hebrew verb that is normally translated as "judge" has two basic meanings: to exercise the function of a judge (in the context of a court or in private judgment) and to rule. None of the judges are ever associated with any function of judgment or arbitration except for Deborah (4:4-5); but this is before she is called by God. Rather, the major judges are shown exercising a specifically military role and sometimes acting as civil rulers. No information is provided on the activity of the minor judges.

Another title that is used for several of the judges is "savior," probably the original title of at least some of the judges. The major judges are presented as charismatics, i.e., people who are raised up by the spirit of the Lord to deliver the people from oppression. Whatever power is given to them is seen as an exceptional measure.

Composition of the book

The book is a series of stories about Israelite heroes who had delivered the people from oppression. The stories originally told of the deliverance of individual tribes and so were limited in their geographical scope. Only later were the heroes made into deliverers of all Israel. These heroic tales from the folklore of the people were meant to entertain and edify, and had been collected together before the Deuteronomistic Historian (D) decided to make use of them. (On the work of the Deuteronomistic Historian, see the introduction to the Book of Joshua, p. 229.)

It was probably D who gave these heroes their pan-Israelite orientation. D also imposed a theological framework on the stories of the major judges. This framework provides an introduction that describes how the people have sinned; how God has allowed them to fall into the hands of their enemies; and how, when the people cried out, the Lord sent a savior to deliver them. Each story ends with a note about how long the land was at peace as a result of the deliverance effected by each savior-judge. D's framework provides the key for interpreting the stories of the judges, i.e., how sin leads to punishment, but repentance leads to deliverance.

The purpose of the Book of Judges

The Book of Judges must be read in the context of the Deuteronomistic History. The author's purpose is to present a basic theology of history: sin leads to punishment, but repentance brings forgiveness and deliverance. This message was meant for the people in exile who had recently lost their land. The author is explaining to them that they had lost the land because of their sinfulness; but if they now repent and turn back to the Lord, the Lord will once again forgive them and deliver them. While a message of hope is present, the book as a whole shows the progressive intensification of the sin of the people. The occasion of this sin is what is presented in the first chapter, namely, that Israel did not drive out of the land the nations with their idolatrous practices. As one goes through the book, the disastrous consequences of this situation become more and more apparent.

Historical accuracy

The basic traditions about the major judges, the material about the conquest in chapter 1, and the reports on the activities of the tribes of Dan and Benjamin in the appendix are quite old. The later Deuteronomistic editors did not significantly rework these stories, but confined themselves to adding comments at the beginning and end of them and inserting connectives between the stories.

There is no reason to deny that the stories are based on real events, though each tradition must be studied separately in terms of its historicity. Just because the stories are old does not mean that they can be accepted uncritically as historical.

Later editors modified two aspects of the stories by imposing the "pan-Israel" perspective on them and by adopting an artificial chronology. As we mentioned above, the "pan-Israel" perspective was introduced at a later time on stories that originally spoke of the deliverance of a limited number of tribes. The chronology found in the book is another matter. If one counts up all the years mentioned in the text, then the period of the judges would cover 410 years, obviously much too long, since the evidence available places the period of the judges somewhere between 1200 B.C.E. and 1050 B.C.E., approximately 150 years. A close reading clearly shows that the chronology in the book is stereotyped and artificial. D has imposed the chronology to support the comment in 1 Kgs 6:1 that there were 480 years between the Exodus and the beginning of the construction of the Jerusalem temple. Though the book shows the judges as following one after the other, in reality some of the major judges could have been contemporaries. The sequence chronology is demanded by having each of the judges be a deliverer of all Israel.

COMMENTARY

PART I: THE CONQUEST

Judg 1:1–2:5

This section presents a different view of the conquest of Palestine from the one presented in Josh 1–12. Here there is no acquaintance with the idea of a comprehensive conquest of Palestine by a united army of Israel. Rather, the picture is that of each tribe, alone or with one or two others, struggling to carve out a territory for itself.

The chapter is not a unified literary composition, but has been built up from separate traditions, many of which are quite old, and which come from different sources than the traditions used in Josh 1–12. The material has been arranged to describe the activity of the various tribes on a line from south to north. The Israel presented here is unable to occupy the coastal plains either in the south or in the central part of the country, and is unable to control the plain of Jezreel. As a result, the people are cut off from the great fertile areas of the land. This seems to be more in keeping with the archaeological evidence than the picture presented in Joshua.

However, it is important to see that the editor has not introduced this material either to counter or correct the picture in Joshua, but rather as a report on the activities of the generation after the death of Joshua but during the lifetime of the elders who outlived him. This is clear from the fact that 1:1-3, which come from D, presuppose the singular view of the conquest found in Joshua and the allotment of the land reported in Josh 13–22, and that the material in 2:10 refers to the generation that followed after the elders who survived Joshua. The editor, then, has introduced this prologue to prepare for the negative evaluation of the period that is found in 2:1-5. Chapter 1 is, therefore, intended to provide the basis for the explanation in 2:1-5 of why the Israelites would not be able to clear out the inhabitants of the land from their midst, namely, because they had disobeyed the Lord by making pacts with the inhabitants of the land, and by not pulling down their altars. As a result the Lord will not clear these nations out of Israel's way but will leave them in the land so that they can oppose Israel, and

so that their gods will become a snare for Israel (2:3).

As the book opens, the editor seems to presuppose that Israel is still at Gilgal (see 2:1 and Josh 4:19; 10:43; 14:6; and the comments on Josh 18:5). Now that the land has been subdued and apportioned among the tribes (see Joshua), it is necessary for each tribe to lay claim to its territory. They consult the Lord to see who will be the first to attack the Canaanites (1:1). The Lord's response is that Judah shall be first, and Judah invites Simeon to join them (vv. 2-3). This association shows that the tribe of Simeon was absorbed into the tribe of Judah at a very early period, and had no territory of its own (see Josh 19:1-9).

Verses 4-36 present the successes and failures of the various tribes. The fact that Judah is presented first and given such a large amount of space (vv. 4-20) shows that the editor presupposed the preeminence of the tribe of Judah. To a large extent Judah is successful in its encounters with the inhabitants of the land, but not completely (see vv. 18-20). The Perizzites (v. 4) were part of the indigenous population of Palestine (see Josh 17:15 and Gen 34:30). The incident with Adonibezek at Bezek is reminiscent of the story of Adonizedek in Josh 10 and may be related. The location of Bezek is uncertain. Adonibezek's mutilation is intended to humiliate him and render him incapable of war in the future. Verse 8, concerning the capture of Jerusalem, appears to be a later insertion into the text and does not agree with verse 21. The material in verses 10-15 is basically a duplicate of Josh 15:13-19, and is meant to explain why the Othnielites had access to the pools of water that should have belonged to the Calebites in Hebron. The reference to the Kenites in verse 16 explains their presence among the tribes of Judah. Judah is unable to take control of the southern coastal plain because the people there had iron chariots (vv. 18-19). The Benjaminites are mentioned next (v. 21) because of their close association with the tribe of Judah. Jerusalem will not be taken until David personally conquers it.

The editor now presents the attack on the central part of the country by the house of Joseph (vv. 22-29). Note that the house of Joseph is shown capturing Bethel, even though the city has been allotted to Benjamin (Josh 18:22). The story (vv. 22-26) is probably meant to illustrate how Israel made pacts with the inhabitants of the land. Verses 27-29 tell of the tribes being unable to take control of the central coastal plain or the plain of Jezreel. These verses, along with the references to the failures in the north (vv. 30-35), are reported as examples of how Israel sinned by living among the original inhabitants of the land instead of driving them out. Notice that it is not said that they could not drive out the natives but that they did not; rather, they put the natives into forced labor.

In 2:1-5 the editor gives the reason for the survey in chapter 1, namely, to explain why in the stories that follow, Israel will be unable to drive out the native inhabitants of the land: because Yahweh will not be with them, since they have been disobedient (see Josh 23:12-13). These verses, composed by D, are the key to the whole section, and send a clear message to the exiles. D is explaining that they have lost the land because they have been disobedient, and have not lived up to the demands of the reform of Josiah (see 2 Kgs 22:1–23:30). The location of Bochim is unknown. Many surmise that the text here originally read "Bethel" (see 20:18, 26; 21:2). The change to "Bochim" in verse 1 supports the etiology of verse 5, where it is explained that the place came to be called Bochim (weepers) because the people wept there. The angel or "messenger" of the Lord is the envoy of the Lord who can speak in the name of the Lord.

PART II: THE JUDGES

Judg 2:6–16:31

2:6–3:6 Introduction. These verses provide the specific introduction to the stories of the judges. Several hands have shared in the formation of this text, which falls into three sections: the report of the death of Joshua (2:6-9); the specific introduction to the stories of the judges (2:10-23); and a list of the nations that remained in the midst of Israel (3:1-6).

2:6-9 The report of the death of Joshua. These verses parallel Josh 24:28-31, but in a different sequence. The repetition shows that Judg 1:1–2:5 is a later insertion into the text for the reasons already given, and to provide a background for understanding the sinfulness of the people and the Lord's judgment upon them as described in 2:10-23. The report of Joshua's death and burial is repeated here to show that a new era has begun.

2:10-23 The specific introduction to the stories of the judges. This material is not unified. It is highly repetitious with an almost identical content found in verses 11-17; 18-19; 20-23. More than likely verse 10 and verses 20-23 were original, D having inserted verses 11-19 later. Their purpose is to show the tremendous apostasy within Israel during the period of the judges. The gods of the native inhabitants have truly become a snare for Israel (see 2:3). Hence, the need for the "saviors," the judges. The verses make clear that in spite of the deliverance that will be brought by the judges, one should not be misled into thinking that the Israelites truly repented of their sinfulness. Rather, the whole period is described as a time of ever-increasing apostasy (2:19).

The author points out that a new era has begun. There is now a generation that has not experienced the Lord's saving deeds on behalf of Israel nor the law of the covenant (v. 10). Rather they have served the pagan god Baal and the Ashtaroth (plural form for various manifestations of the goddess Astarte), abandoning the God of their ancestors who had led them from Egypt, thus provoking the Lord (vv. 11-12). Baal and Astarte (v. 13) were the embodiment of the idolatrous Canaanite cult. The use of the plural "Baals" and "Ashtaroth" does not indicate many deities bearing these names but rather the various local forms of them.

This abandonment angers the Lord, and so the Lord allows the people to fall into the power of their enemies (vv. 13-15; see Josh 23:11-13). Even when the Lord raises up judges to deliver them, the people do not listen to them or follow their example of obedience, but continue to worship other gods. And when the judge dies the people relapse and do even worse than before (vv. 16-19). Most scholars believe that D introduced verses 11-19 here to serve as an introduction to the stories of the judges, and that the elements of the theological framework for the stories may be found in them, i.e., the sinfulness of the people, the Lord becoming angry with the people and allowing them to fall into the hands of their enemies, the cry of the people, and the Lord's deliverance. Notice, however, that the third element of the framework, the cry of the people, is only mentioned in passing (v. 18). Also notice that the cry of the people is not one of repentance, but only a cry of distress under affliction (but see 10:6-16). The Lord seems moved more by the suffering of the people than by their repentance. What is revealed here is the Lord's love for and dedication to the people.

The people's sinfulness is so great, however, that the Lord must pass judgment on the people; so the Lord swears not to clear away any more of the nations that Joshua left when he died. These nations will test the Israelites and make them prove again their fidelity to the Lord (vv. 20-23).

The message in all of this for the exiles is clear: Israel lost the land because of continuing infidelity to the covenant. However, there is still hope because, as the Lord responded to the cries of distress of the people in the past, so the Lord may do again now. Also, the idea of testing that is emphasized in verse 22 leaves a door open for the exiles—perhaps they can pass the test. The one thing that becomes quite clear from this passage is that God's salvation is a gift; it is not a mechanical response to an action on the part of the people, not even an act of repentance (see 10:10-17).

3:1-6 The nations who remained. These verses give two lists of the nations who remained in the midst of Israel, as well as later reflections on the reason why the Lord left them. The classical listing of the nations who lived in Palestine before the conquest is given in verse 5 (see Josh 3:10). The "five lords of the Philistines" (v. 3) refers to the five cities inhabited by the Philistines (non-Semites who entered Palestine at about the same time as the Israelites) on the southern coastal plain. The added reasons for the Lord leaving the nations in Israel's midst (3:1-2) are intended to be more benevolent than the ones already seen.

3:7-11 Othniel. This report on the first of the judges appears to be constructed by D, and presents an ideal example of D's theology. Because of the generalized nature of the story it is difficult to pin it down to any place or time. Being so short, it helps one to understand clearly the basic elements of D's theology of history.

Israel, forgetting the Lord, serves the Baals and Asherahs (v. 7). This angers the Lord, who delivers the people into the power of Cushan-rishathaim, king of Aram Naharaim. When the people cry out to the Lord, the Lord sends them a savior, Othniel, son of Caleb's younger brother, Kenaz (see Josh 15:17). Here in all their simplicity are seen the introductory formulas of D's framework. The location of Aram Naharaim is unknown. The spirit of the Lord that comes upon the judges in these stories connotes an impersonal power or force that so envelops a person that he or she becomes capable of extraordinary deeds. Verse 11 presents D's normal concluding formula.

3:12-30 Ehud. In the story of Ehud one is able to detect for the first time the existence of an ancient tradition that has been taken up and used by the editor. The story begins with D's framework in which Israel sins, the Lord raises up an oppressor, the people cry out, and the Lord sends a savior (vv. 12-15). The story is filled with humor. The oppressor is "Eglon," which means something like "young bull" or "fat calf" (see v. 17). This king with the ridiculous name is slain by the left-handed Benjaminite (Benjamin literally means "son of the right hand") and the king is so fat that the foot-long dagger gets lost in his belly. The story gloats over how the Israelite hero outsmarts the oppressor and his guards. As a result of the deliverance through Ehud, the land is at rest for eighty years (v. 30).

Moab (v. 12) is situated on the southeastern shore of the Dead Sea. Here the king of Moab is shown in alliance with the people from the north (Amorites) and with southern nomads (Amalekites). The setting for this story, however, is the western shore of the Jordan around Jericho (v. 13), confirmed by the reference to the "cool upper room" (v. 20), appropriate to the desert area around Jericho. The location of Seirah (v. 26) is unknown. Thrown into confusion by the discovery of their dead king, the Moabites attempt to cross the Jordan and return to their home; but the Israelites are ready for them at the fords (vv. 26-29). The story originally dealt only with the tribe of Benjamin in the neighborhood of Jericho (v. 13 "the city of psalms").

3:31 Shamgar. Both the origin and the reason for this reference to Shamgar here in the text is unclear. The reference has no parallel either to the stories of the major judges or to the references to the minor judges. Moreover, it seems to be a late insertion, since 4:1 seems to follow directly on 3:30. The reference to the Philistines as the enemy of Israel is strange here, since they didn't become a problem to Israel until late in the period of the judges. The slaying of the Philistines with an oxgoad recalls the exploits of Samson (15:14-17). Shamgar does not seem to be a Semitic name, and some have surmised that he was really a Canaanite who defeated the Philistines and so delivered Israel.

4:1–5:31 Deborah and Barak. The story of Deborah and Barak is told twice. Chapter 4 is a prose account, while chapter 5 contains a poem celebrating the same victory. Both texts are concerned with a battle between Israel and a strong coalition, perhaps made up of Canaanites and Philistines, near the Wadi Kishon in the valley of Jezreel. Chapter 4 locates this battle on the northern edge of the valley of Jezreel in the neighborhood of Mount Tabor, but chapter 5 locates it more toward the southeastern side of the valley.

4:1-24 The prose narrative. The prose narrative begins with the regular D framework (vv. 1-3). This time the oppressor is the Canaanite king, Jabin, who reigns in Hazor and has a general named Sisera, who lives in Harosheth-ha-goiim. The real actor is Sisera, and the mention of Jabin seems to be secondary, a reference perhaps related to Josh 11:1f. The location of Harosheth-ha-goiim is uncertain, but it would have been in the northern part of Palestine.

Verses 4-10 report the call of Barak through Deborah and his summoning of the tribes of Zebulun and Naphtali for battle. Deborah is described as a prophetess and one to whom people came for judgments (vv. 4-5). She is a judge, then, in the forensic sense. Ramah and Bethel are just a few miles north of Jerusalem. The tribal connections of Deborah are not clear. While she may pass judgments in the mountain regions of Ephraim, she is connected here with the tribes of Zebulun and Naphtali. Barak is from Kedesh, north of Hazor, in the territory of the tribe of Naphtali. The figure of ten thousand men (v. 10) from only two tribes appears to be an exaggeration.

Verse 11 acts as a footnote to prepare for verse 17, explaining how a group of Kenites, who should be located much farther to the south, were to be found in this region.

The battle proper is described in verses 12-16, but there is little detail in the report. God is shown as being responsible for everything that happens. The Lord alone is deserving of glory.

The killing of Sisera (vv. 17-22) is a flagrant violation of the law of hospitality. It also appears that Hazor and the clan of Heber, the Kenite, had an alliance with one another! For whatever reason Jael, wife of Heber, decides to stand with the Israelites. Verses 23-24 are the normal D conclusion, though a partial one. D postpones a final chronological reference until 5:31 so as to present chapters 4 and 5 as a unit.

5:1-31 The Canticle of Deborah. Considered one of the oldest texts in the Bible, this poem, because of its age and the condition of its text, is notoriously difficult. The meaning of many early Hebrew words is uncertain and some verses are nearly incomprehensible. Moreover, the connections with chapter 4 are not always clear. In its present form the poem is a song praising Yahweh, the God of Sinai and the conquest, for what the Lord accomplished through Deborah and Barak.

Originally, verse 1 may have been directly linked to the prayer in verse 31 before the song was inserted. Verse 2 introduces the subject of the song, namely, the chiefs of Israel and the noble deeds of the people, i.e., what was accomplished by Deborah and Barak. Verse 3 is an invitation to listen to this hymn to the God of Israel. Verses 4-5 recall how Yahweh led Israel into Palestine accompanied by a series of cosmic events. Verses 6-8 describe the situation before Deborah: it was not safe to travel the roads, people were worshiping new gods, and Israel was unarmed before foreign armies. Verses 9-11 extend another invitation to sing about the leaders of Israel and about Yahweh. Verses 12-18 describe the muster of the tribes for the battle that is to come. Verse 12 describes the general call to Deborah and Barak to muster the tribes. The gathering of the tribes is described in verse 13, and verses 14-17 describe those tribes that responded positively to the invitation of the Lord and those that did not. Special praise is given to Zebulun and Naphtali in verse 18. Verses 19-22 describe the battle. Behind verses 20-22 there is the idea of a sudden storm that trapped and bogged down Sisera's chariots so that his army was easily defeated.

The events surrounding Sisera's death are reported in verses 23-30. First, the town of Meroz is cursed because, unlike Jael, it did not offer any aid to Israel, perhaps by ignoring the fleeing Sisera. Verses 24-27 gleefully describe the death of Sisera at the hand of Jael. This account is a bit different from what is reported in 4:21. Here Jael appears to hit Sisera as he was drinking the milk. Verses 28-30 report in a mocking way the concern of Sisera's mother over the delay in his return and the response she receives from her wisest princess. Verse 31 summarizes the poem's theology and presents the concluding part of D's framework.

For the exiles the episode of Deborah and Barak is a strong motivation to hope and trust in the Lord, who can destroy Israel's enemies and grant freedom from oppression if Israel will only cry out to the Lord.

6:1–8:28 Gideon. These chapters reiterate the basic cycle of sin, punishment, repentance, and deliverance. This time it is the Midianites who oppress Israel, and the savior sent by the Lord is Gideon. Gideon destroys the altar of Baal at Ophrah, erects an altar to Yahweh in its place, and receives a new name, Jerubbaal. With a few men he wins a great victory over the Midianites, but will not accept the kingship when it is offered to him. While the narrative appears basically clear and consistent there are many tensions within it. First of all, there is the double name for the hero, Gideon and Jerubbaal. Secondly, chapter 6 is obviously made up of a series of different traditions (vv. 11-24; 25-32; 33-35; 36-40). There is significant tension between 6:33-35, where all the tribes are mustered, and 7:3-6 where almost immediately most are sent back home for purely theological reasons. In 8:1-3 Ephraim is angry with Gideon because he had not called them, but this seems directly opposed to what is said in 7:24f. Finally, Gideon is presented not only as a champion of the people, but also as a man set on vindicating the death of brothers. All this suggests that the chapters are a collection of originally independent traditions that have been edited into a continuous whole, but not skillfully enough to rid the stories of all inconsistencies. Many of the stories originally concerned only the family of Abiezer from the tribe of Manasseh, but they were later made to refer to all Israel.

Most scholars accept the historicity of the oppression of the Israelites by the Midianites, a people from the desert region southeast of Palestine. Gen 25:2ff. points out that Midian was a son of Abraham who was sent eastward so as not to interfere with the inheritance of Isaac. It is not clear here if the chapters describe just isolated raids, the movement of a seminomadic people into cultivated areas at certain times of the year, or a full-scale invasion akin to Israel's own invasion of the land. This issue cannot be solved, but what is clear is that the editor was more interested in presenting a theological message to the exiles than in recounting a political and military event.

These chapters fall into four main sections: the call of Gideon (6:1-40); the defeat of the Midianites (7:1–8:3); the pursuit of the kings of the Midianites (8:4-21); and the offer of kingship (8:22-28).

6:1-40 The call of Gideon. The story of Gideon begins with the standard framework for the stories of the judges. The Midianite oppression is described as being very critical and widespread, extending from central and northern Palestine to the southwest. The Midianites, together with other nomadic peoples, the Amalekites and Kedemites, were rapidly and indiscriminately plundering the countryside. The Israelites were forced into hiding, where they established a series of strongholds and invented a way to signal the approach of the Midianites (vv. 2-5). Reduced to utter misery, the Israelites cry out to the Lord (v. 6). A new element now appears: in response to Israel's cry the Lord sends a prophet to remind the people of all that the Lord had done for them and how the Lord had commanded them not to venerate the pagan gods of the Amorites. But Israel disobeyed the Lord and had indeed worshiped the pagan gods. The point of these verses (vv. 7-10) is the indictment that the Israelites had brought on their own suffering through disobedience, an important message for the audience of the book, the exiles.

The call of Gideon is reported in what appears to be two variant traditions in verses 11-24 and verses 25-32. The first is a cultic legend explaining the origins of the sanctuary at Ophrah, and shows Gideon, a farmer, threshing his wheat in a concealed wine press, in order to hide it from the plunderers. An angel of the Lord appears to Gideon and commissions him to save the people (v. 11). The angel here, as in other places in the Old Testament, represents Yahweh and is interchangeable with Yahweh. Gideon, obviously unaware of the prophet's explanation in verses 7-10, challenges the angel's greeting with a sarcastic remark, claiming that rather than being with him, the Lord has abandoned the people (vv. 12-13). Despite Gideon's sarcasm, the Lord appoints him to save Israel (v. 14) and assures him of success because "I will be with you" (vv. 15-16). This interchange reinforces the idea that God alone is responsible for what is about to happen (see ch. 7). Gideon, still not satisfied, asks for a sign, which the Lord gives (vv. 17-21). The sign here is a cultic one in which the deity consumes the offering in a particular way. Consecrated by the fire from the rock, Gideon builds an altar there and calls it "Yahweh-shalom" (vv. 22-24). "Shalom" is a complex word that expresses ideas of peace, cooperation, and agreement between two parties. The idea that seeing Yahweh can be fatal (v. 22) is found several times (e.g., Exod 19:21; 33:18-23).

The story of the destruction of the altar to Baal and the building of a proper altar to Yahweh (vv. 25-32) is a variation of the previous story. The editor has included it here for two reasons: to show that Gideon cannot hope to defeat the enemies of Israel unless he purges out the worship of the foreign gods; and to explain Gideon's other name, his "baal" name, "Jerubbaal," the explanation of which is connected with the people's reaction to Gideon's tearing down the altar of Baal. They want Gideon's father, Joash, to hand him over so they can kill him (vv. 28-30). Joash's response (v. 31) is that if the people act in Baal's place by taking action against Gideon without Baal's authorization, they, too, will be put to death, and if Baal is really a god, he can take care of himself. Gideon's second name is a pun on the Hebrew word which means to "litigate, take action against, sue." Hence, his name means something like "let Baal sue" or "take action."

Verses 33-40 form the transition into the battle with the Midianites described in chapter 7. The Midianites and their allies come across the Jordan from the desert on one of their raids and take control of the valley of Jezreel (v. 33). Originally the story dealt only with the family of Gideon and the family of Abiezer from the tribe of Manasseh, but at some stage in the editing of the material it has become a story about all Israel. Hence, the references here to the tribes of Asher, Zebulun and Naphtali are secondary. Before going into battle Gideon seeks reassurance of divine approval through an oracle (vv. 36-40). Oracles before battle are commonplace in the Old Testament (see e.g., 4:6-7; Josh 6:2-5; 7:10-15; 8:1-2). The use of the fleece may have been an accepted practice. Gideon asks for a second proof, since the first one may have been inconclusive, i.e., because the fleece could have collected dew even though the ground appeared dry.

7:1–8:3 The defeat of the Midianites. Assured of divine approval for entering into battle, Gideon encamps on a hill above the Midianites' camp. Topographical details in verse 1 are not too clear, but it appears that the opposing forces were encamped toward the southeastern end of the valley of Jezreel. Though the Lord said nothing when Gideon first mustered his troops (6:34-35), the Lord now tells him to reduce the size of his army so that the Israelites will not take credit for the forthcoming victory. The point of 7:1-8 is to show that it is the Lord who is responsible for the victory over the Midianites. The original story described the victory of only three hundred Abiezerites over the Midianites. Later, when the victory was attributed to all Israel, the editors took the opportunity to make the point that God had brought about the victory by having Gideon send all but three hundred warriors home. There are two troop reductions (vv. 3-6). The nature of the test in verses 4-6 is unclear. Why pick the soldiers who lap up the water with their tongues like dogs? It may have been an arbitrary test to provide a means by which God can make a selection. Verse 8 explains how the three hundred get enough jars and horns for use in the battle strategy (see vv. 16-22).

Knowing Gideon's need for continued assurances of success, the Lord now takes the initiative and tells him to sneak down to the Midianite camp with his aide and hear what they are saying (vv. 9-11). What is revealed, in contrast to the weakness and fear of Gideon, is the power of the Lord. What Gideon overhears is one man telling another about his dream (vv. 13-14). The point of the loaf of bread symbolizing Israel is to show how small and inadequate the breadloaf is in relation to what it is capable of doing. Once again the point is made that it is the Lord who will be responsible for the victory.

Verses 16-22 describe the attack against the Midianites. Notice that Gideon and his men are not engaged in any fighting; rather, it is the Lord who sets the Midianites against one another (v. 22). Israel divided the night into three watches of four hours apiece. The attack begins at the beginning of the middle watch, about 10:00 p.m. (v. 19). It is hard to imagine how the Israelite soldiers could simultaneously carry out the actions described in verses 19-20. More than likely several different traditions have been combined here. Frightened by the sudden burst of light all around their camp and the noise created by the breaking jars and the horns and the shouts, the Midianites are thrown into disarray and take off toward the east and the Jordan River.

Gideon once again musters the tribes for battle and sends them down to the river fords to intercept the fleeing Midianites as they try to cross the Jordan. Logistically, Gideon's procedure here does not make much sense. He gathers all the tribes and sends all but three hundred home. Then, almost immediately, he turns around and summons the other tribes back. This would have taken time and is not compatible with the speed needed to reach the river fords that is presumed by the text. This tension in the text is the result of making what was originally the victory of one tribe into a victory of all Israel. The summoning of Ephraim in verse 24 does not fit well with the complaint of Ephraim in 8:1-3. Seemingly, the Ephraimites are complaining about the lateness of their summons to battle. The text presupposes that Ephraim was the most important tribe at the time. With good oriental diplomacy Gideon calms down the Ephraimites by quoting a proverb that says how little the family of Abiezer has been able to achieve when compared with what Ephraim has done (vv. 2-3).

8:4-21 The pursuit of the Midianite kings. The focus in this section shifts from the actions of God to the actions of Gideon. Yahweh does not appear in this chapter except for a reference in Gideon's speech (v. 7 and v. 19).

The editor may only have wanted to show what became of Gideon. It is not a complimentary picture.

The section begins with a flashback to the situation at 7:22 with Gideon chasing the fleeing Midianites. Both Succoth and Penuel were cities in the Jordan valley, but east of the Jordan River. The reference to the two Midianite kings in verse 5 is surprising, since there has been no previous mention of them. It appears that 8:4-12 may be a variant on 7:22–8:3. The names of the kings are distorted and mean something like "sacrificial victim" and "protection withheld," obvious references to what is going to happen to them. The occupants of Succoth and Penuel are not too convinced that Gideon is going to be victorious and so are not ready to help him, lest they later suffer reprisals from the Midianites (vv. 6-8).

Gideon captures the two kings as they flee from a surprise attack on their camp (vv. 10-12). The location of Karkor is uncertain, but it may have been the central camp from which the Midianites made their periodic raids on Palestine. There is no real proportion in verses 13-17 between the crime and the punishment. Obviously Gideon is attempting to give a message to other people in the area. The "elders of the city" (v. 16) were the governing body when there was no king.

Verses 18-21 come as a real surprise but they explain why Gideon was chasing the two Midianite kings, namely, blood vengeance. They had killed his blood brothers and so now they must be killed. Nothing is known of the incident at Tabor (v. 18) that gave rise to this vendetta.

8:22-28 Offer of kingship. Originally, Gideon (vv. 22-23) would not have been offered kingship by all of Israel as presented here, but by a more limited group or particular city. As a good follower of Yahweh Gideon refuses the offer and states an orthodox Yahwistic principle: the Lord must rule over you. Though Gideon refuses the title of king, it seems clear from 8:24f. and 9:2f. that he accepts power over the people and demands the trappings of a judge. The ephod made from the booty was a cult object used in obtaining oracles (see Exod 28:15-30). This ephod became an object of idolatrous worship, a practice the editor blames for the eventual downfall of Gideon's family (see ch. 9). Notice how the editor stresses that "all" Israel paid idolatrous homage to the ephod (v. 27). The sinfulness of Israel continues.

8:29–9:57 Abimelech. Though there are some tensions in this material, for the most part the story proceeds with a series of clearly defined scenes. Abimelech, one of Gideon's sons, manages to get himself accepted as king over the city of Shechem by killing all of his brothers except one, Jotham, who invokes a curse upon the city and Abimelech. Tension soon develops between Abimelech and the citizens of Shechem and, as a result of a conspiracy headed by a man named Gaal, military conflict breaks out. Abimelech is victorious, but it is an empty victory. In putting down the revolt he destroys the city, wipes out its citizens, and is killed himself. There is no reason to deny the historicity of the story told here. Shechem was on the southern border of the territory of the tribe of Manasseh in the central highlands and had become part of the Israelite confederacy in the twelfth century. Archaeology confirms a significant destruction of the city toward the end of the twelfth century.

The story of Abimelech does not fit the pattern of the other stories of the major judges. First of all, Abimelech is not portrayed as a hero who saves Israel from oppression. Secondly, the D framework is missing, except for the opening statement on the sin of Israel. This passage (8:33-35), along with the conclusion to the story (9:56-57), provides the key for understanding the story. In 8:33-35 Israel is indicted for sinfulness and for being ungrateful to the family of Jerubbaal (Gideon); and in 9:56-57 is found the explanation of the story: it is to show how God requites the evil of Abimelech and the citizens of Shechem who have turned to idolatry and destroyed Gideon's family. In other words, the story is about Israel's sinfulness and punishment. Because it comes immediately after Gideon's refusal of the crown, the story of Abimelech stands out as the tale of the wicked son who accepted the crown—in fact sought it. The story also has a strong anti-monarchy sentiment. The emphasis on sin and punishment is meant especially for the exiles: the reason for the destruction of Jerusalem and the loss of the land in their own time is their sinfulness, especially their following after strange gods.

The all-Israel emphasis in the story is clearly secondary, i.e., added after the fact. Abimelech never ruled over all Israel, but only over the city-state of Shechem and its territories.

The description of Gideon's sons and the note on Gideon's death in 8:29-32 acts as a transition to the story of Abimelech. A concubine (v. 31) is a legitimate wife, but a wife of second rank. The god Baal of Berith (v. 33) was the patron deity of Shechem. By accepting him the people returned to the pre-Israelite form of governance known at Shechem, the monarchy. Rejection of Yahweh is also rejection of a social-political system.

Because Abimelech did not have any right to rule over Shechem, he had to approach the citizens of Shechem through intermediaries, namely, his mother's kinsfolk in Shechem (9:1-3). The "citizens," the prominent people of Shechem who formed a civic assembly, had the power to appoint a person king. Behind the story lies the fact that even though Gideon did not accept kingship, his sons exercised considerable influence after his death and the citizens of Shechem were unhappy with such a situation. They are willing, therefore, to give Abimelech the money to hire the ruffians he needs to kill his brothers (vv. 4-5). The reference to the "one stone" (v. 5) suggests a public execution of all of them at the same place. The number seventy is a round figure for many. For the sacred oak (terebinth) at Shechem see Gen 12:6; Deut 11:30; Josh 24:26.

Jotham's fable (vv. 7-15) has been made to fit here by the addition of verse 15, and reflects a strong rejection of the institution of the monarchy. While the olive, fig, and vine are typical and prized trees in Palestine, the buckthorn, aside from producing beautiful flowers in the spring, seemed worthless to the ancients and a real nuisance because of its thorns. The point of the fable is that only the worst and least qualified are disposed to accept the crown. Jotham's speech (vv. 16-21) is aimed at the citizens of Shechem who have not acted honorably in making Abimelech king, and he utters a curse against both of them. Verses 17-18 are a later addition to the text to explain the statement in verse 16.

After only three years the citizens of Shechem rebel against Abimelech. The author attributes this to the action of God (v. 23) so as to bring on the succession of events that lead to the destruction of Shechem and the death of Abimelech. The civic assembly could depose the king as well as appoint him. What really brings things to a head is the arrival of Gaal, who instigates a full-scale rebellion against Abimelech (vv. 26-29).

When Abimelech hears of these matters from the ruler of the city, he arrives with his army and defeats Gaal (vv. 30-41). Notice that Abimelech does not live in Shechem but at Arumah, a town nearby. Tabbur-Haares means "navel of the world" and Elon-Meonenim means "diviner's oak." They refer to places near Shechem. Once Gaal is defeated Zebul will not allow him to continue to use Shechem as his base of operations, and Gaal disappears. The next day Abimelech returns and ambushes the people of Shechem as they come out to investigate the damage to their crops. Sowing a site with salt (v. 45) is an ancient rite of cursing. From verses 46-49 we learn that Abimelech has destroyed only the lower part of the city. The upper city stood on an artificial platform of earth that supported the ruler's palace and the temple of Baal Berith (also known as Beth-millo; see verses 6 and 20). The remaining citizens take refuge in the "crypt" of the temple of El-Berith. The true meaning of the Hebrew word translated "crypt" here is unknown. Some would translate it by "citadel." The reference is to some part of the fortified temple that Abimelech sets on fire, killing those who had taken refuge there (vv. 46-49).

Abimelech's end comes when he attacks Thebez, a town northeast of Shechem (vv. 50-55). Seemingly, Thebez had taken part in the revolt. Death at the hand of a woman was considered a disgrace (v. 54). With his death the first attempt at initiating the monarchy in Israel fails.

10:1-5 Tola and Jair. These are the first of the "minor" judges. There is a regular pattern followed in the descriptions of these men: name, origin, length of time in office, death, burial, and family. Since the numbers of years of their time in office are not stereotyped, they are probably original to the tradition. Though now they are said to have judged all Israel, their original sphere of influence was probably limited to a particular area. Also, their terms may have been contemporary with other minor judges or even one of the major judges. Their role is unclear. We have already explained in the introduction to this book that

the Hebrew word meaning "to judge" can also mean "to rule." It is possible, then, that they were a type of local administrator. Tola is said to have "saved" Israel, perhaps meaning that after the confusion and unrest of the time of Abimelech, Tola brought some stability through his administration.

10:6-12:7 Jephthah. The story of Jephthah is a composite of various traditions to which some later additions have been made. The story proceeds as follows: a prologue (10:6-16); the recall of Jephthah (10:17-11:11); Jephthah's negotiations with the Ammonites (11:12-28); Jephthah's vow and defeat of the Ammonites (11:29-40); and the defeat of the Ephraimites (12:1-7).

10:6-16 Prologue. These verses introduce the story of Jephthah and contain an expanded version of the D framework. What is interesting here is how this framework has been expanded: first by inserting the list of deities in verse 6; then the list of Israel's opponents, past, present, and future in verses 11 and 12; and the discussion between Yahweh and the people regarding Yahweh's response to their cry in verses 10-16. By recapitulating 2:6–3:6 and referring to the past and future enemies (Philistines) of Israel, this section becomes a theological introduction to the second half of the Book of Judges. The point is that there is nothing automatic about Yahweh's response to Israel's cry (see vv. 11-14). More than words admitting guilt are necessary. What eventually moves the Lord to grieve over the misery of the Israelites (v. 16) is that aside from admitting their guilt they also show themselves ready to accept punishment (v. 15) and, most importantly, to cast out the foreign gods from their midst (v. 16). The author is telling the exiles what is expected of them.

The oppressors this time are the Ammonites, who occupied the territory of the Moabites east of the Jordan River. They especially afflicted the Israelites in Bashan, east of the Jordan near the Sea of Galilee, and in the southern part of Gilead, which belonged to the tribe of Gad. At times they crossed over the Jordan and harried the southern tribes of Judah, Benjamin, and Ephraim.

10:17–11:1 Recall of Jephthah. It is obvious from 10:17-18 that none of the princes of Gilead wanted to begin the war against the Ammonites. Hence, attention turns to Jephthah, the chieftain of a group of brigands who plundered the area (vv. 1-3). Because of his illegitimate birth he had been driven out from his own land by the same people who now want him back to lead them in battle. Unlike the stories of the other judges, Jephthah's calling to be a judge does not take place in a single moment; rather, it takes place through negotiation. In negotiations with the elders (vv. 4-10) the elders first offer him only the role of commander (v. 6). When Jephthah does not immediately accept, they raise the ante to being "leader of all of us who dwell in Gilead" (v. 8). This seems to imply that the office of judge included administrative as well as military responsibilities. Verse 11 is about a certain form of investiture.

11:12-28 Negotiations with the Ammonites. Before rushing into battle Jephthah attempts to clarify the reasons for the Ammonite hostility and discovers that the Ammonites want back the land that they claim Israel took from them when they came up from Egypt (vv. 11-13). Jephthah then gives historical and theological justification for Israel's occupation of the disputed land east of the Jordan. The material in verses 13-27 is no doubt a later insertion to justify Israel's possession of the land between the Arnon and Jabbok rivers. The historical argument is that the territory in dispute did not belong to either Ammon or Moab but was part of the former kingdom of Sihon, which Israel had conquered under Moses. The theological argument is that territories belong to those who received them from their particular deity and the Israelite God had given them this territory. The historical survey in verses 15-22 is in basic agreement with Num 20-24.

11:29-40 Jephthah's vow and defeat of the Ammonites. The spirit of the Lord now comes upon Jephthah and he inflicts a severe defeat upon the Ammonites. The center of attention in this scene is Jephthah's vow that if the Lord will deliver the Ammonites into his power, he will offer up to the Lord as a holocaust whoever comes out of his house upon his return (vv. 30-31). The one who comes out is his daughter. There are a number of parallels to this event in comparative folklore. The surprising thing is that the author has not censored this report of human sacrifice! Elsewhere in the Old Testament it is condemned (Lev 18:21; 20:2-5; Deut 12:31; 18:10; Mic 6:7). The fact of human sacrifice here is

secondary, however, to the theme of the irrevocability of Jephthah's vow. The vow, once it has been made, must be kept. What complicates the situation is that the story is now used as an etiology for a defunct lamentation festival in Israel (vv. 39-40). Some see the story as a myth passed off as history to explain the festival. Perhaps the story is meant to show the lamentable effects of not trusting in the Lord's willingness to save Israel. There is no need for such pagan practices.

12:1-7 Defeat of the Ephraimites. This story, which preserves memories of frontier conflicts between Gilead and Ephraim, is loosely joined to the rest. As in the story of Gideon (8:1ff.) the Ephraimites are upset because they had not been summoned to help in the battle against the Ammonites. Jephthah claims that they had been invited but had not responded (vv. 1-3). In the dialect spoken by the Ephraimites the initial sibilant of "Shibboleth" could not be pronounced correctly, thus giving them away. The meaning of the taunt in verse 4 is not clear.

The conclusion to the story of Jephthah in 12:7 is from the formula used for the minor judges, leading some to see Jephthah as a later development of one who was originally only one of the minor judges. This idea is supported by the fact that the story of Jephthah stands between the two lists of the minor judges (10:1-5 and 12:8-15).

12:8-15 Ibzan, Elon and Abdon. This is the second and final list of the "minor" judges, following the pattern of the first list (10:1-5).

13:1–16:31 Samson. The Samson stories contain the most extensive cycle of traditions in the Book of Judges. Though there is no reason to deny their historicity, it is clear that these traditions have been deeply colored by legendary, cultic, and folklore elements—possibly even by ancient solar myths. Samson's name is related to the Hebrew word for sun, and he comes from an area not far from Beth-shemesh (temple of the sun).

There are some significant differences between the Samson traditions and the other material in the book. The D framework is reduced to a report on the sin of the people and the Lord's deliverance of them into the power of the Philistines. Nothing is said of a cry to the Lord. Also, Samson never commands an army and he does not liberate Israel either from the Philistines or from any other oppressor. His relations with the Philistines appear to be on the level of a private feud. However, the editor sees these exploits as the beginning of Israel's deliverance from the power of the Philistines.

Each of the various traditions had its own prior independent existence. However, the editor has artfully woven them together into a coherent whole. The material falls into four sections: the birth of Samson (ch. 13); the marriage of Samson (ch. 14); Samson's defeat of the Philistines (ch. 15); and the capture and death of Samson (ch. 16).

13:1-25 The birth of Samson. The chapter begins with a short form of the D framework (v. 1). The Philistines had entered Palestine about fifty years after the Israelites as part of the migration of the sea peoples from the Aegean and Crete. Repulsed by the Egyptians around 1200 B.C.E., they had settled on the southern coast of Palestine.

Verses 2-5 report the angel's announcement of the forthcoming birth of Samson to his unnamed mother. His father is from Zorah, a town in the territory originally allotted to the tribe of Dan and the point of departure for the migration of the Danites to the extreme northern part of Palestine (ch. 18). Barrenness is a common theme in the Old Testament (see Gen 11:30 and 1 Sam 1:2f.) and is used as an occasion for a miraculous divine intervention whereby a child is born to undertake a unique mission. In verses 4 and 5 the nazirite rule (Num 6:1-8) is adapted for the consecration of a person in the womb. Normally nazirites were adults who voluntarily consecrated themselves to the Lord for life or for a particular period. Samson is consecrated from his conception, so the rites before his birth apply also to his mother. The regulations that Samson will live under are: abstaining from wine and strong drink, not shaving his head, and avoiding all contact with the dead. Verse 7 adds that he will be a nazirite until his death.

Because the following chapters do not refer to the nazirite vow that Samson is under, it is possible that this chapter was composed as the introduction to the cycle later on in order to make the story of Samson a narrative of the violation of the nazirite vow. It is this sinful person whom the Lord uses to begin the deliverance of the people from the power of the Philistines (v. 5).

In verses 6-23 Samson's father, Manoah, shows typical Semitic caution about the testimony of a woman and so needs to hear for himself what he and his wife must do for the boy who will be born (vv. 8-14). Manoah, in his conversation with the angel, is looking for a sign, which he receives in the consumption of the holocaust by fire and the ascent of the angel in the flame (v. 19). Only then is he convinced that the messenger is from God. When Manoah asks his name, the angel does not reveal it, saying that it is "mysterious," i.e., incomprehensible, like the works of God (see vv. 18 and 19).

14:1-20 The marriage of Samson. Samson's first exploits take place in the context of his marriage. At Timnah, a Philistine town a few miles from Zorah, Samson falls in love with a Philistine woman and asks his parents to obtain her for his bride (vv. 1-3). Normally, marriage negotiations were carried out by the bridegroom's father. Samson's parents are displeased because she is not an Israelite; a foreign wife was considered dangerous to security. "Uncircumcised" (v. 3) is used only of the Philistines in the Old Testament, pointing to the fact that they were the only ones in the region who did not practice the rite of circumcision. Perhaps the editor did not approve of this marriage either, but in verse 4 he provides the interpretative key for the rest of the chapter: what is about to take place is part of God's plan. Though not explicit, it appears that the editor sees the events here, especially those in verses 19-20, as the way the Lord begins the deliverance of Israel from the Philistines (13:5).

The whole process of Samson's coming and going to Timnah (vv. 5-9, 10) is obscure, and the references to his parents in verses 5 and 10 are awkward. These references might be later additions to show that Samson's parents went along with him and set up the marriage in spite of their opposition. The important issue, however, is the killing of the lion and later finding the honey in its carcass. It is the spirit of the Lord that gives Samson the strength to deal so easily with the lion (v. 6). Notice that Samson breaks the nazirite vow by eating the honey, which is impure because it has been taken from a corpse.

Samson's riddle (vv. 10-18) is impossible to solve unless one knows about the private actions of the hero. The Philistines are able to answer it only by threatening his new wife (v. 15). This treachery causes Samson to perform one of his feats against the Philistines (v. 19). Ashkelon was a Philistine stronghold on the coast, southwest of Timnah.

15:1-20 Defeat of the Philistines. After his anger subsides Samson goes to visit his wife, taking along the gift of a kid (v. 1). However, he is refused entrance to visit her because her father has already given her to Samson's best man, having interpreted Samson's abrupt withdrawal (14:19) as a repudiation and divorce of her. The father proposes an alternative, but Samson departs in anger (v. 3).

The incident with the foxes is difficult to visualize (vv. 4-5). It is obviously intended to be some sort of guerilla tactic. In all of this Samson seems to be overreacting, since he had been offended by only one family.

The Philistines retaliate swiftly against Samson's wife and her family, and Samson takes revenge against the Philistines (vv. 6-8). Having escaped to Etam in the territory of the tribe of Judah, the Philistines pressure Judah to turn Samson over to them (vv. 9-10). The sites of both Etam and Lehi are unknown. Lehi means "jawbone," its presence here preparing us for the wordplay in verse 17. Men of Judah now go down to capture Samson and, to their surprise, find him ready to surrender (vv. 11-13). That they did not expect such an easy time is reflected in the large number who set out for him (v. 11). When Samson sees the Philistines the spirit of the Lord comes upon him, moving him once again to extraordinary action (vv. 14-16), another deed by which the Lord begins to deliver Israel from the Philistines (see 13:5).

Notice that Samson again violates the law of the nazirite by touching an animal carcass. Verse 17 tells us that the name of the site "Ramath-lehi" (throwing of the jawbone) is explained by Samson's action of discarding the weapon. Verses 18-19 present the etiology of a spring at Lehi called "Enhakkore," that is, "spring of one who called."

The notice about Samson's judgeship in verse 20 probably indicates a conclusion to an early edition of the Samson stories and that chapter 16 was added later (see 16:31).

16:1-31 The capture and death of Samson. This chapter has three separate episodes: Samson and the harlot (vv. 1-3); Samson and Delilah (vv. 4-22); and the death of Samson (vv. 23-31). While the last two episodes are clearly related, the first one appears to be independent. However, because of its emphasis on Samson's strength, it is a good preparation for the question in verse 5.

The episode with the harlot (vv. 1-3) takes place at Gaza, one of the Philistine cities on the southern coast of Palestine. The city gates at that time had a tunnel-like opening that was flanked by guardrooms. Samson was able to escape the ambush at the gate by leaving at an unexpected time when the men were waiting in the guardrooms, since they did not expect Samson to leave until the morning. The distance from Gaza to Hebron is about 38 miles and uphill.

Samson now falls in love with Delilah. This episode (vv. 4-22) is a series of stereotyped scenes in which Samson is shown as so infatuated with Delilah that his behavior is ridiculous and abnormal. A strong element of magic runs through the episode. First of all, the Philistines appear to believe that some magical or supernatural force gives Samson his strength (v. 5). Samson's first three explanations of his strength are also based on magical ideas (vv. 6-14). Bowstrings (v. 7) were made from the tendons of slaughtered animals; hence, once again Samson disregards the nazirite rule by coming into contact with part of a corpse. Finally, the fourth time that Samson gives the explanation for his strength he tells the truth (vv. 15-17). This is the first time that Samson's strength is presented as something permanent and residing in his unshorn hair. In the other stories his strength is given only on specific occasions as a gift of the spirit of the Lord (14:6, 19; 15:14). The story in 16:1-3, however, presumes some kind of permanent strength, as does 15:8. The ominous note in verse 22 prepares for verses 28-30, where Samson's strength is again the result of a gift of the Lord. One can see the tension between the older stories about Samson's extraordinary strength and the later editor's theological explanation of his strength as a gift of the Lord for the deliverance of Israel. Samson is unable to escape after his hair has been cut off (v. 20) because the Lord has left him. The final breaking of the nazirite rule— once too often—occurs with the shaving of Samson's head.

Perhaps the reason that the death episode

(vv. 23-31) was added was to show that though Samson had squandered away his strength out of his own self-interest, in the end he turned to the Lord (v. 28) and died honorably by bringing about God's justice on the Philistines. Dagon (v. 23) was an ancient agricultural deity of the West Semitic world. In the Bible he appears exclusively as a Philistine deity. Dagon means "grain." The number three thousand in verse 27 seems an exaggeration, and was probably the editor's intention in view of the statement in verse 30.

The chapter concludes (v. 31) by repeating the length of time that Samson judged Israel (see 15:20). No reference is made to any peace in the land, since the editor realized that Samson's exploits were only the beginning of the deliverance from the Philistines.

PART III: APPENDIX

Judg 17:1–21:25

The appendix to the Book of Judges contains two episodes that have been placed here because they deal with the period before the monarchy: the migration of Dan to the north (17:1–18:31); and the civil war against Benjamin (19:1–21:25).

The statement, "In those days there was no king in Israel; everyone did what he thought best," appears at the beginning (17:6) and at the end of the appendix (21:25). In both 18:1 and 19:1 there is the reminder that "at that time there was no king in Israel." These are really pro-monarchy statements that the editor has inserted because he did not see the events narrated in these chapters as commendable. They could only have happened because there was no king in the land. The editor saw the monarchy as a necessary stabilizing factor in Israel.

17:1–18:31 The migration of Dan. The purpose of these two chapters is not merely to report on the history of the tribe of Dan, but to give information about the origins and nature of the sanctuary of Dan. This sanctuary had become important in 922 B.C.E., when the northern tribes had broken off from the southern tribes and formed the kingdom of Israel. As a result of this break, the sanctuary at Dan had become the national sanctuary of the northern kingdom along with the sanctuary at Bethel. The priests in Jerusalem

frowned upon the Yahweh cult at the sanctuary of Dan. These two chapters argue against this sanctuary by pointing out that its cult there represented a merger of disparate worshipers, and that the silver used for making the sacred object kept there derived from stolen money. The priesthood there, although having a noble lineage, is also shown as having been compromised.

Chapter 17 is a background for the events in chapter 18. Note that the carved idol (vv. 3-4) is an idol of Yahweh, something that is strictly forbidden by the Mosaic law (see Exod 20:4-6). Micah also makes an ephod (see 8:24-27) and household idols, i.e., items used for divining (v. 5). In the beginning he makes one of his sons the priest, i.e., one who took care of the sanctuary and gave oracles.

A young Levite from Bethlehem comes looking for a better situation, and Micah convinces him to be his priest (vv. 7-13). Micah's concern to have a Levite priest suggests that Levites were already known for being more skilled in cultic matters. The title "father" (v. 10) emphasizes the priest's role as cultic diviner and oracle giver.

Chapter 18 begins by stating that the Danites were searching for an area in which to live, since they had received no heritage among the tribes of Israel (v. 1). This statement is difficult to accept in light of Josh 19:40-48. They had been allotted territory to the west of Benjamin and south of Ephraim and north of Judah. However, they were so restricted by the Amorites and Philistines (see 1:34) that they could not control their territory, so they sent out scouts to look for a better district. Zorah and Eshtaol (v. 2) are cities from the old Danite territory that were encountered in the Samson stories. The scouts probably recognized the Levite by his accent as coming from the south (v. 3). One of the primary roles of the priest was to consult God on behalf of the people (v. 5). The priest's favorable response will be used later to justify the conquest of Laish and the slaughter of its inhabitants (v. 10).

Laish (v. 7) was a city at the northern extremity of the land, near the sources of the Jordan River. The place is rich in resources, and the people, quiet and trusting, live in an unwalled city. The statement that the people lived "after the manner of the Sidonians" seems to indicate that the city followed Phoenician customs. The scouts justify their recommendation to attack the city by saying that God has given it into their power (vv. 8-10 and see v. 6). "Mahaneh-dan" (v. 12) means "camp of Dan."

The Danites put their little ones, their livestock, and their goods at the head of the column (v. 21) because they expect to be attacked from the rear as soon as Micah discovers that they have stolen his idols and priest. Micah does chase after them but, when he discovers how strong a force they are, he returns home (vv. 22-26).

The slaughter of the people of Laish (v. 27) is unjustifiable. What sin has led to! The Danites rebuild the city, name it after their ancestor, and set up the carved idol that was Micah's (vv. 28-30). In verse 30 the Levite suddenly has a name, Jonathan, son of Gershom, son of Moses. The "time of the captivity of the land" (v. 30) refers to the year 734 B.C.E., when northern Palestine came under the Assyrians and the temple at Dan was destroyed. Verse 31 mentions that the Danites had preserved their sanctuary at Dan during the same time that the real house of God was at Shiloh (v. 31).

19:1–21:25 Civil war against Benjamin. These three chapters are made up of a number of originally independent narratives that have been skillfully combined into a continuous story. They present another example of how things could go wrong because "in those days there was no king in Israel; everyone did what he thought best" (21:25). A hideous crime is committed, and Israel so overreacts to it that they bring on a full-scale civil war.

These chapters fall into three scenes: the episode with the Levite and his concubine (19:1-30); the assembly of Israel and the resultant war against Benjamin (20:1-48); and the getting of wives for the surviving Benjaminites (21:1-25).

19:1-30 The Levite and his concubine. The story of the Levite who goes to Bethlehem to retrieve his wife, and who then suffers a gross indignity on his return, is told to explain why war breaks out between Benjamin and the other tribes of Israel. The story is full of dramatic irony: the father-in-law's hospitality so delays the Levite's return that he cannot make the trip back home in one day; had he stopped in Jebus, the Canaanite city, he would have avoided the outrage; he is offered hospitality in Gibeah, not by a Benjaminite but by another sojourner.

That the man is a Levite is not important for the purpose of the story. Though the editor identifies "Jebus" as "Jerusalem" (v. 10), Jerusalem, in fact, never bore that name. Perhaps Jebus was a suburb of Jerusalem. At this time Jerusalem was still a Canaanite city. Gibeah was about three miles north of Jerusalem, and Ramah was about two miles further north.

Entering Gibeah, the Levite receives no offers of hospitality from the Benjaminites there, but is taken in by another stranger, an old man who, like the Levite, also came from the mountain region of Ephraim. The old man shows the Levite the same hospitality that his father-in-law had shown him in Bethlehem. The verb "abuse" in verse 22 is an attempt to translate the Hebrew verb that means "to know," a verb used euphemistically in the Old Testament to denote sexual intercourse. It is used here in a deliberately ambiguous way.

The gruesome act of cutting up the dead woman and sending pieces of her to all the tribes serves the purpose of arousing the tribes against Gibeah for the outrage they have committed (see 1 Sam 11:7). The implication is that the tribes must help the Levite take revenge on Gibeah or suffer a like fate.

20:1-48 War against Benjamin. In response to the call of the Levite the Israelites gather at Mizpah, about eight miles north of Jerusalem (vv. 1-2). "Dan to Beer-sheba" is a phrase that represents the northern and southern boundaries of ancient Israel. The Israelites on the eastern side of the Jordan River (land of Gilead) also come to the assembly. The size of the armies (vv. 8-10) is exaggerated. Perhaps the Hebrew word for "thousand" refers to a particular military grouping or contingent, as we saw in the Book of Joshua.

In verse 16 the narrator seems to suggest that one reason why the Benjaminites will endure and be able to inflict great losses on the Israelites is because of the seven hundred sharpshooters. The Israelites go over to Bethel, a few miles away, to consult the Lord on who should attack first. The lot falls to Judah (vv. 17-19).

The first two attacks against Gibeah are repulsed, and the Israelites suffer some significant losses (vv. 20-25). After the second loss the Israelites consult the Lord, they fast, and offer holocausts and peace offerings (vv. 26-27). This time they are told that they will be successful because the Lord will deliver the Benjaminites into their power (v. 28).

Verses 29-43 are two accounts, clumsily combined, of the same event. The account in verses 29-36 describes more the field tactics of the troops, while the account in verses 37-43 describes the victory from the perspective of the successful ambush. Both have a resemblance to the capture of Ai in Josh 8. Notice that in verse 35 it is the Lord who defeats Benjamin. Verses 44-48 give the statistics on the fallen. In the end there remain only six hundred, who escape to the rock Rimmon (v. 47). The location of Rimmon is unknown. Though the tradition of war against Benjamin may be early, the story as we have it here has been revised to make it fit. The original tradition probably dealt with a war between Benjamin and its northern neighbor, Ephraim. It is unlikely that such a near obliteration of a tribe ever occurred.

21:1-25 Wives for the Benjaminites. Having almost wiped out an entire tribe, the Israelites realize that if that tribe is going to survive they must obtain wives for the six hundred male survivors. This chapter presents two accounts of how they obtained wives. The separate accounts have been harmonized by the explanation that each stratagem provided only a partial solution to the problem (v. 14).

The first account (vv. 1-14) states the underlying problem, namely, that at Mizpah the men of Israel had sworn that none of them would give their daughters in marriage to anyone from Benjamin (v. 1). The solution that they eventually hit upon was to see if anyone had not come up for the assembly, since a solemn oath had been taken that anyone who did not come up would be put to death (vv. 2-5). Jabesh-gilead was east of the Jordan.

The second stratagem has parallels in Roman and Greek folklore (vv. 15-23). The elders remember the yearly feast at Shiloh when the girls of Shiloh came out to dance. Each Benjaminite is told to seize one of them for a wife. The elders promise to intercede for the Benjaminites when the fathers or brothers of the girls complain. Because they have been stolen from them, not given to the Benjaminites, the men of Shiloh will not be guilty of breaking their vow not to give their daughters in marriage to a Benjaminite (v. 22). The great assembly, called in 20:1, is now dispersed and the Israelites return to their own heritage (v. 24).

The narrator concludes by saying again that all these sad goings-on took place because "in those days there was no king in Israel; everyone did what he thought best" (v. 25). Israel's history of sin has begun. Eventually that sinfulness will lead to the destruction of the northern kingdom of Israel in the eighth century and the destruction of the southern kingdom of Judah in the sixth century. However, the book has pointed out more than once not only the saving power of the Lord, but also the Lord's will to save the Israelites when they cry out to the Lord.

1 AND 2 SAMUEL

Paula J. Bowes

INTRODUCTION

1 and 2 Samuel were originally one book, as were 1 and 2 Kings and 1 and 2 Chronicles. These were divided into two in the Greek translation of the Hebrew Bible known as the Septuagint, from which early translations into Latin and English were made. The Books of Samuel are the centerpiece of a larger collection of narratives which span Israel's history from their entrance into Canaan in about the twelfth century B.C.E. to the Babylonian Captivity (587–586 B.C.E.). This Deuteronomistic History, so called because the writers based their theology on the teachings of the Book of Deuteronomy, was compiled about the seventh century B.C.E. Its basic message was that God has chosen Israel as a special people and has through Moses redeemed them from slavery in Egypt and made with them a covenant on Mount Sinai. God's word which came to Israel through Moses continues to guide and correct the people as well as their kings through the prophets. If they are faithful to the covenantal laws, they will have prosperity and peace; if they disobey, they can expect punishment through natural disasters, invasion, and even exile. They should therefore, out of loyalty and gratitude, keep the commandments of the Lord who has shown them so much favor and grace. The Books of Samuel, then, are not history in the modern sense but theological history—narrative accounts of God's dealings with the chosen people.

The protagonists

Personalities are important in these books, especially three: Samuel, the prophet of their title; and the first two kings of Israel, Saul and David, whom Samuel anointed as king. The account of the miraculous birth of Samuel, so like other portentous births in the history of Israel, sets the tone for the whole. God has intervened to bring another savior in answer to Israel's need for the Word of God. Like most of Scripture, the Books of Samuel tell of God's care and correction of this special people, and of God's justice and mercy toward them.

Disasters and deliverance

It is noteworthy that the deliverance which comes to Israel at the beginning of Samuel's prophetic mission is accompanied by the ruin of the priestly house of Eli and the loss of Israel's most precious possession, the ark of the covenant, the sign of God's dwelling among them (1 Sam 2–4). Out of this national disaster, it is God who is portrayed as causing the Philistines to return the ark (1 Sam 6). Samuel's covenant with the Lord at Mizpah (ch. 7) would seem to bring satisfaction to the people, but they still fear the Philistines enough to ask for a human king like other nations. In Num 11, God answered the people's demand for meat with quail until they were sick of it. Here God gives them what they want despite the disadvantages of a human king and their rejection of the divine. Over Samuel's objections, God commands the prophet to anoint Saul, with the implicit expectation that the king will always be under prophetic direction and required to obey the Mosaic law.

Israel gets a king

The first king, Saul, although gifted and acceptable to the Israelites, proves to be unacceptable to the Lord, who then determines to try again with a man after God's own heart, David (1 Sam 13:13-14). There now ensues the puzzling situation (for us) of two anointed kings, one of whom is in hot pursuit of the other lest his throne be taken from him. Throughout Saul's persecution of David, the fugitive receives help from various quarters, even from Saul's own children, Jonathan and Michal.

A few years later Saul's career comes to its end in a disastrous battle with the Philistines (1 Sam 31). David is eventually made king, first by the Judahites (2 Sam 2:11) and then, at the death of Saul's last eligible heir, by the Israelites (2 Sam 5). This separate anointing by the two major factions in Israel shows the religious and political division that was to last as long as the monarchy, that is, until 586 B.C.E., when Jerusalem was sacked by the Babylonians.

David's rise

The period from Samuel's first anointing of David (1 Sam 16) until his actual enthronement over both houses of Israel (2 Sam 5) is usually designated as the account of David's rise. Just as Samuel's rise at the beginning of the First Book of Samuel was concomitant with the downfall of the Elides, so David's rise is concurrent with Saul's demise. The Second Book of Samuel contains the accounts of David's accession (ch. 5), his bringing the ark of the covenant to Jerusalem (ch. 6), the promise of a lasting succession (ch. 7), and the engrossing story of David's life as king (chs. 9-20).

The peaceful kingdom and the troubled family

Much like Adam's peaceful life in the Garden of Eden (Gen 2), David finds himself with his enemies subdued on all sides (2 Sam 7:1) and a prosperous and enlarged kingdom (2 Sam 8). As did Adam, David disobeys God's word, bringing unexpected sorrows. True to Nathan's prophecy in 2 Sam 12, a sword will always trouble David's house, for four of his sons will die untimely and violent deaths. These trials chapters 9 to 20 recount for us in dramatic realism. The use of dialogue to portray character and move the action forward provides some of the most fascinating reading in the whole Bible.

Although the unknown author uses techniques of the novel in his writing, these accounts are not products of his imagination. They show, by vivid stories, that God works with human freedom, caring for the people with a love that continually forgives and saves.

OUTLINE OF THE BOOKS OF SAMUEL

COMMENTARY: 1 SAMUEL

I. SAMUEL AND THE HOUSE OF ELI

1 Sam 1–3

The First Book of Samuel opens with a double need: the longing of Hannah for a son and the counterpart, Israel's spiritual need for the word of God. This word of the Lord, so necessary for Israel's life, is, according to the Deuteronomistic tradition, Israel's greatest blessing, just as the greatest blessing of a woman in Israel is a child. Israel's need is not disclosed until readers have first savored Hannah's suffering. Understanding this will prepare them to appreciate the magnanimity of the Lord in supplying both needs.

1:1-8 Hannah asks for a son. As is true for other birth announcements in the Bible, this one begins with a short genealogy of Hannah's husband Elkanah (compare Manoah's in Judg 13 and Joseph's in Matt 1). None of these is the protagonist; instead their wives carry the action. Here the barren, despised (by all but Elkanah) wife Hannah is set over against her fertile and scornful rival Peninnah. Just so did Hagar gloat over Sarah (Gen 16:4) and Leah struggle with Rachel (Gen 30).

Another characteristic of biblical birth narratives is the portrayal of the particular child's parents as devout and observant of the commandments of the Lord (1 Sam 1:3; Luke 1:5-6). Elkanah's and Hannah's yearly pilgrimages and sacrifice show them to be worthy parents of a specially favored son, Samuel.

Mentioned also in verse 3 are Eli and his sons Hophni and Phinehas, all priests at the shrine in Shiloh, the center for Yahweh worship before the city was taken by the Philistines (see ch. 4). Although Eli's sons do not yet figure in the story, their presence early in the narrative suggests a connection between Hannah and the larger problems of Israel.

While she bears her reproach, not even Elkanah's patient, loving attempts to comfort Hannah can stop her from weeping and being unable to eat. From these depths, the action can only rise, in hope of change and relief.

1:9-19a Hannah prays for the Lord's gift. The biblical author has described what happens in this family year after year. Now he narrows to a particular day in Shiloh. Eli, from his seat by the door of the temple, observes the distraught Hannah at prayer. She bargains: if she is given a son, she will consecrate him to the Lord as a nazirite. Such a vow entailed abstinence from wine, strong drink, the cutting of the hair and contact with a dead body (see Num 6; Amos 2:11-12). Samson (Judg 13–16) was under this vow, but in his case the angel announcing his birth, not his mother, required it. Hannah offers this condition of her own accord, showing considerable renunciation, since the child would be with her only three years.

It is ironic that abstinence from drink is what Hannah offers, while it is drunkenness that Eli suspects from her movements. Once Hannah is able to satisfy Eli that such is not the case, Eli endorses her request. Since he has not heard any words, he does not know that, in effect, he asks for the one who will replace him in the priesthood. After the prayers of Eli and Hannah, there is a noticeable change in the latter. Now she no longer weeps but can eat and drink (v. 18)!

1:19b-28 Samuel is born. When Hannah bears her son, she names him Samuel, explaining that she had asked him of the Lord. The name Samuel however means "he who is from God" and not "asked." The name Saul would be closer to that. This kind of ambivalence is not unusual for biblical names.

Elkanah is characteristically kind in excusing Hannah from the next three pilgrimages until Samuel is weaned. The parents' concern for the worship of the Lord is underlined by its prominence in the story and in the generous details of offerings and customs at that time (eleventh century B.C.E.).

When she at last brings Samuel to the temple, it is natural for Hannah to let Eli know that her prayer has been answered, since he had supported it (see Judg 13 and Matt 1). The key words: "ask," "give," and "pray," repeated in 1 Sam 1:17-28; 2:1, give evidence of divine answer to persistent prayer. Hannah little suspects that the boy Samuel will supply not only her need to be a mother but also Israel's need for a prophet to bring the people the word of the Lord.

2:1-10 Hannah's song. The canticle the biblical author has put into Hannah's mouth finds a counterpart in the New Testament in Mary's Magnificat (Luke 1:46-55). Both hymns express joy at the birth of a special child; both praise God's power, holiness, and salvation. In both the proud rich are cast down and the humble poor are raised up. Hannah's poem reminds of God's justice; Mary's of God's mercy. The Magnificat only hints at enemies, but Hannah's song begins and ends with their discomfiture and derision (vv. 1,10).

In this poem the Lord is seen as holy, omnipotent, omniscient, and in control of all the life events of all creatures. There are strong contrasts between the hungry and the well-fed, the barren and the fertile, the faithful and the wicked. The theme of the Lord's protection of the people, including the foreshadowed king and anointed one of verse 10, pervades the section.

2:11-21 The sins of Eli's sons and the blessings of Samuel. In these verses the approved service of Samuel, even from childhood, is contrasted with the profligacy of Eli's sons. They are characterized as worthless fellows (literally "sons of Belial"), the same designation Hannah hoped Eli would not level against her in 1:16. The summary indictment against Hophni and Phinehas is that they did not know the Lord, a knowledge which meant experience of and obedience to God.

Normally, Israelite priests were allotted portions of the sacrificial animal, in particular the breast and right leg (Lev 7:29-36). But Eli's sons demanded their share before the ritual burning of the fat had taken place, and even before the meat had been cooked—hardly the dignified control one would expect of priests.

The story of their cultic irreverence is immediately followed by the idyllic picture of the boy Samuel wearing the ephod, a foreshadowing of his future role. Eli's grateful blessing to Samuel's parents results in the birth of five more children, God's most welcome gift to the Israelite (see Gen 18:13-14; 21:5-8; Ruth 4:11-15).

2:22-26 Eli rebukes his sons. In remonstrating with his sons, Eli asks the question David will fail to ask his son Adonijah when the latter declares himself king in his father's lifetime: "Why have you done these things?" (1 Kgs 1:6). Intercession can be made for their fornications, but their sins against the Lord,

those connected with the sacred sacrifice, have no mediator. Eli warns to no avail, but Hophni and Phinehas cannot cry ignorance. Because they refused to obey their father, the author lets us know they deserved their punishment, since the Lord had decided on their death. Verse 26 underlines again the contrast between Eli's unfaithful sons and Samuel, who as he grows earns the approval of both the people and the Lord (see Luke 2:52).

2:27-36 The prophecy against Eli's house. The accusation by the man of God begins in the traditional prophetic pattern of recalling the Lord's former benefits to the accused, listing their duties, their transgression, and finally their punishment. Eli is implicated along with his sons in verse 29 for enjoying the spoils which they had seized. The heart of the matter is that he had preferred his sons to the Lord. Therefore, their office as priests is for the most part cancelled, and those who do minister will have a miserable existence, begging for some employment which will bring them a stipend.

Nathan's encounter with David (2 Sam 12) after his adultery with Bathsheba and the murder of Uriah, has several parallels here. For both Eli and David, the punishment will be worked out within their families. Like Hophni and Phinehas, David's son by Bathsheba will die (2 Sam 12:19; 1 Sam 2:34), but, unlike Eli, David is forgiven and allowed to continue as king (2 Sam 12:13). The key to the different treatments of Eli and David may lie in 2:25, which states that sins against the Lord have no intercessor. While David's sin was against Uriah, Eli's sons have sinned directly against the Lord by profaning divine worship. Therefore David's kingship remains, but the priesthood of the Elides is replaced. The new priest, who will do what is in God's heart and mind, will have a sure house and will minister before the Lord's anointed (1 Sam 2:35). The prophecy is fluid enough to include as the faithful priest (the same adjective in Hebrew as that for "sure" house) Samuel, the anointed king Saul, Zadok, David or even the Messiah, whose name means "the anointed one."

3:1-18 Samuel's call. The prophecy which removed Eli and his house from the priesthood is not immediately implemented. Samuel was in training and not yet aware of his future role. Although at this time direct word from the Lord was rare, Israel longed for her God as much as Hannah longed for a son. The Lord now moves to remedy this just as Hannah's barrenness was reversed, both through the instrumentality of Samuel.

The picture of Eli asleep and practically blind describes Israel's state in relation to the Lord. The lamp of God, that is, God's word, is almost extinguished through the unworthiness of the officiating priests. The Lord ignores Eli and calls directly to the boy Samuel to receive this divine word. There is humor in Samuel's naive running to Eli three times before the old priest realizes that it is the Lord calling. The fourth call brings Samuel's willing response, "Here I am," the same made by Abraham when the Lord called him to sacrifice Isaac (Gen 22:1-2). Samuel's readiness contrasts with the priests' unwillingness to hear (1 Sam 2:25). Samuel is the faithful, chosen priest who will soon replace the unfaithful and rejected house of Eli. Later a similar drama will be played out between the rejected first king of Israel, Saul, and the chosen king David.

The chapter begins with the notice that visions from the Lord were few and ends with Samuel receiving frequent revelations at Shiloh. In between, Eli and Samuel speak to each other twice (vv. 4-9, 16-18). The center of the chapter is given to the Lord's words to Samuel alone (vv. 10-14). The Lord says nothing about Samuel's future but concentrates on the condemnation of Eli's house, adding that there is no chance for expiation. Eli's resignation under this sentence is an exemplary acknowledgment of the divine sovereignty and justice.

When Samuel opens the doors of the temple in the morning light, he enacts the bursting forth of the word of the Lord to the people after a long silence. For Israel as for Samuel, it is to be a new day.

II. THE ARK OF THE COVENANT

1 Sam 4–7

Ever since their journeyings in the desert of Sinai, the Israelites were accompanied by the ark of the covenant, the tangible symbol of the Lord's presence dwelling among them (Exod 37:1-9). This was a gold-plated wooden box said to contain the tablets of the law given to Moses on Mount Sinai (Exod 19–20). The traditions of chapters 4–7 bridge the gap between the ministry of the Elides and the formal inauguration of Samuel as prophet. During this time leadership of Israel is centered in the ark, for despite the silence of the word, the Lord remained with Israel. Even when captured the ark works against the enemy for the good of Israel. This section of the narrative shows the Israelites, greatly disadvantaged before their Philistine enemy and attempting to use the presence of the Lord to bring them victory.

4:1-11 Israel brings the ark into battle. After their disastrous defeat at Aphek (vv. 1-2), the people of Israel look for a more efficacious defense against their most dangerous enemy, the Philistines. These "Sea Peoples" had entered Canaan from the west and had settled along the coastal plain about 1200 B.C.E. They were non-Semitic, worshipers of the grain god Dagon, and were militarily and culturally superior to the Israelites.

The usual battle strategy having failed, the Israelites send for the ark of the Lord. The Lord is described (v. 4) as seated upon cherubim, representations of winged mythological beasts which guarded pagan temples. These cherubim were positioned on the cover of the ark as emblems of God's ministering spirits. The ark's presence in the Israelite camp disappoints the Philistines but induces them to fight with extraordinary bravery out of fear that they might become slaves of Israel. Not only were thirty thousand Israelites slain (v. 10), but the ark itself is captured—an event that causes all ears to tingle when they hear of it (3:11).

4:12-22 The glory of Israel departs. With the capture of the ark, the ministry of the house of Eli comes to an end in the death of Hophni, Phinehas, and their father. The shock of loss is such that Phinehas' wife dies giving birth (v. 19). Her son, whom she names symbolically Ichabod, meaning "Where is the glory?," lives and is mentioned in 1 Sam 14:3 as the uncle of Ahijah, a priest in Saul's camp. (Giving a name from the circumstances of a child's birth is common in the Bible. Sarah's son Isaac bears such a name [Gen 21:3-6], as do the sons of Jacob [Gen 30:6-24; 35:18]. It is particularly applicable in the case of Rachel who, like Eli's daughter-in-law, dies in the distress of childbirth.)

5:1-5 The humiliation of Dagon. As a relief from the sad events of chapter 4, this account introduces a lighter note. The Israelite audience is assured that though the ark was lost, the Lord whose presence it represented has not lost divine power. Here the Philistine god Dagon is disdained in two increasingly demeaning episodes. In the first he seems to be worshipping before the ark which had been moved into his temple. In the second he is dismembered before it. We are not told if he was ever able to be mended. Such is the fate, says the story, of gods made by human hands.

5:6-12 The ark afflicts the Philistine cities. In the previous section the ark had made trouble for the god Dagon in his temple at Ashdod, one of the five principal Philistine cities. Now it makes trouble for the Philistines themselves. There is a plague of mice in Ashdod, hemorrhoids in Gath, and death in Ekron. Four times (vv. 6, 7, 9, 11) we are told that this happens because the hand of the Lord is heavy upon the Philistines. With the same repetition, this time of the Hebrew verb "to go around," the biblical author emphasizes that the ark was sent around from one city to another (vv. 8, 9, 10). In each city the suffering is escalated, as was the indignity of Dagon. There was a similar escalation during the ten plagues in Exodus 7–12 and in the pressures brought on the captors of Sarah and Rebecca before their release (Gen 12, 20, and 26). We may smile with the Israelite hearers that the Philistines were thus bested, but also that their cry of pain went up, not to Dagon, but to the God of Israel in the heavens.

6:1-9 The Philistines plan to send back the ark. In this theological narrative, the Philistines implement their desire to send back the ark. After consulting their advisors, they let the direction taken by the calfless cows point to the originator of their plagues. The normal response would be for the cows to return to their calves. But if they head toward the Israelite border, it would mean that it was the Lord who had brought their troubles upon them.

The Philistines know enough Israelite history to see a parallel between this event and the plagues brought on the Egyptians before the Exodus, and they are determined not to repeat the Pharaoh's stubbornness nor its consequences. In a kind of sympathetic magic, they shape their conciliatory gifts of gold into five hemorrhoids and five mice, one for each of their cities. With the departure of the symbols of their plagues, they hope to eliminate them from their land.

6:10-18 The ark returns; some unexpected consequences. The cows hitched to the ark perform in exemplary manner as if leading a procession to Beth-shemesh, probably the Israelite town nearest to Ekron, where the ark was last kept. The Israelites rejoice to see it and celebrate by offering a sacrifice, much as Elisha will sacrifice his oxen, using the plowing equipment for the fire (1 Kgs 19:19-21). As often happens, a large stone marks the place of the sacrifice and of the divine intervention.

6:19-21 Trouble for Israel. The ark's homecoming is marred by the death of seventy who failed to greet it and thereby committed a sin of irreverence (compare Uzzah's plight in 2 Sam 6:6-8). The Lord's power and holiness represented in the ark become as frightening to the Israelites as they had been to the Philistines. Without divulging their reason, the people of Beth-shemesh send word to the inhabitants of Kiriath-jearim, about eight miles north of Jerusalem, to come for the ark. The chapter ends as it began with the ark, unwelcome to both Philistines and the Lord's own people.

7:1-6 Samuel begins his ministry. Except for the ark's transfer to Jerusalem in 2 Sam 6, the story of the ark concludes with verse 2. Despite its doubtful welcome and the absence of a fitting shrine as had existed in Shiloh, the Israelites are satisfied that it is at least in their own land once more. Its stay in Kiriath-jearim has positive results, for verse 3 tells of the people's desire to return to the Lord. Twenty years later, they are willing to affirm this publicly before Samuel at Mizpah, probably the site north of Jerusalem. (The scene is reminiscent of Jacob at Bethel [Gen 35:1-7] where the Lord asked him to make an altar. There as here the putting away of all foreign gods was required.) Samuel explicitly mentions Baals and Ashtaroth, fertility objects used in idolatrous worship.

The Israelites express their submission in a ceremony of atonement, which involved the pouring of water, fasting, and the confession of sin. Samuel's leadership in this inaugurates his active ministry in Israel. Hophni and Phinehas were priests who had no knowledge of the Lord (2:12). Now Samuel comes in their place as priest and judge, in that knowledge, and through him Israel receives blessing and victory.

7:7-17 Samuel's leadership. The gathering of Israel at Mizpah was for religious purposes, but the Philistines use it for a military confrontation. Once again Samuel intercedes, and before it is necessary to fight, the Philistines are routed by their own fear of thunder. Israel seizes the opportunity to pursue. The victory is credited to the Lord and duly marked by Samuel with a stone. This "stone of help" (Ebenezer) is not the same as in 4:1, though both show the Lord as helping Israel, the one through the ark, the other through Samuel's intercession.

The presence of Samuel now replaces that of the ark. While among the Philistines, the ark went around their cities; now it is Samuel who goes around judging in the four cities mentioned.

For now, the Philistines are no longer a threat to Israel. David will have to fight them later (chs. 17, 23 and 2 Sam 5:17-25), but at this point the cities which the ark had visited come under Israelite control.

In building an altar to the Lord, Samuel is in the tradition of Noah (Gen 8:20), Abraham (Gen 12:7; 22:9), Isaac (Gen 26:25), Jacob (Gen 35:7), Moses (Exod 17:15; 24:4), Aaron (Exod 32:5), and Joshua (Josh 8:30). Samuel is a prophet like Moses, and like Joshua, is both priest and judge. He is the only biblical figure who is priest, prophet, and judge. After him the priestly and prophetic callings begin to separate. However, even Samuel, with the fullness of authority and charism, does not satisfy the people, who long to be like other nations led by a king.

III. SAUL, THE FIRST KING

1 Sam 8–15

These chapters recount the turbulent change from the rule of leaders like Samuel to that of a king. With the loss of the ark and the ever-present threat of the Philistines as background, the Israelites increasingly see a solution to their weakness in the establishment of the monarchy. Samuel resists at first, but at the Lord's command, he anoints Saul (8:22). After being chosen by lot (10:21) and

defeating the Ammonites, Saul is officially inaugurated at Gilgal (11:15). In a negative vein, Samuel warns the people of a king's prerogatives (ch. 12). Monarchy may bring advantages, but they must be ready for side effects.

Samuel's warning finds a certain fulfillment in the Lord's later rejection of Israel's first anointed king. Saul fails, the text indicates, because he disobeyed the word of the Lord mediated to him through the prophet Samuel (chs. 13 and 15). Neither extenuating circumstances nor zeal for the worship of the Lord can overrule this crucial test of obedience to the word, for the king as well as every Israelite.

8:1-5 The people demand a king. The Hebrew text uses the noun or verb for the making of a king a dozen times in this chapter, with the word "judge" a close second. Kingship is about to replace the old system of governing in Israel. Up to this time, charismatic heroes sent by the Lord had led the people in battle against their enemies. Now, instead of praying for a new judge, the people ask Samuel to appoint a king.

8:6-22 The price of kingship. Hardly flattered by this request, Samuel is angry on behalf of the Lord whom he recognizes as the true and only king of Israel. In the revealing conversation between Samuel and the Lord, Samuel is faced with the reality of a people who have been continuously disloyal despite great favors. Verse 8 is encapsuled in a double command to Samuel to obey the people. After Samuel outlines for them what their king will do, the command of verses 7 and 9 is repeated a third time in verse 22. If the sons of Samuel *took* bribes, the king will *take* everything they value including their liberty (vv. 11, 13, 14-17).

The warning is not heeded despite the reminder that there is no way back (v. 18), for once the king is installed, it will be useless to complain. Sometimes God gives us that for which we ask before we know whether or not we really want it.

Verses 11-17 may have been written in hindsight, after the Israelites had learned all too well what it meant to have a king. The description is of a well-established, flourishing kingdom, hardly comparable to Saul's early and simple reign.

9:1-2 Saul is introduced. Twice we are told that Saul is a Benjaminite from the north in contrast to David whose origins are in Judah in the south. This distinction will mean more as the story unfolds. Saul's entrance into it is auspicious. He is handsome, taller than most, and the son of a man of substance. "Handsome" and "stalwart" are also used to describe David (16:18), whose ancestor Boaz was also a man of substance (Ruth 2:1). In the Books of Samuel there are a number of beautiful or handsome people: David, Bathsheba, Amnon, Absalom and Adonijah, but more often than not they come to an unhappy end (see 2 Sam 11, 13; 1 Kgs 1–2). The author seems to warn that such external gifts do not necessarily indicate divine approval and that they can be a source of pride and disobedience to the law. It is not the externals that God approves, but what is in the heart (16:7).

9:3-10 The unsuccessful search. Here we see Saul in action. He is an obedient son, diligently seeking his father's lost asses. Saul and his servant go through four different regions in their wide-ranging but fruitless search. Just as they are ready to give it up, the servant's suggestion leads them to the man of God in Zuph. It is not revealed until verse 14 that the man of God is Samuel. In the discussion whether and how to go to the man of God and what gift to bring for the advice about the asses (vv. 3-10), the verb "go" is used in Hebrew eleven times. The action verbs convey the intensity of the search.

9:11-13 Samuel presides over the sacrifice. Now the verbs change from going to going up, showing that Saul and his servant must not only climb to reach the city but, once within it, they will go up again to the high place where the seer was to officiate at the sacrifice. The high place here is a place of worship of the Lord, but later such places were condemned for idolatrous worship (Jer 2:20; 3:6).

Instead of "man of God," they ask for the seer, that is, one who sees more perceptively either the present or the future. The narrator interjects the information that at his time of writing the proper epithet for both was "prophet" (v. 9).

Verse 13 is important for not only does it include all the action words of the chapter: go, go up, find, eat (three times) and call or invite, but it contains the carefully stated prohibition against eating until Samuel comes and blesses the sacrifice. Knowing this will help

the reader understand the significance of Saul's failure to wait for Samuel's arrival in chapter 13. Also, the mention of invited guests implies that the sacrifice was not a public ceremony but by invitation only. The girls who give directions do not seem to be participants.

9:14-25 Samuel and Saul meet. In the revelation in which the Lord prepares Samuel for the arrival of Saul, the word "king" is never used. Saul is to be a military commander who will rescue Israel from the Philistines. Though this had not been the practice with the judges, Samuel is instructed to anoint Saul. This anointing and the special portion Saul is given to eat (vv. 23-24) are indications of the religious character of the newly instituted monarchy.

Without knowing what is ahead of him and before he is anointed, Saul finds himself the guest of honor at Samuel's banquet. Saul objects humbly to Samuel's praise, insisting, as had Gideon, that his family is the least of his tribe (Judg 6:15). Samuel promises to tell all that is in Saul's heart. With this prophetic backing, Saul begins a process of self-discovery as the Lord makes his will known to Samuel. In view of the previous revelation to Samuel that Israel had rejected the Lord in favor of a king (8:7), it is pure irony for Samuel to describe Saul as one ardently desired by Israel (9:20). Both Samuel and Saul in their different roles answer a need of Israel, one for a prophet and the other for a king. Which one will be the real leader of Israel?

9:26-27 After the feast. It is a surprise that the anointing is not public. If all Israel awaited a king, why this secrecy? It may be a way of reminding the people that the Lord works in his own time and in his own hidden way.

10:1-8 The signs of Saul's anointing. Samuel provides Saul with three signs to confirm his anointing as Israel's commander. Each occurs in a different place and each answers a future need of Saul. The first is at Zelzah, a name derived from the Hebrew verb "to rush upon." The verb appears twice in this chapter and refers to the spirit's rushing upon Saul (vv. 6, 10). This sign points to the location of the asses and to Saul's life-work as well. The second sign, the provision of kids, bread and wine, supplies the sustenance for his task. Because the gifts are consecrated as offerings to God, they indicate divine approval. The third sign connects Saul's kingship with the gift of the spirit and the ability to prophesy. The existence of a Philistine garrison (v. 5) at Gibeath-elohim recalls Samuel's prediction (9:16) that Saul will save Israel from this troublesome enemy.

Despite the positive signs, that is, Saul's change into another man and Samuel's promise that the Lord is with him (vv. 6-7), Saul is to undergo an immediate test: he must wait for Samuel for seven days in Gilgal, and then the prophet will tell him what to do. From the beginning Saul is "another man," but he is not his own man.

10:9-13 Saul as prophet. It is easy to see that Saul's prophetic abilities do not win him the respect accorded to Samuel. At this time prophecy was a more common phenomenon in Israel than would be the case later. The early prophets traveled in bands headed by their "father" (v. 12) and were given to ecstatic states often brought on by music (v. 5). (Elijah and Elisha [1 Kgs 17–21; 2 Kgs 1–9] were of this sort.) Saul's experience here foreshadows a similar event in 1 Sam 19:22-24.

10:14-16 Saul's silence. Was it natural modesty that caused Saul to omit the news of his anointing when his uncle questioned him? Or was it that Saul needed the ratification of his kingship by the people before it could be made public? In any case ratification does take place later at Mizpah (vv. 20-24). Much the same will happen in the case of David who will be anointed by Samuel (16:1-13) long before he becomes king over Judah (2 Sam 2:4). A future king of Israel, Jehu, will also be anointed years before he ascends the throne (2 Kgs 9–10). Saul did not in fact become king until after he had proven himself victorious over the Philistines.

10:17-27 Saul is chosen by lot. As happened in 7:5, Samuel once again calls all Israel together at Mizpah for the formal selection of the new king by lot. The Lord's message begins like a treaty between a lord and his vassal, recalling the good the Lord had done for the people in the past. Although the Lord had delivered them from oppressors, the people have rejected the divine king in favor of a human king. Samuel's tone is one of rebuke and chastisement rather than rejoicing over an awaited gift. The choice of Saul proceeds in the manner of an inquisition. Again and again little embarrassments cloud the ac-

cession of Saul, hinting that all was not well with his kingship from the start.

In answer to the people's cries in the desert, God had given both quail and manna (Num 17). Eating the quail answered the people's desire for meat but brought them death. Manna was God's answer to their need for food; they soon tired of it, but it kept them alive. In like manner, Saul was what the people wanted but he failed as king. The worthless fellows' question whether Saul could save them will be answered by Saul's deliverance of the men of Jabesh (11:9).

11:1-11 The challenge of the Ammonites. These were ancient and troublesome neighbors of Israel who settled along the northeastern shore of the Dead Sea. Nahash's answer to the request for a treaty with Jabesh is cruel, especially to modern ears. While it terrifies all who hear it, Saul's response would be equally abhorrent today. What is interesting is that Saul, anointed king, has no knowledge of the event because he has been plowing (!) and must be informed by the people. Only then does the spirit rush upon him and impel him to military action.

Saul's gory call to arms carries with it a terrifying threat of punishment, bringing thousands out for battle. A similar dismemberment and sending of parts to all the tribes of Israel is told in Judg 19–20, this time to punish an Israelite atrocity.

Beyond Saul's charismatic leadership, there is no special sign of divine intervention in the battle with the Ammonites (v. 11). The Jabeshites had lulled the Ammonites into expecting surrender (v. 9), a successful trick which the Israelite hearers must have reveled in. Saul's zeal brings the victory which confirms his kingship.

11:12-15 Renewal of Saul's kingship. Although the people ask Samuel to produce the men who challenged Saul's rule, it is Saul who makes the decision to pardon them. However, Samuel's initiative brings about the renewal of the kingship at Gilgal. Samuel retains his role as religious leader and kingmaker, but Saul has emerged as a triumphant military hero worthy to be king.

12:1-5 Samuel asks for an accounting. As Samuel's life comes to a close, he demands an evaluation of his ministry, an unusual event in biblical history. His list of possible infractions would make a fitting examination for any politician's career. Samuel is completely exonerated from fault. He has taken nothing, in contrast to the king who, as predicted in 8:11-18, will take everything the people value. The rule of a prophet, Samuel implies, is just, compared with that of a king.

12:6-12 A history of Israelite infidelity. His own record cleared, Samuel launches into Israel's continued ingratitude to the God who brought their ancestors out of Egypt and saved them from their enemies. Previously Israel had been given a judge in time of oppression, but now the fear of Nahash the Ammonite is great enough to make them demand the permanent rule of a king. Although Saul is now that king, Samuel still smarts under the people's rejection of the Lord as the true king of Israel. Verse 10 explicitly mentions Israel's perennial temptation: the trusting in and worship of other gods.

12:13-18 A sign of the Lord's displeasure. If the people think they can rest easily as far as obedience and worship of the Lord is concerned, they are wrong. Samuel warns them again that the Lord their God is the Lord of history with or without a human king. The king is not above the divine law. The sign of the divine sovereignty comes with Samuel's request for thunder and rain during a season when these almost never occur. The harvest is ruined; in anger the Lord has done the people's will.

12:19-25 Samuel intercedes for the people. While the people admit they have sinned in asking for a king, they cannot undo their act. When they ask Samuel to intercede with the Lord, he gives them support and encouragement but warns against idolatry. Such will be the typical message of later prophets, despite the people's infidelity. They will be punished if they do evil, but, like Samuel, the Lord will never abandon them. For their part they must fear and worship the Lord or else they will be swept away.

13:1-7 Jonathan's victory over the Philistines. After the Ammonite victory (11:11), Saul faces a far superior enemy in the Philistines. Without chariotry and cavalry his three thousand are pitifully outnumbered. The only cheerful note is Jonathan's successful attack on the Philistine garrison in Gibeah (v. 3). After it, Saul claims the victory (v. 4), causing the Philistines to renew the fight. The frightened soldiers desert in large numbers

(vv. 6-7) while Saul, holding on to those who are left, awaits Samuel to preside over the sacrifice which will prepare them for the battle.

13:8-18 Saul's test. With his scattered troops deserting, there was enormous pressure on Saul to keep his army from disintegrating. Samuel's failure to arrive on time is puzzling, since delay was demoralizing the soldiers. The point has been made that the people were required to wait for the priest to sacrifice (9:13). It is then disobedience for Saul to usurp Samuel's role and offer the sacrifice himself. Saul's trust was in the "magic" of the offerings—and perhaps the strength the food would give—more than the God to whom the offerings were made and who would decide the outcome of the battle.

This was a test that the impulsive Saul failed, and the failure resulted in the loss of his kingship. Saul is a tragic figure whose story has several portents of an unhappy end. Samuel's rebuke suggests this and points to a new divine choice, a man after the Lord's own heart (v. 14). Samuel departs, leaving Saul with a decimated army to face a threefold attack from the Philistines.

13:19-23 The Philistine advantage. The Philistines controlled not only the price of sharpening tools but the manufacture of iron. The Israelites had to be content with bronze plowshares and weapons which could only be sharpened by the Philistines. If Saul and Jonathan, the only ones who possessed weapons, would attempt battle under such disadvantages, it is because victory in war was seen as belonging to the Lord. If Israel lost, the reason was that the Lord had departed from the people in anger. If they won, the Lord was with them. An important aspect of Israelite warfare in Samuel's time was the ban, which required that all the spoil taken in victory be devoted to the Lord, that is, be completely destroyed as a holocaust or sacrifice. This question of destruction of a conquered people provides a second test for Saul in chapter 15.

14:1-15 Jonathan causes a Philistine panic. The presence of Ahijah (v. 3) associates Saul's efforts with the rejected Elide priesthood. Jonathan, who dominates this chapter, is an exception to this rejection, for, in contrast to his father, nothing adverse is ever reported about him. Jonathan's faith is behind his attribution of his success to the

Lord (v. 6). The armor-bearer's loyalty recalls the loyalty the Lord had expected and not received from Saul. In this awareness of the Lord, Jonathan is like David, who will regularly inquire of the Lord before going into battle (see 23:2, 4; 30:8; 2 Sam 2:1). In Jonathan's exploit, the Philistine panic and the ensuing earthquake are clearly acts by the Lord. Jonathan's trust is a foil for the misjudgment and impulsiveness of Saul.

14:16-23 Saul leads the rout. The unnatural confusion in the Philistine camp caused by Jonathan's raid has two results advantageous for Israel: the formerly fearless Philistines begin to slay one another; and the Israelite deserters return to Saul, who again capitalizes on Jonathan's success (see 13:4). The author attributes the victory to the Lord (v. 23).

14:24-30 The rash oath. Saul's ill-considered oath forbidding his weary soldiers to eat is obeyed by all except his son, who had not been informed. Both the soldier who tells Jonathan of it and Jonathan himself are openly critical of the wisdom of Saul's command (vv. 28-30). The soldier points to the weakness of the people; Jonathan tells of his own revival at having eaten a bit of honey, describing his father's action as troublesome to the people and therefore counterproductive (compare Judg 11:29-31).

14:31-36 Saul corrects ritual disobedience. Saul again shows poor judgment when the over-hungry people fail to let the blood drain from the meat before eating, as they were required to do (Lev 3:17). Saul shows himself piously concerned for the proper ritual and, to his credit, quickly makes appropriate arrangements. Although he wants to do the will of the Lord, he is a bungler who puts more faith in ceremony than in the Lord. Even the altar he builds out of devotion seems unnecessary and extra.

14:37-46 Jonathan freed by the people. After Saul, who had to be reminded to consult the Lord (v. 36), receives no answer from the Lord, he concludes that the cause is someone's sin. Even the life of his son is not too small a price to pay to remove the Lord's silence. Failure to know God's will dogs Saul's reign and will herald his death (see chs. 28 and 31). When the people rescue Jonathan from his father's fanaticism, Saul's sanity is put in question.

14:47-54 Saul's wars and genealogy. Despite the above, Saul seems to have overcome militarily his neighboring enemies (v. 47). The chapter concludes with a list of Saul's sons, wives, and generals. This is standard biblical treatment at the end of a reign. Perhaps it also signals the end of Saul's kingship.

15:1-9 Saul "reinterprets" his orders. Samuel's words make it plain that the Lord is supreme and that since he made Saul king, the king must obey the Lord. Saul's sparing of Agag thwarts the divine decree of punishment, which was to recompense Israel for Amalek's cruelty (Exod 17:8-16; Deut 25:17-19) and flouts the ban (see comment on 13:19-23).

15:10-23 Saul's second rejection. When Saul disobeys by sparing Agag and the best of the Amalekite spoil, the Lord repents of having made him king. Saul's rule now takes a noticeably downward course. Samuel, seeking to rebuke Saul, finds that he has gone to Carmel to erect a monument for himself. When they meet, Saul says confidently, "I have kept the commandment of the Lord." These incidents point to Saul's vanity and failure to know the Lord.

Their meeting is both humorous and ironic. The bleating and lowing which Samuel hears, he should not be hearing; the disobedience Samuel comes to castigate is denied by the one who is guilty. Samuel's poetic oracle (vv. 22-23) puts in perspective external sacrifice as related to an interior attitude of obedience. It also connects Israelite practices of divination and idolatry to sin and presumption. In overrating ritual, Saul has fatally confused his values (see 13:11-13; 14:33-35).

15:24-31 Saul repents. Saul admits his guilt, blaming the people, but Samuel neither accepts the explanation nor acknowledges that Saul may have acted in good faith. Saul finds the rejection impossible to bear and begs Samuel to accompany him to the sacrifice. Samuel agrees, but not before another symbolic rejection is enacted: the tearing of Samuel's cloak stands for the tearing away of Saul's kingship.

15:32-35 Samuel does Saul's job. Samuel's sentence on Agag is a restatement of the *lex talionis* which prescribes that punishment should fit the crime (Lev 24:17-21). Just as Agag rendered women childless by his sword, so shall his mother be made childless. It is a terse, incontestable sentence from the Lord (v. 33), who uses human events to accomplish his inscrutable will.

Today's reader may be astonished at the cold-bloodedness of the prophet as he completes the ban with the slaying of Agag, but biblical prophets are not known to shrink from death (compare Exod 32:25-28; 1 Kgs 18:40). There can be no sentimentality in obeying a God who "puts to death and gives life" (2:6).

IV. SAUL AND DAVID

1 Sam 16–31

Just as the Elide priesthood was cut off and replaced by Samuel, so here Saul is rejected and replaced by David. The Elides sinned against the Lord's worship; Saul sinned by not imposing the ban against Amalek and by usurping Samuel's role as priest in offering the sacrifice. Both infractions touch the worship of the Lord and both incurred the destruction of the respective houses.

As Eli functioned as priest after his rejection (1 Sam 2–3), so Saul continues as king though the Lord is no longer with him. Directed by the Lord, Samuel anoints a new king, David, who proves to be an able soldier and successful in all he does. In these chapters Saul pursues David in jealousy over this success, but David handily escapes each time. Saul at last falls victim to the very enemy he was made king to defeat (9:16; 10:1).

David has all the desired characteristics of a biblical hero: pleasing appearance, speech, and musical ability as well. Compared to Saul, David is superior from his first introduction. More important is that the Lord is with him, something said only once about Saul (10:7) and several times about David (16:18; 17:37; 18:12, 14, 28; 20:13).

16:1-13 David's anointing. Samuel's grief at Saul's rejection suggests not only that he had entertained hope for Saul's success as king but was personally attached to him (see 15:11). The brusque intervention of the Lord precludes further mourning: the Lord is determined to choose another king.

We are surprised that Samuel fears Saul will kill him (v. 2), for it negates the impres-

sion that Samuel held authority over Saul. The Lord encourages Samuel by a subterfuge. The new anointing is to be done under the cloak of a sacrifice at the home of Jesse in Bethlehem. The people's question (v. 4), "Is your visit peaceful?" warns that the prophetic word could bring both good and evil (see 1 Kgs 1:9-16; 2:23-24).

Samuel anoints David at a private banquet with little fanfare (compare Saul's in 9:22-27; 10:1). This is Samuel's last recorded prophetic act before his death (25:1; 28:3).

16:14-23 David the future king. In another sign of rejection, the spirit of the Lord now departs from Saul to be replaced by a spirit of melancholy. But Saul is not left without some relief. It can hardly be coincidence that David is the means of banishing the evil spirit, at least temporarily.

David's relationship to Saul has a happy beginning. Saul is immediately attracted to David and gives him the office of armorbearer, which amounts to on-the-job training for kingship. But this very closeness will soon cause problems.

17:1-11 Goliath taunts Israel's army. The challenger who comes out of the Philistine camp is so powerful and magnificently armed that he terrifies Saul and his army that is encamped on the opposite hill. They seem to have forgotten that it is the God of Israel who determines the victory (14:6; 17:47).

17:12-37 David the hero and savior. Without mentioning his previous anointing by Samuel, the author reintroduces David as a younger son sent by his father with provisions for his brothers in the Israelite camp. This inconsistency has been assigned by some commentators to another tradition which has here been interwoven into the text. However, what we today see as contradiction was often not a problem for the Israelite. David's fearless acceptance of Goliath's challenge shines out against the abject terror of the Israelites (v. 11).

The reward Saul has promised to Israel's defender calls to mind fairy tales wherein the hero is promised wealth and the hand of the king's daughter in marriage. A more realistic advantage comes in the form of tax exemption for the hero's family. From this we see how Saul's army and government were funded and that Samuel's warning about the rights of a king was being realized (8:10-17).

Saul's offer to make David his son-in-law gives him a strong claim to succeed to the throne. Jonathan's later prediction that David would become king may reflect this custom (20:12-16; 23:17).

Now a domestic mini-drama takes place in the angry reception David receives from his oldest brother Eliab (v. 28). David's role here is comparable to that of Joseph, who was sent out to his brothers by his father while they guarded the flocks (Gen 37). In both cases a younger brother of extraordinary promise is the object of jealousy and contempt.

17:38-54 The decisive encounter. When David cannot use Saul's armor to fight the Philistine, he resorts to other skills and puts his trust in the Lord. These along with stones and a sling were the simple means of bringing down Goliath. The theology of the event is summed up by David's statement that "it is not by sword or spear that the Lord saves" (v. 47).

There is an obvious anachronism in verse 54, since Jerusalem was not an Israelite city until after David had become king (2 Sam 5). The mention of Jerusalem and of David's tent is a later addition.

17:55-58 Saul meets David for the first time. It is puzzling that Saul, who had made David his armor-bearer and harp player in 16:21-23, knows nothing of the new hero, nor does his general Abner. Commentators suspect that an alternative account may have been superimposed here.

18:1-4 The covenant of friends. Father and son are immediately attracted to David as a result of his victory over Goliath. Saul makes him part of his household and Jonathan strips himself of his royal garments and weapons to clothe David with them. The gift is tantamount to abdication of the throne in favor of David. Theirs is an unsparingly generous friendship, lasting their lifetime, while Saul's less disinterested love of David soon grows sour.

18:5-30 Saul turns against David. When David's popularity grows with his victories so that the women sing of him to Saul's disadvantage (v. 7), Saul in a fit of jealousy attempts to pin David to the wall as he plays his harp. The king's fear increases when David escapes, and he realizes that the spirit of the Lord had departed from him and rested on David (vv. 12, 15). This transfer of the spirit was the biblical explanation of David's continued success against the Philistines (vv. 5, 30).

Saul, who had cause to be grateful to David, three times acts with duplicity against him. First, he offers his older daughter Merob in marriage, only to give her to another man (vv. 17, 19); second, he sends David into battle with the hope he will be killed by Philistines (v. 17), a tactic David himself will use against Bathsheba's husband in 2 Sam 11–12; third, he offers David the status of son-in-law on delivery of one hundred Philistine foreskins, hoping the danger of the undertaking will bring David death instead (v. 25). Although David demurs at becoming son-in-law out of modesty (vv. 18, 23), he is pleased and seems unaware of Saul's animosity (v. 26). On delivery of double the number of foreskins, Saul gives his younger daughter Michal to David in marriage.

David seems already to have surpassed Jonathan militarily, for no other victory beyond that of chapter 14 is reported of him. Jonathan decreases while David increases (compare John 3:30).

19:1-17 Jonathan and Michal help David. In defense of his friend, Jonathan extracts an oath from his father that he will not kill David (v. 6). However, when the evil spirit returns to incite Saul again to spear David, Michal joins Jonathan in protecting David. After convincing him of the danger from Saul (v. 11), and letting him down from a window to safety, she shows inventiveness in deceiving her father's soldiers (vv. 13-16) and courage in facing his rebuke (v. 17). The unhappy Saul thus finds himself alienated from both his children because of his behavior toward David. The fact that Michal's household contained an idol suggests that the worship of the Lord was not as pure in practice as the biblical ideal demanded (compare Gen 31).

19:18-24 Saul joins the prophets. The spirit of the Lord works to frustrate Saul in his attempt to seize David. Bystanders must have laughed to see all Saul's messengers and then Saul himself seized by the spirit when they approached the frenzied prophets among whom David had hidden himself. The scene in which Saul, in a highly undignified state, rolls helplessly about, raving along with his messengers, confirms the popular taunt of 10:11-12, "Is Saul also among the prophets?"

Such a portrayal reinforces Saul's inadequacy and rejection and at the same time reflects popular disparagement of early prophecy. The main point is that the Lord is protecting David against Saul, to the king's discomfiture.

20:1-10 Jonathan pledges loyalty to David. With the same words Saul spoke when sparing the malcontents who had formerly opposed his rule (11:13), Jonathan utters what is almost a royal decree that David will not die at the hand of his father (v. 21). In so doing he opposes his father's will and transfers his allegiance from Saul to David. On his side David's trust in Jonathan is so great that he requests Jonathan to kill him, should he be proved guilty (v. 8), rather than Saul (compare 2 Sam 14:32).

Jonathan seems at first to be an obstacle to David's becoming king, since he is Saul's legitimate heir. Instead he is the means by which David's destiny is achieved. This chapter marks the change in Jonathan's role from crown prince to David's subject. Also, in his success against the Philistines in chapter 14 and his subsequent rescue by the people, Jonathan in effect replaces his father as king. When Jonathan gives David all the trappings of royalty, he abdicates the throne (ch. 18). David's kingship, divinely instituted by Samuel's anointing (ch. 16), is thus humanly mediated by Jonathan.

20:11-17 The oath of loyalty. The pact David and Jonathan make holds two premonitions: Jonathan, the expected heir to the throne, will give place to David, and then he will die (vv. 14-16). Both face death; both stand in line for the kingship. Jonathan's blessing for David (v. 13) acknowledges Saul's rejection and points to David's succession.

20:18-34 Jonathan tests his father. Saul desperately tries to hold back the tide that is coming in for David by killing him. When Jonathan makes excuses for David's absence, Saul's reaction comes with a vengeance. In highly abusive words, Saul attacks not only Jonathan but his mother, hinting at an undisclosed defection on her part. Rather than attempt to win Jonathan to his side, Saul enlarges the breach by lunging at his own son with a spear. For the first time Jonathan is angry and stalks from the room.

20:35-42 Jonathan sends David on his way. Jonathan here joins his sister Michal in courageously defending David against the murderous intent of their father. With Jonathan's departure from Saul, the king's isolation increases and with it his madness. When the elaborate charade of shooting arrows is over, David offers Jonathan the triple homage befitting a royal person. By saving his life, Jonathan has helped David to become king. David will later preserve Jonathan's posterity by saving Jonathan's son (2 Sam 9; 21:7).

21:1-10 Ahimelech helps David. With David's unexpected arrival alone at Nob, Ahimelech has a premonition that not all is well. He is afraid that David is a fugitive and that he and his supposed men are not religiously prepared to eat the bread designated for the priests. By representing himself as on a mission of Saul's and under the rubrics of holy war, which required abstinence from women (Lev 15:18; Deut 23:10), David allays his fears and enlists his help. Convinced that everything is in order, Ahimelech takes no pains to conceal from Doeg, Saul's henchman, his having given bread and weapons to David (v. 8). Doeg's presence will have to be reckoned with later. The episode shows that human needs take precedence over cultic regulations, a point also made at the disciples' pulling ears of grain to eat on the sabbath (Matt 12:3-4; Mark 3:25-26; Luke 6:3-4).

21:11-16 David flees to Achish of Gath. The second person David meets on his flight from Saul is Achish of Gath. With Ahimelech he had played the part of one commissioned by Saul; with Achish he pretends madness, since insanity was looked upon as possession by an evil spirit and therefore made him untouchable. Although David, the hunted, looks mad, he is not; it is Saul, the hunter, who is the true madman.

22:1-5 David provides for his parents. David's refuge at Adullam's cave makes possible the formation of a guerilla band. Now no longer hostile, his brothers join him, and along with some outcasts of society, provide him with protection. It is the beginning of a power base that will lead to David's coronation.

In view of Saul's pursuit, David asks permission for his parents to settle temporarily in Moab. David's doubt as to where he should go next is resolved by instructions from the prophet Gad to go back to Judah—and the dangerous ambit of Saul. Through all vicissitudes, the Lord continues to care for David.

22:6-23 Doeg betrays Ahimelech. The scene shifts to Saul's camp where, spear in hand, he is complaining about the disloyalty of his men. Paranoia is enveloping Saul's appreciation of events, so that even those closest to him are suspect. Doeg's revelation of David's encounter with Ahimelech at Nob propels Saul into action. When Ahimelech appears before him, Saul again makes a charge of conspiracy (vv. 8, 13) and refuses to hear his pathetic but valid defense. Ahimelech's punishment is a foregone conclusion, but the reaction to Saul's command to slay the priests is not. When not one man moves to obey the command, Saul presses the Edomite Doeg into the cruel business, assuming that a foreigner would be less squeamish about executing Israelites.

Doeg's slaughter begins with the priests and extends to the rest of the inhabitants and livestock of Nob. What Saul should have done to Agag and the Amalekites, he does here against his own people (15:3). Although the true target of Saul's animosity escapes, one son of Ahimelech, Abiathar, survives to report the massacre to David (vv. 20, 21). With the arrival of Abiathar, the story returns to the fugitives in the forest. Here David accepts responsibility for the slaughter at Nob, offering Abiathar what protection he can.

23:1-6 David consults the Lord. In contrast to Saul, who had to be reminded to consult the Lord and then received no answer (14:36-37), David, when he asks whether to engage in battle with the Philistines, not only receives a positive answer but can ask a second time for the sake of his frightened men. David's victory is predictable because the ephod is in his camp, brought by Abiathar in his flight from Saul. Now the Lord is with David in a concrete way, for the ephod permits him cultic access to the Lord's will.

23:7-13 Saul frustrated again. Saul reads David's presence in Keilah as a God-given chance to seize his enemy. His plan to pursue him, as well as the treachery of the ungrateful citizens of Keilah, are made known to David by two further uses of the ephod. Because of this knowledge, David and his men, now six hundred strong, make their escape. Again the narrative contrasts Saul and David: the latter is seen as devout, God-fearing and obedient; the former is hobbled by his lack of the knowledge of God.

23:14-18 David and Jonathan meet for the last time. The essential details of David and Jonathan's relationship, sketched in 18:1-4, are here amplified. Jonathan openly acknowledges that David will be king and that his father will be unable to capture him (v. 17). Only the prediction of Jonathan's position as second to David remains unfulfilled, since Jonathan does not live long enough to see David made king. Jonathan's words confirm his loyalty to David and the relinquishment of any claim to the throne.

Jonathan's brief visit strengthens David's resolve and attests to the hidden care the Lord has for this favored king. Their covenant renewed, Jonathan departs from David and, except for notice of his death in 31:6-7, from the narrative.

23:19-28 Saul is distracted from the pursuit. When the Ziphites offer to disclose David's hiding place, Saul unaccountably asks for further inquiry. Earlier when he heard that David had been at Nob, he acted immediately (22:11). Now he proposes a wide-ranging search, which will only give David more time to flee.

Twice since his complaint that no one tells him anything (22:7-8), Saul is given information which almost leads to David's capture (vv. 7, 19). Each time he has had to abandon the chase because of unexpected developments, or divine intervention. However, Saul has no insight into this, nor does he give up the chase.

24:1-16 David asks justice from the Lord. This is the third sighting of David by spies loyal to Saul, whose three thousand men (v. 3) vastly outnumber David's six hundred (23:13). Saul, discovered in the cave by David and his men, is in his most humiliating predicament. The king's embarrassment serves as a foil to heighten two characteristics of David: his restraint when the enemy is in his grasp, and his extraordinary care not to harm the anointed of the Lord. Since piety holds back his hand from killing Saul, David looks to the Lord to vindicate him.

David argues with Saul with considerable wit. By disparaging himself as a dead dog or flea, he tries to show the king the futility of his chase.

24:17-23 Saul admits David will be king. David's skillful speech (see 16:18) proves so persuasive that Saul is reduced to tears. Gratitude and contrition are in Saul's response, but the announcement that he *knows* David will be king is prophetic. Like his son Jonathan, Saul also asks David to spare his posterity, forestalling the accepted custom of a new king's eliminating the previous ruling house.

Saul is here no longer a dangerous pursuer but a beaten captive at the mercy of one who refuses to kill him. The situation is so emotionally charged that, forgetting their enmity for a time, each leads his army off to his own place.

25:1 Israel mourns Samuel. With the death of Samuel, the role of judge in Israel passes to the king. Samuel was also a priest and a prophet, both of which offices now take on increasing importance in providing a check on the power of the king.

25:2-11 David seeks provisions from Nabal (the Fool). Between the two encounters between Saul and David (chs. 24, 26), there is here what amounts to a romantic interlude. If we have wondered how David supplied his men in the desert, this story provides an answer. Nabal offers David a different kind of opposition from Saul's, but one which could be equally life-threatening. Nabal refuses to share food with David and his men at a time of traditional hospitality, the sheep-shearing festival (compare Gen 38:13; 2 Sam 13:23ff.).

When David asks for gifts from Nabal's feast, he does so by artfully leading from polite greetings, a hint at Nabal's probable indebtedness, advertence to the feast, and finally to the request for provisions. In reply Nabal first tries to make David a nonentity and then equates him with a run-away slave. David addresses Nabal as brother (v. 6) and father (v. 8), but Nabal dismisses him as an unknown (v. 11). Although David may have had no strict right to a share in the feast, Nabal, for his part, fails to recognize (know) what is in his best interest.

25:12-35 Abigail (the Wise) saves David. After hearing Nabal's repulse, David in silent anger girds on his sword, ordering his men to do likewise. By repeating the girding three times, the author delays the action to heighten suspense and show the grim determination of David and his hungry men.

Meanwhile, Nabal's servants inform their mistress Abigail of what has transpired and attest to the good David and his men have done them (vv. 14-17). Their openness in describing Nabal as "mean" (literally, "a son of Belial"—Hannah's "ne'er do well" of 1:16) indicates not only that she had their confidence but that Nabal's ill-nature was well known.

Unlike her husband, Abigail knows wherein her best interests lie. She hurries off with gifts just in time to deflect David's growing wrath. In a speech as skillful as David's, she first blames Nabal for acting the fool and herself for not seeing David's men when they came. Pointing out that the Lord has saved David from blood guilt (v. 26), she presents her gifts. A proof of her wisdom is her perception that because David is fighting the battles of the Lord and there is no evil in him, the Lord will establish a lasting dynasty for him (v. 28).

Abigail concludes her speech with a blessing for David (v. 29) in which she uses two metaphors: (1) she refers to the "bundle of the living" into which David will be bound as a promise of life, and (2) she asks the Lord to hurl the lives of David's enemies as from the hollow of a sling, recalling David's victory over Goliath with a sling (17:40, 49f.). Abigail's last wish, that David remember her when all she predicts comes to pass, brings an equally gracious response from David who then lets her depart in peace.

25:36-39 Nabal's feast. In three short verses Nabal's life comes to an end, with a drunken orgy followed by a stroke. He had prepared for himself the royal banquet (v. 36) which should have been prepared for the true king, David. David had appealed to him as a servant; instead Nabal's wife presents herself as a servant (vv. 27, 41) while predicting David's kingship. Thus the good which David did (vv. 15, 21) is rewarded (v. 30), and the evil which Nabal dealt David (vv. 17, 21, 26, 39) is punished.

25:40-43 David's wives. In making Abigail his wife, David receives not only a woman of wisdom, skilled in speech, but very likely the control of Nabal's estate in the Calebite territory of Hebron (Josh 14:13-14). This advantage is offset by Saul's giving of Michal to another. The name Ahinoam, later listed as mother of David's first-born, Amnon (2 Sam 3:2), appears as Saul's wife in 14:50. If she was now David's and had been Saul's, it could relate to Saul's vicious outburst that

Jonathan was the son of a rebellious woman (20:30).

26:1-12 David confronts Saul. This chapter introduces Joab's brother Abishai, who is second in command of David's army and a man consistently ready with the sword (2 Sam 3:22ff.; 8:16). When he pleads with David to finish off the sleeping Saul, David refuses, once again honoring the sacredness of an anointed king (24:7). Instead of taking Saul's life, David takes away his means of defense, his spear, and his life provision, his water jug. The entry and seizure take place successfully because of the deep sleep the Lord had sent over the camp (v. 12). It is another example of the divine helps continually accorded David at the expense of Saul (see 19:22ff.).

26:13-20 A double rebuke. Abandoning the diffidence he used in his previous encounter with Saul (ch. 24), David, from a safe distance on an opposite hill, openly accuses Saul's general, Abner, of neglecting his king. When this draws Saul's attention, David leaves Abner to attack the king with words. David is willing to accept Saul's persecution if it comes from the Lord, but if from men (that is, Saul), he will be forced by it to flee to a foreign land, where he will be tempted to worship other gods (v. 19).

26:21-25 Saul repents again. Contrite and thankful, Saul admits he has been a fool (compare Nabal, ch. 25). David, however, makes no pact with him as he did in their previous meeting (ch. 24). Ignoring Saul's promise not to harm him (v. 21), David reminds the king that the only reason he has been spared is because he is anointed. This reflects badly on Saul, who, in pursuing one he knows will be king, has no such qualms of conscience. Although the two part in mutual blessing, Saul has stretched David's patience to the breaking point.

27:1-4 David leaves Israel. David experiences discouragement similar to that of Abraham after repeatedly being promised a son (Gen 15:4). Although both Saul and Jonathan have foretold that he will be king, while Saul pursues him, David has little hope for his life in the future.

27:5-12 Achish gives David Ziklag. In a mutually agreeable arrangement, Achish finds an able soldier in David, and David is able, through Achish, to provide for himself and his men. We may wonder why there is no indication of their previous meeting, in which Achish showed himself reluctant to harbor another madman (21:11-16). With the information we have, there is no conclusive resolution to this incompatibility.

In both meetings with Achish, David never betrays his steadfast loyalty to Israel. The raids David makes, ostensibly in Achish's behalf, are against traditional enemies of both Israel *and* the Philistines. David is careful to kill all the humans lest, if they returned as prisoners, they betray him. This deception, like others in the Bible, goes unreprehended.

28:1-2 Achish trusts David. When Achish says that David realizes (in Hebrew, "knows") he is to go out with the Philistines against Israel, David answers that Achish will learn (in Hebrew, "know") what his servant can do. David's response is a cover for his loyalty which has never turned from Israel and means that he hopes not to have to betray himself before Achish. The matter is taken out of his hands in the next chapter.

28:3-6 The Lord does not answer Saul. We are again told that Samuel has died, a fact which, along with Saul's banishing of fortune-tellers (according to Deut 18:10-14), severely limits Saul's knowledge of God's will as he faces his enemy. Seeing himself outnumbered, Saul is afraid, something that is never said of David. David is, however, said to be afraid of Saul (23:15). Again, as in 14:37, Saul is left without divine direction, a disadvantage David never had to contend with.

28:7-14 Saul seeks a medium. The name "fortune-teller" in Hebrew is a form of the verb "to know." In contrast to Achish, who will *know* (v. 2) what David will do, Saul does not *know* what the Lord will do and goes to one who *knows* to find out. Although it means breaking his own regulation, Saul in his great fear, seeks out such a medium. At once she parries his request with the statement that Saul—or anyone in Israel—*knows* that it is a capital offense to practice divination. As soon as she brings up Samuel, she *knows* who her petitioner is. Her scream of recognition has echoed down the ages in music and literature.

28:15-19 Saul finds out what he wants to know. Samuel, showing surprise that Saul has not accepted the departure of the Lord from him, repeats the divine rejection of his kingship. Saul is being punished here for the failure to slay Agag (ch. 15). Israel will fall before the Philistines, as will Saul and his sons. The reluctant answer from Samuel tells Saul all that he would rather not know.

28:20-25 The kindness of the medium. Taking a cue from Samuel's declaration that Saul had disobeyed the word of the Lord in verse 18, the author now begins a play on the word "obey." When the woman sees that Saul has fallen to the ground in weakness, she reminds him that up to now she has obeyed him (v. 21). In turn, he must obey her (v. 22) when she insists on preparing him some food. With his companions urging him, Saul obeys (v. 23) and he is given a feast of a fatted calf (compare Luke 15:23, 27). It is Saul's last banquet before his death in the next day's battle.

29:1-11 Achish reluctantly dismisses David. As they had been when the ark was lost, the Philistines are again encamped at Aphek (4:1), ready to fight against Israel. Achish had ordered David and his men to go out with him in 28:21, showing that his trust in David was firm. However, the other Philistine chiefs remember David's history of slaying thousands of their men (v. 5; 18:6-7; 21:11-12) and realistically assess his presence among them as an opportunity for David to ingratiate himself with Saul by turning on them from the rear.

Achish's speech in which he sends David back is flattering, to the point of calling David an angel of God (compare 2 Sam 14:17; 19:28). When Achish finds nothing wrong with David, he is in the tradition of Potiphar and his jailer, both of whom found nothing wrong with Joseph and who trusted Joseph enough to leave everything in his charge (Gen 39:6, 23). David inspires the same confidence in Achish. It is high praise for both David and Joseph from foreigners. Fellow Israelites were not so easily captivated.

David asks Achish why he cannot go out to fight against "the enemies of my lord the king" (v. 8). His words can refer to Achish or to King Saul (compare 28:2). Here David has again adroitly escaped with his friendship with Achish intact.

30:1-10 The Amalekite raid on Ziklag. Although Saul's devastation of the Amalekites in chapter 15 should have rendered them powerless, they now take their revenge by

sacking the city Achish had given David. Instead of being put under the ban, as Saul had been ordered to do, Ziklag's occupants were fortunately taken alive. Before they know this, the narrative builds the sorrow of the returning soldiers to a crescendo with the recounting of their weeping until exhausted, the information that David's two wives were among the captured, and finally the extreme bitterness of the men toward David to the point that they were ready to stone him, a rare sign of popular disenchantment with David. In turning to the Lord, David acknowledges that God is the source of his strength and success.

In obedience to the oracle received through the ephod (v. 8), David pursues Amalek, leaving two hundred of his weariest soldiers guarding the baggage. They will have a significant role in the distribution of the spoil (vv. 21-25).

30:11-16 The abandoned Egyptian. David receives providential help in the person of the sick Egyptian slave left behind by the Amalekites. In return for food, drink, and asylum, the Egyptian brings him to the carousing Amalekites. He joins a lengthening list of David's helpers: Michal, Jonathan, and Ahimelech, all of whom appear at the crucial moment.

30:17-25 David recovers the Ziklag captives. After an untold number of Amalekites are slaughtered, all the captives and possessions from Ziklag are rescued. David immediately faces another challenge from his own men in their unwillingness to share the spoil with those left behind with the baggage (v. 10). The ones who complained are called stingy and worthless (v. 22), but it is of such that David's small army was made (22:2). He must continually encourage them to trust in the Lord (23:1-5) and do good to their fellow soldiers out of gratitude to him (30:23). David's quick, sure decision to share the spoil among all members of his army becomes a precedent for Israel (v. 25).

30:26-31 The division of the spoil. David shows himself an astute politician by sending gifts from the booty to the Judean settlements in the Negeb where David was already known. These gifts could be means of gaining acceptance later when David is considered for the kingship after the death of Saul (2 Sam 2:1-4).

31:1-8 How Saul and Jonathan died. The happy picture of David sharing the spoils of the Amalekite victory gives way to the darker picture of Saul and the Israelite army fleeing and falling wounded before the Philistines. Once again David's fortunes rise as Saul goes into decline, both as king and human being.

Ignoring battle details, the narrative section, which begins and ends on Mount Gilboa (vv. 1-8), repeats its notice of the slaying of Saul's three sons and the finding (hit) of Saul (vv. 2, 3, 8), the coming of the uncircumcised/the Philistine (vv. 4, 7, 8), the fleeing of the Israelites (vv. 1, 7), and the discovery of Saul's death first by the armor-bearer and then by the Israelites (vv. 5, 7). In concentric fashion these events enclose the central message of Saul's death (v. 6). The literary embellishment heightens the pathos and significance of the event.

31:9-13 Mercy for the bodies of the slain. The Philistines desecrate Saul's body in three ways: they cut off his head, knowing that any mutilation of a corpse is a horror to Israelites; they strip him literally and figuratively of his glory as a soldier by taking his armor and putting it in their temple; lastly, they do the unforgivable: they impale his body on the city wall. Trophies of war hung in a house of worship apparently credit the god with victory (compare 5:2; 21:10).

While the burning of the bodies is usually abhorrent, it is here a mercy since no further atrocities can be done with them. Their proper burial (v. 13) means they are in peace.

Saul's body returns to Jabesh, the scene of his first victory after being anointed king (ch. 11). The man who was to save Israel from the Philistines (9:16) has himself fallen into their hands.

COMMENTARY: 2 SAMUEL

V. THE STRUGGLE FOR THE KINGDOM

2 Sam 1–8

After the death of Saul, David does not seize power, but waits for the Lord to give him the kingship. David rejects Saul's crown offered by the Amalekite messenger, but after being anointed by the Judeans (ch. 2) does accept the allegiance of the north brought him by Abner, Saul's former general. Although this plan is frustrated by Abner's death at the hand of Joab, the last obstacle to kingship over a united Israel is removed by events beyond David's control (chs. 4–5). Once king, David consolidates both his religious and political position by bringing back the ark of the covenant to the new capital in Jerusalem. All Israel is then a divine gift to David who, despite temporary setbacks, prospers under God's blessing and protection.

1:1-16 The Amalekite's report to David. "Death" is a word used eight times in this section, beginning with the death of Saul and ending with David's execution of the Amalekite who brought him Saul's crown and armlet as testimony of his death. If the Amalekite expected a reward from a man he supposed ambitious for the kingship, he is gravely mistaken. Instead of gratitude, he earns death for claiming to have slain an anointed king. David is here consistent in his remarkable reverence for anyone the Lord had anointed, as he demonstrated in 1 Sam 24:7 and 26:9.

1:17-27 The fall of the mighty. The Hebrew word for "warrior," which also appears in translation as "valiant" (v. 22) or "stronger" (v. 23), is the key word for David's elegy. The repeated "fallen" and "slain" underline its somber mood, while David's special love for Jonathan is emphasized in verse 26. Instructions to keep the news from the Philistine women who might rejoice over the slain is contrasted in verse 24 with orders for the Israelite women to weep over Saul and remember his kindnesses to them. Dew and rain are summoned to share the mourning by not appearing on the mountains where the slain lie (v. 21). Saul's neglected shield, no longer anointed with oil, symbolizes the rejection of Saul's own anointing.

2:1-7 David's announcement of kingship. Instead of his birthplace, Bethlehem (1 Sam 16:1), the Lord directs David to Hebron from where he includes, in a message of gratitude, the announcement that he has been anointed king over Judah. Since the area around Hebron was part of the traditional Calebite allotment, David may have gained control of property in Hebron through his marriage to Abigail, widow of the Calebite Nabal (Josh 14:13; 1 Sam 25:3).

2:8-11 Israel follows Saul's son Ishbaal. Not the Lord, but Abner, his own general, makes Ishbaal king over all Israel, except for David's territory in Judah. Such political weakness in Ishbaal is portentous for David's future.

2:12-24 The three sons of Zeruiah. A symbolic but indecisive combat between the Israelites under Abner and the Judahites under Joab, David's general, escalates to full battle. After the Israelite defeat, Asahel, brother of Joab and Abishai (v. 18), refuses to give up. Compulsively, he pursues Abner who tries to dissuade him, knowing that if he kills Asahel he will be liable to blood vengeance. When Abner is forced to stop Asahel with his javelin, Joab and Abishai continue the pursuit. The introduction of the three brothers, cousins to David, begins in violence and is associated with it throughout their lives.

2:25-32 Benjamin and Judah count their losses. The story has moved from one bloody confrontation in Gibeon to another in Geba. Although the losses of Benjamin are far greater than those of Judah, both sides are grateful to return to their respective camps.

3:1-6 The house of Saul and the house of David. The house of Saul weakens as the house of David grows stronger, a process marked by the death of Saul's sons in contrast to the fertility of David, whose six wives produced as many children. Only three of these—Amnon, Absalom, and Adonijah—will figure in the biblical narrative.

3:7-11 The matter of Rizpah, the concubine. Abner's relationship with Ishbaal's concubine Rizpah, more than an insult to a superior, could be read as a bid for the throne. However, Abner refrains from a coup, recognizing David as the predicted leader of Israel (vv. 9-10).

3:12-21 Abner and David make a covenant. With Abner's defection, all the tribes of Israel associated with Saul are ready to come under David's rule. But David makes the return of his wife Michal, Saul's daughter, the condition of his agreement. Without any compassion for Paltiel, to say nothing of the feelings of Michal, the painful deed is done,

clearing the way for serious negotiations between Abner and David. Abner refers to no known biblical passage when he quotes the Lord as saying David will deliver Israel from the Philistines (v. 18). Rather this was promised of Saul (1 Sam 9:16), had he obeyed the Lord (1 Sam 13:13-14). The narrative underlines that Abner departed in peace (vv. 21-24), but it was not a peace that was to last.

3:22-30 Joab's zeal. Abner's insubordination to Ishbaal (vv. 8-10) is mild compared to Joab's attack on David for making an agreement with Abner. Joab says in effect, "How could you let an obvious enemy get away?" Then, without orders, Joab dispatches Abner in cold blood (v. 27), not the last time Joab will act with violence for the good of the state. Substituting vindictiveness and frustration for actual punishment, David delivers a dire curse on Joab and his posterity (v. 29). Presumably impressed by David's outburst, Joab submits to David's order to mourn Abner publicly.

3:31-39 The burial of Abner. David's distress over Abner's death can be felt in the bitter elegy he composed for the funeral. This and the king's extravagant mourning (v. 32) convince the people that David had not ordered Abner's execution. David's acknowledged weakness before Joab is a persistent puzzle in the narrative (v. 39). It required him to endure a man who was a continual thorn in his side at the same time that David owed Joab much of the success of his wars and his rule.

4:1-4 The successors of Saul. With only the crippled grandson Meribbaal left to the house of Saul, besides the frightened Ishbaal, the Israelites can look for no effective leadership from within the northern tribes. Little seems to stand in the way of David's kingship.

4:5-12 The murder of Ishbaal. With Ishbaal demoralized and security lax, it is easy for the two murderers to enter the royal bedroom. Understandably, they see Ishbaal's rule as effectively ended, but they hardly expect David not to welcome their gift of his head. It is a second example of David's refusal to seize the kingdom through violent means (compare 1:1-16).

The execution of the two men, cruel to us, is done according to the law in Deut 21:22f. As the Philistines treated Saul (1 Sam 31:9), so are the slayers of his son treated.

5:1-5 King of all Israel. When the Israelite (northern) tribes come to anoint David king, they have two motivations. First, they claim him as brother (their bone and flesh), a condition for kingship required to prevent foreign rule (see Deut 17:15). Second, they recall David's military leadership (1 Sam 18:16) and the divine promise that David's throne would be established over both Israel and Judah (3:10). Thus he becomes king over an externally united nation, but one whose internal conflicts are never very far below the surface.

5:6-16 A city and a house for the new king. The account of how David made Jerusalem, previously held by pagan Jebusites, his capital is truncated and confused. Despite Jerusalem's reputation of being impregnable (the blind and the lame could defend it), David is able to take it after Joab courageously climbs the water shaft to gain access to the city. This information comes from 1 Chr 11:6, which adds that David rewarded Joab for his bravery by making him commander of his troops.

David's new capital is, for political purposes, ideally situated, since it is on the border between two chief tribes of his kingdom: Judah and Benjamin. Once settled, David has the leisure and resources to build himself a palace. From his friend Hiram of Tyre, David sends for cedar and workmen, just as his son Solomon will later do for the building of the temple (1 Kgs 7).

5:17-25 The Lord goes before David in battle. Success has not yet gone to David's head, for he continues to consult the Lord before going into battle with the Philistines who now seem to resent David's new power. After the first rout of the enemy, David names the place Baal-perazim (literally, "lord of the breaking through"), a play on words referring to the Lord's breaking through the enemy lines so that both the Philistine soldiers and the gods they left behind are scattered (vv. 20-21; compare Gen 38:29).

At the Philistines' second attack, it is the Lord who directs the defense by ordering a rear attack by Israel and by giving an audible sign (v. 24) that the Lord is leading the march. Saul never had the advantage of such tangible support.

6:1-10 The striking of Uzzah. The transfer of the ark is told in fuller detail in 1 Chr 13 and 15, whence we learn in 13:6 that Baala of Judah is another name for Kiriath-jearim, where the ark was left (1 Sam 7:1-2). The joyful procession of thirty thousand (!) is interrupted by the unexpected death of Uzzah when he touches the ark (v. 6). David, upset by the event, leaves the ark at the home of Obededom, significantly identified as from the Philistine city of Gath. If the ark is to bring destruction to the Israelites, let it stay with the Philistines, David's action seems to say. Although this account makes no attempt to explain Uzzah's death, in 1 Chr 15:13 David attributes the Lord's anger to the absence of the priests and Levites.

6:11-19 David brings the ark to Jerusalem. When the king hears of the blessings to Obededom's house, he ventures another transport. In the festal procession David, clothed only with the linen ephod used by priests at liturgical functions, distinguishes himself by his energetic dancing (v. 14). It is a time for joy, music, and the giving of gifts (v. 19). By the transfer of the ark to Jerusalem, that city is established as the religious and political capital of Israel.

6:20-23 The scorn of Michal. For the third time, the presence of the ark brings trouble (1 Sam 6:19; 2 Sam 6:6-7). The Lord, whose presence is said to dwell in the ark, indicates in this way that he is free to dwell wherever he will and not necessarily at the desire of the king. Now David meets another reversal: the scorn of Michal for what she considers his immodest dancing (v. 20). David's wounding retort reminds her that the Lord has rejected her father's house. Her punishment is to remain childless, in that society a woman's greatest reproach (compare 1 Sam 1).

7:1-17 The house of the Lord and the house of David. In peace with all the nations round about, David has the leisure to turn to internal matters, including the public worship of God. In the ancient world a god was truly established when he had a fitting house. Nathan's immediate approval of David's plan to build the Lord a house is revoked by a nocturnal oracle. That the Lord does not communicate directly with David but through Nathan underlines the continued importance of prophecy in relation to the monarchy.

Pointing with pride to his simple tent-dwelling while Israel sojourned in the desert, the Lord turns David's good intentions around. The Lord himself will build a house for David, a house in the sense of dynasty, one that will rule forever (v. 13). In an elaborate play on the word, "house" means palace (v. 1), a dwelling (vv. 2, 5, 6, 7), royal dynasty (vv. 11, 16), and temple (v. 13). Reminding David of his humble beginnings, the Lord unconditionally promises him a great name (v. 9) and a firmly established throne (vv. 13, 16). The prediction that David's son will build a temple comes to realization under Solomon (1 Kgs 8). For another account of the dynastic promise, see 1 Chr 28:1-10.

This passage has been interpreted as the Lord's personal covenant with David. By it the Lord's direct rule over Israel is replaced with a human king, chosen by God, whose posterity will continue to occupy the throne for all generations. Samuel's previously hostile attitude toward allowing Israel to be like other nations has been changed to divine endorsement of the Davidic kingship as well as the establishment of its sure dynastic succession. This text, along with Ps 89 and 1 Chr 17, is the biblical rationale for the royal theology according to which the king was the Lord's representative in bringing Israel victory and blessings.

7:18-29 David praises the Lord. In grateful response to the Lord's promise, David contrasts his own littleness to the Lord's greatness (vv. 18, 19, 22). The Lord is the only God and Israel is his specially favored people (vv. 22, 23). As the Lord did in verse 6, David also recalls Israel's deliverance from slavery in Egypt (v. 23). Then, in a covenant renewal, David reaffirms Israel as the Lord's people and the Lord as their God (v. 24), closing with a prayer for the Lord's blessing (v. 29).

8:1-14 David's victories. This chapter could be called "David strikes" because the verb, variously translated, "defeat," "attack," and "slay," appears in verses 1, 2, 3, 5, 9, 13. The list of victories begins with the Philistines and continues through the countries bordering Israel. The range of conquests includes Moab, Aram (Syria), and Edom.

That David had use for only one hundred chariot horses shows his army inferior in equipment to those of his enemies. However, the plentiful booty enriched David with shields (v. 7), articles of gold, silver, and bronze (vv. 8, 10), all of which were consecrated to the Lord (v. 11).

8:15-18 The heads of government. Besides being a military leader, David governs and administers justice (compare 15:1-6). Joab commands the army and Benaiah the Cherethites and Pelethites, believed to be Cretans and Philistines (see 15:18). By using foreign mercenaries, ancient kings knew how to protect themselves from palace coups.

VI. DAVID THE KING

2 Sam 9-20

David sits on the throne in Jerusalem at peace with his neighbors. Assured of a lasting dynasty (ch. 7), he seeks to do good with his increasing power and wealth. In a moment of passion David breaks the law, bringing on himself divine punishment which escalates from his family to threaten even his throne. These chapters comprise a narrative unit, called the Court Narrative because it tells the story of David's life as king. It is thought to be a separate tradition from those about Saul and David called the Late Source. There are however narrative links in chapters 9-20 to earlier themes, for example, the influence of Joab on David and the recurrent division between the northern and southern tribes, which speak against complete independence of the sources.

9:1-13 David fulfills his oath. A prosperous David remembers his covenant and friendship with Jonathan by looking for descendants to whom he may show kindness. With such close ties to Saul's house, it is strange that David should have to ask if there were any Saulides alive. However, if the events recorded in chapter 21, where David spared Meribbaal when he handed over two sons and five grandsons to the Gibeonite vengeance, took place before those recorded in chapter 9, we can more easily understand why only Meribbaal was left.

When the crippled son of Jonathan, Saul's grandson, is brought to David's court from the house of Machir (see 17:27), David goes out of his way to make Meribbaal feel welcome. Although he protests he is a dead dog—an expression of political and psychological inferiority—Meribbaal becomes part of David's household and has the honor of eating at his table. Ziba, his servant, is assigned to run the family farm, which would provide for them all, including Ziba's fifteen sons and twenty servants.

In doing this David fulfills his oath and shows that he has little to fear from this Saulide. Twice the narrator mentions that Meribbaal is crippled, saying in effect that he is unqualified for kingship (vv. 3, 13). It is then doubtful that making Meribbaal part of his household was a means of keeping an eye on a possible conspirator to the throne. Against this is the allegation of treason that Ziba implies when David's throne is in jeopardy (16:1-4).

10:1-5 David and the Ammonites. David continues his good works, here extending condolences to the Ammonite king on the death of his father. But things turn out adversely due to the negative advice of the young king's advisors. By shaving the beard and exposing the nakedness of David's emissaries, Nahash delivers the ultimate insult. David is considerate and allows the men to stay in Jericho until their beards grow again.

10:6-12 Joab leads the defense against Ammon. Expecting reprisal, the Ammonites prepare to attack first, with the help of Aramean mercenaries. After skillfully arranging his troops for defense, Joab encourages them to fight bravely and leave the outcome to the Lord. The success of battle will then be the typical biblical combination of human effort and the power of God.

10:13-19 The defeat of the Ammonites and Arameans. When the Arameans flee before Joab, their Ammonite allies do likewise before the rest of the troops under Joab's brother Abishai (v. 10). The victory is only temporary, for the Arameans, having gathered fresh recruits from sympathetic rulers beyond the Euphrates, try again to conquer Israel. David now takes the field himself, wipes out the enemy and makes subjects of the Arameans. This account marks the high point of David's military exploits.

11:1-15 David and Bathsheba. While the army is besieging Rabbah, David has little to do but take naps and walk about on his roof. On one such idle afternoon, he sees the beautiful Bathsheba and sends for her. In an extended play on the word "send," the author has David "send" frequently in chapters 10 and 11, alerting the reader to his full royal powers. However, Bathsheba also sends when she informs David she is pregnant (v. 5), and

Joab, too, sends Uriah back from the front lines (v. 6).

Not even the information that Bathsheba was the wife of one of his army officers deters David from possessing her. Once he knows she is pregnant, he begins an elaborate intrigue to cover his paternity. When he asks Uriah the triple question about how are Joab, the people, and the war, it is so much talk masking his real purpose to make Uriah go down to his house to his wife.

This attempt is made for three nights (vv. 8, 10, 13), but Uriah sleeps with the king's servants instead. When David asks why, Uriah's amazing answer painfully contrasts the king's evil designs with the moral uprightness of his loyal soldier. On the third evening, although David has made Uriah drunk, he persists in avoiding his house. The frustrated David then devises a way out of his dilemma by instigating Uriah's death under cloak of battle. The irony is that David sends the instructions to Joab in a letter carried by the victim himself.

11:16-27 David arranges Uriah's death. The instructions David gives Joab are not carried out exactly as given. David had intended for Uriah alone to be slain and for the deed to look like an accident. Joab, understandably concerned for his reputation as military tactician, entices the men of Rabbah to attack, causing some Israelites to be slain, among them Uriah.

Now Joab, anticipating the wrath of David for the deviation, prepares his messenger carefully for a possible angry reaction. What David does say gives not only a look at how wars were then fought but what was going on in Joab's mind. For example, the warning about letting the troops go too near city walls recalls Abimelech's shameful death in similar circumstances at the hand of a woman (v. 21; Judg 9:50-54). Joab may be letting David know how Uriah's death actually took place.

David's response is unexpectedly mild. Things like this happen in war, he says, and the sword devours indiscriminately (v. 25). David will later be very much concerned whom the sword devours when it is a matter of his sons. Here he responds as to a run-of-the-mill war report, with appropriate messages to keep up the siege and be of good courage.

After delaying over the scene between the messenger and David, the narrative regains speed at the telling of Bathsheba's mourning for Uriah, her marriage to David and the birth of their son, all in verses 26-27. The adultery and murder completed, the Lord's judgment comes at last: the thing David did was evil in the Lord's eyes (v. 27). This judgment is the key for what follows.

12:1-7a "You are the man!" Now it is the Lord's turn to send. The power-drunk David is about to be brought to his senses. Nathan, the prophet who brought the promise of David's lasting kingdom (7:16), now conveys the Lord's disapproval. In a parable Nathan tells of a poor man (Uriah) whose beloved lamb (Bathsheba) has been appropriated by a rich man (David). The picture of the lamb's intimate daily life with its master reflects the happy marriage David has usurped in selfishness and cruelty. Although nothing is said in the parable about murder, David breaks in with a decree that the rich man shall die. When he adds that the thief shall make fourfold restitution, he inadvertently foreshadows the loss of his own four sons (12:18; 13:28; 18:15; 1 Kgs 2:24-25).

12:7b-15a The sword over David's house. Nathan, reporting the words of the Lord, recites all the benefits given David: the kingship over both Judah and Israel, the harem of the deceased Saul, a fact not made known before. Was this not enough? The Lord would have added more, had David asked (v. 8), so pleased was the Lord with this divine favorite. David was like a spoiled son for whom not enough can be done. Now he has betrayed the Lord's generosity by despising his word (v. 9).

The punishment Nathan outlines comes in reverse order to the deeds. Because of the murder, the sword will not depart from David's house. Because he took Bathsheba, his friend (identity not disclosed) will lie with the king's wives. As David had done this secretly, the punishment will take place before all. At David's humble admission of sin, Nathan replies that the Lord has already forgiven him. The death David deserved will not be his but that of Bathsheba's yet-to-be-born child.

12:15b-25 David prays for his son's life. Although David adds to his prayer fasting and sleeping on the ground (an ironic touch in view of David's concern for sleeping in chapter 11), the child becomes ill and dies. David in effect has mourned in advance and when death is confirmed, surprises his household by rising, washing, dressing, and eating. From all these an Israelite in mourning ordinarily abstained; by ignoring them David shows his independence of established ritual as well as his acceptance of the child's death (compare 1 Sam 21:1-7).

After David consoles Bathsheba, now his wife, the Lord blesses their union with another son. The divine approval is signaled by the sending of Nathan to add the name Jedidiah, or "beloved," to the name already given him, Solomon. The Lord's love for Solomon will be proved by his accession to the throne after David (1 Kgs 1).

12:26-31 David conquers Rabbah. Rather than take the besieged city of Rabbah himself, Joab sends for David to claim it. Along with the gold crown of the Ammonite deity Milcom, David takes much booty and many captives whom he puts into service. From David's military victories, the story now turns to David the king and father.

13:1-22 The rape of Tamar. Absalom, David's third son, dominates the chapter because of his relationship to Tamar, whom his half-brother Amnon loves. The "love" turns out to be an irrational passion that has made Amnon ill. Taking his cue from this, Amnon's clever advisor Jonadab urges him to use the "illness" as an excuse to bring David to visit him.

David suspects nothing in Amnon's request to have Tamar bake cakes for a sick brother. Once Tamar has the food ready and the room has been cleared (v. 9), Amnon, instead of eating, demands that she lie with him. By using the word "lie" in verses 5, 6, 8, 11, 14, the narrator recalls David's lying with Bathsheba and Uriah's refusal to lie in his own house (ch. 11). The reiteration of "brother" and "sister" stresses the evil that is corroding David's own family.

Tamar makes a poignant and eloquent plea to Amnon not to commit an intolerable crime (literally "folly") in Israel, but Amnon will not listen to her sensible arguments. His passion spent, Amnon's underlying hatred surfaces. Where before he had sent all his servants out (v. 9), now he calls his servant to throw Tamar out (v. 17). Tamar pleads not to be humiliated further; again Amnon refuses. His sending her *away* is the reverse of David's sending *for* Bathsheba (11:4). In grief,

Tamar tears the special garment that marks her a princess and ultimately finds a home with Absalom. David, though very angry when he hears of the deed, makes no move against his first-born. Absalom's silent anger however has an air of foreboding.

13:23-39 Absalom punishes Amnon. Patient but determined, Absalom waits two years to settle the score with the hated Amnon for a crime his father had failed to punish. As Absalom usurps his father's prerogative, David is seen as gradually losing his control over his children.

A false report that all the sons were slain (v. 30) causes David to fear the worst. The strangely knowledgeable Jonadab explains that only Amnon was killed. Here David is typical of many powerful leaders who suffer isolation from their subordinates' plans. As with Amnon (v. 21), David does nothing to Absalom who is allowed to flee unchecked to his paternal grandfather in the non-Israelite region of Geshur (compare Gen 34).

14:1-24 The wise woman of Tekoa. When Joab judges the time is right, he engages a woman skilled in speech and acting to instigate Absalom's return. Like Nathan's parable (12:1-6), her story must bring David to make a judgment on a case close to the king's actual situation but with enough difference to offset suspicion until it is too late. Like David's, the woman's story includes two sons who have quarreled and as a result one has been killed. There are two differences: her son's death was not premeditated murder as was Amnon's, and her family is demanding blood vengeance, as David's is not. Both have the problem of saving the surviving son, in the woman's case because he is the only one to provide posterity, and in David's, Absalom is the heir to the throne.

When David promises to protect her son, she immediately makes a correlation with David's situation. Unaware, the king has judged himself, because what he will do for her son, he will not do for his own (v. 13). The woman presses her point: God does not bring the dead to life but devises ways of returning the banished. If the king would protect her son from death by an avenger, so should he provide a home for Absalom (v. 17).

To win David over, the woman has used disguise (v. 2), homage (v. 4), metaphor (v. 7), and outright flattery (vv. 17, 20). (Compare 1 Sam 29:10; 2 Sam 19:27.) At last David recognizes the hand of Joab in the charade, but he is not angry. Joab's ruse permits him to bring back Absalom for the face-saving reason that the country needs the heir to the throne. However, Absalom returns to Jerusalem not completely reconciled to his father, for David refuses him presence at court.

14:25-27 Absalom's beauty. To fill in the passage of time before David's next contact with Absalom, the narrator concentrates on Absalom's beauty and the weight of his hair. This should alert us to possible trouble, because Bathsheba and Tamar were also beautiful and both had trouble because of it.

14:28-33 Absalom reconciled to David. Once again Absalom bides his time for two years (compare 13:23) before bringing his frustration into the open. We are not told the reasons why Joab who engineered Absalom's return should refuse to come when summoned or why Absalom chose to resort to aggressive means to bring Joab to him. The violence of Absalom's character is apparent in this and in his willingness to have David kill him should the king find him guilty (v. 32).

In Absalom's reunion with his father, there is not a word of welcome or forgiveness, only a kiss. Is it the kiss of one who will betray him (compare Luke 22:48)?

15:1-6 Absalom the politician. Absalom now adopts a high profile with chariots, horses, and men to run before him. By touting himself as a judge for litigants who come to Jerusalem, and by fawning on those from the northern tribes, Absalom works to widen the breach between the North and the South in Israel. The picture is of a person of great vanity and treachery.

15:7-12 David tricked a third time. As he was duped in allowing Tamar to go to Amnon (13:5-7) and Amnon to Absalom (13:26-27), David again lets the sword threaten his house by permitting Absalom to go to Hebron. Absalom's reason for going, the fulfillment of a vow he made in Geshur, is one with which the king can hardly quarrel (v. 8). Why Absalom could not have worshiped in Jerusalem, David never challenges, possibly because Hebron was the place of Absalom's birth (3:2-3) and where David was made king over Israel (5:3). These considerations make Hebron both a logical and ironic place for Absalom to rally his followers. When David's counselor Ahithophel defects to Absalom, the conspiracy is launched.

15:13-18a The loyalty of David's officers. The gravity of Absalom's threat is reflected in David's immediate decision, on hearing of the treason, to flee Jerusalem. All David's officers prepare to depart. By noting that ten concubines are left to guard the house, the narrator anticipates another fulfillment of Nathan's prophecy (12:11). On David's sorrowful journey out of Jerusalem, the party stops first opposite the ascent of the Mount of Olives (the scene of Jesus' *via dolorosa*, compare Luke 22:39). It is the first of seven stations.

15:18b-23 The loyalty of a foreigner. As his people pass before him heading east out of Jerusalem, David stops to urge Ittai of Gath to go back to the king, referring not to himself but to Absalom in Jerusalem. Ittai's loyal determination to stay for life or death (v. 21) counterbalances Absalom's treachery. After this second station, David crosses the Kidron (compare John 18:1).

15:24-31 The arrival of the ark. The sorrowful procession is brought to a halt a third time when the priests Zadok and Abiathar appear with the ark. Perhaps with Shiloh in mind (1 Sam 4:4-11), David sends the ark back in the hope that the Lord will once more let him see it in Jerusalem (v. 25). Resigned though he may be to whatever is in store for him, David does not fail to use the priests and their sons as a source of intelligence about Absalom's activities in Jerusalem.

David continues up the Mount of Olives, weeping and barefoot. The heads of all are covered as a sign of deep sorrow. When the king is told that his advisor has joined Absalom, David for the first time prays publicly for Ahithophel's counsel to be frustrated (v. 31).

15:32-37 Hushai sent on a mission. David and the people have now reached the summit of the Mount of Olives where we are told, significantly, that people used to worship God (v. 32). At this fourth station help comes to David in the form of his friend and confidant Hushai (see 1 Chr 27:33). As with the ark, David does not keep him by his side but sends Hushai to counter Ahithophel's counsel to Absalom.

16:1-4 Ziba brings gifts. The tide of adversity begins to turn for David as he descends from the mountaintop. Stopping for the fifth time, David is met by Meribbaal's servant Ziba (9:2-4; 9-10) with three kinds of provisions: transport, food, and drink. Offering no sign of gratitude, David on inquiring learns that Meribbaal is waiting in Jerusalem to be made king. Without further investigation of this treasonous charge, David impulsively gives all Meribbaal's estate to Ziba. Later Meribbaal will attempt to exonerate himself (19:25-31), but David's touchiness at what may be a resurgence of the house of Saul underlines the persistent threat of secession by the North.

16:5-14 Shimei curses and stones David. The sixth stopping place on David's flight from Jerusalem brings the king into confrontation with another Saulide, also treacherous but more hostile. Shimei of Bahurim brings on David the greatest public humiliation he has yet suffered, but to David none of the cursing and stoning compares with the pain of Absalom's rebellion (v. 11). Shimei rejoices that David's bloody history (referring perhaps to the events of 21:1-14) have brought him the Lord's punishment (v. 8), while David, refusing Abishai's offer to behead Shimei, accepts patiently what the Lord has allowed, hoping his trial will win compensation later (v. 12). Mourning, humiliation, doubt, and betrayal have dogged David's journey since leaving Jerusalem. The support of his people, the loyalty of Ittai, and the promise of help from Hushai and the priests' sons (15:36) are the only bright spots. Exhausted, king and people arrive at the Jordan, the seventh station.

16:15-23 Absalom and his counselors. Back in Jerusalem, Absalom holds a council of war. Hushai joins the enemy camp with cries of "Long live the king!" Absalom's vanity urges him to assume "the king" means himself, but he nevertheless questions Hushai's transfer of loyalty. (For a similar play on misunderstood words, see 1 Sam 28:1-2.)

The devotion Hushai now offers to the one "whom the Lord and all Israel have chosen" (v. 18) is likewise understood by Absalom to mean himself. With these two seeming assurances, it needs only Hushai's pledge to serve Absalom as he did his father to convince Absalom of Hushai's sincerity.

Before Hushai's counsel is sought, Absalom obeys Ahithophel's instructions to take David's concubines. This astute political move to claim the kingship will deal a death blow to any hope of reconciliation between father and son (compare 3:6-11). The tent on the roof recalls David's portentous stroll on the roof of his palace (11:1) and the prophecy that David's neighbor would take his wives in broad daylight (12:11). With tongue in cheek, the narrator comments on the high regard both David and Absalom had for Ahithophel's counsel (v. 23).

17:1-14 Ahithophel and Hushai counsel Absalom. Perceptively analyzing David's situation, Ahithophel advises Absalom to move quickly and silently against the weary king. The discouragement of David's followers will cause panic and flight, leaving the king alone and exposed. With David out of the way, the people can be brought over to Absalom in peace. Ahithophel's apt simile for this, the return of a bride to her husband, is the only flattery for Absalom's swollen ego, but it brings initial agreement for his plan.

As if to show off his new counselor, Absalom asks Hushai to speak as well. Making the most of his chance, Hushai diplomatically suggests that while Ahithophel usually gives good counsel, this time it falls short. Hushai describes effusively David's prowess in war, his tactical skill, the courage of his men, warning that failure on the first attack will discourage Absalom's men. All Israel should therefore be called out and Absalom himself lead the army. Since Ahithophel's plan had not given the prince a role in the pursuit, this alternative must have proved highly attractive to Absalom.

Hushai's elaborate picture of a victory in which all Israel falls upon David and drags the city harboring him into a gorge blinds Absalom and his followers to the unreality of the scheme. The narrator comments that Ahithophel's effective plan was rejected because the Lord planned Absalom's ruin (v. 14).

17:15-22 David crosses the Jordan. Hushai must have feared that Ahithophel's plan could still be adopted, for he urges David not to tarry on this side of the Jordan. The two priests' sons, with the help of a clever woman much like Rahab (see Josh 2), are able to deliver the message in time. David and his people spend the night crossing the Jordan, a move that means both separation and safety.

17:23-29 Help for David. Ahithophel knows that Hushai's plan will bring defeat for Absalom and the rebels. It is not the disappointment of personal rejection that leads him to suicide. Ahithophel is a realist who gambled for high stakes and lost. His is not a shameful death, since he was buried in the family grave. Malefactors earned a pile of stones (compare Josh 7:25-26; 2 Sam 18:17).

Well ahead of Absalom, David reaches Mahanaim (see Gen 32:1-3, 11). Necessary and welcome provisions for David's weary men are brought by the Ammonite prince Shobi, by Machir who had housed Meribbaal before David brought him to Jerusalem (9:4), and by Barzillai, a wealthy adherent of Saul's. This unexpected support from non-Judahites helps restore the strength and courage of the fugitives.

18:1-5 David pleads for Absalom. David's battle preparations include dividing the army into three commands: Joab, Abishai, and the newly arrived Ittai of Gath with his men (15:18-22). Ittai's support may have been decisive because of the large number of soldiers lost to Absalom.

David's bid to lead the soldiers into battle is politely refused, either because they were aware that the king was a target for capture or because they wanted to spare him a confrontation with Absalom. David, who was once praised for slaying tens of thousands (1 Sam 18:7; 29:5), is touchingly told he is worth tens of thousands—behind the lines. Before departing, the soldiers and their commanders hear David's clear request not to harm Absalom.

18:6-18 Absalom defeated. The brief notice of the battle in which David's men are victorious (vv. 6-8) tells of heavy casualties caused by the treacherous forest more than by actual fighting. As with many biblical battles, natural forces—mud, hornets or disease—often bring hostilities to an end. The victory is not to those who fight as much as to the Lord who moves events according to the divine will.

The aftermath is far more dramatic than the battle itself. Absalom is caught by his head in a tree, as the loyal soldier and the disobedient Joab argue about who will kill him (vv. 11-14). The soldier's reminder of David's charge fails to deter Joab, who like a matador places his darts in Absalom and lets his picadors finish him off. As was true with Abner (3:22-27), Joab cannot tolerate a threat to the throne. He is a man of action operating under human counsels; David, more sensitive to the will of God in his life, loves his son more than royal power. Here he is made increasingly aware of the punishing sword that Nathan predicted would never depart from his house (12:10).

With the blowing of the ram's horn (v. 16), the battle for the throne is over. The Israelites flee and Absalom is covered with a mound of stones, a malefactor's burial (compare Josh 7:26). The pillar Absalom built for himself recalls the memorial trophy of Saul (1 Sam 15:12). The notice that Absalom had no son is a direct contradiction to 14:27, which gives him three.

18:19-32 Bringing the news to David. Joab may have had in mind David's execution of the Amalekite who brought news of Saul's death (1:13-15) when he keeps Ahimaaz from running to tell David that Absalom is dead. Although Ahimaaz outruns the Cushite, he is unable on reaching David to relay the bitter truth (v. 29). With distractions about runners sighted and formal greetings (vv. 24-28), the narrative delays tantalizingly for some thirteen verses before the blow of Absalom's death crushes the king.

19:1-5 Joab reproves the grieving David. The simple repeated words "My son, Absalom my son!" convey the depths of David's grief more than any description. As before David had wept and covered his head while ascending the Mount of Olives (15:30) because of Absalom's rebellion, here he weeps with covered head (v. 5) because Absalom is dead. Instead of victory songs and rejoicing, the people have stolen back into the city like a defeated army (v. 4). The use of "stole" recalls that Absalom had stolen the hearts of the people in his attempt to win the throne from his father (15:1-6).

Joab's is the voice of reason, and of the state, in contrast to David's absorption in the death he had so hoped to avoid. Disregarding the king's grief, Joab reminds David that he is insulting the very people who have saved his life. David responds to the threatened loss of support by forcing himself to greet his people. The effects of David's sins here pass beyond his family to touch the throne. He is a beaten man, no longer the self-satisfied monarch of chapters 9 and 10, who enjoyed doing good deeds. Now he is forced to do them.

19:10-15 The return of the northern tribes. The narrative leaves the scene at Mahanaim with its half-hearted victory procession before David to what is left of Absalom's fleeing army. Leaderless and divided in their loyalties, they slowly realize that David was not the failure as king that they had once thought. When David hears they want to restore him (a frequent word in vv. 11-15), he becomes the persuasive politician, reminding them of their common kinship and promising to give Joab's command to Absalom's former general Amasa (17:25). This demotion will rankle the hot-headed Joab until he brings about his own restoration (ch. 20).

19:16-24 The apology of Shimei. This will be the first of three meetings which parallel those of David's descent from the Mount of Olives (16:1-14). The Benjaminite Shimei who had cursed and stoned David hurries to be first in bringing the king across the Jordan. The narrative by repeating the words "cross" and "escort" (the same word in Hebrew) conveys the urgency of the king's crossing.

Ziba comes with Shimei (v. 18), showing that his loyalty was with the Saulides all along. At Shimei's plea for forgiveness, Abishai again offers to take off his head, but David will suffer no vengeance on his day of victory (compare 16:9; 1 Sam 11:13). David refers to Abishai as a satan, or adversary, as Jesus did of Peter (Matt 16:21-23).

19:25-31 Meribbaal explains his absence. Blaming his delay on Ziba's betrayal, the crippled Meribbaal shows his loyalty by appearing as a mourner. Although Meribbaal claims Ziba has slandered him and flatters David by calling him an angel of God (v. 28), David answers him brusquely and reassigns him half the estate he had previously given Ziba (16:1-4). This encounter does not prove Meribbaal's loyalty, but it is telling that Meribbaal is willing to let Ziba have the whole property as long as David is safe (v. 31).

19:32-41a David tries to reward Barzillai. Although he is a Benjaminite, Barzillai has shown his allegiance to David in his gift of supplies at Mahanaim (17:27-29). Although he is a man of substance, like Nabal (1 Sam 25:2), the wise, generous Barzillai is a pleasant opposite to the foolish, stingy Nabal.

From Barzillai's protest that he is too old to enjoy life at court, we learn how ancient kings spent their days.

19:41b-44 The smoldering division. By this time all of Judah and half of Israel are with David. The Israelites, who had been reconsidering their position, accuse the Judahites of stealing David away, perhaps in an attempt to cover their own indecision. The Judahites defend themselves vigorously, despite Israelite protests that they have a greater share in the king (v. 44). David's return to Jerusalem cloaks a deeper division between the two parts of the land which will erupt decisively under David's grandson Rehoboam (1 Kgs 12).

20:1-3 Israel follows Sheba. A new leader for the dissatisfied Israelites who had recently brought David across the Jordan appears in a Benjaminite named Sheba, whom the narrator labels a rebellious individual (literally, a "son of Belial" as in 1 Sam 1:16; 10:27; 25:17; 30:22). With Sheba's cry "Every man to his tent," the men of Israel again desert David (compare 1 Kgs 12:16). Once in Jerusalem, David puts the ten dishonored concubines who had been left behind to guard the house (15:16; 16:21-22) into a guard-house (confinement) for the rest of their lives.

20:4-13 The pursuit of Sheba. David in addressing the new threat from Sheba, assigns Amasa to muster the Judahite army. When Amasa fails, David, bypassing Joab, sends Abishai in pursuit. Suddenly we find (v. 7) Joab and his men marching behind Abishai. For all David's reluctance to deal with him, Joab seems too powerful to be suppressed.

On the way, at Gibeon, Joab interrupts the pursuit to eliminate his rival Amasa with characteristic ruthlessness. By killing Amasa, Joab has rid David of one more political problem; this time we do not hear that David wept. The people standing about the dead soldier wallowing in his blood are dismayed. Only after the body is covered and removed from the highway can the pursuit of Sheba continue.

20:14-22 The wise woman of Abel Bethmaacah. When Joab called on a wise woman before in chapter 14, she was told what she was to do and say. Here a wise woman tells Joab what to do (v. 16). Their conversation is about his planned destruction of a city which is a mother in Israel, that is, a place to

which Israelites in trouble can resort for advice. To prevent this, the woman is willing to sacrifice one life for her people. With the bloody murder of Amasa just accomplished, it is high irony for Joab to deny so vehemently that he wants to ruin or destroy anything (v. 20). When the woman delivers Sheba's severed head, Joab can sound the horn for retreat.

20:23-26 Government leaders. Joab is securely in command with the restored government in Jerusalem, but Abishai is strangely missing. With this list of officials, the long narrative segment contained in chapters 9 to 20 ends.

VII. APPENDICES

2 Sam 21–24

These chapters supply information about David which does not fit well into the continuous narrative of 2 Sam 9–20. David's devotion to the Lord is here highlighted so that his loyalty to the divine covenant recalls the Deuteronomistic theme of obedience to the Lord and its attendant blessings. David's life story is concluded in 1 Kgs 1–2 with Solomon's accession to the throne and David's death.

21:1-14 David relieves the famine. These events may have preceded David's taking of Meribbaal into his house (ch. 9). Here after consulting the Lord according to his usual practice (see 1 Sam 23:2, 4, 9-12; 30:7-8; 2 Sam 2:1), David is told that the blood vengeance incurred by Saul in an otherwise unknown attack must be avenged. Saul had apparently violated the covenant which the Gibeonites had tricked the Israelites into making (Josh 9:3-27) by wholesale slaughter. It is not the surviving Gibeonites but the Lord who demands restitution. The Gibeonites, however, decide the means of atonement, for which David chooses two sons of Saul and five grandsons for execution.

With a devotion like that of Antigone to her dead brother, Rizpah guards the bodies of the slain, two of whom are her own sons (v. 8). A death which involved exposure to the birds of the air and beasts of the field was considered a horror in Israel. Report of this kindness to the dead arouses David's sympathy so that he has all seven, as well as the bodies of Saul and Jonathan (1 Sam 31:11-13) buried in the tomb of Saul's father Kish (v. 14).

The account of their deaths includes two foreshadowings of the end of the famine: the barley harvest is about to begin (v. 9) and the rain is about to come (v. 10). The bodies are sacrifices to plead with the Lord for a good harvest by means of expiating past unrepented sins. The incident is an example of the Israelite idea of collective guilt for which the people suffer along with the king when he has offended God.

21:15-22 David and his heroes. There follow four short accounts of battle with Philistine giants who are equipped like Goliath (1 Sam 17:4-7). The story of Abishai's rescue of David (v. 17) shows how necessary to him were the "ruthless" sons of Zeruiah (3:39). The reference to David as the lamp of Israel indicates the soldiers' affectionate regard (compare 18:3-4). The confusion between verse 19, with its attribution of Goliath's slaying to Elhanan, and 1 Sam 17:48-51, where David is the hero, finds resolution in 1 Chr 20:5. There Elhanan is said to slay Goliath's brother, thus giving David and Elhanan one giant each.

22:1-51 David's rock of deliverance. In a majestic poem, a duplicate of Psalm 18, David praises the Lord in humility and gratitude for having saved him from his enemies. The opening verses offer seven synonyms for the Lord as savior: rock, fortress, deliverer, shield, horn, stronghold, refuge. The Lord keeps David from violence (v. 3) and rescues him from the violent man (v. 49). The Lord hears the psalmist's voice (v. 7), but foreigners hear the same voice, now clothed with power to subdue other nations (v. 45).

The Lord's action in David's life is compared to the action of nature: breakers surge and floods overwhelm (v. 5); the earth sways, quakes, trembles, shakes (v. 8); fire, wind, darkness, cloud, lightning, waters appear in tumultuous action to portray the Lord's response to the cry of the persecuted one (vv. 5-17). The Lord's rescue is described in mythological terms: The Most High mounts a cherub and flies, borne on the wind (v. 11; compare 1 Sam 4:4; 2 Sam 6:2; Exod 25:10-22). The reasons for the rescue are the Lord's love (v. 20) and because David was found free of guilt (v. 21), loyal (v. 22), and innocent (v. 25).

In the center of the psalm, the poet addresses the Lord directly. "You are faithful . . . you are wholehearted . . . sincere . . . astute . . . you save . . . you are my lamp . . . you brighten the darkness" (vv. 26-29). The Lord deals with people according to their righteousness. Note the contrasts: the sincere vs. the crooked (v. 27), lowly vs. lofty (v. 28), darkness vs. light (v. 29).

Resuming the third person, God is presented again as rock (v. 32), the poet's way is unerring and his feet are swift (v. 34). Preparing for war, God trains David to use the bow and girds him for battle (vv. 33, 35, 40). With this God-given strength, the poet overcomes his enemies, who flee and are destroyed (v. 41), are forsaken (v. 42), ground to dust and trampled (v. 43), enslaved (v. 44), obedient (v. 45), fawning and cringing (v. 46). The poem ends with praise for the Lord's kindness to the anointed king, "to David and his posterity forever" (v. 51; compare 1 Sam 2:10).

23:1-7 David praises God. These "last words" of David begin in the style of the oracles of Balaam (Num 24:3-4, 15-16; Gen 49; Deut 33). After describing himself as raised up, anointed, and favored by the Mighty One of Israel, the poet attributes his words to the spirit of the Lord (v. 2). A just and God-fearing ruler is compared to the action of morning light playing on wet grass (compare Hos 6:3). David's rule has been established in an eternal covenant (2 Sam 7), for he has seen salvation and the fulfillment of every desire (vv. 5-6). By contrast the wicked are dangerous to the touch and like thorns destined for the fire (compare Ps 118:12).

23:8-39 David's heroes. David has attached to himself a loyal group of outstanding warriors. Three are singled out for strength and bravery (vv. 8-12). Together they risk their lives to draw water for David from a well guarded by the enemy (v. 16). David's pouring out of the water before the Lord links their dedication to him with an act of worship. Of the remaining warriors cited, only Abishai and Benaiah have significant roles in David's story.

24:1-9 David's temptation. Ancient Israelites saw the anger of God in every calamity. Here the pestilence in Israel begins because of David's curiosity to know how great his people were, knowledge evidently reserved for the Lord alone. Joab tries to dissuade David from taking a census but fails (vv. 3-4). His subsequent journey through the land gives an idea of the extent of Israel during David's reign. The kingdom is bordered by the Mediterranean on the west, Gilead on the east, Dan in the north, and Beer-sheba in the south. By counting women, children and the aged, the total population could be as much as five times the one million three hundred thousand listed (v. 9).

24:10-17 David repents. Once again David regrets an impulsive act (compare 1 Sam 24:6). The prophet Gad offers a threefold expiation, all of which contain three time units. Seeing the Lord as more merciful than humans, David chooses the three-day pestilence, the shortest but the most intense.

As the famine of 21:9 ended at the beginning of the barley harvest, so here the plague breaks out at the time of the wheat harvest, both signs of divine mitigation. These, with the Lord's merciful staying of the destroying angel's hand before Jerusalem (v. 16), are lessons of God's love in the midst of trial. David sounds a progressive note in ancient theology when, instead of the accepted collective atonement, he asks the Lord to punish him and his family alone.

24:18-25 The threshing floor of Araunah. The command to build an altar in Jerusalem, with the promises to make a lasting house for David (7:8-16), is the basis for Israel's Zion theology which celebrates God's holy mountain Jerusalem as the focal worship place for all humankind (see Isa 2–4; Psalms 46, 47, 76, 84, 87, 122).

David's need to purchase the threshing floor of Araunah means that he did not own all the land in his capital and that Canaanites shared the land with Israel. As Abraham made his ownership of Sarah's grave in Machpelah legal by buying rather than accepting the site as a gift (Gen 23:10-16), so David refuses Araunah's offer and insists on paying a high price for land that will later become the ground for the temple.

Epilogue

The Lord has satisfied the people with two important needs: a prophet to deliver the divine word and a king to govern them. These are the leaders by whom the Lord guides their history, punishing them or delivering them as required. God exacts obedience, loyalty, and gratitude, but does not abandon the sinner. The lives of all are bathed in God's goodness and love.

1 AND 2 KINGS

Alice L. Laffey, R.S.M.

INTRODUCTION

The two books of Kings are, properly speaking, the final chapters of a larger section of the Old Testament known as the Deuteronomistic History. This history also includes the books of Deuteronomy, Joshua, Judges, and 1 and 2 Samuel.

In Deuteronomy the law is set forth. Fidelity to the law is to be Israel's response to its covenant relationship with Yahweh, its God. The book details the responsibilities of the people once they have entered the land promised by God to their ancestors.

The Book of Joshua describes Israel's successful conquest of the land of Canaan under the capable leadership of Joshua, a conquest easily and speedily accomplished because of the faithfulness of the people to Yahweh.

The Book of Judges gives a more realistic account of the Israelites' entrance into Canaan. Progress was slow and not always totally successful. Because the people were not always faithful to Yahweh and often worshiped idols, the Lord left Canaanites to dwell alongside the Israelites in the land. During this period of approximately 240 years of Israelite history, leadership in the land took the form of judges—military leaders or prudent advisors whose governing role was not hereditary.

The Book of Samuel introduces Samuel, the last of Israel's judges, the prophet who will anoint Israel's first king. Despite some opposition, Saul is named Israel's first monarch. However, his unfaithfulness to Yahweh leads to his downfall, and he is replaced by David, the Lord's servant, on whom God's spirit rests. The Second Book of Samuel continues

the account of David's rise to power and records his covenant with Yahweh, in which he is promised a dynasty.

The two books of Kings tell the story of David's dynasty. David's son Solomon succeeds him as king and the dynasty is initiated: the Lord's promise is fulfilled. Moreover, Solomon builds a temple for Yahweh, also in accord with the Lord's promise to David.

The First Book of Kings details Solomon's reign, the building of Yahweh's temple, and Solomon's eventual degeneration into unfaithfulness. Solomon's sin and his son's stupidity lead to the division of the kingdom into north and south—Israel and Judah. Much of the remainder of this first book deals with the northern kingdom, especially its idolatrous leaders; for them there can be no lasting dynasty.

The Second Book of Kings continues to assess Israel's and Judah's monarchies. Judah weaves an intricate pattern among its more or less good and bad kings, in contrast to the consistent pattern of evil found in the northern kingdom. Finally the evil northern kingdom is definitively punished; the Lord sends Assyria to conquer it, and the Israelites are taken into exile. Eventually the southern kingdom follows a similar path. Because of infidelity—most explicitly because of the sins of the evil King Manasseh—the Babylonians destroy the temple and lead the people of Judah into exile. Thus do the Second Book of Kings and the Deuteronomistic History end, except for the hopeful note of Yahweh's continued faithfulness in the final three verses of 2 Kings. There it is recorded that Judah's exiled king, Jehoiachin, is released from prison and receives kindly treatment from Babylon's new king.

The Deuteronomistic editor

Most scholars agree that these seven Old Testament books—Deuteronomy, Joshua, Judges, 1 and 2 Samuel, 1 and 2 Kings—originally existed in fragments written at different times by different people in different places. These sources were combined by one or more editors into a literary and theological unity. Some of the material may be as old as the tenth century B.C.E., dating back to the reign of King Solomon; other material, such as the account of Judah's destruction, cannot be dated before the sixth century B.C.E. A final author, usually named the Deuteronomistic editor or the Deuteronomistic historian and referred to as "Dtr" by scholars, wove together the sources at his disposal into a unified, interpreted account of Israel's past.

The Deuteronomistic theology

A consistent theological thread, the perspective from which the entire Deuteronomistic History is recorded, delineates the basic postures between God and the people. Yahweh initiates good for the people, but they turn from God and worship idols. This evil provokes the Lord's anger, and God's response is to punish the people, for example, by selling them into the hands of their enemies. The oppression the people experience leads them to turn again to their God and to ask for forgiveness and deliverance. The Lord hears the people's prayer and saves them, only to have them soon afterward turn from the Lord once again. The pattern—God's good, Israel's sin, God's anger and punishment, Israel's affliction and prayer, God's forgiveness—repeats itself frequently throughout the History.

This theology surfaces in the books of Kings in the form of blessings for kings' fidelity (for example, Solomon's wealth and honor because he sought wisdom to govern the Lord's people) and punishment for kings' sins (for example, the denial to Jeroboam of a dynasty because he caused Israel to sin). Consistently, fidelity issues in well-being, while unfaithfulness leads inevitably to ruin.

As one reads through the History and recognizes this frequently repeated pattern, one wonders if they (we) will ever learn.

Themes

1. **The Davidic covenant.** 2 Sam 7 introduces a special relationship between the Lord and King David. This special relationship, often called the Davidic covenant, is a further explication of the Lord's covenant with Israel. David is "the Lord's servant," "a man after the Lord's own heart." Because the Lord is with David, he is victorious over the Philistines; the Lord grants him rest and enables him to build for himself a palace of cedar. David sins, but he acknowledges and repents of his sin; though he is punished, he is forgiven, and the Lord neither rejects him nor revokes the covenant. Thus David becomes a model—one who walked in the ways of the Lord.

This theme of the Lord's special love for David, and David's faithful response, continues to appear throughout the books of Kings. The fidelity of Yahweh to Solomon and to Judah's kings is very often explained as a consequence of David's intimate relationship with the Lord; David's was a proven faithfulness from which others benefited. We note, then, that Judah's good kings are "like David" in their obedience to the Lord's commands and the evil kings are "not like David." Solomon and Judah's kings are buried "with their ancestors in the city of David." A special effort is made to show that each successive king of Judah is the son of his father, that is, a direct descendant of David. In fact, the Lord relents of the punishment that his people deserve and postpones the end of the kingdom "for the sake of David, his servant."

2. **The Davidic dynasty.** As a consequence of the Lord's covenant with him, David, unlike Saul, will have a dynasty; his sons will rule after him. This theme underlies much of the books of Kings. The promise is fulfilled when Solomon succeeds David. Again, according to the theology of the Deuteronomistic editor, fidelity leads to blessing, wealth, and prosperity for the king and for the people, while unfaithfulness brings ill. Solomon's fidelity leads to wisdom, wealth, honor, and the temple, but his infidelity leads to the division of the kingdom. Yet David's dynasty

remains intact. One tribe, Judah, remains loyal to David's descendants. For some four hundred years, and until the final chapter of 2 Kings, there is a son of David on the throne of Judah.

3. **The Lord's temple.** David is willing to build the Lord a temple, but the Lord prefers that David's son Solomon build it. Its construction is described in the early chapters of 1 Kings. If Yahweh is important, then the dwelling place of his presence must be grand. Three chapters are devoted to elaborate descriptions of the temple's construction, and finally, in 1 Kgs 8, Solomon dedicates it.

The temple figures prominently in the remainder of the History. The major sin of Jeroboam, Israel's first king, was that he built shrines at Bethel and Dan to prevent the people from going south to Jerusalem to worship. Those kings of Judah judged by the Deuteronomistic editor to be "good in the eyes of the Lord" are those who elaborately adorn the temple, who bring offerings to it, who order its restoration, and who remove the idols brought there by their evil predecessors. When Judean kings form alliances with foreign nations, the temple is pillaged and stripped of its treasures. Inevitably, the destruction of the kingdom of Judah and the demise of Yahweh's temple go hand in hand.

4. **Prophecy and fulfillment.** Throughout the books of Kings we find many examples of the editor's conviction that God is faithful. God's word, spoken through chosen representatives, is effective; it always comes to fulfillment. Because the Deuteronomistic editor viewed Israel's history as the lived-out expression of the Israelites' fidelity or infidelity to their covenant relationship with Yahweh, prophets promise, warn, and threaten. They reveal the future consequences of present attitudes and action. They do not speak the word of the Lord in vain. The power of God will bring that word to pass, and the History records explicitly that it does.

5. **The law.** Leadership's fidelity to Yahweh, or lack thereof, is expressed throughout the Deuteronomistic History, including the books of Kings, in terms of Israel's obedience to Yahweh's law. The Mosaic law and the response of David's descendants are the measurements by which to evaluate the monarchy. The Deuteronomistic editor interprets the events of Israelite history according as the kings and people obey or disobey these laws.

These five themes—covenant, dynasty, temple, prophecy, and law—are interdependent and pervade the History. They are key instruments in the Deuteronomistic editor's exposition of his theology, and central to the unity of the books of Kings.

Women and the books of Kings

Many commentators do not notice the significant roles played by women during the period of Israel's monarchies and how these figures have been incorporated into the books of Kings. It is important not only to recognize the evil leadership of a Jezebel, who even outdid her husband in idolatry, malice, and deceit, but also to note other female characters who significantly affected the course of Israel's history: Bathsheba, the queen of Sheba, Jeroboam's wife, the widow for whom Elisha multiplied oil, the Israelite servant girl and Naaman's wife, who together with Elisha made possible his cure. This commentary will make a special effort to point out the contributions of women.

In a similar vein, one cannot accept unqualifiedly that the Deuteronomist—or the Chronicler either, for that matter—was a man. However, considering the period in which the texts were produced, as well as their content and style, I am inclined to attribute them to male authorship.

Then and now

Though the final editing of the books of Kings took place no later than the late sixth century B.C.E., we, as a believing community, regard their word as sacred and as meaningful to us. It is important that we understand the context in which these books were written—by whom and for whom—and that we seek to understand what they meant to the people to whom they were originally addressed. But we must go further. If these texts are to have meaning for twentieth-century Jews and Christians, we must dialogue with the texts against the socio-political and cultural situations in which we find ourselves. We must together seek to understand what constitutes twentieth-century covenant fidelity and, conversely, what forms our idolatry takes.

COMMENTARY: 1 KINGS

PART I: THE REIGN OF SOLOMON

1 Kgs 1:1–11:43

To better understand many of the allusions given in the introductory chapters of the First Book of Kings, some insight into the life of the Israelites in their land in the first millennium B.C.E. might be helpful. First, let us consider the problem of syncretism (the fusion of different religious practices) and foreign women. The Israelites worshiped Yahweh, the God whose marvelous acts in history on their behalf had brought them out of Egypt and into a land that had become their own. But once in this land, they were frequently tempted to incorporate into Yahwism the fertility cults of their Canaanite neighbors. This can be partly explained by their new dependence on agriculture and by their need to guarantee a fertile land and a prosperous harvest. Yahweh had done wondrous things, but could Yahweh make the crops grow?

The infiltration of pagan fertility practices into the Israelite religion was often occasioned by the marriage of Israelite men to Canaanite and other "foreign" women. These women would retain their belief in fertility gods and goddesses after their marriage to Israelite men and were, consequently, often accused of leading Israel into idolatry. That is why the Deuteronomistic historian warns against intermarriage (for example, Josh 23:12) and why, in the text, marriage to foreign women is frequently a foreshadowing of doom.

One must keep in mind, also, that the text we have as Scripture is theologized history; that is to say, history has been shaped here by a theological perspective. A twentieth-century interpreter of history may expect documents to convey what really happened and may facilely label as untrue the shaping of events (for example, by deliberate omissions, emphases, editorial comments, even literary constructions). Yet, are we really so different when we differentiate between an economic history and a political history (with appropriate emphases and omissions), or easily recognize that a Southern interpretation of the American Civil War may read very differently from one produced in Massachusetts?

Applying this principle to the books of

Kings, one can only presume that things may not have actually happened precisely as they are here described. In keeping with the intention of the final editor to show how fidelity to Yahweh led to success and the converse, the characters' actual history—what really happened to them and to Israel during their reigns must be interpreted as the consequence of their fidelity or infidelity to Yahweh. This commentary will look closely at how the text portrays the characters and will suggest, when there is obvious inconsistency, what was probably happening in Israel's history.

The first chapters of 1 Kings connect the previous two Old Testament books, 1 and 2 Samuel, to what follows. The "hero" of 2 Samuel, King David, dies and bestows the kingship on Solomon, the son of his favored wife, Bathsheba, despite the fact that an elder son, Adonijah, is a lively contender for the throne. The chapters that follow emphasize that Solomon's reign is characterized by devotion to the Lord, thereby explaining its political and economic success. Solomon begins by acknowledging his fidelity to the covenant, his reverence for the Lord. It is *for the Lord* and because of the Lord's gift that he will succeed as king. The last chapters (11–12), however, show a shift in Solomon's loyalty. He who had "loved the Lord" now "loves foreign women" (11:1), who lead his heart astray. This judgment accounts for the fact that Solomon, because he oppressed his own people (for example, by taxation and forced labor), lost their support—so much so that the kingdom is split after his death.

1:1-4 David on his deathbed. Most scholars believe that this incident—David, now old and "cold," that is, unable to engage in sexual intercourse—functions as an inclusion. (Inclusion is the technique of framing a literary unit by using the same or a similar word, phrase, or episode at both the beginning and end of it.) David's first sin was his sexual encounter with Bathsheba (2 Sam 11). There he took for himself a woman who already belonged to another. Here, ironically enough, Abishag, a "beautiful girl" legitimately his, is not able to warm and arouse him. In this patriarchal society a woman is understood to be the possession first of her father and then of her husband; yet these women—Abishag and

Bathsheba—significantly affect the life of the king, the well-being of the kingdom, and even the circumstances surrounding the king's death. The verses also point out that David, who had stayed home "in the spring when kings go out to war" (2 Sam 11:1), will not die in battle like his predecessor Saul. The kingdom, by the time of David's death, is well established and at peace.

1:5-10 Ambition of Adonijah. One might expect that David's elder son Adonijah would succeed his father as king. Even before his father's death and, seemingly, with his father's tacit approval, Adonijah prepares to take over. He acquires chariots, drivers, and henchmen, the appropriate possessions of one who will soon "lead in warfare and fight the people's battles" (see 1 Sam 8:20). He rallies support, yet he lacks crucial support from Yahweh's spokesman, the prophet Nathan. This, surely, is an evil omen.

1:11-53 Solomon proclaimed king. Nathan supports Solomon as Israel's future king and plans accordingly. Nathan served as the Lord's spokesman to David at least twice before. It was he who communicated to David the Lord's promise of a dynasty (2 Sam 7), and he who communicated the Lord's judgment of David's sin with Bathsheba (2 Sam 12). David has every reason to take Nathan's word seriously. Now, to convince David that Solomon should reign after him, Nathan arranges a meeting between David and Bathsheba. She is to remind David of his promise to her that her son will succeed to the throne. Nathan assures Bathsheba that he, too, will try to persuade David that Solomon should be king.

Bathsheba and Nathan execute their plan successfully. David names Solomon as his successor, orders Solomon to ride on his mule, to be anointed king, and to sit on his throne. The contender, Adonijah, now has no chance. His only hope is that Solomon will spare his life, which, at least for now, he does.

Was this text written during Solomon's reign, at his court? Is it, in fact, the legitimation of a conspiracy? From a historical perspective, perhaps one must answer in the affirmative; yet, from a theological perspective, the spokesman of Yahweh, supported by David's wife, has indeed revealed Yahweh's will.

2:1-11 David's last instructions and death. David's last advice to his son has to do, first and foremost, with covenant fidelity. Solomon is to revere the Lord as David has done; only thus will Solomon be guaranteed success in his undertakings; only thus can it be guaranteed that a descendant of David will remain on the throne. This is the first time explicit conditions are made regarding the dynasty; its continuance is dependent on faithful response to the covenant.

David's other advice regards specific persons: Joab, Barzillai's sons, and Shimei. Because Joab, David's general, had, without David's knowledge and consent, stabbed Abner (see 2 Sam 3) and Amasa (see 2 Sam 20), David wants Solomon to punish Joab. (One must ask here whether Solomon wants Joab out of the way because he had supported Adonijah, whether this request of David legitimates Solomon's decision to kill a political enemy.)

Barzillai, in contrast, represents loyalty. He had helped David flee from Absalom, and such faithfulness merits reward. Twice elsewhere in the Deuteronomistic History (2 Sam 9:10; 2 Kgs 25:29) eating at table with the king is an explicit sign of favor.

Finally, Shimei should be punished. David has kept his promise and has not put him to death, as his treason deserves (see 2 Sam 19:24). On the other hand, such infidelity cannot be ignored. Solomon's reign must not be thwarted by potential conspirators.

Having spoken his last, David dies. He had reigned seven years in Hebron and thirty-three years in Jerusalem, that is, a total of forty years. Whether these numbers denote historical accuracy or are used symbolically is uncertain. (In many biblical texts, including the Deuteronomistic History, as will become evident, the numbers three, four, seven and twelve [thirty, three hundred, and the like] express totality or completion.) David is laid to rest with his ancestors and buried in the City of David. This assertion is the first of many similar expressions that occur throughout the Deuteronomistic History with reference to the Davidic kings. The Deuteronomistic editor explicitly refers to the place of burial to emphasize the close connection between David and each king of Judah.

2:12-46 The kingdom made secure. David legitimated Solomon's elimination of Joab and Shimei as political opponents. Solomon must now legitimate his removal of

Adonijah, his half-brother, for Adonijah will be a potential threat to the throne as long as he lives. Adonijah asks for Abishag, the woman who had "warmed" the dying David (1:3). Recognizing Bathsheba's influence with Solomon, Adonijah petitions her to intercede for him that he might take Abishag for his wife. Solomon's response is a vehement refusal, for he recognizes such a request as a clear bid for the throne (note again the indirect but very real importance of Abishag; compare 2 Sam 16:22). Solomon is now justified in ordering his brother's death.

Solomon next removes the priest Abiathar from his position of prestige (v. 27). After all, he had supported Adonijah. The text legitimates this decision by a reference to the prophetic denunciation of Eli's house (see 1 Sam 2:30-36). The word of the Lord is thus fulfilled.

Another threat to Solomon's throne is David's general, Joab. Joab deserves death for killing two men without David's knowledge, and David himself had wished it, or so we are to understand. Coincidentally, it just so happens that Joab, too, had been one of Adonijah's supporters! Once Abiathar is out of the way, Solomon replaces him with Zadok; once Joab is out of the way, Solomon replaces him with Benaiah (v. 35). Obviously, both Zadok and Benaiah had been strong supporters of Solomon (see 1 Kgs 1:8).

Finally, some excuse has to be found to make Shimei's death legitimate. David had wanted Shimei to be punished for his disloyalty, and Solomon has only to find a way to eliminate him. Solomon creates circumstances conducive for Shimei to violate a sworn oath, and then Solomon waits. His patience is rewarded, and eventually Shimei is put to death (v. 46).

Having removed all the opposition, Solomon is now secure on the throne. The theological perspective of the text's author has established that Yahweh's will, expressed through the prophet Nathan and through David, has been accomplished. If we are to interpret verse 39 historically, it took three years to make the kingdom fully secure.

3:1-15 Wisdom of Solomon. With political threats removed, political alliances are in order. Solomon wastes no time in securing the "friendship" of Egypt by marrying the daughter of Pharaoh. This removes the possibility

of invasion from the south and creates the peaceful climate in which Solomon can build his palace, the Lord's temple, and the walls of Jerusalem. Though he has intermarried, no mention is made of idolatry. In fact, his worshiping at the high places—activity that is later associated with infidelity to Yahweh—is explained by the fact that the temple had not yet been built (v. 2).

The first part of Solomon's reign is characterized by covenant fidelity to the Lord, by love and obedience. He worships at the best shrine and, from the abundance of prosperity with which the Lord has blessed him, he makes generous sacrifices to Yahweh. Often, as here, dreams occasion an encounter with Yahweh (note, for example, Nathan's dream in 2 Sam 7). In the ensuing dialogue, Solomon perceives himself as Yahweh's servant and requests from the Lord an understanding heart by which to govern the people and to distinguish right from wrong.

Yahweh responds generously. Solomon's request will be granted, and, in addition, he will receive the standard blessings of covenant fidelity—riches and glory and a long life. (When these texts were being written, the Israelites did not believe in life after death. Therefore, for the Deuteronomistic historian, reward for covenant fidelity took the form of material prosperity, a long life, and progeny to continue one's life.) Solomon's reverence for the Lord, proven by his altruistic request, would merit him wisdom in addition to the usual covenant blessings. Solomon awakes from his dream and again sacrifices to the Lord (an inclusion).

3:16-28 Solomon's judgment. Solomon immediately begins to make judgments with the understanding heart the Lord has given him. Cleverly, he sets forth the condition that will enable him to determine the real mother of the living child, and his insightful decision wins the awe of the people, that is, the glory that the Lord had promised.

4:1-6 Chief officers of the kingdom. Solomon's cabinet, if we can call it that, was composed of Jehoshaphat, who had supported David (see 2 Sam 8:16; 20:24); Abiathar (the same Abiathar rejected in 1 Kgs 2:27?); Benaiah and Zadok, who had supported Solomon in his bid for the throne (see 1 Kgs 1:8); sons of Solomon's supporters (Azariah, son of Zadok, and two sons of Nathan); and, finally, some unknown men not referred to elsewhere in the Bible.

4:7–5:14 Solomon's royal state. Just as there had been twelve sons of Jacob and twelve tribes of Israel, so now the land is divided into twelve parts. This time each commissary is to contribute one month's supply of provisions to the king's household. This is the first textual evidence that Solomon used the people for his own benefit. What Samuel had warned—that the king would set the people to do his plowing and his harvesting, that he would tithe crops and vineyards and flocks (see 1 Sam 8:12, 15, 17)—is here acknowledged.

Each commissary has a leader, but the identity of the leader seems to be of no particular interest. Seven men are named, as if to distinguish them from other persons similarly named. Five are identified merely as the son of somebody. None is delineated elsewhere in the History in greater detail. Nevertheless, one may safely conclude that what these men have in common is loyalty to Solomon.

The shrewd organization of Solomon's empire ensures peace and prosperity in the land. For this reason Solomon continues to be characterized by the God-given gifts of wisdom, exceptional understanding, and knowledge. Further, his political savvy is complemented by his literary and musical talents, as well as by his expertise in biology. No wonder he wins international acclaim!

[The editors of the New American Bible have rearranged several verses of the original Hebrew here and elsewhere for the sake of better comprehension. It is for this reason that verse 7 begins chapter 5 and verse 20 follows verse 8.]

5:15-32 Preparations for the temple. Solomon builds alliances wherever he can (see 1 Kgs 3:1), and the one he continues with the Phoenicians stemmed from David's time (see 2 Sam 5:11). Appealing to his father's past history of good relations with Hiram, Solomon obtains Lebanese lumber and workers for the construction of the temple. Solomon's kingship is from the Lord, and the building of the temple will fulfill Nathan's prophecy (see 2 Sam 7:13). In this way the text justifies the consolidation of kingship and religion in Jerusalem.

The first stages of temple-building are marked by cooperation between the two countries. The terms of their agreement or "covenant" are observed by both parties. But is there internal cooperation? Or, to put the question another way, under what conditions and obligations do the Israelites participate in the building project? Do the thirty thousand workmen, in relays of ten (note the numbers!) represent forced labor? Does their resentment cause some of the hostility the dynasty experiences at the end of Solomon's reign (see 1 Kgs 11–12)?

Scholars suggest that there was an anti-temple faction in Israel, just as there had been an anti-monarchy faction (see 1 Sam 8). According to this view, a conservative group—how extensive we do not know—resisted a permanent dwelling for Yahweh's presence in their midst. To join temple and king would be to become even more "like the other nations." The presence of such a conservative element would explain why David had not built a temple. It would also explain a certain resistance to temple-building during Solomon's reign. Moreover, the resistance would have been compounded by inhumane treatment of the temple workers.

6:1-38 Building of the temple. The specific dating we encounter here relates this new and important event to two other major events in Israel's history: the Exodus and Solomon's accession to the throne. This dating pattern is common in the Old Testament, including the books of Kings. Dating is never given by year (for example, 964 B.C.E.), but by relating an event to other significant events.

Next follows a detailed description of the temple. The sacredness of the temple is attested to by the statement that as much work as possible is done at a distance from the building site (v. 7). Its magnificence is asserted by the frequent references to fine woods (olive, fir, and imported cedar), finely carved stone, and an abundance of gold and other decoration. The holy of holies, which would contain the ark of the covenant, is singled out by its elaborate wealth of ornamentation.

Inserted into the account of the building of the temple is a prophetic word that sets conditions for Yahweh's fulfilling his promise to David (the lasting dynasty?), as well as for Yahweh's dwelling in the midst of Israel and not forsaking them: Solomon must observe the Lord's statutes, ordinances, and commands (vv. 11-13). This text is a strong echo of Deuteronomistic theology: obedience will yield good, but the blessings are dependent on fidelity. The chapter ends with the assertion that the temple was completed seven years after it was begun.

7:1-12 Building of the palace. Immediately after saying that it took seven years to complete the Lord's dwelling the text tells us that it took thirteen years to complete the king's dwelling. Are we to conclude that "seven" is meant to be symbolic for the completion of the temple, while "thirteen" is intended as an accurate estimate of the time it took to build Solomon's palace? Or are we to conclude that the king cared more for the grandeur of his own house than he did for the Lord's dwelling? Whereas the Lord's temple measures 60 by 20 by 25 cubits, the palace is larger: 100 by 50 by 30 cubits (a cubit varied from 15 to 22 inches). And, in addition, Solomon builds a tribunal, and separate living quarters for himself and Pharaoh's daughter. Everything is well made; he makes a court and a porch for his own palace similar to those made for the temple.

7:13-51 Furnishing of the temple. These verses form an inclusion—temple, palace, temple. Although the temple itself, including the altar, the table for the showbread, and the lampstands, is heavily laden with gold, many of the articles made for use inside the temple quarters—the columns, the water tank, the stands, basins, pots, shovels, and bowls—are shaped from bronze. Hiram, king of Tyre, had been contracted to provide cedar for the temple; now Hiram, a skilled metalworker and an Israelite whose father had been from Tyre, is contracted to help with the furnishings.

David's act of dedicating offerings to the Lord becomes a precedent for Solomon and future kings (v. 51). Such gifts to God are safeguarded in the temple treasury. Whether this treasury was also the palace treasury is uncertain, but pillaging valuables from the Lord's dwelling would certainly be regarded as a serious offense. When everything is completed, the temple is dedicated.

8:1-21 Dedication of the temple. Verses 1-4 bring together the old and the new: the elders, the tribal leaders, the princes of the ancestral houses, the ark and the tent of meeting, the Levites and the priests, the City of David. Whether the text reflects a combination of sources or a later effort to win all to Solomon and the temple is uncertain. In any case, the past—Israel's former leadership and Yahweh's former dwelling place—comes now to the temple at Jerusalem.

The entire community of Israel, Solomon included, is said to have sacrificed sheep and oxen to the Lord and to have watched the priests march in procession with the ark, bringing it to its resting place in the temple's holy of holies. The reader is explicitly reminded that the ark contains the two stone tablets, which symbolize the Lord's covenant with Israel (v. 9). What better way to connect king and Yahweh, to show Solomon's fidelity to the Lord (compare 1 Kgs 3:4, 15), and to express the approval of the people for what Solomon had built? The cloud that filled the temple is a clear indication of the Lord's approval (compare Exod 16:10; 40:38; Num 9:18; and many similar texts). Again, validation is made for king and temple. The prophetic promises made in 2 Sam 7 that David's son would sit on the throne and that David's son would build a temple for the Lord have now both been fulfilled.

8:22-66 Solomon's prayer. The remainder of this long chapter is constructed as Solomon's prayer to the Lord at the time of the temple's dedication. Verses 22-26 are similar in form to David's prayer in 2 Sam 7:22-29: first the singularity of the Lord is extolled; then Yahweh is thanked for the blessings already bestowed and for future divine promise; finally the Lord is asked to effect the remainder of the promise. Here the specific request is for Solomon's sons and the continuation of the dynasty. Solomon then cleverly brings together pro-temple and anti-temple sentiments. He affirms that no place, not even the highest heavens, can contain Yahweh, yet he also affirms that the temple which he has built is the very place in which Yahweh wants to be honored (vv. 27-30).

Many scholars believe that verses 33-34 and 46-51 are later additions to the original prayer because they suggest a condition of exile. This is quite possible, since the original prayer understands the temple as the appropriate place toward which to petition for forgiveness from sin, sin that results in any of a variety of punishments—defeat, drought, famine, pestilence, blight, and the like. The temple is also understood to be the place of just judgment and the place toward which Israel is to pray for victory in battle (the ark will no longer be taken into battle).

Verses 41-43 and 60 suggest an openness to foreigners, which may originate either in Solomon's policies of imperialism or simply in his foreign diplomacy. These verses may even be an exilic addition dating to a time when nationalism was no longer a possibility.

Israel's election as the Lord's chosen people is explicitly and repeatedly given as the reason why the Lord should listen to Israel's prayer.

Solomon's address to the people (vv. 56-61) repeats the form of the opening of his prayer to Yahweh: he praises Yahweh for fulfilling the divine promises and then petitions for the Lord's continued blessings into the future. Again, the text connects Israel's obedience to the Lord with the Lord's not forsaking the people. The dedication concludes the same way it began, with Solomon and the people sacrificing to the Lord. Only after seven days do the festivities end. The people return home contented with king and temple.

9:1-9 Promise and warning to Solomon. The dialogue continues. Solomon has spoken in prayer to the Lord; now the Lord again speaks to Solomon (compare 1 Kgs 3:10-14). Whereas the Lord had previously required obedience for continuing the divine presence in the temple and to Israel, the Lord now sets forth conditions for the continuation of David's dynasty (compare 1 Kgs 6:12-13). Further, the text explicitly names the sin of idolatry (v. 6). The punishment for Solomon's and his descendants' infidelity will include destruction of the temple, loss of nationhood, and exile. The text here foreshadows what is to come.

9:10-18 Other acts of the king. This text suggests Solomon's additional failings. He conscripted his own people to build the temple (see 1 Kgs 5:27-31), and later he dealt unjustly with Hiram. The twenty Galilean cities that Solomon gave to Hiram amounted to less than adequate payment for the materials he provided for the temple and the palace. Moreover, Solomon forced the non-Israelites living in his dominion to help not only in the building of the temple and the palace, but also in

the construction of Jerusalem's walls, several cities, and a fleet. Nevertheless, Solomon, at this time in his reign, is still faithful to Yahweh, as attested by his concern for the temple and by his offerings.

10:1-13 Visit of the queen of Sheba. A wealthy woman submits to Solomon's superior wisdom and is duly impressed by his grand style and by his fidelity to God. The two exchange an abundance of precious gifts. Verses 11 and 12 seem misplaced, belonging rather with 1 Kgs 9:26-28. In any case, they attest to the close cooperation between the fleets of Hiram and Solomon, to Solomon's benefit. The gold from Ophir is now supplemented by precious wood and stones.

10:14-29 Solomon's wealth. Solomon is ostentatious with his wealth; he uses gold everywhere. His drinking vessels and utensils are of gold, and he puts gold shields and gold bucklers on display in his palace. Every three years his ships bring a new cargo of precious metals. Solomon seems to have everything: the Lord's wisdom, peace in his land, abundant wealth, recognition by everyone. Perhaps his fame leads to envy and resentment, since part of his wealth comes from annual tribute. One must also ask whether the text describing Solomon's chariots is a subtle allusion to the condemnation of kingship in 1 Sam 8:11-12.

11:1-43 The sins of Solomon. Solomon has married Pharaoh's daughter and loved the Lord (see 1 Kgs 3:1-3). Now he loves foreign women, and in symbolic abundance (seven hundred and three hundred!). Because marriage to foreign women inevitably led, in the judgment of the Deuteronomist, to the worship of their gods, Solomon merits the Deuteronomist's stereotypical condemnation of idolatry. Solomon's heart, therefore, is no longer like his father David's, fully faithful to the Lord. His disobedience is explicit. The Lord had promised the continuation of the dynasty on the condition that the people worship Yahweh and Yahweh alone. The Lord's response to Solomon's sin can only be anger and punishment. And so the Lord again speaks to Solomon (vv. 11-13). One notes the absence of prophetic mediation here; the Lord personally names the punishment. The kingdom will fall not to Solomon's son but to Solomon's servant; yet, "for the sake of David," this will not happen during Solomon's lifetime, nor will the entire kingdom be taken away.

During the latter part of Solomon's reign, political adversaries abound: Hadad and the Edomites to the southeast; Rezon of Syria to the northeast; and even his own servant Jeroboam from the north of Israel. And the king of Egypt gives refuge to Jeroboam! The text vindicates Jeroboam's rebellion with a prophetic word (vv. 31-39). Ahijah delivers to Jeroboam basically the same message the Lord gave to Solomon: the kingdom will be divided, and part will be given to Solomon's servant. Because of David, this will not happen until after Solomon's death.

If ten tribes are given to Jeroboam and one to David's descendant, what happened to the twelfth tribe? Most scholars conclude that the reference here is symbolic (the numbers ten and one can each represent the whole) rather than historical. By this time certain tribes had been incorporated into others; for example, Simeon and Levi into Judah and perhaps part of the tribe of Benjamin as well (compare 1 Kgs 12:21).

The Deuteronomistic editor, whose words are put in the mouth of the prophet Ahijah, is swift to make conditions for Jeroboam's future reign and dynastic potential; they will depend on fidelity to Yahweh's commands. David has become the model *par excellence*. For his sake his descendants will continue a dynasty; only if Jeroboam is faithful to Yahweh, as David was, can he hope for a lasting dynasty. David's descendants will indeed be punished, but the Deuteronomist sees an end even to that.

The record of Solomon's death (vv. 41-43) is similar to that of most Judean kings. Reference is made to a source, no longer extant, where more information can be found regarding Solomon's reign. Reference is also made to the duration of his reign—in this instance forty years (a generation), the same number of years as his father's reign. Further, Solomon is buried with his ancestors, including David, in his father's city. Finally, the text notes that his son Rehoboam, in dynastic fashion, reigned after him.

PART II: JUDAH AND ISRAEL TO THE TIME OF AHAB

1 Kgs 12:1–16:34

This section chronicles the history of a divided kingdom between approximately 930 B.C.E. and 870 B.C.E. During that time three of David's descendants reigned in the southern kingdom of Judah: Rehoboam, Solomon's son; Abijam, Rehoboam's son; and Asa, Abijam's son. A dynasty could not be sustained in the northern kingdom. The house of Jeroboam endured only until Jeroboam's son Nadab was murdered. The house of Baasha endured only until Baasha's son Elah was murdered. Zimri held the throne only seven days until he himself was murdered. The house of Omri succeeded in maintaining a dynasty of four generations. Because the biblical text deems Ahab the most evil king of the north—the king whose wife, Jezebel, killed the prophets and led Ahab to ruin—the Deuteronomistic historian incorporates into his History an entire section devoted to Ahab's reign and his confrontations with the prophets Elijah, Micaiah, and Elisha.

12:1-25 Secession of Israel. Ahijah's prophecy to Jeroboam (11:31-39) is fulfilled. Had Rehoboam been politically shrewd, he might have avoided the split. As it happened, brash self-confidence led to authoritarianism and ultimately to defeat. Solomon's reign produced a rival, but a leader with few followers. Rehoboam's reign produces the followers and the revolt. The Lord warned Solomon of the division to come; Ahijah prophesied to Jeroboam; now Shemaiah tells Rehoboam and his people the same thing. Three times the kingdom's division is explained by the infidelity of the Davidic kings.

Because Jeroboam lacks a geographical center like the one David and Solomon established at Jerusalem, he moves about during the first years of his reign. From this time onward in the books of Kings, the term "Israel" refers only to the northern segment of what had been David and Solomon's united kingdom. "Judah" now refers to the southern kingdom, that part of the land ruled over by a descendant of David.

12:26-32 Religious rebellion. Could there be a religious solution to Jeroboam's political dilemma? Creating a new king demands a new capital and, so it would seem, a new temple. How else can the political-social-religious unity of the people be maintained? Their very identity as a people and a nation is intricately bound to belief in, and worship of, Yahweh, even if idolatry and syncretism are sometimes practiced. Is Jeroboam really guilty, or is he guilty only in the eyes of the Deuteronomistic historian, for whom all the northern kings, without exception, do evil in the eyes of the Lord?

Whatever the true answer to that historical query may be, Jeroboam, from the perspective of the biblical text's author, does the very things that can only merit condemnation: he makes golden calves for the people to worship (v. 28; compare Exod 32); he builds temples on the high places (v. 31); he ordains non-Levitical priests (compare Exod 28ff.); and he arbitrarily establishes a pilgrimage feast (v. 32).

12:33–13:34 Message of the prophet from Judah. It is no surprise that a prophetic condemnation follows. As Jeroboam is offering sacrifice on the altar at Bethel, he is confronted by a Judean prophet, who condemns not only the altar but also the priests whom Jeroboam has created. Later, during Josiah's reign in Judah, the illegitimate priests of the high places will be sacrificed. (Was the text written during Josiah's reign to legitimize the purge?)

The truth of this prophetic word is confirmed by the fulfillment of another of the prophet's words—the destruction of the altar (see 1 Kgs 13:5). The prophet of God is in touch with the power of God. When Jeroboam begs him to ask the Lord that his outstretched, withered hand might be restored, he does so, and the king recovers (13:6). Yet, in spite of his experiences of the power of God, Jeroboam does not repent.

God's power can work through God's representative even when that agent is not obedient to God. Students often ask why the old prophet tricked (deceived!) God's envoy. Should not prophets be believed and obeyed? Prophets are to be believed and obeyed by those who hear the word of God through them, but prophets are to be obedient to the word of God that they themselves have heard. One must not trust a human being—even God's messenger—when one has heard God. The younger prophet is now confronted with

God's condemnation of his disobedience by another prophet: he will not be buried with his ancestors. Again, the text records that the prophetic word is fulfilled. The prophet of God dies and is buried, but he is not buried with his ancestors. Yet, he was a true prophet; the word that he spoke against Bethel will be fulfilled. ("Samaria" is used in verse 32 as a synonym for "Israel.")

14:1-20 Death of Abijah. When in trouble, consult God; when all goes well, do as you please—such would seem to be the philosophy of Jeroboam. The sickness of his son brings him to the same prophet whose promise of kingship to him has been fulfilled (see 1 Kgs 11:30-39). Now Jeroboam seeks out Ahijah to learn the fate of his son. Why doesn't Jeroboam himself go to see Ahijah? Why must Jeroboam's wife disguise herself? Is it because the king does not want his people to know that he needs a prophet's help? Just as the prophets in the previous section remained nameless, so does Jeroboam's wife. Abijah is named once. The text deliberately highlights Jeroboam as the central character—Jeroboam, the unfaithful king.

Jeroboam's son will die—such is the word of the Lord. One could have expected as much (compare 2 Sam 12:14). Moreover, the same prophet through whom God conditionally gave Jeroboam a dynasty now removes it. Of Jeroboam's children, only Abijah will not suffer a violent death. Jeroboam is so evil that even the burial of Abijah has to be justified: there is something in him pleasing to the Lord (v. 13)!

Just as the chronicles of Solomon are no longer extant (see 1 Kgs 14:41), neither are the chronicles of Israel (v. 19) nor, for that matter, the chronicles of Judah (v. 29). The length of Jeroboam's reign, his burial, and his son's accession to the throne tie him to the succeeding Israelite reign.

14:21-31 Reign of Rehoboam. The text alternates its accounts of the reigns of the kings of Judah and those of the kings of Israel. Along with the stereotypical notice of Rehoboam's age when he began to reign and the duration of his kingship, his mother's name, Naamah, is given. This pattern is common for most of the kings of Judah. Because the kings had many wives, it was important to record in which house a new king had been raised. For Rehoboam, the detail that his mother was an Ammonite (v. 21) recalls 1 Kgs 11:1-6, where we are told of Solomon's marrying foreign women and his consequent practice of idolatry.

Verses 22-24 tell how Judah under King Rehoboam succumbs to idolatry. This explains the warfare that Judah experiences with both Egypt and the northern kingdom of Israel. Under Rehoboam's leadership Judah becomes like Israel. The books of Kings here begin to depict a proportionate relationship between the quality of the king and the condition of the temple, a thread woven throughout the remainder of the Deuteronomistic History.

In spite of his evil, Rehoboam is David's descendant; therefore, he is buried with his ancestors, and his son Abijam replaces him on the throne.

15:1-8 Reign of Abijam. The description of Rehoboam's son given here is totally stereotypical: What year of whose reign in the north was it when so-and-so began to reign in the south? How long did he reign? Who was his mother? How is his reign to be evaluated from a covenant perspective and in comparison with David's? If the judgment is that the particular king of Judah was unfaithful to the Lord, then the fact that he endured on the throne is explained by a reference to the Lord's faithfulness to his servant David.

If nothing of particular import occurred during a particular king's reign, from a theological perspective, then a reference is made to the king's death and burial with his ancestors. The name of his successor is given. If one should want further information regarding the king, the reader is referred to the court chronicles.

15:9-24 Reign of Asa. Asa reverses his father's reign. Whereas Abijam reigned for only three years, Asa reigns for forty-one. Whereas his father was not entirely with the Lord like David, Asa, like David, pleases the Lord. Whereas Rehoboam allowed the cult prostitutes (see 1 Kgs 14:24), Asa banishes them. Whereas Abijam made idols, Asa removes them. Whereas Maacah, the queen mother of Abijam's reign, venerated a Canaanite goddess, Asa banishes her. Further, Asa brings to the temple precious offerings, appropriate gifts from himself and even from his father. Asa's reign endures through the reigns of at least five northern kings; he has

many accomplishments and has built many cities, blessings of Yahweh for fidelity.

The only shortcoming Asa seems guilty of is letting the high places remain (v. 14). Does this mean he tolerates the idolatry of others within his kingdom? Is this the cause of the continued warfare between the south and the north? On the other hand, is Asa's overwhelming fidelity and resemblance to David the Deuteronomistic historian's explanation of why Asa is able to summon Aram to his defense against Israel (compare 2 Sam 10:19 and 1 Kgs 10:29)? Later the text condemns foreign alliances because they evidence a lack of trust in Yahweh.

15:25-32 Reign of Nadab. The reign of Jeroboam's son, concurrent with the first years of Asa's reign in the south, is similar, from a theological perspective, to his father's. On him and on the entire house of Jeroboam the prophetic word of Ahijah is fulfilled (see 1 Kgs 14:10-16). Verse 32 duplicates verse 16. Scholars usually explain such repetitions as the products of multiple sources. The emphasis that repetition gives is often deliberate.

If the historical reality was constant warfare between the northern and southern kingdoms, then the truth must be acknowledged, in spite of the theological judgment that Baasha was evil and Asa good. History can be shaped by Deuteronomistic theology only so far.

15:33–16:14 Reign of Baasha. The capital of the northern kingdom is not yet Samaria but Tirzah, the city in which Jeroboam eventually settled (compare 1 Kgs 12:25 and especially 1 Kgs 14:12, 17).

The Lord, through his prophet Jehu, condemns Baasha. Baasha's evil, like Jeroboam's, will merit for him the same end: his house will be destroyed; only one son will reign, and that son will meet a violent death. From a historical perspective, written discreetly into the text, one may conclude that Baasha's reign was relatively stable. He survived for twenty-four years on the throne, and his son was able to succeed him. Yet, from a theological perspective, his covenant infidelity made eventual punishment inevitable.

16:8-14 Reign of Elah. The Deuteronomistic historian records only one thing about the reign of Elah: Jehu's prophecy is fulfilled. Elah is murdered and the house of Baasha destroyed. His successor is his servant and murderer, Zimri.

One cannot help but note of the instability of the northern kingdom. The house of Jeroboam reigned for twenty-four years before Nadab was murdered; the house of Baasha reigns for twenty-six years before Elah is murdered. In both instances the murderer becomes king. Neither house reigned a full generation.

16:15-22 Reign of Zimri. Elah's murderer lasts only seven days on the throne before he commits suicide (compare 1 Sam 31:4) and is supplanted by the army general, Omri. Omri apparently has more popular backing than either Tibni, another contender for the throne, or Zimri. The Deuteronomistic historian-theologian blames Zimri's short reign and fate on his sin. No sin is imputed to Tibni, and therefore no explanation is given for his death. In accordance with the violence of the period, a likely historical explanation is that Omri's supporters removed his opposition.

16:23-28 Reign of Omri. Omri moves the capital from Tirzah to Samaria—no small accomplishment in Israel's political history. He dies a natural death and is buried with his ancestors. His son Ahab succeeds him on the throne. Nevertheless, punishment will inevitably come for his idolatry and other sins.

16:29-34 Reign of Ahab. Whereas other kings of the north are compared with Jeroboam and may even have done "more evil" than their predecessors, Ahab is clearly cited as being guilty of evil far beyond that of any of the others. His specific sins are marrying Jezebel and worshiping Baal; he even builds a temple for Baal in the capital.

Moreover, Hiel's rebuilding of Jericho during Ahab's reign merits the fulfillment of the curse in Josh 6:26. He loses his first son when he lays the foundation, and his youngest son when he sets up the gates. Whatever the relative dating of these texts (whether Hiel built Jericho and sacrificed his children—historical events condemned in the later text from Joshua—or whether the passage from Joshua represents an earlier tradition that was inserted into 1 Kings to further document Ahab's evil), there is no doubt that 1 Kgs 16:34 serves as an additional indication of Ahab's sin.

PART III: STORIES OF THE PROPHETS

1 Kgs 17:1–22:54

The remainder of 1 Kings is composed of ancient legends about prophets and their disciples. The content is episodic, inserted into the reign of Ahab in Israel and, indirectly, into the reign of Jehoshaphat in Judah. Throughout the narrative the nature of prophets that has thus far been delineated is further emphasized. The word that God proclaims through a prophet will be fulfilled; more powerful than the king is the prophet.

17:1-6 Drought predicted by Elijah. The word of Elijah to Ahab is a warning of drought and an assertion that Elijah will control its duration. The word of the Lord to Elijah is a promise of protection: food and water and a place of safety. Implicit in the word of the Lord to the prophet is the power of Yahweh; implicit in the word of the prophet is Yahweh's punishment for Ahab's sin.

17:7-24 Elijah and the widow. The miracles of the multiplication of oil and flour and the raising back to life of a widow's only son are the second and third accounts of acts of the Lord's power through Elijah; he has already caused the drought. Ahab's sin brought suffering for the people of Israel; Elijah's fidelity brings nourishment, as does the woman's faith. The power of Yahweh to take away life and to restore it is here demonstrated, as is Elijah's confidence in the Lord.

18:1-46 Elijah and the prophets of Baal. The reader should not be surprised at another miracle, certainly not when an episode is meant to contrast the power of God with the power of no-god. The Lord will bring rain after three years of drought and famine.

Elijah emerges as Yahweh's representative, while Ahab and Jezebel are devotees of the Baals. Obadiah functions as their intermediary. Although he is faithful to the Lord, even to the point of risking his well-being to hide the persecuted prophets, Obadiah nevertheless works for and fears the evil king. However, because Obadiah is faithful to the Lord, he obeys Elijah and occasions the meeting, after three years, of Ahab and Elijah. Each experiences the other as the "troubler of Israel." Who, ultimately, caused the drought—the prophet Elijah or the evil King Ahab?

Mount Carmel becomes the place of confrontation: Elijah, Yahweh's prophet, against

850 false prophets. In a text similar to Deut 30:15-20 and Josh 23:14-16, Elijah exhorts the people to choose Yahweh (v. 21). Next follows a demonstration of the power of Yahweh. One prophet against 850, two bulls prepared for sacrifice, extensive intercession (three pourings of four jars of water over the twelve-stone altar), and a single request. Yahweh's sacrifice catches fire. When Yahweh's supremacy has been securely reestablished, drought gives way to rain (v. 45). The incident is meant to teach Ahab the evil of his ways and to teach the reader the power of Yahweh.

Students often comment on Elijah's killing the Baal prophets. The text is not about killing people; it is about the power of Yahweh. Within that context evil must be removed from the midst of Israel.

19:1-18 Flight to Horeb. Elijah's encounter with God on Mount Horeb has been the subject of much study and reflection. Horeb is another name for Sinai, the mountain of God where the Lord spoke to Moses through a burning bush (see Exod 3) and later gave Moses the Decalogue (see Deut 4-5). The episode is artistically constructed. Before the encounter with the Lord, Elijah is discouraged and almost despairing. The land is evil, the king is evil, the prophets are dead, and Elijah's life has been threatened by Jezebel. He wishes he could die.

But just as Elijah was nourished during the drought and famine, so now he is likewise protected. Twice an angel awakens him to eat, the second time suggesting the journey he is to undertake (v. 7). Just as the Israelites wandered forty years in the desert, so now Elijah takes a journey into the desert for forty days and forty nights. Elijah's complaint to God (v. 10) elicits the Lord's invitation to meet him, an encounter that takes place, not where the power of God is most expected—in heavy winds, an earthquake, a fire—but in a tiny, whispering wind, a noisy silence.

No time now for sulking. Elijah states his plight to Yahweh, but God seemingly ignores his problem and addresses him immediately on another issue. Elijah is a prophet, and as prophet he is commissioned to leave the desert and to anoint three people: Hazael as king of Aram, Jehu as king of Israel, and Elisha as his own successor. These men together will effectively remove all those persons who have

been unfaithful to Yahweh. However, a faithful remnant (seven thousand) will be spared.

19:19-21 Call of Elisha. Elijah first calls his successor. The function of the cloak may be symbolic (compare 1 Kgs 11:30-31) or at least an allusion to Elijah's encounter with Yahweh (v. 13). Elisha recognizes the subtle call and follows, symbolically putting an end to his former life.

20:1-43 Ahab's victories over Ben-hadad. That the northern kingdom of Israel was at war with Aram during much of Ahab's reign is certain. There had been hostility and intermittent fighting between the two countries since Baasha's time. But the historical fact is that Israel was victorious over Aram during Ahab's reign. How could the Deuteronomistic theologian account for this? How could Ahab's evil merit victory? Remember the power of Yahweh's prophetic word, especially when a prophet is listened to and obeyed? The first encounter results in an Israelite victory because Ahab seeks the prophet's word and acts accordingly. The second encounter also results in an Israelite victory, this time because the Arameans stupidly believe that Israel's god can be conquered in the plain. The disproportion between the two armies is designed to show the power of Yahweh. Victory is the Lord's.

According to the rules of Israel's "holy war" theology, Yahweh is the warrior who fights for Israel, and, consequently, all spoils belong to Yahweh. Yahweh was victorious over Aram; it was the word of the prophet that directed Ahab's strategy in the first battle; the word of the prophet also warned of a second attack. Yahweh showed great power in achieving Israel's victory over the exceedingly larger forces of Aram. Therefore, Ben-hadad belongs to Yahweh, and Ahab has no right to set him free (v. 34). (The growing power of Assyria in the ancient Near East may be the historical explanation behind the interim peace between Aram and Israel. Shalmaneser's Assyrian Annals refer to an alliance between Aram and Israel toward the end of Ahab's reign [compare 1 Kgs 22:1].)

From a theological perspective, the reference to a prophet's companion who refuses to obey a prophet and is consequently killed (v. 36) is a fitting introduction to the prophetic condemnation of Ahab. Ahab condemns himself in his encounter with the prophet (compare 2 Sam 12). Just as the soldier must bear the penalty for neglecting his charge, Ahab's sparing King Ben-hadad (compare 1 Sam 15:8-9) would lead ultimately to his own death.

21:1-29 Seizure of Naboth's vineyard. To understand why Naboth would not sell or exchange his ancestral heritage, one must refer to such texts as Lev 25 and Josh 13. The interaction of characters shows Ahab accepting traditional values and Naboth's verdict, however unwillingly.

Jezebel, on the other hand, who has appeared in the text only minimally until now—she had killed the prophets and threatened Elijah—does not respect Naboth's decision and ridicules her husband for doing so. She therefore usurps Ahab's power, that is, his name and his seal, and successfully plots Naboth's death. Ahab tacitly cooperates with Jezebel and reaps the benefits. Or so it would seem, until Ahab is again confronted with Elijah! Prophetic condemnation is in order; murder and theft will not go unpunished. Elijah now pronounces a condemnation similar to the ones Jeroboam and Baasha had heard—the violent end of Omri's dynasty. Ahab's body will lie at the very site of his sin. And the evil Jezebel will likewise be destroyed.

Because Ahab hears the word of the prophet for what it is—Yahweh's word of power—he repents. One can expect the prophetic word to be fulfilled, but here as elsewhere (compare 2 Sam 12:13-14) it is mitigated; the punishment owed him is delayed until his son's reign.

22:1-40 Campaign against Ramoth-gilead. Probably at some earlier stage in the text's compilation, notice was given that Jehoshaphat had succeeded Asa on the throne of Judah (see 1 Kgs 22:41-45) before this account of an Israelite-Judean alliance against Aram. Jehoshaphat is here depicted as recognizing the former unity and the potential for unity between Israel and Judah. He therefore seeks to help the northern king regain territory. Though never named in the chapter, that king is Ahab. Perhaps he fades into the background when compared with Jehoshaphat! Whatever happened to Asa's treaty with Aram? Did Aram become greedy and begin to infiltrate southward? Did Jehoshaphat see an alliance with Israel as strategically more important than an alliance with Aram? Israel was, after all, a closer northern neighbor than Aram.

In any event, Jehoshaphat wants the prophets to be consulted (v. 6). The northern king sends for the compromised prophets, those who maintain favor by saying precisely what the king wants to hear. He will go through the motions, but he dare not risk the truth lest the word of the Lord be adverse. Jehoshaphat presses for a more trustworthy prophet, one who will say "whatever the Lord tells" him (v. 14).

Ahab recognizes Micaiah's first sarcastic word to him as untrue (v. 16). The true prophet could only condemn the wicked Ahab. Micaiah's real response is a prediction of Ahab's death in battle: the sheep (see 2 Sam 7:8 and 24:17) will be without a shepherd. Ahab's evil has been so great that the Lord's judgment against him is final. To guarantee that Ahab will not listen to the prophets' prediction of his death and be delivered, Micaiah says that Yahweh has even allowed a lying spirit within the prophets' mouths. Whether Ahab seeks consolation in the deceitful assurance of the false prophets or takes seriously the word of Micaiah, his end will not change. The Lord has decreed evil against him (v. 23).

Micaiah's being sent to prison is not the first reference in the books of Kings to the persecution of a prophet. Jezebel killed many, and Elijah fled for his life from her.

With Ahab's death (v. 35) comes the fulfillment of several prophecies, including Micaiah's. Moreover, Aram has helped to wipe evil out of Israel (compare 1 Kgs 19:17). Ahab is buried, and his son Ahaziah succeeds him (compare 1 Kgs 21:29).

22:41-51 Reign of Jehoshaphat. Jehoshaphat's twenty-five-year reign is relatively uneventful from the perspective of the Deuteronomistic historian. Like his father Asa, he does good in the eyes of the Lord. He continues his father's good practice of removing the cult prostitutes (see 1 Kgs 15:12). Yet, like his father, he also allows the high places to remain active as places of worship (see 1 Kgs 15:14). The reference to Edom and a fleet (vv. 49, 50) implies relative power and prosperity.

22:52-54 Reign of Ahaziah. Like the other kings who end dynasties in the north, Ahaziah reigns for only two years. His evil is compared not only to Jeroboam's and to his father Ahab's, as we might expect, but also to his

mother's. We conclude that his mother was the evil Jezebel, especially since his idolatry is specified as Baal worship.

COMMENTARY: 2 KINGS

PART IV:
THE KINGDOMS OF ISRAEL AND JUDAH

2 Kgs 1:1–17:41

1:1-8 Ahaziah consults Baalzebub. A new opening and a new king of Israel. Immediately the reader knows what kind of king the Deuteronomistic theologian judges Ahaziah to be—he consults an idol! What follows immediately is prophetic judgment and condemnation.

1:9-12 Death of two captains. For the Deuteronomistic theologian, the power of the prophet far surpasses the king's. No mere soldiers can overpower the power of God. Rather, Elijah pronounces doom on the soldiers sent to capture him, the two groups of fifty and their captains (compare 1 Kgs 18:13). The word of God through Elijah cannot be silenced; it is effective.

1:13-18 Death of the king. The third captain sent by Ahaziah recognizes Elijah's power and pleads for his own safety. He knows what the king has failed to understand: Yahweh, God of power, is with Elijah. When Elijah meets Ahaziah in person, he repeats Ahaziah's fate: the consequence of idolatry is death.

2:1-8 Elijah and Elisha. Elijah's departure is developed literarily with great detail and leads to a climax. Elisha knows of their imminent separation and wants to be with Elijah as long as possible. Elisha follows the prophet southward, from Gilgal to Bethel, to Jericho, and even to the Jordan. Other prophets testify to Elijah's departure and even follow the two as far as the Jordan. The symbolic role of Elijah's cloak as an instrument of power again surfaces when it is used to divide the waters.

2:9-18 Elisha succeeds Elijah. The other side of the Jordan is the place of God's intervention. Elijah is taken up in a flaming chariot drawn by flaming horses. When Elisha sees this, he knows that, according to Elijah's word, prophetic power in good measure will be bestowed upon him. He tears his own cloak

in two; he picks up Elijah's and uses it to recross the Jordan, where he meets those who will now become his followers. Elijah is not to be found; the power of God that had been in him is henceforth to be sought in his successor, Elisha.

Many historical-critical scholars have suggested historical and literary confusion between the two men. This is partly because God had told Elijah to anoint Hazael and Jehu (1 Kgs 19:15-16), but the texts later record that Elisha directs the anointing (see 2 Kgs 8:13 and 9:6). It is sometimes conjectured that the miracles now attributed to Elijah were originally ascribed to Elisha and that they have been altered, repeated, and rearranged in order to heighten the literary contrast between Ahab and Elijah.

2:19-22 Healing of the water. Proof of the efficacy of Elisha's prophetic word is recorded immediately. Potentially fertile land needs pure water if the harvest and the people are to be healthy. Therefore, at the request of the people, Elisha throws salt into the water, and it is henceforth considered a source of well-being. The power of the prophet effects good.

2:23-25 The prophet's curse. The power of the prophet can also effect harm, especially for those who do not take the prophet seriously. Such is the common interpretation of this episode: the cursing of small boys, leading to their death. The writer does not intend to depict the prophet's heartlessness but rather the gravity of taking a prophet lightly.

3:1-27 Campaign of Joram against Moab. Ahab's son Joram succeeds his brother to the throne, another "chip off the old block." Though not as evil as his mother (Jezebel) and his father, in the Deuteronomist's judgment, nevertheless, Joram is evil, like all the northern kings.

Continued peace between Judah and Israel during Jehoshaphat's reign occasioned their alliance, this time along with the Edomites, against Moab (compare 1 Kgs 22). Faced with a water shortage, the kings, at the request of the king of Judah, consult a prophet about

311

their dilemma. They approach Elisha. He rejects Joram, who is too much like his father for Elisha's taste, but for the sake of the king of the south he consults the Lord: they will have sufficient water and even be victors over the Moabites (vv. 17-18). Yahweh effects the victory. Through the miraculous misperception of the Moabites, the promise of the prophet is fulfilled.

Defeat in battle causes the Moabite king to seek Syrian aid, and when that recourse fails, he sacrifices his own child in hopes of winning his god's favor over Israel. This horrifies the Israelites, who return to Israel. Perhaps even they fear the power of the Moabite god in his own land!

4:1-7 The widow's oil. Multiplication of a widow's oil—a miracle Elijah had performed (see 1 Kgs 17:14-16)—is performed also by Elisha. Her own husband had been a prophet, and she trusts the prophet's power. Her complaint brings her deliverance.

4:8-37 Elisha and the Shunammite. Yahweh's prophet has power over life and death. Elisha promises the barren Shunammite a child, and later raises that dead child back to life (compare 1 Kgs 17:21-23). The woman had recognized Elisha as a prophet and had volunteered to provide for his needs; he rewarded her with a child. Now she seeks the prophet after her child's death, again showing confidence in God's representative; again she is rewarded. Gehazi, Elisha's servant, is introduced here. He was unable to bring life back into the child (v. 31).

4:38-41 The poisoned stew. A famine (compare 1 Kgs 18:3) occasions Elisha's next miracle. Just as salt had purified contaminated water (2 Kgs 3:19-22), now meal purifies a poisoned stew. In each case the prophet intervenes and effects miraculous good on behalf of his people's health.

4:42-44 Multiplication of loaves. This miracle complements verses 1-7, and together they parallel 1 Kgs 17:14-16. Twenty barley loaves and ears of grain—food for the prophet, yes, but hardly enough to feed a famine-stricken people. Hardly enough, that is, unless the power of Yahweh is with you.

The close literary connection between the miracles performed by Elijah and Elisha, especially the multiplication of food and the raisings from the dead, and similar miracles of Jesus recounted in the synoptic Gospels cannot be ignored. The New Testament writers seem to have selected particular acts of Jesus to assert, especially to their Jewish converts, that the power of God worked through him.

5:1-27 Cure of Naaman. Five persons are introduced in this episode: Naaman's wife; the Israelite servant girl of Naaman's wife; Naaman himself; Naaman's master, the king of Syria; and, finally, the king of Israel. Four are identified by their relation to the leper, and they all support a request that the king of Israel cure him. Israel's king, however, is powerless, as he himself admits. In contrast, Elisha, the prophet of God with the power of God, can heal.

Elisha commands Naaman to wash seven times in the Jordan, but the leper had washed in other rivers before and refuses. He does not yet realize that the word of the prophet contains the power of God. He ignores the word of the prophet but later is persuaded by his servants, who re-echo the prophet's words. He does what Elisha ordered and is cured (v. 14).

Naaman's physical cure becomes the basis of faith in Israel's God. He wishes to repay the prophet, or at least to buy some of Israel's soil, on which he can, in the future, worship Yahweh in Syria. Elisha refuses the gifts but commends Naaman's conversion.

Gehazi, however, is another story. The power of Yahweh had worked through Elisha to effect Naaman's cure, but why not reap personal benefit from Yahweh's power? Such would seem to be Gehazi's motivation in asking Naaman for the silver talents and the festal garments—motivation strong enough to allow Gehazi to lie, first to Naaman, then to Elisha. But God's knowledge and God's power are both present to God's prophet, who denounces Gehazi's deceit and condemns him to Naaman's leprosy. Infidelity can only yield a curse!

6:1-7 Recovery of the lost ax. Elisha performs another miracle, this one on behalf of one of the prophets. The prophet of God has the power of God and the knowledge of God (see 2 Kgs 5:26-27) to effect good for those who are faithful to God.

6:8-13 Aramean ambush. Elisha is here depicted as a prophet of God with extraordinary knowledge, which he puts to good use on Israel's behalf and against the Arameans.

Proof of his power is the fact that the Arameans want to take him captive.

6:14-23 Blinded Aramean soldiers. The prophet of God can overcome any obstacle with the power of God. He can inspire confidence in his otherwise frightened servant; alone against an Aramean army, he can mediate their being blinded; he can himself lead a blinded army into their enemy's capital; he can even persuade an Israelite king to feed and free Arameans. Further, he can so frighten the Arameans that he causes the raids to cease—raids whose effectiveness the knowledge of God is preventing in the first place. Elisha is in control—or so the Deuteronomistic theology of prophecy would have us believe.

6:24–7:2 Siege of Samaria. War with Syria and famine in Israel describe a country under curse, a land far from fidelity to its God. Sometimes idolatry prompted child sacrifice; now the imminence of starvation has prompted even child cannibalism. The Israelite king blames Elisha for the famine and tries to kill him. Elisha's response is to reassert the power of God: the famine will end the following day, yet the king's adjutant who questioned the prophet's word will die.

7:3-13 The lepers at the gate. What great option is there between death by starvation and death by the sword? Such is the thinking of the lepers as they flee to the Aramean camp. Their courage is rewarded. The power of God, this time giving the impression of a large army and causing the enemy to flee, works on behalf of his people.

7:14-20 End of the siege. The flight of the Arameans signals the end of Israel's captivity in Samaria and, in consequence, the end of their hunger. The Arameans' supplies become spoils of war. Moreover, the word of Elisha to the king's adjutant (see 2 Kgs 7:2) is fulfilled; he is trampled at the city's gate.

8:1-6 Prediction of famine. The woman who had been good to Elisha, to whom he had given a child and for whom he had raised her child back to life, again believes the prophet. Elisha warns of a famine and she flees the land. The famine lasts seven years, after which time she returns to claim her property in Israel. The encounter with the king reveals a believing king. Hearing Gehazi's testimony and the woman's own account, the king returns the woman's possessions. Though al-

ways unnamed, she is a model of one who takes God and God's word seriously.

8:7-15 Death of Ben-hadad foretold. Aram has to have taken notice of the power of Yahweh's prophets before now. Elisha had thwarted the Aramean raids into Israel (see 2 Kgs 6:12) and had led the Aramean army into Samaria (see 2 Kgs 6:19). Now the king of Aram consults the prophet of Israel about his health (compare Ahaziah's consulting idols in 2 Kgs 1:2). Elisha uses this occasion to prophesy to Hazael that he will replace Ben-hadad as king.

The historical fact is that Ben-hadad was murdered by his servant, Hazael, who usurped the throne of Aram. The historical fact is, also, that Hazael waged war against Israel (see 1 Kgs 18:17). However, the Deuteronomistic theologian does not accuse Elisha of precipitating the murder. Elisha merely names the end result and Hazael chooses the means.

8:16-24 Reign of Jehoram of Judah. Though king of Judah, Jehoram is like Ahab. He is married to Ahab's sister (implied is the fact that she is "a chip off the old block," just as his sons Ahaziah and Joram were). Jehoram's reign, judged on its own terms from a theological perspective, deserves termination, but God preserves the dynasty for the sake of Jehoram's faithful ancestor, David. There are hard times, however, like the war with the Edomites and the loss of Libnah, political difficulties interpreted as religious condemnation. In spite of his sin, Jehoram is buried with his ancestors in the City of David, and his son Ahaziah succeeds him.

8:25-29 Accession of Ahaziah. Ahaziah's mother was Ahab's sister. Knowing only that, one can predict the Deuteronomist's judgment on his reign! He does evil and is like Ahab. The Judah-Israelite alliance against Aram results in Joram's being wounded in battle (1 Kgs 18:17 predicted that Hazael would kill many Israelites). This occasions a visit by Ahaziah to Joram at Jezreel.

9:1-15 Anointing of Jehu. The story line is interrupted to legitimize Jehu as the successor of Joram. The prophetic message, this time delivered for Elisha by a guild prophet, places Jehu, Joram's servant, on the throne of Israel. The prophetic pronouncement against the house of Ahab (1 Kgs 21:21-22) and Jezebel (1 Kgs 21:23) will now be fulfilled. The other army commanders affirm the anointing and form a conspiracy with Jehu against Joram.

9:16-26 Murder of Joram. Drama accompanies Joram's murder. While being comforted by Ahaziah, king of Judah, his own army commander betrays him. But treason is easy, as attested by the fact that Jehu can so easily win over Joram's drivers. The encounter of Jehu and Joram is depicted as the encounter of good and evil. Jehu, having been anointed by Elisha, vindicates the Lord for the evil that the house of Ahab has done. Moreover, Joram's blood is spilled in a place symbolic of Ahab's guilt, the vineyard of Naboth (see 1 Kgs 21:21).

9:27-29 Death of Ahaziah. Ahaziah, whose mother was Athaliah, Ahab's evil sister, must also be removed. Jehu orders his death and it is accomplished. Yet, because he belonged to the line of David, his body is returned to Jerusalem and buried there with his ancestors in the City of David.

9:30-37 Death of Jezebel. Punishment comes, finally, to the evil Jezebel. Just as Jehu won over Joram's drivers, so now he wins over two or three eunuchs, who throw Jezebel out the window to her death. The manner of her death and the decomposition of her body are fitting theological judgments for evil such as hers. The word of the prophet—the power of Yahweh—is thereby executed (see 1 Kgs 21:23).

Jezebel addressed Jehu as Zimri. Zimri was a chariot commander who killed his master, Elah, the king of Israel, thus terminating the house of Baasha (see 1 Kgs 16). Now Jehu has terminated Ahab's house. Yet Jehu is here understood as the Lord's instrument in purging both Israel and Judah of their evil leadership.

10:1-11 Killing of Ahab's descendants. Jehu is not content to have killed Joram, Ahaziah, and Jezebel; he must rid Israel of all the house of Ahab, seventy descendants. Just as the other army commanders joined Jehu in conspiracy (2 Kgs 9:13-14), the drivers joined him (2 Kgs 9:18-20), and the eunuchs supported him (2 Kgs 9:33), so now the leaders in Samaria do his bidding by slaying all Ahab's living relatives. Jehu sees their deaths—and the extermination of all of Ahab's supporters—as the fulfillment of Elijah's prophecy against the house of Ahab (1 Kgs 21:21).

10:12-14 Ahaziah's kinsmen. The termination of Ahab's house and of the evil king of Judah, Ahaziah, is still not enough. Ahaziah was Athaliah's son, and there were other sons; and Athaliah was Ahab's sister. These are still living. The relatives going to visit Ahaziah's family must also be terminated— all of them.

10:15-17 Jehu in Samaria. These verses reemphasize Jehu's gathering of supporters (see 2 Kgs 9:18-19, 32; 10:5), his killing of those who supported the house of Ahab (see v. 11), and the editor's understanding that these deaths were a fulfillment of Elijah's prophecy (see v. 10). Whether in Jezreel or in Samaria or elsewhere in Israel, all who supported the evil machinations of the house of Ahab are destroyed.

10:18-36 Baal's temple destroyed. This is not the first time a character has used trickery to accomplish God's purpose. Remember the prophet who lied (1 Kgs 13)? Jehu must accomplish his mission to rid Israel of the evil that the house of Ahab has perpetrated in Israel, and this he does (see 1 Kgs 19:17). His reward is that his sons will reign on the throne of Israel to the fourth generation.

But Jehu is also guilty of walking in the sin of Jeroboam by tolerating the shrines at Bethel and Dan. The text judges that sin with reference to loss of the eastern segment of Israel's land to Aram.

11:1-20 Rule of Athaliah. Even those who know the books of Kings will fail to take serious note of Athaliah. In a patriarchal period such as this, no woman could legitimately rule. Jezebel may in fact have been stronger than Ahab (see 1 Kgs 21), and Athaliah, Ahab's sister, may in fact have ruled Judah for seven years, but the house of the male, be it Ahab or David, is always credited.

Just as the courage of certain women saved Moses (Exod 2), so now Jehosheba, Ahaziah's sister, saves Joash (the Davidic dynasty) from Athaliah's murderous hand. The place of protection is none other than the temple, and the protector is the priest Jehoiada, who anoints Joash king of Judah. When Athaliah realizes what has happened—that a male descendant of David has been anointed king—she, and those who support her, are powerless. The death she inflicted on Ahaziah's other sons now becomes her own fate.

Restoration of the Davidic line demands

covenant renewal, a recommitment of king and people to the Lord, and a recommitment of the people to the king. Once Baal's temple is destroyed (compare 2 Kgs 10:18-28) the king, having reestablished the appropriate covenant relationship, moves from the Lord's temple to his own palace and throne.

12:1-22 Reign of Joash. Joash was seven when he began to reign, and he reigns for forty years. The Deuteronomist credits the good of his reign to the guidance of Jehoiada.

The account of the temple's repair during Joash's reign describes priests who are not administrators. Apparently Joash's rapport with the priests leads to what he considers a convenient agreement: you keep whatever monies you receive, but you also keep up the temple. For twenty-three years the priests keep the money—period! Called to render an accounting, they beg off responsibility; they will no longer accept the funds, but neither will they be responsible for temple repair. Jehoiada's leadership effects a compromise; he facilitates the collection of the money and its use for temple repair.

Joash's reign has a flaw, however—the high places remain. Usually the high places that the Deuteronomistic historian condemns are associated with Israel. But Athaliah had been Ahab's sister . . . In reality, the continued existence of syncretism in Judah, as well as remaining traces of the idolatry that had existed under Ahaziah, can be presupposed. Furthermore, there may still have been resistance in the countryside, even among Yahwists, to the centralization of worship in Jerusalem. The reader should not be surprised, then, to discover a limited punishment for Judah: Aram poses a threat to their well-being.

The fact that Judah buys off Aram with tribute may be a historical fact, as is Joash's violent death. One may suggest, however, that the juxtaposition of the statements is intended to assert an implicit cause-and-effect relationship, from the theological perspective of the Deuteronomistic historian. Whatever his sins, Joash is David's descendant; he is buried with his ancestors in the City of David, and his son Amaziah succeeds him.

13:1-9 Reign of Jehoahaz of Israel. One might think that this text was lifted from the Book of Judges. Jehoahaz's sin leads to the Lord's anger and oppression by Samaria.

However, Jehoahaz entreats the Lord, who sends a deliverer, and the Israelites are liberated from Aram. The pattern, however, will quickly repeat itself (compare Judg 2:11-19). Once back in their land with relative security, the people continue to sin; their fate is lack of prosperity. When Jehoahaz dies, Jehu's descendant continues the line (see 2 Kgs 10:30).

13:10-25 Reign of Joash of Israel. If one were to read these verses logically, one would place verses 22-23 after verse 7; verses 24-25 after verse 19; and verses 12-13 after verse 21. Thus, the Israelites who did evil during Jehoahaz's reign would merit the continued oppression of Aram; yet, the fact that Aram did not totally destroy Israel would also be theologically explained.

Joash's encounter with Elisha again demonstrates the power of the prophet. That Joash takes the prophet seriously is a good sign (though he is desperate) and merits Israel's military successes over Aram; on the other hand, his carrying out of the prophet's word with less than full obedience—thus Elisha interprets the three arrows—accounts for the fact that the victory is limited. The text also hints of conflict between Israel and both Judah (compare 2 Kgs 14:8-14) and Moab.

In spite of Joash's encounter with Elisha, or perhaps because of his less than full success, he receives the traditional Deuteronomistic judgment for a northern king: he is evil, like Jeroboam. Joash is buried in Samaria, and his son succeeds him (see 2 Kgs 10:30).

There is a certain confusion regarding this king's name—Joash or Jehoash; the Hebrew text varies. The accounts recorded here about the king come, most probably, from at least two sources (note, for example, the duplication of verses 12-13 in 2 Kgs 14:15-16).

Elisha, unlike Elijah, dies and leaves no specific successor. Yet, as with Elijah, an aura of the miraculous attends his passing. Because the power of the prophet is in his person—in his life and in his bones—one should not be too surprised that, for the Deuteronomistic historian, even contact with Elisha's bones can restore life. To the end Elisha functions to mediate the power of God.

14:1-22 Amaziah of Judah. Amaziah's mother, Jehoaddin, was from Jerusalem. She, like Joash's mother, Zibia, from Beer-sheba, was of southern origin, which suggests that

Amaziah's may be a more positive reign. He is victorious over the Edomites. Yet, like his father, he allows the high places to remain. He engages in an unsuccessful battle against Israel, which depletes the treasuries of both the temple and the palace. Jehoash's advice to Amaziah—don't fight with me because you'll lose—given as an allegory, recalls Jotham's parable (Judg 9:7-15).

Despite Amaziah's violent death outside Jerusalem, he was of David's line. Amaziah is buried in the City of David with his ancestors, and his son Azariah succeeds him.

14:23-29 Jeroboam II of Israel. Jeroboam II, like his namesake, is an evil northern king. Yet his reign is long and prosperous (we know this from 2 Kings and from the prophets Amos and Hosea). This combination of evil and a long prosperous reign is inconsistent with traditional Deuteronomistic theology, where prosperity is normally a consequence of good, and suffering a consequence of evil. However, the long prosperous reign of an evil king can be explained if it fulfills a prophetic promise: the power of the prophet's word will always be accomplished. An interesting thing about verse 25, however, is that it notes the fulfillment of a prophecy that no preceding text has made. This is the first time in the Deuteronomistic History that Jonah, son of Amittai, is mentioned.

15:1-7 Azariah of Judah. The Deuteronomist's judgment of Azariah's reign, like the reign of his father, is mixed. His mother, Jecholiah, is from Jerusalem. Azariah does good in the Lord's eyes; his reign is long (through the reigns of five northern kings). But the high places remain, and he becomes a leper. Azariah, of David's line, is buried with his ancestors in the City of David and is succeeded by his son Jotham.

15:8-12 Zechariah of Israel. Jeroboam's son stands in contrast to his strong father; he maintains the throne for only six months before falling victim to a conspiracy. The Deuteronomistic historian sees both his reign and its termination as the fulfillment of the Lord's word to Jehu (see 2 Kgs 10:30).

15:13-16 Shallum of Israel. Not much can be said about Shallum's one-month reign. The instability of the throne is obvious. Another conspiracy and another king. Even before the Deuteronomistic theologian can evaluate Menahem, Shallum's murderer and successor,

the reader can predict what the judgment will be for a king who cruelly takes revenge on the innocent and on those who had been faithful to their king.

15:17-22 Menahem of Israel. Menahem receives the Deuteronomist's condemnation, as one would expect. He is evil, like Jeroboam. He postpones the potential Assyrian threat and secures his throne by paying tribute to the Assyrian king—tribute he has exacted from his own people.

15:23-26 Pekahiah of Israel. Pekahiah is not spared the Deuteronomistic judgment accorded all northern kings. Menahem's son maintains the throne for two years but is then murdered by his adjutant, Pekah.

15:27-31 Pekah of Israel. Pekah is also evil and is compared to Jeroboam. During his reign Israel continues to be troubled by Assyria. Tribute is no longer sufficient; Assyria takes over some Israelite land. Pekah is not strong enough to withstand Hoshea's conspiracy.

15:32-38 Jotham of Judah. The first thing to note is another confusion in names—Azariah and Uzziah as designations for Jotham's father—probably caused here, too, by the presence of two sources. Jotham, like his father, does good in the eyes of the Lord; he survives a sixteen-year reign and builds one of the gates of the temple. Yet the high places remain; Aram and Israel oppress Judah. When Jotham dies, he is buried with his ancestors in the City of David and is succeeded by his son Ahaz.

16:1-20 Ahaz of Judah. Ahaz merits condemnation of the Deuteronomistic historian for his idolatry and child sacrifice (compare Gen 22). Judah is significantly weakened at this time. The Edomites have recaptured territories, and the Aram-Israelite coalition has attacked Judah, with the intention of removing Ahaz from the throne. Though their plan is unsuccessful, it forces a Judean-Assyrian alliance that, for all practical purposes, makes Judah a vassal of Assyria. The prophet Isaiah warned against such an alliance (Isa 7:1-16). The increase of Assyrian influence means not only the continued presence of syncretism, the high places, and idolatry, as well as the pillaging of the Lord's temple, but also the replacing of Yahweh's altar with an Assyrian one. From the Deuteronomistic theologian's perspective, what greater insult could Yahweh be rendered?

Yet, in spite of everything, Ahaz is David's descendant. Therefore, he is buried with his ancestors in the City of David and is succeeded by his son Hezekiah.

17:1-41 Hoshea of Israel. Assyria destroyed the northern kingdom of Israel once and for all about 721 B.C.E. (see 2 Kgs 18:9-12). It was standard Assyrian policy to take into exile many of the leading citizens of a conquered nation (for example, the priests) and to transplant foreign peoples into the subjugated territory. The aim was to prevent the development of opposition capable of effecting a conspiracy.

The text notes three stages in the development of postexilic syncretism in Israel. Since Yahweh is the God of the land, appropriate worship need be rendered to Yahweh alone. However, since the dominant population, at least in influence, is now non-Israelite, Yahweh is ignored. A compromise is reached when Yahwism is combined with the idolatrous practices of other peoples.

The Deuteronomistic theologian interprets Israel's demise as fitting punishment for all the evil committed against the Lord. Both Israel and Judah have constantly and consistently turned a deaf ear to prophetic warnings. Now Israel, at the hand of Assyria, has paid for its infidelity. Moreover, the future seems ominous for Judah. The dynasty of David remains, but if it has more kings like Ahaz (see 2 Kgs 16), one must ask, "For how long?"

PART V:
THE KINGDOM OF JUDAH
AFTER 721 B.C.E.

2 Kgs 18:1–25:30

18:1-12 Hezekiah. Hezekiah is very unlike his father; he is even compared to David! Not only is Hezekiah credited with destroying the remnants of Ahaz's idolatry, but he even removes the bronze serpent that Moses made (see Num 21:9). His fidelity is rewarded with a twenty-nine-year reign, prosperity, victory over Philistine cities, and the securing of independence from Assyria in the early stages of his reign, at the very time when Israel is conquered.

18:13-37 Invasion of Sennacherib. Yet, Assyria remains a serious threat. The dialogue recorded here focuses on whom to trust: Hezekiah and his God, or the powerful king of Assyria (compare Isa 36 and 1 Kgs 18). Hezekiah is made to look weak, whereas past Assyrian victories are recounted. By now the reader can predict the Deuteronomist's judgment. Fidelity to the Lord and the covenant will yield success, no matter what the odds. Trust in a foreign power and an idolatrous people, however, can only bring doom.

19:1-19 Hezekiah and Isaiah. Having heard the message of the Assyrian king, Hezekiah proceeds to the temple of the Lord and consults Yahweh's prophet Isaiah. Before Hezekiah has even heard the prophet's consoling word, he imagines a happy outcome: Yahweh angry at Assyrian pride and punishing them accordingly. Isaiah confirms that there is no reason for Hezekiah to fear the Assyrian king. When the king of Assyria repeats his threats, Hezekiah again seeks the Lord (compare Isa 37:1-20).

19:20-37 Punishment of Sennacherib. Isaiah again consoles Hezekiah. "For the sake of David," the Deuteronomistic historian reminds the reader, Assyria will not destroy Jerusalem.

The power of the prophet's word is quickly effected. Yahweh, Israel's warrior, destroys many Assyrian troops, and the survivors flee. Nor does the Assyrian king escape punishment; rather, his own sons kill him. Whereas Yahweh's temple had been a source of deliverance for Hezekiah and Judah, Nisroch's temple becomes the site of Sennacherib's murder (compare Isa 37:21-38).

20:1-21 Hezekiah's illness. Hezekiah's relationship with the Lord is further developed by his cure. Although Isaiah had prophesied that Hezekiah would die from his illness, Hezekiah entreats the Lord, who hears his prayer and adds fifteen years to his life. The sign that the prophet's revised word would be fulfilled is the miraculous movement of a shadow (compare Isa 38:1-8), an immediate indication of the effective power of Yahweh (compare 1 Kgs 13:3-5).

With the emergence of Babylon as a world power, Assyria ceased to be a major threat to the nations of the ancient Near East. Such was the political reality. The Deuteronomistic History, however, uses this opportunity to foreshadow Babylon's eventual victory over Judah with a prophetic proclamation to Hezekiah. Friendliness to Babylon, whether now by Hezekiah or later by Josiah, will not prevent Judah's demise at their hands. Yet, Hezekiah himself will continue to be rewarded for his own fidelity; the doom will come only after his death (compare Isa 39). Hezekiah, of David's line, is buried with his ancestors and is succeeded by his son Manasseh.

21:1-18 Reign of Manasseh. Manasseh's desecration of Jerusalem with innocent blood and his violation of the Lord's temple with every possible expression of idolatry are unforgivable. The promise made to Solomon of the Lord's continued presence in his temple and a Davidic descendant continually on the throne of Israel (see 1 Kgs 9:3-5) was conditioned on the kings' adherence to covenant fidelity. The Deuteronomistic theologian now calls on the word of God, through the prophets, to condemn Manasseh's sin and to predict the dire consequences it will have on Judah. The end is coming.

The Deuteronomistic historian acknowledges the fact that Manasseh survived on the throne of Israel for fifty-five years, the longest recorded reign of any Davidic king, yet he was also judged theologically to be the most evil of them. Perhaps the subtle note that Manasseh was buried "in the palace garden, the garden of Uzza" (v. 18) rather than an explicit statement that he was buried with his ancestors in the City of David is his way of judging Manasseh most harshly. To be buried, first of all, and then to be buried with one's ancestors was of prime importance to the Israelites. In spite of Manasseh's evil, his son succeeded him; a Davidic king remained on the throne as long as the nation of Judah existed.

21:19-26 Reign of Amon. A "chip off the old block," Amon is condemned for doing evil similar to that which his father had done. However, Amon falls more easily into the curses such sin merits: his reign lasts only two years; he is murdered; and he is buried, like his father, in the garden of Uzza. The instability of the people can be seen by the murder of those who murder. In any case, Amon's son Josiah is able to succeed him as king.

22:1-7 Reign of Josiah. Josiah, like Hezekiah, merits comparison to David. Moreover, just as Joash restored the temple after the evil Athaliah's reign, so Josiah sets out to do likewise (compare 2 Kgs 11–12).

22:8–23:30 The book of the law. Josiah is in the process of renovating the temple when the book of the law is found. When he hears its content, he judges his own ancestors by its standards and becomes fearful for Judah's future; the nation merits Yahweh's curses. To further evaluate the book's potential impact on Judah, he sends it to the prophetess Huldah, who will render the Lord's judgment. The word she speaks is twofold: yes, Judah will be punished for its history of sin; however, because of Josiah's distress over the Lord's word, the nation will not be destroyed until after the king's death (compare 1 Kgs 21:29).

The reading of the book of the law in the presence of all the people recalls Moses' command that such a reading be done (Deut 31:9-13). The covenant renewal ceremony recalls both Josh 24:25-27 and 2 Kgs 11:17-20. The covenant ceremony and the proclamation of the law symbolize Israel's recommitment to Yahweh.

Josiah's purification of the temple is as extensive as Manasseh's desecration of it. Specific comment is also made concerning the removal of all the idolatrous remnants left over from the reigns of Solomon, Ahaz, and Manasseh in Judah, and even from that of Jeroboam in Israel. Josiah does, in fact, fulfill the word of the prophet recorded about him in 1 Kgs 13:2. Moreover, the celebration of Passover—a return to the nation's roots—is here reestablished (compare Exod 12; Num 9; Deut 16; Josh 5).

How can the Deuteronomistic theologian accommodate the good that Josiah effected in Judah with the imminent fall of the nation to Babylon? He repeats the prophetic condemnation of Manasseh (see 2 Kgs 21:10-15), reminding the reader of the curses Judah would suffer for its neglect of the covenant (2 Kgs 22:16). And Josiah dies before his nation falls.

Josiah dies at the battle of Meggido (609 B.C.E.). Judah has aligned itself with Babylon against an Egypt-Assyrian coalition; thus the king is killed at the hands of Egypt. This historical truth cannot be denied, in spite of the Deuteronomistic judgment of Josiah's reign. However, Josiah is returned to Jerusalem to be buried and is succeeded by his son Jehoahaz.

Many scholars question whether the book of the law was found in the temple or compiled for the first time, from ancient laws, at this period. They also question whether Josiah established—again, for the first time—or reestablished the Passover. For the purposes of this commentary, it suffices to know that there are good arguments to support both positions.

23:31-35 Reign of Jehoahaz. The Deuteronomistic judgment on Jehoahaz is quite simple: he does evil, for which he is punished. His punishment is a three-month reign, exile to Egypt, and death in exile. His successor, although a Davidic descendant, is not his son but one of the sons of Josiah, his half-brother. Egypt's power over Judah's king is symbolized by the change in name—Eliakim to Jehoiakim; he is not to be understood as a servant of the Davidic covenant and of Yahweh but of Egypt. He does what a vassal should do: he collects tribute from the people to placate Pharaoh Neco.

23:36-24:7 Reign of Jehoiakim. With Babylon's decisive victory over Egypt at the battle of Carchemish (605 B.C.E.), Judah's enemy changed names. The threat that had been Egypt-Assyria was now, decisively, Babylon. In fact, Judah became Babylon's vassal.

Jehoiakim's vain attempt to overthrow the power of Babylon could only yield disaster. The Deuteronomistic historian uses this opportunity to explain Judah's fall as prophetic fulfillment. The Lord has changed sides; God now supports all those nations that are against Judah, and this because of Manasseh's sins (see 2 Kgs 21:10-15). Yet, in spite of Jehoiakim's evil, he is of David's line; he rests with his ancestors and is succeeded by his son Jehoiachin.

24:8-17 Reign of Jehoiachin. Jehoiachin, whose mother, Nehushta, is from Jerusalem, himself does evil in the Lord's eyes. His reign lasts only three months. Isaiah had foretold Jehoiachin's exile to Babylon, along with the exile of others and the confiscation of the temple and palace treasuries (see 2 Kgs 20:17-18). Again, the word of the Lord is effective. When Nebuchadnezzar places Jehoiachin's uncle as puppet king on Judah's throne, he changes his name, the same thing Pharaoh

Neco had done to Eliakim and for similar reasons. Mattaniah (Zedekiah) is fully under Babylonian control.

24:18-25:21 Reign of Zedekiah. Zedekiah does evil in the Lord's eyes as his predecessor had done. In fact, he functions as Nebuchadnezzar's puppet for a while, in spite of Babylon's harsh treatment of Judah, but then he rebels. He is not strong enough, however, to rebel, either militarily (from a historical perspective) or by way of fidelity to Yahweh (from a theological perspective). The consequence is, as one might expect, disaster. Zedekiah is captured and blinded, his sons slain. Moreover, Jerusalem is totally devastated: the temple is dismantled and burned, as are the palace and the other large dwellings. The city walls are destroyed, and another wave of people are taken into exile. In addition, the exiles close to the king are killed.

25:22-26 Governorship of Gedaliah. Nebuchadnezzar's delegate, according to this testimony, wants a peaceful situation in Judah and is willing to abide Judah's former army commanders and the citizens who remain in the land. Among these, however, is one Ishmael, who leads a rebellion; a takeover, however, is impossible. As a result, since they have murdered the Babylonian governor, the Judeans are forced to flee to Egypt, for fear of Babylonian retaliation (compare Jer 40–44).

25:27-30 Release of Jehoiachin. The granting of amnesty on the occasion of a new king's inauguration was a relatively common practice in the ancient Near East. For this reason many think that the notation that Jehoiachin was released from prison is historically accurate. But, even so, why should these verses, a duplication of which is found at the end of the book of Jeremiah, end the Deuteronomistic History? Some scholars believe that the History was written to explain why Judah fell. Others hold that the History is a call to future fidelity: learn from the past for the present. Those who prefer this latter interpretation see these final verses as open to a new future. Yes, Judah had been destroyed; yes, the temple had been burned; yes, the Davidic dynasty, as it had been known, was at an end. But . . . the king had not been killed; the Davidic promise had not been totally snuffed out. In fact, Jehoiachin is given a seat above other kings and eats daily at the Babylonian king's table. That this assertion has symbolic significance—whether or not it is historically true—is clear from a similar reference in the Deuteronomistic History (compare 2 Sam 9:7).

If we were to follow the inspired record of Judah's history further, we would see that hope does lie, long after the Exile, in a Davidic successor. The Gospel of Matthew, for instance, is quick to name Jesus as "son of David" (Matt 1:1).

1 AND 2 CHRONICLES

Alice L. Laffey, R.S.M.

INTRODUCTION

Scholars believe that the books of Chronicles are a rewriting of Israel's history from the perspective of postexilic priests. It is commonly agreed that these books were written after the Deuteronomistic History, probably even after the exiles had returned to Judah. Generally speaking, the unique texts and the additions describe matters of particular interest to priests, including sabbath observance, ritual specifications, descriptions of various temple accessories, and the like. Because much of the content of these books is identical to the content of the Deuteronomistic History, and since space is limited in a commentary such as this, only those passages which are unique to the books of Chronicles and which, by the nature of their content, shed light on the Chronicler's particular theological purpose will be commented on here.

Yahweh's temple and Israel's postexilic identity

Yahweh's chosen people, those for whom Yahweh had been warrior and king (see Exod 15:3, 18; compare Zeph 3:15, 17), the recipients of the Lord's promises of land, progeny, and prosperity, are now deprived of national independence. The glorious promises lie in Israel's past; the present is haunted by Persian domination. If there is to be hope for the future, it must be found in Israel's identity as Yahweh's people and, consequently, in conscientious and enthusiastic dedication to the Lord's presence in their midst—thus the importance of Yahweh's temple and Yahweh's priests for postexilic Israel and for the Chronicler. The Chronicler encourages a downtrod-den people. All is not lost. They remain the Lord's people, and in that very bond is their future.

The monarchic ideal

Reading through the books of Chronicles, one notes radical differences between the Deuteronomist's and the Chronicler's portrayal of Judah's kings. David and Solomon are idealized by the Chronicler. There is no lust for Bathsheba, no prophetic condemnation, no betrayal by one's son, no potential conspiracy. David emerges as the model monarch. And the same can be said of Solomon. One never learns from the Chronicler of Solomon's seven hundred foreign wives and consequent idolatry. Solomon, like his father, is fully faithful to his God. Pride in one's past is hope for one's future; fidelity is the foundation on which to build the future. The God of David's covenant, the God who continues to give life to postexilic Israel, needs fully faithful followers, and they, in turn, need the memory of model monarchs.

The northern kingdom, condemned by the Deuteronomist from Jeroboam I onward, does not even merit mention in the Chronicler's account. There is no time for their infidelity, no place for memories best forgotten. The Chronicler deemphasizes the two kingdoms of Israel's sinful past in order to highlight the one chosen people of the Lord.

The Deuteronomistic theology

While the Deuteronomist understood well-being and prosperity as God's blessing and reward for covenant fidelity, while curses of one kind or another were God's punishment for infidelity, the Chronicler makes the relationship even more precise. He makes no mention of Hezekiah's possessing any shortcomings. The evil Manasseh receives not only immediate condemnation but also immediate punishment. And for the Chronicler, it is not Manasseh who causes Judah's downfall (compare 2 Kgs 23:26), since he is succeeded by the noble Josiah; rather, Judah's fall is fitting recompense for cumulative evil, and especially for the sinfulness of Judah's last kings.

COMMENTARY: 1 CHRONICLES

PART I: GENEALOGICAL TABLES

1 Chr 1:1–9:34

The first section of Chronicles has no parallel in the Deuteronomistic History. Genealogies are normally associated, however, with the Priestly writer of the Pentateuch. For example, Gen 5:1-28 traces the lineage from Adam to Noah (compare 1 Chr 1:1-4); Gen 11:10-17, 31-32, the lineage from Shem to Abraham (compare 1 Chr 1:10-27, 31-32); and Gen 25:12-17 traces the sons of Ishmael (compare 1 Chr 1:29-31). Moreover, a table of nations compiled by the Priestly writer in Gen 10 indicates where the families in the patriarchal line settled (compare 1 Chr 1:4-23 and 4:1–8:40).

The Priestly writer has a penchant for order. Creation, in his account, takes place in climactic order within six days (Gen 1:1–2:4); there is a census taken of the Israelite tribes before their departure from Sinai (Num 1:1-54; compare 1 Chr 4:1–8:40), and the tribes are arranged for departure (Num 2:1-34); a separate census is taken of the Levites (Num 4:1-49); and, finally, a list of the scouts sent to spy out Canaan is enumerated (Num 13:16).

The line of descent from Jacob to David consists of ten men: Perez, Hezron, Ram, Amminadab, Nahshon, Salmah, Boaz, Obed, Jesse, and David (1 Chr 2:3-25). One notes also how tersely the Davidic line is summarized (1 Chr 3:1-24) with an indication that Judah is carried into captivity in Babylon because of its rebellion (1 Chr 9:1). Those who return, those with whom the Chronicler is most familiar, are lay Israelites, Levites, priests, and temple slaves (1 Chr 9:2).

In postexilic Jerusalem the remnants of the tribes, those originally both from northern Israel and from southern Judah, dwelt together. Yet those most influential in the land were the priests and those associated with them.

PART II: THE HISTORY OF DAVID

1 Chr 9:35–29:29

The remainder of the first book of Chronicles is devoted to David. The text is similar to, yet different from, the books of Samuel. First of all, there is no elaborate description of the pros and cons of kingship; monarchy is a given. King Saul functions here—his genealogy and the account of his death and burial—as no more than a context in which to introduce David. In contrast, the role of priests, sacred objects, and sacred places is emphasized. Though 1 Chr 15 in many ways parallels 2 Sam 6—David's bringing the ark of the covenant up to Jerusalem—the following chapter in Chronicles, an addition, is dedicated to the Levites who minister at the ark and their prayers. Moreover, toward the end of David's reign, he himself begins preparations for the temple (1 Chr 22:2-5).

Similarly, the Chronicler notes that before David's death, he organized the Levites into classes (1 Chr 23): the priests (1 Chr 24); the singers (1 Chr 25); the gatekeepers, the treasurers, and the magistrates (1 Chr 26); the army commanders, the tribal heads, and the overseers (1 Chr 27). These chapters have no counterparts in the books of Samuel.

10:13-14 Judgment of Saul. This small addition to the account of Saul's death in Kings is a good example of how the author of Chronicles makes even more explicit the Deuteronomistic theology. Saul's death is explained as a consequence of his rebellion against the Lord (compare 1 Sam 13:13-14 and 15:22-23) and of his consulting the witch of Endor (1 Sam 28).

11:42–13:5 David's mighty men. Typical of the Chronicler, he lists names in great number. In addition to the military supporters enumerated in 1 Chr 11:10-41 (compare 2 Sam 23:8-39), additional names are here given. Except for this mention, we know nothing of these men.

David's army is described in ideal terms: the bowmen can shoot arrows and sling stones with both hands (12:2); the warriors are experts with shield and spear. Men from all Israel—all the tribes—support David. Everyone recognizes that God helps David (1 Chr 13:18); his great army is like an "army of God." David is anointed king over Israel in Hebron (1 Chr 11:3) and gradually wins support for kingship over all Israel (1 Chr 13:38).

15:1-24 The ark brought to Jerusalem. This is a more extensive version of 2 Sam 6. Again, emphasis is given to the Levites. They alone may transport the ark, and they are to direct the appropriate musical accompaniments for the occasion.

16:37-42 Attendants before the ark. Having brought the ark to Jerusalem and having celebrated its presence there, David commissions certain men to remain with the ark. These will offer appropriate sacrifices and make appropriate thanksgiving, while others will serve as gatekeepers and musicians.

21:26–22:19 The altar, the temple, and Solomon. The text asserts that the site of Ornan's threshing floor became the site of Jerusalem's temple. It was more appropriate than Gibeon because the Lord had heard David's prayer here.

Chapter 22 builds on chapter 17. The promise announced there to David—that his son would build the temple—is here developed. David collects materials and workers for the temple and commissions his son. In contrast with David, who fought wars and shed blood, Solomon is to be a man of peace. Whereas 1 Kgs 3 explains that there was not yet sufficient peace in Israel during David's reign for him to build the temple, the Lord now grants this peace to Solomon. Postexilic Judah longs for peace. *Shalom* means much more than an absence of fighting; the term refers to the fullest possible well-being.

23:1-32 The Levitical classes. In contrast with the account in 2 Kgs 1–2, the Chronicler does not depict Solomon as having any rivals to his throne.

All Levites thirty years old and older (v. 3; but see v. 24) are to serve the Lord's temple, the courts, and the chambers. Whether by their presence at the sacrifices, their care of the sacred vessels, or by prayer, their lives are to be devoted to the temple.

24:1-19 The priestly classes. At the time of David there was no distinction between the Levitical and priestly classes. Here lies an anachronism. These men are also temple officers, whose functions are assigned impartially by lot.

24:20-31 Other Levites. The men whose names are listed in typical priestly fashion also served the temple and, just like Aaron's descendants, they too are assigned temple tasks impartially.

25:1-30 The singers. One notes here a reference to David's musical talent (compare 1 Sam 16:18). The music ministers also cast lots to determine their functions in non-hierarchical fashion: young and old, master and apprentice—twenty-four lots in all.

26:1-19 Classes of gatekeepers. The families of Kore and Merari provide the gatekeepers. Again, lots are cast to determine the watches and the gates. No preference is accorded larger families over smaller ones, or vice versa.

26:20-28 Treasurers. All the temples of the ancient Near East had treasuries, and the temple at Jerusalem was no exception (compare 1 Kgs 14:26). These treasuries contained the valuable offerings from previous kings as well as the treasures of the present ruler.

26:29-32 Magistrates. David also appoints civil officials, judges, and police officers to ensure the efficient and effective administration of his kingdom.

27:1-15 Army commanders. Twelve groups of twenty-four thousand men, with each group having its own commander, form David's standing army.

27:16-24 Tribal heads. There is also a leader for each of Israel's twelve tribes. A census is not permitted, since the Lord had promised that Israel would be numerous beyond counting (compare 2 Sam 24 and 1 Chr 21).

27:25-31 Overseers. David also appoints administrators over his treasury, the storehouses, farm workers, the vineyards and their produce, the olive and sycamore trees and the oil, over the cattle, camels, she-asses, and the flocks.

27:32-34 David's court. Jonathan and Jehiel tutor David's sons. Ahithophel (compare 2 Sam 16:23), Jehoiada, and Abiathar (compare 1 Sam 22:20-23) are counselors; and Hushai is David's confidant (compare 2 Sam 17:1-23). Joab commands the king's army (compare 2 Sam 8:16 and 20:23).

28:1-10 The assembly at Jerusalem. 1 Chr 17 (compare 2 Sam 7) promises David a dynasty; the prophet further proclaims that David's son will build the Lord's temple. 1 Chr 22 gives a further explanation of why David will not build the temple—he has shed too much blood. But Solomon must be careful to observe the precepts and decrees that the Lord gave Moses for Israel (1 Chr 22:13). Now, in chapter 28, David commissions Solomon as his successor and reasserts Solomon's role in establishing David's dynasty and in building the Lord's temple. More explicitly than in the other texts, however, the author warns of the consequences of Solomon's infidelity: if he abandons the Lord, he will be cast off forever (1 Chr 28:9).

28:11-21 Temple plans given to Solomon. In contrast with the account in 1 Kings, in which David is already dead before Solomon initiates the building of the temple, here David does the planning and lays most of the groundwork. By the time of the writing of Chronicles, David is clearly understood to be Israel's ideal king.

29:1-9 Offerings for the temple. The temple, the house of the Lord, deserves the most exquisite adornments. Therefore, as a statement of David's wholehearted commitment to the Lord and his dwelling place, David freely gives his personal treasury to enhance the future temple. In so doing,

David becomes a model for all wealthy Israelites.

29:10-22 David's prayer. 2 Sam 22 is a thanksgiving prayer attributed to David and inserted into the Deuteronomistic History. The Chronicler parallels this prayer with a shorter one of his own. Not only do his sentiments include praise, but David here adds typical self-abnegation formulae with appropriate petitions (compare 2 Sam 7:18-19 and 1 Chr 17:16-27).

29:22-25 Solomon anointed. David had named Solomon his successor (1 Chr 23:1). In contrast with the first chapters of 1 Kings, this account presents no struggle; here there are no contenders for David's throne; here no enemies or potential conspirators need be removed. This latter account is, of course, an idealization. Anything needlessly problematic, anything that would show either David or Solomon in less than favorable light has been omitted.

29:26-30 Death of David. The Chronicler accords David a slightly more expanded death notice than that which he receives in 1 Kgs 2:10-11. It resembles those given by the Deuteronomistic historian to the other kings of his line. However, here three sources are named—two of the allusions are probably the creations of the Chronicler—from which one is supposed to be able to secure further information about David's reign. The Book of Samuel is a legitimate source familiar to readers of the Old Testament, but what about the histories of Nathan and of Gad? Did those prophets, like the Chroniclers of Israel and Judah, once compose written records that now are lost? Or is the allusion meant merely to call one's attention to these three men of God who validated David as Yahweh's chosen servant and Israel's king?

COMMENTARY: 2 CHRONICLES

PART I: THE REIGN OF SOLOMON

2 Chr 1:1–9:31

The first nine chapters of 2 Chronicles closely parallel 1 Kgs 3–11 and describe the reign of Solomon. More attention, however, is paid to priestly things, as one might expect. For example, in 2 Chr 1:2-5, the narrator makes a special point of distinguishing between the tent of meeting at Gibeon, where Solomon went to pray and to offer sacrifice, and the ark of God at Jerusalem, in the tent that David had pitched for it. No attempt is made in 1 Kings to explain why, if both the ark and the tent were in Jerusalem (see 2 Sam 7:2), Solomon went to Gibeon to worship (see 1 Kgs 3:4). The Chronicler notices the inconsistency and provides an explanation. Although Gibeon no longer functioned as an appropriate place for David to worship (see 1 Chr 21:28–22:1), the tent of meeting still remained there; thus it was appropriate for Solomon to go there.

In a similar way, Solomon, in appealing to Hiram of Tyre for aid in building the Lord's temple, adds a far more detailed explanation than is found in 1 Kgs 5:1-12 of the functions to be performed in the future temple: the burning of incense and sweet spices (compare Exod 30); the continual offering of the show-bread (compare Lev 24:5-9); the burnt offerings—morning and evening, on the sabbaths, on the new moons, and at the appointed feasts. The Israelites who were ordered to help with temple building were "aliens living in the land" (1 Chr 22:2; 2 Chr 2:17-18; but compare 1 Kgs 9:15-22 and 2 Chr 8:7-9).

The Chronicler specifies what the Deuteronomistic historian had only suggested: that the site purchased by David where he had offered sacrifice after the census (see 2 Sam 24:18-25 and 1 Chr 21:16-30) became, in fact, the location of the temple. The only other reference to Moriah in the Old Testament occurs in Gen 22. There it is the mountain on which Abraham almost sacrificed Isaac to the Lord. The Chronicler here connects the fidelity of Abraham and the sacredness of his sacrifice with Israel's new cultic site.

After the temple had been built, the ark was brought into it in procession (compare 1 Kgs 8:1-9). To the Deuteronomist's description the Chronicler adds further detail: the priests present sanctified themselves without regard to divisions (compare 1 Chr 24); all the Levitical singers stood with their cymbals, harps, and lyres alongside the priest trumpeters east of the altar, and they all praised the Lord in unison (compare 1 Chr 25). The words of their song echo Psalms 118 and 136.

7:1-3. After Solomon's prayer dedicating the temple, the Chronicler adds that God's acceptance of it took the form of a fire coming down from heaven and consuming the offerings (compare 1 Chr 21:26; Lev 9:24; and even 1 Kgs 18:38-39). The people responded by rendering adoration to the Lord. The musical instruments made by David for the Lord's praise are used at the dedication (compare 1 Chr 17:41-42).

7:13-15. The Chronicler inserts into the Lord's response to Solomon's prayer an affirmation that Solomon's requests will be granted. After drought, locust plague, and pestilence—the Lord's punishments for Israel's sins—if the people repent and seek the Lord, God will forgive them and restore their health and the well-being of their land. Yet, the same conditions set forth in 1 Kgs 9 are included here: Fidelity to the Lord like David's will ensure the continuation of the dynasty; idolatry, however, will lead to the temple's destruction and to exile.

8:11. Solomon had married Pharaoh's daughter, and, according to the account in 1 Kings, she lived in the City of David until Solomon built her a home. The Chronicler, subtly emphasizing the taint of a foreign woman, acknowledges her role as Solomon's wife, but points out that she does not live in the house of David. The place where the ark of the Lord had been is considered holy; therefore, it is inappropriate for her to dwell there.

8:12-15. The Chronicler establishes Solomon as a model worshiper. According to the duty of each day—the sabbaths, the new moons (compare Num 28:14; 29:6), the three annual feasts (compare Lev 23)—Solomon offers appropriate sacrifices; he also appoints the divisions of the priests (see 1 Chr 24), the Levites (see 1 Chr 23), and the gatekeepers (see 1 Chr 26). The Chronicler idealizes Solomon;

contrary to the Deuteronomist's record, there is no mention of Solomon's infidelity.

9:29. Just as the Chronicler names sources for further information about David and his reign (compare 1 Chr 29:29), so here mention is made of records containing more information about Solomon: the history of Nathan, the prophecy of Ahijah, and the visions of Iddo.

PART II:
THE MONARCHY BEFORE HEZEKIAH
2 Chr 10:1–27:9

10:1–12:16 The reign of Rehoboam. The Chronicler adds to the Deuteronomist's account of Rehoboam's reign the building of several fortified cities. He further reports that the priests and Levites who had been in the north came south to Judah and Jerusalem, having been expelled by Jeroboam. In addition, those who sought the Lord also came south to Jerusalem to sacrifice.

The first three years of Rehoboam's reign are secure not only because he administers well but, more importantly, because he is faithful to the Lord (no such testimony is given in Kings!). The Chronicler gives an account, omitted from Kings, of Rehoboam's family: eighteen wives, sixty concubines, twenty-eight sons, and sixty daughters. Rehoboam wants Abijah, the eldest son of his favorite wife, Maacah, to succeed him (in 1 Kgs 1–2 Solomon, the eldest living son of Bathsheba, is David's choice).

The second part of Rehoboam's reign is characterized by infidelity to the Lord. The Chronicler's insertion here is consistent with Deuteronomistic theology: the Lord sends Shishak, king of Egypt, to punish Judah's sin (12:1-2). The Lord, however, sends Shemaiah to Rehoboam to interpret for him what is happening. Rehoboam has abandoned the Lord, so the Lord is abandoning Rehoboam. Repentance leads to a mitigation of the intended and deserved punishment; though Shishak attacks Jerusalem, Judah is not completely destroyed.

More information about Rehoboam can be found in the chronicles of Shemaiah and of Iddo (12:15). Again, we note a priestly alteration of the text of Kings, which says that further information about Rehoboam can be found in the chronicles of the kings of Judah.

13:1-22 The reign of Abijah. Whereas Rehoboam's son Abijah (Abijam in Kings) is dispensed with in a brief eight verses of the Deuteronomistic History, the Chronicler devotes considerably more attention to him and characterizes him very differently. In 1 Kgs 15:3 he walks in the sins of his father, and his heart is not wholly true to God. For the Chronicler, he is a foil for Jeroboam. Abijah, in contrast to Jeroboam, has fallen heir to the covenant of salt (compare Lev 2:13). The two fight, and despite Jeroboam's larger army and shrewder military strategy, Abijah's trust in the Lord is rewarded with victory. The Chronicler also adds a note about his family: fourteen wives, twenty-two sons, and sixteen daughters. More information can be learned about the ways of Abijah by consulting the story of the prophet Iddo (v. 22).

14:1–15:19 The first part of Asa's reign. A mere fifteen verses describe Asa's reign in 1 Kgs 15; in contrast, the Chronicler elaborates for almost three chapters. Though nowhere in the Chronicler's account of the previous kings of Judah does it say that they worshiped idols, the Chronicler, nevertheless, praises Asa for removing the foreign altars, the high places, the pillars, the Asherim, the incense altars. Moreover, the earliest part of Asa's reign is blessed with peace, and when there is war with the Ethiopians, the Lord rewards Judah's faithfulness and brings victory.

The prophet Azariah, introduced as Asa's counselor, warns Asa to be faithful. Again, there is explicit reference to the theology of the Deuteronomist: If you seek the Lord, you will find the Lord; if you forsake the Lord, the Lord will forsake you. The prophet's words spur Asa on to greater fidelity, evidenced by the removal of idols, the repair of the temple, and even a recommitment to covenant fidelity. (Joash and Josiah are the only kings of Judah in the books of Kings who explicitly make a covenant with the Lord [compare 2 Kgs 11:17 and 23:3].)

16:1-14 Asa's infidelity. The latter part of Asa's reign meets with political, personal, and theological disaster. Asa turns from trusting God to trusting human forces; for protection against Israel he makes an alliance with Aram instead of trusting in God. Hanani the seer (missing from the Deuteronomistic History) condemns Asa's sin, suggests the happy outcome that would have accrued to Judah had

Asa not sinned, and names the punishment. Asa does not repent and imprisons Hanani. Later, when the king's feet become diseased, Asa does not seek relief from God but consults physicians. Such lack of fidelity can only lead to trouble. The Chronicler makes explicit Deuteronomistic theology: the latter part of Asa's reign suffers from instability and war.

17:1–21:3 The reign of Jehoshaphat. Just as the Chronicler's accounts of most of the kings of Judah contain more detail than their Deuteronomistic counterparts, so likewise the Chronicler gives a more extensive record of Jehoshaphat's reign. He is introduced as a king zealous for the law (compare 1 Kgs 22:43, 47). But then he makes a marriage alliance with Ahab. Anyone familiar with the books of Kings knows that, in the Deuteronomist's judgment, Ahab is a very evil king of Israel. One waits for further judgment on Jehoshaphat. When Ahab and Jehoshaphat fight against Ramoth-gilead, Jehoshaphat wishes to consult the Lord; he therefore escapes theological condemnation. The Chronicler's account of Ahab's and Jehoshaphat's encounter with the lying prophets and Micaiah is very similar to the narrative of 1 Kgs 22.

Added to the Deuteronomistic account of Jehoshaphat's reign is another narrative about battle, this one with the Moabites and the Ammonites (20:1). Jehoshaphat seeks the Lord and is rewarded; Jahaziel, a Levite, proclaims the assuring word of the Lord. The Lord will fight for Judah, and Judah will be victorious. The Chronicler is consistent with only part of the traditional holy-war theology, however. Yahweh wins the victory, but whereas customary holy-war theology demanded that all the spoils of the battle be sacrificed to Yahweh, here all the enemy soldiers are dead (they have killed each other), but the spoils of war—cattle, clothing, and precious things—are, without any later theological reprimand, seized by the Judean army.

Although Jehoshaphat's first alliance with Israel had not caused theological condemnation, his latter alliance with King Ahaziah does. According to the Chronicler, the two of them built ships together. The prophet Eliezer condemns the alliance and predicts the ships' destruction (20:37).

21:4-20 The reign of Jehoram. Both the Deuteronomist and the Chronicler judge Jehoram to be an evil king. The Chronicler justi-

fies his judgment with further elaboration of Jehoram's wrongdoing. He, the first-born of Jehoshaphat's six sons, has killed his brothers and other princes of Israel. And if that were not enough, he has built high places and has encouraged idolatry. The prophet Elijah is inserted into the Chronicler's account with the kind of condemnation one might expect: the Lord will bring a great plague on Jehoram's family, and he himself will suffer from a severe disease of the bowels. Elijah's prophecy is fulfilled when the Philistines and the Arabs take into exile all Jehoram's possessions, including his family, with the exception of his youngest son. Jehoram himself is stricken with the predicted terminal disease.

A major change made by the Chronicler is to note that Jehoram was buried in the City of David, but not in the tomb of the kings (compare 2 Kgs 8:24).

22:1-9 The reign of Ahaziah (Jehoahaz in 2 Chr 21:17). Ahaziah is an evil king in the judgment of both the Deuteronomist and the Chronicler. He is, after all, related to Ahab through his mother, Athaliah. Consequently, it is appropriate for both the Deuteronomistic historian and the Chronicler to associate Ahaziah's downfall at the hands of Jehu with his visit to the Israelite King Jehoram.

No mention is made of the place where Ahaziah is buried. In fact, the only reason the Chronicler's account buries him at all is that he was Jehoshaphat's grandson!

22:10–23:21 The reign of Athaliah. The Chronicler adds very little to the Deuteronomist's portrayal of Athaliah's reign. Simply put, the priests play a larger role, as one might expect. Jehosheba, the woman who saved Joash from Athaliah, is, in this account, the wife of the priest Jehoiada, in addition to being the daughter of King Jehoram (north) and the sister of King Ahaziah (south). In the Chronicler's account, the captains summon the Levites and elders and make a covenant with the king (Joash) in the temple. The priests and Levites arrange the king's debut to the people; they alone are allowed to enter the temple; "they are holy" (23:6).

After Athaliah's death, one of the first things Joash does is to post watchmen under the direction of the Levites and the priests. They are to see to it that no one who is unclean enters the temple (23:19).

24:1-27 The reign of Joash. The Deuteronomistic historian attributes the good that Joash did to Jehoiada's counsel, and the Chronicler specifies this judgment even further. Joash sets out to repair the damage done to the temple by Athaliah. Under Jehoiada's and the priests' leadership, money is collected from the people, and the restoration is accomplished. Jehoiada was so faithful, from the Chronicler's theological perspective (he had saved Joash and had restored the Lord's dwelling), that he is reported to have been buried with the kings. No similar reference is made regarding any non-king in the Deuteronomistic History.

After Jehoiada's death, Joash is influenced toward evil by the princes of Judah and he succumbs. In spite of prophetic warning, idolatry prevails. The Chronicler inserts another priest who prophesies—this time Jehoiada's son, Zechariah. Zechariah predicts that Joash's rejection of the Lord will have dire consequences, but Joash's response is to silence the bad news; he whose life had been saved by Jehoiada now kills Jehoiada's son. Punishment for such sin is inevitable and comes in the form of Aram. The fact that Judah has a larger army means nothing; Judah has forsaken the Lord. Moreover, Zechariah is avenged: Joash's own servants slay him.

For the Chronicler, such an evil king cannot be buried in the tombs of the kings. This is the first mention of the "midrash of the book of the kings" (24:27). Because the Chronicler omits accounts of the northern kings of Israel, he has no need to distinguish the chronicles of Judah from those of Israel.

25:1-28 The reign of Amaziah. The Deuteronomist accorded Amaziah a mixed judgment, and the Chronicler does likewise. The Chronicler inserts two episodes; one speaks of Amaziah's fidelity, and the other speaks of his infidelity. Amaziah has mustered a large army—so large that it includes Israelite mercenaries. But when a prophet cautions him not to include Israelites in his army—because God's strength is far superior to those men, and God is not with them—Amaziah obeys the prophet, takes the financial loss, and dismisses the Israelites. Amaziah is victorious against the Edomites, although the mercenaries' anger causes them to plunder several Judean cities.

After that victory, however, Amaziah does an about-face, in the Chronicler's judgment. He begins to practice idolatry, worshiping the gods of the people he has conquered. He ignores prophetic wisdom—after all, those no-gods have proved powerless; they are unable to secure victory for their own people. Punishment for his infidelity is inevitable, and it comes in the form of a serious military defeat and the consequent pillaging of Jerusalem.

26:1-23 The reign of Uzziah (Azariah in 2 Kgs 15). Like his father, Uzziah gets a mixed rating from both the Deuteronomist and the Chronicler. For the Chronicler, as long as Uzziah seeks the Lord and listens to Zechariah's counsel, he is faithful and all goes well. His successes are both military (a well-equipped army and victories over the Philistines, the Arabs in Gurbaal, and the Meunites) and domestic (cisterns, and towers in Jerusalem and in the wilderness), and he is very prosperous.

However, the Chronicler condemns Uzziah's pride. He records an episode in which Uzziah attempts to usurp the prerogative of priests by burning incense at the altar of incense in the temple. His punishment is leprosy. The Deuteronomist had indicated Uzziah's leprosy but had not explained, from a theological perspective, its cause.

27:1-9 The reign of Jotham. The Chronicler adds little to the Deuteronomist's account of Jotham's reign. He is like his father, but he does not sin by presuming for himself any priestly function. Consequently, the Chronicler emphasizes a prosperous reign for him "because he lived resolutely in the presence of the Lord, his God." He builds cities, forts, and towers; he is victorious over the Ammonites and, consequently, he receives from them substantial tribute.

PART III:
REFORMS OF HEZEKIAH AND JOSIAH

2 Chr 28:1–36:1

28:1-27 The reign of Ahaz. The Chronicler adds to the Deuteronomist's description of Ahaz's reign the fact that he makes molten images for the Baals and burns incense in the valley of the son of Hinnom (vv. 2-3). Additional sin merits additional punishment: the Lord gives him into the hand of the king of

Aram and into the hand of the king of Israel. Further, an Ephraimite kills the king's son, the palace commander, and the king's assistant. Both the Arameans and the Israelites take captives from Judah, and the Arameans retain theirs. The Israelites, warned by the prophet Oded, know that taking the Lord's people captive can only lead to their own punishment. They therefore return the people of Judah to their own land.

Ahaz's sin, from the perspective of the Chronicler, leads to even further punishment. The Edomites, the Philistines, and even the Assyrians, to whom Ahaz pays tribute, pillage Judah. To depict the extent of Ahaz's evil, the Chronicler comments that Ahaz's ill fortune leads, not back to the Lord and to repentance, but to further idolatry. Although he sleeps with his ancestors and is buried in Jerusalem, he is not brought to the tombs of the kings of Israel. (Postexilic Judah is also called Israel.)

29:1–32:33 The reign of Hezekiah. Hezekiah's reign begins with a commission to the Levites and priests to purify the temple. This they complete in seven days. Hezekiah then commands that burnt offerings and sin offerings be made for all Israel: seven bulls, seven rams, seven lambs, and seven he-goats. The burnt offering is made amidst the music of harps, cymbals, and lyres, amidst singing and rejoicing, while both king and people worship. The people add to these offerings more burnt offerings, peace offerings, and thanksgiving offerings.

The Chronicler describes Hezekiah's next reform as the reintroduction of Passover (ch. 30). Hezekiah calls large numbers of the people to Jerusalem for the celebration, and encourages those who have avoided exile to Assyria to return to the Lord; perhaps the Lord will even return the exiles to their homeland. Included in this feast are Israelites from the north, from Ephraim, Manasseh, Issachar, and Zebulun. The Chronicler, as might be expected, emphasizes the priests' and Levites' role, especially their killing of Passover lambs for those who have not sanctified themselves—the northerners and the unclean. The feast lasts seven days, and then another seven days. According to the Chronicler, Hezekiah reestablishes the Passover, a feast that had not been so celebrated in Jerusalem since the reign of Solomon. (The Deuteronomistic historian credits Josiah with reestablishing this feast; it had not been celebrated since the period of the Judges; compare 2 Kgs 23:21-23.)

The Chronicler inserts more information about the priests and Levites (31:2ff.). Hezekiah divides them into classes, according to the service they will perform—offering holocausts and peace offerings, ministering in the gates of the camp of the Lord, and giving thanks and praise. Both king and people contribute generously, so that the priests have more than enough to offer and to eat; there is even an abundant surplus.

When the Assyrians come against him (ch. 32), Hezekiah prepares for combat; he is confident that the Lord is with Judah and will fight for it. Although other gods have not been able to save their people against the superior strength of the Assyrian army, Yahweh can and will save Judah. Thus Hezekiah believes, and his faith is rewarded.

Hezekiah does what is good and right and faithful in the eyes of his God. Everything he does he does with his whole heart, and he becomes very prosperous. Yet the Chronicler alludes to Hezekiah's illness (compare 2 Kgs 20:1-11) and to his insufficient gratitude for the Lord's response to his prayer (32:24-25). This provides an occasion for the Chronicler to refer to Hezekiah's humbling himself and to punishment that will come upon Judah and Jerusalem after Hezekiah's death. A foreshadowing of the form this punishment will take may be seen in the envoys who arrive from Babylon. The Chronicler comments that the Lord will test Hezekiah through them, to see what is in his heart (compare 2 Kgs 20:12-19).

In addition to the book of the kings of Judah and Israel, the Vision of Isaiah has more to say, according to the Chronicler, about the reign of Hezekiah (32:32). He is buried in the ascent of the tombs of the sons of David. Hezekiah merits the note that all Judah and the inhabitants of Jerusalem honor him at his death.

33:1-20 The reign of Manasseh. Contrary to the account of Manasseh's reign as given in the Deuteronomistic History, the Chronicler inserts into Manasseh's reign an account of his being taken into exile to Assyria, his petitioning the Lord for help, his deliverance, and his reformed lifestyle. Perhaps the Chronicler is, with this very unusual addition, trying to account for the fifty-five-year duration of Manasseh's reign. How could such an evil king have reigned so long, unless at some point he had repented? Perhaps the Chronicler is simply explaining why the kingdom of Judah did not fall during or after Manasseh's reign.

The chronicles of the kings of Israel and the chronicles of the seers contain a more detailed account of Manasseh's life (33:18). No mention is made of his burial with the other Judean kings; rather, he is buried in his house, or "in the garden of his house, in the garden of Uzza" (2 Kgs 21:18).

33:21-25 The reign of Amon. The Chronicler adapts the reign of Amon to his purposes. Amon is more evil than his father, Manasseh, had been; he sacrifices to the images his father had made, which suggests that Manasseh's idols remain in place. His father's repentance, also added by the Chronicler, was therefore incomplete. The Chronicler makes no mention of Amon's burial. The Deuteronomistic historian states that he was buried in the same garden as his father (2 Kgs 21:26).

34:1–35:27 The reign of Josiah. An interesting contrast can be drawn between the character of Josiah as depicted in 2 Kgs 22:1–23:30 and in 2 Chr 34–35. Though the events recorded are basically similar, the order of the events is significant. The Deuteronomistic historian portrays Josiah as purging idolatry from Judah *after* the restoration work in the temple had recovered the book of the law, while the Chronicler has the purging of idolatry in Judah and parts of Israel as the first act of Josiah's reign; only after such purification does he commission the Levites and priests to oversee the repair of the temple, and only subsequent to that is the book of the law discovered (34:14). Further, to the Passover account of 2 Kgs 23:21-25 the Chronicler adds copious priestly detail (35:1-19).

In contrast with the account in 2 Kings, the Chronicler makes no mention of Manasseh, nor does he associate the doom to come with delayed punishment for Manasseh's evil reign. For the Chronicler, Manasseh's son Amon was even more evil than his father. While both the Deuteronomist and the Chronicler mention the battle of Meggido, during which Josiah is mortally wounded at the hands of Egypt, only the Chronicler

(35:20) mentions Carchemish (605 B.C.E.), where the Babylonians were victorious over Egypt.

Josiah, like Hezekiah before him (2 Chr 32:33), receives honor from the people at his death. The Chronicler even comments that Jeremiah made a lament for him (2 Chr 35:25); no such allusion is found in 2 Kings. Josiah is accorded burial among the tombs of his ancestors (2 Kgs 23:30 notes: "in his own burial place").

PART IV: END OF THE KINGDOM

2 Chr 36:2-23

36:1-4 The reign of Jehoahaz. The reign of Jehoahaz is short. The Egyptians had slain Josiah at Meggido. Now they force Judah to pay tribute, exile the reigning king, and replace him with his brother, Eliakim (Jehoiakim). Whereas the Deuteronomist compares Jehoahaz's evil to the wrongdoing of his ancestors, the Chronicler makes no such comparison. Jehoahaz simply does evil and is exiled.

36:5-8 The reign of Jehoiakim. Jehoiakim lasts for a while as Egypt's vassal. When Egypt is conquered, he becomes Babylon's vassal. The Chronicler adds that, eventually, Jehoiakim is exiled to Babylon. In contrast with the Deuteronomist, the Chronicler does not explain the present evils in Judah as a consequence of Manasseh's sins (compare 2 Kgs 24:2-4).

36:9-10 The reign of Jehoiachin. Jehoiachin, Jehoiakim's son, reigns for only slightly more than three months before he is exiled to Babylon, and before his uncle Zedekiah replaces him on Judah's throne.

36:11-14 The reign of Zedekiah. For the Chronicler, one of Zedekiah's major sins is his refusal to defer to the spokesman of Yahweh. Zedekiah revolts against Babylon, in spite of the fact that Jeremiah has interpreted Nebuchadnezzar as the Lord's servant who is executing God's just judgment on Judah's sin; Jeremiah counsels the people to submit to Babylon (compare Jer 21:7). Zedekiah is also guilty of other infidelities, though the Chronicler omits any description of his fate (compare 2 Kgs 25:4-7).

36:15-21 Dissolution of Judah. Nebuchadnezzar destroys Judah and Jerusalem, sparing neither city walls nor Yahweh's temple. The people are slaughtered or exiled. Yet, unlike the Deuteronomistic historian, the Chronicler does not bring his history to an end until the end of Judah's exile.

36:22-23 Decree of Cyrus. The word of the Lord is effective. The seventy years prophesied by Jeremiah are completed (compare Jer 25:11-12 and 29:10). In the first year of the reign of King Cyrus of Persia, he commissions the Jews to go up to Jerusalem to build a temple to the Lord God of heaven.

CONCLUSION

The Deuteronomistic historian chronicled Israel's history from the perspective of fidelity to Yahweh, to the obligations of the covenant, to the word of the Lord through the prophets. Infidelity meant punishment and, eventually, the destruction of the temple, the loss of the land, and exile. No king is supreme. Yahweh is king, and a human king is faithful only to the extent that he observes the covenant. The rulers are male, except for the brief reign of Athaliah. In contrast, the prophets are no respecters of sex, as Deborah (see Judg 4–5) and Huldah illustrate. Only the king who obeys the words of the prophet—the words of the Lord through the prophet—is faithful.

For the Deuteronomistic historian, the person who does not know history is bound to repeat it. Therefore, he retells Israel's past so that those living in the present and in the future may learn from it. These are "the facts"; this is the "theological interpretation" of the facts. If you do not want a future of condemnation and exile, you must take God seriously. There is no substitute for obedience and covenant fidelity. Many of the historical circumstances have changed since the Deuteronomist wrote, and all interpretation must take this into account; yet, even now, many of his insights remain valid.

The Chronicler, with a different audience, different leadership, and a different historical situation, also recalls Israel's past, this time ending explicitly in a new beginning. If the priests are to lead a postexilic people to fidelity, they must have credentials, and these the Chronicler provides.

The theological purpose of the two interpretations of Israel's history is quite similar: Learn from the past for the present. Leaders and people alike must observe covenant fidelity and listen attentively to Yahweh's word through the prophets.

EZRA AND NEHEMIAH

Rita J. Burns

INTRODUCTION

HISTORICAL BACKGROUND

The setting for the Books of Ezra and Nehemiah is the two-hundred-year period in which God's people were citizens of the Persian Empire. The Persian period began in 539 B.C.E. when Cyrus the Great of Persia (Iran) wrested control of the ancient Near Eastern world from the Babylonians. It ended in 333 B.C.E. when the same area fell into Greek hands under Alexander the Great.

More specifically, events narrated in the Books of Ezra and Nehemiah fall within the first part of the Persian period, from 538 B.C.E. to shortly after 400 B.C.E. For the Jews this was a time of return and restoration. Over the course of several generations, groups of Jewish exiles in Babylonia made their way back to their homeland of Judah in southern Palestine. There they undertook the work of restoration. They began by rebuilding the temple in Jerusalem and reviving its worship. Later, under Nehemiah's leadership, they rebuilt the walls of the city of Jerusalem and repopulated the city. Nehemiah and Ezra also initiated reforms based on the law of Moses and aimed at restoring the identity and integrity of the Jewish people. The return and restoration, then, were gradual, interwoven processes which together pressed toward revitalization. The temple lay at the center. Around it grew the city with protective walls. Within and around Jerusalem a people was fashioned anew through the influence of the law of Moses.

Our knowledge of this period in history is, in some cases, sketchy. From the Bible we rely primarily upon the Books of Ezra and Nehemiah, but we also turn to other works relative to the period, including Isaiah chapters 40–66, the Book of Haggai, and the Book of Zechariah. Some extra-biblical documents from the Persian period supplement our understanding of this period.

The writers of the Books of Ezra and Nehemiah were selective in the events they chose to narrate. They focused upon two periods: (1) the early period (538–515 B.C.E.) when the first exiles returned to Judah under the leadership of Sheshbazzar and rebuilt the temple under the leadership of Zerubbabel and Jeshua, and (2) the period marked by the restoration of the wall of Jerusalem and religious reforms under the leadership of Nehemiah and Ezra (445–c. 398 B.C.E.).

Before reviewing these periods in greater detail, it is fitting to set the scene which gave rise to the return of the Jews to Judah and the need for restoration.

The early years of the sixth century B.C.E. marked the end of a four-hundred-year period in which the religious identity of the people of God was intertwined with their existence as an independent nation. A little over one hundred years after the northern kingdom of Israel had been swept away by the Assyrians, the tiny kingdom of Judah in the southern part of Palestine fell into the power of a major ancient Near Eastern empire centered in Babylonia. The final blow came in the year 587 B.C.E.

when Babylonian armies destroyed the capital city of Jerusalem. Many citizens of the country, including civic and religious leaders, were taken to Babylonia. The temple, which had served as the religious center since the days of Solomon, was demolished, and its precious furnishings were stolen. The broken land was left in the hands of powerless people, the country's poor.

Forty-six years after the fall of Jerusalem the Babylonian Empire itself capitulated to Cyrus the Great, head of an expanding Persian Empire. This turn of events was interpreted by an anonymous poet in Exile as the beginning of a new era for the captives from Judah. In the Book of Isaiah, chapters 40–55, the writer whom we know only as Second Isaiah speaks of Cyrus as the one through whom Yahweh was doing a new thing. With the advent of Cyrus, wrote Second Isaiah, there would be a new Exodus in which the chosen people, like their ancestors of old, would be led out of bondage back to their land (Isa 43:1-7; 44:24-28; 45:1-3, 11-13).

Indeed, it was the policy of Cyrus to allow peoples exiled by the Babylonians to return to their homelands and build new lives by reviving their native customs and religions. In a document dating from this period (the so-called Cyrus Cylinder), the Persian king describes his policy:

> I returned to (these) sacred cities on the other side of the Tigris, the sanctuaries of which have been in ruins for a long time, the images which (used) to live therein and established for them permanent sanctuaries. I (also) gathered all their (former) inhabitants and returned (to them) their habitations.

It has been suggested that the Persians may have gone so far as to allow the freed exiles a limited recovery of national identity as well. Two leaders in the Jewish return and restoration, Sheshbazzar and Zerubbabel, seem to have been descendants of the pre-exilic royal family. No doubt their authority was limited, but it is significant that they were appointed and patronized by Persian rulers. Such treatment of exiled peoples was almost certain to win Persia the trust and loyalty of subjects who, through securing their own welfare, could live as productive and content citizens of the empire.

Return and restoration of the temple (538–515 B.C.E.)

The edict which authorized the return of Jewish exiles to Judah is said to have been issued in the first year of the reign of Cyrus (over Babylonia), that is, 538 B.C.E. Not all of the exiles, however, chose to return. The relative freedom they experienced during their years in Babylonia had afforded them the opportunity to become settled and, in some cases, prosperous. Judah, on the other hand, was still marked by devastation and poverty, so few Jews returned in the initial contingent, although others would follow over the course of the next few generations.

The far-flung empire of Persia was divided into several administrative units called satrapies. Each of these units was governed by a satrap or governor who was responsible for several smaller territorial districts which fell under his jurisdiction. Although the Persian rulers maintained a firm hold on the empire, they seem to have upheld a policy of non-interference in the internal affairs of the satrapies as long as taxes were paid and the governors maintained peace and order within their respective regions.

Within this imperial system, Judah belonged to the satrapy called "West-of-Euphrates," an area extending from the Euphrates River westward to the Mediterranean Sea. Its headquarters were in Samaria. In the Books of Ezra and Nehemiah, Samaritan leadership figured prominently in hardships facing Jews who returned to Judah. Samaritan governors may have feared the political rivalry of a restored Jewish community to the south. In addition to political concerns, religious animosities contributed to the tension between the Jews and Samaritans. Samaria had been the capital of the ten tribes which constituted the kingdom of Israel until it fell to the Assyrians in 721 B.C.E. In accord with Assyrian policy, some of its inhabitants were deported while peoples of other conquered areas were transported into Samaria to settle. Such mixing of populations was aimed at breaking the solidarity of captured peoples. Although the Samaritans continued to claim a place among God's people, leaders in the community of Jews who returned to Judah after the Exile did not consider the Samaritans to be truly Jewish because they had intermarried with foreign peoples. When the people of Samaria offered to help rebuild the temple of Yahweh in Jerusalem, they were rejected by the returning Jews.

Cambyses came to the throne of Persia after the death of Cyrus in 530 B.C.E. During his brief reign he succeeded in bringing Egypt under the umbrella of the Persian Empire. Cambyses, however, is passed over in the Books of Ezra and Nehemiah. It may be that the next two Jewish leaders to figure prominently in the biblical record, Zerubbabel and Jeshua, came to Judah during the reign of Cambyses, but the Bible describes their activities within the context of the reign of Darius I (522–485 B.C.E.). Although the change of power from Cambyses to Darius was marked by turmoil and revolution, the greater part of the reign of Darius saw the Persian Empire at its height.

Exiles who accompanied Zerubbabel (a civic leader) and Jeshua (a priest) to Judah bolstered the numbers and strength of the restoration community. Perhaps because uprisings in other parts of the empire sparked hopes in Jewish circles for political independence, there seems to have been a movement afoot to establish Zerubbabel as king on the throne of his ancestor, David. At least this was the vision of two prophets from this period, Haggai and Zechariah (see Hag 2:20-23 and Zech 6:9-15). Although these prophets' messianic hopes were not realized, the strongly nationalistic spirit fostered by the two prophets together with international unrest must have contributed to the rebuilding of the temple. Darius himself supported the temple project, perhaps because he wanted the allegiance of those who lived on the borders of recently conquered Egypt.

Whatever the reason, the reign of Darius was a time of growth and progress for the Jewish community in Judah. Under the leadership of Zerubbabel and Jeshua, the temple was completed and dedicated in solemn ceremony in the year 515 B.C.E. This second temple served as a center for Jewish life in Judah until its destruction by the Romans in A.D. 70. Its reconstruction was the first major achievement and the foundation stone of the restoration community.

Restoration of the wall of Jerusalem and reforms (445–c. 398 B.C.E.)

The Books of Ezra and Nehemiah are virtually silent about the seventy-year period between the dedication of the temple (515 B.C.E.) and the beginning of the mission of Nehemiah (445 B.C.E.). The successor of Darius, Xerxes (485–465 B.C.E.), is mentioned only in Ezra 4:6 where he is called Ahasuerus. (He is given the same name in the Book of Esther.) Xerxes was followed by Artaxerxes I and his reign (465–425 B.C.E.) was a second period of significant progress for the restoration community.

By the middle of the fifth century B.C.E. the Persian Empire had lost some of the strength it had enjoyed under the leadership of Darius I, and revolts in Egypt may have motivated Artaxerxes to try to insure the strength and loyalty of his subjects in Judah, the region which bordered Egypt. Nehemiah was a high-ranking official in the Persian court, and we are told that in the twentieth year of the reign of Artaxerxes (445 B.C.E.) the emperor sent Nehemiah to Judah to serve as leader in the Jewish community (Neh 2:1). There is little doubt that the biblical witness about the date of Nehemiah's mission is historically accurate. The Book of Nehemiah tells us that Sanballat was leader of the province of Samaria in Nehemiah's day (Neh 2:10, 19; 3:33-34). That Nehemiah and Sanballat were contemporaries is confirmed by papyri from a Jewish colony at Elephantine in Egypt. From this extra-biblical material we learn that Sanballat's two sons were governors of Samaria at the end of the fifth century B.C.E. Moreover, the Jewish high priest at the end of the century was Johanan, a grandson of the high priest Eliashib who served during Nehemiah's time. On the basis of the Elephantine texts, it is reasonable to date the beginning of Nehemiah's mission at 445 B.C.E., the twentieth year of the reign of Artaxerxes I.

During his first term as governor of Judah, Nehemiah oversaw the rebuilding of the wall around Jerusalem in spite of considerable opposition from Sanballat and others. Having completed the project, Nehemiah returned to Persia in 433 B.C.E. A short time later, however, he returned to Judah. During this second period he initiated several reforms designed to strengthen the solidarity of the restoration community, a positive effort not only for the Jews but also for the Persian throne which was eager to bolster the strength of the western edges of its empire.

The place of Ezra in the chronology of the restoration period continues to be a question among scholars. The biblical text presents Ezra before Nehemiah. Moreover, the appearance of Ezra within the Book of Nehemiah (Neh 8) creates the impression that the respective missions of the two overlapped. Ezra 7:7 tells us that Ezra came to Judah from Persia in the seventh year of Artaxerxes. If the reference is to Artaxerxes I (465–425 B.C.E.), then Ezra arrived in Judah in 458 B.C.E. and began his work thirteen years prior to the arrival of Nehemiah.

However, there are difficulties with this understanding of the biblical witness. Ezra 10:6 says that Ezra was a contemporary of the Jewish high priest Johanan. If Johanan, Ezra's contemporary, was the grandson of Eliashib (as discussed above) whom we know to have been a contemporary of Nehemiah (Neh 3:1, 20-21), then it is clear that Ezra did not precede Nehemiah but came two generations after him. Therefore, the emperor named in Ezra 7:7 might be Artaxerxes II (405–359 B.C.E.) in which case Ezra's mission is dated 398 B.C.E., the seventh year of the reign of Artaxerxes II.

A third proposal on the date of Ezra's mission is that it began in 428 B.C.E., the thirty-seventh year of Artaxerxes I. Some scholars have suggested that the text of Ezra 7:7 contains a slight scribal error in which the first number of the year ("thirty") was omitted. According to this view, Ezra came to Jerusalem a few years after the beginning of Nehemiah's second mission in Judah.

Although the exact date of Ezra's mission is still a topic for discussion, most scholars agree that Nehemiah's mission preceded that of Ezra. This helps to explain why the Nehemiah material in the Bible acknowledges no awareness of the reform of Ezra which, if Ezra had come first, would have occurred less than thirteen years before Nehemiah arrived in Judah. It is possible that the persons who were responsible for the composition of the Books of Ezra and Nehemiah were simply in error about historical sequence. It is more probable, however, that the overall arrangement of these two biblical books was designed with theological purposes in mind rather than to serve as an accurate historical chronicle of the period (see below on Theological Interests).

Because we do not know the exact dates of Ezra's activity in Judah, we cannot be certain where to end the timeline of historical events which form the background to the Books of Ezra and Nehemiah. We adopt the widely accepted view that Nehemiah preceded Ezra. For purposes of this commentary, we also follow the scholarly opinion that places Ezra's mission in the initial years of the fourth century B.C.E. We do so, however, with full awareness of the uncertainty which remains on this question.

The historical relationship between Persian rule and Jewish restoration can be seen at a glance in this outline:

Persian Emperors	Jewish Restoration
Cyrus the Great (539–530 B.C.E.)	Return to Judah
Cambyses (530–522 B.C.E.)	
Darius I (522–485 B.C.E.)	Rebuilding of temple
Xerxes (485–465 B.C.E.)	
Artaxerxes I (465–425 B.C.E.)	Nehemiah's mission including restoration of wall of Jerusalem and reforms
Darius II (425–405 B.C.E.)	
Artaxerxes II (405–359 B.C.E.)	? Ezra's mission including promulgation of the law and reform

THEOLOGICAL INTERESTS

History and biblical accounts

The Books of Ezra and Nehemiah appear within one of three great blocks of material in Hebrew Scripture which present successive events in Israel's history. The first four books of the Bible (Genesis through Numbers) cover the period from the beginnings of humanity to the time when the children of Israel stood on the borders of the Promised Land ready to inherit that space which God had promised to their ancestors. A second block of material sketches Israel's story from the entrance into the Promised Land through the era of the monarchy to the fall of the nation and the Babylonian Exile (see Deuteronomy through the Second Book of Kings). The First and Second Books of Chronicles and the Books of Ezra and Nehemiah trace the last part of Israel's story from the rise of King David (although this is prefixed in chapters 1–9 of the First Book of Chronicles with genealogies which trace Israel's roots back to Adam) through postexilic reconstruction efforts ending shortly after 400 B.C.E.

All of these writings are actually theological interpretations of events rather than historical annals. Each school of writers sets forth its theological reflections on Israel's experience. Readers of the Books of Ezra and Nehemiah must keep this in mind. While the two books contain historical information about the restoration period, the primary aim of the writers was not to present a disinterested chronological account of events. The writers were theologians who carefully selected and arranged materials in accord with theological interests.

Arrangement of materials

A theological order is evident in the present arrangement of the Ezra-Nehemiah materials:

Part I Ezra 1–6
    Restoration of the temple
Part II Ezra 7–10
    Restoration of the worshiping community
Part III Neh 1–7
    Restoration of the wall of Jerusalem
Part IV Neh 8–13
    Restoration of the community around the law

The foundation of postexilic Judaism in Judah was the temple and its worship. Thus Part I of the Ezra-Nehemiah material centers around the rebuilding of the temple even though neither Ezra nor Nehemiah was involved in this initial phase of restoration. Legitimate temple worship required that the worshipers themselves be pure, a people set apart. Part II describes a reform initiated by Ezra to set Jews apart from foreign influence. The city made holy by God's presence in the temple had to be strong and secure. To this end the city wall was rebuilt under Nehemiah's leadership (Part III). All of these works of restoration prepared for and culminated in the restoration of the Jewish community under the law (Part IV). Since both Ezra and Nehemiah were instrumental in restoring the Jewish community, it is theologically appropriate (although perhaps not chronologically accurate) that both be presented as participants in the culmination of their work.

Theological emphases

Just as theological considerations gave direction to the final arrangement of materials in the Books of Ezra and Nehemiah, so certain theological emphases can be seen in the books.

a. God's work and Persian help. Like writers before them, the theologians who composed the Books of Ezra and Nehemiah presupposed that Yahweh, the God of Israel, directed world history. The fall of the nation and the Exile had been Yahweh's doing. Now the same God was bringing the purged people to new life. In the Books of Ezra and Nehemiah, the Persian rulers' ongoing support for the restoration of the Jewish people is traced to God's hand. Likewise, the Jews call upon God to help them in the work of reconstruction and attribute their success to God's gracious aid.

b. Temple and cult. The Books of Ezra and Nehemiah give much attention to the temple and its worship. They present the restoration of the temple as the primary goal of the return from Exile. Moreover, the writers are eager to show that a full life of worship (including sacred festivals and sacred offerings) was an important part of the restoration movement. The writers also show special concern for cultic personnel, priests and Levites.

c. A people set apart. Prior to the Exile, Israel had a national identity, political independence in a land of its own with a capital in Jerusalem, its own king descended from David, and a temple where they thought God was accessible in a special way. The Exile had destroyed all of that. Without land, independence, temple, or king, the postexilic community searched for a new identity which was one with the Israel of the past and yet appropriate for drastically different circumstances.

Membership in the restoration community was limited to those who had been purified through the experience of Exile and who sought to maintain their purity and uniqueness by setting themselves apart from foreigners. Pure blood lineage was especially important, and marriages with foreigners were regarded as threats to the integrity of the restoration community. The objection to marriages with foreigners rests on an identification of holiness with separation—a physical separation from people and things which were not exclusively dedicated to Yahweh. While this perspective might be jarring to today's ecumenically-minded readers who long to reverse centuries of human intolerance based on religious loyalties, the biblical writers reflect a different world and different concerns. The exclusivist policies of the restoration period must be viewed within the context of a community struggling for self-preservation in the rubble of questions of identity occasioned by the experience of Exile.

d. Continuity. The biblical writers sought to show that postexilic Judaism was an authentic extension of pre-exilic Israel. Members of the restoration community had to prove that their ancestors came from pre-exilic Israel. "All Israel" is frequently symbolized by the number twelve, representing the twelve tribes who constituted ancient Israel. For the most part, those who returned from Exile settled in regions their pre-exilic ancestors had inhabited. The temple was restored on its ancient foundations and Jerusalem's wall was rebuilt from the charred stones of the pre-exilic wall. Leadership in worship was reserved to the descendants of pre-exilic Israel's cultic officials. The worshiping community resumed ancient festivals and offerings. The law which gave direction to the community's life was the ancient law of Moses.

LITERARY CONSIDERATIONS

Author and date of composition

We do not know all of the details about the composition of the Books of Ezra and Nehemiah. Contemporary scholarship is virtually unanimous in attributing a significant part of the composition to the Chronicler, that is, the circle of tradition which is responsible for the First and Second Books of Chronicles. In support of this view, one can see points of continuity in the Books of Chronicles, Ezra, and Nehemiah. First of all, the fact that the opening verses of the Book of Ezra duplicate the final verses of the Second Book of Chronicles reflects a deliberate effort to connect the works. Secondly, some of the thematic concerns which come to the fore in Chronicles recur in the Books of Ezra and Nehemiah. These include the prominence given to the temple, the city of Jerusalem, and the cult together with its leading personnel. The manner in which lists and other sources are used has been cited as additional evidence for connecting the author of Ezra and Nehemiah with that of Chronicles.

Despite this, we must guard against imagining that in one sitting a single author composed the final text of Chronicles, Ezra, and Nehemiah from start to finish. Chapters 1–6 of the Book of Ezra bear the strongest traces of the Chronicler's hand. It might be that the rest of the Ezra-Nehemiah materials (Ezra 7–10; the Book of Nehemiah) was subsequently incorporated into the Chronicler's work, perhaps in separate stages.

Although many of the details elude us, it is safe to say that the Chronicler played a significant part in the composition of the Books of Ezra and Nehemiah although the final text probably includes accretions and editing which came from other hands. Thus, when we speak of the authors/editors of the Books of Ezra and Nehemiah, we shall refer to the Chronicler but we do so with the understanding that other unknown writers also contributed to the work of composition.

The language of the books bears the marks of Persian but not Greek influence which suggests that the Books of Ezra and Nehemiah originated prior to the beginning of the Greek period (333 B.C.E.). The latest Persian emperor to be named is Darius II (425–405 B.C.E.) and the latest high priest included is Johanan who is known to have held that position until at least 410 B.C.E. Johanan's son, Jaddua, also appears in Neh 12:23, but we are not told if he yet exercised the office of high priest. For these reasons, most scholars hold that the bulk of the Books of Ezra and Nehemiah was completed in the early years of the fourth century B.C.E. although some additions to the books may have been made later.

Sources

Like many other biblical works, the Books of Ezra and Nehemiah represent a compilation of materials of diverse origin. Because of this, it is proper to regard the Chronicler as a compiler and editor as well as author of biblical tradition. Since the sources used by the Chronicler are no longer available to us in other biblical or extrabiblical works, in most cases it is difficult to judge their historical authenticity. It is possible that previously existing materials were incorporated into the Books of Ezra and Nehemiah exactly as the Chronicler found them. However, it is also possible that the Chronicler altered the materials, shaping them in ways which would serve the theological purposes of this particular part of the biblical tradition. The Chronicler is thought to have used three types of materials: (a) memoirs of Ezra and Nehemiah, (b) official records and correspondence, and (c) lists.

a. Memoirs. Parts of the Books of Ezra and Nehemiah which contain descriptions of the activities of the two main figures are written in the first person. This has led to the suggestion that those parts represent firsthand reports of the activities of Ezra and Nehemiah. It is uncertain whether these sections should be regarded as memoirs (written by the chief figures themselves) or memorials (written by others about the chief figures). Other inscriptions from the ancient Near Eastern world are similar to the Ezra and Nehemiah memoirs. In these inscriptions the first person is used, and their contents typically recount the accomplishments of an individual. Scholars think that these inscriptions were intended as testimony to a deity about the loyalty of a devoted worshiper.

The memoirs of the two biblical figures constitute the most extensive independent sources utilized by the Chronicler in the composition of the Books of Ezra and Nehemiah.

The Ezra memoirs appear in Ezra 7:27-9:15. This section contains two lists (8:1-14 and 26-27) which may have been added to the memoirs from separate sources. Although Ezra's prayer (Ezra 9:6-15) also appears in the first person and so may have belonged to his memoirs, it is possible that this was the composition of another writer, since prayers are known to have been placed on the lips of biblical figures by writers in a later period (see, for example, Dan 3:24-45, 51-90; 9:4-19).

The parts of the Book of Nehemiah which appear in the first person are referred to in many circles as Nehemiah's memoirs. These sections constitute a sizeable portion of the book (Neh 1-7; 12:27-13:31). These texts contain a record of restoration efforts under Nehemiah's leadership. They include two lists which may have been added to the memoirs at some later stage of composition.

b. Aramaic source. For those who read biblical texts in the languages in which they were originally written, the most obvious clue to the diversity of sources in the Book of Ezra is that Ezra 4:8-6:18 and 7:12-26 are in Aramaic while the rest of the Books of Ezra and Nehemiah is written in Hebrew. The bulk of the Aramaic material in Ezra 4:8-6:18 claims to be a record of official correspondence between governors in West-of-Euphrates and two different Persian emperors. It also includes a version of the edict in which the Persian monarch Cyrus authorized the rebuilding of the temple in Jerusalem (6:3-5). The Aramaic section of Ezra 7:12-26 contains a copy of the official papers regarding Ezra's mission authorized by the emperor, Artaxerxes.

It is commonly accepted in scholarly circles that these Aramaic sections represent material from separate sources, perhaps records which were retained in official archives either of the Persian emperors or of Jewish leaders.

c. Lists. A number of lists in the Books of Ezra and Nehemiah probably came from records preserved in Jewish archives. The lists include the names of persons and regions as well as records of temple vessels and community responsibilities.

While it is impossible to know the sources and degree of authenticity of the above-mentioned official correspondence and of the numerous lists, it is likely that they represent materials which originated independently of the narratives which now appear in the Books of Ezra and Nehemiah. It is possible that different records were adopted into the Ezra-Nehemiah traditions at different stages in the composition of the biblical books.

SIGNIFICANCE

The Books of Ezra and Nehemiah are important to contemporary readers for several reasons. First, they are our chief source of information about the restoration of the Jewish community following the Exile. Even though some of the historical details in the books are puzzling to contemporary biblical scholars, nevertheless they provide the best data at hand for our understanding of this period.

Second, we see in these books a community's courage in picking up the pieces of a shattered past and arranging them in creative ways, even in the face of considerable opposition. We encounter a community willing to engage the slow, gradual process of rebuild-ing. The community succeeds through God's protection, its own fierce resolve, properly focused efforts, and good leadership.

Finally, in the figures of Ezra and Nehemiah, contemporary readers see models of piety. Both men depend upon and recognize God's help, but they work without the spectacular interventions which characterize God's gracious presence in much of the rest of the biblical tradition. In their time true piety required human initiative and human effort. Ezra and Nehemiah were marked by devotion to their community, and out of that zeal flowed their commitment to the task of recovery. They saw what situations demanded and devised constructive ways to promote the life of the fragile community. Nehemiah was a model organizer resolute in restoring life to a city in ruins. Ezra founded postexilic Judaism in the law. Jewish tradition would eventually compare him to Moses. Both put their talents and efforts at the service of the tradition that had shaped them. They are models of how to be faithful to one's heritage in creative ways required by new situations.

COMMENTARY: EZRA

PART I: RESTORATION OF THE TEMPLE

Ezra 1:1–6:22

The first six chapters of the Book of Ezra contain an account of events beginning with the return of the exiles from Babylonia (ch. 1) and ending with the completion of the temple (ch. 6). The initial return (during Cyrus' reign) is said to have been led by Sheshbazzar, "the prince of Judah" (1:8). Shortly thereafter Zerubbabel (a royal prince) and Jeshua (a priest), with the support of the Persian king Darius, led the community in completing the reconstruction of the temple.

These chapters seem to be carefully documented. Attention is given to personal and place names, and inventories of goods and offerings, frequent dates, and records of official documents including the edict of Cyrus and correspondence between officers of West-of-Euphrates and Persian emperors.

On the other hand, this is a highly selective account. While it covers events spanning a period of twenty-three years (from the edict of Cyrus in 538 B.C.E. to the dedication of the temple in 515 B.C.E.), it is clear that the writers neglect to mention many aspects of life during the return and restoration. We see a preoccupation with the cult: altar, temple, sacrifices, offerings, temple vessels and utensils, religious feasts, and temple personnel. The writers view the restoration of temple worship as the goal of the return and the foundation of the restoration community.

Special concerns are evident in the writers' portrayal of the Jewish community. There is no hint of poverty or internal tension. According to the account, the only hardship facing the second generation of the restoration movement was the opposition of Samaritan leaders and peoples of the land. We see an idealized community: large in number, great in wealth, single-heartedly dedicated to restoring the life of worship with the help of able leaders of legitimate royal and priestly lineage and the patronage of the Persian throne. Moreover, just as the return is said to have been inspired by God (1:1-5), so the pursuit of a restored cultic life is said to have been carried forward by the community's faithful response to religious traditions begun by Moses and David, as well as to prophetic inspiration of its own day.

1:1-11 The decree of Cyrus. The three opening verses of the Book of Ezra repeat the closing verses of the Second Book of Chronicles. In concluding the record of Israel's life as a nation, with reference to the edict of Cyrus the Persian (2 Chr 36:22-23), the Chronicler testifies that the fall of the nation is not the end of Israel's story. The conclusion to Chronicles then forms a fitting background and introduction to the same writers' view of the period of return from Exile and restoration of the people.

A Jewish perspective pervades this account. The subject of the opening sentence (1:1) is Israel's God. Yahweh is said to have inspired Cyrus to issue the edict of release from Exile. Although the Chronicler does not cite the poet of the Exile, Second Isaiah, their theological perspectives are similar. Second Isaiah regarded Cyrus as Yahweh's "anointed" (Isa 45:1; compare 44:28), the one through whom Yahweh's plan for Israel's release would be realized. Moreover, the biblical writers connect the edict of Cyrus with God's word as spoken through the prophet Jeremiah (Ezra 1:1). This is consistent with what the Chronicler recorded in 2 Chr 36:21. It is a reflection on Jeremiah's earlier prophecy about Israel's release from Babylonian captivity after a period in which God's purpose in allowing the Exile would have been realized (see Jer 25:11-12; 29:10). Although the prophet spoke of this period lasting seventy years, we, like the biblical writers, must understand seventy as a symbolic number suggesting fullness or completion. In calling attention to the fulfillment of God's word, the Chronicler shares with other exilic and postexilic writers (for example, Second Isaiah and the priestly writers) the view that events of salvation history take momentum and direction from God's power-filled word.

A Jewish perspective is also evident in the date which appears in the opening verse. The "first year of Cyrus" refers not to Cyrus' ascent to the throne in Persia (c. 557 B.C.E.), but to his conquest of Babylonia and the beginning of his rule over the Jews. For the biblical writers, the "first year of Cyrus" is 538 B.C.E.

The citation of the edict of Cyrus represents the first of the writers' frequent use of documentation. An Aramaic version of the edict appears in Ezra 6:3-5. Most scholars agree that the edict quoted in Ezra 1:2-4 represents a Jewish version of the Persian document and not a verbatim record. Several details support this view. First, it is extremely unlikely that the Persian emperor would have regarded his power as having come from Yahweh, the God of Israel. In fact, in the record preserved in the Cyrus Cylinder the ruler cites Marduk, the god of the Babylonians, as the one who gave Babylonia into his hand. The record in Ezra 1:2-4 is similar to other Jewish theological perspectives, for example, that of Second Isaiah (see Isa 45:1). Second, it is also unlikely that Cyrus expected the Babylonians to contribute provisions for the travelers as well as free-will offerings for Yahweh. It is possible that the writers of Ezra 1:4 were seeking to parallel this return from Exile with the Exodus from Egypt when the Israelites took with them goods contributed by the Egyptians (see Exod 3:21; 11:2-3; 12:35-36).

While the particular Jewish view of the edict cited in Ezra 1:2-4 should be recognized, it is true that in some ways the biblical testimony is true to the spirit of Cyrus' policies. The Cyrus Cylinder includes the emperor's mandate that the restoration of Babylonian captives on their native soil include the rebuilding of shrines to their local patronal deities. In accord with that policy, Second Isaiah prophesied that Cyrus would authorize the rebuilding of Jerusalem and its temple (Isa 44:28). The writers of Ezra 1:2-4, however, have assigned prime importance to this particular detail of Cyrus' overall policy. In their view, Yahweh commanded Cyrus to rebuild the temple in Jerusalem, and that is why the emperor released the Jewish captives and called upon the support of the Babylonians.

The section which follows (vv. 5-11) is a narrative beginning with preparations for the return to Judah and ending with an abrupt notice about the return itself. Verses 5-6 clearly flow from verses 1-4. We see that as God had inspired Cyrus (v. 1), so God inspired those Jews who chose to return (v. 5). The returnees left Babylonia enriched by the donations of their neighbors who had complied with the directive cited in verse 4. And, in accord with God's plan and Cyrus' edict (v. 2), the exiles' purpose in returning was to rebuild the temple (v. 5). Thus, the writers tell us that it was a wealthy, inspired, temple-oriented community that returned.

The Jews who had been taken into Exile were Judahites along with members of the tribe of Benjamin with whom they were closely associated. Therefore, the returnees belong to these two clans. The Chronicler's interest in worship prompted the specific mention of priests and Levites along with the tribal heads (v. 5). Since the restoration of the temple is said to have been the goal of the return, it is appropriate that this preparation for the return emphasize the collection of temple utensils which had been taken by the Babylonian Nebuchadnezzar as trophies of his victory over Judah (compare 2 Kgs 24:13; 25:13-16; 2 Chr 36:10, 18; Jer 52:17-20). The Chronicler's concern for the continuity of Israel's religious tradition required this note. Vessels for the restored worship were those which had been used in pre-exilic worship.

According to verses 8 and 11, Cyrus entrusted the temple vessels to Sheshbazzar who was leader of the initial return. Very little is known of Sheshbazzar, since he is only mentioned here and in Ezra 5:14-16 where he is credited with having laid the foundations for the temple in Jerusalem. Many scholars link him with Shenazzar who is described in 1 Chr 3:18 as son of Jeconiah (that is, Jehoachin, the last king of Judah) and therefore a member of the royal family during the generation in Exile. In Ezra 1:8 Sheshbazzar is called "prince of Judah" (compare Ezra 5:14). We cannot be certain of the meaning of this title. It may refer to his royal lineage and be used here as nontechnical terminology designating his civic leadership among the returnees.

The biblical writers complete their account of preparations for the return with an inventory of vessels taken back to the land by Sheshbazzar. Readers will note the discrepancy between the tally of individual pieces and the total given in verse 11.

2:1-70 Census of the province. After the brief notice at the end of chapter 1, Sheshbazzar's return to Jerusalem, the scene shifts to the land of Judah where the former exiles settled. Ezra 2 is only one of many examples of the Chronicler's fondness for lists and other official documentation. An introduction (vv. 1-2) is followed by a census of the people by families and towns (vv. 3-35), a listing of special groups within the community (vv. 36-58), those without proof of lineage (vv. 59-63), numerical totals (vv. 64-67), and a concluding description of gifts brought to the temple and of the geographical distribution of the settlers (vv. 68-70). Scholars generally regard the list as a composite of the records of various groups (probably from different time periods) which have been brought together. The numbers are suspiciously large.

The introduction to the census (vv. 1-2) neglects to mention Sheshbazzar, the leader of the earliest return (see ch. 1), and includes instead Zerubbabel and Jeshua who are described in Ezra 3–6 as active in the temple building project around 520 B.C.E. The list of leaders in verse 2 also includes Nehemiah. It may be an anachronism or it may refer to a different person from the one who is the chief figure in the Book of Nehemiah.

In verses 3-35 the census of the laity alternates between listing people by families (vv. 3-19 or 20, 30-32, 35) and by locale (vv. 20 or 21-29, 33-34). In some cases (particularly vv. 19 and 20) it is difficult to know if the name refers to a person or place, though the designation "men of" instead of "sons of" would appear to signal town names (but compare vv. 21 and 33-34 where "sons of" is used for citizens of particular places).

The numbering of members of special groups (vv. 36-58) includes priests, Levites, singers, gatekeepers, temple slaves, and the descendants of the slaves of Solomon. All appear to designate groups of people who exercised functions within the temple, although virtually nothing is known of the group called "descendants of the slaves of Solomon." The special listing of temple personnel witnesses to the cultic orientation of the writers.

Verses 59-63 include the names of lay people who were unable to prove that their lineage was truly Israelite (vv. 59-60) and priests who could not produce records to show that they were legitimate heirs to the rights and privileges of Israel's priestly family (vv. 61-62). We are not told of the resolution of the confusion over the families of lay persons, but verse 63 indicates that the questions surrounding the validity of priests could be settled by casting lots with the Urim and Thummim, two sticks or dice which served as primitive means for consulting the will of

God (see 1 Sam 14:41). Late biblical tradition says they were carried in the breastplate of the high priest (see Exod 28:30; Lev 8:8). We are told that until this judgment was made, "His Excellency" (that is, some civic leader; the same title is applied to Nehemiah in Neh 8:9 and 10:2) prohibited the priests without credentials from sharing consecrated food (see Lev 2:3; 7:28-36), a privilege of the priesthood.

Readers will note that the total number given in verse 64 is greater than the sum of the parts tallied in the preceding verses, a discrepancy which we cannot explain. The total number of slaves and animals (vv. 65-67) is impressive and does not harmonize with the humble beginnings of the restoration community nor with the hardships of the Jews in Nehemiah's day (see Neh 5:1-5).

Just as the newly freed slaves contributed to the construction of the tabernacle when Israel came out of Egypt (Exod 25:1-6; 35:4-9), so verses 68-69 portray a people zealous for the restoration of Israel's cultic life. The closing verse of the second chapter (v. 70) describes the settlement of the returnees. Cultic and civic leaders and others who probably assisted them in their duties naturally settled in the religious and civic center, Jerusalem. Those Jews whose performance of cultic functions rotated and those who had no official duties probably returned to regions which had been their ancestral homes prior to the Exile.

The order in which the Chronicler presents materials is important. The census in Ezra 2 is followed by an account of the restoration of the altar in Jerusalem and a celebration of the feast of Booths (Ezra 3:1-6). A parallel arrangement appears in Nehemiah chapters 7 and 8. The census of Ezra 2 is repeated in Neh 7:6-72a where it is followed by the promulgation of the law (Neh 8:1-12) and the celebration of the feast of Booths (Neh 8:13-18). The restoration of the altar and the promulgation of the law were two very important moments of the restoration period according to the biblical writers. By preceding accounts of the restoration with a census list, the writers sought to emphasize that the groups who took part in these events were truly the people of God, people purified by the experience of Exile whose ancestral roots linked them with earlier generations of Israelites.

3:1-6 Restoration of the altar. The primacy of the cult is clear in this account. It is an idealized picture of the apparent haste and ease with which Israel's elaborate life of worship was restored.

As David had built an altar prior to the construction of the first temple (2 Sam 24:25; 1 Chr 21:26; 22:1), so the returned exiles began by restoring the altar. The entire community worked together, supervised by the families of priestly and civic leaders (vv. 1-2). The writers underscore the importance of continuity with past religious tradition by saying that the altar was rebuilt on its old foundations (v. 3) and by noting that the reestablished cult was in accord with ancient religious practice: they offered holocausts "prescribed in the law of Moses" (v. 2), they celebrated the feast of Booths "in the manner prescribed," and "they offered the daily holocausts in the proper number required for each day" (v. 4; see also v. 5).

The high point of communal worship in the postexilic period was the offering of sacrifice, and this required a legitimate altar. Holocausts (burnt offerings) were sacrifices which were completely burned, a symbolic expression of the totality of the gift. According to Exod 29:38-42 two lambs were offered as holocausts daily, one in the morning and another in the evening. Sacrifices prescribed for other sacred feasts (v. 5) are described in the legislation of Num 28 and 29. Free-will offerings (v. 5) could be brought at any time by worshipers. In verse 4 the writers speak of the restoration of the feast of Booths (Hebrew *sukkot*, "booths" or "huts"; Latin *tabernacula*, "Tabernacles"), a seven-day festival which for much of the biblical period was the most prominent of Israel's religious festivals. From earliest times it marked the harvest of grapes and olives (see Exod 23:16; 34:22) and was characterized by great rejoicing and thanksgiving (Deut 16:14-15; Lev 23:40). In this passage we see that Israel's liturgical calendar also included a special observance to mark the beginning of each month ("new moon", v. 5; see Num 10:10; 28:11-15).

Ezra 3:1-6 raises some chronological questions. First, verse 1 places the efforts to reestablish the life of worship in "the seventh month" although the year is not designated. Most scholars suggest that in both verses 1 and 6 the reference is to the seventh month of the year of the earliest return, that is, 538 B.C.E. If this is the case, however, a second question of chronology arises. Verse 2 attributes leadership in the rebuilding of the altar to Jeshua and Zerubbabel. Their leadership is problematic in light of the fact that chapter 1 names Sheshbazzar as leader in the return of 538 B.C.E. whereas chapters 4–6 connect Zerubbabel and Jeshua with the temple building activity which occurred between 520 and 515 B.C.E. Thus, distinctions in the chronology of Sheshbazzar, Zerubbabel and Jeshua have been blurred.

3:7-13 Founding of the temple. Confusing Sheshbazzar's work with that of Zerubbabel and Jeshua continues in the present section. Here we are told that Zerubbabel and Jeshua oversaw the laying of the foundations of the temple. But Ezra 5:16 attributes the same role to Sheshbazzar. The vagueness of the date in verse 8 does not shed light on the matter. The work is said to have begun in the "year after their coming to the house of God in Jerusalem." The pronoun "their" could refer to Sheshbazzar and the earliest returnees in which case the year was 537 B.C.E. But if "their" refers to Zerubbabel and Jeshua it would have been somewhat later. The former possibility is to be preferred because Ezra 4:5 says that delays in temple reconstruction lasted from the final years of Cyrus until the time of Darius. Since Sheshbazzar was a contemporary of Cyrus (see 1:8-11) and Zerubbabel and Jeshua were contemporaries of Darius (see Ezra 5:1-5 and Hag 1:1), we conclude that it was the earliest returnees who laid the foundations of the temple building. If Sheshbazzar is identified with the Shenazzar who appears in the genealogy of 1 Chr 3:18 (as many scholars suggest), then Sheshbazzar was the uncle of Zerubbabel (see 1 Chr 3:18-19). It is reasonable to view the situation as follows: Sheshbazzar led an initial contingent of Jews back to the land where he began work on the temple building in Jerusalem. His nephew Zerubbabel led a second group to Judah some years later, and he resumed work (perhaps virtually started over) on the temple which his uncle had begun in the earlier period but which had been stopped by Judah's opponents.

Although the description of the laying of the temple foundations and the accompanying celebration narrated in verses 7-13 has the appearance of an eyewitness record of events, a careful examination of the details suggests that, to a large extent, this account was shaped by community tradition. First, the returnees are said to have planned carefully for the building project by securing proper materials and craftspersons (v. 7). The details of their preparation parallel the Chronicler's version of preparatory efforts undertaken by David (1 Chr 22:2, 4, 15) and Solomon (2 Chr 2:1-15) for the construction of the first temple. Second, beginning the work "in the second month" is in chronological accord with the beginning of construction of the first temple in Solomon's day (see 1 Kgs 6:1; 2 Chr 3:2). Finally, the account of the celebration which followed the laying of the temple foundations accords with the Chronicler's tendency to highlight both the cultic and musical, and it is consistent with other cultic occasions narrated in the Books of Chronicles. For example, trumpets are assigned to the priests (v. 10) as in 1 Chr 16:6 while the Levites play the cymbals (v. 10; compare 2:41 where the "sons of Asaph" are singers) as in 1 Chr 25:1, 6 (compare 2 Chr 29:25-26). The refrain of the hymn which is included in verse 11 likewise appears in 1 Chr 16:34 and 2 Chr 5:13 and 7:3 (see also Pss 106:1; 136:1). It is clear that the writers of Ezra 3:7-13 were eager for events in the early period of the reconstruction to appear continuous with Israel's past.

According to these verses those who laid the foundations of the temple were "all who had come from the captivity to Jerusalem" and we are told that the priests and Levites directed the exiles' labors (vv. 8-9). Here again the writers underscore the importance of legitimacy. The core of the restoration community consisted of those who had been purged by the experience of Exile, and their efforts to reestablish the cult were directed by those who held legitimate authority in cultic affairs. The writers' idealized view of matters is probably responsible for the notation that the whole community of returned exiles participated in the founding of the temple.

The writers include a tender scene of the community's mixed response following the laying of the temple foundations. Some of the Jews were sad, some joyful (vv. 12-13). The Chronicler's picture of the sorrow of those who remembered the glory of the first temple has probably been influenced by familiarity with the witness of Hag 2:3 which says that the temple rebuilt during the second year of Darius (that is, in 520 B.C.E.) was a disappointment to the older generation.

4:1-5 Samaritan interference. Chapter 3 ends with the completion of the foundations of the temple presumably during the second year of the return in 537 B.C.E. (see our discussion on 3:7-13). Chapter 5 opens about seventeen years later with resumption of work on the temple building during the reign of Darius. In chapter 4 the biblical writers account for the intervening delay by describing the opposition of the returnees' neighbors, the Samaritans and the "people of the land." Opposition which had only been hinted at in Ezra 3:3 comes into full view in chapter 4.

According to verses 2-3, the controversy began when descendants of the mixed populations of Samaria expressed a desire to be part of the rebuilding project. In offering their help, they refer to the reign of the Assyrian Esarhaddon (681-669 B.C.E.) although 2 Kgs 17:24-41 links the Assyrian mixing of populations in the northern kingdom of Israel with the reign of Shalmaneser V (726-722 B.C.E.) while Assyrian records credit Sargon II (721-705 B.C.E.) with the repopulation of defeated Israel. We do not know where the writers of Ezra 4:1-5 turned for their information; although the population to the north does seem to have been mixed, we know very little of what went on there after its final capitulation to Assyria in 721 B.C.E. The petitioners base their desire to assist in the temple reconstruction on their fidelity to Yahweh. The Judeans, however, thought that they alone were orthodox, and they dismissed the request by referring to the mandate of Cyrus. The Judeans' rebuff of the Samaritans stems from their concern for cultic purity among the Jews, an issue which comes to a head during Ezra's leadership and is narrated in subsequent chapters.

Verse 4 (and 5) traces the hostility to the "people of the land." We cannot be certain whether this refers to Samaritans from the north, to people of mixed blood who had moved from the north into Judah, or simply to residents of Judah who had remained in Judah during the Exile and hence, in the eyes of the returnees, had not undergone the purging required of those who, in their view, constituted the orthodox community. Whatever

the case, these opponents intimidated and discouraged the returnees and subverted their progress. The end of verse 5 describes this state of affairs as lasting from the days of Cyrus (539-530 B.C.E.) to the reign of Darius I (522-485 B.C.E.).

4:6-23 Later hostility. Chronological shifts as well as changes in content mark verses 6-23 as a unit which interrupts the flow from 4:5 to 4:24. First of all, with regard to chronology, verse 6 jumps from the reign of Darius (v. 5) to that of his successor, Xerxes (here called Ahashuerus). Verses 7-23 take readers forward another generation into the reign of Artaxerxes I (465-425 B.C.E.). Secondly, although the particular issues over which there is controversy in verses 6 and 7 are unclear, the matter of concern in verses 8-23 is the rebuilding of the wall of the city of Jerusalem. This sets these verses apart from the concern of verses 1-5 and verse 24 where the issue is the rebuilding of the temple. This change in topic along with the chronological shifts in verses 6-23 show us that these verses interrupt the flow of the narrative. Presumably they have been inserted into this account about the rebuilding of the temple as additional examples of the kind of opposition which hampered the restoration efforts of the postexilic community.

Verses 6 and 7 are related to verses 8-23 insofar as they witness to written statements composed by the enemies of the restoration community and designed to obstruct their efforts. The enemies of verse 6 are the anonymous "they." Those named in verse 7 (Mithredath and Tabeel) appear to have some official roles but we know nothing further about them. In verses 8-23 the enemies are clearly designated as the governor and officials in the Persian province of West-of-Euphrates.

Verse 8 is the beginning of the Aramaic section of the Book of Ezra which continues until Ezra 6:18. An editor prepares the reader of the Hebrew text for the shift in verse 7b. The contents of verses 8-23 claim to be a record of official correspondence to (vv. 8-16) and from (vv. 17-22) the Persian king. This demonstrates the writers' characteristic style of documenting their accounts with what appear to be official records. The question of whether or not the correspondence recorded here is, in fact, an authentic record remains open, since we have no extrabiblical evidence with which to verify it.

The letter to Artaxerxes reports the rebuilding of Jerusalem (v. 12) as a threat against the Persian throne (v. 13). In verse 14 the writers declare that their report is an act of loyalty. Partaking of the "salt of the palace" refers to an ancient custom wherein sharing salt with another symbolized alliance (see Num 18:19; Lev 2:13; 2 Chr 13:5). In verse 15 the composers of the letter suggest to the Persian emperor that their accusation against Jerusalem can be substantiated by an investigation of the city's past. Jerusalem, they say, has a history of rebellion which is documented in Persian records and which will lead to Persia's loss of the entire province of West-of-Euphrates if the rebuilding of the city is not stopped (v. 16).

The letter from Artaxerxes (vv. 17-22) shows that the enemies of the restoration community achieved their desired result: the suspicions of the accusers were substantiated, and the Persian emperor ordered that the rebuilding of Jerusalem be stopped. The truth of the matters which the Persian emperor said were documented in his records is difficult to assess. That any foreign king ever ruled the territory from the Euphrates River to the Mediterranean Sea (the area subsequently called West-of-Euphrates) from Jerusalem is especially questionable. Whatever the case, verse 23 narrates that Artaxerxes' orders were carried out and the rebuilding of Jerusalem stopped.

4:24–5:17 Rebuilding of the temple. Verse 24 of chapter 4 is a transitional statement which resumes the narratives of verses 1-5 of the same chapter and leads into the materials contained in chapters 5 and 6. Verse 24 takes readers back to the later years of Cyrus and the first years of Darius when the concern was not the restoration of Jerusalem (as in 4:8-23) but the reconstruction of the temple.

In Ezra 5:1-2 renewed efforts to rebuild the temple are traced to the inspiration of two prophets from the early years of Darius' reign, Haggai and Zechariah. The Books of Haggai and Zechariah tell us that during the period extending from the second to the fourth year of Darius (between 520 and 518 B.C.E.) these two prophets were concerned about the ne-

cessity, even urgency, of rebuilding the temple. Haggai and Zechariah corroborate the witness of Ezra 5:1-2 that Zerubbabel and Jeshua were leading figures in the restoration community during this period.

Having briefly reported the resumption of work on the temple, the biblical writers divert our attention to the question of proper authorization for the project, a concern which continues throughout the remainder of chapter 5 and throughout the bulk of chapter 6. Regional officials representing Persian interests came to Jerusalem to conduct an investigation regarding the temple project. The blatant hostility which marked the narrative of chapter 4 is absent from the present inquiry (vv. 3-5) and from the subsequent correspondence with the Persian emperor (vv. 6-17). We are not told what precipitated the investigation; although it may have constituted a subtle form of harassment, the text offers no clear indication that this was its purpose. The officials simply inquire regarding proper authorization for the temple reconstruction and the identity of those involved in the work. Verse 5 reports that, unlike the incident reported in Ezra 4:1-5 and 24, the present investigation did not retard progress on the rebuilding and that this was due to God's protective presence. At this point in the narrative the "elders of the Jews" appear to take the lead in the temple project and in dealings with the Persian officials (see Ezra 5:9; 6:7, 8, 14).

The remainder of chapter 5 and 6:1-12 reflect the Chronicler's fondness for including documentation, this time in the form of official correspondence between officers of the Persian province West-of-Euphrates and the Persian emperor. Verses 7-17 claim to be a copy of the letter sent by the provincial officers to Darius. Their report on the rebuilding in Jerusalem (vv. 7-8) and the nature of their inquiry (vv. 9-10) is in accord with what had been narrated in verses 3-4 except that the report contains additional information about building materials and the spirit and progress which marked the Jews' work (v. 8). Verses 11-16 contain a relatively lengthy response on the part of the Jews (a response which is missing from the incident as narrated in verses 3-5). The Jews address only the question about authorization for the rebuilding of the temple. The names which had been requested are not given. (Some have suggested that the list which now appears in Ezra 2 may originally have served this purpose.)

The Jews' response is set within the context of a brief review of history from the beginnings of the first temple. The language of the historical review makes concessions to the fact that this report was prepared for foreigners. The specific identity of the builder of the first temple would have been of no interest to Persian authorities, so Solomon is referred to simply as "a great king of Israel" (v. 11). For the same reason, the personal name of the God of Israel, Yahweh, does not appear, and instead the Jews refer to their God with a more general designation ("the God of heaven and earth" in verse 11 and the "God of heaven" in verse 12) which would have been more familiar to foreigners. At the same time, a specifically Jewish view of history surfaces in verse 12 where we read that the fall of Israel into Babylonian hands was not simply a human exchange of power but an act of God following upon the sinfulness of the covenanted people. The abbreviated report of the fall of the temple and the captivity agrees with longer witnesses to the same events which appear in 2 Kgs 25:8-21 and 2 Chr 36:17-20.

Persian authorization for the rebuilding of the temple appears in verse 13 where Cyrus the Persian is called "king of Babylon." Verse 13 neglects to mention that Cyrus' decree mandated the return of the Jewish exiles. It limits itself to the part of Cyrus' edict which relates to the matter at hand, that is, the rebuilding of the temple (compare the decree as cited in Ezra 1:2-4). Verses 14-15 extend the discussion to some degree by including Cyrus' decree providing for the recovery of sacred temple vessels which had been confiscated by the Babylonian captors.

When we are told in verse 14 that Cyrus appointed Sheshbazzar "governor," the meaning is unclear. The same word was used to describe Tattenai, the non-Jewish official of West-of-Euphrates who sent the letter (see 5:6; compare Ezra 1:8 where Sheshbazzar is called "prince of Judah" and Hag 1:1 where Zerubbabel is called "governor of Judah").

We have said that verse 16 attributes the laying of the foundations of the temple to Sheshbazzar even though Ezra 3:8-10 (and Zech 4:9) gave credit for its beginning to Zerubbabel (see our discussion on Ezra 3:7-13).

The officials' letter ends with their request that Darius verify Cyrus' authorization of the rebuilding of the temple as the Jews had reported and that Darius tell the officials what he wants them to do about this matter.

6:1-18 The decree of Darius. The opening verses of chapter 6 are a further example of the biblical writers' fondness for including official documentation. The statement by Cyrus which Darius found in Ecbatana, one of the imperial centers of Persia, also underscores Persian patronage of Jewish efforts—a consistent witness throughout the Books of Ezra and Nehemiah except for Ezra 4:8-23. The text confirms that the rebuilding of the temple in Jerusalem was authorized, and as such it serves as a response to the inquiry which was the subject of chapter 5. It is presented as an edict issued by Cyrus in the first year of his reign, so it is an alternate witness to the edict cited in Ezra 1:2-4. Although the exact wording of the edict is not the same in the two texts, the content of 1:2-4 is in essential agreement with that of 6:3-5 with the following exceptions: (a) 1:2-4 includes permission for the exiles to return to their land along with permission to rebuild the temple while 6:3-5 confines itself strictly to the temple restoration; (b) 6:3-5 provides for the return of the temple utensils while the document cited in 1:2-4 does not mention them (compare 1:7 and 5:14-15); (c) 6:3-5 contains specific information about the construction of the temple which does not appear in the copy of the edict in 1:2-4. The building materials specified in verse 4 are the same as those used in Solomon's temple (see 1 Kgs 6:36), but there is a significant discrepancy between the proportions of the temple in verse 3 and the size of Solomon's temple recorded in 1 Kgs 6:2. Scholars, citing Ezra 3:12 and Hag 2:3, are skeptical that the second temple was larger than the one which Solomon built.

Having documented the claims of the Jewish leaders, in verses 6-12 the biblical writers cite Darius' response to the final request of the provincial officials that Darius voice his own directives on the matter under investigation. Darius tells the local officials not to interfere with the rebuilding of the temple. He also orders them to facilitate the work with monies collected through taxation within the province and to provide materials for the daily temple offerings required by the Mosaic law (see Exod 29:38-42). Verse 10 makes clear that the Persian emperor's directives are not without self-interest.

In the face of the long delays which mark the biblical writers' account of the rebuilding of the temple, the brief account of the completion and dedication of the temple and the restoration of cultic service (vv. 13-18) may strike the reader as abrupt. Work on the temple went forward in accord with the promptings of the God of Israel, the Persian emperors (Artaxerxes is a later gloss added to verse 14), and prophets of the period, Haggai and Zechariah. It was completed in the spring of 515 B.C.E. The temple was dedicated by a legitimate community of faith defined in verse 16 as priests, Levites, and other Jews who had been purified by the experience of Exile. The offerings for this occasion are relatively modest compared to the sacrifices at the dedication of Solomon's temple (compare 1 Kgs 8:5, 63) and probably reflect the poverty of the struggling community. Finally, we are told that priestly and Levitical personnel assumed their traditional cultic offices (see Num 3; 1 Chr 23-24). Thus the writers establish continuity between ancient practice and the worship of the postexilic community in Jerusalem.

These verses mark the end of the Aramaic section of the Book of Ezra. The concluding verses of the first section (6:19-22) appear in Hebrew.

If the witness of Ezra 6:15 is correct, that is, if the second temple was dedicated in the month of Adar (the twelfth month), then it is realistic to expect that Passover was celebrated soon after, for according to the legislation of Exod 12 Passover was held on the fourteenth day of the first month (Nisan). In including the account of Passover after a description of the temple dedication, the writers are presenting what appears to be a historically reliable account. At the same time, when we note that the Chronicler presents the feast of Booths (Ezra 3:1-6) following the dedication of the altar and that the celebration of Passover followed the reconsecrations of the temple which were part of the reforms of King Hezekiah (2 Chr 29-30; compare 2 Kgs 18-20) and King Josiah (2 Chr 34-35; compare 2 Kgs 22-23), we wonder if the biblical writers offer more of a theological construct than historical fact in Ezra 6:19-22. Whatever the case,

a celebration of Passover is presented as following the rededication of the temple, and Passover observance is linked with the feast of Unleavened Bread as it is in the priestly legislation of Exod 12:1-20. Because the law permitted non-Jews to join in the celebration of Passover (Num 9:14), outsiders are invited to join in the celebration described here. However, the biblical writers' inclusiveness on this occasion is restrained by the repeated reference to members of the legitimate community (those who had been purged by the experience of Exile) and by the qualification that those non-Jews who celebrated Passover had separated themselves from the cultic uncleanness of the "peoples of the land."

The concluding verse of this first section of the Book of Ezra reminds readers of the aim of the entire account of these early years of the restoration. The biblical writers recall that it is Yahweh ("the Lord") who controls history and made the Persian king (certainly this is the intent of the expression "king of Assyria" in verse 22) facilitate the rebuilding of the temple which, according to the view of the writers (see Ezra 1:2), was the primary goal of the return from Exile.

PART II: RESTORATION OF THE WORSHIPING COMMUNITY

Ezra 7:1-10:44

Chapters 7 through 10 of the Book of Ezra constitute the second major part of the Ezra-Nehemiah materials. The chief figure in these chapters (and in chapter 8 of the Book of Nehemiah) is Ezra, a reformer important in the reconstruction, whose name was given to the biblical book. Chapters 7 and 8 introduce Ezra and describe the return from Exile which he led. Chapters 9 and 10 narrate the marriage reform which Ezra is said to have initiated within the restoration community. Much of the material was taken from Ezra's memoirs. Ezra 7-10 and Nehemiah 8 credit Ezra particularly with zealous efforts to establish the law of Moses as the center around which Jewish life was reconstructed. This is the foundation for the postbiblical view of Ezra as a second Moses.

Readers must be aware of the chronological, theological, and literary complexities woven into the Ezra materials. Although the exact time of Ezra's mission is unknown, we accept the scholarly opinion which places Ezra within the reign of Artaxerxes II (405–359 B.C.E.). Thus, a lengthy historical gap separates the materials of Ezra 1–6 (ending with the dedication of the temple in 515 B.C.E.) and the mission of Ezra (about 398 B.C.E.) as described in Ezra 7–10. In the intervening years, Nehemiah led the community in the reconstruction of the wall of Jerusalem and in cultic reforms (see Neh 1–7, 9–13).

The present arrangement of the text is understandable if one recalls the theological interests of the writers (see Introduction, (p. 336). They present community purity, the goal of Ezra's marriage reform, as the second stage of the restoration movement, following the reconstruction of the temple. True worship required not only a legitimate temple with proper rituals and feasts (Ezra 1–6), but also worshipers made cultically pure by their separation from foreigners (Ezra 7–10).

Ezra's proclamation of the law (Neh 7:72b–8:18) is now separate from the biblical writers' account of the rest of Ezra's mission. If one sought to reconstruct an accurate chronology of events, one might read Neh 7:72b to 8:18 between chapters 8 and 9 of the Book of Ezra. However, the present arrangement of the text stresses that the proclamation of the law was the theological culmination of all other works of restoration, the event which marked the full restoration of the Jewish community. Therefore, Ezra's reading of the law is presented in the Book of Nehemiah as part of the fourth and final stage of restoration.

7:1–10 Ezra the scribe. With the simple phrase "after these events," the biblical writers span the years which lay between the dedication of the temple and Ezra's mission. The genealogy of verses 2-5, which in part parallels 1 Chr 5:29-40, is not so much concerned with factual data (it is a historical impossibility that the time period between Aaron and Ezra was only seventeen generations) as with Ezra's priestly legitimacy. He is presented as a descendant of the precursor of all Israel's priests, Aaron. If Seraiah is the same person mentioned in 2 Kgs 25:18, Ezra is also presented as son of the last official high priest before the fall of the temple to the Babylonians (see 1 Chr 5:40; since the fall was in 587 B.C.E., it is clear that Ezra was not, in fact, Seraiah's son). The biblical writers use the genealogy

not only to tell us that Ezra was a priest but to underscore the legitimacy of his priestly lineage and to emphasize that his leadership in the restoration community was an authentic extension of priestly leadership in pre-exilic Israel.

Ezra's more significant role was that of scribe, a term which originally designated an expert in writing who exercised a significant role, politically. In later periods scribes were experts in the law. That is the meaning of scribe as it is used here although Ezra's close relationship with King Artaxerxes also suggests that, prior to being sent to Jerusalem, he held a position (secretary for Jewish affairs?) in the royal court of Persia. It is difficult to know with certainty what constituted the "law of Moses" in which Ezra was well-versed. It may have been the Pentateuch as we know it or some portion of the law contained therein.

According to the biblical writers, Ezra had other credentials for his mission: he was favored by God and by the Persian king. This is consistent with Ezra 1–6 where God showed graciousness to the Jews by providing the generous patronage of the Persian kings.

Having introduced the chief figure in the second stage of the restoration, the biblical writers offer an overview of his return from Exile, a journey which will be considered in greater detail in Ezra 8. The writers' concern for worship in the restoration community led them to include references to the cultic officers who accompanied Ezra (v. 7). They also provide dates for the journey. It seems to have taken about four months. It is interesting that Ezra left Babylon during the first month of the year, the same month which the priestly writers assigned to the Exodus journey (Exod 12:2; Num 33:3). It is difficult to know whether or not the biblical writers were suggesting a theological parallel between the two events.

The introductory verses to the second stage of the reconstruction close with a portrait of Ezra as one who not only studied and taught the law but also zealously practiced it (v. 10).

7:11–26 The decree of Artaxerxes. Interested in including official documentation for various parts of the return and restoration, the biblical writers offer what claims to be a statement by the Persian emperor which (a) authorized a return under Ezra's leadership, (b) commissioned Ezra to establish the law as the basis for life in the restoration community in Judah, and (c) put Ezra in charge of monetary and other gifts for the temple in Jerusalem. The fact that the decree (vv. 12-26) appears in Aramaic gives it the appearance of authenticity. Yet some of its details (such as the list of offerings in verse 17 and the list of temple personnel in verse 24) suggest that it was written by someone with considerable knowledge of cultic affairs in the Jewish community. Some scholars have proposed that it was drafted by a Jewish member of Artaxerxes' court, while others think that an authentic letter of appointment was amplified by the biblical writers.

The opening (vv. 11-12) and closing (vv. 25-26) of this section echo the main emphasis which appears in the introduction to Ezra in 7:1-10, Ezra's authority with regard to the law. Following his commission to lead a group of exiles back to Jerusalem (v. 13), Ezra's basic role in the restoration community is to be guardian of the law of God within the Jewish community. This role represents an extension of the authority of the Persian government (v. 14).

The remainder of Artaxerxes' decree orders Ezra to obtain sufficient provisions to establish full worship in the temple in Jerusalem. The king and his officers not only contributed silver and gold for temple worship out of their own treasuries but also authorized Ezra to take to Jerusalem any gifts which he could collect from Jews living in Babylon. In addition, Artaxerxes sent utensils for temple worship with Ezra, just as Cyrus had done when Sheshbazzar led an earlier return (see 1:7-11; 5:14-15). As a further gesture of generosity, Artaxerxes promised to provide from the royal treasury whatever else was needed for proper worship and included explicit instructions for his officers in the province to which Ezra travelled. Finally, he declared all cultic personnel in West-of-Euphrates tax-exempt. In verse 23 we see that Artaxerxes' magnanimity toward the Jews and their worship was not without self-interest: proper worship was to be conducted in order to secure Yahweh's favor for the Persian king.

The conclusion of Artaxerxes' decree (vv. 25-26) returns to Ezra's role as chief caretaker of God's law. Like Moses (see Exod 18), Ezra

is authorized to appoint administrators of justice within the restoration community. Ezra's own role is to offer instruction in the law. Finally, the Persian emperor provides for the punishment (even the death) of those who fail to obey "the law of your God and the law of the king."

7:27–8:14 Ezra and his companions. The biblical text returns to Hebrew in verse 27. The same verse marks the beginning of what scholars call "Ezra's memoirs," the first-person account which extends to Ezra 9:15 (see our discussion of sources, p. 338). Verses 27-28a are a blessing placed on the lips of Ezra. Its contents reiterate the notion expressed in 7:6 that the generosity of the Persian officials was ultimately an expression of Yahweh's graciousness to the Jewish community. In the remainder of verse 28 Ezra also connects his own work with the providence of God.

Just as the biblical writers included a list of the names in conjunction with an earlier return to Judah (Ezra 2), so the narrative about Ezra's return is delayed by a similar listing which appears in the initial verses of chapter 8. The list begins (v. 2) with the names of returning descendants of ancient Israel's priestly leaders (Phinehas and Ithamar) and of the royal house of David. Verses 3-14 list the names of the heads of twelve lay families who returned along with the total number of returning males belonging to each group. In naming twelve families the biblical writers suggest that "all Israel" returned, that is, representatives from all the twelve tribes of Israel. Nearly fifteen hundred males returned with Ezra—a sizeable number especially if one adds the women and children who must have returned with them. Family names in this list also appear in the longer list in chapter 2, although in a different order.

8:15-36 The journey to Jerusalem. The account of Ezra's journey to Jerusalem is marked by an order similar to that of a religious service. There is (a) an initial gathering of returnees at a location ("by the river that flows toward Ahava") unknown to modern scholars and a three-day rest which will be repeated when the journey to Jerusalem has been completed (see 8:32), (b) recruiting of cultic personnel (Levites and temple slaves), (c) a fast and prayer for a safe journey, (d) the consignment of temple treasures to cultic personnel, (e) the journey itself which unfolded in accord with the prayer of verses 21-23, (f) the delivery of gifts for the temple which in part repeats verses 24-30, and (g) sacrificial rituals to Yahweh and a visit to local civic officials. The biblical writers devote much attention to preparations for the journey and to activities which occurred upon Ezra's arrival in Jerusalem. Among these, interest is particularly focused on cultic concerns. Events during the long journey are only hinted at in verse 31.

Verses 15b-20 contain a record of Ezra's attempts to include cultic personnel in his return. We do not know why Levites did not originally join his group. Some scholars have suggested that not many Levites had gone into Exile because earlier shifts in their cultic duties at the temple had led to their dispersal among outlying cities and towns prior to the fall of Jerusalem. Others suggest that Levites had gone into Exile but had taken up non-cultic professions while they were there. Whatever the case, the recruiters that Ezra sent to Casiphia (Levites were apparently concentrated in this city the location of which is not known) brought a few Levites and a greater number of temple slaves into the caravan. This, like much else in the present account, is attributed to God's guidance. The emphasis upon divine protection likewise appears in the fast and prayer which preceded the journey (vv. 21-23) and in the notation that the group and its many treasures arrived safely in Jerusalem despite the fact that they had neither requested nor received military protection along the way.

Ezra selected twelve priestly leaders and twelve of the cultic personnel recruited from Casiphia to take care of the temple gifts from Persian officials and from Jews in Babylon. The appointment of cultic leaders for this role is in accord with ancient tradition, since Num 3-4 tells us that priests and Levites were appointed to attend to sacred objects on the journey that Moses led through the Sinai wilderness when ancient Israel journeyed toward the Promised Land after the Exodus. The fact that it was twelve priests and twelve other cultic leaders who were guardians of the sacred offerings and utensils again reflects the biblical writers' propensity for the number which symbolized the ideal, "all Israel." Immediately following a brief summary of the journey (v. 31), the biblical writers tell us that

the sacred gifts arrived intact and were delivered to the proper officials as Ezra had directed. Cultic matters were most important to them; this priority given to cult led the biblical writers to suggest that, following the standard three-day rest period, the first activity of the returnees was to offer sacrifices to Yahweh.

9:1-2 Denunciation of mixed marriages. Ezra's work in the restoration community (decrying mixed marriage) is narrated in chapters 9 and 10 of the Book of Ezra and in chapter 8 of the Book of Nehemiah (Ezra's ceremonial reading of the law). Some scholars propose that Neh 8 was originally part of the Ezra materials which appear in the Book of Ezra. Accordingly, they have suggested that Neh 7:72b–8:18 be read between the end of Ezra 8 and the beginning of Ezra 9. While this proposal has merit because of the somewhat nebulous opening of Ezra 9 ("when these matters had been concluded"), for purposes of this commentary we shall follow the text as it has come down to us. In view of the reply that Artaxerxes sent to Ezra, the learned scribe, to "supervise Judah and Jerusalem in respect of the law of your God" (7:14), it is surprising that the first reported incident involving his leadership is the dissolution of mixed marriages and not the reading of the law.

The biblical position on marriages with foreigners is not consistent. While some prominent biblical figures (for example, Joseph, Moses, David) had foreign spouses and the Book of Ruth witnesses to the blessings God bestowed on the Hebrew community through the Moabite woman who married the Hebrew Boaz, the prohibition of mixed marriages which appears in the Book of Ezra has precedents in earlier stages of Israelite tradition (see Exod 34:16; Deut 7:1-4). Marital practices in different ages were shaped by changing social, political, economic, and religious situations. In Ezra's time concern for cultic purity and for securing the identity of the Jewish people required pure blood lines.

The situation is reported to Ezra: laymen and clergymen alike have taken foreign wives, and the worst offenders are community leaders. The "people of the land" with whom they were joined are defined by an editor who had access to the lists of Deut 7:1; Josh 3:10; 24:12. The transgressors are also linked with the "abominations" of their spouses; that is, their marriages had brought them into contact with the worship of other gods.

9:3-15 Ezra's exhortation. Ezra was distressed by the report. In a traditional expression of grief, he tore his clothes and pulled out his hair. As the smoke of the evening offering marked the hour of community worship in the temple, Ezra fell on his knees and stretched out his hands.

Ezra begins praying in the first person singular but changes immediately to the first person plural, which he uses consistently throughout the remainder of the confession of guilt.

Ezra states that Israel's entire history has been characterized by sin which brought on the downfall of the nation and the Babylonian Exile (v. 7). This sinful past provides the perspective within which Ezra interprets Israel's present situation. In the present era the punishment of captivity which was an expression of God's justice has given way to God's mercy. A remnant of the Jewish people was spared and brought once again to Jerusalem. As elsewhere in the Book of Ezra, this mark of divine favor is brought into conjunction with the kindness of the Persian emperors toward the exiles. The end result of these divine and human mercies is that the temple was rebuilt and Jerusalem and Judah were made secure (vv. 8-9). But the present favor is now in jeopardy. The land and its peoples are impure (see Lev 18:24-25), and Israel has transgressed God's commandment by intermarrying with foreigners (Deut 7:1-4). (It is noteworthy that the Deuteronomic tradition cited by Ezra prohibits the marrying of Israelite women to foreign men as well as the marrying of Israelite men to foreign women, a more inclusive view than Ezra's own reform which deals only with marriages which Jewish men had contracted with foreign women.)

While Ezra explicitly addresses his questions to God in verses 13-14, the reader senses he has also aimed them at the Jews assembled for worship in order to call to their attention what was happening in their midst. Have they not learned from experience that punishment follows sin? If God were to punish the present guilt, would not the Jews now living in Israel be completely destroyed? Justice is certain, but mercy is a gift. The fragile remnant of Jews in Jerusalem exists only because of

gift. Their sin of marrying foreigners will require that God act justly with them.

10:1-15 The people's response. The dramatic confession of chapter 9 serves as the background for the decisions and actions reported in chapter 10. The use of the third person suggests that the report in chapter 10 did not come from Ezra's memoirs but from another source.

Ezra had attracted a very large crowd of men, women and children. A layman, Shecaniah, was stirred by Ezra's speech to confess the community's guilt ("We have indeed betrayed our God"). To ward off the possibility of total destruction, a punishment of which Ezra had warned, Shecaniah proposed that Jewish men dismiss their foreign wives and their children.

Shecaniah's exclamation, "Let the law be observed!" (v. 3) is something of a puzzle. While Pentateuchal law prohibited marriage with foreigners (see Exod 34:16; Deut 7:1-4), it did not make provision for what to do in cases where mixed marriages already existed. In other words, the law did not require divorce in cases of mixed marriages. It is possible that what we see here is the beginning of a new practice adopted to meet the demands of a situation not addressed by tradition. Whatever the case, Shecaniah's proposal makes clear that Ezra's condemnation of mixed marriages in chapter 9 was accepted by the community and required the dissolution of already-established families. Concerns about religious tradition took precedence over regard for the sacredness of family bonds. At once, action to dissolve mixed marriages begins. Ezra demanded that the priests and people of the community swear to act. All exiles in the country (that is, all legitimate members of the Jewish community) were required to come to Jerusalem within three days under threat of dispossession and excommunication.

Meanwhile Ezra retires to the temple quarters of Johanan (v. 6). This brief note has played an important part in biblical scholars' discussions about the dates of Ezra's mission. Johanan is described here as son of the high priest Eliashib. However, Neh 12:10-11 and 22 are probably more accurate in presenting Johanan as Eliashib's grandson. Now Eliashib is known to have served as high priest during the time of Nehemiah (445–433 b.c.e.; see Neh 3:1, 20-21). Most scholars conclude from this that, contrary to the chronological witness of the present arrangement of the Ezra-Nehemiah materials, Nehemiah preceded Ezra in the work of restoration. The biblical writers do not tell us whether or not Johanan served as high priest in Ezra's day. (Extra-biblical sources indicate that Johanan held the high priestly office near the end of the fifth century B.C.E..) He did, however, have his own quarters in the temple.

When the biblical writers say that "all the men of Judah and Benjamin" appeared as ordered (v. 9), they refer to "all Israel" by naming the two ancient tribes who constituted the southern part of the country during much of its history. The biblical writers describe a scene both grave and comic. It was Israel's rainy season and those who gathered on the temple mount shivered—over the seriousness of the matter at hand and "because it was raining" (v. 9). Apparently oblivious to their pathetic condition, Ezra (now specifically described as priest instead of scribe) began accusing those gathered before him in the rain. Without awaiting response or confession, he gave the order for separation. The assembled community acknowledged that it was their duty to obey Ezra but pointed out that because of their numbers and the rain it was both humanly impossible and uncomfortable to proceed immediately. They suggested that appointed leaders could handle the matter for the whole community, in light of the numbers involved, and establish a more realistic deadline for the dissolution of mixed marriages.

Verse 15 notes some dissenting voices among those gathered, but the subject of their disagreement is left ambiguous. We do not know whether they objected to the decision to divorce foreign women or to the procedures designed for the reform.

10:16-44 The guilty. Verses 16-17 report that the leaders appointed by Ezra judged the legitimacy of marriages of Jews with foreign women. These hearings took three months. Most of the remainder of the chapter is a list of the offenders, beginning with priests and other cultic personnel and concluding with members of the laity named by families. The list has some parallels with those in Ezra 2 and 8, although it is not a duplicate of either. It contains only 111 names, a surprisingly small total in view of the thousands who constituted the community. This may have been only a partial listing of the people involved. An alternate explanation is that if mixed marriages were widespread only a few people responded to the action taken by Ezra.

COMMENTARY: NEHEMIAH

PART III: RESTORATION OF THE WALL OF JERUSALEM

Neh 1:1–7:72a

Drawing heavily upon Nehemiah's memoirs, chapters 1–7 of the Book of Nehemiah narrate events of the two-month period from the beginning of Nehemiah's mission to shortly after the reconstruction of the wall around Jerusalem, the third major achievement during the restoration period. Work on the wall presses on in spite of both continuous opposition from Judah's neighbors and tensions within the Jewish community itself. Throughout the chapters there is an underlying parallel drawn between the welfare of the city and the welfare of the Jewish community. The restoration of the city wall in Part III thus functions as a fitting preparation for the full restoration of the community under the law in Part IV.

In these chapters we find the biblical portrait of Nehemiah. Throughout, he is presented as a pious Jew, prayerful and dependent upon God's help. His initial fears are transformed to fearlessness before all but God, and he counsels the Jewish community not to capitulate through fear to the evil designs of its enemies. Other prominent characteristics of Nehemiah's piety are the initiative and zealous effort which mark his mission. His oneness with the Jewish people sparks his decision to act when he hears of the brokenness of Jerusalem and its people. He gives practical matters his full attention, assessing situations carefully before acting.

Nehemiah's mission to Judah was authorized and patronized by the Persian throne, as were the missions of Sheshbazzar (Part I) and Ezra (Part II). Nehemiah's appointment as governor over the province of Judah put him in a position to deal firmly with rulers of neighboring regions and with leaders in the Jewish community who needed to be called to account for their acts. With the community at large, he was consistently decisive but not coercive. He was attentive to their needs, even to the point of self-sacrifice. His view of community included women as well as men.

1:1-11 Nehemiah's vocation. The opening chapter of the Book of Nehemiah falls into two sections: (a) a report about the Judean Jews and the city of Jerusalem (vv. 1-3) and (b) Nehemiah's response to the report (vv. 4-11). Succinctly the chapter presents the roots out of which the remainder of the book will grow. First of all, we learn that it is 445 B.C.E. (the twentieth year of the reign of Artaxerxes I) and that, even though nearly a century has passed since the Jews returned to Judah from their captivity in Babylon, they continue to live as a broken people, a plight symbolized by the brokenness of the wall around the city which is their center. Secondly, this first chapter introduces us to Nehemiah, a Jewish official in the Persian court ("cupbearer to the king"), who has both a strong sense of identification with the Jews in Judah and a recognition that the brokenness in Judah constitutes a call to action on his part.

As the book opens we find ourselves in the memoirs of this Jewish layman. Nehemiah was in Susa, a winter residence of King Artaxerxes whom he served. He met with a group of men from Judah whose mission is not stated. They could have come to solicit help from the Persian throne or from Nehemiah. Or, they may have been on a routine business trip within the empire and secondarily functioned as part of an informal network of communication between Jews in Judah and those scattered abroad. Whatever the case, the group included Hanani, a "brother" to Nehemiah, that is, either a blood relative or perhaps just a fellow Jew. In answer to Nehemiah's inquiry, Hanani reports both about the Jews and about the city of Jerusalem. The fact that Nehemiah is reported to have asked about both the people and the city signals a perspective which flows through the work of Nehemiah. We shall see that for him the welfare of the two are closely intertwined. For Nehemiah, the restoration of the people and the restoration of the city are somehow two sides of the same concern.

The news from Judah is bad, and it grips the spirit of Nehemiah (v. 4). The disgraceful situation of the Jews in Judah and of the city of Jerusalem becomes his own diminishment. In the prayer of verses 5-11 we see the strong bond between Nehemiah and the Jews: their sin is his sin (vv. 6-7); their need for God's favor is his need (v. 11). Into his confession and petition Nehemiah weaves words pushing God to act. He politely reminds God of exactly who is speaking to whom. He and the sorrowing Jews in Jerusalem—those who beg for a hearing—are, like Moses before them, God's own servants (vv. 6, 7, 8, 10, 11). At the same time, he reminds God that God is the one who chose and bought this people for the divine self (v. 10), who preserves a "covenant of mercy" for faithful servants (v. 5), and who, after all, has promises to keep (vv. 8-9).

The prayer of Nehemiah is shot through with elements firmly rooted in Israel's religious tradition. In verse 10 he refers to the Exodus from Egypt. Nehemiah's restatement of God's promise (vv. 8b-9) is a paraphrase of Deut 30:1-5 which Nehemiah freely interprets not simply as God's commitment to bring the Jews back to the land of Judah but specifically to bring them back to "the place which I have chosen as the dwelling place for my name," a Deuteronomic way of referring to the city of Jerusalem.

Much takes place in this seemingly simple chapter. Nehemiah has moved from his initial inquiry about Jerusalem to grief, prayer, and a decision to act. It is a fitting introduction to Nehemiah, a man of action who identifies deeply with his fellow Jews. He hears a vocational call: the Jews and Jerusalem are in distress and he is in a position to help. Empathy and prayer are not enough. The closing words of the chapter (v. 11b) reflect his decision to help Jerusalem.

2:1-10 Appointment by the king. The memoirs resume four months later when Nehemiah is in a position to do something about the vocational call narrated in chapter 1. While Nehemiah performed his duty as cupbearer, Artaxerxes noticed that something was wrong with his servant. Nehemiah reports (v. 2) that he was "seized with great fear" when Artaxerxes inquired about the reason for his sadness. To understand Nehemiah's fear we must recall the incident described in Ezra 4:8-23. At some time earlier in his reign Artaxerxes had halted Jewish efforts to reconstruct the wall of the city of Jerusalem. He did so out of a conviction that the restoration of Jerusalem was tantamount to rebellion against the Persian throne. Hence, Nehemiah was fearful because, in effect, he had to tell the king that his sadness was due to a decision that the king himself had made.

The exchange between Nehemiah and the king constitutes a masterpiece of diplomacy. Politics is left out of the conversation. The personal concern which started the discussion ("Why do you look sad?" v. 2) carries to its end. Nehemiah avoids the word "Jerusalem" and instead speaks of the devastation of "the city where my ancestors are buried" (vv. 3, 5). Thus, his request to go and rebuild the city is made only on personal grounds. The king does not refer to his earlier decision either, although he must have been aware that he was being asked to reverse his decision regarding the reconstruction of Jerusalem. It may be that doing so now was politically expedient. In the earlier period there had been much unrest in the area of the empire surrounding Judah, and the reconstruction of a fortified city in Judah may have only fed fires of revolt. But by 445 B.C.E. revolts in that part of the empire had died down, and entrusting Nehemiah (whose loyalty the king knew personally) with the task of fortifying Jerusalem might indeed enhance imperial strength and security in the area. If politics motivated Artaxerxes to grant Nehemiah's request, we are never told so. Instead, the permission to return to Jerusalem is cast as a personal favor to one who had endeared himself to the king. The permission, however, constitutes a political appointment. In Neh 5:14 we are told that Nehemiah went to Judah as governor. The length of his appointment is only alluded to in Neh 2:6, but Neh 5:14 shows that Nehemiah left to begin a term of office which would last twelve years.

Neh 2:6 implies that Nehemiah's commission came from both the Persian king and queen. The inclusion of the queen (whose name, Damaspia, we know from extrabiblical documents) is an unusual but interesting detail. Queens exercised considerable influence during some periods of the Persian Empire (see the Book of Esther) and this was especially so during the reign of Artaxerxes. In addition, we shall see that the Book of Nehemiah frequently includes the role of women as well as men (see Neh 3:12; 5:1-5; 8:2-3; 10:31; 12:43).

The account of Nehemiah's appointment by the king is consistent with the first chapter's portrayal of Nehemiah as a pious believer. At the same time that he asks

Artaxerxes for help, he calls upon God's help (vv. 4-5), and the favor of Artaxerxes is interpreted by Nehemiah as an expression of God's favor (v. 8). Nehemiah is a man of decisive action who links his efforts at reconstruction to the generative presence of God in the situation (see also Neh 4:3).

Nehemiah shows himself to be a practical man. He secures an official letter of appointment from Artaxerxes and a letter granting him access to the royal supply of wood which he will need for the work he is undertaking (vv. 7-8). Moreover, he receives a military escort for the journey (v. 9).

Verse 10 is a warning of things to come. Nehemiah's reconstructive efforts will consistently be undermined by Sanballat and Tobiah, two officials who appear here for the first time. Sanballat was governor of the province of Samaria to the north of Judah. Readers will recall that his predecessor, Rehum, had successfully blocked the reconstruction of Jerusalem's city wall in an earlier period (see Ezra 4:8-23). Tobiah appears to have been governor of the province of Ammon in the Transjordan area east of Judah. No doubt they viewed Nehemiah's appointment and the restoration of Jerusalem as threats to their own political power in the area of Judah. It is also possible that there was more at stake than political jurisdiction. Extra-biblical documents from the end of the fifth century B.C.E. suggest that Sanballat may have considered himself a worshiper of the God of the Jews because the names of his sons (Delayah and Shelemyah) contain elements of the divine name Yahweh. Neh 6:17-19 and 13:4-9 show that Tobiah was related to some of Judah's most influential people, and he, too, may have been a Yahwist or considered himself so. Thus, in addition to their political concerns, Sanballat and Tobiah may have claimed that they had a legitimate voice in the religious interests of the Jews in Judah. The Book of Nehemiah is unclear about their motivations. We only see their consistent opposition to Nehemiah.

2:11-16 Circuit of the city. Upon his arrival in Jerusalem, Nehemiah rested for three days (compare Ezra 8:15, 32) and then conducted a firsthand assessment of the actual condition of the city wall. The account from his memoirs bears all the intrigue of a modern mystery novel. He set out in the darkness of night with only a few companions and one animal so as not to attract attention. He told no one of his plans (vv. 12, 16). By his secrecy he delayed the interference of those who were hostile toward the restoration of Jerusalem. Although he was convinced that his mission was prompted by God (v. 12), he was practical enough to want to assess exactly what needed to be done before prematurely presenting a plan to the Jews.

Verses 13-15 form one of three texts in the Book of Nehemiah which offer some description of Jerusalem during this period. Like Neh 12:31-39 the present text contains only a partial description whereas Neh 3:1-32 is more complete. In a general way the information in all three is consistent, and, taken together, the three texts constitute an important resource for study of the city's history. At the same time, the picture offered in these texts is not perfectly clear to modern scholars because the exact locations of the landmarks named by Nehemiah are not certain.

According to Neh 2:13-15 Nehemiah left and re-entered the city through the Valley Gate, so named because it either faced the central valley of the city (the Tyropoeon Valley) or because it opened onto the Valley of Hinnom. Nehemiah's inspection took him past the Dragon Spring, the Dung Gate, the Spring Gate, and the King's Pool, sites which are no longer certainly identifiable. At some point the ruins of the wall were so bad that passage was impossible for the animal on which Nehemiah rode so he proceeded on foot "up the wadi" which is generally identified with the Kidron Valley. No further sites are mentioned so some scholars suggest that Nehemiah soon turned around and retraced his steps to the Valley Gate, while others think he forged ahead until he had completed a circuit which brought him back to his starting point.

2:17-20 Rebuilding Jerusalem's walls. Up to this point Nehemiah has shown himself to be a pious, practical man of action. Now we catch a glimpse of his qualities as a leader.

Some time after Nehemiah inspected the condition of the city wall, he addressed the Jews (presumably those mentioned in v. 16). First he articulated succinctly and clearly what they knew to be true: "You see the evil plight . . . Jerusalem lies in ruins . . ." (v. 17). He then challenges them to correct that situation by doing something about it, but he does so through words of invitation: "Come, let us rebuild . . . ." Finally, he identifies the brokenness of the city with the brokenness of its people when he speaks of the purpose and goal of the work: "so that *we* may no longer be an object of derision" (v. 17 emphasis added). The invitation to rebuild the city is at the same time an invitation to restore themselves as a people deserving respect. Throughout his short speech Nehemiah's use of the first person plural shows his identification with his fellow Jews, a trait demonstrated in the previous chapter as well. Nehemiah invites the Jewish community of Jerusalem to acknowledge the relationship between their city and themselves, to face the situation squarely, and then to undertake bold measures to act in a constructive way. All the while, he speaks as one who is with them in brokenness and in the effort to rise up. He assures them that this effort is indeed a call from God and that it has imperial endorsement as well (v. 18a). The people respond wholeheartedly (v. 18b).

Nehemiah's enemies respond as well. In verses 19-20 Sanballat and Tobiah are joined by Geshem who, some say, headed a group of Arabs controlling the Transjordan region of Edom and the Negeb area to the south and southeast of Judah. The three opponents, then, represent Judah's neighbors to the north, east, and south. They surround Judah and encircle the Jews. Through mockery and ridicule they attempt to undermine the spirit of renewal among the Jews. In charging them with revolt, the enemies no doubt intended to haunt the Jews by recalling the past. In an earlier period, work on the city had been called revolt and that had been enough to halt the effort (see Ezra 4:8-23). In the present situation these enemy leaders probably were well aware that Nehemiah's project was authorized by Artaxerxes, so their charge of revolt was in all probability merely an empty accusation aimed at intimidating the Jews.

Nehemiah stands his ground with them. He ignores their charge and the reference to imperial authority. The work will go on not because of Artaxerxes' patronage but because of God's. Moreover, he defines the position of Sanballat, Tobiah, and Geshem with regard to the project. In effect he tells the three that what the Jews are doing is none of their business. They are not part of the Jewish people. They have no authority over the Jews. They are not part of the Jews' religious community. It is a bold declaration of the Jews' independence from those who seek to keep them under control. They take their stand in God alone.

3:1-32 List of workers. The memoirs of Nehemiah are interrupted by a list which was probably borrowed from the temple archives. It describes the entire circuit of the wall around Jerusalem. The naming of strategic landmarks (gates, towers, barracks, arsenal) reflects a sense of order and orientation. Many of the workers on the wall are identified by name or family while others are described by role (priests, members of professional guilds) or residence (Tekoites, Gibeonites). The text conveys the impression that this was a precisely organized effort: identifiable workers are linked with identifiable sections of the wall. This well-ordered sense is enhanced by frequent repetition of words which describe the work itself (see vv. 1, 3, 6, 13, 14, 15) and which link the workers with one another (see "at their side . . . next to them/him" in verses 2-12 and "after him/them" in verses 17-31). As in chapters one and two of the Book of Nehemiah, the text portrays the relationship between city and people.

This section of the Book of Nehemiah is the Bible's most comprehensive description of the wall of Jerusalem. Although efforts have been made to link the picture presented here with modern archaeological data, extensive correlation between this text and the findings of archaeology eludes us. Some portions of the wall built under Nehemiah's leadership have been recovered. They are about eight feet thick and their rough construction might suggest that the rebuilding of the wall was a hurried effort (compare Neh 6:15). Modern archaeology has also discovered that the city enclosed by the wall in Nehemiah's time was much smaller than once thought. It seems to have comprised only a part of the pre-exilic City of David on the southeastern crest of the hill facing the Kidron Valley, the Ophel area connecting the City of David with the temple area to the north, and the temple area itself. It is generally believed that the wall constructed during Nehemiah's time did not encompass the entire populated area of Jerusalem. Some people probably lived to the west of the rebuilt wall.

The description of the building effort

begins at the Sheep Gate in the temple area (v. 1), proceeds in a counterclockwise direction around the contours of the city, and finally returns to the starting point (v. 32). Most of the landmarks on the north and west sides of the wall are various city gates (vv. 1-16). The remaining sections of the wall (vv. 17-32) are described in terms of both public sites (vv. 19, 24, 25, 26, 28, 31, 32) and private homes (vv. 20, 21, 23, 24, 28, 29, 30). Archaeological evidence suggests that although the pre-exilic City of David extended downward onto the slopes of the city's southeastern hill facing the Kidron Valley, during Nehemiah's time the slopes of the hill were abandoned and the city wall was constructed instead along the top ridge of the hill. Thus, some of the work on the wall was probably new construction while part of it was undoubtedly an effort to reconstruct the ruins of a more ancient wall.

The high priest Eliashib, the grandson of Jeshua (who was high priest during Zerubbabel's time), and other priests were appropriately assigned to work on the part of the wall around the temple area (v. 1). The compiler of the list gives priority to this area by making it the beginning and end of the circuit. All in all, there seems to have been widespread participation in the rebuilding effort, including citizens from nearby towns and villages. The text even notes that one of the workers was assisted by his daughters (v. 12). Only in verse 5 do we encounter a slight hint that not all the citizens of Judah were in total agreement about the project.

3:33–4:17 Opposition from Judah's foes. Nehemiah's memoirs resume with a scene similar to the one which immediately preceded the list of workers in chapter 3. By now the reader detects a regular rhythm in the book: Nehemiah's mission meets with opposition from Judah's neighbors at every step. Nehemiah's arrival in Judah met with displeasure (2:10), the community's decision to rebuild Jerusalem met with ridicule (2:19), and now Judah's enemies meet the workers' progress with anger and contempt. Neh 3:33–4:17 is preoccupied with the dangers posed by enemies. It is a series of three escalating tensions for the Jewish community.

In 3:33-38 we are faced for the third time with Sanballat, the Samaritan instigator of troubles for the Jews, and his Ammonite collaborator, Tobiah (compare 2:10, 19). Sanballat appears to be addressing an official assembly in Samaria, and, as was the case in 2:19, he and Tobiah speak words aimed at undermining the rebuilding effort. Sanballat asks questions. Tobiah gives answers. Both ridicule. Sanballat minimizes the worth both of the Jews themselves ("these miserable Jews") and their work ("Will they recover these stones . . . from the heaps of dust?"). Tobiah limits himself to a verbal attack on the city wall. Ancient city walls were ordinarily penetrated by siege weapons only after considerable effort, but Tobiah sarcastically says that the wall of Jerusalem could not withstand the force of a fox hurling itself against it!

Apparently Nehemiah was aware of what was being said and responded to their hostile words with words of his own (vv. 36-37). As in 2:20 Nehemiah does not dignify the enemies' remarks by correcting what they say. Rather, once again he turns his attention to God. He prays for God's vengeance on these enemies in much the same way other believers had (see Jer 12:3; 17:18; 20:11-12; Ps 137:7-9). It is noteworthy that he identifies their crime not as an insult against the city (compare vv. 34-35) but against the people themselves (v. 37). Once again, the text presupposes a close bond between city and people. In spite of enemy hostility, however, the builders are indomitable. They continue work on the wall and at this point have half completed it.

A second, more threatening stage of opposition is narrated in 4:1-5. The host of Judah's enemies has increased. They now include Samaria to the north, Arabs to the south, Ammonites to the east, and Ashdodites (from what had been Philistine territory along the Mediterranean coast) to the west of Judah. In other words, Judah is now encircled by groups poised to launch a common attack on Jerusalem. Hostile words had not been enough to stop them, for the wall was now half complete. Their enemies prepare to use military might. The Jewish response is consistent with what we have seen in Nehemiah before: in the crisis situation they pray and take action (see Neh 1:11; 2:4-5) by posting a watch. But fatigue and despair have taken hold among the builders. Nehemiah quotes what may have been a chant commonly heard in the community (v. 4). In Hebrew the verse rhymes and flows with the distinctive rhythm of chants used by mourners. Meanwhile the enemies conspire to attack.

According to verses 6-17, a third and final threat shows itself in the fear that had taken hold of the community. The Jews came "from one place after another" (that is, from all directions) and reported "ten times over" (that is, repeatedly) that an enemy attack was imminent. The enemies had succeeded in breaking the spirit of the Jewish community. City and people alike were now very vulnerable and Nehemiah took concrete measures to address both problems. He organized the Jews to defend the city against attack. At the same time he addressed their fear by challenging them to fear only God. Once again we see the two sides of Nehemiah's religious zeal: depend upon God and fight for yourselves. He pointed out that defending the city was indeed defending their own people. Again, the city and its people are one.

The measures taken by Nehemiah met the enemies' challenge, and he interpreted that as God's work (v. 9). Freed from the grip of helplessness, the community again gave itself to the rebuilding of the wall. From now on, however, the work of rebuilding and the work of defense go hand in hand. Half of a special group around Nehemiah (the "able men") worked on the wall while the rest stood ready to defend the city. Those who could work with one hand ("the load carriers") did so and held a weapon in the other. Those whose work required the use of both hands kept swords at their sides. Nehemiah watched over the whole procedure accompanied by a trumpeter who could summon the workers scattered along the circumference of the wall to the place of attack if one should come. Nehemiah took an additional security measure: he directed workers not to return to their homes outside the city at night. No doubt this was intended for the protection of the city and the protection of the commuters as well. The long days of work on the wall continued, and even at night Nehemiah and his company were ready for battle.

5:1-5 Antisocial conduct. Chapter 5 puts aside concerns about the restoration of the city wall and turns instead to the brokenness which exists within the community itself. Men and women alike (one translator says especially the women) call some errant Jews to justice. The charge was exploitation. The times

were hard, especially for those who made their living from the soil. Verse 3 mentions a famine but it is also likely that the demands of the restoration project in Jerusalem kept farmers from their work. Certainly this was the case if they remained within the city during work on the wall (see 4:16). The issue raised here, however, was not with the project nor with Nehemiah's directives. Rather, it was with those affluent Jews who used this situation to exploit the needy. The situation is described in verses 2-4. The farmers could not raise their own food which meant they had to buy it. In order to pay for it they had to pawn their own children (v. 2) or mortgage their property (v. 3). Others had to borrow money to pay their taxes (v. 4). Presumably their creditors were other Jews. The charge is levied in verse 5: the standard of the community members' fundamental equality had been broken. Community bonds were supposed to be like family ties (see v. 5 "these are our own kinsmen"). Yet some Jews were victimizing other Jews, and the daughters of the poor suffered the most violent indignities. (One translation says that they were raped.)

Once again there are parallels between the city and its people. Just as opposition threatened efforts to rebuild the wall of Jerusalem, so now injustice threatened the strength and integrity of the community. But in this case the attack does not come from foreigners. It comes from within the community itself.

5:6-13 Nehemiah's action. Nehemiah responds immediately even though as in 2:11-16 he does not take action before carefully assessing the situation (vv. 6-7a). He charges corrupt leaders (the Hebrew root "called . . . to account" has legal overtones) with breaking the law by charging interest to other Jews. This is clearly prohibited in Jewish law (see Exod 22:24-26; Deut 23:20; Lev 25:35-38). The New American Bible continues: "I then rebuked them severely" (v. 7c), but this is better translated: "I brought them before a great (official) assembly." In other words, he first accused the nobles and magistrates privately and then brought them to court. In court Nehemiah addresses the buying and selling of members of the community. He attests that the community had made a concerted effort to redeem those poor Jews who had been sold to foreigners (an effort not mentioned elsewhere in the Book of Nehemiah). The honor of the Jewish community required this. (On the practice of paying a ransom for fellow Jews whose dire circumstances had forced them to sell themselves as slaves see Lev 25:47-55.) Now that honor is even more severely offended by the fact that Jews are enslaving other Jews.

The silence of the accused pronounces their guilt. As he had done in the past, Nehemiah calls them back to the only honorable posture for Jews, to stand right before God (compare 4:8). This travesty within the Jewish community invites ridicule from non-Jews just as the brokenness of Jerusalem had.

Verse 10 is difficult. The New American Bible translation seems to exonerate Nehemiah, and in doing so, it follows the witness of the Latin Vulgate translation. A better textual tradition, however, omits "without charge." In other words, Nehemiah confesses that he himself and his closest associates had also broken the law by exacting interest. This seems to flow more naturally into the exhortation which follows: "Let *us* put an end to this usury!" (emphasis added). He proposed measures of reform which were to be taken at once (v. 11), and these were accepted (v. 12).

Finally, Nehemiah put the whole matter in an explicitly theological context by convening a religious service. Priests were called to administer an oath while Nehemiah ritually acts out, then speaks, a curse upon those who do not uphold their oath: may your pockets be emptied if you are unfaithful to your promise.

As the city wall was being restored out of stones left over from a past age, so Nehemiah laid the foundation for a restored people by rooting them in ancient social and religious law.

5:14-19 Nehemiah's lack of self-interest. In the present text the architect of the restored people embodies an ideal of community which goes beyond the strict requirements of the law. As a government official Nehemiah was entitled to appropriate for his own use a portion of the local taxes collected for the Persian throne. But he testifies that, unlike his predecessors (probably the governors from Samaria whose jurisdiction formerly included Judah), he had not used the allowance due him. Moreover, he had contributed to the work on the wall even though he was not a

citizen of Judah and at his own expense had extended hospitality as circumstances warranted. He reports the motivations for his actions: he feared God (v. 15) and he had compassion for his people (v. 18).

In verse 19 Nehemiah prays that God remember his service. This and similar prayers (13:14, 22, 31) echo the contents of ancient memorial inscriptions which presented to a deity the righteous deeds of a faithful believer.

6:1-14 Plots against Nehemiah. For the fourth time the enemies of Judah conspire to subvert the work of restoration. Verbal intimidation, ridicule, and rumors of war had been ineffective; the city wall was nearly finished now. The enemies' final assault was to destroy the Jewish leader or, better yet, to trick him into destroying himself. Through it all, Nehemiah remains intractable. His vision and purpose are fixed on restoration.

By now the conspirators are familiar to us (see 2:10, 19-20; 3:33–4:17). Their initial tactic (vv. 1-4) was to lure Nehemiah out of Judean territory (into the plain of Ono) on the pretext of conferring with them. Whatever their real intent (assassination?), Nehemiah viewed the invitation as a trap though his reply to them reveals nothing of his suspicions. He simply says, "I have more important things to do" and points to the work of restoration. One can hardly imagine a response which would arouse more ire in opponents whose sole aim was to prevent the restoration of the wall of Jerusalem. Repeated invitations got the same reply. Nehemiah refused to divert any energy in their direction.

Lack of success in the first plan precipitated a second one (vv. 5-9). It, too, was an invitation to meet. This invitation, however, is attached to news of a widespread rumor that Nehemiah was spearheading a revolt against the Persian throne. The rumor is a covert accusation and threat. It is the same charge which had been issued against the whole of Jerusalem in 2:19 except that here Nehemiah is singled out as the instigator of the treason. Nehemiah dismisses their words with his reply: "It's a lie, and you have fabricated it." As often happens in cases of harassment, the enemies' designs only gave momentum to Nehemiah's resolve.

The final attempt to do away with Nehemiah (vv. 10-13) is more subtle than the first two. The voices of the familiar foes speak deceptively in the words of a prophet, Shemaiah, who appears to be a member of the Jewish community in Jerusalem. There is no agreement among scholars regarding what lay behind the note that Shemaiah was "unable to go about." Whatever the case, Nehemiah sought out the prophet who said he had Nehemiah's best interests in mind when he counseled the Jewish leader to take refuge from his enemies within the sacred space of the temple. As he had done before (see 2:11-16; 5:7), Nehemiah carefully considered the matter and discerned that this one who pretended to deliver God's word had been bought off by Sanballat and Tobiah. The man counseled not just cowardice (seeking refuge) but also sacrilege, for the temple precincts into which Shemaiah urged Nehemiah were reserved for priests alone. A layman like Nehemiah would have been subject to the death penalty for entering them (see Num 18:1-7), or just as effective in his enemies' eyes, such an abomination would have undermined Nehemiah's credibility within the Jewish community. To follow the prophet's advice would have been to fly in the face of hallowed religious practice. One way or another, Nehemiah was being enticed by Shemaiah to bring his influence to an end. In response to Shemaiah, Nehemiah curtly refused cowardice and sacrilege alike. Once again, we witness his fearlessness and his piety.

In the final verse of this section we see Nehemiah's brief petition that God remember. Like 3:36-37 it asks that God make note of the enemies' work. Tobiah and Sanballat are mentioned by name. Alongside them Nehemiah names prophets whose aim was also to divert his energies from the work of restoration. Of these one might expect that Shemaiah be singled out. Instead the name of a prophetess, Noadiah, appears. The Bible offers no other information about her, but she must have been part of a group within Jerusalem who sought to subvert Nehemiah's efforts. The appearance of her name indicates that women served in religious capacities within Judaism during this restoration period as they had during pre-exilic times (see Exod 15:20; Judg 4:4; Isa 8:3; 2 Kgs 22:14).

6:15–7:3 Conclusion of the work. The announcement of the completion of the city wall of Jerusalem is registered with some solemnity in the memoirs of Nehemiah. The date (both day and month, early October of 445 B.C.E.) is precisely chronicled (compare 1:1 and 2:1). It had been only a few months earlier in Susa that Artaxerxes' cupbearer had heard of the sad state of affairs in Jerusalem and only fifty-two days since the rebuilding project had begun. Such an amazing feat seems incredible, and some scholars accept as more likely the witness of the first-century A.D. Jewish historian Josephus, who reported that the wall was constructed over a period of two years and four months. Others, however, point to the relatively small circumference of the city, the probability that a significant portion of the project simply entailed repair or reconstruction of a damaged wall, and the recent findings of archaeologists that the (only) new section of the wall (that on the eastern ridge of the hill facing the Kidron Valley) was very crudely constructed and conclude that, amazing as it is, the biblical text is probably accurate in saying that the task was completed in fifty-two days.

One is somewhat taken aback that immediately following the notice of completion there are no words of relief or exultation. Instead Nehemiah registers the effect upon Judah's enemies (they "lost much face in the eyes of the nations" v. 16). The completion of the wall is foremost a vindication of the Jews over their enemies. God had indeed been the power within this movement, and now that was clear to all. The enemies' effort to frustrate the work had been there through all stages of Nehemiah's mission (2:10, 19-20; 3:33–4:17; 6:1-14), and the Jewish leader triumphantly attaches a pronouncement of their judgment to his announcement of the Jews' success.

One would expect verses 15-16 to bring to an end the ongoing controversy with the opponents and the text to continue with the contents of 7:1-3 and perhaps the account of the dedication of the city wall (which now appears in 12:27-43). Instead we hear about the enemy Tobiah. Some scholars suggest that verses 17-19 have been misplaced from their original position after verse 14. Whatever the case, we learn that Tobiah was related by marriage (his own and his son's) to very influential Jews in Jerusalem and that in his struggles with Nehemiah, Tobiah had won the support of these Jews so that his subversive influence continued. Viewed together with the witness of 13:28 (that Nehemiah's other enemy, Sanballat, had marital ties with the Jewish high priestly family), Neh 6:17-19 cautions us that even though the Jerusalem wall is complete, the work of the restoration of the Jewish people itself will have to deal with the continuing presence of Nehemiah's opponents.

In 7:1-3 Nehemiah reports that he has arranged for proper leadership and security for the city. Guards were stationed at the city gates. ("Singers and Levites" is very likely a gloss which was mistakenly added to verse 1. They were officials in the temple.) Nehemiah appointed Hanani and Hananiah as administrators over the city of Jerusalem. Both were dependable and apparently not susceptible to the influence of Nehemiah's opponents. It had been Hanani who had first informed Nehemiah of the distress of Jerusalem and the Jews (see 1:2), and Hananiah possessed a quality valued by Nehemiah: the fear of God (see also 4:8; 5:9, 15). Although the Hebrew text of verse 3 is troublesome, it appears that Nehemiah directed that guards carefully watch the city gates and open them only during daylight hours. Nehemiah arranged for another precaution: security guards were stationed at various places within the city. It is clear from these verses that Jerusalem continued to be threatened and that the Jews needed to continue to protect what they had accomplished.

7:4-72a Census of the province. The beginning of this section appears to be a continuation of Nehemiah's memoirs. It describes the Jewish leader's effort to strengthen the city of Jerusalem by addressing the problem of its small population. It was this concern that led Nehemiah (with God's coaxing) to call an assembly in the city. An editor's insertion interrupts the account, however, and Nehemiah does not take up his concern about the smallness of Jerusalem's population again until his memoirs resume in chapter 11.

The contents of verses 4-72a are virtually the same as those in the list of Ezra 2. The few minor discrepancies are probably slight emendations which crept in through the copyists' transmission of the text. As in Ezra 2, we find in the present text an early population listed according to family or places of residence, a listing of liturgical officials and of some who could not trace their ancestry, and a total tally of the people and their belongings as well as

a list of gifts contributed by these people. As in Ezra 2 the list concludes with a single sentence about where the citizens took up residence. A careful comparison of Ezra 2:70 with Neh 7:72a shows that the latter text diverges slightly from the former in omitting reference to any settlement in Jerusalem. No doubt this represents a slight editorial change designed to fit the list of Neh 7 into the concern for increasing the population of the city.

The exact purpose of the insertion of the ancient census list is puzzling, especially since it apparently played no role in the repopulation of Jerusalem. What it does, however, is temporarily draw attention away from the city itself to the other effort which was part of Nehemiah's mission, that of rebuilding the Jewish people themselves. The city wall had been rebuilt on the stones of ages past. Now an editor recalls for us those who had pioneered the effort to restore God's people in the land of Judah. Just as the list of Ezra 2 precedes the restoration of the altar as the center of Israel's worship, so now the same list precedes a service in which God's people once again gather to commit themselves to what had from ancient times been the center of their life as a community, the law of Moses.

PART IV: RESTORATION OF THE COMMUNITY AROUND THE LAW

Neh 7:72b–13:31

In this final section of the Books of Ezra and Nehemiah the biblical accounts of the restoration period come to an end. The text begins with Ezra's proclamation of the law (ch. 8). The community acknowledged its dependence upon God's help (ch. 9) and agreed, communally, to abide by the law of Moses (ch. 10). Jerusalem's population is restored, and the completed city wall is dedicated in solemn ceremony (chs. 11–12). Finally, Nehemiah initiated several reforms to maintain the community's fidelity (ch. 13).

This section is something of a patchwork quilt incorporating in its complex design elements which had appeared in earlier sections. Ezra and Nehemiah are both present, Ezra in chapter 8 and Nehemiah in chapters 11 through 13. In an effort to lessen the jarring impact of the sudden appearance of Ezra in the Book of Nehemiah, an editor has added the name of Nehemiah to the Ezra materials in chapter 8. Ezra's name was also appended to the lengthy prayer in chapter 9, and he was added to the account of the dedication of the city wall narrated in chapter 12. Both Ezra and Nehemiah have been editorially inserted at the end of the list of priests and Levites in chapter 12. In all of this we see an effort to bring together two great leaders who were probably separated from one another chronologically but who were alike in their commitment to the restoration of God's people.

As in earlier sections, the cult and its personnel receive much attention. We see religious festivals and prayer as well as concern for offerings, observance of the sabbath, cultic personnel, and the purity of the temple and of the worshiping community.

In these final chapters, we see the Jewish community of the restoration period mooring itself in pre-exilic Israel. The law which brought to completion the restoration of the community is the ancient law of Moses. The terms of the community's pact are founded on that law, as are Nehemiah's reforms. The community's prayer reviews the past relationship between God and Israel and that past relationship is the basis for their present reforms.

The entire community, including women and children, is restored in the law and in its commitment to the law. Near the end of the book the city of Jerusalem, made secure by a sizeable population and sure city walls, is whole. The community is restored through the law of Moses and through its attentiveness to the cult. All of this is celebrated at the temple, the place where the work of restoration began.

It is worth noticing that the Book of Nehemiah ends in reform. The story ends not at the temple nor at the city wall but in the community and its struggle to be faithful. The temple building and the walls of Jerusalem were concrete realities. They were externals around which the religious identity of the Jewish people centered. But true religion is dynamic; it is a continual process which takes place not in stones but in the hearts of people. Perhaps in ending their narrative as they did, the biblical writers were suggesting that the work of restoration is a continuing one.

7:72b–8:12 Ezra reads the law. Concerns about Nehemiah and the wall of Jerusalem give way to a description of a solemn religious service led by the priest-scribe, Ezra. The entire community gathers in a public square in Jerusalem. It is the beginning of the seventh month, the high point of Israel's liturgical year, at least in a late period. (According to Num 29, the religious festivals of the seventh month included the Day of Atonement on the tenth day and the feast of Booths from the fifteenth to the twenty-second days of the month. In addition, there seems to have been a regularly recurring festival on the first day of the seventh month, but the feast is unnamed both in Num 29:1 and Lev 23:23-25.)

Even though Ezra proclaimed the law, several details in the account suggest that the biblical writers sought to emphasize the community-centeredness of this event. First, we are told explicitly (twice) that the assembly consisted of the entire community—men, women, and children (vv. 2-3). Second, the writers pay close attention to the community's role in the service. Members of the community initiated the service by summoning Ezra to proclaim the law (v. 1) and then they "listened attentively" as he read (v. 3). They saw the scroll as he opened it and stood for the reading (v. 5). They accepted the proclamation with their "amens" and performed ritual gestures of raising and lowering their hands and bodies (v. 6). They responded with tears which gave way to festive celebration (vv. 9-12). From beginning to end the rhythm of the service is marked by the community's participation. The biblical writers repeatedly show that the Jewish community knowingly and willingly accepted the law of Moses. We see this in the description of the children present at the reading of the law of Moses. They were those "old enough to understand" (vv. 2-3). We see it also in the stress given to the interpretation of the law. Verse 8 assigns the interpretive role to Ezra, emphatically stating the goal that the community understand the law. An editor supplemented Ezra's interpretive role by adding that he was joined by Levitical assistants (vv. 7, 9; compare 2 Chr 17:7-9 and 35:3; the Hebrew verb in verse 9 is singular, which suggests that originally Ezra was the only subject. Nehemiah's name was also a later addition). Some scholars think that the Levites' task was to translate the Hebrew words of the law into the community's vernacular tongue, Aramaic. Others suggest that the Levites explained the meaning of the law. Whatever the case, verse 12 states that the goal was successful. We see that the community which actively sought the law not only saw and heard it but also understood it.

The law which was solemnly proclaimed was probably taken from what now constitutes the Pentateuch of the Hebrew Scriptures. The present text suggests that the law directed the community's attention to the life of worship. This is signalled by Ezra's words of verse 10 (where "rejoicing in the Lord" probably refers to worship) and by the editorial addition in verse 11 which refers to the holiness of the day. (Moreover, see the restoration of the liturgical feast which follows immediately in 8:13-18.) The reading of the law must have exposed their failures for the community responded with tears. (Compare Josiah's response to the reading of the law and the liturgical reform which follows in 2 Kgs 22:8–23:24.) However, Ezra counseled the community to view the liturgical reading of the law not as a source of condemnation but as a source of life and strength. A full-fledged holiday followed the reading of the law. The people brought out their best food and drink and shared them with the needy. (The practice of sharing on festive occasions also appears in Deut 16:9-12; 26:11; 2 Sam 6:19.)

8:13-18 The feast of Booths. On the day following the proclamation and celebration of the law, the community gathers to study its contents further. Lay leaders, priests, and Levites join Ezra, and together they find legislation for the feast of Booths. (On the feast of Booths see our comment on Ezra 3:1-6.)

To observe the feast of Booths the community dwells in makeshift huts. This ritual may have originated with the custom of harvesters living in temporary quarters of branches and leafy boughs constructed in the orchards and vineyards where grapes and olives were harvested in the fall of the year, the season of the feast of Booths. Lev 23:42-43 assigns religious significance to the practice by comparing it with the time the ancient Israelites lived in makeshift dwellings while they wandered in the wilderness between Egypt and the Promised Land. Verses 16-17a report that the community immediately prepared to observe the feast of Booths as the law prescribed. The notice in verse 17b is probably not to be taken literally, especially in light of the witness of 2 Chr 8:13 and Ezra 3:4,

which attest to the continued observance of the feast of Booths. Comparison with 2 Kgs 23:22 and 2 Chr 35:18 indicates that this was a stylized way of relating a current festival to the past. The writers of verse 17b want to convey the idea that a new age of religious observance is beginning, but they stress that the newness is actually a revival of authentic ancient practice. The community once again restores itself in continuity with the practices of their ancient ancestors in faith. Their foundation is in the law, the prescriptions of which are followed exactly (compare vv. 15-16 with Lev 23:39-42; also compare v. 18 with Deut 31:10-13).

9:1-37 Confession of the people. Chapter 9 reports a community penance service (vv. 1-5) and a long prayer that includes a summary of the relationship between God and Israel (vv. 6-37). Although they are adjacent to one another in the present text, there is little direct connection between the contents of the two parts of the chapter. They may have originated independently of one another and been inserted here by an editor.

As in the services described in chapter 8, the law stands at the center of the service in 9:1-5. The penitential character of the service is clear from the traditional gestures of repentance and mourning, which include fasting and the wearing of sackcloth and ashes (v. 1). Public confession of guilt and prostration also occur (vv. 2-3). It is noteworthy that Ezra does not appear here. Leadership in prayer belonged to the Levites whose role included leading the community in antiphonal responses of blessing and praise (v. 5).

We cannot be certain of the particular occasion for this service. Because the authors mention in verse 2 that the Jews separate themselves from foreigners before their confession of guilt, some scholars suggest that this service originally followed the Jews' divorce from foreign wives described in Ezra 10.

The prayer of 9:6-37 is a beautifully woven tapestry of threads of tradition from other parts of the Hebrew Scriptures, especially the Pentateuch. In its historical orientation it is similar to other prayers in the Bible (see Pss 78, 105, 106, 135, 136). It offers an overview of God's longstanding relationship with Israel. The biblical view of a God of both mercy and justice is carefully intertwined with a portrait of an unfaithful Israel.

Ezra's prayer begins with the acknowledgement of God's creative activity in heaven and on earth (v. 6) and ends with the political distress of the writer's own day (vv. 36-37). Within these boundaries Ezra rehearses salvation history. It began when God chose Abraham and was faithful to the promise that Abraham would have many descendants who would inherit the land of Canaan (compare vv. 7-8 with Gen 12 and 15). The prayer recites Israel's bondage in Egypt and God's redeeming activity through the plagues and the rescue at the Red Sea (compare vv. 9-12 with Exod 1-15). God's continuing gifts included the law given to Moses at Mount Sinai (vv. 13-14), sustenance during the wilderness journey, and the invitation to inherit the land which had been promised (v. 15). (These traditions run through the Books of Exodus, Leviticus, Numbers, and Deuteronomy.) Up to verse 15 the recital summarizes God's activity, consistently gracious. Israel's response was unfaithful all along the way, but in spite of that, God was "a God of pardons," merciful (vv. 16-22).

Israel's life in the Promised Land is summarized in verses 23-31. As in the earlier traditions, God continued to give, and Israel continued to be unfaithful. In the face of Israel's response, God executed justice against the chosen people while extending divine mercy toward them as well. (Essentially, this is a capsule form of the Deuteronomic history which appears in the Books of Joshua, Judges, Samuel, and Kings.) Hardly a mention is made of the monarchy and the traditions of God's covenant with David through which the Davidic dynasty was established.

The "Now, therefore . . ." of verse 32 signals a change from a recital of salvation history to petitionary prayer. The writer asks God to take into account the hardships that the Jewish people have suffered for several hundred years. (Although the exact reference is unclear, "from the time of the kings of Assyria" may point to the fall of the northern kingdom into Assyrian hands in 721 B.C.E.) In verses 33-35 the writer acknowledges that God has been just in allowing disasters to befall the chosen people but suggests that now is a time for mercy. God's graciousness in giving Israel the Promised Land is compromised by the fact that its rich gifts flow through their hands into the coffers of foreign rulers. They

are slaves once again, not in Egypt but in their very own land.

As in 9:1-5, the particular occasion for the prayer of verses 6-37 is not clear. Verses 36 and 37 describe an oppressive situation although it is unspecified. If Persian authorities are the offenders, this is an unusual witness, since most of the Ezra-Nehemiah materials witness to gracious patronage of the Jewish people by the Persian throne. Some scholars have suggested that the prayer of verses 6-37 originally belonged to the prayer of Ezra reported in Ezra 9. (Specifically, some would have us read Nehemiah 9:6-37 between verses 7 and 8 of Ezra 9.) Ancient Greek tradition connected this prayer with Ezra, for in the Greek translation known as the Septuagint the prayer was attributed to Ezra. Translators of the New American Bible have followed this tradition (see v. 6). However, in the official Hebrew text Ezra's name does not appear with the prayer.

Whatever the origin of this text, the lengthy prayer of verses 6-37 reflects the views of a Jewish community which turned to the past and found insight into the present. As in other parts of the Books of Ezra and Nehemiah it shows us a postexilic Jewish community mooring itself in pre-exilic Israelite religious tradition.

10:1-28 Agreement of the people. The community which stood primarily as receiver of God's gifts and mercy in chapter 9 adopts a different stance in its relationship with God in chapter 10. Now it commits itself to responsibility. It solemnly swears to fashion itself according to the law of God given through Moses. No leader administers the oath. Rather, through mutual consent, members of the community bind one another to the requirements of the law.

The bulk of chapter 10 appears to be official documentation of those who entered into the agreement (especially vv. 2-28) and of the contents of the oath (vv. 31-40). This material may have come from records preserved in the temple archives.

The text opens with a connecting verse probably supplied by an editor (v. 1). The introductory phrase, "In view of all this," is vague and functions as a transition to the record which follows. The editor then summarizes the groups who entered into the agreement to live by the law although the order in verse 1 (princes, Levites, priests) differs slightly from the order of the list itself (civic officials, priests, Levites, community leaders). Nehemiah's name heads the list, and it is accompanied by the name of Zedekiah who may have been the secretary who recorded the names (v. 2). Priests are listed according to family (vv. 3-9) while the Levites appear to be listed as individuals (vv. 10-14). We know some of the leaders of the people (vv. 15-28) from the lists of Ezra 2 and Neh 7, although new names also appear here.

10:29-40 Provisions of the pact. Before recording the obligations of the pact (vv. 31-40), the biblical writer stresses that this was a commitment of the entire community. All, including women and children, assume equal responsibility for community life (compare Neh 8:2-3). The obligations of the pact are taken from Pentateuchal tradition. The restoration community adopts ancient law as its own charter thereby establishing itself as a legitimate continuation of pre-exilic Israel. (A number of the obligations listed here will surface again in chapter 13 as the concerns of Nehemiah's reform.)

Preserving the integrity of the community is the first obligation mentioned. The community agrees to be a people set apart by not contracting marriages with foreigners. (Here, unlike Ezra 9–10, there is no provision for what to do in cases where mixed marriages already exist.) It secures the place of daughters as well as sons in the community (v. 31).

According to verse 32, the community also promised to forgo commercial dealings on the sabbath and holy days in accord with Pentateuchal law (see Exod 20:8-11; Deut 5:12-15). The land, too, shall rest every seven years (see Exod 23:10-11; Lev 25:2-7), and those burdened by debts shall have relief in accord with Mosaic law (Deut 15:1-3).

Earlier, the Persian kings had provided materials necessary for the temple cult. Now the community pledges to maintain supplies for regular worship out of its own resources. These included monetary contributions as well as offerings of bread, grain, and meat which were needed for rituals prescribed for daily temple service and also for special days. (For a list of prescribed offerings, see Num 28–29.) In addition, verse 35 describes the arrangement for provision of the firewood needed for temple sacrifice. According to

verses 36-38a, the community promises to continue ancient Israel's practice of recognizing that all things which are given to them for their sustenance and growth come from and ultimately belong to Yahweh. They offer back to Yahweh the first of everything—products of the soil as well as the first-born of animal and human life (see Exod 23:19; 34:26; Deut 26:1-11). The community will contribute tithes for the support of temple personnel (vv. 38b-39). All the cultic pledges are summarized in the final sentence of the chapter: "We will not neglect the house of our God."

11:1-2 Repeopling of Jerusalem. Chapter 11 returns our attention to the city of Jerusalem and specifically to a concern first addressed in the opening verses of Nehemiah chapter 7. The city wall had been completed, Jerusalem's officials appointed, and precautionary measures taken to protect the city in case of enemy attack. Only one point of vulnerability remained: the smallness of the city's population (Neh 7:4). The author says Nehemiah convened a meeting "to examine their family records" (7:5a). Presumably Nehemiah was initiating steps to address the population problem. At that point, however, the text digresses. We see a list of those who first returned from Exile (7:6-72a), Ezra's proclamation of the law (7:72b–8:18), prayer (9:1-5, 6-37), and the community's solemn pact (10:1-40). Finally, chapter 11 returns to the population issue. It is reasonable to assume that, prior to the final editorial arrangement, the present text originally followed Neh 7:4-5a.

To solve Jerusalem's population problem, community leaders settled in Jerusalem as did one family in ten chosen by lot. Those who willingly became this "tithe" of the entire community were endorsed by the rest (v. 2). Just as the rebuilding of the temple and the city wall physically restored Jerusalem, so now the "holy city" (as Jerusalem was frequently called in the postexilic period) restored its population.

11:3-24 The residents of Jerusalem. Those chosen by lot from outlying areas are passed over, and we are given a record of the leaders who took up residence in Jerusalem. The list of verses 4-19 is enveloped by reminders that the rest of the population was settled in cities in the surrounding region of Judah (see verses 3b and 20).

The people living in the region of Judah traced their ancestry to two of the sons of Jacob, Judah and Benjamin, so the list begins with names and totals of Judahites (vv. 4-6) and Benjaminites (vv. 7-9) who moved to Jerusalem. There follows a list of cultic leaders: priests (vv. 10-14), Levites (vv. 15-18), and gatekeepers (v. 19). A comparison of this list of settlers with the list of 1 Chr 9:2-18 shows that, while the two are not identical, they have much in common. It is possible that one was taken from the other or that both were taken from a list preserved in the temple archives. The list of 1 Chr 9 claims to be a record of those who settled in Jerusalem following the return from Exile. Here a somewhat parallel list is said to be a record of those who settled in Jerusalem following the completion of the city wall.

As mentioned above, verse 20 notes that the remainder of the population was scattered throughout Judah and to this was appended the miscellaneous information which appears in verses 21-24. There we learn the names of various officers residing in Jerusalem: leaders of the temple slaves (v. 21) and singers (vv. 22-23) and a Jewish ambassador to the royal court of Persia (v. 24).

11:25-36 The other cities. The closing verses of chapter 11 spell out in greater detail what had been said in summary fashion in 11:3b and 20. They list towns and regions outside Jerusalem where Jews resided. Verses 25-30 name seventeen places (many the same as in Josh 15) as far south of Jerusalem as Beersheba where Judahites lived. Verses 31-36 list sixteen areas (some the same as in Ezra 2 and Neh 7) to the north and west of Jerusalem where Benjaminites lived. The entire area is suspiciously large. Scholars suggest that the list may include some cities which lay beyond the provincial borders of Judah but which nevertheless had sizeable Jewish populations.

12:1-9 Priests and Levites under Zerubbabel. These verses constitute the first of a series of lists of cultic personnel from different periods in the restoration movement. They are a record of the priests (vv. 1-7) and Levites (vv. 8-9) who were part of the earlier return to Judah from Exile when Zerubbabel was civic leader and Jeshua was priestly leader (see Ezra 1-6). Some of the priestly names here also appear in the list of those who signed the community pact (see especially 10:3-9). Like-wise, some of the Levites named in 12:8-9 appear in other lists in the Books of Ezra and Nehemiah (see, for example, Neh 7:43 and Ezra 2:40). The Levites are temple singers, and here they seem to be arranged in choirs for antiphonal singing.

12:10-11 High priests. Verses 10-11 are a record of those who served as high priests from around 538 B.C.E. to sometime in the early 300s B.C.E. The high priesthood was an inherited office. Little is known of these men except that Jeshua is clearly from an early stage of the restoration shortly after 538 B.C.E. (see his role in Ezra 1-6) and that his grandson Eliashib was Nehemiah's contemporary and thus held the high priestly office during 445-433 B.C.E. (see Neh 3:1, 20, 21). If Johanan, the high priest listed here as Eliashib's grandson, is identical with the Johanan who appears in Ezra 10:6, then he was in office around 400 B.C.E. and was a contemporary of Ezra.

12:12-26 Priests and Levites under Joiakim. The editor's fondness for archival lists again shows itself. Here we find a list of priests who purportedly served during Joiakim's term as high priest, that is, after the dedication of the second temple (in 515 B.C.E. when Jeshua held the high priestly office) but before Nehemiah came to Judah (in 445 B.C.E. when Eliashib was high priest). There is close similarity between the families listed here and those who purportedly belonged to the previous generation (see the list of Neh 12:1-7) although slight differences in names and spellings have crept in, probably as a result of scribal error. The Levitical names in verses 24-25 are also similar but not identical to the families of Levites said to have been from the previous generation (see Neh 12:8-9; also compare the Levitical lists of Neh 7:43-45; Ezra 2:40-42; and Neh 11:15-19). As in verses 8 and 9, the Levitical singers seem to have been arranged in antiphonal choirs. Other Levites served as gatekeepers.

Verses 22-23 suggest that these records agreed with the temple records. (Verse 23 is in error in describing Johanan as Eliashib's son. Verses 10-11 clearly present him as Eliashib's grandson.) The official register of priests and Levites is referred to as the Book of Chronicles but one must not identify these records with the biblical books which bear the same title.

The parenthetical note which concludes this section (v. 26b) is an editorial addition designed to relate the list of cultic leaders from the time of Joiakim to the chief figures of the two biblical books under consideration. It is not chronologically accurate, for all other evidence firmly presents Nehemiah as a contemporary of the high priest Eliashib (see Neh 3:1, 20, 21).

12:27-43 Dedication of the city wall. This account opens with the gathering of the Levites from surrounding villages into the city of Jerusalem for the solemn dedication of the completed city wall. As such, it bears some connection with the note at the end of chapter 11 (v. 36) which told where the Levites settled.

A more logical progression might juxtapose this account of the dedication of the city wall to Neh 6:15, the notice that work on the wall was complete. In the present arrangement of materials, however, a compiler thought it fitting to address other concerns before describing the solemn dedication of the completed wall. Among these concerns were a city strengthened by security measures (7:1-3) and a larger population (7:4-5a and 11:1-2), and a Jewish community restored through the law (ch. 8), prayer (ch. 9), and commitment (ch. 10). Throughout the Book of Nehemiah we have seen that Jerusalem and its people are inextricably linked. The welfare of one somehow signals the welfare of the other. Therefore, it would have been inappropriate to dedicate the restored city wall before the restoration of the people was complete. With the pact described in chapter 10, the people have been restored in the ancient law of Moses. Now the wall, restored from ancient ruins, can be dedicated.

According to verses 27-29 the Levitical musicians (instrumentalists and singers) came to Jerusalem. The first act in the dedication service was purification both of the community and of the city gates and wall (v. 30). The community then formed a grand procession which moved in opposite directions on top of the city wall toward the temple area. Half moved toward the right. The choir was followed by a civic official, half of the community's family leaders, the priests with trumpets, and Levites with musical instruments. (An editor, eager to coordinate the

missions of Ezra and Nehemiah, has added Ezra's name as leader of this group.)

A similar group moved in procession toward the left. Nehemiah was part of this group (vv. 38-39). By verse 40 the two groups have converged in the temple where the ceremony continues. There was singing (some have suggested that Psalm 147 might have been used in this service), elaborate sacrificial rituals, and so much festive noise that it could be heard far off (vv. 40-43; compare the clamor at the service marking the laying of the foundations of the temple in Ezra 3:13). As he has done in other parts of his memoirs, Nehemiah specifically notes the presence of women (and children). It was a community, whole and entire, which now dedicated its own restored wholeness in dedicating the wall.

12:44-47 Offerings for priests and Levites. The community's provisions for cultic personnel has been appended to the account of the dedication of the city wall. Many scholars regard this part as the composition of the Chronicler, for like the Chronicler, it features cultic personnel (especially the Levites) and paints a picture of the ideal workings of the community, especially with regard to the cult and its personnel.

The sections open with information about the storage of goods brought to the temple (v. 44a). These were the "wages" of the temple officials contributed by the community in accord with the law (see Neh 10:36-40a). Then the writer subverts any suspicions that these tithes for the clergy's use were obligations imposed on a reluctant community. Indeed, "Judah rejoiced in its appointed priests and Levites" who had a prestigious tradition of service extending back several hundred years to the original design of King David (vv. 44b-46; compare 1 Chr 23–26). Having described the collection of goods (v. 44a) and their recipients (vv. 44b-46), the writer concludes that the system of providing for the cultic personnel functioned with smooth regularity (v. 47). The original writer attested that this was the case in the early days of the return when Zerubbabel was governor. Another writer added a gloss to bring this information up to date. We are told that it was also the case during the time of Nehemiah.

13:1-3 Separation from aliens. Once again the text calls our attention to the prohibition against mixing with foreigners. The topic comes to the fore at a public reading of the law (vv. 1-2). The prohibition is taken from Deut 23:4-7 which, in turn, has its background in the incident recorded in Num 22–24. Ammonites and Moabites are to be excluded from the "assembly of God," an expression which may be technical terminology referring to the worshipping community or it may, by extension, encompass the whole of the Jewish community. It is unclear whether the law excluded Ammonites and Moabites only from the temple or from all contact with the Jewish community. If verses 1-3 were intended as a basis for the reforms described in verses 4-31, both meanings apply. Nehemiah threw the Ammonite Tobiah out of the temple precincts (vv. 4-9), and he also denounced marriages with Ammonites, Moabites, and other foreigners (vv. 23-27). Whatever the case, the community responded immediately to the demands of the law. It set itself apart from all foreign elements (v. 3).

13:4-14 Reform in the temple. We now return to the memoirs of Nehemiah. His first term as governor of Judah had ended in 433 B.C.E. when he returned to the service of Artaxerxes. The monarch is referred to as "king of Babylon" in verse 6 when, in fact, he ruled the Persian Empire. But, like Cyrus before him (see Ezra 5:13), Artaxerxes adopted the title of the king of the empire which the Persians had conquered.

During Nehemiah's absence from Judah, contaminating influences and lax observance compromised some of the Jewish community's earlier accomplishments. Nehemiah held Jewish leaders responsible for the backsliding. After some time (we are not told how long) Nehemiah returned to Judah and initiated a series of reforms aimed at correcting abuses which threatened the purity and smooth functioning of the temple cult (vv. 4-14), restoring strict sabbath observance (vv. 15-22), and maintaining the purity of the Jewish community by strict separation from foreigners (vv. 23-31).

During Nehemiah's absence Tobiah the Ammonite had made his way into the temple precincts and had his own quarters there. Offerings and utensils for use in the temple worship as well as material goods contributed by the community as payment to cultic officials had been removed from storage areas in the temple, and the space was given over for Tobiah's use. Tobiah had not seized the area. It was given to him by the priest in charge, Eliashib (who is not to be identified with the high priest). Nehemiah immediately ousted Tobiah from the temple chambers. The area was then purified and restored to its proper use (vv. 4-9).

Another problem came to Nehemiah's attention; the Levites had abandoned temple service and Jerusalem itself (vv. 10-14) out of necessity. For some reason the tithes contributed to cult officials by the community in return for their service had ceased, so the Levites were forced to move to the country to make their living by farming. (Note how far this situation is from the ideal described in Neh 12:44-47.) Nehemiah held the leaders responsible for this neglect of temple worship. He called the Levites back to their regular service in the temple and resumed the practice of tithing whereby the people brought offerings of food to provide the Levites and singers with a steady income. He placed trustworthy men in charge of the storage and distribution of these goods.

In verse 14, in a manner similar to that found on ancient Near Eastern memorial stones, Nehemiah asked God to remember this proof of his deep concern for the temple and its services (compare 5:19; 13:22, 31).

13:15-22 Sabbath observance. Strict observance of the rules for sabbath rest was an important feature of postexilic Judaism. The sabbath was a day set apart—holy. Through sabbath rest Jews witnessed that their lives and livelihood ultimately were gifts of God. Just as the sabbath was a day set apart, so sabbath observance set Jews apart from others. It was a distinguishing feature of their identity as a religious people. Profanation of the sabbath was a threat to the distinctiveness and integrity of Jewish life.

When Nehemiah returned to Judah to undertake his second term as governor, he saw Jews conducting business as usual on the sabbath. They made wine and transported their produce to Jerusalem to sell it in the marketplace. There they encountered Phoenician traders selling their imported merchandise. Nehemiah instructed the people to stop trading on the sabbath (v. 15) and issued a weightier accusation against the Jewish officials (v. 17). The prophets Jeremiah and Ezekiel had attributed the fall of Jerusalem and the Babylonian Exile to Jewish profanation of the sabbath (Jer 17:19-27; Ezek 20:12-24). Now Nehemiah tells Jewish officials that their neglect of the sabbath might well have the same result (v. 18).

Nehemiah was a man of action. Not content with warnings and accusations, he had the city gates closed on the sabbath (which began near sundown one day and continued until sundown the following day; see v. 19). When vendors continued to appear at the city gates, perhaps hoping to lure some customers outside, Nehemiah drove them off with threats of violence (vv. 20-21). He appointed Levites to monitor the gates so that the sacred character of the day would be maintained (v. 22a). Once again, he asked that God remember what he had done (v. 22b).

13:23-31 Mixed marriages. Mixed marriages seem to have been a recurring problem in the restoration period, for concern about them appears here for the fourth time in the Books of Ezra and Nehemiah (see Ezra 9–10; Neh 6:18; 10:31 and now 13:23-27). During Nehemiah's absence the practice of marrying foreigners had returned (or perhaps continued). Nehemiah saw the consequences of this transgression in the voices of the community's children: some of them spoke Ashdodite and none of them knew Hebrew. The language of Ashdod (a Philistine area near the Mediterranean coast) was Aramaic, probably not too different from the speech of the Jews at this time. The difference that came to Nehemiah's attention, then, may merely have been particular accents or pronunciations. But Hebrew was the Jews' distinctive religious language, and not understanding it was tantamount to a breakdown of their identity as a people.

Nehemiah's reaction to the situation was violent: he beat the guilty. Unlike Ezra, he did not demand divorce in cases of mixed marriages. He did, however, strictly reiterate the requirement to which the community had already agreed (see Neh 10:31). As was his method in the argument with violators of the sabbath (13:18), he recalled an incident in their history from which they should have learned. King Solomon had contracted mar-

riages with foreigners and this had led to sin (see especially 1 Kgs 11:1-10). Could they not see that they were making the same mistake? Women were an essential part of the Jewish community. Jewish daughters were not to be married off to foreigners and foreign women were not to take their places in the community.

Once again, community leaders were among the worst offenders. The high priestly family itself was now related through marriage to Nehemiah's archenemy, Sanballat the Horonite (see Sanballat's role in Neh 2:10, 19; 3:33-38; 4:1-5; 6:1-14). One of Eliashib's grandsons, the son of Joiada the high priest, had married Sanballat's daughter. If the Jewish high priestly family was on such familiar terms with Sanballat who had opposed Nehemiah's mission from the very first, surely this was a serious threat to Nehemiah's earlier success in strengthening the Jewish community. Enemy influence now lived in the leading house of the religious community. Moreover, according to Lev 21:14, the high priest was forbidden to marry outside the Jewish community. Although Joiada's son was not yet the high priest, he was a potential candidate for the office and that may account for part of Nehemiah's reaction. Whatever the considerations were, Nehemiah ousted the young Jew from the community.

In the final verses of the book (vv. 30-31), Nehemiah once again asks that God remember his efforts. The summary of his works seems modest. Essentially, it is a summary of the terms of the community agreement described in Neh 10:31-40.

Nehemiah does not ask to be remembered for having engineered the rebuilding of the wall of Jerusalem which, ironically, is the accomplishment for which most students of the Bible remember him. In 5:19 he asked God to remember his refusal to impose greater financial hardship on an already burdened people. Here, in 13:30-31 as in 13:14 and 22, he asked God to remember that he had abided by the pact that the community had made (compare 10:31-40). It appears that Nehemiah wanted to be remembered only as a faithful member of the community for which he spent himself.

1 MACCABEES

Alphonse P. Spilly, C.PP.S.

INTRODUCTION

This work, originally written in Hebrew, survives only in a Greek version. It mentions John Hyrcanus' leadership at the end, so the earliest date for the book would be sometime during his reign (129–104 B.C.E.). The friendly attitude toward the Romans would indicate that the book was written prior to Pompey's invasion in 63 B.C.E. Most scholars date the book during the reign of John Hyrcanus or his main successor, Alexander Jannaeus (103–76 B.C.E.).

Hellenization

The book depicts the confrontation between traditional Jewish religion and Hellenistic culture. The latter was a mixture of Greek and Near Eastern culture, and it had a very important impact on the Near East from the death of Alexander the Great in 323 B.C.E. well into the Roman period. After the death of Alexander, his empire in the Near East was divided between the Ptolemies in Egypt and the Seleucids in Syria. Jerusalem was under the influence of the Ptolemaic kingdom until 198 B.C.E. Under the Ptolemies, there was some Hellenistic influence, but Judaism was able to conduct its affairs in relative freedom.

When Jerusalem fell under the rule of the Seleucids, however, there was increasing confrontation with Hellenism. Segments of the Jewish community actively promoted the Hellenization of Judaism, and Seleucid rulers such as Antiochus IV were more aggressive than their predecessors in spreading Hellenistic culture throughout the empire.

Civil war

Events within the Jewish community led to a civil war between the orthodox and the Hellenizers. When the Seleucids threw their weight into the struggle, the balance was clearly in favor of the Hellenizing party. At stake was the very survival of Judaism as it had been known up to that time. The struggle between Judaism and Hellenism is reflected in other Jewish literature of the period. Earlier influence of Hellenism on Jewish culture is reflected in the Book of Sirach, written to persuade Jewish youth of the value of their traditions. When the Hellenization process entered a much more aggressive phase (167–164 B.C.E.), the Book of Daniel was written to encourage faithful Jews to persevere despite the defilement of the temple and religious persecution. Non-canonical Jewish literature also survives from this period and provides further perspective on the confrontation with Hellenistic culture (for example, the Book of Jubilees, the Testament of Moses, and parts of 1 Enoch). The first-century (A.D.) Jewish historian Josephus also chronicles this period of Jewish history, but with a rather sympathetic view toward the Hellenization process.

Seleucid domination

The Seleucid empire gained control over Palestine in 198 B.C.E. after the battle of Panium (Baniyas). At first the Jewish population welcomed Antiochus III, the Seleucid

370

king. He, in turn, showed them great consideration and made some improvements in their lives. Antiochus III was succeeded in 187 B.C.E. by Seleucus IV, who appears in the narrative about Heliodorus in 2 Macc 3. The Heliodorus incident portrays increasing conflict between the Seleucids and at least part of the Jewish populace.

The conflict escalated during the reign of Antiochus IV Epiphanes, who ruled the Seleucid empire from 175–164 B.C.E. His policies seem to have been determined by two major considerations: he needed money to finance his military endeavors, and he needed the people under his rule to be unified for defensive purposes. In 169 B.C.E. he plundered the temple in Jerusalem, returning in 167 B.C.E. to put down a rebellion that had been based on false rumors of his death. He set up a citadel at one corner of the temple precincts and manned it with Hellenist soldiers. He forbade the practice of Judaism and set up an "abomination of desolation" (an altar to Zeus) in the temple itself. These are the events that sparked the Maccabean resistance and rebellion.

The Maccabees

The First Book of Maccabees tells the story of a particular family who decided to rebel against the forced Hellenizing of Judaism, first under the leadership of their father, Mattathias, and then successively under the leadership of three brothers. Unlike the Hasideans who preferred a non-violent resistance, the Maccabean family decided to meet force with force. It is difficult to date the brief activities of Mattathias, but they probably took place in late 167 or early 166 B.C.E. Upon his death, Judas assumed control of the rebellion until his own death in 160.

Judas won a series of victories against the Seleucid generals and was able to purify and rededicate the temple in 164 B.C.E. The narrative first recounts his early successes in primarily defensive campaigns, but a turning point occurred when he began to take the offensive against neighbors who were persecuting the Jewish people. Although he was able to restore a measure of religious freedom for his people, his work was often frustrated by the intrigues of the high priest Alcimus. Judas died in battle and was succeeded by his brother Jonathan (160–142 B.C.E.).

Under Jonathan's leadership, political activity began to supplant military efforts. When Antiochus V (164–162 B.C.E.) died, two rival claimants to the throne emerged—Alexander Balas and Demetrius I. Both courted Jonathan's favor because they needed his support, and he alternated in receiving honors and gifts from both of them. In 152 B.C.E. Alexander Balas appointed Jonathan high priest; he assumed the office on the feast of Tabernacles. Jonathan was able to regain parts of the territory of the old Davidic-Solomonic empire, but, in the end, his involvement in Seleucid politics led to his own death at the hands of a treacherous Seleucid general, Trypho.

The third Maccabean brother, Simon (142–134 B.C.E.), followed closely in the footsteps of Jonathan, not only accepting the high priesthood from Demetrius II, but also involving himself in Seleucid politics. He was relatively successful as a leader and further expanded the territory over which he governed on behalf of the Seleucids. He called his family "Hashmonay," and historians refer to the dynasty he established as the "Hasmoneans." Simon and two of his sons were murdered at a banquet by one of his sons-in-law, the assassin in turn being killed by John Hyrcanus, Simon's second son.

John Hyrcanus I (134–105 B.C.E.) continued the Maccabean/Hasmonean agenda by accepting the high priesthood, distinguishing himself as a military leader, and expanding the territory under his control. In 109 B.C.E. he took Samaria and destroyed the Samaritan temple on Mount Gerizim, attempting to force the Samaritans to worship in Jerusalem. The Hasideans, who were basically supporters of the Maccabees (although reluctant supporters because of Maccabean assumption of the high priesthood), seem to have definitively broken with Hyrcanus over his Samaritan policies. The Sadducees, the priestly aristocracy who often seem to have been favorable toward Hellenization, backed Hyrcanus. Although he did not take the title of king, there seems little doubt that Hyrcanus understood himself as restoring the Davidic-Solomonic empire by his expansionist policies.

John Hyrcanus was succeeded by his eldest son, Aristobulus I, in 104 B.C.E. He was quite friendly to Hellenism but unfriendly to his mother and brothers. He imprisoned them and let his mother starve to death. After taking the title of king, he died suddenly and was succeeded by Alexander Jannaeus (103–76 B.C.E.), the oldest surviving son of John Hyrcanus and an avid promoter of Hellenistic institutions. His very name betrays what had happened to the Maccabean rebellion by this time. We might wonder what Mattathias or Judas Maccabeus would have thought of one of their descendants named Alexander, after the famous Greek who started the Hellenization process! The Pharisees, successors of the Hasideans, openly opposed Jannaeus and his policies. The rebellion had come full circle.

The First Book of Maccabees

1 Maccabees differs from 2 Maccabees in several important regards. Clearly all the Maccabees are featured as heroes in 1 Maccabees, whereas 2 Maccabees recounts the deeds of Judas alone and tends to relegate him to the role of a mere agent of God. From what can be compared with other sources from this era, the author of 1 Maccabees is rather reliable when describing the events that took place, although he clearly does so from a Jewish point of view. He tells of Maccabean successes *and* defeats. With regard to the latter, he tells the story succinctly, not glossing over or altering the facts, but without attempting to develop a theology of defeat.

This book gives the impression of agreeing with the pragmatism of the Maccabees (as opposed to the idealism found in 2 Maccabees). When Judas and his brothers find that military operations are less feasible, they engage in typical Hellenistic political and diplomatic maneuvers to achieve their goals. They take the same pragmatic attitude toward the law; they are very flexible in applying it to various situations. Their attitude toward the sabbath provides a key example of this (they are willing to defend themselves on the sabbath), as is their approach to the high priesthood. They are concerned about the Jewish people perhaps more than about the temple as such (unlike 2 Maccabees, which centers attention consistently on the temple). 1 Maccabees covers a much broader time period than 2 Maccabees, which limits itself to part of the story of events that took place while Judas was still alive and the leader of the rebels.

The theology of 1 Maccabees

The theology of 1 Maccabees might be called covenantal. The people are expected to observe the law, the Torah. When they fail to do this, God punishes them. Those within Judaism who are called breakers of the law or non-observers of the law are the ones considered responsible for the disasters that Judaism experiences during the Seleucid period. They include people within Jerusalem, the priests of the temple, and, at times, the high priest himself. 1 Maccabees clearly condemns them and their activities.

At the same time, the book focuses attention on the aggressive and oppressive policies of the Seleucid regimes. There are repeated invasions of the land and attempts to prevent the Jewish people from observing the law, especially regarding worship in the temple.

One of the most important contributions of the Maccabees was their restoration of the temple, the memory of which is still celebrated by Jewish people as the feast of Hanukkah. The Maccabees are described as observers of the law, although they apply it flexibly to particular situations. The Hasideans, or pietists, are presented in 1 Maccabees as rather naive and simplistic in their rigid adherence to the law, especially by not defending themselves on the sabbath and thereby perishing.

The Hasideans were among those who were at first skeptical about the methods of the Maccabees but supported them for a time, after seeing some of their successes. Later a rift occurred when Jonathan Maccabeus became the high priest. There were serious obstacles to recognizing the legitimacy of his claim to that office: he was a warrior with blood on his hands, and he was not of the high priestly family. Onias IV, the son of the last fully legitimate high priest, was living in exile in Egypt. There were probably some within Judaism who favored bringing him back to Jerusalem to serve as high priest. Jonathan, however, was able to remain in office because he was the leader of the people at the time and had great power. Simon, his brother, and his dynastic successors also became high priests and remained in office for the same reasons.

Although the author of 1 Maccabees shows considerable respect for the Maccabees, at times the reader may get an impression that the author did not approve of everything they did. The narrative is very blunt about the fact that violence leads to further violence. The more the Maccabees engage in political and diplomatic maneuvering, the more they find themselves betrayed. At times it costs them their lives. As the narrative unfolds, each of the brothers comes to a tragic end. The reader may wonder whether the author might not be addressing the then-current Hasmonean ruler, subtly recommending that he learn from the mistakes of his predecessors.

Theologically, the author makes clear that all of the victories and successes in the narrative are due to the help and beneficence of God. He tells the story with frequent allusions to Jewish tradition, often comparing the Maccabees with heroes of old, such as Joshua and the judges, David, and others. This he does especially when the Maccabees engage in a controversial action, such as in 2:23-26, where Mattathias slays a Jew about to offer sacrifice in obedience to a Seleucid command, Mattathias being compared with Phinehas of old (see Num 25:6-14). We can presume that the author was trying to influence those who did not fully support Maccabean actions or their assuming the high priesthood.

Theologically, the Seleucids may be considered to be the instruments of God, who is punishing the people for breaking the covenant. However, the arrogance of some of the Seleucid leaders, whether kings or military commanders, is such that it mocks the power of God. These leaders develop their own plans, which often conflict with the plans of God. The reader may anticipate who wins in such a struggle with the divine.

In the story of Israel, and especially among its prophets, there is an important theme of a remnant who remain faithful to God and to the Torah. The Maccabees are presented as the leaders of those within the community who remain faithful despite persecution and constant threats to survival. In the end, despite the deaths of the Maccabees, the people are relatively free to live in accordance with their ancestral customs and their law. God is once again shown to be faithful to the people.

OUTLINE OF 1 MACCABEES

COMMENTARY

INTRODUCTION

1 Macc 1:1–2:69

The first two chapters of 1 Maccabees set the scene for the rest of the book by describing the events that led up to the Maccabean rebellion.

1:1-9 Alexander and his successors. The book opens with a brief description of the career of Alexander the Great, who seemed determined to impose Greek culture on the peoples of the Near East. The mention of his pride and arrogance (v. 3) is quickly followed by the notice of his impending death. After his death in 323 B.C.E., his generals divided up the empire. The two most important divisions in terms of Jewish history were the Ptolemaic kingdom (with its capital at Alexandria in Egypt) and the Seleucid kingdom (with its capital at Antioch in Syria).

Palestinian Jews found themselves situated between these rival kingdoms, and the history of Judaism during this period is closely interwoven with that of the Ptolemies and the Seleucids. The latter kingdom began to dominate the area of Palestine after 198 B.C.E. A Jewish interpretation of this course of events (v. 9) suggests that the Jews' troubles are to be blamed primarily on the Greeks. The association of the Kittim (v. 1) with the "cause of distress" (v. 9) may be an allusion to Num 24:24.

1:10-15 Antiochus and the lawbreakers. In 175 B.C.E. Antiochus Epiphanes became the Seleucid king and greatly influenced Jewish history. Although 1 Maccabees chronicles historical events, it does so from the viewpoint of Jewish tradition and theology. One of the early themes in these first chapters is the tension between the plans of Antiochus and those of God, a familiar theme in Jewish tradition (see Exod 5–15 for a similar contest between Pharaoh and God).

Antiochus is described in these early chapters as arrogant, a second Alexander. The name he chooses for himself, Epiphanes, may indicate that he thinks of himself as the manifestation of a god, or at least as "illustrious." Arrogance is one of the most serious sins according to Jewish tradition. It seems to be a key to understanding the story of the tower of Babel (Gen 11:1-9) and may be related to the motivation that led the Man and the Woman to sin in the story of the Garden (Gen 2-3). Readers familiar with Jewish tradition, therefore, are forewarned in these early chapters that they can expect Antiochus to fall eventually, just as Alexander the Great did. This must be kept in mind, even though at various points in the narrative Antiochus may appear to be winning in his struggle with God's people.

At the same time, it is clear that not all the problems facing Judaism are originating from outsiders such as the king. There are those within the Jewish community itself, "breakers of the law" (v. 11), who find Hellenistic culture attractive and perhaps also convenient, especially those engaged in trade and commerce with Hellenists. Their seduction consists in making foreign alliances, probably to improve their economic circumstances. However, in Jewish tradition, making foreign alliances or covenants always endangers Israel's covenant with its God (see Deut 7:2, for example). It brings Israel into close association with neighboring peoples, an association which can—and which, in fact, often did—lead to worshiping the gods of their neighbors.

The Hellenistic gymnasium (v. 14) was not only a place of recreation, but a center of Hellenistic culture and ideas; it was a rival, therefore, to the dissemination of Jewish tradition among the young. Exercise was taken in the nude, and this seems to have caused embarrassment for circumcised Jewish youths, who consequently took measures to cover over this sign of God's covenant with the people. (For the implications of such an action, read Gen 17:9-14).

Jewish tradition is clear that all will go well for God's people as long as they remain faithful to the covenant and observe the law. On the other hand, when the law is not kept and the covenant is broken, disaster can be expected to follow. Therefore, readers familiar with Jewish tradition will expect from what is described in verses 10-15 that crises will arise within Judaism because of the lawbreakers.

1:16-40 Punishment of the Jews. We do not have to wait long to encounter such crises, punishments for the sinfulness of some within the community: Jerusalem is despoiled, its walls torn down, the sanctuary defiled, and a citadel housing foreigners and apostates established in one corner of the temple area. There is an implicit irony in the telling of the story. Antiochus invades Egypt in 169 B.C.E. and plunders Jerusalem on his way back to Antioch, possibly to help finance his adventures. One might presume that Antiochus is conducting these activities simply on his own initiative. However, for our author, looking at these events with the eyes of faith, what is really happening is that God is allowing the people to be punished for the sinfulness in their midst. It is not surprising that Antiochus is described like a second Nebuchadnezzar because of his profanation of the sanctuary and of sacred things (see 2 Kgs 25).

Antiochus comes to Jerusalem a second time in 168 B.C.E., perhaps in response to a threat of civil war between the Hellenizing Jews and those who are resisting Hellenization. The building and staffing of the citadel, in effect, give control of the city to the Hellenizing party.

The narratives describing these events are interspersed with two laments (vv. 24-28 and 36-40) resembling those that were sung after the destruction of Jerusalem by the Babylonians in 587 B.C.E. (see the Book of Lamentations). They contain many allusions to Old Testament passages and follow a traditional style.

1:41-61 Hellenizing policies of Antiochus. Conditions deteriorate further for the Jewish community. According to the author's view, Antiochus wants to unite all peoples of his kingdom by having them abandon their particular traditions and religious practices and adopt the king's religion. The remainder of the chapter describes the reactions of two groups of Jews: those who comply with the king's edict (vv. 41-61) and those who do not comply (vv. 62-64).

Those who comply are closely associated with the dismantling of Jewish religion: Jewish religious practices are forbidden, objects associated with Jewish worship are destroyed, the observance of the sabbath and feast days is proscribed, circumcision is forbidden, dietary laws are not to be observed, and Jewish sacred books are burned. The temple itself is defiled and turned into a typical gentile sanctuary, in violation of Jewish law. This crisis, in the author's view, is precipitated by the sins of the apostates and any who tolerate them.

1:62-64 Jewish resistance to Hellenization. Although many Jews cooperated with this dismantling of their religion, some—the heroes and heroines of this book—resolve to maintain their fidelity to the covenant at the risk of their lives. The theme of a remnant of the people remaining faithful to God and to the covenant is a cherished aspect of Jewish tradition. Especially from the time of the Babylonian Exile and its aftermath, keeping themselves separate from other peoples is understood as essential for their survival as God's people.

There is a second classic struggle, therefore, being outlined in this first chapter—the tension between the breakers of the law who adopt Hellenistic ways and those who remain faithful to the covenant and Jewish tradition. Again, for those familiar with the tradition, the outcome of this struggle is already known, but the story is still worth telling. God will win a great victory for the people, accomplishing this through human instruments— the Maccabees. It is time for the author to introduce us to this family of heroes.

2:1-14 Mattathias and his family. Mattathias and his family are of priestly descent. Their initial reaction to the Hellenizing policies of Antiochus and to the Jewish collaboration with the Hellenists is mourning and lament. This first reaction is somewhat passive and is expressed in the traditional language and gesture of lamentation.

2:15-28 Incident at Modein. What happens next, however, is decisive in their adopting an aggressive response of resistance to the Hellenization process. At Modein representatives of the king attempt to force Jews, including Mattathias and his sons, into apostasy. Mattathias is singled out as a person of some prominence in the community and is invited to be the first to obey the king's edict by offering sacrifice (vv. 17-18). Despite flattery and attempts to persuade him with privileges and wealth, Mattathias answers for himself and his family by utterly refusing to comply with

a request that would imply abandoning the law and covenant (vv. 19-22). The refusal is in accordance with Jewish tradition and gives evidence of great fidelity to, and zeal for, the tradition.

Not everyone in the crowd, however, is disposed to follow his example by resisting the king's officers and risking death. When someone comes forward to comply, Mattathias kills him (v. 24). The author recalls the example of a priestly predecessor (see Num 25:6-15 for a similar action by Phinehas during the wilderness wandering period of Jewish tradition) and thereby justifies the violent deed. Mattathias and his family now have no alternative but to flee to the wilderness to protect their lives and prepare their defenses. They invite all who intend to remain loyal to the covenant to join them (vv. 27-28).

2:29-41 Early example of Jewish resistance. Evidently not all who go to the wilderness in resistance to the king's policies and edicts immediately join the Maccabees. We are told about some rebels who are destroyed because they refuse to defend themselves on a sabbath. Whereas the Maccabees flee to the mountains, where it is safer, this other group merely goes out into the desert. The Maccabees leave their possessions at home in order to move more quickly, but the others take their families and possessions with them. In addition to these encumbrances and vulnerability, this latter group also interprets the sabbath law in a rather extreme way—all of which leads to their destruction (vv. 37-38).

The Maccabees, by way of contrast with these martyrs, decide to fight even on the sabbath in their resistance to Hellenization. Their realism is not only practical (they see their actions as necessary for the survival of the people) but also theologically based (the law is for the people, not the people for the law).

2:42-48 Organization of Jewish resistance under the Maccabees. Those who are faithful to the covenant join the Maccabees and begin to attack the lawbreakers. The Hasideans are probably members of the scribal class, hence interpreters of the law, but here they are described primarily as mighty warriors. These verses describe in summary fashion and with theological nuance the classic struggle between the faithful and the apostates: faithful Jews are successful over arrogant sinners. We are thus given a preview of the victory that God will eventually win for the people through the agency of the Maccabees.

2:49-69 Farewell discourse of Mattathias. The remainder of the chapter describes the last days of Mattathias, especially his farewell address to his family. Farewell discourses are found elsewhere in Jewish tradition (see Gen 49, for example). The fact that Mattathias is a venerable and faithful patriarch adds weight to his words, but they are even more important because they are his last words before he dies. The words put on his lips are a summary of Maccabean theology, deeply rooted in Jewish tradition and focusing on the importance of remaining faithful to the covenant and the covenant God. Various models of such fidelity are raised up from Jewish history, implying by these references that remaining faithful will result in victory. Those under duress who remain faithful to the law and the covenant will be rewarded. (For a similar list of heroes, see Sir 44–49).

It is significant that military leadership is passed on to one of the brothers, Judas, with the charge to inflict vengeance on the Gentiles (Hellenists) who have caused the people such suffering (vv. 66-68). The farewell discourse ends in a traditional way with a description of Mattathias' death and burial. We are at a transition point in the story.

PART I: JUDAS MACCABEUS

1 Macc 3:1–9:22

Judas is the first of the Maccabean brother-heroes to begin turning the tide against the Hellenists and the Hellenizing Jews. Our author again uses traditional language to sing Judas' praises, often comparing him to the judges and King David—Jewish leaders who were victorious against the enemies of God's people because the spirit of the Lord empowered them in battle (see, for example, Judg 3:9-10).

3:1-9 Introduction to Judas' career. Mattathias' choice of a leader to succeed him is confirmed by his family and their supporters. In song the author summarizes Judas' career, describing him as a giant and as a lion, winning victories on behalf of God's faithful people against their enemies (see Sir 46:1-6 for a similar poem and description of Joshua).

The language is as theological as it is military. This may help explain the "joyful" waging of war for the preservation of Judaism and the covenant (v. 2). God's plan is being carried out against the Hellenizing Jews and their Seleucid supporters, and Judas is God's instrument.

3:10-26 Early victories of Judas. Judas' first victory is achieved against Apollonius. After defeating him, Judas takes his sword, just as David took Goliath's (see 1 Sam 17:51).

Seron, a commander of the Seleucid army, is the next one to encounter Judas in battle. Motivated by ambition as well as perhaps by duty, Seron makes plans for battle. The author subtly forewarns the reader that, because Seron's plans are not the plans of God, they are doomed to failure. Seron is joined by many renegade Jews who have suffered from Judas' earlier attacks, but Judas is fearless in this encounter, despite the superior numbers of the enemy. Being so clearly outnumbered by the enemy is an opportunity to show that God is the one who achieves the victory, not the human soldiers or their commander (see Judg 7 for a similar concept). Those who attack Judas and his troops are arrogant and non-observers of the law. The outcome can be predicted easily by a believer.

Judas responds with a similar theological assessment of the situation when he is confronted with the fear of his guerrilla companions, who have been weakened by lack of food. Echoing David's friend Jonathan (see 1 Sam 14:6), Judas encourages his men with the assurance that God will help those who fight on behalf of the law. He then immediately takes the initiative and defeats Seron (v. 23). The enemies who survive the defeat retire to the region known in tradition as Philistia, recalling the enemies of God's people who dwelt there and fought Israel during the days of Saul and David. Judas has told his soldiers not to fear the godless; but now the godless begin to fear Judas because God is on his side (see 1 Chr 14:17 for a similar statement about David, or Exod 15:15-16 and Josh 5:1 for similar statements about Israel as a people).

3:27-37 The reaction of Antiochus. Antiochus is understandably angry at this defeat of his armies. His reaction is swift and predictable: he begins to build up a full-scale army to defeat Judas. As is usually the case, however, this requires a substantial financial outlay. The author of 1 Maccabees explains, perhaps with some amusement, that Antiochus is short of money because of his mismanagement and foolish policies that have disrupted the kingdom (v. 29).

Before he goes to Persia to raise the needed monies, Antiochus places Lysias in charge of his kingdom and his army, with the order to destroy Jerusalem and Judah and to settle colonists in the land (vv. 32-36). Again, even though such threats of annihilation seem particularly ominous for the Jews, a believer will rest secure that somehow God will not allow Lysias to be successful against the covenanted people.

Antiochus relies on collecting sufficient revenue for his armies and making alliances with his neighbors. In what follows, Judas' reliance is primarily upon prayer.

3:38-59 Preparation for war. Lysias moves against Judas and Jerusalem with a large army of infantry and cavalry. Slave traders of the region prepare for the enslavement of the Jews, who, they presume, will lose the war. For the Jews, such an enslavement would be tantamount to negating the Exodus and returning to Egypt. Lysias is joined by people from "the land of the Philistines" (v. 41). The author identifies the region in such a way that his readers' memories are turned to the days of old when it seemed certain to all except God's faithful people that the Philistines would dominate them for all time. In those days God raised up David, who definitively defeated these enemies of God's people. Without having to be explicit, the author once again points to Judas as a kind of new David (there are echoes, in this narrative, of 2 Sam 5:17-25 and 1 Chr 14:8-17).

Judas' preparation seems to be primarily liturgical. He and his forces gather at Mizpah, a site famous in the early history of the judges and Saul, but not mentioned again until this passage (v. 46). When Israel was afraid of the Philistines on a particular occasion, the prophet Samuel gathered Israel at Mizpah and prepared them for battle by fasting and acts of penitence (see 1 Sam 7:5-12). Judas' preparation is similar: prayers, fasting, and acts of penitence. In another place in the tradition, all Israel was summoned to Mizpah to combat an enemy; those who did not come were to be put to death (see Judg 20:1, 3 and 21:1, 5, 8).

While their enemies consult the images of their gods, Judas and his followers seek direction from their sacred writings, which have been outlawed by the king (v. 48). The law reserves the use of priestly vestments, the presentation of tithes and first fruits, and the presentation of nazirites for the temple. However, even though the temple has been defiled, it remains a center of focus in this narrative. The people's prayer of lamentation in the face of such severe danger is accompanied by traditional liturgical preparation for war: blowing trumpets and raising a "loud shout" (see Josh 6, for example).

Judas then organizes his army in a manner similar to that of Moses (see Deut 1:15 and 20:5-8) and reduces the size of his already small force by sending home those who were in the process of building new homes, those who are engaged to be married, and those who were planting vineyards (v. 56). He also dismisses the fainthearted, those who perhaps do not have enough faith in God's power to save them all. Victory will come from God, not from the army.

Judas' final prayer focuses the attention of his troops not only on the nation but on its primary symbol, the temple of the Lord in Jerusalem. The last verse is the key to the whole section: "Whatever Heaven [that is, God] wills, he will do" (v. 60).

4:1-25 Gorgias attacks Judas. The account of the first stage of this battle demonstrates Judas' superior strategy and tactical maneuvers. Despite the treachery of renegade Jews who serve Gorgias as guides, Judas is able to elude his adversary. Later, when Judas' forces encounter Gorgias' army, Judas reassures them by recalling what happened under similar circumstances during the Exodus from Egypt, when the people were trapped and in danger of being enslaved once again (see Exod 14). His further words of encouragement echo such passages as 2 Kgs 19:19 and others that refer to the rescue of Jerusalem on another occasion when the Assyrian general Sennacherib besieged the city—unsuccessfully. Judas also recalls for his troops the Jews' covenantal election.

In the ensuing battle the Gentiles are defeated and lose about half of their troops (vv. 12-15). Judas does not allow his own troops to take time out for plundering what is left of the enemy's camp because he does not want them encumbered with booty. There are still contingents of Gorgias' army in the vicinity. When these see what has happened to the rest of their army, however, they flee once again to the land of the Philistines. After Judas' troops plunder the enemy camp (v. 23), they go away singing hymns of praise (see Ps 136 for a similar song). The preparation for battle was primarily liturgical, and the celebration afterward partakes of the same quality.

4:26-35 Battle with Lysias. Lysias' discouragement at being defeated by Judas prompts him to raise a much larger army and to head it in person. The year is probably 165 B.C.E. Lysias moves toward Jerusalem from the south this time, from Idumea.

Judas, too, has a much larger army but is still outnumbered about seven to one. In the face of such odds, he once again prepares for battle by prayer (vv. 30-33), recalling earlier successes of Israel against the Philistines: David over Goliath (see 1 Sam 17) and Jonathan against the Philistines (see 1 Sam 14:1-15). Drawing on consistent Jewish tradition, Judas asks God to destroy the Jews' enemies, who are presumed to be the enemies of God as well.

The tide of battle once again goes against Lysias (v. 34), who then returns to the capital city, Antioch, to raise an even larger army. A more complicated picture is painted in 2 Maccabees, suggesting that Lysias was persuaded that Judas' increasing support from the Jewish population would dwindle once the pressure of persecution was eased. However, the author of 1 Maccabees omits any details in the story that might reflect poorly on his hero. At any rate, Lysias' withdrawal to Antioch provides an opportunity for Judas and his supporters to take control of the temple in Jerusalem.

4:36-59 Rededication of the temple. Although the text may give the impression that Judas proceeded directly to the purification of the temple after the battle with Lysias, a careful reading shows that this did not happen for nearly a year, not until 164 or even 163 B.C.E. The delay may have been caused by those who were concerned that contemporary apocalyptic writings contained predictions for the near future, and only after the passage of time had shown that these predictions were not accurate could Judas proceed with the purification of the temple.

In the ancient world, people faced issues of order and chaos in a religious way. The Jews understood God's work of creation primarily as making order out of chaos. They thought of the wilderness as the place of chaos farthest removed from order. On the other hand, the city (especially Jerusalem with its temple) was the place of greatest order. When the temple is described as a wilderness (v. 38), it symbolizes the great chaos or undoing of creation that the people were experiencing during the Hellenization process. What is needed is a new creation—setting the temple in proper order, following the guidelines of the law.

When Judas and his supporters arrive at the temple, they find it much like a typical Syrian-Canaanite sanctuary, the kind of worship space condemned in Jewish tradition (see Deut 12:2, for example). Their first response is one of lamentation in word and gesture (vv. 39-40). But before they can proceed with the work of purification, they first have to attack the citadel, staffed with government forces, presumably to neutralize it.

Judas selects blameless priests for the work of purification (v. 42). We know from 2 Maccabees that many of the Jerusalem priesthood had been supporters of the Hellenizers. When the carefully chosen priests begin the task of purification, a dilemma arises regarding the altar. Because it has been used for idol worship, the law commands that it be destroyed (see Deut 12:2-3). However, the same law forbids destruction of the Lord's own altar (Deut 11:4). The priests work out a compromise: they tear down the altar to make room for its replacement, but carefully store the stones of the altar until a prophet indicates what God wants to be done with them (v. 46).

Then, in accordance with the ancient law, they erect a new altar, make new vessels and furnishings, and restore the temple to its status before its defilement by the Hellenists. The rededication probably took place in December 164 B.C.E., three years to the day when the first heathen sacrifice had taken place. This is the origin of the annual feast of Hanukkah, a feast of joy and praise because the "disgrace" (v. 58) was removed from among the people. Order is once more established; they have experienced an act of new creation.

4:60-61 Defensive fortifications. Judas fortifies the temple mount and stations a garrison there to protect the temple from any future incursions by the Hellenists.

5:1-8 Judas on the offensive. In areas outside Maccabean control or influence, the Gentiles grow angry at the turn of events and begin to exterminate the Jews who live in their midst. The theme of gentile opposition to the temple is a familiar one in Judaism (see Ezra 4 and Ps 47). Judas moves first against the Idumeans (identified here in somewhat archaic terms as the "sons of Esau," possibly alluding to Obad 15-21, and seeing Judas' action as fulfilling that prophecy).

Judas next turns his attention to the "sons of Baean," whose identity continues to elude us. The Ammonites lived east of the Jordan River. This is the first time that Judas takes the offensive, but it is in defense of Jewish lives that are being threatened.

5:9-54 Deliverance of Jews in Galilee and Gilead. Although the author describes real events in this section, the narrative develops in such a way that Jewish readers would recall Joshua's rescue of the Gibeonites (see Josh 9) as well as Jephthah's deliverance of Gilead (Judg 12:1-7).

Jews whose lives are threatened in Gilead (the territory east of the Jordan River) and Galilee are unable to defend themselves without help from the Maccabees. Ptolemais is the city of Acre (Acco) in the northwest corner of Israel. Tyre and Sidon are towns along the Phoenician coast just north of the Galilean border.

Judas' brother Simon is sent with troops to aid the Jews in Galilee (v. 21), while Judas himself goes to rescue those in Gilead. Joseph and Azariah are left in charge of Judea. Although Azariah is not mentioned elsewhere, Joseph is mentioned in 2 Macc 10:19-22 in unfortunate circumstances.

Simon's campaign is quite successful, but he cannot guarantee the safety of the Jews in Galilee and therefore evacuates them to Judea. Judas and Jonathan cross the Jordan River into Gilead (v. 24). The Nabateans (v. 25) were an Arab people who played an important role in the life and politics of the region from the fourth century B.C.E. until the Muslim conquest. Although our author says that they were peaceable with Judas, 2 Macc 12:11-12 states that they became peaceable only after

being defeated in a violent skirmish. The skirmish was probably unimportant for our author's purposes, so he omits it.

Judas' opponent in these Transjordan battles is Timotheus, who rallies many Gentiles to his cause and hires Arab mercenaries as well. Judas wins the battles through superior tactics, including taking the initiative away from Timotheus. The gentile survivors take refuge in a temple (v. 43), either because they think the Jews will respect it as a place of asylum or because they think their goddess (probably Astarte) will save them. Judas evacuates the Jews from the area, probably for the same reason that Simon evacuated people from Galilee. When they return to Judea, they proceed at once to the temple to offer sacrifice and celebrate the victories that God has given them.

5:55-64 A defeat for the Jews. The author draws attention to something that happened while Simon was in Galilee and Judas and Jonathan were in the Transjordan. Joseph and Azariah, left in charge of Judea and motivated by ambition, attack the Gentiles around them, violating their orders, which were defensive rather than offensive. Making a name for oneself in battle is a familiar theme in the Hellenistic world, but it is not acceptable motivation for action in Jewish tradition. These two are defeated because they did not obey Judas' orders. God's salvation is to come through the Maccabees, and other efforts that are not consonant with theirs will not succeed.

5:65-68 Judas attacks Edom and Philistia. Problems accompany Judas on his next campaign. Some priests seem to have ambition similar to that of Joseph and Azariah, and they too are killed in battle. The headiness of victories won by the Maccabees should not distract them or the reader from the real purpose of the military operations: to bring salvation to God's people, not to provide opportunities for individuals to realize personal ambitions.

6:1-17 Death of Antiochus IV Epiphanes. Our author is taking us back to 4:35, resuming the narrative after the defeat of Lysias. We know from other sources that Antiochus IV Epiphanes died in December, 164 B.C.E., around the time of the rededication of the temple. Our author implies that Antiochus died only after he had heard about the rededication of the temple. 2 Maccabees says that

Antiochus died after unsuccessfully attempting to plunder the temples of Persepolis. The Seleucids had a reputation for robbing temples, and Antiochus was no exception.

The narrative states that Antiochus realizes that his defeat at Elymais and his impending death are the consequences of the way he has treated the Jews (vv. 12-13). The news of Lysias' defeat and the taking of Jerusalem and Beth-zur provide additional support for this assessment. However, what seems to surprise Antiochus is no surprise to the reader, who has been expecting such a fall since 1:10 above. The fact that he is going to die in a foreign land (v. 13) would be seen by the Jews as further evidence of the severity of his punishment.

The narrative may be historically correct when Antiochus is described as saying that he is "kindly and beloved" in his reign (v. 12), because his son is called "Eupator" (someone with a good father). In appointing Philip as regent of his son Eupator, Antiochus IV probably means to demote Lysias. Eupator is only a boy at this time, somewhere between the ages of nine and twelve. Antiochus gives Philip the insignia of royal office—the crown, the purple robe, and the signet ring, with which he seals important documents (v. 15). However, even this plan of Antiochus is not to be fulfilled exactly as he has decided. His son Eupator is with Lysias, who appoints the boy king (Antiochus V Eupator) and assumes the regency himself, thereby becoming Philip's rival.

6:18-63 Campaigns of Antiochus V against Judas. Although we have witnessed Judas' successes against nearly all the enemies of the Jews, the only territory that he actually controls is the temple area and Beth-zur. The garrison in the citadel is still intact, despite the attack just prior to the rededication of the temple. Judas will find it difficult to meet other challenges if the citadel is able to force him to reserve part of his troops for the defense of the temple area. Judas and his supporters are still probably only a militant minority in the country.

Judas, therefore, decides to attack the citadel (v. 20), garrisoned by troops of the king and by some Hellenizing Jews. From what has been related so far in this book, the reader may presume that Judas will be successful; however, that is not the case. What is strik-

ing about the rest of this chapter is that it contains no theology of defeat. It tends to accentuate the positive by noting Maccabean courage and bravery. The siege instruments that Judas uses demonstrate that he is now in a position to challenge the government seriously. The siege probably begins in the autumn of 163 B.C.E.

Some of the garrison in the citadel escape (v. 21) and report to Antiochus V what is happening in Jerusalem, apparently exaggerating the situation enough to motivate him to take action against Judas. Although Judas could make a case for attacking Jewish apostates (in view of Jewish law) and of defending Jews who are being persecuted in the neighboring territories, his siege of the citadel and fortification of the temple and Beth-zur are clearly rebellious acts against the kingdom.

The boy-king decides, probably with the guiding hand of Lysias, to raise an enormous army to fight Judas (vv. 28-30). There will be no more underestimation of Judas' military abilities. In the Jewish tradition, Gideon slew one hundred twenty thousand Midianites with a force of only three hundred men (see Judg 7). Lysias' army is similar in size, and our author may be suggesting that Judas' defeat came about because he had too many soldiers! The text focuses attention, however, on the enormous size of the Syrian army and on Maccabean courage.

The Syrians attempt to take Beth-zur before advancing on Jerusalem. Judas has to lift the siege of the citadel to confront the Syrian army. Not to do so would not only endanger Beth-zur but would also involve the risk of eventually being caught between the Syrian army and the citadel garrison.

The exact significance of verse 34 has long been debated. Ancient sources tell of other occasions in which elephants were intoxicated, but this was a dangerous tactic, because they could easily turn on their own troops in such a wild state. Presumably they were given something to rouse them for battle. The phalanx, a distinctively Greek military formation introduced by Philip of Macedon and his son Alexander the Great, was particularly difficult to penetrate and hence successful. This battle is described in more detail than other battles, probably to underline the near invincibility of the Syrian force and to help explain Judas' defeat.

Eleazar (v. 43) is a younger brother of Judas. His act of heroism and courage is remembered with good reason; his success in penetrating the phalanx is itself a remarkable feat (vv. 43-46). His motive in killing the elephant seems to be to kill the king (who because of his age is probably not actually involved in the battle, however). Eleazar gives his life to "save the people and win an everlasting name for himself" (v. 44). This may mean that he gave his life for his people and hence won everlasting renown as a martyr. It is not the same kind of making-a-name-for-oneself encountered in the cases of Joseph and Azariah (see ch. 5).

Judas is defeated. Beth-zur is taken by the Syrians, who station a garrison there. Beth-zur could not withstand a siege because of a food shortage. During a sabbatical year crops were not sown. The campaigns of earlier Syrian generals had probably also disrupted agricultural work and storage in the preceding year. Moreover, we learn in verse 53 that supplies were also short because of the number of refugees that had been brought to Jerusalem from Galilee and the Transjordan. Judas is being defeated by lack of supplies as well as by the strength of the Syrian army.

The Syrians turn their attention to the siege of the temple area. We are told that few Jews remained in the sanctuary (v. 54), while the rest were scattered, some of them going home. Judas, curiously, is not mentioned during this siege. He may have avoided the trap of being cornered in the temple and may have fled to the hills or even back to Modein. The author is silent on the matter. To admit that Judas was not a part of the defense of the sanctuary would have been embarrassing to his hero, but his silence about the matter also obviates any difficulties that might arise when we learn about the negotiations with the Syrians and their subsequent treachery.

Jerusalem had been under such a siege before; in 701 B.C.E. the Assyrian general Sennacherib besieged it and then had to lift the siege in order to put down a rebellion in the eastern part of the empire. Something similar occurs here, but the author does not exploit the similarity. Lysias, who is clearly in charge of the entire military operation, learns of a challenge to his authority by Philip, who had been appointed regent by the dying Antiochus IV. Lysias sues for peace with the Jews

(v. 58) so that he can return to Syria and defend his position against Philip. His words, designed to convince his fellow officers of the rightness of this move, tactfully leave out his personal concerns. Seemingly, the sabbath-year shortage of food is affecting the Syrians as well, but taking care of the "affairs of the kingdom" (v. 57) is the primary motive for the withdrawal.

The terms offered the Jews amount to a repeal of the decree outlined above in 1:41-50. We are simply told that the Jews accept. Again, Judas is not specifically mentioned in the account. Lysias treacherously reneges, however, when he enters the temple area and orders that its fortifications be destroyed (v. 62). He also leaves a military garrison behind, although the Jews presumably are free to go to the temple and to conduct their worship according to their own law. We might think that the problems are over for the Jewish faithful, but we will learn that the truce is an uneasy one.

No high priest has been mentioned so far in the narrative. We know from other sources that Menelaus was the high priest up to this point. His Hellenized name gives us a clue as to which side he was on in the civil war. According to 2 Macc 13:3-8, Lysias arranged for his execution. The absence of a high priest at this point in Jewish history is a further complication in the story.

7:1-4 Demetrius I becomes king. Demetrius, a cousin of Antiochus V, had been a hostage in Rome. When a Roman delegation came to Antioch, the head of the delegation was murdered. The Romans retaliated by allowing Demetrius to return home as a rival claimant to the throne with the support of the army, and his rivals were killed. The Maccabean story becomes more complicated from this point on because of the internal struggles within the Seleucid kingdom.

7:5-20 Bacchides is sent to Judea. We do not know much about Alcimus' background, but he was of a priestly family. Menelaus, the previous high priest, and other Jerusalem priests were prominent in the Hellenizing party within Judaism. It is not surprising then to find Alcimus in the company of people who make charges against Judas (v. 6). We know from other sources that Demetrius was preoccupied with the rebellious province of Babylonia, and this explains why he entrusted the Judean matter to someone else. Bacchides seems to have been given wide discretionary powers.

Once again, the Seleucid king does not underestimate Judas' capabilities, and Bacchides is sent to Judea with a large army. This large force belies Bacchides' offers of friendship and peace. Judas and his brothers are evidently strong enough to resist or ignore such offers.

The scribes (v. 12) are probably the same group as the "Hasideans" (v. 13). These scholars of the law are duped by Bacchides and Alcimus, the newly appointed high priest. The Hasideans are caught in some theological dilemmas. On the one hand, Menelaus had not been a member of the high priestly family, but Alcimus was. For the Hasideans, this was something very much in his favor. They also believed, on the basis of their tradition, that a high priest was to be appointed by a legitimate king, so placed by God. Was not Demetrius the lawful ruler of the land, and was not Alcimus his choice for high priest? The Maccabees might argue theologically, on the other hand, that the victories given them by God showed that the period of Israel's subjugation by the Seleucids was over; therefore Demetrius was not the divinely appointed ruler over the Jews.

At any rate, the Hasideans are portrayed as naive in trusting Alcimus and Bacchides. The treachery of Alcimus must have been a rude awakening for many of the people, but not for the Maccabees. The fulfillment of Scripture alluded to in verse 17 is a quote from Psalm 79. After Bacchides makes Alcimus the ruler of Judea and Jerusalem and assigns troops to him, Bacchides returns to Antioch. The problems have multiplied for the Maccabees. The high priest has the authority to regulate temple worship and also has civil authority, with troops to back him up. From the author's viewpoint, this is clearly a low point in the Maccabees' career.

7:21-25 The intrigues of Alcimus. The enemy, at this point in the narrative, becomes the high priest and his supporters, highly placed fellow Jews. Evidently they control Jerusalem, while Judas seems to be strong in the countryside. He begins to retaliate against these enemies, who are worse than the Gentiles (v. 23), while Alcimus seeks his primary support from the Syrian king.

7:26-50 Nicanor battles Judas. Nicanor is an archvillain in 1 Maccabees, described as someone who hates all Jews, including perhaps Alcimus and his allies. A somewhat different portrait is painted in 2 Maccabees, where Nicanor and Judas become friends for a time (see 2 Macc 14:18-28). Nicanor might have come to Judea to work out a reconciliation with Judas rather than commit his troops to the difficult task of subduing a guerrilla force. According to 2 Maccabees, he persuades Judas to settle down and marry. Later the Hellenizing party forces his hand by complaining to the king that Nicanor is not carrying out the task for which he was sent. Judas is warned and refuses to associate with Nicanor any longer. In our narrative these events are telescoped (vv. 28-30).

When Nicanor loses some men in his first skirmish with Judas, he does not defeat or capture Judas, but his attitude toward Jews hardens. The sacrifices being offered in the temple for the king would be supported not only by the Hellenizers but by all Jews who recognized Demetrius' authority as coming from God. Nicanor's behavior is particularly tactless at this point, and his demand that Judas be delivered to him is impossible to carry out. His threat to destroy the temple prompts the priests to sing a lament once again (vv. 37-38). The prayer borrows heavily from Solomon's prayer at the dedication of the temple (see 1 Kgs 8:29, 33-34). We can safely presume that Nicanor will be punished for his blasphemies against the temple.

As both sides prepare for battle, Judas prays, alluding to what happened to Sennacherib when he besieged Jerusalem in 701 B.C.E. (see 2 Kgs 19:32-36 and Isa 37:33-38). The implication is clear: God is asked to do to Nicanor what he did to Sennacherib. Judas' forces are considerably fewer than on earlier occasions. However, when the people of the countryside see that he is being victorious against Nicanor, they seem to realize that God is with the Maccabees, so they come out to help Judas defeat the enemy (v. 46).

The treatment of Nicanor's corpse (v. 47) may offend more sensitive readers, but such gloating over a defeated enemy is commonplace even in our contemporary world. The author sees a fitting irony in Nicanor's severed arm being put on display in Jerusalem near the temple against which he had raised the same arm. The feast commemorating this event was still being celebrated in the first century A.D.

The author concludes this chapter with the notice that for a short time there was peace in the land (v. 50). The battle is probably to be dated in March, 161 B.C.E., and Judas will die in battle nearly a year later. The Maccabees have risen somewhat in the estimation of the people of the countryside, but they are a long way from solving the Hellenization problem.

8:1-16 Reputation of the Romans. Judas attempts to break the stalemate of power among the Jews by engaging the Romans as allies. The description of the Romans is decidedly positive in tone. The author has not yet had direct experience of them. He is at pains to point out how similar the Romans are to the Jews! He especially respects their renowned organization and military power as well as their longstanding opposition to the Greeks.

8:17-32 Embassy of Eupolemus and Jason. The Romans seem to have been disposed to allow the Jews to live according to their own law. No doubt there were Jews among Judas' supporters who were favorably disposed toward Rome. However, there were potential theological problems involved in what Judas was attempting to do. The prophets had often warned the people against making foreign alliances rather than trusting God. We can assume that Judas probably would have made appeal to the foreign alliances contracted by Solomon (see 1 Kgs 3:1) as a way of preserving and expanding his empire and influence.

Rome, on the other hand, was probably willing to support the Maccabees against the Seleucids to keep a balance of power in the area. Demetrius had become king against Rome's wishes. Rome had nothing to lose in this arrangement with Judas, and, to a great extent, neither did he. Although Rome pledged to defend Judas and his supporters, they did not interfere in the affairs of the region until much later, when Aristobulus II invited Pompey into Palestine in 63 B.C.E.

It is interesting that the two ambassadors sent to Rome have Greek names (v. 17). No doubt they are also fluent in Greek, the popular language used in Rome at the time. Judas is shrewd and pragmatic. Although he prays

in preparation for battle, he also is willing to use whatever seems necessary to achieve victory.

The brief speech of the ambassadors before the Roman senate is noteworthy because it singles out Judas and his brothers as the leaders of the Jewish people (v. 20). Alcimus and his supporters are no longer considered part of the Jewish people, at least not by our author. The agreement that is made requires Rome and the Jews to come to one another's help should someone attack either of them. The wording is rather loose, however (see v. 30 in particular), and the treaty is made specifically with "the Jewish nation," not with Judas or his brothers. The author refers to a threatening letter allegedly sent by the Roman senate to Demetrius (vv. 31-32). However, the wording of the letter seems to be more Jewish than Roman. At any rate, Demetrius (if he did in fact receive such a letter) does not seem to have been very concerned about such a threat.

9:1-22 The death of Judas. The narrative resumes with events after the defeat of Nicanor (see 7:50 above). Despite the important defeat of Nicanor and even after the return of the ambassadors from Rome, Judas still does not seem to enjoy wide support among the people. In the first part of this chapter morale seems very low. Demetrius sends reliable Bacchides into the land, presumably to reinstate Alcimus as high priest and to destroy Judas.

The situation is precarious. The Syrian army attacks a city in Galilee, far from the influence of Judas, and kills the inhabitants. Judas is not in Jerusalem at this time, so Bacchides does not seem to spend much time there. When the Syrian army does encounter Judas' forces, it is clear that once again he is greatly outnumbered. Desertions leave him with a greatly reduced army (v. 6). It is strange but probably true that Judas did not have more support from the people after his brilliant career and the definitive victory over Nicanor.

What is even stranger is his statement just before the battle is joined (v. 10). So often on earlier occasions he had seemed pleased with the fact that he did not have many troops, because then it would be clear to all that the inevitable victory came from God. His preparation for battle on earlier occasions was primarily prayer. This time he adopts a fatalistic approach and speaks about dying with bravery, sounding more like a Hellenistic warrior than the man of faith we encountered earlier.

As was his usual tactic, Judas takes the initiative, but despite a long-fought battle, he is killed. His brothers bury him, and his supporters mourn his passing. Verse 21 is a brief lament recalling David's words of grief at the death of his close friend Jonathan (see 2 Sam 1:17-27).

PART II: JONATHAN MACCABEUS

1 Macc 9:23–12:53

9:23-27 Aftermath of Judas' death. With Judas no longer a threat, the supporters of Alcimus are given the opportunity to reestablish their control of the country. The agricultural situation probably had been greatly affected by the series of wars. During time of famine the government (under the leadership of Alcimus) probably controlled the distribution of food, so it is not surprising that people desert the remaining Maccabees at this time. Those who do not desert are derided and punished. The country is once more in a crisis, as though all that Judas had fought for now eludes his supporters. At this low ebb in Maccabean fortunes Jonathan's career begins to emerge.

9:28-31 Jonathan takes Judas' place. Maccabean supporters choose Jonathan, the youngest of the brothers, to be "ruler and leader" in terms that are reminiscent of the selection of Jephthah, the judge of long ago (see Judg 11:4-11).

9:32-53 Bacchides opposes Jonathan. Jonathan inherits less power, fewer friends, and more enemies than Judas had. In the eyes of Bacchides, Jonathan is a rebel against a king who has ceased persecution of the Jews. Jonathan has to withdraw from the area that had once been controlled by Judas and retires to a wilderness area southeast of Jerusalem, the same area to which David fled when he was being pursued by Saul (see 1 Sam 21–29).

Verse 34 is omitted in this translation, as in others, because it is merely a repetition of verse 43 and out of place here. The Nabateans (v. 35) could be expected to befriend the Maccabees and oppose the Seleucids. Jonathan, in

expectation of a Seleucid attack, does not want to be burdened with too many possessions. The "sons of Jambri" (v. 36) are a tribal group; the author does not identify them as Nabateans. Jonathan and Simon decide to carry out revenge against this tribe, which had stolen their baggage and kidnapped or killed their brother John. The bride's father is identified in a curious way as a prince of Canaan (v. 37). Canaan no longer existed as a political entity, but the identification of such an ancient enemy might help explain the violence that ensues.

Bacchides will not let the attack go unpunished and seeks out Jonathan on a sabbath. Jonathan's rousing cry to his troops is an echo of Josh 3:4. Jonathan, like his father, Mattathias, on a previous occasion, decides that it is more important to survive than to observe the sabbath (v. 44). The punishment spelled out in Deut 28:7 affects, not Jonathan, but Bacchides. Jonathan, like Judas before him, counsels prayers to God for deliverance as preparation for the upcoming battle. However, Jonathan seems to be defeated, although the narrative does not say so directly. Bacchides loses many soldiers, while Jonathan and his men escape. There are echoes in this passage of the exploits of David's general, Joab (see 1 Chr 19:10-15).

Bacchides then sets out to consolidate his control of the country by building fortresses (v. 50). He garrisons them, takes the sons of leading families as hostages against their good behavior, and turns the citadel in Jerusalem into a kind of prison. Jonathan and his supporters are conceded the wilderness and probably considered adequately neutralized.

9:54-69 Death of Alcimus and a plot against Jonathan. In 159 B.C.E. Alcimus decides to tear down a wall in the temple. It is not clear exactly which wall, but it may have been one that kept Gentiles away from the inner courts, thus making it possible for them to enter the previously forbidden area. At any rate, he joins the list of people in the Maccabean books who sin against the temple and suffer punishment accordingly. There is some irony in his loss of speech; he can no longer give orders about the temple. Eventually he dies "in great agony" (v. 56).

Once again there is no high priest, and so the Hellenizing party is without a leader. Bacchides returns to Antioch either because his presence is perhaps no longer needed or merely to get new instructions from the king. A period of relative calm seems to take place at this point.

But the peace is not to last. Some of the Hellenizers develop a conspiracy against Jonathan. Peaceful coexistence is not their way. They persuade Bacchides to return and capture Jonathan. Bacchides prefers to have his allies capture Jonathan even before he arrives, but it is difficult to keep such conspiracies secret. Jonathan learns of the plot and kills the ringleaders (v. 61). Jonathan then prepares for a siege by developing fortifications at Bethbasi in the desert, probably two miles southeast of Bethlehem and eight miles from Jerusalem itself.

Bacchides has no choice but to besiege Jonathan. The latter escapes and annihilates some nomadic tribes that evidently were planning to join Bacchides in the siege. Simon and Jonathan take the initiative, attack Bacchides, and overcome him. By now the Syrian's patience with the Hellenizers has come to an end. The Hellenizers are the ones who invited him to capture Jonathan; so, in a sense, they are responsible for Bacchides' present situation. He has some of them executed and prepares to return to Antioch.

9:70-73 Jonathan makes peace with Bacchides. Jonathan is probably the only Jewish figure of any importance with whom the Syrians could make peace. Despite earlier attempts at peacemaking and subsequent treachery on the part of the Syrians, Jonathan offers to make peace, and Bacchides accepts. The text makes it clear that this time the Syrians prove trustworthy. Jonathan, the guerrilla chieftain, becomes in effect a judge, similar to leaders in the days of old (see the Book of Judges). His "judging" amounts to ruling the people, but it is unclear exactly what his authority was. He receives no specific office from the Syrians at this point and does not live in Jerusalem. The reference in verse 73 may be more theological than political in its intent. Meanwhile, there are still Jewish hostages in the citadel at Jerusalem.

10:1-14 Alexander Balas challenges Demetrius. Jonathan's fortunes change rather dramatically in 152 B.C.E., when a rival claimant to the Syrian throne challenges Demetrius by setting up a throne in Ptolemais, a seaport easily defended. Alexander (known as Balas)

claims to be the son of Antiochus IV Epiphanes. He is supported against Demetrius not only by the Roman senate, but also by the kings of Cappadocia, Pergamum, and Egypt. Demetrius' problems are multiplied by his unpopularity with his troops. In the ensuing narrative, both Alexander and Demetrius attempt to acquire Jonathan as an ally. He in turn is able to play them off against each other, accepting the best offer in typically pragmatic Maccabean style.

Demetrius is the first to approach Jonathan, giving him permission to raise an army (v. 6)—as though he needed such authorization! Jonathan does not object to this, but he uses Demetrius' letter to arrange the release of hostages from the citadel in Jerusalem. He then takes up residence there and sees to the restoration of the city and the fortification of the temple area. The Hellenizers realize that Jonathan is no longer vulnerable and they flee, some of them taking up residence at Beth-zur.

10:15-21 Jonathan becomes the high priest. Alexander in turn writes a flattering letter and designates Jonathan high priest. Two factors militate against Jonathan's accepting the appointment: it is made by a king whose legitimacy is still a matter of dispute, and Jonathan is not of the high priestly family. On the other hand, expediency gives way to principle, and Jonathan accepts the high priesthood (as well as membership on Alexander's council), thereby consolidating his power (v. 20).

Throughout their history, theological problems concerning their accession to the high priesthood will continue to plague the Maccabees (or Hasmoneans, as they are later called). At this time, however, Jonathan was the only person with so much power and authority within the Jewish community, and it is not clear whether he was seriously challenged for accepting the high priesthood. However, it may have been this event that led to the establishment of the Essene group at Qumran, a group that became alienated from the temple and its "wicked priest." 1 Maccabees does not raise these theological problems, of course, because the Maccabees are its heroes.

The price to be paid for the honors bestowed on Jonathan is loyalty to Alexander. In October, 162 B.C.E., at the feast of Tabernacles, Jonathan assumes the office of high priest. We are not told how the people receive him.

10:22-47 Demetrius attempts to win back the Jews. In a letter to the Jewish nation, Demetrius, Alexander's rival, pointedly does not mention Jonathan. The two references to the high priest in verses 32 and 38 presumably refer to someone yet to be appointed *by Demetrius*. The letter outlines financial arrangements he is willing to make, arrangements extraordinarily favorable to the Jews. In short, Demetrius seems to be making a very attractive offer to the Jewish people, with the intention of wooing them away from Jonathan. This probably would not have been too difficult; there were those who opposed Jonathan and the Maccabees, and those who did not like his accession to the high priesthood.

Demetrius' opening words (v. 22) seem to imply that he either does not know of Alexander's arrangement with Jonathan (which is very unlikely) or that he is presuming he can count on the nation to respond favorably after the people have heard his terms: exemptions from certain taxes and tithes, special tax status for Jerusalem, turning the citadel over to a high priest, and release of Jews taken into captivity in the various battles. Moreover, he names Jewish feasts as tax-exempt days, makes it possible for Jewish mercenaries to be hired for his armies at favorable conditions, and offers to include Jews in prominent places within his kingdom.

Verses 38-39 are somewhat problematic, for Demetrius offers what he probably cannot deliver. He seems unaware of the centuries of hostility between the Samaritans and the Jews. Because Alexander holds Ptolemais, Demetrius can hardly deliver it for the benefit of the temple. He may be implying that he will take Ptolemais soon and overcome Alexander, but such a prediction is seldom wise.

Demetrius makes provisions for royal revenues to be donated to the temple (v. 41) and seems willing to consider it a place of asylum for those who are in debt to the crown. He is not the first king to make provisions for restoring the temple (Cyrus and Antiochus III had done this earlier [see Ezra 6:3-5 and Josephus, *Antiquities*, XII.3.3]). But it is quite extraordinary for a Seleucid king to be willing to finance the fortification of Jerusalem. These extraordinary measures show to what extent Demetrius is determined to win the support of the Jews, and possibly how desperate his situation is.

Jonathan and his supporters do not accept Demetrius' offer (v. 46). The Hellenizing party is ignored. It is not surprising that Jonathan rejects an offer designed to turn the people away from his support!

10:48-50 Alexander defeats Demetrius. The manuscripts vary in their reading of verse 49, and it seems (from other sources) that the confusion is due to the seesaw nature of the battle, with Demetrius gaining the upper hand at first and later being defeated, falling from power in 150 B.C.E. Alexander then takes measures to develop foreign alliances.

10:51-58 Alliance with Egypt. Alexander's request for an alliance with Egypt, sealed by marriage with the Ptolemaic royal family, is probably motivated by a concern that Egypt not ally itself with Demetrius' family. Demetrius has sent his sons abroad for their safety, and Alexander can expect a later challenge to his rule from them. Ptolemy VI responds somewhat cautiously and requests that the marriage be celebrated in Ptolemais, a city named after an Egyptian king.

10:59-66 Alexander honors Jonathan. The gathering for the royal wedding becomes the occasion for both Hellenistic kings to court Jonathan. Alexander still needs his support, and it is possible that Ptolemy has designs on recovering Palestine as part of his empire. Jonathan, on the other hand, also has reasons for going to Ptolemais with gifts. Onias IV, a rival claimant for the high priesthood, is in Egypt. Jonathan's "friendship" with Ptolemy can neutralize Onias and his supporters.

Jonathan's lavish gifts may well be at the expense of the Hellenizers—booty taken from them. Those who come before Alexander to protest against Jonathan are not heeded. Jonathan is in a position of great power and influence.

If there is any doubt among his enemies about Jonathan's current status, the clothing with royal purple and the invitation to sit at the king's table dispel such notions (vv. 62-63). The Hellenizers, the supporters of Onias, and the Hasideans (who seemingly object to Jonathan's assumption of the high priesthood because he is not of the high priestly family) are all effectively silenced by these actions and the royal proclamation that no one should interfere with Jonathan.

Jonathan returns to Jerusalem not only as high priest but also as military and civil governor. He has reason to be pleased. The civil war seems to be over, with the Maccabees the clear winners. However, there are still garrisons of Syrian troops in parts of Judea, including the Jerusalem citadel. The Jews are not yet an independent nation.

10:67-89 Jonathan is victorious in battle. Nothing is said about the years 150–147 B.C.E., presumably a time of Judea's settling down under the rule of Jonathan. In 147 B.C.E. problems develop with the return of Demetrius II to challenge Alexander's rule. Demetrius II, the son of Demetrius I, is still a teenager. What makes his challenge possible is the ineptitude and unpopularity of Alexander. The Syrians are ready for a new ruler.

Demetrius appoints Apollonius as governor (v. 69). Apollonius realizes that before he can successfully attack Alexander, he will have to deal with Alexander's faithful ally, Jonathan. The letter he allegedly sends is modeled on 1 Kgs 20:23-32, dealing with an earlier Syrian invasion. Apollonius' intention is to lure Jonathan into battle by taunting him. The approach works, and Jonathan sets out with a large army and his brother Simon. Jonathan is bound to defend the southern coastal cities by his alliances with Ptolemy and Alexander.

Jonathan is able to drive a strategic wedge between Apollonius and Demetrius by taking Joppa (v. 78), which might have been Apollonius' main supply port (there are not many harbors along the Palestinian coast). Apollonius' retreat southward might have been a ruse to lure Jonathan into the kind of terrain that would favor Apollonius' cavalry (see his taunt in 10:70-73). The ruse works, and Jonathan soon finds himself surrounded by the cavalry. At the same time, Jonathan's forces outnumber the Syrians. By sheer courage and determination, Jonathan's forces hold their ground and wear down the Syrians. When the cavalry weakens, Simon attacks the infantry successfully. When this happens and the cavalry flee, Jonathan is not able to follow them because he has no cavalry. The Syrian infantry seek refuge in the temple of Dagon (v. 83). Jonathan does not honor its status of asylum but destroys the temple and the men who are in it. The neighbors in Ashkalon decide to honor Jonathan, as does his ally, Alex-

ander. Jonathan's rank is raised still further to "Kinsman" of the king (v. 89), and the rest of "Philistia" is given to him. In short, he survives Apollonius' challenge very well.

11:1-19 Ptolemy VI plots against Alexander. Although ancient sources differ about Ptolemy's motives in the actions that follow, 1 Maccabees remains favorable to Alexander and his son against both Ptolemy and Demetrius. Ptolemy may have been merely acting as though he were a faithful ally, coming to Alexander's rescue against Apollonius and Demetrius II. In reality, he may have been taking advantage of the weakness and unpopular position of his son-in-law and attempting to reestablish Egyptian control over Palestine and perhaps Syria as well.

In 145 B.C.E. Ptolemy VI Philometor begins a march toward Syria, probably moving along the Palestinian coast. The fact that he leaves garrisons in each of the cities along his route gives us a hint at his motivation (v. 3). Although some people try to turn Ptolemy against Jonathan, the king needs his support—or at least he does not want to antagonize such a powerful person. Jonathan's behavior is very correct toward this ally. He tactfully withdraws to Jerusalem, leaving Ptolemy and Alexander (both of whom are his allies) to settle their own disputes.

Ptolemy invites Demetrius to form an alliance with him (v. 9) and offers to give him his daughter, Cleopatra, who is Alexander's wife! Ptolemy's intention is probably not so much to underwrite Demetrius' claim to the throne as to undermine Alexander. Ancient sources make clearer the accusation of attempted assassination (v. 10). According to the Jewish historian Josephus, Ammonius, a minister in Alexander's court, tried unsuccessfully to kill Ptolemy while he was enroute to Antioch. Our author, however, defends Alexander and provides us with Ptolemy's "real" motivations.

While Alexander is out of the capital, Ptolemy arrives and assumes the kingship of "Asia," that is, Syria (v. 13). So much for his support of Demetrius II! Ptolemy, however, for all his boldness, does not make a wise decision because he cannot count on Jonathan's support. Moreover, he can expect the opposition of Demetrius II and the Romans, who had kept Antiochus IV from uniting Syria and Egypt in 168 B.C.E. We are told that Alexander

387

was in Cilicia putting down a rebellion (probably fomented by Demetrius, who seems to have been there at the same time). Alexander's immediate return to Syria leads to direct conflict, which ends in the death of both antagonists (vv. 17-18). The populace, not favorably disposed to the Egyptian occupational forces, eliminate them. The way is now open for Demetrius II to assume the Seleucid throne.

11:20-38 Jonathan and Demetrius II. Jonathan has wisely stayed out of the conflict between Ptolemy and Alexander. Before Demetrius has a chance to consolidate his position, Jonathan moves against the citadel in Jerusalem. Both men will need the support of each other, and Jonathan's move against the citadel probably puts him in a stronger bargaining position with Demetrius. Naturally the Hellenizers, who may have become a minority by now, complain to the new king about Jonathan's actions.

What happens next is a lesson in Maccabean diplomacy. Although Demetrius reacts angrily to Jonathan's move, he proceeds more carefully in dealing with him. Demetrius moves south with a threatening army but requests a conference and the lifting of the siege. Jonathan does not honor the request regarding the siege but approaches Demetrius with important Jewish leaders and gifts (vv. 23-24). This pleases Demetrius, who inherited financial problems brought on by a series of wars and fiscal incompetence.

Demetrius confirms Jonathan in the high priesthood and in his status as a Chief Friend. Nothing is said about the citadel at this point, but we will learn later (v. 41) that the siege was lifted. Presumably in return for this "favor," Demetrius agrees to the same basic financial favors that had been offered by his father (see 10:30, 38). Demetrius' letter (vv. 29-37) is addressed both to Jonathan and to the Jewish people. The letter is basically a copy of what Demetrius had sent to his chief minister, Lasthenes, who as a general had helped Demetrius press his claims to the throne.

The letter in effect gives Judea a favored status and increases its territory with the addition of the three Samaritan districts. Taxes previously sent to Antioch now go to Jerusalem for the support of the temple and its priests. However, Judea remains a Syrian possession, and the Syrian garrison remains in the citadel. Afterward Demetrius makes a serious blunder in demobilizing his troops. We know from other ancient sources that he led a dissipated life, and his minister, Lasthenes, was very corrupt. The peace that Demetrius believes he has brought to his kingdom is not to last.

11:39-56 The revolt of Trypho. The next episode in our narrative seems extraordinary when the reader remembers the earlier struggles of the Maccabees against the Hellenizers and the Hellenists. In this segment of the story, Jonathan sends Jewish troops in an attempt to save Demetrius!

Trypho's career is interesting. He first came to public notice as a soldier of Demetrius I; then he became a governor of Antioch under Alexander; he was, perhaps, one of the two courtiers who crowned Ptolemy VI in Antioch; and later he became one of the "Friends" of Demetrius II. Such shifts in loyalty help explain his next adventure—rebellion against Demetrius II and installation of a new king in the person of Antiochus VI, a mere boy. Antiochus VI would have been well advised not to trust such a person.

Meanwhile Jonathan again requests that Demetrius remove the garrison from the Jerusalem citadel (v. 41). Demetrius I had agreed to such an action but did not implement it. Perhaps Jonathan is aware that Demetrius II could use the additional troops in Antioch to shore up his own faltering position. Demetrius agrees to arrange the move later, but after he is secure once again, he also reneges (see vv. 52-53). But, at this point in the narrative, he requests Jewish troops to help defend him.

Demetrius' unpopularity reaches alarming proportions, and the Jewish mercenaries ruthlessly put down a rebellion of the populace. The reader may be excused for wondering what is happening to the Maccabean religious revolution at this point. Demetrius does not become wiser from this experience. He alienates his sole ally, Jonathan, not only by reneging on his promises but also by causing Jonathan new problems, revoking the provisions of the letter found in verses 29-37.

11:57-62 Antiochus VI and Jonathan. Trypho now returns to Antioch with Antiochus VI, who was probably about four years old. Demetrius' army rebels against him and enthrones the boy-king, who promptly confirms Jonathan in the high priesthood and sends him lavish gifts. The letter alluded to in verse 57 was probably ordered by Trypho and drawn up for the young king by royal secretaries. Jonathan's allegiance is once more being courted by restoring the rank he had held under Alexander (see 10:89).

Simon Maccabeus is made governor of the coastal area from Tyre in the north to somewhere between Gaza and the Nile in the south, including some Hellenistic towns that were not pro-Jewish. Jonathan sets out on a tour, ostensibly to develop support for the new regime, but probably in reality to ensure his own control over the area. He is well received at Ashkalon but rebuffed at Gaza (v. 61). Significantly, after he overcomes the dissidents at Gaza, he takes hostages back to Jerusalem rather than send them to Trypho.

Meanwhile Demetrius II counterattacks by sending a large force to confront Jonathan in Galilee and, presumably, to prevent him from organizing forces loyal to Antiochus. Simon Maccabeus takes Beth-zur, the place of refuge for Hellenists who had escaped from Jerusalem (see 10:14). When Jonathan meets the enemy armies, he is defeated in an ambush (v. 68). His expressions of grief—tearing his clothes and throwing earth on his head—are expressly forbidden activities for a high priest (see Lev 10:6; 21:10). Seemingly, there were exceptions to the rule. Verses 71-74 echo Josh 7:5-9, implying that God has listened to Jonathan's prayers. (See also 1 Sam 14:21-22 for a similar victory by an earlier Jonathan.) Jonathan's troops rally to him, and after decisively defeating the enemy, he returns to Jerusalem.

12:1-23 Alliances with Rome and Sparta. According to 2 Macc 11:34-38, there had been diplomatic activity between the Jews and the Romans in 163 B.C.E., and, as we have read earlier (see 1 Macc 8), Judas had contacted the Romans in 161 B.C.E. It is not surprising, therefore, that Jonathan also makes diplomatic overtures to the Romans. What is less clear is why the Romans or the Spartans would consider embroiling themselves in Jewish matters in the Near East. Perhaps they have no intention of actually doing so. Jonathan may simply be seeking international recognition and status, as well as giving Trypho and Demetrius pause before attacking a people who have become friends of

Rome. The Romans seem to receive the Jewish embassy courteously and, presumably, at least renew their friendship with the Jewish people.

Although there may be reasons for questioning the authenticity of Jonathan's letter to the Spartans as presented in verses 5-18, the basic contents of the letter might be authentic. The date of the letter seems to be 144 B.C.E. Sparta had become independent two years earlier when the Romans helped it defeat Corinth and the Achaean League. The Spartans might be expected to understand Jewish nationalism and would provide an example of how an ally of Rome had benefited when attacked by neighbors. Undoubtedly, the example would not be lost on Trypho or Demetrius. In other words, in this chapter we probably have two more examples of Jonathan's political and diplomatic maneuvering that at the same time demonstrate his adaptation to Hellenistic ways. Eventually this approach will cost him his life.

The letter to Sparta is sent by Jonathan, the "senate" (the Sanhedrin), "the priests, and the rest of the Jewish people" (v. 6). The reference to not needing such an alliance or friendship because of the "sacred books" (v. 9) is not very tactful or diplomatic in a letter such as this and raises questions about the authenticity of the letter. Jonathan sends emissaries with Greek names; no doubt they are also fluent in the Greek language.

Although there is clear precedent for approaching Rome, Jonathan and his followers need something to establish bonds with the Spartans. That is why they recount a legend about the common origins of both peoples and quote earlier correspondence between Arius, a Spartan king, and Onias, a Jewish high priest (vv. 19-20). Identifying these people is a problem because there were at least two people each with the names of Arius and Onias during the period in question.

The Hebraic nature of verse 23 provides further complications regarding the authenticity of the letter. There are indications, however, that at times the Greeks were interested in associating themselves with ancient Egypt and the Near East. Perhaps the legend that both the Spartans and the Jews were descended from Abraham would have impressed the Spartans at this point in their history. No response is recorded from Sparta, however, and perhaps the very mention of such an embassy has already achieved the author's purpose of increasing Jonathan's prestige.

12:24-34 Demetrius again attacks Jonathan. Jonathan is currently loyal to Antiochus VI and his general, Trypho. When he learns that Demetrius has prepared a large army against him, Jonathan once again takes the initiative by leaving Jerusalem and crossing the border into Syrian territory (Hamath). When the enemy discover how prepared Jonathan and his troops are, they flee (v. 28). While Jonathan is in the territory, he attacks a group of Arabs. His motive is not clear, but they may have been at least partly responsible for the assassination of Alexander Balas, who had been friendly toward the Maccabees. The reason for Jonathan's march to Damascus (v. 32) is also unclear, but he may have had some dreams about restoring the Davidic empire, which at one time included Damascus (see 2 Sam 8:5-7).

Meanwhile Jonathan's brother Simon moves to the coastal area to prevent any active support of Demetrius among its inhabitants. Once again a threat to Maccabean supremacy has been overcome.

12:35-38 Jonathan builds up Judea's defenses. Jonathan seemingly has control of the Sanhedrin (the assembly of elders) and secures their agreement to build up the defenses of Judea. Part of this program includes the attempt to isolate the citadel in Jerusalem from the rest of the city because it is still held by foreigners. In effect, this initiates another siege.

12:39-53 The deceit of Trypho. The general Trypho decides to realize his ambition to become king. According to the author, Trypho thinks that Jonathan, the faithful ally of King Antiochus, will prevent such a move. That is why he now sets out to destroy Jonathan. We are not told what Jonathan knew of this plot, but he goes out to meet Trypho and his army with a large force of his own (v. 41). Trypho, deceitfully changing tactics, flatters Jonathan and gives him gifts. Jonathan makes the fatal mistake of accepting both, along with the advice to allow all but a few of his troops to return home. In past Maccabean history, a small army and prayer were adequate for defense or victory. Such is not the case at this point in the narrative.

Jonathan is invited to Ptolemais, the place where he had been honored by Ptolemy of Egypt and Alexander of Antioch (see 10:59-66). However, this time there is no Egyptian king to protect him, nor is there a Syrian king who needs his support. The inhabitants of Ptolemais seize Jonathan and kill many of his troops (v. 48). When Trypho attempts to destroy Jonathan's remaining troops in Galilee, he is not successful, and Jonathan's men return to Judea to mourn the loss of Jonathan. We are not told whether he is still alive or not. Perhaps they do not know his fate at this time.

The closing verse of this chapter (v. 53) reminds one of Psalm 2, which describes the temptation of surrounding peoples to rebel and attack the Jewish nation when someone (God's anointed) is assuming a new leadership role in Israel. The full psalm in Jewish tradition, however, assures us that these matters are ultimately in God's hands, and God will take care of the people.

PART III: SIMON MACCABEUS

1 Macc 13:1-16:24

13:1-11 Simon becomes the new leader. When Trypho prepares to invade Judea, Simon delivers an address to the people in Jerusalem, drawing upon such familiar themes of 1 Maccabees as devotion to the law and the temple and also commitment to the nation. The author, of course, does not mention any self-interest on the part of his heroes, the Maccabees. Simon appears to believe that Jonathan is already dead (v. 4). As had happened on previous occasions, the people accept a Maccabee as their leader (see 1 Macc 2:65ff. and 9:29-31). It is noteworthy that the people accept Simon as their leader but not as high priest. Perhaps this is an indication of the popular belief that only the legitimately reigning Seleucid king could appoint a high priest. Simon's first task is to complete the defensive measures begun by Jonathan.

13:12-24 Trypho kills Jonathan. Trypho invades the land of Judah, bringing Jonathan along as a prisoner. The offer he makes Simon involves a clear dilemma. If Simon refuses Trypho's offer, the people will hold him responsible for his brother's death. If he accepts the offer, he is taking a major risk with the deceitful, treacherous, and ambitious

Trypho. In effect, however, he has no choice but to pay the ransom money and deliver Jonathan's children to the Syrian general. True to form, Trypho reneges on his offer (v. 19).

As Trypho marches deeper into the land, ravaging it as he goes along, Simon counters his every move and prevents him from taking a direct approach to Jerusalem itself. Trypho becomes a natural ally of the Syrian garrison in the Jerusalem citadel, who accordingly appeal to him for help. But Trypho is prevented from coming to their aid by a seasonal snowstorm; he turns back to Syria, but first he kills Jonathan and probably his sons as well.

13:25-30 Jonathan is buried at Modein. Jonathan's body is buried in the family tomb at Modein. He does not receive the eulogies that Judas had (see 3:1-9) or that Simon will later receive (see 14:28-47). Jonathan's deeds were more political than military. He seems to have been working toward the independence of the Jewish nation but was captured and killed before he could accomplish this. The stage has been set, however, for Simon to realize that dream.

A careful reading of Simon's burial procedures for his brother reveals an astonishing borrowing from Greek or Hellenistic ways (vv. 27-30). The practice of setting up pyramids is borrowed from the Egyptians (and Hellenistic Ptolemies). The setting up of carved suits of armor (trophies) is a Greek burial custom for victorious warriors. The Greeks also had the practice of setting up victory monuments near the sea in memory of sea battles. Simon adopts the practice, even though the Maccabeans were not seafaring. They had no fleet and had won no naval victories. Perhaps the capture of the port town Joppa may have triggered some Maccabean dreams about the potential of developing a navy. At any rate, we seem to have come some distance from Mattathias' zeal and passion for matters Jewish! On the other hand, this cultural adaptation is often found at some point in revolutions throughout history.

13:31-42 Simon and Demetrius become allies. Predictably, Trypho kills the young Antiochus VI and assumes the royal throne. Simon's response seems limited primarily to further defensive measures in Judea. He was probably fairly independent of Trypho, who had demonstrated his vulnerability earlier (see vv. 12-24).

Although the Maccabees had not been on good terms with Demetrius II, Simon now turns to him in order to form an alliance. Trypho was probably already in trouble with the Syrian populace for assassinating Antiochus VI, and there is some indication that his dictatorial ways had also alienated his army. That is why Demetrius was probably in a position to regain the Seleucid throne. The gifts that Simon sends him imply allegiance.

The response of Demetrius seems gracious enough, but he probably has little choice but to respond positively. He addresses Simon as "high priest" (v. 36). Although it is quite likely that the populace or the Sanhedrin had already chosen Simon as high priest, the author of 1 Maccabees is careful to call him by this designation only after it is at least confirmed by a king with some semblance of legitimacy to his reign. The favors Demetrius bestows on Simon are not all they may appear to be at first reading. He has little choice but to revalidate grants he had made earlier (see 1:24-37), to agree to Simon's retaining control over the fortifications over which he already has control, to pardon any acts of rebellion on the part of the Maccabees, and to exempt the Jews from all taxes. At the same time he is also willing to take Jews into his service.

Although verse 41 implies a kind of independence of gentile "yoke," full political independence will not come until later.

13:43-53 Simon captures Gazara and the citadel. Simon now moves to assure complete military control over all Judea and the coast by capture of the remaining Syrian garrisons there. First he takes Gazara, resettles it with Jews who observe the law, and builds himself a residence there.

Jonathan had begun the siege of the citadel two years earlier (see 1 Macc 12:36), and Simon brings it to a successful end in 141 B.C.E., when the garrison surrenders. The citadel is entered with great jubilation and rejoicing (v. 47). For the first time since 169/168 B.C.E., the temple area is free from the menace of the citadel (see 1 Macc 1:33-37). Verse 53 introduces Simon's son John, who is later known as John Hyrcanus, Simon's successor, who ruled from 134 to 104 B.C.E.

14:1-3 Demetrius is captured. According to the author, Demetrius II marched into Media to get help in his campaign against Trypho. However, it is possible that Trypho was fairly immobilized at this point and that Demetrius turned his attention to Media because of the threatening progress of the Parthian empire there. At any rate, the Parthians capture Demetrius, Simon's ally, and imprison him. Arsaces (v. 2) is probably Mithradates I, who actually treated Demetrius fairly well, even giving him his own daughter in marriage.

14:4-15 Song of praise to Simon. At this point in the narrative, the author inserts some poetry that sums up the praises of Simon in much the same way as he did earlier with the praises of Judas (see 3:3-9). The song recounts some of Simon's important military accomplishments, notably the capture of the port of Joppa and the citadel in Jerusalem. It is interesting that Simon Maccabeus is praised for capturing Joppa (v. 5), the gateway to commerce and communication with the Greek isles. Such contact with Greeks was not where this story started! At the same time Simon is described in language that is reminiscent of the reign of Solomon (see 1 Kgs 5:5, for example).

The second part of this song of praise seems to describe Simon's reign as a kind of messianic age, a familiar theme in intertestamental literature. The poem contains several allusions to Old Testament texts (see Lev 26:4; Zech 8:4, 12; Ezek 34:27; Isa 52:1; 1 Kgs 4:25; Mic 4:4; and Isa 27:5-6). The Jewish apocalyptic movement, especially during the second century B.C.E., looked forward to a period of peace for God's people, a time when they would be ruled by someone who was just, someone who would see to it that everyone, including the poor, had enough to eat—that they could eat their bread in security.

Despite what one might think of the political and religious developments in Judaism during the period of the Maccabees, it must be admitted that, under Simon, the Jewish people in Judea experienced their first quasi-independence since the fall of Jerusalem in 587 B.C.E. We might excuse some people of the time, including our author, who might have thought that the messianic prophecies and apocalyptic predictions were indeed being fulfilled under the Maccabees—especially under Simon.

14:16-24 Rome and Sparta renew alliances with Simon. Rome and Sparta learn of the death of Jonathan and express their interest in renewing alliances with Simon. Numenius, the Jewish emissary who had been sent to Sparta and Rome by Jonathan, figures prominently in this narrative also. The full chronological sequence of events is not clear at this point because of the way the author has schematized and telescoped events. Simon responds to the Romans' offer of friendship by sending a significant gift, a golden shield weighing nearly half a ton—an expensive gift from a small nation struggling to stay alive.

14:25-49 The Jewish people honor the Maccabees. We have heard the author's summary praise of Simon as well as the offers of friendship from Sparta and the important ally, Rome. Now it is time to hear what the people themselves thought of the Maccabees. Setting up a memorial inscription to record the great deeds of leaders was a familiar practice in the Hellenistic world. The inscription in this part of the narrative is dated September, 140 B.C.E.

What is curious is what the inscription does *not* say. Although Mattathias, the father, is mentioned (v. 29), Judas' name does not appear, and Jonathan's role is described cursorily. The majority of the praise, of course, is heaped upon Simon, who is the current ruler. Perhaps it was considered impolitic to praise his brothers while he was ruling. Perhaps also the manners in which Judas and Jonathan came to their deaths was a cause of some embarrassment, and therefore not suited to the author's purpose of praising his heroes.

As a result of all that he had done on behalf of the nation, the people acknowledge Simon as permanent leader, high priest, and governor general, implying military, spiritual, and civil authority. His power is just short of royal, as is his official clothing. In effect, we have here a new constitution that outlines Simon's responsibilities and his acceptance of them, as well as the implied responsibilities of the people who have offered these positions to him.

15:1-9 Antiochus VII and Simon. Antiochus VII, the younger brother of Demetrius II, was called "Sidetes" by the people, because he was born at Side in Pamphylia. When he decided to wrest control of the

Syrian kingdom away from the unpopular Trypho, he sought the friendship of Simon. Although Antiochus probably would not have embarked on such a venture without adequate financial and moral support, Simon was nevertheless someone to be reckoned with.

In his letter to Simon (vv. 3-9), he may be exaggerating the conditions in Syria somewhat to enhance his claim to the throne. Although he seems to grant Simon what had been granted by others (or simply taken by the Maccabees), his concessions or privileges make it clear that he considers Judea to be a Syrian province. The authorization to coin money is a new privilege, however. Presumably the coinage was in bronze, because silver and gold were reserved to the king. Since he withdraws most of these concessions a few months later, it seems probable that Simon did not mint any coins.

15:10-14 Antiochus VII invades Syria and Judea. In the autumn of 139/138 B.C.E., Antiochus invaded Syria, forcing Trypho to flee to Dor, a city south of Mount Carmel. In our narrative Antiochus pursues him and besieges this port city. Since Antiochus has moved south into Judea, we might expect some encounter with Simon. However, the author inserts a notice about renewed friendship between Simon and the Romans before resuming the narrative about Antiochus' relationship with Simon.

15:15-24 Rome renews alliance with the Jews. Numenius, the Jewish legate to Rome, brings a letter addressed to such neighboring kings as Ptolemy and Demetrius. The latter, perhaps, had not yet been captured by the Parthians when the letter was written, or perhaps the Romans simply were not aware of his fate. The renewal of friendship is expressed especially in the acceptance of the large golden shield that Simon had sent to Rome (v. 20). The letter provides for a kind of protection of the Jews from their neighbors and includes provisions for extradition to Jerusalem of all troublemakers who seek refuge in neighboring countries. It is not clear why this letter is included precisely at this point in the narrative, but it does in fact provide a kind of contrast between the way the Romans deal with the Jews and the way the Syrians do. The various kingdoms mentioned in verses 22-23 are primarily independent states of the eastern

Mediterranean, an area of increasing interest to the Romans.

15:25-41 Antiochus attacks the Jews. The narrative resumes with the story of Antiochus' pursuit of Trypho. Although Antiochus besieged the city of Dor by land and sea (v. 25), Trypho was able to escape (v. 37); however, he has no further influence on the development of events in this area. Antiochus is already in control as this part of the narrative begins. Simon sends some troops to help Antiochus, presumably as a way of indicating his acceptance of Antiochus' offer (see vv. 3-9).

The situation has changed, however—Antiochus no longer needs Simon's help. He refuses to accept the assistance and reneges on his earlier agreement. Moreover, he demands the return of Joppa, Gazara, and the citadel in Jerusalem, all of which formerly belonged to the Syrian kingdom. Simon, in effect, is being asked to make recompense for the cities taken by force. The substitution of a financial arrangement instead of returning the cities or the citadel demonstrates that the matter is open to some negotiation. Although the sum of money is high, Simon can probably afford it.

Simon receives the Syrian envoy, Athenobius, in full Hellenistic splendor at his court (v. 32). Again, the picture given suggests that we have traveled far from where Mattathias and his family began in the revolt against the Hellenization of Judaism. Instead of impressing the envoy with his wealth, however, Simon unwittingly makes it clear that he can in fact afford the recompense demanded by Antiochus. His refusal to pay can now be taken as an indication of his intransigence and rebellion.

Simon's formal response, however, appeals to Greek international law which provided, for example, for one's right to retake ancestral lands that had fallen into the hands of others. The Jews' claim to their land is based on divine promises to their ancestors. Likewise, Greek international law provided for conquest of territory outside the ancestral land through just wars of retribution. Accordingly, Simon argues that the citizens of Joppa and Gazara were doing harm to the Jews (v. 35), and that is why those cities were taken. His willingness to pay a mere tenth of what Antiochus demands as recompense is perhaps an attempt to show that the Jews are willing to make some concessions in the negotiations. On the other hand, the amount is so small that its offer seems to indicate defiance.

The Syrian response is anger. Antiochus appoints Cendebeus as commanding officer of the coastal region to succeed Simon, thereby in effect removing him from office. Cendebeus is also sent to Judea and Jerusalem to prepare for an attack on the Jewish people, while Antiochus himself continues to pursue Trypho. (Trypho died eventually at Apamea, a Phoenician city.) The situation described in verses 40-41 reminds us of earlier days when the Maccabees fought the Syrians and the Hellenists in the heart of Judea. The peace and security that Simon seemed to have achieved have been short-lived.

16:1-10 John Hyrcanus attacks the Syrians. The narrative is nearing its end. Simon, the last of the Maccabean brothers to rule over the Jewish people, is getting too old to lead the troops into battle. He passes on the Maccabean military leadership to his sons Judas and John (Hyrcanus), while retaining other power and authority (v. 3). John attacks Cendebeus with a large army and with cavalry as well, the first reference to cavalry in the Maccabean narrative. Although Judas is wounded in battle, John is victorious and brings peace to the land once again.

16:11-17 Simon and his two sons are murdered. We are now introduced to Simon's son-in-law, Ptolemy, son of Abubus. Ptolemy's name might be a surprise even among the in-laws of the Maccabees. The name Abubus is a Hellenized form of a Semitic name. We have become familiar with Maccabean behavior, which so closely parallels and resembles Hellenistic leaders' actions—their drinking parties, their mistresses, and their tendency to eliminate rivals. This latter tendency emerges in Ptolemy, who decides to succeed his father-in-law and become an ally of Antiochus VII.

Ptolemy invites Simon, Judas, and Mattathias to his home at Jericho and provides a sumptuous banquet for them. One might expect Jewish hospitality and table fellowship, but instead there is treachery and assassination. Simon's death is described very briefly and without comment (v. 16). He joins his brothers in an ignominious death—dying while drunk at the hand of his own son-in-law. We do not know how many Jewish people supported Simon, but a return to Syrian vassalage and taxation probably would not have been very acceptable to them. This may explain why Ptolemy writes to Antiochus and requests troops to help him in ruling the country.

16:18-24 Conclusion. Ptolemy has a traitor in his own midst. Someone warns John of what has happened to his father and brothers and of Ptolemy's intention to have him murdered as well. John has his would-be assassins killed and returns to Jerusalem before Ptolemy can arrive there. The rest of the story is merely summarized in our narrative. We learn that John also became high priest. The book ends on a note similar to that found so often in the books of Kings, referring the reader to the chronicles of John's pontificate.

The book ends somewhat abruptly. The Maccabees have clearly been considered heroes by the author. However, the way the book is composed may provide a clue as to the author's final verdict. Most of the songs of praise about the brothers come at the beginning of their respective narratives rather than at the end. All three brothers died because of treachery. All three fully and freely engaged in Hellenistic diplomacy and became more and more Hellenistic in their ways. One wonders whether the author is not saying that, although they did great deeds on behalf of the nation and had great potential for leadership, there was a flaw in each of their characters. Most of what they gained was soon lost.

On the other hand, Jewish independence became a reality under John Hyrcanus, who seems to have dreamed of restoring the Davidic-Solomonic empire. Perhaps this is what prompted the author of 1 Maccabees to tell the story of the Maccabees' heroism.

2 MACCABEES

Alphonse P. Spilly, C.PP.S.

INTRODUCTION

This book, originally written in Greek, is said to be a summary of a five-volume work written by Jason of Cyrene (2 Macc 2:23). Although it is difficult to date the work, it may be from the reign of John Hyrcanus (129–104 B.C.E.) or later, but before the arrival of Pompey in 63 B.C.E. The work differs from 1 Maccabees in many ways, but significantly in its not being pro-Maccabean or pro-Hasmonean. Because some of its main tenets were contrary to the policies of John Hyrcanus, some date the book to the early years of his reign, a time when the author might have tried to influence a policy debate. Although it might well have been written in Jerusalem (because of its emphasis and propaganda regarding the temple), some would place its origins in Egypt, and more specifically in Alexandria (in part, because of its occasional confusion of Palestinian geography). It may have been written as a corrective to 1 Maccabees (or vice versa). The two books clearly have different purposes and different points of view and thereby complement each other.

The theology of 2 Maccabees

From the prologue to the epilogue, the book's primary concern is with the temple in Jerusalem. It covers a period of the Hellenistic age when the temple experienced profanation, purification and restoration, and renewed attacks, primarily during the reigns of Antiochus IV and his son. The temple is a symbol of what happens to the nation as a whole: the people suffer persecution, followed by liberation and restoration.

The book's theology is primarily Deuteronomic: sin leads to punishment, repentance leads to salvation. Sin means a failure to observe the law, and it breaks the covenantal relationship between God and the people. One of the limitations of this theology is that it has no explanation for innocent suffering and can lead one to think that all suffering is a punishment for sin.

Unlike 1 Maccabees, this book sees the main problems as beginning within the Jewish community. Individuals, including high priests, introduce Hellenistic ways into Judea, Jerusalem, and even the temple—practices that are considered incompatible with the authentic exercise of Jewish religion. The sins of these few bring God's punishment on the community, symbolized especially in the profanation of the temple and experienced in the proscription of Jewish religion.

The reader encounters martyrs here, those especially singled out as models of perseverance and fidelity to the law and religion. Persecution is God's way of purifying the people because of the sin that has been found in their midst. It is not simply punishment but discipline or correction. Remaining faithful during persecution, even to the point of giving one's life, has important effects on the course of events and hastens the people's restoration.

The Gentiles also play an important role in this book. In a manner well known within the Deuteronomic tradition, they become the instruments of God's punishment. However, as is also the case in that same tradition, they frequently become arrogant and step beyond their role as God's instruments to challenge divine authority and power. This results in their fall. The higher they attempt to raise themselves in their arrogance, the lower they seem to fall.

What underlies the theology of this book is the divine control of events. If the Gentiles are mere instruments of God's punishment, then leaders such as Judas are mere agents of God's salvation. Before each major confrontation, Judas prays with the people for divine protection; victory is always attributed to God. Frequently heavenly manifestations and mysterious figures appear to bring about the victory or at least to guide and encourage the people.

The theological viewpoint of the author controls the unfolding of the narrative. Where this calls for modification of historical events, the author does not hesitate to gloss over unpleasant facts or simply to change the presentation of the facts. Whereas 1 Maccabees at times admits that Judas occasionally lost a battle, he does not lose any ground in 2 Maccabees after the rebellion has begun. Characterization is done, not on the basis of historical facts known about the actors in this drama, but in terms of the demands of the author's theological bias. Enemies are archvillains, and heroes and heroines are also much bigger than life. This gives some of the major episodes in the book their legendary quality.

The relevance of 2 Maccabees

The stark nationalism of the book, its earthiness and violence, its near delight in gory details, and its simplistic theology of retribution may not attract the reader to return often to this narrative for spiritual reading. However, there is something valuable in its theology of martyrdom for a world that experiences so much oppression of individual and religious freedoms. The martyrs provide us with striking examples of courage in the face of immoral coercion and of the willingness to sacrifice even life itself rather than deny something as sacred as human and religious rights.

OUTLINE OF 2 MACCABEES

COMMENTARY

INTRODUCTION

2 Macc 1:1–2:32

The first two chapters of 2 Maccabees provide an introduction to the thought of the book with two letters and the author's own prologue.

1:1-10a Letter of 124 B.C.E. The Jewish people in Palestine are writing to their co-religionists in Egypt, primarily about the observance of the feast of the rededication of the temple (Hanukkah). The dating of the letter (v. 10) is significant in the history of Egyptian Jews because it was in 124 B.C.E. that Ptolemy VIII (Euergetes II) and his sister Cleopatra II agreed to end their civil war. The Jewish populace in Egypt had supported Cleopatra and might have needed some encouragement in the face of possible retaliation by Ptolemy VIII. The reference to a "time of adversity" in verse 5 might refer to this specific historical context.

The first six verses contain a typical greeting and prayer for the welfare of the addressees. Noteworthy are the senders of the letter—no high priest, Sanhedrin (senate), or member of the Maccabean family is mentioned. This may be in keeping with a tendency within the book to downplay leadership (with the exception of Judas Maccabeus) and to highlight the common people, who are the real heroes and heroines of the book.

The religious content of the letter centers on God's covenant with the patriarchs of Israel. God's "remembering" this special relationship with the people is not so much a matter of divine memory as God's continuing commitment on behalf of the people—not only those in Palestine but those in Egypt as well. This divine commitment includes rescuing them in their present distress.

The covenantal relationship also has implications for the people's behavior: they are to observe the Torah, the law, the manifestation of God's will for the people. Even their capacity for observing the law is attributed to God's gift. There may be a subtle hint in verse 5 that the reason for their present distress is their sinfulness, but this is not clear.

The next part of the letter (vv. 7-8) alludes to an earlier letter, sent in 143 B.C.E., which chronicled their problems with Jason, a high priest who bought the office from the Seleucid king. Jason and his associates rebelled and brought violence and destruction to the land, as 2 Maccabees will detail later. Prayer led to God's rescuing the people from these calamities.

The letter ends with an exhortation to celebrate Hanukkah, called here the feast of Booths because of its resemblance to that great feast commemorating the years of wilderness wandering after liberation from the slavery of Egypt and its Pharaoh.

This letter may at first seem a strange introduction to a book, but it outlines themes that will run throughout the ensuing narrative: the attacks against Jerusalem and God's rescue of the people. The festival that is to be celebrated is the rededication of the temple, and the rest of the book will continue to focus our attention on that sanctuary. The theology is, as we have noted, basically Deuteronomic: sin leads to punishment, but repentance to salvation.

1:10b-2:18 Letter of 164 B.C.E. The focus of this second letter is also the temple and the feast of Hanukkah. In this letter both the Sanhedrin (senate) and Judas Maccabeus are included among the senders, but the people themselves retain the first place in the greeting. Aristobulus may be a second-century B.C.E. Jewish philosopher who lived in Alexandria and whose writings have survived as fragments preserved in the writings of early Christian writers. He was at the court of Ptolemy VI and, according to this letter, was a member of the high priestly line.

The allusion to historical events in verses 11-12 is vague, although verses 13-16 refer to the death of Antiochus at the temple of Nanea. The author seems to be referring to Antiochus IV, although it was Antiochus III who died in a raid against a temple. This family, at any rate, was known for its raiding of temples. The pretext for the visit to the temple was the ceremonial marriage of the king with the goddess of fertility, but the real intention, according to this author, was his greed for money. This motif will reappear later in the book. The priests at the temple seemingly were aware of the purpose of the king's visit, and became responsible for his death and that of his associates.

Verse 17 contains the moral of the story: this is how God deals with the wicked, especially those who attack temples. The next part of the letter contains five subdivisions, connected primarily by association of ideas rather than by logical development.

Verses 18-36 demonstrate the continuity between the temple of Nehemiah and that of Solomon through the telling of a legend, according to which the fire used for sacrifices in Solomon's temple was hidden at the time of the temple's destruction in 587 B.C.E. and turned to liquid. Nehemiah directed the priests to find the liquid and, in actions that resemble those of Elijah on Mount Carmel (see 1 Kgs 18:30-39), ignited the sacrifices through the power of the sun enflaming the liquid, identified as naphtha. We know, however, that the temple was rebuilt by Zerubbabel many years before Nehemiah arrived on the scene. The point of the story is less historical accuracy than theological highlighting of the importance of the temple in the eyes of the Lord.

The prayer recited on this occasion is notable for its numerous attributes of God, who is designated as the only king of Israel (v. 24). The prayer asks two things of this beneficent God: acceptance of sacrifice and restoration of the people (that is, liberation from the Gentiles who oppress them). This language is appropriate, given the date of the letter—a year or so after the writing of the Book of Daniel.

The next section (2:1-8) centers attention on Jeremiah, who is reputed to have been the one who told the priests to hide the fire in the first place. Although the letter of Jeremiah to the exiles in Jer 29 does not mention the fire, it does mention the observance of the law and contains warnings against idolatry (as in 2 Macc 2:2). The legend continues with a description of Jeremiah's alleged journey to Mount Sinai, where he hid the tent, the ark, and the altar of incense until such time as the Lord would reveal to the people where they could find these objects. The expectation of the glory of the Lord manifesting itself in the cloud (2:8) would remind the Jewish readers of the Lord's presence in the wilderness and especially at Sinai, and also at the dedication of Solomon's temple.

The mention of Moses and Solomon in 2:8 introduces another section of this letter (2:9-12), comparing the roles of these two leaders. Both prayed and fire is said to have come from the heavens to light the sacrifice, just as happened with Nehemiah. This led to the celebration of a dedicatory feast for a whole week—similar to the feast of Hanukkah.

The mention of celebrating a feast for eight days leads back to the days of Nehemiah, who is said to have collected some of the scriptures just as Judas Maccabeus is alleged to have done (2:13-14). These scriptures are made available to the addressees of the letter (2:15).

The last part of the letter perhaps contains its real purpose: notice of the celebration of Hanukkah, celebrating God's deliverance of the people (presumably through Judas Maccabeus' ability to take control of the temple, to purify it, and to reestablish Jewish worship there). However, Judas is not mentioned as the agent of God here; instead, God alone is said to be the one who has had mercy on the people and brought them back together so that they could worship God in the temple. This is consistent with the theological emphasis of the book. Whereas 1 Maccabees highlighted the human agency of the Maccabean family in achieving independence, 2 Maccabees insists upon the ultimate causality of divine favor and intervention.

2:19-32 Author's preface. The author now presents his own introduction, noting that this is the story of the Maccabees, but also of heavenly manifestations. Emphasis is put on the temple and altar once again. It is clear that God has accomplished all this (2:22). The author also identifies his source, a work by Jason of Cyrene, condensed in the present version.

It is remarkable that a book that is so preoccupied with Jewish matters and opposed to Hellenizing efforts is so consciously written with Hellenistic historiographical principles! The analogies of festive banquets and the adornment of houses are also more Hellenistic than Jewish. There is even what approaches humorous self-consciousness at the end of the preface (2:32). With this we are ready to begin the narrative proper.

PART I: HELIODORUS

2 Macc 3:1-40

The introduction has focused attention on the temple and God's protection on its behalf, and has also promised to tell about heavenly manifestations. The story of Heliodorus is a dramatic narrative that delivers on this promise. Although there is a historical core to the story, it is told with great literary license in order to highlight the theological viewpoint of the author.

Events center on two Jews: Onias III, the high priest, and Simon, a wicked schemer. There are also two Hellenistic characters: the greedy king Antiochus and his minister Heliodorus. The story follows the basic outline of a well-known literary type from this period in which a deity defends his or her temple with whatever means are necessary, and so commentators often refer to this narrative as a blend of historical information and pious legend.

3:1-6 Onias versus Simon. Jerusalem is described as living in "perfect peace" because of two factors: the high priest Onias is pious, and the people observe the Torah. Antiochus III was generous in donating sums of money to temples within his domain, and we have no reason to think that Jerusalem would fare any differently. The money donated by the king was meant to underwrite the temple's expensive sacrificial system. However, this royal donation is not the money which will figure in the story that follows.

Simon, the brother of Menelaus (whom the reader will meet in the next chapter), is an official of some standing in Jerusalem. It is not clear what his quarrel with Onias was (v. 4), but there is some evidence that Onias was pro-Ptolemaic (pro-Egyptian) while Simon was pro-Seleucid (pro-Syrian). The politics of the day may lie behind this narrative, as is the case with so many others in the Maccabean books.

Simon's subsequent actions would be considered treasonous as well as illegal by upright Jews and Gentiles. His approach to the governor may be seen as an attempt to ingratiate himself with the Syrian authorities. Antiochus III needs finances to pay a tribute levied against his kingdom by Rome. Simon alleges that there are excess funds in abundance in the Jerusalem temple (v. 6). He says that not all of the funds are needed for the sacrificial system and that the king could have easy access to them. (Later in the narrative we will learn the nature of these excess funds.) The effect of Simon's treachery will be seen in the sub-

sequent narratives in 2 Maccabees. Whereas 1 Maccabees suggests that the Jews' difficulties were primarily caused by the Hellenists, 2 Maccabees focuses the blame on wicked people among the Jewish populace.

3:7-14 The mission of Heliodorus. The governor reports the financial good news to the king, who immediately sends one of his ministers to appropriate the excess funds for royal use. What follows makes it clear that the major difficulties between Jerusalem and Antioch have not yet developed, and relationships between the two are primarily cordial. Heliodorus' subterfuge (taking an indirect route) may have been designed to prevent any depositors from withdrawing their money before his arrival at the temple.

Heliodorus is direct with the high priest, asking him about the excess revenues in the temple treasury (v. 9). Onias' response is probably accurate: some of the funds have been collected to help care for widows and orphans, as Jewish law prescribes in so many places (see, for example, Deut 16:12-13), and some of the money has been deposited by a certain Hyrcanus, son of Tobias.

During the Hellenistic period, the Tobiads were a powerful and wealthy Jewish family. Their initial holdings were in Transjordan, but they also had residences in Jerusalem and Alexandria. They were pro-Hellenist merchants who were primarily pro-Egyptian. During the course of their history, they were often at odds with the high priestly family of the Oniads, although that does not seem to figure in the present narrative. The Hyrcanus of this narrative had earlier collected taxes for the Ptolemies and had remained pro-Egyptian after the Seleucids had taken control of Palestine (after 198 B.C.E.). During this latter period he had maintained a territory in the Transjordan almost independent of Seleucid rule, and evidently had deposited his earnings and family fortune in the Jerusalem temple for safekeeping. He and Onias III probably shared pro-Egyptian sympathies.

At stake in the Heliodorus incident are some legal questions. Because Hyrcanus is pro-Egyptian, he can be considered a rebel by the Seleucids, and his rights could be considered nil. On the other hand, Onias appeals to both Jewish and Greek law regarding the inviolability of a sanctuary and the safety of any funds deposited there. Heliodorus, rather than trying to sort out the legal moral dilemma, relies instead on his orders from the king (v. 13) and makes preparations to defraud the temple. In the dramatic account that follows, the reader may have recourse not only to law but also to the theology of this book: God will defend the temple. The only question that remains is how it will be done.

3:15-21 The reaction of the faithful Jews. With great dramatic strokes, the author describes the impact Heliodorus' mission and intent have on the Jewish faithful. They are helpless in resisting Heliodorus and his royal mandate, but they turn to God with prayer and gestures of mourning and lament. Can God fail to hear the prayers of a people in so much anguish?

3:22-34 God's response to Heliodorus and the Jews. When Heliodorus approaches the temple with his associates and retinue, God is manifested in such a powerful way that Heliodorus' associates are thrown into panic and fainting. A mysterious rider on a magnificent horse charges Heliodorus, and the rider's two companions whip Heliodorus, who falls to the ground, seemingly unconscious (v. 27). His bold approach to the temple precincts ends dramatically with his being ignominiously carried away on a stretcher, utterly helpless. The Jewish people change their prayer from lament to praise at this mighty manifestation of God's power and protection.

The story is not yet over, however, in accordance with this literary genre. Fearful for his death, Heliodorus' associates intercede with Onias, asking him to pray for Heliodorus to the God who has so awesomely struck him down. Perhaps they are already worrying about what they are going to explain to the king about Heliodorus' condition, presuming the king might be somewhat skeptical if they describe what occurred.

Onias' motives in what follows may be equally pious and political. How will he explain to the king that an important minister on an equally important mission has met with such grief in Jerusalem? While Onias prays on behalf of Heliodorus, the young men appear once again to Heliodorus with a message of salvation (because of Onias' prayer) and a mandate to proclaim God's power and majesty. They disappear as mysteriously as they appeared.

3:35-40 The witness of Heliodorus. Heliodorus' offering of sacrifice is not against temple practice. Although Heliodorus bears witness to the power of the God of the Jews as commanded, the king understandably remains skeptical, for he has not shared Heliodorus' experience. The king, by asking who might be better qualified for such a mission (v. 37), appears to accuse Heliodorus of incompetence. Heliodorus replies with some irony: send your worst enemy or someone who plots against your government and he will be appropriately punished. The irony stems from the fact that later in history Heliodorus *did* plot against Antiochus and brought him to his death. The narrative ends with a suitable summary statement about the "power" that is present in Jerusalem, power that will destroy whatever or whoever tries to harm the temple or the people.

PART II: PROFANATION AND RESTORATION OF THE TEMPLE

2 Macc 4:1–10:9

A. Profanation and Persecution

2 Macc 4:1–7:42

The events described in 4:1–7:42 cover the period from 175 to 167 B.C.E. and tell the story of the assault of evil on the Jewish nation and their religion.

4:1-6 Simon continues to oppose Onias. Simon accuses the high priest Onias of treason, a charge that the author of 2 Maccabees is quick to deny. Onias proceeds to the Syrian court to defend himself, probably in the eyes of both the Seleucid king and his own people. His mission is aborted, however, by the king's death.

4:7-22 Jason purchases the high priesthood. With the accession of Antiochus IV Epiphanes to the Seleucid throne, Onias' own brother, Jason, promises the king money in return for being appointed high priest and introducing Hellenistic practices into Jerusalem. The gymnasium and youth club were basic institutions of Greek education. Enrolling the men of Jerusalem as Antiochene citizens probably meant a shift of power to Jason's supporters. All these actions demonstrated a shift away from Jewish values and practices to a Hellenistic way of life.

At the new gymnasium Jason introduced Jewish youths to Hellenistic training. The Greeks exercised naked, wearing only broad-brimmed hats to shield their heads from the hot sun. The author's lack of esteem for Jason is found in verse 13, where he is described as "outrageous," "wicked," "ungodly," and "pseudo-high priest." The temple priests are themselves caught up in Hellenistic fashions and ways. There will be a price to pay for abandoning Jewish practices, especially worship.

The competitive games played every five years were similar to the Olympiad, and Jason, with his predilection for matters Hellenistic, sends a delegation to Tyre. It is not clear how he understands the offering of sacrifice to Hercules, but the delegation has qualms about this and instead donates the money to the building of Antiochus' fleet.

Later Antiochus himself visits Jerusalem, where he is received with great pomp and celebration. This was quite possible because Onias was in exile and Hyrcanus was dead; hence the pro-Ptolemaic party was powerless.

4:23-29 Menelaus supplants Jason. Jason makes a tactical error by sending Simon's brother Menelaus to deliver the promised money to the king. Menelaus betrays Jason by outbidding him for the office and supplants him as high priest. Jason had not proved himself to be a loyal brother to Onias, but at least he was of the high priestly family. Menelaus is not of the high priestly family and can be expected to encounter opposition among the Jewish populace. Further opposition might also be expected because of the high rate of tribute promised by Menelaus. The date is 172 or 171 B.C.E.

Jason becomes a fugitive in the Transjordan (Onias is presumably still in Syria), and Menelaus cannot make good on the money promised to the king. Accordingly, he is summoned to appear before the king.

4:30-38 Andronicus murders Onias. When some important cities in the northwest part of his kingdom rebel, Antiochus marches to pacify them, leaving Andronicus in charge. This man had assassinated the son of Seleucus IV, making it possible for Antiochus IV to succeed to the throne. This perhaps helps to explain the power he wields in this narra-

tive. Menelaus lives up to his wicked reputation and, after stealing some golden vessels from the temple, gives them to Andronicus (v. 32). He also sells some along the way, but we are not told what he did with the money.

Onias III, still in exile in Syria, denounces Menelaus' actions and implicates Andronicus in the deed—the one who is acting in the place of the king! Onias, realizing the seriousness of his accusations, takes refuge in a sanctuary, albeit a Greek one. (Jerusalem, the nearest Jewish sanctuary, was inaccessible.) Menelaus and Andronicus conspire, and Andronicus treacherously persuades Onias to leave his place of refuge, whereupon he is immediately killed (v. 35). The author is quick to point out that this terrible deed prompts a response of outrage among both Jews and Gentiles. Even Antiochus is said to have been remorseful and angry over this action. At any rate, by executing Andronicus, Antiochus also removes a possible threat to his own throne. The author points out that the punishment fits the crime.

4:39-50 Menelaus plots evil against his fellow Jews. The scene shifts back to Jerusalem, where Lysimachus, with the connivance of Menelaus, further plunders the temple of its golden vessels. The people begin to riot and are opposed with Hellenistic armed force. In the battle that ensues, the people are victorious and kill the perpetrator near the treasury, where he committed the crime.

The people bring charges against Menelaus. He in turn promises a bribe to the new governor, Dorymenes (v. 45), who promptly intercedes with the king on Menelaus' behalf. Menelaus is acquitted and his accusers are punished instead. Menelaus remains in power, but the reader will have to ask how long it will be before he is punished for his wickedness, especially his crimes against the temple.

5:1-10 Jason dies in exile. Antiochus invades Egypt in 169 and again in 168 B.C.E. The appearance of mysterious horsemen in the sky for forty days indicates that an event of special importance is about to happen. The motif is frequently found in Greek and Roman literature. Here it would be interpreted as a portent that God is about to act. Although the people pray, hoping that the omen will prove to be a favorable one, that is not how the narrative unfolds.

It was not unusual in ancient (or modern) times for people to attempt rebellion upon the death of a sovereign. If Antiochus had actually died, Jason's acts would not take on the character of treason, because there would be no legitimate king. If that were true, it would also imply that Menelaus was no longer the high priest until reconfirmed in office by a subsequent king.

However, Jason's assumptions are incorrect, and Antiochus is very much alive. Before he finds that out, Jason attacks Jerusalem to regain the high priesthood (v. 5). We are not informed of the role of the people in the matter, but Menelaus takes refuge in the citadel. Jason slaughters his fellow citizens, but is unsuccessful in the venture and has to flee for his life. For a time he becomes a man without a country. His first place of refuge is the Transjordan, but there he is called to account by Aretas, the king of the Nabateans. He might have expected to find refuge eventually in Egypt because he was anti-Seleucid at this point, but he does not find a home there. Eventually he takes up residence in Sparta, where he eventually dies and is buried as an exile. Again the punishment fits the crime.

5:11-27 Antiochus IV attacks the Jews. Even though it is doubtful that the majority of people in Jerusalem defended Menelaus or sided with Jason, neither do they seem to have accepted Menelaus as their high priest. To Antiochus this means rebellion, and he moves swiftly to put it down. He is described in somewhat exaggerated terms to underline his ruthlessness and his pride.

The depth of Antiochus' arrogance is demonstrated by his decision to enter the temple precincts, something we know from ancient historians as historically accurate (v. 15). The traitor Menelaus, who should be expected to know and enforce the Jewish law regarding foreigners' being forbidden to enter the temple, instead leads the way and serves as a guide! Antiochus dares to lay his impure hands on sacred vessels and to remove them for his own use. The actions remind the reader of the impious activities of Nebuchadnezzar and Belshazzar in the Book of Daniel.

Antiochus is contrasted with Heliodorus (5:18); the latter was merely on an inspection tour when he was flogged by the mysterious horsemen. Antiochus could have expected much worse treatment for his looting of sacred vessels—had it not been for the sins of the people that led to this event. The appearance of the heavenly horsemen at the beginning of this chapter is now clear: they came to show that God is about to punish his people for the sins connected with Hellenization, especially those committed by Jason, Menelaus, and their followers.

This is not a new biblical theme. Earlier the Assyrians and the Babylonians were described as being the instruments of God's punishment because of the people's sins. Nevertheless, the Assyrian and Babylonian kings often thought that they were acting on their own, as does Antiochus, and eventually they were brought down because of their pride and arrogance. The reader can expect the same fate to befall Antiochus, but that will not happen until chapter 9.

The author makes clear why, despite the theme of divine protection of the temple, Antiochus is successful against the temple and the inhabitants of Jerusalem (vv. 17-20). Divine protection of the temple is conditioned by the people's observance of the law and their fidelity to the covenant relationship. When the broken relationship is restored, the temple will return to its former glory.

Antiochus is described as being so high and mighty that he thinks he can sail on land and walk on the sea (v. 21). When he leaves Jerusalem and Judea, he leaves behind tyrants such as Philip, Andronicus, and Menelaus. The reference to Mount Gerizim (v. 23) means the Samaritans. Perhaps the overbearing attitude of a governor like Philip caused the people to rebel once again; otherwise it is not clear why Antiochus sends Apollonius to punish the people further.

Apollonius deals treacherously with the populace, seeming to be peaceable until the sabbath, when he parades his men through the streets; those who leave the relative safety of their homes to view the parade are then massacred. The reader is now introduced to Judas Maccabeus, who escapes to the wilderness with a few companions (v. 27). The date is probably early 167 B.C.E. There is no suggestion in 2 Maccabees that Judas does not observe the sabbath (contrary to what 1 Maccabees states). Here there is only a brief mention of Judas, but the keen reader will remember that Judas is waiting in the wings for his day of vengeance on the Hellenists. For now the deliverance of the people remains in the future. Things will get worse before they get better.

6:1-5 Antiochus profanes the temple. Antiochus III had granted the Jews freedom to worship in their own manner and according to their own law. Antiochus IV in effect now abrogates the earlier decree. Although it is not clear exactly what Antiochus has in mind, it is clear that the Jews are no longer free to worship as they wish. The first change is profaning the temple and dedicating it to Zeus, the head of the Greek pantheon. Introducing prostitution into the temple precincts would recall for the Jews their past history when sacred prostitution, an important part of Canaanite ritual, was introduced into the temple despite the repeated condemnation of the prophets. Because it was considered to be one of the reasons for the downfall of Jerusalem in 587 B.C.E., verses 4-5 would have special meaning for the Jewish people.

6:6-11 Antiochus proscribes Jewish practices. The next changes are prohibitions regarding the celebration of the sabbath and Jewish feasts. Then the Jews are forced to observe Hellenistic customs relating to the monthly celebration of the king's birthday and participation in Dionysiac processions. These decrees are adopted by other cities in the area as well. According to verse 10, circumcision is outlawed, and two women who have circumcised their sons are killed. Those hiding in caves are burned to death because they do not defend themselves on a sabbath.

6:12-17 A theology of persecution. The reader was advised earlier that the reason for the ills that befell Jerusalem and the people was that the people had sinned by engaging in various Hellenizing activities. The author now explains that the punishment was not meant to be destructive but corrective, like a parent disciplining a child. In effect, the author states that God gives other nations enough rope to hang themselves; with Israel, God punishes them before they reach the fullness of their sinfulness so that they can then experience God's mercy. The assertion that God does not abandon the covenanted people is found throughout Jewish tradition.

6:18-31 Eleazar becomes a martyr. The narrative now includes a typical account of a martyr's death. These verses describe Eleazar's joyful acceptance of death rather than doing anything—even something trivial—against God's will, the dialogue between the person and the tormentors, his sufferings, his perseverance to death, and the reactions of the tormentors.

There may be an implied contrast between the Eleazar of 2 Maccabees and the Mattathias of 1 Maccabees. Both are priests, and both assess the persecution for its true intent. But whereas Mattathias defies the king's orders and defends the right to observe Torah, Eleazar refuses to violate the law and instead goes to his death. (There are also interesting parallels between this story of Eleazar and that of Socrates.)

In the course of the narrative, Eleazar seems to believe that judgment or punishment takes place after death (v. 26), but he does not mention a resurrection of the body. Besides keeping his integrity before the Lord, Eleazar hopes that his witness will provide a helpful example to youth. The next episode in the narrative demonstrates youth's response to Eleazar's wish.

7:1-42 Seven youths and their mothers become martyrs. This narrative is skillfully written, with each character providing another element of the theological argument in favor of martyrdom. The number seven, in Jewish tradition, symbolizes perfection; accordingly, the reader may look upon this as a "perfect" family. The story, despite its gruesome details, is meant to edify. It underlines the premise that observance of the law is more important than life itself. The presence of the king adds further import to the story.

Each of the seven sons presents a part of the theological argument: (1) it is better to die than to transgress the law; (2) the king may take their lives, but God will raise them up again; (3) the king may dismember them, but God will restore their limbs; (4) they will be restored to life, but the king will not be restored; (5) God will not forsake the people but will torment the king and his nation; (6) they are suffering because they have sinned as a people.

The mother exhorts her sons to remain faithful by recalling for them God's power to create and to restore life (v. 23). When the king intercedes on behalf of the youngest boy, the mother returns to the theme of God's creation and re-creation, arguing that if God can make the whole universe and humanity out of nothing God can also restore life. The last son then sums up all the preceding arguments, adding a new one at the same time: the martyrs' deaths play a role in bringing to an end the divine discipline that the people are undergoing. Martyrdom makes a difference in the life of the people. In the end the mother also becomes a martyr. Eleazar's example has been followed, and it is time to move on in the narrative to demonstrate the effects of the martyrdoms.

B. Restoration

2 Macc 8:1–10:9

In rapid succession Judas Maccabeus defeats an important adversary, Antiochus IV dies a horrible death, and the people purify the temple and Jerusalem. God brings this about, partly because of the faithful witness of the martyrs. The text moves from the assault of evil to its elimination.

8:1-36 Judas defeats Nicanor. We are at the midpoint of the book. The narrative again is skillfully written; the author does not give many details of the battle in order to highlight his theological emphases: God's help in achieving the victory, the disposal of the booty, and Nicanor's fate.

Judas first gathers associates and prays to God, asking for God's favor on the people, their temple, their city, and the blood of the martyrs (vv. 2-3). Verse 5 makes it clear that the tide has turned—God's anger has changed to mercy. The Gentiles and Hellenizers will be helpless now. Judas attacks cities of the Hellenizers and gains a reputation that attracts the attention of Philip, the commissioner in Jerusalem. He contacts Ptolemy, the son of Dorymenes (4:45) and the governor of the area, requesting assistance. Ptolemy in turn sends Nicanor, a skilled general and trusted official of the royal court, to put down Judas' rebellion.

According to 2 Maccabees, the Seleucids still owe considerable tribute to the Romans, dating from an agreement in 190 B.C.E. (It is possible that the tribute had been paid in full by 173 B.C.E., and that the author of 2 Maccabees is mistaken.) At any rate, Nicanor plans to raise money by selling the Jewish populace into slavery (v. 10). Although in 1

Maccabees the slave-traders take the initiative and follow Nicanor's army like vultures, in this narrative Nicanor invites them because he is presumptuous about a victory over the Jews.

Although some of Judas' troops desert at the advance of the enemy army, the rest prepare for battle. Selling whatever property that is left, they show their determination and make themselves less vulnerable to later reprisals. Judas sums up their theological position before the battle succinctly: the Gentiles trust in weapons and strategy, whereas the Jews simply trust in an all-powerful God (v. 18). He further recalls the famous defeat of Sennacherib (recounted in many places in the Old Testament; see, for example, 2 Kgs 19:35-36) and another battle not known from existing sources—both of which demonstrate what happens when the people trust in God rather than in themselves.

The battle is described in a single verse (v. 24), but the accumulation and distribution of booty receive more attention. First of all, scrupulously observing the sabbath, Judas' men do not pursue the enemy as far as they might have otherwise. After observing the sabbath, they distribute the booty not only to the soldiers who had participated in the battle (as was the custom) but also to the widows, orphans, and those who had been tormented (perhaps referring to the surviving members of the martyrs' families). Taking care of the widows and orphans is a key responsibility in the law.

Those who persecuted the people receive their deserved punishments: those who set fire to the temple gates are themselves destroyed by fire; Nicanor, who sought to enslave the people, flees the country dressed like a runaway slave. Verse 35 describes his defeat with sarcasm: he was "eminently successful"—in destroying his own army! He who had promised to enslave the Jews has to acknowledge them as champions instead—because of their observance of the law. The tide has clearly turned.

9:1-19 God punishes Antiochus IV. This narrative follows the typical story about the death of those who set themselves against God, especially with arrogance. The description of the death of Antiochus IV at this point in the narrative differs somewhat from that in chapter 1, but its development and details enable the author to make the appropriate points that fit the overall theology of the book.

Although there is no way of confirming the story that Antiochus attempted to despoil a temple in Persepolis, such an action would not be out of character for this family. As he heads home in disgrace after his unsuccessful raid on the Persian temple (vv. 1-3), he learns of Nicanor's defeat and plans to achieve a definitive victory against the Jewish people. He drives his chariot with determination, but God's condemnation rides with him (v. 4)! He is struck down with a terrible malady, experiencing great pains in his bowels (again the punishment fits the crime). That does not deter him from his plans against God's people, but then he is thrown from his chariot, suffering racking pain throughout his body. Like Heliodorus, despite his great pride and arrogance, he is ignominiously carried away on a stretcher, helpless. His condition worsens with the onslaught of worms and putrefaction. The turning point is described in verse 11: he begins a personal transformation from arrogance to understanding. From this point of the narrative on, it is difficult to verify the historicity of his deathbed conversion. It fits the author's theme well, however, and may be primarily a theological write-up.

What happens next is ironic: Antiochus makes vows to God and writes a surprisingly cordial letter to the Jewish people. However, God will no longer have mercy on him (v. 13). In the end he remains, in the mind of the author, a "murderer and a blasphemer" (v. 28). It is possible to read verses 14-27 as the feeble attempts of Antiochus IV to reverse the inevitable end he is fast approaching. In turn, he promises to set Jerusalem free (despite earlier threats to turn it into a graveyard); to give the Jews full-citizen status (despite earlier judgments that they are not even worth burying); to donate to the temple and restore what had been stolen (despite earlier thefts); and even to become a Jew himself (v. 17)! Like Heliodorus, he is also willing to proclaim the power of God to all. Again, the judgment that frames this part of the narrative is repeated: his promises do not bring any relief from his suffering (v. 18).

Antiochus then composes a supplicating letter to the Jews (vv. 19-27). Jewish gloating over the hideous details of his suffering perhaps gives way to laughter at the words that are said to come from his hand. He addresses them as "esteemed citizens," sends them "hearty greetings and best wishes." Piously he asserts that his hopes lie in heaven (which the reader knows has already condemned him and which will not relent). He tends to gloss over details of his terrible illness, which the reader already knows is serious and nearly unbearable. He speaks of hope for recovery, but commends his son, who, he suggests, will treat the Jews "with mildness and kindness"! Another possible purpose of the letter is to make clear to the reader that the problems Antiochus faces are of his own making. The Jews are good citizens, reliable people who can be trusted.

Antiochus is trying to ingratiate himself with the Jews, according to the letter, and is also attempting to arrange for his successor. According to 1 Maccabees, his son, Antiochus V, was only a boy at this time. Antiochus designated Philip as regent, but Lysias assumed the regency in opposition to Philip (1 Macc 6:12-17).

Antiochus dies in the mountains on foreign soil, while Judas and his associates celebrate in Jerusalem. The archenemy of the temple has been disposed of.

10:1-9 Purification of temple and city. The purification of the temple becomes a symbol of God's mercy, signaling that the period of God's wrath has clearly come to an end. The purification is possible only because of God's help; the providential nature of the action is also alluded to by the notice that the purification takes place on the very anniversary of its defilement.

After restoring the furniture of the temple (v. 3), Judas and his followers pray to God, asking that any future punishment for their sins come directly from God rather than through the mediation of a foreign enemy. Again, the rededication of the temple is compared with the feast of Booths.

This entire section comes to an end in verse 9 with the notification that "such was the end of Antiochus."

PART III: DEFENSE OF THE TEMPLE

2 Macc 10:10-15:36

A. Events Under Antiochus V

2 Macc 10:10-13:26

10:10-13 Lysias becomes commander-in-chief. Although the narrative states that Antiochus V put Lysias in charge of the government and the military, it would be more accurate to say that Lysias made the boy Antiochus king. The first activity under the new regime consists of accusations of treason against Ptolemy Macron, who had treated the Jews with fairness. This possible ally commits suicide. Thus the first section of this narrative opens on an ominous note. The reader will learn that the problems with Hellenization are not over; the temple needs to be defended by Judas and his associates.

10:14-23 Victory over the Idumeans. The Idumeans are harassing the Jews and welcoming fugitives (Hellenizers) from Jerusalem. Responding to these provocations, Judas and his forces attack the Idumeans successfully. When the survivors withdraw to two large towers, Judas leaves some lieutenants, including at least one of his brothers, in charge of besieging the towers. The author of 2 Maccabees dares to write what would not be found in 1 Maccabees: some of Simon Maccabeus' men accept a bribe and commit treason. Judas returns, puts them to death, and successfully completes the siege of the towers.

10:24-38 Judas defeats Timothy. When Timothy approaches Judea with a large force, Judas and his followers pray, as is their custom, before advancing to meet the enemy. After Timothy's forces are overcome, he flees to a stronghold called Gazara (v. 32), which is promptly besieged by Judas. The defenders blaspheme with impunity because of their reliance on the strength of the fortress. Eventually, however, Judas and his associates overcome their resistance and kill Timothy. (However, a Timothy will reappear [see 12:10-25] and fight Judas once again. Presumably it is a different Timothy.) Judas' troops praise and thank God for the victory.

11:1-12 Judas defeats Lysias. The previous attacks were primarily local skirmishes, but now Judas and the main minister of the kingdom engage in battle. Lysias has three ob-jectives in mind in his expedition against Judas: (1) to make Jerusalem a Hellenistic settlement, (2) to levy a tribute or tax against the temple, and (3) to continue to sell the high priesthood to the highest bidder. Although none of this is new in the Maccabean books, at this point in the narrative it demonstrates that the problems of the faithful are far from being over.

Lysias makes the same mistake as his Seleucid predecessors did: he relies on his military might and does not take God's power into consideration. When he begins to besiege Beth-zur, Judas goes to its defense, after having prayed for an angel to help the Jews. He barely leaves Jerusalem when a mysterious horseman appears at the head of the army (v. 8), encouraging Judas' forces. Needless to say, they are once again victorious, and Lysias escapes in shame.

11:13-38 Peace with the Syrians. There follow four letters that purport to give the terms of the treaty arranged between Lysias and the Jewish people (vv. 17-21; 22-26; 27-33; and 34-38). According to the dates given in the letters, three of them are from the reign of Antiochus IV, and only the second letter is from the time of Antiochus V. All the letters may be authentic. Their order and placement at this point in the narrative fit the author's objectives. Antiochus IV was the archenemy of the temple and of the Jews. Conciliatory correspondence is not to be attributed to him but will fit his son's reign.

The intent of the earlier correspondence may have been to undermine Judas' rebellion. The letters might be addressed to the Hellenizing party and those Jews (probably a majority) who had not yet allied themselves with the Maccabees.

The second letter (vv. 22-26), which may be from Antiochus V, is particularly conciliatory. If it is authentic, the reader will wonder what happened in the meantime to break the truce. Perhaps it was the activities of Judas Maccabeus.

The third letter (vv. 27-33) grants a kind of amnesty to those who had rebelled against the proscription of Jewish practices and the forcing of Hellenistic ways. The letter says they acted out of ignorance; the king is clearly not apologizing for the Hellenization process. The reader may wonder whether the recipients of the letter were reassured by the return of

Menelaus, the high priest who was not of a priestly family and who had purchased the office.

The fourth letter (vv. 34-38) is the earliest evidence we have of relations between the Romans and the Jews.

12:1-37 Renewal of hostilities. Although 2 Maccabees goes to great lengths to insist that the Jews want to live in peace, hostilities between the Syrian government and the Jewish people resume. The problems are said to have been caused by some of the local governors and some of the Jews' neighbors. Some of their neighbors may have been fearful that the Maccabean revolt might spread.

The people of Joppa (near present-day Tel Aviv) deceitfully invite some of the Jews for a boat ride and murder them (vv. 3-4). Judas' response is quick and decisive. Although he does not have access to the city itself during his night attack, he destroys the port and boats that are outside the city walls. The people of Jamnia are reported to be considering a similar stratagem, and Judas deals with them in the same way.

The attack by Arabs (12:10-12) is probably geographically displaced. With the help of God once again, Judas is victorious. The battle against Caspin (vv. 13-16) involves themes encountered elsewhere in the book. The inhabitants, relying on the supposed strength of their fortifications, blaspheme. Judas, with the help of God similar to that experienced by Joshua in the battle for Jericho (see Josh 6), overcomes their resistance. A terrible slaughter follows. From this point on, Judas takes the initiative, moving from a defensive to an offensive strategy.

Judas next marches into the Transjordan in search of a certain Timothy, presumably a Syrian military commander (vv. 17-18), but finds that Timothy has already departed from the area. Two of Judas' commanders attack the garrison that Timothy left behind and successfully overcome it (vv. 19-20). Judas continues his pursuit of Timothy, who is accompanied by a large force, and eventually engages him. Once again, despite their overwhelming numerical superiority, the Syrians encounter a mysterious being ("the Allseeing") and flee. Predictably, Judas follows up the rout with slaughter, but Timothy bargains for his freedom and escapes (v. 24).

Judas next marches against Karnion, Ephron, and Scythopolis. The Jews living in the last city testify to their good relations with the citizens of that town, and Judas spares the town (vv. 26-31).

Judas and his soldiers go to Jerusalem for the feast of Pentecost, or feast of Weeks, as it is called in the Hebrew Bible. Afterward they once again take the initiative and march off in search of Gorgias, the governor of Idumea, to the south of Jerusalem. They encounter Gorgias and his army, and a fierce battle ensues. Gorgias escapes capture through the agency of a Thracian mercenary and flees to an Idumean town, Marisa (v. 35). Judas rallies his troops by raising a Hebrew battle cry, perhaps from one of the psalms, and they put the Syrians to flight. Judas retires to a nearby town not far from Marisa, but far enough not to be surprised by an attack on the sabbath. He and his troops purify themselves there and observe the sabbath.

12:38-46 Atonement for the dead. On the day after the sabbath, Judas and his associates prepare to bury those who fell in battle. However, they find forbidden amulets in the clothes of each who died in battle. Whether they wore the amulets because they believed they had special protective qualities or whether they had simply been part of the booty taken during the battle, either action was against the law. The judgment is made that they died because of their sins. This incident resembles the battle at Ai recorded in Josh 7.

The occasion is used to warn the living to avoid such a sin in the future. Judas and his troops pray that the sinful deed be removed, perhaps so that the community would not suffer any further setbacks. However, he then collects money to underwrite an expiatory sacrifice on behalf of those who died in their sins (v. 43). According to the author, Judas was thinking of the resurrection of the dead. Presumably this means that he was praying so that, released from their sins, they would enjoy the rewards of the resurrection with all those who fought on behalf of the Jewish cause.

13:1-2 The Syrians invade Judea again. In the autumn of 163 B.C.E., not quite a year after the rededication of the temple, Antiochus V and Lysias invaded Judea with a very large, well-equipped army. The king was about twelve years old at this time; presumably the invasion was due to complaints about Judas' attacks on the citadel and other offensive activities (see 1 Macc 6:21-27).

13:3-8 The death of Menelaus. With the rededication of the temple under Judas' leadership, Menelaus probably was excluded from functioning as high priest. On the other hand, it is not clear that Antiochus V confirmed him in the high priesthood after the death of his father, Antiochus IV. At any rate, Menelaus wants to return to Jerusalem and resume the privileges of office. God intervenes, and the young king turns against Menelaus (v. 4). The irony in the story is that Menelaus, a leader among the Hellenizers, is executed by the Hellenistic Syrians.

Lysias may have realized that a military solution or a policy of force was not resolving the problems in Judea. He may also have realized that the populace did not consider Menelaus to be fit for the high priesthood because he was not a member of the high priestly family and because of his high-handed manner of carrying out the office. Antiochus V condemns Menelaus to death by asphyxiation. The author of 2 Maccabees once again points out that the punishment fits the crime.

13:9-26 Judas attacks the invading army. Antiochus V is probably unfairly depicted in this narrative, but the Syrian army poses a serious threat to Judea's security. Judas fights on behalf of the country, the temple, and the law. The people prepare for this important battle with prayer, weeping, fasting, and prostrations, in typical Maccabean fashion. Judas moves his troops north of Jerusalem to block access to the city and pitches his camp near Modein, the Maccabean family home (v. 14).

As is often his strategy, Judas attacks at night and begins to rout the Syrians. At dawn he withdraws, and the Seleucid king counterattacks, attempting to draw Judas into battle in another location. Antiochus attacks Beth-zur unsuccessfully, and Judas provides the garrison there with supplies. (According to 1 Macc 6:31, 49-50, Beth-zur capitulated because it did not have adequate supplies. The author of 2 Maccabees overlooks the problems involved and simply presents Judas as a hero in this incident.)

After a second unsuccessful attack, the king turns his attention directly upon Judas. Verse 23 may refer to Antiochus' attack on the temple (1 Macc 6:51-52). But internal affairs of the kingdom turn the king's attention back to Antioch, where Philip is said to have been left in charge and to be in rebellion. This is probably not true, because Antiochus IV had designated Philip to be regent, but Lysias, who had Antiochus V in his care, usurped the office. Antiochus V would hardly have put Philip in charge while he went off to Judea. Philip is simply in rebellion, and the king must return to Syria to defend his throne.

Before he does so, he reaches a truce with the Jews (v. 23). He appoints Judas as military and civil administrator of the territory between Ptolemais (modern Haifa) and the Egyptian border. Not everyone is pleased with the outcome of this expedition (vv. 25-26), but Lysias defends the treaty. However, the opposition to the treaty and the particular circumstances that brought it about may alert the reader that Judas' troubles are not yet over.

B. The Final Defeat of Nicanor

2 Macc 14:1–15:36

14:1-11 Alcimus is antagonistic toward Judas. In 162 or 161 B.C.E., Demetrius, son of Seleucus IV, arrived in Syria to challenge Antiochus for the throne. A change in government could be expected to prompt new requests from the Hellenizing party in Jerusalem. A possible spokesman for this group is Alcimus, who seems to have been appointed high priest by Antiochus V to succeed Menelaus. Once Antiochus was no longer the king, Alcimus would have to be confirmed in office by Demetrius, the new king. 2 Maccabees accuses Alcimus of willfully incurring defilement at the time of the revolt, but no specifics are given.

Alcimus approaches Demetrius with gifts but keeps silent (v. 4). Later when he is invited to a council meeting by the king, he names the Hasideans, led by Judas, as the ones who consistently foment rebellion. (Elsewhere the Hasideans and Judas do not always agree on goals or strategies.) Alcimus objects that they are the ones who keep him from exercising his high priesthood. His speech to the king covers all the rules of Greek rhetoric, including the explanation that his first concern is for the king's interests, and his second, for his people's interests. He gives the king the opportunity to make an independent evaluation of the situation, but at least some of the people attending the meeting heartily agree with Alcimus' assessment of the Judean problem.

14:12-25 Judas and Nicanor. Nicanor, someone familiar with the Judean scene, is sent to kill Judas and restore Alcimus to the temple. Once again, the author makes clear that the violation of the treaty does not come from Judas but from a sinner within the community, in collusion with Syrian authorities. There will be another attack on the temple and its territory. The Gentiles in Judea rally to Nicanor, while the Jews lament and pray for God's help. Judas takes the initiative and decides to encounter Nicanor, but, after a brief skirmish, Nicanor (perhaps like Lysias on an earlier occasion) opts for a non-military solution to the problem. Working first through emissaries, the two leaders finally meet and agree to a truce.

At this point something curious occurs in the narrative. Nicanor moves to Jerusalem, where he behaves quite appropriately. He develops a fondness for Judas and keeps him in his company (vv. 23-24). Judas even follows Nicanor's suggestions, marries, and settles down. Although 1 Maccabees presents Nicanor as a crafty, untrustworthy foe, 2 Maccabees first describes him as fond of Judas, and only later does he become untrustworthy and dangerous.

14:26-36 Alcimus plots against Judas. Naturally Alcimus is not pleased with the progress of events. Taking a copy of the agreement between Nicanor and Judas, Alcimus goes directly to Demetrius and tries to convince the king that Nicanor and Judas are plotting against the throne. The king is understandably angry, but rather than accuse Nicanor of treason, he simply demands that he capture Judas and transport him to Antioch.

This puts Nicanor in a difficult position, and he wrestles with the dilemma long enough for Judas to realize that something amiss is developing. He gathers some associates and escapes (v. 30). Nicanor becomes very angry that Judas has outwitted him and at the same time put him in a very difficult position with his king. Ignoring the right of sanctuary, Nicanor looks for Judas in the temple

precincts and, not finding him there, raises his right hand and his voice against the temple, threatening it with destruction. The reader, remembering the opening chapters of this book and the story line to this point, can readily anticipate the outcome of Nicanor's threats.

14:37-46 The story of Razis. Razis, a man of important standing in the community, becomes Nicanor's next intended victim. Despite his status in the community and his reputation as one who stood up to earlier persecution, the reason why he is singled out is not clear. Perhaps Nicanor suspects that Razis knows where Judas is to be found. Although he sends a sizable force to arrest Razis, the effort fails because Razis commits suicide rather than allowing himself to be taken (v. 4). (He may have done so to avoid revealing under torture where Judas was hiding.) Although suicide was not common in ancient Judaism, neither was it unknown (see 2 Sam 17:23). Seemingly, it was not considered sinful, and in desperate situations might have been thought of as morally allowable. In this narrative, Razis' defiance of Nicanor fits the tenor of these chapters, despite the gruesome details.

15:1-5 Nicanor blasphemes against the sabbath. The reader learns that Judas has escaped to Samaria. Nicanor decides to attack on the sabbath, but some Jews in his party plead with him not to act like a barbarian but to respect this day of rest. His answer is filled with arrogance, implying that the one who decreed the sabbath should keep to heaven while Nicanor is ruler on earth. In effect, Nicanor has challenged the God of Israel. Such arrogance is a prime target for God's punishment.

15:6-16 Onias III and Jeremiah appear to Judas in a dream. Judas, meanwhile, rallies his troops in a way reminiscent of the holy war, while adding the story of a dream he had in which Onias III, a respected former high priest, appeared praying for the Jewish community. When another figure also appeared, Onias introduced him to Judas as the great prophet Jeremiah, who also was praying for the people and Jerusalem. Jeremiah gave Judas a golden sword, in accordance with his frequent threats of sending a sword against Israel or its enemies (see Jer 50:35-37, for example). The sword comes from God, he says, and with it Judas would destroy his enemies. This is a familiar motif in ancient literature; the offer of the special weapons gives divine assurance of ultimate victory.

15:17-35 Defeat of Nicanor. With such backing the Jewish forces decide to attack the enemy, primarily to defend the city, the temple, and its sacred vessels. In reality they are also concerned about the Hellenizing party's gaining control once again over Jerusalem and the temple. In proximate preparation for the decisive battle, Judas prays for divine help, reminding God of the defeat of Sennacherib by Hezekiah (2 Kgs 18:13–19:35; Isa 36–37). Martial music accompanies Nicanor's troops; liturgical prayer accompanies Judah's (vv. 25-26). The Jews fight the enemy with hands and hearts, and they are once again victorious, with God's help. Gloating over the dead Nicanor follows; his head and right arm are displayed opposite the temple, against

which he had risen both in defiance and blasphemy.

The narrative ends with the celebration of a festival in honor of Nicanor's defeat, similar to the feast of Purim or Mordecai's Day.

EPILOGUE

2 Macc 15:37-39

The epilogue matches the preface. Despite the subject matter, the author states his intention: to delight the ears of the readers. The author, who consistently has argued that the main problems arose within the Jewish community rather than from the Gentiles, ends his book in fairly typical Hellenistic fashion, demonstrating how far the Hellenization process had developed by the time the book was written.

ISAIAH

John J. Collins

INTRODUCTION

The Book of Isaiah presents in a particularly acute way two problems that confront the Christian interpreter of the Old Testament. The first concerns the discrepancy between the surface impression of the text and modern critical reconstructions of its history and meaning. Christian tradition, like Jewish tradition, long regarded the entire book as the work of a single prophet, Isaiah of Jerusalem. Critical scholarship, however, has taught us to distinguish First Isaiah (chs. 1–39), Second Isaiah (chs. 40–55) and Third Isaiah (chs. 56–66). Second and Third Isaiah are now dated to the late sixth century B.C.E., two hundred years after Isaiah of Jerusalem. Moreover, it now appears that less than half of First Isaiah actually contains words of the prophet himself. The remainder was added by anonymous scribes over several hundred years. Jewish legend had it that the prophet Isaiah met his death by being sawn asunder during the reign of the impious King Manasseh. Some conservative Christians have felt that his book has suffered a like fate at the hands of the critics.

The second problem concerns the Christological interpretation of the Old Testament. The Book of Isaiah has been treasured by Christians because it seems to predict crucial elements in the life of Jesus; the most striking examples are the virgin birth in Isa 7 and the passion and death in Isa 53. The book is cited or alluded to more than three hundred times in the New Testament. Jesus himself claimed to fulfill a text from Isaiah (61:1–2) in his sermon at Nazareth (Luke 4:18). Yet, critical scholarship has insisted that we must first understand the biblical texts in their own historical context. Isaiah had a message for the people of his own time, and this message did not require foreknowledge of events that would happen several hundred years later. The use of Isaiah by the Gospel writers tells us about the faith of the early Christians rather than the prophet's own message.

Critical scholarship, then, has cast doubt on the unity of the Book of Isaiah and on the Christian belief that it predicts Christ. Both these points have been shocking for Christians, although the shock has worn off, except in very conservative circles. Yet, the critical approach to the Bible should not be seen as a negative development. It has enriched our understanding of the Scriptures by showing how "the word of the Lord" is rooted in and speaks to concrete historical situations. The Bible is not a book of dogmatic propositions to be learned and believed, but a moving illustration of the faith of a people in ever-changing circumstances. If we know how an oracle conveyed its message in its original setting, we then have a guide to the way it should be understood in other settings. We cannot fully appreciate Matthew's use of the Immanuel prophecy (Matt 1:23) unless we understand the message Isaiah was delivering to King Ahaz when he originally spoke it (Isa 7:10–17).

For those who have mastered it, historical criticism has been a tremendously liberating force, for it has brought to light many aspects of biblical faith that had been submerged by the dogmatic theology of a later age. We now recognize, however, that a purely historical approach is also limited. In the case of Isaiah, we simply do not know the historical setting of some oracles, or we know it only in a very general way. Besides, the power of some passages lies in the fact that they transcend their original situations; they express fundamental hopes, fears, or insights that are applicable in recurring situations. The great messianic prophecies of Isaiah fall into this category. A passage like Isa 11, which dreams of a day when the wolf will lie down with the lamb, articulates a universal yearning for peace that is not peculiar to any historical situation. In this commentary we will try to do justice both to the historical particularity and to the universality of Isaiah's prophecies.

The composition of the book

Fundamental to the critical understanding of Isaiah is the insight that chapters 40–66 cannot be the work of Isaiah of Jerusalem but come from a much later time. Not only do these chapters *predict* the restoration of Jerusalem after the Babylonian Exile, but they *presuppose* the Exile itself. Second Isaiah *presupposes* that the Exile is already at an end. Third Isaiah (chs. 56–66) *presupposes* that the Jewish community has already returned to Judea. The issue, then, is not whether the prophet Isaiah could have predicted events of a much later time; the fact that the later events are presupposed is a sure indication of the time when these chapters were written.

Even within First Isaiah there is much material that was added later. Chapters 13–23 consist of oracles against various nations. Only a few passages in these chapters (for example, ch. 20) are likely to have come from the time of Isaiah himself. Chapters 24–27 constitute the so-called "Apocalypse of Isaiah." These chapters are no earlier than the Babylonian Exile and may even be later than Third Isaiah. Chapters 34–35 come from the sixth century, about the time of Second Isaiah. Finally, chapters 36–39 are taken, with very little modification, from 2 Kgs 18–20. The original oracles of Isaiah are found primarily in chapters 1–12 and 28–33 (plus a few passages in chapters 13–23). Even these chapters have come to us through the hands of editors who left their mark by the arrangement of the material and by minor insertions. (Most of the editorial work can be placed after the Exile,

but some may have been associated with the reform of King Josiah in 621 B.C.E.) The Book of Isaiah, then, is not a monograph by an individual author but the collection of an ongoing tradition that spanned more than two hundred years.

The prophet Isaiah

At the origin of this tradition stands Isaiah of Jerusalem. The superscription in Isa 1:1 tells us that he prophesied "in the days of Uzziah, Jotham, Ahaz and Hezekiah, kings of Judah." The great vision in chapter 6, which is usually thought to mark the beginning of his prophetic activity, is dated to the year of Uzziah's death, probably 742 B.C.E. We know that he was active late in Hezekiah's reign at the time of an Assyrian invasion in 701 B.C.E. (described in Isa 36–38). His career, then, spanned roughly the second half of the eighth century B.C.E. His contemporaries included the prophets Amos, Hosea, and Micah.

Isaiah's career was marked by a series of crises caused by the military encroachment of the great superpower of the East, Assyria. The first great crisis, in the years 735–733 B.C.E., was the Syro-Ephraimite war. Syria joined forces with the northern kingdom of Israel (Ephraim) to form an alliance against the Assyrians. When King Ahaz of Judah refused to join, they mounted a campaign against him with a view to deposing him and installing a more cooperative king. This was the occasion of Isaiah's famous Immanuel prophecy. Ahaz appealed to Assyria for help. In 733 B.C.E. Samaria, the capital of northern Israel, was forced to submit. Ahaz remained king in Jerusalem as a subject of Assyria.

The next great crisis came about a decade later. The northern kingdom of Israel rebelled against Assyria, and in 722 B.C.E. Samaria was destroyed. Its population was deported and foreign settlers were brought in. The northern kingdom of Israel ceased to exist. This catastrophe may be prophesied in Isa 28:1-4.

Judah was again in danger in 713 B.C.E., when the Philistine city of Ashdod rebelled against the Assyrians. Isa 20 records the activity of Isaiah on this occasion.

Finally, in 701 B.C.E., Hezekiah of Judah revolted and provoked the famous campaign of Sennacherib. Most of the southern kingdom was ravaged. The Assyrian king boasted that he shut up Hezekiah in Jerusalem "like a bird in a cage." Yet Jerusalem was not destroyed, and Hezekiah remained on the throne. The prose account in Isa 36–38 attributes the deliverance of Jerusalem to "the angel of the Lord" (37:36).

This succession of crises plays some part in the ordering of the material in First Isaiah. Chapters 6–8, which are widely thought to be a memoir from Isaiah himself (see 8:16), clearly belong to the early period. Some material in chapters 10–23 can be attributed to the middle period, between 722 and 701 B.C.E. The oracles in chapters 28–32 relate to the time of Sennacherib. Some scholars think that the oracles in chapters 2–5, which deal primarily with social abuses, belong to the earliest period of the prophet's activity, before the Syro-Ephraimite war, at a time when Amos was making similar charges in northern Israel, but there is no clear evidence of their date.

The politics of Isaiah

Isaiah's preaching is directly concerned with the events of the day. He denounces the luxury of those who join house to house and field to field and of the women who parade in jewelry. His ideal seems to be the simple way of life in which people can live on curds and honey, the natural produce of the land. He does not see the loss of the vineyards—a source of wealth and luxury—as a great catastrophe. He certainly does not urge his people to fight to defend them; rather, he advocates a quietistic, pacifistic stance in the face of the Assyrian threat.

Isaiah's ideal of social simplicity was not conceived in rustic isolation. He was an urban prophet familiar with the temple (ch. 6). He had access to the king as a kind of political advisor, both in the early days of the Syro-Ephraimite war and in the time of Sennacherib at the end of his career. He was an educated man, as we can see from his mastery of Hebrew verse and from his familiarity with international politics. His social and political vision did not arise from naïveté but from his fundamental theological convictions.

Theological principles

At the heart of Isaiah's prophecy is his vision of God as "the Holy One of Israel," which is presented most vividly in chapter 6. The holiness of God shows up the inherent sinfulness of humanity. The power of the spirit contrasts with the powerless flesh (Isa 31). The emphasis on God's holiness is rooted in the praise of God's glory in the temple cult (compare Psalms 29, 93, 96–99). For Isaiah, the exaltation of God is the corollary of human finitude. Human pretensions to power are pathetic and doomed to failure. Consequently, Isaiah is very critical of the attempts of the Judean kings to play power politics or even to control their own destinies. He is in conflict with the sages, the professional advisers of the king, whose plans are overridden by the "plan of the Holy One of Israel" (5:19).

The central demand of Isaiah is for faith in this God. "Unless your faith is firm," he tells Ahaz, "you shall not be firm!" (7:9). Faith here means trust and reliance on God rather than on one's own resources. The context for this faith is provided by the royal ideology of the Davidic house. The divine charter of the dynasty is provided by the oracle of Nathan to David, recorded in 2 Sam 7. There the Lord promises David:

> I will establish a house for you. . . . I will raise up your heir after you, sprung from your loins, and I will make his kingdom firm. . . . And I will make his royal throne firm forever. I will be a father to him, and he shall be a son to me. And if he does wrong, I will correct him with the rod of men and with human chastisements; but I will not withdraw my favor from him as I withdrew it from your predecessor Saul, whom I removed from my presence. Your house and your kingdom shall endure forever before me; your throne shall stand firm forever (2 Sam 7:11-16).

One of the terms used to express the "firmness" of the dynasty is derived from the same root as the word for "faith."

The promise to David is the basis for a theology of kingship found in the psalms. The essential points are found in Psalm 2. If the kings of the earth rise up against the Lord and "his anointed" (the king), God will laugh at them, for "I myself have set up my king on Zion, my holy mountain" (Ps 2:6). The decree of the Lord is then proclaimed: "You are my son; this day I have begotten you" (Ps 2:7). This special father-son relationship is reaffirmed in Psalm 110, where the king is invited to "Sit at my right hand till I make your enemies your footstool" (Ps 110:1). The king can even be addressed as "God" (Ps 45:7), although he is clearly subordinate to the God who blesses him. The king is hailed as God's representative without reservation.

This glorification of the monarchy presumes certain responsibilities. The king is supposed to act "in the cause of truth and for the sake of justice" (Ps 45:5), to defend the afflicted and crush the oppressor (Ps 72). The whole ideology assumes and demands a very high degree of trust and reverence for the kingship (compare also Pss 89, 132).

Trust in the kingship goes hand in hand with trust in Mount Zion, the site of the temple in Jerusalem, as the dwelling place of God. Later Jewish theology might qualify the idea that God actually lived in the temple (1 Kgs 8:27; compare Isa 66:1; Acts 7:48), but Psalm 46 declares that it is "the holy dwelling of the Most High. God is in its midst; it shall not be disturbed" (Ps 46:5-6). The people of Jerusalem need not fear, "though the earth be shaken," because "the Lord of hosts is with [them]" (Ps 46:3, 8; compare Psalm 48). The worshiper in the temple could hope to see God's power and glory (see Ps 63:3), as indeed Isaiah does (Isa 6). The rhetoric of the temple worship, then, proclaims that the people need fear no adversary, because they have God's presence in their temple and God's support for their king.

This theology of kingship and temple provides the context for Isaiah's faith. (Unlike his contemporaries Amos and Hosea, Isaiah does not draw upon the tradition of the Exodus.) Isaiah demands that king and people alike live by the faith they profess. But this was not so easy when the Assyrian army was at the door. Isaiah is not so naive as to think that God will obligingly protect the people from all harm. He recognizes the extent of the suffering and destruction that will be inflicted, but he insists that life will go on. God will leave the people a remnant.

This theme of Isaiah's message, proclaimed in the name of his son Shear-jashub ("A remnant shall return," 7:3), is at once both good news and bad news. The remnant will ensure the survival of the people, but only after widespread destruction; it will be like the survival of a stump when a tree has been cut down. From this stump will come an ideal ruler in a future time (ch. 11), and Mount Zion will be exalted as a center for all peoples in days to come (ch. 2).

The ideal king and ideal temple are future ideals for Isaiah. They highlight the shortcomings of the present rulers and present cult. Isaiah affirms his faith in the royal theology but prevents it from serving as political propaganda for the kings of his day.

The political theology of Isaiah uses the popular traditions in an ironic way. The irony is best captured in the symbolic name Immanuel. "God is with us" was the professed faith of the Davidic line. For Isaiah, however, this is not a guarantee of easy salvation. The presence of God can be mediated by the sword of the Assyrian, the rod of Yahweh's anger (10:5). Salvation, for Isaiah, is not identical with wealth and prosperity, but with the purified worship of God. The people might, ironically, be better off when reduced to a remnant, stripped of their vineyards and forced to rely on curds and honey like the first Israelites.

Isaiah's quietistic stance goes hand in hand with his social criticism. The people who tried to survive by alliances with Egypt or who relied on horses, the armaments of their day (Isa 31), were the same people who joined house to house and field to field and got drunk on the produce of their vineyards. These were the people who stood to gain from national independence, who had something to fight for. Ironically, Judah and Israel were vulnerable to Assyrian greed because they had a measure of wealth and luxury. If they lived the simpler life, without wealth or power, they would be left in peace. The ideal kingdom sketched in Isa 11 is not a powerful empire, but one of peace and simplicity.

We can appreciate why the early Christians saw correspondences between Isaiah's prophecies and the kingdom proclaimed by Jesus. Two thousand years later Isaiah's political ideals have lost none of their relevance to the issues of international politics and the welfare of society.

Second Isaiah

The prophet we know as Second Isaiah worked in a very different situation. In the early years of the sixth century B.C.E., the kingdom of Judah had finally collapsed. In 586 B.C.E. Jerusalem was destroyed by the Babylonians. King Zedekiah had seen his sons slain before his eyes and was then blinded and taken in fetters to Babylon with the leaders of his people. The Jewish people were decimated, and the survivors humiliated. Some Jews saw this catastrophe as a punishment for their sins, but many must have wondered whether their God enjoyed any control over the course of events at all.

Then hope came from an unexpected quarter. The Persian king Cyrus entered Babylon as conqueror in 539 B.C.E. Within a year he had authorized the Jewish exiles to return home. This decree was consistent with Cyrus' generally tolerant policies toward subject peoples. He presented himself to the Babylonians as a liberator who was granted his triumph by the god of the Babylonians, Marduk. To the Jews he proclaimed that it was the Lord, the God of heaven, who had sent him, and that the Lord had also charged him to rebuild the temple in Jerusalem (so Ezra 1:1-4). Second Isaiah, elated at the unexpected deliverance, gladly proclaimed that Cyrus was the anointed ("messiah") of Yahweh (Isa 45:1).

The oracles of Second Isaiah are written in celebration of this deliverance and attempt to reformulate the faith of Israel in light of it. They consist of short hymnic units. It is not clear whether they have been arranged in a deliberate order. Chapter 40 is certainly an introduction to the collection and establishes several of its main themes. Some scholars find a shift at chapter 49. Chapters 49–55 are somewhat more sober in tone than chapters 40–48. They abandon some characteristic themes of the earlier chapters, such as the polemic against idolatry and disputes with the Babylonians. The later chapters show a strong interest in Zion. The differences, however, do not lead us to suppose that chapters 49–55 have a setting different from that of chapters 40–48. All these oracles were delivered after the rise of Cyrus and before the practical problems of the restoration had become apparent. They were probably written in Babylon.

Four of the short poems that make up Second Isaiah are commonly set apart as the "Servant Songs": Isa 42:1-4; 49:1-6; 50:4-9; 52:13–53:12. These passages are distinguished by their focus on the figure called "the Servant of Yahweh." Scholars of an earlier generation thought that these oracles were the work of a different prophet, but that view is now widely rejected. It is also doubtful whether they even represent a distinct, late stage in the composition of the book, as is sometimes claimed. Rather, they should be seen as an integral part of the collection that makes up Second Isaiah and interpreted in that context.

Theological themes

Second Isaiah, no less than Isaiah of Jerusalem, celebrates the transcendent power of God, before whom all flesh is like grass. He relates this to two distinctive themes.

First, Yahweh, God of Israel, is the Creator of all, the first and last, and there is no God besides Yahweh. Second Isaiah affirms that Yahweh alone is God in a more emphatic manner than any other biblical writer. Earlier biblical writers admit the existence of other gods but forbid the Israelites to worship them. Even Second Isaiah does not deny the existence of Babylonian gods (for example, Bel and Nebo—46:1), but he views them as helpless idols that have no power to save, and so they are in effect "no-gods." The monotheism of Second Isaiah is the basis for his highly sarcastic polemic against the worship of idols. All nations are obligated to serve Yahweh, since Yahweh is Creator of all.

Second, this Creator-God is the redeemer of Israel who buys it back from a state of slavery. This theme is based on the idea that Yahweh is bound to Israel by bonds of kinship. It also goes hand in hand with the prophet's view that the liberation from Babylon is a new Exodus.

The theme of the new Exodus is introduced already in 40:3: "In the desert prepare the way of the Lord!" The prophet is not interested in the Exodus as ancient history but as the myth or paradigm that reveals what God is like in the present. Yahweh is a God who liberates slaves, who overturns the status quo. Yahweh is a hidden God (45:15) whose ways may be obscure for a time but who will then be revealed in unexpected ways.

Undoubtedly the best known theme of Second Isaiah is the portrayal of the figure of the Suffering Servant, especially in the great Servant Song of Isa 53. This passage has attracted much attention because it has traditionally been taken as a prophecy of the passion of Jesus, and indeed it played some part in the early Christian understanding of

Jesus' death. The original significance of this figure for the Jews of the sixth century is still in dispute. The Servant has been identified with a wide range of historical figures from Moses to Zerubbabel (the governor at the time of the restoration and heir to the Davidic throne) or even the prophet himself. More probably, however, the Servant was not a historical individual but an idealized representation of the faithful Jews in exile.

The Servant poems, then, can be read as Second Isaiah's explanation of the Babylonian captivity. The view that the Jews were being punished for their sins is inadequate. They had received double for all their sins (40:2). Rather, their suffering had a positive purpose; they were to serve as a light to the nations. It was the infirmities of the other nations that they bore. Their lives were an offering for the sins of the Gentiles. Second Isaiah believed that the unexpected restoration of the Jews would bring the other nations to their senses and lead them to acknowledge Yahweh as the true God. In this he was disappointed, but the Suffering Servant persisted as a model of piety that has had profound influence on both Jewish and Christian spirituality.

Third Isaiah

Isa 56–66 is closely related to Second Isaiah but comes from a slightly later period, after the exiles had returned to Jerusalem and discovered the harsh realities of the situation. Some of the oracles, especially chapters 60–62, still resound with the enthusiasm of Second Isaiah; other passages, however, attest to deep divisions within the postexilic community and a sense of near desperation on the part of the prophet (chs. 63–66). Yet, out of these circumstances emerged the powerful vision of a new heaven and a new earth (65:17) that would be picked up later by the author of the Book of Revelation in the New Testament. These chapters raise fundamental issues concerning the priorities of a community in difficult times and the nature of true worship.

The so-called "Apocalypse of Isaiah"

The oracles that were inserted into First Isaiah at chapters 24–27 resemble Third Isaiah in their sense of near desperation with the present and desire for a radically different future. They are called "the Apocalypse of Isaiah" because of their heavy reliance on mythological symbols, which is a well-known feature of apocalyptic literature. They are not cast in the particular form of an apocalypse, however, which is a supernatural revelation, usually a vision mediated by an angel (see Dan 7–12). These chapters are prophetic oracles from an unknown prophet. They are often thought to reflect the further deterioration of the postexilic community after the time of Third Isaiah, perhaps about 500 B.C.E. Some scholars put the date much later, even as late as 300 B.C.E.

The difficulty of establishing a firm date for these chapters in itself tells us something about their nature. The heavy reliance on mythical symbols has a generalizing effect. These oracles provide a cluster of metaphors for a recurring type of situation. (This is also true of some of the oracles against the nations in Isa 13–23.) The portrayal of cosmic devastation in Isa 24 is as apt in an age of ecological crisis and nuclear threat as it was at any time in the ancient world. The hope that God "will destroy death forever" and "wipe away the tears from all faces" (25:8) remains the ultimate human aspiration.

Within the Book of Isaiah these chapters form a conclusion to the oracles against the nations by moving away from particular denunciations to more general, cosmic descriptions of judgment and salvation.

The unity of Isaiah

It is easier to show that the various parts of the Book of Isaiah come from different periods than to provide an explanation as to why they were all combined under Isaiah's name. Some scholars are willing to suppose that it was sheer accident, that material copied on a single scroll came to be regarded as a single book. The more plausible suggestion is that the later writers considered themselves part of an Isaianic tradition. Despite the differences between the various sections, there are some basic themes that run throughout. These include:

—the centrality of the holy mountain of Zion;

—a reliance on mythical symbolism to express the hopes (and fears) for the future;

—a yearning for universal peace that involves not only Israel but the right ordering of all nations.

All these themes are related to the cult of the Jerusalem temple. It may be that the continuity of the Isaianic tradition is simply that it is a Jerusalem tradition and that "all the Isaiahs" drew on a tradition of cultic piety. We will find that this is true even when the prophets were sharply critical of current cultic practice, for example in Isa 1 and 66. There are also some indications that later "Isaianic" writers drew motifs and allusions from the earlier Isaianic corpus; for example, the oracle on the vineyard in Isa 27 builds on the "song of the vineyard" in chapter 5. In the "new creation" of Isa 65 the wolf and the lamb will graze together, as in the messianic prophecy of Isa 11.

The fondness for mythical symbolism and ideal representations throughout the Book of Isaiah has lent itself to reinterpretation by subsequent generations. The general character of the messianic prophecies allowed the early Christians to see their fulfillment in Jesus. This classical Christian reinterpretation of Isaiah should not, however, cause us to ignore the fundamental messages of these writings in their historical contexts; nor should it distract us from seeking analogies between the prophet's situation and our own or from asking how his religious ideals can be correlated with our modern problems.

COMMENTARY: FIRST ISAIAH (Isa 1–39)

INTRODUCTORY PROPHECY

Isa 1:1-31

The opening chapter singles out the themes of judgment and salvation, which are characteristic of the whole book. It contains some oracles of the original Isaiah but has been edited as an introduction to the collection of oracles. The editor probably wrote after the fall of Jerusalem in the sixth century B.C.E. His message is simple: Whatever disasters befell Jerusalem are a punishment for infidelity; but if the people repent and are obedient, they will again eat the good things of the land.

1:1 The superscription. The "vision" here refers to the entire revelation of Isaiah, most of which is in verbal form. The prophet's father, Amoz, should not be confused with the prophet Amos, whose career overlapped Isaiah's. The reigns of the kings listed cover most of the second half of the eighth century. If Isaiah's career began in the year of Uzziah's death, the probable dates are 742–701 B.C.E.

1:2-8 Judah devastated. The description of Zion, "left like a hut in a vineyard" (1:8), recalls the boast of the Assyrian king Sennacherib that he had shut up Hezekiah of Judah "like a bird in a cage," and may refer to the same situation in 701 B.C.E. Isaiah, however, does not put the blame on the Assyrians but on the Judeans themselves: "They have forsaken the Lord, spurned the Holy One of Israel" (1:4). The opening line, "Hear, O heavens, and listen, O earth" (1:2), introduces an indictment for breach of covenant in Deut 32:1. In this case, however, there is no appeal to the Sinai covenant or to the Exodus from Egypt. Instead, the prophet appeals to an instinctive natural law: if an ox and ass can know their master, then Israel should know its God and know what is right. The prophet's concern is not merely with the breach of specific laws but with the lack of a proper religious attitude that should inform all of life.

Verse 9 introduces the theme of the remnant. It is a small remnant, ensuring survival, but little more.

1:10-16 An oracle on true worship. This oracle begins with a mention of Sodom and Gomorrah, and is placed here because the same cities are mentioned in verse 9. Sodom and Gomorrah were the cities of the Plain, destroyed by fire from heaven because of their corruption (Gen 19). In verse 9 the analogy was with the total way in which they were destroyed. In verse 10 the Judean leaders are addressed as "princes of Sodom" because they are equally corrupt.

The theme of this oracle is true worship. God professes no pleasure in the constant sacrifice of animals or even with the observance of the new moon and sabbath, because "your hands are full of blood!" (1:15), not only because of the sacrifices but because of the violence of their lives. Isaiah is not opposed to ritual as such. He says they need a ritual of

417

washing to symbolize repentance and purification. Ritual, however, is only as good as the intentions it expresses. What matters is how people treat the widows and orphans, not how often they go to the temple or offer sacrifice. A very similar critique of the cult and plea for justice is found in Amos 5:18-27, also from the eighth century B.C.E.

1:18-20 Call to repentance. This brief insertion has the tone of the law in Deuteronomy and expresses succinctly the message of the editor. Rather than just proclaim judgment or salvation, as the prophet typically does, it sets a goal for repentance and so emphasizes human responsibility. The assumption that obedience ensures prosperity is naive, however, and was sharply criticized in the later biblical tradition, most obviously in the Book of Job but also in Second Isaiah.

1:21-31 Redemption by judgment. The chapter concludes with a threat of punishment for political and social corruption. The main point to note is that the punishment is seen as redemptive, like the refining of metals by fire. Zion will be purified. The experience will be severe, but it is necessary if the cherished claims to justice and faithfulness are to be rendered appropriate.

ORACLES AGAINST JERUSALEM AND JUDAH

Isa 2:1–12:6

These chapters are given a new introduction in 2:1 and gather oracles that are mainly from the early period of Isaiah's activity. We may distinguish the rather general social oracles of chapters 2–5, the memoir of Isaiah in chapters 6–8, the messianic oracles in chapters 9 and 11 (separated by oracles on Samaria and Assyria), and a concluding psalm in chapter 12, which may have marked the conclusion of a distinct collection.

2:2-5 The future of Mount Zion. Verses 2-4 are duplicated almost exactly in Mic 4:1-3. Micah, like Isaiah, was an eighth-century prophet of the southern kingdom. We do not know which prophet, if either, composed this oracle. The prospect of nations streaming to Mount Zion is often related to the pilgrimages of Jewish exiles to Jerusalem in the postexilic period. Even in the pre-exilic period, however,

Mount Zion was considered to be a sacred mountain, the center of the earth, and important for the whole world (see Psalms 46–48).

In the lifetime of Isaiah, King Hezekiah is said to have tried to destroy the "high places" where people worshiped outside of Jerusalem and to centralize the cult (2 Kgs 18; 2 Chr 31). Samaria and the northern kingdom had recently been destroyed, and Hezekiah was trying to rally the survivors to Jerusalem. Isa 2:2-5 would make good sense in this context. The "house of Jacob" that is invited to walk in the light of the Lord (v. 5) certainly includes the northern kingdom of Israel.

This vision of the future of Zion already contains the idea that Israel is a light to the nations, a theme we will meet again in Second Isaiah. The Israelites are not told to go out to convert the nations but to attract them by their worship on Zion. In the ideal world of the future time, all nations will come together to the central city of Jerusalem. Recognition of the claims of Jerusalem is the converse of recognition of Yahweh as sovereign. This recognition and the acceptance of Yahweh's instruction are seen as the keys to world peace, when swords will be beaten into ploughshares.

Whatever the origin of this oracle, it introduces themes we will meet repeatedly in the Book of Isaiah and is in harmony with the great messianic prophecy of Isa 11. We should note that the prophet Joel (Joel 4:10) inverts the great vision of peace and bids the nations beat their ploughshares into swords in anticipation of battle on the day of the Lord. Neither prophecy should be taken as a prediction of the future; both are projections of basic human hopes and fears.

2:6-22 The Day of the Lord. This long oracle begins by giving reasons why God has abandoned the people, the house of Jacob (probably the northern kingdom, which was conquered by the Assyrians in 733 B.C.E. and again decisively in 722 B.C.E.). The offenses include idolatry and pursuit of treasures and armaments. All are symptoms of human pride. In response, God will manifest his majesty "on that day" (v. 11). The "Day of the Lord" is known from a famous passage in Amos 5:18-20. There it appears that most people look forward to the Day of the Lord, but Amos says that it will be "darkness and not light." Most probably it was a festival day (perhaps during the fall festival of Tabernacles) when God was supposed to be manifested to the cultic community.

Amos suggests that when God is really manifested, most people will not be able to endure it. Similarly, in Isaiah the "day" takes on the character of a battle day when God will rout any foes. The description of the divine manifestation echoes the cultic celebration of the psalms (for example, Psalms 29 and 97) and is related to the tradition of God's kingship. Isaiah is thinking not only of a theophany in the cult, however, but of an occasion when all will flee to caves from the terror of the Lord. It is possible that the terror will be conveyed through the Assyrian invasion, but Isaiah sees it as the manifestation of God. Humanity will then recognize its puny nature before the overwhelming power of God, and the folly of human ambitions to wealth and power will be exposed.

3:1-12 Anarchy in Jerusalem. "That day" will also have effect in Jerusalem. Isaiah sketches a breakdown of the social order. "Hero and warrior," anyone who could lay claim to power is removed. The people will be ruled by mere boys (v. 4), women, or even a babe in arms (v. 12). That "a little child" should be leader may sound idyllic in Isa 11, but here (v. 5) it is a symptom of chaos. There was no such breakdown of order in Isaiah's time. The prophecy is partly a wish and partly an assertion that such a breakdown *could* happen, and that the pride of the leaders has a shaky foundation.

3:13-15 The accusation. The formal accusation in verses 13-15 focuses on one aspect of that foundation. The political leaders, the elders and princes, have built their wealth by appropriating land and exploiting the poor. A similar theme is characteristic of Amos. We will meet it again in Isa 5.

3:16–4:1 The women of Jerusalem. Isaiah is especially severe on the women. He provides an impressive inventory of their finery. He seems to relish the prospect that their heads would be shaved and they would be led away in sackcloth by the Assyrians (they were not, but it was a distinct possibility). He treats the women as the representatives of the culture of luxury and pride, and therefore especially ripe for a fall. We find a similar attitude in Amos, who called the women of Samaria "cows of Bashan" (Amos 4:1).

4:2-6 The glorious remnant. The final oracle relating to "that day" is probably the work of a later editor. Elsewhere in Isaiah the remnant is not portrayed in such glorious terms. The signs of God's presence—the smoking cloud by day and the flaming fire by night—recall the Exodus tradition, which is also out of character for Isaiah. Yet the passage is developing a genuine theme of Isaiah: Jerusalem must be purged if it is to be holy, but the purge is ultimately the means to salvation.

The "branch of the Lord" here is a general reference to whatever God will cause to grow, synonymous with "the fruit of the earth." The same word is used for a messiah in Jer 23:5; Zech 3:8; 6:12.

5:1-7 The song of the vineyard. This famous poem is a parable, like Nathan's parable in 2 Sam 12 or some of the parables of Jesus. The speaker does not at first disclose his true subject but leads his listeners to pass judgment before they realize that they are condemning themselves. The vineyard involves a double allegory. On the one hand, there is the obvious agricultural sense of the words. On the other hand, the fact that the song is said to be a love song, sung for a friend, suggests that the friend's vineyard is really his wife. There is a hint, then, of marital infidelity as a second level in the allegory. The song is not very explicit about the sins of Israel, except that they involve bloodshed and injustice. The indictment draws its force from the analogy with the unproductive vineyard and the less obvious analogy with marital infidelity. It appears that both kingdoms, Israel and Judah, stand accused.

There is yet another nuance to the allegory. The vineyard was very valuable property that contributed greatly to the life of luxury. It symbolized the wealth of the land. The parable suggests that this wealth has not produced a just society. The threat that the vineyard would be overgrown by thorns and briers was fulfilled rather literally after the Assyrian invasions.

The entire poem may be compared to Hos 2, where God threatens to make the land a wilderness and the analogy with marital infidelity is again present. The vine is a favorite symbol for Israel in the Old Testament: compare Hos 10:1; Jer 2:21; Ezek 15:1-8; 19:10-14. Compare also the parable of the vineyard in the New Testament: Matt 21:33-42; Mark 12:1-10; Luke 20:9-18.

5:8-16 Denunciation of social abuses. These oracles are proclamations of woe and have a dirge-like effect. They do not invite the wicked to repent but are announced as certain and unavoidable. They paint a vivid picture of Israelite society in the eighth century. The large landowners add house to house by foreclosing on debtors or pressuring the smaller farmers off the land (see the story of Naboth's vineyard in 1 Kgs 21). The large estates could then be turned into profitable vineyards, which supported the luxurious (and drunken) lifestyle of the rich rather than supplying the staples of life for the poor. Isaiah insists that those who exalt themselves in this way will be humbled before the majesty of God.

5:17-25 Denunciation of the wise. Isaiah is especially angry at the professional sages, the political advisers of their day. They are skilled in political rhetoric, call evil good and good evil. They indulge in petty corruption, acquitting the guilty for bribes. Besides, being "wise in their own sight" (v. 21), they do not allow for God's control of events or for the ability of a prophet to discern it. Isaiah insists that the "Holy One" has a plan, which will humble human pride. The sages doubt this and challenge God (and Isaiah) to get on with it. They are pragmatic politicians. Isaiah can only retort by proclaiming the wrath of God.

5:26-30 The Assyrian danger. Isaiah's threat that Yahweh would disrupt the plans of the wise was not totally lacking in practical reason. He does not simply envisage a miracle. God would act through a "far-off nation" (5:26). Isaiah was an astute political observer who saw the menace of Assyria and had no illusions that Judean diplomacy would be able to avert disaster. The complacency of the wise and their self-indulgent lifestyle left them vulnerable to a changing political situation.

6:1-13 The call vision of Isaiah. Isaiah's vision, reported in chapter 6, is usually thought to mark the beginning of a memoir (6:1–8:20) that was recorded in the time of the prophet himself. The vision is dated to an early point in his career (742 B.C.E.). Since it involves the commissioning of the prophet, it is usually regarded as his inaugural vision. Hebrew prophets were thought to receive their message in the heavenly council (compare Jer 23:19, which claims that Jeremiah's opponents have not had this experience). Such visions were not necessarily confined to the beginning of a prophet's career. The closest parallel to Isaiah's vision is attributed to a prophet named Micaiah ben Imlah in 1 Kgs 22, and it is not an inaugural vision.

Isaiah makes the astonishing claim that he has seen the Lord. There is some ambiguity in the Bible as to whether a person can see God. In Exod 33:11 we are told that God used to speak to Moses face-to-face, but also that Moses was only allowed to see God's back, since "my face you cannot see, for no man sees me and still lives" (Exod 33:20; compare Isaiah's fear that he is doomed in 6:5). The prophet Ezekiel sums up his own introductory vision as "the vision of the likeness of the glory of the Lord"—a very circumspect claim (Ezek 1:28). Isaiah, by contrast, is perfectly direct: "I saw the Lord" (6:1). The parallel with the vision of Micaiah ben Imlah in 1 Kgs 22 suggests that there was a prophetic tradition that prophets could indeed see God.

Here it must be said that what a prophet sees in a vision is inevitably conditioned by his preconceptions and by the beliefs of his contemporaries. A prophet in the eighth century B.C.E. *could* have a vision of God because it was believed to be possible, and the report would be accepted by a significant number of his contemporaries. God is envisaged as a king because the king was the most powerful and majestic figure in the prophet's experience. (The similarity between the heavenly and earthly courts is more obvious in 1 Kgs 22.) The seraphim in Isaiah's vision are evidently inspired by the cherubim, the hybrid figures in the Jerusalem temple above which Yahweh was supposed to be enthroned.

Isaiah apparently had this vision in the temple, possibly on a cultic occasion when the house was filled with the smoke of incense. Such an experience may not have been unique to prophets. The psalmist speaks of gazing toward God in the temple "to see your power and your glory" (Ps 63:3). It may be that worshipers hoped for such a vision when they attended worship in the temple. In any case, the claim to have seen God lends considerable authority to the prophet's message. If it comes directly from God, it takes precedence over the claims of any human institution.

The cry of the seraphim expresses Isaiah's central affirmation about God: "Holy, holy, holy" (6:3). The significance of God's holiness is shown in the prophet's immediate confession of impurity. Isaiah does not recall a specific sin. The impurity is inherent in his human condition and endangers him in the presence of God. The remedy is a drastic one: his lips are purified with a burning coal. An analogous remedy will be prescribed for the whole people.

The prophet's vision is never an end in itself. He is not practicing a life of contemplation. Instead, he is given a message that bears on the political situation in Jerusalem. This message is not to save the people; on the contrary, it ensures their doom by making their hearts sluggish. The prophet's job here is to announce the coming judgment, not to bring about the conversion, at least not directly. We may compare Exod 7:3, where God hardens Pharaoh's heart, thereby setting him up for further destruction.

It would seem, then, that the judgment on Judea cannot be avoided. The question raised by the prophet is not "whether" but "how long?" The answer involves the familiar theme of the remnant. Israel will be like a tree that has been cut down, so that only a stump remains. The editorial gloss, "Holy offspring is the trunk" (6:13), gives the prophecy an upbeat ending. It also is in keeping with the thought of Isaiah that this remnant does indeed have a future. Yet the emphasis in chapter 6 is overwhelmingly negative. The good news of the remnant is overshadowed by the destruction of the majority. The destruction will presumably purify the remnant, as the burning coals purified the prophet's lips.

7:1-25 The prophecy of Immanuel. The opening verse of chapter 7 refers to the campaign of Syria (Aram) and northern Israel (Ephraim) against Judah in the reign of Ahaz. The campaign in question took place between 735 and 733 B.C.E. (see 2 Kgs 16) and is known as the Syro-Ephraimite war. Syria and Israel had already been paying tribute to Assyria since 738 B.C.E. but had now decided to revolt by withholding payment. Judah had refused to join the alliance. As yet Ahaz had no quarrel with Assyria, and in any case hopes of success were remote. Israel and Syria then attempted to overthrow Ahaz and replace him with a king more amenable to their wishes.

The royal ideology of the Davidic dynasty professed a sublime confidence that God would protect his chosen king and city. Recall Ps 46:1-4:

> God is our refuge and our strength,
>   an ever-present help in distress.
> Therefore we fear not, though the earth
>   be shaken
>   and mountains plunge into the depths
>   of the sea . . . .
> The Lord of hosts is with us;
>   our stronghold is the God of Jacob.

Such a profession is easily made when there is no immediate danger. Faced with an actual invasion, however, "the heart of the king and the heart of the people trembled, as the trees of the forest tremble in the wind" (7:2).

At this juncture Isaiah goes to meet Ahaz, who is apparently checking his water supply in anticipation of a siege. Isaiah is accompanied by his son, whose name, Shear-jashub, means "a remnant shall return." His advice to the king is startling. He does not suggest the course that Ahaz would eventually take, to appeal to Assyria for help (2 Kgs 16:7). Instead, he tells him to "remain tranquil and do not fear" (7:4) because the attack will not succeed and the state of northern Israel will soon come to an end. (The reference to "sixty years and five" (7:9) has puzzled commentators. It is too far away to have immediate relevance for Ahaz, and besides, Israel was effectively terminated in 722 B.C.E. Some scholars suggest that this verse is a gloss added in 671 B.C.E. when further settlers were brought to Samaria by the Assyrian king Esar-haddon [see Ezra 4:2]. Others suggest that the original text read "six years or five" [so the Jerusalem Bible], but there is no textual evidence for this reading.) The divine commitment to make the Davidic line "firm" (2 Sam 7:16) is conditional on the faith of the king. (In Hebrew the words for "firm" and "believe" are derived from the same root.)

The birth of a child. Isaiah then offers Ahaz a sign and proceeds to give it even when the king refuses to ask for it. The sign is that a young woman will bear a son who will be "living on curds and honey by the time he learns to reject the bad and choose the good"

421

(7:15). The mother is called an *almah* in the Hebrew, that is, a young woman of marriageable age, though not necessarily a virgin. The Greek translation of Isaiah used the word *parthenos*, which means "virgin" unambiguously, and this translation is cited in Matt 1:22-23 and formed the basis of the traditional Christian interpretation of this text as a prophecy of the birth of Christ. The Hebrew, however, does not suggest that the birth in itself was miraculous.

Since the sign was given to Ahaz, we must assume that the young woman in question was known to him. There are two possible identifications. The first is the prophet's wife. We know that the prophet gave symbolic names to his children. The second is the king's wife. The name Immanuel, "God is with us," could serve as a slogan for the Davidic house. While the prophet could predict the name of his own child more confidently, a royal child would be the more effective sign for the king. While either identification is possible, it seems more probable that the woman in question was one of Ahaz's wives.

The child about to be born will be "living on curds and honey by the time he learns to reject the bad and choose the good" (7:15). The translation of this sentence is disputed. It could be that he will live on curds and honey *so that* he may learn (so the Vulgate). The age of moral discrimination is usually put at about twenty years. According to this interpretation, Immanuel would be brought up on a diet of curds and honey in order to form his moral discrimination. Some scholars, however, think that the age in question may be much lower—three to five years of age. The lower figure seems more probable in view of 7:16: "For before the child learns to reject the bad and choose the good, the land of those two kings whom you dread shall be deserted." If this sign has any urgency, the interval can be no more than a few years.

The meaning of the sign. The diet of curds and honey is evidently part of the sign and illustrates the ambiguity inherent in this whole passage. The land of Israel was proverbially "a land flowing with milk and honey" (Exod 3:8; 13:5; Num 13:27; Josh 5:6). Such food would appear abundant to nomads from the wilderness; it would surely seem spartan to a king accustomed to live in luxury. The im-

plications of the diet of curds and honey can be seen in 7:21-25: those who remain in the land will have to live on its natural produce, since cultivation will be impossible. Curds and honey will be the only available food. The phrase "On that day" (7:20, 21) suggests that the coming destruction is "the day of the Lord," but it is clear that the instrument of destruction is "the razor hired from across the River" (7:20)—the Assyrians.

Isaiah not only predicts that Syria and Israel will be destroyed but also that Judah will suffer "days worse than any since Ephraim seceded from Judah" (7:17). It would seem from 7:18-20 that the real menace to Judah is seen to come from the Assyrians rather than from the Syro-Ephraimite coalition.

What, then, is signified by the birth of Immanuel? Evidently the name "God is with us" is *not* a promise that God will shelter the king from all harm if only he has faith; rather, it is an ambiguous sign. The presence of God is not always protective. It can also be destructive, as on the "day of the Lord" (see above, chapter 2). Yet it is not entirely destructive. The birth of a child is perhaps the most universal and enduring symbol of hope for the human race. The newborn child does not contribute to military defense or help resolve the dilemmas of the crisis, but he is nonetheless a sign of hope for a new generation. The prophet predicts that he will reach the age of discernment, however bad the times may be. Even if cultivation becomes impossible, people will survive on curds and honey. Moreover, they can recall a time at the beginning of Israel's history when such a diet was seen as a bountiful gift of God. Isaiah prophesies that the vineyards, worth thousands of pieces of silver, will be overgrown with thorns and briers (see the Song of the Vineyard, Isa 5:6). This would be a loss to the ruling class but not necessarily to the common people. The demise of the vineyards might mark a return to a simpler lifestyle, in which Israel and Judah would be less wealthy, but also less torn by social oppression and less entangled in international politics.

Isaiah's advice to Ahaz, then, is to wait out the crisis, trusting not for miraculous deliverance but for eventual survival. The prophet probably feels that there is no need to fight against Syria and Israel, Assyria will take care of them. Sending for aid to Assyria is probably also unnecessary and would bring Judah directly into subjection. In the meantime Judah might be ravaged and reduced to near wilderness, but life would go on, and the society would be purified in the process.

Ahaz, of course, does not follow Isaiah's advice. He sends gold and silver to the king of Assyria and becomes his vassal. Damascus is destroyed. Samaria survives only because a coup puts a new king on the throne, but even then it survives for a mere decade. The politics of Ahaz seem to work well enough for the present, but Isaiah would surely hold that they do not go to the heart of the matter.

The figure of Immanuel in Isa 7 is not presented as a messianic figure, although he probably was a royal child. Nothing is said of his future reign. Instead, he is a symbol of hope in weakness, of new life in the midst of destruction. When early Christianity read this passage as a prediction of the birth of Jesus, it implied an analogy between the two births. In the Gospels, too, a birth in inauspicious circumstances was nonetheless taken as a sign of the presence of God.

8:1-15 Prophecies concerning Assyria. A series of short oracles in chapter 8 throws some light on Isaiah's stance in the crisis of 735–738 B.C.E.

First, the prophet has another child, who becomes a living sign that the Assyrians will plunder Syria and Israel. Unlike Immanuel, this child is explicitly said to be the prophet's son. His relevance to the prophet's prediction, however, is similar: Damascus and Samaria will be destroyed before he begins to talk. The time period is presumably not much less than was implied in the case of Immanuel.

A second short oracle is found in verses 5-10. The people have rejected the waters of Shiloah (a stream in Jerusalem) by not trusting in the divine promises to David and succumbing to fear. The waters of Shiloah flow gently; they are not mighty or threatening. Because the Judeans have not been content with such a passive role, the great river of Assyria, the Euphrates, will flood them. There is pointed irony in this. Ahaz has appealed to Assyria for protection, but the protection of Assyria is overpowering and oppressive in itself. Isaiah is adamant that anyone who resists will be crushed (as indeed they were). The plans of the counselors are in vain, for "With us is God!" (v. 10). Here again the prophet

is playing on the name of Immanuel. God is present in the Assyrian onslaught, not with those who resist it.

A third brief oracle in verses 11-15 dismisses political alliances as futile and says that the fear of the people is misplaced—they should fear the Lord. The point here is not only that they should fear the Assyrians as God's weapon but concerns a basic religious attitude. Isaiah renounces all political intrigue and its goal of international power. Yahweh becomes a stumbling block, frustrating the designs of the counselors in Jerusalem as well as Samaria. Isaiah seems to regard political intrigue as sinful in itself. In the context of the Assyrian crisis, he had, at least, good reason to regard the intrigue of the Israelites as ineffectual.

8:16-20 Conclusion of the memoir. This passage gives a rare glimpse of the formation of a prophetic book. The prophet gives instruction that his words be recorded and preserved by his disciples. The memoir (probably chapters 6–8) is, then, a testimony, a public reminder of the prophet's message, like the symbolic names of Isaiah's children. It will be available for consultation, so that people will not need to resort to mediums and fortunetellers (compare the story of Saul in 1 Sam 28). Such signs are necessary when God is "hiding his face from the house of Jacob" (v. 17). At this juncture God was most obviously hidden from the northern kingdom, but Isaiah apparently thinks of all Israel as one people, subject to the God who dwells in Jerusalem on Mount Zion.

8:23–9:6 A new king. The famous prophecy of the birth of a child is properly called a "messianic" prophecy because it describes an ideal king whose reign is still in the future. There is disagreement as to how the oracle was originally understood. It could refer to the birth of a royal child (compare Vergil's famous *Fourth Eclogue,* which was written to celebrate the birth of the Roman emperor's son). More probably it was a hymn in honor of the enthronement of a new king (compare Ps 2:7, where the king is told the decree of the Lord: "You are my son, this day I have begotten you"). Apparently the king was adopted as "son of God" when he came to the throne. The king in question in Isa 9 is surely Hezekiah, Ahaz's successor, who became king in either 725 or 715 B.C.E. (the evidence is inconsistent). The earlier date would make better sense here.

Isa 8:23 refers to the dismemberment of northern Israel by the Assyrians in 733–732 B.C.E., when three districts were taken away from Samaria and made Assyrian provinces. It is disputed whether the text should be translated as "he has glorified the seaward road" or "he has oppressed" it. If "glorified" is correct, the prophet is anticipating something that has not yet happened. In any case, chapter 9 announces light for those who live in darkness—new hope for the people of northern Israel oppressed by the Assyrians. The prophet says that God has smashed the oppressor "as on the day of Midian" (a battle described in Judg 7). He probably says this in anticipation, because of his confidence in the new king. The hope for northern Israel is found in the arrival of a new Davidic king in Jerusalem and involves the reunification of Israel.

The titles given to the royal "child," especially "God-Hero" (9:5), suggest that he is more than a human being. There can be no doubt, however, that the prophet Isaiah is thinking of an actual king in Jerusalem in the late eighth century B.C.E. The divine titles are part of the royal ideology. Ps 2:7 declares that the king is the begotten son of God, although this is probably understood as a formula of adoption. Ps 45:7 addresses the king as *elohim*, "god." The king is not considered equal to Yahweh, but he is regarded as a superhuman being.

This king is expected to bring about an era of peace. He will be able to do this because God will give him all the empire governed by David. This, of course, did not come about in the time of Hezekiah, nor has it ever come to pass since then. In the context of Isaiah's message, this is a vision of hope. The glory of the king is still in the future—it is a matter of potential and possibility, not of accomplished fact. The oracle has endured because it formulates a goal of universal peace, which is still desired by humanity.

Christianity applied this prophecy to the birth of Jesus. In doing so, it disregarded the real political concern of Isaiah for the land of Israel. It picked up instead the fact that these wonderful attributes were attached to a child, to one who has no real power in this world. As in chapter 7 the birth of a child symbo-

lizes the hope of humanity for a brighter future. The prophecy affirms that the key to this future lies in justice and innocence rather than in military might.

9:7–10:4 Judgment on the northern kingdom. We have seen that Isaiah is concerned with the northern kingdom of Israel as well as with his own state of Judah. This series of oracles announces God's judgment on the north. The time in question is not clear; it may have been as early as the Syro-Ephraimite war (see 9:20). The grounds for the judgment are partly arrogance (9:8), partly the social injustice implied by the pursuit of luxury, and partly the failure of the Israelites to turn to Yahweh, who, in Isaiah's view, dwells in Jerusalem (8:18). Since no conversion follows the early setbacks of Israel, Yahweh's wrath is not turned back, so worse destruction is to come. The series concludes with a woe-oracle on social injustice that is closely related to the woe-oracles in chapter 5. Some scholars think that material has been displaced and that some verses from chapter 5 originally belonged in chapter 9 (compare the formula in 5:25, which corresponds to 9:11, 16, 20, and 10:4).

10:5–34 The role of Assyria. Pagan Assyria is the rod with which Yahweh chastises Israel. Yet, Assyria is not itself exempt from judgment, since its intention is not to serve Yahweh but to wreak destruction. This oracle is somewhat later than the passages in chapters 7–9. It comes from a time when Jerusalem rather than Samaria was being threatened, either in 713 B.C.E. on the occasion of a revolt by Ashdod or in the better-known invasion of Sennacherib in 701 B.C.E.

The pattern of this oracle is a familiar one in the Bible (see Isa 14; Ezek 27–28). The king of Assyria is guilty of excessive pride, or *hybris*: "By my own power I have done it, and by my wisdom, for I am shrewd" (v. 13). In Isaiah's view, human power and wisdom accomplish nothing. Assyria is an unwitting helper in the plan of God. The prophet's conviction that Assyria would be broken appears to be based on the divine commitment to Mount Zion. Zion can be struck with a rod (10:24) and so is not protected from all harm. Yet, the ironic quotation of Assyria's claims in 10:8-11 clearly implies that Jerusalem is not like Samaria or other cities and cannot be completely destroyed. So the threatening advance of the Assyrians in verses 28-32 comes close to Jerusalem but stops short of the city. The final assertion of God's majestic power (vv. 33-34) is ambiguous. It is manifested in the subjection of Judah by the Assyrian advance, but it also casts a shadow on the Assyrian success and suggests that it too will be cut off.

The passage on the remnant in verses 20-21 is inserted here because of the occurrence of the word "remnant" in verse 19. The insert shows the typical ambiguity of the remnant: the survivors will be purified and learn to rely on the Lord, but *only* a remnant will be left. This idea is consistent with the message of Isaiah throughout his career.

11:1-9 The ideal king. The messianic prophecy in chapter 11 refers more obviously to a future time than was the case in chapter 9. It is not apparent that the king in question has even been born. He is described as "a shoot from the stump of Jesse," that is, from the Davidic line (compare Mic 5:1, where the lineage is expressed through a reference to Bethlehem, the home of Jesse). This description does not presuppose that the line had been broken: "stump" is roughly equivalent to "roots" in the parallel line.

The oracle that follows falls into two parts. Verses 2-5 describe the attributes of the king. The spirit of the Lord will be upon him, and he will do all that a righteous king should do. Verses 6-9 describe a transformation of nature in his reign. This description is quite fantastic, as it concerns a transformation of animal nature that no king could achieve. It is like a return to the garden of Eden. The reference to "all my holy mountain" in verse 9 suggests that the whole earth will then partake of the sanctity of Mount Zion.

It should be obvious that this is a poetic passage, a fantasy of an ideal world rather than a prediction of the future. Such friendship between wolf and lamb has never come about, and there is no reason to think that Isaiah expected it would. Rather, the purpose of this passage is twofold. On the one hand, it is a beautiful picture that comforts the reader in the midst of the turmoil of the Assyrian crisis. On the other hand, it paints a picture of what an ideal world would be like. As such, it presents a challenge for any king. Perhaps Isaiah had come to realize that Hezekiah was not an ideal king, despite the hopes

expressed in Isa 9. Indeed, what king could possibly measure up to the ideal presented here? Yet the ideal is important. It reminds us of the imperfections of the present and gives us a goal to work toward, even though we may never fully attain it.

The goal expressed in Isa 11:1-9 is perfect peace, without "harm or ruin"(11:9). In such a world "a little child [will] guide them" (11:6). The motif of the child was prominent in chapter 7 and in the imagery of chapter 9 (but see also 3:12). The child as leader is a contradiction of political and military reality. In Isaiah's view, the power and supposed wisdom of human rulers are of little account. What matters is "the knowledge of the Lord" (v. 9) that goes hand in hand with "the fear of the Lord" (v. 2)—single-minded devotion to justice and abandonment of human pretensions and ambitions.

11:10-16 Reunification of Israel. This oracle of restoration comes from a later time when not only Israel but also Judah had been scattered in exile. The point of contact with Isaiah's prophecy lies in the opening reference to the root of Jesse. The image of the "signal" or standard for the nations recalls how the nations are said to stream to Mount Zion in chapter 2, but of course the motif of "a light to the nations" is also prominent in Second Isaiah in the exilic period. Here the restoration is presented as a new Exodus (a motif also repeated by Second Isaiah). By contrast, there are no references to the Exodus in those oracles that are ascribed with any confidence to Isaiah himself. The ideal situation envisaged, however, is quite compatible with the hopes of Isaiah. It looks for a reconciliation of Israel and Judah, and their joint sovereignty over the other nations.

12:1-6 A song of thanksgiving. This short hymn of thanksgiving probably concluded an independent booklet of Isaiah's prophecies. The hymn is the work of an editor, despite the use of the characteristically Isaian phrase "the Holy One of Israel" (12:6). The psalmist looks back on hard times but can now praise God, since the crises are past. The judgment oracles of Isaiah are thus put in perspective, for the editor can view these events with hindsight. The reader, too, is encouraged to put the words of Isaiah, bound as they were to specific situations, in a broader, long-term context.

ORACLES AGAINST VARIOUS NATIONS
Isa 13:1–23:8

The oracles in this section are addressed to various foreign nations but include an oracle against Judah and Jerusalem in 22:1-14 and an oracle against a particular official in 22:15-25. Similar collections of oracles against foreign nations are found in Jer 46–51 and Ezek 25–32 (see also Amos 1:3–2:6; Nahum; Obadiah). The number of such prophecies that have survived shows that it was traditional for prophets to predict doom on other nations (and perhaps thereby bring it about—compare the role of the Moabite seer Balaam, who is called on to curse, or prophesy against, Israel in Num 22–24). Usually the prediction of doom on a nation's enemies carries the implication of blessing for the nation itself.

At least some of these oracles come from a time long after Isaiah (for example, the oracles against Babylon in Isa 13–14). Chapter 20 describes an action in Isaiah's own career, and a few passages may be original oracles of the prophet (for example, 14:24-27; 17:1-11). In several other cases there is no clear evidence of origin. We must allow that Isaiah delivered some oracles against foreign nations, that this collection was expanded, and that much of the present collection may not be from the prophet himself.

The oracles against the nations are of historical interest but offer relatively little religious guidance for the modern reader. Here we will comment only on the more notable passages.

13:1-22 The destruction of Babylon. The occasion envisaged by this prophecy is the fall of Babylon to the Medes and Persians, so it was probably composed about 540 B.C.E. Here the destruction of Babylon is "the day of the Lord," a phrase that can be applied to any manifestation of God in judgment. In verses 10-13 the heavens are darkened and the earth shaken. Yet it is apparent that what the prophet has in mind is a military event, described in gruesomely realistic terms in verse 16. The cosmic effects are metaphorical. They provide vivid images of the collapse, not of the world at large but of the world of the Babylonians. This metaphoric use of cosmic imagery plays an important part in other sections of the book and in later apocalyptic literature.

14:1-22 The king of Babylon. The taunt-song against the king of Babylon is famous for its comparison with "Lucifer, Son of Dawn." The comparison is drawn from an ancient Canaanite myth, where Attar, the Daystar, tries to occupy the throne of Baal. The pattern of the story is a very popular one in the Bible. Whoever tries to rise too high will be cast down lowest of all. In a sense this was already the pattern of the story of Adam and Eve, who were cast out of the garden because they wanted to be like God (see Isa 14:14). The same pattern is found in Ezek 27 and 28. By contrast, the pattern is inverted in the case of Jesus, according to Phil 2. Because he did not deem equality with God something to be grasped at, he received a name above every other name. The model of Lucifer can obviously be applied to many figures in history besides the king of Babylon. (Lucifer in this context is simply the Daystar, a heavenly being, but is not identified as Satan. This model, however, played a part in the popular legend of the fall of Satan from heaven, which was developed by John Milton in *Paradise Lost*.)

One other aspect of these chapters should be noted. The prophet evidently delights in the overthrow of Babylon. There is a certain amount of vengefulness here and considerable resentment toward the overlord—an emotion that superpowers often arouse in less powerful people. This aspect of the prophecies may not be to everyone's taste, although anyone engaged in a struggle for liberation will surely resonate with it. It may not be the ideal attitude toward our enemies, but it is at least realistic. Few people get through life without such sentiments. It is better to express them than to deny them hypocritically. The taunts against Babylon are echoed in the New Testament Book of Revelation (chs. 17–18) to vent the feelings of some early Christians against Rome.

14:24-27 The destruction of Assyria. This brief oracle appears out of context here. It suggests that God will allow the Assyrian to invade Israel and will break him there. It raises the question of how Isaiah envisaged God's overall plan for Israel and Assyria. We will return to this question later (p. 432).

17:1-11 Oracle against Syria and northern Israel. This passage is an authentic oracle of Isaiah from the time of the Syro-Ephraimite war. The prediction is that Syria and northern Israel will be brought low, so that they will come to respect the Holy One of Israel.

17:12-14 The turbulent nations. Chapter 17 concludes with a general statement on the nations, which has many parallels in the psalms (for example, Psalms 2, 48). The viewpoint in these verses is that of the Jerusalem cult, which Isaiah shared only with qualifications. The presupposition is that Yahweh and the nations are in opposition. The conflict is expressed through a metaphor drawn from Canaanite myth. The Canaanites had a story in which the god Baal, the god of fertility, is challenged by the unruly figure of Yamm (the Sea) but proceeds to trounce him with two clubs. Here the nations are like Yamm, turbulent rebels, but the same fate will befall them. God's ability to rebuke the sea is given as testimony to the divine power in the Old Testament (Nah 1:4; Ps 106:9). The same motif is used to show the divinity of Jesus in the New Testament (Matt 8:23-27 and parallels).

19:1-15 Oracles against Egypt. It is uncertain whether any of these oracles actually come from Isaiah. We should note at least that the taunts against the sages of Egypt in verses 11-15 recall Isaiah's quarrel with the sages of Jerusalem (5:18-25). Isaiah's interest in Egypt comes from the fact that Egypt is a potential ally, and Judah might be tempted to rely on Egyptian aid.

19:16-24 The future of Egypt. The short oracles with which the chapter concludes are less likely to come from Isaiah. They fantasize how in the future Egypt will fear Judah and come to worship the Lord. Here we must recognize the desire of the powerless little state to get the upper hand over its powerful neighbor. We know that there were Jewish temples in Egypt at Elephantine (about 400 B.C.E.) and at Leontopolis (about 150 B.C.E.), although this was contrary to the law in Deuteronomy. It is unlikely that the passage in Isaiah had either of these in mind. It is simply indulging in a fantasy about the conversion of the Gentiles. Verses 23-24 add another fantasy—that one day Israel will rank as a third world power with Egypt and Assyria. This fantasy was never realized (at least until modern times!). It is strangely in contradiction to the ideals of Isaiah as we have seen them in chapters 2–11, where he held that Judah would be better off to renounce all ambition in the international arena.

20:1-6 A naked prophet. Symbolic actions were a favorite device of the prophets to dramatize their message. Hosea married a harlot. Ezekiel performed numerous strange acts, including the use of dung to cook his food (Ezek 4). Here we find that Isaiah went naked for three years at the time of the rebellion of Ashdod (713 B.C.E.). This was a sign that Egypt and Ethiopia would fall to Assyria, and the captives would be led away naked.

The symbolic action is a kind of street theatre. It grabs the attention and presents the passerby with a visual image more powerful than any speech. How the people react is, of course, up to them. First they must find out what the sign means, then decide what to do about it. In this case the sign is not performed for the benefit of Egyptians or Ethiopians; rather, it is meant to show the people of Judah and the coastland the folly of relying on Egyptian aid. Egypt was not in fact conquered, but it did not protect the rebels either. Isaiah's warning was justified.

21:1-10 The fall of Babylon. Yet another oracle on the fall of Babylon in the sixth century is inserted here. Two points should be noted. The phrase "Fallen, fallen is Babylon," (21:9) is picked up and applied to Rome in Rev 18:2. The significance of this message for the Jews is underlined in verse 10. Judah has been threshed and winnowed by Babylon—she can hardly fail to delight in the fall of the oppressor.

22:1-14 The fall of Jerusalem. This lone oracle against Jerusalem is included in the oracles against the nations, perhaps to make the point that Judah, too, is subject to judgment (compare the treatment of Israel in Amos 1–2). Much of this oracle presupposes the actual fall of Jerusalem to the Babylonians in 587–586 B.C.E. (so 22:4-11). Some scholars, however, recognize an oracle of Isaiah in verses 1-3 and 12-14, which presuppose that the city did not fall. This oracle may have been delivered on the occasion of Sennacherib's campaign against Jerusalem, which we will examine below in Isa 36–39.

In verses 1-3a the prophet chides the people of Jerusalem for their panic and lack of trust. Then in verses 12-14 he rebukes them because they turned too easily to celebrating instead of taking their narrow escape as an occasion for repentance. The slogan attributed to the revelers, "Eat and drink, for tomorrow we die!" (22:13), is often quoted (see Isa 56:12; Wis 2:6; 1 Cor 15:32). The force of the prophet's criticism may be that the people in Jerusalem did not show enough concern for the sufferings of their fellow Judeans and did not take the lesson of the folly of rebellion to heart.

22:15-25 Rivals at court. The two officials who are the subjects of verses 15-25 are also mentioned in Isa 36 and 2 Kgs 18, where Eliakim is called "master of the palace." The oracle cited here may have been setting a seal of divine approval on a reorganization of the royal cabinet. The wrath of the prophet is aroused by the luxury of Shebna, especially the tomb he has prepared for himself. The prophet sees this as an attempt to control his fate, which will be frustrated by God. He also objects to Shebna's delight in chariots. It is interesting to see the prophet engaging in day-to-day politics and endorsing one official against another. Such participation in political life is necessary for anyone who seriously wants to influence public policy.

THE APOCALYPSE OF ISAIAH

Isa 24:1–27:13

These chapters stand out from their context, as they are much less specific than the oracles against foreign nations which precede them. They are loosely structured and were not necessarily composed as a coherent unit. Attempts to tie them to a specific historical setting have usually focused on allusions to the destruction of a city (24:10-12; 25:1-5; 26:5; 27:10-11). The city in question has been identified with a whole spectrum of cities from Babylon in the sixth century B.C.E. to Samaria in the second. It is not certain, however, that all references are to the same city or that all passages envisage a specific city at all. If the references are to a single city, the most likely referent is Babylon, but the lack of specific detail makes these chapters into a general description of a desolate world and the hope for definitive salvation through the power of God.

24:1-20 The desolation of the earth. This passage reads like a ritual mourning for the land. We may compare Joel 1-2, but there the occasion is quite specific—it is a plague of locusts. In Isa 24 the occasion is not clear at all.

It may have been a severe drought or some unspecified historical crisis. Some scholars identify the "city of chaos" in verse 10 as a particular city (for example, Babylon, when it was destroyed by Xerxes of Persia in 482 B.C.E.), but it may also be read as a more general reference. Just as the whole land is turned upside down, cities too are reduced to chaos. Special attention is paid to the lack of wine, which dampens festivity (v. 11). The disorders extend also to social relations. Distinctions in status break down. Servant and master are on equal footing. The prophet is developing themes which we have seen already in Isa 2-3 and which were associated with the "day of the Lord" (see also Joel 1-2). The destruction of the earth and the breakdown of social order are seen as manifestations of the majesty of God and correctives to human pride. Hence the surprising call to give glory to the Lord in verses 14-16 (compare Psalm 29, which takes the thunderstorm as an occasion to give glory to the Lord).

Only two verses give a reason for the desolation of the earth. Verses 5-6 lay the blame on humanity. The offenses are stated in very general terms: they have transgressed laws, broken an everlasting covenant (v. 5). The covenant in question is not necessarily the one made with Moses at Sinai. The phrase "everlasting covenant" (our text reads "ancient covenant") is used in Gen 9:16 for the covenant with Noah, which was a covenant with all peoples, not just Israel. The disruption of the earth, then, may be due to a breach of natural law. The underlying idea is that the order of nature is directly affected by human behavior. This idea was common in ancient Israel, especially in the temple cult. We can appreciate it anew in modern times as we observe the effects of technological progress on the environment or contemplate the threat to nature from the development of nuclear power.

The desolation of the earth redounds to the glory of God, but it is nonetheless a hardship for humanity. Verses 16b-20 evoke the sense of terror for humanity in the manifestation of God's majesty (compare Amos 5:19 on the impossibility of escaping from God's judgment; also, more directly, Jer 48:43-44). Verses 18b-19 describe the destruction of the world. The "windows on high" will let in the floodwaters that have been restrained since creation (compare Jer 4:23-26, where the whole earth is returned to its primeval state and creation is undone). Both in Isa 18–20 and in Jeremiah this total destruction is still in the future. It should not be taken literally as a prediction of the end of the world but as a vivid metaphorical way of conveying a sense of impending desolation.

24:21-23 The final judgment. The last oracle in chapter 24 picks up explicitly the motif of "the day of the Lord." The judgment described, however, has no parallel in the Old Testament, for it includes the punishment of the host of heaven—that is, the stars, which were regarded as angels (see Judg 5:20) or as pagan gods (Deut 4:19; Jer 8:2). The story of rebellious angels who are then punished by God is told in detail in the apocalyptic book of *1 Enoch* in the second century b.c.e. This passage in Isaiah raises the possibility that some mythological notions that first appear in post-biblical Jewish literature had in fact been current at a much earlier time.

The parallel punishment of the host of the heavens and the kings of the earth suggests that the two are closely related. The kings of the earth have their heavenly patrons (compare the notion of guardian angels), who are the real source of their power. This idea was widespread in antiquity. We will meet it again in Isa 36–37.

The culmination of the entire "day of the Lord" is that the Lord of hosts will reign on Mount Zion. The basic concepts in these oracles are drawn from Jerusalem cult traditions. The goal is the veneration of God on Mount Zion. This goal is to be reached through widespread destruction that will bring all peoples, including the Jews, to their knees. It is assumed, however, that life will go on on earth. God is to be glorified in Jerusalem, not in heaven. Christian readers may have difficulty with the prophet's insistence on the particular place, Mount Zion. They can at least appreciate some of the implications. The God of Mount Zion is the God of all the earth, and the frailty of humankind is the converse of the majesty of God.

25:1-5 A hymn of thanksgiving. This short hymn would appear to be written to celebrate the fall of a particular city (the most obvious candidate is Babylon). The lack of specificity, however, makes it possible to reapply it to any other city, or even to take

it as a general affirmation of God's ability to upset the status quo (see the song of Hannah in 1 Sam 2).

25:6-8 The final banquet. The image of the great banquet is taken from ancient mythology and has a long history in the folklore of the world. The motif is developed in the "wedding feast of the lamb" in Rev 19 (see also the parable of the great supper in Matt 22:2-14; Luke 14:16-24). The banquet suggests a celebration after the victory is won. In this case the banquet is given "on this mountain," presumably Mount Zion. It is, however, a feast for all peoples, in accordance with the tradition that all the nations would flock to Zion. The feast is described with mouthwatering vividness. This is not the heaven of a disembodied soul but probably reflects the desire of impoverished people for a bountiful meal. The salvation desired goes beyond this, however. God will destroy death forever. In Canaanite mythology, Death (Mot) was the name of a god, the opponent of Baal, god of fertility. The prophet is probably alluding to that myth. The resurrection of those who have already died is *not* implied here. Rather, the point is that God will ultimately remove every threat that hangs over humanity, including the ultimate one. God will also remove all sorrow and the humiliation of the Jewish people during the Exile. The prophet may have hoped for such salvation after the end of the Exile, but the destruction of death remains, inevitably, a distant horizon. Christianity transferred the land without tears to heaven; for Judaism it remains a utopian ideal for life on earth. (For the destruction of death, see Rev 20:14.)

25:9-12 Oracle against Moab. The specific reference to Moab here is usually taken to indicate a date after the Exile when relations were bad between Judea and her neighbors. (The oracle in Isa 24:17-18 is cited as an oracle against Moab in Jer 48:43-44.) Moab was located east of the Dead Sea.

26:1-19 Song of trust. Isa 26 begins as a standard psalm of trust in God, affirming that God vindicates the life of the righteous poor. Verses 11-19 proceed to contrast the other lords who have ruled over Israel with the people of God. The other lords are dead; they cannot rise. The allusion here is probably to Babylon, which was indeed dead as a world power. The Israelites had long labored in vain, failing to achieve salvation. But now, "your dead shall live, their corpses shall rise" (26:19). Some scholars take this verse as the earliest attestation of belief in resurrection in the Hebrew Bible. In view of the context, however, that is unlikely. The point is that Babylonian power is broken and will not be revived. Israelite power, which had been broken, will be revived. The resurrection involved is probably another formulation of the increase of the nation noted in verse 15 (compare Ezekiel's vision of the valley full of dry bones in Ezek 37, which is explicitly interpreted to refer to "the whole house of Israel"). It is the resurrection of a nation through a new generation, not the resuscitation of those who are already dead. Of course, the use of resurrection language to describe the restoration of the Jewish people helped to pave the way for the eventual emergence of a belief in the resurrection of the dead (which is first attested in Judaism in the second century b.c.e.).

26:20-21 Hiding from the wrath. This short oracle suggests that Israel (or perhaps the remnant) is exempt from the wrath of God. The idea that some people can hide from the wrath recalls the Exodus story in which the Lord passes over those houses that have been properly marked (Exod 12). For God going forth to judge the world, the reader should compare the theophanies in Judg 5; Deut 33; Hab 3; also Psalm 98. The prophet also assures the people that the time of God's wrath is a brief moment. If they can wait out the bad time, they will yet be glorified. This idea also plays an important role in Second Isaiah's explanation of the Exile.

27:1 Leviathan. A number of passages in the Bible allude to a battle between God and a monster (variously called a dragon or Rahab; see Isa 51:9; Job 26:12). Usually this battle is in the past. The story of this battle is not told in Genesis or Exodus, and we have only recently come to understand the allusion. The Canaanite myths (which were discovered at Ugarit in northern Syria in 1929) include the story of a battle between the god Baal and the Sea. Associated with the Sea are monsters called Lotan, the dragon, and the crooked serpent. All these are probably the same figure, called by different names. The dragon is a symbol of chaos—all the forces opposed to peace and order. The battle between a god and a dragon was a Canaanite story and symbolized the victory of life and order over chaos. For the Canaanites, Baal was the god who slew the monster and made civilized life possible. When the biblical authors referred to this story, they substituted Yahweh for Baal. For them, it was their God who slew the dragon when the world was created or Israel was led out of Egypt.

Leviathan in Isa 27:1 is the Lotan of Canaanite myth and another name for the sea dragon. This passage, however, suggests that he has not yet been slain. The decisive battle for the welfare and salvation of the world has not yet been won. It remains in the future, to be fought on the "day of the Lord." This expectation of a decisive action by God in the future becomes increasingly prominent in later biblical writings and in the apocalyptic literature. The symbolism of the sea monsters plays a prominent part in Dan 7 and in the Book of Revelation, especially chapters 12 and 13.

The symbol of the monster, Leviathan, is exceptionally powerful. Traditional Christianity would relate this figure to Satan, but the original symbol could be used for any threat to human welfare. "Doing battle with the monster" remains a useful metaphor for our various struggles in life.

27:2-13 The restoration of Israel. This section of Isaiah concludes with a series of oracles introduced by the phrase "On that day." The first picks up the motif of the vineyard from Isa 5. Now Yahweh is no longer angry. Briers and thorns are no longer means of punishment; rather, God will burn them.

The restoration of Israel is conditional, however, on cultic purity—essentially observance of the reform carried out by King Josiah in 621 b.c.e. (see 2 Kgs 22–23), which involved the destruction of altars and places of worship outside of Jerusalem, in accordance with the law of Deut 12.

The "fortified city" (v. 10) and "not an understanding people" (v. 11) would seem to refer to a specific city and people. Many scholars identify the city in this case as Samaria. The allusions to Jacob and Israel, then, should be read as "the northern kingdom," and the implication would be that Israel should find its center in Jerusalem and not in Samaria. The passage is obscure, however. Both its origin and its reference are uncertain.

The last two oracles refer to the gathering in of Jews from the Diaspora. As we have come to expect in the Book of Isaiah, they are to worship on the holy mountain in Jerusalem. Part of the editor's program was apparently to reunite the whole people with Mount Zion as the place of worship for all. In this respect he was probably in continuity with Isaiah of Jerusalem.

POLITICS AND SALVATION
Isa 28:1–33:24

With chapter 28 we return to a cluster of oracles from Isaiah himself. The core of this cluster comes from the time of Hezekiah's decision to revolt against Assyria in 701 B.C.E. A major factor in Hezekiah's decision to revolt was the hope that Egypt would support the various rebel states. Many of Isaiah's prophecies are concerned with the folly of that hope.

These chapters have come to us through the hands of an editor. The oracles are arranged so that judgment and salvation alternate. Many of the oracles of salvation may come from a later time. Nearly all of chapters 32–33 consist of later material. The final editing of this material probably took place after the Babylonian Exile.

28:1-4 The fall of Samaria. The first oracle of this section comes from an earlier period of Isaiah's career, before the fall of Samaria in 722 B.C.E. It is included here partly to ensure that the prophet's word will be seen to address all of Israel and partly because drunkenness is also a theme of the following oracle in verses 7-22. The oracle in verses 1-4 recalls Isaiah's preaching in Isa 5 and that of the prophet Amos. The downfall of Samaria comes from the lifestyle of the upper classes, symbolized by their drunkenness. The "garland" in verse 1 refers to the city of Samaria, perched like a crown on a hill.

28:5-6 The remnant. These verses are the work of an editor who wants to give a positive connotation to the image of a crown. The remnant here has a purely positive meaning. For the prophet Isaiah it was always ambiguous.

28:7-22 Judah's covenant with death. Verses 7-13 refer to Isaiah's dispute with the priests and the other prophets. The heavy drinking may have been in the context of a cultic celebration of Canaanite origin. People drank themselves into a stupor in a celebration of fellowship with the dead. It was an ex-

pensive practice that only the rich could afford. Whether Isaiah is referring to this ritual or not, the drunkenness of the priests implies social irresponsibility.

Verse 9 is presumably a quotation of Isaiah's opponents. In verse 10 they mock his preaching as if it were the stammering of a child. (The Hebrew makes no real sense.) Isaiah retorts that his speech sounds strange because they do not listen (see Isa 6:9 and, more directly, Ezek 3:5-9). The word of the Lord becomes nonsense to them, so that they stumble without guidance.

Verses 14-15 are addressed to the rulers of Jerusalem, probably including the religious leaders. They are arrogant because they think they are secure. The "covenant with death" probably refers to an alliance with Egypt. The rulers think that the scourge of Assyria will not touch them because of this alliance. Isaiah, however, sees it as a covenant with death. Death (Mot) was the name of the Canaanite god, enemy of Baal, the god of fertility. Egypt, the traditional enemy of Israel, is called "Death" here, as it is given the name of another Canaanite deity, Rahab, in Isa 30:7. The point is that the attempt to secure life ends in death (see the story of Adam and Eve, and also Hos 13:1, where the Israelites who worship Baal find Mot [Death] instead). Isaiah says that the rulers have made lies their refuge. The lies are the double-talk inherent in diplomacy, but also the hope for Egyptian protection, which was only an illusion.

The cornerstone that God lays in Zion (v. 16) is either God or righteousness and justice. It implies a reference to the Davidic covenant, but the security of Zion depends on its adherence to justice (compare the oracle to Ahaz in Isa 7:9: "Unless your faith is firm you shall not be firm"). Those who trust in anything other than God will be swept away by the flood of Assyria (see Isa 8:8). The saying about the short bed in verse 20 means that there will be no place to rest or hide. The Assyrian invasion is the "strange deed" of God, just as surely as David's victory over the Philistines at Mount Perazim (2 Sam 5:17-25) or Joshua's victory over Gibeon when the sun stood still (Josh 10:1-15). The oracle ends with a definitive assurance that Isaiah has heard of the coming destruction directly from God.

28:23-29 A parable of salvation. The severe proclamation of judgment is followed by a promise of relief. The argument is based on analogy from nature: there is a season for everything, destruction cannot go on forever. Whether Isaiah spoke this oracle is disputed. It accords well with his overall message. He never predicted that Judah would be left without any remnant. It is unlikely that he delivered this oracle together with the preceding one, since it would have undermined the threat, but he may well have spoken it later, when the Assyrian invasion was underway or already past. An editor placed it here to show that the threat of destruction was ultimately modified and should not be taken as final.

29:1-8 Ariel, Ariel. Ariel is evidently a name for Jerusalem. Its meaning and origin are obscure. It may be derived from a word meaning "altar."

Verses 1-5a represent God as attacking Jerusalem (presumably through the Assyrians) just as David did long ago. Verse 1 gives the impression that the festivals are observed in a mindless manner and to no avail. Verse 4 vividly describes how Jerusalem will be brought low, but it stops short of saying that the city will be captured.

The sudden visitation by God in verse 6 is ambiguous here. On the one hand, it completes the humiliation of Jerusalem; on the other hand, it is also a saving act. The enemy will be frustrated at the last moment and will vanish like a dream of the night. This passage strongly resembles the Zion ideology presented in the psalms. According to Ps 48:5-6,

. . . the kings assemble,
    they come on together;
They also see, and at once are stunned,
    terrified, routed.

The psalm attests the belief in the inviolability of Zion, a popular belief in Jerusalem that was later sharply criticized by Jeremiah (Jer 7:4). Many scholars question whether Isaiah would have endorsed such a belief. Yet, we have found throughout that Isaiah's message was double-edged. First, Judah would be brought to its knees, but it would not be utterly destroyed. Isaiah modifies the Zion theology by insisting that Jerusalem is not protected from humiliation. The "strange deed" (28:21) of the Lord, then, includes both extensive destruction and ultimate deliverance, and is presumably meant to teach Judah a severe lesson.

29:9-16 Criticism of the "wise." These verses continue the critique of 28:7-22. The

blindness of the leaders recalls the prophecy of Isa 6:9-10. The reasons for the criticism are twofold: superficial worship (v. 13; compare Matt 15:8; Mark 7:6) and the attempt of the king's advisers to control their destiny by devious diplomacy. Isaiah's ideal of simple submission to the plan of God would, of course, eliminate Judah's ambitions as a state.

29:17-24 Prophecy of salvation. In some respects, the predominant optimism of this prophecy is closer in spirit to Second Isaiah than to Isaiah of Jerusalem (compare 29:18 with 42:7). Yet, much of what it anticipates concerns the internal reform of Judah, especially the removal of the arrogant rulers. This theme follows well enough on verses 9-16. It may be that an original oracle of Isaiah was recast by the editor to provide a counterpart to the negative oracles of verses 9-16.

30:1-18 Alliance with Egypt. Isaiah again castigates the Judeans for relying on international intrigue and especially on the promise of Egyptian help. The gifts given to Egypt are wasted. Egypt is called "Rahab," a name for the chaos monster (see Job 26:12), but it is a subdued Rahab, not only evil but useless. The prophet is irate at the unwillingness of the people to listen to his own message or to consider the Holy One as a factor in their plans. The king's counselors found prophets useful enough when they spoke flattery and were willing to spread propaganda; the prophet who had an independent point of view was merely a nuisance.

Isaiah's message to Hezekiah was essentially the same as his advice to Ahaz: "By waiting and by calm you shall be saved." First, they should not provoke the Assyrians by revolting. Second, they should not compound the problem by alliances and attempts at resistance. Isaiah makes no allowance for national pride, nor even for the natural instinct to provide for one's own protection. The *trust* is that God will protect them, not indeed from all harm, but from being wiped out. This passive approach might mean accepting much suffering, but Isaiah could validly argue that the alternatives were worse. They could not hope to flee from the Assyrians. Patient trust here becomes the cornerstone (Isa 28:16) of the hope for salvation in Zion. We may compare Isaiah's stance with the ethic of nonresistance attributed to Jesus in the Sermon on the Mount (Matt 5:38-42).

We should emphasize, however, that for Isaiah nonresistance was a political tactic that might lessen the danger of outright destruction.

30:19-26 Salvation for Zion. Verses 19-26, probably the work of an editor, expand on the idea that God is willing to show favor. The concern for the destruction of idols (v. 22) and the transformation of the high places (v. 23) point to the time of King Josiah's reform, when the cultic sites outside Jerusalem were destroyed (2 Kgs 23). Verse 21, "This is the way . . . ," is the fulfillment of the promise of Isa 2:3 that God would "instruct us in his ways."

30:27-33 Judgment on Assyria. This oracle, too, may be a later addition, from the time when Assyria fell to the Babylonians in 612 B.C.E. The idea that Assyria would eventually be destroyed had its precedent in Isa 10. The manifestation of God in the thunderstorm is the image used throughout Isaiah for destruction, whether of Israel or of Assyria. The prophet points out that the oppressors of history eventually fall. Even though the prophets use historical crises as occasions to press for the reform of their own people, it is important that they do not thereby endorse the actions of the superpowers.

31:1-3 Flesh and spirit. Yet another indictment of the alliance with Egypt puts the matter in a new way: the Egyptians are human and not divine, their horses are flesh and not spirit. The contrast here is not between body and soul but between human power and divine power. The Egyptians have only fallible human power; they are not supernatural and can work no miracles to save Judah from Assyria. The point is that Judah overrates Egypt. Similarly the horses, a crucial element in the armaments for the day, are only flesh; they cannot withstand what Isaiah sees as the plan of God. This contrast of flesh, as mere humanity, to the spirit or power of God will play an important role in the theology of St. Paul in the New Testament.

31:4-6 Deliverance of Zion. As in the preceding chapters, an editor has balanced the prophet's indictment with an oracle of salvation. The image of God sheltering Jerusalem like a flock of birds fits well with the popular Zion theology but is far too simple for Isaiah, who preached consistently that only a remnant would survive. The reference to idols in verse 7 again shows the concerns of King Josiah's reform.

31:8 Fall of Assyria. Like the preceding chapter, chapter 31 ends with a prediction of the fall of Assyria, to set the record straight. When Assyria did fall, the sword was wielded by the Babylonians, but a Jewish prophet would still see that event as the work of the Lord.

32:1-8 A just king. Unlike the messianic prophecies in Isa 9 and 11, this passage does not refer explicitly to the Davidic line or the royal ideology; therefore it has been thought to come from a later hand. It does presuppose the existence of the monarchy, however, and so must be preexilic. The contrast of the fool and the noble is typical of the wisdom literature. Verse 3 would seem to deliberately revoke Isa 6:10. The concern of the passage is with justice in the land, with feeding the hungry and giving drink to the thirsty. It implies a criticism of the rulers of the day, who are branded as fools for their neglect of the Lord and for social injustice. The oracle is in continuity with the preaching of Isaiah, but the generalized references to the fool and the trickster lack the specificity of a passage like Isa 5.

32:9-13 Prophecy of impending destruction. This passage picks up motifs from earlier prophecies of Isaiah (see the oracle against the women of Jerusalem in 3:16-26 and the briers and thorns in 5:6; 7:23-24). Here, however, the address is to women of the countryside, in view of the references to fields and harvest. It does not indict them for luxury but wants to alert them to imminent danger. The occasion of this oracle is unknown.

32:14-20 A rustic utopia. The New American Bible has transposed verse 19 and placed it before verse 15, thereby altering the sense of the passage. In the Hebrew the transformation of the desert goes hand in hand with the destruction of the city. When the city is destroyed, the people will live in the quiet countryside, imbued with the spirit of the Lord. This passage does not accord well with either the message of Isaiah or with most of the tradition in this book, all of which had an important place for a purified Jerusalem in any final utopia (see especially 2:1-5, but also 33:17-24). The New American Bible solves the difficulty by moving the last verse and so allowing that the city may share in the restoration. Others suggest a different translation (for example, the "cities shall lie peaceful in the plain"—New English Bible), but even this contrasts with the exaltation of Zion in Isa 2. We may at least see some continuity between Isaiah's disdain for the luxury of the upper classes and the negative attitude toward the city here. The blooming of the desert appears again in 35:1 and 43:19-20.

33:1 Oracle against an enemy. This very brief oracle is addressed to Assyria or Babylon or some other enemy. The logic is the same as in Isa 10 or 30:27-33: the day of the oppressor will come.

33:2-16 Prayer for God's manifestation. This section is made up of smaller units that alternate between distress and hope for the manifestation of God. Verses 2-4 pray for God to be revealed on Zion and terrify all enemies. Verses 7-9 describe the breakdown of the country. Verses 10-13 are an oracle proclaiming the theophany. Verse 14 states the initial human response: who of us can live with the consuming fire? The manifestation of God is terrifying even for God's own people. Verses 15-16 give the answer: the virtuous can stand in the presence of God. This whole passage would seem to be derived from a liturgy in the Jerusalem temple (see Psalm 24).

33:17-24 The restoration of Zion. This passage may well have concluded one edition of the prophecies of Isaiah. The editor promises a full restoration of the monarchy and of Zion, which had been major points of reference in the prophecy of Isaiah. Compare the earlier prophecies in Isa 2, 9, and 11.

POSTEXILIC ORACLES

Isa 34:1–35:10

These two chapters are generally believed to belong together. The deliverance of Jerusalem is the counterpart of the destruction of Edom. There are also similarities of language in the two chapters. The setting is after the Exile, when the Jewish community experienced much tension with all its neighbors. Edom lay immediately south of Judah.

34:1-17 Oracle against Edom. This oracle begins with a call to judgment (see Deut 32:1) against all nations and then moves to the specific case of Edom. The presuppositions of the judgment are drawn from the royal ideology:

the Lord is Zion's defender and defeats all nations that oppose it. The passage is notable for two reasons. First, it uses the imagery of cosmic destruction—the heavens will be rolled up like a scroll. This imagery is obviously metaphorical here. It is a poetic evocation of utter desolation, which attests the absolute power of God over the world. In the later apocalyptic literature this imagery is used in a more literal way.

Second, we cannot overlook the fact that this is a rather gory fantasy of vengeance. It is true that the vengeance of the Lord is closely related to the idea of justice. It is a matter of punishing the oppressor and vindicating the oppressed (see Deut 32:34-43). Yet, it is no less true that this oracle expresses the frustration and resentment of the Jewish community in the hard times of the postexilic period. The sentiments expressed are less than admirable, but they are certainly an honest expression of human nature. Religious people have often expected their God to satisfy their desire for vengeance. The expectation, however, is seldom fulfilled.

35:1-10 A triumphal procession. Chapter 35 provides the positive counterpart to chapter 34 by focusing on Israel's liberation. The imagery is closely related to that of Second Isaiah: there will be a highway in the desert (see Isa 40:3), the desert will bloom and burst forth with springs (see Isa 43:19). Verse 10 is repeated directly in Isa 51:11. The liberation involves opening the eyes of the blind and the ears of the deaf (see Isa 42:7). The theme of the procession, which is also fundamental to Second Isaiah, is probably derived from the temple cult. The message is one of comfort and hope. Undoubtedly the author of these chapters saw the destruction of enemies like Edom as a necessary precondition for the transformation. In both cases we must recognize the role of fantasy, but the images of chapter 35 have lasting power to console and encourage those in need of liberation.

STORIES FROM THE TIME OF KING HEZEKIAH

Isa 36:1–39:8

The prose narrative that concludes First Isaiah is paralleled, almost word for word, in 2 Kgs 18:13–20:19. Since the account fits into the ongoing narrative of Kings and is written in the style of that work, we may assume that it was borrowed from there by the editor of Isaiah.

The narrative is made up of three episodes: the invasion of Sennacherib in chapters 36–37, the sickness and recovery of Hezekiah in chapter 38, and the Babylonian delegation in chapter 39. The stories in chapters 38 and 39 qualify the miraculous deliverance in chapter 37. Chapter 38 suggests that Hezekiah is a special king in any case, and chapter 39 warns that the deliverance from the Assyrians will not be repeated when the Babylonians attack.

36:1–37:38 The invasion of Sennacherib. The narrative in Isa 36 differs from that of 2 Kgs 18 in one major respect. It omits 2 Kgs 18:14-16, which says that Hezekiah submitted and paid an exorbitant tribute to the king of Assyria, including even the gold overlay from the panels of the temple. The accuracy of that passage in 2 Kings is confirmed by an Assyrian account, which boasts that Hezekiah was shut up in Jerusalem "like a bird in a cage," his territory reduced, some two hundred thousand of his people taken into slavery, and the tribute increased. The account in Isaiah (like 2 Kgs 18:17–19:37) makes no mention of this humiliation but ends instead with a miraculous deliverance by the angel of the Lord.

There are other difficulties in the narrative. 2 Kgs 18:9 puts the accession of Hezekiah before the fall of Samaria, in 725 B.C.E. His fourteenth year then would be 711 B.C.E., but we know that Sennacherib's campaign took place in 701 B.C.E. The dates have been somehow confused in the transmission of the text. Tirhakah, mentioned in Isa 37:9, did not become king of Egypt until 690/89 B.C.E. He is named here by mistake, by an author who evidently wrote long after the events. Moreover, the narrative is not really one account but two—the first in Isa 36:1–37:9a, the second in Isa 37:9b-36. The second account repeats part of the words of the Assyrian messengers from the first account but gives a slightly different account of the role of Isaiah. The main problem, however, concerns the relation of the incident described here to that in 2 Kgs 18:14-16.

Some scholars resolve this problem (and the mention of Tirhakah) by supposing that there was a second invasion by Sennacherib

about 688 B.C.E. There is no extrabiblical evidence for this. It is simpler to suppose that a single invasion was remembered in different ways, as indeed there are differences between the two accounts in Isa 36–37. In that case, we must assume that Hezekiah was forced into submission. The cost to Judah was enormous, but Jerusalem was spared and Hezekiah was allowed to continue on the throne. Even this much must have seemed like a miraculous deliverance to the people of Jerusalem, since they had little hope of withstanding the Assyrian attack.

The reason for Sennacherib's *relative* leniency is not clear. Isa 37:7 suggests that he was eager to return home to forestall conspiracy. Isa 37:9 suggests that he was threatened by an Egyptian advance. There is a report in the Greek historian Herodotus that an Assyrian army was overrun by field mice near the Egyptian border. This report has the appearance of a legend, but some have supposed that it arose from an outbreak of bubonic plague in the Assyrian army, and that this in turn was perceived by the Jews as the work of the angel of the Lord. In any case, Judah had not escaped unscathed. The description of the ravaged land in Isa 1:2-8 probably refers to this time.

36:1–37:9a The first account. The first account is largely taken up with the speech of the Assyrian messengers. The capture of Lachish, southwest of Jerusalem, is known from an Assyrian wall relief and from excavations at the site. The speech of the messengers is probably a creation of the Jewish author, inspired perhaps by Isaiah's oracle against Assyria in Isa 10:5-11. The unreliability of Egypt might indeed be a theme of Assyrian propaganda, as it was of Isaiah's preaching. The suggestion that Hezekiah had alienated Yahweh by tearing down some altars presupposes knowledge of Hezekiah's reform (2 Chr 29:3-31:21). The claim that Yahweh sent the king of Assyria anticipates the propaganda of Cyrus of Persia at a later time. In all, the speech reads like clever propaganda, although it may tell us more about Jewish perceptions than about Assyrian views. The punch line comes in verse 18: "Has any of the gods of the nations ever rescued his land from the hand of the king of Assyria?" The success of a nation is taken to reflect the power or weakness of its God. In

Jewish eyes, the assault on Jerusalem was a direct affront to Yahweh (see Ps 79:10: "Why should the nations say, 'Where is their God?'").

The response of Isaiah (37:6) in the first account recalls his advice to King Ahaz in Isa 7:4: "Do not fear." The advice to remain calm was not, of course, easy advice in the circumstances, but it was consistent with the prophet's stance throughout his career.

37:9b-36 The second account. The second account elaborates on the role of Isaiah. First, he recites a lengthy psalm, affirming that an attack on Jerusalem is an insult to the Holy One of Israel and is doomed to defeat (see Psalms 2, 48). Some of the wording of the psalm recalls Second Isaiah (37:26; see also 45:21; 46:10), and this contributes to the impression that it does not come from Isaiah himself (also compare 37:29 with Ezek 38:4). In verses 30-32, however, we may well have an authentic prophecy of Isaiah, since it recalls his position in Isa 7. Cultivation will not even be possible for two years. Only a remnant will remain, but it will be the bearer of God's promises to Zion. Here the full cost to Judah is acknowledged.

Isaiah's prophecy of the remnant is overlaid here, however, with pious legend. First, in verses 33-35 Isaiah is said to prophesy that the Assyrians would not even reach Jerusalem. The Assyrian account, by contrast, explicitly claims to have cast up earthworks against the city. Then comes the action of the angel of the Lord. Even if we assume that a large number of Assyrians died in a plague (185,000 is impossibly high), attribution of this to the angel of the Lord requires a leap of faith and is the stuff of legend.

What actually happened is far from clear. Sennacherib must have offered Hezekiah terms that did not require his abdication, and he accepted. Whether Isaiah approved of the surrender is not reported. The occasion can hardly have aroused much rejoicing in Jerusalem. Yet, with the passage of time the humiliation was forgotten, and the fact that Jerusalem was not destroyed was seen as proof of God's protection. In one sense this showed a proper appreciation of the gift of life, which was preserved against all expectations. On the other hand, it surely contributed to the complacent belief that Zion could never fall, a be-

lief that Jeremiah encountered with much frustration a century later.

The violent death of Sennacherib is also reported in nonbiblical stories.

38:1-8 The sickness of Hezekiah. The king's own experience parallels the deliverance of Jerusalem. At first his death seems certain; then he gets a reprieve. The reason is apparently his wholehearted piety. We may infer that this is also why Jerusalem was reprieved. Things might be different under another king. This story, too, has a legendary quality in the supernatural sign of the reversal of the sun. Such stories are meant to arouse wonder, not to report fact. Note that Hezekiah is not criticized for asking for a sign, as Ahaz had been.

38:9-20 Hymn of thanksgiving. Hezekiah recites a psalm of a type that is well-attested in the Psalter (see Psalms 6, 13, 22). It begins by describing the plaintiff's distress and then moves to thanksgiving for the Lord's deliverance. The moral in 38:16 applies also to the experience of Jerusalem in the preceding chapter. Note that this psalm entertains no hope for God's favor beyond death. The finality of death made the plight of Hezekiah and of Jerusalem all the more urgent.

39:1-8 The delegation from Babylon. The story of the delegation from Babylon prepares us for the transition to the Babylonian era. The fall of Jerusalem to the Babylonians is never described in the Book of Isaiah, but it is the presupposition of Isa 40–55. The editor of the book fills the gap by having Isaiah prophesy it here in the story taken from 2 Kgs 20. At the same time, the prophecy corrects the impression that Zion cannot fall, which might be derived from chapters 36–37.

Hezekiah's action in displaying his treasures is typical of ancient diplomacy and was designed to impress his visitors. Babylon at that time was a rising power eager to foster rebellion against Assyria. That such a delegation should have visited Hezekiah is not in itself implausible. Hezekiah's reaction to Isaiah's prediction smacks of Louis XIV's famous dictum "Après moi le déluge." The author probably meant only to emphasize that Hezekiah ended his days in peace because of his piety. (Compare the idea that the punishment of King Ahaz was deferred until the time of his son because he repented [1 Kgs 21:29].)

COMMENTARY: SECOND ISAIAH (Isa 40–55)

At Isa 40:1 we move to a new setting at the end of the Babylonian Exile (539 B.C.E.), and the oracles that follow are very different from those of Isa 1–39 in tone. They are often called the "Book of Consolation." Unlike chapters 1–39, all the oracles in these chapters are likely to be the work of a single prophet. They may be divided into two parts: chapters 40–48 deal predominantly with liberation from Babylon; chapters 49–55 with the restoration of Zion. The difference between these parts, however, is a matter of degree of emphasis and cannot be taken to indicate different origins or settings.

LIBERATION FROM BABYLON

Isa 40:1–48:22

The first part of Second Isaiah takes the good news that the Exile is at an end as the occasion to contrast Israel and Babylon and their respective gods.

40:1-11 The proclamation of release. This passage serves as an introduction to all of Second Isaiah by specifying the occasion of the oracles—the release of Israel from the Babylonian Exile. In Ezra 1 this event is attributed to a decree of Cyrus, king of Persia. The prophet, however, claims that there is a more fundamental cause, namely, a decree of Yahweh in the heavenly council. The idea of a heavenly council of gods was widespread in the ancient world and was based on the assumption that God has a royal court like any great king. Vivid biblical illustrations are found in Psalm 82, 1 Kgs 22, and Isa 6. The scene in Isa 40 may be viewed as a counterpoint to that of Isa 6. In the earlier chapter the decree was one of judgment on Israel; here it is one of consolation. (Note that Jerusalem can stand for the people as a whole.)

Verse 2 presupposes the usual view that the Exile was a punishment for Israel's sins, but adds that Israel has received "double for all her sins." The implication is that the suffering is not fully explained as punishment. We will find later that Second Isaiah finds a more positive way to understand the experience of the Exile.

The voice in verse 3 is the voice of an angel implementing the divine decree. The "way" is analogous to the great ritual processions of the Babylonian gods, but also the triumphal procession of Yahweh from Mount Sinai at the time of the Exodus (compare Ps 68:8-9; Deut 33:3). The Exodus motif is made explicit by the location "in the desert." The return from Babylon is seen as a reenactment of the original liberation of Israel out of Egypt. The hope for a new Exodus was found as early as Hosea (ch. 2) in the eighth century, but now Second Isaiah claims that it is actually taking place.

The liberation of Israel is viewed as a revelation of God. In the first Exodus, Israel's God went before the people in a pillar of cloud or a pillar of fire. Now all flesh would see the glory of God. The prophet is told to proclaim the difference between the passing power of humanity and the unshakable word of God. The power of the Babylonians, which had seemed so great, had now faded like the grass of the field.

In verses 9-11 Zion/Jerusalem is told to proclaim the good news to "the cities of Judah." (The familiar translation "O thou who bringest good tidings to Zion" is possible but improbable, since the verbs are feminine in agreement with Zion.) Here again Jerusalem is an ideal figure, representing the community of exiles who would join the prophet in returning to restore the actual city. We should bear in mind that not all the Jews who were in Babylon took the opportunity to return; many decided that they were better off in exile. The prophet is not only proclaiming deliverance but urging the people to accept it. He bases his exhortation on the assurance that God is with them with power, but also with loving care, suggested by the popular image of the shepherd (compare Psalm 23 and John 10).

This passage of Second Isaiah is best known to Christian readers from the citations in Matt 3:3 and John 1:23, where Isa 40:3 is taken to mean "the voice of one crying in the wilderness" and applied to John the Baptist. The citation is not quite accurate and does not give the original meaning of the passage. The application to John was apt enough, however, since he too was proclaiming a new act of salvation like the Exodus, and he set himself to prepare for it.

40:12-31 The incomparable God. The threefold oracle in verses 12-31 follows naturally from the declaration "Here is your God" in verse 9. The first stanza (vv. 12-17) asks a series of rhetorical questions reminiscent of Job 38–41. The implied answer is that it is Yahweh alone who has created the earth. The nations are as nothing before Yahweh, since the whole earth is in this God's grasp.

The second stanza (vv. 18-24) begins with another rhetorical question: To whom can God be likened? Second Isaiah mocks the statue-makers, as he will do at much greater length in chapter 44. (The New American Bible unnecessarily inserts verses 6-7 of chapter 41 here.) The initial question is balanced by another: "Do you not know? Have you not heard?" (40:21). What has been told from the beginning is the sovereign power of Yahweh to bring princes to nought and make rulers as nothing (40:23; compare Psalm 107). Yahweh's ability to overthrow the Babylonians comes from the fact that it was Yahweh who created the earth, as the cult tradition of Jerusalem had long claimed (for example, Psalms 93, 95).

The third stanza (vv. 25-31) closely parallels the second in form. The introductory question, "To whom can you liken me . . . ?" (40:25), is followed by a command to look up at the stars, which were often honored as divine by Babylonians. The prophet shares the common belief that the stars are a heavenly host of supernatural beings but insists that they are subject to Yahweh, who keeps them in order. At this point the prophet directly reproaches the Israelites for their despair in feeling abandoned by their God. The second half of the stanza, "Do you not know, or have you not heard?" (40:28), responds directly to this despair. The Creator is everlasting. Not only does God not grow faint but the Creator is a source of renewed power for those who are attentive to the divine will. Hope did not come easily to the Jews during the Exile. It was only possible for those who deeply believed that their God was indeed the supreme God. Second Isaiah was convinced that his faith was now vindicated by the fall of Babylon. Note that in verse 25 God is called "the Holy One," a title often found in First Isaiah.

41:1–42:9 Judgment and election. Many commentators divide this long passage into several short oracles. In particular, 42:1-4 is commonly set apart as one of the so-called "Servant Songs." The key to understanding the passage, however, is to recognize that there are two parallel and complementary trial scenes in 41:1-20 and 41:21–42:9. In each case there is:

—summons to trial	41:1	41:21
—legal questioning	41:2-4	41:22-29
—election and reassurance of Israel	41:5-20	42:1-9

In the first scene the nations are summoned for judgment. The issue to be decided is: Who raised up Cyrus of Persia, the "champion of justice," who overthrew Babylon? The answer is given unequivocally: Yahweh, first and last, is responsible for all developments in history. Verses 5-7 (verses 6-7 are inserted after 40:20 in our text) parody the reaction of the Gentiles. They have to encourage one another in making their idols, since the idols cannot encourage them. By contrast, Israel is chosen as the Servant of the Lord. However despised Israel may be in the Exile as a "worm" or "maggot" (compare Ps 22:6), there is no reason to fear. Yahweh is the servant's redeemer (41:14), buying his freedom from slavery. This section concludes with a prophecy of the transformation of the desert with water for the needy. The reference to the desert suggests that the Exodus theme is implied here and that the poor and needy are Israel. The transformation, however, is also for the Gentiles, so that they will recognize the work of the Holy One of Israel.

The second section has a long series of questions and constitutes a more coherent trial. The challenge is: Which of the gods had foretold the rise of Cyrus, and, more crucially, had heralded good news for Israel? The answer is a resounding "Not one." The conclusion is that "all of them are nothing" (41:29). Second Isaiah is more emphatic in denying the power of pagan gods than any earlier biblical book. The argument presupposes the prophet's faith that it is Yahweh who is responsible for the collapse of the power of Babylon. Anyone who did not already share that faith would hardly be persuaded.

The so-called Servant Song in 42:1-4 corresponds to 41:8-9 in singling out a chosen Servant. In both passages the Servant is Israel, conceived in terms of its ideal destiny. The mission of the Servant is specified much more fully in chapter 42 than in chapter 41. The spirit of the Lord is upon him, as on the messianic king in Isa 11. He is to bring justice to the nations, but in a nonviolent, nonaggressive way. The role is further elaborated in 42:6-7. The Servant is a covenant of the people, a light to the nations. We may recall the portrayal of Mount Zion as a center for the nations in Isa 2:2-4. The precise understanding of "a covenant of the people" (42:6) is disputed, but the idea seems to be that God makes a covenant with the nations through the mediation of Israel. The Servant is also sent to open the eyes of the blind and liberate the imprisoned. In the following passages the "blind" refers to Israel (42:16) and specifically to the Servant in 42:19! The most obvious "prisoners" in this context are the Jewish exiles in Babylon. Yet, the Servant Israel is being sent to help the blind and imprisoned.

Some scholars have drawn the conclusion that the Servant in this passage is not Israel but an individual, and that the passage comes from a different hand than the surrounding oracles. We will see in Isa 42:18–43:8, however, that there is considerable ambiguity in the idea of the Servant. There is tension between the ideal of what Israel is supposed to be and what the community actually is. It is Israel's destiny to be a light to the nations, but in order to fulfill this, the blind among the people must recover their sight and the exiles must be liberated.

The section concludes with affirmations that God does not give divine glory to idols (compare 41:6-7) and that "the earlier things have come to pass" (42:9; compare 41:22-23, 26). In this way the prophet concludes this long section by referring back to two important themes of chapter 41.

42:10-17 A hymn to Yahweh the warrior. The "new song" (v. 10) is a hymn of praise like Psalms 96 and 98, which begin with the same invitation. The reason for praise is given in verses 13-17: Yahweh the warrior, who has held back for a time, will let loose divine anger. Here again there is reference to the Exodus, when Yahweh was first recognized as a warrior (Exod 15:3). The divine warrior was traditionally supposed to have a destructive effect on nature (Isa 42:15; compare Judg 5:4-5; Hab 3:5-15; Nah 1:2-6). In Exodus 15 God leads the people to their triumphant occupation of the land; here too God will lead the "blind" Jews on their return journey. The confusion of idol worshipers in verse 17 is the corollary of the recognition of Yahweh as the true God.

42:18–43:8 The deaf and the blind. Despite his general euphoria, the prophet has moments of dejection. The address to his people as "blind and deaf" betrays some frustration on his part. The problem is not only that they are despoiled and plundered but they have become indifferent. So the prophet insists that even their humiliation in the Exile was the work of their God and was a punishment for sin. Yet Israel is still the Servant (42:19). The tension between Israel's vocation as Servant and its present reality is most obvious in this passage. Despite the past divine wrath, God has now redeemed Israel and promises to protect it in any ordeal, be it fire or water. The Holy One is identified as the savior of Israel, which is more precious than Egypt or Ethiopia. The implication is that the Persians will be allowed to conquer other countries in return for the release of Israel. The reason given in 43:4 is simply "because I love you" (compare Deut 9, which insists that the original gift of the land was not merited by Israel). The new Exodus is an Exodus of the blind.

There is some vacillation in Second Isaiah's portrayal of Israel. Some passages emphasize the ideal, what Israel is called to be, and minimize the people's sin. This passage is exceptional in its frank criticism of their shortcomings. The apparent inconsistency comes not only from the emotional intensity of the prophet but also from the nature of his program, which was to project an ideal of Yahweh's Servant that was not fully realized in the exilic community.

43:9-12 The Servant as witness. This brief trial scene repeats some of the motifs of the longer unit in 41:1–42:9. Again the issue is who is the true God, and the test is the ability to foretell the future. A new motif is introduced with the idea that the Jewish people are witnesses. They are called "my servant" collectively (the Hebrew reads the singular; the New American Bible changes it to "my servants"). The mission of witnessing is the same as being "a light for the nations" (42:6). Whereas in earlier times the Davidic king was Yahweh's representative on earth, that role has now passed to the people.

Isa 43:10 is exceptionally strong in its denial of the other gods and may be taken to mean that they do not even exist. The prophet is not a philosopher, however. What concerns him is not the existence of the gods as such but the power to save. He is completely unequivocal in his assertion that there is no savior but Yahweh.

43:14–44:5 Exodus and election. The immediate point of reference in this oracle is stated at the outset: the release of the Jews from Babylon. Isa 43:15-21 puts this event in context. Yahweh is the creator of Israel by virtue of the Exodus, yet the Jews are told not to remember the things of the past. The Exodus is not past history! It is something new, something that is happening in the present. The present tense in verse 16 ("opening a way") is quite deliberate. God's saving action, summed up in the Exodus story, is not all past but is repeatable. Exodus is a pattern in history. What matters is not so much whether it happened in the time of Moses but whether it is happening in the present. Second Isaiah thus points the way to using the Exodus story to throw light on a new situation. In our own time the Exodus story has been appropriated in a similar way by the liberation theologians of Latin America.

The original Exodus was followed by failure on Israel's part (see especially the indictment in Deut 32). Second Isaiah acknowledges this and even asserts that the destruction of Jerusalem was a punishment for Israel's sin. (The "first father" in 43:27 is probably Jacob; compare Hos 12:3.) Yet Jacob is also the Servant, formed from the womb (44:2; compare 49:5). The descendants of Israel will fulfill their destiny by the help of the spirit (compare 42:1), which will vitalize them as water brings life to dry ground. Compare the transforming power of the spirit in Ezek 36, where there is also an analogy with water, and in Joel 3. Here again we find a contrast between Israel's sinful history down to the present and its future as the Servant of the Lord.

44:6-23 The futility of idols. The comparison of Yahweh with the other gods begins by touching on some themes that are now familiar. Yahweh alone can predict events, and Israel is Yahweh's witness. The passage continues with a scathing attack on idolatry. The prophet is engaging in polemics. He is not attempting to give a sympathetic or even fair presentation of the idol-makers. The idol is only a piece of wood, such as one burns in the fire. It can have no power to save. Of course, the pagans probably looked on their idols much as Roman Catholics have looked on statues of saints—not as the actual sources of power but as representations that are helpful to the worshiper's imagination. The point of the polemic, however, is that the pagan gods are fittingly represented by pieces of wood, because they have no more power than their idols. The God of Israel, by contrast, is represented by a living people, whose resurgence from the Exile witnesses to God's vitality.

The polemic against the idols, then, culminates in the contrast with Israel, whom God has formed to God's own glory. Israel is not an icon but a Servant, a living representative. The "fashioning" of Israel entails wiping out its sin and redeeming it. The liberation from the Exile, then, is the occasion when Israel is to be remade into an appropriate reflection of the glory of God.

44:24–45:13 The Persian messiah. The central contention of this oracle is that Yahweh is creator of all, and therefore the fall of Babylon and the rise of Persia are God's work. The prophet's primary purpose is not to convince the Gentiles of this but to convince the Jews. So he begins by affirming that Yahweh is the redeemer of Israel and by highlighting the restoration of Jerusalem and Judah. The novelty of this passage, however, is the explicit statement that the decree to rebuild Jerusalem will come through the mouth of Cyrus, who is God's anointed king, or messiah (45:1).

The idea that God's purposes are achieved through pagan kings is not a new one. Isaiah of Jerusalem had said that Assyria was the rod of Yahweh's anger (Isa 10:5). Jeremiah declared the Babylonian king Nebuchadnezzar to be the servant of God (Jer 27:6). Unlike the Assyrian of Isa 10, Cyrus is not accused of pride or arrogance. He fulfills every wish of God. One purpose of his mission is that he himself may come to know that Yahweh is God. The prophet is preaching here a thorough universalism. Pagans may serve Yahweh even though they do not know the God of Israel. Ultimately Yahweh must be known from the rising of the sun to its setting (compare Mal 1:11).

The basis for this universalism is a thorough monotheism, which emerges here more clearly than in any earlier biblical book. There is no God beside Yahweh. Persian religion was dualistic: there was a god of light, responsible for the good, and a god of darkness, responsible for evil. Second Isaiah holds that one God creates both light and darkness, good and evil (45:7). (Compare the rugged insistence of Amos 3:6 that if evil befalls a city, Yahweh must have caused it.) The evil that befell Jerusalem was Yahweh's work; so now it is the rise of Cyrus that brings its restoration.

Not all the Jewish exiles could so readily accept a Persian messiah. The "woes" of verses 9-10 are addressed to those doubters who question whether this can be the work of God. All humankind is created by God and counts as children of God (v. 11). Yet, Second Isaiah has by no means abandoned the special place of Israel. The hand of God can be seen in Cyrus' career because he liberates the Jews and mandates the rebuilding of Jerusalem. It is for the sake of Jacob that Cyrus is called (v. 4). It is in the interest of the Jews themselves to accept the Persian sovereignty as the work of their God.

45:14-25 The hidden God. Nations may serve God without knowing it, but Second Isaiah believed that the time had come for universal recognition. People from the ends of the earth would bring gifts to the temple in Jerusalem. Verses 14-17 formulate a confession for these Gentiles. Verse 15 can also be translated "You are a God who hides yourself." The point is that until now the Gentiles would not have suspected that Yahweh controls all history. What has been hidden, however, is now made manifest. Yet the notion of a hidden God is important. What is going on in history may not always be obvious. We should not jump to conclusions because one party is prospering for a time while another is down; we must wait and see how things come out in the end. The prophet assumes that the humiliation of Israel was temporary and is now over. Its exaltation, which is now beginning, will be lasting and definitive.

The Gentiles say that Yahweh was a hidden God. Yet Yahweh protests that the word of God was not spoken in hiding but in the Jerusalem temple, the sacred space that is the very opposite of an empty waste. The predictions to which Second Isaiah repeatedly refers are the claims traditionally made in the Jerusalem cult that Yahweh is king of all the earth

(compare Psalms 93, 96-100). Yahweh has been hidden from the Gentiles only because they have not sought God in the right place. Now, claims the prophet, they are like fugitives from a battle, forced to acknowledge Yahweh by the course of events.

We must observe at this point that the prophet's expectations were not fully realized by the Jewish restoration. Other nations did not feel compelled to acknowledge that Yahweh was responsible for the rise of Persia. Israel would suffer further humiliations in future ages. The aspect of the prophecy that has enduring validity is that Yahweh is a hidden God. Only on rare occasions, like the fall of Babylon, does Yahweh appear to be in control of history. The challenge of Jewish and Christian faith has been to wait for such occasions, to affirm that Yahweh is God even in the depths of the Exile, and to hope that the day of liberation will finally come.

46:1-13 The gods of Babylon. Bel and Nebo are gods of the Babylonians. They are being carried on pack animals in flight from the fallen city. By contrast, Yahweh has carried Israel from its birth. Once again, the release from Babylon is seen as evidence that the God of Israel has power over and above the people of Israel, while the Babylonian gods are no more than their wooden statues.

The warning to the rebels, both Jewish and Gentile, is reminiscent of Psalm 2. God is established on Mount Zion. From there God summons Cyrus from a far land. The "former things" are the events by which Yahweh was first established on Zion (see Exod 15) and which are now being reenacted in the return from the Exile.

47:1-15 A taunt against Babylon. The taunt-song against a fallen enemy was a convention of ancient warfare. In this case the gloating is intensified by the fact that Babylon had humiliated Jerusalem. Two charges are brought against Babylon. First, there is the lack of mercy toward the Jews. The Exile was indeed a punishment designed by God, but Babylon was guilty too. We may compare the indictment of Assyria in Isa 10, even though it was "the rod of Yahweh's anger." Second, Babylon was guilty of hybris, the pride that sets itself equal to God. The boast, "I, and no one else!" (47:8) echoes a claim only Yahweh can make, and is therefore blasphemous. The taunt against Babylon here is similar to Isa 14, where it is called "morning star, son of the dawn," and to the taunts against Tyre in Ezek 27 and 28. Babylon's wisdom led it astray, as the pursuit of wisdom misled Adam and Eve in Gen 2–3. Babylon was famous for astrologers, who claimed they could predict the future by observing the stars, but they have no power to help.

This poem is imbued with a spirit of vengefulness that may be distasteful to modern Westerners. It was fully endorsed, however, in the Christian Book of Revelation, where Babylon is used as a symbol for Rome and is taunted bitterly in Rev 17–18 and contrasted with the new Jerusalem. The vengefulness must be seen in context. It is the outpouring of resentment by the oppressed. It is not love of one's enemy and it is not the noblest human emotion, but it is certainly understandable. The fall of Babylon was a necessary part of the liberation of the Jews. The taunt-song plays a part in rebuilding the self-esteem of a Jewish community that had been humiliated by Babylon. It can still strike a sympathetic cord with any people who are oppressed by an arrogant overlord and whose resentment is too deep to be glossed over by professions of charity.

48:1-22 Rebukes and exhortations. The oracle that concludes the first part of Second Isaiah is exceptional in the severity of its tone. We get the impression that the prophet is exasperated by the people's failure to respond. Many scholars have questioned the unity and authenticity of this chapter. There are indeed problems of coherence and consistency, but the chapter is held together by a number of recurring motifs (for example, the allusions to "stock" and "name" in verse 19 refer back to verse 1).

The prophet begins by establishing the reliability of God's word by referring to the "things of the past" that were foretold long ago. He then proceeds to argue for the need for a prophet, since he is now proclaiming something that has not been previously predicted. The denial that anyone could have heard of these things before is hard to reconcile with a passage like 45:21 ("Who announced this from the beginning. . . . Was it not I, the Lord?"), but compare the emphasis on novelty in 43:19. It may be that only the fall of Babylon is regarded as foretold, while the actual return is absolutely new (as in

43:18-19, "Remember not the events of the past . . .").

Verses 9-11 appear as a digression that affirms God's motive for action: for his own sake. This motivation is well established in the tradition (see already Deut 32:27 and several psalms and prayers). Despite the apparent scorn for Israel here, this passage lays a secure foundation for the restoration, since it does not depend on human merit. Verses 14-15 reaffirm that Cyrus will do God's will against Babylon. Verse 16 makes an unusual assertion of the prophet's own authority. Just as the word of God has been public in the past, so the prophet is sent openly now. Verses 17-19 follow with an appeal for obedience. Finally, in verse 20 we get the climactic command, which is the real "new thing" proclaimed by the prophet—the actual command to flee from Babylon. This command comes as the climax not only of chapter 48 but of the first half of Second Isaiah. It is echoed, appropriately, in Rev 18:4, where flight from another imperial city is demanded of Christians in the time of the end. The flight from Babylon becomes a metaphor for liberation from imperial power in any age.

Despite the severe rebukes of the preceding oracles, the prophet concludes that the Lord has redeemed the Servant. Israel's status as Servant is not something established by its past actions but something that is now being brought about by a new creative act of God. It is an ideal on the verge of realization.

THE RESTORATION OF ZION
Isa 49:1–55:13

49:1-7 The call of the Servant. Here, as in Isa 42, we have a direct reflection on the mission of the Servant. (The unit is often identified as 49:1-6, since a new oracle begins in verse 7, and distinguished as one of the Servant Songs.) The Servant is explicitly identified as Israel in verse 3, yet many commentators have argued that this identification cannot be original, for two reasons: first, the statement "from my mother's womb he gave me my name" strongly suggests that the Servant is an individual; second, in verse 5 the Servant appears to have a mission to Israel, and therefore to be distinct. Some commentators, then, have argued that the Servant in this passage is the prophet himself. The passage is indeed problematic, but there is no warrant for rejecting the clear identification with Israel or for supposing that the Servant here is different from other passages in Second Isaiah.

The statement that the Servant has been called "from the womb" echoes the call of Jeremiah (Jer 1:5: "Before I formed you in the womb I knew you"), and indeed Jeremiah appears in many ways to be a model for understanding the Servant. More broadly, the commissioning of the Servant here follows a traditional pattern already found in the call of Moses in Exod 3:1-4:17. God makes the commission, Moses protests his inadequacy, but God reassures him. The call from the womb is a way of saying that the mission of the Servant is like that of a prophet or Moses.

The apparent distinction between the Servant and Israel in verses 5-6 is more difficult. It is not absolutely certain that it is the Servant who is to raise up the tribes of Jacob; it is possible that God is the subject and that the restoration of Israel coincides with the realization of its mission as Servant. The more common understanding, however, sees the Servant as the subject. In this case we must recognize that the prophet has a special role in the transformation of Israel. He has to live out the role of the Servant and persuade the rest of the people to follow him. He and his followers represent the new Israel, and they still have a mission to their fellow countrymen. Isa 49:4 reflects the discouragement of the prophet, which we have already seen in chapter 48. The reassurance, however, is not only that he will be able to persevere (compare Jer 15:19-21) but that the model of Israel which he represents will prevail.

The mission of the Servant is not only concerned with the restoration of Israel; he must also be "a light to the nations" (v. 6), as in 42:6. Jeremiah, too, was appointed as a prophet to the nations (Jer 1:5). The way in which the mission is to be carried out is clarified in the supplementary oracle in 49:7. The "one despised . . . the slave of rulers" (v. 7) is surely Israel in exile (compare Isa 53:3). When Israel is restored, however, the kings of the earth will be astonished by the transformation and will be led to acknowledge the sovereignty of Yahweh. In this way Israel can be to the nations what the individual prophet was to the Jewish people.

Needless to say, princes did not prostrate themselves as readily as the prophet expected. What is significant, however, is the universal breadth of the mission. Israel remains a chosen people, but salvation must reach to the ends of the earth.

49:8–50:3 Consolation for Zion. This passage has a well-balanced structure. It begins with the triumphal procession back to Israel, as in chapter 40. The central part of the prophecy is a reassurance for Zion. Then the prophet returns to the gathering in of the exiles, viewed this time from the vantage point of Zion (compare Isa 11:10-16). Finally, it concludes with two short oracles affirming Yahweh's power to save.

The most striking lines in this passage are surely those in 49:15: "Can a mother forget her infant . . . ?" Female experience, as well as male, can serve as analogy for God. The analogy of the mother is then transferred to Zion. The abundance of children is indicative of the Hebrew idea of salvation—abundance of life in the land of Israel.

The tenderness toward Israel in this passage is in sharp contrast to the vindictive statement in 49:26: "I will make your oppressors eat their own flesh . . . ." The reference is to cannibalism in a besieged city. Yet, even this atrocious situation has a positive purpose, namely, that all flesh may come to know the Lord. The repetition of the word "flesh" is significant, and it highlights the condition of humanity over against the power of God.

The point of 50:1-3 is that the rejection of Zion was only temporary (for the metaphor of divorce, compare Hos 1–3). It was not that Yahweh was overcome by any other power. How could it be, when Yahweh even overcame the primeval power of the sea? Accordingly, no one should doubt Yahweh's ability to save.

50:4-11 The faithful disciple. This unit is often defined as 50:4-9 and distinguished as a Servant Song (although the word "servant" only occurs in verse 10). The reason it is set apart is that it is written in the first person, like 49:1-6, and appears to describe the sufferings of an individual, as does chapter 53. The "well-trained tongue" of verse 4 is literally "a disciple's tongue." The notion of disciple may be picked up from Isa 8:16, where the prophet's message is entrusted to his disciples.

The portrayal of the disciple here recalls

the confessions of Jeremiah (Jer 11:18-23; 15:10-21; 20:7-18). Jeremiah was "like a trusting lamb led to the slaughter" (Jer 12:19), and his pain was continuous (Jer 15:18), yet God made him "a solid wall of brass" (Jer 15:20; compare also Ezek 3:9, where the comparison with flint is used, as in Isa 50:7). The disciple here, like Jeremiah and Ezekiel, is upheld by God in the face of adversity. Moreover, the disciple appears to accept his afflictions willingly, although 50:10-11 may invoke evil on his adversaries, as Jeremiah also did. (Verses 10-11 are very obscure. "Kindle flames" may refer to a Persian ritual or may be merely a metaphor for trying to provide human solutions rather than wait for God.)

The "servant" mentioned in verse 10 is presumably the speaker in verses 4-9. Here again there is some ambiguity as to whether the reference is to the prophet himself or to the community of Israel. The passage makes good sense as an account of the hardships of the prophet, but it could also speak metaphorically of the mission of Israel to the nations. It may be that the prophet and his disciples represent the true mission of Israel, although they meet resistance even within the Jewish community. The enduring significance of the passage is ultimately independent of the historical reference. It paints a picture of the true disciple as one who perseveres in the face of adversity without concern for self-preservation. Christians have appropriately seen a correspondence between this model and the conduct of Jesus in his passion.

51:1-8 Exhortations to trust. The prophet recalls how Abraham was promised numerous descendants while Sarah was yet barren. During the Exile, Zion was as barren as Sarah, but it too will become fertile. Isa 51:4-5 alludes to the oracle in Isa 2:2-4 ("from Zion shall go forth instruction"—the same Hebrew word, torah, is used in both passages). The light to the peoples, associated with the Servant in 42:6 and 49:6, is here the justice of God, manifested from Zion. The permanence of God's justice is then contrasted with the potential transience of the earth and the actual transience of humanity. The power and justice of God cannot be judged on the basis of passing circumstances but only in view of the long-term outcome of events.

51:9–52:12 A rousing call. This long oracle is structured by a triple call of "Awake,

awake." The first is addressed to "the arm of the Lord," urging God to repeat the wonderful deeds of old. The Bible has no story of a battle between Yahweh and Rahab or a dragon. The battle with the sea monster was part of Canaanite mythology. It is taken over by the Israelites as a metaphor for the work of creation, when God reduced order to chaos (see Job 26:12). Here it also serves as a metaphor for the Exodus, when God "dried up the sea." The prophet is not interested in verifying the historical facts of the Exodus—"slaying the dragon" and "drying up the sea" are equally appropriate ways of referring to God's ability to overcome any enemy or obstacle. What matters is not what God did in the past but what God is doing in the present.

The second call is addressed to Jerusalem. Ezekiel had said that Jerusalem would drink the cup of her sister Samaria, a cup of grief and destruction (Ezek 23:32-33; Jer 25:15-29 uses the image of a cup for the destruction to come upon the nations). Now Second Isaiah proclaims that the cup has been drunk and is being taken away and given to Jerusalem's enemies. We may note that the image of Jerusalem giving her back to her enemies to walk on resembles the Servant giving his back to the smiters in Isa 50:6.

The final call (52:1) urges Zion to put on strength (like the arm of the Lord in 51:9) and promises redemption. In the future, Jerusalem would be pure—free from the uncircumcised. The apparent exclusion of the uncircumcised here serves as a reminder that the universalism of the prophet is not religious pluralism but requires the conversion of the Gentiles to the religion of Israel.

The concluding oracle of this section develops the theme of the new Exodus in a manner reminiscent of Isa 40. This Exodus will not be in haste, as was the first one. God will go before and after, like the pillars of fire and cloud. The joy of liberation is coupled with the call for those who carry the sacred vessels to purify themselves. The return to Jerusalem has the character of a religious procession from the profane place of Babylon to the sacred area of Jerusalem. There God is proclaimed king, just as in the psalms of the old Jerusalem cult.

52:13–53:12 The Suffering Servant. The so-called fourth or last Servant Song is Second Isaiah's best known contribution to

Judeo-Christian spirituality, and deservedly so. Christianity has traditionally seen here a prophecy of the passion of Jesus. Historical criticism, however, proceeds on the assumption that the prophecy made sense to the people of the prophet's time, whatever further levels of meaning were later found in it. The original meaning is inevitably bound up with the identification of the Servant. Scholars who distinguish the Servant Songs as separate compositions usually identify a historical figure here—often the prophet himself or Sheshbazzar, the heir to the Davidic throne. In the context of Second Isaiah as a whole, however, the Servant must be identified as Israel, although the prophet holds an idealized view of the Servant's role, and not all the exilic community lived up to it.

The significance of this passage goes beyond the historical identification of the Servant. It presents a model of piety which allows that suffering can have a positive purpose. As such it broke with a long biblical tradition that regarded suffering as a punishment for sin. It laid the foundation for one of the basic ideas of Christianity.

Isa 52:13-15 is presented as an utterance of God. It focuses on the coming transformation of the Servant from extreme humiliation to glory. Since this change will be witnessed by kings and nations, we must assume that the Servant is the Israelite nation or someone who represents it.

In 53:1 the speaker changes. Chapter 53 expresses the astonishment of the "kings" and the "nations" mentioned in 52:15. It attributes to them a startling affirmation: "it was our infirmities that he bore, our sufferings that he endured . . ." (53:4). The Servant, we are told, was delivered up to death and was counted with the wicked, although he had done no wrong. His life was given as a sacrifice for the sins of others. The concluding verses in 53:10-12 are apparently spoken by God and confirm this affirmation.

The statement that the Servant had done no wrong appears to contradict other statements in Second Isaiah (for example, Isa 50:1: "It was for your sins that you were sold."). The contradiction is only apparent. Isa 53:1-10 is not giving a factual account of Israel's experience but is presenting a model for understanding it. The guilt of Israel is not important for this model. Relative to the nations,

Israel was innocent. As we were told in chapter 40, the punishment exceeded the guilt in any case. Here the prophet is concerned with the excess of punishment.

The model of the Servant is indebted to the precedent of the prophet Jeremiah. Jeremiah was like a lamb led to the slaughter (Jer 12:19); so also was the Servant in 53:7. More generally, the experience of Jeremiah showed that a faithful prophet might have to suffer to fulfill his mission. As Jeremiah was a prophet to Israel, so Israel is to the nations.

The model of the Servant goes beyond Jeremiah insofar as the Servant is apparently put to death (53:8-9) and yet will prolong his days and see his descendants. The people of Israel were said to die in the Exile and rise again at its end in Ezekiel's vision of a valley of dry bones and in Isa 26. That is also the original meaning of chapter 53. It is not difficult, however, to see how Christianity could claim that this model was again exemplified in the death of Jesus of Nazareth.

The key notion in chapter 53 is that the sufferings of the righteous can bear the sin of others. This idea is based on the analogy of sacrifice. The logic of the procedure can be illustrated by the famous ritual of the scapegoat in Lev 16. Aaron confesses the sins of the Israelites over the goat and puts them on its head, and then it carries the sins off to the wilderness. This ritual is evidently a symbolic act. It can have a powerful effect on the people, but only if they participate actively in it. They must understand the symbolism and intend to express their separation from sin. The mere performance of the ritual will not of itself transform the people without their involvement.

The dynamic interaction involved in bearing the sin of others can be seen even more clearly in a symbolic action of the prophet Ezekiel. Ezekiel was famous for his insistence on individual responsibility (Ezek 18:4: "only the one who sins shall die"). He clearly defined the role of the prophet as that of a watchman (Ezek 3:17; 33:1-9). His job is to warn the people. They have to save themselves by their reaction. Yet this prophet is told to lie on one side for 390 days, and on the other for forty days, to bear the sins of northern Israel and Judah respectively (Ezek 4:1-8). In Ezekiel's case, bearing the sin is clearly a symbolic act. The strange posture of the prophet is meant to attract attention, give rise to reflection, and lead people to recognize the gravity of their situation. Only if they do this can they hope to be saved. The suffering of Ezekiel does not automatically prevent the destruction of his people. There is not a set amount of suffering that he can undertake instead of them. His suffering is only a sign to them. Whether they then escape their doom depends on how they heed his warning.

The suffering of the Servant in chapter 53 can be understood most satisfactorily on the model of Ezekiel. The Servant is a light to the nations. The experience of Israel is to catch the attention of the other nations, lead them to reflect on their situation, and realize that they are even more deserving of such punishment. The purpose of the Exile was ultimately to bring about the conversion of the Gentiles. The mission of the Servant, to which the Jews were called, was to accept unmerited suffering in patient fidelity and so to serve as an example for the nations.

The Gentile nations did not react to the Jewish experience in the way the prophet hoped. Yet the model of the Servant has endured. It provides a way of making positive sense of suffering, which is always a challenge to the human spirit. It also suggests a style of evangelizing, not by conquering others but by bearing their burdens and setting an example. For Christians this model was intensified by the example of Jesus, whose suffering and death were also understood as a sacrifice for the sins of others.

54:1-7 A promise to Zion. The prophet resumes the joyful proclamation to Zion that was the theme of Isa 52:1-12. Two motifs are especially important here. First, Zion is the wife of God. The prophet Hosea used this metaphor to great effect and suggested that God was divorcing Israel. Second, Isaiah insists that Zion was only cast off for a moment (compare Isa 50:1 for the motif of divorce). Moreover, the abandoned wife will have more children than one who has a husband. (This is a favorite biblical theme. To illustrate how God can reverse any situation, compare the Song of Hannah in 1 Sam 2.) Underlying the metaphor of marriage is the idea of a covenant, a binding mutual commitment. The language of marriage, however, adds an emotional dimension to the covenant and

deepens the commitment by arousing feelings of love.

The second theme is the analogy with the days of Noah. After the flood God guaranteed the future of life on earth: "Never again will I doom the earth because of man . . . . As long as the earth lasts, seedtime and harvest, cold and heat, summer and winter, and day and night shall not cease" (Gen 8:21-22). That promise had been kept since the days of Noah. The promise to Zion is equally sure. Second Isaiah is reaffirming the traditional Zion theology found, for example, in Ps 46:3: "Therefore we fear not, though the earth be shaken . . . ."

Here we cannot fail to observe that Zion was destroyed again. On a literal level the promise would seem to be broken. Yet, both Judaism and Christianity continue to affirm that "my love shall never leave you nor my covenant of peace be shaken" (v. 10). The peace must be understood as an inner peace that can survive not only the shaking of the hills but the destruction of Zion itself. The restoration from the Exile had shown that God was with the people even in the darkness. The moment of clarity enjoyed by Second Isaiah would have to be remembered as a witness again in darker days ahead.

55:1-13 Call to a feast. The invitation to eat and drink resembles the call of Wisdom to her feast in Prov 9. The prophet suggests that wisdom lies in heeding his words and returning to Zion. The feast is identified with the promises of the covenant to David. As the king was a witness to other nations, so now the restored people is to assume that role. The prophet does not anticipate a renewed Davidic dynasty; his messiah is Cyrus of Persia. Yet the Davidic covenant is not broken. It is fulfilled through the restoration of the Jewish people. Such transformations are possible because "my ways are not your ways." Second Isaiah maintains the contrast made by First Isaiah between the power of the Holy One (spirit) and mere human flesh (compare Isa 31:1-3).

Isa 55:10-13 provides a fitting conclusion to Second Isaiah by affirming the effectiveness of the prophetic word. The triumphal procession back to Jerusalem with which the prophet began in chapter 40 is the crowning validation of the reliability of prophecy and the power of the God of Israel.

COMMENTARY: THIRD ISAIAH (Isa 56–66)

Chapters 40–55 were set in Babylon on the eve of the return from the Exile. Chapters 56–66 are slightly later in date and reflect the problems of the Jewish community after the return. It is possible that they are the work of Second Isaiah, at least in part, that is, if we allow that his style of prophecy was altered by the new circumstances. It is more probable, however, that they are the work of his disciples, who emerged as a distinct group in the returned community. These disciples are referred to as the servants of the Lord in chapter 65. Presumably they saw themselves as carrying on the mission of the Servant, which played such a prominent part in Second Isaiah.

56:1-8 Qualifications for admission to the temple. Only two things are necessary for admission to the rebuilt temple—observance of the sabbath and fidelity to the covenant. The prophet does not spell out what the latter requirement entails. The point of the oracle is to insist that two classes of people, eunuchs and foreigners, are not automatically excluded. Eunuchs had been specifically excluded according to Deut 23:1: "No one whose testicles have been crushed or whose penis has been cut off, may be admitted to the community of the Lord." Some high officials at royal courts in the ancient world had to be eunuchs so that they could be trusted with the royal harem. Some people castrated themselves in the worship of pagan gods. At least some of these people could not subsequently be circumcised, and Third Isaiah does not appear to insist on circumcision as a requirement. "To hold fast to my covenant" (v. 4) appears to be a broad moral attitude rather than a matter of specific rituals, except for the case of sabbath observance.

The second class in question is that of foreigners (v. 6). The prophet is speaking here of converts who want to join themselves to the Lord. The point is that people who were not born Israelites can become servants of the Lord. The significance of this oracle can be seen by contrasting it with Ezek 44, which presents a different program for the postexilic temple, according to which "no foreigners, uncircumcised in heart and in flesh, shall ever enter my sanctuary; none of the foreigners who live among the Israelites" (Ezek 44:9).

It is evident that there was disagreement within the Jewish community as to whether foreigners should be allowed to worship in the temple. What is remarkable is that both sides of the debate were preserved in the canon of the Scripture. The authors of Isa 56 and Ezek 44 were both sincerely concerned with the welfare of their community, and both were trying to be faithful to older traditions. The exclusivist viewpoint of Ezek 44 received powerful support from Ezra in the following century and may be credited with strengthening the distinctive identity of Judaism. Christianity has undoubtedly found the inclusive vision of Third Isaiah much more congenial in this matter.

56:9–57:21 Denunciation of abuses. There is no agreement among commentators about the unity, origin, or meaning of this passage. Since it resembles preexilic oracles against idolatry, some scholars think that this material is preexilic too. Others read the whole passage as an attack on the postexilic priestly leaders of the community and think that idolatry here is a metaphor for a style of religion of which the author did not approve. Very likely neither of these extremes is correct. The oracles are evidently directed against religious leaders—compare the use of watchman (as prophet) in Ezek 3:17; 33:1-9; Jer 6:17 and of shepherd (as leader) in Ezek 34. We must assume, however, that the charges are meant literally. The leaders are at best negligent, and there is widespread pagan worship. (Isa 57:9, which speaks of sending ambassadors to the "king," *melek*, even down to the netherworld, probably means that people offered human sacrifice to the Canaanite god *Molech*.) The people who engaged in these practices were certainly not the more exclusive faction whose views are represented in Ezek 44 and with whom Third Isaiah had a different quarrel. Much of the Jewish community after the Exile was quite lax in its religious observance, as we can see from the tirades of the prophets Haggai and Malachi, and from the reforms that were necessary in the time of Ezra and Nehemiah.

The rhetoric in much of this passage is simply abusive. The prophet was unlikely to win over the leaders by calling them "dumb dogs" (56:10) or the like. This is the language of polarization, which presumes that the situation is beyond remedy. Such language can only seldom be justified.

Chapter 57 concludes with a more positive attempt "to revive the spirits of the dejected" (57:15) and seems to hold out the prospect of forgiveness. Even the sinners are souls that God has made. In 57:14 ("prepare the way") the prophet seeks to recapture some of the initial enthusiasm of Second Isaiah. The final verse, however, maybe added by an editor, dampens this spirit of reconciliation by insisting that there is no peace for the wicked.

58:1-14 The value of fasting. After the fall of Jerusalem in 586 B.C.E., it became customary to observe four fast days, in the fourth, fifth, seventh, and tenth months (Zech 8:18; compare Zech 7:5). Third Isaiah denies that this observance has any intrinsic value. He does not object to ritual as such—he complains of inadequate observance of the sabbath. Ritual only has value, however, when it is the expression of a just society. Self-affliction is not a good in itself; feeding the hungry is. Verses 6-7 give a concise summary of the essentials of true religion: free the oppressed, feed the hungry, shelter the homeless, clothe the naked. The prophet anticipates the criteria for the final judgment in Matt 25:31-46, but he is drawing on a long tradition of prophetic criticism (compare Amos 5:18-27, which insists that worship without justice has no value). The problems of injustice were apparently as great in Third Isaiah's time as before the Exile, although we might have expected a more close-knit community after the return (the prophet refers to the poor as "your own" in 58:7).

The postexilic community experienced much difficulty after the return. The prophet Haggai attributed their lack of prosperity to their tardiness in rebuilding the temple. Third Isaiah attributes it to the lack of social justice. In this he was the more typical of the older prophetic tradition.

59:1-21 A promise of divine intervention. Chapter 59 continues the theme of chapter 58. Lack of prosperity is not due to Yahweh's weakness but to human sin. In this case the prophet goes on to predict a divine response. Yahweh would be girded as a warrior, as at the time of the Exodus and the Conquest. Underlying this prediction is the prophet's faith that God has the power to punish the wicked

and the hope that God will do so immediately, within the course of human history.

There was no miraculous transformation of Jewish society after the Exile. Later biblical literature would increasingly postpone God's judgment to an end-time or until after death. Belief in an eventual judgment remained vital, however. The hope and concern for justice in this world is an important part of the prophetic legacy and is inseparable from belief in the sovereignty of Yahweh.

We should note that Yahweh is expected to take vengeance on a segment of Jewish society, not on foreign nations. Those who will be redeemed on Zion are "those who turn from sin" (v. 20). We find here a division within the Jewish community and a distinction between the servants of God and the members of the Jewish nation as such.

60:1-22 Restoration of Zion. Chapters 60–62 stand out from the rest of Third Isaiah by their exuberant tone, which is very similar to Second Isaiah. Perhaps these chapters were written shortly after the return, before the problems that dominate the other chapters had developed. Jerusalem is seen as the focal point of the nations. The prospect of caravans coming from such places as Sheba (v. 6) recalls the glory of Solomon. The foreigners and their kings will be subject to the Jews and be their servants, but they will be welcome in Jerusalem and their offerings will be accepted in the temple. The vision of the new Zion is universalistic in this sense, in contrast to the exclusive vision of Ezek 44. The prophet envisages a wonderful transformation—the people will all be just, and Yahweh will give light to the city by means of the divine presence. This vision of the new Jerusalem is echoed in Rev 21:22-27 in the context of a new creation after the end of this world. The idea of a new creation is also found in Third Isaiah (65:17). The prophet knew that such a wonderful state is not the stuff of history or of human experience but represents an ideal goal that can serve as a guide for our values.

61:1-11 Good news for the poor. The opening verses are very similar to the so-called Servant Songs in Isa 42 and 49. The prophet sees himself as realizing the mission of the Servant. The prisoners in question are the Jewish exiles in Babylon. The year of favor is the sabbatical year, traditionally the time for the cancellation of debts and the release of Hebrew slaves (see Deut 15; compare Lev 25). The anointing is probably metaphorical (virtually meaning "appointed"). Prophets were not usually anointed, although Elijah was told to anoint Elisha in 1 Kgs 19:16.

In the context of Third Isaiah, this passage illustrates again the concern of the prophet for the poor, a concern that was prominent in Isa 58 and 59. The importance of the passage transcends its historical context, however. It presents a concise summary of the mission of a servant of God in any age. It is a mission to raise up the lower strata of society. The Gospel of Luke has Jesus read this text, with minor variations, at the outset of his career (Luke 4:17-19).

The prophet is here the bearer of good news, like Zion itself in Isa 40:9. Verses 4-9 repeat the universalistic vision of Isa 60 but add a note of concern for justice in verse 8 and a promise of an everlasting covenant, presumably a renewal of the promise to David, as in Isa 55:3. Now all the people are the beneficiaries of that promise. Further, all the people will be named priests of the Lord (v. 6). The prophet sees the whole Jewish people as priestly mediators between God and the Gentiles. This extension of the priesthood inevitably dilutes the role of the official hierarchy and contrasts very sharply with the program for the restoration in Ezek 44, which assigns a very special role to the Zadokite priests. (Compare the dispute in Num 16, where Korah rebels against Moses and Aaron, contending that the whole people is holy, but is swallowed alive by the earth for his impertinence!) The canon of Scripture has preserved both sides of this debate without resolving it. In the New Testament, Rev 20:6 says that all the martyrs who are raised in the first resurrection will serve God as priests for a thousand years, without distinguishing a special priestly class. This, of course, is resurrected life, but it presents an ultimate ideal for the people of God.

62:1-12 Reminding the Lord. Chapter 62 retains the positive tone of chapters 60–61, but it also reflects some initial disappointment after the return to Jerusalem. It is necessary to "remind the Lord" because God does not appear to be fulfilling earlier promises. The prophet insists that all will yet be well, because the Lord has sworn. The purpose of this oracle is to encourage the returned exiles to plant grain, in confidence that it will not all go in taxes, and to build up the city. We may compare the oracles of Haggai of about the same time, when he promised that all would be well if they built the temple.

The assurance of a divine oath, or promise, is a powerful motivating factor. There is a risk in such rhetoric, however. If the land remains relatively desolate, the discrepancy between the promise and the reality can breed extreme disillusionment. The prophet was attempting to use the power of positive thinking (unlike most other prophets!) to raise the morale of the people, in the hope that their efforts would be blessed. Even if the result fell short of the ideal, the efforts of the prophets may have borne fruit insofar as they inspired people to work at rebuilding their community.

63:1-6 God the warrior. The mood changes abruptly in chapter 63. The warrior imagery picks up from Isa 59 (63:5 corresponds very closely to 59:16), but the imagery is much more violent here. The violence is directed against the Gentiles, specifically against Edom and its capital Bozrah. Edom, Judea's southern neighbor, had become a major enemy during the exilic period. It is possible that this oracle was evoked by some hostile action taken by the Edomites, although many commentators assume that Edom is representative of all hostile nations. We met another violent oracle against Edom in Isa 34.

The image of God as warrior is deeply entrenched in the oldest traditions about the Exodus and the Conquest (for example, Exod 15). The God of Israel was never a pacifist, although the people are often urged to take a submissive stance. The assumption here is that Edom and some other neighboring states were impeding the restoration of Judah. The prophet does not call on the Jews to make war on them, but he hopes that his God will remove the offenders by whatever means are necessary.

63:7–64:11 A plea for God to act. This passage is virtually a psalm and especially resembles the communal laments of the Psalter (for example, Psalm 44). It reflects a traditional pattern, which begins by recalling God's saving deeds in the past (especially the Exodus and the Conquest), acknowledges the sin of Israel, and ends with a plea for mercy (compare Deut 32, which ends with a promise rather than a prayer, and such postexilic prayers as Neh 9 and Dan 9). In part it also resembles the laments for the temple in the period of the Exile (for example, Psalm 79). The prayer that God "rend the heavens and come down" (63:19) has a ring of desperation to it. The main problem in interpreting the passage is to determine why the author was moved to such desperation.

Two verses are especially important for the author's situation. One is 63:18. The first half of that verse is translated in the Revised Standard Version as "Thy holy people possessed thy sanctuary a little while," and this rendering is more probable than that of the New American Bible. Does this mean that the whole duration of Solomon's temple—about 350 years—seems short in retrospect? Or does it mean that one Jewish party occupied the sanctuary for a short time after the return from the Exile and was then ousted by its enemies? (Some scholars think here of Ezek 44, which makes the Levites subordinate to the Zadokite priests, and suggest that chapter 63 was written by Levites.)

The second relevant verse is 63:16: "Were Abraham not to know us . . . you, Lord, are our father." This translation suggests a purely hypothetical situation—compare Isa 49:15: "Can a mother forget her infant . . . ? Even should she forget, I will never forget you." The Hebrew, however, could be translated more naturally as "for Abraham has not known us." This understanding of the text has prompted the view that the author of chapter 63 belonged to a party that was rejected by the official leaders of the community, represented here as Abraham and Israel. The passage, then, can be understood in either of two ways: either it reflects a bitter struggle within the Jewish community after the Exile, or it more simply reflects the initial failure of the returned exiles to rebuild and restore the holy place. In view of the other indications in Third Isaiah (especially in chapters 56 and 66), it seems more probable that the prophet's desperation arose from conflict within the Jewish community.

Whatever the precise origin of this passage, it is clearly a prayer for a time of despair. Two features should especially be emphasized. The first is the frank admission of sinfulness: "all of us have become like unclean men" (64:5). Even if there is a split in the community, no party can claim complete innocence. Second, when no human aid is forthcoming, the prophet appeals directly to God. It was God who brought them out of Egypt (63:9: "It was not a messenger or an angel but he himself" can also be phrased differently and understood to say that "the angel of his presence" saved them. In either case the point is the same: it was no human resource). The plea to rend the heavens forcefully (63:19) expresses the need for help from beyond (compare Isa 59:16 and 63:5: "there was no one"). The plea is based, not on the justice of God, but on God's mercy; he is the Father of all. The idea of God as Father assures the right of even outsiders and castaways to invoke God, irrespective of their standing in the community. The motif is used in a similar way in Mal 2:10 in an argument against divorce. The fatherhood of God was a characteristic motif on the lips of Jesus, who argued that the one Father made the sun shine and rain fall on the just and the unjust (Matt 5:45).

65:1-16 My servants will eat. The division within the postexilic community is more explicit here. The prophet evidently identifies with the "servants" who continue the mission of the Servant of Second Isaiah. This group is at odds with another party, which is accused of a range of idolatrous practices. Yet these people claim to be holy and warn others not to touch them. This puzzling passage reminds us of Ezek 44:19, where the Zadokite priests are told to change their vestments when they leave the altar so that they will not transmit holiness to the people. Some scholars read the grotesque practices of 65:3-4 as a parody of the official cult of the legitimate priests (see the commentary on Isa 66). It is more probable, however, that chapters 65 and 57 show that there was actual idolatry going on. The fact that the idolaters think they are holy only adds to the grotesque character of their abuses.

We must also assume that the idolaters enjoyed the main power in the postexilic community. They have now inherited the land. The "servants" are outsiders, who are powerless for the present. The prophecy in 65:13-16 anticipates the beatitudes of Jesus, especially in the Lukan version: "Blest are you poor; the reign of God is yours. Blest are you who hunger; you shall be filled" (Luke 6:20). A major function of religion has always been to give hope to the hopeless. The prophet merely asserts that fortunes will yet be reversed. He offers no evidence for his claim. Neither does Jesus in the beatitudes. The only evidence for such a claim is faith in the power of a God who will ultimately set things right and the knowledge that all human power and wealth must eventually pass.

65:17-25 A new creation. The prophetic dissatisfaction with the present is even more evident in 65:17, in the oracle about a new creation. The idea that God would do something radically new was familiar from Second Isaiah (compare Isa 43:18-19). The replacement of heaven and earth, however, goes far beyond the earlier concepts. This prophecy is picked up in Rev 21:1 ("Then I saw new heavens and a new earth") and is often thought to be typical of apocalyptic literature. In chapter 65, however, the new creation is remarkably similar to the old one. Life will go on on earth. People will still die, and there is no promise of resurrection or immortality, in sharp contrast to the apocalyptic literature. Rather, the prophet presents his ideal of earthly life: freedom from grief, from premature death, from oppression and exploitation.

The concluding mention of the wolf and the lamb (v. 25) very deliberately recalls the messianic prophecy in Isa 11. Both prophecies are fantasies, although chapter 65 is more restrained in its imagery. Both provide consolation and relief from the distress of the present. The ideal presented must also be taken seriously, however, as a portrayal of the goal toward which we strive, even if we cannot fully attain it.

66:1-6 True and false worship. The interpretation of these verses has been greatly disputed. Some scholars contend that the prophet is rejecting temple worship as such; others hold that the issue is how much importance should be attached to the temple. The second point of view is the more probable. Third Isaiah seems to presuppose a temple in other passages (including 66:6). Even Solomon's prayer at the dedication of the temple (1 Kgs 8:27) had declared: "If the heavens and the highest heavens cannot contain you, how much less this temple which I have built!" The point is that the temple must be seen in perspective. It is not the most important thing in the religion.

Third Isaiah's perspective on the temple here contrasts sharply with that of Haggai, who preached that rebuilding the temple was the primary requirement for prosperity in the postexilic community. Here again, the canon of Scripture has preserved both sides of a heated debate. The temple was very important for the morale of the community, and we can appreciate why a prophet like Haggai insisted on thinking positively about it. On the other hand, Third Isaiah walks in the footsteps of the great prophets, including Isaiah of Jerusalem, when he points out the danger of trusting too completely in an institution and reminds people of the ethical demands of their religion.

The interpretation of 66:3 is even more controversial. The Hebrew juxtaposes four pairs of actions, indicated by participles: "slaughtering an ox, slaying a man," etc. These pairs can be understood in either of two ways: "one who slaughters an ox *is like* one who slays a man" (so the New American Bible and the Revised Standard Version), or "one who slaughters an ox *also* slays a man." The first interpretation empties the sacrificial cult of all value; even a cereal offering is no better than swine's blood. If the second interpretation is correct, the problem is syncretism: those who offer the sacrifices to Yahweh also engage in pagan practices. In either case, there is a division within the community, and the prophet and his followers find themselves rejected. The understanding of this passage depends on our understanding of other passages, such as Isa 57. It seems more probable that pagan worship was the issue. The evidence does not warrant the drastic conclusion that the prophet totally rejected the sacrificial cult.

66:7-24 The Lord's power shall be known. The book concludes with a twofold oracle of judgment. On the positive side, the prophet points out how far the postexilic community has already come. Would God have brought them so far only to abandon them? The prophet cloaks his message in plentiful metaphors of childbirth and mother love. At verse 14, however, the negative side of the judgment appears. Power for the servants of God is wrath for God's enemies. The fiery coming of the Lord resembles the coming of God's messenger in Mal 3:2: "For he is like the refiner's fire."

The conclusion, then, has two aspects.

The exiles will return from all the nations. Some will even serve as priests and Levites. All humankind will worship in Jerusalem. This bright prospect has a dark side too. The corpses of the wicked will burn and be eaten by worms forever, as a spectacle for the rest of humanity. The wicked will not be alive to feel the pain of this punishment. The idea of hell did not emerge in the Jewish tradition until about three hundred years after Third Isaiah, yet this passage is rightly seen as a precedent for hell, because it attempts to describe an unending punishment of the wicked.

The lurid spectacle of 66:24 is a rather unpleasant note on which to close the Book of Isaiah. The idea was surely born of the resentment of the prophet's followers, who were excluded from power in the postexilic community. It expresses their hope for justice, but seems excessive in its prolonged torture of dead bodies. It does, however, provide a powerful closing image for the Book of Isaiah. Much of the book was concerned with salvation on Mount Zion. This theme was repeated in chapters 65–66 and reinforced with the theme of a new creation. The final image does not detract from these themes, but it adds a reminder that salvation cannot be achieved without judgment. The wolf will not lie down with the lamb until human evil is eradicated. The smoldering fire of Gehenna stands as a reminder of the reality of evil and its inevitable unpleasant consequences.

JEREMIAH

Peter F. Ellis

INTRODUCTION

Jeremiah the man

Jeremiah lived in changing times. He grew up in the best of times and died in the worst of times. He grew up during the reign of King Josiah (639–609 B.C.E.), when Judah was at peace and when king, priests, and people were engaged in a revitalization of Mosaic faith and worship. He died around 580, an exile in Egypt in the worst of times, when Judah was no longer a nation, Jerusalem was in ruins, the temple had been burned to the ground, and the Jews had been deported into exile in Babylon. His life spanned the last twenty years of the Assyrian empire (destroyed by the Babylonians between 612 and 605) and the first twenty years of the neo-Babylonian empire (605–539). He was and had to be "a man for all seasons."

Jeremiah was born in Anathoth, a few miles north of Jerusalem, belonged to a priestly family, and was called to the office of prophet at an early age (c. 626). During the forty or so years he served as a prophet (626–580), the kingdom of Judah went through one religious reformation (626–609); three wars (against Egypt, 609; against Babylon, 597 and 587); three exiles (597, 587, and 582); and five Davidic kings (Josiah, 639–609; Jehoahaz, for three months in 609; Jehoiakim, 609–597; Jehoiachin, for three months in 597; and Zedekiah, 597–587). During these years Judah went from one of the brightest periods in its history (under King Josiah from 639–609) to the darkest (609–587) in all the 443 years of the Davidic dynasty (1025–587).

Few people in history have been involved so crucially in the fate of a nation as Jeremiah

was. He preached the renewal of the covenant under King Josiah in 621. He lived through the first (597) and the second siege (587) of Jerusalem. He saw the temple destroyed, Jerusalem devastated, and his people marched off into exile in Babylonia. At the end he himself was forced into exile in Egypt. There he died, stoned to death, as the legend goes, at the hands of his own people.

With the exception perhaps of Jesus and St. Paul, we know more about Jeremiah as an individual than about any other person in the whole history of Israel. We know from his own words that he was a quiet, peace-loving mystic sent by God, against his inclinations, to rebuke kings, accuse his fellow Jews of infidelity to the covenant, and draw upon himself in return the scorn, contempt, and homicidal hatred of his enemies.

Jeremiah did not want to be a prophet. The prophetic office guaranteed trouble. Jeremiah wanted peace. He had no peace. His own relatives plotted his death (11:18–12:6). Pashhur, the high priest, had him scourged and thrown into the stocks overnight (20:1-2). He preached against abuses in the temple, was put on trial for his life and barely acquitted (ch. 26). He had to go into hiding during most of the twelve-year reign of King Jehoiakim. When a book of his sermons was read before the king, the king fed the manuscript page by page into a fire (ch. 36). During the siege of 588–587, he was first arrested and thrown in prison. Later he was dropped into a cistern to die. He was rescued only at the last minute by his Ethiopian friend, the eunuch Ebed-melech (ch. 38). When the Babylonians captured Jerusalem, they found Jeremiah in chains with other Jews, awaiting deportation to Babylon (44:1-6). Jeremiah describes his internal sufferings in his famous confessions (11:18–12:6; 15:10-21; 17:12-18; 18:18-23; 20:7-18).

All in all, no one in the history of Israel was more like Jesus than Jeremiah. Jesus taught in parables; so did Jeremiah. Jesus was rejected by his own people; so was Jeremiah. Jesus wept for his people; so did Jeremiah. Jesus was scourged, imprisoned, and put on trial for his life; so was Jeremiah. In the end the tragedy of Jerusalem in the time of Jesus paralleled the tragedy of Jerusalem in the time of Jeremiah. Jesus prophesied the destruction of Jerusalem and the temple by the Romans; Jeremiah prophesied the destruction of Jerusalem and the temple by the Babylonians. In each case the prophecy was fulfilled: in 587 B.C.E. by the Babylonians, in A.D. 70 by the Romans. Jeremiah resembled Jesus in so many ways that the Jews of Jesus' time wondered if Jesus might not be Jeremiah come back from the dead (see Matt 16:14)!

It is perhaps too much to say, as Ernest Renan said, that "without this extraordinary man, the religious history of humanity would have taken another course." It certainly is not too much to say that without Jeremiah the mystical side of human nature and the unfathomable capacity of the human heart for unselfish suffering might have lain hidden until the coming of Jesus. The theology Jeremiah lived, more than the theology he preached, influenced the ages that followed him and produced psalmists and wisdom writers who sounded the depths of Jeremiah's heart. His life more than his teaching was a ferment and a fire that permeated the bones of Israel after the Exile and prepared the way for him who came to cast a similar fire on earth and to see it kindled in the lives of innumerable saints.

Jeremiah's message

Jeremiah's message as a prophet to his people was at the same time the most pessimistic and the most optimistic that could be conceived. When he looked at the abysmal state of Judah's covenant relationship with God, he sank into pessimism. When he looked at the patient and long-suffering God of Israel, he was filled with optimism. His God was a God of hope, of promise, of power, and of an indomitable will to make the people of Israel a holy people.

In typical prophetic fashion, Jeremiah accused his people of sins against the covenant and predicted God's judgment upon them. But he did more than just accuse and condemn. He raised the consciousness of his people. He made them see that crimes against each other were crimes against God. He made them see that God loved them even when he chastised them. Finally, when he saw that destruction was inevitable, that Israel was not responding to God, and that the old covenant was finished, he predicted a new covenant (31:31-34). This was the covenant inaugurated by Jesus on the night before his death (see Luke 22:20 and 1 Cor 11:25).

The Book of Jeremiah

In 604 B.C.E. while in hiding, Jeremiah dictated to his secretary, Baruch, the gist of what he had preached during his past twenty-three years as a prophet (see ch. 36 and 25:1-14). When the king had Jeremiah's manuscript burned (36:21-23), Jeremiah had Baruch compose a new manuscript (36:32). Scholars believe that the greater part of this second manuscript has been preserved in chapters 1–20 and chapter 25 of the present Book of Jeremiah. Verses 1-14 of chapter 25 appear to be the conclusion of the manuscript written in 604. The rest of the book (chs. 26–52) is made up of biographical material about Jeremiah (chs. 26–44), a collection of Jeremiah's prophecies against the pagan nations (chs. 45–51), and a final chapter (ch. 52) taken from 2 Kgs 25.

What confuses the reader of Jeremiah is the lack of chronological sequence in the book. The siege of Jerusalem in 588–587 B.C.E. is first mentioned in chapter 21. In chapter 25, however, the reader is back in the year 604 B.C.E. This happens regularly. What is the explanation? The best explanation is that the editors of the prophetic books had before them several collections of material dealing with the preaching of Jeremiah, stories about him, and historical accounts of the last days of Judah. They had the manuscript dictated in 604, together with collections of prophecies against the kings of Judah (chs. 21–23) and against the false prophets (23:9-40). In addition, they had a collection of prophecies dealing with the new covenant (chs. 30–33), a large collection of biographical material (chs. 24; 26–29; 34–45; 52), and a collection of Jeremiah's prophecies against the pagan nations (chs. 46–51). Instead of placing all this material in chronological order, a task that would have been extremely difficult, they put it together more or less end to end and thematically, so that events mentioned earlier in the book in one collection are sometimes duplicated later in another collection of material. An example of this confusion is Jeremiah's famous temple sermon. Jeremiah gives his version of the sermon in chapters 7 and 8; someone else gives another, abbreviated version in chapter 26.

All this is the fault—if we can call it that—of the third-century editors. Nothing can be done now to change it. The best the reader can do is to try to read each collection of material *as a collection*, asking of each collection what its message as a whole is. This is the way we shall deal with the book in this commentary. It is not the only way, but it is the least confusing way. Reading the book in its present order, we shall comment on its message under the following headings:

THE LAST KINGS OF JUDAH
Josiah (639–609)

Jehoahaz (609)	Jehoiakim (609–598)	Zedekiah (597–587)
	Jehoiachin (597)	

THE KINGS OF BABYLON

Nabopolassar (626–605)

Nebuchadnezzar (605–562)

Evil-merodach (562–560)

Neriglissar (560–556)

Labashi Marduk (556)

Nabonidus and Belshazzar (556–539)

Reading Jeremiah

Understanding Jeremiah, or for that matter any of the prophets, can sometimes be difficult. Jeremiah frequently repeats the expression "The word of the Lord," then speaks in the first person as if he were God speaking. He accuses Israel of crimes as if he were a prosecuting attorney in a courtroom. He then delivers God's judgment on Israel for its crimes, as if God were a judge in a trial that ends with the condemnation of the accused. Surprisingly, while he claims to speak as God's messenger and supports his claim by describing the vision in which God commissioned him as a messenger, he sometimes speaks in his own name (see Jeremiah's confessions in 12:1-6; 15:10-21; 17:12-18; 18:18-23; 20:7-18). These apparent inconsistencies call for an explanation.

First, the reader should understand that the primary way in which a prophet sees himself (his self-image or job description) is as God's messenger, sent to the covenanted people Israel to announce to them God's judgment on how they have failed to live up to the norms of behavior demanded of them by their covenant relationship with God.

An understanding of the prophet's role as messenger helps to explain why he speaks so often as if he were actually God speaking, and why he describes his experience of a vision in which he was called by God and commissioned as God's messenger. Once the art of writing came into existence between 6000 and 4000 B.C.E., communication over a distance could be accomplished by letter. Before the invention of letters, that is, in the preliterary age, communication over a distance could only be accomplished by means of messengers, who served as "living letters." The messenger memorized the message, physically bridged the distance between the sender and the addressee, and ultimately delivered orally the message he had memorized. In the case of a king's message, for example, the messenger would say: "The king sent me. The word of the king: 'I your king say to you . . . .'" In short, since the prophet was God's messenger, he spoke, as a messenger would, in the first person because he was speaking for God who sent him.

Second, behind the concept of God sending the prophet as messenger and with roots in very ancient mythology lay the scenario of the king's council. The pagan mythmakers imagined the world of the gods to be similar to royal society on earth. Such a scenario posited a world populated with gods, goddesses, and sons and daughters of the gods. In heaven as on earth, one god was high god or king over other gods. When the high god wished to legislate, he gathered round him his council of lesser gods. After the meeting messengers were sent out to bear tidings of the council's decisions to the other gods.

Israel took over this scenario from the mythmakers, kept the lesser gods of the council but demoted them to the status of messengers (angels), and envisioned Yahweh and the divine council in the same way that the pagans envisioned their high god and his council (see 1 Kgs 22:12-23). The plurals of Gen 1:26 ("Let *us* make man in *our* image") and Isa 6:8 ("Whom shall I send? Who will go for *us*?") reflect the scenario of God consulting this divine council. Jeremiah saw himself as one who had "stood in the council of the Lord, to see him and to hear his word" (23:18; see also 23:22). The role of the prophet, as we know it from Israel's history, was born when God sent humans rather than angels to be the messengers from the divine council.

The role of the messenger and the scenario of the king's council also explains why a prophet sometimes describes his inaugural vision. Anyone can *claim* to be God's messenger, but only the messenger sent by God can truly claim to speak God's word. Whoever has not been sent and nevertheless claims to be God's messenger is by definition a false prophet. It is a matter of great importance, therefore, for the truth of a prophet's message that he be able to authenticate his position by testifying to his experience of having been directly commissioned by God as a messenger. Jeremiah so testifies (1:1-10); so also do Isaiah (Isa 6:1-13) and Ezekiel (Ezek 1–3). Without the certainty such an experience provides and without such a positive commission, it is hard to see how Jeremiah, Isaiah, Ezekiel, or any of the other true prophets could have sustained for so long the burden of so unpopular a role. Such an experience is popularly referred to as a prophet's inaugural vision.

Third, the role of messenger explains the first-person form of speaking and the purpose of the prophet's inaugural vision experience. It explains as well why he so frequently uses such words as: "The Lord sent me" and "This is the word of the Lord." What it does not explain is the nature of the message that the prophet brings from God. To understand the prophet's message, the reader needs to advert to the accusations against Israel that make up so much a part of the prophet's message. These accusations and the judgments that follow them are all related to the demands of Israel's covenant relationship with God.

These demands are summed up in the ten commandments of the Sinai covenant, which in turn are summed up in the two great commandments: You will love the Lord your God with all your heart, and you will love your neighbor as yourself.

When Israel fails to fulfill these demands either by turning to the idol worship of the pagans (see Hos 1–3) or by committing crimes against the neighbor (see Amos 2:6-16; 3:9-15; 4–6; 8:4-9 for oppression of the poor by the rich viewed as a crime against the demands of the covenant), God sends a prophet-messenger to announce to them divine judgment of condemnation.

Thus, the major part of the prophetic message has to do with Israel's failure to live up to the demands of the covenant relationship with God. This explains why the prophets so often accuse and condemn. It explains as well why covenant theology constitutes the heart of the prophetic message, just as new-covenant theology constitutes the heart of the gospel message.

Fourth, the reader will understand the prophet's prosecuting attorney role if he or she recalls the well-known scenario of a court trial with its defendant, accusations, indictment, defense and prosecuting attorneys, and judge. God, of course, is not really a judge in our sense of the term, nor are the prophets prosecuting attorneys. But the rhetorical use of such an imaginative confrontation between accused and judge—between Israel and God—serves to dramatize for the prophets' audience the seriousness of their relationship with God and the seriousness of their crimes against the God who so lovingly initiated that relationship. Such an imaginative confrontation is popularly known as a trial or controversy and is reflected in the prophet's language whenever, as so often happens, a prophet accuses and condemns either Israel as a whole or particular individuals (see the frequent accusations in Jer 2:1–4:4 and the judgments, frequently introduced by the word "therefore" in Jer 5–9).

In summary, the reader will understand Jeremiah and any other prophet if he or she sees the prophet as one who saw himself as: (1) one who had been present at meetings of the divine council; (2) one who had been commissioned as God's messenger (inaugural vision); (3) one who accused and condemned Israel for crimes against the covenant God; (4) one who played the role of prosecuting attorney when speaking in the name of God and the role of defense attorney when speaking in his own or in his people's name; and (5) one whose concern, above all other matters, was to bring Israel to appreciate and treasure its unique relationship with God. The prophets, and Jeremiah in particular, had what might be called a passion for God and for God's people: for God, that God be truly loved and praised; for the people, that they be, in God's own words to them, "my people, my renown, my praise, my beauty" (see Jer 13:11).

COMMENTARY

PART I: JEREMIAH'S CALL

Jer 1:1-19

1:1-3 The editor's introduction to the Book of Jeremiah. These verses summarize Jeremiah's career from the time of his call in 626 B.C.E. to the fall of Jerusalem in 587. They constitute as well a heading for the collection of materials put together by an editor to make up the Book of Jeremiah as we have it now. Similar editorial headings occur at the beginning of other prophetic books, for example, Amos 1:1; Hos 1:1; Isa 1:1; and Ezek 1:1-3. The editor's heading for the book helps the reader to situate in history the career of each of the prophets.

1:4-10 The call of Jeremiah. Unless a prophet is truly called by God and sent as God's messenger to the covenanted people, there is no good reason why the people should listen to him. Speaking about false prophets, God says through Jeremiah: "I did not send these prophets, yet they ran; I did not speak to them, yet they prophesied" (23:21). To establish his credentials as a prophet, Jeremiah, along with Amos (Amos 7:14-15), Isaiah (Isa 6:1-13), and Ezekiel (Ezek 1:4-3:15), reminds his readers that he was called directly by God and commissioned to be God's messenger to them, the covenant people. That God "knew," "dedicated," and "appointed" Jeremiah to be "a prophet to the nations" even before he was born is the prophet's symbolic way of declaring that God had a role for him to play not only in the history of Israel but in the history of the gentile nations as well (v. 5).

Jeremiah's excuse, "I know not how to speak; I am too young" (v. 6), recalls Moses' attempt to escape the difficulties of the prophetic office (see Exod 4:10-13). Jeremiah knows that prophets lead a lonely life, are frequently scorned, often persecuted, and with few exceptions rejected during their lives. God, however, commands (v. 7). Jeremiah's only comfort is God's promise, "I am with you to deliver you" (v. 8). It is consoling to observe that God regularly promises to be "with" those who have been commissioned for difficult tasks in his service (see Exod 4:12; Josh 1:5, 9; Judg 6:16; 1 Sam 3:19; 16:13; Matt 28:20).

God's touching of Jeremiah's mouth (v. 9) is the prophet's metaphorical way of expressing that what he preaches to the people is truly the word of God and not any human word (compare Isa 6:6-7; Ezek 3:1-4, 10-11). Verse 10 indicates the scope of Jeremiah's message: he will deal not only with Israel but with other nations as well, and his message will be both negative and positive. He will prophesy the end of the old covenant and the existing dynasty of David, but he will also prophesy a new covenant (see chs. 30–33) and a new David.

1:11-16 Two visions. The visions of the branch of the watching-tree (almond tree) and the boiling cauldron may be later than Jeremiah's inaugural vision. They are placed here because they foreshadow the fulfillment of Jeremiah's prophecies concerning the Babylonian invasion and the destruction of Jerusalem and the kingdom of Judah. Jeremiah may have been out in the field in early February when the almond tree first blossoms, and he appears to be watching the still wintry landscape. God too is "watching"—watching over the divine Word to bring it to fulfillment (vv. 11-12). The boiling cauldron tipped to the north indicates the direction from which the invading Babylonian armies will come (v. 13) when they besiege and destroy Jerusalem (vv. 14-16 and see ch. 39).

1:17-19 God encourages Jeremiah. These verses conclude Jeremiah's call. God reminds him that he is not alone in the face of his enemies (v. 17), that it is divine power that strengthens him (v. 18), and that ultimately he will win out over his enemies because God is with him (v. 19). Jeremiah's need for such divine assurance is borne out by the despairing tone of the prophet's famous "confessions" (see 12:1-6; 15:10-21; 17:14-18; 18:19-23; 20:7-18).

PART II: JEREMIAH'S PREACHING FROM 626 to 604 B.C.E.

Jer 2:1–20:18

In all likelihood the major portion of the material in chapters 2–25 comes from the book dictated by Jeremiah to Baruch in the year 604 B.C.E. (see 36:28-32). Scholars debate about where and when Jeremiah preached what is in these chapters and even whether everything in these chapters comes from Jeremiah himself and not perhaps from the editors of the book. These questions have their place, but the when, the where, and the who are not nearly as important as the what of the prophet's message. It is because God spoke to Judah and to us through the mouth of Jeremiah that the Book of Jeremiah has entered the Bible. What God says, therefore, is the important thing, and it will be the aim of this commentary to concentrate on that divine message.

A. Jeremiah's Earliest Sermons (2:1–6:30)

When Jeremiah dictated to Baruch his book of sermons in 604 B.C.E. (see 36:28-32), he began by summarizing the gist of his message in 2:1–6:30. The message is that Judah has been unfaithful to God and therefore deserves a judgment of condemnation and punishment. Since this judgment is based on crimes against the covenant, Jeremiah, like all the prophets, begins by preaching God's accusations against Judah and concludes by threatening Judah with judgment and punishment. Chapters 2:1–4:4 deal mainly with accusations; chapters 4:5–6:30, with judgment and punishment.

2:1–3:5 Accusations. This collection of accusations begins and ends in the same way with the use of Hosea's marriage analogy for the Sinai covenant (see Hos 1–3), in which God is the bridegroom and Israel the unfaithful bride (compare 2:2 and 3:1-5). In verse 5 the people are accused of infidelity to God, a crime against the first commandment of the covenant. Verses 6-9 accuse them of ingratitude for forgetting the great things God did for them at the time of the Exodus and the conquest of the Promised Land. Verses 10-13 continue the accusations of ingratitude, contrasting the fidelity of the pagans to their gods, who are no gods at all (vv. 10-11), with the infidelity of Israel to the true God. Their crime is twofold. They have abandoned God, "the source of living waters," that is, water that flows naturally from the earth in springs and brooks and can be depended upon, and have chosen instead pagan gods, "broken cisterns, that hold no water," and therefore cannot be depended upon (vv. 12-13).

2:14-19 "Is Israel a slave, a bondman by birth?" Jeremiah demonstrates the evil of forsaking "the living waters" for the "broken cisterns" by reminding his listeners how they were punished by their Egyptian and Assyrian allies—"the waters of the Nile" and "the waters of the Euphrates"—(vv. 14-18) when they forsook God, their source of strength (v. 19).

2:20-28 "Long ago you broke your yoke." Jeremiah utilizes the language of Hosea's marriage analogy again to accuse his people of breaking their "yoke" of marriage to God by giving themselves to harlotry, that is, infidelity (v. 20). In verse 21 he uses the Isaian covenant analogy (see Isa 5:1-7), in which God is the owner of the vineyard and Israel is the vineyard, to again accuse them of infidelity. Verses 22-28 continue the accusations with Hosean language likening Israel's rampant infidelity to the covenant to the sexual ardor of a "frenzied she-camel" (vv. 22-25) and to the shame of a thief caught red-handed in his thievery (vv. 26-28).

2:29-32 "How dare you still plead with me?" Despite medicinal punishment, the way of divine pedagogy, Israel continues to rebel (vv. 29-30) and to act as if God had no interest in her (v. 31). Unlike a bride who never forgets her bridal jewelry, Israel has forgotten God.

2:33-37 "How well you pick your way when seeking love!" The indictment continues with accusations of crimes against the innocent (v. 34) and hypocritical avowals of innocence (v. 35). For such crimes God threatens the shame of subjection to Egyptian and Assyrian conquerors (vv. 36-37).

3:1-5 "If a man sends away his wife." Jeremiah concludes this collection of accusations by returning to the theme with which he began it, namely, the theme of the unfaithful wife (compare 2:2 and 3:1, 5). According to Deut 24:1-4, a divorced and remarried wife was forbidden to return to her original husband. Israel in her infidelity has sinned with many lovers and like a harlot refuses to blush (vv. 1-3). Even more, she hypocritically continues to call upon God as "My father . . . the bridegroom of my youth" (v. 4) and to expect forgiveness, all the while committing all the evil it can (v. 5).

3:6-10 "See now what rebellious Israel has done!" This prose passage both summarizes the accusations of 2:1–3:5 and at the same time takes up and develops the theme of 3:1-5: the return of the divorced wife who has rebelled against her husband—God. The key words "rebel" and "return" recur regularly (see 3:1, 7, 8, 10-14, 22; 4:1). The comparison (to the detriment of Judah) with the rebellious northern kingdom of Israel (vv. 6-10) suggests that this sample of Jeremiah's preaching dates to the reform of King Josiah (2 Kgs 22–23), which began in 626 B.C.E. and ended with Josiah's death in 609 B.C.E.

3:11-18 "Rebel Israel is inwardly more just than traitorous Judah." The theme "inwardly more just," which recurs in 4:3-4, frames 3:6–4:4 and summarizes the purpose of Jeremiah's preaching: guilty Judah, like guilty Israel, is called upon to confess its guilt and return to God not just externally but internally (v. 13). God will richly reward such a return (conversion) by bringing back the exiles of Israel (and Judah, if verses 14-18 do not come from editors during or after the Babylonian Exile) and making Jerusalem the special center for the worship of all the nations (vv. 17-18).

3:19–4:4 "How I should like to treat you as sons." This section begins with God's plaintive pleas for Israel to return (vv. 19-22a), continues with a suggested confession similar to the confession in Hos 14:2-4 (vv. 22b-25), and ends with a conditional absolution (4:1-2) and a final appeal for genuine inward conversion: a circumcision of the heart, that is, an inward rather than just an outward sign of commitment to God (vv. 3-4, and see 3:11, where the theme of "inwardly just" is first mentioned).

4:5–6:30 The judgment against guilty Judah. In this section Jeremiah summarizes God's judgment against Judah, the judgment first mentioned in 1:13-17, namely, that enemies will come from the north and destroy Jerusalem and Judah.

4:5-18 "Proclaim it in Judah." In verses 5-8 Jeremiah dramatizes the reaction of the people when they hear that invaders from the north have come to destroy the nation (vv. 6b-7). Verses 9-13 describe the dismay and desperation of the king, the princes, the priests, and the false prophets (vv. 9-10) when they witness the imminent fulfillment of God's judgment upon them (vv. 5-13). Finally, in

verse 14 Jeremiah appeals to Jerusalem to "cleanse [its] heart of evil" in view of the disaster (vv. 15-17) about to take place because of its misdeeds (v. 18).

4:19-31 "My breast! my breast! how I suffer!" Jeremiah's grief as he anticipates the judgment and condemnation of Judah (vv. 19-21) is expressed in his repugnance for what his people have done (v. 22), in his horror at the approaching scourge (vv. 23-29), and in his repugnance for their attempt to prostitute themselves before their conquerors in order to stave off destruction (vv. 30-31).

5:1-31 Universal corruption. Combining accusations with judgment, Jeremiah complains to God that he cannot find even one upright person in Judah (v. 1); that all, from the lowliest to the greatest, are guilty (vv. 2-5); they will be punished (vv. 6-10) because they have openly rebelled (v. 11), denying God, as if God were powerless or nonexistent (v. 12), and rejecting the prophets (v. 13). For all this, God threatens destruction by a nation from afar (vv. 14-15), which will destroy their crops, their children, their flocks, and the "fortified city" (Jerusalem) in which they trust (vv. 16-17). Following a gloss from postexilic times (vv. 18-19), Jeremiah urges his people to pay attention (vv. 20-21) and to fear the all-powerful Lord of nature (v. 22). Verses 23-31 further accuse Judah and prepare the way for the climactic judgment that follows in 6:1-30.

6:1-30 The invaders from the north. Verses 1-5 ring with the cries of the invaded and the invaders, followed by a first series of accusations (vv. 6-10) leading up to God's judgment on young and old (vv. 11-12), small and great, false prophet and priest (vv. 13-15). A second series of accusations begins with an exhortation to remember "the way to good, and walk it," followed by Israel's reply, "We will not walk it" (v. 16), and its refusal to hearken to the warnings of God's "watchmen," that is, the prophets (v. 17). Verses 18-26 continue with further accusations and judgments, mentioning again the people "from the land of the north" (v. 22) and the destruction that the invading armies will bring (vv. 23-26). The section concludes with Jeremiah's evaluation of his ministry as a failure (vv. 27-30). He has been sent as a "tester" of his people (v. 27), and he has found them "silver rejected" (v. 30).

B. The Temple Sermon (7:1–8:3)

The temple sermon is the most memorable of Jeremiah's sermons. It is dated (see 26:1) early in the reign of King Jehoiakim (609–598 B.C.E.) and is written in Deuteronomic style, the style of the Book of Deuteronomy, which was found in the temple in 621 B.C.E. and with which Jeremiah was certainly acquainted. Like the material in chapters 2–6, the temple sermon is filled with accusations and condemnations.

7:1-15 Hear the word of the Lord. Standing near the gate to the temple area (v. 2), Jeremiah excoriates the Jews for their superstitious belief that the presence of God's temple will protect them (see Isa 36–37) from their enemies (v. 4) and calls them to reform their lives (vv. 5-7). In verses 8-11 he accuses them of crimes against the covenant, coupled with the hypocritical conviction that they can turn the temple into "a den of thieves" and still escape punishment. He reminds them that the Shiloh temple was destroyed in the time of Samuel (1050 B.C.E.) and that the same thing can now happen to Solomon's temple in Jerusalem (vv. 12-15). As chapter 26 explains, Jeremiah's threat leads to his trial for blasphemy against the temple, a crime of which he is acquitted only when someone reminds the judges that the prophet Micah made the same threat against the temple in the reign of King Hezekiah (715–687 B.C.E.) and was not condemned.

7:16–8:3 "You, now, do not intercede for this people." The sermon continues with accusations dealing with liturgical abuses (7:16-31) and concludes with a long description of the punishment that will be visited upon the people who have made God's temple a "den of thieves" (7:32–8:3).

C. Accusations and Judgments (8:4–10:25)

This section continues in different ways the accusations and judgments of chapters 2–6.

8:4-7 "Tell them." Here Jeremiah bemoans the unnatural conduct of people who, unlike the "Turtledove, swallow and thrush [which] observe their time of return, . . . do not know the ordinance of the Lord" (v. 7).

8:8-12 "How can you say, 'We are wise . . .'?" There is no true wisdom where the word of the Lord is rejected (vv. 8-9). The judgment introduced as usual by the word "therefore" is a just sentence on priests and prophets who in their greed for gain defraud the people (v. 10) and promise peace when there is no peace (vv. 11-12).

8:13-23 "I will gather them all in." The threat of punishment (v. 13) returns to the theme of invasion (vv. 14-17) and concludes with Jeremiah's soliloquy, in which he expresses his uncontrollable grief over the downfall of his people (vv. 18-23).

9:1-21 "Would that I had in the desert a traveler's lodge!" Jeremiah's soliloquy is followed by God's soliloquy (9:1-5). God would like to depart from this people and live alone in a desert lodge (v. 1), free of their lying, deceptions, and violence (vv. 2-5). The soliloquy is followed by a judgment and threat of punishment (vv. 6-8) and concludes with a long dirge that serves as a funeral song lamenting the destruction of Jerusalem and Judah (vv. 9-10), asking and answering why such calamities have come about (vv. 11-15), and calling upon the wailing women to come and intone a dirge (vv. 16-17) over the devastated land and the corpses of the slain (vv. 18-21). The dirge, which asked the question "Who is so wise . . . ?" in verse 11, concludes with a definition of true wisdom (v. 22), which consists in knowing God as the only source of "kindness, justice and uprightness on the earth" (v. 23).

9:24–10:16 "See, days are coming, says the Lord." Like the surrounding idol-worshiping nations, the whole house of Israel is circumcised in the flesh, that is, outwardly but not inwardly in the heart, the only place where true commitment to God counts for anything (vv. 24-25). Israel, therefore, is no different from the idolatrous nations. Its idolatry, the prophet declares in language similar to that of Isa 40–66, is pure foolishness (10:1-11), and its gods are not to be compared with the true God (vv. 10-13), whose greatness highlights the inanity of idolatry (vv. 14-15) and who is "the portion of Jacob," that is, the God of Israel (v. 16).

10:17-25 "Lift your bundle and leave the land." Jeremiah concludes this collection of accusations and judgments (8:4–10:25) with a poem that probably dates from 597 B.C.E., when the Babylonian armies first invaded and defeated Judah and Jerusalem. The opening lines (vv. 17-18) advise the people to prepare for deportation. In verses 19-21 Jeremiah puts into the mouth of the nation a brief soliloquy lamenting its defeat (vv. 19-21) and blaming this defeat on the shepherds (the kings) who did not seek the Lord and thus brought about the defeat and deportation of the people (v. 22). The whole section concludes with Jeremiah's prayer of intercession for his wayward people (vv. 23-25).

D. Deuteronomic Sermons, Confessions, and Parables (11:1–20:18)

This section continues Jeremiah's accusations and judgments against Judah. It varies their presentation, however, by dramatizing them in different ways, for example, by introducing more Deuteronomic sermons (chs. 11; 16; 17; 19; 20), a number of parables (chs. 13; 18; 19), and Jeremiah's five famous confessions (12:1-16; 15:10-21; 17:12-18; 18:18-23; 20:7-18).

11:1-18 The covenant sermon. In the year 621 B.C.E., in the course of cleaning and reforming the temple and its cult, the priest Hilkiah discovered a manuscript presumed to be the Book of Deuteronomy and had it read before King Josiah (see 2 Kgs 22:8–23:25). Josiah, who had begun his reform some years earlier, used the book to further his reform by sending preachers to the cities of Judah and even to the cities of the defunct northern kingdom. The reform failed, but presumably 11:1-18 is an example of the kind of sermon Jeremiah preached when he took part in the abortive reform.

12:1-6 The first "confession." The five "confessions" of Jeremiah consist of soliloquies in which Jeremiah carries on intimate conversations with God. He laments his misfortunes, considers giving up his hopeless mission, pleads with God to avenge him against his enemies, and in the end rests his hope in God alone. Few people in the history of religion have exposed with such nakedness their inmost objections to God's way of dealing with them. Jeremiah's complaint in the first confession is the age-old complaint that God appears to reward opponents and to ignore those who are loyal (vv. 1-3a). He begs God, therefore, to show preference for the righteous by punishing the wicked (vv. 3b-4). God's reply (vv. 5-6) provides no comfort: Things will get

worse not better (v. 5), and even Jeremiah's own relatives will betray him (v. 6).

11:19-23 "Yet I, like a trusting lamb." These verses fit better here after 12:6 and describe Jeremiah's reaction to his relatives' plot to kill him (v. 19). He entrusts his care to God (v. 20), who promises to punish the inhabitants of Anathoth (vv. 21-23).

12:7-17 "I abandon my house." The oracle declares that just as Jeremiah's relatives have turned on him, so his "heritage" has turned on God (vv. 7-8). For this they are punished, as Jeremiah's relatives were punished (vv. 9-13). Verses 14-17, which refer to the possible conversion of the neighboring kingdoms that turned against Judah at the time of the Babylonian invasions of 598 and 588 B.C.E., echo the universalism of the promise to Abraham (Gen 12:1-3) and the later universalism of Isa 40–55. Some consider these verses to be an exilic gloss.

13:1-11 The parable of the linen loincloth. Parables are extended similies in story form. The important element is the central point of likeness. The details are secondary and pertain only to the fleshing out of the story. Most parables, like those of Jesus, are purely literary, that is, made-up stories; for example, the good Samaritan, the prodigal son, Dives and Lazarus. Some parables are acted out; for example, Jesus' washing of the feet of his disciples at the Last Supper. They are called parables in action. In each parable the reader should search out the nature of the parable—literary or in action—and the covenant themes, usually inherent in the accusations and judgments.

In the parable of the loincloth, the central likeness is the closeness of one's underclothes to one's person as the measure of the closeness intended to exist between God and the people (v. 11). The burial of the loincloth in a cleft of the rock by the Parath (Euphrates), where it rots (vv. 1-7), signifies the punishment of Israel for refusing to obey God and following strange gods instead (vv. 8-11). The nature of the parable is probably that of a parable in action. The Parath (Euphrates) is probably not the great river that runs through Babylon but a stream with the same name not far from Jerusalem, used here as a symbol of Babylon and the Exile there. Watching Jeremiah's parabolic burying of the loincloth in a cleft of rock by the Parath would excite curiosity and the question "Why?" Jeremiah answers by telling the parable (vv. 1-7) and then giving the answer (vv. 8-11).

14:1–15:4 The great drought. In the Middle East, when the winter rains fail for two or three years, drought and famine are sure to follow. The drought described in verses 2-6 caused a national emergency. What follows in 14:8 to 15:4 is Jeremiah's intercessory prayer for the nation (vv. 8-9) and God's command to him not to intercede for these people (vv. 10-12). Jeremiah then blames it all on the false prophets (v. 13). God answers him by condemning both prophets and people to sword and famine (vv. 14-16). In the lament that follows, Jeremiah again attempts to intercede for his people (vv. 17-22) and is again rebuffed (15:1-4). God is watching over the divine word (see 1:12) and is determined to see it fulfilled! It is impossible to date this section, but the frequent references to the "sword" (vv. 12-13, 15-16, 18; 15:2-3) suggest a time of war, perhaps the Babylonian invasion of 598 B.C.E.

15:5-9 "Who will pity you, Jerusalem?" This lament follows naturally upon God's determination to fulfill the word of judgment against Jerusalem in 15:1-4.

15:10-21 Jeremiah's second "confession." The mention of a mother of seven swooning away in 15:9 leads Jeremiah to think of his own mother and his own situation as "a man of strife and contention to all the land" (v. 10). Almost in despair he argues with God to avenge him on his persecutors, reminding God how he, Jeremiah, interceded for his enemies (vv. 11, 15), how he delighted in God's word (v. 16), and how this led to his unbearable loneliness (v. 17). Jeremiah concludes by accusing God of betraying and abandoning him like "a treacherous brook, whose waters do not abide" (v. 18). God's reply is a rebuke and an implied accusation. Jeremiah himself needs to repent (return to God) and weigh well his own response to God (v. 19a). If he does, he will continue to be God's "mouthpiece," and God will be with him against his persecutors (vv. 19b-21 and compare 1:18-19).

16:1-21 Jeremiah's celibacy. God commands Jeremiah to be celibate, not because celibacy is better than marriage but because in the days of thirst, starvation, and destruction that would accompany the siege and destruction of Jerusalem, Jeremiah would be spared the anguish of witnessing the terrible suffering of a beloved wife and children. In addition, like the children of Hosea (see Hos 1:4-9) and Isaiah (see Isa 7:3; 8:1-4), Jeremiah would be a living symbol of the unhappy fate of Judah and Jerusalem (vv. 1-4). He is not to mourn with the mourners (vv. 5-7) nor celebrate with those who sit eating and drinking (vv. 8-9), because Judah and Jerusalem are to be punished for forsaking God and God's covenant law (vv. 10-13). Verses 14-15 do not harmonize with the message of destruction in verses 10-13 and probably represent a post-exilic gloss. Verses 16-18 continue the message of doom. Like verses 14-15, verses 19-21 probably also represent a postexilic gloss. They speak of the conversion of the pagan nations and ridicule idolatry, two popular themes of exilic and postexilic literature.

17:1-13 "The sin of Judah is written with an iron stylus." This series of sayings contrasts the true and the false Israelite. Sin begins in the heart, and Judah's guilt is undeniable (v. 1). For its sin it will be punished (vv. 2-4). The wicked trust in human beings and are cursed (vv. 5-6); the just trust in the Lord, and their future is assured by God (v. 8 and see Ps 1:1ff.). Verses 9-10 return to the mysterious workings of the human heart (see v. 1) and avow that only God can probe its incalculable ways (v. 10). An example of such incalculable ways is the one who acquires wealth unjustly (v. 11 and see Luke 12:13-21). Jeremiah's observations on the human heart conclude with a declaration of doom for those who forsake God (vv. 12-13).

17:14-18 Jeremiah's third "confession." This confession should be interpreted in the light of Jeremiah's observations concerning mysterious workings of the human heart mentioned in 17:1, 5-10. As in his first and second confessions, Jeremiah begs God to heal him (v. 14), to observe the blasphemous scoffing of his enemies (v. 16), and to remember how he did not press for his enemies' total destruction (v. 16). Naturally, he prays that his enemies and not he himself be confounded (vv. 17-18), for only thus will it be seen that God is a just God.

17:19-27 Desecrating the sabbath. Here, as in his Deuteronomic temple sermon (see 7:1–8:3), Jeremiah attacks those who sin against God's covenant commandment of keeping holy the sabbath day. All prophetic accusations and judgments deal in one way or another with crimes against the ten commandments. This sermon is notable in that it deals specifically with only one commandment and shows that although Jeremiah is against the hypocrisy of those who make an outward show of piety (see 7:1ff.), he is not against the temple cult in itself (compare Isa 1:12-17). When commanding "Keep holy the sabbath day," God meant what the words say. As with all the commandments, God promises blessings for those who observe them (vv. 24-26) and curses on those who do not (v. 27).

18:1-12 The parable of the potter. The potter with his wheel—one wheel at the top holding the clay and the other at the bottom rotated by his feet—is master of what he will create (vv. 1-4). So is God the master of Israel's fate (vv. 5-6). But God is not a tyrant and leaves the last word to Israel. The divine blessings are conditional, and so are the threats (vv. 7-10). The message of the parable is clear: all depends on Israel. But, as verses 11-12 make clear, Judah has no intention of repenting, and therefore its fate is certain (v. 12).

18:13-17 Judah's unnatural apostasy. Jeremiah's conviction that Judah will not return to God fills him with horror (v. 13). It should be as natural for Judah to be faithful to God as it is for the snow to remain on the mountains of Lebanon and as it is for the mountain streams to run steadily down (v. 14). Yet Israel has done the unnatural thing: it has forgotten God and turned to idolatrous worship (v. 15). In view of what God the potter declared in 18:10, therefore, Judah's fate is certain (vv. 16-17).

18:18-23 Jeremiah's fourth "confession." As in his earlier confessions, Jeremiah is outraged with his enemies because they have not only persecuted him but now even plot his death (vv. 18-19). He argues with God (v. 20a), reminds God how he, Jeremiah, prayed for his enemies (v. 20b), and then launches into a bitter prayer for the destruction of those enemies (vv. 21-23). Since Jeremiah's enemies are God's enemies, it is not unlikely that Jeremiah prays for their destruction in order that all might see that God is not impotent before apparent foes. Jeremiah had, after all, interceded for them, so he could hardly have hated them.

19:1-20:6 The symbolic earthen flask. This episode cannot be dated, but the references to Babylon in 20:4-6 indicate that it occurred sometime after Babylon came to power in 605 B.C.E. The earthen flask, a clay water jar, symbolizes Judah and Jerusalem (v. 3). Jeremiah takes it with him to the valley of Ben-hinnom, the valley on the southwest side of Jerusalem later turned into a garbage dump and called Gehenna (vv. 1-2). At a Baal fertility-cult temple there in the valley, Jeremiah delivers a bitter sermon against Judah and Jerusalem, accusing it of flagrant idolatry (vv. 3-5) and threatening it with total destruction (vv. 6-9). At the end of the sermon, he hurls the earthen flask to the ground, smashing it to bits, thus indicating by a parable in action the destruction of the city and the nation (vv. 10-15). Baruch, his secretary and biographer, or perhaps Jeremiah himself, then describes what happened. Pashhur, chief officer in the temple, has Jeremiah scourged and then placed in the stocks overnight (20:1-2). The next morning Jeremiah, filled with indignation, predicts a bitter end for Pashhur (vv. 2-4a) and for the whole nation (vv. 4b-6). The prophecy is fulfilled when the Babylonians capture Jerusalem in 587 B.C.E. and deport king and citizens into captivity and exile in Babylon.

20:7-18 Jeremiah's fifth and last "confession." Goaded almost to despair, Jeremiah, in a magnificently passionate soliloquy, accuses God of seducing him into accepting a mission that brings only "derision and reproach all the day" (vv. 7-8). He contemplates abandoning his office of prophet but then, in almost a paroxysm of revulsion, admits that God's word is like a fire in his bones that he can neither hold in nor endure (v. 9). God's word brings him only denunciation, the loss of friends, and the threat of death (v. 10). Despite all this, he knows that God is with him and that his persecutors will not triumph (v. 11). With a burst of confidence, he then calls upon God to avenge him on his enemies (vv. 12-13). Finally, emotionally drained, he despairingly curses the day he was born (vv. 14-18). As many have observed, this confession says more about the nature of inspiration and the hardships of the prophetic mission than a dozen learned treatises.

PART III:
PROPHECIES AGAINST THE KINGS AND THE FALSE PROPHETS

Jer 21:1–25:38

In the book that Jeremiah dictated to Baruch in 604 B.C.E. (see ch. 36), it is probable that chapter 20 was followed immediately by chapter 25, a chapter whose content sounds very much like the conclusion to that book (see 25:1-3, 13). Later, when editors put the whole book together in the form in which we have it now, they interpolated between chapter 20 and chapter 25 a collection of Jeremiah's prophecies against the kings and the false prophets. They did so in all probability because the content of these prophecies contains the overall theme of chapters 1–20, namely, accusations against and condemnations of those who have been unfaithful to the covenant.

In chapters 21–24 the editors are concerned more with content than chronology. The collection begins and ends with a prophecy against the last king of Judah, King Zedekiah (597–587 B.C.E.). By repeating the same names, Zedekiah (21:1 and 24:8) and Nebuchadnezzar (21:1 and 24:1), and the expression "sword, famine, and pestilence" (21:7, 9 and 24:10), the editors make the collection begin and end the same way, thus creating a frame or, as it is technically called, an inclusion-conclusion for the whole section.

A. Prophecies Against the Kings and False Prophets (21:1–24:10)

21:1-10 Against King Zedekiah. Following the siege of 598 B.C.E. and the deportation of the reigning king, Jeconiah, to Babylon as hostage royalty, Nebuchadnezzar placed Jeconiah's uncle, Zedekiah, the third son of Josiah (639–609), on the throne of Judah. In return Zedekiah rebelled. Infuriated, Nebuchadnezzar besieged Jerusalem for the last time in 588 B.C.E. King Zedekiah, a believer in Jeremiah, seeks from the prophet a good word from the Lord (vv. 1-2). Jeremiah's response provides little comfort: the city will fall to the Babylonians (vv. 3-7), and only those who surrender will save their lives (vv. 8-10).

21:11–22:9 Against the whole royal dynasty of David. In the section that follows, Jeremiah will deal with each of the kings in chronological order, beginning with Jehoahaz. Here he twice gives warning against the Davidic dynasty as a whole, first in 21:11-14 and a second time in 22:1-9. Each warning begins with a reminder of what God expects of the kings (21:11a and 22:1-4) and ends with a threat of destruction (21:11b-14 and 22:5-9). The whole section breathes disillusionment with the messianic dynasty of David (see 2 Sam 7 for the promise of perpetuity to the dynasty) and leads up to the promise of a future successful Davidic king (the Messiah) in 23:1-8.

The "Valley-site" (v. 13a), another name for Jerusalem, which is surrounded by valleys, is considered impregnable (v. 13b), but God will "kindle a fire in its forest," probably a section of Solomon's palace called "the Forest of Lebanon" (1 Kgs 7:2), and destroy it (v. 14). In 22:1-9 the prophecy of destruction is conditional (vv. 4-6), but with little hope that the condition will be fulfilled (vv. 7-9).

22:10-12 Against Jehoahaz. When his father, King Josiah, died in battle against the Egyptians at Megiddo in 609 B.C.E. (see 2 Kgs 23:28-30), Jehoahaz ascended the throne of Judah. He reigned three months, was deposed by Pharaoh Neco of Egypt, and led into exile, never to return. His throne name was Jehoahaz; his personal name, Shallum (v. 11).

22:13-19 Against Jehoiakim. Enthroned as vassal king by the Egyptians, Jehoiakim paid a heavy tribute to Egypt (see 2 Kgs 23:24ff.). Jeremiah accuses him of engaging in vast building projects and refusing to pay his laborers (vv. 13-15a), and contrasts him for the worse with his pious father, King Josiah (vv. 15b-17). The judgment against him is harsh: no one will mourn him (v. 18), and he will be buried as ignominiously as an ass (v. 19). It should be noted that Jehoiakim murdered prophets (see 26:20-24), forced Jeremiah and Baruch into hiding, and was so contemptuous of Jeremiah that he callously fed into the fire the first of Jeremiah's two manuscripts dictated to Baruch in the year 604 B.C.E. (see 36:20-26). Jeremiah had ample justification for his harsh judgment against Jehoiakim!

22:20-30 Against Jehoiachin. Jeremiah's longest prophecy against a king is leveled at Jehoiachin, also known as Coniah and

465

Jeconiah (v. 24). He succeeded Jehoiakim in 598 B.C.E., reigned three months, and was then deported to Babylon as hostage royalty along with his family and many of the nobles and priests. He is mentioned as still living in Babylon in 562 B.C.E. (see 2 Kgs 25:27-30). The prophecy against him begins with the accusation that he has from his youth refused to listen to God (vv. 20-21). It continues with the threat of exile (vv. 22-23) and concludes with a long denunciation (vv. 24-30) predicting his defeat by Nebuchadnezzar (it happened in 597 B.C.E.) and exile with no hope of return (vv. 24-27). It concludes with a bitter tirade not only against Jehoiachin but against his descendants as well (vv. 29-30). Verse 30 is important because it shows Jeremiah's complete disillusionment with the Davidic dynasty, a disillusionment that leads up to his prediction in 23:1-6 of a future successful descendant of David whom Israel would look forward to as the Messiah! The prediction that Jehoiachin will be "childless" does not mean that he will have no sons (he had seven) but that none of them will ever reign as king of Judah.

23:1-8 A future son of David who will succeed. The prophecy of a future successful son of David begins with the accusation that the "shepherds," that is, the kings, have been responsible for the exile of the nation (vv. 1-2) and the promise that God will be the Good Shepherd who gathers the dispersed sheep and brings them back to their meadow, a symbolic way of speaking about the return from the Babylonian captivity (vv. 3-4 and compare Ezek 34). This promise is repeated in verses 7-8 and thus forms a frame around the messianic promise in verses 5-6. The future ideal king is described as "a righteous shoot [descendant] to David," who unlike his predecessors will reign and govern wisely (v. 5). He will be the savior of Judah and will be called "the Lord our justice." This prophecy, along with the prophecy of Isaiah about "a shoot [that] shall sprout from the stump of Jesse" (Isa 11:1ff.) fueled the messianic hopes of Israel in the centuries that followed and was fulfilled with the coming of Jesus, "the son of David," five centuries later.

23:9-40 Against the false prophets. Besides true prophets, Israel also had to deal with false prophets, those who falsely claimed to have been sent by God as messengers to the people of Israel (see 29:1-17 for an example

of a false prophet who told the people the opposite of what Jeremiah told them). In verses 9-14 Jeremiah describes the depravity of some of the false prophets. In verses 14-24 he repeats many of the charges he had made against the false prophets who opposed him. He then concludes with a long deuteronomically styled diatribe against those prophets and their insolent claims (vv. 25-40).

24:1-10 Against Zedekiah. Jeremiah frames the whole section against the kings and the false prophets (21:24) by ending as he began (see 21:1-10)—with a prophecy against Zedekiah and renewed remarks about Nebuchadnezzar and the scourges he would bring: sword, famine, and pestilence. The prophecy is dated to 598 B.C.E. and deals with the fate of the exiles of 598 B.C.E. (vv. 1-7), whom Jeremiah designates symbolically as "the good figs" (vv. 4-7), and with the fate of King Zedekiah and the remaining Jews in Jerusalem, whom he designates symbolically as "the bad figs" (vv. 8-10). Undoubtedly the editors placed this prophecy last in the collection of prophecies against the kings because it not only serves to frame the whole collection but also introduces and foreshadows what will follow: God's promises for the future for "the good figs" (chs. 29–33) and God's threats of doom for "the bad figs" (chs. 34–39). The passage is doubly important because it contains the first promise of what will constitute the heart of "the new covenant" in the words: "I will give them a heart with which to understand that I am the Lord" (v. 7 and compare 31:31-34).

B. The Conclusion of Jeremiah's Book (25:1-38)

Originally this chapter followed chapters 1–20. It formed the conclusion of the manuscript that Jeremiah dictated to Baruch in 604 B.C.E. (see 36:27-32). In 605 B.C.E. Nebuchadnezzar had made himself master of the Middle East from Mesopotamia to Egypt. Jeremiah now knew that "the wind from the north" that would devastate Judah and Jerusalem (see chs. 1–6) would be the armies of Babylon. Writing in Deuteronomic style, he reminds his readers that what he has written constitutes a summary of twenty-three years of preaching (v. 3), which they have rejected, as they rejected the preaching of all the prophets (vv.

4-7). Since they will not listen, their doom is sealed. God will send "the tribes of the north" (Nebuchadnezzar's armies) to devastate the land (vv. 8-10). The nation will be in exile for seventy years (vv. 11-14).

This is the first reference to the seventy years of the Babylonian captivity, which ended in 539 B.C.E. with the destruction of the Babylonian Empire by Cyrus the Great of Persia. However one counts the seventy years, whether from 604 B.C.E., when Jeremiah first spoke of them, or from 597 B.C.E., when the first group was deported to Babylon, or from 587 B.C.E., when the major deportation took place, it is impossible to get exactly seventy years. The figure is best interpreted as a round number signifying a long time. Although Jeremiah did not know it, it was during those seventy years that his book was read, pondered, and heeded. Too late the exiles realized that Jeremiah's preaching made sense, that his enemies had erred, and that God had justly punished them. But it was not too late to return to God, from whom alone, as Jeremiah had so many times insisted, they could confidently expect forgiveness, security, and a future. Out of the ashes of the Exile came a fire, and Jeremiah's book was the spark that ignited it.

The reference in verse 14a to the nations that would destroy the kingdom of Judah leads Jeremiah in verses 15-38 to predict the future downfall of those same nations. In the Greek text, but not in the Hebrew, there follow here the prophecies against the nations in chapters 46-51. The "cup" (vv. 15ff.) symbolizes destiny. The destiny can be good, as in Ps 23:5 ("my cup overflows"), or bad, as in Matt 26:39 ("My Father, if it is possible, let this cup pass me up"). In this case the "cup" is a cup of wrath for the nations that have oppressed God's people.

PART IV: BIOGRAPHICAL MATERIAL AND THE NEW COVENANT

Jer 26:1–33:26

This section of the book comes from sources that contained biographical material about Jeremiah. Like the following chapters (chs. 34–39), it is long on narrative and short on sermons. The narrative material would seem to come from a biography of Jeremiah

by his secretary Baruch. Whatever the original source or sources, it is clear that the editors did not arrange the material in chronological order. Chapter 26 deals with the temple sermon dated to 608 B.C.E. Chapters 27–29 date to 593, and chapter 36 dates to 604 B.C.E. More than likely the editors chose to arrange the material according to theme. Thus chapters 26–29 deal with the truth and efficacy of Jeremiah's prophetic words; chapters 30–33, with Jeremiah's predictions of hope for the future and a new covenant for Israel; and chapters 34–39, with the rejection of both Jeremiah himself and his word by kings and commoners.

A. The Temple Sermon (26:1-24)

The hand of the biographer (Baruch?) is evident here in the dating (609–608 B.C.E.), the beginning (v. 1) of the reign of King Jehoiakim (609–598 B.C.E.), and in the pervasive third-person narrative account. The biographer summarizes Jeremiah's famous sermon (see 7:1–8:3) predicting the destruction of the temple (vv. 2-6) and then goes on to tell what the results were for the courageous prophet. He is accused of blasphemy against the temple and threatened with death (vv. 2-6). Jeremiah responds to the charge (vv. 7-11) by declaring that it was God who sent him to prophesy against the temple and the city, and only their repentance (see ch. 18) can save both city and temple (vv. 12-13). If they execute him, they will bring down upon themselves, their city, and its citizens "innocent blood" (vv. 14-15 and see Matt 27:24-25).

In the informal trial that follows, Jeremiah is defended by some of his friends among the elders (v. 16), who remind Jeremiah's accusers that the prophet Micah a century earlier, in the reign of King Hezekiah (715–687), made the same prediction (Mic 3:12) and was not condemned to death (vv. 17-19). Jeremiah is acquitted, but his biographer highlights the danger to the prophet by telling the story of a less fortunate prophet, Uriah, who fled into Egypt, was brought back to Jerusalem, and there executed and thrown into the common grave (vv. 20-24). By placing these episodes here at the beginning of the biographical section of the book, the editors emphasize the nature of the true prophet—one whose prophecy is fulfilled. The readers know how well Jeremiah's prophecy was fulfilled, and the editors leave no doubt about it in the following chapters, especially chapter 39.

B. Jeremiah Against the False Prophets (27:1–29:32)

As in chapter 26, the editors' concern in chapters 27–29 is to emphasize the truth and fulfillment of Jeremiah's prophecies, despite the opposition of his enemies—in this case the false prophet Hananiah in Jerusalem (see ch. 28) and the false prophets in Babylon (see 29:20-32). The biographer begins by explaining the background of Jeremiah's conflict with Hananiah. In 593 B.C.E., only four years after the first siege and capture of Jerusalem, King Zedekiah of Judah, who had been put on the throne by Nebuchadnezzar, plots against Nebuchadnezzar by calling to Jerusalem the ambassadors of the kings of Edom, Moab, Ammon, Tyre, and Sidon (vv. 1-3). Using an ox yoke as a parable in action, Jeremiah declares to the assembled ambassadors and Zedekiah that it is God's will that they all bend their necks under the yoke of the king of Babylon (vv. 4-8). They must not listen to false prophets who predict a successful revolt (vv. 9-22).

What follows in chapter 28 is a vivid account of the face-to-face meeting of the true prophet and the false prophet. Hananiah predicts success (28:1-4). Jeremiah counters with a declaration that implicitly accuses Hananiah of prophesying falsely (vv. 5-9). Hananiah throws Jeremiah's ox yoke to the ground and repeats his prediction of a successful revolt (vv. 10-11). Finally Jeremiah receives word from the Lord and prophesies Hananiah's death within a year for having prophesied falsely in the name of the Lord (vv. 12-17). Once again as in chapter 26, the editors have highlighted the veracity of the true prophet by chronicling these unique encounters between the true prophet and the false prophet.

Chapter 29 continues the theme of Jeremiah's battle against the false prophets. This time the opposition comes from Babylon, where false prophets are assuring the exiles of 597 B.C.E. that they will soon return to Jerusalem. Jeremiah refutes their claims by sending a letter to the exiles via friends sent on a diplomatic mission to Nebuchadnezzar (vv. 1-3).

The letter (vv. 4-23) urges the exiles to expect a long stay in the land of their conquerors, to settle down there (vv. 4-6), to pray for the welfare of Babylon (v. 7), and to pay no heed to the false prophets (vv. 8-9). In verses 10-14 Jeremiah assures them that after seventy years God will reverse their fortunes and bring them back to their own land. The letter continues with a threat against Jerusalem and King Zedekiah (vv. 15-20) and against two false prophets in Babylon (vv. 21-23). It concludes with a threat of death for Shemaiah, who had written from Babylon to the high priest urging him to arrest and silence Jeremiah (vv. 24-32).

The editors placed this letter-writing episode here not only because it continues the theme of Jeremiah's battle with the false prophets but also because it serves as an excellent preamble to the theme of the following chapters—the theme of hope for the future and the promise of a new and successful covenant (chs. 30–33).

C. Jeremiah and the New Covenant (30:1–33:26)

The editors of Jeremiah's prophecies grouped in these chapters material from different sources dealing with the prophet's predictions of hope for Israel and Judah in the future. The prophet who predicted with such certainty the fall and exile of Judah and Jerusalem with equal certainty predicted its return from exile and the inauguration of a new and successful covenant in the future. The prophet whose mission was "to root up and to tear down, to destroy and to demolish, to build and to plant" (see 1:10) here builds and plants. The hopes he plants and the future he begins to build take root during the long years of exile and come to fulfillment at the Last Supper, when Jesus declares, "This cup is the new covenant in my blood, which will be shed for you" (Luke 22:20). The editors wisely placed this collection of prophecies of hope after Jeremiah's encouraging letter to the exiles of 597 B.C.E. (see ch. 29) and before the dismal account of the last days of Judah and Jerusalem (see chs. 34–39).

30:1-24 Prophecies of hope. Chapter 30 begins with a statement of hope for the future (vv. 1-3), the general theme of chapters 30–33. Jeremiah's words are directed to Israel, the defunct northern kingdom, and Judah, the soon-to-be-defunct southern kingdom (v. 4). This statement makes applicable to Judah the prophecies of hope in 30:1–31:14; these originally were directed only toward the defunct northern kingdom, which suffered destruction and deportation under the Assyrians in 722 B.C.E. Jeremiah speaks of Israel, therefore, not so much as a national entity, but as that entity better known as the people of God, a moral entity which no national catastrophe can destroy and which exists today and will always exist despite all the vicissitudes and debacles of history.

The prophecies of hope begin with the cries of dismay and fear (vv. 5-7) that fill all hearts when it becomes obvious that the fearful "day of the Lord," the day when God will fulfill earlier threats of destruction for Judah and Jerusalem, has arrived. Bondage to pagan masters, however, will not last. In the future, Israel will serve God and its messianic king (vv. 8-9). This reversal of fortune will be the work of God (vv. 10-23), a work described in language that will be echoed thirty years later in the soaring poetry of Deutero-Isaiah (see Isa 40–55).

31:1-40 The new covenant. Chapter 31 might well be described as Jeremiah's "Hosean" chapter. It shows Hosea's influence on Jeremiah's theology, language, and style (see chs. 2–3 for earlier examples of Hosean chapters). The linguistic and stylistic similarities are obvious (compare vv. 2-3, 9, 18, 20 with Hos 2:16; 11:1-4; 14:2-8). The theological similarities become evident when the reader compares Jeremiah's and Hosea's emphasis on God's love for Israel, and Jeremiah's prediction of a new and eternal covenant (31:31-34) with Hosea's prediction of a new and eternal marriage (Hos 2:18-25).

Verses 1-6 announce the good news of return from exile, emphasizing God's love for Israel (v. 3: "With age-old love I have loved you"). Verses 7-14 rhapsodize over the joy of the returned exiles. Verses 15-20 call upon Israel to end its mourning. Verse 15 calls poetically upon Rachel, the long-dead matriarch of Israel, to cease her cries of mourning for her exiled children. They will return from exile (vv. 16-17), repentant (vv. 18-19) and assured of God's loving forgiveness (v. 20 and see Hos 14:3-9). In the New Testament, Matthew uses this same poetic allusion to Rachel in his story

of Herod's slaughter of the innocents (see Matt 2:18).

In 31:21-22 Jeremiah begins to speak about the new covenant. Calling poetically upon the exiles to set up roadmarkers as they go into exile so that they can follow them on their return (v. 21), he asks dramatically, "How long will you continue to stray, rebellious daughter?" (v. 22a) and then answers his own question with the mysterious statement of verse 22b. Scholars do not agree on the exact meaning here of the verb "encompass," but most agree that the "new thing" that God "has created upon the earth" is a responsive and loving Israel, which, unlike the faithless woman of the Hosean marriage analogy (see Hos 1–3), "will encompass the man [God, in the Hosean analogy] with devotion." This is Jeremiah's indirect way of speaking about the new covenant he will describe in 31:31-34.

Verses 23-30 apply to Judah directly all that Jeremiah said about Israel in 30:1–31:22. Verse 28 repeats what was said about the positive aspect of Jeremiah's mission (see 1:10). Verses 29-30 assure the Israelites that God will judge them according to their own merits and not according to the sins of their ancestors, whose wickedness brought down upon the nation destruction and deportation.

31:31-34 The new covenant. This famous prophecy provides the foundation and the core of the central theological teaching of the New Testament. St. Paul in 2 Cor 3:1–5:21 and the author of Hebrews in Heb 8:6–9:15 explicitly expound this prophecy in relation to Christ. It underlies, but without explicit references, much of the "new life" theology of St. John and is central to the teaching of Jesus in John's Last Supper discourse (John 13–17).

What is "new" about the new covenant is not the God who makes it nor the people with whom it is made—the true Israel—nor the will of God expressed in the Sinai commandments, but the results of the new covenant and the means by which those results are brought about. In contrast to the old Sinai covenant, which failed because Israel did not respond to God's love, the new covenant will be successful. It will be successful because it will be God and God alone who will put into the hearts of the people the power to respond with love. We call this power "grace," and as the books of the New Testament, especially the Pauline letters and John's Gospel, insist, it comes to us along with forgiveness of sins through faith in Jesus who died for love of us.

Although Jeremiah speaks only here of a "new" covenant, he speaks of it implicitly in many other places: in the promise to the exiles of 597 B.C.E. to give them a "new heart" (24:7; see also 32:38-40); in the hope-filled letter to the "good figs" in exile in Babylon (29:5-14); and in the new thing that God will create on earth: "the woman [who will] . . . encompass the man with devotion" (31:22). In the years that follow, Jeremiah's prophecy will be echoed by Ezekiel (see Ezek 16:59-64; 36:25-30) and Deutero-Isaiah (see Isa 55:3; 59:21; 61:8). For Jesus, six hundred years later, the making of the new covenant will become the aim and the focus of his passion, death, and resurrection.

The remainder of the chapter emphasizes the certainty of the promise of God to Israel (vv. 35-37) and of the promise to rebuild Jerusalem (vv. 38-40).

32:1-44 More on the new covenant. This chapter, from a biographical source, was added here by the editors because its theme fits with the theme of chapters 30-31—Israel's return from exile and the new covenant. The episode described took place in the tenth year (587 B.C.E.) of the reign of King Zedekiah, when Nebuchadnezzar's armies were besieging Jerusalem and after Jeremiah had been imprisoned in the quarters of the guard (vv. 1-5 and see 37:21). Ostensibly Jeremiah purchases his cousin Hanamel's field in Anathoth because the Mosaic law demanded that the nearest of kin purchase such property in order to keep it within the clan (vv. 6-9 and see Lev 25:25). Since property during a siege is worth nothing (see vv. 24-25), Jeremiah actually buys the field not as an asset but as another way of professing his faith in God's promise of restoration (vv. 10-15). Thus his purchase of the property amounts to a parable in action. His long prayer in verses 16-44, especially verses 24-25 and 36-44, explains the central point of the parable in action. Verses 38-41 repeat in similar words the substance of what Jeremiah said about the new covenant in 31:31-34 and account for the inclusion of chapter 32 in the collection of Jeremiah's prophecies of hope in chapters 30-33.

33:1-26 More on Israel's hope. Like chapter 32, this chapter contains another prophecy of hope made by Jeremiah during the siege of Jerusalem and at a time when the prophet was imprisoned in the quarters of the guard (vv. 1-13). A second prophecy dealing with the future of the Davidic dynasty follows (vv. 14-18) and presents another version of Jeremiah's prediction of a future Davidic Messiah given more succinctly in 23:5-6. Israel's future rests on firm foundations—a new covenant and a new David (vv. 19-26 and see 31:35-37).

PART V:
DISOBEDIENCE AND DESTRUCTION
Jer 34:1–39:18

As in the rest of the book, the editors arranged the material in chapters 34-39 in a thematic rather than chronological order. Chapters 35-36 date to 598 and 604 B.C.E., respectively, in the reign of King Jehoiakim (609-598 B.C.E.) while chapters 34 and 37-39 date to the last years of King Zedekiah (597-587 B.C.E.). The theme of disobedience to God and God's prophet—a disobedience that results in destruction—clearly dominates and unifies the whole section.

A. The Broken Pact with the Slaves (34:1-22)

34:1-7 "This word came to Jeremiah from the Lord." The chapter begins with Jeremiah's announcement during Nebuchadnezzar's siege of Jerusalem (v. 1) that the city will fall and King Zedekiah will be captured (vv. 2-3). A promise is made to Zedekiah that if he *obeys* (the key word in this whole section), he will die in peace (vv. 4-5). He does not obey, however, and does not die in peace (see 39:4-7). Verses 6-7 indicate that the siege is far advanced, since only two of Jerusalem's fortress towns, Lachish and Azekah, remain. Interestingly enough, one of the twenty-nine Lachish letters (messages to the garrison commander at Lachish written on broken pieces of pottery discovered by archeologists when they excavated Lachish) contains the words: "Let my lord know that we are watching for the signals of Lachish . . . for we cannot see [the signals] of Azekah." The message would seem to indicate that Azekah had fallen and only Lachish remained.

34:8-22 "This is the word that came to Jeremiah from the Lord." The episode of the broken covenant with the slaves accounts for the inclusion of this chapter in the section that runs from chapter 34 to chapter 39. During the siege the king and the nobles freed their slaves, in accordance with the provision of the Sinai covenant that slaves were to be freed every seventh year (Exod 19:4-6; Deut 15:12-15). However, later they went back on their word and reenslaved their compatriots (vv. 8-11), probably when an Egyptian army arrived and forced the Babylonian armies to lift the siege temporarily (see vv. 21-22 and 37:4-5). By breaking their covenant with the slaves, they also broke their covenant with God (vv. 12-20). As verse 17 puts it: "You did not obey [the key word in this section] me by proclaiming your neighbors and kinsmen free. I now proclaim you free . . . for the sword, famine, and pestilence." The chapter concludes as it began (see vv. 1-7) with a renewed threat of destruction (vv. 21-22).

B. The Rechabites Obey but Israel Does Not (35:1-19)

The editors included this chapter for the same reason they included the previous chapter: it testifies to Israel's disobedience. Jeremiah contrasts the obedience of the Rechabites to their founder, Jonathan ben Rechab, with the disobedience of the Israelites to their founder, God. Founded in the ninth century (see 2 Kgs 10:15-17), the Rechabites, a reactionary group of Israelites, disdained the settled and luxurious life of their kinsfolk who accepted the way of life of the Canaanites. They insisted on going back to the desert way of life of the time of Moses and the Sinai covenant, electing a nomadic life, living in tents, planting no crops or vineyards, and drinking no wine (a vice of the Canaanites).

35:1-19 "The word came to Jeremiah from the Lord in the days of Jehoiakim." This episode (v. 1) occurred at the end of the reign of King Jehoiakim (609–598 B.C.E.), when the Babylonian invasion of 598 B.C.E. had begun (see v. 11). Using the equivalent of a parable in action, Jeremiah tempts the Rechabites to drink wine in order to demonstrate by their refusal their staunch obedience to their founder (vv. 2-5). In justification of their refusal, the Rechabites dutifully recite the commands of their religious founder (vv. 6-11). The key line is verse 10: "we obediently

do everything our father Jonadab commanded." In verses 12-17 Jeremiah draws the moral of his parable, contrasting the obedience of the Rechabites to their father with the disobedience of the Israelites to their Father and repeating four times the key word "obey" (see vv. 13-14, 16-17). The lesson concludes with Jeremiah's promise of a blessing on the Rechabites (vv. 18-19).

C. Contempt for the Word of the Lord (36:1-32)

Continuing with source material demonstrating Israel's disobedience, the editors include an episode from the fourth year (605 B.C.E.) of King Jehoiakim (609–598 B.C.E.). The Israelites not only reject God's covenant (chs. 34–35), but they reject as well the words of God's prophet (ch. 36) and the prophet himself (chs. 37–38).

36:1-4 "In the fourth year of Jehoiakim." Why Jeremiah decided to put his prophecies in writing is not clear. Probably it was because under King Jehoiakim he was forbidden under penalty of death to preach; possibly it was because Babylonian armies were in the area, and he feared the end might come sooner than he had expected. His written words read to the people might still bring them to their senses (v. 3). If he died his words would outlast him (as they did) and might eventually bring about Israel's repentance and return (as they did). Baruch the scribe writes from Jeremiah's dictation and the book is done (v. 4).

36:9-19 "In the ninth month." Jeremiah sends Baruch to read his book publicly in the temple area (vv. 5-10). Some of the nobles hear the reading and call upon Baruch to read the book before the king's assembled counselors (vv. 11-16a). The nobles decide that the king should hear about the book but fear for the author and his scribe, and urge them to go into hiding (vv. 16b-19). When the king hears the words of the book, he shows his contempt for the word of the Lord by cutting it into strips and feeding it into a fire (vv. 20-23) and by ordering the arrest of Baruch and Jeremiah (vv. 24-26). The king, however, cannot so easily destroy the word of God. Jeremiah dictates a second scroll (vv. 27-32) and adds to it a searing condemnation of the contemptuous king (vv. 29-31).

D. Contempt for the Lord's Prophet (37:1–38:28)

Chapters 37 and 38 have much in common and may even be two different versions of the same episodes. This would not have bothered the editors, who were intent on demonstrating that the people of Jerusalem not only scorned the commands of the covenant (chs. 34–35) and the written words of the prophet (ch. 36) but the prophet himself (chs. 37–38). Such contempt for the covenant, the prophetic word, and the prophet himself proved how richly deserved was the destruction of Jerusalem described in chapter 39.

37:1-10 "Coniah, son of Jehoiakim, was succeeded by King Zedekiah." The formal introduction (v. 1) suggests that this section belonged to an independent source before it was taken up by the editors and incorporated into the Book of Jeremiah. The words "Neither he, nor his ministers, nor the people of the land would listen to the words of the Lord spoken by Jeremiah the prophet" (v. 2) more than adequately express the theme of chapter 37 and its counterpart, chapter 38. Weak and irresolute and unwilling to abide by Jeremiah's advice, the king sends again and again to Jeremiah, seeking a good word from the Lord (v. 3). This particular appeal to Jeremiah is made during the break in the siege occasioned by the arrival of an Egyptian army in the spring or summer of 588 B.C.E. (vv. 4-5). Jeremiah's reply is consistent: Jerusalem will fall despite the help of the Egyptians (vv. 6-10).

37:11-21 "When the Chaldean army lifted the siege of Jerusalem." In the time between the raising and the resuming of the siege, Jeremiah attempts to go home to Anathoth but is arrested at the city gate as a deserter (vv. 11-14). He is tried and thrown into a dungeon (vv. 15-16). The king has him brought to the palace, hoping that Jeremiah will have good news for him. Jeremiah's reply gives no hope (vv. 17-18). In obvious pain and anguish, Jeremiah pleads with Zedekiah to be released from the dungeon located in the house of Jonathan the scribe (vv. 18-20). He is subsequently imprisoned in the quarters of the guard, presumably a more benign prison (v. 21).

38:1-28 "Shephatiah, son of Mattan." Presumably Jeremiah has greater freedom in the quarters of the guard (see 32:6-15). What-ever the reason, his advice to the people to flee the city is construed as treason. He is handed over to his enemies, thrown into an empty cistern, and left to die in the mud of starvation and thirst (vv. 1-6). Fortunately Ebed-melech, a friend, is able to persuade the king to have him rescued from the cistern (vv. 7-13). Meeting with Jeremiah, the king again asks for a good word from the Lord (vv. 14-16) and again is rebuffed (vv. 17-27). After the meeting Jeremiah remains in the quarters of the guard until the city falls (v. 28).

E. The Fall of Jerusalem (39:1-18)

The editors append here a succinct account of the fall of Jerusalem. Whether it is from Baruch's biography of Jeremiah or freely composed by the editors, it serves the editors' purpose of showing that despite all the opposition of kings, false prophets, nobles, and common people, the word of Jeremiah has been vindicated. God has watched over the divine word and brought it to fulfillment (see 1:11-19).

39:1-18 "In the tenth month of the ninth year of Zedekiah." The siege that began in January of 588 B.C.E. ends with the fall of the city in July of 587 B.C.E. (vv. 1-3). The king tries to escape by fleeing down the Jericho road toward the Jordan. He is captured in the desert near Jericho, taken to Nebuchadnezzar's headquarters at Riblah in Syria, and condemned (vv. 4-5). Before having his eyes gouged out, he is forced to witness the execution of his sons, thus ensuring that the last event he sees by the light of day is the death of his own children (vv. 6-7). In the days that follow, the Babylonians burn the palace, the temple, and many homes and then deport into slavery and exile the cream of the population (vv. 8-10). Jeremiah, probably because he has so often counseled submission to Babylon, is spared (vv. 11-14). The account ends with Jeremiah's promise to Ebed-melech, the eunuch who saved him from death in the miry cistern (see 38:7-13), that his life will be spared (vv. 15-18).

PART VI: DISOBEDIENCE TO THE END

Jer 40:1–45:5

The editors included this section in the book of Jeremiah for two reasons. First, it continues the theme of Judah's disobedience to God and to God's prophet, the theme that dominated chapters 34–39. Second, it proves conclusively that Jeremiah was right when he called the inhabitants of Jerusalem "the bad figs" and predicted (see 24:1-10) for them only sword, famine, and pestilence (see 29:16-19).

A. Jeremiah at Mizpah (40:1–42:22)

40:1-6 Jeremiah in prison at Ramah. This version of Jeremiah's release from prison differs from the version given in 39:8-14. Either the editors used two different sources, or, as seems more likely, Jeremiah was released twice. After his release in Jerusalem, he could easily have been swept up along with others and sent to Ramah, about five miles north of Jerusalem, to await deportation. There Nebuzaradan gave him the choice of accompanying him to Babylon or staying with Gedaliah in Mizpah (vv. 4-6).

40:7-12 Gedaliah at Mizpah. After the destruction of Jerusalem and the deportation of the most prominent citizens, Nebuchadnezzar appointed Gedaliah governor of the conquered territory. He belonged to an old noble family, and his father, Ahikam, had helped save Jeremiah from execution after he preached his famous temple sermon (see 26:24).

As governor Gedaliah sets himself up at Mizpah, a little town about eight miles north of Jerusalem. Jerusalem after its siege and fall is no doubt uninhabitable. To Mizpah come soldiers and their commanders who have successfully hidden in the hills during the last days as well as the poor of the land, whom the Babylonians did not deport (vv. 7-8). To these Gedaliah promises his intercession with the Babylonians (vv. 9-10). Later on those who hid out in Moab, Ammon, Edom, and other countries come to join the others at Mizpah. Gedaliah and his community offer a glimmer of hope in an otherwise dismal situation. But it is not to last.

40:13–41:3 The assassination of Gedaliah. Johanan, one of the army commanders who joined the group at Mizpah, warns Gedaliah that the Ammonite king Baalis has persuaded Ishmael to assassinate him (vv. 13-14). Ishmael is a royal prince. Why he would join in a plot against his own people

is hard to explain. He makes no attempt to take Gedaliah's place, and he must know that killing both his own people and the Babylonians will make him an outlaw in his own land. Johanan's suggestion that he kill Ishmael and forestall the assassination attempt shows that he is well aware of the consequences that will follow upon the assassination of a governor appointed by Nebuchadnezzar (v. 15). Gedaliah's refusal to believe in Ishmael's treachery costs him his life (41:1-3).

41:4-10 More murders. Ishmael's slaughter of the eighty pilgrims to Jerusalem is as difficult to explain as his assassination of Gedaliah (vv. 4-7). His release of the ten men with the hidden store of food assures that the slaughter cannot be kept secret (v. 8); so does his imprisoning of the other people at Mizpah (v. 10). However one looks at Ishmael's actions, they remain an enigma.

41:11-18 Rescue of the prisoners. Fortunately for Ishmael's prisoners, Johanan and other military commanders arrive on the scene before Ishmael gets too far, and they liberate the prisoners (vv. 11-14). Ishmael escapes to Ammon (v. 15), but he leaves Johanan and the others with a major problem. Should they wait at Mizpah and hope that the Babylonians will not avenge the murder of Gedaliah and the Babylonian garrison, or should they escape to Egypt and thus evade Babylonian vengeance? They opt for Egypt, heading south and camping near Bethlehem (vv. 16-18). There they will consult with Jeremiah before going on to Egypt.

42:1-6 Consulting the prophet. Jeremiah's presence at Mizpah at the time of the assassination of Gedaliah (41:1-3), the massacre of the pilgrims from Shechem, Shiloh, and Samaria (41:4-9), and the subsequent rescue by Johanan and the others (41:11-18) is presumed but not proven by his presence among the group led by Johanan and the others. He could have joined them later. The story in chapter 42, like so many of the stories in chapters 34-44, centers on the theme of the Jerusalem inhabitants' continued, and by now habitual, disobedience to God and to God's prophet. Here the biographer emphasizes not only their disobedience but their hypocrisy as well. They approach Jeremiah (vv. 1-4) and swear to abide by his word from the Lord (vv. 5-6), when, as will become abundantly evident (see 43:1-7), they are already determined to flee into Egypt no matter what Jeremiah says.

42:7-9 "Ten days passed." If Johanan and the other commanders were already determined to flee into Egypt, Jeremiah's delay of ten days could only have aggravated them and perhaps even incensed them against him. Possible and even probable Babylonian reprisals for the assassination of Gedaliah and the Babylonian garrison made delay agonizing. What Jeremiah did during the ten days is not explained. He probably prayed and just waited. His waiting tells us something about the nature of prophesying. The prophet cannot turn on prophecy like tap water. It is not a human activity. Only when God speaks can the messenger speak God's word to others.

42:10-12 Jeremiah's word from the Lord: Remain and trust in God. Jeremiah's reply, in language that is by now almost stereotyped (compare 25:3-14; 26:2-6; 27:4-15; 29:16-19), calls upon Johanan and the others to do what they fear in their hearts to do: remain in the land and put their trust in God's promise to build them up (v. 10) and to save them from the reprisals of the Babylonians (vv. 11-12).

42:13-22 "But if you disobey." The rest of Jeremiah's reply to Johanan and his followers emphasizes the necessity of obedience (v. 13), anticipates their by now habitual disobedience and their decision to flee to Egypt (v. 14), and concludes with two long warnings on the dire consequences of their anticipated disobedience (vv. 15-22).

B. Jeremiah in Egypt (43:1–44:30)

43:1-7 As expected, they do not obey. Even the people's disobedience needs a hypocritical defense. Despite their solemn protest that they would abide by Jeremiah's word (see 42:1-6) and the implicit belief in the prophet that such a protestation implies, they now accuse him of lying and, equivalently, of being a false prophet (vv. 1-2). The attack on Baruch, Jeremiah's secretary (see 36:4, 16-19), is probably for the sake of the crowd, in order to take their attention off the commanders' refusal to accept Jeremiah's word (v. 3).

In verses 4-7 the narrator spells out the disobedience of the commanders. Against the word of the prophet, they lead the remainder of the group left in Judah into exile in Egypt.

It is impossible to tell how large the group was. It contained the leaders, Jeremiah and Baruch, and some princesses from the royal family (v. 6), all important people, most of whom had much to fear from the Babylonians. The arrival at Tahpanhes (probably modern Tell Daphneh, a city at the eastern edge of the Nile Delta) closes the story and provides a transition to the account of Jeremiah's last days among the exiles in Egypt.

43:8-13 A symbolic act in Egypt. The narrator has almost nothing to say about the situation of the exiles in Egypt. He is intent instead on emphasizing and reemphasizing what has been his constant theme: the persistent and hard-hearted disobedience of the people right down to the end. He begins and ends this section (43:8–44:30) in the same way—with a prediction concerning the defeat of Egypt by Nebuchadnezzar (compare 43:8-13 and 44:29-30). In between he gives an account of Jeremiah's last words to the exiles in Egypt.

The symbolic act consists of building a throne for Nebuchadnezzar at the entrance to the royal building in Taphanhes, which was used as Pharaoh's residence when he visited the city (vv. 8-9). Since it is unlikely that a refugee from Judah would be allowed near the palace, it is quite likely that Jeremiah's act was done in pantomime. The throne, as the explanation that follows in verses 10-13 makes clear, symbolizes the future conquest of Egypt by Nebuchadnezzar. (For similar symbolic language, see 1:15; for the actual setting up of such a throne or judgment seat, see 39:3.) The point of Jeremiah's symbolic act is that flight to Egypt against the word of God will not save the people. The Babylonians will catch up with them in Egypt and there have their vengeance upon them. They cannot flee from God or escape God's word of condemnation upon them.

Nebuchadnezzar's devastation of Egypt is described in stereotyped language based upon the typical destructive acts of conquerors (v. 11). Burning temples and despoiling them of their idols were practices well-known (v. 12). Nabonidus, the last king of Babylon, was a fanatic about burning the temples of conquered peoples and carrying off to Babylon their idols and cultic accoutrements. The reference to the sacred pillars of Beth-shemesh (house of the sun) probably refers to Heliopolis, a city about five miles northeast of modern Cairo, famous for its temple to Ra, the Egyptian sun-god (v. 13). Nebuchadnezzar invaded Egypt in 567 B.C.E. (see Ezek 29:17-20). He did not fulfill Jeremiah's prophecy literally. The fact that he came at all, however, was sufficient to verify the substantial truth of Jeremiah's prediction.

44:1-14 Jeremiah's last words. This section summarizes and closes the preaching of Jeremiah. The setting is someplace in Egypt, probably Tahpanhes; the audience, the exiles living in different cities throughout Egypt (v. 1). The sermon resembles and repeats much that Jeremiah said earlier (see chs. 7 and 25). It begins with warning words from Jeremiah (vv. 2-14), continues with the self-justifying response of his stubborn audience (vv. 15-19), and closes with Jeremiah's final condemnation of those now residing in exile in Egypt.

Jeremiah begins by reminding his audience that Judah and Jerusalem were destroyed because of the sin of idolatry (vv. 2-6). That, however, was not enough—they have continued their idolatry in Egypt (vv. 7-8). They have forgotten the sins of their ancestors that brought about this destruction (vv. 9-10), and therefore they are condemned to suffer in Egypt the same condemnation and destruction as their ancestors suffered in Jerusalem (vv. 11-14). Jeremiah had said that the future of Israel lay with the exiles of 597 B.C.E. and not with those who remained in Jerusalem after that deportation. He had called the exiles of 597 B.C.E. "the good figs," and those who remained in Jerusalem "the bad figs" (see chs. 24 and 29). The exiles in Egypt are from those who remained in Jerusalem. They are "bad figs" to the end.

44:15-19 Stubborn self-justification. Deluded people find it easy to justify themselves. Nevertheless, the exiles' self-justification is both subtle and mischievous. Jeremiah blamed the destruction of Jerusalem and Judah on Judah's idolatrous infidelity to God and to the covenant. The exiles blame it on their "mistake" of not continuing their idolatrous practices! Their argument is based presumably on the history of the last one hundred years of the kingdom of Judah (687-587 B.C.E.). During the long reign of Manasseh (687-640 B.C.E.), they practiced idolatry and, despite the idolatry, lived in peace (vv. 16-17). When, how-

ever, they discontinued their idolatrous practices, beginning with the reign of the pious King Josiah (639-609 B.C.E.), disaster followed upon disaster (vv. 18-19), beginning with the conquest of Judah by the Egyptians in 609 B.C.E., continuing with Nebuchadnezzar's invasion of the country in 598 B.C.E., and concluding with the death and exile of the nation in 587 B.C.E. In short, they were better off as idolaters! The argument is plausible; the theology is outrageous.

44:20-23 Jeremiah's response. Jeremiah ignores the deluded logic of the argument and reiterates his contention that idolatry, and idolatry alone, explains the national disasters (vv. 20-23).

44:24-30 The last word. Jeremiah tells the stubborn and self-justified people: "You and your wives have stated your intentions, and kept them in fact" (v. 25). The future will tell who is deluded and who is truly justified, and the future Jeremiah predicts is destruction (vv. 26-28). They have trusted in the protection of Pharaoh, but Pharaoh will be handed over to his enemies. As events turned out, Pharaoh Hophra was supplanted and executed by Amasis, the general of his army, who succeeded him as Pharaoh. In addition, Nebuchadnezzar invaded Egypt. More than that we do not know. But it was enough to verify Jeremiah's word. When Judah became reestablished in Palestine after the defeat of Babylon by Cyrus the Great in 539 B.C.E., it was reestablished by exiles from Babylon. Little is known about the exiles in Egypt. The Elephantine letters testify to their continuance in Egypt in later years and to the half-pagan form of worship they practiced in their temple on the island of Elephantine in upper Egypt. Beyond that nothing more is known about them for certain.

With Jeremiah's last words in Egypt, we come to the end of what we know for certain about this extraordinary prophet. Jewish legend has it that Jeremiah was stoned to death by the exiles in Egypt. That is the legend, and no one would be surprised if it was more fact than legend.

C. A Message for Baruch (45:1-5)

When Baruch the scribe wrote down, at Jeremiah's dictation, the summary of Jeremiah's preaching from the year 626 to 604

B.C.E. (see 36:1-4, 27-32), he evidently shared Jeremiah's own dismay and depression when confronted by the dire future in store for his people, his nation, and himself (vv. 1-3). Jeremiah now has a personal word of comfort for his disheartened friend. God would indeed tear down what had been built and uproot what had been planted (v. 4), but Baruch himself will escape death (v. 5b). He is told not to seek great things for himself—as well he might, since he is a professional scribe and an educated man, and his brother (see 51:59) is an officer of importance in the entourage of King Zedekiah. Whatever great things Baruch might have sought for himself, he certainly had to give them up when he associated himself with the prophet so much opposed by the kings and the nobles of Judah.

It is a matter of speculation just how much Baruch had to do with the source materials of the Book of Jeremiah. The material in chapters 34-44, however, has all the signs of an eyewitness account. It is very specific about dates and names and frequently tells of conversations that could only have been known by one extremely close to Jeremiah. Of all the people mentioned in the book, no one seems to have been closer to the prophet than Baruch. It is not idle supposition, therefore, to credit to Baruch the major part of the material found in chapters 34-45.

Nor is it surprising, if Baruch wrote these chapters, that he should have reserved to the end, almost as his signature, this long-remembered word of comfort from his friend Jeremiah. Some authors insist that this chapter is chronologically out of order, belonging more properly at the end of chapter 36. They may well be correct, but only if Baruch intended his book to be a chronological account of the last years of Jeremiah. If he intended it, however, to constitute a theological testimony to Judah's rejection of both God and God's prophet, then the present thematic rather than chronological order would much more effectively have fulfilled his purpose. In that case he might well have reserved this early word of comfort from Jeremiah and used it, as we have suggested, as the equivalent of an author's signature on his work.

PART VII: COLLECTED ORACLES AGAINST THE NATIONS AND CONCLUSION

Jer 46:1–52:34

A. Oracles Against the Nations (46:1–51:64)

Like chapters 25–32 in the Book of Ezekiel and chapters 13–23 in the Book of Isaiah, chapters 46–51 form a distinct section in the Book of Jeremiah. In the Septuagint (Greek) translation of the book, they are placed after 25:13a and conclude with 25:15-38, and the nations are arranged in the order of their political importance. In the Hebrew they follow a geographical order moving from west to east. These variations indicate that the oracles formed an individual collection that was introduced into the book in different ways according to the tastes of the third-century editors of the prophetic books. With few exceptions, which may come from later oracles mistakenly attributed to Jeremiah, most of the oracles date to the decades immediately before and after the fall of Jerusalem in 587 B.C.E.

The basic theme of the oracles against the nations both here and in the other prophets is that God is the God of all the nations and that their destinies, like Israel's, lie in the hand and design of God. In reading the oracles, the reader should be aware of the fact that Semitic poetic expression revels in the symbolic, indulges in gross exaggerations, and frequently sees things only in black and white, with no regard for fine distinctions and careful qualifications. The universal extent of God's power, majesty, and sovereignty is what the poet strives to impress upon the readers. To this all the language, symbolism, and details are subservient. In short, the oracles against the nations are impressionistic rather than realistic.

46:1-12 Egypt defeated at Carchemish. This oracle is dated to 605 B.C.E., when the Babylonian army under Nebuchadnezzar defeated the Egyptian army under Pharaoh Neco at Carchemish on the Euphrates (vv. 1-2). It was a humiliating defeat for the Egyptians and should have taught the king of Judah and the neighboring kingdoms of Palestine to think twice about allying themselves with Egypt. Shortly after this battle Nabopolassar, the father of Nebuchadnezzar, died, and Nebuchadnezzar hastened back to Babylon to take over the reins of the neo-Babylonian empire. His defeat of Pharaoh Neco avenged the death of King Josiah (639–609 B.C.E.) at Megiddo just four years earlier.

46:13-28 Nebuchadnezzar's conquest of Egypt. After his coronation as king, Nebuchadnezzar led several campaigns against Egypt, this one in 568 B.C.E. The Pharaoh referred to in verse 17 is probably Pharaoh Hophra. He is here given the derogatory name "the noise that let its time go by" because he was noted for promising much to his allies and delivering little. Verses 25-28 represent Jeremiah's final words against Egypt.

47:1-7 Against the Philistines. The land of the Philistines lay on the coast bordering the Mediterranean Sea. Since the coast route was the easiest route from north to south and vice versa, the Philistines had the misfortune of being in the way when Egyptian armies moved north or northern armies moved south. In this case it appears that Babylonian armies were moving south against Egypt and overran the coastal cities and Philistia. The oracle cannot be precisely dated.

48:1-47 Against Moab. Moab was directly east of the Dead Sea. Lack of information about the history of Moab makes it difficult to date this oracle. Moab plotted against Babylon in 593 B.C.E. (see 27:3), escaped disaster in 587, but was eventually punished by Babylon, probably in 582, when Nebuchadnezzar marched for a third punitive raid into Palestine. Later, Arab invaders destroyed Moab completely, bringing to an end the ancient nation so long an enemy of Israel and so closely associated with the history of Israel from the beginning (see Num 22–24).

49:1-6 Against Ammon. Located east of the Jordan and just north of Moab, Ammon, like Moab, was a longtime enemy of Israel (see 2 Sam 10). And like Moab, Ammon was a member of Zedekiah's conspiracy against Babylon (see 27:3). It too escaped disaster in 587 B.C.E. but was overrun first by Nebuchadnezzar's armies in 582 and later by Arab invaders. Like Moab, it ceased to exist as a nation.

49:7-22 Against Edom. Edom lay south and east of the Dead Sea. It was remembered with bitterness by Judah not only for the long-lasting enmity between the two nations beginning at the time of the Exodus (see Num 20:14-21) but for its callous and treacherous treatment of Judah at the time of the Babylonian invasion of 587 B.C.E. It not only refused to help the Jews but collaborated with the Babylonians and cheered the downfall of Judah and Jerusalem (see Ezek 35:12-14; Obad; Ps 137:7). Later, when the Arab invaders arrived, the Edomites moved into southern Judah and occupied territory as far north as Hebron, just thirty miles south of Jerusalem. This occupied territory became known as Idumea. The oracle was probably occasioned by a Babylonian raid on Edom sometime after 587 B.C.E., but it echoes with the remembrance of earlier bitter encounters between the two longtime enemy nations.

49:23-27 Against Damascus. Northeast of the lake of Galilee, Damascus paid tribute to Nebuchadnezzar after the battle of Carchemish in 605 B.C.E. The oracle probably refers to a disaster following this date, but it cannot be dated with assurance.

49:28-33 Against the Arab tribes. In 599 B.C.E., on his way south to attack Judah, Nebuchadnezzar led a punitive raid against the Bedouin tribes in the desert area of eastern Syria. This brief oracle probably dates to that event.

49:34-39 Against Elam. Verse 34 dates this oracle to the year 597 B.C.E., the beginning of the reign of King Zedekiah of Judah. Elam lay east of Babylon in the southern part of modern Iran. Elam clashed with Babylon about this time, and Jeremiah may well have intended the oracle to quash any hopes the exiles of 597 B.C.E. had that Elam would save them from a long exile.

50:1–51:64 Against Babylon. Not surprisingly, the longest of Jeremiah's oracles against the nations is against Babylon. No other nation had such a lasting influence on the kingdom of Judah. Babylon invaded Judah in 605, 598, 588, and 582 B.C.E. As a result of the invasion of 588 B.C.E., the nation ceased to exist, its capital was destroyed, its temple burned to the ground, and its people led off into exile. Babylon was the burial ground of the Israelite nation, and only the resurrection of the nation after 539 B.C.E. kept Babylon from being its perpetual tomb. However much Judah deserved the treatment meted out to it by Babylon, it never ceased to consider Babylon its archenemy.

Since no internal evidence points to the rise of Cyrus, the conqueror of Babylon in 539 B.C.E., and since the description of the fall of

Babylon differs greatly from its actual fall (it fell peacefully from within as a result of treachery), the oracle cannot be dated after 539 B.C.E. How long before that date it was composed is difficult to tell. The oracle deals not only with the fall of Babylon but with the return of the people from exile as well (vv. 4-8 and *passim*). Since the oracle against Babylon terminates the collection of Jeremiah's oracles against the nations, it is not improbable that the editors added to it much that had been said against Babylon by Jeremiah himself as well as oracles against Babylon spoken by others during the long years of the Babylonian captivity.

B. Conclusion of the Book (52:1-34)

This chapter is an appendix. It draws upon 2 Kgs 24:18–25:30, the last chapters of the Deuteronomist's history of Israel's covenant relationship with God, a history that runs from Deuteronomy through Joshua, Judges, 1-2 Samuel, and 1-2 Kings. The history was written after 562 B.C.E., the last date mentioned in 2 Kings. Since this chapter repeats much that was already said in chapter 39, one must ask why the editors added it. The best explanation would be that it was added to reinforce both the negative and the positive messages of Jeremiah. By once more describing the fall of Jerusalem (52:1-30), the editors remind the reader how unerringly Jeremiah's predictions of destruction came to pass. By including the good treatment accorded Jehoiachin, the last king of Judah, by the king of Babylon (52:31-34), the editors remind the reader that Jeremiah predicted not only destruction and exile but return from exile and the rebuilding of the nation. Jehoiachin's release from prison in Babylon was a clear sign of hope for the future.

52:1-16 The fall of Jerusalem. Zedekiah, the third son of Josiah and the uncle of Jehoiachin, who was exiled as hostage royalty in Babylon in 597 B.C.E., is judged by the author of 2 Kings to have done "evil in the eyes of the Lord," as had so many kings of Judah, thus bringing about the end of the kingdom (vv. 1-3). The siege began in January of 588 B.C.E. and ended in July of 587 (vv. 4-6). The escape, capture, and blinding of Zedekiah (vv. 7-11) repeat what was said in 39:5-7. A month after the fall of the city, Nebuzaradan,

Nebuchadnezzar's general, arrived to overlook the destruction of the city and to supervise the deportation of the citizens (vv. 12-16).

52:17-23 The looting of the temple. The Babylonians first looted the temple in 597 B.C.E. (see 27:16 and 2 Kgs 24:13). It had been refurbished in the intervening ten years. The looted items are for the most part those bronze, silver, and gold items described in Exod 25–30 and 1 Kgs 6–7. Following the first looting of the temple in 597 B.C.E., Jeremiah warned the people that what was left would be carried off later. After the looting the temple was burned to the ground.

52:24-30 Deportation into exile. Deportation of conquered peoples as the most effective means to prevent further rebellion had long been practiced by the Assyrians (see 2 Kgs 17). Babylon continued the practice, and it would have a long history in the centuries that followed. It did not mean deportation of all the people but only those influential persons, leaders, bureaucrats, and the intellectual elite whose presence might sustain or rekindle the fires of rebellion. Some were executed (v. 27), either as examples or for their known part in the rebellion.

The numbers given in verses 28-30 cover three groups of exiles: those of 597, 587, and 582 B.C.E., respectively. The figure of 3,023 mentioned here (v. 28) differs from the 10,800 mentioned in 2 Kgs 24:14, 16. A possible explanation is that the figure mentioned here represents only the males, while the figure mentioned in 2 Kgs 24 represents the total of men, women, and children. The 745 men of Judah mentioned in verse 30 as deported in the twenty-third year (582 B.C.E.) of King Nebuchadnezzar may be those deported after a punitive raid on Judah following the assassination of Gedaliah and the slaughter of the Babylonian garrison by Ishmael (see 40:13–41:3).

52:31-34 The release of King Jehoiachin from prison. The young king who succeeded his father, Jehoiakim, in 598 B.C.E. and reigned only three months before being deported to Babylon as hostage royalty was released from prison in 561 B.C.E. by Evil-merodach, the successor of Nebuchadnezzar (v. 31). Since many people both in Babylon and back in devastated Judah considered Jehoiachin rather than Zedekiah their legitimate king, his release from prison was a sign of hope for the future.

Receipts for supplies given to the king and his entourage have been found in the Babylonian chronicles. Significantly they refer to him as "Yaukin, *king* of Judah."

The favors accorded Jehoiachin (vv. 32-34) may or may not have amounted to special treatment beyond that given to other hostage royalty. For the editors of the Book of Jeremiah, however, this was surely interpreted as special treatment. It was meant to remind the reader that Jeremiah had predicted an end to the Exile and the return of the exiles to their land (see chs. 25; 29; 32; 33). Thus the concluding chapter records the fulfillment of Jeremiah's predictions of disaster as well as a presage of the fulfillment of his predictions of return and rebuilding.

C. The Influence of Jeremiah

There is no simple measure of the influence of Jeremiah. In time his words, like a two-edged sword, penetrated the marrow of Israel, stirred the heart of the nation in exile, and reverberated through sacred writ even into the books of the New Testament.

Like Moses before and Jesus after him, Jeremiah lived at a turning point in his people's history and bridged the gap between the old and the new. In his inaugural vision he was set "over nations and over kingdoms, to root up and to tear down, to destroy and to demolish, to build and to plant" (1:10). He fulfilled his mission to the letter. He saw Assyria disappear from the stage of history and Babylon take over center stage. He preached the funeral oration for Judah and the Sinai covenant and at the same time foretold the institution of a new covenant. He declared the Davidic kings rejected but heralded the coming of a new David.

Of Jeremiah it can be said: no man did more for his nation and was treated worse. The mystery, however, is not in the prophet's suffering but in the resurrection of the nation that died and was buried in Babylon in fulfillment of his prophecies.

Israel's resurrection from national death in Babylon is one of the wondrous works of God. But God works through human beings, and of all those who worked for Israel's resurrection, none did more than Jeremiah. When he arrived on the scene in 626 B.C.E., there was hardly an Israelite alive who would admit that the city of Jerusalem could be taken and the temple destroyed. In the popular mind, God was bound to Jerusalem and to the Davidic kings, and Jerusalem was inviolable because God had chosen it. The defeat of Sennacherib in the time of Isaiah only confirmed the average Israelite in this false theology. More than anything else, it explains the senseless revolts against Babylon and the childish expectation, even in the last months of the siege, that God would intervene and destroy Nebuchadnezzar, as happened with Sennacherib.

Jeremiah's thankless task was the destruction of this false theology. He reminded the people in his temple address that God was not bound to the temple but could and would destroy it as Shiloh had been destroyed in times past. He insisted repeatedly that Jerusalem would be destroyed, that the kings, though they might be as the signet ring on God's finger, could nevertheless be taken off by God and cast away.

Jeremiah tried to make the Jews understand that the fall of Jerusalem would not be the work of Babylon but the work of God using Babylon as a juggernaut. He was derided, mocked, and scorned. His enemies, the false prophets, carried the day.

But when the Day of Yahweh came for Jerusalem, the nation, and the kings, there were those who remembered. *Then* the parables of the loincloth and the potter and the broken flask were seen in a new light. *Then* the temple address was seen to make sense. The false prophets were proved false, the childish optimism groundless, the popular theology a trap.

If that had been all that the people learned from Jeremiah's preaching, it would have been enough to vindicate the prophet, but at the terrible price of national despair. There was more, however. In exile the people remembered that Jeremiah had spoken of the "good figs" that would one day return to Judah and to whom the Lord had said: "Only after seventy years have elapsed for Babylon will I visit you and fulfill for you my promise to bring you back to this place" (25:10). They remembered his sermons of consolation (chs. 30-31), his buying of property in the last days of the siege, and his promise from God: "Houses and fields and vineyards shall again be bought in this land" (32:15). They remembered most of all his promise of a new covenant for Israel

(31:31-34; 32:40) and his promise of a new David in days to come (33:14-26; 23:5-6).

The downfall of Jerusalem, the temple, and the kings came as Jeremiah had predicted. But when it came, some at least were prepared to understand it as it should have been understood—in the light of the covenant between God and the people of God, according to which the nation's future depended on its loyalty or disloyalty to the stipulations agreed to on Sinai. For these at least, the tragedy was explicable, and explicable in terms of the faith by which Israel lived. Among these, too, faith continued to live, through the dreadful days of siege and destruction and through the long years of exile. That faith was the link that joined the Israel of old to the Israel that arose from the grave of the Exile to become a nation again in 539 B.C.E. And it was Jeremiah who forged the link.

BARUCH

Peter F. Ellis

INTRODUCTION

In the years that followed the catastrophic destruction of Jerusalem in 587 B.C.E., some Jews were deported to Babylonia, others fled into Egypt, still others remained in the devastated homeland. In 539 B.C.E. Cyrus the Persian defeated the Babylonians and established Persian rule over what had been the empire of Babylon. As one of his first acts, Cyrus decreed the return of conquered peoples to their homelands. Thus it came about after 539 B.C.E. that the Exiles were free to return to their homeland.

Many returned, but many more remained in the land of the conquerors. Those who remained formed what came to be called the Diaspora—the Jews of the dispersion or permanent exile who never returned to their homeland but remained in colonies situated for the most part in Mesopotamia and Egypt. While many of them no doubt defected from their ancient faith, many more remained faithful. In the centuries that followed, the Diaspora Jews flourished both spiritually and temporally.

Fortunately for Israel's religious future, many of the exiles came from the influential and intellectual circles of the people—priests, scribes, and prophets. From these the exiles received instruction and encouragement. With the temple and its sacrifices so far away, the cult of the exiles came to be localized in the synagogues and centered upon the inspired writings. Thus in the course of time, they came to be the people of the book. Faithful to Jerusalem and the rebuilt temple of Zerubbabel, completed between 520 and 515 B.C.E.,

the Diaspora Jews gathered in their synagogues, read and studied the law and the prophets, and in due time produced their own inspired books. Among these were the books of Lamentations, Tobit, Esther, Judith, Wisdom, and Baruch.

Diaspora writings, as might be expected, dealt with Diaspora situations and challenges. This is eminently true of the Book of Baruch. It deals in its successive parts with the exiles' relations with Jerusalem, with hope for the future, and with resistance to the idolatrous worship of the surrounding pagans.

Since the material in the book reflects events late in the Exile and shows some dependence on the writings of Deutero-Isaiah (550–540 B.C.E.), it seems reasonable to believe that editors are responsible for the attribution of the Book to Baruch. Baruch had been Jeremiah's secretary (see Jer 36). He had perhaps accompanied the prophet into exile. In addition, he was well acquainted with Jeremiah's letter to the exiles (see Jer 29) and with Jeremiah's message of hope (see Jer 30–33).

It was customary in ancient times to attribute works by unknown authors to more famous authors of previous centuries. Thus many psalms written by nameless authors were attributed to David, and several wisdom books were attributed to Solomon (for example, Proverbs and the Book of Wisdom). It must have seemed fitting to the third-century editors of the prophetic books to attribute to Baruch, Jeremiah's famous secretary, this collection of writings dealing with the situation and challenges of the exiles.

COMMENTARY

A. Introduction (1:1-14)

1:1-4 Baruch's scroll. This section begins in the style typical of Baruch in the Book of Jeremiah (see the opening verses of Jer 32; 36; 38; 39)—with specific names and dates. It makes a bow toward Jer 36 by attributing this second book to Baruch (vv. 1-2). The "fifth year" (v. 2) is perhaps meant to be the fifth year of the exile (582 B.C.E.). Baruch is pictured reading his scroll before the exiled king, his courtiers, and the exiles in Babylon, somewhat as he had read Jeremiah's scroll in Jer 36:8-19 (vv. 3-4).

1:5-9 Concern for temple worship. The weeping, fasting, and praying, in addition to the taking up of a collection for the temple, provide a program for the readers that will keep their hearts centered on the temple and on their traditional Yahwistic faith (vv. 5-7). Nothing is known about a restoration of the cultic vessels taken from the temple after the Babylonian invasion of 597 B.C.E. (v. 8). That new cultic vessels were made to substitute for the looted vessels can be taken for granted (v. 9). It is mentioned no doubt as a reminder to the reader that supporting temple worship was the duty of every true Israelite. At the time the Book of Baruch was put together, the new temple of Zerubbabel had long been in existence. It was completed in 516 B.C.E. (see Ezra 1-6).

1:10-14 A message for the high priest. The message testifies to the exiles' concern for divine worship (v. 10) and concern for good treatment by their Babylonian overlords (vv. 11-12). The juxtaposition of Nebuchadnezzar, the second king of the Babylonian empire, and Belshazzar, the last king, indicates a late date for the book. Belshazzar was coregent with his father, King Nabonidus, when the armies of Cyrus the Great conquered Babylon in 539 B.C.E. No son of Nebuchadnezzar by the name of Belshazzar is known to history. The last two requests—a request for prayers for the contrite exiles and a request that Baruch's book be read publicly on feast days—emphasize what is central to the purpose of the editors: true contrition and a firm purpose of amendment (vv. 13-14). In one way or another, it will be the purpose of every section of the little book of Baruch to arouse and sustain in its readers these sentiments so critical for the spiritual health and the national survival of Israel.

B. A Penitential Prayer (1:15-3:8)

Penitential prayers such as the one preserved here are typical of exilic literature (see Neh 9:6-37; Dan 9:4-19). What the exiles refused to learn from Jeremiah, they learned from the hardships of the Exile. Prayers such as this were a feature of the synagogue services that originated in exilic times.

1:15-22 "Justice is with the Lord, our God." The prayer begins with an acknowledgment of national guilt that embraces the sins of the author's contemporaries (v. 15) and their ancestors (vv. 16-17). It then traces Israel's guilt back through history to the time of Moses and the Exodus (vv. 18-22). Mention of the curse that the Lord enjoined upon Moses (v. 20) reflects the curses of Deut 28 and prepares the way for the just fulfillment of these curses that the author acknowledges in 2:1-10.

2:1-10 Just retribution. All the evils are summed up in the two most horrible of all: the cannibalism of children in the last days of the siege of Jerusalem (v. 3) and the degradation of the nation as a whole following the fall of Judah and Jerusalem to the Babylonians in 587 B.C.E. (vv. 4-5). That all this has been just retribution for the sins of the nation is honestly acknowledged in verses 6-10.

2:11-15 An appeal for mercy. What has preceded has been preamble to the prayer that properly begins here. Firmly believing that God is just, in the sense that God is ever merciful and faithful to earlier promises to save the covenanted people, the author of the prayer, who has already confessed his people's guilt (1:15-22) and their justly deserved punishment (2:1-10), now enters his plea for mercy (vv. 11-13). He appeals to God's honor to show the whole earth, by merciful treatment of the exiles, that God is Lord of Israel and Lord of all (vv. 14-15).

2:16-18 The nether world. Up to the second century before Christ, Israel had no clear knowledge of the future life. In its prayers, therefore, it believed that praise could be given to God only by the living (vv. 17-18).

Clear revelation concerning the future life begins with Dan 12 and 2 Macc 7.

2:19-35 Hopes based on God's unfailing mercy. This section of the prayer begins with an admission that the punishment Israel suffered was deserved because the people refused to listen to the warnings of the prophets (vv. 19-20), and especially the warnings of Jeremiah (vv. 21-26). Verse 23 combines two typical Jeremian warnings (see Jer 7:34 and 27:12). Verse 25 mentions the stereotyped Jeremian trilogy of sword, famine, and pestilence (see Jer 32:24, 36; 34:17). Verses 27-35 recall the unfailing mercy of God (v. 27), who despite Israel's failure to heed the warnings of Moses (vv. 28-29) will deal mercifully with it in the time of its captivity (vv. 30-32), bring it back to the land promised to its ancestors (vv. 33-34), and establish with it the new covenant (v. 35) promised by Jeremiah (Jer 31:31-34).

3:1-8 A concluding plea for mercy. These verses sum up the heart of the whole long prayer (2:11–3:8), emphasizing again God's mercy (vv. 1-4), God's honor (vv. 5-6), and the gift of fear of the Lord, which enables the people to call upon God in praise, even in the land of their captivity (vv. 7-8). The prayer is long and repetitious but filled with a true spirit of penitence and hope. It represents Israel at its best.

C. A Poem in Praise of Wisdom (3:9–4:4)

Modern readers can understand this poem easily if they recall that for the Jews wisdom is equivalent to fear of the Lord (that is, obedience to the will of God) and that the will of God is found in the revelation of God's will contained in the Scriptures, preeminently in the books of the Pentateuch (the Torah). In brief, only God is the ultimate source of true wisdom, and God has chosen to reveal this in the Torah. As a consequence praise of wisdom is indirectly praise of God. Doing God's will, moreover, is the way of the wise; not doing it is the way of the fool. A prayer for wisdom is a prayer for the grace to do God's will. The reader should note that wisdom is personified in the poem from 3:15 to 4:4, just as it is personified in Prov 8:1-36 and Sir 24:1-31.

3:9 "Hear, O Israel, the commandments of life." This beautiful prayer begins with an exhortation to Israel to hear, that is, to obey God's commandments. It ends in 3:37–4:4 with the declaration that God has given wisdom to Israel (v. 37) and that that wisdom is found in the book of the precepts of God, that is, the Torah-Pentateuch (3:38–4:4). As a result, the whole poem is an appeal to Israel to do God's will and thus to be both wise and blessed (4:4).

3:10-14 The consequences of not hearing. Israel is asked how it came about that it is in exile (vv. 10-11). The answer: The people have forsaken wisdom (vv. 12-13 and see Jer 2:13). The admonition "Learn where prudence [that is, wisdom] is" (v. 14) leads into the question of where wisdom can be found (3:15-36), a question that will be answered in 3:37–4:4 with the declaration that wisdom is found in "the book of the precepts of God" (4:1).

3:15-23 Wisdom is not found among the Gentiles. Since by definition only Israel possesses God's revelation, it is clear that true wisdom cannot be found among the Gentiles. Here the author means the wisdom that comes from God, since wisdom and wisdom literature were well known and cultivated among Judah's neighbors, the Egyptians, the Mesopotamians, and many of the smaller nations of the Middle East. The rulers of old who heaped up wealth have not found wisdom (vv. 17-19), nor have the later generations: the Canaanites (vv. 20-22), the Midianites, the Temanites, the children of Hagar (Arabic tribes descended from Abraham and Hagar), and their pagan wisdom writers (v. 23). Human beings on their own are not able to find true wisdom!

3:24-36 Wisdom is found only with God. In all of God's creation (vv. 24-25), no human being has discovered wisdom or found the way to her (vv. 26-31). Only God, who created and established the earth and to whom no other is to be compared, knows wisdom (vv. 32-35).

3:37–4:4 Wisdom is the law. Only God knows the way to wisdom, and God has given her to Israel (v. 37) in the book of the precepts of the law, the Pentateuch. Let Israel cling to wisdom, "walk by her light" (that is, live according to God's law), and Israel will live and be blessed (vv. 1-4). Israel's "glory," which God gives to Israel and not to pagans, is the law (v. 3).

D. A Poetic Plea for Return from Exile (4:5–5:9)

In this beautiful poetic discourse, very much indebted to the poetry of Deutero-Isaiah (Isa 40–55), the speaker personifies Jerusalem as the mother of the nation, explaining to the nearby nations and to her exiled children the reason for her exile and encouraging the exiles to look for an early return home. The discourse has four parts: introduction (4:5-8); Jerusalem's explanation to the nations (4:9-20); Jerusalem's encouraging discourse to her exiled children (4:21-29); the poet's address to Jerusalem to rejoice in the return of her exiled children (4:30–5:9).

4:5-9 "Fear not, my people." The speaker begins by reminding Israel that it went into exile because of its infidelity. Verse 4 introduces Jerusalem, who will be the personified speaker in 4:9-29, as the grief-stricken mother of Israel and the exiles.

4:9-20 Jerusalem's address to her neighbors. Jerusalem mourns for the captivity of her sons and daughters (vv. 9-11), whose sins have brought upon them punishment (vv. 12-14) by a nation from afar (Babylon), which has exiled them and left their mother, Jerusalem, widowed and solitary (vv. 15-16). The widow symbolism in verses 12 and 17 flows from the Hosean symbolism of the marriage between God and the people Israel (see Hos 1–3). Jerusalem asks herself what she can do for her children. She acknowledges that only God can deliver them from the Exile (vv. 17-19). She herself will pray (v. 20) and call upon her children to pray with her. Verse 20, with the mention of crying out to God, provides a transition to verses 21-29.

4:21-29 Jerusalem trusts in God's mercy. Jerusalem calls upon her children to pray (v. 21) and speaks about her trust in God's mercy (v. 22) and her confident expectation that God will bring her children back to her (vv. 23-24). In verses 25-29 Jerusalem concludes her address. She counsels patience and promises God's vengeance on her persecutors (vv. 25-26). Her last words are a plea for repentance (vv. 27-29)—a repentance that has been a goal of the discourse from the beginning.

4:30–5:9 The poet's address to Jerusalem. Now that mother Jerusalem has finished her discourse (4:9-29), the speaker addresses her in soaring language and bids her prepare for the end of her mourning and the joyful return of her children. She should not fear (v. 30), because God will destroy Babylon, "the city that rejoiced at [her] collapse" (vv. 31-35). She should look to the east and see her sons returning home (vv. 36-37). Babylon was due east of Jerusalem, and the poet envisions God leading the exiles back across the desert, as in Isa 1:4-11. Jerusalem, which had taken off her robe of peace in 4:20 for a robe of mourning, is now told to remove the mourning robe and put on the splendor of God—the manifestation of God's saving action in returning her children from exile (5:1-4). In a final apostrophe (5:5-9), Jerusalem is called to stand upon the heights and watch her exiled children come marching home on the road laid out in the desert (see Isa 1:3-5) and led by none other than God (see Isa 1:9-11).

E. The Letter of Jeremiah (6:1-72)

Chapter 29 of the Book of Jeremiah contains a letter written by the prophet to the exiles carried off to Babylon following Nebuchadnezzar's invasion of Judah and Jerusalem in 597 B.C.E. Sometime in the centuries that followed, an unknown author wrote this long satire against the idol worship of the pagans and attributed it to the great prophet of the last days of Judah. Editors included it at the end of the collection of writings now found in the Book of Baruch. Although it exists only in a Greek translation, it was originally composed in Hebrew. Critics believe it cannot be the work of Jeremiah for several reasons, the strongest being that: (a) the editors of the Book of Jeremiah did not include it in the book; (b) it shows a strong dependence on the satires against idol worship in Isa 40–55; (c) it speaks in verses 27-31 of practices of the Mosaic law that never were of any concern to Jeremiah.

All things considered, the letter constitutes a long sermon attacking the foolishness of idol worship and exhorting the exiles not to be taken in by it. The modern reader may consider such an attack superfluous. Few today believe in idol worship. In the ancient world, however, it was otherwise. Few believed in one God. The overwhelming majority believed in many gods and worshiped them in many forms. They not only worshiped them but they built magnificent temples for them, supported a rich and powerful priesthood to serve them, and celebrated a multitude of feast days with processions, sacrifices, the singing of psalms, and elaborate spectacles.

For the Jewish exiles from a tiny Middle Eastern nation with a small unpretentious temple and a modest priesthood and cult, the power, the wealth, and the magnificence of the pagans' idol worship, especially in such a great metropolis as Babylon, must at times have seemed overwhelming. True believers, of course, would not have been impressed. Many others, however, may well have felt that truth was determined by power, magnificence, and numbers. Deutero-Isaiah as early as 550 B.C.E. feared the attraction of idol worship for lukewarm exiles and lambasted idols and idol worshipers in a series of satirical comparisons between the nature and power of Israel's God and the nature and impotence of the pagan gods (see Isa 40:18-20; 41:21-24; 44:6-20; 46:1-7). The idol-worship religion of the pagans was no mean adversary to the revealed religion of Israel!

The letter of Jeremiah proves that the idol worship attacked by Deutero-Isaiah in the first fifty years of the Exile continued, in the centuries that followed, to have a powerful attraction for the exiles who remained in pagan countries. The letter attacks idol worship with scorn, invective, mockery, and incredulity. Its message is summed up in the recurring refrain: "Thus it is known they are not gods; do not fear them" (see vv. 14, 22, 28, 39, 44, 50, 56, 64, 68, 71).

The letter reads easily, is patent in its satirical intent and requires only a few brief comments. **6:3 you will see borne upon men's shoulders gods of silver . . . :** This is a reference to the great processions that were part of the pagan cult. **6:6 my angel:** Symbolic of God's protective presence, the angel here recalls the angel of Exod 23:20-21. **6:10 the harlots:** Sacred prostitution, that is, intercourse with priestesses in the temple precincts, was a prominent feature of pagan worship and was particularly offensive to Israel because of its prevalence in the Baal fertility cult of the Canaanites (see Deut 23:17-18). **6:12 the house:** This means the pagan temple. **6:19 their hearts are eaten away:** The idols were made of wood covered with gold or silver. The wood frequently rotted away or was eaten by insects. **6:25 displaying their shame:** It could be that the idols were naked figures, or it could be that they displayed their weakness by having to be carried. **6:27-31 Unclean practices.** Jewish law considered menstruating women unclean (see Lev 12:2-3). It was forbidden for priests to bare their heads, shave their beards, or rend their garments (see Lev 21:5-10). **6:42 girt with cords:** This is another reference to sacred prostitution (see v. 10). An unbroken cord signified that the woman had not fulfilled her obligation of sacred prostitution in the temple. **6:72 the better for the just man:** This final verse, following so powerful a denunciation of idolatry, is surely a provocative understatement!

CHRONOLOGICAL CHART*
for
AMOS, HOSEA, MICAH, NAHUM, ZEPHANIAH, HABAKKUK

JUDAH	*ISRAEL*	*ASSYRIA*
Uzziah 783–42	Jeroboam II 786–46	
	AMOS	
	HOSEA	
	Zechariah 746–45	Tiglath-pileser III 745–27
	Shallum 745	
Jotham 742–35	Menshem 745–37	
ISAIAH	Pekahiah 737–36	
Ahaz 735–15	Pekah 736–32	
MICAH	Hoshea 732–24	Shalmaneser V 826–22
	Fall of Samaria 722/1	
		Sargon II 721–05
Hezekiah 715–686		
Manasseh 686–42	*Babylon*	Sennacherib 705–681
		Esarhaddon 680–69
		Ashurbanipal 668–27
Amon 642–40		
Josiah 640–09		
JEREMIAH	Nabopolassar 626–05	Sin-shar-ishkun 629–12
ZEPHANIAH		
NAHUM		
		Fall of Nineveh 612
Jehoahaz 609		
Jehoiakim 609–598		
HABAKKUK	Nebuchadnezzar	
	605–582	
Jehoiachin 598/7		
EZEKIEL		
Zedekiah 597–87		
Fall of Jerusalem 587		

Exile

*Dates are dependent upon John Bright, *A History of Israel*. 3rd ed. Westminster Press, 1981.

AMOS

Carroll Stuhlmueller, C.P.

INTRODUCTION

The fierce champion of justice

The prophet Amos spoke plainly to the Israelites, even fiercely so. The Hebrew text, moreover, is well preserved. If some sentences seem vague or confusing, the fault lies at our doorsteps, due to our ignorance of ancient times and the ancient way of life. While Amos' words ring with the crystal tones of a bell, the person of Amos is lost in the echo. A few facts are obvious enough. He was from the village of Tekoa (1:1), some ten miles south of Jerusalem in the tribal portion of Judah. Again according to the opening verse, he prophesied during the long, prosperous reign of King Jeroboam II (786–746 B.C.E.), "two years before the earthquake," therefore around 760. We find his shaggy figure in the capital city of Samaria as well as at the venerable sanctuary of Bethel. At the instigation of the high priest, he was expelled from the northern kingdom of Israel and was sent packing back to Judah (7:12). The name Amos means "burden," and the name Tekoa probably means "to sound the [ram's] horn." His message carried a burden of destruction; it was sounded loud across the northern kingdom and was remembered long afterward at Jerusalem (1:2).

Other information about Amos has to be pieced together from details scattered throughout the book. Some of these fragments are distinct, others remain blurred. Twice Amos is described as a shepherd, yet each time the common Hebrew word for "shepherd" is not employed. Instead, in 1:1 the word is the same one used of a Moabite king in 2 Kgs 3:4; in 7:14 the word refers more to the breeding of cattle (Gen 33:13). This fact, along with Amos' acquaintance with the vocabulary and style of the wisdom literature, associates him with nobility. The prophet, moreover, shows himself an absolute master of the Hebrew language; his writing is characterized by structural unity and momentum toward a climax (1:3–2:16); the blending of irony and seriousness (4:1-5); rhetorical questions (at least thirty—2:11; 3:3-6); haunting sounds that speak a message even without words (2:16); the up-and-down, staircase style of literary chiasm (5:4-6).

Yet, any number of other details point to a person economically poor, with neither clout nor prestige. According to 7:14, Amos was forced to take a second job as a "dresser of sycamore trees" (moonlighting to make ends meet?). He worked in dangerous association with lions, bears, and snakes (3:4, 8, 12; 5:17); he knew the groan of heavily laden wagons (2:13) and was desperate about locust plagues (7:1-2). His caricature of women in 4:1-3 smacks of a rough herdsman; he spits disdain at wealthy men lying on ivory couches in their massage parlors (6:3-6). Therefore, we place Amos in the ranks of the poor. He was born brilliant and was desert-trained to perceive color, sound, grandeur, and wonder in contemplative silence. He quickly absorbed the patterns of temple worship, legal proceedings at the city gate, and the sophisticated ways of the sages.

487

Historical setting

Amos learned much from the market-places of Israel's larger cities. As he sat on the ground with other shepherds, displaying his wool, cheese, and leather goods, he swapped news from Tyre, Damascus, Moab, and Gaza. All the while he angrily detected the flagrant injustices of society: extensive international commerce for the benefit of the wealthy; deceitful business practices not only to cheat the defenseless poor but also to seize their land; the amassing of natural resources for sensual pleasure. Some documentation found amid the ruins of Samaria tells of large shipments of oil and wine for the royal court; these were paid from taxes squeezed from the poor. The country was basking in the military victories of King Jeroboam II, who had successfully completed the military plans of his father, King Joash (2 Kgs 13:24-25; 14:25, 28). Israel's long-time enemy, Damascus, had been leveled to the ground by the Assyrians around 800 B.C.E., leaving Israel free to extend its territory and privileges. Such material blessings, the people thought, proved God's good pleasure with them.

Amos' sermons and oracles were radically destructive, that is, cutting to the *roots* of Israel's life. All God's ancient promises to the Israelites and the divine presence among them would end. Whatever survived would be "like a brand plucked from the fire" (4:11), like the shank bone of a sheep that "the shepherd snatches from the mouth of the lion" (3:12). Yet Amos was addressing that part of the twelve tribes most directly linked with Moses' exodus out of Egypt and Joshua's settlement of the land. The promises of the covenant resided among these people of the northern kingdom.

Typical of prophecy, Amos accepted the reality of historical changes, such as the forthcoming onslaught of the Assyrian army against Israel or the earlier inauguration of the Davidic dynasty at Jerusalem. This latter fact is witnessed to in the conclusion of the book (9:11-15), composed by a disciple of Amos if not by Amos himself. In fact, Amos had politics and international affairs at his finger tips (1:3-2:16). God was mysteriously present, at work within this real world. For this reason Amos ends up far ahead of his Old Testament times, for he glimpsed the role of the nations in God's plans for salvation, especially in the one-liner of the appendix (9:7).

A person of tradition

Amos was radical in another way. His roots (the Latin word is *radix*) were firmly set in Israel's traditional institutions and memories. He spoke positively of prophets and nazirites (2:11-12). He did not condemn liturgy, only the selfish spirit of the devotees (4:5). He based his reflections upon the Exodus (2:11; 3:1; 9:7), Israel's hopes for the future (5:18), and its special election (3:1-2; 5:15), even though he reversed the conclusion against what the people expected from these ancient promises. Wisdom traditions show up rather abundantly: didactical questions; numerical sequence (three plus one); themes of good and evil. His morality reached back into ancient norms of the early clans or tribes.

Most of all, in Amos' eyes Yahweh was the God of the poor, as was the case when Yahweh delivered slaves out of Egypt and gave dispossessed people their own Promised Land.

Literary form

Amos is the first prophet with a book to his name. Earlier prophets, like Elijah and Elisha, Gad and Nathan, strongly influenced Israelite policy but left no books. There is no satisfactory explanation for this radical change, only some guesses. Did written scrolls become popular because of a notable advance in literacy among the people? Or did Amos' announcement of destruction point up the necessity of writing down whatever was to be preserved? Or did the sweeping internationalization of Israel, with its extensive correspondence, stir the prophets to communicate with written documents?

The book is arranged with all the neatness of a good household. After a historical and religious introduction (1:1-2), four major presentations of Amos are to be found: oracles against the nations (1:3-2:16); three judgment speeches, which begin with "Hear this word" (3:1-5:6); three collections of Woe Sayings (5:7-17; 5:18-27; 6:1-14); and four visions (7:1-9; 8:1-3). It is possible that the book ended here at one time, especially when we note that the story of Amos' final day of preaching at Bethel was inserted into the vision narratives (7:10-17), stitched in by the mention of Jeroboam in 7:9 at the end of the third vision and in 7:10 at the beginning of the biographical account of Amos' expulsion from Bethel. Later two longer portions were added—a judgment speech (8:4-14) and a vision story (9:1-4), each somewhat different in style from others in the book. Still later an appendix of four "one-liners," with each verse being a separate entity (9:10-14), was tacked on. Liturgical fragments in the style of a hymn were woven into the text (4:13; 5:8-9; 9:5-6). The final addition came during or after the Babylonian Exile, announcing the revival of the Davidic dynasty at Jerusalem (7:11-15). Typical of biblical prophecy, Amos' book thus ends with an upbeat note.

COMMENTARY

INTRODUCTION

Amos 1:1-2

1:1 Historical introduction. The editor situates Amos during the prosperous, heady days of King Uzziah of the southern kingdom of Judah (783–742 B.C.E.) and King Jeroboam II of the northern kingdom of Israel (786–746 B.C.E.). The historical orientation is from the south, where Amos' preaching was edited and preserved; Uzziah's name is given first. **The words of Amos . . . received in vision:** The words contain a divine message, perceptible only in mysterious moments when one is absorbed in God. **shepherd from Tekoa:** See p. 487. **two years before the earthquake:** This earthquake did severe damage to Israelite cities like Hazor in northeast Galilee; it is dated 760 B.C.E. and was still spoken of several centuries later (see Zech 14:5). Dating Amos' preaching by the earthquake may have this fearful insinuation: Soon after Amos the earth and the foundation of Israel will collapse. The rumbling theme of earthquakes spreads fear throughout the book (4:11; 6:11; 7:7-8; 8:8; 9:1).

1:2 Religious introduction. The orientation is again from Jerusalem or Zion, confessing that God's mysterious providence directed the destruction of the north, even of beautiful Mount Carmel, which juts out on the northern coastline. This "antiphon" is repeated again in Jer 25:30 against foreign nations (after the announcement of Israel's and Judah's deportation) and once more in Joel 4:16 against the foreign nations but also as a word of protection and refuge for Israel. Evidently editors in biblical times felt free to adapt ancient inspired texts to new circumstances. The setting of the preacher added a necessary ingredient to the interpretation of God's word.

ORACLES AGAINST THE NATIONS

Amos 1:3–2:16

This section is composed in a style reminiscent of sanctuary oracles and of the wisdom school. Oracles originated in the sanctuary when a person with serious difficulties came either for a blessing and solution or for protection against an enemy. Oracles designate a communication from God to one or more persons gathered in prayer, frequently at a sanctuary (Gen 26:24; 28:13; Ps 12:6). Prophets adopted this style to indicate their conviction that their words expressed a conscience formed from an immediate experience of God. The schema here of three + one consists of the sacred numbers three, four, and seven, each in some way denoting completion—no more crimes will be tolerated. The arrangement also reflects a practice within the wisdom literature of the Bible (Prov 30:15-16, 18-19; Sir 26:5-6). For Amos, the numerical sequence infers God's patience in putting up with three crimes and God's equal determination to put an end to the crimes; yet even in this last instance God is present in the act of punishment. The Hebrew word for "crimes" occurs only once in the Pentateuch (Exod 22:8), where it recalls pre-Mosaic clan traditions. Amos, therefore, may be reaching into basic human nature to judge right and wrong.

Many of Israel's neighbors, frequently hostile to Israel, are named: Aram or Damascus, to the northeast; Philistia, on the seacoast to the southwest; Tyre, on the northwest coast; Edom, south of the Dead Sea; Ammon, east of the Jordan River; and Moab, east of the Dead Sea. The prophet would have received a roar of applause after each oracle. The compact and well-coordinated style of each oracle locks the people and their enthusiasm still more firmly into the discourse. When Amos comes to the oracle against Israel (2:6-16), the audience cannot escape—they must listen in stunned silence!

Each foreign city is condemned for "crimes against humanity," such as acting as middle-persons in selling captive soldiers into slavery, waging war with excessive cruelty, and profaning the bones of the dead. While each oracle is strikingly vivid, that against Judah (2:4-5) appears dull and colorless, making us suspect its genuineness. It is probably a later addition from someone at Jerusalem not nearly as eloquent as Amos. Israel, too, is condemned for crimes against humanity rather than for violating cultic or refined religious norms.

2:6 sell [into slavery] the just man for silver . . . for a pair of sandals: This refers to the brutal enforcement of laws to pay one's debts—only a small amount for the wealthy but the total possessions of the poor—or to the seizure of ancestral lands for flimsy reasons.

Land was normally marked off by the length of one's sandals (see Deut 25:5-10, which deals with the marriage of a relative's widow in order to preserve the name of the husband and to protect the latter's property for the son bearing his name).

2:7 Son and father go to the same prostitute: This alludes either to the degradation of domestic servants in a wealthy household (the Hebrew does not use the word "prostitute") or else to an insidious, lustful father who interrupts a legitimate romance of the son.

2:8 Upon garments taken in pledge they recline: According to Exod 22:25-26 and Deut 24:11-13, the long, flowing outer cloak taken in pledge of the future payment of a debt was to be restored at each sundown, lest the person have insufficient protection against the cold evening air. In making sure that the poor fulfill their obligations, the wealthy priests

break the law themselves and commit further sexual sins under the influence of alcohol.

2:16 shall flee naked on that day, says the Lord: The sound of this phrase in Hebrew is haunting, evoking the desperate, silent agony of people led off captive totally naked, to be sold for whatever purpose along the way until the remnant are resettled in a foreign land. The person's shame becomes the instrument of pleasure for the gloating conquerors. There was no need to mention the dreaded name of Assyria.

JUDGMENT-ADDRESSES AGAINST ISRAEL

Amos 3:1–5:6

This section is addressed exclusively to Israel, frequently in the form of judgment speeches. This style is modeled upon that used in Israel's law courts, presided over by elders at the city gates (Deut 16:18-20; 21:19; 25:7; Amos 5:10). A typical example is 4:1-3, which consists of: summoning of the defendant (v. 1a); listing the crimes of the defendant, who is referred to in the third person (v. 1b); words of the judge as a messenger of Yahweh (v. 2a); verdict and punishment (vv. 2b-3). See also 8:4-8. Amos, as mentioned already, remains in masterful control of style. Other literary forms are found in this section. All are linked together by the introductory formula "Hear this word" (3:1; 4:1; 5:1).

3:1-2 This oracle is rooted in Israel's election as the Lord's chosen people. **You alone have I favored:** The Hebrew verb means literally "to know," not in the sense to know about, but to experience and therefore to know with sensitivity, concern, and intimate love (Gen 4:1; Jer 1:5; Ps 1:6). At this time people would then conclude from Israel's election that God will bring a blessing or a happy conclusion. Amos reverses what is expected by declaring: "I will punish you." Neither blood lineage with those who came out of Egypt nor good theology ensures Israel's well-being. To be truly Israel, the people must continue the liberation of the poor, as God once liberated them from bondage in Egypt. Yet, Israelite priests and nobles are using their privileged positions to enslave other Israelites. Religion has become a veneer for supporting the upper class. By comparing Israel with other nations, here as in the oracles against the nations, Amos arrives at common basic human norms for judgment.

3:3-8 The sequence here mounts to a crescendo of strength: first it is animals against animals (v. 4), then humans against animals (v. 5), and finally humans against humans. Not only is there a purpose in each event, but there is also the insinuation that humans turn up no different from animals in their violent state. Verse 7 is probably a later reflective addition. In verse 8 Amos feels the animal urge to roar against human injustice.

3:9-10 The key word here is "castles," those of foreigners and those of Israel, citadels of extortion and robbery where Israel is no different from any other nation. How can Israel strut around as a chosen people?

3:12 This independent oracle combines a moment of shepherd existence with theology and sarcasm! **A pair of legs or the tip of an ear of his sheep:** These words indicate all that is to be left of Israel, hardly enough to reconstruct a sheep or the people. The few Israelites who escape with their life and are marched into exile, nakedly the butt of jokes and selfish desires (2:16), are pictured with mock pathos as clutching a piece of their ivory couch, a remembrance of their lost opulence (see 3:15; 6:4). It is as though people today, in being driven away from their homes, would treasure most their transistor radios! Implied here is Amos' intuition of the "remnant," which we will discuss at 5:15.

4:1-3 As at the beginning of chapter 3, a new subdivision is introduced with the formula "Hear this word." With brutal, even crude language, Amos likens the opulent ladies of the capital city of Samaria to the large, well-fed cows of Bashan, prized for their quality milk and meat (Deut 32:14). They grazed in the open area between Israel and Damascus, presently called the Golan Heights, then as now bitterly fought over. In this area the cattle roamed freely, munched the luscious, dew-laden grass, and became fiercely temperamental. Amos foresees a long siege, the eventual, angry capture of the capital, then the mopping up process. Amos portrays the bloated corpses of these presently pampered women pitched onto a dung heap outside one of the city gates. **the last of you:** The Hebrew may refer either to the very last

corpse or more likely to the posterior part of the anatomy whereby barbed poles inhumanly lift the body from the streets.

4:4-5 Similar to 1 Sam 15:22-23; Ps 50:14; Hos 6:6; and Matt 9:13, these verses are not condemning liturgical worship as such but the unworthy motives of the worshipers. **for so you love to do:** "You get a kick out of it, don't you, folks!" Strange for the Bible but typical of Amos, these sarcastic words are placed within the literary form of a solemn liturgical oracle from God!

4:6-13 A rhetorical momentum sweeps us forward by one type of natural catastrophe after another, with the continuous refrain "you returned not to me," and at the end the fearful climax, "prepare to meet your God." Amos' striking images communicate the taste and smell of disaster. Drought is spoken of as "teeth clean of food" and pestilence as the stench of dead horses!

The transition to a historical recollection in verse 11 seems like an editorial addition; part of the verse is identical with Hos 11:8; Isa 13:14b; and Jer 50:40, a "floater" that can end up almost anywhere! Verse 13 is cast in the form of a hymn with participles that bring the excitement of creation into the present moment: "Your God, O Israel, forming the mountains, creating the wind . . . turning dawn into darkness, striding upon the heights of the earth." This verse belongs to a longer hymn, whose fragments are found as well in 5:8-9 and 9:5-6, similar to others in Jer 12:13, 16; Isa 42:5. These were added to the canonical texts as congregational refrains when the Scripture was proclaimed in synagogue worship. Theologically this section confesses the directive hand of God in nature and history, fulfilling a divine purpose for Israel.

5:1-6 This is the final sermon of Amos in the second major division of his prophecy (3:1–5:6). The editor combines a funeral dirge over dead Israel with an exhortation to "seek the Lord" (v. 6) while there is still time. In the dirge the people are sorrowfully addressed as "virgin Israel," stricken before appreciating the joys and fulfilling the hopes of life (Gen 15:2-3; Judg 11:38). As used by Jeremiah, this title indicates new hope. The sinful, barren people, described as the "adulterous spouse," miraculously return to the condition of the Lord's virgin spouse as at the moment of marriage (Jer 31:4, 21-22; see 1 Sam 1; Isa 54:1).

5:4-6 An excellent example of the literary form of chiasm (the word derives from the Greek letter "chi," written as an "x"). The sequence of words in the downward stroke (a-b-c) is followed in reverse order in the upward stroke (c-b-a), as here:

a—Seek me that you may live	a—seek the Lord that you may live
b—not Bethel	b—Bethel become nought
c—not Gilgal	c—Gilgal shall go into exile
	not Beer-sheba

PROPHETIC WOES

Amos 5:7–6:14

A new major section in the Book of Amos begins here, a series of three speeches whose opening word is "Woe!" (5:7; 5:18; 6:1). (We note that the Hebrew word for "Woe" is present in 5:7 only by amending the text.) In his use of this literary form, Amos is at a major turning point of its evolution; he may even be responsible for this change. Earlier passages consider "Woe!" as a way of mourning the dead at funerals (1 Kgs 13:30). Gradually it became a curse with scorn and bitterness at what ought to be dead or is already morally dead (Isa 33:1; Jer 48:1). Later "Woe!" becomes a taunt over someone's foolishness (Isa 45:9).

5:7-17 This passage condemns blatant social injustices. Small landowners are being taxed into bankruptcy and forced to become serfs on their former family homesteads or even slaves somewhere else (see 2:6). The extension of international trade and the craze for foreign luxuries by the powerful clique of noble people have bled the land of its natural resources, just as foolish military ventures will leave the country heavily in debt to pay indemnities to the conquerors. This enforced payment falls heaviest upon the poor. Even archaeology has disclosed a marked tendency by which palaces became larger as peasant dwellings became smaller! Amos does not condemn liturgy as such but the spirit with which it is performed and its split from the people's daily morality. So, too, Amos is not against politics and commerce but calls down "Woe!" upon "those who turn judgment to

[bitter-tasting] wormwood" (compare Deut 29:17; Lam 3:15, 19), upon those who exact levies of grain, build sumptuous houses, and accept bribes.

5:15 remnant of Joseph: For Amos, this phrase may mean simply the few who survive, but it became a technical theological term, prominent in the Book of Isaiah (Isa 7:3; 10:19-22). Even for Amos, "remnant," is not to be interpreted externally, in this case numerically. Rather, "remnant" may designate that fragile, delicate but essential aspect of what it means to be an Israelite and a true follower of Moses, the faithful adherence to godly ideals, the courageous search for the mysterious way of the Lord, the strength to give up everything for "the pearl of great price" (Matt 13:46).

5:18-27 The second "Woe!" discourse repeats a very traditional religious idea, God's promises for the future at the heart of the Mosaic exodus out of Egypt, and then reverses what the people normally conclude from it (see 3:1-2). While the normal answer ought to be light and joy, Amos declares that the "day of the Lord" will mean "darkness and not light" (5:18). **day of the Lord:** This phrase already had a long history in extrabiblical documentation. In the Akkadian literature of southern Mesopotamia (modern Iraq) over a millennium before Amos, the "day of the god" indicated a special feast honoring the god with elaborate liturgical ceremonies. For Israel in Amos' time, "Yahweh's day" was characterized as a glorious celebration of the Lord's presence when ancient redemptive acts were renewed liturgically (see 5:21-25).

Amos, however, announced the opposite. After his time, "day of the Lord" came to mean a day of the Lord's wrath against Israel (Zeph 1:15), or later, during the Exile, against Israel's enemies (Isa 13:6, 9; Jer 46:10, 21); still later there was a return to the ancient idea, a day of salvation for Israel (Joel 3:4), and eventually a day of final judgment (Mal 3:19-23; Matt 24:1). Amos gave this phrase its permanent place. He relied upon a most ancient tradition, creatively challenged its misrepresentation in his own day, and thereby attempted to restore the original thrust of Israel, the liberation of oppressed people and the condemnation of oppressors.

5:25-27 These verses are plagued with textual and interpretive difficulties. Against verse

25, the Bible makes it clear that Israel offered sacrifice to Yahweh at every period up to Amos' time: Abraham (Gen 12:7-8; 15:7-21); Moses (Exod 18:12); Joshua (Josh 5:10-12); Samuel (Judg 13:16). The identity of Sakkuth and Kaiwan is uncertain.

6:1-14 This is the third and last "Woe!" statement. To manifest that the Lord can and will send devastation, Amos ticks off in verse 2 the names of once prosperous cities in north Syria, already severely weakened by Assyria and soon to be completely destroyed. He has only contempt for the soft, effete men and women of Samaria (see 4:1-3), who at times talk grandly of patriotism and religion yet remain blind to the misery of the poor, all the while luxuriating in their "massage parlors."

Verses 9-11 recall a plague in which only a single person survives in an infested house, and even that one leaves us with the haunting sound of "Silence!" (see 8:3). Verse 12 is a typical paradox from the wisdom school: Israel's situation is as unnatural as plowing the sea with oxen. In verses 13-14 Amos deflates the false hopes that surged with Jeroboam II's conquests to the east of the Jordan River and even those further north into Syria. Amos' bleak outlook is deliberately modified, almost reversed, with new but futile hopes in 2 Kgs 14:24-27.

THE VISIONS

Amos 7:1–8:3

This new major section in the Book of Amos consists of four visions, into which a biographical account of Amos' expulsion from the northern kingdom has been inserted. The visions follow a careful pattern, easily observable despite the editorial additions. In the initial two visions Amos speaks first, asking for divine patience, and the Lord relents. In the third and fourth visions the Lord speaks first and thereby settles the matter. The refrain rings out: "I will forgive them no longer" (7:8; 8:1). The Hebrew language is marked with literary devices such as question and answer, onomatopoeia, and paronomasia, so that a slight change of consonants or vowels in the Hebrew produces a new, dramatic meaning ("ripe grapes" or *qais* in Hebrew becomes "the end" or *qes* in 8:1-2).

These visions, therefore, were intended for public communication. Each centers on an object clearly visible to others: locust, fire, plummet, and ripe fruit. The vision also includes a secret or symbolic meaning, communicated individually to Amos. Because a vision or a mystic communication from God frequently occurs in the commissioning of a prophet (1 Sam 3; Isa 6; Jer 1; Ezek 1), it is possible that the vision became a normal literary style to indicate God's choice of a prophet. Thereafter the prophet will speak with the personal strength of having stood in the council of the Lord (Jer 23:18-22). The momentum within the four visions leads up to the certitude that the balloon will burst and prosperous Israel will disintegrate as much from internal decay as from external military invasion.

7:1-3 The first harvesting of a crop belongs to the royal treasury (money did not yet exist). Even the poor will be swept into the consuming mouth of destruction. In this experience of mystical prayer and of compassion for the poor, Amos is commissioned as a prophet.

7:10-17 A biographical account is stitched into the account of the visions by the repetition of the name of the king, Jeroboam, in verses 9 and 10. Such biographical accounts do occur elsewhere in prophecy (Hos 1; Isa 7; Jer 26–29 and 34–45); they were composed to provide religious insights into the prophet's mission or else, as here (and with Jeremiah), to justify its divine origin and eventual fulfillment.

7:10 The sanctuary of Bethel, sixteen miles north of Jerusalem, was one of the most ancient, existing before the patriarchs (Gen 12:8; 13:3); it was closely associated with Jacob's dream of a ladder between heaven and earth (Gen 28:10-22). Jeroboam I, founder of the northern kingdom at the death of Solomon, restored Bethel as a prominent place of assembly and worship (1 Kgs 12:26-33). The priesthood of Bethel derived independently of the Mosaic Levitical priesthood, just as the Zadokites, once pagan priests when the Jebusites controlled Jerusalem, were installed by David to officiate with Levites of Mosaic background (1 Kgs 12:21). Amaziah's worry over a revolt was not unfounded; the very dynasty of Jeroboam II was inaugurated through a bloody coup d'état at the instigation of the prophet Elisha (1 Kgs 9–10).

7:12-13 to the land of Judah! There earn your bread by prophesying: Amaziah is insinuating that Amos prophesies for a living (see 1 Sam 9:7-9; 2 Kgs 5:5, 15, 22-27; Mic 3:5). Amos will retort sarcastically that he is no prophet but works for a living as a shepherd and dresser of sycamores! In verse 13 the narrator, by a play on words, points up the obsequious surrendering of temple and priesthood to royal wishes: "never again prophesy in Beth-el" (literally, "house of God"); "for it is the king's sanctuary and a royal temple" (in Hebrew, *beth mamlakah*).

7:14 I am no prophet, nor a member of a prophetic guild: While some translations favor the past tense or a question ("I was no prophet" or "Was I not a prophet?") in accord with the past tense in verse 15, the present tense (which we prefer) harmonizes with verses 12-13 and also with a similar passage in Zech 13:5. Northern prophecy had sufficiently discredited itself in Amos' eyes that he repudiated any association with it. As in 3:1-2 and 4:4-5, Amos is not totally rejecting the institution but its degenerate form. In fact, in verse 12 he seems to accept the title "visionary" or "seer," a title used in the south, Amos' homeland (2 Sam 24:11; Isa 30:9-10). **shepherd and dresser of sycamore trees:** See p. 487.

7:15 The Lord took me from following the flock: The phrase is drawn almost literally from 2 Sam 7:8 and the story of David's call to kingship, another sign of Amos' roots in tradition, and the word "took" in Hebrew frequently signifies a radical, abrupt transfer into another way of life (Gen 5:24; 2 Kgs 2:3; Ps 49:16). **Go, prophesy:** While Amos rejects the categorization of prophet, or at least Amaziah's concept of prophet, he obeys the Lord's command to reinvigorate and transform the ancient institution of prophecy by doing it.

7:16-17 Even in his final words Amos remains bitterly sarcastic as he enumerates with crescendo the punishments to come upon the high priest: his wife a harlot and his children dead; then, what's worse, loss of family property; and, worst of all for a priest so finicky over ritual, death and burial "in an unclean land," without the proper blessing upon a grave in the Holy Land.

The visions and the biographical account complement and support each other. One provides the origin and the other the end of Amos' career as a prophet; each concludes with an unequivocal announcement of Israel's end in exile and of Amos' vindication as God's spokesman. While Israel collapses into exile and oblivion, Amos' words become a permanent book, remembered today as God's word.

ADDENDA

Amos 8:4–9:10

A prophetic judgment speech and a vision, each somewhat different in style from the earlier speeches in 3:1–5:6 and the visions in 7:1-9 and 8:1-3, are added to the book. Similar themes recur: dishonest commerce by which the poor become poorer, ever more dependent and even reduced to slavery (see 5:7-12); darkness as on the day of the Lord in 5:18; destruction and exile. Verse 9 of chapter 8 may be alluding to an eclipse of the sun on June 15, 763; there was another total eclipse in 784. Verses 11-12 make it clear that Israel does not decide on its own terms when and how to return to the Lord; they may "wander from sea to sea . . . and not find" the word of the Lord. Unless the journey is undertaken at God's prompting, it will lead only further into desert waste and famine.

9:1-6 While the earlier visions simply announced the end, this new vision elaborates on the end of Israel with imagery and style that match the catastrophic dimensions of Israel's collapse. Amos' words sweep through the universe, reach into the nether world, summon the sea and its monsters to undo the work of creation. The text not only alludes to the opening antiphon and its reference to beautiful Mount Carmel (1:2 and 9:3), but it also concludes with a continuation of the fragments of an ancient hymn (4:13; 5:8-9) that perceives God as once again subduing the angry sea and putting boundaries to its waves, extending the heavens and regulating the good order of nature: "I, the Lord by name" (9:6).

APPENDIX OF ONE-LINERS

Amos 9:7-10

These four verses, each seemingly an independent unit, share features of Amos' style (rhetorical questions, catchwords, disputation). Even the ideas are not as divergent from those found elsewhere in Amos' prophecy as some scholars infer: Amos saw hope for a remnant in 5:15 as here in 9:8b, 9. The minicreed about the Exodus in 2:10 and 3:1 is repeated verbatim in 9:7. Amos is not thoroughly at home with the traditions of the Exodus; after all, he was a southerner from Tekoa, while the Exodus and other Mosaic traditions were more deeply rooted in the northern kingdom. Therefore, these four oneliners circulated separately among his disciples, who may have modified them; after the main part of the book was edited, they were added here as an appendix. Other biblical appendices are found in 2 Sam 21–24; Isa 36–39; Jer 52. Short appendices are added to chapters like Isa 1:27-31.

Verse 7 may be one of the most radical, universalist statements in the entire Hebrew Scriptures, similar to Isa 19:24-25; 66:21. Amos compares Israel's Exodus to the migrations of the other nations: the Arameans swept out of the Syrian-Arabian desert in the twelfth century B.C.E., the Philistines possibly from Crete in the eleventh century B.C.E. Amos' statement implies that Israel is no different from any other people in the external pattern of its origin and history. It was Israel's faith, formed through God's inspired word and through the leadership of faithful servants like Moses and Joshua, that transformed a secular migration into a sacred exodus. Amos is implying that the history of other peoples can also be spirited by faith in Yahweh and can become the external form and symbol for believing in Yahweh and worshiping the Lord.

RESTORATION

Amos 9:11-15

This positive, even glorious conclusion to the negative, destructive oracles of Amos not only conforms to the style of editing prophetical books with an upbeat momentum, but it also presents an important norm for our interpretation of prophetic literature.

The section is divided into two oracles, each with its introductory and concluding formulas: verses 11-12 about the revival of the Davidic empire; verses 13-15 about the abundant re-creation of Israel's cities and farmland. Stylistic and logical links bind this final set of oracles to the Book of Amos: verse 13 picks up phrases from 8:13; verse 14 repeats, only to reverse, 5:11. The Exile, so clearly announced in 2:16; 4:2-3; 5:27, will be turned around in Israel's restoration (v. 14).

The composition of this section belongs after Israel's return to its homeland from Babylonian exile. Comparisons with Joel 4:18-21 tilt toward a common date, around 500 B.C.E.

Surprisingly, this affirming, enthusiastic view of the future never permeated the rest of the book; the editors respected the dire threats and stern sarcasm of Amos, even though they saw the future differently. The future generations of Amos' disciples realized that: (1) sin and punishment could come again, so that Amos' warnings remained valid, even though the distant future will eventually turn out bright; (2) while reading of condemnation and desolation, we ought not to forget God's mercy and fidelity; (3) we need to decide whether threat or promise is more appropriate pastorally and spiritually, for "there is an appointed time for everything, . . . to kill and to heal, . . . to rend and to sew" (Eccl 3:1-8). Jerusalem and the Davidic family were the line of continuity, the inheritors of the Mosaic promises, originally received by the ancestors of the northern kingdom. The future was to be considered more a creation of God, generously given in view of just and compassionate relationships among God's people, than a human achievement at Israel's beck and call (see 8:11-12).

The apostle James, as cited in Acts 15:15-17, draws upon Amos 9:11 when approving Paul's apostolate to the Gentiles. David's empire will extend to the world, not by the sword, but by confessing Jesus as Lord and Savior. At this moment the prescriptions of the Mosaic law will not be a prerequisite for baptism. Even the Mosaic covenant is fulfilled beyond its own dreams, certainly beyond the human works of a law-abiding Jew. Amos' words receive an interpretation still more radical than that of the first disciples and editors. Yet, in quoting from Amos, James declares how necessary and valid the Hebrew Scriptures remain for appreciating faith in the new Son of David.

HOSEA

Carroll Stuhlmueller, C.P.

INTRODUCTION

Hosea was a contemporary of Amos. Both prophesied in the northern kingdom of Israel during the reign of Jeroboam II (2 Kgs 14:23-29), yet Hosea's ministry was not abruptly cut short as was that of Amos' (Amos 7:12-13). Rather, according to the scholarly position followed in this commentary, Hosea's words reflect the chaotic, mad, and finally destructive years after Jeroboam II's death. There are other differences. Hosea was a citizen of the north, stressed far more than Amos the intimate love of God for Israel, continuously inserted his own personal feelings, developed and applied such northern traditions as Exodus and wilderness experiences from Mosaic times, and moved within agricultural rather than desert images.

While Amos goes down in biblical annals as the prophet of divine justice—justice in the strict modern sense of punishment equal to the seriousness of the crime—Hosea is known as the prophet of divine love, love ever willing to suffer in order to win back one's beloved. Yet, no justice is fiercer than tender love that has been betrayed and attacked, and so Hosea ends up far more certain and definitive about the destruction of Israel: "I will attack them like a bear robbed of its young, and tear their hearts from their breasts" (13:8). "Where are your plagues, O death! . . . My eyes are closed to compassion" (13:14).

The chaotic times of Hosea

This agonizing reversal from forgiveness to angry rejection parallels the history of Israel from the prosperous years of Jeroboam II's reign to the chaotic years that followed. Hosea began announcing "the word of the Lord . . . in the days of Jeroboam, son of Joash, king of Israel" (1:1; 2 Kgs 14:23-29). As described in the introduction to the prophecy of Amos (p. 488), these were heady years of success and plenty, hard years of indifference toward the poor, years bloated with sensuality and laziness. Amos' sarcastic, even crude sketch of women fat as Bashan cows (Amos 4:1-3) and of men pampered by the sweet scent and tingling touch of massage parlors (Amos 6:4-6) says it all! While Amos viewed the sickening scene with stern eyes from a distance, Hosea experienced its poignant, cruel thrust into the heart of his marriage. Chapters 1–3 and 4:1–5:7 carry the jagged scars of Hosea's heart against the frolic and degradation of Jeroboam II's years as king.

The death of Jeroboam II in 746 B.C.E. also struck a mournful toll over the prosperous land of Israel. Flowers cut in full bloom quickly lose their lovely petals, so that only the dark stem and malodorous water remain. The succinct record in 2 Kgs 15:8-31 captures the style of newscasting on television—one stroke after another without time to breathe: "Zechariah, son of Jeroboam, . . . was king . . . for six months. . . . Shallum, son of Jabesh, . . . attacked and killed him. . . . Shallum reigned one month, [till] Menahem came up, attacked and killed Shallum. . . . Menahem punished the city of Tappuah, even to ripping open all the pregnant women. . . .

During his reign Pul (Tiglath-pileser III) invaded the land and Menahem gave him a thousand talents of silver." The two-year reign of Menahem's son, Pekahiah, was ended by the insurrection of his adjutant, Pekah. During Pekah's reign a new revolt brought the Assyrian army again; the northern provinces were enveloped in darkness (see Isa 8:23) and lost forever to Israel. Hoshea conspired against Pekah, killed him, and reigned in his stead with Assyria's blessing, only to revolt against Assyria and so bring on the end, absolutely and unconditionally. The ten northern tribes totally disappear to history. Each word of this account in 2 Kings lunges, gasps, and collapses, only to start the dreadful process once more. The details can be outlined this way:

Jeroboam II (786–746)
  free and prosperous
Zechariah (746–745)
  compromising and ineffective (assassinated)
Shallum (745)
  anti-Assyria (assassinated)
Menahem (745–737)
  pro-Assyria, paying tribute
Pekahiah (737–736)
  pro-Assyria (assassinated)
Pekah (736–732)
  anti-Assyria (assassinated)
Hoshea (732–724)
  pro-Assyria; then anti-Assyria (captured and executed)

Clearly, the anti-Assyrian policy, to align with Egypt and other smaller states in military revolt against the feared monster to the east, was suicidal. Prophetically, in the evaluation of 2 Kings or in the preaching of Amos and Hosea, destruction was already determined by infidelity and injustice that had corroded the moral fiber. Military adventures were condemned, not simply for their foolish miscalculation, but principally for the smokescreen they provided for condoning social injustices.

The period from the death of Jeroboam II until Hoshea's seizure of the throne is reflected in many ways within 5:8–8:14 in Hosea's prophecy. (*Note:* the prophet Hosea is not to be confused with King Hoshea.) The violent rise and quick demise of dynasties tumble through the lines of 7:5-7: "They are all heated like ovens, and consume their rulers" (see 8:4).

The abrupt change of policies—first an alliance with Egypt, then one with Assyria—provokes Hosea's disdain: "Ephraim is like a dove, silly and senseless; they call upon Egypt, they go to Assyria" (7:11; see also 5:13; 8:9). When Assyria pounces upon the prey and rends it mercilessly, God wants no mistake about it: "I carry it away and no one can save it from me" (5:14; also 7:8-9).

Chapters 9–12 reflect the false quiet and deceptive hope for peace and relief shortly before and immediately after the succession of Shalmaneser V to the throne of Assyria in 726 B.C.E. Hosea warns: "Rejoice not, O Israel . . . . For you have been unfaithful to your God, loving a harlot's hire" (9:1). When King Hoshea revolts, Assyria's short fuse of patience ignites and its anger explodes against Israel. After King Hoshea has been captured ("Where now is your king, O Israel?"—13:10) and the fury is roaring south against the capital city of Samaria, Hosea's reaction is recorded in 13:1–14:1. He summons the plagues and the deadly sting of destruction and declares on God's part: "My eyes are closed to compassion" (13:14).

The prophet must have escaped before the capital city was burned to the ground, leaving the charred remains of ivory inlaids for later archeologists to discover, and from Jerusalem he composed the finale (14:2-9). Hope triumphs as he writes: "Return, O Israel, to the Lord, your God, . . . [who] will heal . . . defection, [and] will love . . . freely" (14:2, 5). Most probably it was later disciples who added the editorial allusions to Judah found throughout the book (1:1, 7; 4:14; 5:5; etc.). In 12:3 the name "Israel" was replaced with "Judah," but the word "Israel" is now restored by many translators, as in the New American Bible. Finally, the admonition to "understand these things" in the book of Hosea was inserted at the very end (14:10), probably by someone of the school of wisdom that produced such books as Proverbs.

The passionate character of Hosea

The history of the times and of the text has already provided us with biographical information about the prophet Hosea. The sorrows, frustrations, and renewed hopes of his marriage supplied the major image for chapters 1–3 about the sins and infidelities of Israel, and contributed intense passion to important lines in the rest of the book. Hope and agony, springing from strong emotions, characterize not only the book but the person of Hosea. These rise prominently to the surface, as God cries out impassionately: "I will not give vent to my blazing anger. . . . For I am God, no human person" (11:9). Hopes spilling over with compassion induce Hosea to moderate the punishments of Deuteronomy, a book otherwise close to him in spirit and vocabulary. While Deuteronomy legislates the punishment of death by stoning for a stubborn and unruly son (Deut 21:18-21) and for an adulterous wife (Deut 22:13-24), Hosea pulls back from such harshness.

Comparing Hosea with Amos, we discern a whole new set of images. While Amos draws upon his experience of shepherding a flock in the desert wilderness, Hosea frequently refers to agricultural scenes. These he adduces, whether as peacefully present in their rich produce, indicative of the new espousals of Israel with God (2:23-25), or as painfully absent when "the land mourns and everything that dwells in it languishes" because of Israel's sins. While the wilderness is the haunt of lions and bears for Amos (Amos 3:8, 12; 5:19), for Hosea it can be the idyllic place of Israel's honeymoon with God (9:10; 13:4-5). Hosea's appreciation of fertility in the family, in the farmland, and in the folds of livestock should have been soured, one would think, by his wife's infatuation with fertility rites in the temple (2:4-9); yet his estimate of the dignity before God of life and sexuality won the day. He not only received back his wayward wife but responded with heroic compassion in the end.

The covenant theology of Hosea

What secured this triumph in Hosea's soul and writings can be traced back to the covenant between Yahweh and Israel in the days of Moses. Hosea even stresses the two outstanding qualities of this covenant: *bonding in love* and *sturdy trustworthiness*. These are the two words that Yahweh pronounced with dramatic compassion as Moses stood atop Mount Sinai with the two stone tablets of the law in his arms (Exod 34:6-9). Through the heartrending experience of his broken and healed marriage, Hosea transforms the somewhat legal framework of the Mosaic covenant

into the intimately personal and loving contract of marriage. Hosea's remembrance of the covenant shows up in his allusion to the Decalogue in 4:2. While the covenant enables Hosea to suffuse the note of compassion, it also provides a straightforward way to brush aside flimsy excuses and to call sin by its honest name—swearing, lying, murder, stealing, and adultery.

Just as sketching the times and sequence of chapters in the book has already introduced us to the person of Hosea, so the preceding biographical details have led us into the major theological lines of this prophecy. Mosaic traditions are not only present in an impressive way, but ancient customs and inspired attitudes (about five hundred years old by now) were seen as a living, motivating force. Unlike Amos, who talked *about* the Exodus as a point of comparison with the present moment (see Amos 2:9-12; 3:1-2; 9:7), Hosea sees it happening right now. Israel's sins bring the people back to Egypt (8:13; 9:3; 11:5), not geographically, because they either remained in the Holy Land or were taken eastward into exile; nor politically, because Egypt pretended to be a friendly state and a place of asylum; but typologically, because Egypt was a symbol or type of sin and bondage. In this regard we note the frequent use of the word "now" in Hosea's preaching (4:16; 5:3, 7; 7:2; 8:8). This ability to see a contemporaneity in ancient redemptive acts of God was probably inherited from Deuteronomy, another ancient northern tradition (see Deut 5:1-5).

One final aspect of Hosea's theology cannot be passed over. Hosea could not refer to God simply and generally as God; at least forty-five times he uses the sacred name Yahweh (Exod 3:11-15), and if he refers to God as Elohim or El, it is almost always as "*your* God" or "*my* God" (2:25; 3:5; 4:6; 12).

The disturbed text of Hosea

The Hebrew text of Hosea seems very disturbed. Various explanations are offered: it reflects a northern style instead of the more customary Hebrew of Jerusalem; Hosea himself was emotionally disturbed and this fact leaves its scars upon the book; or later scribes handled the text with less than satisfactory care. The following variations are to be noted in the numbers for chapters and verses:

Hebrew; NAB	Greek; Vulgate; RSV
1:1-9	1:1-9
2:1-2	1:10-11
2:3-25	2:1-23
chs. 3–10	chs. 3–10
11:1-11	11:1-11
11:12	12:1
12:1-14	12:2-15
13:1-15	13:1-15
13:16	14:1
14:1-9	14:2-10

COMMENTARY

INTRODUCTION

Hos 1:1

The introduction or superscription to the book of Hosea is less elaborate and less informative than that found in the Book of Amos. Although Hosea prophesied in the northern kingdom of Israel, more attention is given here to the kings of the southern kingdom of Judah whose reigns extended beyond that of Jeroboam II. This fact hints at the book's redaction at Jerusalem, capital of the southern kingdom.

The introduction accentuates the theological or inspired quality of Hosea's preaching. While Amos' book begins with "the words of Amos," Hosea's opens with *the word of the Lord* that came to Hosea." The name Hosea means "the act of saving" or simply "Savior." In Greek, the initial "h" was reduced to a small apostrophe, called a "rough breathing." These were customarily dropped when writing with only capital letters. The final "a" of the Hebrew name would have indicated feminine gender in Greek and so was changed to an "e." From the Greek came the spelling of this prophet's name in the Latin Vulgate and in older Roman Catholic editions of the Bible, namely, Osee.

Hosea was "the son of Beeri." The name Beeri is not otherwise found for a person in the Old Testament, although a village located near Bethel had this name. Beeri means "my fountain" or "O fountain." Only here in the entire book is the prophet's name recorded for us!

YAHWEH, SPOUSE OF ISRAEL

Hos 1:2–3:5

The first three chapters center upon Hosea's marriage, the infidelities of his wife Gomer, the doubtful paternity of the second and third children, and the application of this situation to Israel's covenant with Yahweh. It is important to note at the outset that in real life Hosea was the faithful spouse and Gomer the adulterous sinner, but in the application of this background to Israel, the ones targeted most as unfaithful harlots were the religious and civil leaders (particularly the former), all of the male sex (see 4:4-11; 5:1-3)!

Each of the three chapters tells basically the same thing, yet never as a story for its own sake but as a religious symbol about Israel— and for that matter, about what can happen to any one of us. Many important details are missing for a good story: the name of the paramour (or were there many?), the place of their rendezvous (at the temple for fertility rites? secretly in a private dwelling?). While chapter 1 speaks *about* Hosea and the children, chapter 2 consists mostly of Hosea's speech, and chapter 3 follows in an autobiographical style. Chapter 3 is the most succinct, possibly the oldest. Closest to the domestic tragedy, chapter 3 could not humanly sustain long explanations. Chapter 2 represents an outburst of violent emotion, again very near to the raw memory of what happened; chapter 1, written from a distance by a disciple, can afford to be the most explicit about the meaning of the episode.

1:2-8 A similar style is used to tell about the conception, birth, and naming of all three children. **1:2 the Lord said to Hosea:** The marriage of Hosea was probably arranged in the normal way of the time by the parents, yet, viewed from the faith that God's providence covers especially significant events of human life, the Lord is said to *order* it. **take a harlot wife and harlot's children:** The grammatical form of the noun "harlot" (in Hebrew, masculine plural) indicates a woman of such tendencies. Hosea did not look for a prostitute to marry; his wife may have experienced strong temptations due to her initiation at the sanctuary's fertility rites. **1:3 Gomer:** The proper name of the woman, without any significance for the story of Hosea, argues for a real marriage rather than a piece of fiction or allegory. **conceived and bore him a son:** This is the only time Hosea is clearly said to be the father of the child.

1:4 the name Jezreel: Each of the three children's names has a double meaning, good in itself but also bad for Israel. Jezreel refers to the fertile valley stretching from Mount Carmel in the west to the hills above the Sea of Galilee in the east, literally a breadbasket of nourishment. Jezreel was also the site of many bloody battles beginning with the Book of Judges (Judg 4–5). **1:6 Lo-ruhama:** Hebrew for "No pity," a name that could have indicated a child able to hold her own against injustices; theologically, it negates one of the key qualities of the Mosaic covenant, the Lord's compassion (see p. 498). In the singular the Hebrew word denotes the mother's womb, where a child develops in warm security; derivatives like *ruhama* show the feminine, motherly side of God. Hosea eventually interprets the child's name as an end to the covenant. **1:8 Lo-ammi:** Hebrew for "Not my people," a name that originally alluded to the boy's illegitimacy and to his ability to survive alone in this world despite all odds against him. Religiously, the name announces the end of Israel's special privileges and reduces Israel to the status of all other nations. **1:9 I will not be their God:** The Hebrew refers to the divine name as revealed by God to Moses, "I am who I am." When spoken by Israel, it was read in the third person: "He who is [always there with you]," or Yahweh (Exod 3:14-15). Literally verse 9 reads, "No longer am I 'I am' for you."

2:1-3 These verses are frequently placed after 2:25 or, as in the New American Bible, after 3:1-5. The Revised Standard Version, following the ancient Greek and Vulgate enumeration, lists these verses as 1:10-11 and 2:1.

2:4-25 While the overall impact of these lines is unmistakable, the grammar, the emotions, and the sequence of verses are confusing; the New American Bible adjusts the verses in a new sequence. Some scholars claim that verses 18-25, or at least verses 21-22, are editorial additions. Perhaps the editor responsible for the biographical section in 1:2-8 drew verses 18-25 from a treasury of Hosea's speeches.

At first Hosea speaks *to* the children (vv. 4-5) and then *about* them (vv. 6-7); he explodes with vitriolic disdain (vv. 5-6, 11-12) and peacefully settles with nostalgic memories (v. 10 and the end of v. 15, into vv. 8-9); he is at the point of divorce (v. 4) and reverts to reconciliation (vv. 16-17). While bitterly denouncing Canaanite fertility rites at the sanctuaries, Hosea employs the language of this ritual to appreciate the luscious beauty of the landscape. The Hebrew word for "allure" (v. 16), describing God's way of drawing Israel closely into loving covenant bonds, is also the word for sexual seduction. **2:17 the valley of Achor:** This valley southwest of Jericho was once surrounded with sinister memories of military defeat and deceit in the days of Joshua (Josh 7:24-26); now Israel is invited to reenter the Promised Land through it and take possession of its rich source of life. The days of the Exodus are now gloriously repeated and the covenant is enhanced by comparison with matrimonial bonds, as Israel calls the Lord "my husband." True love (v. 20) is never selfish, and so Hosea sees the good effects of Israel's new espousals with Yahweh spiraling outward, even to protect birds and crawling animals.

2:21-22 These lovely lines need to be unpacked for their theological richness. In this marriage between Yahweh and Israel, the Lord offers the dowry "in right and in justice" ("right": a moral rectitude that brings peace and satisfaction; "justice": a public, authoritative declaration that such is true); "in love and in mercy" ("love": affection between those bonded by blood or treaty; "mercy": see above 1:7); "in fidelity" (sturdy reliability in one's relations). **you shall know the Lord:** The Hebrew word for "know" is the one most frequently used for marital intercourse (Gen 4:1, 17, 25) and stresses the experiential or intuitive aspect.

2:23-25 Again intimate love reaches outward toward a new creation. The bonding between Israel and Yahweh hints at its repercussions upon people everywhere; universal mission is already being signaled from afar. Difficult or seemingly impossible, whether for adulterous Israel or for unsuspecting foreigners, God's love acts miraculously, so that Jezreel is once again a fertile breadbasket, and Lo-ruhama and Lo-ammi are to become the Lord's legitimate children. What is biologically impossible—changing a child's natural parentage—now happens. These lines are applied to the Church's universal mission in 1 Pet 2:9-10; Rom 9:25-26; 11:32.

3:1-5 This passage retells the story of Hosea's reconciliation with Gomer. For the application to Israel's covenant with Yahweh, an application continuously being made by Hosea, it is important that Hosea never divorced Gomer nor is he marrying someone else. Here we note several, very human phases in the return of Gomer. Three times verse 1 uses the Hebrew verb "to love," which denotes normal physical and emotional attachment. After Hosea obeys the Lord and brings Gomer back to his home, he still cannot consummate the marriage. After such a severe estrangement, intercourse would be too much a routine physical act, not a full expression of human love. He says to her: "Many days you shall wait for me . . . I in turn will wait for you" (3:3). Verse 5 applies the lines to the southern kingdom of Judah, probably after the destruction of the north in 721 B.C.E., reaffirms the promises to the Davidic dynasty at Jerusalem, and then extends the promises into "the last days" (3:5), a phrase also found among the southern prophets in speaking of the new Jerusalem of peace (Isa 2:2-5; Mic 4:1-5; Jer 23:5-6, 20; Ezek 38:16).

2:1-3 The New American Bible transfers these verses here; for an explanation, see the commentary on 2:23-25. Hosea seems to reach back behind the Mosaic covenant to the earliest memories of Israel with the ancient patriarchs and their wives, to whom were promised offspring "like the sand of the sea" (Gen 22:7), "children of the living God," born

of parents too far advanced in age for conception or else barren for a long period of years. Yahweh is not dead like the false fertility gods of the Canaanites. **2:2 one head:** Hosea avoids the title of king, perhaps out of disdain for the reigning monarchs, perhaps too as a way of uniting Israel with the premonarchic days of Abraham and Moses.

CRIMES OF LEADERSHIP IN JEROBOAM II'S REIGN

Hos 4:1–5:7

As already explained in the introduction, this section belongs to the final years of Jeroboam II's long reign (786–746 B.C.E.) and in that sense is a continuation of chapters 1–3. Although promiscuity was involved in the sanctuary fertility rites, the crime of adultery is attached to all serious offenses against the Lord and the neighbor because of the intimate love of Yahweh, which every sin violates.

4:1-3 This section is composed in the style of a legal proceeding at the city gate (see Deut 25:7; Ruth 4:1) and includes a summons of the defendant (v. 1a), evidence of crimes (vv. 1b-2a), verdict of "Guilty!" (v. 2b, literally "blood upon blood," meaning that the crimes are written across the hands), and the consequent punishment (v. 3). For other examples of this type of judicial speech among the prophets, see: Amos 4:1-3; 8:4-8; Isa 1:2-16. The crimes represent a mini-decalogue (Exod 20:1-17; Deut 5:1-21). They are all crimes against basic relationships and human trust: cursing by ritual language, lying, premeditated murder, kidnapping (the original meaning instead of "stealing"), and adultery. In order to challenge a false trust in later theologies and rituals that developed out of the Mosaic covenant, Hosea goes back to the basic ABC's of humanity as reflected in the Ten Commandments. Prophets condemn covenant religion by appealing to precovenant expectations enfleshed in all men and women, and even in "the beasts of the field" and "the birds of the air," which also suffer the effects of human selfishness. For 4:1b, see 2:21-22.

4:4-19 Here are graphic details about fertility rites, even at such ancient sanctuaries as Gilgal (Josh 4:19–5:15; 1 Sam 15:12-33) and Bethel (= "house of God," which Hosea contemptuously calls *Beth-aven*, or "house of emptiness"; for Bethel, see Gen 28:10-22; 1 Kgs 12:29-33). Verse 4 is a very difficult verse to translate confidently from the Hebrew; in any case the accusation is targeted not so much against the ordinary Israelite but against "you, O priest" (in the singular according to the Hebrew and therefore aimed at the high priest legitimately installed but morally corrupt).**4:6 want of knowledge:** See 2:22. **4:8 feed on the sin:** The ritual law of sin-offerings prescribes a stipend for the livelihood of the priests (see Num 5:8-10). Hosea implies that the priests tolerate sin or sharpen the sense of guilt among the people, who then feel compelled to bring more generous offerings. The word "greedy" implies lust or an unusually strong desire. Verse 9a is a proverb found verbatim in Isa 24:2a; it reads literally: "and it will be like people like priest." The priests imitate the worldliness of people about them, and people shelter themselves under the priests' example.

5:1-7 The reference is to the continuation of the lascivious rituals in such renowned sanctuaries as Mizpah (1 Sam 7:5-14) and Tabor (Judg 4:14). The play on words in verses 1-2 makes the lines difficult to translate into English: "a snare *(pah)* are you at *Mizpah*," or in English, "a snare are you at Miznare." In verse 3, Ephraim is the name of a son of the patriarch Joseph (Gen 41:52; 48:1). Verse 7 refers to children conceived through the fertility rites.

ASSASSINATIONS, INSTABILITY, LOSS

Hos 5:8–8:14

These chapters rumble and tumble with the assassination of kings and their royal families, pro-Assyrian and anti-Assyrian policies, treaties with Egypt against Assyria, and with Assyria against Egypt, big promises and meager delivery, politics in place of moral reform, and distracting military adventures that lead to heavy losses, which again distract the people to seek remedy in new assassinations. We are living through the period from the death of Jeroboam II in 746 to the seizure of royal power by King Hoshea in 732. The period covers only fourteen years, yet it produced seven kings, five dynasties, a major war from 736 to 732, and the loss of the north-

east section of the kingdom to Assyria (2 Kgs 15:27-31; Isa 8:23).

5:8-14 The various allusions are difficult to identify; the whirl of events and the tragedy of malfeasance in leadership disrupt any orderly discussion. At one point Menaham captures the throne in the north and tilts in favor of Assyria; at another time Ahaz, king of Judah, in a panic to save his throne, declares himself a vassal of Assyria, sacrificing the independence of his country and enmeshing it in international turmoil. **5:13 cannot heal you:** One of Hosea's favorite words is introduced into the text here and again in 6:1; 7:1; 11:4; 14:5, generally with the other key word, "return," so that interior return or conversion becomes an absolute condition for healing the injuries of any individual or the nation. Verse 14 states that even though Assyrian armies inflicted the mortal wound, God wants no misunderstanding: "I am like a lion . . . I rend the prey and depart." The Assyrians are following through with God's plan! Implicit in such a seemingly cruel interpretation of divine providence is the consoling fact that moral conversion, not military action, can heal Israel for new life.

5:15–6:7 The centerpiece here is a prayer (6:1-3), lovely in itself, stitched carefully into the context by word play and parallel ideas, and then rejected because of Israel's insincerity. The most beautiful words cannot save an ugly heart. While the words speak of conversion, Israel refuses the consequence of adequate repentance. As one author commented, the transition from conversion to repentance is as crucial as waking up without getting up!

The words "heal" in 5:13, "rend" in 5:14, and "go back" in 5:15 are identical with "return," "rend" and "heal" in 6:1. The phrase "look for" in 5:15 is of the same Hebrew root as "dawn" in 6:3 ("dawn" is the first light that we "look for" in the early morning). As mentioned already, the prayer in 6:1-3 is carefully inserted into place. **6:2 third day:** This is a technical phrase in the Bible, symbolic of the Lord's extraordinary appearance as Savior: in Exod 19:11, 16, when the Lord came down to Mount Sinai; in Gen 42:18, when Joseph said to his brothers, "Do this and you shall live"; in Jonah 2:1, Jonah's deliverance from the belly of the whale (see also Josh 3:2; Ezra 8:15; Isa 16:14; 37:30). This long tradition of "three days" converges gloriously in the New Testament doctrine of Jesus' resurrection and is enshrined in the Church's creed.

In verse 4, as in 11:8-9, we eavesdrop on the compassionate heart of God struggling against the inevitable destruction of Israel. **6:5 smote them through the prophets:** A long series of non-writing prophets have been warning Israel, such as the elders in Num 11:16-30, Samuel in 1 Sam, Elijah and Elisha in 1 Kgs 17–2 Kgs 13:20. A conscience that is stirred and challenged becomes a destructive force for revenge and self-justification if one does not obey it. **6:6 love . . . not sacrifice:** This is a classic text (see 1 Sam 15:22; Ps 50:14; Matt 9:13; 12:7). Ritual acts like sacrifice and holocaust were intended to externalize in a sacred assembly the interior spirit of obedience and adoration before God. Without love and knowledge of God they are a sham, or, in Ezekiel's words, a "whitewash" (Ezek 22:28).

7:3-16 Deceitful and cruel dynasties rise and collapse, as though moral turpitude is remedied by military excitement. Kings, after stirring the passions of the people to revolt in order to capture the throne, are themselves the victims of these overheated ovens as people "consume their rulers" (7:7). **7:8 Ephraim, a hearth cake unturned:** Hosea evokes the image of dough being baked on burning coals, unturned, so that it remains raw and cold on one side, burnt to charcoal and reeking with smoke on the other. Hosea refers to social conditions, with half the people too rich and half too poor; religious conditions, with excessive ritualism but no spirit; political busyness, with no consistency or thoroughness; cultural veneer, pretentious and overdone in contrast to the dirt and hunger of the poor; a country of half-fed people, half-cultured society, half-lived religion, half-hearted policy, half-baked cakes.

8:1-14 This poem is carefully crafted with key words stitching the lines together and with major themes in balanced repetition, and at the center the haunting sound of a proverb (v. 7). While verses 1-6 and 11-14 modulate from frantic misdirection in politics to feverish ritualism in worship, verses 8-10 point to the disastrous effects. Such a frenzied whirl of activity can only foment more intense movement until all disintegrates. **8:1 A trumpet . . . You who watch:** The latter phrase remains better in its original He-

brew, "like a vulture": first, because of the repetition of the particle "like" (in Hebrew, an emphatic, dramatic word); second, the vulture signals a field of dead bodies—carcasses of animals for immolation on the altar (?) or the bloated bodies of dead soldiers and of city inhabitants after a long siege. Sacrificial animals, sanctifying the altar in signs of adoration, now contaminate the house of the Lord in their rotten state. **8:2 "O God of Israel, we know you":** Israel rejects and yet calls upon the Lord. **8:5 Cast away your calf:** The golden calves set up by Jeroboam I at the sanctuaries of Bethel and Dan (1 Kgs 12:26-33) were originally considered the pedestal or throne for God's invisible presence like the ark or chest surrounded by cherubim wings at the Jerusalem temple (Exod 25:10-22; 37:1-9). Soon the symbol became an idol so as to divinize human talents and work, and to focus on the calf or bull in its fertility symbolism.

8:7 When they sow the wind, they shall reap the whirlwind: This proverb echoes in every language of the world. The three couplets in Hebrew resound with the same sounds and even rhyme at the end. Not only do the words and ideas fit compactly together, but, once begun, they rush like a whirlwind to their destruction. **8:9 Ephraim bargained for lovers:** No longer attractive and with little to offer any more, Ephraim pays her lovers (foreign nations whose assistance she courts) for their sensuous enjoyment of herself—lines bitterly true of the rape and destruction that accompany military invasion. **8:13 they shall return to Egypt:** see the introduction (p. 497). Although Egypt is actually a friendly nation, coaxing the revolt against Assyria, Hosea views Egypt as a type of oppression since the days of Moses. Israel's sins have reversed the covenant at Sinai and have driven Israel back to pre-Mosaic days. Beneath the surface, however, is the assurance that what God did once can be done again if Israel converts sincerely.

INTERLUDE OF FALSE HOPES

Hos 9:1–13:8

As noted in the introduction, these chapters bring us into the reign of the last king of the north, Hoshea (732–724 B.C.E.). After the

Assyrian army had broken the back of the revolt instigated by King Pekah and lopped off the northern provinces of Israel, Hoshea was placed upon the throne with Assyrian help. This period of time represents Israel's last chance at conversion, healing, and survival. The nation failed to realize the futility of seeking salvation by intrigue, treaties, and military armaments. They paid little or no attention to Hosea's threats and previously to those of Amos. Perhaps they felt that they had suffered enough (or too much) and so could settle down to business as usual in the sanctuary worship and in their social injustices now that King Hoshea was enthroned and peace had returned.

Chapter 9 has more than its share of textual difficulties in a book beset with many disturbed Hebrew readings; there are also a number of puns and like-sounding words, which are always difficult to translate into another language. We spot various allusions to the autumnal feast of Tabernacles, at times simply called "the feast," as in verse 5 (see 1 Kgs 8:2; Ezek 45:25; Neh 8:14). Tabernacles was the final harvest festival, in thanksgiving especially for grapes and olives (see 9:2). Several references to dwelling places in this chapter may allude to the practice of dwelling in tents during the octave of this feast (Lev 23:42). This chapter of Hosea witnesses to the prophet's keen awareness of the Exodus traditions. In his prophecy, accordingly, Hosea is not condemning sanctuary worship in itself, because this was one of the principal means of his learning the Mosaic traditions; like Amos, he is against *that* worship rendered evil by its tolerance or active support of sensuality and social injustices.

9:1-2 The references to threshing floor and wine press, along with other details to follow in this chapter, place us within the eight-day festival of Tabernacles; these phrases are also used in Deut 16:13 in reference to the final harvest and the feast of Tabernacles. Harvest is normally symbolic of life. Yet the carousing and excesses even at Israel's sanctuaries contradict God's holiness and concern for the poor. The feast that celebrates God's tabernacling presence among Israel is driving God out. We are reminded of Jesus' reaction when he drove the money-changers out of the temple (John 2:13-22). Once again Egypt is a type of oppression and sin (v. 3); the people's

offenses have transformed their own land into "Egypt" (see 7:16).

9:4 mourners' bread that makes unclean: As in Amos 7:17, the people and priests may be violating social justice and turning the sanctuary into a business, even for the sale of sex, yet they can still be scrupulous over fine points of the law such as unclean food or burial in an unblessed or unclean grave! *Mourners' bread* was unacceptable because of the mourners' contact with a corpse (Deut 16:14); strict rules isolated people mortally or contagiously ill as well as those who cared for them (Num 19:11-22; Lev 21). People of nomadic background, occupying an arid area, develop strict rules concerning contagious diseases. Israel, moreover, with very little understanding of the physical body and with little or no appreciation of the healing profession, evolved a system of health care that combined common sense with strange concoctions (see the rules for the purification of leprosy and skin diseases in Lev 14). Israel's legitimate offerings of wine become unclean like mourners' food because sensuality has reduced Israel to a state of being dead, and its sinfulness is contagious! **9:6 Weeds . . . thorns:** The inhabitable oasis where tents are pitched quickly reverts to wild growth; Israel's sins corrupt the earth (4:3), and the harvest festival is replaced with weeds and thorns.

9:7-9 The play on words and sounds in the Hebrew verses carry the enigmatic touch of prophecy as well as its poetic mystique, yet the sense becomes clear enough when we read from the background of prophecy's history. Already from the start, prophecy could turn into a self-serving business for pay (Num 22:17). Even in the days of Moses prophecy needed correction, in this case because of jealousy (Num 11:26-30; 12:6-8). In a later episode we stand by, scandalized and disillusioned, as prophet argues against prophet in 1 Kgs 22 or Jer 28. Amos, we recall, refused to be associated with the prophetic guilds (Amos 7:14) once honored by the presence of Elijah and Elisha (2 Kgs 2). Hosea resounds with his own "Amen!" in declaring that the professional "prophet is a fool!" Moreover, their craft or employment has become a snare for them so that they are sinking to the sexual degeneracy of "the days of Gibeah," the site of a vicious form of homosexual activity and a hideous type of revenge (Judg 19–21).

9:10-17 These lines dramatize the meaning of the word "Ephraim" in reverse. It means, as we read in Gen 41:52 about Joseph's naming his second son Ephraim, "God *has made me fruitful* in the land of my affliction." Though the second-born son, Ephraim was to receive the first-born's blessing from Jacob (Gen 48:12-20), as specially precious to the Lord (see Jer 2:3). Yet the people of Ephraim (= northern kingdom of Israel) have "consecrated themselves to the Shame" (9:10), as happened when Israel was first initiated into the fertility rites at Baal-peor at the instigation of a prophet named Balaam (Num 25; 31:8, 16). The people Ephraim, whose name declares the fruitfulness of the womb, by their sexual excesses will become "childless" (9:12) through the cruel excesses of the military conqueror Assyria. The final verse begins with the formula of a blessing only to end with a curse. Verse 16 reminds us of the deep weariness of sated lust.

10:1-15 This series of short, disparate oracles may date to the early years of King Hoshea. King Pekah has been assassinated (v. 3). The land is again producing its fruit as it recovers from the disastrous war against Assyria. Yet the hopes for moral reform and for a return to social justice have turned into empty words and false promises (v. 4). The idolatrous rites continue, as indicated by the worship of stone pillars, which are representative of the male god Baal and are usually joined by wooden pillars for the female goddess Astarte (see 3:12-13).

Verses 5-8 anticipate a new and worse invasion by Assyria if Samaria continues in its promiscuous rites. Bethel is singled out, referred to as Beth-aven (v. 5) or just Aven (v. 8); the latter word stands for emptiness or shame, a sarcastic way of alluding to the famous sanctuary (see the commentary on 4:5-6). The new king will endure the same fate as Pekah (v. 7; see 13:10 for the actual event). The destruction will be so cruel and complete that people will "cry out to the mountains, 'Cover us!'" (v. 8), words repeated in Luke 22:30 and Rev 6:16. Verses 11-13a draw upon the image of harvest, as in chapter 9, only to see that Israel "reaped perversity." Israel trusted in the military; it will be destroyed by the military (vv. 13b-15). The records about Salman's ravage of Beth-arbel have been lost; the event cannot be documented. Twice the word "chastise" occurs (v. 10); its Hebrew form indicates disciplinary punishment, suffering that purifies and strengthens and so transforms. An elusive element of hope abides in lines sweeping toward destruction.

11:1-11 This chapter seems like an island around which runs the current of Hosea's preaching from chapter 10 to 12:1. The image of Israel here modulates from the adulterous spouse to the wayward child. While the rest of Hosea increases the momentum toward death, dramatically summarized in 13:14, chapter 11 draws from the intuitive hope deep within the heart of Hosea, like an island whose roots extend beneath the river currents.

Grammatically, chapter 11 is divided between verses 1-7 and 8-11. The opening section refers to Israel in the third person; the other part uses the second person. The first verses reflect Israel's wandering in the Sinaitic wilderness, while verses 8-11 reach forward to Israel's settled life in the land of Canaan. Yahweh speaks throughout in the first person singular. If ever there was an Old Testament discourse wrapping God in the warm flesh of human parenthood, this is it—the supreme revelation of divine love in the Hebrew Scriptures. To compose it, Hosea had to overcome the angry disappointment of illegitimate children from his own wife; he had to cleanse from view the lascivious excesses of Canaanite fertility rites. Reaching into the depth of his own human compassion, he recognized God's presence as the source of such heroic love.

The opening line stresses that God loved the child before Israel knew how to respond (see 1 John 4:7-11). When Matthew sees the fulfillment of this line in Jesus' infancy, Hosea's prophecy enables us to recognize the passover mystery in Jesus: through the Red Sea, across the wilderness, toward new life (Matt 2:15). "Israel [as] my firstborn child" was already revealed to Moses (Exod 4:22-23); here it is reaffirmed with stronger personal bonds. The actions described in verses 3-4 are maternal; here we have one of the most striking feminine images of God in the Hebrew Scriptures. *"Healer"* is one of Hosea's persistent titles for Yahweh (see 5:13). **11:5 return to . . . Egypt:** The typology is evident here. Sin and slavery, even in Assyria, are considered a return to Egypt. According to the Hebrew verse 7 should read: "My people are in suspense about returning to *me*"; the second line of verse 7 is almost unintelligible in the Hebrew and is variously reconstructed.

In verses 8-11 God speaks ever more passionately, convulsing within by the contrasting demands for death as humanly required (Deut 21:18-21), and for forgiveness and another chance to be loved yet again (see 3:1) as divinely expected. In the Hebrew verse 8 begins with a strong phrase like "but on the contrary" (Gen 39:9; 44:34). Admah and Zeboiim are the names used in northern traditions, while southern traditions referred to Sodom and Gomorrah (Gen 19:28; Isa 1:9-10). Both sets of names occur in Deut 29:22. With verse 10 the pattern is broken; this verse refers to the Lord in the third person (otherwise in chapter 11 in the first person); the reference to roaring lions is typical of Amos, not of Hosea (Amos 1:2, 3:4, 8). This verse is usually considered a later addition from an anonymous but inspired source.

12:1-13:8 (RSV: 11:12-13:8) Typical of so much of prophecy, this section of Hosea (a) reverts to an ancient tradition, only to reverse the people's easygoing understanding of it; (b) makes an effective use of wordplay; (c) detects a new appreciation of the present situation; and (d) has undergone later revision and application.

The charge of "lies" and "deceit" against contemporary Ephraim in 12:1 is drawn from the ancient story of the patriarch Jacob, who lied to his blind and aged father Isaac in order to acquire the birthright (Gen 27), and again to his uncle Laban, whom he "hoodwinked by not telling him of his intended flight" (Gen 31:20) after Laban had deceived Jacob about the identity of his wife (Gen 29:23-25). While the traditions in Genesis absorbed these lies and deceit into the larger theology of God's mysterious providence, Hosea lifts them out to be seen for what they were—lies! Hosea states how he himself has been victimized by lies that "surround me."

Verse 1b about Judah is a later adaptation to the southern kingdom. The application to Judah continues in verse 3a. Here where the text reads "Israel" (correctly according to Hosea's original intent), the Hebrew text reads "Judah." In verse 3b Ephraim is clearly identified as a chip off the old block continuing to lie and deceive like his grandfather Jacob!

12:4-7 The references to Jacob are intensified: "In the womb he supplanted his brother" (Gen 25:26; 27:36); the word "supplant" (*'akab*) is the origin of Jacob's name. "He contended with God" refers to Jacob's wrestling with the angel at the river Jabbok, where God changed the patriarch's name to Israel (see Gen 32:23-33, especially verse 29, where we read: "You shall no longer be spoken of as Jacob, but as Israel, because you have contended with the divine"). The word *sarah* ("contend") contains the central consonants of the word "Israel." It was at Bethel that God appeared to Jacob atop the ladder on which divine messengers ascended and descended (Gen 28:13). Verse 6 is an addition adapting the passage for a liturgical setting, like Amos 4:13; 5:8-9; 9:6b. In verse 7 Hosea's deeply embedded optimism surfaces again.

12:8-13:8 These lines thrice modulate from difficulties to a divine intervention and back again to worse difficulties (12:8-12; 12:13-13:1; 13:2-8). **12:8 merchant:** The Hebrew word is also the proper name "Canaan"; from its origins Israel has been Canaanite—deceitful, covetous, and sensual. **12:9 fortune:** The Hebrew word is spelled almost the same as the words translated "man" in verse 4 and "falsehood" in verse 12. Ancestor Jacob, kindred Canaanites, present Ephraimites—all are marked by greed and deceit.

Verses 10-11 speak of a new beginning with the Exodus, new reformation with the prophets. "Gilead" is possibly a reference to the pact between Jacob and Laban (Gen 31:46-54), solemnized at Galeed (Gal + ed = "hill of witness"); it is very similar to "Gilgal," the site of an ancient sanctuary whose licentious style of worship now witnesses against Israel. **12:12 heaps of stones:** The phrase possibly recalls the stones of witness set up near Gilgal in Joshua's days (Josh 4). In verse 14 Moses is honored by the title of prophet (or is it vice versa?—see Num 12), yet in this section from 12:1 onward Jacob is criticized much more negatively than the traditions in Genesis.

The third poem in this subsection (13:2-8) again opens with the continuation of sin despite all warnings. For Hosea, the principal offense is idolatry and its sensual rites, prompting the scornful gibe "Men kiss calves," which refers to the golden calves that were considered pedestals for Yahweh at Bethel and Dan (see 8:5). Hosea contrasts Yahweh's shepherding of Israel in the wilderness (vv.

4-5) with the gluttonous banquets at the sanctuaries (v. 6). The divine shepherd turns into the bear or lion now attacking the flock (see Amos 3:12).

THE STING OF DEATH

Hos 13:9–14:1

This final preaching of Hosea begins as abruptly as the message is final: "Your destruction, O Israel!" **13:10 Where now is your king:** King Hoshea has been captured by the Assyrians, who are now proceeding southward toward Samaria to besiege and destroy the capital city and deport whatever population remains after war's fatalities and the Assyrian executions at the captured city gate. "That he may rescue you" is a cruel pun on the name of the last king, Hoshea; in Hebrew, *yoshiah* reads "rescue" or "save." **13:11 I give you a king . . . and I take him away:** There were four kings in the space of two years, 746–745: Jeroboam II, Zechariah, Shallum, and Menahem! Is there another sting of irony in the prophet's summoning the Canaanite god Death to condemn the Israelites for their fertility rites honoring the gods of death and life, Muth and Baal (v. 14)? Beyond a doubt, in Hosea's mind is the certainty of total destruction.

The compassion of chapter 11 is reversed unconditionally only to be reversed again by St. Paul, who combines the passage with Isa 25:8 and reads the words as a question that expects the answer "No!" (1 Cor 15:54-55). In his resurrection, Jesus Christ has overcome the sting and plague of death.

CONVERSION, HEALING, AND NEW LIFE

Hos 14:2-9

If this optimistic conclusion clashes with the absolute doom in the preceding section, such an upbeat ending is typical of prophecy. We noticed a similar finale to the Book of Amos. Whether it be the entire Bible or individual books, the beginning and the conclusion generally center on hope; in between is the superhuman struggle to sustain such ideals within the absorbing challenges of Planet Earth. As a matter of fact, Hosea has frequently hinted at the positive side of a strong faith in God as healer and savior underlying his negative, severe condemnations. He continually recognizes a redeeming quality in the worship of Israel, even in its fertility rites, for he makes abundant use of its themes and vocabulary. All the while he condemns the excesses so painfully experienced in his own marriage (5:15–6:7). Whether it is sin or virtue, each has immediate repercussions across the world of vegetation and livestock (2:20, 23-25; 4:3).

Either Hosea himself or a disciple drew upon earlier preaching to end the prophetic book, possibly at Jerusalem after the fall of Samaria (721 B.C.E.). The opening lines follow the style of a prophetic exhortation (vv. 2-3a) and a prayer composed by the prophet for the people (vv. 3b-4). The following verses (vv. 5-9) present God's reply. Each of the two sections—Hosea's preaching in verses 2-4 and God's response in verses 5-9—opens with a favorite word of Hosea, usually linked closely together: "return" and "heal" (5:13; 6:1; 7:1; 11:4-5). Physical healing depends upon moral conversion.

14:2 Lord, your God: Hosea does not speak about the nature of God from any philosophical background but from a personal experience and a liturgical memory of the Lord's intimate sharing in Israel's life (see the Introduction, p. 498).

14:3 render as offerings: The Hebrew text is somewhat disturbed. The prophet has suffered severely from the sexual aberrations at the sanctuaries on the part of his wife and others, but he still speaks positively of ritual and worship. These are the source of his hope in a God who called the people out of Egypt, taught them to walk, and formed a covenant of love with them in the wilderness (2:18-22; 11).

14:4 the orphan finds compassion: The immediate reference is Israel, yet we wonder if there is not also an allusion to Hosea's own second and third children, probably illegitimate (1:6, 8), whom he sees as fully his own, just as God accepts Israel (2:1-3, 24-25).

14:6 like the dew: Dew is a symbol of the divine gift of life. It appears without rain and is an important source of nourishment for vegetation during the long dry season in a land of cold nights and excessively warm days (see Judg 6:37-40; Pss 110:3; 133:3; Job 38:28). Verse 9 is like a divine soliloquy upon which we eavesdrop, as in 11:8-9.

CONCLUDING RECOMMENDATION

Hos 14:10

A scribal annotation—or perhaps a spontaneous exclamation in a public assembly—is attached to the book. As an accepted part of the Bible, the verse is truly inspired and comes from an anonymous inspired writer. It has the hallmark of the sapiential movement as witnessed to by Psalm 1. As the conclusion of Hosea's preaching, it reminds us that our response, too, is an integral part of the prophetical book of Hosea. The Bible remains incomplete without our listening and reflecting, our adapting and assenting within our life-setting today. Yet the Bible remains the basis and support of this reflection. It is our guide toward a conclusion; we must be true to its message and inspiration, in this case to Hosea.

As we look back over the fourteen chapters of the Book of Hosea, the concluding recommendation in 14:10 seems right at home. In his preaching, the prophet shows many other touches that relate to the sapiential movement: Hosea's high appreciation of the knowledge of the Lord (3:22; 4:1); the disciplinary role of suffering (5:9); the impact of good living across the earth (2:19-20; 4:3; 10:1). These are all important motifs in the books of Proverbs, Job, and Sirach, which are later books, of course, but representative of a movement that existed from the time of Solomon. Our adaptation to life today places us within a centuries-old tradition and shows the blending of many traditions in the Bible, traditions that include the patriarchal narratives, covenant laws, settlement in the land, scribes and wisdom, prophecy and its challenges, liturgy and its symbolic power to unite over the centuries.

MICAH

Carroll Stuhlmueller, C.P.

INTRODUCTION

Micah of Moresheth, especially when compared with Amos and Hosea, turns out to be an elusive prophet. Unlike the prophecy of Amos, the Book of Micah provides no visions about a personal call to be a prophet (see Amos 7:1-9; 8:1-3), nor any episode like Amos' tryst with the high priest Amaziah in defense of his divine summons (see Amos 7:10-17). Micah's preaching does not depend upon any highly charged emotional experience as was the case with Hosea and his tragic marriage with Gomer. The poor condition of the Hebrew text of Micah, moreover, and its successive re-editing over the centuries by a "school" of disciples cloak the prophet in a series of textual and editorial disguises. The frequent plays on words that intrigued and enticed his listeners, as they do modern students of his Hebrew style, wove its own puzzling web around the prophet from Moresheth. In this short introduction, therefore, we approach *the man* Micah gradually through an appreciation of the book, its literary style, and its major religious topics.

The Book of Micah

The book, as canonically accepted in its final form, is simple enough in its subdivisions, with its double sequence of threats and promises: chapters 1–3, a series of threats, and chapters 4–5, promises; 6:1–7:7, again threatening poems, followed by promises in 7:8-20. Our commonsense hunch says that Micah did not speak in such a neatly balanced way. If he had, the elders in Jer 26:18 would

never have quoted the menace of 3:12; it would have been canceled out at once by the glorious promise in 4:1-5.

The preaching of Micah was re-edited on several occasions: for instance, the final lines of 1:5 were redirected to Judah and Jerusalem; 2:12-13 come from the Babylonian Exile and announce a new ingathering in the Promised Land; 4:4-5 represent two different applications of the vision of the new Jerusalem where foreign nations gather in the holy temple (see commentary below).

The style of Micah

Micah's style as a preacher is being more and more appreciated. No longer is he put down as a country bumpkin, blushing easily and embarrassed in public. He displays an unusual directness. Who can match his condemnation of animal sacrifice at the cost of overlooking the hunger and sickness of the poor in 3:2-3? Stylistically we detect a shrewd and quick turn of phrase in his frequent plays on words (see the commentary on 1:10; 2:4, 6, 11; 4:14; 5:1). Micah kept his listeners guessing, smiling, and intrigued as he enticed them into a devastating conclusion.

Along with these general stylistic qualities, Micah also displays an unusual versatility. He moves easily among: lamentations (1:8-16); question-and-answer repartee (1:5; 2:7); Torah speech, summarizing the Lord's expectations (6:6-8); personal confessions of faith, introduced by "as for me" (3:8; 7:7); oracles of judgment (2:3; 5:10-15) and of promise

509

(4:1-4); a longer judgment speech, modeled upon legal procedures at the city gate (ch. 6).

The major topics of Micah's prophecy are to be distinguished according to the stage of preaching or editing already alluded to in this introduction. Before and during his preaching, Micah had witnessed severe, even wantonly cruel suffering on the part of the poor. Their land had been violated in order that the Jerusalem government might build defenses in such outposts as Moresheth overlooking the Mediterranean plains and then embark upon reckless military adventures. Several times, as we shall see, the dark and ominous cloud of the Assyrian army swept through the pass of Megiddo and down the coastal plain against Philistine cities or Egypt or Jerusalem, and earlier against the city of Samaria, whose three-year siege left the army time for savage entertainment and sadistic diversion in neighboring areas like Moresheth. Little wonder that Micah spoke with outrage against the social injustices and religious sham by which the administration at Jerusalem sought to distract the country from the dangers of war and the plight of the poor.

The "original" Micah leveled his criticism principally against religious and civil leaders for tolerating these excesses and then gaining financially from it all (see the commentary on 3:5-8). No hope was left when the defenders of religion and morality were themselves corrupted by pleasure and greed.

Micah's continuous interaction with temple and religious traditions, with social justice and civil leadership, points up a person with keen penetration into present reality and long roots into "ancient times" (5:1). Although he was oriented toward Jerusalem and the Davidic dynasty (4:14–5:4), he draws near at times to the style of the more northern traditions of Deuteronomy and is seriously concerned about the northern kingdom of Israel or Samaria (1:2-7; 6:16). He makes poignant use of the Exodus tradition in 6:1-5, again a more northern motif.

Micah's heirs kept his prophetic words closely in touch with the ever new "present reality," now the Babylonian Exile, a century and a half later. In fact, Babylon, the place of exile, is named in 4:10. One of the two closing psalms offers the discouraged people of postexilic times a prayer for rebuilding the walls of Jerusalem (7:11).

The person of Micah

From the background of the Book of Micah, we have already begun to appreciate his character and person. Micah hails from the village of Moresheth (1:1). This city is also considered in some way a dependent of the Philistine city of Gath. The phrase "Moresheth-gath" (1:14) means "property of Gath." Originally Gath belonged to the Philistine Pentapolis of Gath, Gaza, Ashkelon, Ekron, and Ashdod, all in the southwest coastlands. These cities passed in and out of the control of the Israelites and at this time contained a strong contingent of Israelites. It is not at all impossible that Moresheth was administered through Gath. Moresheth was about twenty miles southwest of Jerusalem, nestled in the foothills overlooking the Mediterranean.

Moresheth influenced the language of Micah. His was not the desert imagery of Amos nor even the strong agricultural or rural setting of Hosea, and certainly not the cosmopolitan sophistication of Isaiah. Micah refers to the fields owned by the villagers (2:2, 4-5), the threshing floors on the hillside (4:12). More attention is given to the greedy plans and rapacious actions of people who come from the larger Jerusalem and who, in the comfort of their rented homes at Moresheth, covet and cheat (6:11) and take possession of whatever they desire (2:1-2; 6:9-11). They take over fields because of unpaid debts (2:2, 4). They strip off the mantle of debtors, which the law prescribed always to be returned at sundown (2:8).

The question is raised whether or not Micah belonged to the class of elders at Moresheth, for it was a group of "elders of the land" who recalled his words in Jer 26:17-18. In this case he would have been one of the judges at the city gate (Deut 17:5; 21:19; Ruth 4:1), responsible as well for defending the rights of the small town against the royal officials from Jerusalem. Another suggestion links Micah with "the people of the land," a group who reached back to the early days of David and always remained loyal to the ancient family. They were suspicious of others who manipulated the throne and its power for their own benefit (2 Kgs 11:18-20; 14:21; 21:24). Micah does not oppose the dynasty but wants to see it restored to its pristine purity and purpose, as when he sees its future no longer in Jerusalem but in ancient Bethlehem (Mic 4:14–5:4).

Micah and Isaiah

Both Micah and his contemporary Isaiah interacted vigorously with the Davidic dynasty but with a number of differences. While Isaiah's interests remained with the capital city of Jerusalem (Isa 1; 2:1-5; 4:2-6; 8:5-10), Micah's sympathies gravitated toward Bethlehem. Isaiah was the aristocrat, firmly attached to Jerusalem and its temple, a brilliant poet, a politician with international perspective; Micah was a countryman, less suave, brutal at times in his language, a poor person suffering with the poor rather than a wealthy person defending their rights. Sin for Isaiah turned out to be the sacrilegious act of polluting the temple (Isa 4:4); for Micah it was the callousness of stripping a man of his mantle and driving "the women of my people . . . from their pleasant homes" (Mic 2:8-9). Isaiah was the herald of a faith that demanded respect for the mysterious holiness of Yahweh; Micah was the prophet of divine justice for the inviolable rights of the poor.

Micah and Isaiah were contemporaries. It seems, however, that Isaiah began the prophetic ministry earlier, for he interacted vigorously with the king's policies at the time of the Syro-Ephraimite crisis (735–732 B.C.E.). Syria (or Damascus) and Ephraim (or Israel) had formed a coalition against Assyria; they marched against Judah when its King Ahaz refused to join (Isa 7:1-2; 22:1-14). Micah does not seem to allude to it. King Ahaz's pro-Assyrian policy was reversed into active revolt by King Hezekiah, much to the dismay of Isaiah. The king's bad politics led to an invasion by Sennacherib around 701 B.C.E. In preparation for this invasion, King Hezekiah had taken over landed property in the foothills to the west of Jerusalem. Was it at this time that many of the people of Moresheth lost their property? In this case Hezekiah may go down in the annals of the books of Kings and Chronicles as a very pious reformer of idolatrous and insincere worship (2 Kgs 18–20; 2 Chr 29–32), yet he would have remained insensitive or blind to the many social injustices left unchecked in the midst of the feverish liturgical reform or later in the all-absorbing preparations for war.

We place Micah at the earliest around 727 B.C.E., certainly before the collapse of Samaria (721 B.C.E.); his ministry would have extended into 701, the time of Sennacherib's invasion of Judah.

COMMENTARY _____

INTRODUCTION

Mic 1:1-2

1:1 Historical introduction. As in the case of Amos, this book too begins with some historical orientation and then with a religious, melodic opening. The editor lists Micah as prophesying under three kings, from Jotham through the reign of Ahaz into the time of Hezekiah (742–696 B.C.E.). Because the book says little or nothing about the great crisis during the reign of Ahaz, we confine his ministry to the time of Hezekiah. The editor may be thinking of Micah's earlier activity as an elder defending the rights of the dispossessed before his preaching came to the attention of many others.

Clearly enough, Micah's ministry is linked with the flow of history, particularly that of his own time. The Bible points out that God does not create the ideal setting for redemptive activity; God accepts us as we are in our total environment. The prophet's word is the product of its own age. Eternal truths emerge from the prophets, not as generic predictions of the future but rather as ideals and hopes rising from the trials and triumphs of the moment. The editor refers to "the vision he [Micah] received." Prophets peered beneath the surface to the ancient covenant, its laws and hopes, and to the merciful God who made Israel a special people. From this perspective came forth ideals and expectations for the present into the future.

1:2 Religious introduction. This verse seems to have been added somewhat late. It has all the marks of non-Mican authorship: Yahweh as accuser-witness is not found until Mal 3:5, in the postexilic age; "holy temple" is an expression not normally used at this time; "peoples, all of you" is a phrase from later literature like Lam 1:18; Ps 67:4, 6; and the use of 'adonai or "Lord" as a title for Yahweh does not occur again in the Book of Micah. Other aspects of this opening verse link it with other familiar introductions, such as the canticle of Moses in Deut 32:1 and the prophecy of Isaiah in Isa 1:2. The later editor is adapting Micah's book to a common style. While these pieces of biblical literature are directed rather exclusively to Israel, this open-

ing or formal prelude has a universal ring ("O peoples . . . O earth") and touches everyone with faith in God, regardless of religious differences. **all that fills you:** This refers to the abundant gift of life across the earth, vegetation, animals, birds, fishes, and humanity. **his holy temple:** See the commentary on 1:3-4, below.

THREATS AGAINST SAMARIA AND JUDAH

Mic 1:3–3:12

The principal sermons of Micah against social injustices are gathered in this initial collection. The opening poem rivals some of the best in Isaiah. It comprises a theophany introducing Yahweh the Judge (vv. 3-4); presentation of the evidence (v. 5) and sentencing of the culprit (vv. 6-7); after these judicial procedures, mostly related to the final years of Samaria, a long lamentation is added as the same fate strikes Judah in the Assyrian invasion under Sennacherib in 701 B.C.E. (vv. 8-16).

1:3-4 Micah begins the trial of defendant Israel with a solemn entry of the divine Judge; the language here is that of a theophany (meaning "God's manifestation"). We are reminded of the fragments of hymns in Amos about Yahweh forming the mountains, declaring to people their inmost thoughts, and treading upon the heights of the earth (Amos 4:13; also 5:8-9; 9:5-6). Although the passage infers Yahweh's presence in earthly sanctuaries, the primary residence or throne is located above the waters of the heavens, as any number of biblical passages indicate (see Pss 11:4; 19:2; 29:9; Hos 5:15; Isa 29:21). The trembling and even the melting and collapsing of the earth at the touch of the Lord's presence are literary devices for inculcating the Lord's awesome wonder, mighty power, and transforming force upon human life, as declared at Mount Sinai (Exod 19), at the crossing of the Red Sea and the Jordan River (Psalm 114), at Israel's wandering through the wilderness (Ps 68:8-11), at Yahweh's response to the king (Ps 18:8-20).

1:5 Crimes especially of ritual immorality are brought against the defendant, the northern kingdom of Israel, under the name of its ancestor Jacob. The nation's religious and civil leaders, as we saw also in the Book of Hosea, bear the brunt of the responsibility for tolerating and even encouraging such gross transgressions of Yahweh's holiness. **house of Judah . . . Jerusalem:** After the collapse of the northern kingdom, a later editor, applies the statement to the southerners. The verdict of "Guilty!" leads to the harsh sentencing of total destruction (vv. 6-7); for a similar outcome, see Amos 4:2b-3; Hos 4:3. **1:7 idols:** These include not only the golden calf at Dan and Bethel, originally the pedestal for Yahweh's invisible presence but superstitiously turned into an object of worship (see Hos 8:5; 13:2), but also the symbols of male and female deities of fertility (Hos 9:10-14). **wages:** The term refers to the "gifts" to the prostitutes in fertility rites, what Deut 23:19 calls "a harlot's fee or a dog's price" (also Hos 2:11, 14; 9:1). **shall they return:** What the Assyrian soldiers looted from Israel's temples will be returned to Assyrian sanctuaries as favors for their own sacred prostitutes.

1:8-9 This lament is prompted by the agony experienced by Micah's own country of Judah, which has imitated the sin of Samaria and must therefore suffer the same punishment. Several serious theological issues emerge here:

1) Must God inflict such horrendous pain as a military invasion with plunder, rape, fire, and deportation? While there is no satisfactory answer for what remains a mystery of faith, there are several "fixed spikes" (Eccl 12:11) on which to hang our reflections. Military invasion as "evil [that] has come down from the Lord" (Mic 1:12) results from God's willingness to work out our salvation in the midst of human history. Here God's presence can function quietly within our slow process of reasoning and decision-making, but it can also function within other, more violent forms of human reaction. Secondly, when the reward from God is superhuman, even though accomplished on a human level, the struggle turns out superhuman as well, as we recognize in the cross of Jesus.

2) Another theological issue centers on Micah's participation, already by premonition, in the savage outcome of military invasion: "I go barefoot and naked" (v. 8; see Amos 2:16; 3:12). He imitates the action of the prophet of Jerusalem who around 713 B.C.E. went about "walking naked and barefoot . . . as a sign" (Isa 20:2-3). Why must the innocent suffer? Why must the wicked suffer, as Habakkuk will ask (1:13), when they are still "more just" than their conqueror? The presence of the innocent—in this case a prophet like Micah and the small villages in the way of the Assyrian army—provides the only hope for arriving at peace and human dignity as God wants.

1:10-16 In naming the cities leveled by Sennacherib on his way to Jerusalem in 701 B.C.E. Micah chooses small ones, for the most part clustered around his own village of Moresheth; some are not mentioned elsewhere in the Bible, not even in the listing of cities "in the foothills" (Josh 15:22-47). Often he announces the sorrow to be inflicted on the city by a play on words. Every Hebrew word has a meaning. At times the text has been tampered with and at other times poorly preserved.

1:10 publish it not in Gath: These words were taken from 2 Sam 1:20, part of David's dirge over Jonathan, where he mentions Philistine cities in the area of Moresheth. In Hebrew, "publish" begins with the word "Gath" spelled backward. **weep not at all:** This probably ought to read "weep not at Ko," so that the phrase "at Ko" *(bako)* relates to the Hebrew word for "weep," *bakah*. **In Beth-leaphrah roll in the dust:** the word *aphrah* in the name of the village signifies "dust"; *beth* means "house." The phrase might be read: "In the house of dust roll in the dust." The word for "roll" in Hebrew contains sounds similar to the Hebrew word for "house" and for "Philistine."

1:13 Harness steeds to the chariots, O inhabitants of Lachish: Not only do the words "chariots" and "Lachish" sound alike in Hebrew, but the entire line has a continual interchange of the letters.

1:14 Give parting gifts to Moresheth-gath: Because Moresheth, as already mentioned, denotes gift (received) or dowry, the play on words implies, "Give a gift to the gift of Gath."

2:1-5 Micah loved the pleasant fields of the Shephelah, the name given to the rolling, falling hills between the central mountain range and the Mediterranean coastland (in Hebrew *shephal* means "to fall"). Micah mourned, even cursed their loss. By contrast,

Amos never felt the same attachment to the fierce silence of the desert that Micah did to the Shephelah. Micah detests the way in which the fields were coveted at night and seized in the morning. People were not even ashamed of carrying out their evil dreams in open daylight.

The sacrilegious nature of the action becomes clear from such texts as Lev 25:23-24, in which God declares that "the land shall not be sold in perpetuity; for the land is mine, and you are but aliens who have become my tenants. Therefore . . . [every jubilee year] you must permit the land to be redeemed." Wealthy landowners, perhaps from the powerful city of Jerusalem, confiscated whatever they wished for it "lies within their power," words found identically in a long series of texts: Gen 31:29; Deut 28:32; Neh 5:5; Prov 3:27. The problem existed a long time and was always detestable to the Lord. **2:3 from which you shall not withdraw your neck:** The first words are an alliteration in Hebrew. **2:5 you shall have no one** to redistribute the land to the rightful owner once the exile sets in.

From the literary viewpoint, these verses carefully complement each other: what the people carefully plan and quickly accomplish in verses 1-2, God just as quickly reverses in verses 3-5.

2:6-11 Ancient and modern translators come up with different versions and interpretations. Is verse 6 ridiculing or affirming Micah? Is verse 10a spoken by the greedy despoilers ordering the poor from their ancestral land, or is it a command from foreign soldiers to depart for exile? Yet we may be able to detect a balanced structure: verses 6-7, an accusation against Micah and God, with a short reply from God; verses 8-11, spoken by Micah, recounting the people's sins (vv. 8-9), their punishment (v. 10), and finally a repetition of the accusation against Micah, now turned against the people (v. 11).

2:6 preach: The Hebrew verb can be taken in a derogatory sense suggesting saliva dripping out of the mouth of a prophet stirred into a rabid, ecstatic spasm (consider 1 Sam 10:10-12 and 19:22-24; 1 Kgs 18; Acts 2:13). The people consider themselves pious sanctuary-goers, so how can "the Lord be short of patience" (v. 7a)? God quickly replies that divine words promise good things only

to those who act uprightly (v. 7b). Verses 8-9 are an eloquent condemnation of those who keep what the law clearly stipulates is to be returned to the poor man at sundown lest he contract intestinal colds (see Amos 2:8). Women and children are deprived of their inalienable honor and their right to the land. The culprits are ordered into exile because of their cruelty and greed. **2:10 rest:** The word may refer to their once happy and peaceful lodging in the land (Ps 95:11; Deut 12:19). **2:11 futile claim:** The phrase can be translated more literally, as in the Revised Standard Version, as "wind and lies." The people's mockery of Micah during their drunken revelry in the sanctuary (see Amos 2:8) ricochets upon themselves.

2:12-13 This passage is generally considered an exilic or postexilic addition, a minor upbeat note in the midst of Micah's condemnations. Verse 12 refers to the gathering of Israel safely within the sheepfold; verse 13 to Israel's breaking loose into a new freedom toward the Promised Land. In this case the king is Yahweh. According to another explanation, the verses are spoken by the false prophets of verse 11, who make use of liturgical language to reassure Jerusalem that all is well. Verse 11 attributes these false hopes to the euphoric effects of strong drink. Verses 12-13 present a liturgical procession with the solemn opening of the gates of city and temple as the ark is carried through the city back again into the holy of holies (see Psalm 24). A third possibility remains, namely, accepting both interpretations according to different periods when Micah is being read.

Chapter 3 counters the greed of Israel's leaders with some of the most violent language in prophecy. Living during the Assyrian epoch of international history, Micah and his neighbors in the villages of the Shephelah will experience the atrocious cruelty of the Assyrian army. Again the question is raised about Yahweh's interaction in history (see 1:8-9). The chapter is carefully structured: verses 1-4, against civil rulers in the northern kingdom of Israel (spoken between 727 and 721 B.C.E.); verses 5-8, against prophets, seemingly closer at hand in Judah of the southern kingdom; verses 9-12, a conclusion that condemns all categories of leadership but focuses upon Jerusalem and its impending destruction. The literary device of "inclusion" (repetition of key words) binds together verse 1 and verse 9, so that verse 9 and the following three verses bring the poem to a strong ending. They apply emphatically to Jerusalem what verses 1-4 had been directing toward the northern kingdom of Israel, an area that now lay in ruins with its population in exile.

3:1-4 These words are addressed to the "leaders of Jacob . . . the house of Israel." The opening phrase, "And I said," denotes an emphatic reversal—"But on the contrary I say!" This fact endorses the second of the interpretations for 2:12-13 (see above). The word "rulers" shows up in Isa 1:10; 3:6, 7; 22:3 for other incapable and venal leaders.

3:2b-3 The language is graphic, even crude, drawn from the action of preparing an animal for ritual sacrifice (see Lev 1:3-9). In a milder form it appears in Pss 14:4; 53:5, and with agonizing moan in Ps 79:1-4. **3:4 cry to the Lord:** In the Bible civil leaders are responsible both to God and to those they govern (Rom 13:1). These leaders, however, deliberately use their divine origin as a club over the people. **hide his face:** The phrase is repeated in Ps 10:11 by wicked rulers as an excuse to proceed in their wickedness; and in Ps 13:2 by persecuted people appealing to God to make the divine presence felt. Micah invokes the phrase as punishment upon the evil rulers.

3:5-8 Micah is not condemning all divination, only that directed by greed, which included most of it in his day. Again the language is graphic and eloquent: feed them well and they declare *shalom*; fail to be generous to their rapacious appetite and (literally) "they sanctify a war against that one." As in Jer 6:4 and Joel 4:8, the word "holy" or "sanctify" occurs, stirring the whole discussion of what is called a "holy war," well known in the history of religions. **3:7 cover their lips:** This is a sign of mourning (Ezek 24:17-22) and of being contagiously unclean (Lev 13:45). Verse 8 provides the purpose of Micah's ministry and clearly states its credentials. **with the spirit of the Lord:** This translation may not be the best. The Hebrew word for "spirit" was used by Micah in a pejorative sense in 2:11, "wind and lies." The Hebrew word can mean both "wind" and "spirit." Micah was completely disillusioned by the sensual, greedy prophets, who were driven by "wind" (see 1 Sam 10:10-13; 19:22-24).

3:9-12 A conclusion in verse 9 repeats key ideas of verse 1; verse 10 relates to the bloodshed in verses 2-3. Verse 11 condemns all leaders with the single charge of greed, yet they have the audacity to claim that God is on their side as they repeat sacred language found also in Amos 5:14 and Isa 7:14. Verse 12 will be cited by the elders of the land in Jer 26:16-19 to protect Jeremiah from being put to death for declaring that Jerusalem can be destroyed "like Shiloh." Shiloh once housed the ark of the covenant and had been the center of Mosaic religion (1 Sam 1-3), yet it was destroyed by the Philistines who captured the ark (1 Sam 4). Micah is said to have spoken these words "in the days of Hezekiah" (Jer 26:18), a king zealous for the reform of the liturgy (2 Kgs 18-20; 2 Chr 29-32) but evidently blind to other abuses against the poor. Because of Hezekiah's piety, the leaders claimed "the Lord in the midst of us" (Mic 3:11).

As we reflect on chapters 2-3, we ponder the cost in human misery because of greed and sensuality in leadership, first driving the people from their pleasant houses (2:9), finally reducing Jerusalem to rubble (3:12).

GATHERING OF THE POOR
AND THE OUTCASTS

Mic 4:1–5:14

During the time of the Babylonian Exile, the material in chapters 4-5 was gathered from a reservoir or treasury of prophetic material, some from the prophet Micah, some attracted to the Micah texts by association of words or themes. The purpose of the editor seems clear enough by comparing 3:12 and its view of Jerusalem "reduced to rubble" with 4:1 and its vision of Jerusalem to which "peoples shall stream." The violent devastation of chapters 1-3 is reversed in a peaceful reconstruction. Although familiar historical names like Assyria and Babylon (4:10; 5:4), Jerusalem and Bethlehem (4:2; 5:1) reappear, they also seem to merge with other legendary names like Nimrod (5:5), are caught up in idyllic vision (4:1-3), or else are placed in perplexing parallel, like Bat-gader and Bethlehem (4:14; 5:1). Enough of Micah's style is preserved to ground us in his legitimate school of prophecy, yet too much of the visionary or symbolic is spread through the chapters for us not to strain our eyes beyond Micah's time into the "messianic" future.

Perhaps Israel's liturgical tradition is the most responsible agent for this blending of antiquity with the messianic future. Liturgy has a knack of extracting the best from historical reality, separating it from its political and military context, and highlighting God's concern—in this case, to create a new Jerusalem. This process was already at work in such pre-exilic psalms as Psalms 46–48, and it reaches sublime prophetic expression in Isa 65:17–66:24. As we will see below, the association of the Isaiah tradition suffused a new hope and grandeur about the text of Micah.

4:1-5 A number of oracles from a large prophetic repertoire reappear here. It is difficult to know who is the author, but it is certainly not Micah, for the passage would have neutralized his angry condemnation of Jerusalem in 3:12. Lines reappear in Isa 2:2-4, Zech 3:10; 1 Kgs 5:5; Joel 4:10, never with exactly the same meaning.

4:1 In days to come: The Greek text and the Aramaic Targum make it read: "at the end of days," that is, in the messianic age. **higher than the mountains:** This is to be understood only religiously, for even the Mount of Olives, just to the east, reaches a higher altitude than Jerusalem. A similar idea occurs in Pss 68:16-19; 89:13; Isa 60:1-3; 66:23. These texts already hint at the universal outreach of verse 2: "many nations . . . shall come and . . . climb the mount of the Lord." A lovely counterpoint is perceived here: while nations stream up the mount, instruction flows down and goes forth.

4:3 He shall judge: The subject is not clear, but it is probably Yahweh. Joel 4:10 quotes from this vision, only to reverse it into a statement of war. Earlier, in Joel 4:1-2, the nations are assembled for judgment in the Valley of Jehoshaphat (the word means "Yahweh judges"). For this reason many Jews, Christians, and Muslims today want to be buried in this valley between Jerusalem and the Mount of Olives.

Verse 5 draws our eyes away from the glorious liturgy on the temple mount to the homey setting of each one's vine and fig tree—a warning against liturgical excesses! Verse 6 was added last, correcting what seemed to be the overenthusiastic "ecumenism" of verses 1-3. This text in Micah at least

leaves the pagans at peace with their paganism (see Deut 4:19-20; 29:25; 32:8-9 for a similar reaction). The conversion of the nations and their dignified and equal reunion with Israel waited for St. Paul to argue the case in the letter to the Romans (Rom 9–11).

4:6-8 Someone in the days of exile looks back upon "the former dominion" (v. 8)—either the days of Micah or better the kingdom of David and Solomon—and recognizes the Lord as King (notice the end of the Davidic dynasty) over the remnant of people who are lame, outcasts, and afflicted. This scene of Jerusalem is considerably different from that in 4:1-3. We recognize the influence, or at least the parallels, joining the passage to Isa 35:4-6, 10; 41:17, from the time of the Babylonian Exile or later. **Magdal-eder:** The name means "tower of the flock," and is another name for the temple as a home and refuge for the flock of Israel.

4:9-10 As it stands, this poem seems to reflect best of all the period of the Babylonian Exile. Even if the poem was further refined during the Exile, its original composition may reflect King Hezekiah's agreement with Babylon, through its representative Merodach-baladan, against Assyria; the prophet Isaiah had reacted strongly against the negotiations. The solution to Judah's troubles was closer to home in remedying its social injustices (see 2 Kgs 20:12-19, repeated in Isa 39). **Writhe in pain:** The language of childbirth implies that new life lies hidden beneath the suffering of the people. **the Lord redeem:** The Hebrew word for "redeem" implies a blood bond and its consequent obligations of family love (see Lev 25:23-55).

4:11-13 The language of harvesting is applied to Israel's victory over hostile nations. This short poem may have been composed, possibly by Micah, for a harvest festival. Yet Micah's more persistent attitude of repudiating a military solution in favor of internal moral reform points to another author. The poem was stitched in here by the reference to Israel's enemies at the end of verse 10.

4:14–5:5 The play on words in verse 14 makes it difficult to be certain of the text and of the historical circumstances; the setting is probably the time of the Assyrian siege of Jerusalem under Sennacherib in 701 (see 2 Kgs 18:13–19:37; Isa 36–37). Theologically Micah and Isaiah realize the hopelessness of the current Davidic kings; even pious King Hezekiah proved ineffective in stemming the country's immorality but sought a military solution by revolting against Assyria. Both prophets begin to look to a *future* Davidic king. For his part, Micah indicates this by shifting attention from strong, cosmopolitan, and permissively immoral Jerusalem to small, honest, and God-fearing Bethlehem, where the prophet Samuel went to choose a king (1 Sam 16:1-13). The Lord's favor rested on young David.

4:14 The Hebrew word for "fence yourself in" is the same as *gader* in *Bat-gader;* the word for "rod" sounds very much like that for "ruler." *Bat-gader* harmonizes with *Bethlehem.*

5:1 Ephrathah: This is a place-name for a spot north of Jerusalem near Ramah where Rachel died (1 Sam 10:2; Jer 31:15); it is also the name of a clan, descendants of Ephrathah, the second wife of Caleb (see 1 Chr 2:18-19, 50-55, where reference is made to people called Bethgader and Bethlehem). These people settled around Bethlehem, south of Jerusalem, and also at Jaar, or Kiriath-jearim, west of Jerusalem (Ps 132:6). Later tradition confusedly located Rachel's tomb near Bethlehem (Gen 35:19; Ruth 4:11), where it is venerated today as a popular Israeli shrine. **whose origin is from of old, from ancient times:** The Hebrew text uses the plural, "origins," referring to the long, three-hundred year history of the Davidic dynasty with its accumulated promises and hopes; "ancient" does not necessarily mean eternal, but far away in the very distant past or future (see the final verse in the Book of Micah; also Isa 51:9).

5:2 she who is to give birth: Similar to Isaiah (7:14), Micah highlights the mother of the future Davidic king; in Old Testament times the queen-mother occupied an important place at court (1 Kgs 1:11-37; 2 Kgs 10:13). The silence about the father in this verse is interpreted by early Christian writers as an indication of the virginal conception of the promised Messiah. Verse 3 reflects the aura of mystery and promises surrounding the Davidic dynasty, as in Psalm 72.

5:4 he shall be peace: The New American Bible and the Revised Standard Version connect this line with the preceding description of the new Davidic king from insignificant Bethlehem. The Hebrew text joins the line with the following announcement of future shepherds and leaders whom God will raise up to deliver Israel from Assyrian domination. In this latter case a better translation would be: "this [plan] will be peace." Christian tradition certainly favors the former position. Nimrod, ancestor of Mesopotamian peoples (Gen 10:8-12), surrounds the text with mystery. **seven shepherds, eight men of royal rank:** Although rabbinical sources identify these persons, Micah is probably speaking symbolically, as Amos does in 1:3, 5.

5:6-8 Typically un-Micah in style and ideas, this military solution is from the time of the Exile. **remnant:** By now this is an important prophetical theme (see Amos 3:12, 5:15; Isa 7:3; 10:19-22). **Like dew coming:** The dew appears without rain, almost miraculously, a symbol of God's gift of life (Pss 110:3 [Hebrew text]; 133:3; Job 38:28), mentioned in many blessings (Gen 27:28; Deut 32:2; Isa 45:8).

5:9-14 This section ends with vintage Micah, with the destruction of Israel's military forces (vv. 9-10) and idolatrous sanctuaries (vv. 11-13). The final verse, however, condemns "the nations," so that the final word in chapters 4–5 turns in Israel's favor. "Sacred pillars" and "sacred poles" (vv. 12-13) refer to stone pillars and wooden poles representing the male and female fertility deities (Exod 34:13; Deut 16:21-22).

NEW THREATS

Mic 6:1–7:7

The second major section of threats (6:1–7:7) and promises (7:8-20) repeats the sequence of the first. The threats occupy less space than in the first section, and the Hebrew text is even more disturbed; the promises come from the period of the Exile or still later. Memorable lines occur, to resonate again in the New Testament and in the liturgy.

6:1-8 As the Hebrew word for "plea" in verses 1-2 clearly denotes, these verses follow the sequence of a legal procedure: verses 1-2, summoning the court, particularly the witnesses, and naming the defendant; verses 3-5, cross-questioning the defendant; verses 6-7, the defendant's reply and final statement; verse 8, the judge's verdict—probation—as in Isa 1:16.

The appeal in verses 1-2 to the universe as the courtroom and to the mountains and the earth's foundations as star witnesses follows a biblical pattern already found in Mic 1:2 but also in Deut 32:1; Ps 50:1-6. In the questioning of verses 3-4, not only is there an appeal to the Lord's gracious deeds, but we also glimpse God's personal agony over Israel's apostasy. These lines inspired the *Improperia* sung during the veneration of the cross on Good Friday. The abrupt "Answer me!" puts a limit on God's patience. The text of verse 5 is defective.

Miriam, seldom alluded to in the Bible, is accorded honorable mention with Moses and Aaron. The story of King Balak's summoning of the seer Balaam to curse Israel and his act of blessing Israel instead, is told in Num 22-24. Shittim (the word means "acacia tree") was the final stage of the journey from Egypt to the eastern bank of the Jordan River (Num 33:49); Gilgal was the famous sanctuary on the western banks near Jericho (Amos 4:4). This entire history from the Exodus out of Egypt to the settlement in the Promised Land is encapsulated as "the just deeds of the Lord," that is, God's complete or just fulfillment of every promise (see Josh 23:14).

6:7-8 The people seek shelter in feverish ritual actions as in Hos 6:1-7; 7:8; they even sacrifice their first-born, as was done by King Ahaz (2 Kgs 16:3) and King Manasseh (2 Kgs 21:6). They ritually slaughter their own children, imagining to appease God against their oppression of the poor. God's verdict, nonetheless, allows a second chance: "to do the right," as stipulated in the laws of the covenant; "to love goodness" according to bonds attaching them to one another and to Yahweh in the covenant; and "to walk humbly" by realizing that God's compassion is their only hope. This advice is addressed to "you . . . O man"; the Hebrew word *'adam* includes men and women in a very generic sense, reaching outward to all humankind as in Gen 1-3.

6:9-16 The trial scene continues. In verses 9-12 Israel's crimes of greed and injustice are made public (see 2:1-3; 3:11). Verses 13-16 pronounce sentence against the defendant. Yet, because of the poor condition of the Hebrew text, we cannot be sure. Notice how the New American Bible juggles the verses to make better sense! The statements can easily

be from Micah, assembled here somewhat freely as though for an appendix (see Amos 9:7-10). **6:9 cries to the city:** Without doubt the city is Jerusalem. **6:10-11 criminal hoarding . . . meager ephah . . . criminal balances . . . false weights:** The repetition is devastating—how low the wealthy stoop in swindling the poor and illiterate! As a result, they themselves and the entire country are completely out of balance, their delicate bonding with the Lord is upset, and their family life is torn apart (see Mic 7:5-6). **6:13 I will begin to strike you:** Here the New American Bible follows the ancient versions of the Greek and Syriac by slightly modifying the Hebrew from *halah* ("to become sick") to *halal* ("to begin"). The Hebrew reveals God's anguish (as in 6:3 and especially in Hos 11:8-9): "On the contrary *it is I myself*, sickened [by the fact that I] must strike you with devastation . . . ." **6:14 food that will leave you empty:** The meaning is not clear; it is possibly a reference to dysentery, weakness, and shame. Verse 16 is addressed directly to the northern kingdom, where Omri achieved fame by building the new capital city of Samaria (1 Kgs 16:23-28) and Ahab by defeating Damascus (1 Kgs 20), yet both were condemned for their religious indifference and social injustice. In this case verses 9-16 represent the early preaching of Micah; or else Micah applies to Jerusalem, at a later date, the lesson of the northern kingdom, whose magnificence collapsed into ruins as a "reproach of the nations."

7:1-7 This lamentation finds Micah sharing the sorrowful destruction of his own people, caused by their interior disintegration, yet in the end he says, "I look to the Lord" (v. 7). Again the Hebrew text is plagued by less than careful transmission. With a touch of pathos, Micah identifies with the vineyard far more completely and personally than Isaiah in Isa 5:1-5. This section about deception and betrayal in family and nation begins with "Alas!" in verse 1 and with "the faithful" in verse 2, the latter word denoting the blood bond and its normal obligations (see Hos 2:21-22). This passage may have influenced Jesus' cursing the fig tree that failed to provide fruit (Mark 11:12-14) and his statement about division in marriage and family (Matt 10:34-37; Luke 12:52-53). The selfish destroy themselves from within.

REBUILDING FROM ANCIENT PROMISES

Mic 7:8-20

Like other prophetical books, Micah's ends happily. In the final verse Micah reaches into the earliest traditions about the patriarchs to assure us of God's faithfulness in the future. A series of allusions to the time of the Exile help establish the date: a final collapse in darkness (v. 8); admission of guilt in experiencing the wrath of God (v. 9); wishing shame upon the enemy (v. 10); the walls of Jerusalem are still in ruins (v. 11). Verses 11-13 were added in the early postexilic Judah, but before the rebuilding of the walls by Nehemiah in 445 B.C.E. (Neh 2:17-20; 6:15).

7:8-10 An address by Jerusalem, possibly against Edom, which plundered the city, or what was left of it, after its destruction by the Babylonians in 587 B.C.E. Hatred rose to white heat against Edom, as we observe in Isa 63:1-6 and in the entire Book of Obadiah. "Fallen, I will arise" overturns the dire statements of Amos 5:12 over the "house of Israel . . . fallen, to rise no more"; "in darkness, the Lord is my light" reverses Amos 5:18: "day of the Lord . . . darkness and not light." Verse 10 is a filigree of customary formulas: "cover with shame" (Pss 35:26; 44:16; 89:46); "Where is the Lord?" (Pss 42:4, 11; 79:10; Joel 2:17); "trampled underfoot" (Isa 5:5; 7:25; 28:18). When we are numbed by pain and despair, we can only fall back upon customary or memorized prayers in order to discover thereby a new hope from the faith of our ancestors.

7:11-13 Now that the empire of David and Solomon is only a memory, hope transforms it into a new universal kingdom, to be achieved by God's mysterious power "from sea to sea." When the theology and legal system of postexilic Israel tended to become ever more narrow and exclusive, the liturgy drew upon memories to dream what God will do and so prepared for the universal apostolate of Christianity. Verse 12 is an allusion to the theme of the day of the Lord, derived from Amos as a time of overwhelming darkness for Israel (5:18) but in later tradition changed into a day of victory (Isa 11:10-11; 12). **they shall come:** The subject is left vague. Is it foreign countries coming to worship Yahweh? Or to pillage Jerusalem? Does "they" refer to the Diaspora Jews returning to Jerusalem from their homes in foreign countries? **7:13 land shall be a waste:** Possibly this is the devastated appearance of Yehud (or Judah) upon the first return (see Haggai).

7:14-17 This prayer of confidence asks God to bring back the idyllic days "when you came from the land of Egypt." Mount Carmel is to the west, Bashan and Gilead to the east (see Amos 4:1). Nations shall stand or collapse in awe and subjugation, with their hands over their mouths (Judg 18:19; Isa 51:15) or licking the dust (Gen 3:14). This is ecumenism or universalism at its worst!

7:18-20 The opening phrase, literally "Who is God like you," may have inspired the name of this book—Micah. Yet the phrase is somewhat elaborate compared to Micah's short name ("who is like" God). Verse 18 is possibly a renewal of the covenant (Exod 34:1-9). **7:20 faithfulness . . . and grace:** These words repeat the great virtues of the Mosaic covenant (see Hos 2:21-22; 4:1; Ps 89:2-3, 25, 34), which are seen to reach back to the patriarchs. Just as the mention of Miriam in 6:4 is rare in the Old Testament, the name of Abraham appears here in somewhat isolated splendor in the Hebrew Bible. Micah can look hopefully to the future because of his loyalty to tradition.

NAHUM

Carroll Stuhlmueller, C.P.

INTRODUCTION

Historical setting

Nahum, one of the most eloquent orators in the Bible, shouts, sings, and celebrates: "Nineveh is destroyed!," and he adds at once, with a play on his own name (Nahum means "the one consoled"): "Where can one find any to console her?" (3:7). For over three hundred years Assyria had controlled the Near Eastern world; the capital city had been Nineveh for over one hundred years (see the attention given to Nineveh in Gen 10:11-12). Assyria ruled by calculated terror and brutality (see the comments on Amos 2:16; 3:12), exacting heavy tribute, permitting no compromise nor repudiation of treaty, deporting entire populations, as in the case of the kingdom of Israel in 732 and 721 B.C.E., and moving new groups of people into the former territory. With clenched fist and fiery despair, people shouted at the silent skies: "How long, O Lord? Will you hide yourself forever?" (Ps 89:47), words still echoing in the New Testament: "How long will it be, O Master, . . . before you judge our cause and avenge our blood?" (Rev 6:10). Nahum's book is the Hallelujah chorus of triumphant relief. In his final verse he writes of Nineveh's destruction, "All who hear of this news of you clap their hands over you" (3:19). Details about the disintegration of Assyria are provided in the introduction to the Book of Zephaniah (p. 524).

Nineveh (in northern Iraq) was destroyed in 612 B.C.E. by a coalition of Babylonians (in southern Iraq) and Medes and Persians (in present-day Iran), with the help of smaller tribes. The leveling was so complete that when Xenophon passed by the site of Nineveh in 401 B.C.E., he was able to learn from the local inhabitants only that a great people had once occupied the site and had been destroyed (*Anabasis*, Bk. III, ch. IV, 10-12). Nahum composed this rhapsody of excitement and grandeur after 663 B.C.E., when Assyria captured and looted Egypt's sacred city of Thebes (see 3:8), probably after 627 B.C.E., when Babylon successfully revolted and achieved independence, but before the fall of Nineveh in 612 B.C.E.

Nahum writes so vividly that some claim that his native city of Elkosh was near Nineveh (where the Iraqi locate it today), but everyone even in far-off Judah knew about Nineveh, a city of 1800 acres with a population possibly as high as 288,000. A double line of fortifications lay to its east, the Tigris River to its west. The city had a circumference of eight miles, with moats sometimes 150 feet broad and colossal walls, some of whose ruins rise 25 to 60 feet above the surface today. While its armies cannibalized the world, its rulers patronized the arts. Ashurbanipal collected the "ancient classics," which provide entry for us today into the myths, folklore, religion, and legal systems of the area.

Style and theology

Nahum not only writes as an eyewitness of the destruction, but he also pretends to be inside the city in its last hours. In chapter 2 his sound pictures boom, with a two-beat cadence for alarm, a four-beat for marching, and a five-beat for wailing. His rhythm rumbles and rolls, leaps and flashes, like the horsemen and chariots in his poetry. If Nahum had written more, he would surpass Isaiah as the poet laureate of the Hebrew Bible.

His theology is focused upon one consuming topic: God does not tolerate injustice forever! Nahum draws upon the vocabulary of the "holy war," as it is called in Mic 3:5; Jer 6:4; Joel 4:9. Here the traditional oracle against the nations (see Isa 13–23; Jer 46–51; Ezek 25–32; Amos 1:3–2:16), always an exceptionally brilliant piece of writing, reaches white heat.

The book is subdivided as follows: 1:1, introduction; 1:2–2:1 (RSV, 1:2-15), hymn to Yahweh; 2:2-14 (RSV, 2:1-13), siege and capture of Nineveh; chapter 3, funereal epitaph.

COMMENTARY

INTRODUCTION

Nah 1:1

1:1 Unique among the prophets, Nahum's work is called a "book." Typical of other prophetical writings, his work is also designated a "vision" (Amos 7:12; Hab 1:1; Isa 1:1; 2:1; especially 13:1), stressing a unique revelation. Elkosh is a city some twenty miles southwest of Jerusalem.

HYMN TO YAHWEH

Nah 1:2–2:3

This section is textually disturbed; many translations, including the New American Bible, revise the order of verses, generally to systematize the persons addressed as "you" in 1:9–2:1; others seek to reconstruct better the alphabetic or acrostic poem at the beginning. Keeping verses 2-11 together (the New American Bible does not), we are able to arrive at an alphabetic sequence for most of the lines, including *mem* (the letter "M"), in which case the author stopped short of *nun* (the letter "N"), which would stand for Nineveh, a city not to exist any longer.

1:2-3a These verses draw principally upon Exod 34. While this chapter stresses the Lord's compassion, Nahum underlines the other theme, also present in a more muted way in Exod 34—the Lord's jealous revenge upon evildoers. Three times Nahum acclaims the Lord as "avenging"; the Hebrew for this word sounds almost like his own name. To be "jealous," in its etymological sense, means to love dearly and so to tolerate no rivals.

1:3b-8 The prophet refers to terrifying desert storms, particularly the fall sirocco. Nahum weaves into the picture the language of other storms in which Yahweh battles monstrous forces of evil, sometimes called by the names of pagan deities, as in Pss 74:13-14; 89:11-12; Isa 51:9-10. The names Bashan, Carmel, and Lebanon in verse 4 recall violent moments in nature (Amos 1:2; Ps 29:5) or moments of new peace (Mic 7:14; Ps 46). Just as the storm in Psalm 29 circles around the land of Israel to spend itself at Kadesh, Nahum allows a harbor of peace for Israel in verses 7-8.

1:9-2:3 Except for 2:2, these verses can be read more clearly by keeping in mind either the city Nineveh, addressed in verses 9, 10, 11, 14; 2:2, or the city of Jerusalem, described in verses 12-13 and 2:1; 2:3. This sophisticated procedure is forced upon us by the disturbed state of the Hebrew text. Verse 9 picks up the phrase "he . . . will make an end" from verse 8 and applies it specifically to Nineveh and adds a definitive end in verse 9c. In verse 11 "scoundrel" translates the Hebrew word *belial*, which comes from the root "to swallow" into the grave so that no descendants will be seen (v. 14; 2 Sam 22:5).

1:12 Speaking for the first time in his own name, the Lord assures Jerusalem, "I will humble you no more." Would that these words were true, for in 587 B.C.E. Jerusalem was not only to be humbled but even leveled to the ground by the Babylonians! Prophecy needs to be interpreted in its setting, at times according to the enthusiastic rhetoric of the speaker. In verse 13, again speaking to Jerusalem, Yahweh assures the city that the yoke of Assyria will finally be broken after more than a hundred years of oppression. Little wonder for the mighty relief, the prophetic eloquence, the angry jealousy.

2:1 This language will be taken up by Second Isaiah to announce the return from exile by "the bearer of good news" (Isa 40:9; 52:7). **Celebrate your feasts:** Some say the reference is the feast of Tabernacles, which later commemorated Yahweh as King and Creator at the new Jerusalem (Zech 14:16). Perhaps the interchange of speakers and addresses in this section may be explained by a ritual of blessing Judah and cursing the enemy, as we see in other biblical passages such as Num 22-24 and Joel 3-4. "The bearer of good news, announcing peace" in 2:1 ought to assuage our fear of ruthless warfare. The Hebrew for "bearer of good news" lies behind the Greek word for "gospel."

2:3 This verse foresees the restoration of the northern tribes, deported by Assyria in 733 and 721 B.C.E. Like Jer 31:1-22, it is one of the unfulfilled prophecies of the Hebrew Bible.

FALL OF NINEVEH

Nah 2:2, 4-14

These lines of attack (vv. 2, 4-6), conquest and looting (vv. 7-10), and mock lamentation (vv. 11-14) deserve first place in the hall of literary fame of biblical Hebrew. On a par with it are Ezekiel's extended image of shipwreck for the collapse of the seaport city of Tyre (Ezek 27) and Isaiah's hushed silence in Sheol as "Lucifer—the morning star" of Babylon enters "the recesses of the pit" (Isa 14:12-19).

2:2 After losing the battle in the approaches to the city, Nineveh girds itself for the fierce final assault. In quick succession and with abrupt commands the enemy sets up the battering rams and other machinery of war at key spots around the city; inside, the defenders are ordered to take their positions on the walls. For the importance of watchmen on the city walls, see 2 Sam 18:24-27 and Ezek 3:16-21; 33.

2:4-5 These verses describe by anticipation the presence of the enemy troops already within the city, or else the frenzied movement and countermovement within the city as parts of the city walls crumble under attack and

emergency signals are sounded hither and thither.

2:7-10 These verses describe the collapse and plundering of the city, one of the wealthiest in the world, filled with the loot of world resources. **The river gates are opened:** This may refer to the river Choser, which entered the city at its northeast corner. The Medes and Babylonians may have dammed its water to empty some of the moats around the city in preparation for the moment when the dam was opened and a deluge of water crashed against the walls, flooding the city. Its muddy waters buried the palace treasuries. **mistress . . . and her handmaids:** These words signify the statue of the goddess Ishtar, "queen" of Nineveh, and the priestesses who serviced her fertility rites.

2:11-14 Wailing and judgment. The Hebrew of the opening lines sounds like the wind howling at night through a graveyard. Verse 12 is a cruel question when its only answer is "Nowhere!" The "lion" Assyria, which plundered the world and tore the flesh of its victims and dragged them away from their homeland for its own selfish pleasure and well-being, is "consumed in smoke." The oracle of judgment in verse 14 is spoken in the name of "the Lord of hosts" who went into battle (Exod 15; Num 10:35; 1 Sam 4:4-6; Ps 24:7-10), through his lieutenants, Cyaxares, king of the Medes, and Nabopolassar, king of Babylon.

ASSYRIA IS DESTROYED! CLAP THE HANDS!

Nah 3:1-19

While reflecting upon the fate of Assyria, this chapter is taut with excitement. It erupts with anger, smirks with pent-up revenge, moves with unbelievable cruelty, and ends with a clap of victory over the dying victim. To express one's fury this artistically, each sound and word had to be carefully crafted. Psychologically, anger has a necessary role in our life; nationally and internationally we badly need a way to release desperation and hatred and to be healed of our torturing scars; spiritually we have the inspired prophecy of Nahum. While not the height of perfection nor the only step leading to this height, it may be a necessary step somewhere along the way.

At best, it is a warning that the "Assyria" of any age and place, or the brutal despot within each of us, will not be tolerated by God. If we combine Nahum with other prophecies like that of Hosea or Jeremiah, the Bible recognizes a disciplinary or purifying power in the suffering that even "Assyria" endures.

This final chapter can be divided as follows: the siege and capture are relived (3:1-3); the guilty are punished (3:4-17); victory is celebrated over the dying tyrant (3:18-19).

3:4 Woe! This is a form of speech already encountered in Amos 5:7, 18; 6:1. Witchcraft was punished by death (Deut 18:9-12; 1 Sam 28:8-25).

3:5-7 Assyria, whose divine patroness, Ishtar, governed war and fertility with cruelty and licentiousness, is treated as a harlot (see Hos 2:4-15; Isa 47:1-3); in Assyrian law, an adulteress, found guilty, was stripped and handed over to anyone's pleasure. **any to console?** reverses Nahum's name, which means "the one consoled." Nineveh is compared to cities like No-Amon (religious name for Thebes), over four hundred miles south of Cairo, and to peoples allied with Egypt, such as the Ethiopians, Put (Somalia?), and the Libyans, conquered by Ashurbanipal and now an example of what is happening to Assyria.

3:11-13 The punishment of war includes accepting a place in enemy brothels just to stay alive.

3:18-19 Instead of ending with a pall of silence over the dying victim, Nahum calls for a final, triumphant clap of hands!

ZEPHANIAH

Carroll Stuhlmueller, C.P.

INTRODUCTION

Historical setting

Zephaniah breaks the prophetic silence that hung over Judah since Isaiah and Micah disappeared toward the end of Hezekiah's reign (715–686 B.C.E.). Hezekiah's son, Manasseh, reversed what seemed to be the hopeless anti-Assyrian policy of his father. Hezekiah and Jerusalem may have survived, but the rest of the countryside had been devastated and the country's resources depleted. Manasseh even introduced fertility rites into the Jerusalem temple (2 Kgs 21:7); "he immolated his son by fire" (2 Kgs 21:6). Rabbinical tradition holds that Isaiah was martyred at this time. Zephaniah may have been the first to speak out against such "abominable practices" (2 Kgs 21:2), early in the reign of Manasseh's grandson, Josiah (640–609 B.C.E.).

Several factors prepared the way: first, a conversion experience late in life for Manasseh (2 Chr 33:12-13); second, a strong movement by the "people of the land," with whom Micah had been associated, to revive ancient loyalties and morality (see introduction to Micah, p. 510). This group rose up to suppress a palace revolt that had assassinated Manasseh's son Amon (2 Kgs 21:24); the "people of the land" not only placed a legitimate heir of the Davidic line on the throne, but they also surrounded him with advisers who would eventually undertake the great "Deuteronomic reform" in 621 B.C.E. (2 Kgs 22:3–23:30). Still another condition not only made possible the revival of prophecy but also provided a setting of cosmic upheaval for

Zephaniah's literary style, namely, the imminent collapse of the Assyrian Empire.

Even though the last great king of Assyria, Ashurbanipal (669–627 B.C.E.), had marched south into Egypt, captured its magnificent city Thebes, and profaned its most sacred temple in 663, the empire was heaving under symptoms of serious disease. Babylon revolted twice—the first time in 652, only to be cruelly brought back into line; the second time in 633, successfully. Coincidentally (?) King Josiah was publicly converted to the Lord in 633 B.C.E. In 629/28 Josiah began the purge of idolatrous worship across the land of Israel where Assyrian occupation forces were crumbling.

An eerie foreboding spread a mysterious suspense and a weird nostalgia over the Near East. The new twenty-sixth dynasty in Egypt revived many aspects of the age of pyramids, almost two thousand years earlier. Ashurbanipal had been gathering ancient documents at Nineveh and so made it possible for archeologists to recover them in the nineteenth and twentieth centuries A.D. Babylon began to use the Sumerian language in its official archives, thus reviving the initial dominant culture in southern Mesopotamia around 3000 B.C.E. Zephaniah's terrifying "day of the Lord" was a legitimate offspring of this world of colossal change, unbelievable upheavals, shifts of world power, dark clouds of war and destruction, and surprising rebirths from the ashes.

Zephaniah's announcement "A day of

wrath is that day" (1:15), through Jerome's Latin Vulgate translation, provided the script for the famous composition of Thomas of Celano, *Dies irae, dies illa* (ca. 1250 A.D.), formerly sung or recited at Roman Catholic funeral masses. Zephaniah called for silence as before a solemn ritual (1:7), as princes and even royalty were tried and found guilty (1:8-9), to be driven away like chaff (2:2). Zephaniah's way of handling offenses enabled prophecy to take its first steps toward the apocalyptic style, more evident in such writings as Ezek 38–39 and fully developed in Dan 7–12.

The historical background of Zephaniah's preaching is to be located in the early years of King Josiah (640–609 B.C.E.), before his vigorous "Deuteronomic" reform (621–609 B.C.E.). Scholars once associated Zephaniah with a so-called Scythian raid which, according to the ancient historian Herodotus, swept through the Assyrian empire down into Syria and Israel around 630 B.C.E. Yet there is no corroborating evidence, and the opinion is now generally discounted. Josiah inherited not only the social injustices that Micah denounced but also the open idolatry of Manasseh's reign. Much like the Deuteronomic reform, Zephaniah focused only upon false and sensual worship and paid little attention to social injustices. Unlike Amos, Zephaniah was not a spokesperson for the poor; and unlike Micah, he never belonged to their ranks. The opening verse makes him

a second cousin of King Josiah, and in 1:8 he speaks familiarly about "the king's sons." He was at home in Jerusalem (1:4, 10).

Style and structure

Stylistically, Zephaniah appears in a steady line of continuity with prophecy of the south. With Amos and Isaiah, he centers upon the remnant, the day of the Lord, sin and chastisement. Other phrases link him with Amos, for example "seek the Lord" (Amos 5:4-7, 14-15; Zeph 2:3) and the customary form of the curse (Amos 5:11; Zeph 1:13). There is scant evidence of stylistic elegance; the language is clear, correct, and sincere. We detect: little perception of the anguish of God, noticeable in Hosea and Micah (only Zeph 3:7a); no vignettes of the wealthy as in Amos, nor of the poor as in Micah; no echoes of the desert sounds that punctuate Amos' words, nor the agricultural landscape that adorns Hosea's preaching. Not even the sharp, bitter tones of satire are perceived here. Besides sincerity of heart and outrage over idolatry, Zephaniah manifests the booming sound of dissolution in the day of the Lord (see 1:14-16) and a courageous vigor to speak out even against royalty.

The plan of the book is what we will come to recognize as more and more typical of prophecy: oracles against Judah and Jerusalem (1:2–2:3); oracles against foreign nations (2:4-15); statement of hope or renewal (3:1-19).

COMMENTARY

INTRODUCTION

Zeph 1:1

Zephaniah's father is called Cushi, which is an Ethiopian name. Zephaniah refers to Ethiopians negatively in 2:12, but more positively in 3:10. While his father mixed African blood into Zephaniah's Israelite origins, his other ancestors reach back four generations to Hezekiah, very likely the king at Jerusalem. Zephaniah is the only prophet whose pedigree is recorded so extensively (normally only the father's name is provided), perhaps to offset the jealousy caused by his Ethiopian father. The name Zephaniah means "Yah(weh) protects or conceals" and was common enough (see Jer 21:11 and Zech 6:10-14).

SILENCE! THE FEARFUL DAY OF THE LORD

Zeph 1:2–2:3

This section can be subdivided for our better appreciation: a cosmic setting for the charges against Jerusalem (1:2-6); silence before the "liturgy" commences (1:7-13); the fearful day of the Lord (1:14-18); probation, perhaps, for the poor (2:1-3).

1:2-6 The opening verses direct our vista across the earth, as God sweeps away every sign of life; the story of creation in Gen 1–2 is told in reverse. Three times the Hebrew word for "sweep away" occurs, canceling out earlier promises expressed by this same word, as in Gen 8:21 after the great flood: "Never again *will I sweep away* the earth because of humankind." Zephaniah reneges on the benefits of the earth celebrated during the feast of Ingathering (Exod 23:16). Liturgy is no guarantee of happy results unless words and actions come from a sincere heart (see Hos 5:15–6:7).

Verses 4-6 explain why Yahweh, "a jealous God" (Exod 34:12-16), never tolerates what the same passage calls a "wanton worship" with sensual fertility rites and child sacrifice. **the very names of his priests:** The Hebrew text uses a rare word for "priests" (Hos 10:5; 2 Kgs 23:2), common in other Semitic languages; here it has the derogatory sense of "priestling." **host of heaven:** Assy-

rian deities (Jer 8:1-3; Ezek 8:16-18); **Milcom:** He was the god of the Ammonites, who inhabited Transjordan (1 Kgs 11:5); the Hebrew text refers to him under the name *malcom* ("their king"), poking ridicule at the king who tolerated such worship. Verses 5-6, particularly in the Hebrew, show how the people assuaged their conscience, for they also "adore the Lord"; these two-timers were long ago condemned by the prophet Elijah (1 Kgs 18:21).

1:7-13 This section opens with a call for silence in the final preparations for the liturgy of this "day of the Lord," once a time of light and joy, now a time of darkness and death (see Amos 5:18). The repetition of "day of the Lord" (vv. 7, 8, 9, 10) unites all other observations: "slaughter feast," not the animals for the sacred banquet but the inhabitants and worshipers; "foreign apparel" for the heathen ritual (2 Kgs 10:22); "leap over the threshold" superstitiously to avoid the demons there (1 Sam 5:5), yet acting deceitfully once inside the temple.

Different parts of Jerusalem are cited: "Fish Gate" (on the northwest—Neh 3:3); "New Quarter" (location uncertain); "hills" (reaching north, the area of any attack upon the city); "Mortar" (more to the south, at a "quarry," as the word means); "merchants" (or "Canaanites," if we keep the Hebrew word as a proper name), an area of Jerusalem for foreigners.

1:12 explore Jerusalem with a lamp: Like Diogenes in search of a single just person or of the wicked in their secret haunts of sin. **thicken on their lees:** Like undrawn wine, sweet and syrupy, such people are solicitous only for their bodily comfort. Verse 13 is from Amos 5:11 or from a repertoire of prophetic memories.

1:14-18 This *Dies irae* (see p. 525) receives its best commentary in the terrifying booming and rhythmic sound of the Hebrew words. One must listen to the Gregorian plainchant of the *Dies irae* to appreciate this plaintive but triumphant victory song of the grave.

2:1-3 Zephaniah recognizes a possibility— "perhaps" in verse 3—of shelter in the devastating day of the Lord for "the humble of the earth." Zephaniah inaugurates the long development of the theological meaning of humility, poverty, and lowliness as contained in the Hebrew word 'anawim. Some religious significance was already attached to the state of being economically poor or socially deprived (Prov 15:33; 18:12). Yet, Zephaniah recognizes these as the only ones to be saved. Military invaders executed the wealthy and powerful. During the Exile, Second Isaiah addresses all the people to be reassembled by God in their own land as poor and lowly (Isa 41:17). In the postexilic age, the promised savior is said to belong to the lowly (Zech 9:9). Still later some Jewish people deliberately embraced poverty as a godly way of life, as in the case of the Pharisees and also the covenanters along the Dead Sea (who were to produce the Dead Sea Scrolls). New Testament saints, like Mary, see in poverty an interior attitude of dependence upon God (Luke 1:48).

ORACLES AGAINST THE NATIONS

Zeph 2:4-15

For the meaning and scope of the oracles against the nations, see the commentary on Amos 1:3–2:16 (p. 489). While prompted more immediately by God's designs for punishing Israel, these sections signal God's control over foreign nations, a control that can eventually embrace their salvation. Zephaniah even states such a wild possibility at the end of verse 11 but seems to take it back in verse 15! Yet, even in verse 11 "ecumenism" is toward captured people (see Mic 7:16-17), different from the more open view in Mic 4:1-3 (yet, see Mic 4:4-5). The citation of nations moves from the western shore of Philistine territory to Moab and Ammon, east of the Jordan River and the Dead Sea, from south of Israel in Egypt, under the control of an Ethiopian dynasty (see 1:1), to the north, the route taken by Assyria to invade Israel.

AFTER REPENTANCE NEW HOPE

Zeph 3:1-20

Typical of Zephaniah's negative disposition, even the characteristically happy ending for prophecy starts with a renewed condemnation of leadership, civil and religious (vv. 1-5) and a reiteration of the destruction of the

nations (vv. 6-8). Salvation is promised only to the remnant of the lowly (vv. 9-13); two psalms of rejoicing close the prophecy (vv. 14-18a; 18b-20).

3:1-5 These verses resound with themes and even lines heard elsewhere in prophecy. Verse 2a is found again in Jer 7:28; verse 4b, in Ezek 22:26. Condemnation of leaders, civil and religious, in quick succession was already heard in Mic 3:11 (see Jer 2:26). The object of this *Woe!* is Jerusalem. According to the Hebrew word in verse 2, the suffering is said to be disciplinary and corrective (see Isa 53:5). Verse 5 begins emphatically with "The Lord within her is just," in contrast to the other insolent leaders.

3:6-8 These verses intimate that a serious transition is underway. In a divine soliloquy (v. 7) we hear that Jerusalem will now accept the disciplinary correction repulsed in verse 2. **3:8 wait for me:** Waiting upon the Lord is the prophetic posture for salvation, as in Hab 2:3 and Isa 30:15-18 before the Exile, or in Isa 40:31 during the Exile. **I arise as accuser:** The phrase might also be translated "as a witness." **my decision to gather together:** Here we meet the Hebrew word repeated negatively three times in 1:2-3, with the meaning "to sweep away," but now positively in Jerusalem's favor. **3:11 the earth be consumed:** This should not be taken literally, for Jerusalem must survive! Texts like this one always need interpretation.

3:9-13 A strong transition appears here in the Hebrew text. In verse 9 a promise to "purify the lips," reminiscent of Isaiah at the time of his call (Isa 6:5) intends that the deceit and falsehood, as witnessed by Psalm 12, be removed. To "call upon the name of the Lord" (v. 9) imparts many rights and privileges, just as in the case of a child who can call someone mother or father. In verses 12-13 salvation is promised to "the remnant . . . a people humble and lowly." As mentioned in the commentary on 2:3, the humble are already on the way to being the assembly whom God saves as a special people. The Gospel of Matthew makes use of the Greek version of Zephaniah in recording Jesus' words to disciples to "Learn from me, for I am *gentle and humble of heart*" (Matt 21:29).

3:14-18a This first psalm, a hymn of praise, is ready to be sung "at festivals" (v. 18a). In many ways it reminds us of the many jubilant lines in Isa 40–55, particularly in chapters 40–48. Here we draw attention to a number of phrases that cluster again in Luke's presentation of the annunciation to Mary that she was to become the mother of Jesus: "Be glad," "The Lord is in your midst," "Fear not," "mighty savior" (see Luke 1:26-38). Mary, tabernacling Jesus within herself, is thus presented as the new Jerusalem, the model for the poor and lowly.

3:18b-20 As elsewhere in prophecy, the "lame" and the "outcasts" are assembled (see Mic 4:6-7), the very ones rejected from the temple, even if they were priests, by the legislation of the Torah (Lev 21:16-23). Verse 20 was probably added during the time of the Exile. As Israel is assembled, its salvation will strike the attention of "all the peoples of the earth," a hint that universal salvation is possible.

HABAKKUK

Carroll Stuhlmueller, C.P.

INTRODUCTION

Style

Habakkuk and Jeremiah inaugurate a new attitude in prophecy. Up until now, for the most part, prophecy consisted in delivering the oracle of God to Israel; now the prophet's question to God becomes for us the word of God, in some real yet mysterious way revealing God's word in our own challenge to God! Nothing as fully developed as this questioning style in Habakkuk and Jeremiah ever comes totally new. Here or there prophecy has been interrogating God, but never so extensively as to become the gist of the entire prophecy. Even Moses differed with God (Exod 32:11-14); and further back still, Abraham argued with God about the fate of the five cities (Gen 18:22-33). We find Amos putting a question to God in his first two visions (Amos 7:1-6). This style, however, will almost dominate the prophecy of Jeremiah, particularly in his famous confessions (Jer 12:1-5; 15:10-21; 17:14-18; 18:19-23; 20:7-18). In all these cases the starting point is a strong faith in God's fidelity; and at the end God closes the conversation when and how God wishes. God remains God!

Person

Little if anything is directly known about Habakkuk. The name never occurs again in the Hebrew Bible. The deuterocanonical section of the Book of Daniel refers to him as bringing some bread and boiled stew to Daniel in the lion's den at Babylon; this Habakkuk is carried by an angel, who seizes him by the crown of his head and afterward returns him to his own place (Dan 14:33-39), an episode generally considered a popular story of much later vintage. Some explain the name Habakkuk as the intensive form of a Hebrew word meaning "to embrace." Jewish tradition, other than the one in Dan 14, links the prophet with the childless woman at Shunem, to whom the prophet Elisha promised a child. The word "to embrace" occurs in the story (2 Kgs 14:8-37). Other scholars derive the prophet's name from a bulbous plant, known from an Assyrian root word but not found in the Bible. The Greek Septuagint adds to his name in 1:1, "son of Jesus of the tribe of Levi," an identification prompted, no doubt, by the liturgical poem in chapter 3.

Date

The prophecy is to be dated sometime after the Babylonians became an active threat against Judah but before their destruction of the city of Jerusalem in 587 B.C.E. Habakkuk's serious complaints about violent injustice among the people in Judah suggests sometime in the reign of Jehoiakim (609–597 B.C.E.), a king despised by Jeremiah for his abuse of power at the cost of much suffering by the poor and defenseless. Jeremiah declares that he will be given "the burial of an ass" (Jer 22:13-19; see also 2 Kgs 23:37). Certainly chapter 3 qualifies Habakkuk to be numbered among the "cult prophets," who functioned at the temple; chapters 1–2 may leave us some clues for a liturgical ceremony.

529

Themes

Several major religious motifs thread their way through the prophecy: God's absolute trustworthiness; God's control of the universe; our inability to understand adequately the mysterious ways of God; our failure to fathom the mysteries of the universe and the colossal struggles of nature and politics; God's determination not to tolerate violence, begotten by pride.

COMMENTARY

CROSS-QUESTIONING GOD

Hab 1:2–2:5a

This section consists of a double series of question and lament (1:2-4 and 12-17), each followed by an oracle or reply from God (1:5-11 and 2:1-5a). Such question-answer style follows a pattern that surfaces in some psalms of lament and supplication (see Pss 12; 45; 79). Doubts arise, however, if King Jehoiakim would have permitted Habakkuk, any more than he did Jeremiah, to speak in the temple against the country (Jer 26). Verses 2-4 of chapter 1 place the theme and two key words of Habakkuk before us: the question *Why?* (vv. 3 and 13b) and the situation of violence (1:2, 3, 9; 2:8, 17). *Why* does a God who "comes forth to save [the] people" (3:13) tolerate violence against the innocent? **1:4 the law (torah) is benumbed:** What the prophecies of Micah and Isaiah see streaming down from the temple mount (Mic 4:1-3; Isa 2:2-4) is silenced by "leaders [who] render judgment for a bribe" (Mic 3:11).

1:5-11 God's reply is: "I am raising up Chaldea," that is, the Babylonians, who will punish Jerusalem's wicked leaders, civil and religious. From the beginning of Israel's occupation of the land of Canaan, god is said to have summoned other nations to punish the people for their sins. This theme preoccupies the Book of Judges, whose introduction offers a theological explanation: the abundance of good things induces Israel to sin; sin brings weakness and military invasion; such sorrow moves Israel to pray to God, who sends a "judge," or military leader, to liberate them; and a new prosperity sets in, almost so that the cycle can repeat itself (Judg 2:6–3:6).

Prophecy gradually recognized a more positive attitude toward the nations: in Amos 1:3–2:16 God cares enough to punish them for their offenses against humanity (they are not judged according to the Torah), and in Isa 10:5-15 they are "my rod in anger," directly called as God's instrument in determining the long-term fate of Israel. Only much later does prophecy consider the nations to have a share in Israel's light and salvation (Isa 49:6). Habakkuk's statement is an important link in this development of an ever more positive regard toward the foreigner.

Verses 8-11 reflect the swift maneuvering and sudden success of the Babylonian forces. In verse 11 we encounter the problem of translating the Hebrew word either as "wind" (NAB) or as "spirit" (see the commentary on Mic 2:11, p. 514). In the latter case the same line could read: "[God's] spirit passed by and so he [King Jehoiakim] passed onward" and continued to reign as king. Even though Jehoiakim was installed by the Egyptians, he was wily enough to win the approval of the Babylonian king Nebuchadnezzar.

1:12-17 God's answer is unacceptable, not because Habakkuk lacks faith, but rather because his faith in God is pure, strong, and elevated. *Why* does a God who is "from eternity . . . holy . . . immortal . . . a Rock . . . pure . . . [compassionate toward] misery . . . gaze on the faithless in silence while the wicked man devours one more just than himself" (vv. 12-13)? The Babylonians are more wicked than the wicked leaders of Jerusalem. **1:12 immortal:** This verse contains a scribal correction. The Hebrew reads literally "you do not die," but since it seemed improper to associate death in any way with Yahweh, the Hebrew text was changed in its written form to "we do not die"! **1:13 devours:** The word implies a voracious, even ruthless, appetite. The earth swallowed the Egyptians (Exod 15:12); the fish swallowed Jonah (Jonah 2:1); the Lord "destroys (literally "swallows up") death forever" (Isa 25:7). **1:14-17** Habakkuk strengthens his case against the Chaldeans: they undo God's work of creation by treating human beings like fish and animals (vv. 14-15); they offer up ritual sacrifice to their instruments of war (v. 16).

2:1-5a The Lord's reply is elegantly introduced as awaited from a "guard post" or watchtower (Hos 9:8; Mic 7:7; Isa 21:6-21; Ezek 3:17-21; 33). Already the importance of waiting is stressed. The prophet feels an obligation to find an answer for his troubling questions. He has not only a heritage to guard but a present responsibility to discharge.

The Lord's answer is immediate and clear, so precise that it is to be written down (a rare command for a prophet who at best dictated, as in Jer 36, or confided to disciples, as in Isa 8:16) in letters so large as to be read on the run, and so consoling that one runs with eagerness to report it ("run" is the emphatic word here). Verse 3 stresses the need to wait with patience, for it will come true at the "end"—the Hebrew word here does not mean "fulfillment" (see Dan 8:19; 11:27, 35; 12:4).

2:4 the just man, because of his faith, shall live: The word "just" stresses the fulfillment in oneself of the Lord's promises (see Hos 2:21-22; Zech 9:9); "faith" puts the emphasis upon fidelity, sturdiness (Exod 34:5-8); "lives," while the faithless are reduced to silent inactivity (Isa 14:15-20; 38:18-19). **Wealth . . . is treacherous; the proud, unstable:** These words reverse the idea of faith or sturdiness in the preceding line and link with verse 4a about the rash person without integrity. Verse 4b becomes the keystone in Paul's theology of the justification of *all* people by faith in Jesus, whether they have been initiated into the Mosaic covenant or not (Rom 1:17; Gal 3:11); the letter to the Hebrews links the passage with the need for patience, (Heb 10:37-38). The commentary on Habakkuk found in the Dead Sea Scrolls refers the passage to "those who fulfill the law in the house of Judah, whom God will free at the tribunal of justice on account of their labors and their faith in the Teacher of righteousness [their founder]."

ORACLES OF WOE

Hab 2:5b-20

These five oracles of woe do not name any foreign nation; in many ways they address the evils within Judah at the time of Habakkuk.

Yet, because of the familiar way of editing prophetic books (oracles or sermons against Israel or Judah, followed by oracles against nations), and because the crimes in the first and fourth oracle seem to be on an international scale, this section is frequently entitled "Oracles Against the Nations." No clear pattern emerges in the five oracles, except for the format of: (a) Woe! with a statement of offenses; (b) the Hebrew word *ki* at the beginning of verses 8, 11, 14, 17, introducing a punishment. Yet verse 14 is not a punishment, and there are other verses out of step!

Woes such as these already occurred in a major section of Amos (5:7, 18; 6:1) and appear elsewhere in prophetic literature in a series of judgments and condemnation only in Isaiah. The style is more common in the Torah (Deut 27-28) and in sapiential books. The section here is subdivided: introduction (vv. 5b-6a); five woes (vv. 6b-19); conclusion (v. 20).

The introductory verses (vv. 5b-6a) stress the unquenchable appetite of death. The inhabitants in the nether world, the foreign nations, take up a taunt against Judah (or Assyria? or Babylon?) in a way similar to their satire against Babylon in Isa 14. The words "satire" and "epigrams," again in Mic 2:4 and Jer 24:9, indicate a message of general import, worthy of serious study.

Verses 6b-8 attack unjust and greedy ways of lending to others (Ps 15:4-5; Exod 22:25; Amos 2:6-8). Verses 9-11 are directed against proud and heartless wealthy people who construct spacious homes, whose "stone in the wall shall cry out" against them with the groaning of the poor and destitute (see Jer 22:13-19 against King Jehoiakim, who "works his neighbor without pay" as he constructs his "airy rooms" and cedar-paneled walls). Verses 12-14 speak against building "a city by bloodshed" (Mic 3:10 has identical words and even names the city), perhaps a reference to the unnecessary bloodshed in the cities of the Shephelah, or low-lying hills where Micah lived, pillaged by foreign troops because of the reckless and selfish policies of Jerusalem. Verse 14 seems to be a familiar refrain; it occurs also in Isa 11:9. Verses 15-17 might reflect the violent forms of sensuality and war among the Assyrians and their allies whose fertility rites entailed drunkenness and nakedness (see Gen 9:20-25) and who deserved the cup of the

Lord's wrath (see Obad 16; Isa 51:17; Jer 25:15). Verses 18-19 rail against idolatry. Verse 20, the conclusion, prepares for the liturgical prayer by placing us silently in the Lord's holy temple.

CANTICLE

Hab 3:1-19

This final canticle moves with the momentum of Israel's most ancient hymns, like the Song of Moses in Exod 3, of Deborah in Judg 5, again of Moses in Deut 32, or the magnificent Psalm 68. Dramatic moments in Israel's history are told against a background of cosmic upheavals, so fiercely does Yahweh battle for the safety and well-being of the people. Even though quite different in style from chapters 1-2, this canticle could have come from Habakkuk. Yet the links are somewhat fragile. If not only 1:2-5 but also 2:5b-20 were directed against Judah's religious-civil establishment, then it is difficult to accept Habakkuk's authorship of chapter 3 with its friendly reference to the king or "anointed one" in 3:13.

3:1 Similar to many psalms, the canticle is introduced with a "title," with liturgical indications. **Prayer:** The Hebrew word, repeated five times in the psalms, indicates a supplication or lament, which this canticle or hymn of praise is not! Is this word a rubric, adapting the canticle to the more normal style of the prophecy of Habakkuk? **a plaintive tune:** This Hebrew word, often left untranslated, is not found elsewhere in the Bible, but because of a similar Babylonian word, it is considered a plaint or lament.

3:2 This introductory verse reminds us of the opening stanza to Ps 44:2-9, "O God, our ears have heard, our ancestors have declared to us . . . ." God is asked to remember (that is, repeat) the great redemptive acts from Israel's origins. "In the course of the years" indicates Israel's optimistic openness to the future, but also a real ennui with the length of time involved.

3:3-7 The poet's gaze sweeps from Teman and Paran, Cushan and Midian, an area to the far south where the Negeb turns into the Sinai desert; other songs like Judg 5 and Psalm 68 recognize the Lord coming up from here at the head of a victorious people: fear (symbolized by pestilence and plague) and earth-shattering victories accompany the journey into the Promised Land. Similar imagery is used in Psalm 46 to prepare for a temple liturgy at Jerusalem.

3:8-15 Yahweh's victory over world forces is told with imagery from Canaanite mythology as found already in Pss 29; 77:14-20 (introduced also by "remember" in verse 12); 89:6-19. Verse 15 seems to refer to the Lord's triumph at the Red Sea and the Jordan River (Psalm 114). Only in verses 16-20 does the element of lament for a plaintive tune (v. 1) appear. Yet the canticle may be using "fear" more as a literary device, as in verse 2, to communicate a sense of awe at what the Lord will do to "the people who attack" (v. 16). "In the course of the years" Israel must turn to the Lord and live in faith (2:4b), and if victory is delayed, must wait for it (2:3b). In verse 16b "decay" can just as correctly be translated "trembling."

Verses 18-19 begin emphatically in the Hebrew, with the meaning "But I, on the contrary." Verse 19bc is very similar to Ps 18:34, a psalm with which the canticle of Habakkuk shares other stylistic features. The psalmist moves with the swift and victorious step of the Lord. The final line, "For the leader; with stringed instruments," is a liturgical rubric, also found at the beginning of many psalms. That liturgical notes are part of the inspired word of God shows that the way in which a later generation used the canticle in its worship belonged to the essential inspiration of the psalm; the psalm will not release its full meaning until it is relived liturgically, as the opening lines of this canticle pray.

EZEKIEL AND DANIEL

Toni Craven

INTRODUCTION

Outline of contents

The Book of Ezekiel is an orderly five-part collection or anthology of writings by the prophet and his followers. Chapters 1–3 tell of the prophet's call; chapters 4–24 contain prophecies about the fate of Jerusalem before its fall in 587 B.C.E.; chapters 25–32 are prophecies against the foreign nations; chapters 33–39 encourage the hope of restoration after the fall of Jerusalem; and chapters 40–48 present a vision of the new temple and the restoration of the cultic and political life of the people in the land of Israel.

The Book of Daniel is a three-part collection containing short stories written by unknown authors about Daniel and his companions (chs. 1–6; and the deuterocanonical Greek chs. 13–14) and apocalyptic visions written in the first person and fictitiously attributed to Daniel (chs. 7–12).

Kind of literature

Form and content define the literary type or genre of Ezekiel as prophetic literature (with some apocalyptic sections, notably chs. 38–39), and Daniel as both edifying short story and apocalyptic vision.

Prophetic literature

Ezekiel, like the other classical Old Testament prophets, is a passionate, uncompromising spokesperson for God. He announces words of judgment and encouragement to his particular community as it faces a crisis in its religious and political existence. Ezekiel makes the sixth-century Jewish community in Judah and Babylon mindful of its false hope in Jerusalem and its false despair after the fall of the city in 587 B.C.E. In a variety of ways, including visions (see chs. 1–3; 8–11; 37; 40–48), symbolic actions that concretely dramatize the message (see chs. 4–5), allegories (symbolic stories with an interpretation, see ch. 16), and judgment speeches (often introduced by the oracle formula "thus says Yahweh" and closed with the recognition formula "that you may know that I am Yahweh"), Ezekiel calls for individual responsibility, repentance, and submission to the sovereignty of God. He does not predict a timetable for the distant future, though he does give voice to a poetic vision of a community restored, for the sake of the divine name, to a new national identity in a new and restored Israel.

Edifying short story

Like Ruth, Esther, Tobit, and Judith, parts of the Book of Daniel (chs. 1–6; 13–14) are self-contained short stories with distinct beginnings, middles, and endings. The nine narratives in Daniel are tales of biblical heroes who cope successfully with difficulties, survive the terrible oppression, and in the end triumph gloriously. In an entertaining fashion, the stories teach that good prevails over evil and that God rewards faithfulness. Daniel, Shadrach, Meshach, Abednego, and Susanna are portrayed as inspiring models of courage and virtue.

Apocalyptic literature

A kind of literature that flourished from 200 B.C.E. to 100 B.C.E. (see, for example, Isa

24–27; Ezek 38–39; Dan 7–12; Joel 3; 2 Esd; Rev), apocalyptic (Greek for "unveiling," "uncovering," or "revelation") works always contain some revelation of information hidden from ordinary human understanding. Through the medium of angels, visions, and bizarre symbolism, special knowledge is revealed. In the Book of Daniel, the special revelations in chapters 7–12 take the form of a kind of resistance literature that encouraged those experiencing persecution under Antiochus IV to persevere because the end of the time of tribulation was at hand. These apocalyptic predictions about the exact time of God's intervention and the heavenly events accompanying the establishment of the divine kingdom on earth are unique in the Old Testament (compare the New Testament Book of Revelation).

Geographical and historical background

Babylon, which was over 750 miles from Jerusalem, is the presumed geographical setting for Ezekiel and much of Daniel. Both books refer to the Babylonian Exile and the fall of Jerusalem in 587 B.C.E. to Nebuchadnezzar. This traumatic event occurred during the lifetime of Ezekiel; for the authors of Daniel it was a remembered event that served as a springboard for their veiled discussions of the repressive rule of Antiochus IV Epiphanes (175–163 B.C.E.).

Four centuries separated the composition of the books of Ezekiel (sixth century B.C.E.) and Daniel (second century B.C.E.). Ezekiel described the Exile prophetically as an occasion that demanded the conversion of a sinful, rebellious people and their acquiring of a "new heart" (Ezek 36:26). Daniel interpreted the Exile retrospectively as a time in which heroes of faith successfully resisted religious and political oppression. In Daniel, the Exile and the subsequent dominion of the Persians and the Greeks were understood apocalyptically as signs of promised reward for those who also resisted oppression and patiently awaited God's dramatic transformation of the course of history.

Historical outline

The major dates, events, and personages associated with the Books of Ezekiel and Daniel are summarized in the following historical outline.

B.C.	EGYPT	PALESTINE	MESOPOTAMIA
		THE BABYLONIAN EMPIRE	BABYLONIA
		Jehoiachin (Jeconiah), 3 mos., 598–597	Nebuchadnezzar, 605–562
		First Deportation to Babylonia, 597	
	Apries (Hophra), 589–570	Zedekiah (Mattaniah), 597–587	
		FALL OF JERUSALEM SECOND DEPORTATION, 587	
		BABYLONIAN EXILE Ezekiel, c. 593–573	
			Nabonidus, 556–539 (his son: Belshazzar) RISE OF PERSIA Cyrus II, 550–530 Defeat of Media, c. 550
600 to 500			Invasion of Lydia, c. 546
		(Second Isaiah, c. 540) Edict of Cyrus, 538	FALL OF BABYLON, 539

B.C.	EGYPT	PALESTINE	MESOPOTAMIA

THE EMPIRE OF PERSIA

B.C.	EGYPT	PALESTINE	MESOPOTAMIA
	Conquest by Persia, 525	THE RESTORATION JUDAH Return of exiles Rebuilding of Temple, 520–515 (Haggai) (Zechariah)	Cambyses, 530–522 Darius I, 522–486
500 to 400	Egypt under Persian rule, 525–401	(Malachi, c. 500–450) Ezra's mission, 458(?) Nehemiah arrives, 445 Ezra's mission, c. 428(?)	Persia Xerxes I (Ahasuerus), 486–465 Artaxerxes I (Longimanus), 465–424 Xerxes II, 423 Darius II, 423–404
		Ezra's mission, c. 398(?)	Artaxerxes II (Mnemon), 404–358) Artaxerxes III, 358–338 Arses, 338–336 Darius III, 336–331

EMPIRE OF ALEXANDER THE GREAT, 336–323

B.C.	EGYPT	PALESTINE	MESOPOTAMIA
400 to 300	*Ptolemaic Kingdom* Ptolemy I, 323–285	Egyptian Control	*Seleucid Kingdom* (Mesopotamia and Syria) Seleucus I, 312/11-280
300 to 200	Ptolemy II, 285–246 Ptolemy III, 246–221 Ptolemy IV, 221–203	Egyptian Control	Antiochus I, 280–261 Antiochus II, 261–246 Seleucus II, 246–226 Seleucus III, 226–223 Antiochus III, 223–187
200 to 100	Ptolemy V, 203–181 Ptolemy VI, 181–146 MACCABEAN REVOLT, 168 (167) Ptolemy VII, 146–116	Syrian Conquest, 198–200 <hr> MACCABEAN REVOLT, 168 (167) Judas, 166–160 Jonathan, 160–143 Simon, 143–134 John Hyrcanus, 134–104 Conquest of Shechem, 128	Seleucus IV, 187–175 Antiochus IV (Epiphanes), 175–163 Antiochus V, 163–162 Demetrius I, 162–150 Alexander Balas, 150–145 Demetrius II, 145–138 Antiochus VI, 145–141 Antiochus VII, 138–129
100 to 30 A.D.	Roman Conquest, 30	Pompey captures Jerusalem, 63	Roman occupation of Syria, 63

THE EMPIRE OF ROME

The historical outline above is taken from: Bernhard W. Anderson, *Understanding the Old Testament*, © 1986, pp. 650, 651. Reprinted by permission of Prentice-Hall, Englewood Cliffs, New Jersey.

COMMENTARY: EZEKIEL

PART I: CALL OF THE PROPHET

Ezek 1:1–3:27

The opening chapters ascribe this book to Ezekiel ben-Buzi, who had an extraordinary vision in Babylon in the year 593 B.C.E. According to the sixteen dates attached to the book, he remained active as a prophet at least until 571 B.C.E. (see the last dated oracle in 29:17). We know little about this man except that he was married and that his wife died during the siege of Jerusalem (see 24:15-18).

It is generally assumed that Ezekiel was exiled from Judah to Babylon in the first deportation of 597 B.C.E. Together with other exiles skilled in crafts, commerce, and agriculture who settled in Tel-abib, Nippur, and Babylon itself, Ezekiel took up residence in an alien land. On the banks of a river in Babylon, Ezekiel saw a vision which convinced him that God called him to speak as a prophet to the exiles.

The strange imagery of the opening chapters poetically dramatizes a new vision of God's mobile holiness suitable to the difficult times of the Exile. Ezekiel is called to submit his life to the majesty of God and is commissioned to speak a harsh word of judgment and warning to the rebellious people of Israel. The prophet is commanded to eat a scroll covered with lamentation and woe (2:9-10) and to stand as a watchman or pastor over the house of Israel.

1:1-28 The vision: God on the cherubim. Two superscriptions open the book. In the first (v. 1), Ezekiel recounts his visionary experience by the Babylonian river Chebar. In the second (vv. 2-3), the collector of his words and deeds provides information about the beginning of the prophet's career, his name, family, and position in Israelite society.

The reference in the first superscription (v. 1) to the "thirtieth year" is an enigma. The date cannot refer to either of the kingships that might have influenced Ezekiel. More than

thirty years had passed from the beginning of the reign of Nabopolassar of Babylonia in 626 B.C.E., and less than thirty years had passed from the beginning of the reign of Josiah of Jerusalem in 621 B.C.E. (2 Kgs 22:23). Though interpreters have variously taken the "thirtieth year" as a reference (1) to the age of the prophet (according to Num 4:30, the minimum age for ordination was thirty), (2) to the date when Ezekiel first published his work, or (3) to thirty years from the time when the high priest Hilkiah found the book of the law in the temple during the reign of Josiah (2 Kgs 22:8ff.), no satisfactory explanation of this date has been discovered. It is even said that the ancient rabbis forbade persons under thirty to read the opening of this book lest they be led astray by Ezekiel's strange vision.

Also problematic is the incomplete date in the second superscription (v. 2). It refers to the year 593 B.C.E., but it does not specify a particular month. Both the first and the second superscriptions specify the fifth day, but neither contains full reference to a year, a month, and a day.

Verse 3 is a kind of heading found frequently in prophetic books (compare Hos 1:1; Joel 1:1; Mic 1:1; Zeph 1:1; Jer 1:2-3). Although syntactically the word "priest" in verse 3 can refer to either Ezekiel or his father Buzi, the phrase has traditionally been interpreted as an indication that Ezekiel was a priest in Jerusalem before he was called to be a prophet in Babylon. Actually, there is no information in the text about Ezekiel's homeland, although it seems highly probable that he came from Jerusalem with the first exiles deported to Babylon in 597 B.C.E.

The vision of Ezekiel is the most detailed account available to us of the call of a prophet. It is similar in many details to Isaiah's call and commissioning (Isa 6), like Jeremiah's call (Jer 1:9-10) in the one respect of the eating of the scroll, and clearly related to the type of call known from the vision of Micaiah (1 Kgs 22). Ezekiel's call combines an earthly setting with a heavenly vision. Like Isaiah and Micaiah, Ezekiel sees God seated on a throne. Ezekiel is near the river Chebar, a canal along the Euphrates River in the vicinity of Babylon, when the heavens are opened and he sees a strange and dazzling vision of God's maj-

---

Parts of this commentary on the Book of Ezekiel were prepared as a co-authored revision of Walter Harrelson's *Interpreting the Old Testament* (New York: Holt, Rinehart and Winston) and are used with permission.

esty. It is in the land of exile that "the hand of the Lord came upon" the prophet (v. 3).

Ezekiel sees a great cloud with fire flashing about it swept along from the North. Within the cloud a bronze object appears. As the cloud draws nearer, strange living creatures are distinguishable, each with straight, human-like legs and hands, feet like those of calves, four wings, and four faces (one of a human, one of a lion, one of a bull, one of an eagle). With one pair of wings each figure modestly covers its body (compare Isa 6:2). The tips of the other pair of wings join the four figures together, so that they shield the object they carry in their midst. The motion of their wings makes a deafening sound, and flaming torches, burning coals, and fire dart out from behind the creatures. Ezekiel sees four wheels, one beside each of the beings (possibly a later expansion of the vision—1:15-21). And looking upward, he sees a firmament (a kind of platform), upon which is a throne. On the throne is a likeness of a man, although the fire and the gleaming bronze make it impossible for Ezekiel to see this figure clearly. The brilliant colors of the rainbow mark the entire scene, and its splendor overwhelms the prophet.

Ezekiel describes the strange details of his experience with care. In the midst of the cloud he sees something that gleams "like" electrum (v. 4). Within the cloud he sees figures "resembling" four living creatures (v. 5), whose four faces are "like" burning coals of fire (v. 13), and over their heads something "like" a crystal firmament (v. 22). He hears something "like" the sound of water, "like" the voice of the Almighty (v. 24). Above the firmament, on something "like" a sapphire throne, is one who has the "appearance" of a man (v. 26), who gleams from the waist up and looks "like" fire from the waist down (v. 27). Such, says Ezekiel, is the vision of the "likeness" of the glory of Yahweh (v. 28). Though this vision is not easily comprehended, it is clearly a sign that God has not abandoned the people. In the land of exile, where the ruling nation honors other gods, Yahweh comes to call a prophet for the community. The Jerusalem temple is over 750 miles away, but Yahweh's relationship to the covenant people continues.

(Fourteen passages in the Book of Ezekiel have been rearranged in the New American Bible translation. To alert the reader to these changes when they occur, comments like the one that follows will be enclosed in brackets.)

[This first chapter is one of the most difficult to translate in the entire Old Testament. The New American Bible translation deletes verses 14, 21, and 25 and transposes the order of the verses that describe what Ezekiel first sees as the stormwind approaches (notice that the text reads 7, 10, 9, 12, 8, 11, 13). The deletions are made on the grounds that certain verses repeat information already given. The transpositions are seemingly made to keep like descriptions together. In the Hebrew text, mixed gender references to the living creatures complicate translation. In verse 5 the references are grammatically feminine, and the New American Bible sensitively translates "their form was human." In verses 7-8 all the references are masculine. Since the New American Bible inserts verses 10, 9, and 12—in which grammatical vacillations are extreme—between verses 7 and 8, the reference to the faces of the creatures in verse 10 is translated "like . . . the face of a man." The Jerusalem Bible better translates, "As to what they looked like, they had human faces" (1:10a). Similar ambiguities occur in verses 23-25, and again the New American Bible reorders and omits certain verses for the sake of smooth reading.]

2:1–3:15 Eating of the scroll. The Israelites who have been taken into exile are to learn that in the alien land "a prophet has been among them" (2:5). Those who have given up hope in the Lord's guidance and who are ready to make a new life for themselves in the land of exile are reminded that even in an alien land God calls them to fidelity. Those who fix their hopes upon the homeland and expect God's deliverance to come from there are assured that God's purpose for the covenant people can be accomplished wherever the people may be. In short, God's active presence in exile is the fundamental import of Ezekiel's vision. In response to the greatly varied hopes and fears of the exiled community, the chief message of the vision is that the Lord is still with the people. Exile in Babylon does not put them outside the range of either God's mercy or God's judgment.

The words heard by Ezekiel (ch. 2) are strange and vague. He is addressed as "son of man" (2:1), an address that occurs over eighty times in this book and is regularly best translated as "human being" or "man" (compare Ps 8:5, where "man" and "son of man" are synonymous terms). In the Book of Daniel (7:13-14), this phrase refers to a special human figure who receives the heavenly gift of dominion. And in the Gospels "son of man" refers variously to a coming heavenly judge and savior; to sayings about the suffering, death, and resurrection of Jesus; or simply to Jesus himself. But in the Book of Ezekiel, "son of man" is used as an address that contrasts Ezekiel's human frailty with God's divine majesty.

God summons Ezekiel to stand up (2:1) and then commissions him to speak a prophetic word (2:4) to the Israelites. Repeatedly God says that the covenant people are a "rebellious house" (see vv. 3, 5, 6, 7, 8), but God does not explain what wrong the people have done. Ezekiel is not told what he is to say to these rebellious people, only that he must speak what God commands whether they heed or resist the message. The prophet is not to fear the looks or the words of the people (2:8) but is to obediently speak the word that God will put into his mouth (2:9). Then the prophet sees a hand extended from the midst of the fiery throne. In the hand is a scroll with terrible words written upon it, front and back (2:10). He is told to eat the scroll, does so, and finds that the scroll is as sweet as honey (3:1-3). Like Jeremiah (Jer 1:9) and Moses (Deut 18:18), Ezekiel is commanded to speak the words that the Lord has put into his mouth (3:4).

Ezekiel is reminded (as was Jeremiah, ch. 1) that the people are stubborn and will not heed the divine message (3:5-11). He is to persist, however, in speaking, letting nothing deter him from his task. He is to say, "Thus says the Lord God" (3:11), whether or not the people listen to his words. Though commissioned to speak the divine word, Ezekiel delivers no oracle until chapter 6. Instead, in the opening chapters of the book he tells how the Lord, seated upon a throne-chariot, came to him in a resplendent vision, how a hand unrolled before him a scroll with "woes, mourning, and lamentation" written upon it, and how he ate the word that the Lord God brought to him on the banks of the river Chebar in the land of Babylon.

Some interpreters believe that the vision of the throne-chariot and the giving of the scroll are two separate acts on two different occasions. They argue that the vision came to Ezekiel during the Exile in Babylon, while the giving of the scroll occurred when he was still in Jerusalem, prior to the Exile. In the present text, however, the two acts are part of one event. In exile, Ezekiel has seen a powerful vision of God that brings to him a divine word and symbolic authorization to speak God's word to the rebellious house of Israel.

The effect of the experience upon Ezekiel is now reported (3:12-15). Hearing the loud rumblings of the departure of the living creatures and the glory of the Lord behind him, the prophet is transported by the spirit from the site of the vision to Tel-abib, one of the exilic settlements beside the river Chebar. For seven days he sits among the exiles, overwhelmed and unable to speak.

3:17-21 The prophet as watchman. The solemn portrayal of the prophet as a special mediator of God's word for the people (ch. 3) relates to other passages in the book (chs. 14, 18, 33). Ezekiel's charge in 3:17-19 to warn the wicked for both their sake and his own is identical with that in 33:7-9. Chapter 33 marks an important shift of emphasis in Ezekiel's prophecies after the fall of Jerusalem in 587 from words of judgment to words of hope. It is likely that later editors of the Ezekiel tradition inserted this passage about the prophet as watchman in the opening section of the book in order to indicate that from the start Ezekiel was appointed to protect the covenant people, to watch over Israel, to turn the evildoer from evil and to confirm the righteous in righteousness. Implicit in this passage about the prophet as a lookout is a break with the narrow idea that the sins of the people in former times have brought God's judgment upon the present generation.

Especially after the fall of Jerusalem, Ezekiel was concerned with convincing the people that they must not interpret God's actions in this way. Each individual stands before the present claim of the covenant God. The prophet is charged with seeing that the individual who is condemned for faithlessness hears the word of condemnation. Though the faithless person is individually responsible for breaking the covenant, Ezekiel, too, will be punished if that person is not warned. In discharging his prophetic responsibility, Ezekiel will save his own life, and each person who heeds his warnings will also live (v. 21). The treatment of chapter 33 will enable us to see more clearly what the brief oracle in chapter 3 means.

3:22-27 Ezekiel's dumbness. This passage, like the preceding one about the prophet as a lookout, seems to belong to a time later in the prophet's career. The portrayal of the prophet as one unable to speak freely (v. 26) contradicts the sentiment of earlier passages in which Ezekiel is commissioned as God's spokesperson (2:4 and 3:4). Later in the book (24:17-23 and 33:22), a period of symbolic silence is observed by the prophet shortly before the fall of Jerusalem.

The scene portrayed in 3:22-27 (the restraining of the prophet by the people after he returned from his overwhelming encounter with the Lord) may be a symbolic act, or it may be an actual occurrence. If it is a symbolic act, its meaning is that the population in Judah will shortly be invaded, bound, and led captive into exile. Perhaps it did happen that the people restrained the prophet, thinking him to have gone mad, and that Ezekiel interpreted this act as a sign of the people's refusal to hear him and as a sign of the coming captivity of Judah. Most likely, however, 3:17-21 and 3:22-27 were later editorial additions.

PART II: BEFORE THE SIEGE OF JERUSALEM

Ezek 4:1–24:27

Chapters 4–24 record the actions and words of Ezekiel before the fall of Jerusalem in 587 B.C.E. These first six years of Ezekiel's prophetic career, according to the highly edited chronology of the final form of the book, were directed to calling the people who remained in Judah as well as those in Babylon to right knowledge of God. In symbolic acts, allegorical stories, visions, parables, and judgment speeches, Ezekiel describes the imminent, irrevocable doom about to befall the chosen people on account of their idolatrous behavior. They have profaned God's holiness by turning to false gods and false prophets, and there can be no peace for them.

The divine presence has been so badly profaned in Jerusalem that in 592 B.C.E. (see 8:1), five years before the temple is to be destroyed,

Ezekiel sees the glory of the Lord abandon the temple, moving first to the main entrance of the temple (10:2-4), then to the east gate (10:18-19), and finally to the Mount of Olives (11:22-23; relocated in the New American Bible to the end of chapter 10). The place of the divine presence becomes a scene of divine judgment. And Ezekiel voices God's indictment of the people for their failure to live according to the ethical requirements of the law. In his attempt to call the people back to God, the prophet speaks out against false prophets, calls for personal responsibility, and retells the disastrous history of Israel, tracing Israel's infidelity back to its very beginning in Egypt (ch. 23:3).

3:16–5:17 Acts symbolic of siege and exile. [The New American Bible text for this section has the following alterations: (1) 3:16a is inserted before 4:1; (2) 4:12-15 is placed after 4:17; (3) 5:13-15 is placed after 5:17. The rearrangements are seemingly made to untangle the text; they do not alter the sense of the passage.]

Four symbolic acts in 4:1–5:17 enact the fate of the Judeans who have not gone into captivity. Ezekiel acts out variously the role of God toward the people of Judah and the circumstances of those who will be punished. In the first symbolic act (4:1-3), the prophet draws upon a brick of the sort used in Babylonia for building purposes a picture of Jerusalem under siege. By unflinchingly "fixing his gaze" (4:3) on what he has sketched, Ezekiel dramatizes God's active power against Jerusalem.

In the second symbolic act (4:4-8), Ezekiel lies for a certain number of days on his left side facing north, then for a shorter number of days on his right side facing south, to indicate the number of years that North Israel and Judah must endure exile. Judah's exile is here fixed at forty years (4:6). The reference to God's binding Ezekiel (4:8) is a metaphor for the oppression experienced by the prophet on behalf of the people.

The third act (4:9-17) illustrates the scanty food rations in Jerusalem during its siege. The prophet is allowed only meager allotments of food and water. He eats carefully weighed-out mixed grains, which he is instructed to cook using human excrement as fuel (4:12). Such an act is so repulsive to Ezekiel that God relents and permits him to use cow dung, the more common fuel for cooking (4:15).

The fourth symbolic act (5:1-17) represents the death and hardships the people will experience at the hands of the enemy. Ezekiel cuts hair from his head and beard, and divides it by weight into three parts. One part is burned in the fire, another part is thrown into the air and scattered by a flashing sword, while the third part is blown away by the wind. Complete disaster will befall the inhabitants of the besieged city. The detailed interpretation of this symbolic act is probably very largely an expansion by the later community. The cannibalism suggested in verse 10 is elsewhere attested in the Old Testament as an expression of God's most severe punishment (see Lev 26:29; 2 Kgs 6:29; Jer 19:9).

Some interpreters have suggested that Ezekiel engages in these symbolic enactments of the divine word while still deprived of the ability to speak following his vision. This interpretation may indeed be correct. The visible acts of a prophet unable to speak would be an impressive way of communicating God's message. Yet, the appearance of the four symbolic acts together in chapters 4–5 and the fact that other prophets performed symbolic acts suggest that this interpretation is not necessarily correct. This collection was most likely made by some of Ezekiel's followers, who editorially grouped the traditions that represented the siege of Jerusalem. These dramatic enactments are reminiscent of the actions of Isaiah, who walked about Jerusalem "naked and barefoot for three years as a sign and portent" that the inhabitants of Jerusalem should not trust Egypt and Ethiopia (Isa 20:2-6); and of Jeremiah, who was instructed to buy a loincloth, wear it for a time and bury it, and then dig it up, rotted and good for nothing, to symbolize the corruption of "the pride of Jerusalem" (Jer 13:1-11). Prophets regularly use actions as well as words, visions, and dreams to symbolically portray the divine intent. In the Book of Ezekiel, this grouping of symbolic actions precedes the prophet's utterance of the divine word.

There is still no direct word or oracle from Ezekiel indicating what sins within the community are prompting God's threatened judgment. The elaboration of the last symbolic act (ch. 5) does refer to Israel's rejection of God's statutes and ordinances (5:6) and to the defiling of the sanctuary (5:11), but it is likely that these references come from the later tradition. It appears, therefore, that Ezekiel has first performed certain grim symbolic acts describing the fate of Jerusalem and Judah without having indicated why God is bringing ruin. Chapters 6–11, however, lay out in vivid detail the corruption of Israelite life and worship which, in Ezekiel's view, is leading God to complete the destruction of the holy city and its surroundings.

6:1-14 Against the mountains of Israel. Two oracles (vv. 1-10 and vv. 11-14) describe God's unrelenting anger at the inhabitants of the Promised Land. The reason for the judgment is no longer left in doubt: Israel has turned to idols, has committed abominations on high places, has forsaken God, and has become proud and arrogant.

Each oracle opens with an instruction that Ezekiel perform a gesture ("turn toward the mountains of Israel," v. 2; "clap your hands, stamp your feet," v. 11) and deliver a message in God's name ("Thus says the Lord God," vv. 3 and 11) that death and desolation will befall the entire countryside. The address to "the mountains of Israel" (6:2, 3) is meant in the Book of Ezekiel as an address to the whole Israelite people (see 19:9; 33:28; 34:13, 14; 35:12; 36:1, 4, 8; 37:22; 38:8; 39:2, 4, 17). Because of the sins committed on high places, where Israel has worshipped other gods, all Israel will experience destruction. Those who are permitted to escape the divine wrath (vv. 8-10) will be scattered in foreign lands, where they will remember their pasts with remorse. From this remnant will come those who understand the discipline of God's destruction as they turn from evil "to know the Lord."

The recognition formula "know that I am the Lord" appears over sixty times in the Book of Ezekiel and functions both as a word of judgment and of consolation. Its four occurrences in this chapter (6:7, 10, 13, 14) are harsh predictions that idol-worshipers will be slain and that those who live will remember the calamity and desolation that befell the land. The entire community will experience severe punishment for forsaking the covenant with God. Through the prophet, God here speaks a merciless word that promises utter destruction. In disaster, "then shall you know that I am the Lord."

7:1-27 The end has come. A revelation formula, "thus the word of the Lord came to me" (v. 1), and the recognition formula "thus they shall know that I am the Lord" (v. 27) set the boundaries of an exquisite poem that describes the disaster soon to befall the Promised Land. Though textually difficult to decipher because of duplications and shifts in voice, this poem sounds an alarm of imminent, irreversible doom for those who dwell in the land (verses 2-4 are repeated in a slightly more elaborate form in verses 5-9).

On "the day of the Lord" (v. 10; compare Amos 5:18), the life of the community will come to an end. The dissolution of the community (vv. 10-27) is described as a time when commerce will cease (vv. 12-13), the people will be under siege (vv. 14-16), and grief will be everywhere apparent (vv. 17-18). Wealth will be useless to those who have made idols (vv. 19-20), as God hands over the land to disaster (vv. 21-24). There shall be no peace when God's judgment comes (vv. 25-27). The community will crumble as individuals, prophets, priests, those who counsel, and those who rule can no longer do their jobs rightly. Anguish will replace peace (*shalom*: personal, economic, social wholeness or well-being) when God comes to punish the people.

8:3, 5-18 Vision of abominations in the temple. [The New American Bible text of chapters 8-11 has been extensively rearranged. In this section on the abominations in the temple, 8:1, 2, and 4 have been omitted. In the next section, "Slaughter of the Idolaters," 9:1-11 is followed by 11:24-25. And in the section "God's Glory Leaves Jerusalem," the text reads: 8:1, 2, 4; 10:1-22 (internally reordered); 11:22-23. These changes affect the meaning of chapters 8-11 in a variety of ways, as illustrated by comparison with translations that preserve the canonical order of the Hebrew text, such as the Jerusalem Bible or the Revised Standard Version. Instead of one transportation from Babylon to Jerusalem (8:1-4) and one return from Jerusalem to Babylon after God's departure from the holy city (11:22-25), the New American Bible suggests two round trips (one in what is basically chapters 8-9, another in what is basically chapters 10-11). Other alterations of meaning will be noted in the discussion.]

Ezekiel has a vision in which the spirit carries him from Babylon to the north gate of the Jerusalem temple (8:3). There the prophet is shown four successive acts of abomination taking place in the temple, each more offensive than the last. In 8:5-6, Ezekiel arrives at the gate of the inner court of the temple and looks out to see an altar set up before the image of a deity (perhaps Asherah, the goddess of love). The holiness of God is defiled by this abomination at the entrance to the sanctuary itself, but still greater evils are to be shown to the prophet. In 8:7-13, Ezekiel is led to a hidden room, where he sees seventy elders, including a certain Jaazaniah, the son of Shaphan (perhaps the Shaphan of 2 Kgs 22, who had been a leader in the reforms of Josiah), presenting incense offerings to loathsome creatures and beasts whose representations are inscribed on the walls of the hidden room. In 8:14-15, Ezekiel goes into the temple court, where he comes upon some women weeping for Tammuz, the Babylonian vegetation god, whose death signaled a dry season of infertility during the summer month that bore his name (June-July) until his sister, the goddess Inanna, brought him back to life in the spring. In the last scene, 8:16-18, Ezekiel is taken to the inner court between the vestibule of the temple and the altar of burnt offering, where he finds the worst blasphemy of all: twenty-five men have turned their backs on the temple where God is enthroned to worship the sun.

For Ezekiel the priest, these four acts represent complete apostasy from God and mean that the entire temple area must be violently cleansed of such abominations.

9:1-11; 11:24-25 Slaughter of the idolaters. In 9:1-11, six executioners and a man dressed in linen (linen is prescribed for priestly garments in Lev 16:4) and carrying a writing case are summoned to destroy the city. The origin of these seven figures from the north is obscure. Their job description is like that of God's destroying angel (Exod 12:23; 2 Sam 24:16-17; 2 Kgs 19:35). Their number is fixed at seven for the first time in the Old Testament in this text (compare the later usage of this number in Tob 12:15; Rev 8:2, 6; especially 15:1, 6-8, where the seven angels are dressed in white linen; 16:1-21). Perhaps the seven are an allusion to the seven Babylonian planet-gods, one of whom served as a heavenly scribe and compiled a Book of

Fate. In this text the man in linen is charged with the responsibility of marking the foreheads of those to be delivered.

Only those who "moan and groan over all the abominations that are practiced" in the city are to be spared (9:4). Without pity or regard for sex or age, all others are to be smitten. As the severe punishment is being carried out, Ezekiel asks God if all Israel must be destroyed (9:8). God answers that the evil deeds of the people cannot go unpunished. Then the man in the linen garment returns (the text does not mention the return of the six executioners) and says that God's commands have been accomplished (9:11). The New American Bible here inserts 11:24-25, which tells of the return of the prophet to Babylon and his report to the exiles about everything he has seen in Jerusalem.

8:1, 2, 4; 10:1-22; 11:22-23 God's glory leaves Jerusalem. [The text of the New American Bible differs here from the Hebrew original. Verses within chapter 10 have been rearranged, and verses from chapters 8 and 11 have been added. The text thus reads: 8:1, 2, 4; 10:20-22, 14-15, 9-13, 16-17, 1-8, 18-19; 11:22-23.]

This section opens with a date (17 September 592) and the notice of a transportation from Babylon to Jerusalem (8:1, 2, 4 transposed). Ezekiel's strange guide on this occasion is described in terms much like those used to describe the mysterious figure that appeared to him by the river Chebar (compare 1:27 and 8:2-4). The prophet is seized by the hair of his head and taken to the court of the temple (compare Habakkuk's mode of travel in Dan 14:36).

Once in the temple precincts (10:20-22), Ezekiel fixes his attention upon the glory of God and the same four-faced, four-winged living creatures he had seen in Babylon (see ch. 1). Beside each of the creatures he sees "a wheel within a wheel" (10:10), rimmed with eyes (10:12; compare 1:18). These wheels, which Ezekiel now learns are called "wheelwork" (10:13), are moved by the locomotion of the living creatures' wings (10:16-17).

Above the cherubim Ezekiel sees a throne-chariot like the one he saw in chapter 1 (the notable difference is that the living creatures of 1:26 are named "cherubim" in 10:1). But this throne-chariot is empty, because the glory of the God of Israel has gone up to the threshold of the temple (10:4). The man in linen is instructed to take fire from within the wheelwork and to scatter it over the city of Jerusalem. But before the city is destroyed, God's glory must leave the temple. Thus it happens that the glory of the Lord leaves the threshold of the temple to rest in the throne-chariot, which the cherubim carry to a mountain east of the city. The divine presence departs from the sanctuary and the city. Jerusalem is now without God's protection.

11:1-13 Judgment of the princes. The prophet is transported in an ecstatic vision to the east gate of the temple, where he pronounces an oracle against Jaazaniah (a man mentioned in 8:11, but with a different father) and Pelatiah. As he prophesies the coming death of these men who are misleading the people, Pelatiah falls dead.

It is difficult to know how this story is to be understood. Presumably the exiles later heard of the death of Pelatiah and fearfully assumed that he died just as Ezekiel related his vision of Yahweh's judgment. The section ends with the prophet's haunting cry, "Alas, Lord God! Will you utterly wipe out what remains of Israel?" Ezekiel grieves over the destruction of the people (11:13), just as he did over the fate of Jerusalem (9:8), but he cannot stem God's vengeance.

11:14-21 Restoration of the exiles. A word of promise closes Ezekiel's vision (11:14-21). The people in Jerusalem say that the Lord has sent the exiles into captivity and thereby turned over the land of promise to those who remain in the land. Not so, says this passage; God will punish those who remain in the land for their abominations, while the exiles will be delivered at a later time. This entire section, including the reference to the giving of a new heart and a new spirit to the restored community (vv. 19-20), seems to belong to the later period of Ezekiel's prophecies of hope (see 36:22-32).

12:1-28 Acts symbolic of the Exile; prophecy ridiculed. Two additional symbolic acts (vv. 1-20) and two independent sayings (vv. 21-28) condemning the people's rejection of the divine word are reported in chapter 12. Though Ezekiel dwells in the midst of a rebellious people who refuse to see or heed his message (12:1), he is instructed to perform symbolic acts reminiscent of those described in chapter 5, in the hope that perhaps the people may yet "see" (12:3) and repent of their rebelliousness.

As part of the first symbolic act (12:1-16), Ezekiel is instructed to prepare an exile's baggage and to leave at night by digging through a wall (12:1-7). Though this act symbolizes the fate of the inhabitants of Jerusalem, the verbal interpretation of it that follows (12:8-16) is directed to the exiles, who are warned not to put their hope in the holy city or in a quick end to the Exile. The event is interpreted as referring to Zedekiah, who left Jerusalem at night by making a breach in the walls of the city and fleeing into the hands of the Babylonians; they captured him and took him to Riblah, where he was blinded and led into captivity (see 2 Kgs 25:4 and Jer 39:4). The explanation of Ezekiel's symbolic act found in 12:8-16 is quite clearly a later reworking of the event.

As part of the second symbolic act (12:17-20), Ezekiel is told to eat his food with quaking and trembling as a sign of the panic that will seize the inhabitants of Jerusalem when their city is surrounded. The two sayings at the close of this chapter (12:21-28) prepare the way for the section against the false prophets (13:1–14:11). Those who think that the words of the prophets have lost their power are condemned (12:22-25), as are those who insist that the words of judgment apply only to a far-off day (12:26-28). The Lord's word is sure, and its fulfillment is even now ready at hand.

[Note that the New American Bible text of the two sayings reads 12:21-23, 25, 24, 26-28, presumably for the sake of smooth reading.

Chapter 13, which in its difficult and clearly layered original contains two sayings against false male prophets (vv. 1-9 and 10-16) and two sayings against false female prophets (vv. 17-21 and 22-23), has been extensively rearranged in the New American Bible. The two sayings against false male prophets are given in 13:1-2, 5, 7-8, 10-16 and 13:3-4, 6, 9, and the two sayings against false female prophets in 13:17, 22-23 and 13:18-21. Such radical reordering results in virtually rewriting the chapter. Unfortunately, there is no explanation in the notes to explain these changes.]

13:1-16 Against the prophets of peace; against false prophets in Chaldea. Thematic unity, an introductory revelation formula

(v. 1), and a concluding recognition formula (v. 23, displaced in the New American Bible translation) distinguish chapter 13 (compare 12:26 and 14:2). The chapter opens with a word of denouncement for men who prophesy falsely out of their own thoughts (v. 2) when they have seen nothing (compare the parallel passage in Jer 23:9-32). Their unauthorized words are simply an adornment for the desires and wishes of the people, like whitewash placed upon a wall (vv. 10-12, 14-16). The message of these prophets is worthless. They offer hope that rests upon illusion (vv. 10, 16). God intends judgment, not peace, for the covenant people. Prophets who insist that Jerusalem and Judah will be spared have had false visions and speak lies (vv. 6-9). God's judgment is that these false prophets and their works will be utterly destroyed (vv. 15-16).

13:17-23 Against false prophetesses; against sorceresses. Ezekiel also condemns women who prophesy falsely out of their own thoughts (v. 17). These women undermine the faith of all by capitalizing on the dangers of the times to frighten people into paying for good omens (compare 1 Sam 9:7, where bread is the payment for an oracle). The women are involved with sewing magic bands and making veils for every head (v. 18), though it is unclear whether they or their clients wear these objects. They dishonor God by prophesying for venal motives, determining life or death according to the price paid them (v. 19; compare Mic 3:5). Their lies have disheartened the righteous and encouraged the wicked (v. 22). The judgment is that these false female prophets will no longer see visions or practice divination when God rescues the people from their power (v. 23).

It is sometimes suggested that these women should not be classified as "prophets," a title that the Old Testament uses for only a very few women (Miriam in Exod 15:21; Deborah in Judg 4:4; Huldah in 2 Kgs 22:14 and 2 Chr 34:22; the wife of Isaiah in Isa 8:3; and Noadiah in Neh 6:14). Instead they ought to be thought of as "sorcerers" (so the New American Bible heading) because they engage in strange acts of magic (compare the story of the medium at Endor in 1 Sam 28:7ff.). Since the text does not specify these women by the noun "prophets" but rather by a feminine plural participle—"those who play the role of the prophet" (v. 17)—their name has allowed some ambiguity about their role. But the compositional arrangement of the chapter is not ambiguous. In context, the women are understood as false prophets.

Chapter 13 is a two-part structure in which verses 2-16 are remarkably similar in form to verses 17-23. Internal symmetries and carefully drawn parallels between men (vv. 2-16) and women (vv. 17-23) who have misused their prophetic authority demonstrate an intended equation of the two groups. In each half of chapter 13, Ezekiel is instructed as "son of man" (vv. 2, 17) to deliver God's word (vv. 3, 18). Both the oracle to the men and the oracle to the women open with an unusual cry of dismay (vv. 3, 18; used elsewhere only in 34:2 in an oracle against false shepherds, the Hebrew interjection *hoy* expresses pain, "ah" or "alas," which is to be distinguished from the more regularly used *'oy*, translated "woe"). Both the men and the women are accused of prophesying their own thoughts (vv. 2, 17), of having delusive visions and practicing false divination (vv. 6-9, 23). And both oracles contain two recognition formulas (vv. 9, 14, 21, 23). Through the word of the prophet, males and females are denounced for speaking lies that have dishonored God and disheartened the people.

If practicing acts of magic accounts for understanding the women in chapter 13 as sorcerers, then the men must also be so understood. Both groups are accused of practicing "divination" (the men in verses 6-9; the women in verse 23), an act of magic specifically prohibited in Deut 18:10. More likely Ezekiel used a participial circumlocution to address women "who play the role of the prophet" in order to condemn them for practices as abominable as those of their male counterparts (compare also the women and the men singled out for dishonoring the sanctity of the temple in chapter 8).

14:1-11 Prophecy useless for idolaters. As in 8:1 (which was transposed to chapter 10), so here in 14:1 (and again in 20:1) the elders of Judah exiled in Babylon come to consult Ezekiel. Following the revelation formula (v. 2), God explains to Ezekiel that these men are syncretists who have consulted idols and questions whether such as these should be allowed to seek an oracle of the Lord (v. 3). Through the prophet, God warns that those who consult idols before coming to a prophet will not receive a word of the Lord but rather an answer from God in person (vv. 4-5). Again the prophet is instructed to caution the people not to seek a prophetic word of the Lord while they follow idols (verse 7 is a variant of verse 4) lest they personally encounter God, who will make of them an object lesson for others by excluding them from the community. The recognition formula (v. 8) rounds out this word of warning to syncretists.

There follows a word to the prophet who responds to the requests of idol-worshipers, detailing his offense and punishment (vv. 9-10). The prophet who deludes and those who are deluded by other gods will be equally punished (compare Jer 14:15-16; 27:15). The divine purpose is to educate both the people and the prophet who might stray from an exclusive relationship with God (v. 11). Even though they are in a foreign land where Babylonian gods whose power is manifest in the achievements of Nebuchadnezzar are worshiped, the people are not permitted to give allegiance to any god other than the God of Israel without grave consequences.

14:12-23 Personal responsibility. In the remainder of this chapter and in the following nine chapters (14:12–23:49), Ezekiel's message for Israel is related to various events from its past history. Ezekiel, like Jeremiah and Second Isaiah, recounts the history of God's dealings with the people in order to draw a contrast between past acts of mercy and present experiences of judgment, and also to testify to the graciousness of God.

In a two-part oracle (vv. 12-20, 21-23), the prophet declares that even pious intercessors from Israel's past like Noah, Daniel, and Job could not divert God's wrath against the land (compare the parallel text in Jer 14:19–15:4). Four acts of judgment are about to befall its inhabitants as the sword, famine, wild beasts, and pestilence (v. 21) come upon Jerusalem. The sons and daughters who survive will serve as an object lesson justifying God's destruction of Jerusalem (vv. 22-23). Righteousness will save individuals but not the city. The prophet is insisting here on individuals' responsibility and accountability. Each must choose to act righteously and live, or to act faithlessly and die, a theme more fully developed in chapter 18.

15:1-8 Parable of the vine. In this short

allegory on the wood of the vine, the prophet declares that in God's eyes the inhabitants of Jerusalem have become unproductive and valueless, like a useless vine that no longer produces fruit. Like wood that is good for nothing, the homeland will be thrown into the fire. Later on the prophet will return to this image of Israel as the vine of the Lord (19:10-12).

16:1-63 The faithless spouse. In this the longest chapter of the book, Ezekiel narrates the beginning of Israel in an allegory about Jerusalem as the unfaithful wife of the Lord. Ezekiel is regarded as the Old Testament father of allegory, a literary form in which a story is told and then application is made to the contemporary situation (see also chs. 15, 17, 19, 23, 31, 34). Ezekiel is instructed to recount this figurative story so that Jerusalem will know its abominations (v. 2).

Verses 1-14 describe Jerusalem as an unwanted orphan, born from the union of the Amorites and the Hittites, and cast aside at birth by its parents. Neither midwife nor parents cared for Jerusalem. The child lay beside the road, unloved and untended, when God came by and performed the duties of a midwife. God saw to the needs of the child and then left. When Jerusalem came of age, God returned and betrothed the city, showering presents upon it and taking it as a bride. Jerusalem was "renowned" among the nations for exceeding "beauty," queen-like dignity, and the splendid gifts that God had bestowed upon it (v. 14).

Reversing the terms of adornment that closed verse 14, verse 15 opens a section (vv. 15-34) that describes how the "beauty" and "renown" of the city led it astray. Jerusalem's harlotry was idolatry played out with passers-by (v. 16) and with self-constructed male images (v. 17; compare 23:14). Jerusalem sacrificed her children to these images (vv. 20-22). She spread her legs to all, including Egyptians (v. 26), Assyrians (v. 28), and Babylonians (v. 29). So insatiable was Jerusalem's lust that she scorned payment and even stooped to paying lovers to come to her (vv. 30-34).

Verses 35-43 tell how God sentenced Jerusalem to a violent death. The harlot is summoned (v. 35) to hear an oracle that first restates the cultic sins she has committed by turning to other lovers and idols (v. 36), and then lists the consequences she will suffer on account of these sins: she will be stripped naked by her lovers (v. 37), sentenced by God as an adulterer and murderer (v. 38; see the death penalty prescribed in Deut 22:22 and Lev 20:10), and horribly executed by the assembly (vv. 39-40). While many women (a figure for the other nations) look on, Jerusalem will be punished, so that never again will she give payment to other lovers (v. 41). Then God's wrath will be satisfied (v. 42). Jerusalem will have been justly punished according to her own conduct for forgetting her origins and for adding immorality to her other abominations (v. 43).

Verses 44-58, a diatribe comparing Jerusalem to her sisters, opens with an epigram, "Like mother, like daughter," restates Jerusalem's Amorite and Hittite parentage, and moves quickly to an unfavorable comparison of Jerusalem to her two sisters, Samaria and Sodom (vv. 44-46). Jerusalem, the most wicked of the three, is called to blush for her sins (vv. 47-52). Then follows a sequence (vv. 53-58) describing the restoration of Sodom, Samaria, Jerusalem, and their daughters (neighboring cities), and the enduring sense of shame that Jerusalem will experience in the restoration.

A messenger formula (v. 59) introduces the climactic closing section (vv. 59-63) of chapter 16, which includes a dramatic restatement of all that has preceded and the astonishing declaration of an everlasting covenant (compare v. 60 and 37:26). Verses 60-61 recall the covenant God made with Jerusalem in her youth (compare vv. 3-43) and her relationship to her sisters (compare vv. 44-58). Verses 62-63 promise a reestablished covenant between God and Jerusalem. Reconciliation will bring with it sober shame and right recognition of God for Jerusalem. No longer will the city be oblivious to its abominations (see the charge of v. 2). With exceeding graciousness, God will pardon the iniquity of Jerusalem. This closing section of promise may be from Ezekiel, but the likelihood is that it comes from the hand of an editor. In the later chapters (34–37), where Ezekiel sums up his hope for Israel, he uses different language and imagery.

17:1-24 The eagles and the vine. The allegory of the eagles and the cedar (vv. 1-10) and its interpretation (vv. 11-21) comment

545

upon the political disquiet experienced in the land of Judah. In 597 B.C.E. Nebuchadnezzar ("the great eagle," v. 3) came to Judah and took King Jehoiachin (the "topmost branch" of the cedar, v. 4) and the leading citizens to Babylonia. Zedekiah ("seed of the land," v. 5) was then appointed head of the Judean state by the Babylonians. Yet, in 588 he rebelled against Babylonia by turning to Psammetichus II of Egypt ("another great eagle," v. 7).

Ezekiel's message is that the Egyptians will not be able to save the king or the land of Judah. Like Jeremiah (see Jer 37–38), Ezekiel insists that Zedekiah should have submitted to the rule of Babylonia. Ezekiel even declares that the oath and the covenant between Zedekiah and Nebuchadnezzar were as binding as the oath and covenant between the people and the Lord (see v. 19). Rebellion against Babylonia is actually rebellion against God, who had brought Nebuchadnezzar against Judah.

Like chapter 16, this chapter also closes with a word of promise (vv. 22-24). God will plant a sprig from the high cedar, care for it, and cause it to grow. The future of Israel is entirely in the hands of God, who can make a high tree low and a low tree high (v. 24). These closing words of promise may be an addition, although in this instance they are more in keeping with Ezekiel's own style. Perhaps the prophet added this section about the mystery of God's sovereignty to the prophecy at a subsequent time.

18:1-32 Personal responsibility. Following the revelation formula (v. 1), God questions Ezekiel about the proverb "Fathers have eaten green grapes, thus their children's teeth are on edge" (v. 2). Some of the more cynical exiles may have repeated this proverb in order to blame others or God (vv. 25, 29; compare 33:17, 20) for their sufferings. Ezekiel passionately argues that each generation is responsible for its own actions (vv. 3-20). He declares that the judgment of God falls only upon the sinner. The present generation is in no better or worse position before God on account of the sins of the previous generations. God will not destroy Israel for past sins, only for present ones. Each generation receives life or death according to its own actions (vv. 21-31). If the wicked should now turn from their evil ways, God would forgive them, and

the present generation would live (see Deut 30:15-20). The prophet appeals to the people to turn back to God, declaring that God takes no pleasure in anyone's death (see vv. 23 and 32). The chapter closes with God's cry to the house of Israel, "Return and live!" (v. 32).

19:1-14 Allegory of the lions; allegory of the vine branch. The tragic end of the princely offspring of a lioness (vv. 2-9) and of a vine (vv. 10-14) is told in two allegorical lamentations. The subject of the first lament is the exile of two royal lion cubs of Judah— one to Egypt and the other to Babylon. Since only one king contemporary with Ezekiel was taken captive to Egypt, the identity of the first lion cub (vv. 3-4) is unquestionably Jehoahaz, the son of Queen Hamutal and King Josiah. After only a three-month reign in 609 B.C.E., Jehoahaz was taken captive by Pharaoh Neco and deported to Egypt, where he died (see 2 Kgs 23:30-34).

The identity of the second lion cub (vv. 5-9) is more difficult, since two kings contemporary with Ezekiel were taken captive to Babylon. If the same mother lion (v. 2) bore both cubs, then the second king is Queen Hamutal's son Zedekiah (2 Kgs 23:31; 24:18), who was taken captive by Nebuchadnezzar in 587 B.C.E., blinded, and led in chains to Babylon (see 2 Kgs 24:18–25:7). If, however, the mother lion is a metaphor for Judah (compare Gen 49:9), from whom many princes emerged, then the second king might well be Jehoiachin, the son of Queen Nehushta, who after a three-month reign in Jerusalem was led away captive to Babylon in 597 B.C.E. and kept prisoner by Nebuchadnezzar (see 2 Kgs 24:8-15).

The subject of the second lament (vv. 10-14) is the annihilation of Zedekiah (compare chs. 17 and 31) and the mother vine. This allegory tells how the vine and its strongest stem were plucked up, exposed to the weather, and burned (v. 12). Then transplanted to a desert land (taken to Babylon; see Jer 52:1-11), this once stately vine had no branches and no fruit. The strength of the royal vine was destroyed (v. 14).

The fate of Judah's royalty is thus the subject of mourning and lamentation (see vv. 1 and 14c). The two historical allegories in chapter 19 are both dirges in five-beat lament meter. Three beats followed by two give the poems a limping, halting rhythm in Hebrew (compare 2 Sam 1:17-21; Isa 14:4-21; Amos 5:1-3). Form as well as content effectively show that, for Ezekiel, nationalistic hope in the Davidic line was virtually dead.

20:1-44 Israel's history of infidelity. Chapter 20 opens with a specific date (August 591, eleven months after the last date given in 8:1, which was transposed in the New American Bible to chapter 10) and presents a familiar scene of certain elders of Judah gathering at Ezekiel's house (compare 8:1 and 14:1). The exiles come to ask that Ezekiel inquire of the Lord for them. As in chapter 14, so too here, following the revelation formula (v. 2), God questions whether the elders should be permitted to seek an oracle (v. 3). Instead of an oracle, Ezekiel is charged to deliver a jarring historical retrospective (vv. 4-31) that underscores the sinfulness of the chosen people from their very beginning in Egypt (vv. 5-9), through the rebellious first generation (vv. 10-17) and second generation (vv. 18-26) in the wilderness, even to the present generation (vv. 27-31). All have profaned God by going after idols (see vv. 7, 16, 18, 24, 30, 31).

Israel can take no delight in its past. As Ezekiel tells the story, there never was a time of right relationship between God and the people (compare the more usual interpretation that once the people entered the land of Canaan, syncretism caused a strain in their relationship with God; see Hos 2). Ezekiel claims that from the moment of the Exodus onward, there has been disharmony between God and the idolatrous chosen people. For the first time in the book, Ezekiel presents the important theological rationale (further developed in chapters 36 and 39) that God has extended mercy to the people, not for their own sake but for the sake of the holiness of the divine name (vv. 9, 14, 22, 39). Deliverance is inextricably bound to God's holiness, reputation, and character in the world. And now, at the conclusion of the historical account, to be true to the divine identity and presence, God refuses an oracle to the idolatrous elders (v. 31).

In the course of the historical recitation, Ezekiel speaks of statutes given by God that were "not good" (v. 25), laws that contributed to the defilement of those who sacrificed their first-born to God (v. 26; compare Exod 22:28-29). Retribution seemingly takes the form of God's misleading the people. Law,

more ordinarily understood as a light of guidance (Ps 119:105), is here a cause for stumbling. God deals perversely with this rebellious people (compare Ps 18:26) as a mysterious, incomprehensible judge.

A disputation (vv. 32-44) following the historical recitation reiterates the charge that the present generation is idolatrous. In its first section (vv. 32-38), God promises harsh treatment for those who serve "wood and stone" (v. 32). As a wrathful king (v. 33), God will assemble the exiles and lead them to the desert in a new exodus (v. 34) for a severe "face to face" judgment (v. 35; compare the "in person" encounter promised to idolaters in 14:4). Like a shepherd, the Lord will use a staff to count out the small number of faithful people from the rebellious ones. The transgressors will never again be permitted to return to the land of Israel (vv. 37-38). Thus God promises that the exiles will know the Lord (see the recognition formula, v. 38).

The dispute then continues with a word to the members of the house of Israel urging them to put away all idols (vv. 39-44). Authentic worship requires complete awareness and renunciation of past evil conduct and actions. Then an unexpected word of genuine hope mitigates the severe judgment: God promises to bring Israel back into the land, to receive the offerings of the people, and to accept their repentance (vv. 40-44). By such means the mystery of God's holy name will be made manifest to the nations. Restoration will bring with it true recognition of the Lord (see the recognition formula repeated in verses 42 and 44).

21:1-10 The sword of the Lord. In chapter 21 Ezekiel's voice grows more strident as he warns that the sword of destruction is unsheathed and ready to strike. First the prophet is instructed to deliver an allegory against the forest of the south stating that God is kindling a fire that will devour all the trees (vv. 2-4). Ezekiel protests that the people mock him when he speaks in parables (v. 5), so he is given an interpretation of the allegory to proclaim (vv. 6-10). God is coming with an unsheathed sword, which will not be sheathed again, to destroy the wicked and the virtuous of Jerusalem.

21:11-12 Act symbolic of the city's fall. As in 6:11; 9:8; and 11:13, the prophet expresses grief over the coming suffering of his people. He is instructed to groan with deep emotional sadness as a sign that the end has come.

21:13-22 Song of the sword. Ezekiel engages in a kind of sword dance. He sings a song about a sharpened, ready sword of destruction (vv. 14-15) and performs a number of symbolic actions (vv. 16-22). He cries aloud and slaps his thigh (v. 17), claps his hands (v. 19), and brandishes the sword to the right and to the left (v. 21). He announces that the sword has been put in the hand of an unidentified slayer (v. 16) and that God approves (v. 22). God, the divine warrior, will execute fierce judgment against the people, not for them.

21:23-32 Nebuchadnezzar at the crossroads. Next Ezekiel is instructed to draw a map indicating two possible paths from Babylon (21:23-28), one leading to Rabbah in Ammon (the modern city of Amman, Jordan) and the other to Jerusalem (compare the symbolic acts in 3:16–5:17). In 587 B.C.E. these two small nations joined in an alliance against the threatening power of the Babylonian empire. In verse 26, by three methods of divination (shaking marked arrows and drawing one by lot; consulting teraphim, which were small images of household gods; and interpreting markings on the entrails of a sacrificed victim), Nebuchadnezzar determines that Jerusalem will be punished first (v. 27). Though the people may wish to dismiss this warning, their fate is marked by the arrow in Nebuchadnezzar's hand (v. 28).

Zedekiah is addressed as a depraved and wicked prince whose end is coming (vv. 29-32). A triple repetition, "twisted, twisted, twisted will I leave it" (v. 32), expresses the utter chaos about to befall the city. The sign is thus made clear that Jerusalem and its ruler are doomed to destruction.

21:33-37 Against the Ammonites. In this difficult passage, which may come from a later period, the Ammonites are depicted as wielding a sword against Israel (vv. 33-34). God stays their hand (v. 35) and declares that these people will themselves be judged and destroyed (v. 36). So complete will be their destruction that they will no longer be remembered (v. 37). No worse punishment than this could be imagined.

22:1-31 Crimes of Jerusalem. Three oracles on the common theme of the defile-

ment of Jerusalem have been grouped together in chapter 22. Verses 1-16 attack the violence and idolatry of the bloody city (notice the sevenfold repetition of the word "blood/bloodshed" in verses 2, 3, 4, 6, 9, 12, 13). Verses 17-22 describe Israel as scrap metal of no value. And verses 23-31 condemn the princes (v. 25), priests (v. 26), nobles (v. 27), prophets (v. 28), and people of the land (v. 29) who have turned to sinful ways. The destruction of Jerusalem is inevitable, given the universal corruption of the city (compare Zeph 3:1-8).

23:1-49 The two sisters. In chapter 23 the prophet concludes his grim picture of Israel's past (see 14:12–23:49), using the coarsest language found in the prophetic literature. God tells Ezekiel an allegory about North Israel and Judah, portraying the two nations as harlots (compare ch. 16) who seek to outdo one another in their sins.

Verses 1-4 introduce the two sisters and tell of their immoral childhood in Egypt. Despite their sins, Oholah (Samaria) and Oholibah (Jerusalem) were taken as brides by the Lord and bore many sons and daughters. The names of the two whores can be translated as "(she who has) her own tent" (Oholah) and "my tent (is) in her" (Oholibah). Since the "tent" was a place of meeting with God in the wilderness (see Exod 33:7), the names may be cultic allusions. Another possibility is that the words are simply sound-alike names with a foreign flavor. Though the meaning of the names is now obscure, the symbolism of the two harlot sister cities wed to God as representatives of Samaria (the capital of Israel) and Jerusalem (the capital of Judah) is clear.

Verses 5-10 describe the depravity and punishment of the older sister, Oholah-Samaria, who offered herself to Assyrian lovers. Verses 11-21 describe the even more vile harlotry of Oholibah-Jerusalem, who made open advances to Assyria and Babylonia. In four divine sayings (vv. 22-35), each introduced by the formula "thus says the Lord God" (vv. 22, 28, 32, 35), God declares that on account of her sins Jerusalem will be punished. Original to the text is the judgment that Jerusalem will be handed over to her lovers, who will now unleash violence against her. They will mutilate her so horribly that she will never again be able to play the harlot (see v. 25: "cutting off your nose and ears," a punishment found in both Egyptian and Assyrian texts). Most likely secondary to the text are verses 28-34, which state that Jerusalem will be handed over to those she hates (vv. 28-30) and that she will be judged by sharing her sister's cup of dismay (vv. 31-34).

Verses 36-49, a later retelling of the allegory of Oholah and Oholibah, summarize the sins of the sisters (vv. 36-44) and describe their punishment (vv. 45-49). The women sin simultaneously and will be punished simultaneously. Added here is a warning to individual women not to imitate the lewdness of the two sisters (v. 48). Finally, the recognition formula appears, signaling that judgment is an experience through which God's sovereignty will be known (v. 49).

24:1-14 Allegory of the pot. The siege of Jerusalem by Nebuchadnezzar, king of Babylon, began on the tenth day of the tenth month in the ninth year of Jehoiachin's captivity (v. 1; see also 2 Kgs 25:1). On this very day, which would fall toward the end of the year 588, Ezekiel, who was in Babylon, was commanded to write down the date and to deliver an allegorical oracle to the rebellious people (vv. 1-2). Ezekiel describes the coming fate of those left behind in the city of Jerusalem as the destruction of an unclean and rusty cooking pot (vv. 3-14). God avenges the crimes of the city and its inhabitants in a fire that consumes not only the contents of the pot but the pot itself. God had wished to spare the city, but now the end has come. No one need hope, for God will not relent.

24:15-21, 24, 22-23 Symbol of the destruction of the temple. [For some unexplained reason, the New American Bible translation places verse 24, which contains a recognition formula, before verse 22. There is no change in meaning with this move, but the regularity of the pattern in which the phrase "thus you shall know that I am the Lord" closes a section is here broken.]

Since the Jerusalem temple fell in the summer of 587 B.C.E., God's shocking word to Ezekiel in this passage probably took place sometime after the preceding dated allegory (vv. 1-14). The prophet is told that his wife, who is "the delight of his eyes" (v. 16), will suddenly be taken from him and that he is not to mourn her death publicly (v. 17). Ezekiel proclaims this strange message to the people, and on the evening of the same day (v. 18)

his wife dies, just as the Lord had said. The people ask for an explanation of these strange acts from the prophet (v. 19), who proclaims that the death of his wife is a sign of the death of Jerusalem. As he has been commanded not to weep over the loss of his beloved, so too must the people not weep over the destruction of their delight and desire, the sanctuary of Jerusalem (vv. 20-24).

24:25-27 End of Ezekiel's dumbness. It appears that Ezekiel neither laments his wife's death nor speaks at all until word reaches him that the city has fallen. Most likely an editor added these words to relate the preceding passage about the destruction of Jerusalem to 33:21, in which a fugitive from Jerusalem (first mentioned in 24:26) arrives in Babylon to announce that the holy city has been taken. As the text now stands, chapters 25–32 have been inserted between these two significant passages about the fate of Jerusalem (compare 24:26 and 33:21).

PART III: PROPHECIES AGAINST FOREIGN NATIONS
Ezek 25:1–32:32

Chapters 25–32 form a unit clearly distinct from the chapters before the siege of Jerusalem (3–24) and those after the fall of the city (33–39). In some of the most exquisite poetry in the book, Ezekiel declares God's vengeance against neighboring countries that have violated the covenant people. Seven groups of foreign people are singled out for judgment: the Ammonites, the Moabites, the Edomites, the Philistines, the inhabitants of Tyre, the inhabitants of Sidon, and the Egyptians. According to six of the seven dates listed in these chapters (see 26:1; 29:1; 30:20; 31:1; 32:1; 32:17), the oracles were delivered within the space of three years, between 585 and 588 B.C.E. A seventh date (29:17) describes a time fifteen years later. It is likely that Ezekiel himself is the author of these important oracles against the foreign nations. International as well as national concerns occupy the interest of the prophet in these chapters.

25:1-7 Against Ammon. The Ammonites are condemned for having exulted over the fall of Jerusalem and the conquest of the land. The defeat of Ammon at the hands of the people of the East is promised. God will bring destruction upon the Ammonites because they have delighted in the ruin of Israel. They will come "to know the Lord" (vv. 5, 7) in their own destruction.

25:8-11 Against Moab. Moab's fate is to be the same as that of Ammon and for the same reason. Moab, too, is to learn that the Lord alone is God (v. 11) and that the fate of Judah and Jerusalem does not mean that Israel is like all the nations.

25:12-14 Against Edom. Judgment is levied against Edom for having taken part in the destruction of Judah and Jerusalem, apparently by rounding up the fugitives and turning them over to the Babylonians and then infiltrating the land of Judah and claiming ownership (see Obadiah). The fate of Edom is different in that the vengeance of the Lord will be executed by the people of Israel. Chapter 35 expands the details of the devastation of Edom.

25:15-17 Against the Philistines. The oracle against Philistia is similar to that against Edom. The Philistines also appear to have harassed the fugitives and taken advantage of them in their plight. Although there is no indication of the means of God's punishment of Philistia, historically it almost certainly was destroyed at the same time as the campaigns of the Babylonians against Judah and Jerusalem.

26:1–28:19 Against the city of Tyre. The next three chapters are devoted to oracles against the famed commercial center Tyre, the chief city of Phoenicia. This city, located on almost impregnable rock at some distance from the Mediterranean shore, withstood the efforts of Nebuchadnezzar to capture it. In 586 B.C.E. the Babylonians began a thirteen-year siege, which ended inconclusively. Not until the time of Alexander the Great (fourth century) was part of the island itself destroyed.

The four oracles in 26:1-21 are of two types. The first two units (vv. 1-6 and 7-14) are oracles similar to those against the other nations. Because Tyre exulted over the fall of Jerusalem, it too will be punished by Nebuchadnezzar. The second units (vv. 15-18 and 19-21) are laments over the death of Tyre and its descent into the nether world. The fall of Tyre will cause all the princes of the sea to gather trembling on the shore, lamenting the death of Tyre and the threat to their own

kingdoms. Tyre will be placed in the underworld, there to remain forever.

In chapter 27 Ezekiel portrays Tyre as a great ship beautifully fitted out and proudly sailing the seas. He relates the extraordinary range and variety of Tyre's trading activities (27:12-25a). Then he details the end of this great commercial city as it is destroyed by God's east wind, which wrecks Tyre's exquisite ship, much to the mourning and consternation of the people on the shore (27:25b-36).

Chapter 28 is a second oracle about the ruin of Tyre (vv. 1-10) and a lamentation over the demise of its king (vv. 11-19). Tyre is cast down for misusing its divine position, wisdom, and wealth. Ezekiel grants that God created the king even wiser than Daniel (compare 14:14) but declares that his pride is the undoing of the city. God will cause it to die at the hands of foreigners (vv. 9, 10).

The lament in 28:11-19, seemingly based on a variant version of the Eden story, is a judgment against the king of Tyre. On the holy mountain of God (v. 14) a city was established which Ezekiel calls Eden, the garden of God (see Gen 2–3). The king, the first human being, was created perfect, wise, and beautiful, and was clothed and adorned with precious stones. A cherub guarded the king (compare Gen 3:24), who was blameless until he spurned his beauty and wisdom by acts of violence and arrogance. For his sin he was cast out of the mountain city by a guardian cherub and humiliated before the nations.

Ezekiel recasts this myth to make it portray the imminent ruin of Tyre. The old story probably related the sin of the first king, leading to his expulsion from the mountain city. The mountain thereafter was the dwelling place of El, the high god, and entrance to it was barred to earthly residents. But for Ezekiel, the historical sins of Tyre constitute the real corruption of the city. God executes judgment upon Tyre by stripping away all its treasures, won through its maritime trading, and humbling the people for their pride and injustice. Ezekiel does not contest the truth of the myth of Tyre's origin; he states it in order to dramatize the reversal of Tyre's fortunes.

28:20-26 Against Sidon. A brief oracle against Sidon (vv. 20-24), the other great city of Phoenicia, and a general promise of restoration for Israel following God's judgment of the foreign nations (vv. 24-26) complete the chapter. The composite nature of this section is indicated by the four recognition formulas in verses 22, 23, 24, 26.

The oracles against Egypt (29:1–32:32) are even longer and richer in mythological imagery than were the oracles against Phoenicia. The pride of Pharaoh, who considers himself a god, constitutes the chief sin of Egypt. Repeatedly this theme recurs in the following seven sections.

29:1-16 Egypt the crocodile. In a composite of several brief oracles (vv. 3-6a; 6b-9a; 9b-12; 13-16), dated January 587 B.C.E. (v. 1), Pharaoh is chastised for thinking himself maker and master of the Nile. On account of his sin, Egypt will be reduced to the most lowly of kingdoms.

29:17-21 The wages of Nebuchadnezzar. An oracle dated April 571 B.C.E. (v. 17; this is the latest dated oracle in Ezekiel) refers to the costly siege of Tyre by Nebuchadnezzar and promises the Babylonian king that he will recoup his spent treasures by the plunder of Egypt. Nebuchadnezzar is named as God's agent, and his wages are listed as the riches of Egypt.

30:1-19 The day of the Lord against Egypt. This section, which is the only undated oracle in the collection against Egypt, is clearly a composite (introduction formulas occur in verses 2, 6, 10, and 13; recognition formulas occur in verses 8 and 19). It elaborates the theme that the day is coming when God will devastate Egypt and its southern neighbor, Ethiopia. Nebuchadnezzar will invade Egypt (v. 10), and God will dry up the Nile (v. 12). These punishments will lead to international recognition of the Lord.

30:20-26 Pharaoh's broken arm. The fourth section against Egypt is dated April 587 B.C.E. (v. 20), just a few months before the fall of Jerusalem. About three months earlier, Pharaoh Hophra had come to the aid of Jerusalem, which was under siege by the Babylonians (see Jer 37:5). In this oracle all hope in Egypt's help is crushed. God declares that the arms of Pharaoh will be irreparably broken (v. 22), while the arms of the king of Babylon will be strengthened (v. 24). God will put a sword of destruction in the hand of Nebuchadnezzar (v. 25) and scatter the Egyptians among the nations (v. 26). Thus will the Egyptians know and recognize God.

31:1-18 Allegory of the cypress. The fifth section, dated June 587 B.C.E. (v. 1), is a three-part prophecy addressed to Pharaoh and his retinue (v. 2). A description of a great tree, more beautiful than any tree in the garden of God (vv. 3-9), opens the poem. Then follows a prose account describing the fall of the great tree on account of its pride (vv. 10-14), and its consignment to the nether world (vv. 15-18).

32:1-16 Dirge over Pharaoh. Dated March 585 B.C.E., this composite section opens with a fragment of a lament (vv. 1-3) over the destruction of Pharaoh, here symbolized as a lion and a sea monster. It continues as an oracle of judgment (vv. 3-8) against Pharaoh, allegorically portrayed as a sea monster that God will catch and throw upon the shore, where the beasts of the earth will devour the carcass. Then follows a series of later expansions that abandon the sea-monster imagery completely. First a prose interpretation of the grief that the nations will feel in seeing God's sword brandished against Egypt (vv. 9-10) is added. Next an oracle about Nebuchadnezzar as God's agent in bringing a sword of destruction against Egypt (vv. 11-14) appears. Then, closing the section is a brief prose subscription (vv. 15-16) which first reiterates the claim that the desolation of Egypt will be a means through which the nations will know the Lord and then concludes with an instruction to the daughters of the nations to take up a lament over Egypt's demise (on the role of women in mourning, see Jer 9:16-19).

32:17-32 Dirge over Egypt. [The New American Bible text reads 32:17-18, 20, 19, 21-32. The transpositions were seemingly made to achieve a smoother reading of this difficult passage.]

This seventh oracle opens with a date that most likely is April 586 B.C.E. (the Hebrew text lacks a month). The prophet is told to wail (v. 18) over the condemnation of Egypt to the underworld. Egypt's comfort will consist in the fact that its descent to Sheol has been preceded by that of other great world powers. Already gone down to the underworld from the Mesopotamian region are Assyria (v. 22), which fell to Babylonia in 612 B.C.E.; Elam (v. 24), a country east of Babylon, which was conquered by the Assyrian Ashurbanipal in 650 B.C.E. (see Jer 49:35-39); and Meshech and Tubal (v. 25), two tribes in Asia Minor that traded slaves with Tyre and terrorized As-syria. From the Palestinian region, Edom (v. 29) and the Sidonians (that is, Phoenicians; v. 30) lie among the slain in the pit with Egypt.

Ezekiel's prophecies against Egypt were probably the most important of all for the in-habitants of Judah and Jerusalem. Several of these oracles are dated prior to the fall of Jerusalem in 587 B.C.E. (see 29:1; 30:20; 31:1). Ezekiel tried to convince the leaders of Jerusa-lem that Egyptian help was a delusion, but his words, like those of Jeremiah, went unheeded. From this group of seven oracles against Egypt (29:1–32:32), the entire cycle of oracles against Israel's seven neighbors (25:1–32:32) may then have grown as Ezekiel and his followers reflected on the worldwide significance of God's judgment of the covenant people Israel.

PART IV: SALVATION FOR ISRAEL

Ezek 33:1–39:29

The fall of Jerusalem marks the turning point in Ezekiel's message. Following the hor-ror of 587 B.C.E., the prophet turns from dire predictions and condemnations of false hope to a radical revival of the spirit of the people. In chapters 33–39 Ezekiel and his followers counter false despair in a series of sermons that project new and renewed forms of life for the community, which doubts its ability to survive. Significantly, this section on salva-tion for Israel opens with God's demand for personal responsibility both for Ezekiel as a lookout for the people and for every indi-vidual.

33:1-9 The prophet as watchman. Chap-ter 33 resumes the theme of the prophet as God's lookout within Israel (compare 3:17-21). Ezekiel has the responsibility of declaring to the wicked their sins (vv. 8-9). If he fails to do so, the wicked will receive punishment for their misdeeds, and his own life will also be required. Ezekiel's warnings and judgments are designed to lead Israel to the knowledge that God stands ready to for-give those who have turned from their wicked ways. As the lookout, Ezekiel has assumed an awesome responsibility, greater than that of any other prophet in Israel. His duty to watch and to warn the wicked and the faithful must weigh heavily upon him, especially as the end of Jerusalem draws closer and closer.

33:10-20 Individual retribution. This sec-tion, which is a disputation on individual re-sponsibility, also resumes an earlier theme (see ch. 18). The prophet seeks to overcome the despair of those who resign themselves to their just fate and to refute the bitter anger of those who hold that the Lord is punishing Israel un-justly for the sins of previous generations. Ezekiel maintains that God longs to forgive the wicked and awaits their repentance (see vv. 11, 19). The prophet also argues that the virtuous will live (v. 13), though just how Ezekiel supposed God would spare the righ-teous in the coming devastation is not indi-cated. Presumably he counted upon the preservation of a righteous remnant in exile, with whom the Lord would make a fresh start.

33:21-22 The fugitive from Jerusalem. This brief section reports the arrival of the fu-gitive who brings the news that Jerusalem has fallen (compare 24:25-27). The date listed in verse 21 is about eighteen months after the ac-tual fall of Jerusalem. The fugitive arrives "on the fifth day of the tenth month in the twelfth year of exile." According to 2 Kgs 25:2, 8-9, Jerusalem fell on the seventh day of the fifth month in the eleventh year of Zedekiah (com-pare Jer 52:12, which lists the same year and month but specifies the tenth day of the month). The journey from Jerusalem to Baby-lon would be expected to take about four months (see Ezra 7:9). Even allowing for ex-haustion or a circuitous route, the fugitive's traveling time seems unreasonably long.

The evening before the fugitive arrives, Ezekiel experiences the hand of the Lord upon him (compare his similar experience in his call to be a prophet in 1:3 and 3:14). At the same time, Ezekiel recovers his ability to speak (v. 22; compare 3:22-27). The prophet is freed to new action on behalf of the Lord. He begins a new phase in his prophetic career, and from this point onward in the book, he delivers a more hopeful message to the people.

33:23-29 The survivors in Judah. The judgment against those in the ruined land of Judah who assumed that God would restore the land through them probably belongs to the period just after the fall of Jerusalem. Since those who remain in the land continue to practice the same sins that led to the ruin of Israel, further devastation awaits them. The implication of this oracle is that the Lord's fresh start will be made with the exiles, not with those who remain in the land of Judah. The judgment is therefore an implicit word of hope for the people in exile.

33:30-33 The prophet's false popularity. In this section God speaks directly to Ezekiel about his effectiveness as a prophet. Even though Ezekiel is popular, his message is not heeded (v. 32). To the exiles he is only a clever entertainer (compare Ezekiel's complaint that the exiles regarded him as "one who is forever spinning parables," 21:5). God declares that in the near future the exiles will recognize the accomplishment of the words the prophet has spoken; then they will recognize that a prophet has been among them (compare 2:5). This word is therefore an implicit word of encouragement for Ezekiel. His effectiveness is not to be measured by his present reception in the community.

34:1-16 Parable of the shepherds. In a composite oracle (notice that following the revelation formula in verse 1 there are three introductory formulas in verses 2, 10, 11) against wicked shepherds (= rulers; see Ps 78:71; Isa 44:28; 63:11; Jer 2:8; 10:21; Zech 11:4-17), God declares their end. Because the shepherds of the past have failed in their responsibilities to the sheep (vv. 2-6), God is coming against them to punish them and to rescue the sheep. God will take over the shepherd's responsibilities (vv. 11-16). God will be the good shepherd (compare Gen 48:15; Psalm 23; Jer 31:10; Mark 6:34; John 10:1-18), tending the sheep, rescuing the scattered of the flock, bringing them to rest in good pastures in their own land, where the lost will be sought out and those who stray brought back, where the injured will be bound up and the sick healed.

34:17-31 Separation of the sheep. Sayings related to the shepherd theme are grouped here, though the emphasis shifts from the shepherd who has failed the sheep to judgments against sheep who have misused their power. In verses 17-19, which open with an introductory formula, God addresses the sheep with words of judgment, saying that callous self-interest will be punished. Verses 20-22, which also open with an introductory formula, continue the theme of the strong versus the weak sheep. In verses 23-24 there is an abrupt shift in content from the theme of sheep against sheep to the theme of the appointment of a messianic prince. A human

shepherd is promised who will feed the sheep (v. 23; compare vv. 2-10, where God was personally to fulfill this task). David, the great ancestor of the royal house in Jerusalem, is to be the future shepherd/prince, and the Lord will be God.

In verses 25-27, which end with a recognition formula, shepherd imagery is abandoned completely as the passage shifts to an elaboration of the covenant of peace between God and the people. Verses 28-30, which also end with a recognition formula, provide information about the security and prosperity the restored house of Israel will experience. Verse 31 reintroduces the sheep imagery in a closing formula that emphasizes God's desire for the salvation of the people.

The many seams in this section demonstrate the importance of the concept of God's desire for the future salvation of the covenant people to both Ezekiel and his followers.

35:1-15 Against Edom. Continuing the denouncement begun in 25:12-14, Ezekiel here repudiates the hope of the Edomites that they will take over the former land of Israel and Judah. He attacks Edom for its enmity against its neighbor nation Israel at the time of Jerusalem's fall in 587 and for its effort to settle in the land (v. 10). Ezekiel denounces Mount Seir, the high place of Edom, and declares that God will not permit the land of Israel and Judah to pass into the hands of the Edomites. Because Edom has cherished enmity toward Israel, it is to suffer a fate worse than that of Judah: Edom is to become a perpetual desolation. And as the four recognition formulas in verses 4, 9, 12, 15 underscore, thus will Edom know the Lord.

36:1-15 Regeneration of the land. The oracle against Mount Seir of Edom prepares the way for the promise of restoration now delivered to the exiles. The mountains of Israel are told a word that explicitly draws a contrast between the destruction promised the high places of Edom and the future restoration of Israel.

In this complex section, which contains six introductory "thus says the Lord" formulas (vv. 2, 3, 4, 5, 6, 13), a displaced concluding recognition formula (v. 11) before the end of the passage, and two closing "says the Lord" formulas (vv. 14, 15), the mountains of Israel, condemned earlier in chapter 6, are promised regeneration. The promise of restoration that was begun in chapter 34 with the announcement of new leadership (the Davidic Messiah) gains momentum with the promise of a new land. Verses 1-7 promise that the nations which have ridiculed Israel, particularly Edom, will suffer reproach. Verses 8-15 promise prosperity to the mountains of Israel when the exiles return to repopulate the land.

36:16-38 Regeneration of the people. The second half of chapter 36, which develops God's reasons for the repopulation of the land, divides into five subsections defined by formulas and shifts in address. In verses 16-21 God speaks to Ezekiel about the cause of the Exile. In God's sight the defilement of the land by the chosen people was "like the defilement of a menstruous woman" (v. 17; compare Lev 15:19). Personal responsibility, as Ezekiel had earlier said, explicitly required that a virtuous person "not defile his neighbor's wife, nor have relations with a woman in her menstrual period" (18:6; see also 22:10). Because of their reprehensible defilement of the land and their idolatry, the people were scattered. Yet, even in other lands they continued to profane God's holy name (v. 20). Now grief over the preservation of the holiness of the divine name motivates God to tell Ezekiel that the Exile will end (v. 21).

In verses 22-23, which are framed as a subunit by an introductory formula and a recognition formula, God speaks directly to the house of Israel. God rehearses their wicked history and emphasizes that it is not for their sakes that the Exile will end. Zeal for the holiness of the divine name motivates God to return the people to the land. Here, as in chapter 20, the dominant motivation for restoration is concern for the preservation of God's holiness.

Verses 24-32 list a series of individual acts that God will initiate so that the people can live in the kind of obedience that will preserve the holiness of God's name. God will gather the chosen people from their exile and lead them back to their own land (v. 24). Then, in a three-stage purification, God will create a new, radically reordered human harmony. First, God will ritually cleanse the people from their past impurities and idols (v. 25; on washing as a means of purification, see Num 19:9-21; Ps 51:3-4). Second, God will transplant new hearts and spirits into the people (v. 26; compare Jer 31:31-34). And third, God

will animate their human hearts with the divine spirit, so that the people will have the inner power to live by God's statutes and decrees (v. 27). Verses 28-32 describe the material prosperity God will give the people when they return to the land, and they close with a sober reminder that these benefits are given, not for the sake of the people, but to set forth God's glory in the world.

Verses 33-36, which open with an introductory formula, promise that when Israel is rebuilt, the neighboring nations will recognize God's power. And verses 37-38, which open with another introductory formula, promise that in the future restoration to the land, Israel will be abundantly repopulated.

37:1-14 Vision of the dry bones. Ezekiel's vision in the valley (or the "plain," which is the same location as that in his call, 3:22) filled with dry bones is perhaps the best known section of the book. It is composed of a dramatic report of a vision (vv. 1-10) and its interpretation (vv. 11-14). The occasion is a time when the exiles have lost all hope in the future. The people who had once hoped falsely in the inviolability of Jerusalem and their past history now despair falsely, saying, "Our bones are dried up, our hope is lost, and we are cut off" (v. 11).

The prophet experiences the hand of the Lord upon him (see our comment at 33:22) and is led to the center of a place filled with numerous dry bones (vv. 1-2). In this place filled with countless signs of death, God puts the question to Ezekiel, "Can these bones come to life?" The prophet surrenders to God the power to make such a decision about life and death, and with reserve replies, "You alone know that" (v. 3).

God then instructs Ezekiel to prophesy to the dead bones so that a new spirit, sinews, flesh, skin, and breath will revive the bones (vv. 4-6). Ezekiel does so and hears a great noise as sinews, flesh, and skin cover the bones, but no spirit comes into them (vv. 7-8). In a second instruction God tells him to call the spirit from the four winds to come and breathe life into the slain (v. 9). Again Ezekiel does as commanded, and the spirit revives a great upright army of live bodies (v. 10).

In the interpretation that follows, God declares that those whose hope has turned to despair will be led from their experience of death to new life in the land of Israel (vv.

11-12). This interpretation of resurrection employs a different picture of the place from which the dead bones are reassembled. Here the bones are raised from proper graves (v. 12), not from a valley strewn with unburied bones. The Lord will burst the bonds of the grave to restore the people to new political existence. Verses 13-14, which contain two recognition formulas, emphasize that the new life that the Lord will grant the people will revive both their understanding of God and their life in the land. The picture in Ezekiel is not that of individual resurrection from the dead. This is a visionary description of a new corporate political beginning for Israel.

37:15-28 The two sticks. A symbolic action (vv. 15-17; compare chs. 4–5; 12; 24:17) and its interpretation (vv. 18-28, to which later materials have been added; see the two introductory formulas in verses 19, 21) portray the reunion of North Israel and Judah. Ezekiel hopes not only for the restoration of the Judean exiles in Babylon, but also for the reassembly of the exiles of Israel who were carried away by the Assyrians in 721 B.C.E. to a location most likely unknown to Ezekiel. Though the exiles from Israel have long since ceased to be a recognizable entity, Ezekiel envisions that in the sovereign purpose of God they are destined to return to the land along with the exiles from Judah. The restored people will be ruled by one prince (v. 22), whose identity (v. 24) is the same as the Davidic shepherd-prince described in chapter 34. God promises to dwell among the people and to make an everlasting covenant with them (vv. 26-27). Thus shall the nations recognize that it is the Lord who makes Israel holy (v. 28).

38:1–39:29 Prophecy against Gog. [The New American Bible divides these chapters into three prophecies against Gog by rearranging the text of chapter 38 to read 38:1-13, 17-23 as a first prophecy against Gog, and 38:14-16 as a second prophecy against Gog. These chapters are complex, yet content and the appearance of only one messenger formula in 38:1 suggest that chapters 38–39 are a unity composed of four subsections: 38:2-13; 38:14-24; 39:1-16; 39:17-29, each of which is marked by an instruction to Ezekiel to speak.

The first three subsections have Gog as their subject; the last subsection is directed to birds and wild animals.]

The clue to understanding these strange chapters, which are unlike the other materials in Ezekiel, is in 38:17. The question there occurs as to whether the enemy who comes from the land of Magog is that enemy whom the prophets spoke of in former days. This verse suggests that the chapters originated in later speculation concerning the great enemy from the north referred to in Jer 1:13-16; 4:5-8; 6:1-8, 22-26. The enemy here is called Gog, a name that probably does not refer directly to any world power, just as the land named Magog does not refer to any particular land (this vague enemy from the north is allied to Meshech and Tubal; compare 38:2 and 27:13).

This is an apocalyptic vision, similar to that found in Isa 24–27. It tells of the coming of a massive force against Israel, after Israel's restoration to the homeland (38:12). The enemy comes at the will of God, who is about to display a mighty show of power before all the nations. The Lord will defeat the forces of Gog, scattering the slain over the entire land of Israel. It will take seven months to gather up the bones of the slain and bury them (39:12). This carnage will have the double purpose of causing Israel to know that the Lord is their God (39:22) and of causing the nations to see the saving power of God, who exiled the people for their sins but has now secured their lives from harm (39:23-29).

These chapters may have been produced by Ezekiel (the language of 39:21-29 is quite similar to that found elsewhere in the book). More likely, however, they are the product of some of Ezekiel's disciples. The notion of a massive battle at the last day seems not to have entered Ezekiel's thoughts elsewhere in the book. It may be that some of his disciples had portrayed in veiled language the coming destruction of Babylonia. Yet, the fact that Israel will already have been liberated from exile when the enemy arises would seem to make such a view implausible. Gog seems better considered as a mythical world power invented by the disciples to emphasize God's protection of Israel.

PART V: THE NEW ISRAEL

Ezek 40:1–48:35

The closing section of the Book of Ezekiel contains an architectural sketch of the temple complex in Jerusalem (40:1–42:20), a description of restored worship in the temple (43:1–44:3), laws regarding temple personnel and practices (44:4–47:12), and the boundaries for a reapportionment of the land (47:13–48:35). These chapters are an idealized vision of the restoration of a new Israel to the homeland (compare chs. 34, 36, 37). Renewed life is now rightly centered on the temple. And the name of the new city is appropriately "The Lord is here" (48:35).

The New Temple

40:1-5 The man with a measure. Only one date, April 28, 573 B.C.E. (v. 1), appears in chapters 40–48. On this day Ezekiel is transported (compare 8:3) to a high mountain in the land of Israel, where he sees a divine vision of a city being rebuilt. He observes a celestial man at the gate of the city with two measuring devices in his hand—a linen cord and a measuring rod (six cubits long = about 10½ feet; v. 5). The divine messenger explains that he is Ezekiel's guide and cautions the prophet to pay close attention to all that he is to see. Then the guide proceeds to measure the width and height of a 10½-foot-wide by 10½-foot-high outer wall that surrounds the temple.

40:6-16 The east gate. Beginning at the east gate (which is the gate through which God departed the city in 10:19), the guide climbs its steps (there are most likely seven steps—see 40:22, 26) and measures the gate's threshold, or entrance hall, which is 10½ feet long (v. 6). Then he goes into a long corridor that is flanked on each side by three 10½-foot-square roomlike recesses (v. 7a). At the end of the corridor of the gateway is another threshold, or entrance hall, which is also 10½ feet long (v. 7b). This symmetrical entrance way leads to a roomy vestibule (about 14 by 35 feet), which opens onto the outer court of the temple.

40:17-19a The outer court. Thirty rooms occupy the north, south, and east inside perimeter of the outer wall of the temple. A pavement in front of these rooms connects the three sides of the outer court. Verse 19 fixes the distance between the outer and inner east gates as one hundred cubits (a distance of about 175 feet).

40:19b-23, 24-27 The north gate, the south gate. Built into the north and south outer walls are two gates identical in construction with the east gate (see vv. 6-16). Steps, a threshold, a corridor flanked by three rooms, and another threshold lead out to a vestibule. As decorative features, each of the gate structures has recessed windows, palm-tree reliefs on the jambs, and pilasters (rectangular columns set into the walls as an ornamental motif).

40:28-29, 31-37 Gates of the inner court. [The New American Bible omits verse 30 on the grounds that it duplicates verse 29. It should be noted that the dimensions of the vestibule are altered from 50 by 25 cubits in verse 29 to 25 by 5 cubits in verse 30. Most likely verse 30 is corrupt, since verses 29, 33, and 36 agree on the longer dimensions.]

The guide next takes Ezekiel across the outer courtyard (a distance of about 175 feet, according to verse 19) to measure the south, east, and north gates in an inner wall. These gates are duplicates of the outer gates, except that their vestibules are on the outside of the gate structures, so that they face the vestibules of the outer gates. The only difference in these reversed structures in the inner wall is that they have eight steps, not seven (compare vv. 31, 34, 37 and 22, 26) leading to them.

40:38-47 Side rooms. In verses 38-39 it is not clear exactly which gate contains the described sacrificial equipment. Perhaps the vestibules of all three inner gates are furnished with a room for washing burnt offerings (see the requirement of Lev 1:9, 13) and two tables on each side, upon which are slaughtered sin offerings and guilt offerings (see 45:13-17).

From verse 40 to the end of this section, Ezekiel sees twelve tables, which seem to be described from the perspective of the north gate. According to verse 40, two tables stand on each side of the outside wall of the vestibule of the inner gate, which most likely means that these four tables are in the outer court at the foot of the steps leading up to the north inner gate. According to verse 41, another four tables, which are used for slaughter, stand in the vestibule of the inner gate (also described in verse 39). Verses 42-43 describe four small cut-stone tables, which are intended to hold the instruments of slaughter and are most likely located near the slaughter tables on either side of the vestibule.

Verses 44-46 explain that two rooms occupy the inside of the inner court wall, beside the north and south gateways. These rooms face each other, though it is unclear whether they are located to the right or to the left of the gates. The room by the north gate is for the use of the priests who care for the temple. The room by the south gate is for the priests who sacrifice at the altar (Zadokites, according to 44:15-21).

The inner court is next measured as a perfect square (about 175 feet square), and the altar is described as standing in front of the temple (v. 47).

40:48–41:15a The temple building. From the inner north gate, the guide next takes Ezekiel across the inner court to the vestibule of the temple building. Ten steps lead up to the temple vestibule, which measures about 35 by 21 feet. The exterior of the vestibule area is described as featuring wall pillars (pilasters), two columns beside the jambs (compare 1 Kgs 7:15-22), and a wide doorway (40:48-49). Beyond the doorway is the nave, a room that measures about 35 feet wide by 70 feet deep (41:1-2). Ezekiel remains in this area while the heavenly guide proceeds to measure the holy of holies, a 35-foot-square room (41:3-4).

The architectural details of the measurements taken in chapter 41:5-15 are obscure. The guide first measures the wall of the temple, then ninety rooms built in three stories outside the temple with some kind of stairway connecting them, and finally a large structure behind the temple that is simply called "the building" (41:12).

41:15b-26 Interior of the temple. This section resumes the description of the outer vestibule and inner nave of the temple, where Ezekiel was left standing in 41:1. High windows allow light to enter the nave. Ornamental wood carvings of palm trees and two-faced cherubs, each with a human and a lion face, cover the wood-paneled walls of the nave and the vestibule (vv. 15b-20). A 5-foot 3-inch-high, 3½-foot-square table stands before the entrance to the holy of holies (v. 22; compare 1 Kgs 6:21). And two sets of double doors decorated with the same design as that on the walls separate the vestibule from the nave, and the nave from the holy of holies (vv. 23-25).

42:1-14 Other structures. This section is extremely difficult to interpret. Apparently the guide takes Ezekiel to a square area behind the west end of the temple building, where he measures two building complexes on the south and the north sides of the western square. These buildings serve as sacristies for the priests; here they eat the sacred meals, store cereal, sin, and guilt offerings, and vest for temple activities.

42:15-20 Measuring the outer court. The guide takes Ezekiel from the nave to the outer east gate and there begins the final measurements of the external east, north, south, and west walls. The perimeter of the exterior walls forms a square 500 cubits, or about 875 feet on a side. The purpose of this outer wall is to separate the holy area of the temple complex from its profane surroundings.

Restoration of the Temple

43:1-9 The return of the Lord. When full measurements have been completed, the guide takes Ezekiel to the east gate, where the prophet sees the return of God's glory to the reconstituted temple. God, who departed the temple on the throne-chariot by the east gate as a sign of judgment (11:22-23), now returns through this same gate as a sign of restoration (43:1-5). Ezekiel is overwhelmed and falls to his face (compare 1:28b), but the spirit (not the guide; compare 8:3) takes him to the inner court, where God speaks to the prophet, promising to dwell in the midst of Israel forever (vv. 7-9).

43:10-12 The law of the temple. God instructs Ezekiel to describe the measurements and design of the temple and to teach the house of Israel the law, or *torah* (instruction), of the temple, that the "whole surrounding area on the mountain top shall be most sacred." Ezekiel is charged with the priestly duty of making known to the people the *torah* about God's possession of this high mountain (compare 40:2) and the divine presence which sets this area apart as holy. Israel is to be ashamed of its sins in the face of the majesty of God.

43:13-27 The altar. Ezekiel receives detailed instructions about the dimensions and consecration of the altar. The altar of burnt offering is described as a large structure 18 cubits square at its base, with successive layers 16, 14, and 12 cubits square (vv. 13-17). At each of the four corners of the top layer are horns, vertical protrusions about 20.4 inches high (v. 15; traditionally these were places of utmost sanctity and refuge—see Exod 21:13; 27:2; 29:12; and 1 Kgs 1:50; 2:28). In an elaborate seven-day ritual, the Levitical priests are to consecrate this altar to God by ritually sacrificing young bulls, unblemished he-goats, and rams, and by scattering salt (vv. 18-27).

44:1-3 The closed gate. The heavenly guide takes Ezekiel from the inner court (43:5) to the outer east gate, which has been closed. The guide explains that this gate is to remain perpetually shut as a sign that God returned to the temple through it. Only the prince may sit in the vestibule of this gate structure when he eats his sacrificial meal.

The New Law

44:4-9 Admission to the temple. Next the guide leads Ezekiel to the inner court (v. 4; compare 43:5, where the spirit took him to this same place). The prophet observes God's glory filling the temple and once again falls to his face (compare 43:3). In a manner closely dependent on 40:4, the guide urges Ezekiel to listen closely to all he will hear about the statutes and laws of God's temple (v. 5).

The house of Israel is charged as a "rebellious house" (compare chs. 2; 12; 17:12; 24:3) that has in the past admitted foreigners to service in the sanctuary (vv. 6-8). The first law of the restored temple prohibits foreigners from entering the sanctuary (v. 9).

44:10-14 Levites. The next regulation limits the service of the Levites to that of temple servants and gatekeepers. Their duties include guarding the gates (perhaps they stood in the square, roomlike recesses in the corridors of the gate structures—see 40:10) and slaughtering sacrifices for the people (v. 11). This demotion to menial tasks (once performed by foreigners, according to verse 8) has come about because of the Levites' own sins (v. 12). They are now prohibited from the priestly ministries that involve handling the most sacred things of the temple (v. 13).

44:15-31 Priests. Because of their faithfulness, the Zadokites are elected to full priestly service (vv. 15-16). In a composite section, various regulations about their dress (vv.

17-19), personal conduct (vv. 20-22), duties (vv. 23-24), purification after mourning (vv. 25-27), and benefits (vv. 28-31) have been assembled. Within the sacred precincts priests are required to wear linen garments (v. 17; compare the man dressed in linen in 9:2, 11; 10:2, 7; and the vestry described in 42:14). Priests are required to keep their hair carefully trimmed (v. 20), to refrain from drinking before entering the inner court of the temple (v. 21), and to marry virgins or the widows of other priests (v. 22). Their responsibilities include teaching (v. 23) and juridical decision-making (v. 24). Should a priest become unclean by coming near a dead person, he must be ritually cleansed (see Num 19:11-12) and wait an additional seven days before entering the inner court (vv. 25-27). Priests are to own no land (v. 28; contradicted in 45:4; 48:10-12). Their income is a portion of the sacrifices (vv. 29-31).

45:1-8 The sacred tract of land. These verses detail the dimensions of a three-part division of a square area of land, about 43,750 feet on a side, into east-to-west strips (compare 48:8-22). The northernmost strip is assigned to the Levites, the middle strip to the sanctuary complex and the Zadokites, and the southernmost strip to the city and the people. An area on the east and west fringes of these strips is allotted to the prince. This idealized scheme places the temple at the center of the reapportioned land in an area separate from the city and the royal dwelling.

45:9-12 Weights and measures. Verse 9 is a self-contained oracle with its own introductory and concluding formulas. Addressed to the princes of Israel, it warns against violence and oppression. According to verses 10-12, the princes are to see that correct weights and measures are honestly regulated.

45:13-17 Offerings. Two offering ordinances have been combined detailing the contributions required from the people for the support of the temple (vv. 13-15) and from the people to the prince, who in turn is obliged to provide for the support of the temple (vv. 16-17). The original ordinance is most likely the one according to which the people support the temple directly.

45:18-25 The Passover; the feast of Booths. Three seven-day festivals are listed here. The first is an annual rite of purification of the temple (vv. 18-20). The second is the celebration of the Passover (vv. 21-24). And the third is the celebration of Booths, or the Ingathering of the crops. Passover, traditionally celebrated at the beginning of each year, and Booths, in the middle of the year, become occasions on which the prince offers sacrifices to ensure the purity of the community.

46:1-7 Sabbaths. Though the outer east gate is perpetually closed (44:1-2), the inner east gate may be opened on sabbaths and on new moons (and on other special occasions—see v. 12). The prince is permitted to enter through this gate to take sacrifices to the doorpost of the gate on behalf of the people who remain in the outer court. Listed here are the requirements for sabbath and new-moon sacrifices, which the prince presents to the priests, who alone are allowed to enter the inner court to sacrifice to the Lord (vv. 4-7).

46:8-15 Ritual laws. Ritual requires that the people enter the temple area by either the north or the south gate and that they leave by the gate opposite the one they entered (v. 9). Ritual also prescribes that the prince enter and exit in this same manner on nonfestal days (v. 10) and stipulates the offerings the prince is to take on solemn feasts as freewill offerings and as daily offerings.

46:16-18 The prince and the land. The prince's right to the land is strictly regulated. He can give land as a permanent inheritance to his sons and as a temporary gift to his servants. He is forbidden to seize land from others.

46:19-24 The temple kitchens. Once again resuming Ezekiel's tour of the temple (see chs. 40–42; 44:1-9), the heavenly guide takes the prophet first to the kitchen on the west side of the temple, where the priests eat their portions of the sacred offerings (vv. 19-20; not mentioned in the description of the priests' chambers in 42:1-14). Next they go to see four kitchens, one in each corner of the outer court, where the laity eat their sacrificial meals, which are prepared by the Levites (vv. 21-24; also not mentioned in the description of the outer court in 40:17-19; 42:15-20).

47:1-2 The wonderful stream. Ezekiel and his guide return to the front of the temple, where the prophet notices water trickling from below the south wall of the temple (v. 1). As the guide leads Ezekiel through the north outer gate, the prophet sees that the water has changed course and is flowing beneath the south wall of the temple toward the east (v. 2). The farther east the prophet goes, the greater the flow of water becomes. Four times the guide measures the water, and each time its depth increases dramatically until it has become a torrent (vv. 3-5). Ezekiel sees wonderful trees on both its banks (vv. 6-7). The guide explains that the life-giving waters of this river that springs from the throne of God will make the salt waters of the Dead Sea fresh, and barren places fertile with trees whose fruit is good for food and whose leaves drive sickness away (vv. 8-12).

Thus the measurements of the heavenly guide are finished in this climactic vision of the temple in Jerusalem as the source of a great river that flows out to the east, emptying into the Dead Sea and bringing life wherever it goes. This closing motif derives from the ancient myth of the mountain city from which the rivers of the earth flow (see Gen 2:10-14) and reappears in later apocalyptic literature (see Zech 14:8; Rev 22). It fittingly concludes Ezekiel's vision of revitalized worship in a restored temple.

The New Israel

47:13-20 Boundaries of the land. Inserted between an opening oracular formula (v. 13) and a closing formula (v. 23) is a description of the boundaries of the restored land. These boundaries portray no vast expansion of Israelite territory, but they break the old tribal boundaries by providing land in equal measure to each tribe, with little regard to the territory formerly occupied. The northern boundary is fixed as the frontier of Hamath, the pass between the Lebanon and Hermon mountains, and the southern boundary as Kadesh and the Wadi of Egypt. The Mediterranean provides the western border, and the eastern boundary is the Jordan River and the Dead Sea. The extent of this land is no greater than that held under David.

47:21–48:7 The northern portion. Before the distribution of the land begins, the notice appears that resident aliens, like native Israelites, are to have equal rights of ownership (vv. 22-23). Then, beginning in the north, the land is apportioned in equal east-to-west strips to seven tribes: Dan, Asher, Naphtali, Manasseh, Ephraim, Reuben, and Judah (48:1-8).

48:8-22 The sacred tract. The southern boundary of Judah's territory is the land set apart for the Levites, the temple, the Zadokites, and the prince. The details listed here accord with those specified in 45:1-8.

48:23-29 The southern portions. Below the sacred tract the following five tribes will settle: Benjamin, Simeon, Issachar, Zebulun, and Gad.

48:30-35 The gates of the city. The book closes with a reference to the twelve gates of the city of Jerusalem, one named for each of the tribes (the name of Joseph now appearing in place of Ephraim and Manasseh so as to make room for a Levi gate), to the city's circumference, and to its new name, "The Lord is here."

COMMENTARY: DANIEL

PART I: DANIEL AND THE KINGS OF BABYLON

Dan 1:1–6:29

The first section of the Book of Daniel is a collection of six independent, edifying short stories about Daniel and his companions. According to these chapters, Daniel was taken as a youth into Babylonian exile in 606 B.C.E. (see Dan 1:1), where he lived as a pious and loyal Jew who possessed the power to interpret dreams and visions. Purportedly telling of events that occurred in the court of Babylonia and Medo-Persia during the period of exile in the sixth century B.C.E., these stories are of two types: tests of loyalty (chs. 1, 3, 6) and displays of wisdom (chs. 2, 4, 5). They teach that through obedience to the law the faithful will triumph over adversity and convince foreign powers of the sovereignty of Yahweh.

These chapters raise troublesome issues about the date of composition, unity of authorship, and original language of the Book of Daniel. Most scholars are agreed that the Book of Daniel is the work of more than one author and that it took its present form around the year 165 B.C.E., toward the end of the oppressive reign of the Seleucid king Antiochus IV Epiphanes, who persecuted the Jews of Jerusalem and Judah (175–163 B.C.E.). The opening chapters, however, seem to be earlier compositions. Since the tales in Dan 1-6, with the possible exception of chapter 2, do not contain veiled apocalyptic historical references and do not explicitly refer to the persecution of the second-century community, they are likely from a time earlier than that of Antiochus IV. Their vocabulary, knowledge of Persian and Hellenistic customs, and fundamentally inaccurate descriptions of major sixth-century historical events and personages make it equally unlikely that the chapters come from their purported time of the Babylonian Exile. For instance, the historical Nebuchadnezzar attacked Jerusalem and led Jehoiachin, not Jehoiakim, into exile in 597 B.C.E., not 606 B.C.E., as claimed in 1:1; Belshazzar was the son of Nabonidus, not Nebuchadnezzar, as stated in 5:11; and Babylon was conquered by Cyrus, not Darius the Mede, as credited in 6:1. Chapters 1–6 employ a common folklore plot of the success of the uncompromising wise courtier, and thus contain a message for those who are living in oppression or in times when accommodation to foreign culture is a danger. Though there is room for debate, the chapters seem best to fit the need of the third-century community to resist assimilating too much Greek culture into Judaism.

That our final form of Daniel is written in three languages is an additional complication. The book begins in Hebrew (1:1–2:4a), shifts to Aramaic (2:4b–7:28), and then back to Hebrew for the remainder of the protocanonical chapters (8:1–12:13). Deuterocanonical Greek additions consisting of the "Prayer of Azariah and the Song of the Three Young Men" (inserted into the story of the fiery furnace in chapter 3) and "Susanna," "Bel," and "The Dragon" (appended in chapters 13:1–14:42) further testify to the complex compositional history that lies behind the present text.

The Book of Daniel as a whole is a religious tract written to encourage people faced with difficult choices. The opening chapters were likely told to encourage the Jewish people to stand firm in the midst of alien pressures, as Daniel and his friends had done.

Told first most likely in the third century B.C.E. and then retold in the second century B.C.E. by the redactor/author who gave shape to the final protocanonical text (chs. 1–12), these chapters set the tone for what follows.

1:1-21 The food test. The first short story introduces Daniel and his companions, tells of their training in Nebuchadnezzar's court, and recounts their struggle with the compromises required by life in a foreign culture, particularly the dilemma involved in being required to eat and drink ritually impure food.

Verses 1-2 set the story in Babylon in the year 606 B.C.E., identified here as the year in which Nebuchadnezzar laid seige to Jerusalem and led Jehoiakim to exile in the land of Shinar (an ancient name for Babylonia; see Gen 11:2; Zech 5:11). In actuality, Nebuchadnezzar attacked Jerusalem in 597 B.C.E., when Jehoiachin was on the throne, and it was this king who was led into exile when Zedekiah was appointed to rule Jerusalem (see 2 Kgs 24:10-17). Though historically inaccurate, the opening verses create a time of exile in a foreign setting as the scene of the narrative.

Verses 3-7 define the situation and characters involved in this story. Nebuchadnezzar instructs Ashpenaz, his chief chamberlain (=chief eunuch), to choose some talented, noble young Israelites for probationary training in the king's service. During the three years of their education, the candidates are to be fed from the royal table. Among those chosen by Ashpenaz are four young men from Judah, to whom Babylonian names are assigned: Daniel becomes Belteshazzar; Hananiah becomes Shadrach; Mishael becomes Meshach; Azariah becomes Abednego. In addition to a change of name, another historical source, Josephus, explains that selection for the king's service involves being rendered a eunuch (compare Esth 1:10; Deut 23:2). Without question, the identity and destiny of these four young men are altered by their training.

Verses 8-21 show that Daniel and his companions do not completely assimilate Babylonian ways. Daniel asks the chief chamberlain to allow him to eat food other than that from the royal table (the ritual regulations about meat are found in Lev 11:2-47; Deut 12:23-24; 14:3-21; there are no ritual laws concerning wine, though mention of wine as well as food is made also in Jdt 10:5; 12:1-4; on food as

a sign of obedience and separation, see Tob 1:10-11; 1 Macc 1:62-63; 2 Macc 5:27). When Ashpenaz refuses out of fear of royal retribution (v. 10), Daniel makes the same request of the steward, this time asking for a ten-day trial on vegetables and water for himself and his three companions (vv. 11-13). The steward agrees, and when the four young men flourish, he allows them to continue a diet of vegetables (vv. 14-16). God rewards the faithfulness of the four by granting them such success that at the end of their time of training the king finds them ten times more knowledgeable than anyone in Babylonia. They enter the king's service, where Daniel remains until the first year of Cyrus (v. 21; 538 B.C.E.). For these four youths, loyalty to the Lord is rewarded with success in the foreign court.

2:1-49 The king's dream. The second short story is a suspenseful tale of God's disclosure to Daniel of mysteries not known to others in Nebuchadnezzar's service. The three companions figure in only a secondary fashion (see vv. 13, 17-18, 49) in this story, which is primarily a demonstration of Daniel's great wisdom.

A brief introduction (v. 1) sets the date as 603 B.C.E., the second year of Nebuchadnezzar's reign (which contradicts the three years of training required in 1:5), and establishes the situation as Nebuchadnezzar's decree that an interpreter from his kingdom tell him the details of a disturbing dream he had dreamt and explain the meaning of the dream.

In the first episode (vv. 2-13), magicians, enchanters, and sorcerers are summoned before the king, who explains that he wants them to help him understand a terrible dream that has robbed him of rest. The first response of the interpreters (the language of the text shifts from Hebrew to Aramaic for 2:4b–7:28) is that they need only be told the dream and then they will give the king its meaning. Nebuchadnezzar commands that they tell both the dream and its meaning, or they will die (v. 6).

A second time the interpreters ask for the details of the dream (v. 7), and a second time Nebuchadnezzar refuses, claiming that he cannot trust their interpretation if they cannot tell the dream (vv. 8-9). In their third word to the king (vv. 10-11), the interpreters declare that no human being, only a god, can tell a dream. Nebuchadnezzar is so angered that he decrees the death of all the wise interpreters of Babylon (v. 12). The threatening note that Daniel and his companions are sought out as members of this condemned company closes the section (v. 13).

The second episode (vv. 14-24b) involves Daniel and Arioch, the captain of the king's guard, who has been sent to execute the wise interpreters. Though there are inconsistencies in this episode (notably between verse 16, where Daniel goes freely to the king and asks for time to discover the dream's interpretation, and verse 24, where Daniel asks Arioch to arrange an audience with the king) which suggest editorial additions, the basic story line is coherent. Daniel goes to Arioch and asks why the wise interpreters of Babylon have been sentenced to death (v. 15). Then Daniel returns home to tell Hananiah, Mishael, and Azariah about the failure and fate of the interpreters, and the four young men pray for deliverance from the God of heaven (v. 18; compare Tob 10:11; Jdt 5:8; 6:19; 11:17). Their prayer is answered during a nocturnal vision, in which God reveals the mystery of the king's dream to Daniel (v. 19). Daniel blesses the name of his God (vv. 20-23) and returns to Arioch, requesting a stay of execution for the wise interpreters and an audience with Nebuchadnezzar (v. 24a, b).

In the third and final episode (vv. 24c-45), Arioch takes Daniel to Nebuchadnezzar (vv. 24c-26), and Daniel tells the king both the dream and its interpretation. In the dream, Nebuchadnezzar saw a huge, human-like statue made of various metals that crumbled when it was struck at its feet by a mysterious stone (vv. 31-35). The symbolism of the destruction is explained as the demise of four successive empires, beginning with Babylon (vv. 36-45). Since this is the only place in the Old Testament where the ages of human history are described by symbolic metals, the kingdoms have been variously interpreted. Most likely, however, the head of the statue, which was made of gold, represented Babylon; the chest and arms, which were made of silver, represented Media; the belly and thighs, which were made of bronze, represented Persia; the legs, which were made of iron, represented Greece; and the feet, which were made of iron and tile, represented Alexander's divided empire ruled by the Ptolemies in Egypt and the Seleucids in Syria (the dynasty to which the hated Antiochus Epiphanes belonged). Daniel confirms as correct Nebuchadnezzar's revelation that the smashing of the statue by the stone cut by no human hand is a sign of the end of the present age and the coming of an indestructible kingdom that the God of heaven was establishing (vv. 44-45).

In a surprising conclusion (vv. 46-49), Nebuchadnezzar falls at Daniel's feet and worships him, readily acknowledges the superiority of Daniel's God (for other instances of royal conversion, see 3:95-96; 4:31-34; 6:26-28), and rewards Daniel for his great display of wisdom in telling the dream and its interpretation (a feat thus greater than that of Joseph, who interpreted the dream that Pharaoh *told* him—Gen 41) by promoting him to the highest office in the kingdom. The chapter closes with the note that Daniel requests administrative posts in the provinces for Shadrach, Meshach, and Abednego, while he himself remains at the king's court (v. 49).

3:1-97 The fiery furnace. The third short story is a dramatic contest about the identity of the true God, in which Shadrach, Meshach, and Abednego show their willingness to suffer death rather than worship a god other than the God of Israel. Daniel plays no part in the story of the fiery furnace (his brush with martyrdom occurs in the lions' den, ch. 6).

No date opens this story (though the Septuagint specifies "the eighteenth year of the reign of Nebuchadnezzar," 587 B.C.E.; compare Jdt 2:1). Instead, verses 1-7 deftly sketch the cause of the crisis. Nebuchadnezzar has set up a huge golden statue (87.5 feet tall and 8.75 feet wide) in the plain of Dura (an unknown Babylonian location) and has ordered an elaborate dedication ceremony, at which all are required to fall down and worship the golden statue or be cast into a white-hot furnace.

The conflict develops when some of the Babylonians approach Nebuchadnezzar and denounce the provincial administrators, Shadrach, Meshach, and Abednego, for refusing to serve the king's god (vv. 8-13). Enraged, Nebuchadnezzar sends for the three and demands that they worship the statue, saying, "Who is the God that can deliver you out of my hands?" (v. 15). Shadrach, Meshach, and Abednego refuse (to do otherwise would violate the commandments—see Exod 20:3-6), expressing both their hope that their God will deliver them and their willingness to die if necessary (vv. 17-18; compare Jdt 8:15).

The punishment is carried out in verses 19-90b. Nebuchadnezzar orders that the furnace be heated seven times more than usual (seven is used as a symbol of fullness and totality; see also 4:13, 20, 22, 29; 9:25). So hot is the furnace that the men who bound and threw Shadrach, Meshach, and Abednego into the flames are consumed themselves (for others who suffer the penalty they seek to inflict, see Dan 6:25; 13:62; Esth 7:10). But the three walk about in the flames, singing to God and blessing the Lord (v. 24).

Verses 24-90b, found only in the Septuagint, detail what happens while the three are in the furnace. Included here are two prayers (vv. 26-45, 51-90) and a brief connective narrative (vv. 46-50) known in the Apocrypha as the Prayer of Azariah (= Abednego) and the Song of the Three Young Men. Though supplements to the Hebrew Bible, these verses are considered fully authoritative, deuterocanonical portions of the story by Roman Catholics. In the first prayer (vv. 26-45), which makes no mention of the fiery furnace, Abednego praises God's wisdom and justice and confesses the sinfulness of his own nation (his petition for deliverance in verses 34 and 43 for the sake of the divine name is reminiscent of Ezek 20; 36:21; 39:25). While Abednego prays, the king's men continue to stoke the furnace, and its flames devour those nearby (vv. 46-48; compare v. 22). An angel of the Lord comes down to drive the flames from the furnace (vv. 49-50). In response to their miraculous deliverance, the three young men sing a song of praise and thanksgiving to the Lord for saving them from the raging fire (vv. 51-90; compare Ps 148).

Astonished to hear the singing and bewildered at seeing four men in the midst of the flames, Nebuchadnezzar calls Shadrach, Meshach, and Abednego out of the furnace (vv. 90c-97). When the king sees that they are unharmed, he blesses their God for sending them an angel of deliverance and decrees that any persons who blaspheme the God of Shadrach, Meshach, and Abednego will be cut to pieces and their houses destroyed, for "there is no other God who can rescue like this" (v. 96). Following this testimony, Nebuchadnezzar promotes the three, men-

tioned here for the last time in the Book of Daniel, to higher positions in the province of Babylon. As in chapter 2, faithfulness and loyalty to the Lord are rewarded with professional advancement.

3:98–4:34 Vision of the great tree. The fourth short story is written in the form of a testimonial letter from Nebuchadnezzar to his subjects (see 3:98-100). A dream and experiences of madness and restoration have convinced the king that the God of the Jews governs all human kingdoms and determines who will rule them. In this undated narrative, the king of Babylon recounts a lesson in humility taught him by the King of heaven (see 4:34). Daniel figures only in the portion of the story dealing with the interpretation of the king's dream (see 4:1-24).

The story opens with Nebuchadnezzar's account of his interpreters' failure to explain a frightening dream (vv. 1-4; the situation is similar to that of chapter 2, except that here the king will tell his dream). Daniel comes before the king, who graphically describes his dream (vv. 5-15) of a great, flourishing tree (compare Ezek 31:1-9) and the coming of a heavenly sentinel (a designation found only in Dan 4:10, 14, 20; used as a synonym for "angel" in 1 Enoch 1:5; 20:1; 2 Enoch 7:18; Book of Jubilees 4:15; Testament of Reuben 5:7; Testament of Naphtali 3:5). The heavenly sentinel announced that the tree would be cut down, leaving only its stump bound with a band of iron and bronze, and that a man would be struck with a disease that would make him like an animal for seven years.

With polite reserve, Daniel explains to Nebuchadnezzar that he is the tree that will be cut down and he is the man who will become like an animal if he fails to realize that "the Most High rules over the kingdom of men and gives it to whom he will" (v. 22). The stump will recover when the seven years of punishment have passed, but Daniel appeals to the king to atone for his sins by good deeds and thus avoid punishment (vv. 16-24; compare Sir 3:30).

Twelve months later, according to a narrative note about the king in verses 25-30, Nebuchadnezzar is struck down for pride in thinking that Babylon was built by his own achievements. As predicted, the king goes mad and eats grass like an animal (historically this is most likely a reference to Nabonidus, not Nebuchadnezzar).

In verses 31-34 Nebuchadnezzar, speaking in the first person again, says that at the end of the seven years of punishment his health, sense, and kingdom were restored and he blesses the Most High. He closes his letter to his subjects, not denying the existence of the Babylonian gods, but explaining that he now praises and exalts "the King of heaven, because all his works are right and his ways just; and those who walk in pride he is able to humble" (v. 34). In this story, acknowledgment of the Lord brings health and prosperity to a foreign king.

5:1–6:1 The writing on the wall. The fifth short story is a simple one-scene mystery story about a swiftly punished sacrilege committed by King Belshazzar, here described as Nebuchadnezzar's son (the historical Belshazzar was only a crown prince, since his father, Nabonidus, was the last king of Babylon). At a great royal banquet, under the influence of wine, Belshazzar calls for the sacred gold and silver vessels from the Jerusalem temple and uses them as goblets for himself and his guests to toast the Babylonian gods (vv. 1-4). His desecration is dramatically halted when a human finger, unattached to a body, appears and writes a mysterious message on the wall (vv. 5-6). The terrified king offers a reward to the wise interpreter of Babylon who can read the message, but none can be found (vv. 7-9; compare chs. 2 and 4). Hearing of the king's distress, the queen comes before him and suggests that Daniel be summoned (vv. 10-12).

In verses 13-16 Daniel is brought and offered the same reward as the others if he can interpret the writing (compare vv. 7 and 16). In verses 17-23 Daniel refuses the reward (though see v. 29) but agrees to interpret the message on the wall. First Daniel delivers a brief homily about the lesson of humility the Most High had taught Nebuchadnezzar (vv. 18-21; compare ch. 4). Then he accuses Belshazzar of rebelling against the Lord of heaven by profaning the temple objects that evening (vv. 22-23) and declares that the writing translates as a divine declaration of the end of the Babylonian empire (vv. 24-28). Belshazzar rewards Daniel as promised (v. 29). And later that same night the king is slain (v. 30). So it happens in this story that Daniel's wisdom is displayed and a foreign king is eliminated for failing to respect God's sovereignty. A historically confused note that Darius the Mede succeeded to the throne closes the story (6:1; at issue here is the fact that Cyrus the Persian captured the Babylonian throne of Nabonidus in 539 B.C.E.).

6:2-29 In the lions' den. The sixth short story is a dramatic test of loyalty involving King Darius, Daniel, and officials in the Medo-Persian court (compare ch. 3). Verses 2-10 describe an intrigue in which Daniel, who is one of the three supervisors of the one hundred and twenty provinces of the empire, is entrapped by jealous court rivals, who get the king to issue an immutable, irrevocable decree that for thirty days anyone who petitions a god or a person will be cast into a den of lions. Even though Daniel hears of the prohibition, he continues his customary practices of prayer (v. 11), thus violating the king's decree. Three times a day (see Ps 55:18) Daniel withdraws to an upper chamber in his home (compare 1 Kgs 17:19; Jdt 8:5) to kneel in prayer (see also Ezra 9:5; Ps 95:6; Luke 22:41; Acts 7:60; Jewish prayer postures also included standing with hands lifted toward heaven and prostration). The officials catch Daniel offering his petitions to God (v. 12) and hand him over to King Darius, who reluctantly sentences Daniel to the lions' den (vv. 13-16). Before sealing the den, the king says to Daniel, "May your God, whom you serve so constantly, save you" (vv. 17-18).

After a sleepless night, Darius returns to the den and calls out, "O Daniel, servant of the living God, has the God whom you serve so constantly been able to save you from the lions?" (vv. 19-21). Speaking the only words he utters in the entire story, Daniel replies, "O king, live forever! My God has sent his angel and closed the lions' mouths so that they have not hurt me. For I have been found innocent before him; neither to you have I done any harm, O king!" (vv. 22-23). The king orders Daniel taken out of the den, and his accusers and their families cast in (vv. 24-25).

Then Darius sends an edict (vv. 26-28) throughout his kingdom testifying to the power and sovereignty of the living God of Daniel (compare 3:95-96). A narrative note that Daniel fared well during the remainder of the reign of Darius and the reign of Cyrus (v. 29) closes the story.

PART II: DANIEL'S VISIONS

Dan 7:1–12:13

In this section the genre changes from short stories about Daniel and his three companions to apocalyptic visions (revelations; see the introduction) written in the first person and attributed to Daniel. In this series of four visions concerning the course of world history, Daniel is not the interpreter of mysteries but rather the recipient of secret revelations. Through symbolic visions (chs. 7, 8) and direct revelations (chs. 9, 10–12), Daniel learns of divine actions soon to occur. Through the mediation of angels, it is revealed that in the immediate future God will judge and destroy Antiochus IV Epiphanes. Because the chapters anticipate the death of Antiochus, it is likely that they were composed sometime late in his reign when he had turned to persecuting the Jews (around 168 B.C.E.), before his actual death (163 B.C.E.).

7:1-28 Vision of the four beasts. Still in Aramaic (as is 2:4b–7), this dream tells of a mysterious symbolic vision (vv. 1-14) and its interpretation (vv. 15-28) which were revealed to Daniel in the first year of King Belshazzar of Babylon (v. 1; compare ch. 5; Belshazzar ruled only as a regent for his father, Nabonidus, from 549 to 539 B.C.E.). In the first scene (vv. 2-8), the four winds stir the waters surrounding the earth (compare Gen 7:11), causing four horrible, evil beasts to rise from the chaotic waters: one like a lion with eagle's wings, which has its wings pulled off and is given human-like legs and a human mind (v. 4); a three-fanged animal like a ravenous bear (v. 5); a four-winged, four-headed animal like a leopard (v. 6); and a ten-horned, ravaging beast with great iron teeth and trampling feet, which is too horrible to be likened to any animal on earth (v. 7). As Daniel watches, three of the horns of the fourth beast are torn away by the emergence of a little horn with human-like eyes and a mouth that speaks arrogantly (v. 8).

The second scene of the dream is a heavenly judgment scene (vv. 9-12) in which Daniel sees the Ancient of Days (God, portrayed as an old, white-haired man dressed in white) presiding from a fiery throne with wheels (compare Ezek 1:26; 10:1) over a court of thousands of servants (on the heavenly court, see 1 Kgs 22:19; Job 1:6). When the

books are opened (v. 10; compare Isa 65:6, Mal 3:16), the four beasts are brought to trial. The fourth beast is sentenced to death, and its body is cast into the fire (v. 11). The other three beasts lose their power but are permitted to live (v. 12).

In a second event in the part of his dream about the heavenly court (vv. 13-14), Daniel sees "one like a son of man" (see comment at Ezek 2:1) coming on the clouds to the court of the Ancient One. This special human figure (a symbol for the "holy people of the Most High," according to verse 27) receives the heavenly gifts of everlasting dominion, glory, and kingship over the nations.

In his dream Daniel is bewildered by the vision of the trial of the four beasts in the heavenly court and the inheritance of the one like a son of man. He seeks the meaning of his vision from "one of those present," presumably an angel interpreter (vv. 15-28). He is told that the four beasts symbolize the four kingdoms over which the holy people of the Most High will triumphantly rule (vv. 17-18; Babylon, Media, Persia, and Greece; compare ch. 2). The ten horns of the fourth beast represent the divided Greek empire of Alexander the Great, and the blasphemous little horn represents the ruler Antiochus IV Epiphanes, who persecuted the Jews of Jerusalem and Judea (see 1 Macc 1:20-63). The angel assures Daniel that though the little horn wars against the holy ones, its triumph will be brief. Dominion over it will soon be given to the holy ones of Israel (vv. 19-27). The son of man here represents God's own people, to whom victory will be given in the immediate future (v. 27). Daniel records that the dream-vision ended and that he kept what he had seen to himself because he was terrified (v. 28).

8:1-27 Vision of the ram and he-goat. Written in Hebrew, this vision, which is dated two years after chapter 7 (see v. 1), tells of a battle between a two-horned ram (representing the Medo-Persian empire) and a he-goat (Alexander the Great). Using another set of symbols, this vision recapitulates the historical story told in chapter 7. The he-goat easily defeats the two-horned ram (v. 7; reference to Alexander's defeat of Persia in a series of battles between 334 and 331 B.C.E.). Then, at the height of the he-goat's power, its great unicorn is broken off (v. 8; reference to Alexander's early death in 323 B.C.E.) and four horns sprout in its place (v. 8; symbols of the four areas into which Alexander's kingdom was divided: Macedonia, Asia Minor, Syria-Babylonia, and Egypt). One of the horns sprouts its own little horn (v. 9; Antiochus IV Epiphanes). This little horn attacks earthly and heavenly powers, coming into combat with the prince of the host (seemingly God, though possibly the high priest, Onias III, who was assassinated in 170 B.C.E. by Antiochus) and desecrating the temple (vv. 10-12).

For this vision, Daniel (who is awake) is transported (compare Ezek 3:12; 8:3; 40:1) to Susa, the capital of Persia, to the banks of the river Ulai (vv. 1-2). There he meets the angel Gabriel (one of the archangels, according to 1 Enoch), who reveals that the appointed time of God's wrath is drawing near when Antiochus will be overthrown (vv. 15-25). The vision of the two thousand three hundred evenings and mornings that are to pass before the purification of the temple (vv. 13-14; 26) is confirmed as true (these 1150 days equal three years and seventy days, which is remarkably close to the actual time that elapsed between the desecration of the temple by Antiochus in 167 B.C.E. and its reconsecration on the twenty-fifth of Chislev in 164 B.C.E.; see 1 Macc 4:52-59; compare 2 Macc 10:3). Daniel is enjoined to keep secret all that he has seen. The note that he felt weak and ill for some days afterward and that he did not fully comprehend all that he had experienced closes this second vision (v. 27; compare 9:22, where Gabriel gives Daniel understanding).

9:1-27 Gabriel and the seventy weeks. The third vision of the divine mysteries concerning the end of time takes the form of a direct revelation to Daniel through the mediation of the angel Gabriel (see ch. 8). This narrative is set in the first year of the reign of Darius the Mede, the son of Ahasuerus (v. 1; no historical Ahasuerus ever had a son Darius; Darius I of Persia had a son Ahasuerus; Darius the Mede in Daniel is not a historical figure; the year according to the chronology of the book is 538 B.C.E.; compare 5:30–6:1). The chapter divides into two parts: Daniel's prayer (vv. 3-19) and God's answer as delivered by Gabriel (vv. 20-27).

Daniel's prayer is occasioned by his meditation on Jeremiah's prophecy that seventy years would pass while Judah remained desolate and its people captive (v. 2; see Jer 25:11-12; 29:10). As he puzzles over the truth hidden in this prophetic text, Daniel does penance and fasts (v. 3; on fasting as an appropriate way to prepare for a revelation, see 10:2-3; Exod 34:28). Then he offers a prayer that opens with a frank confession of the disobedient sinfulness of the covenant people (vv. 4-14); recalls God's graciousness in leading the people out of Egypt and God's justice in punishing Jerusalem (vv. 15-16); and petitions God to deliver the holy city and the nation that bears God's name (vv. 17-19). A threefold request (often called the Old Testament *Kyrie eleison* = "Lord, have mercy") summarizes and concludes the prayer: "O Lord, hear! O Lord, pardon! O Lord, be attentive and act without delay, for your own sake" (v. 19; compare 3:43).

Gabriel is sent by God to instruct Daniel on the meaning of Jeremiah's prophecy (vv. 20-27; cherubim had two wings—see Exod 25:20; seraphim had six wings—see Isa 6:2; but Gabriel is the first angel to travel by wings in the Old Testament; other angels simply appear). Daniel is given a reinterpretation of Scripture. He is told that not seventy years but seventy weeks of years (= 490 years) must pass before desolation will come to an end. The seventy weeks of years are divided into three segments: seven weeks (49 years) until an anointed leader (v. 25; that is, 587 B.C.E., the second deportation, to 538 B.C.E., the arrival of Cyrus the Persian); sixty-two weeks (434 years) until an anointed shall be cut down (v. 26; from the end of the Exile in 538 to the assassination of the high priest Onias III in 170 B.C.E.; historically not 434 but 368 years, an understandable mistake, since the precise length of the Persian period was not known to later Jewish writers like the author of Daniel); and one week (v. 27; 7 years; 170 to 163 B.C.E.), broken at the half-week when sacrifice will be abolished (presumably Antiochus IV's desecration of the temple in 168 B.C.E.). Thus, the fulfillment of Jeremiah's prophecy is at hand for Daniel.

10:1–12:13 Vision of the Hellenistic wars. The fourth and final vision divides into three parts: a lengthy introduction describing the appearance of God's emissary to Daniel and their conversation (ch. 10); a revelation that rehearses the history of the relationship between the Ptolemies in Egypt and the Seleucids in Syria and ends with the death of Antiochus (11–12:4); and an epilogue that closes with the sealing of God's secrets until the end of time (12:5-13). Chapters 10–12, which are actually a historical retrospective written in the form of prophecy, were most likely composed shortly before the death of Antiochus (163 B.C.E.), since the details of his death are inaccurately predicted (see 11:40-45).

Fictitiously dated 536 B.C.E., the third year of Cyrus, chapter 10 finds Daniel on the banks of the Tigris River (he is physically there, not transported as in 8:2). Following a three-week period of penance and fasting, Daniel is granted a revelation (vv. 2-3; compare ch. 9:3). A heavenly emissary appears to him on the twenty-fourth day of the first month (v. 4; it is unusual that Daniel fasted for much of the first month, since Exod 12:1-20 specifies it as the month during which Passover is celebrated; perhaps the author is alluding to the time when this celebration was suspended in 168 B.C.E. on account of a decree issued by Antiochus IV abolishing Jewish religion). Described in language reminiscent of Ezekiel, the angel-interpreter, a gleaming man dressed in linen with a belt of fine gold around his waist (vv. 5-6; compare Ezek 1:27-28; 9:2-3, 11; 10:2, 6, 7), is seen only by Daniel, who faints at the sight (vv. 7-9). Those who are with Daniel flee in terror.

In verses 9-14 the angel raises Daniel to his knees, addresses him as "beloved" (the title given by Gabriel in 9:23), and urges him to stand up and hear the message the angel has been sent to speak (compare Ezek 2:1). Assuring Daniel that he need not fear (v. 12), the angel explains that he was delayed in answering Daniel's prayer because for three weeks he was involved in a heavenly opposition with the patron angel of Persia, until finally Michael, the patron angel of Israel, came to his aid (v. 13; compare 10:21; 12:1). The angel reveals that he has come to tell Daniel what will happen to Israel in the days to come (v. 14).

Daniel responds by falling forward in stunned silence (v. 15). A second time the angel reaches out to comfort and reassure him. When the angel touches his lips, Daniel recovers his ability to speak (compare Isa 6:7; Jer 1:7) and says that he is seized with pangs of labor (v. 16; so also 1 Sam 4:19). Daniel wonders where he will get the breath to speak to the angel (v. 17). A third time the angel touches Daniel (v. 18), again addressing him as "beloved" and reassuring him that he need not be afraid (v. 19). And this time Daniel is strengthened and ready to hear the truth.

The revelation of what is written in the book of truth (11:2–12:4; compare 7:10) includes a brief account of the historical events from the time of Cyrus the Great to Antiochus IV (vv. 2-20) and a lengthier description of the reign of Antiochus IV (vv. 21-45). Much of the detail here is veiled and difficult to decipher. Perhaps the three kings of Persia (v. 2) are the successors of Cyrus: Cambyses, Darius I, and Xerxes. The great king of Greece (v. 3) is clearly Alexander the Great, whose empire was divided into four kingdoms after his sudden death in 323 B.C.E. (v. 4). The king of the south (v. 5) is Ptolemy, one of Alexander's generals, whose descendants controlled Egypt until 30 B.C.E.

After 248 B.C.E., Ptolemy II gave his daughter, Berenice, in marriage to Antiochus II (the grandson of Seleucus, who was king of the north) on the condition that Antiochus II divorce Laodice and disinherit their two sons. Laodice avenged herself and her disinherited children by poisoning Antiochus II and murdering Berenice and her child (v. 6). In retaliation, Ptolemy III, Berenice's brother, put Laodice to death when he invaded and plundered the Seleucid kingdom (vv. 7-8). Then Seleucus Callinicus invaded Egypt in 240 B.C.E., but he was defeated (v. 9). His sons, Seleucus Ceraunus and Antiochus III, continued the fight with Egypt (v. 10). But in 217 B.C.E. Ptolemy IV soundly defeated Antiochus III at Raphia on the southern border of Palestine, and Egypt gained control over Palestine (vv. 11-12). When Ptolemy V acceded to the throne at age five (203 B.C.E.), Antiochus III again attacked Egypt and recaptured Palestine (vv. 13-16).

In 193 B.C.E., hoping to gain control in Egypt, Antiochus III gave his daughter, Cleopatra, in marriage to Ptolemy V (v. 17). His plan failed because Cleopatra encouraged an alliance between Egypt and Rome. In 197 B.C.E. Antiochus III had invaded Asia Minor; in 192 B.C.E. he invaded Greece. The Romans defeated him in 191 B.C.E. at Thermopylae; and in 190 B.C.E., after the defeat at Magnesia near Smyrna, Rome forced Antiochus III into a treaty of subservience, imposed an enormous indemnity upon him, and took his son (Antiochus IV) as hostage (v. 18). In order to pay the tribute to Rome, Antiochus III tried to plunder the temple of Bel in Elymais, but its inhabitants killed him in 187 B.C.E. (v. 19). His successor, Seleucus IV (187–175 B.C.E.), attempted to plunder the temple treasure in Jerusalem but was murdered in a conspiracy led by Heliodorus, possibly abetted by Seleucus IV's younger brother, Antiochus IV (v. 20; compare 2 Macc 3:1-40).

Shortly before his death, for reasons that are now obscure, Antiochus II negotiated an exchange of hostages with Rome. In place of his younger son, Antiochus IV, he sent his older son, Demetrius. Thus in 175 B.C.E. when Seleucus IV was murdered, Antiochus IV, "a despicable person," usurped the throne from Demetrius and seized control of the Seleucid empire (v. 21). After Antiochus IV came to the throne, various parties in Jerusalem began to compete for appointment as high priest (from this time on, Seleucid and Roman leaders assumed the right to appoint and depose the Jewish high priest). First, in 174 B.C.E. Jason, the brother of the legitimate high priest, Onias III, bribed Antiochus IV for the appointment. Then, in 172 B.C.E. Menelaus offered a bigger bribe and secured the office. Menelaus not only bought the high priesthood but he had the deposed Onias III murdered (170 B.C.E.; vv. 22-23; compare 9:26; 2 Macc 4:32-43).

Details of the two Syrian-Egyptian wars are supplied in verses 24-35. In the first campaign (169 B.C.E.) against Ptolemy VI Philometer (the son of Antiochus's sister Cleopatra), Antiochus IV succeeded in taking captive Ptolemy VI, who had been given very poor strategical advice by his counselors (vv. 25-26; compare 1 Macc 1:16-19). When nobles in Alexandria filled the throne by crowning Ptolemy VII, Antiochus IV pretended to ally himself with his prisoner, Ptolemy VI, against Ptolemy VII (v. 27). If he could not conquer Egypt, Antiochus IV hoped, at least, to keep its royal family divided.

Though not entirely successful in Egypt, Antiochus IV returned home a richer man. But trouble brewed in Jerusalem, where Jason tried to reinstate himself in the office of high priest by murdering many of the supporters of Menelaus. Enraged, Antiochus IV invaded Jerusalem, massacred many Jews, reinstated Menelaus, and looted the Jerusalem temple (v. 28).

When word reached Antiochus IV that Cleopatra had reconciled her two brothers, Ptolemy VI and Ptolemy VII, to reign conjointly, he invaded Egypt a second time (168 B.C.E.; v. 29). But as Antiochus IV marched on Alexandria, he was stopped by a Roman delegation (Kittim = eastern Mediterranean people, here Romans) and was ordered by the legate, Popilius Laenas, to leave Egypt (v. 30a). Frustrated and hearing of further difficulties in Jerusalem, Antiochus IV ordered a bitter and bloody persecution of those who resisted Hellenistic culture and religion in Palestine (168–164 B.C.E.; see vv. 30b-35). In 167 B.C.E. an idol was erected and consecrated to Zeus, and swine were sacrificed on the altar of the Jerusalem temple (this is the "horrible abomination" in verse 31; see also 9:27; 12:11). Antiochus IV behaved blasphemously, even claiming divinity for himself (v. 36; on his coins he added the appellation Epiphanes, meaning "God Manifest"; many in his kingdom, however, called him Epimanes, meaning, "Mad Man"). In turning to Zeus Olympios, Antiochus IV neglected his ancestral god Tammuz (v. 37; compare Ezek 8:14).

The description of Antiochus IV's abominable reign closes with an inaccurate prediction of a successful final campaign against Egypt and an incorrect location of the place of his death as between the Mediterranean Sea and Jerusalem (vv. 40-45). The author of Daniel seems to have been unaware that Antiochus IV died of an undiagnosed disease at Tabae in Persia during an unsuccessful campaign in the fall of 163 B.C.E. (see 1 Macc 6:1-16). On account of this break with accurate historical reporting, critics argue that this apocalypse (chs. 10–12) was composed before Antiochus IV's final eastern campaign and death.

According to the poetic conclusion (12:1-3) to the revelation of what is written in the book of truth (11:2–12:4), the great tribulation of the end times will result in the vindication of the elect of God. Michael, Israel's patron angel, will arise to assist the redemption of Israel (v. 1). Many who sleep in graves will awake to live forever, others to be given to everlasting horror (v. 2). This promise of resurrection for individual reward and punishment is nearly unparalleled in the Old Testament (compare Isa 26:19). The faithful who have stood fast during the times of persecution are promised eternal reward (compare the more widespread Old Testament view that all the dead inhabit Sheol, which, though not a place of retribution, was a place where communion with God was cut off; see Isa 38:18; Ps 88:10-12). The new life described in Daniel exceeds both metaphoric description of political restoration suggested by texts like Ezek 37:1-14; Hos 6:1-2; Pss 80:19-20; 85:7 and hyperbolic expressions about being brought up from Sheol in texts like Pss 30:4; 86:13; 103:4; Isa 38:17.

Verse 4 is an injunction that Daniel keep the revelation secret until the end of time (compare 8:26). Given the fictitious date 536 B.C.E. assigned to the fourth vision in 10:1, the injunction is necessary to complete the narrative's pretended chronology. For the author, application of the revelation belonged to the time after the death of Antiochus, a time that was imagined at hand.

Verses 5-13 are little more than an epilogue that attempts to fix the time of the end. To two angels standing on either bank of the river (v. 5; compare the opening setting in 10:4) the man clothed in linen swears that the time of severe persecution will last for three and a half years (v. 7; compare 7:25; 9:27). Baffled at what he hears, Daniel requests further illumination, but he is denied (vv. 8-10). And in what appear to be two later additions, the time of persecution is extended, first to 1290 days (v. 11), and then to 1335 days (v. 12). In verse 13 Daniel is told to go his way until the end. On this note of imminent relief from persecution, the protocanonical text of Daniel ends.

PART III: APPENDIX

Dan 13:1–14:42

The third section of the Book of Daniel is a collection of three edifying deuterocanonical short stories about Daniel (Susanna, 13:1-64; Bel, 14:1-22; the Dragon, 14:23-42). Found only in the Septuagint, these stories are like those in Dan 1:1–6:29. They, too, teach that faithfulness triumphs over adversity and that foreign powers can be convinced of the sovereignty of the Lord.

13:1-63 Susanna's virtue. In the Greek and Old Latin translations of the Book of Daniel, the story of Susanna is placed before chapter 1, as an introduction (most likely because in verse 45 Daniel is described as a young boy in Babylon). In the Vulgate (the Latin translation of the Bible made by Jerome in about 382 C.E.), the story of Susanna is listed as chapter 13.

This story is different from all others in the Book of Daniel in that the conflict is internal to the Jewish community and the protagonist is a woman. Chapter 13 is a test of Susanna's courage and loyalty to the law in the face of false accusation, as well as a display of Daniel's wisdom and cleverness in solving what is sometimes called one of the earliest detective stories.

Babylon is the setting of the narrative (v. 1; compare chs. 1–5). Verses 1-4 tell that Joakim, a very rich and highly respected Jew, married the very beautiful and God-fearing Susanna (compare Jdt 8:7-8), who had been well trained in the law of Moses by her parents (only her father, Hilkiah, is mentioned by name). Joakim's house and its garden are the scene of the tale (compare the instruction in Jer 29:5 that the exiles build homes and plant gardens in Babylon).

Verses 5-14 introduce the two antagonists and describe the situation that occasions the conflict. Two wicked old men, who are appointed judges of the exiled community, lust for Susanna, who usually came out for a walk in the garden at noon, after the judges had finished trying cases and presumably had left Joakim's garden. Secretly watching her every day, the judges develop a passionate desire to have intercourse with her (v. 11; a variety of Greek expressions for sexual intimacy are used in this narrative: "to be with/have intercourse with," vv. 11, 39; "lay down with," v. 37; "so give in to our desire and be with us," v. 20; and "making love," v. 54). Though both judges pretend to leave for lunch one day, they catch each other spying on Susanna, admit their desire, and agree to watch for an occasion when they might be alone with her.

The dreadful day is described in verses 15-27. On a very hot afternoon, when everyone has supposedly left the garden, Susanna instructs her two maids to shut the garden doors and to prepare a bath for her (v. 17). When the maids have gone, the two elders appear and demand that Susanna lie with them (v. 20), saying that if she refuses, they will testify that they saw a young man with her in the garden (v. 21).

Admitting the dilemma, Susanna chooses to call out for help (see Deut 22:23-27), saying, "It is better for me to fall into your power without guilt than to sin before the Lord" (v. 23). As she calls out, the elders also shout, and one of them runs and opens the garden gate, so as to circumstantially convict her. When those in the house rush out, the elders tell their concocted story about the young man and Susanna. Believing the elders, the servants are very much ashamed of their mistress.

The next day, when the two judges come to hear cases in Joakim's garden, they order Susanna to appear for judgment (vv. 28-41). They are determined that she be put to death. Veiled, Susanna appears with her parents, children, and relatives (her husband is not mentioned until verse 63). The elders order her to show her face, "so as to sate themselves with her beauty" (v. 32), and place their hands on her head (see Lev 24:14) as they make their case against her. Without question, the assembly believes the two respected judges and condemns Susanna (v. 41).

Susanna protests her innocence to the Lord (vv. 42-43), and her prayer is heard (v. 44). God stirs a young boy named Daniel to speak out in her defense (v. 45). Daniel refuses to participate in an execution without clearer evidence (vv. 46-49). The trial is reopened (vv. 52-59), and Daniel examines the judges. He asks each separately under which tree they saw Susanna and her lover. One answers, "Under a mastic tree," and is told he will be "split" in two (v. 55; there is a play on words in the Greek). The other answers, "Under an oak," and is promised he will be "cut" in two (v. 59—another play on words). Though Daniel declares the fate of the two evil judges before both have testified, their own lies seal

their fate. According to the law (see Deut 19:16-21), they must suffer the fate they planned for the one falsely accused (vv. 60-62). Susanna's parents, relatives, and husband praise God because Susanna is found innocent (v. 63). And Daniel becomes famous among his people (v. 64).

Though seemingly trapped in a situation in which social convention allowed men of age and rank to determine her fate, Susanna teaches that purity, truthfulness, and the practice of prayer are rewarded by a God who answers a woman's prayer, inspires Daniel to interrogate her accusers, and holds out a future of hope.

14:1-42 Bel and the Dragon. Two very brief detective stories that ridicule idolatry appear in chapter 14 (compare chs. 3, 6). In the first (vv. 1-22), Daniel convinces Cyrus that the Babylonian god Bel (= Marduk) does not consume the sacrifices that are daily offered to him. By putting ashes on the sanctuary floor, Daniel proves to the king that the priests and their families enter through a secret trap door and take the sacrificial food for themselves.

In the second story (vv. 23-42), Daniel convinces the king that the great dragon is a worthless god. By feeding the animal pitch, fat, and hair, Daniel causes it to burst and die. Angered that they have lost their priests, Bel, and now their dragon, the people of Babylon demand that they be allowed to throw Daniel into a den of lions (v. 31; compare ch. 6). Daniel spends six days in the den with seven lions, but he is unharmed because God had an angel transport the prophet Habakkuk by the hair of his head from Judah to Babylon to bring Daniel food (vv. 33-39). On the seventh day the king comes out and finds Daniel in good health, praises the God of Daniel, and orders those who sought Daniel's death to be put into the lions' den. They are quickly devoured (v. 42). Daniel's wisdom is once again proven and rewarded, and a foreign power is convinced of the sovereignty of Yahweh.

JOEL, OBADIAH, HAGGAI, ZECHARIAH, AND MALACHI

Mary Margaret Pazdan, O.P.

INTRODUCTION

A variety of starting points is available for exploring a text of the Bible. The process of selection is similar to how a viewer encounters snapshots in a photo album. One individual focuses sharply on a single image, while another admires the arrangements or qualities of composition. A third person enjoys the sequence and patterning of several pages, whereas a fourth examines an entire album for imaginative contours. If the snapshots or the album captures the attention of the viewer, they may provide opportunities for additional variations by repeated inspection.

The viewer's experiences also inform what is perceived. A family member, relative, or friend is delighted to find memories suddenly revitalized by significant photos that celebrate life (for example, birthdays, anniversaries, summer holidays). Juxtaposed to these photos, however, are others that remind the viewer of circumstances that have modified the moment captured on film (for example, distance, aging, death). Viewers unfamiliar with the photos need explanations from others to give the photo meaning.

The photographer's experiences direct the selection of the subject. Often the photo represents more possibilities to the viewers than the photographer saw in framing the subject. The understanding of the photo deepens when the viewer and the photographer discuss its importance. The reality of the photo is seldom exhausted, because each viewer sees with limited perception.

Like the viewer and photographer, a number of biblical scholars began to dialogue with persons of other academic disciplines. No longer confined to the historical-critical method of the nineteenth century, commentators cautiously applied the distinctive methods of new literary, canonical, and sociological criticism to broaden the possibilities of interpreting prophecy, including the five books treated in this commentary. The interdisciplinary method indicated in scholarly and popular articles for over a decade may provide insights into the meaning of postexilic prophecy, which had been generalized and undervalued.

Why does prophecy from its early development (about 1000 B.C.E.) through the period of the Exile (586–538 B.C.E.) receive more attention in surveys of the Old Testament?

a) The books that record the growth of prophecy are wonderful literature. Nathan, the court prophet, indicts King David (1000–967 B.C.E.) by means of the parable of the ewe lamb (2 Sam 12:1-15). A cycle of narratives about northern Israel (869–815 B.C.E.) records the adventures of Elijah and Elisha: a contest on Mount Carmel with the prophets of Baal, meeting Jezebel, miracles, experiences of God, involvement with political and religious leaders (see 1 Kgs 17–21; 2 Kgs 1–9).

Prophetic books named for individuals follow the *narratives about* prophets. They offer biographical details, dramatic gestures, and bold prophetic oracles to communicate the word of God. Isaiah, Jeremiah, and Ezekiel appear as inspiring, heroic figures in the struggles of Judah (782–586 B.C.E.). The prophets stimulate interest and imagination for scholars. Concurrently, they appeal to children and adults in catechetical and sermon contexts as well as by their association with literature, music, and art.

b) Many events described by the texts are supported by the parallel literature of the ancient Near East. Archeological data confirms the historical and literary perspectives of preexilic and exilic prophecy. Analysis and comparison with extrabiblical materials generate additional study and discovery.

c) The books indicate common political-religious dimensions of kingship and temple. Fidelity of the king and community to the Jerusalem temple is *the* standard by which northern Israel and Judah are judged (see 1 Kgs 12–2 Kgs 25). The prophets exhort the people to be faithful to the covenant stipulations first formed with God on Mount Sinai through Moses. They develop the ethical dimensions of Torah, images of God and future liberation, often evoking images from Exodus.

d) New Testament authors frequently refer to persons and passages from preexilic and exilic prophecy to describe Jesus, the Jews, and early communities of believers.

When earlier scholars compared postexilic prophecy with the characteristics of preexilic and exilic prophecy mentioned above, the former appeared unimportant and secondary in the prophetic corpus. The narratives are limited, lacking in personal detail, and seldom the subject of art or literature. The historical and literary data is sparse; often reconstruction is contradictory. The political, social, and religious conditions after the Exile do not compare favorably with the symbolic unity of kingship and temple. The texts are quoted infrequently by New Testament authors.

Contemporary scholars do not judge postexilic prophecy by earlier prophecy. Prophetic forms and content aligned to king and temple are no longer considered necessarily normative or significant. What, then, is appropriate for interpreting postexilic writings? In this commentary the central focus is the particular contribution of each book as a witness to restoration after the experience of exile. Information about a particular author,

dating, and composition, together with an outline of the book, is given just before the commentary on each book. Considerations common to Joel, Obadiah, Haggai, Zechariah, and Malachi are described below.

Location in the Old Testament

The Jewish canon and the Alexandrian canon include the Books of Joel, Obadiah, Haggai, Zechariah, and Malachi among the Twelve Minor Prophets. What does the division imply? The designation "minor" has been interpreted as meaning "inferior" or "less important," because the Twelve Minor Prophets follow the Latter Prophets (Isaiah, Jeremiah, Ezekiel) in the Jewish canon, and the Prophets (Isaiah, Jeremiah, Baruch, Lamentations, Ezekiel, Daniel) in the Alexandrian canon. The term "minor" probably refers to the size of the texts compared with the prophetic books that precede them.

In a manner unlike that of the Major Prophets, the historical factors for ordering and collecting the Twelve Minor Prophets remain obscure. Scholars examine the canons and the books for implications of how the process may have occurred. In comparing the canons, the first and the seventh through the twelfth books are identical (Hosea, Nahum, Habakkuk, Zephaniah, Haggai, Zechariah, Malachi), while the second through the sixth books are in different order: Jewish canon (Joel, Amos, Obadiah, Jonah, Micah); Alexandrian canon (Amos, Micah, Joel, Obadiah, Jonah).

Which list is earlier? What accounts for the change of order? There are three suggestions for the ordering of the books in each canon: (a) chronology; (b) repetition of words and phrases between books, for example Amos 1:2 and Joel 4:16; (c) mechanical considerations, for example the length of a scroll. Today the questions and suggestions are unresolved.

How twelve independent prophetic books became a collection that was considered as one book is a puzzle. Often the fact that the Twelve could be written on one scroll is given as a solution. Historically, the process of collection was completed by 300 B.C.E. Sirach, writing a century later, acknowledges the prophets in his praise of Israel's heroes:

Then, too, the TWELVE PROPHETS—
may their bones return to life from their
    resting place!—

Gave new strength to Jacob
and saved him by their faith and hope.
(Sir 49:10).

Sirach's grandson, translating the Hebrew text into Greek after 132 B.C.E., includes the division of prophets in his foreword: "Many important truths have been handed down to us through the law, the prophets, and the latter authors; and for these the instruction and wisdom of Israel merit praise."

The Minor Prophets were also important to the Qumran community, whose scrolls include a commentary on Micah as well as eight incomplete copies of the Twelve Minor Prophets. In Christian tradition the title "Minor Prophets" is attributed to Augustine (*De civitate Dei*, XVIII, 29). Canonical critics observe that the process of ordering and collecting the Twelve Minor Prophets is less important than the factors involved in shaping each book and the way the final form of each book functioned in a particular community of faith.

Historical background

The ministry and textual tradition of Joel, Obadiah, Haggai, Zechariah, and Malachi extended over two centuries of postexilic Judaism. Although the period is poorly documented, some biblical witness and archeological data are available to reconstruct the historical context for the prophets and their literary records.

2 Kgs 23:36–25:30, 2 Chr 36:9-21, and Jer 32–34; 37–39; 52 interpret the final days of Judah and the deportations to Babylon. In 599 B.C.E. King Jehoiakim refused to pay tribute money to Nebuchadnezzar, ruler of the neo-Babylonian empire. Although the biblical texts are unclear about Jehoiakim's fate, they indicate that his son Jehoiachin had ruled for only three months when Nebuchadnezzar forced him to surrender Jerusalem in the spring of 597 B.C.E. Jehoiachin, the royal household, craftspersons, military officials, and prominent citizens were sent into captivity. The sacred vessels of the temple were also transported to Babylon.

To reduce the possibility of further rebellion, Nebuchadnezzar appointed Jehoiachin's uncle, Zedekiah, as king of Judah. For eleven years he wavered between the patronage of the pro-Egyptian party and the protection of Jeremiah. Having chosen resistance as his brother did, he, too, had to surrender to Nebuchadnezzar, who ordered the palace, the temple, and the city destroyed; the ruler and inhabitants were deported to Babylon in 586 B.C.E.

For the few persons remaining near Jerusalem, Nebuchadnezzar appointed Gedaliah as governor. After he was assassinated by a rebel, the Babylonian policy of deportation and division of the land continued in Judah and other parts of the empire. The Edomites, ancient enemies of Israel, seized some territory in Judah. The Book of Obadiah is directed against their treachery. The Book of Lamentations reflects the anguish and tragedy of this period for the Jews.

After Nebuchadnezzar died in 562 B.C.E., the empire gradually declined and Cyrus the Persian seized the opportunity for twenty years of conquest. His success culminated in the surrender of Babylon in 539 B.C.E. Cyrus' liberal attitude toward subject peoples extended to authorizing their return and financing the restoration of temples and cults. The Cyrus Cylinder, an inscription written on a clay barrel and telling of Cyrus' Babylonian triumph and of his policy of allowing captives to return to their homelands, indicates his intentions: "May all the gods whom I have placed within their sanctuaries address a daily prayer in my favor . . . that my days may be long."

Cyrus also issued a decree to the Babylonian Jews. Under the leadership of Sheshbazzar, prince of Judah, a small group returned bringing donations from their neighbors and the confiscated temple vessels (Ezra 1:2–2:70). Meanwhile, large numbers remained in Babylon, preferring their homes, structures of community life, and loyalty toward the lenient government to an uncertain future in ravaged Judah (compare Jer 29:1-9).

The returnees found a decimated land, inhospitable landowners, intermarriage, and syncretistic worship. Sheshbazzar, appointed governor, initiated attempts to restore the sacrificial altar and the foundations of the temple. The confused chronology and narrative detail of Ezra, the only biblical record for the period, do not indicate what happened to Sheshbazzar.

After Cyrus' death, Cambyses, his son, reigned until 522 B.C.E. At his death widespread rebellion occurred in many areas of the empire. Darius, an officer of Cambyses' army, stabilized the empire after two years of fierce battles. During that time another group of Babylonian Jews returned to Jerusalem, including Zerubbabel, appointed governor, and Joshua, the high priest. During their dual leadership there were renewed efforts to rebuild the temple.

Obstacles, however, continued to impede progress. Within the community, antagonism over property claims continued. Droughts and poor soil added to the burden of harsh living conditions. Opposition to the restoration came from neighboring areas under Persian control as well as from the Samaritans to the north. Darius intervened to settle the disputed authorization for rebuilding the temple. Haggai and Zechariah, too, encouraged the residents to persevere in their efforts.

In the spring of 515, nearly twenty-five years after Cyrus' decree, the community offered sacrifice to God and dedicated the temple (Ezra 3–6). There is no evaluation of Zerubbabel's leadership. He, like Sheshbazzar, disappeared mysteriously from the narrative of Ezra. Joshua and the priestly class associated with the temple presumably became the source of political and religious authority for the community.

There is a gap of fifty years in the biblical record, although the undated text of Malachi offers an assessment of community life just before the arrival of Ezra. The author condemns the irresponsibility of the priests in cultic matters, intermarriages with non-Jews, and social injustice.

Ezra, commissioned by Artaxerxes I, initiated a religious reform in 458 B.C.E. by condemning intermarriage, appointing honest magistrates and judges, and assembling the people for the reading of the law (Ezra 7:1–10:16; Neh 8:1–9:37). Nehemiah, cupbearer to Artaxerxes I, was governor of Judah from 445–433 B.C.E. He protected Jerusalem from its enemies by supervising the rebuilding of the city walls. After a brief absence, Nehemiah returned as governor (430–418 B.C.E.) to enforce religious laws regarding the support of temple officials, marriage, and observance of the sabbath (Neh 1:1–7:5; 11:1–13:31).

The undated Book of Joel is considered a witness to the situation of the community after the reforms of Ezra and Nehemiah. The author exhorts the people to public prayer and penance to avert God's judgment. It is a preparation for "the day of the Lord," the ultimate judgment between Israel and the nations.

There is a gap of nearly a century in the biblical record, during which time the Persian empire declined and the Greek empire developed under the leadership of Alexander the Great (336–323 B.C.E.). Second Zechariah (chs. 9–14) is addressed to the Jewish community during this emergence of a new world empire. The oracles describe a cosmic battle, the Messiah, and the new kingdom of God.

Attitudes and perspectives about reconstruction

The Babylonian Jews who returned to Jerusalem in two stages participated in the multiple tasks of reconstruction. What challenges did they encounter together with the group already well established in Judah during the Exile? In addition to the obstacles mentioned above, both groups were confronted with the complex question of identity.

The province of Judah was one of several provinces included in the satrapy "West of Euphrates" (see Ezra 4:17, 20; 5:6), whose administrator, the satrap, probably resided in Damascus. Judah enjoyed the type of independence granted to members of the nearly two dozen satrapies of the vast Persian empire, including freedom for cultic activity. Judah, with Jerusalem as its center, can be identified as a temple-community like others restored and subsidized by the central government. Jerusalem functioned both as a cultic center for prayer as well as an administrative center for the province.

The officials appointed by the central government mediated their authority as governors—for example, Sheshbazzar, Zerubbabel, Nehemiah. In daily affairs, however, the priests exercised authority over the community. They decided on the status of individuals in the community according to their participation in and support of the cult. Their legislation about the standards of purity necessary for worshipers included the condemnation of those who engaged in syncretistic worship, those who married resident aliens, and those who transacted business with non-Jews.

Both residents and returnees were affected by these criteria. Tension developed among the two groups, including the priestly class. The conflict among the priestly functionaries resulted in a division of responsibility. The Zadokite priests (returnees from Babylon) assumed the major position for cult and administration; the Levites were relegated to minor positions with little authority.

Some scholars suggest that two mainstreams of religious authority developed from this situation and that this accounts for the decline of prophecy. The theocratic group was associated with the Zadokite priests and the rebuilding of the temple and the reconstitution of religious life according to the Torah and the vision of Ezekiel (Ezek 40–48). The apocalyptic group was associated with the Levites and a future transformation of the present situation according to the vision of Deutero-Isaiah (Isa 40–55). This assessment, however, is too sharp. It does not allow for the plurality of religious experience and perspective.

The manner of restoration of the community and its identity is related to the interpretation of God's revelation as understood by the individual prophet. Each responded to the needs of a particular community. Each had a provisional proclamation directed toward encouraging that community to be faithful to God:

a) *Obadiah* implored God to destroy the Edomites and to vindicate Israel from their deceit.

b) *Haggai* and *Zechariah* believed that the restoration of the temple would hasten the advent of God for the purpose of dwelling in Jerusalem forever. Zechariah also considered the relationship of God to other nations. Both prophets encountered the resistance of the Jerusalemites due to shattered dreams and oppressive living conditions, which curtailed enthusiasm and stamina for reconstruction. Neither prophet was certain about the role of the governors and the priestly class. Even after the completion of the temple, the past could not be an appropriate model for the present.

The ministry of these prophets was effective because they provided inspiration for a common identity among the residents, that is, a temple-community and the reestablished locus for cultic activity. After their deaths the dilemma of unfulfilled prophecy and unresolved relationships among their neighbors continued. Uncertainty, confusion, and instability characterized the period.

c) *Malachi* addressed abuses in cultic practices. *Joel* admonished the community about its relationship to God and its symbolic expression in worship. Both prophets desired a renewal of dedicated religious life for persons who would accept their message.

d) The writings of *Second Zechariah* stirred dormant hope and dispelled the apathy of the community through visions of climactic struggle followed by the day of the Lord, a day when a kingdom of peace and blessing would be secured forever.

These five prophets may well be remembered for activity during a bleak period of Israel's history. Each prophet with his literary record witnesses to a particular situation somewhat influenced by imperial Persian and Greek policies, yet transcending them with a religious vision related to the experience of the community to whom the message is addressed. Being convinced of the fidelity of God, they spoke a message calling the community to respond appropriately. They exhorted the community to be faithful to God, the constant reality of their past history and their present experience.

The postexilic prophets in this series cannot be judged by whether or not their message was fulfilled in subsequent history. The mystery of the faithful God and the manner in which the individual and the community respond are the perspectives that these books develop. In addition, the fact that communities of believers preserved and edited these proclamations and considered them to be the authentic revelation of God indicates their significance for developing faith in postexilic communities.

Literary forms

The Books of Joel, Obadiah, Haggai, Zechariah, and Malachi contain poetry and prose. There are visions and oracles attributed to the prophets whose names are the superscriptions for the books as well as editorial insertions to consolidate the material and provide interpretation for later communities. The books refer to earlier Scripture (Torah and Prophets) by allusion to and repetition of events and ideas. Occasionally there are direct quotations from earlier prophets.

The literary structure of each book is developed from the particular context in which the message was first proclaimed. Prophetic formulas common to preexilic and exilic books are sometimes located in the postexilic compositions; occasionally they are combined with new patterns. In particular, scholars often regard sections of these books as indicating a new literary form, viewpoint, and content known as "apocalyptic." Since the literary structure of a particular text is a primary indicator for its religious meaning, it is important to understand the structure in order to interpret the significance of the text. A few literary considerations for each book are presented below according to the chronological order already suggested.

Obadiah, the shortest book in the Old Testament, consists of two sets of oracles received in a vision according to the tradition of Jerusalemite prophets. The first set of oracles describes the destruction of Edom (vv. 2-9) in language similar to that of Jer 49:7-22. This neighbor of Israel is condemned for its betrayal of Jerusalem to Babylon (vv. 10-14). The second set was added later to include the day of the Lord as a judgment for all nations (vv. 15-16). The event culminates in the restoration of Israel and the establishment of the universal kingdom of God (vv. 17-21). Some scholars suggest that the structure of the oracles (vv. 2-17) indicates a community at worship proclaiming God's sovereignty through the proclamation of oracles against its enemies.

The two chapters of *Haggai* also contain oracles interspersed with editorial frameworks to interpret them. The frameworks include: (a) the chronology of Haggai's ministry to the residents of Jerusalem (1:1, 15; 2:1, 10, 20); (b) insertions of traditional prophetic formulas to introduce an oracle, such as "the words of the Lord through the prophet . . ." (1:1, 3; 2:1, 10, 20; compare 1:12, 13); (c) a report about the result of Haggai's preaching to the community (1:12, 14). Although words of comfort are included in the oracles, suggesting the judgment of salvation characteristic of classical prophecy (1:13; 2:4, 5), the oracles add a new development—the disputation. Some indications of this pattern are rhetorical questions (1:4; 2:3, 16) and a question-and-answer format (1:9-11).

Oracles do not function as the major liter-ary form of revelation in *First Zechariah* (chs. 1-8); rather, they are a secondary pattern occurring in a collection (chs. 7-8) and attached to visions, which are the primary pattern of revelation (1:7-6:8). The visions constitute some of the most difficult texts to interpret in biblical literature. Some scholars suggest that the significance of the "night" visions consists in providing an alternative to the oracles and visions of Ezekiel (chs. 40-48) and of Haggai about temple reconstruction. Zechariah constructed a theological perspective for fidelity to God in the new situation of "in betweenness."

In the Book of *Malachi* the question-and-answer format that appeared in Haggai (and First Zechariah) becomes the basic structure of the oracles. This catechetical pattern was suitable for exhorting the community and its cult officials to be responsible for their relationships to God. They were urged to revitalize indifferent cultic practices and to observe the laws of marriage and the prohibitions against divorce (1:2-3:21). The two appendices (3:22-24) conclude with an instruction to be faithful to the law and a description of Elijah, God's messenger who will reconcile family members.

The Book of *Joel* is a collection of oracles with two interrelated themes: devastation and salvation. In the first part (1:1-2:17), the prophet functions as a cult figure. He calls the people to repentance in a communal lamentation liturgy intended to avert a disaster far worse than the locust plague. After introducing the concept of "the day of the Lord," Joel admonishes them about their expectations. In the second part (2:18-4:21), the prophet describes the day of the Lord in more detail. Throughout the oracles there is frequent allusion to, or direct quotations of, sayings found in other prophetic collections; for example, Isa 13:6 and Ezek 30:2-3 (Joel 1:15); Zeph 1:14-15 (Joel 2:1-2); Obad 17 (Joel 3:5).

Second Zechariah (chs. 9-14) is separated from First Zechariah by nearly two centuries of political and religious history. The chapters are divided into two sections. Each section has its own introduction (chs. 9-11 and 12-14). Unlike First Zechariah, the oracular structure is prominent. Within the oracles there is no original revelation; rather, the function of the oracles is to collect the expectations of earlier prophets and to indicate how they may be fulfilled; for example, Zeph 3:14ff. (Zech 9:9); Isa 5:26 (Zech 10:8); Joel 4 (Zech 14). Another major difference is the absence of any mention of the temple builders and officials. In addition, there are no chronological indications nor any coherent "historical" framework. Finally, the chapters of Second Zechariah have been assessed for apocalyptic language and viewpoint.

Relationship to apocalyptic writings

In the past fifteen years there has been renewed interest in the origin, language, structure, content, and interpretation of Jewish apocalyptic writings. Postexilic prophecy has been considered a possible source for apocalyptic, since the phenomenon did not parallel the structure and content of classical prophecy. Some scholars constructed a polarity between the "traditionalists" and the "visionaries" existing in the temple-community. Their conflict of interests resulted in the formation of two distinctive groups. The "traditionalists" reaffirmed the position of supporting the temple and its officials. The "visionaries" expressed their radical hopes for a new identity by the transformation of the present situation. Today interdisciplinary analysis with the social sciences, especially cultural anthropology, appears to support this interpretation.

Intra-group conflict and fluctuating circumstances can be catalysts for the formation of apocalyptic groups. The more difficult question is not why *an* apocalyptic viewpoint and literature emerged but why *this particular form* emerged. The religious diversity apparent in postexilic communities suggests that apocalyptic development was not the inevitable result of particular social circumstances.

Most of the present century of scholarship has considered the related question of the origins of apocalyptic language. Did it emerge from prophecy? Is it an adaptation of Persian dualism? Is wisdom literature the matrix? The search for sources appears to be misdirected, since any apocalyptic text combines allusions from a wide range of sources. The meaning of any text is dependent on the sources as well as on the way the sources are combined through the editorial process.

Current investigations of the structure and content of Jewish apocalyptic writings have indicated that some sections of the postexilic prophetic books may be categorized as protoapocalyptic, for instance, Second Zechariah, Joel 3–4; Mal 3–4. Sharing a few structural similarities and features of content, however, does not indicate that some postexilic texts can be interpreted according to apocalyptic world views. The decision to investigate the linguistic affinity and structural parallel of postexilic prophecy to apocalyptic literature underscores the reluctance of some scholars to analyze these prophetic texts for their own contributions.

JOEL

Mary Margaret Pazdan, O.P.

INTRODUCTION

Authorship

What is known about the author of this book is limited to 1:1, which names and identifies him: "The word of the Lord which came to Joel, son of Pethuel." The verse uses a traditional prophetic formula, "the word of the Lord came to . . . ." The name Joel means "Yahweh is God." It is recorded by the Chronicler (see 1 Chr 4:35; 5:4; 7:3; 11:38; Ezra 10:43; Neh 11:9), whose texts were compiled in the postexilic period. Pethuel is mentioned nowhere else in the Old Testament. "Joel ben Pethuel" may designate the author of the book.

Other biographical detail is inferred from the text. Many scholars suggest that Joel was a cult prophet attached to the Jerusalem temple-community. His concern for temple worship and his prophecies in liturgical form may indicate that he was a temple official. He never identified himself, however, as a priest.

Dating of the text

The superscription of the book indicates no chronological setting for Joel. Earlier scholars, however, suggested a preexilic period for the book, noting its position in the Jewish canon between Hosea and Amos, and its repetition of words and phrases from Amos (compare Joel 4:18 and Amos 9:13). Although a minority of scholars still favor a preexilic dating, the majority of them locate Joel in the Persian period. The book suggests some literary dependency of Joel on earlier prophetic traditions (see p. 576). Historical allusions (1:9; 4:6), the absence of earlier administrators (kings and governors), and the lack of internal dissension and internal oppression also imply a late postexilic period. The approximate dating of the text is 400–350 B.C.E. (see p. 574).

Composition of the text

For the past century the unity of the text has been debated. Some scholars maintained that it was a work composed of two parts by two different authors. Others modified this position or emphasized its unity. Recent scholars suggest that the book has a literary unity. They refer to thematic connections, such as "the day of the Lord" (1:15; 2:1; 3:4; 4:14) and parallel expressions (2:27 and 4:17). Commentators debate whether the literary unity is the work of one author or of a few authors who edited the chapters for its present canonical shape.

Outline of the book

There are differences in the numbering of the chapters and verses in the second part of the Book of Joel. This commentary is based on the New American Bible, which uses the Hebrew text; other Bibles and commentaries may use the Greek text. The chart compares the two versions:

Hebrew Text	Greek Text
3:1-5	2:28-32
4:1-8	3:1-8
4:9-16	3:9-16
4:17-21	3:17-21

In this commentary the numbering of the Greek text is given in brackets:

COMMENTARY

PART ONE: THE PLAGUE OF LOCUSTS AND THE COMMUNITY

Joel 1:1–2:17

Situations of catastrophe prompted special liturgies to respond to a particular disaster within the community (see Judg 20:26; Jer 14:2, 7-9, 12). The Book of Joel is developed according to the structure of a communal lamentation. The components of the ritual were expanded for future generations until they attained the present canonical shape. This process broadened the possibilities for interpretation of the book.

Part One consists of two units (1:1-20 and 2:1-17). Both units indicate the structure of the first part of a lamentation liturgy: (a) a call to communal lamentation; (b) a cry and prayer of lamentation. The prophet calls together the Judeans of the temple-community to reflect on the catastrophe of the locust plague. He exhorts the entire community to mourn its devastated land, to repent, and to cry out to God for assistance. The plague is compared to the day of the Lord.

1:1-4 Plague of locusts. After the superscription of the book (v. 1), the setting is introduced. The prophet initiates a summons and exhortation to the community. The elders, leaders of the community in the postexilic era, are addressed (see Ezra 5:9; 6:7-8; compare Joel 1:2, 14; 2:17; 3:1). All the members of the community are called to consider whether the present disaster ever happened to their ancestors (v. 2). The rhetorical question is a common teaching tool, especially in the Writings of the Jewish canon, which preserved the accumulated wisdom of the people. Likewise, the prophet exhorts the community to hand down its experience of the plague to future generations (v. 3).

An initial description of the locusts appears as the climax of the setting (v. 4). "Cutter," "swarm," "grasshopper," and "devourer" may indicate stages of development in the life-cycle of locusts. How they destroy crops is suggested by the triple reference to the fact that *what (is) left* at each stage is *eaten* by the next stage. The damage that the locusts cause is attested to in biblical and extrabiblical literature. The last recorded plague in Jerusalem is reported to have been in A.D. 1915.

1:5-20 Call to lamentation. Verses 5-14 address members of the community for whom the results of the plague are overwhelming. Exhortations to particular actions refer to ritual activities associated with the liturgy of lamentation. Four groups of people are highlighted:

1) Imbibers of wine (vv. 5-7) are enjoined to "weep" and "wail" for the loss of sweet, new wine used to celebrate the autumn harvest festival (Exod 23:16). Like an invading army, the locusts have destroyed the vine.

2) The second group is not specified (vv. 8-10). It is probably a call to the entire community to "lament." The analogy of "a virgin girt with sackcloth for the spouse of her youth" (v. 8) refers to the mourning ritual of a woman after the first stage of relationship. The bridal price has been paid and public vows have been declared (see Deut 20:7; 22:23-24). The second stage, bringing the woman to her husband's home, has not occurred.

The image suggests deep, personal mourning. What type of loss could evoke such grief? Temple sacrifices have ceased because locusts ravaged the harvest (v. 9). The ritual ingredients of grain, wine, and oil are in short supply (v. 10). Significantly, the community's relationship with God symbolized in worship is severed.

3) Field workers and vinedressers (vv. 11-12) are told to "be appalled" and "wail." Their toil is futile. Their harvest, too, has failed. The yield is "dried up" and "withered." In particular, the land often interpreted as a sign of God's blessing for Israel has now become a curse. Like the produce, "joy has withered away" in the community.

4) Priests (vv. 13-14) are exhorted to "gird [themselves] . . . weep . . . wail." The instruction repeats the directives given to the other groups, with additional stipulations: (a) They are to spend day and *night* in sackcloth, a custom invoked only in extreme situations (see 2 Sam 12:16; 1 Kgs 21:27). (b) As "ministers of the altar," their ritual activity is located in the "house of your God," the temple, where sacrifice is no longer held (v. 13; compare v. 9). (c) Their office authorizes them to announce a fast, to summon and assemble the leaders and the entire community. The formal liturgy of lamentation is convened in the "house of the Lord, your God" (v. 14).

Verses 2 and 14 comprise an inclusion mentioning the "elders" and "all who dwell in the land." Its function is to draw attention to a literary unit by separating particular verses from the text. Here verses 2-14 describe the members of the community gathered for lamentation.

A cry and a prayer of lamentation follow (vv. 15-20). An exclamation of sorrow is attached to the day of the Lord, which is identified as "near" and as a day of "ruin from the Almighty" (v. 15). The statement was alarming to the community for two reasons. First, according to prophetic oracles, the day of the Lord meant God's judgment against the enemies of Israel, "the nations" (see Isa 13:6; Ezek 30:2-3; Jer 46:10). Later the oracles included the judgment of Israel for disobeying God (see Amos 5:18-20; Lam 2:22; Ezek 34:12). After the destruction of Jerusalem (586 B.C.E.), the threatening oracles appeared to be fulfilled. Second, according to the postexilic community, the day of the Lord was considered a future event limited to the nations.

In addition, the prophet invites the community to consider its present situation with a rhetorical question regarding the scanty food supply and the absence of sacrifices (v. 16; compare v. 2). Both persons and animals starve because the locusts have devoured their sustenance (vv. 17-18). The joy especially characteristic of the community at harvest festivals and worship is banished (v. 16; compare v. 12). The clear parallelism between the day of the Lord and the devastation of the plague suggests that the prophet may be interpreting the plague as a foreshadowing of the day of the Lord for the community.

A prayer (vv. 19-20) concludes the first unit of Part One. It is structured according to many psalms of lamentation: an invocation to God and a statement of complaint (vv. 19b-20; compare Pss 12:1-3; 74:1). "Fire has devoured" is a repeated metaphor to describe the locusts as the source of the complaint (vv. 19a; 20b).

2:1-11 Great alarm. This section and 2:12-17 constitute the second unit of Part One. The relationship of 1:2-20 and 2:1-17 is problematic. A few commentators state that 2:1-17 is a doublet. Some prefer to draw literary and theological parallels. Others emphasize the differences between the two sections. Canonical critics suggest that the parallels and redaction are clues as to how later communities of believers interpreted the book.

The section compared with 1:2-14 indicates parallels and differences. Some elements are nearly identical. Catastrophe is the focus. While 1:2-14 described the *results* of the locust invasion, 2:1-11 describes the *agents* of the catastrophe. The images that alluded to the relationship of the plague to the day of the Lord (1:15-20) are repeated. The proclamation is addressed to members of the temple-community. The time-sequence, however, is different. The locust plague is an event of the *past*; the day of the Lord is *imminent*. A second difference is the addition of metaphors to indicate other characteristics of the event.

The new section indicates a parallel setting (2:1-3; compare 1:2-4). Approaching danger is announced to "all who dwell in the land" with the blast of the "trumpet" (v. 1; compare 1:2, 14). The *shofar*, or ram's horn, sounded an alarm for battle as well as a call for the community to assemble in worship. The day of the Lord is the source of anxiety. The event is also heralded by cosmic signs (compare Zeph 1:14-15) and an unprecedented enemy (v. 2; see 1:6). Like "devouring fire" (see 1:4, 19), the oppressor transforms the "garden of Eden" into a "desert waste" (v. 3; compare 1:20).

A series of metaphors developed according to strength, skill, and terror identifies the day of the Lord in the context of battle (vv. 4-9). The details may resemble a description of the "holy war." Some scholars consider the event as an early stage of the day of the Lord. The metaphors are: running and leaping horses, dragging chariots behind them (vv. 4-5a); a crackling, devouring flame (v. 5b; compare 1:19; 2:3); a mighty people arrayed for battle (v. 5b); warriors and soldiers running and scaling the wall with disciplined routine, assaulting the city and climbing into the houses (vv. 7-9). Two groups are affected. Anguish colors the victims' faces (v. 6; compare Isa 13:8). The cosmic forces (earth, heavens, sun, moon, stars) quake and darken (v. 10).

The image of the holy war continues with the appearance of the Lord as the leader of the army (v. 11a). The section concludes with an inclusion, the day of the Lord (vv. 1a and 11b). The short comment "who can bear it?" appears to be a postscript, another example of the rhetorical question noted above (1:2b, 16b).

2:12-17 Call to repentance. This section is constructed to provide connections with the first part of the unit (2:1-11). It also indicates structural and thematic parallels and differences when compared with 1:5-20. The verses suggest an immediate response to the day of the Lord (2:1-11), just as the plague of locusts in the first unit demanded a response. Both events are followed by an exhortation to communal lamentation.

Verses 12 and 13 indicate an unusual circumstance to alter the awesome day of the Lord. The revelation reverses the poignant more-than-rhetorical-question of section one, to which it is structurally connected (v. 11b). God's proclamation, "Yet even now, says the Lord" (v. 12a), presents a possibility other than imminent gloom and destruction (2:1-11). It offers hope to the community

trembling from the locust invasion and fearfully awaiting the worse event.

What is suggested? The invitation is to "return to me with your whole heart, with fasting, and weeping, and mourning" (v. 12b; see Amos 4:6-11; Hos 3:5; 14:2). The language indicates a turning toward God with one's whole being, the complete reorientation of thoughts and decisions toward God. Participation in a communal liturgy of lamentation (fasting, weeping, mourning) is encouraged. The ritual will symbolize the process of the community's commitment to God.

Verse 13b is a reaffirmation of the earlier relationship of God and the community revealed in the covenant at Mount Sinai (compare Exod 34:6-7). God is gracious, merciful, kind, relenting in punishment. The members of the present community are dependent upon a new manifestation of God's mercy. God *may* relent. The community is challenged to "return." Only then will there be the restored blessing of "offerings and libations," symbols of the relationship of God and the community (v. 14; compare 1:9, 12, 16).

The new possibility for the community gives a sense of urgency to the ritual of lamentation (vv. 15-17). The ritual actions to initiate the liturgy repeat earlier directions (v. 15; 1:14; 2:1). Additional components comprise this summons:

a) Children, infants, bride and bridegroom are included in the assembly. The gravity of the situation and the witness of "all who dwell in the land" preclude any exceptions for privileges ordinarily given to a young couple (v. 16; compare Deut 24:5).

b) The location for the officials of the service is indicated: "between the porch and the altar" (v. 17a). It is the traditional place for leading the community in lamentation. The distance may refer to the lack of sacrifices due to the locust invasion as well as the symbolic interpretation of strained relationships between the community and God (compare Ezek 8:16).

The prayer of lamentation (v. 17b) that concludes the section differs from the one recorded in 1:19-20. The priests implore God to spare the community, "your people," and to prevent "your heritage" from becoming "a reproach with the nations ruling over them." The plea is a traditional one (Pss 42:4; 79:10; 115:2). Here the collective experience of Israel mirrors the current situation. A rhetorical question is attributed to the nations. It ironically emphasizes their interpretation of the community's plight: "Where is their God?"

PART TWO: THE RESPONSE OF THE LORD TO ISRAEL AND THE NATIONS

Joel 2:18–4:21 [2:18–3:21]

Part One and Part Two constitute identical literary and topical structures. Each part is constructed with two units. Each unit contains two sections. Each part refers to a particular stage of the communal lamentation liturgy. In addition, the ordering of Part One and Part Two follows a chronology of events (locust invasion and imminent day of the Lord); the order of a lamentation service (stage one and stage two); and a development of prophetic revelation.

Part Two consists of two units: 2:18–3:5 [2:18–32] and 4:1–21 [3:1–21]. Both units indicate the structure of the second part of a communal service: a series of oracles containing divine assurance. The proclamations respond to the plea of the community suffering the results of the locusts and fearing the approaching day of the Lord. They promise a *future* of restoration and *new* blessings to reverse the characteristics of the day of the Lord.

In addition to the consistencies in Part One and Part Two, some commentators have identified a new literary genre in Joel 3:1–4:21 [2:28–3:21], namely, proto-apocalyptic (see p. 577). Characteristics of this genre which describe preliminaries to the day of the Lord include: outpouring of the spirit, cosmic signs, judgment against the nations, and blessings for the community.

2:18-27 Compassion for the community. This section describes a restoration of the community's situation by God. Verse 18 provides the transition from Part One to Part Two. God's concerns are the land and the people. The phrase "stirred to concern" is better translated "became jealous" (Revised Standard Version). It indicates the passionate zeal of God *for* the community (see Ezek 39:25; Zech 1:14; 8:2). God responds to the plight of the community with compassion. Subsequent activity is detailed in the assurances about restored life and freedom from enemies.

They are presented in three consecutive oracles:

1) Assurances are introduced (vv. 19-20). God will send supplies needed for sustenance and sacrifice: "grain," "wine," "oil" (v. 19a; compare 1:7, 9-11, 13b, 16-17; 2:14). The community will no longer be "a reproach among the nations" (v. 19b; compare 2:17). Verse 20 describes the "northerner," which may refer to the locusts as well as their symbolic counterpart, the army of invaders (see 2:1-11). Hostile forces often approached from the north (see Jer 1:14, 15; 4:6; Ezek 38:6; 39:2). Here the enemy is destroyed by expulsion to an "arid and waste" land and by drowning in the sea.

2) "Fear not" oracles are addressed to the land and the animals connected with the community (vv. 21-22). Both are assured of verdant and fruitful life (compare 1:10-12).

3) Instruction and promises are announced to the temple-community, "children of Zion" (vv. 23-27; Lam 4:2; Ps 149:2). The group is invited to "rejoice in the Lord, your God!" (v. 23a). The second part of the verse is obscure. The New American Bible has God giving the community a "teacher of justice: he has made the rain come down for you." The Revised Standard Version has God as the giver of "the early rain for your vindication." Both translations point to God who restores a favorable condition for harvest by providing rain at the proper seasons.

This favorable situation, in turn, provides supplies for temple sacrifice. "Justice" and "vindication" suggest the ritual act of worship, which represents the covenant relationship of God and the community. The daily sacrifices at the temple had ceased because of the locust invasion.

The next three verses support the interpretation. God will provide grain, wine, and oil in great abundance as restitution for the destruction of the locusts (vv. 24-25; see 1:4; 2:5-9). Needs for sustenance and for worshiping God will be satisfied (v. 26; compare Ps 126:3).

A recognition formula concludes the section (v. 27). It indicates a new understanding of God for the community. God will be in their midst. No other god is comparable to the God of Israel. The community will "nevermore be put to shame" (compare Exod 20:2-3). The reference may be to the disgrace of the

Exile (v. 26). The revelation of the new relationship is a climax to the section as well as a response to the taunt of the nations: "Where is their God?" (2:17).

3:1-5 [2:28-32] Blessings for the community. These verses are connected thematically to 2:18-27. Both describe the characteristics of future restoration in successive stages. "Then afterward" (3:1) provides the transition to a new time-sequence. It presupposes that the conditions of restoration that God promised (2:18-27) have been fulfilled. It points to an uncertain time in the future when God's new blessings (3:1-5 [2:28-32]) will be realized in the community. The section is structured according to three blessings. Each is outlined in a three-line stanza:

1) Participation in God's spirit (vv. 1-2 [2:28-29]). "All mankind" identifies the members of the temple-community (2:19, 27; compare 4:2, 17, 19-21). The Revised Standard Version translates the Hebrew as "flesh" to emphasize the contrast between human weakness (see Isa 40:6; Ps 56:5) and God's vital power, which will transform their lives. The promise is radical, for Jewish tradition had limited God's spirit to persons with official status: a judge, like Gideon (Judg 6:34); a king, like Saul (1 Sam 16:14); a prophet, like Ezekiel (Ezek 2:2). Although Moses desired a spirit-filled community (Num 11:29), God's spirit had been limited to the seventy elders (Num 11:17, 25).

In these verses God's spirit will empower each member of the community to "prophesy." The activity is further clarified with corresponding terms: "dream dreams" and "see visions." The "prophets" are identified as "your sons and daughters," "your old men," and "your young men" (v. 1b). What is unusual is the mention of "servants" and "handmaids" (v. 2). Although their rights were protected according to the law for the sabbath rest (Exod 20:10) and festivals (Deut 12:12, 18; 16:11, 14), they were not considered members of the community. Participation in God's spirit implies *equal* status for each person in the community.

The author of Luke-Acts quotes and interprets Joel 3:1-5a [2:28-32a] in the account of Peter's discourse at Pentecost (Acts 2:17-21). The risen Lord "received the promise of the holy Spirit from the Father and poured it forth" (Acts 2:33). Greek and Jew alike have access to the Spirit if they believe in Jesus and are baptized (Acts 2:38).

2) Cosmic signs (vv. 3-4 [2:30-31]). The activity of God on behalf of the Israelites during the Exodus (1250 B.C.E.) included wonders with blood (Exod 24:4-8), fire and smoke (Exod 13:21-22; 19:18). These elements (v. 3) and the eclipse of the sun (v. 4a; compare Rev 6:12) also indicate traditional imagery associated with the terrible day of the Lord (see p. 581). The identification of cosmic signs as blessings becomes clear when the verses are considered as portents of the day of the Lord, when something *unexpected* will occur (v. 5).

3) Deliverance (v. 5 [2:32]). Rescue is assured for each person who "calls on the name of the Lord" (v. 5a). The directive includes recognition of God (Exod 33:19) and worship (Isa 12:4; Ps 105:1; compare Zech 13:9) before the nations. Those designated as "the rescued" are further identified in verse 5bc as a "remnant" and "survivors." Their home is located on "Mount Zion" and in "Jerusalem." The descriptions indicate the temple-community of Judah preeminently. Some commentators suggest that the descriptions may include the Jews of the Diaspora (see Isa 27:12-13; 57:19), that is, Jews living outside Israel.

Paul introduces verse 5a in Rom 10:12-13 by interpreting its significance universally: "For there is no distinction between Jew and Greek; the same Lord is Lord of all, enriching all who call upon him" (Rom 10:12). The outpouring of the Spirit at Pentecost is interpreted similarly: ". . . the promise is made to you and to your children and to all those far off, whomever the Lord our God will call" (Acts 2:39).

Recognition of earlier prophetic tradition is acknowledged in the clause "as the Lord has said" (v. 5b). The use of "remnant" terminology interprets Obad 17a: "But on Mount Zion there shall be a portion saved; the mountain shall be holy." The prophet also specified the source of life for the "remnant" by drawing on Ezek 39:29: "No longer will I hide my face from them, for I have poured out my spirit on the house of Israel, says the Lord God."

"Survivors whom the Lord shall call" (v. 5c) is a recognition of the mutual relationship between the Lord and the community that "calls upon the name of the Lord" (v. 5a). In 3:1-5 [2:28-32]there is the recognition that

God's community will continue. A community whose home is in Jerusalem will be given God's spirit to function as prophets.

4:1-17 [3:1-17] Judgment on the nations. This section continues the theme of Part Two: Response of the Lord to Israel and the Nations. The circumstances of the community's suffering at the hands of the nations are reviewed. They prescribe God's action and judgment against Israel's enemies consistent with traditional imagery associated with the day of the Lord. Two later additions occur in the text (vv. 4-8, 18-21).

The introduction for the section (vv. 1-3 [3:1-3]) states the reasons for God's judgment. Verse 1 is a transition linking the theme of restoration for the community (2:17–3:5 [2:17-32]) with the consequences of its enemies (3:2-17 [2:32–3:17]). In verse 1 the community is designated initially as "Judah" and "Jerusalem"; in verses 2 and 3, however, it is described in relation to God: *"my* people" (see 2:17, 27; 4:3); *"my* inheritance" (see 2:17); *"my* land."

God will assemble all the nations for judgment (v. 2a). The "Valley of Jehoshaphat" is probably cited more for its connection to the Hebrew phrase ("Yahweh judges") than for its location as a specific geographical area. In early Christian tradition the historian Eusebius (*Onamastikon*) identified the place as the Kidron Valley. In verse 14b the place is referred to as the "valley of decision."

The nations are indicted for three actions toward the community which occurred during earlier Jewish history and continued through the time of Joel (vv. 2b-3):

1) "Scattered among the nations" refers to the deportations led by Assyria and Babylon from the eighth century through the sixth century. The exilic experience of Judah and Jerusalem, in particular, is recalled here.

2) "And divided my land" describes the immediate accessibility to the land for the conquerors who settled there (see Lam 5:2).

3) "Over my people they have cast lots" indicates how little the victors valued the lives of the deportees (see Obad 11; Nah 3:10). Children, in particular, are described as the victims of their pleasures.

The prose addition (vv. 4-8 [3:4-8]) elaborates the guilt of the nations resulting from their treatment of Israel (vv. 1-3). It suggests a courtroom narrative, with God functioning as accuser, judge, and vindicator of the community. To open the trial, God poses a rhetorical question about taking vengeance and promises swift retribution. Tyre, Sidon, and the regions of Philistia (the addressees) refer to territories of traditional animosity toward Israel. Next, God condemns specific actions against the community: plundering the temple, selling persons as slaves to the Greeks, sending them into exile (vv. 5-6). Finally, God promises exact retaliation for their deeds. For engaging in slave trade (see Amos 1:6-10; Ezek 27:13), they will be sold as slaves to the community. As dealers, the community will exile its former enemies by bartering with the Sabeans. The scene concludes with a statement of divine authority: "Indeed the Lord has spoken" (vv. 7-8).

The third division in the section (vv. 9-16 [3:9-16]) continues the poetic and thematic structure of the introduction (vv. 1-3). The Valley of Jehoshaphat is the site for judgment (v. 12) and for battle (v. 14). Unknown addressees are exhorted to announce war, rouse the soldiers, and assemble the peoples roundabout (vv. 9-11). The dire situation implies additional soldiers. The untrained warriors—farmers and field workers—are urged to respond. The directive is an ironic one that intentionally *reverses* the call to peace declared in earlier prophetic traditions (v. 10; see Isa 2:4; Mic 4:3).

Instructions associated with harvest, "apply the sickle," "come and tread" (v. 13), now identify the ferocious battle waged against the enemies of the community. The event is closely aligned to the imminent day of the Lord (v. 14). Additional cosmic imagery heralds the day (vv. 15-16). The Lord dwelling in Zion "roars" and "raises his voice" (v. 16a; compare 2:11a). The action does not indicate anger but *protection* for the community, for whom the Lord is a "refuge" and "stronghold" (v. 16b; see Pss 31:3-5; 61:4).

The climax to the section is a summary declaration of the oracles of assurance and blessing. The ultimate security for the community is knowing that the Lord is "your God," dwelling among them, providing the source of holiness and protection from all enemies (v. 17 [3:17]).

4:18-21 [3:18-21] Presence of God in Jerusalem. This poetic insertion may be regarded as an appendix to the Book of Joel. It amplifies the major theme of restoration by a series of promises to be fulfilled "on that day":

a) abundant sustenance for the community: wine, milk, water (v. 18; see Amos 9:13b; Ezek 47:1-12);

b) the destruction of Egypt and Edom, enduring political enemies (v. 19; see 1 Kgs 14:25; Obad 8-14);

c) everlasting security for Judah and Jerusalem (v. 20; see 3:5; 4:16);

d) retribution for enemies and the presence of the Lord in Zion (v. 21).

Conclusion

A literary analysis of the Book of Joel suggests the structure of a communal liturgy of lamentation. The format, however, has been expanded and developed by editorial activity. While many commentators recognize the development of the book, there is no consensus about the number of persons involved in this process. Some commentators see no connection between the literary development of the book and its religious meaning. They interpret the book according to a few general perspectives:

a) The book presents a restricted, nationalistic point of view. God's promises of restoration are limited to the Zion community in fulfillment of earlier prophetic traditions. Often Joel is compared unfavorably with the breadth of Isaiah and Micah, who include the participation of the nations in the community of Jerusalem (see Isa 2:2-4; Mic 4:1-3).

b) The importance of the book is virtually dependent on the figure of Jesus. He is the fulfillment of the prophecies by dying for the "nations" and giving the Spirit to all who believed in him.

c) Jews and Christians await a future event that will surpass the expectations of restoration that Joel proclaimed (see Rev 21).

Canonical critics offer a different perspective on the relationship of the literary development of Joel and its religious meaning. *How* the Book of Joel emerged as a canonical text provides clues to its religious significance in future communities.

Sources available for the editorial process included the original prophecy of Joel, presenting the devastation of the locust plague, and images and terms describing the day of the Lord taken from earlier prophetic traditions. In arranging and adding to the sources, the editor(s) shaped the text to provide a message for future communities. References to the new addressees are indicated initially in the introduction to the first part of the book (1:3). The entire second part of the book (2:18–4:21 [2:18–3:21]), with its proclamations about future possibilities, is also fashioned to include them.

The editorial process provided a continuity of religious experience and hope for the original community and for future communities. It shaped the book to declare that God's compassion toward the temple-community of Judah because of their repentance would be possible for any community. Correspondingly, the blessings of restoration would be possible for future communities as well. For both types of community, original and future, neither final judgment nor blessings had definitively occurred.

The perspective of canonical critics appears preferable to the interpretation of other commentators because it assumes that a text can be valuable for its own contribution. Consequently, the methodology does not depend on prophecy-fulfillment in the New Testament or on comparison with other prophetic traditions in the Old Testament to validate the importance of the Book of Joel. Canonical criticism provides a necessary focus on the placement of Joel within the Minor Prophets. It also widens the interpretation of Joel through a different methodology that includes implications for future communities.

OBADIAH

Mary Margaret Pazdan, O.P.

INTRODUCTION

Authorship

What is known about the author of this book is limited to verse 1a, which names and identifies him: "The vision of Obadiah. [Thus says the Lord God:] Of Edom we have heard a message from the Lord." "Vision" is a technical term for prophecy (see Nah 1:1; Mic 1:1), whose contents are described in verses 2-4. "We have heard a message . . .," however, emphasizes that auditory perception is the source for prophetic inspiration. "[Thus says the Lord God:]" and the repetition of the divine name also indicate traditional prophetic formulas. The name Obadiah means "servant of Yahweh." It occurs twelve times in the Hebrew Scriptures. In the Book of Obadiah the name may be used more for its symbolic sense.

Other biographical detail is inferred from the text. Many scholars suggest that Obadiah was a cult prophet attached to the Jerusalem temple before its destruction (586 B.C.E.). The structure of the prophecies reflects a liturgical service in which the sovereignty of God is affirmed through oracles against the nations. Obadiah's connection with the temple in Jerusalem is strengthened by references to God's kingdom and Mount Zion (vv. 17, 21). Other scholars suggest that an unknown prophet utilized a liturgical structure for the deliverance of oracles.

Dating of the text

The superscription of the book indicates no chronological setting for Obadiah. The position of the book in the canons is not decisive for establishing a date. The Jewish canon lists Obadiah after Amos (preexilic), while the Alexandrian canon locates Obadiah after Joel (postexilic).

While most scholars agree that the oracles against Edom were proclaimed after 586 B.C.E., the dating of the final text is disputed. The present discussion involves a consideration of the relationship between Israel and Edom, oral and written traditions, and the process of editorial activity.

According to Jewish tradition, the relationship between Israel and Edom was one of continuous conflict. It is attributed to the fraternal conflict of two brothers, Jacob and Esau (see Gen 25:19-34; 26:34-35; 27:1-44; 32:4; 33:1-17). The hostility developed for several centuries as the descendants of Jacob (Israelites) and Esau (Edomites) refused one another rights of territorial passage (see Num 20:14-21) and freedom (see 2 Sam 8:13-14; 1 Kgs 11:15-18).

Edom revolted against Judah about 844 B.C.E. The animosity between them continued, however, for nearly 250 additional years, culminating in Edom's alliance with Babylon against Judah (see p. 573). Although the extent of Edomite activity against Judah during this period is unclear, the witness of the anti-Edom oracles (see below) indict Edom for treachery and betrayal. There is even a claim that the Edomites burned the temple (see 1 Esdras 4:45). They probably conspired with the Babylonian empire and settled in Judean territory.

A recent archeological investigation supports this position. It uncovered an inscription contemporary with the last days of Jerusalem. A troop commander in Arad sent for additional soldiers to fortify a position against an imminent Edomite attack: "Behold I have sent to warn you: are not the men with Elisha, lest Edom come thither."

Edom, unlike Judah, was independent but not untroubled for over a hundred years after the fall of Jerusalem. Tribes from Arabia frequently raided the land (see Mal 1:2-4). After 450 B.C.E. the name Edom disappeared from historical records. During the reign of Herod the Great (37–4 B.C.E.), however, the territory designated Edom was named Idumea. *Mekiltha*, a Jewish text of the early Christian period, identified Edom as a code name for oppression.

Commentators suggest that the enmity between Israel and Edom was preserved in oral traditions that were later recorded as anti-Edom oracles. While some fragments are located in the Jacob cycle (see Gen 25:23; 27:39-40), the most extensive witness is located outside the Torah (see Isa 21:11-12; 34:5-7; 63:1-6; Jer 49:7-22; Lam 4:21-22; Ezek 25:12-14; 35:1-5; Amos 1:11-12; Mal 1:3-5; Ps 137:7-9). In these passages Edom is condemned for less dramatic but more continuous harassment than burning the temple.

Part of the complexity involved in dating the Book of Obadiah is the relationship of the anti-Edom oracles (vv. 1-14, 15b) to Jer 49:7-22. Some commentators state that Obadiah represented the prior tradition, while others indicate that Jeremiah was the first witness to the tradition. A third group traces both Obadian and Jeremian oracles to a common earlier tradition. Both prophets incorporated the tradition and additional material after the fall of Jerusalem (586 B.C.E.).

Another question is the chronological relationship of the oracles in Obadiah. While condemnations of Edom predominate (vv. 1-14, 15b), there are oracles describing the day of the Lord (vv. 15a, 16-18) and the restoration of Israel (vv. 19-21). The difference of opinion about the approximate date of the oracles and subsequent editorial activity results in a final composition date from early postexilic (535 B.C.E.) to a century later (435 B.C.E.).

In this commentary Obadiah is identified first *chronologically* because of his proximity to the Edomite conspirators and redaction of earlier anti-Edom oracles. In addition, his position as a transitional figure between exilic and postexilic prophecy indicates a singular contribution among the other Minor Prophets. His contribution includes oracles against Edom after the destruction of Jerusalem as well as later oracles about the day of the Lord. These factors indicate that the date for the final edition of the text is a question of secondary importance.

Composition of the text

Although the Book of Obadiah is the shortest book of the Old Testament, discussion about the final dating of the text and related literary questions continues in the literature. There is no consensus about the priority of Jeremiah, Obadiah, or another common tradition for the anti-Edom oracles. In addition, the text has been analyzed according to two extreme positions: a literary unity or a collection of fragments. Presently, several commentators propose a moderate position. The book contains two sets of oracles and an appendix. Thematically, the unity of the oracles consists in Edom's condemnation and future situation in the day of the Lord. The appendix is related to Israel's restoration in that event.

Outline of the book

PART ONE:	Oracles against Edom (vv. 1-14, 15b)
vv. 1-9	Pride and Destruction of Edom
vv. 10-14	Treachery of Edom toward Judah
v. 15b	Condemnation of Edom
PART TWO:	Oracles about the Day of the Lord (vv. 15a, 16-21)
vv. 15a, 16	Judgment of the Nations
vv. 17-18	Return and Restoration of Israel
vv. 19-21	Appendix: Return and Restoration of Israel

COMMENTARY

PART ONE: ORACLES AGAINST EDOM

Obad 1-14, 15b

Part One is a collection of oracles that expand a common tradition of anti-Edom material. The closest parallel is Jer 49:7-22 (see p. 587). Commentators state that no more bitter diatribe exists against Edom in the whole of the Old Testament than what is recorded here.

Two perspectives are prominent about the interpretation of verses 2-9. The context of verses 1b and 7, in particular, is debated. Some suggest that the destruction of Edom has already occurred. The verses are an additional reflection on the event. Others indicate that the verses designate a future destruction. Attempts to establish the context are directly related to considerations of the dating and the composition of the text.

Proposals that seek to identify a specific historical event, that is, an Arabian conquest of Edom, appear to limit the possibilities for interpretation of the section. Although recent archeological discoveries are providing some limited support for this type of analysis, additional research and data are needed.

1-9 Pride and the destruction of Edom. Verse 1 is a prose introduction to the Book of Obadiah. It states his identity and function. It also links him to earlier prophetic tradition: "we have heard a message from the Lord" (v. 1a; see Jer 49:7).

Verse 1b relates the departure of a messenger to proclaim Edom's destruction among the nations: "Up! Let us go to war against him!" It is difficult to determine whether the statement refers to an *actual event*, that is, the approach of the Arabian enemy against Edom, or whether it is a *prophetic formula* of a war summons to the nations (Jer 49:14; Joel 4:9ff. [3:9ff.]; Mic 4:13).

God announces the destruction of Edom (vv. 2-4; see Jer 49:14-16). The dispositions of the nation's heart are condemned. Pride effects Edom's contemptible position among the nations (v. 2). False security arises from dwelling "in the clefts of the rock" and "in the heights." The "rock" refers to the terrain as well as to the Edomite capital, Sela, a nearly impregnable city.

The arrogant challenge "Who will bring me down to earth?" will prove no obstacle to an enemy (v. 3). Even a position as an eagle with a nest among the stars will not thwart God's action: "I will bring you down" (v. 4; compare Amos 9:2; Isa 14:13-14).

God's power of destruction is compared to the strategy of prowlers invading homes in Edom (vv. 5-9). If "thieves," "robbers," or "vintagers" trespassed, they would leave something behind for the household (v. 5; see Jer 49:9; Lev 19:10; Deut 24:21). The destruction of Edom (Esau), however, will be without mercy. The event is described in a traditional cry of lament (vv. 6-7; see 2 Sam 1:19-27; Jer 38:22; Lam 1:1; 2:1; 4:1). It will be as thorough as the forfeit of Jacob's birthright to Esau (v. 6; see Gen 25:27-34). Those closest to the Edomites, allies and relatives, will participate in the devastation. "There is no understanding in him!" indicates the bewilderment and surprise that the event causes among the Edomites (v. 7).

Verse 7 is as difficult to interpret as verse 1. What are the implications of "allies" and "relatives"? Is it an ironic comment on the real but spurned relationships between Edom and Judah, which were completely severed in the fall of Jerusalem? Do the terms relate to the reversal of Judah's situation in the day of the Lord? (see Part Two). Do the bonds of relationship refer to those who supported Edom after the fall of Jerusalem but who later conquered Edom? The comment "There is no understanding in him" is appropriate for each interpretation.

The divine formula "says the Lord" (v. 4) is repeated to form an inclusion expressing God's judgment against Edom (v. 8a). In a rhetorical question God states the disappearance of the "wise" and "understanding" from Edom (Esau). Their demise is related to verse 7, which also commented on "no understanding" (see Jer 49:7). The inhabitants of Edom and Arabia were traditionally considered wise persons (see 1 Kgs 5:10; 10:1-3; Job 1:1; 2:11; Prov 30:1; 31:1).

Warriors will be destroyed with the wise (v. 9). "Teman," an important city in Edom, refers to the whole territory. Another inclusive term is "Mount Esau" (vv. 8b, 9b).

10-14 Treachery of Edom toward Judah. The indictment against Edom is declared:

"violence to your brother Jacob" (v. 10). Specifically, the condemnation is collaboration by passivity toward Babylon's activity, that is, sacking and dividing up the city of Jerusalem (v. 11). A poignant question implied by the arrangement of verses 10 and 11 is: How can you, the "brother," become "one of them," the "aliens"?

Additional details of Edom's behavior during the destruction of Jerusalem imply active participation. They are presented in a series of present-tense protests for what has already occurred. This literary device highlights the sense of irony for the future situation of Edom (vv. 12-14). Although the injunctions repeat sacking the city (v. 13), the more malicious activities are mocking the calamity of "your brother" (v. 12) and hindering the escape of refugees (v. 14).

15b Condemnation of Edom. This statement, which is derived from the traditional Jewish practice of *lex talionis* (an eye for an eye), is the climax to Part One. It summarizes the judgment of retribution against Edom: "As you have done, so shall it be done to you" (see Exod 21:23-25; Lev 24:17-22).

PART TWO: ORACLES ABOUT THE DAY OF THE LORD

Obad 15a, 16-21

The relationship between Part One and Part Two is parallel to the Book of Joel. The plague of locusts in Part One of that book was a foreshadowing of the day of the Lord in Part Two. Similarly, in Obadiah, the anti-Edom oracles in Part One are a foreshadowing of the day of the Lord in Part Two. In addition, the different consequences of the day of the Lord are identical: punishment for the nations (especially Edom) and restoration for Judah (compare Joel 4:1-21 [3:1-21]; Obad 15a, 16-21).

Was one book the model for the other? Since Joel 4:17 [3:17] quotes Obad 17, he may have used the Obadian model with some editorial activity. It is also possible that both books are dependent on earlier traditions that they modified according to a similar structure. Some commentators consider the structure of a communal lamentation to be another convincing parallel for Joel and Obadiah.

15a, 16 Judgment of the nations. The imminent day of the Lord is announced for "all the nations" (v. 15a). The proclamation connects the previous section (vv. 11-14), where the phrase "on the day" was used ten times to detail the guilt of Edom. The proclamation also introduces the prominent theme of the present section (vv. 15a, 16-21).

Verse 16 indicates how the punishment of the nations is related to God's judgment of Judah and Edom. Again, the *lex talionis* is operative: "As you have drunk . . . so shall all the nations drink continually" (vv. 16a, 15b). The metaphor of drinking refers to the cup of God's judgment and wrath (see Jer 25:15-29). Just as the community experienced the bitterness of God's judgment "upon my holy mountain" (Jerusalem) in 586 B.C.E., so all the nations (including Edom) will drink the cup until they "shall become as though they had not been" (v. 16b; compare Jer 50:25-28; Joel 3:4-4:21 [2:31-3:21]).

17-18 Return and restoration of Israel. The nations' judgment (vv. 15a, 16) is contrasted with Israel's future. Jacob (Judah) and Mount Zion (Jerusalem) are emphasized in restoration images (v. 17) corresponding to Joel's vision (Joel 4:17 [3:17]). A "portion" ("those that escape" in the Revised Standard Version) develops the theme of the "remnant" who would escape God's judgment (see Isa 4:3; 37:32; Zeph 2:7-9). Holiness characterizes the group.

Although confirming the tradition of Judah's restoration, Obadiah inserts a new perspective. The prophet includes the *whole* country by referring to Jacob *and* Joseph, who represent Judah and northern Israel respectively (v. 18a). All will share in the possession of Mount Zion. The fate of Esau (Edom) and the other nations symbolized by Esau is quite different. They will not survive (v. 18; compare Joel 1:4, 19; 2:3, 5). The metaphors of "fire" ("flame") and "stubble" indicate God's judgment against the nations through Israel's agency (see Isa 10:17; 29:5-6; Ezek 25:14). Again, the divine formula confirms the judgment (v. 18b; see vv. 4, 8).

19-21 Appendix: Return and restoration of Israel. The additional verses identify the day of the Lord as a day of great blessings for all the people of Israel. The participation of the nations appears to be limited to loss of land. Verse 21, however, suggests a different role.

The appendix outlines the extensive restoration of the boundaries of Israel. Unlike the small territory to which the Judeans returned in 538 B.C.E., their future homeland implies territorial boundaries greater than the ones achieved by King David (vv. 19-20). Precise geographical locations, however, are difficult to establish, since the Hebrew text is obscure. The major emphasis of verses 19 and 20 is to claim for Israel more land than it had possessed before deportations.

The role of Jacob, who "shall take possession of those that dispossessed them" (v. 17b), parallels "occupy," which occurs five times (vv. 19-20). The verbs suggest, in language reminiscent of covenant promises (see Gen 12:7; Exod 3:8; 2 Sam 7:10), how Israel will be restored.

"They shall occupy the Negeb, the mount of Esau" (v. 19a): The Negeb, an area south of Judah, was occupied by the Edomites during their collaboration with Babylon. It is identified by the name Idumea during the rule of Herod the Great. The area is mentioned twice (vv. 19a; 20b) as an inclusion to highlight Israel's restoration as the reversal of Edomite fortune.

Instead of "They shall occupy . . . the foothills of the Philistines," the Revised Standard Version reads: "those of the Shephelah [shall possess] the land of the Philistines" (v. 19a). The Shephelah is a foothill region west of Judah and east of the Philistine coastland. Repossessing the territory of a traditional enemy, the Philistines, is one characteristic of restoration (see 1 Sam 17; Judg 13–16; 1 Sam 31:8-13; 2 Sam 21:15-22).

Ephraim, with its capital Samaria, is a region north of Jerusalem whose traditions are associated with northern Israel. This land, too, will be reclaimed. Benjamin is a territory north of Jerusalem that extends east to the Jordan River. Its inhabitants will extend borders to Gilead, a region northeast of Ephraim and across the Jordan (v. 19b).

Exiles of Israel were scattered in distant regions. Their identity and the geographical locations mentioned in verse 20 are disputed. The first group mentioned is "the captives of this host," which the Revised Standard Version translates "the exiles in Halah" (v. 20a). They may be deportees of northern Israel who were sent to Halah, a city northwest of Nineveh (see 2 Kgs 17:6). The group will occupy "Canaanite" ("Phoenician" in the Revised Standard Version) land along the Mediterranean coast, including the city of Zarephath near the coast, about ten miles south of Sidon (see 1 Kgs 17:9-24; Luke 4:26).

"The captives of Jerusalem" (v. 20b) parallels "the captives of this host" (v. 20a). Some deportees who did not return to rebuild Jerusalem are living in Sepharad. The identity of this city is disputed. Some suggest Babylon as a parallel to Halah, which is located there; others identify it with Sardis in Asia Minor (see Rev 3:1). Several Jewish commentators identify the term as Spain. Most recently it has been identified as Hesperides on the northern coast of Africa. Whatever the precise designation of Sepharad, the verse indicates that exiles far removed from Jerusalem will return to closer proximity by occupying "the cities of the Negeb."

Verse 21 forms an inclusion with verse 17 by returning attention to Mount Zion. Who will exercise dominion on Mount Zion and the mount of Esau (Edom)? The Hebrew is translated here as "saviors" (v. 21a). The people of Israel will function as *judges* and as God's *viceroys* in the kingdom. Sovereignty belongs to God alone (v. 21b). Other scholars interpret the term as God's restoration of the remnant, that is, the people who are "saved." This distinction offers Israel participation in the universal kingship of God. Other nations, however, may ultimately experience God's saving action.

Conclusion

The meager status of the Book of Obadiah among the Minor Prophets has not been transformed by later generations. The text is not listed in a lectionary for reflection on the mystery of God and human response. It is neither utilized for catechetical or preaching events nor suggested for personal or communal prayer. In addition, the book is not generally recognized in extrabiblical literature or contemporary situations. Why, then, was it preserved in tradition?

Commentaries and articles on Obadiah emphasize questions regarding the dating of the text, archeological data, and literary composition. The religious message appears less important in comparison to these considerations. When the religious dimensions of the text are investigated, the results are similar to the analysis about the Book of Joel (see p. 585):

a) The book presents a widely attested Jewish tradition about the relationship of God and the community. Restoration of the land is a symbol of the restoration of a spiritual relationship. Some reflection about the present state of Israel is occasionally related to the same premise.

b) The function of Israel among the nations is to offer witness and an invitation to future possibilities. God's blessing (restoration) can be a sign that judgment (punishment) may not be the ultimate condition.

c) Confidence in God's sovereignty is indicated through the oracles about Edom's punishment and Israel's restoration.

Obadiah's contribution to postexilic prophecy may appear to be a very limited and localized message. In style, too, its bitter invective against Edom may offend believers (although the verses parallel some of the psalms and oracles against other nations).

Nonetheless, Obadiah can be read *in context* as a passionate plea to the God whose sovereignty assures Israel a future. Recourse to this God demands strong faith. The experience of the Exile and the prospect of return have not restored confidence in God nor in the community's self-image. Where else can the community turn? Only this God will forgive and restore Israel. Even more unexpectedly, this God will bless Jacob's (Israel's) estranged brother, Esau (Edom). An invitation will be extended to participate in the universal kingdom of the sovereign Lord.

HAGGAI

Mary Margaret Pazdan, O.P.

INTRODUCTION

Authorship

For the Books of Joel and Obadiah the author's identification was limited to the superscription of each book (v. 1). Additional biographical information was obtained through inferences in the text. For the Book of Haggai, however, there are more citations. The name Haggai appears eight times (1:1, 3, 13; 2:1, 10, 13, 14, 20).

The superscription (1:1) identifies his function as a prophet and names the addressees to whom he proclaims the oracles. Four verses identify Haggai with the word "prophet" and a traditional prophetic formula, "the word of the Lord came to . . ." (1:1, 3; 2:1, 10). Two verses identify Haggai as a "messenger of the Lord [proclaiming] the message of the Lord" (1:13; 2:20). Two verses mention his name as one who proclaims God's oracles (2:13, 14). The absence of any genealogy may be intended to emphasize Haggai's prophetic authority. Outside the text that bears his name, Haggai is linked with Zechariah as a prophet (see Ezra 5:1, 16; 6:14).

The name Haggai means "festival." Other names in the Old Testament are also derived from the same Hebrew root (see Gen 46:16; Num 26:15; 2 Sam 3:4; 1 Chr 3:2). The name may refer to the day of the prophet's birth, that is, a festival. It may designate Haggai's task of restoring the temple for cultic activities that celebrate festivals. While some identify Haggai as a priest, there is no indication in the text for this designation. It is preferable to associate him with cult prophets in Jerusalem. His position in that group, however, is unclear.

Dating of the text

The Books of Joel and Obadiah are difficult to date for three reasons: (a) their different positions in the Jewish and Alexandrian canons; (b) the absence of chronological data in the superscriptions; (c) minimal contextual clues. The dating process for the Book of Haggai presents an opposite situation: (a) an identical position in the canons; (b) clear chronological data in the superscription; (c) five precisely dated oracles.

The Book of Haggai is listed as the tenth Minor Prophet, between Zephaniah and Zechariah in both canons. The superscription and the chronological data of the text indicate that the ministry of Haggai included five proclamations of the word of the Lord from August through December 520 B.C.E.

The addressees are members of the second group of exiles from Babylon, who returned to Jerusalem about 522 B.C.E. under the leadership of Zerubbabel, the governor, and Joshua, the high priest. These two had been appointed to the positions of leadership during the early reign of Darius I of Persia (1:1; see p. 574).

The duration of Haggai's ministry is unclear. Although he is believed to have been a contemporary of Zechariah, there is no acknowledgment in either book of the other's activity. The recorded oracles indicate Haggai's perspective on how to achieve restoration for the Judean temple-community. The final form of the text indicates additional perspectives by the editor. The final date of the text is considered a question of secondary importance among commentators.

Composition of the text

For more than a century questions about the unity of the Book of Haggai have been discussed. The literary relationship between Haggai and Ezra has also been analyzed. More recently, the process of editorial activity has been examined for additional literary forms as well as for the religious significance of the oracles.

Scholars focus attention on one section of the text (2:10-19) in particular. Rearrangement of chapter 2 has been suggested as a partial solution to the difficulties of the verses. The New English Bible prefers this order: 1:14, 15, 13; 2:15-19, 10-14, 1-9, 20-23. Others, including the New American Bible, suggest that 2:15-19 should go after chapter 1. Revision of 2:18 is indicated by brackets. The editors believe that the date of the month is a gloss or that the date should be changed from the ninth month to the sixth month. None of the proposed rearrangements is confirmed in any text or version.

In general, there is a consensus about the structure, which provides a unity to the text, namely, five oracles introduced by editorial frameworks (see p. 576).

Outline of the book

COMMENTARY

PART ONE: RECONSTRUCTION OF THE TEMPLE

Hag 1:1-15a

Part One offers a historical framework for the activity of Haggai by the insertion of chronological introductions and narrative detail. Another component of the oracles is the use of two traditional prophetic formulas: "Thus says the Lord of hosts" (1:2, 5, 7) and "says the Lord" (1:13). The contrast of prose introductions and poetic oracles is also apparent.

1:1 Superscription. This verse is not an introduction to the entire Book of Haggai but is limited to the first oracle (1:2-11). In addition to mention of the date of August 520 B.C.E., the verse identifies the current Persian ruler, Darius I. Since the position of monarch no longer existed for the Jewish community after the Exile, the superscription accommodated the new situation by substituting the name of the foreign ruler.

Zerubbabel and Joshua, the appointed representatives of Darius' government, are the addressees of the first oracle. Their names are repeated in the second and third oracles. Unlike Haggai, both are identified by function *and genealogy:* "the governor of Judah, Zerubbabel, son of Shealtiel, and the high priest Joshua, son of Jehozadak."

Zerubbabel was the nephew of King Jehoiachin, who had been exiled to Babylon in 597 B.C.E. (see 1 Chr 3:17-19). His civic appointment was probably considered a minor position in the extensive Persian empire. In this early stage of restoration, however, his presence was a reminder of the royal Davidic household that had ruled in Jerusalem. Symbolically, he may have been a catalyst for dreams of rebuilding a new kingdom according to the model of the preexilic monarchy (see Hag 2:20-23).

Joshua is named Jeshua in the Books of Ezra and Nehemiah. He was a grandson of the chief priest in Jerusalem. Joshua and his father had been exiled to Babylon (see 1 Chr 5:40-41). The designation "high priest" occurs here for the first time. As the religious leader of the returned exiles, his position may have been more autonomous. After him priestly authority became more significant (see pp. 574–575).

1:2-11 First oracle: Exhortation to rebuild the temple. The oracle consists of three sections related to the problem of temple restoration (vv. 2-4, 5-6, 7-11). Each is introduced by a traditional prophetic formula.

The first section (vv. 2-4) considers the question of the community's attitude toward rebuilding the temple. The initial statement is presented as a quotation from the community: "Not now has the time come to rebuild the house of the Lord" (v. 2). Next, a rhetorical question offers an opportunity to reflect on experience: "Is it time for you to dwell in your own paneled houses, while this house lies in ruins?" (v. 4).

It is clear that the entire community, not just the civic and religious leadership, is being challenged. The repetition of the word "time" (vv. 2, 4) draws attention to the irony of the situation. Who really decides what is the propitious "time" for rebuilding?

In preexilic tradition an interesting parallel suggests a response to the question. God provides the perspective. Recall the encounter between God and David *before* the first temple was constructed. In that situation David confided his worries to Nathan about a dwelling for God, since he, David, lived in a house of cedar (2 Sam 7:2-3). God replied by promising to build David a house! The metaphor of "house" symbolized an everlasting dynasty and kingdom (2 Sam 7:7-17).

Why was Haggai's community waiting to rebuild the temple (v. 2)? The foundations for the temple had been laid in the spring of 536 B.C.E. by the first group that had returned from Babylon (see Ezra 3:7-13). No additional progress, however, had been achieved. What factors impeded the project? Had the community forgotten the edict of Cyrus for the task of restoration? Were the living conditions enervating? Did they experience opposition inside and outside the community? (See p. 574.) Perhaps they were waiting for the literal fulfillment of Jeremiah's prophecy: "Only after seventy years have elapsed for Babylon will I visit you and fulfill for you my promise to bring you back to this place" (Jer 29:10; 25:11; compare Zech 1:12, 16-17). If so, a few years still remain for the fulfillment. There is no specific reason indicated in the text to account for the community's resistance to rebuilding the temple.

The second section, too, invites the community to reflect on its experience (vv. 5-6). "Consider your ways" (vv. 5b, 7b) introduces a series of comparisons between efforts at reconstituting daily living and the results. Although they have labored for food, drink, clothing, and wages, the results are meager and unsatisfying (v. 6).

The third section consists of a command and a judgment from God (vv. 7-11). It indicates the relationship between God's activity and the present experience of the community. The community must obtain timber to build the house of God (v. 8a). The urgency of the task consists in giving glory to God (v. 8b).

The expectations about restoration cannot be met (v. 9a). Why? God has entered into the situation. Efforts are useless, especially in providing homes for themselves while God's house "lies in ruins" (v. 9b). Stark living conditions are the direct result of God's initiative for the drought. The land and its produce, persons and their livestock are affected (vv. 10-11).

The literary form of verses 9-11 is a question-answer pattern. The didactic style of the verses repeats the plight of the community (vv. 4-6). In addition, it emphasizes the need for immediate response on the part of the community. Clearly, the temple must be rebuilt. However, the physical restoration suggests a metaphorical function.

According to Haggai, to rebuild the temple means to restore the relationship of the community with God (compare the commentary on Joel 1:5-20, p. 579). Restoration of God's house is the primary responsibility of the community. Until the task is completed, the community lives under God's judgment enacted through the Exile and continuing in the harsh conditions of their lives. When the temple is completed, blessing will replace judgment. The Lord will dwell in the temple-community again.

1:12-15a Second oracle: Response and assurance. The ordering of the verses is debated (see p. 593). The dating for the oracle does not follow the pattern of the other oracles, that is, a prose introduction (see 1:1; 1:15b–2:1; 2:10, 18, 20). For some commentators, the dating information at the conclusion of the oracle (v. 15) indicates the need for rearrangement. They suggest that the phrase "on the twenty-fourth day of the sixth month" ought to be shifted to 2:15 to provide a chronology for the third oracle (2:15-19). Rearrangement, however, is not necessary.

The prose reflection of verse 12 indicates the importance of Haggai's position in the temple-community. The editor of the text draws attention to his prophetic credentials (vv. 12b-13; see p. 592). In addition, Haggai's proclamation is obeyed by the entire community. "All the remnant of the people" may be inserted to identify the returned exiles as the ones who will receive the blessings of restoration (v. 12a; 2:2; see Isa 10:20-22; Mic 4:7; Zech 8:6, 11-12). This group "listened to the voice of the Lord" (see Jer 23:3; Deut 6:2-3).

The brief oracle is located in the center of the editorial comment (v. 13). "I am with you" is a traditional proclamation of assurance (see Gen 28:15; Exod 3:12; Jer 1:8; 30:10-11; Isa 41:10; 43:5). Here the word is accompanied by action as the Lord "stirs up" the spirit of Zerubbabel, Joshua, and the community for the task of rebuilding the temple (v. 14). The Hebrew verb from which the word for "spirit" is derived is used to describe God's power to activate Cyrus, who authorized the exiles to return (2 Chr 36:22-23) and to activate the exiles themselves (Ezra 1:5).

The phrase "twenty-fourth day of the sixth month" (v. 15a) does not have to be shifted to another place in the text. The date recalls to the community the process involved in their own call to rebuild the temple. Having listened to the proclamations of Haggai (vv. 2-11), they determined to be obedient. God's subsequent word and action of assurance (vv. 13-14) encouraged their response to be faithful. They began the project of restoring the temple.

PART TWO: FUTURE GLORY OF THE TEMPLE

Hag 1:15b–2:23

Part Two refers to future blessings for the Judean temple-community, blessings that were proclaimed before the Exile. It offers hope in present circumstances, blessings for the future, and a role of prominence to Zerubbabel, the civic leader. Four identical structural components link the two parts of the book: chronological introductions; addressees; question-and-answer pattern; assurances. Promises of future blessings are a development of the Lord's assurances (vv. 6-9, 21-23).

1:15b–2:9 Third oracle: Assurance and promises. The chronological introduction (1:15b–2:1) follows the pattern of the first oracle (1:1). The "twenty-first day of the seventh month" indicates nearly one month of work on rebuilding the temple. The date is also important in the Jewish calendar: it is the final day of a week's celebration of the feast of Booths, during which the community would remember its ancestors' living in tents as they journeyed through the wilderness (see Lev 23:33-36, 39-43; Deut 16:13-15). As one of the three pilgrimage feasts (along with Passover and Pentecost), the feast of Booths would draw crowds to Jerusalem.

The addressees of the third oracle are identical with those of the previous oracle: Zerubbabel, Joshua, and the "remnant of the people" (v. 2). Haggai may have chosen the occasion of the festival because of the presence of the civic and religious leaders and other persons gathered in Jerusalem. The celebration provided an association with the period of the first temple. During Solomon's reign the temple had been dedicated on this festival (see 1 Kgs 8; compare Ezek 45:25; Zech 14:16).

The question-and-answer pattern (1:9-11) continues in the first section of the oracle (2:3-5). A series of three questions (v. 3) invites those assembled to reflect on their memories of the temple before Babylon conquered Jerusalem with the probable assistance of Edom (see the commentary on Obadiah, p. 586). The comparison of the Solomonic temple and the sporadic progress of reconstruction since 538 B.C.E. left no doubt about which was a glorious achievement.

A proclamation of assurances links the third oracle to the second oracle. While recorded briefly in the second oracle (1:13), the declaration occurs in an expanded form (2:4-5). Officials and community members are exhorted to "take courage" (three times), and not to fear (v. 4). The Lord is present; God's spirit dwells in all the members of the community (v. 5b; see 1:14).

The traditional language of assurance is developed by an editor in verse 5a. The reference to God's relationship with Israel provides a continuity of experience for the returned exiles. The specific event, "the pact," is the covenant experience at Mount Sinai. "I am with you, says the Lord of hosts" is assurance to both groups (v. 4b; see Exod 29:45-46).

The second section of the oracle announces future blessings for the community (vv. 6-9). The uncertainty of when they will be fulfilled is indicated by "one moment yet, a little while" (v. 6a). The Revised Standard Version, however, interprets the phrase to mean that God will act again in a similar way: "once again, in a little while."

While cosmic shaking is attributed to God in earlier traditions (see Amos 8:8-9; Isa 2:13-21; 13:13; Ezek 38:20; compare Joel 2:10; 4:16 [3:16]), the proclamation here promises a new reality (vv. 6b-7a). The "nations" and their "treasures" will be shaken, too. There is no indication in this verse of "universalism," that is, universal salvation, as some commentators have suggested. They compare this section to Isa 60:5-11, which presents a different concept.

The future action of God will be directed to filling the new temple with "glory" (v. 7b). "Silver" and "gold" from Babylon and the nations will be used for sacred vessels to worship God in glory (v. 8; compare Zech 6:9-15). The Lord's direct intervention, then, will accomplish what no dedicated human effort could accomplish independently. Greater glory will be in the Lord's second temple than in the period of the first temple (v. 9a). The present situation of the community will be reversed.

The section concludes with a comprehensive promise of blessings, "peace" (shalom) in verse 9b (compare Zech 8:12, 19). What constitutes "peace"? Where is it to be located? For whom? The term's multiple interpretation transcends any particular designation. The verse may be intentionally unclear in the Hebrew text. In the Greek text, however, a scribe appended a reflection: "and peace of soul as a possession for all who build, to erect this temple."

2:10-19 Fourth oracle: Decisions and future blessings. This oracle is the most difficult passage to interpret. Commentators debate virtually every perspective: dating indications; the connection between verses 11-14 and 15-19; the placement of the oracle; the addressees (v. 14); the religious significance of the passage. The division of the oracle into two sections (vv. 10-14 and 15-19) is generally agreed upon among scholars.

Verse 10 identifies the date for the oracle (compare v. 18). There are several suggestions about altering the date and the placement of the oracle (see p. 593). Rearrangement, however, is not necessary, since precise dating is not the only factor to be considered for interpretation. The verse indicates that a few months after work had commenced on the temple, Haggai proclaimed another oracle.

In the first section of the oracle, the initial statement in verse 11 exhorts Haggai to consult the "priests" for a "decision" (torah). Priests were the arbitrators for all circumstances of daily life (see Deut 17:8-13; compare Zech 7:2-3; Mal 2:7). Each decision under their jurisdiction was connected with the primary concern of the community: What constitutes holiness, that is, what is involved in purity and defilement? The verses describe a set of circumstances about ritual purity. The situation is formulated in two question-and-answer patterns (vv. 12-13; see 1:9-11; 2:3-5).

The first question is about "sanctified flesh," or roasted meat that had been blessed for ritual sacrifice (v. 12). If a person were carrying the ritual element, would the element effect holiness for other objects that came into contact with it? The priests respond negatively. Holiness is not transferred by contact with a sacred object (compare Exod 29:37; 30:29; Lev 6:26-27).

Another perspective of the first question follows (v. 13). If a person is defiled because of contact with an unclean object, would the defilement be transferred to other objects with which the person comes into contact (see Lev 6:20-21, 25-28; 11:24-28; 22:4-7)? The priests respond positively. Defilement, unlike holiness, is easily transferable. Contemporary sociological analysis of Jewish purity and defilement codes confirms the extraordinary stratification implicit in groups, religious responsibilities, and possibilities of changing one's status of purity and defilement.

The climax of the section occurs in verse 14. It states the judgment of the Lord following the norms of the priests' decisions. To whom is the judgment directed? To "this people . . . this nation." What is the verdict? "All the works of their hands, and what they offer there is unclean." The identity of the addressees and the judgment of the Lord provide the religious significance of the section.

Earlier scholarship suggested that the addressees were the Samaritans or a group later reinterpreted as the Samaritans. According to Ezra, their offer to collaborate with the returned exiles in the restoration of the temple had been spurned. During the leadership of Zerubbabel and Joshua, the Samaritans retaliated, and progress on the temple was hampered (see Ezra 4:1-5). Although the chronology in Ezra is uncertain, the events are part of a reliable tradition. As enemies of Judah, their history indicted them as "unclean." The offerings of the Samaritans would also be defiled.

Contemporary scholarship, however, does not accept the identification of the Samaritans. It prefers to identify the addressees as the temple-community of Judah because (a) the only group that Haggai addresses throughout the book is the returned exiles; (b) the term "this people" refers to the community (see 1:2a); (c) the terms "this people, this nation" are used in prophetic literature to designate Judah in judgments of reproach (see Jer 6:19, 21; 14:10, 11).

What is the indictment against the temple-community? Commentators do not agree. Six interpretations represent the discussion:

a) The phrase "the works of their hands" refers to the yield from agriculture and animals. No ritual offerings are acceptable, because the altar has not been sanctified. Although it is unclear whether the altar was destroyed in 586 B.C.E. (compare 2 Kgs 25; Ezek 43:13-26), restoration of the temple would include a rededication of the altar. Thus Haggai is exhorting the community to attend to the appropriate cleansing of the altar while the work of restoration continues.

b) A similar interpretation proposes that the temple itself may be identified with "sanctified flesh" (v. 12a). Until the temple is restored, the community remains unclean.

c) A third interpretation suggests that the ritual offerings are a symbol of the community's life. Since the group has failed to live according to God's covenant, the offerings are unclean (compare Isa 57:3-10; 65:3-7). The offerings will be acceptable if the community reforms (see Isa 1:15; compare Isa 33:14ff.; Ezek 18:5ff.).

d) Israel had been chosen to be holy (see Exod 19:6), yet subsequent history indicated that it had become defiled. Only acceptance of God's blessings and repentance will redefine the community's status before God (see 2:19).

e) God's future presence in the temple (2:2-9) will not automatically assure that the community is ritually pure for worship. The temple and its ritual are not a guarantee of holiness. Repentance and integrity of life are necessary to give the ritual its context and meaning. This interpretation is based on an addition of the Greek text: "Because of their early profits, they shall be pained because of their toil, and you have hated those who reprove at the gates" (compare Amos 5:10). The addition is the earliest interpretation of the Hebrew text.

f) There is no indictment. Rather, "the works of their hands" refers to the reconstruction of the temple. It is the effort of the community to prepare for the Lord's coming. When the temple is restored, God's presence will fill the temple with glory and renew the community (see Ezek 36:22-32; 43:1-9).

These various interpretations indicate a tension between God's initiative and human effort. They also present the importance of temple restoration and sacrificial worship as symbols of the condition of the community. Both perspectives link the temple-community with the collective experience of Israel. Both realities will continue in future communities.

Verse 15a provides a connection between the first and second sections of the oracle: "But now, consider from this day forward." The directive appeals to the community to reflect on its situation before the task of rebuilding had begun (vv. 15b-16a). The section repeats the comparison in the first oracle between human efforts and results as well as God's intervention (vv. 16b-17; see 1:5-7, 9-11). One new judgment occurs about the community's response to its stark situation: "you did not return to me" (v. 17b).

Although the section repeats the experience of the community, a new emphasis is apparent. Notice that "consider" occurs three times (vv. 15a, 18 [2 times]). The immediate object of the verb is "this day." It is not a reference to an indefinite day but to a precise day, that is, "the twenty-fourth day of the ninth month" (v. 18a). The significance of the date is specified: "a stone laid upon a stone in the temple of the Lord" (v. 15b) and "the temple of the Lord was founded" (v. 18b).

Some commentators propose that the verses identify the day on which the foundation stone of the temple was laid (compare Ezra 3:10-13; Zech 4:9). A sacred place for worship was restored. The formal ceremony of rededication is not described. Rather, the function of verses 15-19 is to compare the situation of the community before and after the event. Beforehand, the community experienced the judgment of God; afterward, however, God transformed judgment into blessing: "From this day, I will bless!" (v. 19b).

Other commentators suggest that the emphasis on "this day" is not directly related to the laying of the foundation stone. Rather, the oracle proclaimed on "this day" reveals the community's need for repentance. Blessing will follow judgment (see v. 17b) if the community returns to God.

2:20-23 Fifth oracle: Future of Zerubbabel. Verse 20 introduces the oracle with the same date as the previous one, which presented the Lord's judgment and blessing on the temple-community. The addressee is "Zerubbabel, the governor of Judah" (v. 21a). The proclamation contrasts the treatment of the nations—judgment (v. 22)—with that of Zerubbabel and the community—blessing (v. 23).

From 522 to 520 B.C.E. Darius I struggled to achieve stability among the rebelling satrapies of the Persian empire (see p. 574). The situation may have been interpreted as a fortuitous one for Judah to achieve political independence as another dimension of restoration. Zerubbabel as a Davidic descendant would restore the hopes of the returned exiles as well as promote the fulfillment of messianic expectations.

The introduction to God's action repeats the cosmic shaking of the third oracle (v. 21b; compare 2:6b). Verse 22 identifies God's action upon Judah's enemies: "overthrow," "destroy," "go down." The terms are found in the Torah and the Prophets to describe the Sodom and Gomorrah tradition (Gen 19:25, 29; Deut 29:23; Amos 4:11); in oracles against the nations (Isa 13:19; 23:11; Jer 51:20-21); and in the Exodus from Egypt (see Exod 14:23; 15:1, 5). There is no indication in the verse of when God will act on behalf of Judah.

Verse 23 describes God's action toward Zerubbabel "on that day." The verbs and titles identify Zerubbabel with other figures who were particularly chosen by God. The first action and title are presented in verse 23a: "I will take you" indicates a special election (see Exod 6:7; Josh 24:3; 2 Sam 7:8). "My servant" assigns Zerubbabel another responsibility to his position as governor. The role especially identified David (2 Sam 7:5; 1 Kgs 11:32, 36; 1 Chr 17:4; Ps 132:10; Ezek 34:23; 37:24-25), Judah, and Mount Zion (Ps 78:68-70).

"I will set you as a signet ring" is the second promise of God to Zerubbabel (v. 23b; see Sir 49:11). The proclamation is a reversal of the one to Jeconiah (Coniah), Zerubbabel's grandfather, just before the Exile: "As I live, says the Lord, if you, Coniah, son of Jehoiakim, king of Judah, are a signet ring on my right hand, I will snatch you from it" (Jer 22:24).

The signet ring contained the king's seal, which was used to stamp important documents with royal approval. The ring is a metaphor to indicate the relationship of the king to God. The king functioned as God's representative. The final phrase of verse 23 appears to confirm the possibility of Zerubbabel's attaining royal status: "for I have chosen you, says the Lord of hosts."

Conclusion

The Book of Haggai has been analyzed according to the perspective of unfulfilled prophecy. Images of restoration were proclaimed during the Exile to revitalize hope (see Ezek 40–48; Isa 40–55). The experiences of the first groups of returnees from Babylon did not correspond to the prophetic oracles. Haggai's contribution about a restored temple and a reconstituted ruler of Davidic ancestry (2:1-9, 20-23) were realized neither in his own lifetime nor in the lifetimes of future communities.

Perhaps the apparent "failure" of Haggai's proclamations accounts for the minimal value given to his book by several commentators. Some commentators, however, assess the value of the book differently. Canonical critics, in particular, present the contribution of Haggai for succeeding generations. It is important to consider his message for contemporaries and for future believers.

Attending to probable expectations of

both groups, one can analyze Haggai's understanding of God's revelation:

a) Haggai's directives to the community addressed both dimensions of restoration, that is, a restored temple and a reconstituted Davidic ruler. He urged the people forward in the immediate task of rebuilding the temple. The process, in turn, facilitated their identity with God as a temple-community. He also warned them that their identity consisted in integrity of life as well as prescribed ritual sacrifice to confirm their covenant relationship with God.

b) Haggai reminded the community that their efforts at restoration would contribute to the fulfillment of visions proclaimed during the Exile. The community needed the motivation to connect their labor, which was so slow and hampered, to their past history and future possibilities.

c) Haggai did not propose that there was a simple relationship between the initiative of God and the response of the community; rather, he respected the mystery of the faithful God and the struggling community. Haggai was convinced that God would never abandon the community. He believed in the God who consistently enters into the human condition, filling it clearly, at times, with glory and presence.

ZECHARIAH

Mary Margaret Pazdan, O.P.

INTRODUCTION: FIRST ZECHARIAH

Zech 1:1–8:23

The introduction indicates that two centuries of political and religious history divide First Zechariah (chs. 1–8) and Second Zechariah (chs. 9–14). As a preparation for the study of Zechariah, then, it is helpful to review the information about First and Second Zechariah, especially the sections on historical background, attitudes and perspectives about reconstruction, and literary forms (see pp. 574–577). In addition, a comparison of the material on authorship, dating and composition of the text, and an outline of the texts will provide a clearer context for study of each section of Zechariah.

Authorship

Unlike Haggai, whose name was supplemented only by his function (prophet), Zechariah is identified by function and genealogy. The superscription (1:1) and the introduction to the first vision (1:7) describe him as "the prophet Zechariah, son of Berechiah, son of Iddo." His identity as a prophet may be inferred from his name, which means "Yahweh has remembered." It occurs about thirty times in the Old Testament.

Outside the text that bears his name, Zechariah is identified with Haggai as a "prophet" and as the "son of Iddo" (see Ezra 5:1; 6:14). The phrase "son of Berechiah" (Zech 1:1, 7) is occasionally considered a gloss (see the note in the Jerusalem Bible; compare Matt 23:25). The phrase, however, may indicate Zechariah's father.

Iddo, the grandfather of Zechariah, was one of the priestly exiles returning from Babylon with Zerubbabel and Jeshua (Joshua; see Neh 12:4, 16). Consequently, some commentators emphasize Zechariah's priestly origin. Others identify him as a priest because of his concerns for the restoration of the temple and cult as well as the priesthood.

Dating of the text

First Zechariah, like Haggai, provides specific dates for oracles and visions. The book, which is found in the eleventh position in both canons, between Haggai and Malachi, is a postexilic text. Exact chronology is established for the beginning of Zechariah's ministry in the superscription: October-November 520 B.C.E., during the second year of Darius' reign (1:1). Zechariah's ministry began two months after Haggai proclaimed his first oracle (see Hag 1:1).

The second date suggests that Zechariah's ministry concluded two years later: November-December 518 B.C.E., during the fourth year of Darius' reign (7:1). Comparing the dates attributed to Haggai's ministry shows that Zechariah's ministry was eighteen months longer (see p. 592).

The civic and religious leaders of the temple-community mentioned in Haggai appear also in First Zechariah: Zerubbabel (4:6-10; 6:11-14) and Joshua (3:1-10; 6:11-14). The addressees of Haggai and First Zechariah are identical, that is, the second group of returned exiles from Babylon.

Nothing in chapter 8 or in any editorial revisions indicates a later chronology for Zechariah's ministry. The final form of First Zechariah is not considered apart from the dating process of the entire text (fourteen chapters) and its canonical placement (see p. 616).

Composition of the text

Visions constitute the major literary genre of First Zechariah (1:7–6:15). They are interspersed with oracles, which function as responses. A separate collection of oracles (7:1–8:23) is also apparent. Additional material has expanded the visions and the oracles to constitute the final form of the text. The motive ordinarily given for the redactional activity is a changing political context.

Scholars discuss two questions about redaction: Who is responsible for the additions? What sources were used? The questions are part of the complex considerations of the relationship of Zechariah (chs. 1–14) to apocalyptic literature (see p. 577). The relationship of First Zechariah to Second Zechariah regarding the editorial process of the book and the development of religious ideas is discussed below (see pp. 616, 623).

Rearrangement of the text is suggested for chapters 3 and 4. The Jerusalem Bible changes verses *within* the chapters: 3:1, 2, 3, 4a, 5, 4b, 6, 7, 9a, 8, 9b, 10; 4:1, 2, 3, 4, 5, 6a, 10b, 11, 12, 13, 14, 6b, 7, 8, 9, 10a. The New English Bible rearranges chapter 4 as frames around chapter 3 (4:1-3, 11-14; 3:1-10; 4:4-5, 6-10). Note that the New American Bible rearranges only chapter 4 (4:4-10, 1-3, 11-14). Rearrangement is one solution to the difficult task of interpreting First Zechariah.

The three-part structure of the text is recognized by most commentators: (a) introduction (1:1-6); (b) visions (1:7–6:15); (c) oracles about fasting and future days (7:1–8:23). Nonetheless, there is little consensus about the interpretation of the visions and oracles. It is no wonder that several contemporary commentators concur with Jerome in their judgment of Zechariah as the most obscure book of the Bible.

Outline of the book

There are two places in the text of First Zechariah where the numbering of chapters and verses is different. This commentary, based on the New American Bible, represents the Hebrew text, while other Bibles and commentaries may use the Greek text. The chart compares the versions:

Hebrew Text	Greek Text
2:1-4	1:18-21
2:5-17	2:1-13

In this commentary the numbering of the Greek text is in brackets.

COMMENTARY: FIRST ZECHARIAH

PART ONE: INTRODUCTION TO FIRST ZECHARIAH

Zech 1:1-6

The introduction establishes a continuity between "your fathers" and the returned exiles. What the Judean prophets had proclaimed about God's imminent judgment had occurred in the destruction of Jerusalem. That experience is a mirror for the next generation who returned to rebuild Jerusalem.

1:1 Superscription. The verse is similar to the superscription of Haggai (see Hag 1:1). It identifies the Persian ruler (Darius I), the year and month, and confirms Zechariah's ministry as prophet.

While the superscription of Haggai emphasizes his prophetic credentials, Zechariah's focuses on a genealogy of a priestly family that survived the Exile. Whereas Haggai's oracle is addressed to the leaders of the temple-community and the returnees from Babylon (see Hag 1:1-2), Zechariah's oracle has no specific addressees (see Zech 1:2ff.); from the context it is inferred that it is addressed to members of the temple-community.

1:2-6 Return to the Lord. Verse 2 is an editorial insertion that interrupts the sequence of the prophetic oracle. The verse links the present generation of returned exiles to their relatives: "The Lord was indeed angry with your fathers. . . ." The connection between the two generations is continued by the repetition of "your fathers" (vv. 4, 5, 6; see Ezek 20:27, 30; Jer 7:25-26).

The divine formulas "Thus says the Lord of hosts" (vv. 3, 4) and "says the Lord" (vv. 3, 4) complete the prophetic formula introduced in verse 1. The title "Lord of hosts," which appears three hundred times in the Old Testament, occurs fifty-three times in Zechariah, fourteen times in Haggai, and twenty-four times in Malachi.

The exhortation of the Lord of hosts is "Return to me" (v. 3a). Specific reasons for returning are not indicated (compare 2 Chr 30:6-9; Isa 44:22; Joel 2:12; Mal 3:7). The community, however, is assured that the Lord will return to them (v. 3b).

The exhortation is strengthened by reference to their ancestors' experience (v. 4a). Previous generations had refused to obey the Lord's warning proclaimed through the prophets (v. 4b). By not listening, the "fathers" refused to turn to the Lord (v. 4c).

The term "former prophets" refers to the preexilic prophets (see Jer 35:15). Later, in the Jewish canon, the term indicates a collection of books describing early prophetic activity in Israel (Josh; Judg; 1-2 Sam; 1-2 Kgs).

Verse 5 consists of two rhetorical questions about the existence of "your fathers" and the "prophets." Their mortality is compared with the eternal power of the Lord's "words and decrees" proclaimed by "my servants the prophets" (v. 6a). It is God's words that "overtake your fathers." The verb "overtake" indicates God's action to impart blessing (see Deut 28:2) or curse (Deut 28:15) on a community. Here the context favors "curse," that is, the destruction of Jerusalem.

The second half of verse 6, an editorial addition, refers to the current situation of Zechariah and the community. They have learned from the past that God is faithful to promises. They have accepted the invitation to return, to restore their relationship to God, to reconstruct the temple.

What does the language of the oracle suggest about Zechariah's function in the community? Zechariah may have used traditional prophetic formulas to strengthen his position in prophetic tradition. The authority of the "former prophets" appears to have nearly canonical status: what they proclaimed was fulfilled in the experience of the Exile. In this perspective Zechariah is continuing an old tradition and contributes nothing new to prophecy.

Zechariah's intent may be to appeal to a collective history and to invite the community to be unlike their ancestors, that is, to return to the Lord and rebuild the covenant relationship. The visions indicate dimensions of that choice. Zechariah builds on the past to create new possibilities for the future. The perspectives are not contradictory. The first represents older scholarship (see p. 572), while the second indicates more recent scholarship.

PART TWO: "NIGHT" VISIONS AND RESPONSES

Zech 1:7–6:15

The "night" visions of First Zechariah are regarded as some of the most difficult passages of the Old Testament. Basic questions that contemporary scholars discuss are: What is the specific function of the visions in regard to the ministry and message of Zechariah? What is the relationship of the visions and the accompanying oracles? What is the literary genre of the visions? Does the literary genre determine the religious message?

Visions are common in prophetic literature (see Isa 6; Ezek 1:1; Jer 1:11-19). The visions of First Zechariah, however, are generally identified with a distinctive literary genre called "apocalyptic." One characteristic of the genre is the presence of a secret revelation of God transmitted through a vision. The images of the vision are not taken literally; rather, each image is a symbol that is interpreted for its own value.

Ordinarily an angel assists in the interpretation of the vision. The Hebrew term for "angel" means "messenger." It is used in connection with many persons in the Old Testament. Even the phrase "messenger of the Lord" does not necessarily designate an angelic being. Prophets are identified with this phrase (see Hag 1:13; 2:20).

Other characteristics of apocalyptic literature are well-defined ideas about God, human beings, good, evil, and the world. Since the visions of First Zechariah are "apocalyptic" in form but not in content, scholars do not situate First Zechariah in that category. Some commentators designate the visions as "proto-apocalyptic."

The visions of First Zechariah may be symbolic representations of what is necessary for the restoration for the temple-community. Each vision generally follows a pattern: introductory statement; description; question about interpretation; the angel's explanation.

1:7-12 First vision: Equestrians. The superscription offers additional chronological data (v. 7). The month Shebat is from the Babylonian calendar adopted by the Jewish community after the Exile. The name that appears here does not occur anywhere else in the Old Testament. That detail and "the second year of Darius" place Zechariah's ministry during the Persian period. The visions occurred about three months after the first oracle addressed to Zechariah.

Verse 8a is an awkward transition between the "word" addressed to Zechariah and written in the traditional third-person prophetic formula (v. 7) and the "vision" proclaimed in the first person. Verse 8a states that Zechariah's vision occurred "during the night." No other time-sequence is indicated in the subsequent seven visions. Although it is possible for all of them to occur in one night, most commentators suggest that they are a succession of "experiences."

The first vision (vv. 7b-13) can be compared to focusing a telescope. One adjustment presents a large picture; additional adjustments reveal more details. Verse 8b depicts a tranquil scene. Evergreen shrubs ("myrtle trees") grow alongside streams. An equestrian stands beside his red horse, and behind him are "red, sorrel, and white horses." An exact location is not specified. The place suggests a garden like Eden, outside Jerusalem or near the entrance to heaven.

Zechariah asks the interpreting angel for an explanation (v. 9a). The angel, however, does not offer one but provides another glance at the scene (v. 9b). The central character *within the scene* identifies the horses: "These are they whom the Lord has sent to patrol the earth" (v. 10). The metaphor could point to the angels of the heavenly council (see Job 1:7; 2:2) as well as to Persian messengers, who provided a thorough communication system in the empire.

A third viewing of the scene follows. The central character ("the driver" in verse 8) becomes the "angel of the Lord" (v. 11a; see the note on "angel" above). Equestrians repeat their function: "We have patrolled the earth" and state their judgment: "see, the whole earth is tranquil and at rest" (v. 11b). Cosmic peace may be a reference to the leadership of Darius, who successfully defeated the rebellious satrapies of the empire.

A fourth glance reveals the climax of the vision. The angel of the Lord petitions the Lord of hosts to relieve the oppression of Jerusalem and Judah (v. 12). The lamentation over the situation of the returned exiles, who "felt your anger these seventy years," is a sharp contrast to the judgment of the equestrians (v. 11). God's intervention is needed if there is to be reconstruction (compare Joel 2:14).

1:13-17 Responses. Responses to the vision function with verse 9 as an inclusion to bracket the visionary scene. Similar to the structure in Joel, a lament (v. 12) is followed by divine assurance (v. 13; see p. 579). Verse 13, however, is a *narrative* comment rather than an oracle of consolation. It serves as a transition to the oracles.

Three oracles of consolation have been appended to the vision. They respond to the lament (v. 12). Each is introduced by traditional prophetic formulas (vv. 14b, 16a, 17a). The interpreting angel exhorts Zechariah to proclaim the first and third oracles (vv. 14-15, 17).

In the first oracle (vv. 14-15), God responds. "I am deeply moved" (v. 14b) is better translated "I am exceedingly jealous" (RSV). As in Joel 2:18, the passionate zeal of God *for* Jerusalem and Zion is clear (compare Zech 8:2-3; 9:9). That zeal takes the form of anger *against* the "complacent nations" (v. 15).

The second oracle proclaims what God's zeal means for the community: "I will turn to Jerusalem in mercy" (v. 16a; compare v. 3b). The temple and the city will be restored through divine initiative (v. 16b; compare the commentary on Hag 1:2-14).

The third oracle describes the care of the Lord of hosts for "my cities" (v. 17a). Goodness, consolation, and election will again be present when God returns to Jerusalem (v. 17b). Two details are absent: the time of God's return and the outcome of the complacent nations (v. 15).

2:1-4 [1:18-21] Second vision: Four horns and four blacksmiths. This succinct vision lacks the details and oracular responses of the first vision. The visionary medium proclaims, "I raised my eyes and looked" (5:1; 6:1) and the first image, "four horns," is seen (v. 1 [1:18]). The interpreting angel is asked for assistance (v. 2a [1:19a]). The horns are identified as those who "scattered Judah and Israel and Jerusalem" (v. 2b [1:19b]).

Verse 3a [1:20a] states that the Lord is the agent who reveals the next image. The prophet asks about the function of the blacksmiths (v. 3b [1:20b]). The Lord responds that they "terrify" and "cast down" the "horns" who "scattered the land of Judah" (v. 4 [1:21]).

In earlier commentaries "horns" was a metaphor for world powers (Mic 4:13). The context would identify them as the enemies of northern Israel and Judah, especially Babylon. In the last decade, however, additional possibilities for interpretation have been suggested: two pairs of animal horns, four horns of the altar, horns in the ground, horn-shaped threshing tools, and horned helmets.

Similarly, "blacksmiths" in earlier commentaries was a metaphor for those who exercise judgment (see Isa 54:16-17), that is, the Persians, who reversed the fortunes of Babylon. In the last decade the term "blacksmiths" has come to identify ploughmen, artisans, constructive or destructive creators.

The thought of earlier commentaries is developed in two ways. Both highlight tasks of reconstruction. One identifies the horns as the horns belonging to animals that have roamed over the ruins of Jerusalem. When the ploughmen guide the animals back to their proper enclosures, there is space to rebuild and reconstitute the community. The other identifies the horns of the altar, which provided sanctuary for those who clung to them. After the Exile, artisans came to rebuild and purify the altar area for sanctuary and cult.

There is no specific oracle that responds to the second vision. Among the three interpretations of the vision, only the earlier one replies to the fate of the "complacent nations," which remained unaddressed in the first vision (1:15).

2:5-9 [2:1-5] Third vision: Measuring line. The third vision is introduced with the same formula as the second vision (v. 5a [v. 1a]). The new image is a man with a measuring line (vv. 5b-6 [1b-2]). This vision develops the image of the measuring device noted in the second oracle of the first vision (see 1:16).

Another new dimension is the introduction of a second angel (v. 7 [v. 3]). This angel exhorts the interpreting angel to give "that young man" (the measurer) a message about how people will live in Jerusalem. They will live "as though in open country." The Revised Standard Version translates this better: "as villages without walls" (v. 8a [v. 4a]). Why "without walls"? "Because of the multitude of men and beasts in her midst" (v. 8b [v. 4b]).

A divine assurance is the climax to the vision. It parallels the oracles in the first vision (see 1:13-17). The Lord promises to be present: "an encircling wall of fire . . . the glory in her midst" (v. 9 [v. 5]).

The third vision is related to the other two visions, functioning as the third adjustment of the telescope. The first focus was cosmic; the second focus was the land of Israel; and the third is the city of Jerusalem. In addition, the third vision specifies how God "will turn to Jerusalem in mercy" (1:16a): God will offer presence and glory (2:9). These gifts suggest "prosperity" (1:17b), that is, all living things will flourish (2:8b).

The third vision is a striking illustration of the use of traditional symbols to proclaim a new reality. The "encircling wall of fire" (v. 9a [v. 5a]), which recalls God's presence as a cloud of fire during the Exodus (see Exod 13:21-22; 14:20; 40:34), is reinterpreted as the protective care of God for Jerusalem. God's initiative in rimming the city offers a perspective to human effort involved in the process of reconstruction.

The rebuilding of the temple in all its complexities is also given a new perspective. The vision of temple restoration that Ezekiel offered to the exiles as hope for the return of God's glory (see Ezek 40–48) is broadened. Zechariah's vision extends God's glory *(kabod)* to all *throughout Jerusalem*.

2:10-17 [2:6-13] Responses. The oracles consist of two sections. The first section (vv. 10-13 [vv. 6-9]) comments on the enemies of Israel mentioned in the first collection of oracles (1:15) and the second and third visions (2:1-4 [1:18-21]; compare 2:9 [2:5]). The second section continues promises of blessings for Jerusalem noted in the first collection of oracles (1:14; 16-17) and the second and third visions (2:4b [1:21b], 7-9 [3-5]). In addition to a thematic division, traditional prophetic formulas separate some of the oracles: "says the Lord" (v. 10ab [v. 6ab]; v. 14b [v. 11b]); "said the Lord of hosts" (v. 12a [v. 8a]).

There is no interpreting angel for the oracles (compare 1:13ff.). Rather, the prophet is clearly indicated as the one commissioned by God (see vv. 12a, 15b [vv. 8a, 11b]). The verses suggest that the fulfillment of God's promises will authenticate the prophet's proclamation.

The first section of oracles contains imperatives for the exiles and warnings for those who conquered them. There is a parallel construction for verses 10 and 11. Those who are living in "the land of the north" (v. 10a [v. 6a]; see Jer 3:18; 16:15; 23:8; 31:8) are identical with the ones "who dwell in daughter Babylon" (v. 11b [v. 7b]).

The exiles are exhorted to "flee" and "escape to Zion" before God "scatters" the inhabitants of Babylon "to the four winds of heaven" (vv. 10-11a [vv. 6-7a]). In these verses the identification of Babylon is probably more extensive than the geographical region designated as exilic territory. It includes all oppressors of Israel.

An ironic punishment is pronounced for the nations that plundered Israel (v. 12a [v. 8a]): "they become plunder for their slaves" (v. 13a [v. 9a]). Why such harsh treatment? "Whoever touches you touches the apple of my eye" (v. 12b [v. 8b]). The metaphor indicates "pupil" or "gate" of the eye, that is, a treasured part or relationship.

The second section, like the third vision (see vv. 8-9 [vv. 4-5]), presents new revelation in traditional terms. Let those in Jerusalem rejoice (see Zeph 3:14-15; Zech 9:9; Pss 9:14; 48:11). The Lord is coming to dwell with the temple-community (v. 14 [v. 10]). The Hebrew of the verse indicates the language of manifestation and abiding presence.

The Lord's dwelling is mentioned in the next verse (v. 15 [v. 11]) with unexpected proclamations. "On that day," referring to the day of the Lord (see the commentary on Joel 2:18–4:21 [2:18–3:21]), the "many nations" shall "join themselves to the Lord . . . and they shall be his people." How the nations will be joined or how Israel and the nations shall become a "people" is not indicated. The concept of the Lord's dwelling among the nations and Israel is remarkable, especially when compared with Zechariah's contemporary Haggai. The latter limited the nations' contributions to their treasures for the temple (see the commentary on Hag 2:7-9).

Covenant language ("choose") is used to indicate the Lord's relationship to Judah and Jerusalem (v. 16 [11]). The designation of Judah as "holy land" appears only here. Everything will be holy because of the Lord's dwelling among the people.

The responses conclude with a fragment of liturgical directive: "Silence . . . in the presence of the Lord!" (v. 17a [v. 13a]; compare Hab 2:20; Zeph 1:7).

3:1-5 Fourth vision: Joshua the high priest. Chapter 3 is presented without any rearrangement of the verses (see p. 601). The vision differs from the first three visions in form. There is no introductory statement, question about interpretation, or explanation by the angel. Some commentators suggest that the unusual form indicates a later vision that was added to an original seven visions.

Verse 1 is an introduction to the vision. The "he" probably refers to the interpreting angel who accompanied the prophet during the first three visions (v. 1a; see 1:9, 14; 2:2, 7 [1:19; 2:3]). Three characters appear in the vision of the heavenly council (v. 1b):

a) "Joshua the high priest" appears for the first time (see p. 593).

b) "The angel of the Lord" who appeared in the first three visions convenes and authorizes the proceedings of the heavenly council (see vv. 2, 4-5).

c) "Satan" is a transliteration of the Hebrew word that means "adversary." It is not a personal name in the Hebrew Bible; rather, it designates a role, that is, accuser (see Job 1:6-12; 2:1-7; Ps 109:6; Rev 12:10).

Verse 2 ironically reverses the roles of Satan and Joshua. Whatever accusations the adversary had spoken against Joshua are abrogated by the double rebukes of the "Lord who has chosen Jerusalem" (see 1:17b; 2:16 [2:12]; compare Hag 2:23). Verse 2 concludes with a rhetorical question: "Is not this man a brand snatched from the fire?" (see Amos 4:11). As Joshua represents the entire community in verse 1, here their communal deliverance from exile is suggested (v. 2b).

The position of Joshua before the angel of the Lord (v. 3a) repeats verse 1a. The "filthy garments" that Joshua wears (v. 3b) are associated with the fire imagery of the Exile experience (v. 2b). The garments could symbolize mourning (see Jer 41:4-5) or the guilt associated with living in Babylon.

The authoritative angel of the Lord directs the angels of the council to reclothe Joshua (vv. 4-5). "Festal garments" and a "clean miter" replace the filthy garments. According to some commentators, the ritual dressing indicates garb of the high priest (see Lev 8:1-9). Others propose a figurative context of acceptance in the court (see Isa 62:3; Job 29:14).

The ritual activity symbolizes the judgment of the angel: "See, I have taken away your guilt" (v. 5b). "Guilt" suggests the association of Joshua with the land of Babylon as well as the transgressions of the temple-community, of which he is the religious leader (see Exod 28:36-38; Num 18:1). To function as high priest, the ritual activity was necessary. The temple ritual for purification is not available.

3:6-10 Responses. A challenge and two oracles of assurance interpret the fourth vision. Each is prefaced by a traditional prophetic formula: "says the Lord of hosts" (vv. 7a, 9b, 10a). Each proclamation is directed to Joshua the high priest by the authoritative angel (v. 6).

The challenge is made in verse 7a: "If you walk in my ways and heed my charge . . . ." The first condition refers to moral integrity (see Deut 8:6), while the second is more ambiguous. The Hebrew term suggests a general obligation or prohibition (see Gen 26:5; Lev 18:30), or a duty (Isa 21:8). It also signifies ritual activity (see Num 3). In this context the faithful cultic service of God is apt.

Acceptance of the challenge results in two areas of responsibility (and blessing) in verse 7b. Each one reflects the situation of a *preexilic monarch.* "Judge my house" indicates judicial functions (see Deut 17:8-13), while "keep my courts" refers to decisions about cultic activity. Both responsibilities are carried out at the temple. The judicial functions *there* are new for a high priest (compare Ezek 44:10-31). "Access among these standing here" describes Joshua's approach to the members of the heavenly council.

The second oracle is an unconditional blessing for Joshua and his associates (v. 8). The identity of the group is unclear. Some commentators suggest additional priests or persons of prominence in the temple-community (see Ezra 2; Neh 7). In what sense are they a "good omen"? They are considered signs of God's blessing (v. 8b; 6:12-13). The "branch" imagery was a traditional one for a just ruler (see Jer 23:5; Isa 11:1). The appearance of a monarch like David is part of the expectation of restoration of the temple-community. Haggai, Zechariah's contemporary, had proclaimed that possibility for Zerubbabel (see Hag 2:23). Verses 7 and 8 suggest some type of shared rule. The high priest (and other priests) functions in the temple, while a Davidic heir functions on the throne.

Verse 9a continues the second oracle with another image: "one stone with seven facets." Attention returns to Joshua (see v. 7) as the one before whom the stone is placed. The stone might be a person; a real stone for temple reconstruction; a stone for ritual purposes; a stone belonging to the garb of high priest.

Verse 9b provides additional details about the stone, which clarify its identity. It probably is the engraved stone that adorned the high priest's turban (see Exod 28:36-38). Its inscription, "Sacred to the Lord" (Exod 28:36), suggests cleansing from guilt (see Exod 28:38).

Something new is revealed. Aaron (and his successors) "*bears* whatever guilt the Israelites may incur" (Exod 28:38a). The Lord of hosts *removes* the "guilt of the land in one day" (v. 9b). This completes the process that the angel of the Lord started by removing Joshua's guilt (v. 5). Now God's initiative cleanses the land.

Verse 10 completes the challenge and oracles of assurance. "On that day" identifies a future possibility wherein the community will be at home and extend hospitality (see 1 Kgs 5:25 [4:25]; Mic 4:4).

4:1-6a, 10b-14 Fifth vision: Lampstand. There is some rearrangement of verses in chapter 4. Note the difference between the New American Bible text and the arrangement of the commentary (see p. 601).

The introductory statement of the fifth vision presents the interpreting angel, who stirs up the prophet (v. 1; compare Joel 4:9 [3:9]). Verse 1 may be a literary device to unify the material between the first vision "at night" (see 1:8) and the present one.

Verse 2a is a departure from the first four visions, where the prophet immediately reports what he sees. This time the interpreting angel asks the question (compare 5:1-4). Zechariah responds with a detailed description of a gold lampstand (vv. 2b-3).

The prophet questions the angel about "these things" (v. 4). The angel responds with another question, implying that the image ought to be clear (v. 5a). After the prophet admits he does not know (v. 5b), the angel explains the scene by first interpreting the lamp (vv. 6a, 10b). The seven "facets" (lights) on the lampstand are "the eyes of the Lord that range over the whole earth."

The prophet inquires again about the "two olive trees at each side of the lampstand" (v. 11). Another question follows: "What are the two olive tufts which freely pour out fresh oil through the two golden channels?" (v. 12). Again, the interpreting angel is surprised that the prophet does not recognize the image (v. 13). When the prophet admits that he does not know (v. 13), the angel explains (v. 14).

How may the major components of the vision be interpreted? A description of the lampstand explains the basic structure of the vision. Within the last century archeological discoveries have classified a number of clay lamps and lampstands conforming to a particular shape. A lampstand is at the base. Resting on the stand is a bowl for oil. On the rim of the bowl are indentations for wicks (usually approximately seven). When the wicks are ignited, they burn because they are draped over the oil.

Although the term for the lampstand is *menorah*, it does not match the description of the seven-branched candelabrum used in ritual contexts (see Exod 25:33). What is unusual in the description of the lampstand in the vision is not its shape but its composition of gold.

What does the lampstand symbolize? The lampstand and lights represent the presence of God, who looks kindly upon all of creation (see 2 Chr 16:9; compare Ezra 5:5). The lampstand and lights parallel and develop two images of earlier visions: the equestrians who patrol the earth (1:10-11) and the encircling wall of fire (2:9).

The olive trees (vv. 3, 11) and the olive tufts (v. 12) are clearly interpreted by the angel as the "two anointed who stand by the Lord of the whole earth" (v. 14). Who are the "anointed"? They are Zerubbabel and Joshua, equal in dignity and importance. Their proposed rule is unexpected because only a monarch like David was anticipated. Nonetheless, for the temple-community there are two who will govern. After Zerubbabel's death the office of high priest grew in prominence (see p. 574).

Many commentators considered Zerubbabel and Joshua as messiah figures because of the "anointed" terminology. The Hebrew phrase translates "sons of oil." In addition, the oil is of the type used for harvest festivals, not for an anointing ceremony. As high priest, Joshua had already been anointed. The two rulers function, however, in a revolutionary role. Although verse 12 is difficult to translate, the imagery suggests that Zerubbabel and Joshua are close to God, who needs their oil for the agency of compassionate presence ("seven facets") for the community. They, in turn, require God's support for leadership. The interdependency is new.

4:6b-10a Collection of responses. If the verses were not rearranged, they would appear between the description of the lampstand and its interpretation. The verses are a poetic insertion consisting of two oracles. Both are introduced by traditional prophetic formulas: "This is the Lord's message" (v. 6b); "This word of the Lord then came to me" (v. 8; see 6:9; 7:4; 8:1, 18). The oracles describe Zerubbabel's leadership in restoring the temple, as an earlier visionary ritual had described Joshua's preparation for the office of high priest (3:1-10).

The first oracle (vv. 6b-7) describes how the work of temple restoration will be accomplished. Neither an "army" (compare 1 Kgs 5:20) nor "might" (see Neh 4:10) is adequate to the task. Divine activity will complete the work (v. 6b).

Since God's spirit is with Zerubbabel, he is the leader in the temple reconstruction. First, Zerubbabel is compared metaphorically to a mountain of obstacles and emerges as the greater one (v. 7a; see Isa 40:4; 41:15). Second, he will bear the "capstone" amid exclamations of the community.

Commentators debate the identity of the capstone. Is it the foundation stone or the final stone on the pinnacle of the temple? Some see the oracles (vv. 6b-10a) and the visionary ritual of Joshua (3:1-10) in the wider context of Mesopotamian services for rededication of the temple. The capstone signifies continuity. It is a stone taken from the earlier temple and positioned in the new one to assure cultic continuity. The "select stone" (v. 10a) refers to another type of ritual—placing an engraved tin tablet into the edifice of the new temple.

Others propose that the capstone is the final piece of the new temple. It is the "select stone" (v. 10a) placed by the hands of Zerubbabel, the civic governor of the temple-community. The Hebrew terms used to describe the stone allow both interpretations. In general, Zechariah was convinced that Zerub-

babel's leadership was necessary for the project (see 6:12-13).

The second oracle (vv. 9-10a) connects the activity of Zerubbabel with the credibility of the prophet. The Lord's proclamation assures Zechariah that Zerubbabel, who began the foundation, will finish it (v. 9a). The completion of the temple will be a sign to the community that Zechariah's proclamations are validated (v. 9b; compare 2:9, 11; 6:15).

Verse 10a describes the general attitude of the temple-community toward the task of reconstruction (compare Hag 2:3-5; Ezra 3:12). Even these scoffers "shall rejoice to see the select stone in the hands of Zerubbabel." The four references to Zerubbabel's hands (4:7 [implicit]; 9 [twice]; 10a) may refer to his royal function in the cultic ceremonies of temple restoration. In ancient Near East traditions the king often assisted in temple reconstruction either actually or symbolically.

5:1-4 Sixth vision: Flying scroll. The spatial quality and movement of the vision parallel the seventh vision: the flying bushel (5:5-11). Both visions are directed to the temple-community. What is necessary to cleanse the community for renewed relationship with God? The theme of renewal, addressed to Joshua with regard to cult (3:1-10) and to Zerubbabel with regard to temple reconstruction (4:6b-10a), has specific implications for the community as well.

Verse 1 is the introductory statement and description of the flying scroll. It repeats the literary form of the second and third visions (see 2:1 [1:18]; 2:5 [2:1]). The short formula will be repeated in the eighth vision (see 6:1).

The question of the interpreting angel (v. 2a) appears redundant, since the prophet had already announced his vision (v. 1). The vision is described with additional detail (v. 2b). While a scroll would be a familiar sight (see Jer 36:1-8) and symbol (see Ezek 2:9-10; 3:1-3), the proportions are unusual. A scroll is much longer than it is wide. In addition, although no one is holding the scroll, it is unrolled and flying in the air!

The dimensions of the scroll match the area of Solomon's temple porch (see 1 Kgs 6:3) and are similar to those of the desert sanctuary, which is half the size (see Exod 26:15-28). However, there is no apparent connection between the flying scroll and either area.

The interpreting angel identifies the scroll as a "curse . . . over the whole earth"; it will sweep away "every thief" and expel "every perjurer" (v. 3). The curse refers to consequences for covenant abrogations that were added to the ceremony by oaths (see Deut 28:15ff.; compare Gen 26:28; Ezek 17:13). The thought in verses 3-4 is a fusion of the covenant stipulations and the Decalogue prescriptions. Specifically, the thief represents the laws regarding human conduct (see Exod 20:15-16), and the perjurer represents attitudes toward God (see Exod 20:7).

Verse 4 is a divine oracle that interprets the vision. It tells of the consequences for thief and perjurer. Their houses and inhabitants will be consumed by the curse that God sends forth (compare Ps 147:15; Isa 55:11).

What is the particular situation in the community that draws attention to thievery and perjury? The perpetrators of these crimes are forbidden to enter the temple (see Ps 24:4). Thievery was a particular problem for the temple-community, especially the usurpation of land tracts by those who remained in Judah during the Babylonian Captivity. Litigation occurred. The charge of perjury is probably related to these occasions.

The curse of the flying scroll may also represent the continuity of judgment and values. Even though the community will be administered by a new model of leadership (Joshua and Zerubbabel), the standards will remain the same as before (compare the commentary on 4:6b-10a). Another factor of continuity is the phrase "the whole earth" (v. 3a). Within both Judah and the Diaspora the same obligations for all Jews will be in force.

5:5-11 Seventh vision: Flying bushel. The vision is inaugurated by a command of the interpreting angel to look up and identify the new symbol (v. 5). The familiar question pattern follows (v. 6a), with the angel's response (v. 6b). The vision reveals another character: "a woman sitting inside the bushel" is "Wickedness," whom the angel thrusts inside, "pushing the leaden cover into the opening" (vv. 7-8).

Next the prophet sees additional characters. Two women with ruffled wings like a stork's lift the bushel into the air (v. 9). The prophet seeks assistance from the angel, who explains the women's action. They are taking the bushel to Shinar, where they will deposit it in the temple when the building is completed (vv. 10-11).

The bushel container and the woman are central to the vision. Their relationship is the key to interpretation. The bushel container functions as the "setting" for both parts of the vision. The term in Hebrew means "container" (see Ruth 2:17) and a "measure" or standardized weight (see Amos 8:5; Ezek 45:10). The prophet's question, "What is it?" refers to content as well as measure.

The question of content is immediately clarified by the angel: "their guilt in all the land" (v. 7b). What is the source of guilt? The woman named Wickedness is the symbol of evil surrounded by guilt (v. 8). Like the genie in the bottle and unlike Pandora and her box, Wickedness and guilt can be controlled by the leaden cover that the angel thrusts into the opening of the container.

Many speculate about why the woman personifies wickedness. Some refer to the feminine gender of the Hebrew word for "wickedness." Others associate it with Israel's sin, which is often described by use of the metaphor of harlotry (see Jer 3:8; Hos 1:2; Ezek 16). A few point to the garden event (Gen 3) as the origin of the personification.

Two figures, half-animal (stork wings) and half-human (women), appear as *deae ex machina* to remove the bushel basket. Stork wings suggest flying animals (see Jer 8:7) and unclean animals (see Lev 11:9; Deut 14:18). Soaring in the wind, they carry the container to Shinar, an ancient name for the land of Babylon (see Gen 10:10; 11:2; Dan 1:2; Rev 14:8). There Wickedness and guilt will have a temple in which to reside.

The image of removing evil and guilt is parallel to the image of Joshua's "filthy garments" (3:3). God initiates the removal of extensive evil ("in all the land") of the community and the impurity of the high priest through agents—two women and the angel (3:5). God is not contaminated by impurity or evil.

The bushel container and the woman are considered non-standards for the temple-community that has returned to restore relationship with God. Covenant obligations (5:1-4) and the removal of evil and guilt are dimensions of reconstruction.

6:1-8 Eighth vision: Four chariots. The final vision forms an inclusion with the first vision (1:7-12). The first verse (1:7) and the last verse (8:8) indicate visionary experience. Details of place (glen, mountain pass) and time (night, sunrise) are different. Important images, however, parallel one another: horses, colors, patrolling functions.

Verse 1 is a short introductory statement with an initial description of the vision; details appear in verses 2-3. Four chariots emerge between two "bronze mountains" (v. 1). Each chariot is numbered and described by a colored horse (red, black, white, spotted) that pulls it. All the horses are "strong" (vv. 2-3).

The question of the prophet (v. 4) is readily answered by the interpreting angel (v. 5). The chariots turn in different directions (v. 6). While anticipating their patrolling function, the "strong horses" are commanded directly by God (vv. 6b-7a). While they are patrolling the earth, God issues a second command to the prophet (v. 8).

The final vision reveals personified "winds" patrolling the earth for the Lord, whose abode is protected by two bronze mountains. The chariots are primary, while the number and color of the horses are secondary details (vv. 2-3). They may resemble military forces (see 2 Kgs 23:11; Ps 104:4) that are eager to facilitate conditions so that the Lord's spirit may "rest in the land of the north" (v. 8b).

The first and eighth visions function as opening and closing scenes of the night visions. In the first vision toward nightfall, the report of the equestrians patrolling the earth indicates that "the whole earth is tranquil and at rest" (1:11). Nonetheless, there is a plea for mercy on behalf of the temple-community, which does not experience that "rest" (1:12). The Lord is moved to compassion for the community but is "exceedingly angry with the complacent nations" (1:16).

The intervening visions present the plight of the community, especially the importance of dual leadership, temple restoration, and purgation. In contrast, the situation of the oppressors of Israel is included briefly (see 2:1-4, 12-13). The phrase "the whole earth" and movement patterns characterize the process of the visions.

In the eighth vision there is tranquility because God's spirit is at rest "in the land of the north." The downfall of the oppressors as well as the return of the exiles to Jerusalem signals a new reality. Exact chronology is not a con-

cern in any of the visionary narratives or oracular responses.

6:9-15 Responses and a crown. The structure of the final section of the eighth vision consists of two oracles. The first oracle (vv. 9-11, 14-15) frames the second oracle (vv. 12-13). The first oracle is a private proclamation to the prophet: "This word of the Lord came to me" (v. 9), while the second oracle is a public proclamation: "And say to him: 'Thus says the Lord of hosts'" (v. 12a). Both oracles respond to the visions whose reality will occur when the temple is completed. The oracles in their final, edited form, however, focus on an indefinite future.

After the oracular introduction (v. 9) the prophet is commanded by God to take something from the "returned captives Heldai, Tobijah, Jedaiah" (v. 10a). What the returnees possess becomes clear in verse 11: "silver and gold." The names are not found in Jewish tradition. Their orthodox position in returning to Jerusalem is indicated by their *theophoric* names, that is, the consonants for Yahweh appear in their names. They also represent others in the Diaspora who contribute materials for temple restoration.

The returnees are commanded to go immediately to the "house of Josiah, son of Zephaniah (these had come from Babylon)" (v. 10b). There may be continuity between the two groups of returned exiles if Josiah had been taken into exile. On the other hand, if he had remained in Judah, there would be continuity in the two groups who now lived on the land restoring the temple.

The silver and gold brought back from exile will be fashioned into a "crown" (v. 11a). Other ancient texts read "crowns." Arguments based on subsequent verses are persuasive for both the singular and plural forms of the noun. The discussion about "crown" is the beginning of many difficult textual decisions in the section.

Who will wear the crown? The New American Bible states: "place it on the head of [Joshua, son of Jehozadak, the high priest] Zerubbabel" (v. 11b). The Revised Standard Version and the New English Bible, however, delete the reference to Zerubbabel and the brackets around the Joshua description. Again, there are persuasive arguments for either Joshua or Zerubbabel and the crown.

Those favoring Joshua note that the fate

of Zerubbabel is unclear in the tradition. The final editor probably inserted Joshua's name to clarify what happened historically, that is, the high priest became the source of authority for the temple-community (see p. 574).

Commentators who propose Zerubbabel's name refer to his function as the temple-builder (see 4:9; compare 4:12). He would be the logical one to be crowned in a royal ceremony, since the installation as high priest would be a separate ceremony. Others argue that the coronation had to be symbolic due to the position of the temple-community of Judah within the Persian empire.

One scholar noted that Zerubbabel's role was diminished in the lampstand vision by its position in the middle of the vision. Now, Joshua's role is similarly diminished by its position in the middle of the final oracles.

Finally, since a two-person rule had been a possibility suggested before in visionary material (see 4:1-5, 10b-14), *two* crowns may be apt for Zerubbabel and Joshua.

A public oracle of the Lord follows the description of the crown (vv. 12-13). Its focus is temple reconstruction (see 4:6-10a), in particular an individual who has an important role in the project. The person is identified as "Shoot," a name used to describe a future Davidic figure (see the commentary on 3:8). Zerubbabel is the logical referent drawn from 3:8 as well as from the additional detail at the end of the verse: "he shall build the temple" (v. 12b).

The choice of Zerubbabel is strengthened by the details of verse 13. The first part repeats the function of temple-builder and adds the royal function of ruling from the throne (v. 13a). The priest mentioned in the second part of the verse is probably Joshua. Both reign from the throne area, yet Joshua appears to claim more status. "Friendly understanding" describes their new model of leadership for the temple-community (v. 13b).

The next two verses are the conclusion of the first oracle (vv. 9-11, 14-15). The symbolic function of the crown (see the commentary on v. 11b) is described (v. 14). While memorial offerings on behalf of the community were known (see Exod 30:16), the crown will immortalize several individuals.

A comparison of the names in verses 14 and 10 indicates that two of the four names are different: Heldai and Helem (Hebrew text); Josiah and Hen (Hebrew text). In addition, the function of Joshua changes from one whose house served as a meeting place (v. 10b) to one who will be immortalized with the other three (v. 14b). Some commentators suggest that Helem and Hen are nicknames for Heldai and Josiah.

Verse 15 reiterates themes mentioned in the visions and response oracles. First, there is an acknowledgment of assistance for temple reconstruction from those "who are from afar." Not only will they send materials (see v. 11), but they will actively engage in the process (v. 15a).

Second, the cooperation in rebuilding will be another sign of the prophet's authentication from God (v. 15b). The other signs described a new relationship between the temple-community and God (see the commentary on 2:13 [2:9]) as well as leadership for the temple reconstruction (see the commentary on 4:9b).

Third, the last part of the verse, which is incomplete, presents a challenge that was neglected by ancestors before the Exile. It suggests that obedience to the Lord is adhering to the visions and oracles of Zechariah. The challenge offers the community a new beginning and an opportunity for returning to God as God desires to return to the community. The final words of First Zechariah, then, form an inclusion with the first divine oracle (see 1:3ff.).

PART THREE: ORACLES ABOUT FASTING AND THE FUTURE

Zech 7:1–8:23

Part Three consists of the final two chapters of First Zechariah. It is a collection of oracles arranged from various contexts to form a coherent message. The sections present hortatory material that could be developed in greater detail for preaching occasions. The tone of the oracles is an interweaving of encouragement and warning, with constant reference to past experience as a model for present and future activity. The basic structure of chapter 7 is a question-and-answer format, while chapter 8 is a series of ten proclamations. It is impossible to separate the prophet's oracles from the elaboration of the editor.

7:1-3 Question about fasting. The superscription combines a traditional prophetic formula and a precise chronology (v. 1). It is one year after the visions and two years after the beginning of temple restoration, that is, November-December 518 B.C.E. The chronology also indicates the ninth month of the year (Chislev). The notation of month occurs in one other superscription (1:7). The mention of Darius as king occurs here and in Hag 1:1.

Verse 2 introduces individuals who are new to the temple at Jerusalem. Scholarly discussion suggests that Bethelsarezer was a Jewish official in Babylon who acted on behalf of his community. He sent Regemmelech and his retinue to Jerusalem with a request. The phrase "implore the favor of the Lord" describes a situation needing immediate attention (see Exod 32:11). Note that the phrase is structurally parallel to "ask the priests of the house of the Lord of hosts, and the prophets" (v. 3a).

The "priests of the house of the Lord" and the "prophets" (v. 3a) describe those who functioned with authority in the temple-community after the Exile (compare Mic 3:11). Since the verse implies that temple restoration had been completed, it may be an editorial remark. Nonetheless, the cooperation of both groups is needed to address the community's plight both in Babylon and Jerusalem. Their response would probably affect Jews throughout the Diaspora as well. Ironically, the text indicates only the response of the prophet.

The question before the authorities concerns ritual activities of mourning and abstaining (v. 3b). The temple had been destroyed in the fifth month (2 Kgs 25:8-9). Consequently, rituals were observed to commemorate that event. Ought any community observe them now that reconstruction on the temple was in progress? According to several commentators, a deeper question is implied. Has the promise of the prophets been fulfilled? Are we living in a new age following upon the restoration of the temple? If so, mourning is transformed by rejoicing.

7:4-7 Responses. The replies are two oracles consisting of rhetorical questions from God and one from Zechariah. The divine-oracle formula is found in verse 4, and verse 5a states that "all the people of the land" (compare Hag 2:4), including the priests, will be the addressees of the proclamation. In verse 5b another time for ritual mourning commemorates the assassination of Gedaliah, the Jewish governor of Jerusalem, who had been appointed by Babylon (2 Kgs 25:22-26; see p. 573).

The first question focuses on intentions for fasting and mourning (v. 5b). The second question follows immediately. Wasn't the opposite situation of eating and drinking also "for yourselves"? (v. 6). Self-centeredness is the attitude challenged in both situations (compare Hag 1:4-8, 10; Isa 58:3-7, 13).

Zechariah's rhetorical question is a comment on the Lord's question (v. 7). He draws attention to the tradition of the community before the Exile. The "former prophets" had spoken God's word when Judah was populated and at peace (v. 7b). Their collective proclamation vindicates his message, too. Zechariah had spoken about a meager population in Judah after the Exile (see 2:10 [2:8]; compare 2:8 [2:4]). He may be suggesting that fasting before and after the Exile is problematic; its focus is on the individual, not God.

7:8-14 Another collection of responses. These verses can be divided according to topic. Verses 8-10 interrupt the response about fasting (vv. 4-7). They present a summary of ethical teaching promulgated by the prophets before the Exile. Verses 11-14 return to the response about fasting.

Verses 8-9a introduce a divine oracle with a traditional prophetic formula. The oracle (vv. 9b-10) states the genuine nature of fasting proclaimed in earlier tradition. The first part is a general maxim for social conduct: be honest in judgment; be compassionate toward one another (v. 9b; see Jer 7:5). The maxim is reinforced by specific prohibitions (v. 10; see Jer 7:6; compare 1:4b).

Verses 11-14 provide a picture of the community before the Exile (compare 1:3b-6) as a model for reflection. The admonitory style is similar to the Chronicler's (see 2 Chr 30:6-9; Neh 9:25-31). The instruction issues warnings and provides hope. The section reinforces Zechariah's and the editor's claim to authority.

Earlier communities had refused to listen to the Lord's imperative about true fasting (v. 11a). Metaphors of body language dramatize their stubbornness (vv. 11b-12a). What were they resisting? "The teaching and the message that the Lord of hosts had sent by his spirit through the former prophets" (v. 12b). No one but the prophets was entrusted with God's teaching and message (compare 1:4). A closer relationship between God and the prophets is indicated by the phrase "his spirit." Since the prophets shared in God's spirit, to reject them is virtually to reject God.

God's response to the community's stubbornness was reciprocal: "he would not listen when they called" (v. 13). The concluding verse extends the consequences of the preexilic community through the Exile and the restoration attempts of the current community. God acted by scattering the community "among all the nations that they did not know" (v. 14a). The land, too, suffered: it became desolate (v. 14b).

8:1-8 Blessings for Jerusalem. Two prophetic formulas introduce the first oracle (vv. 2-3). The omission of "to me" indicates that Zechariah is repeating what he had heard before (v. 1). God's "intense jealousy" of, and "wrath" toward, Zion indicates passion and concern for the returned exiles (v. 2). The proclamation functioned initially as a response to the first vision (see 1:14). Verse 2 also initiates promises of blessings (8:2-23) following the oracles of warnings (7:4-17).

Verse 3 states how God will respond to the community. Again the language parallels the response after the first vision (see 1:16). In both sections God "will return to Zion . . . and . . . will dwell within Jerusalem" (v. 3a). God's dwelling recalls how the people and God lived in tents (see Exod 25:8; 29:46). However, there is a new revelation here. God's *presence* initiates a new name for Jerusalem: "faithful" and "holy mountain" (v. 3b; see Joel 4:17 [3:17]; compare Isa 1:21-26; Ezek 48:35).

The second oracle (vv. 4-5) is introduced with a traditional formula (v. 4a). It specifies two groups of persons who will revel in the Lord's presence. "Old men and old women" (v. 4b) and "boys and girls" (v. 5) will fill the streets of the city and enjoy their activities without fear (see Amos 5:16; Lam 2:11-12; Isa 65:20; Ps 127:3-4; Jer 30:18-21). The two groups are described in harmony and sexual equality. They represent those who would have found the journey back from exile quite difficult. The groups also reverse the anxiety about the present depopulation of the temple-community (see 7:14; compare 7:7).

The third oracle (v. 6) is introduced as the first two oracles were (v. 6a). It presents God's rhetorical question about the expectations of the community toward divine activity (v. 6b). Does the reversal of present circumstances, that is, depopulated city, "remnant" group (see Hag 1:12), appear impossible? (Compare Gen 28:14; Jer 32:17, 27.)

God reassures the community in the fourth oracle (vv. 7-8). After the introduction (v. 7a), God promises to repopulate the city by delivering the exiles from captivity (v. 7b). The "land of the rising sun . . . of the setting sun" refers to Babylon and Egypt (compare 2:10 [2:6]; Jer 31:8). The exiles will share God's dwelling in Jerusalem (v. 8).

"They shall be my people, and I will be their God" indicates that the covenant contracted by their ancestors remains a reality for those returning (v. 8b; see Lev 26:12; Jer 31:33). The phrase "with faithfulness and justice" suggests God's response to the covenant as well as the challenge of mutuality for the community in maintaining the covenant.

8:9-17 Encouragement and challenge for Jerusalem. The section is comprised of two parts (vv. 9-13 and 14-17). Each begins with a traditional prophetic formula as an introduction (vv. 9a, 14a). Each presents past tragedy and develops future possibilities of blessing. Both refer to earlier ethical teaching as well as to earlier verses in First Zechariah.

After the introduction (v. 9a), the first exhortation is "let your hands be strong." The addressees are those who had heard Haggai speak about the necessity of temple restoration, especially the "foundation of the house of the Lord." The term "prophets" suggests that the addressees of that prophet had also heard Zechariah, who was Haggai's contemporary (v. 9b; see Hag 1:6-11; 2:15-19).

Verse 10 describes the situation before temple restoration began in earnest. At that time there was no economic security (v. 10a). In addition, hostile forces precluded security. God initiated the circumstances by setting each person against the neighbor (v. 10b).

Verse 11 introduces a new oracle. God's judgment is reversed. God will act differently: "But now I will not deal with the remnant of this people as in former days . . . ." The expression is similar to covenant language. How will the present situation be different for the temple-community? It is described as "the seedtime of peace," that is, vine and land will be productive; the heavens will water the earth (v. 12a; compare Hag 1:10-11).

Another contrast concludes the first part. As Israel and Judah were "a curse among the nations," now they will be a "blessing" through God's saving intervention (v. 13a; see v. 7b). The oracle concludes with two exhortations: "do not fear, but let your hands be strong" (v. 12b; compare Deut 28:1-28). The second exhortation forms an inclusion with verse 9b, formally closing the oracle.

The second part begins with an introduction to another oracle (v. 14a). The construction "as . . . so" provides the structure for comparing past history and present experience (vv. 14b-15; see 1:6; 7:13). It also repeats previous oracles. *As* God had decided to harm the community because of its ancestral history and "did not relent" (v. 14b; see 1:6b; compare Jer 4:28; 51:12; Lam 2:17), *so* God decided "in these days . . . to favor Jerusalem and the house of Judah" (v. 15).

The oracle concludes with a short summary of ethical teaching about truth and honesty in judgments (compare 7:9); exhortations against evil plans for others (compare 7:10b) and against false oaths (compare 5:3-4). God detests these activities (vv. 16-17).

8:18-23 Responses about fasting and the future. Two oracles conclude First Zechariah. The first one (vv. 18-19) responds to the delegation's question about fasting (7:2-3), while the second is a description of the role of Jerusalem for the temple-community and the nations.

A prophetic formula introduces the first oracle (v. 18). The phrase "to me" is added to indicate that the response to the delegation is mediated through Zechariah and not the priests (see 7:3). The decision begins with a listing of traditional times of fasting: "the fourth, the fifth, the seventh and the tenth months" (v. 19a).

Compared with the other notations (see 7:3b, 5b), this listing has two additional months. The significance for these days of the months is identical with the other months' commemoration: the tragic events leading to the destruction of Jerusalem. The fourth month commemorates the Babylonian attack on the walls (see 2 Kgs 25:3-7; Jer 39:2), while the tenth month marks the beginning of the siege of Jerusalem (see 1 Kgs 25:1-2; Jer 39:1).

Verse 19b dramatically reverses the commemorative status of the collective days of the four months. The days previously given to mourning and fasting are designated as "occasions of joy and gladness, cheerful festivals for the house of Judah" (v. 19b). The expressions in Hebrew identify times of celebratory banquets (see Esth 8:16-17); happiness at social festivities (1 Sam 18:6; 1 Kgs 1:40; Isa 9:2); and happy assemblies for cultic activity (Isa 33:20).

The addition "only love faithfulness and peace" (v. 19c; RSV: "truth and peace") stipulates qualities of living. "Truth," in particular, attends to how community members are challenged to interact with one another and how they regard one another (see vv. 16-17). Can the community be commanded to love truth and peace? The oracle states a promise for a better future if the community responds according to this norm (compare Deut 6:4-5; Amos 5:4; 6).

A prophetic formula introduces the second oracle (v. 20a). "Peoples, the inhabitants of many cities" (v. 20b), will approach Jerusalem (compare 2:11; Isa 2:2-4; 66:18-21; Mic 4:1-3). There will be a mutual interaction among them as they invite one another to approach (v. 21a). The same motivations of the delegation to approach Jerusalem (see 7:2-3) characterize the city-dwellers: "Come! let us go to implore the favor of the Lord . . . I, too, will go to seek the Lord" (v. 21b).

Verse 22 reiterates verse 21b by forming a *chiastic* structure, a literary device resembling an X. The first clause of verse 21b parallels the last clause of verse 22, forming the left stroke of the X. Likewise, the second clause of verse 21b parallels the first clause of verse 22, forming the right stroke of the X.

Verse 23 continues the notion of the repopulated city drawn from persons of the Diaspora and the nations. "Ten men of every nationality" refers to a number of completeness and the number needed to constitute a prayer grouping (v. 23a). What is even more remarkable is how these persons of different nationalities and tongues "shall take hold of every Jew by the edge of his garment and say, 'Let us go with you, for we have heard that God is with you'" (v. 23b).

The term "Jew" appears only in verse 23 and Jer 34:9. Some suggest that the role of invitation to approach Jerusalem gives the Diaspora Jews a significant role. Others find the expression a missionary statement. The proclamation "we have heard that God is with you" is the fulfillment of God's promise to the temple-community: "Return to me . . . and I will return to you" (1:3). The role of the community is twofold: to live with integrity and hasten the return of the Lord to Jerusalem; and to invite others to share in the Lord's blessings by approaching and residing in the city where God dwells.

Conclusion

First Zechariah, like Haggai, has been assessed according to the criterion of unfulfilled prophecy. The perspective is deceptive. It limits any contribution of the prophet to his contemporaries and subsequent communities of believers. When one evaluates the text according to literary form, redaction, and closely aligned religious insights, however, the prophet stands as an exemplary source of how to construct and discover meaning in the process of restoration.

Zechariah, like Haggai, had a few common goals. This is to be expected, since they functioned separately but as contemporaries.

a) Both encouraged efforts at temple reconstruction. Bleak conditions challenged their vision of the future importance of the temple. Its completion would symbolize the restoration of the community's relationship with God. God's presence would provide a new community identity.

b) The prophets proclaimed a necessary ethical component for the restoration of relationship with God and the continuance of this relationship. Yet neither prophet proposed a simple cause-effect relationship between human effort and God's response. They lived in the mystery of the faithful God who continued to reveal mercy within the community through "glory (*kabod*)" and "spirit (*ruach*)."

c) Leadership in the community was shared. Zerubbabel was a clear candidate for leadership, since he symbolized the restora-tion of a Davidic figure and stability to the returned exiles.

First Zechariah also contributes individual insights through the complex "night" visions and interpretive oracles:

a) The visions witness to his broad experience of God, whose presence is not limited to Jerusalem. Interesting characters, angels, and an interpreting assistant interact with him to provide a rich understanding of how and why God continues to be with the temple-community. The oracles added by a final editor bridge the distance between the experience of Zechariah and the interpretation necessary for later communities to understand that experience.

b) The visions are characterized by an indefinite geography, fluidity of movement, and solitary or frequent occurrence through "all the earth." No longer is Israel isolated in its efforts at restoration. The cosmos participates and supports the struggle. This dimension adds mystery and awe to the situation of "in betweenness," that is, a time between promises of a new community proclaimed during the Exile (see Isa 40–55; Ezek 40–48) and fulfillment for the recently returned exiles.

c) The visions are directed to "theological" concerns, that is, God's presence, restored ritual, and purity. God, however, is no longer localized in the temple but is described as "glory" and "a wall of fire" for the community. Restored ritual is dependent upon the purity of the high priest and the integrity of the community.

There is also a close correspondence between these concerns and other factors, including leadership, punishment of evil community members, and the future population of Jerusalem. Leadership is to be equally shared by civic and religious authorities, who assist God in the directives for the new community. "Curses" mete out punishment to those who are irresponsible toward one another. Possibilities of urban dwellers to populate Jerusalem are dependent on the cooperation of the Diaspora Jews.

INTRODUCTION: SECOND ZECHARIAH

Zech 9:1–14:21

The reader is invited to follow the suggestions outlined in the introduction to the Book of Zechariah (see p. 600). Reviewing sections of the introduction and preliminary considerations for First and Second Zechariah will provide a clearer context for the commentary on Second Zechariah.

Authorship

There is no indication of authorship. Although the earliest manuscript of the Minor Prophets from Qumran shows no break between Zech 1–8 and 9–14, modern scholarship does not agree that both parts originated from one author. The history of scholarship from the early 1700's, which includes the linguistic analysis of the past decade, offers the same conclusions.

Three arguments against the unity of authorship are presented:

a) The *content* of First Zechariah, which is concerned with temple reconstruction, historical figures, and dated oracles, contrasts with the material of Second Zechariah, which addresses God's judgments and "eschatological" promises (promises about God's future action). The historical context is obscure.

b) The *style* is considerably different. First Zechariah is a compilation of "night" visions and interpretive oracles written in prose, while Second Zechariah is a series of oracles derived from reference to earlier prophets and written in poetry. First-person references of the prophet are absent.

c) The *vocabulary* is different in introducing oracles. First Zechariah uses traditional prophetic formulas, whereas Second Zechariah uses the phrase "An oracle: The word of the Lord" to introduce the two major sections (9:1; 12:1). The vocabulary of Second Zechariah, like the style, is dependent on earlier prophets.

Dating of the text

There are no verses that contain any specific dates. Possibilities for identifying a historical context are dependent upon internal clues:

a) The use of preexilic and exilic prophecy (Isaiah, Hosea, Jeremiah, Ezekiel, Joel), as well as themes characteristic of Joel, for example "day of the Lord," indicates a postexilic context.

b) Some allusions to events that occur after 333 B.C.E. appear especially in chapter 9 (see the commentary on ch. 9).

c) Apocalyptic style and content, especially in chapter 14, suggest a period later than the early postexilic that characterizes First Zechariah.

The consensus among scholars is to date the text after the conquest of Alexander the Great (333 B.C.E.) and within two decades following his formation of the new empire. The final date for the editorial process of First and Second Zechariah is before 200 B.C.E. There is no agreement, however, about the number of editors, the extent of redaction, and the length of time required for the canonical shaping of Zechariah.

Composition of the text

How the oracles were ordered and edited is unknown. Scholars propose that two units of material, each three chapters long, were arranged with common superscriptions: "An oracle: the word of the Lord" (9:1; 12:1). The same superscription appears in Mal 1:1. The two units of Second Zechariah were appended to First Zechariah because of a perceived relationship. The fourteen chapters became the eleventh Minor Prophet. The one unit of Malachi was added to the other prophetic scrolls, thus constituting the Twelve Minor Prophets (see p. 572).

There are several problem verses in Second Zechariah due to the poetic language. Less rearrangement of Second Zechariah is suggested than for First Zechariah. The New English Bible is the only translation that suggests the following order: 9:1–11:17; 13:7-9; 12:1-14; 13:1-6; 14:1-21.

Outline of the text

PART ONE:	First Oracle: Judgments of God (9:1–11:17)
9:1a	Superscription
9:1b-8	Invasion by the Lord
9:9-10	Coming of the King
9:11–10:1	Victory for the Community

COMMENTARY: SECOND ZECHARIAH

PART ONE: JUDGMENTS OF GOD

Zech 9:1–11:17

Part One is an interweaving of God's judgments: destruction and restoration. All judgments are future-oriented. Unlike the future proposed by First Zechariah, however, this future appears closer and virtually imminent. There is one theme that indicates development among the edited oracles. It is the contrast between the leadership that genuine and false shepherds exercise over the community.

9:1a Superscription. The wording of the superscription, "An oracle: The word of the Lord," has already been noted (see p. 616). The translation is common to most versions. The Hebrew, however, specifies the first word as "burden."

As an introduction to the first and second oracles (9:1–11:17; 11:1–14:21), the superscription suggests that a particular responsibility has been given to the prophet on behalf of God's people. Since the first oracle is equally concerned with God's judgments of destruction and restoration, the unknown prophet might well hesitate to proclaim God's message. Yet God's word must be announced as it was received.

The rest of the superscription directs the Lord's word to "the land of Hadrach, and Damascus is its resting place" (9:1a). Although Hadrach does not occur in the Old Testament, archeological data locates it in Syria north of Hamath (v. 2). Damascus, the capital, is located in central Syria. What is the relationship of God's word to this country? The translation "against the land" suggests God's negative judgment toward Syria, especially Damascus, a traditional enemy (see Amos 1:2).

9:1b-8 Invasion by the Lord. Verse 1b describes additional "cities of Aram" and "all the tribes of Israel" as belonging to the Lord. Verse 1 proclaims God's judgment against northern cities that belong to God just as Israel does. Verses 2 and 3 enumerate additional cities under God's judgment: Hamath (in Syria), Tyre and Sidon (south along the seacoast). Some commentators identify the cities (vv. 1-7) as those conquered by Alexander as he destroyed the Persian empire and promised a new age. Alexander may have raised hopes for the messianic age as he conquered Israel's enemies.

The wisdom and riches connected with Tyre and Sidon (vv. 2b-3) will be useless against the Lord's attack and destruction "by fire" (v. 4). Other southern cities, such as Ashkelon, Gaza, Ekron, will witness the consequences and respond with fear, anguish, and despair. The king will flee, as will the inhabitants, and the "baseborn will occupy Ashdod" (vv. 4b-6a; see Neh 13:24).

A grammatical change to first person singular (v. 6a) heightens the role of the Lord in the invasion. God will intervene to destroy the pride of the Philistines and their abominable sacrifices. Nonetheless, even the Philistines will become part of God's "remnant" and will be "like a family in Judah" (v. 7). The final note promises the Lord's protection for all who will live in Jerusalem, "my house." The designation of the trespassers and the promise of the Lord's watching parallel two passages of First Zechariah (see 7:14 and 4:10b).

9:9-10 Coming of the king. The transformation of God's judgment of destruction to restoration noted in the previous section may be the context for the description of the future king (vv. 9-10). Exhortations to rejoice and shout for joy are addressed to the community named "daughter Zion . . . daughter Jerusalem" (v. 9a; compare Zech 2:10).

The king will be "a just savior . . . meek, and riding . . . on a colt" (v. 9b; compare

617

Matt 21:5; John 12:15). Most commentators identify the figure as a messianic king who is "just," one actively involved in all aspects of vindication. He is "meek" in his corresponding role as "servant" (compare Isa 49:4; 50:8; 53:12). Riding on a colt was a custom of officials (see Gen 49:10-11; Judg 5:10; 1 Kgs 1:33).

Again a grammatical change to first person singular (see v. 6a) emphasizes the Lord's role. All implements of war will be banished: chariot, horse, warrior's bow (v. 10a). Reconciliation of the northern (Ephraim) and southern (Jerusalem) kingdoms issues forth in "peace to the nations" and worldwide "dominion" (v. 10b; compare Ps 78:7-8).

9:11–10:1 Victory for the community.
The section consists of three oracles joined by word associations. The images of return, "theophany," that is, God's manifestation, and restoration of the community and land are highlighted. Earlier history and references to ideas in Second Isaiah are bases for the development of the section.

The grammatical change to first person indicates a new oracle (vv. 11-13). Israel is addressed directly: "As for you, for the blood of your covenant with me . . ." (v. 11a; see Exod 24:8; compare Mark 14:24). The relationship prompts the Lord to initiate a rescue of prisoners from the dungeon of exile (vv. 11-12a; compare Isa 42:7; 61:1b). The exile experience will be reversed: "This very day I will return you double" (v. 12b; compare Isa 40:2; 61:7).

Those who captured Israel will be judged by the captives. Verse 13, which concludes the section, describes how Judah and Ephraim (the totality of Israel) will be as a bow and arrow (RSV) for God's judgment against their enemies (compare Ps 7:13-14). They will be as a "warrior's sword" against "your sons, O Yavan." Although Yavan occurs in the Old Testament to indicate the Greeks (see Gen 10:2, 4; Isa 66:19; Joel 4:4 [3:3]), it probably was added here during the Maccabean era (ca. 167 B.C.E.) to point to current oppressors of Israel.

The role of the Lord as a victorious warrior (vv. 14-15) is the second oracle of the section. It draws on the concept of the holy war (see the commentary on Joel 2:1-11; compare Pss 18:7-15; 77:16-20). The images of lightning, trumpet, and storm correspond to God's theophany on Mount Sinai (v. 14; compare

Exod 24:9-10, 15, 18). God protects the covenanted community as they engage in the battle, overcoming and trampling their enemies (v. 15a; see 2 Sam 22:8-18). The victory is described as a sacrificial ritual (v. 15b; Exod 24:6-8; compare Lev 16:14-15; 17:11).

The victory for the community is described in the third oracle (9:16–10:1). God will save the people, who are "like a flock" and "jewels in a crown raised aloft over his land" (v. 16; compare Zech 6:14). Abundance of grain, new wine, rain, and grassy fields indicates a restored community and land (9:17–10:1; see Joel 2:19, 22-24; compare Hag 1:10-11; 2:19).

10:2–11:3 Shepherd oracles.
This section and the following one (11:4-17) provide different images of shepherds. The theme constitutes over fifty percent of the first oracle (9:1–11:17). Again, the oracles are separated by third-person and first-person grammatical changes. Themes of genuine leadership, restoration, and punishment for Israel's enemies are used.

The Lord speaks (vv. 2-5). Verse 2 is a transition connecting the theme of "grassy fields" for "everyone" (v. 1b) to the shepherd and sheep theme (v. 2b). "Diviners" have duped the community, utilizing "teraphim" or household gods (see Judg 17:5; 18:5) for future speculations, which God judges as "nonsense," "false visions," "deceitful dreams," and "empty comfort" (v. 2a; compare Jer 23:32; 27:9). Many commentators think use of the teraphim was limited to the preexilic period and the chaotic condition of the community before the Exile. To some extent, they were also used in the postexilic community (compare Mal 3:5a; Isa 65:3-5; 66:17).

Earlier tradition claims that treacherous leadership led the community astray (see Hos 4:4-9; Mic 3; Jer 2:26). The shepherd as leader had been a personal symbol of Hammurabi (1728–1686 B.C.E.). Later "shepherd" was used to designate God (see Gen 49:24; Ps 23), as was "just king" (see Isa 44:28; Jer 23:2-4; Mic 5:4; Ezek 34:23-24).

"Shepherds" and "leaders" are parallel terms and the objects of God's wrath (v. 3a). The verb states that God "visits" different persons, God's visitation "will punish the leaders," but the visitation of the flock results in making them a "stately war horse" (v. 3b). The flock, identified as the house of Judah, is the context for the development of the victor-warrior in verses 4-5 (see 9:11-10:1).

Verses 4 and 5 list a number of traditional metaphors which indicate the type of leadership that will come forth from Judah ("from him"—v. 4). The Revised Standard Version and the New English Bible render the sense of the Hebrew better than the New American Bible for both verses. In verse 4a three metaphors occur: "cornerstone" (NAB: "leader") indicates stability (see Judg 20:2; 1 Sam 14:38; compare Ps 118:22); "tent peg" (NAB: "chief") suggests endurance (see Isa 22:23); "warrior's bow" (NAB also) suggests fearless courage (see 2 Kgs 13:17; compare Rev 6:2). Verse 5 identifies the leaders as "warriors" who will be victorious: "the Lord is with them . . . ."

The second oracle, a composite of several divine proclamations, develops the theme of restoration (vv. 6-12). Verse 6 concludes the focus on Judah by noting God's activities of strengthening and saving Judah and the "house of Joseph," that is, the northern kingdom (v. 6a). Judah and Joseph will be brought back and treated with mercy (see Jer 33:26; compare Hos 11; Zech 7:13). A wonderful expression describes the new situation: "They shall be as though I had never cast them off . . . ." (v. 6b).

Verses 7-9 reveal the future of Ephraim (the northern kingdom). As "valiant warriors" (RSV; see Judg 7:24-25; 8:1-3) with cheerful hearts, their children will witness them and "be glad . . . and rejoice in the Lord" (v. 7; compare Isa 29:19). The Lord will bring them back from exile with a "whistle," that is, a signal. It is an ironic expression first used to denote God's "signal" to Israel's enemies (compare Isa 5:26-30). Ephraim will experience the past in a new way (v. 8a; compare v. 6b). Although scattered "among the nations," they "remember" the Lord and "rear their children and return" (v. 9).

Verses 10-12 continue the theme of restoration of the exiles. Egypt and Assyria were countries involved in the destruction of the northern and southern kingdoms (see Isa 7:18). Gilead and Lebanon are fertile, rich areas ideal for restoration. In Egypt, the Nile will dry up and the scepter will be taken away. In Assyria, "pride . . . will be cast down" (v. 11). For those returning from exile, however, God's strength will enable them to continue home (v. 12; compare v. 6; Isa 40:31).

The final section is a "taunt song" against the treacherous shepherds (11:1-3). The literary form was used by earlier prophets to proclaim God's judgment on Israel's enemies (see 5:2; Isa 14:4-21; Jer 6:1-5). Here the enemies of Israel are compared to trees, and their leaders are shepherds (compare Isa 10:33-34; Ezek 31). Lebanon and Bashan are particularly singled out for judgment; they were often linked together in earlier prophecy (see Isa 2:13; Jer 22:20; Ezek 27:5-6).

Lebanon is addressed first: cedars and cypress are destroyed, devastating the wealth of the area (vv. 1-2a). Cedar was a symbol of the royal house of Judah (see Ezek 17:3, 4, 12f.). Next Bashan is considered: "the impenetrable forest is cut down!" (v. 2b). The different trees symbolize various nations. Finally the shepherds lament, for "their glory has been ruined" (v. 3a). "The roaring of the young lions" may suggest other leaders whose territory is devastated "in the jungle of the Jordan" (v. 3b; compare Jer 25:34-37; 50:44; Ezek 19:1-9).

11:4-17 Shepherd allegory. This section is prose except for verse 17, which is poetry. While the themes of shepherd and sheep have been noted above (see 9:16; 10:2, 3, 8-9; 11:3), they are most developed here. Oracles in the first person contain three symbolic acts. Most commentators interpret the section as allegory, proposing that the symbolic acts are a written imitation of earlier prophetic tradition. The section is divided into three parts: verses 4-6; 7-14; 15-17.

The superscription of the first oracle (vv. 4-6) is unusual (v. 4a). The phrase "my God," found in many prayers (see Pss 7:2; 18:3; 22:2; 88:2), suggests a separation of the speaker from the hearers (see Joel 1:3; Josh 9:23). The prophet may be initiating controversy both through use of the phrase as well as through his self-identification as the shepherd of the flock (v. 4b).

The prophet uses the image of a market with buyers and sellers of sheep to condemn the leaders with Israel. The buyers—foreign nations that occupied Israel—"slay them with impunity," while the sellers—religious leaders *within* Israel—"do not even feel for them" (v. 5; compare Amos 2:6; Jer 38:8-22; Neh 5:10-13). God's judgment mirrors the conduct of the shepherds. Neither leaders nor people will be delivered by God (v. 6b).

The second oracle (vv. 7-14) contrasts the prophet as leader with previous leaders (vv. 4-6). Verse 7 parallels verse 4b. The Lord's command to "shepherd the flock" (v. 4b) is obeyed by the prophet, who is employed by the sheep merchants (v. 7a). Staffs in hand, the prophet "fed the flock" (v. 7b).

Verse 8a is a gloss whose meaning is unclear. Who are the "three shepherds"? How did they function? At least forty interpretations have been suggested in the past century. Since there is little information about what transpired in the Jewish community between 350–200 B.C.E. (see p. 574), it is believed that the three shepherds may have functioned during that time either as high priests or as temple officials.

Verse 8b resumes the narrative and indicates the mutual dissatisfaction of shepherd (prophet) and flock (undetermined). The prophet's rejection impels him to withhold leadership from the people. He leaves them to their own resources (v. 9).

The next response of the prophet is to "snap asunder" both staffs. Verses 10 and 14 function as an inclusion for verses 11-13. The literary structure is similar to the "vision within the vision" (see the commentary on 4:1-6a; 10b-14; 6b-10a). Verse 10 describes the prophet's action of breaking his first staff, called "Favor," and interprets it as "breaking off the covenant which I had made with all peoples." The implication is that gentile nations as well had contracted a covenant with God. The second staff, called "Union," is also broken, which is interpreted as "breaking off the brotherhood of Judah and Israel" (v. 14), the period of the divided kingdom before and after the Exile.

The second symbolic act is described in verses 11-13. The prophet indicates through his action that in rejecting him, the people have rejected God (compare Matt 27:4-6). In Hebrew, "treasury" is also translated "to the potter." Artisans worked in the temple area to provide clay receptacles for the treasury, which held sacred objects and served as a bank for private holdings (2 Macc 3:10ff.; compare Matt 27:6-9).

The third oracle (vv. 15-17) includes a command of the Lord to the prophet to perform a third symbolic act. Although the description of the act is omitted, its significance is emphasized: "God will raise up" an utterly incompetent shepherd unconcerned that the flock will "perish," "stray," need healing or food (v. 16a). Who is the foolish shepherd? Again, the verse defies a clear historical context. Some commentators suggest the office of high priest (compare Ezek 34:1-6).

The allegory concludes with a poetic "woe" imprecation to the "foolish shepherd who forsakes the flock" (v. 17a). Curses of a useless arm and blind eye will render the shepherd incompetent and unable to lead (v. 17b).

PART TWO: RESTORATION

Zech 12:1–14:21

Part Two is a collection of edited oracles about God's restoration of the temple-community. Future battles, purification, and blessings will occur "on that day" for the community as well as for the nations. The collection may have been added to restore communal hope after Alexander's career did not fulfill messianic expectations. Part Two, especially chapter 14, contains more proto-apocalyptic characteristics than Part One (see p. 577).

12:1 Superscription. "An oracle: the word of the Lord" repeats 9:1 and introduces Part Two (see p. 616). The phrase "concerning Israel" was probably added by an editor, since Israel is not mentioned again. It may, however, refer to all the inhabitants of Israel (see 1 Chr 21:1; 2 Chr 29:24). Verse 1b is a new introduction: "Thus says the Lord." The description that follows identifies the Lord as creator, similar to other hymnic identifications (see Isa 40:22; 42:5; Ps 24:1-2).

12:2-9 Jerusalem and Judah. This section is a series of divine oracles proclaimed in the first person. The creator God promises prominence to Jerusalem and Judah as victorious over the nations. Traditional metaphors are used frequently. The phrase "on that day" occurs in five verses of chapter 12 (sixteen times in chapters 12–14).

The first oracle is constructed in perfect parallelism (vv. 2-3). God will make "Jerusalem . . . a bowl . . . and a weighty stone for all peoples roundabout" (vv. 2a, 3a). Both will thwart enemies: "stupefy . . . injure themselves badly" (vv. 2b, 3b). The bowl is a symbol of God's wrath toward Israel's enemies (see Jer 25:15-16; Ezek 23:31-34; compare Isa 51:17), while the weighty stone indicates an unmovable barrier for the enemy (see Isa 8:14-15; 28:16; compare Zech 3:9). "For all peoples roundabout" is a repetition of Joel 4:11-12 [3:11-12].

The second oracle presents the Lord as the victorious warrior on behalf of Judah and Jerusalem (vv. 4-5). The third oracle describes the "clans of Judah" taking a more active role in the vindication of Jerusalem (v. 6). Jerusalem, however, will remain "on its own site" (v. 6b).

The next two oracles have a grammatical change to the third person, that is, the prophet speaks of the Lord (vv. 7-8). The Lord's preference for Judah is indicated by saving her "tents . . . first" (v. 7a) in order to prevent the exaltation of the "glory of the house of David and . . . inhabitants of Jerusalem" (v. 7b). It is unclear whether the references to Jerusalem mean that the community also needs purification or that the verse describes the humbled condition of the community in an ironic manner. Either interpretation provides the context for the next verse as well.

The Lord's protective care as "shield" will protect the Jerusalemites (v. 8). The verse recalls the prestigious memory of David, whom supplicants addressed as an "angel of God" (see 1 Sam 29:10; 2 Sam 14:17, 20; 19:28). Was David's line still represented in the community? Were there new hopes and dreams of a final age when David's ancestor would reign? The difficulty of dating the oracle prevents a response.

The final oracle (v. 9) is God's proclamation about the enemies of Jerusalem. It is a summary of the section.

12:10–13:1 Mourning in Jerusalem. The abrupt departure from the scene of the liberation of Jerusalem (12:1-9) to that of murder and mourning prompted some editions of the Bible to transpose the section to the end of 11:4-17. Nonetheless, the context of the previous passage (12:1-9) prepares for this section with its challenge for repentance. Verse 10, especially difficult to interpret, appears in Johannine literature (John 19:37; Rev 1:7), in Handel's *Messiah*, and in Christian devotion to the crucified Jesus.

Verse 10a promises God's gift, "a spirit of grace and petition," to the "house of David and . . . the inhabitants of Jerusalem." In addition to military victory (vv. 2-4; 6-9) and recognition of God's strength (v. 5), the community will participate in an interior renewal of heart (compare Ezek 36:26-27; 39:29; Joel 3:1-2 [2:28-29]). The "grace" of repentance appears to be the focus of the conversion. It is linked to a specific event: "They shall look on him whom they have thrust through." Intensive and extensive mourning follow (vv. 10b-14).

Who has been "pierced" (RSV)? Hebrew and Greek manuscripts differ here. Some read "on him," some read "on me." The more difficult reading ("on me") is preferred. The emendation "on him" denies the possibility that it is God who is pierced. Some commentators also question the translation "thrust through." Is it literal? Metaphorical? (see Lam 4:9; Prov 12:18). The same question arises when comparing verse 10 to Isa 53:5, which parallels the verse exactly.

Most commentators propose a literal interpretation for "piercing." The identity of the pierced one varies. Possibilities include a representative of God; a collectivity, such as the martyrs of Judah in the Maccabean era; a historical figure who had been murdered, for example, Josiah, Onias III, or Simon Maccabeus; a charismatic figure cast out by officials; the good shepherd of Zech 11. The identity remains unclear. The only "facts" from the verse are of a man murdered by the inhabitants of Jerusalem. Mourning and repentance occur afterward.

Verse 10b begins the detailed description of the mourning. The loss is especially poignant. The description recalls the Egyptians grieving over their first-born (Exod 4:22) and David's lament over his first-born (2 Sam 12:15-23) and over Absalom (2 Sam 18:33).

Two images note the intensity of grieving (v. 11). The name Hadadrimmon recalls the lamentation rites associated with the fall and spring seasons ritualized by the pagan weather-gods Hadad and Rimmon. Megiddo recalls the historical site at which the beloved King Josiah was killed (609 B.C.E.). National rites of mourning were conducted yearly (see 2 Chr 35:24-25).

The "land" and all its peoples are involved in mourning. First, royal houses are mentioned (v. 12; see 2 Sam 5:14), then priestly houses (v. 13; see Num 3:18), then everyone else (v. 14). The phrase "and their wives" (5 times) suggests the separation of women and men during mourning.

Mourning "on that day" is connected with the opportunity "on that day" for purification "from sin and uncleanness" (13:1), which include all human misconduct, ritual and sexual impurity. There was a ritual cleansing for Zerubbabel and the community (see Zech 3:4, 9) and a similar promise according to Ezekiel (see Ezek 36:25).

In Isa 53:5 the piercing and death of God's messenger are related to forgiveness of sin. Yet in 13:1 Zechariah does not identify the pierced one as "servant." The identity of the fountain, its relationship to the one "thrust through," and the effect on the community are perplexing. The interpretation is difficult for us because Christian tradition has appropriated 12:10 and 13:1 to refer to Jesus.

13:2-6 Purification in Jerusalem. As Jerusalem would be cleansed of bogus leaders (see the commentary on 11:4-17), so idol worship and false prophets would be purged from the land. Ezekiel had specified that rejection of idolatry was part of the purification of the community (see Ezek 36). Some suggest that even worship of the temple may have been a problem.

Idol worship may have been promoted by dishonest prophets who sought to reclaim the glory of the preexilic era for themselves. The "spirit of uncleanness" associated with them impeded the community's relationship with God. The phrase occurs only here in the Old Testament, while it occurs frequently in the Gospels as something over which Jesus had power.

The punishment accorded to false prophets is described in verses 3-6. Parental accusation initiates the process (v. 3a; compare Deut 13:1-9; 18:19-22). If the son continued to prophesy, the parents were to "thrust him through" (v. 3b). The verb is the same used in 12:10.

Verse 4 suggests that the false prophet is somewhat honest by being ashamed to speak about visions or to assume a "hairy mantle" for leadership (see 2 Kgs 1:8). The irony of verse 5, however, contradicts this. There the false prophet mimics Amos, who preferred to till the soil (see Amos 7:14).

The deception is uncovered in verse 6, where the false prophet explains that his wounds are the result of punishment by his parents (v. 4b). Several suggest, however, that the lacerations were part of a ritual enacted for idols (see 1 Kgs 18:28), and the "dear ones" (RSV: "friends") were associates in the idolatrous worship (see Hos 2:7, 10-12; Ezek 23:5-9).

13:7-9 Sword and fire. The poetic section takes up the theme of shepherd and sheep. In contrast to previous sections (10:3; 11:4-17), where the shepherds were guilty of not fulfilling their duties, this shepherd is not condemned. He is described as the one who "is my associate" (v. 7a). The Hebrew word is otherwise limited to Leviticus, where regulations are given about relationships among the Israelites. "Near neighbor" is the translation there (see Lev 6:2; 18:20).

Who is this shepherd? As is the case with the pierced one, there are several interpretations. Some link the shepherd with the one who appeared before (see 11:4, 17; 12:10). Others suggest a good leader not previously mentioned. However uncertain the identification, the text describes the shepherd as the one against whom the sword is raised (13:7). Consequently, the sheep scatter and God turns a hand "against the little ones." Why the shepherd is struck down is not clear. The act precipitates the dispersal of the Lord's community, that is, the sheep.

The consequences are quite extreme. Two thirds "shall be cut off and perish" (v. 8a; compare Ezek 5:1-12). The remaining one third will be judged again. Traditional metaphors for God's cleansing action describe their plight: "into the fire" (compare 3:2; Ezek 5:4; Mal 3:3); refined "as silver is refined"; tested "as gold is tested" (v. 9b). The result is a reconciled relationship: "They shall call upon my name, and I will hear them . . . They are my people . . . The Lord is my God" (v. 9c).

14:1 Superscription. The ominous note that begins the final chapter of Zechariah parallels the "day of the Lord" (see Joel 1:15; 2:1). Two battles are then described in which the Lord will be present as antagonist against and protagonist for Jerusalem (vv. 2-3).

14:2-5 War and victory. In a first-person oracle God announces plans for "gathering all the nations against Jerusalem" (v. 2a). Grim consequences mark the defeat of the city: capture, plundered houses, ravished women, and half the inhabitants sent into exile (v. 2b). The rest of the people will remain in the city (compare Isa 1:9).

A grammatical change to the third person narrates another battle in which the Lord will fight against the nations (v. 3; compare Isa 43:13). Verses 4-5 contain the only mention of the Mount of Olives in the Old Testament (compare 2 Sam 15:30), while the earthquake is compared to the one attributed to Uzziah's seizure of priestly functions (see 2 Chr 26:16-21). No Davidic figure is mentioned; God's presence is primary.

14:6-11 Transformation of the land. The changes in the land noted in verses 4-5 continue in this section. Vegetation, animals, and persons alike will benefit from the favorable conditions (v. 7; compare Rev 21:23, 25).

According to verse 8, the valuable gift of water will be assured (compare Ezek 47:1-2; John 4:18; 7:37-39). The changes in the cosmos are related to the Lord's kingship "over the whole earth" (see Ps 97:1). It will be recognized and proclaimed in credal formula (v. 9; compare Deut 6:4-5).

Jerusalem will be accorded greater prominence (v. 10a). The territory described is from the reign of Josiah, who ruled twenty years before the Exile. Geba is six miles north of Jerusalem, and Rimmon is thirty-five miles southwest of Jerusalem (see 2 Kgs 23:8). Jerusalem, however, "shall remain exalted in its place" (v. 10b). Unfortunately, the places for the area markers of the city (v. 10c) are difficult to locate. Today they indicate four directions.

14:12-15 Plague and tumult. This section is an addition that enlarges upon the description of verse 3. The style is exaggerated, characteristic of apocalyptic writing. Verse 12 describes how the plague will affect "flesh," "eyes," and "tongue" (compare Ezek 28:21-22; 39:17-20; Rev 16:6; 19:17-18). Verse 13 attributes the "great tumult" among neighbors to the Lord. "Judah also shall fight against Jerusalem" (v. 14) ought to be interpreted as "with" or "in" Jerusalem, which the Hebrew also allows. Verse 15 concludes the section by mentioning a similar plague that will affect all the animals.

14:16-21 Celebration in Jerusalem. The final section of Second Zechariah parallels the corresponding section in First Zechariah (8:20-23). The verses indicate that nations that were Jerusalem's enemies will come to worship and celebrate the feast of Booths (v. 16). A curse will be leveled against "any of the families of the earth" who do not come for worship. "Lack of rainfall" will be the punishment (compare v. 8). The feast of Booths occurred just before the autumn rains.

Because of the Nile River, rain shortage will not be a serious problem for the Egyptians who fail to come to Jerusalem. However, the plague is the potential curse for them and for all the nations that fail to celebrate the feast of Booths (vv. 18-19).

The concluding verses suggest the total dedication of Jerusalem and Judah to God. The temple itself is not the source of holiness. Instead, ordinary objects will become holy because of the persons who own them.

The Book of Zechariah has no conclusion. The editor probably wanted to use Malachi as the final message. For this purpose, the beginning of Malachi parallels Part One and Part Two of Second Zechariah (see pp. 616-17).

Conclusion

The two parts of Second Zechariah develop the future judgment of God upon the temple-community and upon the nations. Chapters 9-11 outline battles against the enemy, consolation of the community, and the concept of shepherd and sheep. Chapters 12-14 use proto-apocalyptic language and content to dramatize what mourning and celebration entail. The second part also broadens the concept of the significance of Jerusalem and Judah for the nations.

Are there points of continuity between First Zechariah and Second Zechariah? The editor of the scroll and the persons responsible for the canonical status of Zechariah used literary devices to ensure that all fourteen chapters would be considered as *one* Minor Prophet (see pp. 601, 616).

Beyond literary considerations, there are religious relationships of continuity and development between the chapters.

a) Historically, First and Second Zechariah addressed communities separated by nearly two hundred years. While the political situation was different in the Persian and the Greek empires, the religious struggles were similar. Who will provide civic and religious leadership? What is required? Can an emperor fulfill expectations?

b) In proclaiming a future in which God would initiate victory, both communities heard about their renewed relationship to

God. God as warrior and protective presence would give them comfort and support for their activities. Before this happened, however, the community would suffer the ravages of war and the comprehensive process of purification.

c) Fidelity to God's covenant through faithful living and restored worship would characterize those who lived in Judah. Evil is not denied but recognized. God assured the communities that evil will not be ultimately victorious. Transgressors could repent or be punished.

d) God's relationship to the nations, as well as their own relationship to traditional enemies, was developed in radically new perspectives. "On that day" Israel and the nations would share in God's compassion. They would live together in a land free from war and for holiness. Communal worship would be one symbol of the new reality.

e) The vision of an unexpected future was offered to both communities while the uncertainties of the present weighed heavily in their daily experience. How would the communities prepare for the blessings of "that day"? Attention to God's word spoken in the past and reinterpreted by the minor prophet Zechariah would provide some direction in living during periods of "in betweenness."

MALACHI

Mary Margaret Pazdan, O.P.

INTRODUCTION

Authorship

What is known about the author of the Book of Malachi is derived from 3:1, where the phrase "my messenger" occurs. An editor probably used the Hebrew transliteration (*mal'achi*) "Malachi" for 1:1, where the proper name appears. The name Malachi does not occur anywhere else in the Old Testament. The absence of any precise chronology and genealogy in the superscription (1:1) lends support to the suggestion that the author was an anonymous prophet.

The superscription includes the word "oracle" (the Hebrew means "burden") rather than a personal name. It parallels Zech 9:1; 12:1, where the literary device marks collections of oracles that were added to First Zechariah (see p. 616). While a common superscription unites Second Zechariah and Malachi, the historical background, literary structures, and religious significance of the collected oracles differ greatly.

Dating of the text

According to its canonical position, the Book of Malachi is the twelfth of the Minor Prophets. This location is not conclusive for establishing a chronology of the text. The Book of Malachi describes situations that place the prophet about fifty years after the completion of the temple (515 B.C.E.) and just before the ministry of Ezra (about 460–445 B.C.E.). For an understanding of the historical context, see pp. 573–574.

The book offers some perspective about the challenges the prophet encountered. Although the community was under the office of a governor (see 1:8; Hag 1:1; Neh 5:14), civic authority had declined. The priests had assumed civic and religious authority for the community. The priests, however, were irresponsible leaders, failing to correct several abuses: worship, moral and social problems, and mixed marriages.

The book offers valuable insights into Jewish communities in the mid-fifth century B.C.E. It corresponds to Ezra and Nehemiah and supplements these books. It is a historical witness to how a community may participate in the process of restoration with a population of about twenty thousand living in an area twenty by twenty-five miles square.

Composition of the text

A collection of oracles has been edited and unified by a literary device called the disputation. It is a catechetical structure consisting of three elements: (a) an affirmation of God or the prophet occurs at the beginning of each section; (b) a question arises from the audience, usually a reproach or a complaint; (c) God or the prophet responds often with an argument.

The prophet and the editor depend on Ezekiel and Deuteronomy for ideas and images for the disputation. The Levitical sermons of the Chronicler are similar in structure and content. The two appendices were added to conclude the Book of Malachi and the scroll of the Twelve Minor Prophets. The identification of the precursor of the messianic day links the collection to the New Testament (see the commentary on 3:23-24).

Outline of the book

Like Joel and First Zechariah, where the numbering of chapters and verses are different, the Book of Malachi has one discrepancy in the numbering. This commentary, based on the New American Bible, follows the Hebrew text, while other Bibles and commentaries may use the Greek text. The chart compares the versions.

In this commentary the numbering of the Greek text is in brackets.

COMMENTARY

PART ONE: ORACLES

Mal 1:2–3:21 [1:2–4:3]

The six sections of Part One are addressed exclusively to Israel and concern its covenant relationship with God. A covenant theme is developed in the first oracle, which proclaims God's love for Israel (1:2-5). It forms an inclusion with the first appendix, where the people are enjoined to "remember the laws of Moses . . . the statutes and ordinances for all Israel" (3:22 [4:4]). Abuses within the community are discussed in connection with covenant stipulations.

1:1 Superscription. For discussion of "an oracle" and "Malachi," see above (p. 625). "Israel" refers to the whole nation, not merely the northern kingdom. The phrase introduces the focus of Part One: concern for the Jewish community and the experiences of daily life. There is no discussion about the role of the nations; neither are there any judgments of future orientation.

1:2-5 First oracle: God's love for Israel. The catechetical pattern, the structure for the oracles, uses language suggestive of an intimate relationship between the dialogue partners. The oracle begins with a statement of the Lord: "I have loved you" (v. 2a). Anticipating the listeners' response, the Lord's oracle continues: "but you say, 'How have you loved us?'" (v. 2b).

The disputation concludes with a response from the Lord (vv. 3-5). The Edomite situation is offered as a vivid memory from tradition. The mutual distrust of two brothers (Esau and Jacob) ignited enmity between their families and descendants, an enmity that grew to an irreconcilable impasse when Babylon invaded Jerusalem (586 B.C.E.). Complicity *with* the enemy and *against* Judah was unforgivable to the exiles and their descendants (for the historical development of the tradition, see p. 586 and the commentary on Obad 10-14.

In verse 3a God asks a rhetorical question to situate the response: "Was not Esau Jacob's brother?" Next, the declaration of God's love identifies Jacob as the special one (v. 3b). The Hebrew verb designates the *elective* sense of "love." The specific meaning was used in the covenantal context when God declared love for Israel (see Deut 4:37; 7:7, 8; 10:15) and extended an invitation to Israel to respond in love (see Deut 5:10; 6:5; 11:1, 13).

The choice of Jacob ought to be seen as an election. This is not clear in the English translation. The election of Jacob rather than Esau does not entail "hatred" toward Esau. It is a matter of choice, of the mysterious decision of God. Ironically, although Jacob was chosen, his family experienced the Exile while Esau's did not. Paul uses verses 2-3 to develop the theme of election and predestination in Rom 9:13. In the present context, however, predestination is not the issue.

Another appeal to the community's experience is remembrance of the fate of Edom after the Exile. The Lord ravaged the area, toppling the mountains (where the tribe lived in safety) and ruining the land (v. 3c). Historically, the event corresponds to the raids of Arabian tribes that greatly diminished Edom's influence in the Negeb about a century after the fall of Jerusalem.

The downfall of Edom appears to be permanent. Even if they attempt "to rebuild the ruins . . . I will tear down" (v. 4a). More devastating than the ruined land is the name that Edom will bear forever: "wicked country" (RSV) and the judgment of the Lord: "the people with whom the Lord is angry forever" (v. 4b).

The oracle concludes with a third appeal to experience (v. 5a). The conviction of being chosen by the faithful God will impel the community to praise (v. 5b; compare Zech 9:1-8). The ironic expectation of the prophet is a hope that the community will become observant; look beyond Israel and acknowledge that God's dominion is greater than the "land of Israel."

1:6–2:9 Second oracle: Sins of the priests. Eight oracles have been combined to disclose the two principal sins of the priests: offering polluted sacrifices (1:6-14) and abrogating the roles of teacher and leader (2:1-9). Each oracle is identified by an introductory or concluding prophetic formula: "says the Lord of hosts." The literary structure continues the disputation format. The characteristic elements indicate expansions.

The sin of offering polluted sacrifices is described in two sections (vv. 6-9; 10-14). The first section begins with a comparison of familial and household relationships with covenant relationship (v. 6a). The Lord questions the fidelity of the covenant partners. The tone of the rhetorical questions suggests that the covenant relationship has deteriorated: "Where is the honor due to me? Where is the reverence due to me?" (v. 6b; compare Exod 4:22; Hos 11:1; Isa 1:2).

The prophetic formula follows (v. 6b). What is unusual here is the addition "to you, O priests, who despise his name." The grammatical change from the third person to the second person suggests that the judgment is that of the prophet who has spoken the Lord's word or of an editor. The charge of despising

the Lord's name is extremely serious. It is equivalent to despising the very being of God.

The next two topics are concerned with priestly matters (vv. 6c-7: see v. 12). There were very strict standards for suitable sacrificial offerings (see Lev 22:18-25; Deut 15:21; 17:1). Contemporary sociological criticism of biblical texts confirms the complexity of standards in regard to purity (holiness) and pollution (sinfulness).

The phrase "table of the Lord" appears only here in the Old Testament, although the idea appears elsewhere (see Ps 23:5; Ezek 44:16). The tables for slaughtering the sacrifices were located at the gates of the inner court of the temple. A single table was located in the sanctuary, where only the priest was allowed (see Ezek 40:39-43).

The questions about sacrifice are answered by additional rhetorical questions of the Lord appealing to priestly experiences (v. 8; see vv. 3-5). Blind, lame, and sick animals constitute "polluted food" (v. 8a). Such offerings would not be acceptable to the governor nor invite his hospitality (v. 8b). The governor's refusal and attitude are the analogy for God's disposition. An ironic question from the prophet concludes the oracle (v. 9; compare Zech 7:2).

The Lord's response to the polluted offerings is developed in the second section (vv. 10-14). Let there be a cessation of all temple sacrifice (v. 10a; see Ezek 40:39-41). God's preference is for *no* sacrifice: "I take no pleasure in you . . . neither will I accept any sacrifice from your hands" (v. 10b). The statement would cause anxiety among the priests. Their function as well as the efforts of the community to restore the temple for worship were being threatened.

The Lord's response continues a contrast between the priests and people of the covenant community and the "nations." There are various interpretations of verse 11. Some commentators suggest that the verse describes imminent expectations of a messianic age when Gentiles will worship with Jews (compare Isa 66:18-21; Zech 14:21). A few Catholic commentators propose that the verse is a reference to the sacrifice of the Mass. Others relate the verse to the situation of the Diaspora Jews and their synagogue activities (prayer and study), which have replaced or substituted for temple sacrifice. The last argument is most probable. However, whatever the particular interpretation may be, the general context identifies a type of activity that is pleasing to God.

The remaining verses of the section continue the contrast between the priests and the nations by indicting priestly thoughts and behavior.

The concluding oracle of the section issues a curse to the priest who deceives himself and the community by offering a "gelding" and holding back a "male" animal (v. 14a; see Lev 22:18). There is an implied contrast between the covenant community and the "nations." The Lord is a "great King whose name will be feared among the nations" (v. 14b). The repetition of "great" (vv. 5, 11, 14) and "name" (vv. 6, 11, 14) throughout the indictment for polluted sacrifices (vv. 6-14) emphasizes the nature of God and how inadequately the priests respond.

The second indictment condemns the failure of the priests as teachers and leaders because they have abandoned personal integrity (2:1-9). The entire section is the Lord's response in covenantal terminology. The priests will be cursed if they do not heed the Lord's warning (vv. 1-2; see Deut 27:14-28:68). "Shoulder" (v. 3) is interpreted literally as the choice portion of animal sacrifices given to the priests (see Deut 18:3). The Revised Standard Version renders "shoulder" as "offspring," implying that the whole priestly lineage will be cut off with no successors, while the New English Bible translates the term as "arm," suggesting that priests will be prevented from officiating at the altar.

God offers a sign to the priests that the commandment is intended for them. It is the "covenant with Levi," whereby "life and peace" were offered. Levi responded by fearing God and standing in awe of God's name (vv. 4-5). In addition, Levi spoke true doctrine (torah) honestly, lived "in integrity and uprightness, and turned many away from evil" (v. 6; compare Deut 31:9-13). While the covenant with Levi (v. 4) is not recorded in the Old Testament, it is presupposed in other texts (see Jer 33:21; compare Num 25:11-13).

The covenant with Levi is the model for the priest, who is to be knowledgeable in the law and is to instruct the community (v. 7a; see Deut 17:9; 33:10). The priest must be faithful to the covenant "because he is the messenger of the Lord of hosts" (v. 7b). This is the one verse in the Old Testament where a priest is given the title "messenger," which traditionally was associated with a prophet. The transfer of title and function from prophet to priest may refer to the historical circumstances of Malachi's experience.

The comprehensive model of the covenant with Levi and the additional role of "messenger of the Lord of hosts" are the basis for the judgment of the priests (vv. 8-9). They have not been faithful to the obligations of the covenant nor to their role as teachers and leaders (v. 8). Since they voided the covenant of Levi, the Lord has stripped them of their status. They have become "contemptible and base before all the people," since they refuse to keep God's covenant and to instruct the community in its stipulations (v. 9).

Some commentators have suggested that the description of the covenant with Levi and its authority may be a reference to the contrast between the Zadokite priests (returnees from Babylon) and the Levites. The latter had been given menial tasks in the service of the temple, while the priests were important functionaries (see p. 575). Malachi may be favoring Levitical rather than Zadokite jurisdiction in the community.

2:10-16 Sins of the community. The community is guilty of breaking covenant with God in different situations. While the section begins with a general admonition (v. 10), the sin that is emphasized is the faithlessness of husbands to wives. Divorce, which Jewish law only permitted husbands to initiate under specific conditions, was becoming troublesome (see Deut 24:1-4; Hos 2:4; compare Ezra 9-10).

The returned exiles were wealthy and may have expected to enhance their position in the community by marrying a local woman. The practice of divorce meant that the community included many single, divorced Jewish women. Intermarriage meant that non-Jewish mothers would be responsible for teaching their children the practices of a religion that was foreign to them. It is not clear from the text what reasons were given for the divorce proceedings.

The prophetic injunction goes beyond earlier Jewish law, which regarded the wife as a possession of the husband (see Exod 20:17). The prophet identifies the relationship between husband and wife as a covenant that affects the partners, the individuals in their relationship to God, their children, and the other members of the community. As in the case of the indictments against the priests, here the covenant is the basis of the indictment against the community.

The prophet poses rhetorical questions that address the reality of the community's experience of common origin to begin a new disputation (v. 10a; compare Deut 32:6; Isa 63:16; 64:8). Referring to a common historical tradition, the prophet points out the "abomination" (RSV) that Judah, Jerusalem, and Israel have committed (v. 11a). "Abomination" is a technical term used to describe idols and the practice of idol worship forbidden by the covenant (see Deut 32:16; Isa 44:19). The present community is guilty of the same offense (v. 11b).

The consequences of the community's action (v. 11b) are interpreted in two ways. Literally, the verse identifies *worship* as unacceptable to the Lord due to the covenant faithlessness of the worshipers. Metaphorically, the "temple," "sanctuary" (RSV), "holiness" (NEB) of the Lord may also identify the *community members*, who are called to belong to God (see Deut 32:9). Whether worship or the members themselves are described, the indictment is the same: members have married "the daughter of a foreign god" (RSV; see 1 Kgs 11:1-8; Neh 13:23-27). Mixed marriages violate the covenant with God *and* the bond that unites the community (see Exod 34:13-16; Deut 7:1-4).

The first section concludes with a threatening curse (v. 12a). The identification of "witness and advocate" is difficult. Most commentators propose a universal meaning, that is, anyone involved in the situation. Exclusion from the community and prohibition to sacrifice in the temple are the closely related civic and religious punishments (v. 12b).

Sacrifices are no longer acceptable (v. 13b; compare 1:10b). Verse 14a is the only occurrence of a community question in the disputation: "Why is it?" The relationship of faithful living to genuine ritual is reiterated for the community as it was for the priests (see the commentary on 1:6b-13; 2:3-9). The prophet responds to the question by identifying the Lord as "witness between you and the wife of your youth" (v. 14a; compare Isa 54:6; Prov 5:18).

The severity of the broken relationship is indicated in verses 15-16. This obscure text may be an addition by scribal editors who disagreed with the prophet's insight. The emphasis is on God who created each person as "one being, with flesh and spirit," who in turn creates "godly offspring." The implication is that according to the model of God who is one, the married partners ought to be faithful to their union as "one" and "not break faith" (v. 15). Synonymous parallelism (vv. 14b, 15b) underscores the importance of fidelity to the marriage covenant.

Verse 16 consists of two divine oracles, which conclude the section. Two situations are hateful to the Lord. The first is divorce. While the English translations concur about the clause "I hate divorce," the Hebrew renders it "if he hates send (her) away" (v. 16a). Perhaps the text was amended by a scribe who desired to bring Malachi's teaching into conformity with earlier permission for divorce (see Deut 24:1). The oracle is attributed to the "Lord, the God of Israel," a phrase used nowhere else in the Old Testament. The title fits the context of continuing covenant relationships.

"Covering one's garments with injustice" is the second object of the Lord's hatred (v. 16b). It is an obscure clause. The "garment" may be a symbol for the divorce partners. The final injunction of the prophet (v. 16c) forms an inclusion with verse 15b, which brackets the Lord's oracles. It is a general exhortation to be faithful in all relationships with others and with God.

2:17–3:5 Fourth oracle: God's justice. Consistent with the focus on Israel, God's justice will be enacted upon that community through a judgment that both eliminates social abuses and purifies the Levites. The section 3:1-21 [3:13–4:6] is characterized as "proto-apocalyptic" because of the imminent judgment of the Lord (see p. 577). Nonetheless, the "nations" are not included in the judgment (compare Joel 3–4 [2:28–3:21] and Second Zechariah).

The disputation begins with a statement from the prophet (2:17a; compare Isa 43:24), followed by a question formulated to anticipate the audience (2:17b). The response identifies two attitudes of the community that are weakening the covenantal relationship. The people assume that evil is pleasing in God's sight (see Jer 12:1; Hab 1:2-4). Their belief in

629

a just God is waning, that is, they are beginning to doubt God's existence (2:17c).

Thus the final verse of chapter 2 provides a transition to the next theme, God's justice. The questions about "wearying God" and the "just God" are repeated (3:13-15) and answered (3:16-18) in the context of the sixth oracle (3:13-21 [3:13-4:3]).

The next section (3:1-5) offers an entirely new focus on the "messenger" who will appear before the Lord's judgment. Verses 1a and 5 are first-person oracles representing God, while verses 2-4 are a third-person narration of the prophet. God announces that "my messenger" will be sent to prepare "the way before me" (v. 1a), while the prophet proclaims the coming of this messenger (v. 1b).

The identity of the messenger of the covenant is unclear. Verses 1b-4 are confusing. Did the editor of the book identify "my messenger" with the prophet Malachi (see p. 625)? Will the "messenger of the covenant" fulfill a Levitical role (see 2:4-8; compare Isa 40:3)? Are "my messenger" and the "messenger of the covenant" different individuals or the same individual? Does the description designate an angelic being? God? Or the imminent presence of God?

The prophet probably envisioned "my messenger" as a Levitical figure. A later editor, however, identified him as Elijah (see 3:23 [4:5]). It is possible that the Levitical figure could also function as the "messenger of the covenant." While commentators are divided about the identity of the messengers in Malachi, the messenger is unanimously identified in the Gospel traditions as John the Baptist (see Mark 1:2-8; Matt 3:1-11; Luke 3:2-16).

Verses 2-4 describe the coming of the Lord as judge in traditional metaphorical language. The double questions about the coming of the Lord refer to battle imagery (v. 2a; see 2 Kgs 10:4; Amos 2:15). "Like a refiner's fire or like the fuller's lye" are consistent images in prophecy (see Isa 1:25; Jer 6:29-30; Ezek 22:17-22). In Malachi the images signify that God will remove all impurities and cleanse the sons of Levi (vv. 2b-3; compare Zech 13:9).

In verse 4 the prophet compares future Levitical sacrifices on behalf of Judah and Jerusalem with the sacrifices that pleased the Lord in the past. The era of Moses is an appropriate identification for that period (see Jer 2:2;

Isa 63:9, 11; compare Amos 5:25; Jer 7:22). The purification and acceptance of Levitical sacrifices (vv. 2-4) present a sharp contrast to the concluding verse of the section, which enumerates the evildoers who will be judged (v. 5; see 2:17c).

Verse 5a presents a court context in which the Lord is both witness and judge (see 2:14). With the exception of sorcerers (see Deut 18:10-11; Jer 27:9), all the groups responsible for social evils are indicted: adulterers and perjurers (compare 2:11-16); employers who defraud (see Lev 19:13; Deut 24:14-15); those who oppress widows and orphans (see Zech 7:10) or maltreat the sojourner (v. 5b). The perpetrators of social evils are described as the ones "who do not fear me" (v. 5c).

3:6-12 Fifth oracle: Ritual offenses. Four oracles of the Lord have been combined in the section to address the community about the quality of their ritual activity. Their deeds indict them when they approach the altar, just as the priestly activities and attitudes condemned the priests earlier (1:6-2:9).

The Lord's statement about the covenant bond initiates the disputation (v. 6; compare 1:2; 3:5; Gen 27:36). Next, there is a judgment about how that relationship was defiled throughout history (v. 7a). A plea to return to the Lord concludes the oracle (v. 7b). Malachi, like Zechariah, does not idealize past generations (see Zech 1:2, 4). Both invoke earlier Jewish tradition in pleading with their communities to return to God (see the commentary on Zech 1:3).

The Lord anticipates the question of the community: "How must we return?" (v. 7c) and responds with instructions about tithing. This is an unusual prophetic injunction, for earlier tradition insisted that community gifts were neither needed (see Ps 50:7-15) nor acceptable (see Amos 5:21-23; Isa 43:23).

Tithes represented one-tenth of an individual's produce; this portion was given to the Levites, who in turn gave a tithe to the priests (see Num 18:23-24, 28). According to the law, tithes were given to the Levites and to destitute members of the community every three years (see Deut 14:28-29). Therefore, if tithes were not given, members of the community suffered (compare 3:5). Offerings were portions of sacrifices and voluntary gifts given to the priests (see Exod 29:27-28; 25:2-7). By "robbing" God, the community is judged:

"you are indeed accursed" (v. 9; compare Prov 11:24).

Three oracles describe blessings promised to the community if they return to God by obeying the law about tithes and offerings (vv. 10-12). This is probably the prophet's response to those members who doubted God's existence (see 2:17).

The imperative "try me in this" suggests God's willingness to be tested. God's fidelity to the community will be seen in the blessings they enjoy (v. 10b). However, an obedient response of the community is a pre-condition for God's blessings. Two images of land harvest describe some of God's blessings: no locusts will "destroy your crops; and the vine . . . will not be barren" (v. 11; compare Joel 1:4; Hag 2:16, 19; Zech 8:12).

Abundant harvests will be evident to the nations, which "will call you blessed, for you will be a delightful land" (v. 12). Unlike Zechariah, there is no indication here that the nations will share in God's blessings bestowed on the community (see Zech 14:16-19).

3:13-21 [3:13–4:3] Sixth oracle: God's servants. The priests had been indicted for their actions and words. The same judgment is passed on the community, who had already been indicted for their actions (3:6-12). This section describes why their words nullify the covenant with God. The first part contains the questions of the evildoers. The second part is a contrast between those who fear God and the evildoers.

The attitudes of the community indicate skepticism. Lack of personal gain in observing the covenant requirements contributes to an apathetic spirit. The description of being clothed "in penitential dress" (NAB), "as in mourning" (RSV), "behaving with deference" (NEB) is difficult to interpret. It may identify a particular group of the community, such as the Levites, who had suffered because the tithes were not sufficient. They dressed in repentance but continued to experience hardships (compare Neh 13:10-13). Not only is the community lacking in fervor, but judgment suffers as well (v. 15; compare 2:17; Ps 73:2-14). Although these attitudes are widespread among community members, the situation is not a definitive one.

A shift from the Lord's oracles to prophetic narration and oracles announces the second part of this section. Responding to the disputation (vv. 13-15), some members seek to "return" to God (v. 16; compare 2:1). To preserve a record of those who "fear the Lord and trust in his name," a "book of remembrance" is compiled (v. 16c; compare 2:4-5). The book is a traditional symbol in Jewish tradition (see Exod 32:32-33; Isa 4:3; Ps 69:29; compare Esth 6:1-2). The phrase "book of remembrance," however, occurs only in Malachi.

God promises the people another blessing. They will be "mine . . . my own special possession," thus reaffirming the covenant with the Lord (v. 17a; see Exod 19:5; Deut 14:2; Ps 135:4). Compassion is another blessing from God (v. 17b; see 1:6a; 3:6). The ability to "again see the distinction between the just and the wicked" (v. 18a; compare 2:17b) will definitively challenge: "Every evildoer is good in the sight of the Lord" (v. 2:17c).

The second distinction that will become clear is between the one who serves God and the one who does not serve God (v. 18b). The approaching judgment of God will satisfy the scoffers' question: "Where is the just God?" (2:17c). The apocalyptic image of judgment as fire describes the separation of the community. Unlike the "refining" fire (3:2), the "blazing" quality will reduce "all the proud and all evildoers" (to) "stubble . . . leaving them neither root or branch" (v. 19 [4:1]).

For "you who fear my name, there will arise the sun of justice with its healing rays" (v. 20a [4:2a]; compare 3:16c; Isa 57:18-19; Luke 1:78-79). This is the one verse where the "sun of righteousness" (RSV) occurs in the Old Testament. Most commentators attribute the symbolism to the Egyptian and Mesopotamian sun-god, who is pictured with a winged solar disc on many Near Eastern monuments. The god functioned as judge among the gods of the pantheon.

Experiencing the "sun of righteousness" will rouse the energies of those who fear the Lord: "you shall break loose like calves released from the stall" (v. 20b [4:2]; NEB) and "tread down the wicked" (v. 21a [4:3a]). Consistent with the image of consuming fire (v. 19), the wicked will "become ashes under the soles of your feet on the day I take action" (v. 21b [4:3b]). God will vindicate those who fear the Lord (see Deut 32:35; Prov 20:22). The clause "on the day I take action" (vv. 17b;

23b [4:3b]) is an inclusion bracketing the Lord's future activities.

PART TWO: APPENDICES

Mal 3:22-24 [4:4-6]

The appendices summarize characteristic teaching, identify the messenger of the Lord, and describe the day of the Lord. There is no consensus about when they were combined, edited, and added to Part One of Malachi. Their inclusion indicates the importance of the closing verses of Malachi, the scroll of the Twelve Minor Prophets, and the conclusion of the Old Testament for future generations of communities.

"Remember the law of Moses . . . all Israel" (v. 22 [4:4]) points to the importance of the first five books of the Old Testament. Each phrase of the verse is an exhortation to be committed to Mosaic law. The phrases are taken from Deuteronomy's covenantal descriptions.

The next verse identifies the mysterious messenger of Mal 3:1 as the prophet Elijah (v. 23a [4:5a]). Descriptions of him in 2 Kings and Sirach correspond to the functions of the messenger (see 2 Kgs 2:11; Sir 48:10-12; commentary on Mal 3:1). "Before the day of the Lord comes, the great and terrible day" repeats the traditional imagery of that "day" (v. 23b [4:5b]; see Isa 3:5; Joel 2:11; 3:4 [2:31]).

Verse 3:23b [4:5b] may have been judged an inadequate conclusion of Malachi. For whatever reason, another verse was appended (v. 24a [4:6a]). It continues the thought of the first appendix (3:22a [4:4a]) in a chiastic structure whereby "fathers" is the left stroke of the X and "children" is the right stroke of the X. The verse offers a comment on the purpose of the covenant law, that is, mutual love among parents and children. The verse concludes with a traditional warning from the Lord: "Lest I come and strike the land with doom" (v. 24b [4:6b]).

The verse that concludes Malachi in the New American Bible is not found in the Hebrew text. Commentators propose that rabbis included it in order to formulate an appropriate conclusion, *not* one of doom. They inserted a repetition of verse 23 [4:5], which associates Elijah with the day of the Lord.

Conclusion

The prophet Malachi ministered to the community of Israel at a "trough" period. The process of rebuilding the temple and reconstituting a religious identity had been completed nearly fifty years beforehand. The glorious visions of Haggai and First Zechariah had not been fulfilled. Expectations of a new age related to the cosmopolitan world-view of Alexander the Great had also been disappointing.

The prophet faced a lethargic priesthood and community in which serious cultic, religious, and social abuses were not examined nor judged adequately. How could he revitalize the situation? He would appeal to the one consistent memory of a faithful God of the covenant! His exhortations would give all concerned a sense of continuity with a faded but glorious tradition. Opportunities to meet the same requirements of faithful living in the present would challenge everyone.

The Book of Malachi emerges as an effective text for rousing the hearts of the disenchanted and disappointed. In an age in which nothing spectacular occurred in religious, social, or political arenas to offer temporary distraction or assistance, Malachi offered a clear critique on the status quo. The prophet presents a creative relationship between the Law and the Prophets that can sustain and carry forth the community. The covenant offers a model of integrity between actions and words that is the basis for worship, leadership, and teaching.

The structure of the book is an effective resource for initial evangelization as well as later situations. The disputation style carefully distinguishes between God's exhortations and comments and the questions of the community. The additional responses offer opportunities for clarification and deeper understanding.

The language combines traditional metaphors and new insights in a clear, direct style. The book is not pedantic, dense, or unappealing. The insights often expressed in ironic phrases, questions, and statements breathe a new spirit into traditional material from the Law and the Prophets.

The Book of Malachi is an appropriate text with which to conclude the Twelve Minor Prophets as well as the Old Testament. It is a witness to the mystery of a faithful God who gives individuals and communities what is needed for the present. It is a perennial call to respond to the God who first loved all of creation and continues to transform the cosmos until the blessings promised "on that day" are no longer expectations.

An Introduction to the Wisdom Literature of Israel

Lawrence E. Boadt, C.S.P.

The nature of a wisdom book

After the Revolutionary War, when the delegates of the thirteen American colonies were writing a constitution, it got to the point where everyone objected to some part of the new document, and it looked as though it might never win approval. During the discussion Benjamin Franklin, the elder statesman of the group, noted that while he also did not agree with all the provisions, he had lived long enough to know that he often changed his mind and would likely do so again. He thought that this probably was not the best document, but it was far from the worst, and he would vote for it. It soon passed overwhelmingly. His good sense, discretion, and prudent judgment gave him the right to the title "Father of American Wisdom."

This same spirit that characterized Franklin also marks the wisdom books of the Old Testament. They are an often neglected part of the Bible but reflect an important insight into Israel's religious ideal, which is certainly not just the same as fidelity to the Mosaic law or obedience to the prophets. The Book of Daniel describes this further dimension of the ideal well when the Babylonian king wants some of the captured Jewish youths brought to his court to study wisdom: "young men without defects, handsome, intelligent and wise, eager to learn, prudent in judgment and competent to serve in the king's palace" (Dan 1:4). Other descriptions of the wise person are found in Gen 39:1-6; 41:8-32 (Joseph), 1 Kgs 4:29-34 (Solomon), and 2 Sam 16:15–17:14 (Ahithophel and Hushai).

The wisdom books are not all alike; they differ in style and content from one another. But certain characteristics do set them off from other biblical books; they show:

1) very little interest in the major traditions of the Pentateuch, such as the law of Sinai, the covenant, the cult, the special call of Israel;

2) little or no concern with the history of Israel as a people;

3) a searching for the meaning of life and the mastery of life as it is known from experience and not from faith alone;

4) an eagerness to explore the unknown and the difficult problems of sickness, suffering, death, the inequality of rich and poor, the seeming arbitrariness of divine blessing on people;

5) a curiosity about the world as a whole and the universal experience of all nations and peoples;

6) a commitment to discovering proper moral behavior, the right way to live.

These concerns invited the wise to be questioning about life while at the same time analyzing and ordering common experience into rules to live by. Wisdom encouraged discipline of thinking, careful reasoning, and the control of passions. "Go not after your lusts, but keep your desires in check. If you satisfy your lustful appetites, they will make you the sport of your enemies," says Sirach (18:30-31). At the same time, the sages were extremely broad-minded about borrowing from other peoples. They were, in short, interested in life in all its dimensions from the very practical viewpoint of "How can I get the best out of it for me and for society as a whole?"

This approach often makes the wisdom writings seem very secular in outlook. Many proverbs are never related to divine law at all. Even a non-believer can heartily agree with the admonition "Consort not with wine-bibbers, nor with those who eat meat to excess, for the drunkard and glutton come to poverty, and torpor clothes a person in rags" (Prov 23:20-21). The Rabbis of the centuries immediately after Christ argued vehemently whether Qoheleth (Ecclesiastes) was an atheist before they decided that the book had to be canonical because Solomon's name was attached to it. Whether optimistic about the world, as is Proverbs, or pessimistic, as are Job and Qoheleth, wisdom looks at the world from a very worldly point of view. The key example of this is Joseph in the Book of Genesis, who acts with discretion and prudence and does God's will without ever receiving any revelation from God at all.

While such qualities are valued almost everywhere in the Old Testament, only a few books can be called specifically "wisdom books" because they maintain the focus on intellectual reflection about the world from a humanist's standpoint throughout. These are: *Proverbs; Job; Ecclesiastes* (or in Hebrew, *Qoheleth); Ecclesiasticus* (or in Hebrew, *Sirach* or *Jesus ben Sira); The Wisdom of Solomon.* Closely related to these is the *Canticle of Canticles (Song of Songs).* Although the Song is love poetry, it is also a confident affirmation of creation and the human capacity for happiness. A number of the psalms may also be listed as wisdom writings: 1, 32, 34, 37, 49, 73, 111–112, 128 and possibly a few others (19:8-15; 119 and 127). Scholars have also pointed to wisdom influences in the prophets, especially Isaiah and Amos, who both place emphasis on knowing the divine "counsel" or wisdom and frequently make use of wisdom expressions. A few echoes of wisdom thinking occur elsewhere, such as in the story of the Garden of Eden (Gen 2–3), the life of Solomon (1 Kgs 3–11), the story of Joseph (Gen 37–49), and the Book of Daniel (chs. 1–6).

Observations on life were not restricted to Israel. Proverbial statements are nearly universal. In the past, biblical scholars often treated the wisdom material almost entirely in relation to other books of the Bible; but in the past few years, the discoveries of wisdom writings from the Egyptians, Sumerians, and Babylonians have increased enormously, and now the evidence points clearly toward how much Israel was indebted to these nations for its wisdom tradition. This should not surprise us. Wisdom's focus on the common questions of human beings everywhere would naturally lead the Israelites to study famous works from other nations.

Egypt, in particular, was a source of study. It produced many collections of proverbs dating from 2400 B.C.E. down to 500 B.C.E. Often these were in the form of a father's instruction to his son, which may well have been a formal way of talking about teacher and pupil. The earliest of these, the *Instruction of the Vizier Ptah-hotep,* gathered advice on how to succeed in life and resembles the older proverbs in the Book of Proverbs. Compare Ptah-hotep's "If you are sitting at the table of one greater than yourself, accept whatever he gives when it is set before your face" with Prov 23:1, "When you sit down to dine with a ruler, keep in mind who is before you." The much later *Instruction of Amenemope,* written sometime between 1000 and 600 B.C.E., has thirty instructions that match very closely the collection in Prov 22:17–24:22. One example is Prov 23:10: "Remove not the ancient landmark, nor invade the field of orphans." Compare this with Amenemope's "Do not carry off the landmark at the boundaries of the arable land nor disturb the position of the measuring cord." The Israelite sage has modified the saying somewhat to apply to the custom of leaving the gleanings for the poor (Deut 24:19; Ruth 2:1-7). For more detail on the relation of Amenemope to Proverbs, see the commentary below on 22:17–24:22.

Egypt's wisdom schools also produced school texts in praise of scribes (see Sir 39:1-11), name lists and classifications of all kinds of things (see the claim for Solomon in 1 Kgs 5:13), pessimistic reflections on life (see Job and Qoheleth), and even a story of honesty and uprightness threatened by lust (the *Story of Two Brothers)* that became the model for Joseph tempted by Potiphar's wife in Gen 39:1-20.

In Sumeria and Babylonia the wisdom tradition was just as developed as in Egypt. Sumerian proverb collections date before 2000

635

B.C.E. and many of their sayings sound like counterparts in Israel. "While your glance flits to it [wealth], it is gone! for assuredly it grows wings, like the eagle" (Prov 23:5) is similar in message to the Sumerian adage "Possessions are sparrows in flight that find no place to land." Interestingly, the Sumerian editors collected their proverbs by topic, while it is very difficult to find any order in Israel's collections. Also, the Sumerians favored nature images and offered a minimum of moral judgment. In this, too, they differed from Israel.

Babylon produced a great number of works dealing with questions of human life. The poem *I Will Praise the Lord of Wisdom* (in Babylonian, the *Ludlul bel nemeqi*) grappled with the question of why the gods allowed undeserved suffering. It is sometimes called "the Babylonian Job." Other works explore the question of meaninglessness, and there is even a *Dialogue of Pessimism* between a man and his slave, ending with a hint of suicide. A work popularly known as the "Babylonian Qoheleth" also explores the problems of theodicy (God's treatment of the innocent sufferer).

Whereas Sumerian proverbs had a harsh side to them—the forces of nature can be brutal and indiscriminate, and so can the gods—Babylonian wisdom tried to grapple with the uncertainties of life and to reconcile the contradictions of experience. They accented the need to understand the universe in terms of moral laws that would guide human behavior. Thus they could produce many reflective proverbs that are not unlike those favored by the sages in the Book of Proverbs. "What your eyes have seen bring not forth hastily against an opponent; for what will you do later on when your neighbor puts you to shame?" (Prov 25:8) is not far from the advice of the Babylonian *Counsels of Wisdom*, "Do not frequent a law court . . . . for in the dispute they will have you as a testifier, and you will be made their witness and they will bring you into a lawsuit not your own to affirm."

Egyptian, Mesopotamian, and Israelite wisdom generally agreed that traditional wisdom, passed down from long ago, had a special value that no individual could match by a single lifetime of experience. Almost all known works emphasized the importance of sitting at the feet of a father or teacher and learning from the past. The introduction to the *Wisdom of Shuruppak*, a Sumerian work, is typical:

> (Shuruppak) offered instructions to his son. . . .
>
> Oh, my (son), instruction I offer you, take my instruction. . . .
>
> My instruction do not neglect, my spoken word do not transgress.

Since both Mesopotamian and Egyptian wisdom writings were well established and highly developed long before Israel existed as a nation, we must conclude that their influence on later Israelite thinking was very deep.

Wisdom's two ways

The Greek philosopher Protagoras said that "man is the measure of all things." The ancient wisdom teachers of the East would have agreed that this is the starting point for the analysis of experience. While the sages were not truly philosophers in the modern sense of seeking a systematic explanation of the first principles of reality, they were keen observers of the world in which they lived and attempted to find patterns and predictable events that would help humans cope with that world. We must remember that they knew little about the causes of disease and sickness, about the causes of weather conditions, and about the extent of civilization except what was nearby. This meant that they could do little to prevent disfiguring diseases or to cure them, to stop floods or predict droughts, to understand the strange ways of far-off peoples. The physical world in which they lived was much more uncertain, and therefore more frightening, than ours. But it was just as interesting, and the curiosity of the wisdom teachers constantly sought interlinking connections between things. Despite the uncertainties, they were convinced that the world is orderly and can be understood well enough to allow the formation of norms for moral behavior.

The wise would observe, classify, reflect, make comparisons and analogies, and finally draw conclusions for daily behavior. Wisdom oriented its disciples to the good order of the universe, whether called *maat* in Egypt, *ME* in Babylon, or *sedeqah* in Israel. Common observation usually supported a world of order—the sun rises and sets daily, the seasons are predictable, but human certainty was also tied to faith in the divine order of creation. The cause of this certainty lay in the goodness of the gods and their plan for the universe. Only the gods fully understood such a plan, but humans could learn of it in a limited way and act accordingly. Thus on one level ancient wisdom was extremely confident and positive about life and the human ability to live successfully according to divine order. The use of proverbs—short sayings that capture the essence of right behavior—reflects this attitude.

On the other hand, tension developed between what was deduced as good order and passed on as true, and people's day-to-day experience of failure and uncertainty. In contrast to the confident wisdom of Proverbs and Sirach, a second stream of skeptical and questioning reflection developed. It wrestled with the human pain and suffering that arose from not understanding why life was often inconsistent with the beliefs based on divine good order. The Books of Job and Qoheleth are vehement at times in their challenges to traditional wisdom. They fully question our capacity to know and understand why nature acts the way it does and what God intends for us to do. Both propose solutions that rely more on a personal relationship with God than on an understanding of reality. Of course, both Job and Qoheleth also begin with experience and use its discovered regularity to present their cases; they only deny its ultimate ability to explain the purpose for which God acts.

Israel's wisdom teachers tried to solve the tension by more and more affirming that there are limits to what humans can know. Sir 3:20 advises, "What is too sublime for you, seek not," while 3:21 adds, "what is hidden is not your concern." God always lets us know enough by which to direct our lives, but the ultimate meaning of each life is hidden in the silence of the divine purpose. In this, wisdom rejoins the faith proclamations of the Law and the Prophets.

The cosmic horizon

Experience is both highly personal and often impersonal. When bad or good fortune happens to me alone, I turn to the intimacy of prayer to praise God or to beg help; but many events, such as war, natural disasters, the oddities of strange animals, or the regularity of the seasons, have little to do with me

personally and raise larger questions about the universe as a whole. It is not at all surprising that wisdom gave great attention to cosmic origins and the wonder of creation itself.

While Israel's Mosaic faith stressed personal salvation by Yahweh for the people, its wisdom circles based their discoveries on the order to be found in the very plan of creation. Hymns in praise of the divine goodness and majesty of God revealed in creation fill the wisdom tradition. Job 28, Prov 8, Sir 16 and 43, and Wis 7 all identify wisdom with the vast and incomprehensible greatness of creation itself. Passages in other parts of the Old Testament (Gen 1, Ezek 28, Isa 40, Ps 8) also praise creation as a sign of God's greatness, but nowhere does it play such a central role in our approach to God as it does in the wisdom tradition. Indeed, many if not all of these other passages may be influenced by wisdom. Even in the short sayings of Proverbs, the Creator plays a focusing role (Prov 14:31; 17:5; Eccl 12:1).

This emphasis on creation places wisdom in the stream of Ancient Near Eastern religion, especially Mesopotamian, in which cultic practice centered on a return to the right order and perfect goodness of the first creation by the gods. The pagan peoples tried to erase the time in between then and now—the sin and the failure—and to restore the wholeness and vitality of that first moment. To a certain extent, Babylonian religion was an escape from the present time to a timeless, ideal world by means of cult.

Israel's attitude differed profoundly on that point. It was convinced that time moved on and one could never return to what was lost. But God would always act again to heal, rebuild, or re-bless the world, and one could trust God completely because God acts unfailingly out of innate goodness. In Gen 1–3 this conviction is expressed by God's blessing of the first humans, their rejection of the blessing, and the divine re-blessing without completely restoring what they had lost. It is expressed in the faith proclamations of the covenant, where God's fidelity to the promise endures despite Israel's infidelity. And it is expressed in wisdom by appealing to the divine act of creation as a source of understanding the goodness of the world. The beauty of divine order and harmony is revealed to our intelligence by reflecting on creation, and al-

637

though we cannot fully grasp its meaning, it shows us the basic options before us: the way of goodness or evil, the way of the wise or the fool; the attitudes of humility or human arrogance. These themes are treated more fully in the commentary on the Book of Proverbs that follows.

Late wisdom, reflected in Sirach and the Wisdom of Solomon, brings faith and creation reflections closer together by affirming that God as Creator is only fully known through obedience to the law (see especially Sir 24 and Wis 18–19).

Where does wisdom find its home?

Scholars have argued for several different sources of the wisdom tradition. One that appears frequently behind proverbial sayings is the *family*. Many proverbs are directed explicitly from father to son (Prov 1:8; 2:1; 10:1) or from mother to son (Prov 31:1-2). But more than that, a significant number of maxims are directed to questions of relations between parents and children, moral instruction of the young, and family manners. Prov 19:26 warns, "He who mistreats his father, or drives away his mother, is a worthless and disgraceful son"; and 20:11, "Even by his manners the child betrays whether his conduct is innocent and right."

Although everyone agrees that some education had to take place at home, not all believe that Israelites attended formal schools. But the many references to masters as "fathers" in Proverbs, as well as the widespread existence of schools in Egypt and Mesopotamia, suggest that Israel, too, had programs of education that at least some boys attended over many years. These included learning the alphabet, followed by writing and mastering short proverbs, and finally studying longer works of literature. The foreword to the Book of Sirach, written about 132 B.C.E., gives one account: ". . . my grandfather Jesus [ben Sira], who, having devoted himself for a long time to the diligent study of the law, the prophets, and the rest of the books of our ancestors, and having developed a thorough familiarity with them, was moved to write something himself in the nature of instruction and wisdom . . . ." This formal education was probably aimed at developing a professional class of scribes and bureaucrats who would serve administrative functions in the temple, the royal government, and houses of business. There are many examples of Sumerian and Egyptian essays in praise of the scribal profession as the highest in the land. A similar passage can be found in the Bible in Sir 38:24–39:11, and there are many hints at the importance of the scribe elsewhere (1 Chr 27:32-33; Isa 8:16; Jer 26:1-21).

Above all, wisdom in the Ancient Near East was associated with kings and royal administration. David is called wise in 2 Sam 14:20, and Solomon's wisdom is described in detail throughout 1 Kgs 3–11. Prov 25:2 declares, "God has glory in what he conceals, kings have glory in what they fathom." 1 Kgs 5:9-14 declares of him:

> God gave Solomon wisdom and exceptional understanding and knowledge, as vast as the sand on the seashore. Solomon surpassed all the Cedemites and all the Egyptians in wisdom. He was wiser than all other men—than Ethan the Ezrahite, or Heman, Chalcol, and Darda, the musicians—and his fame spread throughout the neighboring nations. Solomon also uttered three thousand proverbs, and his songs numbered a thousand and five. He discussed plants, from the cedar on Lebanon to the hyssop growing out of the wall, and he spoke about beasts, birds, reptiles, and fishes. Men came to hear Solomon's wisdom from all the nations, sent by all the kings of the earth who had heard of his wisdom.

This tradition attributes encyclopedic knowledge to the king, as well as the ability to rule successfully and to make good judgment (1 Kgs 3). But kings gathered around themselves skilled advisors to assure that they did as well as possible (see 2 Sam 16:15–17:23; 1 Chr 27:32-33; 1 Kgs 12:6-7; Jer 8:8-9; Isa 31:1-3). The Books of Daniel and Esther portray the royal courts of the Babylonians and Persians filled with wise counselors of the kings. Still other passages in the Bible refer to the fame of sages in the courts of the kings of Edom and Assyria (see Ezek 28:3-4; Jer 49:7).

When David created his empire, he brought Israel from local tribal organization to world power overnight. He needed diplomats, administrators, and recordkeepers quickly. This necessitated borrowing the techniques of neighboring kingdoms, especially Egypt. Under his son Solomon this training became well established, and a burst of literary activity took place, including the first writing down of Israel's religious traditions by the Yahwist, the historical accounts of David's own rise to power, and the cultivation of wisdom as an art. Even the titles of Solomon's government officials—"the one over the house," the secretary, and the herald (1 Kgs 4:1-6)—are borrowed from the top offices in Egypt, corresponding to vizier, royal scribe, and royal announcer. In this situation, schools for the gifted would have flourished. An Israelite youth chosen to study would have seconded the enthusiastic cry of an Egyptian scribe, Duauf: "The scribe—every position at court is open to him!"

There is no statement in the Old Testament that actually says someone made a living as a teacher of wisdom, but it is highly probable. Jeremiah mentions the wise on the same footing as the priest and the prophet: "Come," they said, "let us contrive a plot against Jeremiah. It will not mean the loss of instruction from the priests, nor of counsel from the wise, nor of messages from the prophets" (Jer 18:18).

Although it may be hard to show a full profile of the professional wise person functioning outside of a political role in the palace, there are enough hints in the Scriptures to put together a reasonable sketch. The philosophy of life found in the Book of Proverbs often reflects the concerns of the wealthy and those with leisure time for study. The emphasis on good speech, writing skills, proper manners, and money lending describes a ruling elite rather than the farming or laborer class. The conservative bent of proverbial wisdom is sometimes attributed to the "haves," who value political stability above everything. Thus the wisdom teacher ran classes for upper-class youths. One proverb seems to imply that the wealthy families paid the teacher directly: "Of what use in a fool's hands are the means to buy wisdom, since he has no mind for it?" (Prov 17:16).

The methods of the wise

Part of the task of education was to memorize the valuable teachings of the past; another part was to learn to reason and make associations. To achieve these goals, the sages perfected many distinctive literary forms, the chief of which were the proverb and the comparison. Since education was for the most part

oral, one can well imagine the teacher asking the students questions, and the students answering according to set keys that aided their memories. In light of this, it is surprising how few riddles and fables are found in Hebrew literature. The wisdom teachings of Mesopotamia favored both as teaching aids, but only one or two fables occur in the Old Testament (Judg 9:8-15; Ezek 19:10-14) and a single complete riddle (Judg 14:12-18). The small collection of numerical sayings in Prov 30:15-33 may originally have been riddles, but they now appear in the text as proverbial observations on life.

The *proverb* was an important element in Israelite wisdom because it distilled the lessons of the past in a clever, practical manner, with a touch of the sermon, and in easily remembered form. The popularity of the proverb in Israel was due to its ability to capture both the most commonplace insight into daily life and the most difficult problem of experience in new and interesting ways. In the same way, the *comparison* forced the hearer to make analogies between what was observed in the animal or plant world and human behavior. Neither proverb nor comparison hoped to explain reality fully, but by collecting insights side by side, a richer and more varied picture would emerge.

This search for the multiple faces of life also helps to explain the other literary genres favored by the wisdom schools. They are mostly non-dogmatic and yet educational. The way of wisdom was persuasion, not command, and so the more important genres include *allegory* (Prov 5:15-23; Eccl 12:1-6); *numerical sayings* (Prov 6:16-19; 30:15-33; Sir 25:7-11); *onomastica* (that is, name lists: Ezek 27:12-25; Sir 24:13-17; *hymns* (Prov 8:22-31; Job 28; Sir 24); *dialogues* (Job); *beatitudes* ("Blessed is the one who . . .": Prov 3:13; 8:32ff.; 14:21; 16:20; Eccl 10:17; Sir 14:1-2); *question and answer* formats, especially *rhetorical questions* (Qoheleth); *confessions of praise* (Sir 33:16-18; 51:13-22); *partial riddles* (Sir 39:3; Wis 8:8); *quotations* used as departure for reflections (Eccl 4:8; 10:18; 11:1; 7:3-4; 10:2); and *philosophical reflections* (Wisdom of Solomon). When not using one of the more clever literary forms, the wisdom writers fell back on the straightforward *instruction*, a form borrowed from the Egyptians (Prov 1–9).

Because the wisdom schools developed such effective methods of educating people, the prophets often borrowed their techniques. The rhetorical question was a favorite of the major prophets, particularly Isaiah, as was the dialogue between God and prophet (see especially the so-called Confessions of Jeremiah in Jer 12, 15, 17, 18 and 20). Some prophets, notably Ezekiel, loved the parable and the metaphor as ways to make a point (see Ezek 16, 17, 19, 23, 29, 30, 31, and 32). Amos used the numerical saying as a dramatic device (Amos 1:3–2:6). But whereas wisdom employed these means to open young minds to the world around them, the prophets used them to challenge people's understanding of the covenant. The introduction to the Book of Proverbs (p. 646) discusses many of these in greater detail.

A brief survey of the wisdom books

Solomon's reputation for wisdom was so great in Israel that he was believed to have been the author of the Books of Proverbs and Qoheleth, the Song of Songs, and the Wisdom of Solomon. An amusing legend in the Talmud tells how the great king had written the Song of Songs in his lusty youth, Proverbs in mature middle age, and Qoheleth in his skeptical old age! Proverbs is treated fully in the following commentary, but a brief overview of the other major wisdom books at this point will help to understand their interrelationships.

—Job. The Book of Job uses an old folk tale about an absolutely righteous man who proves faithful under severe trials (chs. 1–2; 42) as the framework for a great dialogue on the question of human suffering and the problem of the human search for personal knowledge of the transcendent God (chs. 3–41). It has many elements of drama, with the outcome uncertain until the end. The Job of the dialogues is neither the patient sufferer of tradition nor the prayerful accepter of his fate found in the folk tale. Instead, the author (seventh or sixth century B.C.E.) had the courage to move beyond simple acceptance of God's will to ask hard questions of the traditional and sometimes overconfident wisdom presented by proverbs and instructions. If God always cares for the just, why do the wicked seem to prosper? Why do the innocent suffer? What hope does uprightness offer?

The book also explores the deeper question of how one can know God. Many of Job's complaints deal with the *silence* of God before the human search for justice and faithfulness. The divine answer, when it comes, denies us any claim to a relationship with God based on our justice but calls for personal knowledge through obedience and reverent worship. As Job finally admits, "I had heard of you by word of mouth, but now my eye has seen you" (Job 42:5). Job's questions are also well known in Babylonian wisdom literature, but the author of Job situates the answer within Israel's commitment to Yahweh's personal self-revelation to them. Job in many ways resembles the psalms of lament with their threefold structure: (1) a cry of pain and lament; (2) a call to God for help; (3) a promise to praise God forever. Job teaches us that ultimately from the midst of doubt and questioning comes trust.

—Qoheleth. The author of this book is the most skeptical writer in the Bible. Like Job, he challenges the traditional certainties of wisdom, examining the same world of experience. "Vanity of vanities, all is vanity," he begins, and he ends no more convinced. It is not for us to understand the meaning of life or to figure out the divine purpose behind events, especially success and failure, reward and punishment of moral behavior, or finally death itself. Instead the writer highlights the transcendence of God, the need to recognize limits to human wisdom, and the ability to accept life as it comes, bearing its pains and enjoying its pleasures in moderation (Eccl 5:17). Everything has a proper time (Eccl 3:2), but it is known only to God in its fullness. Qoheleth's advice to enjoy life as it is given may not seem very religious, but he tempers it with warnings to "fear God" (Eccl 5:6). The outlook is far more pessimistic than that of the optimistic Book of Proverbs, but it stands clearly in the tradition of searching questions directed to all creation on the problems of human justice, the existence of evil, life and death.

—Sirach. Written in the early second century B.C.E., the Wisdom of Jesus ben Sira most resembles the positive outlook of Proverbs. It gathers advice on all the traditional subjects of wisdom by theme and sets them out as a guidebook for young students who want to obtain wisdom. Although wisdom can be attained by study, it is meant to serve as guidelines for human conduct, not as speculation. Sirach makes a special point of identifying sage advice with the religious practices of Judaism, especially linking wisdom with the law of Moses (ch. 24). Wisdom is thus a divine gift to Israel in a unique way. Even more so than for Proverbs, "fear of the Lord" is the way of wisdom. The achievements of the teachers can only be rightly appreciated in the light of divine revelation. Because of its late date, the Book of Sirach was never accepted into the Hebrew canon, but became a favorite part of the Christian Scriptures—hence the later name, Ecclesiasticus, the "church book."

—WISDOM OF SOLOMON. This may be the latest book in the Old Testament and reflects a reaction to Greek philosophy in Alexandria and its challenges to Jewish faith during the first century B.C.E. Because of its date and the Greek language in which it was written, it never entered the Hebrew canon. The main purpose of the book is to reassure the Jewish community in Egypt that keeping their faith is worthwhile despite the hardships met in a pagan culture. It borrows the language of philosophy to achieve this goal. But it also stands out from earlier wisdom books by its intense concern with (1) *salvation history* as a lesson directed to the wise, and (2) *immortality* as an explanation of God's care for the suffering of the just. While it stands in the optimistic tradition of Proverbs and Sirach, it often makes wisdom so abstract that it obscures any practical value for living (see 7:22-25). But it does manifest the ability of Jewish wisdom to creatively meet the challenge of Hellenistic thinking.

—SONG OF SONGS. It is hard to know where to put the Song of Songs among the biblical books. It is frequently included among the wisdom writings because its message is interpreted as an allegory of Israel's loving relationship to Yahweh. Although most scholars today admit that it began as a collection of down-to-earth love songs composed for weddings, it has had a long history of development before reaching its present form. There may have been a stage of application to royal weddings (see Psalm 45), which would have given the songs a religious setting. In any case, it has always invited reflection on the wonder and beauty of divine creation, the mystery of divine (and human) love, and the

ramifications of relationships built on the covenant. It uses the dialogue form, which is one of the techniques preferred by wisdom teachers as a way of challenging students to think. The Song of Songs probably received its final editing after the Exile in circles that knew the wisdom traditions of Job, Qoheleth, and Proverbs well.

—WISDOM PSALMS. No two lists agree on how many psalms belong to the category of wisdom. The problem is deciding on the criteria. The most certain criteria are: (1) the reflective contrast between the just and the wicked person, or between the wise and the foolish—Psalms 1, 34, 37, 49, 73, and 112 all qualify on this ground; (2) the use of special wisdom expressions such as "happy is the one who . . ." or the "fear of the Lord," as in Psalms 32, 111, and 128. Many other psalms make use of wisdom themes but put their major emphasis elsewhere.

The achievement of wisdom

Biblical theology usually gives much less attention to wisdom than it does to the prophets, the history of salvation, or the legal material. Yet wisdom was important through all of Israel's history. Before prophecy was born, wisdom had a long tradition behind it. The prophets themselves often borrowed wisdom's insights and expressions; and when prophecy failed, in the period after the Exile, wisdom was just reaching its peak. Its international character allowed it to bring the best of other cultures into Israel's thinking and gave a broader context to the special covenant theology that prevented a too nationalistic and too narrow idea of God's will.

Some of the major contributions of wisdom thinking to Israel's religion were:

1) *Emphasis on cause and effect.* Acts have consequences, and moral decisions can never be made outside the context of social responsibility and the experience of others before us. Often much that is unexplainable can be partially explained by analogies with common experience.

2) *Appreciation of time.* Israel did not strive to erase time and return to origins. Time moved on and God always acted with the present and future in view. This gave Israel a true sense of history and a confidence that God would always act again. At the same time, Israel could not hope to control the cycle

of time by cult or magic as the pagans did; rather, God alone knew the times and controlled the future.

3) *Confidence in order.* Wisdom believed in the empirical search for the hidden order of divine purpose in the world. It could be studied and reflected upon, and could provide guidelines for conduct. While wisdom therefore gave great value to tradition, it also provided Israelite faith with the confidence to make new applications in changed situations throughout its history.

4) *God revealed in creation.* The Mosaic law and the prophets brought Israel an awareness of God as a personal savior, but wisdom opened up the more universal dimension of Yahweh as the Creator and the only God by pointing to the order and beauty of creation and the divine will revealed in it. It also gave emphasis to the positive role of human understanding and management of the world.

5) *Humans as responsible.* Wisdom is often accused of having a theology of God's justice but none of divine mercy until the latest periods (Sirach). This is not entirely true. Whereas the prophets stressed mercy after sin, wisdom stressed the *continuity* of God's creation, so that after misfortune or failure there was another chance. More than that, humans share the creative power of God and must exercise it responsibly and prudently according to wisdom.

6) *Personification of wisdom.* Several passages treat wisdom as though it were an independent being close to God (Prov 1:20-33; 8:22-31; Sir 24:1-31; Wis 9:9-11). This is primarily a literary device to express how the transcendent God becomes present in a personal and immanent way by communicating himself to our intelligence, understanding, and faith. Without this development, Christianity's theology of Jesus as Son of God and Word-made-flesh could not have found such expression.

7) *Wisdom as divine gift.* While wisdom put high value on human reasoning, it more and more refined its understanding of the limits of human knowledge to give greater emphasis to the divine initiative. Knowing God and divine revelation gave light to human understanding, light unattainable by experience of the world alone. Wisdom was always ethical in orientation, but it developed a richer

stance in which religious knowledge and ethics worked as one.

8) *The meaning of suffering.* Based on experience and reflection, wisdom wrestled with the challenge of suffering and offered several answers that could guide practical decisions of sufferers. None were very adequate (evil as the result of sin, a testing from God, a disciplinary correction of our faults), but neither are most modern answers. It rejected pagan responses of magical protection or legitimate despair and placed evil firmly in the area of ethics. Whatever the reason for a particular evil, the results are always in the hand of a just and merciful God who listens.

9) *Trust as the basic virtue.* Wisdom recognized its limits and emphasized that trust is the basic virtue of the wise. Experience is often paradoxical and seemingly contradictory; fundamental questions of life and death are beyond our control, and God cannot be made to conform to our expectations. Thus the ultimate wisdom looks ahead confidently and bases reasonable hopes and responsible decisions on a firm commitment to Yahweh for better or for worse.

10) *The value of community.* This may seem a strange claim to give wisdom, which so often highlights the *individual* struggle for growth. But it is deserved in the sense that wisdom's concern with the universal human pool of knowledge led it to value other peoples and their contributions, the power of communication and dialogue through words, listening and respecting other opinions, and the need for justice, honesty, and integrity in human dealings. The vision that combined social interdependence and individual worth is far more highly developed in the wisdom writings than in other parts of Scripture.

Wisdom does not stand opposed, therefore, to the teachings of the Pentateuch or the Prophets but serves to unite the teachings of revelation and the obedience demanded by faith with the practical experience of everyday reality in order to enrich both.

Wisdom's relevance today

Religious faith in the modern world has come under increasing pressure from the expansion of human knowledge. Areas of life that were once considered the inviolable preserve of divine action alone are now open to human investigation and even management.

Travel in space, prolongation of life, the creation of human embryos in test tubes, and even genetic engineering of the individual touch on areas that traditional wisdom reserved to the mystery of divine purpose. These are on top of human victories in understanding the factors of climate and weather, the causes of disease and sickness, and the movement of the heavenly bodies that so baffled the ancient thinkers and led them to suggest prayer where human knowledge failed. Many people in our culture no longer see how God impinges on daily life in any meaningful way; their outlook has been, de facto, totally secularized, even if they still nominally profess to believe in God. Their world is a world of human control, and human decisions are all that matter.

Many others, experiencing the horrors of modern war and aggression or living through a personal tragedy of disease or sudden death in the family, wonder why God is silent when most needed. They question the value of creeds and biblical laws, elaborate religious worship, and the theologies of the churches when God seems so distant from human affairs and so unnecessary to solving our worldly problems.

It is here that wisdom has the most to say to us. On the one hand, it affirms that the order, goodness, and beauty of the universe we have discovered and mastered by our powers are really an unfolding of God's own designs. Humans are created in the image of God and given dominion over the universe to govern it wisely by the powers of understanding, prudence, and verbal skills with which God has endowed them. On the other hand, as our own understanding of the world deepens, the wisdom literature assures us that it is natural and permissible to question and to doubt along the way. Job and Qoheleth proclaim that questioning the hidden God often helps us understand better that even in silence God is present.

Above all, wisdom both encourages us to use our human power of reflection and questioning and warns us that today, just as much as in Old Testament times, we run the risk of human pride claiming too much for itself and foolishly, even arrogantly, rushing us toward the destruction of God's good creation.

PROVERBS

Lawrence E. Boadt, C.S.P.

INTRODUCTION

The structure of the book

Proverbs has nine different divisions of varying length. The shortest is seven verses, the longest, thirteen chapters.

1:1-7	Title and general introduction to the whole book
1:8–9:18	The instruction of a wisdom teacher
10:1–22:16	The collected "Proverbs of Solomon"
22:17–24:22	The "Words of the Wise"
24:23-34	Additional "Words of the Wise"
25:1–29:27	Proverbs of Solomon collected under Hezekiah
30:1-33	The collected Words of Agur
31:1-9	The collected Words of Lemuel
31:10-31	"The ideal woman": an appendix to Lemuel

These divisions in turn may well include smaller collections that once stood by themselves, for example 25:2-27 or the group of numerical sayings in 30:10-33. What strikes us immediately, of course, is that this book is a collection of collections. It is substantially different from most other books of the Bible because of the brevity of its single units. The section from 10:1 to 22:16, for example, contains 375 individual proverbs. Even the longest unit, the poem of Wisdom personified as a woman in chapter 8, seems more a series of separate commands and a litany of titles than a strictly integrated work of art. Sayings often stand side by side with no apparent connection to one another. Thus, "Do you see a man hasty in his words? More can be hoped for from a fool!" in 29:20 is followed by: "If a man pampers his servant from childhood, he will turn out to be stubborn." Both are good advice in different circumstances. One can only wonder what brought them together at this point in the text. As a result, many scholars believe that there is no real order in the Book of Proverbs. They suggest that the separate collections were gathered up over a long period of time and loosely joined together by means of the editorial headings that begin each section.

That is far too negative a view, however. While no one denies that many of the short sayings were originally written down as remembered and not necessarily arranged in a set order, signs of organization are everywhere in the book. The instructions of Lady Wisdom in chapters 1–9 clearly parallel the ideal women of chapter 31. The "Words of the Wise" in 22:17–24:23 are modeled on and match the "Thirty Sayings of Amenemope" from Egyptian wisdom literature. And the introductory preface in 1:1-7 sets a clear course that governs the purpose of the whole book. Proverbs is not a novel with a single, carefully written, very dramatic plot, but, as the comments that follow will show, the editors and collectors of Israel's wisdom certainly intended to present a theology in which the great educational tradition of the wise could be understood.

Literary characteristics of the Book of Proverbs

There are two main types of material in the Book of Proverbs. The first is the *proverb* proper, and the second is the *instruction*. Other literary forms also occur here and there but are quite subordinate to the main two. These less frequent genres include riddles, prophetic urgings, admonitions or warnings, personified self-praise, and extended metaphors or model stories. These are discussed where they occur in the text.

—THE PROVERB. While almost all people recognize a proverbial statement when they hear one, few agree on a definition. The most common characteristics include (1) brevity, (2) cleverness, (3) memorable form, (4) rootedness in experience, (5) universal truth, (6) practical aim, and (7) long use (traditional origin). The first three deal with the form, the last four with the content. Thus the proverb is almost always described as poetic or metrical, with terse, vigorous, forceful, striking imagery. Its style is easy to remember and may have originated in oral societies before writing was common.

The content, on the other hand, is often paradoxical at first sight. Proverbs combine real experience of the concrete with general applications to all times and situations. This makes them partially true and partially false at the same time. What one does at one moment may be all wrong at the next. It is no accident that the Book of Proverbs can place contradictory sayings side by side as in 26:4-5: "Answer not the fool according to his folly, lest you too become like him," and "Answer the fool according to his folly, lest he become wise in his own eyes." No generalization ever captures all the human experience for every occasion. The very nature of a proverb forces the hearer or reader to ask, "How does this so-called truth apply to me?" The better the proverb, the more questions it raises along with its apparent answers.

Some writers distinguish between a *proverb*, which has roots in the common people's usage over many, many years and whose origins are unknown, and an *aphorism*, a clever saying invented by a well-known literary figure.

The Ancient Near East was a much more traditional society than modern society, and proverbs are found in all the ancient civilizations, almost always presented anonymously as the lessons of past generations to the youth of today. Israel shared this view completely, and this fact, together with a common tradition of poetic expression, shared cultural values, and identical experience of coping to survive in similar geography makes Israel's Proverbs appear more like the proverbs of Egypt, Sumeria, or Babylon than many modern Jews and Christians feel comfortable with.

—THE INSTRUCTION. Chapters 1–9; 22:17–24:23; and possibly 31:10-31 can be best compared to the well-known Egyptian wisdom form called "Instruction," which is usually framed as the legacy of a father to his son and includes commands and prohibitions along with the reasons why they should be heeded (the *motivation* for obeying). A number of plain proverbs and warnings are thrown in as well. It usually begins with a call, "Listen, my son . . ." The most notable features of this particular kind of wisdom literature are the absolute authority of the father or teacher and the belief that such wisdom can be learned by hearing and doing it. The instructor does not appeal beyond experience nor expect the student to question the truth of the teaching. At the same time, the teacher shows no doubt whatever that the student can master the lesson by understanding and obeying it. Such teaching was based on the conviction that the world is ordered by *maat*, the concept of divine right order (often a goddess), and that the good person can live according to that order and attain success by proper conduct.

Israel saw much of value in this view and made use of the ideas of (1) instruction or discipline (used often, beginning in Prov 1:2); (2) the contrast in the ways of the righteous and the wicked; (3) the conviction that evil deeds reap retribution; and (4) the belief that self-control is essential to success. But while Egyptian literary works such as Amenemope and Ptah-hotep were written only for the professional training of court scribes, Israel's Proverbs opened up the ideal to every youth. What may have started as an elite school program was broadened to become a religious ideal of wisdom for the nation, parallel to the Law and the Prophets.

The artistic beauty of Proverbs

The word for "proverb" in the title of the book, "The Proverbs of Solomon," comes from *mashal*, the Hebrew word for "likeness" or "comparison." But *mashal* has a much wider meaning in the Bible than merely "proverb." It is used in Ezekiel of allegories and stories (Ezek 17:2; 24:3) as well as of short maxims (18:2; 16:44). In several prophetic passages it refers to a taunt song or mocking image (Isa 14:4; Jer 24:9; Mic 2:4). In each case a lesson is to be learned, and so the best interpretation of the term used as a title for the whole Book of Proverbs might be "paradigms," "models," or "examples," as many authors suggest, but always as a work of art. The *mashal* is the product of the skill of the poet and gains acceptance because of its pleasing use of language and imagery.

The chief artistic device is, of course, the good comparison. Often the images are drawn from nature or family life. The aim is to find just the right metaphor or analogy from ordinary experience to capture the extraordinary lesson in the proverb. Thus, in order to describe the evil charms of an adulteress, the teachers compared them to honey-sweet tidbits that cause terrible stomach aches (Prov 5:3-4). Another well-loved tradition was the contrast between the lazy person and the ant. How demeaning to realize that even an ant is better than that (6:6-11)!

More specifically, most of the actual proverbial sayings and many of the instructions in the book are fashioned according to classical Hebrew poetry, with two parallel parts to each verse. This parallelism, or better, use of balanced lines, is the most easily recognized element in biblical poetry. The major types of parallelism employed make the second half of the line say either the same or the opposite of the first half, or else elaborate a part of the first half. These are called:

1) *synonymous parallelism:*

"Even in laughter the heart may be sad,
and the end of joy may be sorrow." (Prov 14:13)

2) *antithetic parallelism:*

"The memory of the just will be blessed,
but the name of the wicked will rot." (Prov 10:7)

3) *synthetic parallelism:*

"Entrust your works to the Lord,
and your plans will succeed."
(Prov 16:3)

In this last case, the second part describes the results of the first action, thus extending the scope of the message instead of repeating it. Other variations occur occasionally, such as:

4) *"better than" comparisons:*

"Better a dish of herbs where love is
than a fatted ox and hatred with it."
(Prov 15:17)

5) *comparisons:*

"Like golden apples in silver settings
are words spoken at the proper time." (Prov 25:11)

6) *numerical series:*

"Three things are never satisfied,
four never say, 'Enough!'
The nether world, and the barren womb;
the earth that is never saturated with water,
and fire, that never says 'Enough!'"
(Prov 30:15-16)

In all these examples a balance is created between the first and second half of a thought. Usually it is expressed in a regular three-beat-plus-three-beat meter that gives the poetry both solemnity and weight:

"The-glóry of-yoúng-men is-their-stréngth
And-the dígnity of-óld-men is-gréy-hair"
(Prov 20:29).

Other poetic devices are also used for effect: *rhetorical questions* (6:9; 23:29); *hyperbole* (2:18; 5:5); *fables* (6:6-8); *irony* (19:24; 23:27; 26:13-15); *chiasmus* (1:16, 29; 2:16); *alliteration* (13:3, 14); *puns* (13:20; 23:5); and *acrostics* (31:10-31—each line begins with the next letter of the alphabet in order). Naturally the last four poetic techniques only appear in the original Hebrew and do not show up in our English translations. How much richer our appreciation would be if we all read Hebrew!

Purpose of the Book of Proverbs

While the Torah and the Prophets stress faith and obedience, wisdom, especially the Book of Proverbs, stresses understanding and obedience. The two poles within which it moves are clearly the intellectual and the ethical. Since the ancient Israelite considered the heart to be the seat of thinking and reasoning as well as of decision, it is to the heart that the teaching of Proverbs is directed. An Israelite would agree with Socrates' maxim "The unexamined life is not worth living." But unlike the great Greek philosopher who asked about the ultimate meaning and nature of life itself, the Israelite sages sought the practical results. They wanted to know how behavior affected the life a person led. They insisted upon *reflection* as the key to understanding, but theirs was not truly a philosophical outlook in the Greek tradition that asks about the origin and why of things. Instead they examined human experience as a series of many different actions that must be sorted out, classified, and their results evaluated. This could not be done by one generation, but required the cumulative verification of many centuries. Thus, while proverbial wisdom is very particular about life, it often seems somewhat rigid and unbending in its conclusions. What is the *same* about life always appeared more important than what *varied* or did not fit established patterns.

The purpose of proverbial wisdom in Israel can be summed up in one word: *education.* Many proverbs originated in family and tribal education of youth, perhaps long before the nation Israel came into being. One can well imagine the village elders advising young farmers-to-be, "He who tills his own land has food in plenty, but he who follows idle pursuits is a fool" (Prov 12:11). Still other proverbs are the products of formal education, oriented toward professional careers in administrative posts or teaching: "By patience is a ruler persuaded, and a soft tongue will break a bone" (25:15). The chapters belonging to the Instruction genre (1–9 and 22:17–24:22) are almost entirely school lessons, whereas the general collections of proverbs in chapters 10–22 and 25–29 contain many more family or folk proverbs, as well as proverbs that have a general social lesson that may or may not stem from a formal classroom.

The vocabulary of the wise

The subject matter of proverbial wisdom ranges over most of the areas of life also met with in other books of the Bible, except for the cultic or legal aspects of the Pentateuch and the events of Israel's history. Thus we regularly find sentences dealing with poverty and evildoing, with mercy and trustworthiness, themes familiar to us from the prophets and the psalms. But there is a whole body of words that occur again and again in Proverbs (and often in Job or Qoheleth) but are rarely used outside of the wisdom tradition. These will be discussed as they occur in the text, but it is worth listing them here to underline how much wisdom is tied to the intellectual activities of intention, understanding, and thinking.

Wisdom	An overall mastery of life through understanding and successful action.
Discipline	Education with a heavy dose of coercion as well as self-control.
Understanding Capacity	
Counsel	Good advice and critical sharpness.
Prudence	Trained cleverness.
Competence	Successful grasp of affairs.
Political expertise	
Resourcefulness	
Intelligence	
Rebuke	

On the negative side, there are special terms for those who reject the learning process or who cannot seem to learn.

Simple	Uneducated and in need of much teaching still.
Fool	Usually lacks self-control and discipline.
Stupid	Intransigently wrongheaded.
Scoffer	One who refuses to listen and reviles the value of wisdom.
Arrogant	Basically conceited and always causing strife.
Godless	No respect for God (found only in 11:9).

Lazy	Lives only for the moment with no thought of tomorrow.
Impious	A stupid person but with a blasphemous attitude.

The theology of Proverbs

The religious teaching of Proverbs reflects a long period of development. Among the lasting values inculcated from the very earliest materials are the ideals of family life and filial obligation, and the absolute place of justice in society. Honesty, truthfulness, and above all integrity are taught in dozens of different ways. Concern for the poor and helpless and the value of hard work are both held up to the reader as good. Self-control and the restraint of desires and passions are a common theme. Also, the contrast between the just person and the wicked is explored again and again. Indeed there is a constant conviction that evil does not go unpunished in the divine order of things, even though in the older wisdom God is not always named as the one who brings justice. In this, Proverbs stands in harmony with the theology of Deuteronomy, which promises blessing for fidelity to Yahweh but curse for infidelity. In many ways this older level of proverbial teaching can be summed up as a guidebook for success in life, where life is seen as divine blessing.

With time the wisdom teachers of Israel drew their lessons ever closer to the specific national traditions of their faith, and much of chapters 1–9 reflects the attempt to identify wisdom with the divine authority of their own God Yahweh. This includes equating wisdom with fear of the Lord (faithful fulfillment of religious duty) in 1:7, 29; 2:5; 9:10; and 31:30; and asserting the divine origin of wisdom before the world began (8:1–36). Many individual proverbs in the great collections of chapters 10–22:16; 22:17–24:22; and 25–29 are directly connected to Yahweh and Yahweh's control of history (see 15:3, 11; 16:1, 4, 9; 19:21; 21:2). All of wisdom is now seen as practical lessons that put us into proper relationship to God as well as to our fellow citizens. The final edition of Proverbs proved to be a great achievement because it united the common wisdom of the Ancient Near East with the special insights of Israel about the God who is really present and caring in the affairs of everyday life.

The final edition

Sumerian proverbs similar to those in the Bible are known in collections as far back as the middle of the third millennium B.C.E. And as discussed in the introduction to wisdom literature, there is good reason to presume that the monarchy of David and Solomon established schools modeled on the wisdom academies in Egypt and to a lesser extent those in Mesopotamia.

Thus we may discern at least three major stages in the formation of the Book of Proverbs. The first is the collection of short proverbs used in traditional teaching of youth, whether in family, village, or tribal settings. Some individual groupings may date back to the time of the Judges or earlier.

A second important stage was the court and temple school founded on Egyptian models in the monarchy period. In this regard, Solomon may indeed have been the original inspiration, although the claim that he authored most of the proverbs in the book is not to be taken at face value. To this period belong the majority of the proverbs and most of the instructions found in chapters 1–9 and 22:17–24:22.

A third stage is represented by the additions and expansions that related these teachings specifically to Yahweh as the single guarantor of world order and justice and as the giver of wisdom to human beings. Not that every mention of Yahweh in individual proverbs is necessarily late. For example, Prov 19:3, "A man's own folly upsets his way, but his heart is resentful against the Lord," is more of an observation on life than a theological attempt to prove that Yahweh is the source of wisdom. But generally proverbs with Yahweh's name (the New American Bible has "the Lord") establish a later context for interpreting the meaning of older wisdom sayings. This level of synthesis and the final editing of the book should be probably dated soon after the Exile, about 500 B.C.E., since the book now conforms well to both the general teaching of Deuteronomy on the right way of life and to the affirmation of the vital creative power of God so evident in the exilic prophet Second Isaiah.

COMMENTARY

PART I: WISDOM'S INSTRUCTIONS

Prov 1:1–9:18

Overall plan

Chapters 1–9 stand apart from the collection of proverbs in chapters 10–22 and 25–30 in several ways. They are first of all written in much longer units than the two-line proverbs that dominate the remaining sections. They are also much more impassioned in tone, more like homilies aimed at persuading young minds of the power of wisdom. And they are not neutral, third-person observations about life and reality as proverbial sayings are, but they frequently address the hearer in the second person and even include long speeches from Wisdom personified as a woman. The arguments and warnings addressed to the seeker after wisdom are bolstered by elaborate motivations and reasons why they should be obeyed and even embraced. These are all characteristics of the international "Instruction" genre of literature (see p. 645). It is aimed at the education of youth, usually for positions as scribes or administrators in government. Chapters 1–9 have broadened this to include all citizens on every corner and in every square of the city (Prov 1:8; 8:1).

There has been much discussion over exactly how many individual instructions can be found in these nine chapters. The structure of the whole is the product of some growth, and clear additions such as 6:1-19 (a group of proverbs) break up and to some extent hide the original plan. Chapters 1–9 certainly were intended as an extended preface to the collected proverbs that follow in 10:1 and the chapters following. The role of wisdom as a speaker in chapters 1 and 8 is essential to the plan, as is the contrast between "Lady Wisdom" and the evil woman who is described sometimes as an adulteress and sometimes as foolishness ("Dame Folly") itself.

Fitting all the instructions into one simple outline has proven a block to all commentators. The number of suggested instructions ranges from seven or eight up to twelve or more. Some scholars have thought that the occurrence of "my son" in direct address marked off the separate passages; but a look at 1:15 will show that some occurrences of this phrase fall in the middle of a speech. The best guide is still the natural sense of when one topic ends and another begins. In this way chapters 1–9 can be divided as follows:

(1:1-7)	(General introduction to the whole book)
1:8-19	First instruction
1:20-33	Wisdom's first speech
2:1-22	Second instruction
3:1-12	Third instruction
3:13-35	Fourth instruction
4:1-9	Fifth instruction
4:10-27	Sixth instruction
5:1-23	Seventh instruction
6:1-19	Proverbial collection (a comment on 5:21-23?)
6:20-35	Eighth instruction
7:1-27	Ninth instruction
8:1-36	Wisdom's second speech
9:1-18	Tenth instruction

As noted in the comments that follow, other structures are also present. Chapter 2 is a theme statement for chapters 3–7, and the first seven instructions together may make up the seven pillars of wisdom's house mentioned in 9:1. But how they developed still remains somewhat of a mystery.

1:1-7 The purpose of the book. What stands out immediately in the search for wisdom is its intellectual quality. It is not vision or smell or skill in a worker's craft that receives praise, but the virtues of studying diligently and developing good judgment. "Discipline" is formal education at the hands of a teacher. It is hard work, requiring lessons and practice. The title announces that what follows are the "proverbs" of the wisest king, Solomon. As pointed out in the introduction (p. 646), the Hebrew sense of *mashal* means more than a saying—it is a lesson or model to be followed. Thus the special wisdom of leadership and judgment proper to kings is being offered to all who submit to disciplined study. Humans can become wise by learning and are capable of growth in understanding, but never simply on their own.

The "simple" in verse 4 are the unlearned, especially the young, but also those who have never had formal education.

The impression that is left when all the nouns about knowledge are piled up together in these few verses matches the intention of the older Egyptian instructions. The teachers want to impress upon open and promising minds that successful careers in public service demand thinking for both decision-making and dealing with people. This is what we might call "old wisdom," a self-confident, positive reliance on human ability to learn and to master the world. Israel shared this view in part, and many sections of Proverbs breathe just such optimism about gaining wisdom through mental ability.

The intellectual aspect is matched by moral conduct. Verse 3 mentions three important qualities of behavior to be seen frequently in the following chapters: it must be right, just, and honest. The ultimate criterion, however, is summed up in verse 7: fear of the Lord, which is both piety and religious fidelity. Without it the search for wisdom becomes folly (see the comments on 9:6). Possibly, too, the editors sum up the entire contents of the book in verse 6: it contains proverbs (chs. 10–22; 25–29); parables (chs. 1–9); words of the wise (chs. 22–24); and riddles (chs. 30–31).

1:8-19 First instruction: A warning against the wicked. As in Egyptian models, the instruction is framed as the address of a father to his son, or since it is really a metaphor, a teacher to the pupil. The most important lesson for the beginner in wisdom is how easily one can be misled by temptation and seductive arguments to do evil. The only protection is a firm adherence to what has been learned about the right way of acting.

The sinners of verse 10 contemplate violence to gain money or wealth. Perhaps verses 10-12 describe a theft in the planning stages, or better, thoughts of a general life of crime and extortion that will prove very rewarding financially. It does not really matter, since a larger lesson is involved here, illustrated by the reference to the nether world. Because Israel had no concept of an afterlife as a place of happiness and vitality, life was for here and now. To destroy the quality of life of the innocent, to harm them, defraud them, or dishonor them was as good as killing them. It was handing them over to the power of death that would destroy a rich and vibrant life. Sin is service to the powers of death. The more people become involved in evil, the farther

from *real* life they travel. They themselves will soon be trapped in the meshes of death. (See a similar thought in Isa 59:7.)

The image of verse 17 is not clear. It means that the traps set by the wicked will hardly entice a youth into them if they are seen being prepared. But some scholars think that the image says the opposite: some birds are so naive that they go after seed even in an easily visible trap.

The teacher promises that obedient learning at home and school will lead to honor and respect in society. These are the real marks of success, described by the image of the royal crown on the head (v. 9). The whole passage argues from common sense and not from any divine commandment of the Lord. It is old wisdom at its best.

1:20-33 Wisdom's first speech: an invitation scorned. The previous section argued from reason; now the authors present Wisdom speaking as a prophet. She calls aloud in public places, as did the classical prophets (Jer 11:6; Isa 58:1), to persuade people to convert their hearts to Yahweh. Verse 32 suggests that the people's "turning away" ("self-will" misses the point) will be the reason for their condemnation, as will be their rejection of Yahweh's "spirit." Both ideas are common in the prophets (see Jer 2:19; 8:5; Hos 11:7 for "turning away," and Isa 40:13; 44:3; 61:1; Ezek 11:5; Mic 2:7; Joel 3:1 for the divine spirit).

In many ways Wisdom is modeled here on the prophet Jeremiah, who by and large also experienced rejection of his message. The expression "How long?" (v. 22) is a favorite in his oracles (Jer 4:14, 21; 12:4; 13:27; 23:26; 31:22; 47:5). And, like Wisdom in verses 26-28, Jeremiah was finally driven by God not to answer the people when they did finally seek help during the catastrophe of the Babylonian invasion (Jer 14:11). The combination of rebuke for sins and veiled threat of punishment, which is proper to prophetic preaching, is here employed as the power of the word of wisdom to offer life. Wisdom promises rest and peace free from fear to those who seek counsel and reproof (vv. 25, 30), knowledge and fear of the Lord (v. 29), and spirit and word (v. 23; see also Deut 12:10; Ezek 34:25).

In contrast, the simple (v. 22) see no value in working for wisdom. They love their simplicity (NAB: "inanity"). "In ignorance is bliss" becomes their motto. The NAB omits the second part of verse 22: "(How long) will the scoffers rejoice in their scoffing, and the stupid hate knowledge?" It may be an added comment, for it is in the third person, unlike the rest of the passage. But it illustrates what is finally made clear in verse 30: the choice of ignorance ends up in deliberate folly and self-destruction.

2:1-22 The second instruction: the benefits of wisdom. Here the wisdom teacher waxes eloquently on the blessings that wisdom can bestow. Clearly a receptive student is in mind, the ideal candidate for instruction. The chapter is chiastic in structure, with the opening theme repeated at the end, and the two middle sections parallel to one another in an A-B:B-A pattern. Verses 1-11 describe wisdom's blessings; verses 12-15 warn against the evil man; verses 16-19 warn against the adulteress; and verses 20-22 return to the promise of blessing. The whole forms a theme statement for the fuller treatment of both the evil man and the adulteress in chapters 3–7. If 1:20-33 sounded prophetic, this passage echoes Deuteronomy and the psalms, especially in the contrast between the ways of the just and wicked, and the call to obey God's commands (see Deut 4; 11; Pss 1; 37).

In 2:1-11 the vocabulary of old wisdom that was seen in 1:1-7 reappears, but this time it is explicitly related to Israel's conviction that all knowledge and blessing come from Yahweh alone. Wisdom is a gift of God and not the product of native human intelligence or ability. There is no rejection of human searching and questioning in this, but a subordination of ends. The source of knowledge, understanding, and intelligence that can guide right conduct is knowledge of God's role in the process. It is the exact opposite of what the proverbs often refer to as the attitude of those "wise in their own eyes" (3:7; 26:5, 12, 16; 28:11).

The first warning in verses 12-15 sketches the way of the wicked. Their thinking is crooked and their speech is crooked. They are the opposite of the upright and honest person of verse 9. Evil is so much their way that they could no longer be straight if they wanted to! The second warning is against the adulterous woman. Sexuality is always an area of temptation, but involvement with a seductress who

is married can lead to grave social consequences beyond merely personal sin. It is the destruction that is death itself. Like Psalm 1, the passage ends by proposing two ways of life to the youth and calling for a decision in favor of wisdom's way.

3:1-12 The third instruction: the blessing of fidelity to God. Verse 1 mentions the Torah and divine commands in the context of a promise of long life. "Kindness and fidelity" (v. 3) also fit into this pattern, which is very close to Deuteronomy's theological view of the covenant on Mount Sinai. Indeed, many aspects of this short section suggest that it is a deliberate attempt to counteract the older concept of a self-reliant wisdom. It twice condemns those who judge themselves wise (vv. 5, 7) and opposes such self-confidence by proposing an ideal of trusting in and fearing the Lord. Although echoes of traditional wisdom are present (long life is also the goal of Egyptian instructions), it has been reworked away from a sharp emphasis on intellectual achievement toward a more meditative and prayerful attitude. This is seen in verse 6: "In all your ways be mindful of him." Even verses 11-12 conclude with a form of reproof that has little in common with the corrections of the teachers and is closer to an explanation of suffering as a way to God (Deut 8:5).

A look at the direct imperatives in these twelve verses shows that not one of them is clearly directed toward the intellectual pursuit of wisdom. In fact, verses 9-10 are close in spirit to Mal 3:10, "Bring the whole tithe into the storehouse, that there may be food in my house, and try me in this, says the Lord of hosts: Shall I not open for you the floodgates of heaven, to pour down blessing upon you without measure?" Among the prophets, Malachi is the most priestly in tone and combines the outlook of Deuteronomy that blessing comes in return for fidelity with a spirituality centered on worship. Not unexpectedly, the priestly-oriented Letter to the Hebrews in the New Testament directly quotes verses 11-12 in Heb 12:5-6, but applies it naturally to Christian believers.

3:13-35 Fourth instruction: wisdom's value in society. Many commentators break up this unit into two parts: a hymn on the worth of wisdom (vv. 13-24) and a collection of short sayings dealing with other people (vv. 25-35). But neither part stands alone. The instructions for social conduct in the second part follow upon the promise of peace and security in verses 23-24. They place human conduct within the context of the divine command to love one's neighbor (Lev 19:18) and thus reveal the real nature of "life" that wisdom offers to those who grasp her (vv. 16, 18). In many ways this entire instruction continues the message of the preceding one in 3:1-12 on the necessity of bringing wisdom under the revelation proclaimed in the covenant with Yahweh.

Some important ideas are raised in this passage. Verses 13-15 hint that wisdom can be personified as an ideal wife (similar to Prov 31:10), more valuable to a young man for success in life than the most costly gems. Verses 16-18 deepen this claim by comparing wisdom to the tree of life at the center of the Garden of Eden in Gen 2:9. At the time of creation it represented the human hope for eternal life; here it symbolizes medicine or balm that gives pleasant help and life to the soul (v. 22). Wisdom also brings peace (v. 17). The Hebrew word *shalom* means much more than our English word "peace." It is wholeness, blessing, prosperity—a full, successful life.

In verse 19, the claim that creation was given order by wisdom prepares us for the full description found in chapter 8. It also reflects Egyptian wisdom's concept of *maat*, "right order," which is at the heart of mastering wisdom. Here Yahweh, the God of Israel, alone gives good order to all things, and not some abstract principle. In the same way, the list of commands about treatment of others in verses 27-31 reflects the universal wisdom of the Ancient Near East, but it is brought under Yahweh's guidance by verses 32-35. There are two ways: one brings friendship with God, blessing, kindness (divine mercy), and honor; the other, curse, retribution, and shame.

4:1-9 Fifth instruction: the summons to get wisdom. In truly traditional fashion, this instruction calls on the pupil or child to receive education eagerly. The terms "instruction," "understanding," and "teaching" in verses 1-2 refer to the lessons of the wise, either passed down in the family or the schools. Here again wisdom is treated almost as a bride to be loved and treasured above all else in life. The strong stress on the home as the source of this insight is probably due to the author's concern to make the point ex-

tremely personal. Wisdom is not just another commodity; it must be loved for its own sake.

There is no mention of the Yahweh of faith in this whole passage. The images and metaphors are borrowed from the remembered joys of a warm and loving childhood, in which education was mixed with affection and concern. Like a deeply devoted parent, wisdom will guard and stand by the individual for life (v. 6); like a friend, she will return favor for favor and honor for honor (v. 8); and like a wife that is herself a jewel, she will give the crowning touch to every aspect of a person's life. Perhaps there is even a hint that wisdom is a queen who bestows royal honors on favored servants and courtiers. But one must first get wisdom, and that requires listening, obeying, and the trusting spirit of a child who heeds the words and commands of the father and teacher (v. 4).

4:10-27 Sixth instruction: the two paths. One of the major themes of wisdom literature is that of the two ways. One leads to light and life, the other to darkness and death. One is straight, the other is crooked and devious. To give the metaphor power, various words for road, path, or highway are used. Each step must be deliberately taken. The passage is very artistically arranged in a chiastic fashion to show how walking is as easy on the one path as on the other, but the decision will lead to major differences. The *way* of wisdom stands opposed to the *path* of the wicked, while the *path* of the just opposes the *way* of the wicked. The A-B:B-A pattern argues against the decision to place verse 18 after verse 19, as in the NAB translation. The contents of the right way or path are the traditional wisdom teachings of the sages. The strong command to shun evil in verse 15 comes from the experience of generations that once a person gets into the grip of temptation to evil, it is harder and harder to free oneself.

Verses 20-27 reinforce this message with a series of warnings against playing the two ways off against one another. It is always a human urge to toy with just a few sinful things or to indulge certain vices no matter what, while trying to keep a basically upright lifestyle. But the masters of wisdom had no use for this indecisiveness or deliberate playing with fire. A choice must be made, and one's whole life must then be directed to attaining wholeness and uprightness.

Above all, speech betrays the real directions of a person's heart. False speech is the chief enemy of wisdom everywhere in Proverbs. The strict command in verse 24 is paralleled by the Egyptian advice of Amenemope: "God hates him who falsifies words; his great abomination is the one contentious of belly" (the belly being the source of speech for the Egyptian as the heart was for the Israelite). An Aramaic work, *The Words of Ahiqar*, reinforces the message: "My son, more than all watchfulness, watch your mouth!" Verses 26-27 return to the two paths with a final warning against any compromise. Heb 12:13 quotes verse 26 as the discipline for Christians.

5:1-23 Seventh instruction: the dangers of the adulteress. If speech can be the greatest internal enemy of a person, the lures of the adulteress are the greatest external enemy. The word for the woman is specifically "foreign woman," and many have thought the entire treatment of this theme in Prov 1–9 is a metaphor for apostasy, expressed by participation in the cults of fertility in honor of goddesses of sexuality such as Ishtar (Babylonian) or Astarte (Canaanite). Given the prophetic condemnations of such cults (Ezek 8; Jer 44), some echo of this may be present in part, especially in chapter 9. But the description in chapter 5 is so vivid and direct that there can be little doubt that real-life marriages are being discussed.

Warnings against violating the wife of another man go back as far as the earliest known wisdom literature. The *Instruction of Ptahhotep* (before 2000 B.C.E.) says, "Beware of approaching women. A thousand men have been led astray from their good; a man is but mocked by their glistening limbs . . . but death is the penalty for enjoying it." The *Wisdom of Ani* (1500–1200 B.C.E.) explicitly warns, "Beware of the woman from abroad . . . a woman whose husband is far away."

This section contains four separate statements that contrast the evil woman with the faithful wife. Verses 1-6 describe her words, which quickly snare the youth's uncontrolled passions and enslave him to death itself. Discretion, that is, prudence, is the only safeguard (v. 2). Verses 7-14 then draw the conclusions of failure. The youth's life and reputation are ruined (v. 9), his position and money are lost (in penalty payments to the

wronged husband? or to the wife for her favors?), and his whole body is diseased and beaten in punishment. Actually, the penalty in the law was death by stoning (Deut 22:23-24; Lev 20:10), but in practice, the text suggests, it was often much milder. Too late the youth wishes he had listened to instruction.

In sharp contrast, verses 15-19 draw upon the age-old metaphor of fresh running water to describe a faithful marriage. Verses 20-23 then draw the moral conclusion from this: why go after forbidden and disastrous pleasure that merits death and loss because of its folly when so much can be found in faithful love? On top of this, a hint is made in verse 21 that God will see and judge evil. But otherwise the lesson is drawn from common experience.

6:1-19 Four lessons about wise conduct. This section is entitled "Miscellaneous Proverbs." But "proverbs" is a misleading term, since in fact there are four extended descriptions here, far from simple two-line sayings. In the first case, a person agrees to back up the loan of another, probably a foreigner, as the Hebrew word for "neighbor" suggests. This is considered rash and foolish because the guarantor can easily be stuck in the deal. The solution proposed is to browbeat and pester the moneylender until he lets you out of the deal. It is similar to Jesus' solution in his parable of the unjust judge in Luke 18:1-5.

In the second case, verses 6-11, a scene from nature becomes a moral. The ant is famed for its constant, busy search for food and its highly organized community life, which makes the most out of collective effort. The lazy person, on the other hand, acts as though no plans ever need to be made for the future. Everything will somehow work out. The authors cite what must have been a very popular saying in verses 10-11, since it is found again in 24:33-34. The message is plain: disaster overpowers those who do not plan ahead—they are as helpless as the victims of vicious armed robbers!

The third example, in verses 12-15, deals with the person who cheats and defrauds others. He talks fast and his line is smooth; he puts his arm around the intended victims' shoulders, gives a knowing wink, and soon has gotten hold of their life savings, with a promise of future wealth that will never be realized. This kind of evil person destroys trust in social agreements and contracts, creates bitterness and strife, and in the end always gets caught in his own trap—at least that is the pious hope of the sages!

Finally, the section ends with a numerical proverb in verses 16-19, similar to those that appear in chapter 30. Seven is the symbolic number for completeness and equals the summary of all the vices mentioned in verses 1-15. Artistically, the authors have arranged them as though they were a list of the parts of the body, but each comes from within an evil mind that rejects the lessons of wisdom.

6:20-35 The eighth instruction: a further warning against adultery. This instruction opens with a call to accept the commandments and teaching of one's parents. The language is the language of Deut 6:7-8 and 11:19 with one difference: in Deuteronomy it is the profession of faith in Yahweh that one is bound to, whereas here it is the moral lessons of Israel's wisdom traditions. Ps 119:105 says, "A lamp to my feet is your word, a light to my path." So, too, here it is discipline, traditional instruction, which is the light that guides rather than divine revelation.

Sexual license is condemned because it results from uncontrolled lust; but even more wrong is violation of another's marriage rights out of such lust. It leads only to terrible consequences that hurt all the parties, including the betrayed husband. The folksy images of verses 27-29 make the point clear. If you do X, you always get Y. Verses 30-35 bring out some of the more practical consequences. A thief who gets caught may be punished or fined until he has nothing left, but at least people will sympathize with the need that led him to steal, and may actually respect him for his desperate solution. But an adulterer is publicly humiliated, and the enraged husband will seek vengeance in every possible way. The young man will never forget this foolish mistake. Beyond the punishments, physical and monetary, he will probably be barred from any hope of obtaining position or respect in the community again.

Akkadian wisdom understood another lesson from such conduct. After the affair, the woman may well let the adulterer take the consequences as she sides with the very husband she has cuckolded: "Do not take a harlot, whose husbands are many, an Ishtar priestess devoted to a god. In your trouble she will not support you, in your conflict she will ridicule you; reverence and humility are not with her!" The youth who gets himself into such trouble is said to be a "fool" in verse 32 (the word actually means "lacking a mind"). Adultery is the shortest-enjoyed and longest-paid-for evil act in the wisdom dictionary.

7:1-27 The ninth instruction: more on the adulteress. That this is an independent instruction is shown by the elaborate introduction in verses 1-5, matching the one in 6:20-24. Both cite Deut 6:4-9 as divine law and urge the readers to make wisdom teaching as much a part of their lives as a sister or close friend would be. The description of the adulteress is much more colorful and detailed than the ones in chapters 5 or 6. Although it seems to stick to the case of a married woman who seduces a young man, several new elements enter the picture. Now the woman acts more like a cult prostitute on the lookout for clients. The young man in turn obviously goes to the area where he knows he will find her waiting as she looks out her window. Shortly after, she suggests a connection between sex and religious duty (vv. 14-15; note also the combination of vow-offerings and peace-offerings in the law of Lev 22:21 and Num 15:8).

Illustrating this scene are the well-known ivory images of the goddess Ishtar at the lattice of a window which have been found at various ancient sites but which all originate in Phoenician (Canaanite) areas. They represent love amulets associated with the temple rites dedicated to the goddess, which often included ritual sexual intercourse between worshipers and priestesses. Deuteronomy itself emphatically warned against the dangers of such cultic infidelity on the part of Israel and promised curse and death for those who fell into it (Deut 11:26-28; 30:15-20). There is good reason to believe that in chapter 7 we are dealing with a warning against cult prostitutes and not just with a wayward wife. But the two images are joined into one, and verses 19-20 return to the explicit image of adultery.

Verses 21-27 describe, in metaphors of dumb animals, the stupidity of the youth who becomes involved. Several times before (2:18; 5:5) the penalty has been described as death. The seductive words of the woman are like the mouth of Sheol itself—a pit or gaping jaws that swallow the guilty alive. It is an image borrowed from Canaan. The Epic of Baal from Ugarit describes the hero-god's descent into the underworld through the mouth of Death, who is said to have "one lip to earth, one lip to heaven, and his tongue to the stars."

8:1-36 Wisdom's second speech: her incomparable value. In sharp contrast to the woman of chapter 7, Wisdom herself now calls for attention and offers a counter-ideal. Again the comparisons to prophecy are strong, especially in the introduction of verses 1-11. Like the prophet Jeremiah, Wisdom opposes her true words to the false and lying words of other prophets (see Jer 2:8; 6:13; 23:13-14). But as in chapter 4, Wisdom does not at first appeal to divine authority but to human reason and the value of wisdom for its own sake (see a similar thought in 3:13-15). Her call lays stress on the power of upright words to help the simple gain sense and competence ("resource" in verse 5).

Wisdom's second claim (vv. 12-16) also comes from the best of old wisdom. She offers the gifts of statesmanship, the skills of public office. Much of the vocabulary of traditional older wisdom is found in verses 12-14. We can note, however, that later passages, such as Job 12:13 and Isa 40:13-14, attribute these qualities only to Yahweh. Here Wisdom claims them for herself, thus suggesting an identity between personified Wisdom and God. The same can be said of the divine power to appoint kings in verses 15-16. Note, too, the titles of Ishtar in Babylonian tradition: "Ishtar, creator and majesty, lady of peoples, goddess of humanity, who gives the sceptre, the throne, the royal insignia to the totality of kings."

Wisdom's third offer is made in verses 17-21: a personal relationship of love. There is no direct mention of God in these verses, but the merely abstract comparisons to gold and wealth hardly do justice to understanding the promise made in verse 17 that Wisdom loves those who love her, and she will be found by all who seek her. Job 28 insisted that for a pious Israelite wisdom cannot be found except when given by God as a gift. In an indirect way, the same view is maintained here, for it is by duty (really "judgment") and by justice that Wisdom is found and in return for which she gives her love. These terms, "judgment" and "justice," are the major terms

of the covenant law (see Isa 1:21; Hos 2:21; Pss 72:2; 85:12; 89:15).

Finally, the greatest of Wisdom's claims appears in verses 22-31. She belongs to the divine world far more than to the human world of the older sages. She claims to have been created before all else, before all those natural wonders of the heavens that aroused Israel to acknowledge God's almighty power over human affairs. Verses 22-29 refer specifically to Israel's literary accounts of creation, with elements drawn not only from Gen 1-2 but also from Job 38:4-18 and Ps 104:1-9. The purpose is to show that if Wisdom took part in God's creative action, she has a right to as much acknowledgment from the Israelites for her value as they give to the heavenly bodies as signs of God's goodness. Verse 30 has always been the key verse. The New American Bible has translated the Hebrew word for wisdom's role as "craftsman," which suggests a very active role for Wisdom in the process of creation. Others think that it may mean "darling" or "beloved" and may refer more to the playful aspect described in the rest of the verse. Both, however, emphasize a similar point, namely, that Wisdom was before God's presence as a model on the day of creation.

Many attempts have been made to identify the remains of a Near Eastern myth about Wisdom as a creation goddess in this passage. The closest parallels are Egyptian descriptions of *maat*, the personified goddess of world order: "Even to the gods she is precious, to her forever belongs the sovereignty; in heaven she is treasured up, for the lord of holiness has exalted her" (from *The Words of Ahiqar*, found in a Jewish colony at Elephantine in Egypt). Israel uses similar language to express how Wisdom mirrors the orderly plan of Yahweh revealed in his creation. In Prov 8 the personification does not suggest that Wisdom exists apart from God, but is instead a way of expressing the *purpose* of the divine will as it is made manifest in the world. The passage ends with a peroration in 8:32-36: to find Wisdom is to find life as well as divine favor. In fact, they are the same.

9:1-18 The tenth instruction: a parable of two banquets. To cap the eight chapters arguing for Wisdom's superiority to folly, the author or authors end by describing two banquets—one given by Lady Wisdom, the other by Dame Folly. Both sit by the road and call people in; both appeal especially to the simple and to those lacking sense (vv. 3-4, 14-16); both offer a rich reward (vv. 5, 17). But Wisdom's reward turns out to be life (vv. 6, 11), while Folly's turns out to be a poison that brings death (v. 18). The two may not seem equal, but since Wisdom's banquet requires a long period of learning, the lure of quick pleasure offered by Folly easily captures many.

The chapter is divided into three sections. Wisdom's banquet takes up verses 1-6, Folly's 13-18. In between stands a section with three proverbs from old wisdom contrasting once again the way of the wicked and the way of the wise. It includes a warning that all that has been said about wisdom in chapters 1–9 is summed up in the theme already announced in 1:7: the beginning of wisdom resides in piety and true fidelity to Yahweh (fear of the Lord). This is Wisdom's final word. The emphasis placed on it indicates that verses 7-12 are not accidentally inserted here. They are intended to summarize Wisdom's offer. The accent on fear of the Lord also suggests that the strange reference to a house of seven pillars in 9:1 and to Folly's house high on a hill in 9:14 contrasts different temples. The Jerusalem temple and its worship of Yahweh stresses the blessing of life that comes to those who search it out (see Pss 15; 24). The temples of the cult prostitutes and their sexual rites confer only death on their devotees.

Wisdom's house of seven pillars is made up of her teachings. The seven may refer to a holy place (main room of the temple) that consists of the instructions in chapters 2 to 7. In this case the vestibule would be made up of chapter 1 and the holy of holies of chapter 8, thus forming a spiritual model of the temple of Solomon. In any case, the nine chapters of Part I continually interrelate priestly *torah* and prophetic challenge with Wisdom's advice. This hints that the authors or editors saw these chapters as an argument for wisdom as an equal source next to law and prophecy for Israel's faith. Jer 18:18 already alluded to such a triple parallel: "Instruction shall not be lost from the priests, nor counsel from the wise, nor the word from the prophets."

PART II: THE PROVERBS OF SOLOMON

Prov 10:1–22:16

This first collection of proverbs attributed to Solomon is the longest section in the Book of Proverbs, but there are no internal subdivisions marked in the text. It consists of 375 single proverbs covering just about every aspect of conduct involving social relationships. Sayings on one topic, such as proper speech, are not all grouped together, however, but are scattered throughout the collection. The same is true of other topics. Scholars have long sought the principles by which individual proverbs were grouped, but no one has yet proposed a convincing answer. We know that *Sumerian* proverbs were often collected by topic. In one tablet, sayings on dogs are in one place, followed by those involving wild oxen, and then those using the metaphor of the ass, etc. Perhaps someone will yet find a key to unlock the secret of Hebrew ordering.

A few clues already exist. For example, chapters 10–15 are very heavy with proverbs contrasting the just and the wicked person. Chapters 16–22, on the other hand, deal more with practical advice on how to be successful. Perhaps these originally represented two separate collections. Certain smaller sections seem to follow special themes: thus 11:4-11 stresses the rewards of the just; 16:1-9 is on God's rule of life; 16:10-15 is on the behavior of kings; and most of chapter 18 is on the use of speech. None, however, can be clearly identified as originally a separate unity.

Many scholars do not believe that we will ever be able to identify the original collections of proverbs. Individual sayings would have been reworked often, and it is better to distinguish those sayings that reflect earlier wisdom thinking from those that show a later, more developed faith in Yahweh. Three stages have been suggested. The oldest accents practical rules for success in life and rarely or never mentions God. A second stage shows concern for the effects of social versus antisocial behavior, and a third stage uses the thought and language of a fully working Israelite piety. The second group could easily be absorbed into the first group, which would leave only two major stages of proverb development: an older, more neutral proverb used for educating the young and the apprentice public servant in the mastery of life; and a later stage when these were modified and "corrected" by sayings which emphasize Yahweh's control over success and failure, and which make a close connection between wisdom and faith. A possible middle stage between older and later wisdom would have been a developing awareness that moral attitudes are basic to divine order and that upright behavior is always rewarded.

In any case, most scholars agree that few of the proverbs actually come from Solomon's time. A long history of development has taken place, and it is only in the final reading of the total collection that the message of proverbial wisdom for Israel is fully seen. The message combines keen observation of both practical moral conduct and the consequences of human decisions with trust in God and reliance on the divine ordering of the world.

In order to gain the most out of reading this section, it is important to look over a chapter or a good part of a chapter at a time, reflect on how the individual proverbs relate to one another or how they differ, and then ask: How do these diverse sayings build up a picture of the wise believer? How do they reinforce one another? The differences and the apparent lack of unity will sharpen our looking—an essential purpose of the proverb form itself!

10:1-32. The major topic that runs through chapter 10 is the role of the just person. Again and again the just are related either to the wise or to the wicked. It is a kind of theme statement for the rest of chapters 11–22. Smaller units can be seen in verses 18-21 on the power of speech, and in verses 27-32 on the rewards of just behavior. Almost all the proverbs are in antithetic parallelism, setting the ideal against undesired foolish or evil behavior. Above all, the foolish or stupid person lacks self-control over speech and over appetites, and it is primarily on these that the sayings focus here.

Verses 1-7 give examples of careful stewardship on the part of the wise in contrast to the lack of foresight and short-sighted cravings of the foolish. Verses 8-17 focus on still another aspect distinguishing wisdom from foolishness—intention. What does the fool or evil person want? Strife seems to be one answer; quick gain at someone else's expense seems to be another. Violence is never

far from the ways chosen by such people, since they want what they want at any cost. These same verses keep returning to the far different goal of the wise—life. It is long-term (v. 14) and requires careful learning (v. 17), careful speech (v. 11), and careful choice of goals (v. 16).

Verses 18-21 illustrate one aspect of wise calculation—the use of speech. Words can destroy and wound, or they can reveal too much and offend against propriety. But they can also contribute advice or comment of value and support others in need of encouragement and recognition. The training of wisdom teachers gave great attention to speech as the means of communicating and revealing wise decisions. (See more on this in chs. 12 and 18.)

Verse 22 asserts the primacy of God's blessing over human effort in the search for success. The following few sayings strengthen this conviction by showing how the upright outlast the wicked.

Verses 27-32 close the chapter by detailing the rewards of God's blessing: long life, joy, security, peace, as well as skill in speaking and a charming manner. In all ways, being just has the advantage over evil behavior.

11:1-31. The proverbs in this chapter continue the theme of uprightness. Verses 2-8 contrast the *personal* attitudes of the just and the wicked, while verses 9-15 describe the *social* implications of the two ways. The remaining sayings are harder to classify, but they generally keep up the opposition between right behavior and evil conduct.

The most common idea in this chapter is that the just person who has virtue expresses most fully the idea of the ideal order (*maat* of the older Egyptian wisdom). This ideal order forms the perfect unifying link between practical wisdom and religious wisdom, since it expresses both good sense and religious obedience to God's will. Closely associated with this concept is the word translated "upright" in verses 3 and 6, and "righteous" in verse 11. It emphasizes the inner, personal commitment to a living out of the divine ideal. It implies the spirituality of a person totally committed to making justice really work.

We can note that this chapter has a strong urban orientation. Verses 9-15 in particular express the ramifications of justice toward one's neighbors. The social community as a whole benefits or suffers from the choices one makes. The chapter opens with a saying on fair scales that typifies the concern for justice. Law and prophets demand just dealings in buying and selling (Deut 25:15; Lev 19:36; Ezek 45:10; Amos 8:5; Mic 6:11). In this they are one with wisdom. But this is part of a larger concern with the evil attitude that is always out to cheat someone else. The Egyptian Amenemope names both false weights and cheating as "abominations" to the god, as does Proverbs in verse 20. The opposite hope is expressed by verse 26: generosity in goods merits divine blessing.

The New American Bible has filled out verse 16 from the Greek Septuagint. Actually the Hebrew text reads: "A gracious woman holds on to honor, but ruthless men cling to wealth." It does not create a perfect contrast, but it makes sense as it stands and did not require a change.

Another small note can be made on verse 22. Nose rings are still known in Bedouin tribes as a sign of beauty, so the point is that a rebellious spirit seems as inappropriate in a woman as putting a sign of beauty on a pig.

Verse 31 can be considered the moral lesson of the chapter. It is quoted in 1 Pet 4:18 as a comfort to Christians under persecution. Indeed, the author of 1 Peter was a great admirer of this section of Proverbs. 1 Pet 4:8 quotes a saying from Prov 10:12.

12:1-28. The education of the beginner in wisdom continues with further examples of the differences between the just and the wicked. Verses 1-3 set the tone by bringing together the older ideal of wisdom through correction and the development of good habits with obedience to Yahweh's will. In verse 5 it is explicitly asserted that the intentions and considerations of the heart are all-important. Those motivated by justice are "legitimate" (NAB), those of the wicked are "deceitful." The word for "legitimate" in this verse might be better translated "good judgment." The sense is taken from legal usage, where the judge must render a decision on a given case. What is justice in this situation? The religious meaning is that the upright do what is just, and God accepts them as legally guiltless. On the other hand, the wicked only produce fraud and dishonesty. The Hebrew word for "deceitful" is the same as that used for "false scales" in 11:1. Legally, the guilty

will be condemned for the concrete acts of fraud that their machinations lead to.

The remainder of the chapter gives various examples of the good habits typical of the just: steady work, prudence, kindliness, and self-control. But the largest emphasis falls on speech and the thoughts that motivate it. Verses 14-15 express it as a mixture of choosing good words that win people over and of listening to others in order to learn rather than speaking before thinking. This is given flesh in the series of sayings in verses 17-23 dealing with thought versus speech. Lying and dishonesty can be destructively powerful uses of the tongue, but their gain is short-lived. Truth endures, and it not only outlasts dishonesty but also brings the benefits of peace, security, and joy to the one who serves it.

Once again the message is drawn from older wisdom but given a specifically Israelite turn in verse 22, where it is God who will demand an answer to the abomination of false speech. Amenemope expressed a similar insight: "God hates the falsifying of words, his great abomination is the one who is sick within." Verse 23 also reflects a saying of Amenemope: "Better is the man whose news stays in his body than the one who speaks it out injuriously." Often in the Old Testament an "abomination" is tied to false worship (Dan 9:27; 11:31; 12:11), but in Proverbs and Amenemope it means a fundamental moral flaw. Further Egyptian influence can be detected in the sayings against anger (v. 16; see ch. 14).

13:1-25. This chapter opens, as does the beginning in 10:1, with a contrast between the wise and foolish son (or pupil). Generally the chapter has two major themes to develop this contrast: the dangers of uncontrolled appetites or desires (vv. 2-12), and the quality of life that results from the choices each person makes (vv. 13-25).

The power of appetites was well known to Israelite teachers. Their instructions concentrated on internal dispositions, however— the longing for what belongs to another, the desire for external show, anger, and above all pride. Verse 10 calls it "insolence," a quality that puffs up one's own importance while seeking to cause embarrassment and shame to others (v. 5). Dishonest and violent behavior is always tempting in order to achieve such goals.

Another area that the sages associated with uncontrolled appetite was money. Wealth can be a sign of divine blessing and success for the good person who follows the path of justice (v. 11), but it also focuses the dreams and hopes of the wicked on acquiring more. With wealth they can receive the external signs of blessing. Verse 8, for example, can make the neutral observation that wealth frees one from many normal worries, while poverty makes instruction almost impossible. A similar thought occurs in 18:23: "The poor man implores, but the rich man answers harshly," and also in 18:11: "The rich man's wealth is his strong city." But the search for wealth as a primary goal of life leads to treachery and fraud, so roundly condemned in the proverbs we have already seen. True wealth is in wisdom (3:14; 8:10; 8:18-19; 16:16); in turn, wise behavior, especially generosity, will lead to wealth (recall 12:24-25). A spiritualized interpretation of this is found in verse 21.

The quality of a life of wisdom is summarized in the choice between life and death. Life is more than mere existence, of course. It is the fullness of blessing now. So it is described as a fountain (v. 14) that brings reward (v. 13), favor (v. 15), healing (v. 17), honor (v. 18), good (v. 21), an inheritance for one's children (v. 22), and a full stomach (v. 25). The sinner, naturally, receives the opposite—misfortune, ruin, poverty, shame, and an empty belly. These belong to the realm of death (v. 14). The fundamental message is to acquire this life quality, best expressed by verse 20. The only way to gain wisdom is to walk with the wise.

14:1-35. The difference between the wise and the foolish continues to occupy center stage in this chapter, especially as the one is prudent and cautious, and the other rash and foolhardy (vv. 3, 6, 7, 16, 24, 33). Discipline is needed (vv. 8, 12, 15, 18) and prudent judgment (vv. 4, 10, 13, 20, 23, 30). All of this fits the tradition of international wisdom, but it is tempered here with two religious convictions proper to Israel. Divine concern for the world means that wicked and foolish behavior can expect punishment (vv. 11, 14, 19, 32), and "fear of the Lord" rules the actions of the just (vv. 2, 26, 27).

This "fear of the Lord" does not imply a frightened obedience in order to avoid punishment. It relates to the awe and reverence one must show before the transcendent power and majesty of God. There is a healthy fear of the consequences of sin, but there is also love and a sense of trust in the divine power that cares for and directs all things in our lives. It can be described as loyalty to Yahweh. It is devotion, fidelity, and obedience at the same time (see Lev 19; Deut 10:12; Ps 34:10-12). In practice, it is piety: the observance of the religious obligations and moral standards of the law. In 2 Kgs 17:25-29 priests had to be sent to Samaria to teach the new settlers how to "fear the Lord," that is, to be good Jews. In the later wisdom tradition, keeping the law was identified with fearing the Lord, which in turn was the same as wisdom (Sir 1:14, 16, 18, 20; 15:1; 19:20; 21:11), and the law is the path to wisdom (Sir 1:26; 9:14-15; 24:22-23; 39:1-3). In Proverbs, fear of the Lord has a strong *ethical* content, whereas in Gen 20:11 and other Pentateuchal passages it seems primarily tied to *cultic* concerns. The development of religious wisdom brought the two into one by the time of Sirach, but in Proverbs the connection to living uprightly is still dominant.

Many of the proverbs echo themes already seen. Lying, arrogance, laziness, refusal to learn from discipline, and rash behavior are all condemned. Resourcefulness, truthfulness, and shrewd planning are all praised. A new theme of anger and quick-tempered behavior appears in verses 17 and 29. It is common elsewhere in Proverbs (12:16; 15:18; 16:32; 17:27-28, etc.). It reflects one of the most frequent topics in Egyptian wisdom: the value of the "cool" versus the "hot" spirit. One Egyptian noble left this epitaph on his tomb in self-praise: "Silent, cool in temperament, calm in expression." It sums up the ideal scribe and statesman for Egypt—indeed, it is exactly the description of Joseph as vizier of Egypt in Gen 37-50! The "hot" man cannot control his speech, his desires, his temper, or his rash decision-making. He expresses everything he feels, and wants all his cravings satisfied. No one is less suited to work with or cooperate with others. Amenemope says of such a person, "Like a storm which arises as fire in the straw is the hot man in his time." A few chapters later, it adds, "Do not make the hot man your companion, and do not hold a conversation with him!"

15:1-33. The proverbs in this chapter typify the conduct of the cool temperament over against the hot spirit. The "ill-tempered man" of verse 18 is literally in Hebrew "a man of heat." The early part of the chapter stresses calm speech, cautious affirmation of "knowledge," and an openness to learning (vv. 1-7). They are themes covered many times before (see 12:1; 13:18, 24; 14:33). Above all, discipline is needed to develop such a cool spirit (vv. 5, 10, 12, 20, 21, 24, 31, 32). "Discipline" and "reproof" are the bases of old wisdom's formula for worldly success. A very intentional effort has been made here to link these to the practice of Israel's faith. Proverbs that name Yahweh as the source of wisdom and judgment are more frequent in this chapter than anywhere else in chapters 10–22 except for chapter 16. In verse 33, "fear of the Lord" is equated with both discipline and wisdom. Verse 8 even mentions the role of worship and prayer, a theme very rare in Proverbs. Verse 9 forms a general conclusion on the mutual roles of worship and wisdom that identifies rejection of Yahweh and evil conduct as equal abominations.

Verse 11 presents the only positive view of the nether world in Proverbs. Usually Sheol is a place cut off from life and from God. Here the saying suggests that God takes a personal concern even for the world of the dead. Verse 12 presents us with the "senseless" person. The characteristic of this type of person is that he or she refuses to change anything. Thus there is no way for wisdom to enter moral decision-making.

The concern of Yahweh for the poor and defenseless is a major proclamation of both the law and the prophets (Deut 10:18; 14:28-29; 24:17-22; Exod 22:21-24; Isa 1:17, 23). It is just as important to the wisdom tradition. Verses 16-17 turn two well-known Egyptian sayings of Amenemope into a statement of faith: "Better is bread when the heart is glad than riches with vexation," and "Better is the poor man in the hands of the god than riches in the storehouse" (see Prov 14:31; 19:17; 22:9; and 29:4). Verse 25 goes on to include the widow among the helpless. This, too, fits the traditional Near Eastern sentiment. An inscription of Pharaoh Amenemhet I says,

> I gave to the poor, I nurtured the orphan,
> No one has been hungry in my years,
> No one has been thirsty.

The *Epic of King Keret* at Ugarit, a Canaanite text of the thirteenth century B.C.E., accuses the king of failing in his duty:

> You do not give the widow her rights . . . .
> You do not overthrow those who oppress the
>   poor.
> The orphans are not fed by you,
> Nor the widows fed behind your back.

Israel has made this a divine obligation placed upon all Israelites and not just upon kings: Pss 72:1-4, 12-13; Jer 7:5-6; 22:2-3; Ezek 22:6-7; Zech 7:10. The wisdom teachers do not extol poverty as a special favor from God, but they acknowledge the priority of faithfulness to Yahweh even in want over material signs of blessing.

16:1-15. These fifteen verses are the center of Solomon's collection in chapters 10–22. Verses 1-9 detail the proper relationship of God to human wisdom, and express mention of Yahweh occurs in eight of the nine sayings! This is followed in verses 10-15 by a mini-guidebook for kings. The two groups belong together, since the king enjoyed a special relationship with God as "son" (Pss 2:7; 72:1) and "shepherd" of the people (Ezek 34:23). Kings, therefore, must embody the divine concern for justice. The thought in these two sections rests squarely on the older wisdom insights, but it has been transformed into a declaration of Yahweh's direct control over every aspect of life and especially over human planning.

Verse 1 affirms that even words, those most intimate expressions of a person's private thought, are directed to effects never dreamed of by the speaker. The Assyrian work *The Words of Ahiqar* (seventh century B.C.E.) likewise declares, "If he were beloved of the gods, they would put something good in his palate to speak." Verses 2-3 extend this insight. Only if God directs human plans will they succeed. Compare the early Egyptian advice of *Merikare:* "If the tongue of a man be the rudder of the boat, the Lord of all is its pilot!" The key attitudes are listed then in verses 5-8: humility rather than pride, kindness, piety, peaceful relations with others, and virtue (that is, uprightness) even in the middle of difficulty. Finally, verse 9 sums up the lesson by repeating the opening insight. Wisdom recognizes its limits. God is beyond human understanding, a mystery not comprehended by the skills of learning, and thus Yahweh ultimately exercises control even over wisdom itself.

Verses 10-15 obviously presume an ideal king. His words share divine authority and uphold the order of both justice and right judgment. But verses 11-12 assert that no kingdom can achieve this unless the people also live by the same qualities as kings. Verses 13-15 concentrate on how to win royal favor. They seem to be directed to the instruction of potential diplomats for the royal service. The advice is purely practical. Success will depend on winning the king's favor, and this is done by catering to his ways. But at least Proverbs keeps such fawning suggestions quite limited in scope. The *Wisdom of Ptah-hotep* (ca. 2450 B.C.E.) and the *Words of Ahiqar* (seventh century B.C.E.) both agree on extensive submissiveness before kings to gain favor. One example from Ahiqar reads: "If a thing is commanded you in the presence of a king, it is a burning fire; hasten to do it!"

16:16-33. The remainder of chapter 16 returns to the general advice on good conduct for everyone. If advancement in the king's service had a certain self-serving pride attached to its practical requirements of bowing and scraping, this should not be carried over as the ideal of every Israelite. They were members of the chosen people who bound themselves in a covenant of worship and obedience to Yahweh alone. These more general sayings, which would have been treasured in Egypt or Babylon as well, extol virtues important to the covenant: prudent speech (vv. 21, 23, 24), respect for elders (v. 31), praise of a cool temper (v. 32), and excoriation of evil words (vv. 27-30). But the spirit of humility before Yahweh and the submission of all human hopes and plans to the divine will are declared the only true road to success.

The combination of healthy respect for the limits of human knowledge with deep trust in the providence of Yahweh is summed up in the final saying of verse 33. Although applied here to the search for knowledge by means of learning, the mention of the lots reminds the reader that all major decisions throughout Israel's history were sought by asking God to indicate the answer through the casting of lots or other divination practices (see examples in Num 26:55; Lev 16:7-10; Josh 7:14; 14:2; 1 Sam 10:20-21; Prov 18:18). Later Egyptian wisdom came to the same realization. Amen-

emope could say, "One thing are the words men say, another is that which the god does." It is a universal insight—there is even a Malay proverb that goes, "Man's designs and God's decrees differ."

17:1-28. Among the general words of advice in this chapter are a number of sayings on strife (vv. 1, 4, 14, 19, 20) and bribery (vv. 8, 23). The first series underscores the importance of social relationships in the thinking of wisdom. The right relations between parents and children (v. 25), servants and employers (v. 2), business associates (v. 18), and friends (v. 17) are constant themes in the Book of Proverbs. Strife breaks down the proper order that exists and creates the sources of future hatred, violence, and lying. As verse 4 puts it, evil seeks ever more evil, and, like a dam that bursts, it becomes a flood (v. 14). The wise also know that evil ways are very hard to dislodge from our thinking. Verse 13 is an Old Testament version of "Those who live by the sword shall die by the sword." The thought of verse 1 agrees with 15:16-17 and the saying of Amenemope, "It is better to be praised as one who loves men than to have riches in the storehouse."

The attitude toward bribery in Proverbs has two sides. In a non-judgmental way, the wise observe that bribes often obtain results (18:16; 21:14). But more often the sayings take a stand against such perversions of justice, not only in this chapter but also in 28:21. In this regard, wisdom condemns bad judges (17:15, 23; 18:5) and perjury (19:5, 9, 28; 21:28) as well. All of these represent the destruction of society's divine order and of law. In this they agree wholeheartedly with the psalms and the prophets (Pss 15:5; 26:10; Isa 1:23; 5:23; Ezek 22:12; Mic 3:11). Deut 16:19 captures the essence of wisdom's position: "You shall not pervert justice or show partiality; and you shall not take a bribe because a bribe blinds the eyes of the wise and undermines the cause of the just."

The fool figures prominently in these sayings (vv. 10, 12, 16, 21, 24, 25). This is not the ordinary foolish person, but one who has too little ability to learn in school and who therefore acts in just the opposite manner out of spite. There is a hard-headed stubbornness in the fool that really tries to break up the accepted order and established ways of human relationships in society.

18:1-24. Several of the proverbs in chapter 18 return to the topic of good speech. This is not surprising in light of the intellectual tradition of wisdom. Even Babylonian wisdom literature gives its greatest attention to the quality of speech. At least ten separate expressions for sinful speech occur in the major Babylonian texts. These include words that are wicked, seditious, offensive, blasphemous, lying, exaggerated, and slanderous. In Prov 18 we meet still other categories of sinful or foolish speech: quarreling (v. 1), vain and empty self-opinion (v. 2), scorn spoken out of contempt (v. 3), creation of strife (v. 6), talebearing (v. 8), and speaking without thinking (v. 13). This reflects wisdom's message elsewhere in the book: empty chatter is foolish (15:2; 14:23); stirring up strife is evil (10:19; 26:21; 29:22 and most of chapter 17); gossip is destructive (11:13; 20:19; 26:20, 22); seeking scandal is wrong (16:27; 17:4).

At the same time, speech rightly used is a powerful tool for the wise person. Frankness and truth can change people (15:32; 24:26); words can heal (12:18; 13:17; 15:1; 16:24); persuasion can win people over (10:32; 11:9, 11); silence or reticence in speaking protects reputations (17:9; 25:8-9); holding back in speech acts shrewdly (12:23; 13:3; 21:23); and patient speech cools tempers (15:18; 17:27; 20:3).

In general, the wisdom teachers valued reserve and careful consideration in speech. It is true that they also had enough of a sense of humor to depict the foolish and stupid in slightly exaggerated cartoons of themselves. But they had a serious purpose in mind, namely, to steer the student through the pitfalls of the most difficult area of human conduct: the impulse to speak out what pops into the mind. The Letter of James in the New Testament is heir to this understanding in its treatise on the use of the tongue in 3:1-12.

19:1-29. No particular theme dominates chapter 19. It has several sayings on the problems of laziness (vv. 15, 24), royal service (v. 12), control of anger (vv. 11, 19), false witnesses (vv. 9, 28), and the training of children through discipline (vv. 13, 18, 25, 27), similar to those in earlier chapters. The most attention is paid to the dangers of wealth. Riches can lead to crooked behavior, false friends, greedy associates, and eventually to dishonesty (vv. 1, 4, 6, 7, 22). On the other side, there is no sign of God's disfavor in being poor (vv. 1, 17), although it leads to all sorts of undesirable difficulties (v. 7).

Wisdom's attitude on the subject of wealth was always ambivalent. Older wisdom saw a definite connection between material blessing and divine favor, while later wisdom developed a piety of the 'anawim, the righteous who have no inheritance in this world except the Lord. This latter theology is found mostly in the psalms, but its beginning can be found in verse 17 and in 22:4. God's special concern for the poor (see the comments on chapter 15 above) guarantees that any generous charity to the poor will be like a loan to God—its repayment is assured! Late Babylonian wisdom developed a similar insight, expressed in the *Dialogue of Pessimism:* "The man who sacrifices to his god is satisfied with the bargain; he is making loan upon loan."

Scattered throughout the proverbs of Solomon are a number of sayings about the value of a good wife (12:4; 18:22; 19:14). As far back as the *Instruction of Ptah-hotep* in Old Kingdom Egypt, this had been a staple of wisdom teaching: "If you are a man of standing, you should establish your household and love your wife at home as is fitting. Make her heart glad as long as you live. She is a profitable field for her lord." While a minor theme in chapters 10–22, it is a major element in the final summation of wisdom in Prov 31:10-31.

The value of "counsel" is emphasized in verse 20. It is above all the quality of shrewd political advice. It frequently appears in contexts in which scribes are called on to advise the king: 2 Sam 8:17; 20:25; 2 Kgs 18:18; 22:8. Perhaps the most famous episode occurs in 2 Sam 16, where the two most famous givers of counsel in David's kingdom, Hushai and Ahithophel, duel against each other. Ahithophel gives sounder counsel, but Absalom follows the deceptive words of Hushai and thus loses his opportunity to win his revolt against his father David. Joseph, too, is portrayed as a wise counselor of Pharaoh in Genesis.

In Proverbs, counsel is often directly equated with wisdom (15:22; 19:20; 21:30), as it is also in certain royal passages of Isaiah (11:2; 19:11) and in an oracle of Jeremiah (Jer 49:7). Verse 21 gives a definite religious response to older wisdom's pride in human cleverness by affirming that God's counsel is greater than ours. This agrees with the polemical stance of prophets such as Second Isaiah who mock the pretensions of human counselors who think that they can figure out what course God is likely to take. See Isa 40:13-14 as a good example. God does not act according to human decisions but establishes the order according to which humans must act.

20:1-30. The proverbs in this chapter are of a general nature. In some cases it seems that later wisdom thinkers have actually tried to soften or correct some of the more optimistic claims of older wisdom. Verse 12 attributes all seeing and hearing (that is, learning) to God's foresight and intention, lest people claim that goodness or justice or integrity or their virtuous conduct from childhood onward came from their own moral uprightness (vv. 6-11). This should be related to the question of intention. Verse 5 describes human intentions as coming from the very depth of our being. The word used is also "counsel," and the lesson is the same as in chapter 19. Right intention draws on the counsel of God, who makes the eye and the ear instruments of learning and communicating wisely.

Several of the proverbs echo themes found primarily in chapters 1–9. Verse 4, on the lazy farmer, reflects 6:6-11, while the warning against standing bond for a neighbor's loan in verse 16 is similar to 6:1-5. The bread of deceit that seduces someone resembles the stolen bread and water of folly in 9:17. The proverb on sleep and wakefulness in verse 13 is the ancient counterpart to our modern saying "The early bird catches the worm." And the very realistic scene in verse 14 still takes place regularly in the bazaars of the Near East, where bargaining over items for sale involves an elaborate ritual of feigning how much one is losing in the deal. The warning against gossips (v. 19) echoes many similar cautions in Amenemope and other ancient sources.

The careful advice in verse 18 illustrates perfectly the proverb found in 1 Kgs 20:11: "It is not for the man who is buckling his armor to boast as though he were taking it off" (1 Kgs 20:11). The explicit sayings about Yahweh's guidance and the need to trust in God found together in verses 22-24 balance those in verses 10-12. The saying about just weights seems somewhat out of place in verse 23, but it is repeated in both halves of the verse and must represent the ideal behavior

of those who trust in the Lord. All the other proverbs in the chapter must be read in the light of these two Yahweh sayings in verses 22-24.

Finally, in verse 29 we come to another saying in praise of old age. Wisdom and age are closely associated in the proverbial literature, and especially in those who serve as town elders. See 16:31 and 17:6 for like sentiments. Ezek 7:26 associates the gift of "counsel" with the elders. Other biblical passages that link age and wisdom are Ezek 27:8-9; Job 26:3; 32:7-9; Eccl 4:13; Ps 105:22.

21:1-31. This chapter opens with three sayings about Yahweh and closes with two more. In between is a body of traditional old wisdom offering advice on a wide range of subjects. Since it is probable that the five sayings on Yahweh are intended to interpret the context for all the others, we can broadly characterize the chapter theme as divine control of events. "Man proposes but God disposes" would be the modern equivalent of the editors' judgments on these proverbs. They are very practical, and some may even be a little offensive to our modern sensibilities (vv. 9, 14). The three opening proverbs stress the major fields of divine action: the king subject to Yahweh, final judgment at death, and the importance of worship to ethical conduct. These symbolize all of life's major moments that fall under divine supervision.

The saying on God as weigher of hearts may be a Hebrew equivalent to the Egyptian belief that the god of wisdom, Thoth, judged the heart of the deceased. The heart is often shown on a balance scale weighed against the feather of *maat*, "right order." If the heart comes out lighter, the soul deserves punishment. Similar references may be seen in Prov 16:2 and 24:12. Generally, Proverbs shows little interest in the question of an afterlife, and so one must be careful not to make too much of this possible interpretation of verse 2. It could mean no more than that Yahweh rewards the just and punishes the wicked in this life. However, verse 3 also has Egyptian parallels on the greater value of right conduct over sacrifice. *Merikare* says, "Righteousness of the heart is more acceptable to God than the sacrifice of an ox by an unrighteous man."

Other interesting sayings include verse 13, which is an equivalent to the modern boy who cried "Wolf!" once too often; and verse 16, which mentions the "shades" (that is, the spirits of the dead) as though they formed a community in Sheol, the land of the dead. Verse 18 seems strange. It may suggest that God often allows enemies to be defeated so that Israel may benefit from freedom, but it may just as well reflect the thought that God forgives the faults of the just by making the wicked bear the punishment for both. It is a reverse atonement. The only other place where a theology of atonement exists in the Old Testament is in Isa 53, the passage on the suffering servant.

Verse 19 returns to one of the favorite themes in Proverbs, the quarrelsome wife (see 6:14; 6:19; 10:12; 18:18-19; 19:13). Verses 30-31 close the chapter by reaffirming the theology of Second Isaiah discussed above in chapter 19. God's counsel and wisdom far exceed all human efforts, and especially in war; only Yahweh decides the outcome of battles. A particularly effective example to illustrate this is the story of Gideon's battle against the Midianites in Judg 7:1-23.

22:1-16. The final group of proverbs in chapters 10-22 deals with general, practical advice more than with any special summary of what has gone before. Education, wealth, laziness, and adultery all make their return appearance in variations of earlier sayings. Indeed, one of the striking features of these verses is how abruptly they end without any notable attempt to sum up or close out the whole.

Since Israel did not have a belief in an afterlife full of blessing for most of the Old Testament period, a good "name" and reputation were highly valued. One lived on after death in the honor and esteem of generations to come. Thus verse 1 places the value of a name above wealth, just as earlier proverbs placed integrity and justice above wealth (15:16; 19:1). The good name, then, must also include a life of integrity and justice. The theology of verses 2 and 4 brings this point out in reference to Yahweh. God values people, no matter whether rich or poor, and will give reward to those who are humble and reverent. The same can be said of the message of verses 11-12, which emphasize Yahweh's approval of integrity and rejection of dishonest plans and calculations.

The cryptic expression of verse 13 shows the humorous side of proverbs. Even in an-

cient Israel, one would be hard-pressed to run across a lion in the street very often! Verse 14 recalls the repeated warnings in chapters 1-9 against the adulteress as the jaws of death—see 3:18; 5:5; 7:27; 9:18. Verse 15 links the values of physical discipline and learning. From what we can gather, no one spared the rod in ancient education. Proverbs such as 13:24; 23:13-14; and 29:15 extol the value of using a stick to teach wisdom. Comparison with verse 6 and other passing references indicate that the philosophy behind its use was to knock foolishness out of the student. If he or she made the association between mistaken ways of thinking and the painful consequences, the lesson would last a lifetime. This type of education was probably closely tied to memorizing proverbs for the teacher. Forgetting one could lead to a swift rap on the knuckles.

PART III: THE THIRTY SAYINGS OF THE WISE

Prov 22:17-24:22

For over fifty years scholars have recognized the close connection between 22:17-24:22 and the Egyptian *Teaching of Amenemope*. Both are classical examples of the Instruction genre, in which commands alternate with motives for obeying. Proverbs 1-9 and 30-31 are also largely in this form. But what sets 22:17-24:22 apart are the extremely close parallels in wording to Amenemope (particularly in 22:17-23:11), sometimes appearing in the same order! Moreover, the general introduction to Amenemope has a decided similarity to the introduction to Proverbs in Prov 1:1-7. Both state the same purpose, as can be seen from Amenemope: "The beginning of the teaching of life, the instruction for success. All precepts for conversation with the great, the rules for courtiers, to know how to answer one who speaks, to return a written message to one who sends it, to direct one on the paths of life, to make him prosper on earth . . . ." The major difference between this stated purpose and Prov 1:1-7 is that the Egyptian work certainly directed its teachings to an elite class of trainees and emphasized the practical success that would result. The Israelite work was ordered more to understanding the meaning of life, particularly the relationship of human knowing to the divine will.

The same is true in Prov 22:17–24:22. While it seems to have known and borrowed from Amenemope, it did not simply reproduce the Egyptian theology. It modified many sayings and added others to give a specifically Israelite faith perspective. The closest parallel to the message of this section of Proverbs is found in Psalm 37. The psalm stresses the salvation of the just and the punishment of the wicked, as does Proverbs, but it places more emphasis on Yahweh as the sole hope of salvation.

Amenemope was composed sometime between 1000 and 600 B.C.E. It is divided into thirty chapters and includes both long and short thought units. In selecting from these, the Hebrew authors left aside many sections that applied only to Egypt or Egyptian beliefs. Thus they eliminated chapter 5 of Amenemope and its long description of the Nile, as well as the extended directive on praying to the sun-god in chapter 7. Israel kept the form of thirty sayings by adding new ideas of its own. In asking why Israel valued this foreign work so highly, the reason must be found in the particular sensitivity of Amenemope toward human dependence on the gods—a characteristic not often prominent in early Egyptian wisdom, which seemed so often to be mostly clever advice on how to get ahead by one's own efforts. Israel's sages obviously felt that much of this material would help deepen their own understanding of Yahweh's action in the world.

22:17-21: The general introduction. The New American Bible translation of these verses is quite radical. The traditional translations do not recognize "Amenemope" or "thirty" sayings, which make the connection clear. But the text of the Hebrew at these points is extremely uncertain and even corrupt. Where verse 19 has "the words of Amenemope" in the New American Bible, the Hebrew today literally reads, "I make known to you today, even to you," which makes little sense. And in verse 20, where "Thirty" stands, the Hebrew suggests "formerly," in the sense that "I wrote to you formerly." Since no one can identify when this former time was, even the ancient Jewish scholars marked this as a corrupted passage. The New American Bible has made only the slightest correction of the

Hebrew and is almost certainly the most accurate reconstruction of the original presently available. Chapter 1 of Amenemope uses almost the same wording: "Give your ears, hear what is said, give your heart to understand it . . . . Let it abide in your breast so that it may be a key to your heart. When there is a whirlwind of words, it will be a mooring-stake for your tongue." In chapter 30 of Amenemope, the author concludes: "See these thirty chapters—they entertain and instruct. They are the greatest of all books, they give knowledge to the ignorant." The Egyptian work then dedicates them to the education of the scribe, while the Hebrew adapter leaves them open for anyone to study.

The message of verses 17-21 follows the traditional methods of the wise. There is first a call to hear and listen to teachings that have been discovered and treasured already by others (see Prov 1:8; 2:1; 4:1; 5:1). This is not an invitation to go out and discover the world for oneself. There is a treasury that has been stored up and is now offered to the minds and hearts of the listeners so that they may own the entire deposit personally.

Verse 18 goes on to indicate that possession is not enough—the wisdom of these words must be communicated and acted upon. For what purpose? To trust in God. This is the ethical dimension of faith. One could be asked to believe in God through sheer faith, to obey God through the commandments, or to fear God through worship. But the author picks the word "trust," used by the psalmists again and again to express their confidence that God is a refuge, a source of strength and protection for the moment of need (Pss 9:11; 22:5; 25:2; 31:15; 52:10; 56:5; at least thirty times in all). An interesting insight into what this trust meant to ancient Israel occurs in 2 Kgs 18:19-24, where the Assyrian general belittles the citizens of Jerusalem for trusting in Yahweh over the gods of Assyria. Jer 17:5-7 presents another parallel from prophecy; the prophet challenges the people to choose: either trust in themselves and be cursed, or trust in Yahweh and be blessed. This passage breathes the spirit of wisdom!

22:22-23 First saying. Amenemope says, "Guard yourself from robbing the wretched and driving away a weak man." The context presumes a legal attempt to cheat the poor of

665

their rights. Trials were held at the city gates (Pss 69:13; 127:5; Ruth 4), where the elders would gather. Like the widow and the orphan, the poor often had few defenders (see the insights of Prov 19:4, 6, 7). But Yahweh had special concern for the poor and the weak and would fight their cause (see Pss 69:19; 103:4; 119:154).

22:24-25 Second saying. Here, too, there is a closely related saying in Amenemope: "Do not associate with the hot man, and do not approach him to converse." The hotheaded have very little control over their temper or their words. Both are anathema to the ideals of the wisdom schools.

22:26-27 Third saying. A bit of humor has been injected into an otherwise serious warning: Even the bed with you in it could go! Cautions against standing as the guarantor of a loan are frequent in Proverbs (6:1-5; 11:15; 17:18). Apparently defaults were frequent, and many friendships no doubt came to an end over bad debts. It is still a common maxim that friends should never lend one another money.

22:28 Fourth saying. This is similar to 23:10. Amenemope also warns against the practice: "Do not carry off the landmark at the boundaries of the arable land nor disturb the position of the measuring cord." Deut 19:14 and 27:17 doubly reinforce this same law for Israel. In rocky and hilly Palestine, it is an easy matter to push the boundaries around by moving the piles of rocks that serve as fences and landmarks for each family's ancestral claims. It is therefore a serious matter.

22:29 Fifth saying. The point is that a person skilled in the art of wisdom and proper behavior will go far in the royal bureaucracy. Amenemope closes with this saying: "As for the scribe who is experienced in office, he will find himself worthy to be a courtier."

23:1-3 Sixth saying. If one wants the king's favor, it is necessary to act with proper decorum and humility. This is common Egyptian advice. Ptah-hotep insists, "If you sit at the table with one greater than yourself, take what he may give when it is set before you." Amenemope suggests, "Do not eat bread before a noble, nor lay on your mouth at first." See also Sir 31:16.

23:4-5 Seventh saying. Amenemope is the source of this saying: "Cast not your heart in pursuit of wealth. They have made themselves wings like geese and are flown away to the heavens." The Hebrew author changed the unfamiliar goose to a familiar eagle, but otherwise kept the saying as is. The first line means, "while your glance flits *away from* it, it is gone."

23:6-8 Eighth saying. The "grudging man" is, literally, a man "of evil eye." This helps make sense of the saying. The meal is a metaphor for involvement with crooked planners. They are either preparing to cheat you or else you will pay a price that poisons you if you join them. Amenemope is clearer: "The property of a poor man is a block to the throat; it makes the throat vomit. If it is obtained by false oaths, his heart is perverted by his belly."

23:9 Ninth saying. Speaking advice to a fool is wasted effort. Compare Amenemope: "Empty not your belly to everybody, and thus damage the regard for yourself."

23:10-11 Tenth saying. This is similar to 22:28 and its parallel from Amenemope. Another saying of the same sage fits here also: "Guard against disturbing the boundaries of the field lest a terror carry you off." It goes on to proclaim that the god protects the land. In Israelite tradition Yahweh is the "redeemer" of the helpless (Prov 19:17; 21:23; 22:9).

23:12 Eleventh saying. This is the standard introduction to the wisdom Instruction form. It seems out of place in the middle here but may introduce a new source for many of the following sayings: *The Words of Ahiqar.* Prov 22:22–23:11 was closely dependent on Amenemope; the remaining sayings are often similar to Ahiqar, but many are independent. Ahiqar was popular among the Jews—a copy was found in the Jewish colony at Elephantine in Egypt (fifth century B.C.E.).

23:13-14 Twelfth saying. Ahiqar 81-82 is very close: "Withhold not your son from the rod or you cannot keep him from wickedness. If I smite you my son, you will not die, but if I leave you to your own heart, you [will not live]." Ignorance puts one into the grip of death's kingdom, and true life is found only in wisdom, "the fountain of life" (13:14).

23:15-16 Thirteenth saying. Again this saying makes a close link between our interior understanding and our public performance, especially in speaking. The teacher's appeal is both intellectual and emotional. Note the artistic arrangement of the two verses in a chiasm: *your—my:my—your.*

23:17-18 Fourteenth saying. There are two antitheses here: (1) the zeal for sin or the zeal for fear of the Lord; (2) a lasting future or a future without hope. The value of sin is short-lived, while fear of the Lord offers a future of blessing. God's promises of security and life will endure. A Christian can understand a fuller sense of eternal life in this passage based on the New Testament and not seen by the writer of Proverbs.

23:19-21 Fifteenth saying. This brings together a group of related vices: gluttony, drunkenness, and sloth, all of which were considered destructive of making a living. They were grave social offenses—see Deut 21:20 and prophetic denunciations in Isa 5:11-12; 28:7-9; Ezek 23:33; Amos 6:6.

23:22-23 Sixteenth saying. This and the following saying deal with the family as source of wisdom. This is sometimes called "clan wisdom," because it is passed down by parents and elders in the tribe rather than in formal schools. The language is the same as for school wisdom, however: truth, wisdom, instruction, and understanding.

23:24-25 Seventeenth saying. Many scholars would consider this to be part of the preceding saying. It moves beyond the older wisdom ideal to exalt the value of justice above everything. Note that all four lines stress the joy that being just will bring.

23:26-28 Eighteenth saying. This instruction is close in spirit to chapter 7. The theme is prominent in chapters 1–9 as the greatest danger to a young man seeking wisdom (2:16; 5:3-6; 6:24-25; 7:5-27; 9:13-18). The "pit" may be Sheol, as noted earlier (ch. 7; see also Ps 30:4), but there may be a *double entendre* here for the sexual role of the female. Hebrew poets loved puns.

23:29-35 Nineteenth saying. This is the longest of the instructions, and the most free in its format. It makes its point about the evils of alcohol by opening and closing with two vividly described scenes of the effects of heavy drinking. Much of the message is carried in rhetorical questions and answers. In fact, verses 29-30 were perhaps originally a riddle and its answer. The warning comes in verses 31-32: wine is great going down, but its effects afterwards! The image of the biting like serpents suggests its fatal results. The authors end on a note of humor that is sadly all too true. The ancients did not know of alcoholism as a disease, but they knew well its symptoms.

24:1-2 Twentieth saying. This proverb echoes Ps 37:1. It is a standard admonition with a standard reason why. Interestingly, this and the next two sayings begin with succeeding letters of the alphabet: aleph in verse 1, beth (v. 3), and ghimel (v. 5). It fails to continue further, but was there perhaps earlier a collection of twenty-two sayings in which each began with the next letter of the alphabet?

24:3-4 Twenty-first saying. Life itself is the house that is furnished by wisdom. A prosperous house is the same as a life full of honor as well as strength. See 9:1 and 14:1.

24:5-6 Twenty-second saying. Wisdom together with strength is the ideal in Israel. See Dan 1:4; 2:23; Isa 11:2, and especially the picture of David and Solomon together. David is the strong hero, and Solomon the wise ruler. Their united monarchy established the pattern of Israel's royal theology. Yahweh, however, is the model for both (see Isa 31:2; Jer 10:12; 51:15; Dan 2:20; Ps 147:5; Job 26:12). Wisdom, though, is superior to strength alone, for it guides strength toward success (see Prov 20:18). The prophets sometimes must condemn human pride in one's own wisdom and strength (see Isa 10:13; Jer 9:23; 51:57).

24:7 Twenty-third saying. The setting for this saying is the city gate, where justice was administered (see the comments on 22:22 above). The NAB translation is strange and somewhat contradictory. The Hebrew text reads more clearly: "Too high is wisdom for the fool; he is not to speak in the gate."

24:8-9 Twenty-fourth saying. The intrigue that is condemned is calculated evil, carefully planned out. A person who plans this is identified with the worst of wisdom's enemies. A literal translation of verse 9 makes the condemnation clearer: "The intrigue is sinful foolishness, and such a scoffer is an abomination to all people."

24:10-12 Twenty-fifth saying. There is some question whether verse 10 belongs with verses 11-12. But it stands as a call to action, which is given concrete application in verses 11-12 for an extreme case. The situation that the proverb writer has in mind is not absolutely certain, although it must deal with the case of an innocent person condemned. Execution was often immediate, so that if a witness knew the truth, the time to act was right away. The reference to God as the tester of hearts is discussed above (p. 663).

24:13-14 Twenty-sixth saying. Honey has always served as the natural sugar and favorite sweet of the Near East. Even today stores throughout the Arab world are filled with pastries smothered in honey. It is very high praise of wisdom to think of it as the honey of the soul.

24:15-16 Twenty-seventh saying. The two parts are not connected by logic. Verse 15 serves as a warning not to do violence against the just person. The reason given in verse 16 suggests that plotting evil soon trips up the plotter in quick ruin, while the upright bounce back from sin. It probably refers the judgment to God, who will forgive the just many times. Note the Aramaic proverb, "Seven parts for the righteous, one part for the wicked."

24:17-18 Twenty-eighth saying. Lev 19:18 commands Israelites not to bear grudges or seek vengeance against their own people. This proverb can be understood as an extension of that law. Its final line, however, gives an unexpected reason: if we do not rejoice in the enemy's downfall, God will assure that it will take place anyway. The ultimate sense must be that we are to leave retribution in God's good judgment.

24:19-20 Twenty-ninth saying. The message of this saying is similar to that of the preceding one, but it is much clearer. Do not be angered yourself nor seek after vengeance (NAB's "envious"). It is God who controls the future and extinguishes the lamp (=life) of the wicked (13:9; 20:20) or establishes it (1 Kgs 11:36; 15:4; Ps 132:17; 2 Sam 21:17—all said of David).

24:21-22 Thirtieth saying. All ancients knew the power of kings to do as they chose. Ahiqar warns his son, "Soft is the tongue of a king, but it breaks the ribs of a dragon!" An example of royal power perverted in the service of evil is found in the story of King Ahab and Naboth's vineyard in 1 Kgs 21. How much more must one fear the judgment and punishment of God!

24:23-34 An appendix: Further sayings of the wise. These twelve verses have a separate heading, indicating that they were attached to chapters 22–24 as a supplement. There are two themes: justice in the law courts and the ethic of responsible work. No special connection to

Yahweh is mentioned, and it is reasonable to assume that these are an older series of proverbs aimed at the student of wisdom in the schools. The two themes are interlocked, so that verses 23-26 deal with false judges, verse 27 with work, verses 28-29 with false witnesses in court, and verses 30-34 with laziness at work.

Society depends on both values—justice and work—for health. The false judge and the lying witness are strongly denounced by citizens because the community's basis of trust is undermined. The kiss on the lips in verse 26 was a sign of trust and friendship. The Gospels confirm how sacred was the symbol when they record that Judas betrayed Jesus with a kiss (Matt 26:48-50; Mark 14:44-45; Luke 22:47-48). Verse 29 cautions against vengeance and gives the same basic advice as verses 20-22: leave the punishment in the hands of God.

The picture of the untilled field is a sharply drawn cartoon of the lazy man. Its theme is much the same as that of 6:9-11, and the technique of education by ridicule is exactly the same as that employed in the instruction on drinking in 23:29-35.

PART IV: HEZEKIAH'S COLLECTION OF OLD PROVERBS
Prov 25:1–29:27

A second Solomonic collection

The title of this section states that officials of King Hezekiah (715–688 B.C.E.) edited and collected proverbs that stemmed from the time of Solomon (or from Solomon himself or from the royal schools founded by him!). Two aspects can be noted from the start. One is that many of the proverbs repeat those in the earlier collection of chapters 10–22. Compare, for example, 25:24 and 21:9; 26:15 and 19:24; 27:12 and 22:3; 28:19 and 12:11; 29:3 and 10:1. The second is that the connection to Yahweh is rarely made. Chapter 25 mentions God once, chapter 28 twice, chapter 29 three times, chapters 26 and 27 not at all. The first three chapters are good examples of older secular wisdom, while the last two provide somewhat more direct reflections on Israelite piety.

25:1-28 An Egyptian-style instruction. It has been shown that this chapter is based on an Egyptian model of instructions for a king and his subjects. It is a mixture of admonitions and practical sayings about life. But it has a clear structure. There is an introduction in verses 2-5 stating the role of the king (vv. 2-3) and then that of the wicked who threaten the king's rule (vv. 4-5). This is followed by an extended section on the king (vv. 6-15) and then on the wicked (vv. 16-26). Each part has six units. A general statement concludes the section (vv. 27-28). The chapter is thought to be a product of the royal schools because of its high regard for the king and for loyal obedience by subjects. It contains very few of the important words that occur regularly in chapters 10–22. This probably indicates that this chapter was edited earlier than chapters 10–22.

This royal instruction opens in verses 2-3 with praise for the special divine favor shown to kings. Kings were invested with greater wisdom than ordinary mortals (see 1 Kgs 3) and were subject only to the vastly greater wisdom of the gods. Ancient kings saw themselves as delegated by the god to govern the divine kingdom on earth. And yet, as verses 4-5 make clear, evil tolerated or allowed to gain power will destroy the blessing from the gods.

The advice in verses 6-15 on how to act before a king and how to speak as a diplomat is generally quite practical if we keep in mind that the student of the scribal school is to master the *art* of speaking well. Verse 6 becomes a parable of Jesus on places of honor at table (Luke 14:7-11). Verse 14 could be summarized as "all talk, no action" in modern idiom. Verse 15 recalls the saying of Ahiqar that a king's speech is soft but is also sharper than a sword and stronger than a club that breaks ribs (see also Prov 15:18).

The more general advice in verses 6-16 concentrates on the contrast between moderation combined with self-control (vv. 16, 17, 21, 22, 25, 27, 28) and the destructive effects of disorder (false witnesses, v. 18; unreliability, v. 19; grief, v. 20; backbiting, v. 23; and weak resolve, v. 26). Verses 21-22 propose treating enemies with kindness as a way of putting them to shame and, by means of the image of coals, to "burn" the lesson into them. It may sound anything but altruistic in spirit, but it is a practical way of reducing the bitter violence that hatred causes. Some schol-

ars would soften the picture a little by translating the first part of verse 22 as "live coals you will *take from* his head."

In verse 28, the New American Bible has "feelings" for the Hebrew *ruah*, "spirit." Someone's spirit is the power of life in "the image and likeness of God" (Gen 1:27; see Ezek 37:1-14). Evil will easily overcome the person whose spirit has not been trained in the moderation and self-control proposed by the wisdom teachers.

26:1-28. There is no specifically religious content in chapter 26. It can be divided into three major topics: the fool (vv. 1-12, using the strong Hebrew sense of the "stupid one"); the lazy person (vv. 13-16); and evil speech (vv. 17-28).

Generally, the wisdom position on the fool can be stated simply: to deal with the fool seriously makes one a fool in turn. Wisdom is perverted by the fool, who does not understand the value of good order, logical thinking, self-control, or self-denial for a larger good. The fool thinks only of what he or she can get right now and interprets everything in that selfish light. The result is a totally unbridled person, badly in need of severe disciplining to get back on the way of social responsibility (v. 3). The opposite advice in verses 4-5 shows the difficulty involved in dialogue with fools. They do not learn, and their speaking endangers all around them. The fool cannot be taught and cannot be corrected, and all who attempt it come to grief themselves (v. 10). Verse 11 illustrates the point graphically and is later quoted by 2 Pet 2:22 in the New Testament.

Verses 13-16 gather together another small section on the lazy. Verse 13 repeats 22:13; verse 15 repeats 19:24; verse 14 is similar in theme to 24:33. Thus these are not a new series of ideas. The attention to laziness was popular among the wise, and there were probably two independent collections that used the same sayings.

The remainder of the chapter deals with the harmful effects of speech wrongly used. It is focused on hypocrisy and deceptive words. A surface seriousness conceals evil intentions in the heart of the speaker. Like glaze on the surface of a pot that has never been fired (and thus is likely to break easily), smooth words conceal much deception that will shortly bring the trusting listener to disaster or loss. Verse 26 suggests that such hidden evil is found out by observing the religious practice of the individual. Verse 27 expresses the traditional Israelite conviction that evil brings evil on itself (the plots of both Daniel and Esther are examples).

27:1-27. The advice covers the full range of wisdom concerns, and the individual sayings are not grouped by themes that can be easily identified. Friendship and neighbors appear the most frequently (vv. 5, 6, 8, 10, 14, 16, 19). Verses 23-27 form a single extended image of agrarian life.

The chapter opens with a saying similar to one in Amenemope, "Man does not know what the morrow is like." A parable of Jesus about the rich man who filled his barns and then died the same night makes the same point (Luke 12:16-21). Verses 3 and 7 both echo imagery used in the words of Ahiqar, "I have lifted sand and carried salt, but there is nothing heavier than debt," and "hunger sweetens what is bitter." While Prov 27 certainly does not use the images identically, it does reflect the influence of international wisdom.

Friendship is extolled when it is frankly honest. Correction and learning can only come from a forthright "telling it like it is" in contrast to the flatterer or liar. The New American Bible translation has lost the analogy of friendship in verse 9 by suggesting the word "grief." The second half of the verse more properly reads, "and the sweetness of friends (is better) than perfumed wood." A friend is valued because he or she is close at hand and presumably concerned enough to give help and support.

Other practical advice warns against anger and jealousy (v. 4), loans to strangers who may leave the country without repaying (v. 13), and excessive curiosity (v. 20), which can be as greedy as death itself, never allowing even one victim to go free from its hold. Finally, verses 23-27 draw for us an ideal farming community that is self-sufficient. Such pastoral imagery occurs occasionally in Proverbs and reflects the predominant occupations of farming and herding. But most of its advice is directed to the urban professional class found in palaces, schools, temples, law courts, and civil government. This reminds us that Israel was also an important trading nation that carried on commerce throughout the Mediterranean world and needed large numbers of ex-perts trained in language and diplomacy, and possessing economic and mathematical skills to work out business transactions. This merchant-orientation of Proverbs also explains the insistence on just weights and honest speech free from any hint of fraud or deceit in negotiations. International trust depended on it.

28:1-28. Although Yahweh is mentioned only in verses 5 and 25, the majority of the proverbs in chapter 28 reflect a very developed piety and morality built around the concepts of care for the poor and obedience to the law. The chapter opens with another saying on the just versus the wicked. Poverty is not extolled as a good, but it is far better to be poor and have integrity than fall prey to the temptations of greed that plague the wealthy, who always seem to crave more.

The major development of this theme is seen in verses 3, 6, 8, 11, 20, 22, 25, 27. Wealth may be a sign of both divine blessing and of industrious behavior (vv. 19-20); it is only greed that runs over others that is condemned. This is not, however, merely a late piety speaking. Care for the poor is the foundation of a king's throne, and a nation without justice will fall. This belief is reflected in all ancient societies around Israel as well. Compare the words of Esarhaddon, king of Assyria (681–669 B.C.E.), explaining why Babylon fell to his armies and was destroyed: "They [the citizens] oppressed the weak and gave him into the power of the strong. Inside the city there was tyranny, the receiving of bribes; each day without fail they plundered each other's goods . . . Marduk, the Enlil of the gods, was angry and devised evil to overwhelm the land and destroy the peoples."

The defense against such rampant injustice, according to the authors of this chapter, is faithfulness to the law (vv. 4, 7, 9). The law of Moses is closely associated with the ideal of justice (see Exod 21; Lev 19; Deut 14–15; Ps 119:142). Thus the common wisdom of ancient nations is given a specifically Israelite framework for putting it into pratice.

Another mark of human wisdom subjected to worship is the concern of verse 13 that everyone needs mercy for sins committed. It can be achieved by an open admission of guilt to God. The Babylonians also recognized the value of confession but were not as confident that it always worked. Verse 26 can be taken as a summary of the Israelite point of view. Humans cannot be truly wise if they trust only in themselves. There are too many evils catalogued in these sayings—fraud (v. 24), greed (vv. 22, 25), flattery (v. 23), and partiality (v. 21)—that will lead them astray. All of them result from pride, and the only safeguard is humble submission to Yahweh (see also 29:23).

29:1-27. Many of the sayings in chapter 29 deal with two themes: the king (vv. 1, 2, 3, 4, 12, 14, 16, 26) and the need for disciplined learning (vv. 15, 17, 19, 21). A subtheme, related to these two, deals with the passion of anger and its subsequent loss of self-control. Much of the wisdom language of Prov 1-9 and 10-22 returns in this chapter: the just, the wicked, the wise, the fool, the upright, and the arrogant, as well as justice, correction, and rebuke. It is the best of old wisdom organized around Yahweh, who gives blessing and life to every individual *equally* (vv. 13, 26).

The proverbs in verses 8-11 center on the wise as peacemakers in the community, and verses 17-22 stress aspects of speaking according to wise training. Verses 13-14 return to the theme of the poor (see chapter 28). Verse 13 in particular reminds one of Jesus' saying, "The sun rises on the evil and the good alike" (Matt 5:45). It is also close to Prov 14:31; 17:5; 22:2. Verse 14 on the responsibility of the king toward the poor is very much like the demands of Psalm 72 and reflects the Israelite ideal of kingship (see the earlier discussion on Prov 15:1-33, p. 660, and the Ugaritic text of *King Keret* quoted there).

Discipline is praised as the means to guide a person on the way of the just. The strong statement on the value of physical beating in verse 15 is based on the need to check our personal urges until we have had a chance to examine and question what we should do. This is the method of the wisdom tradition.

Verse 27 closes this fourth collection of materials with the unmistakable assertion that there can be no compromise between the way of the wicked and the way of uprightness. In this, wisdom is completely equated with moral behavior.

PART V: THE WORDS OF AGUR AND LEMUEL
Prov 30:1–31:31

30:1-9. These nine verses are a single unit attributed to Agur, the son of Jakeh, who is otherwise unknown. If, as the New American Bible translates, he is from Massa, it suggests wisdom from the East beyond Edom. Gen 25:14 identifies Massa as an area in northern Arabia. Edom itself, another north Arabian neighbor, was famed for its wisdom in biblical tradition (see Jer 49:7; Obad 8). However, many scholars doubt that this Massa is meant. The Hebrew word also means "oracle," and is closely followed here by a standard prophetic formula, "The pronouncement (of the Lord)." The second part of verse 1 is also very difficult. It may mean either "I have no God" or "who has no God." Some propose another sense, "one who wearies himself about God." The only translation that is certainly not correct is the traditional literal rendering of the Hebrew, "The man says to Ithiel, to Ithiel and Ucal." Such names are unknown and make no sense in this context.

The meaning of the whole passage, however, is not in doubt. Human knowledge is nothing compared with that of God. It is the same message as Isa 40:12-18, prophetic in spirit, challenging the hearer to learn humility before the mystery of God's transcendence (v. 4). God's word is always to be trusted and stands without need of any help from us. The thought echoes the orthodox defense of the divine word found in Ps 18:30 or Deut 4:2. It concludes in verses 7-9 with a double wish: that God may guard the author both from a lying tongue and from want, so that there will not be any temptation to destroy his or her trust in God's powerful care.

Numerical proverbs in 30:10-33. Most of these verses are in the form of comparisons or riddles. The formula for the riddle is the use of succeeding numbers, "three things and four," or just a set number, "four things there are . . . ." Recall the old English riddle: "Four stiff-standers, four dilly-danders, two lookers, two crookers, and a wig-wag." The answer is a *cow*, and it is gotten by making a relationship between the five descriptive comparisons. Though Proverbs does not ask us to guess the answers, it does force us to figure out what the four given elements have in common in the five examples: vv. 15-17, 18-19, 21-23, 24-28, 29-33. Riddles are fun but also educational, and they help train students in the use of analogy.

30:10-14. The New American Bible places the end of Agur's reflections at verse 6; other scholars see it continuing to verse 10. The answer is according to taste. The slander mentioned in verse 10 may be connected to the lying in verse 8, or else it may introduce the groups named in verses 11-14 who do harm by what they say. Since verses 11-14 belong together as four examples of those who destroy the spirit of trust in a community, verse 10 may be a later addition placed next to verse 11 because it also mentions cursing. Probably the four lines were introduced by a formula similar to the ones that follow: "Three groups, yes, four I disdain" (or something like it). This grouping shows strong overtones of condemnation and is not merely a casual observation of behavior.

30:15-16. An independent saying about the leech introduces this first real numerical proverb. The common element in both this saying and the four examples is an unlimited desire for more—greed. Since the focus in these riddles is on human behavior, the key comparison is not in the images from nature, but the example of the barren womb and what it says about longing for parenthood.

30:17. This short saying returns us to verse 11 and thus rounds out the whole section from verses 10-17. The overall theme has been selfish greed, and its worst form leads to rejection of respect for parents. The law in Exod 21:17 and Lev 20:9 is just as strong!

30:18-20. The key to this comparison is in the mystery of how a thing happens, especially the mystery of love between a man and a woman. Some hold that seduction is the issue, but that would make the comparisons meaningless. Others think it is the attraction of forbidden sex because of verse 20. But that is an addition from later intended as a warning against allowing lust to overcome love.

30:21-23. The four objects of comparison in this riddle are all human stereotypes of arrogance. In a sense they are the standard cast of characters from comedy shows, and more than a little humor is intended here. Each one represents the Peter Principle at its worst—someone who has gone way past ability and

makes up for incompetence by being overbearing.

30:24-28. In contrast to the preceding, the images in this saying are all from the animal world. The ant is famed for its industry, the badger for its tenacity, the locust for its disciplined mass migrations, and the lizard for its resourcefulness under any conditions. Naturally, the lesson of how these weak creatures succeed so well is intended for the human audience.

30:29-31. The Hebrew text is difficult in these verses and so translations differ. The combination of three proud beasts and a human king fits the pattern of verses 18-19, so that the translation in the New American Bible is probably correct. The message is not profound, but it represents well the ancient experience of kings and their splendor.

30:32-33. This summarizes the riddle collection. The major theme has been pride and proneness to easy anger when others disagree. The reader is warned against both by the prophetic tone of the chapter.

31:1 The words of Lemuel. The label in 31:1 presents the same problem as 30:1. Does "Massa" mean an Arab place name or does it mean "oracle"? The New American Bible fudges here by translating it both ways, "king of Massa" and "The advice." At least the sense is not lost by preserving both! A second problem is whether this heading covers both verses 1-9 and 10-31. Most scholars would consider the poem on the ideal woman to be a separate piece attached at the end as a kind of conclusion to the whole Book of Proverbs. This is discussed below.

31:1-9. This piece is written in the traditional Instruction genre for royal officials. Probably the person of Lemuel is a fiction to give weight to the advice that follows. Under the cover of the education of the king-to-be, the author presents practical guidelines for a prudent and wise life. The fact that it is called a mother's advice probably underscores that what is taught here was reckoned as traditional family or clan wisdom. On the other hand, it may indicate a Judean origin in the royal schools. From the Book of Kings we know that the queen-mother was an important position in the royal administration of the southern kingdom (1 Kgs 14:21; 15:2; 1 Kgs 11:1-16).

The lesson comes with three commands:

restrain your sexual appetite, do not become the victim of drink, respect the rights of the poor by doing justice. The first probably refers to harem intrigues—many kings have fallen or been assassinated because of strife that began in the jealousies of the palace. Wine, too, undoes all of the self-control and discipline that wisdom teaches (see 23:29-35). Israel itself records a fanatical group, the Rechabites, who opposed all drinking of wine (see 2 Kgs 9 and Jer 35). But the most important teaching is last. The king represents justice in the land and must be the final refuge and appeal of the poor against corrupt officials. See the earlier discussion at 16:10-15; 28:1-28 and 29:1-27.

31:10-33. Proverbs ends with this acrostic poem of twenty-two lines (each line beginning with the next letter of the Hebrew alphabet). This makes it a highly artistic creation, and more impressionistic perhaps than strictly logical in its order of thought. The good wife has been an important theme throughout Proverbs (11:16; 12:4; 18:22; 19:14), and so it is not surprising that the book should end with the example of a woman as the ideal wise person. In some ways the litany of good qualities resembles the traditional marriage song in praise of the bride, an example of which is found in Song of Songs 7:1-10. These marriage songs describe the physical beauty of the woman from head to foot to show that her beauty is complete. Here it is her wisdom and good management that are complete.

In light, however, of the themes found in chapters 1–9 on Lady Wisdom versus the adulterous woman or the foolish woman, it is probably better to see in this passage more than a picture of the perfect wife. She is wisdom in action—the model of self-control, prudence, understanding, and just behavior. Even more particularly, it is the wisdom who called out at the city gates for people to listen (1:21; 8:3), and wisdom that was manifest in fear of the Lord (1:7; 9:10), just as this woman is marked by fear of the Lord and her praises sung in the city gates (31:30-31). The husband can be identified with the young man of chapters 1–9 who heeds wisdom's call. As a result, he is a man of stature and respect in the community.

The poem opens with a stanza describing how much a man depends on a good wife for prosperity (vv. 10-12). The remaining verses then alternate between her ability as a business woman and her prudent care of her own family. It may seem strange that a woman is praised for her commercial dealings, since this is an area reserved to men in the Old Testament (except for the rare case of a queen in power—for example, the queen of Sheba in 1 Kgs 10). But we should understand "commerce" in verses 13, 14, 16, and 24 as a metaphor for wisdom. The international exchange of wisdom throughout the Ancient Near East is aptly portrayed as a commercial transaction. Israel buys only the best of what will fit its own theology. The search, however, often leads to far places.

An Arab proverb states, "A clever woman is never without wool." This ideal woman is prepared; she is the opposite of the fool or lazy person. She "delights" in her primary responsibility to her family, working late at night, creating things by the skills she has mastered, seeing needs ahead of time. Making clothes is the chief metaphor of such practical wisdom. The clothes cover the body and give it shape, protection, and a liveliness in the same way that wisdom forms, guards, and enriches the mind and spirit. Moreover, verses 23 and 25 promise that the reward of a marriage to wisdom will be respect and honor—the same "weight" mentioned in other proverbs (11:16; 21:21; 22:4; 29:23). The reference to the city gates in verse 23 emphasizes the judicial role of the husband in settling disputes.

The woman's teaching consists of wisdom and mercy ("kindly counsel" in verse 26). It excels all other virtues that one can strive to obtain (v. 29), and may well combine the ideals of prophet and wise person into one, since "mercy" is the central concept of the covenant theology of the prophets. If we can push this mere hint that far, chapter 31 would correspond nicely to the mix of teaching and prophetic exhortation found in chapters 1 and 9, so that the beginning and end balance one another. Then the children and the husband of the ideal woman represent the disciples of wisdom, who have accepted as one the teachings of the law, the prophets, and the wisdom books.

Although the passage most certainly has Lady Wisdom in mind, we must not forget that it also gives a real example of womanly ability and achievement. Rather than being just another passage describing the submissive wife in the ancient world, it reveals the remarkably even-handed approach of Proverbs that recognizes wisdom where it is found—in men and women alike.

JOB

Michael D. Guinan, O.F.M.

INTRODUCTION

One of the most basic characteristics of being human is the capacity to sense injustice and to fight against it. We experience something as unfair and are willing to stand up and say so; we put ourselves on the line rather than submit. The biblical Book of Job is an expression of just such a capacity and just such a stand. Throughout the centuries many have found in it an eloquent presentation of their own pains and sufferings as they have struggled to understand the justice of God in the face of their own broken experience. (In scholarly circles, such an undertaking is known as "theodicy.") To study the history of the interpretation of Job is almost as revealing of human experience as to study the book itself.

The problem is, of course, nothing new. Some of the oldest literature we know from the ancient Near East, from Sumer, wrestles with this question of the suffering of the innocent. In addition, several treatises along similar lines have come down to us from both Mesopotamia and Egypt. As beautiful a voice as it is, then, Job's is not a solo voice but soars over a surging chorus.

When the Book of Job joined the chorus is not an easy question. Scholars have generally been inclined to locate it in the context of the Babylonian Exile. Some would see it more in the struggles and confusion leading up to the destruction of Judah and Jerusalem in 587 B.C.E. Others locate it in the search for meaning and soul-searching during the time of the Exile itself. Still others place it after the Exile in the Persian period (after 538 B.C.E.), reflecting back on the trauma and chaos recently survived. While full certainty about the dating may be elusive, we must admit that the book has such a universal quality to it that ultimately the dating question may not be of great importance.

The question of dating is not the only problematic aspect of this book. Its readers and interpreters face difficulties on almost every page. It may be helpful to sort these difficulties into two broad clusters: (1) difficulties arising from the book itself; and (2) difficulties arising from its social and religious background. In short, we face problems of text and context.

Difficulties arising from the text

The first problem is the received Hebrew text itself. It is very corrupt, many passages being practically unintelligible. Compounding this is the vocabulary of the book. As very elevated poetry, it abounds in rich and diverse expressions, rare words, and words occurring only once in the Bible. Some scholars have even suggested that the composer of Job made up words to convey multiple levels of meaning. All of this means that Job is an exceptionally difficult book to translate. Recourse is often had to the related Semitic languages—Aramaic, Arabic and Ugaritic—in an attempt to elucidate obscure passages. A comparison of modern translations would prove interesting in this regard. A glance at ancient translations (for example, the Greek or Aramaic) assures us that they faced the same basic problems that we do today.

When we move to the next level, that of literary history and composition, problems again abound. A prose, narrative prologue and epilogue encase a long poetic dialogue between Job and his friends. Was the prose story originally older and separate? There seem to be three cycles of speeches between Job and the three friends, but the third cycle is in considerable disarray. How is this to be sorted out? Are the wisdom hymn in chapter 28 and the Elihu speeches (chs. 32–37) original or later additions? Scholars dispute these and many other points of detail. We will be concerned primarily with the Book of Job as we have it and with the translation of the New American Bible (NAB). While at times we will have to refer to disputed points, they will not loom large in our commentary.

A third type of problem involves the overall meaning of the book. It does not seem to answer nor deal directly with the questions Job raises. We will defer our discussion of this until the end of our commentary, until after we have read and studied our way through the book.

Difficulties arising from the context

The Book of Job was written about 2500 years ago within the context of Israelite culture and religion. We can well imagine that ancient Israelites, reading or hearing the story, would respond from within that context and would pick up overtones and undertones that escape us as inhabitants of another space, time, and thought world. While we can never expect to carry ourselves back in such a way as to catch all the nuances, we can discern certain broad aspects of the ancient culture and religion that can help us to situate ourselves and to begin to bridge the culture gap. Here we would highlight three elements of both the cultural and the religious contexts of Job.

Cultural

1) Job lives within a *tribal* culture. He is the patriarch of the tribe and is concerned about its needs, namely its growth, in terms of both his own descendants and his land, possessions, and prosperity. Family ties are close, and he can expect to live on (at this time the Israelites did not have any concept of a life after death) in the presence of his descendants and in their memory.

2) The tribal culture is also an *oral* one. Communication and education depend primarily on the spoken word; it is this that ties society together. As the exchange between Job and his friends heats up, the rhetoric will become more bombastic, even insulting. This is consonant with an oral culture in which the important thing is not simply *that* something be said but also *how* it is said. *What* people say looms very, very large as well, and this leads directly to our third trait.

3) The tribal, oral culture is predominately a *shame* culture. In such a context honor and shame are pivotal values, if not *the* pivotal values. A good name or reputation carries weight and makes one honorable (the Hebrew word for "honor," in fact, means basically "to have weight"). That Job seems to be in the wrong, and is called such by his friends, would have been in itself a source of great suffering and affliction. It is important not only to be right and just but to be recognized as such by others. While such a position may seem strange to us, for whom "being honest" and "doing your own thing" are so important, many other parts of our globe, such as the Mediterranean cultures (Spain, Italy, Greece, the Arab countries) and the Asian cultures of the Far East, still largely convey an honor-shame value system.

Religious

1) According to Jer 18:18, three sources of religious leadership and guidance were available to ancient Israel: the law of the priest, the word of the prophet, and the counsel of the wise. It is to this third category that the Book of Job belongs. It speaks from the context of *the wise* and *wisdom theology*. For our purposes, two aspects of wisdom thought may be singled out: (a) Wisdom depends on and speaks from experience. It is in the everyday happenings of our lives and in our reflection on them—expressed most characteristically in proverbial form—that we find wisdom and God's teaching. (b) According to the common teaching of wisdom, wise, righteous living should, generally speaking, bring with it the rewards of fuller life, especially offspring and prosperity. It is precisely Job's experience (a) which seriously calls the doctrine (b) into question.

2) In presenting Job's argument with God, the Book of Job draws heavily on *legal imagery*. If someone had a complaint against another, that person would first try to settle the issue informally. If this failed, the defendant swore an oath of innocence and appealed to a third party, a judge, who would call on the accuser to present evidence. Legal language abounds as Job protests his innocence and calls for some third party to stand with him (for example, 9:33; 16:19; 19:25).

3) In addition to wisdom themes and legal expressions, the Book of Job is situated within the context and language of *lamentation*. In times of distress and affliction, Israel poured out its lament before the Lord. Lamentation is the spontaneous response to the presence of the realm of death, in whatever manifestation of brokenness, in our lives. It is a loud, religious "Ouch!" When we stub our toe, we cry out in pain; when something in our experience stubs our "religious toe," we lament. Lamentation is present throughout the Bible (the Book of Lamentations, Jeremiah, many of the psalms), but it is something we today have lost touch with and may need to rediscover. We will return to this at the end of our study.

These elements of culture and religion obviously overlap and influence each other. Thus, Job suffers the loss of his family and possessions; he seems to be unrighteous, a conclusion his friends quickly draw. In his shame he pours out his lament to God and calls on God for a hearing that will acknowledge his innocence for all to see. At various points in our commentary we will refer back to these issues.

Outline of the book

The following general outline may guide us as we work our way through the Book of Job:

I. *The Prologue (1:1–2:13)*
There is a wager in heaven and the just Job is despoiled of everything. Three friends arrive to console him.

II. *The Poetic Dialogue (3:1–31:40)*
After Job bitterly laments his lot, the three friends rise to God's defense. They argue back and forth through three cycles of speeches until Job ends with a fervent oath of innocence.

III. *The Elihu Speeches (32:1–37:24)*
A brash youth interrupts and manages to say little that is new or helpful.

IV. *The Yahweh Speeches (38:1–42:6)*
Yahweh finally responds in two long speeches and overwhelms Job into silence.

V. *Epilogue (42:7-17)*
Job's fortunes are restored and they all live happily ever after.

COMMENTARY

I. PROLOGUE

Job 1:1–2:13

A prose prologue in five scenes, alternating between earth and heaven, opens the book, sets the stage, and introduces the characters. From a calm and happy beginning, the action moves quickly, ending in suffering, tension, and confusion.

1:1-5 Scene one: Earth. We meet "a man" (the first word in the Hebrew text) whose name is Job. Although the name was not uncommon in the ancient Near East, its precise meaning is uncertain. The best guess—"where is [my] Father [God]?"—is appropriate but almost certainly coincidental. The figure of Job seems rather to be an old legendary hero of faith (see Ezek 14:14, 20). Uz is certainly located in the broad territory east of the Jordan River, but whether it is in the more northerly Aramean region or the more southerly area of Edom is hard to determine. At any rate, Job is presented as a non-Israelite.

More important, this man is a model of upright and virtuous living. His "fear of God" refers not to a servile emotion but to a response of obedient faith (see Deut 10:12). Within the context of wisdom theology, the fear of God is also the beginning and the essence of wisdom (Job 28:28; Prov 1:7; 9:10) and usually brings with it prosperity and a full life (see Prov 3:13-18). Job is thus blessed with seven sons and three daughters, an abundance of livestock, and male and female slaves (better than NAB's "work animals").

Job's righteousness is highlighted even further. On the chance that one of his children, in the midst of their periodic family celebrations, might have sinned and cursed God, Job intercedes for his loved ones and sacrifices whole-burnt offerings on their behalf. This rosy, idyllic situation is about to end.

1:6-12 Scene two: Heaven. Yahweh (NAB: "the Lord"), like an Oriental monarch holding court, is surrounded by the "sons of God." In ancient mythology these were originally lesser divine beings, but in the Bible they are demoted to the status of servants and attendants of Yahweh (see 1 Kgs 22:19-23). To imagine them as angels, in the sense of later Christian theology, is surely an anachronism. Among them is the Satan. This is not a proper name, as in the same later Christian theology, but rather describes an office and a function: "the adversary." He seems to have been God's CIA agent checking up on things around the world. We, the readers, are aware of Job's integrity; now we learn that God is also aware of it, and in fact takes pride in Job (v. 8). The Satan is skeptical and, in front of the whole heavenly court, suggests that Job is virtuous simply because he gets something out of it. If Job were to lose all these blessings, what would he say then? He would flagrantly curse God. In the context of a shame culture, Yahweh's honor is now involved and has a stake in the outcome. The Satan is allowed to put Job to the test, something he hastens to do.

1:13-22 Scene three: Earth. In quick succession, four messengers rush in reporting disaster. Job's blessings of scene one are stripped away—first his livestock, then his slaves, finally his children. Forces of destruction both human (Sabeans and Chaldeans) and natural (lightning and whirlwind) are let loose by Satan, reducing Job's cosmos to chaos. With dramatic gestures typical of lamentation and mourning, Job tears his garments (see, for example, Gen 37:29, 34), shaves his head (see Isa 15:2; Jer 7:29), and casts himself to the earth from which he was taken and to which he will return. The Satan, however, is frustrated in his hopes. When Job opens his lips to speak, he utters what seems almost a religious proverb and blesses God. He does not say anything to bring shame to God.

2:1-6 Scene four: Heaven. The scene quickly changes; the heavenly court is again in session. God, almost chuckling, is enjoying the vindication of both God's servant and God's honor. Verse 3b is important because it further confirms what we already know—and what Job will staunchly maintain throughout the book: there is no connection between Job's virtuous life and his sufferings. The Satan replies with a proverb so terse (three words in both Hebrew and English) that its meaning almost completely eludes us. It seems to suggest some sort of trade-off. Job has blessed God, it would seem, only in order to protect his own life. If Job's person is attacked as well, he will surely curse God. Thus Job falls into the power of the Satan, who rushes out to do his dirty work.

2:7-13 Scene five: Earth. Job is immediately struck with a repulsive disease whose poetic description, both here and elsewhere in the book (7:5; 19:17, 20), will not yield to more precise medical diagnosis. His wife enters the stage, delivers her one line, and then disappears into the wings, thus creating a vacuum that later tradition would fill by giving her both a name (Sitis) and a more prominent place. Job reproves her for speaking "as senseless women do" (v. 10). He is not implying that women as such are foolish; biblical wisdom recognizes and praises wise women (Prov 31:10-31; Judg 5:29; 2 Sam 14:1-20). In this instance, his wife has offered foolish advice. Folly, the opposite of wisdom (Prov 9:1-12, 13-18), describes primarily the behavioral failure to recognize, speak, and do the right thing at the right time. As such, folly contributes to the breakdown of social and cosmic unity and harmony that God, through wisdom, calls all of us to foster and manifest. Job does not yield to the temptation to speak foolishness. As the Hebrew text says, "in all this, he did not sin with his lips" (v. 10).

Three friends (there is no basis for the later belief that they were kings) hear of Job's plight and gather from their distant homelands, which cannot be identified with certainty. Moved by genuine compassion, they come to offer comfort and consolation, but the sight of his condition, so radically changed, moves them too to traditional expressions of lamentation (see 1:20 above; also Josh 7:16; 1 Sam 4:12). They sit with him in the dust and speak perhaps the wisest consolation, their silence.

And so the prologue ends. Job is left, "a man" now literally on the earth, and God, who dwells in heaven, looks down. How will these two, in their two places, relate and interact? The Satan has loomed large, using natural phenomena, marauders, physical disease, and Job's wife to get him to curse God, to "sin with his lips" (1:11, 22; 2:5, 9, 10). With his failure, the Satan too disappears into the wings; in what follows, his work will be furthered by Job's friends, until now silent. We, the readers, and God know that Job is in fact completely innocent. The issue at stake is: What will Job say? The audience, the listeners—God, the friends, the readers—wait in anticipation. We do not have long to wait.

II. JOB'S MONOLOGUE: LAMENTATION

Job 3:1-26

The proverbial "patience of Job" comes to a dramatic end, never to reappear. So far Job's responses to his various afflictions have manifested a dangerous conflict between his actions (grief and mourning) and his words (praise of God). This dichotomy is now resolved: his words and actions agree as he pours out his lamentation, to no one and to everyone.

Lamentation, as we noted above, is the spontaneous cry of pain when our lives are overwhelmed by chaos, brokenness, and confusion. The common ancient Near Eastern mythology dealt with this struggle between order and chaos, life and death. Chaos is there symbolized in two ways: (1) as a sea monster, variously called Sea, Rahab, Leviathan, the twisting serpent. The storm god (in Canaan, Ba'al) defeats Sea, tramples it in victory, and then reigns/rains life and fertility from his palace in heaven until the arrival of his other foe; (2) as death, manifested in the hot, dry summer and the barren wilderness. There is no rain and everything dies. Ba'al dies, only to revive with the coming of the fall rains, which usually bring life and fertility for another year. Since language borrowed from this mythic complex recurs in the Book of Job (7:12; 9:8, 13; 26:12), it would be well to keep this in mind.

3:3-10 Curse the day and night. Job does not curse God but rather the day of his birth and the night of his conception (v. 3b, better translated: "the night when they said, 'A man is conceived!'"). In language which reverses that of the Genesis creation account (Gen 1:1–2:4), he prays that the day become night, and the night be wiped out of the calendar. In his affliction, Jeremiah expressed a similar wish (Jer 20:14-18). The translation and meaning of verse 8 are obscure. Since Leviathan was thought to cause eclipses by swallowing the sun, this would fit the context of Job's prayer for darkness.

3:11-19 Longing for death. The struggle between light and darkness was part of the cosmic struggle between order (life) and chaos (death). Job has prayed for darkness; now he prays for death: "I wish my womb had become my tomb!" Two common features of lamentation appear: (1) the repeated question

"Why?" (see Pss 22:2; 43:10; 43:2). While this implies, "I do not understand," it is a cry of pain rather than a request for theological or scientific explanation; (2) the focus on "I" (see Ps 77:1-6). In the face of intense suffering, it is hard to look outside oneself. Job looks to death, in which all are equal (vv. 14-19), to bring him tranquility and rest.

3:20-26 Deliver me from God! The "bitter in spirit" (v. 20) refers more probably to profuse weeping. The expression in Hebrew is literally "bitter of throat" and reflects the belief that in times of great distress, the intestines put pressure on the liver and heart, breaking them down ("broken-hearted") and turning them to liquid, which passes through the throat, leaving a bitter taste, and then exits the eyes as tears.

The question "Why?" recurs for those "whose path is hidden from them" (v. 23a). Verse 23b shows a strong ironic twist. In 1:10 the Satan had accused God of "surrounding" Job with blessings; here Job uses the same word to describe his being "hemmed in" by God. For ancient Israel, Yahweh was the God who had delivered them from death; here, in a statement of great irony, Job prays for death to deliver him, the servant (v. 19; see 1:8; 2:3), from God, the taskmaster (vv. 18-19).

III. FIRST ROUND OF SPEECHES

Job 4:1–14:22

Shocked by Job's lament and moved to answer his repeated "whys," the friends abandon their wise silence (see 13:5). It is difficult to characterize the chapters that follow. Discussion? Debate? Dialogue? Perhaps "speech" is helpful, if we think of politicians less interested in really responding to arguments point by point and more interested in playing to an audience and scoring points that way. We, the readers/hearers, are the audience.

The speeches are given roughly through three rounds: (1) 4:1–14:22; (2) 15:1–21:34; (3) 22:1–27:21. In the first two, each of the friends speaks, and Job responds, usually at greater length; the third round is in some disarray, perhaps the result of textual confusion.

4:1–5:26 Eliphaz's first speech. Beginning politely enough, Eliphaz suggests that the "instruction" (an important word in Old Testament wisdom circles) Job has offered to others in the past should not be forgotten now when Job is in need (4:2-5). After alluding to Job's general uprightness of life ("piety" and "integrity" in verse 6 reflect the Hebrew words translated "fear of the Lord" and "blamelessness" in 1:1, 8; 2:3), Eliphaz makes his first main point. Based on experience ("Reflect now" . . . "As I see it"), he affirms the doctrine of retribution: the innocent do not perish (4:7). Only those reap mischief who have previously sown it (4:8). In proverbial fashion (see Prov 28:15; also Pss 17:12; 22:14, 21), the wicked, like the lion, may make a big noise, but in the end they are cut down and their families left destitute.

In remarkable fashion, Eliphaz appeals next, not to wisdom experience, but to a special vision; the eerie description might best fit a nightmare. Preceded by fear and shuddering, a wind blows over his face (a better translation than "a spirit passed before me") causing him to shudder (4:15). He peeks out and perceives *ein Etwas*, a vague something. And then a voice that makes Eliphaz's second, fairly platitudinous point: All humans are sinful; none are blameless! The reference to the imperfections of God's servants and messengers in verse 18 has nothing to do with the later theory of good and bad angels. If the members of God's own court are not blameless, how much less blameless are human beings, creatures of clay who perish quickly without ever knowing wisdom! Eliphaz does not pursue the implications of this last phrase for himself and his own theory. The anthropological view of human existence expressed here (4:17-21 and 11:11; 15:14-16; 25:4-6), while similar to that of many a radio and television preacher, seems almost a parody of the higher anthropology of Psalm 8 and Gen 1:26-31.

Eliphaz goes on to taunt Job (5:1-2): "Do not bother calling on any of the lesser beings in Yahweh's court either!" Since some Near Eastern religions held that everyone had a personal god who would speak his or her case in the heavenly council, some polemic may be involved here. In fact, Job will later call for some kind of mediator to stand between himself and God (9:33; 16:19; 19:25). Insinuating that Job is a fool, Eliphaz uses the proverb in 5:2 to argue that the prosperity of fools is only apparent; their way ends in disaster that affects not only themselves but their whole family. Their children will have no one to speak for them or rescue them "at the gate" (5:4), the place where tribal business and legal matters were handled (see Ruth 4:1; Prov 22:22). In verses 6-7 a third point is made: Whatever mischief and trouble we find in our lives is a human product.

Between his contrasting descriptions of the lot of the fool (5:3-7) and that of the righteous (5:17-26), Eliphaz urges Job to do as he, Eliphaz, would do, that is, appeal to God! A hymn-like section follows, describing God as the creator and source of the life-giving rain (verse 9 is omitted in the New American Bible as a duplicate of 9:10); as the all-wise one who ordains things justly (vv. 12-14); and as the protector and defender of the poor and oppressed (vv. 11, 15-16). All these images are commonplace in Old Testament thought.

Beginning with a beatitude—suffering can be God's parental and ultimately healing correction—the description of the rewards of righteousness falls into two parts, verses 18-22 and verses 23-26. Verses 18-22 present the negative side: basically, God saves from oppression and death. In an oral-shame culture, the tongue (v. 21) could indeed be a terrible scourge, as Job is in fact experiencing! Verses 23-26 present the positive side. The life-giving relationship of humans with both the earth and the animals, fractured by sin (Gen 3), is here restored (v. 23). The power of life is manifested further by begetting many offspring (so important in a tribal society) and by living to a ripe old age. Fidelity to God, then, brings abundance of life.

Having made his four basic points—what innocent person perishes? (4:7); can mortals be blameless against their maker? (4:17); humans themselves beget mischief (5:7); happy those whom God reproves (5:17)—Eliphaz concludes his opening remarks (v. 27) with a ringing appeal to experience: "So it is, and what's more, you should know it!" Unfortunately, Job knows no such thing.

6:1–7:21 Job's reply to Eliphaz. Job responds with a strong emotional outburst. His anguish and calamity may be too great to be measured (vv. 1-2), but they can, even must, be spoken (v. 3). The divine hunter pursues him with poisoned arrows (v. 4). As the rhetorical question in verse 5 suggests, Job is not braying without reason. To add insult to injury, Eliphaz's advice is too much for Job

to stomach (vv. 6-7). The "white of an egg" in verse 6b is a traditional rendering of a very obscure Hebrew phrase.

Job turns to prayer (vv. 8-12). As in chapter 3, he still longs for death to bring relief and consolation, but, as there and throughout the book, this never brings him to contemplate suicide. Job is not an unfeeling statue of stone or bronze (v. 12) but a human being who is being pushed to the limit.

At last Job clearly acknowledges the presence of his friends. Apparently responding only to Eliphaz, throughout Job addresses "you-all" (plural) and gives an object lesson on the meaning of friendship. A friend owes kindness, loyalty, and fidelity to one in despair, even when—or especially when—that one is moved to abandon religion ("fear of the Almighty," v. 14). A friend in need is a friend indeed! Instead, the friends are like the Palestinian wadis (gullies), which fill quickly with rain but just as quickly run dry. They are totally undependable; they cannot be trusted. An ancient caravan, trusting them, would risk not only frustration but even possible death.

This is what Job's friends are; in a way, they came, took one look and ran (v. 21). He had never imposed on them for anything, but he had a right to expect honest words. Job challenges them to show where he has sinned to deserve this treatment (v. 24). Their fear (v. 21) prevents them from hearing the truth in the "sayings of a desperate man" (v. 26). Job's charge in verse 27 would seem as gratuitous as Eliphaz's suggestion that he has sinned. Job resolutely affirms that right and justice are still on his side (v. 29).

To answer Job's first outcry, Eliphaz had painted a fairly unflattering view of human existence (4:17-21). Here Job would seem to agree. Life is a drudgery, and humans are all slaves. The night drags on forever, while life flies by like the wind (vv. 4, 7). Job will soon be gone, descended to the nether world (v. 9). This is one of several statements (10:21; 14:10-12; 16:22) which show clearly that no hope for resurrection or afterlife appears in the book. After death all alike, with no distinction between rich and poor, wicked and upright, go down to the realm of death. But does Job really agree with Eliphaz? It does not seem so. Eliphaz presented a theological view of the way things are; Job is giving an existential description of his experience, which is not the way things should be. If he agreed, why his constant outcry against it as something unjust?

Job will not keep silent. The purpose of the test proposed by the Satan was to see what Job would say, and now he will have his say. Verse 11 is a very important statement in the context of the whole book. God is treating Job like the mythological monsters Sea and Leviathan. Job's struggles stand in the context of the cosmic battle between order and chaos, life and death. Since God has apparently put Job on the side of chaos, he longs to be with the other mythological figure of chaos and oppression, Death (v. 15).

Psalm 8 asks, "What is man, O God, that you watch over him" and concludes to the exalted nature of human existence. Job clearly parodies this. Yes, God watches over him, but like Big Brother in Orwell's *1984* (vv. 17-18, 20). Why won't God leave him alone, at least long enough to catch his breath (v. 19)? Even if he had sinned, why (again that question!) does God not simply forgive? A chasm separates any possible guilt of Job from his sufferings. Job will soon be dead, and then it will be too late (vv. 20-21).

8:1-22 Bildad's first speech. "When are you going to shut up, you old windbag?" (8:2). Thus the second friend jumps with both feet into the fray and comes immediately to a defense of God's justice. While it was implicit before, this is the first time the issue is stated so clearly (v. 3). With logical consistency that allows no room for uncertainty, the death of Job's children (perhaps discreetly alluded to by Eliphaz in 5:4) is attributed to their own sins (v. 4). Still, if Job will only turn and repent (something Eliphaz had likewise recommended, with himself as model, 5:8), he will be restored to his former prosperity (vv. 5-7). This is quite irrelevant, as Job has consistently longed, not for his old possessions, but for understanding and justice.

In the best wisdom tradition, Bildad appeals to the accumulated wisdom of the ages passed down from the ancestors (vv. 8-10). In their name he cites a proverb with Egyptian coloring. Just as plants need water if they are to grow and blossom, so humans need God if they are to grow and prosper (vv. 11-12). Bildad then develops the example of one who forgets God. Forgetting God is not a simple lapse of memory; it is cutting off our

water supply in the middle of the desert! It is a personal amnesia. We forget who we are, where we are from, where we are going, and how we are to live. Such persons might find some prosperity, but it hangs by a thin thread (vv. 14-19).

On the other hand, God does not forsake the upright (vv. 20-22). If only Job will repent, he will again be filled with laughter and rejoicing. Verse 21a recalls Israel's happiness when God returned them from exile (Ps 126:2). In verse 22 Bildad gives an ironic foreshadowing of what in fact is going to happen at the end of the book (42:7-17).

9:1–10:22 Job's reply to Bildad. These chapters are beset with many problems of text and translation, but it is clear that they abound in legal images. At times Job is the plaintiff who wants to haul God off to court (9:3). Unfortunately, since the defendant and the judge are the same, what chance does he have? At other times Job seems to be the defendant who has to answer for his life (9:14). Job's sense of helplessness also keeps coming up, especially in the face of God's awesome creative power. At any rate, it is clear that Job's speech is getting bolder and more outspoken.

The friends had argued, "How can one be justified before God?" meaning "All are sinners" (4:17). Job agrees with the question but with quite a different meaning. One cannot be justified when the judge and defendant are the same and so powerful (vv. 2-3). God can overturn the order of creation (vv. 5-7) just as God first established it. Like a warrior with his victorious foot on the back of the fallen prey, God plants a foot on the back of the defeated Sea (v. 8; see Ps 110:1-2). Later (chs. 38–41) Yahweh will appeal to these same wonders of creation.

Job's utter confusion and helplessness are reflected in verses 11-21. He does not know what to do or say that would make any difference. Verse 13 again alludes to God's defeat of the primal sea monster, this time under the name of Rahab. Throughout these verses a series of "if" questions shows Job turning first one way and then another as he looks for some course of action. There is none. He despises his life (v. 21). Who is there to blame but God (vv. 22-24)?

Job's life is going by swiftly, like a runner, a speedy boat on the Nile, or an eagle.

There is no way that he can win; even should he succeed in cleansing his name, God would just muddy it up again (vv. 25-31). Forsaken by his friends, alone, Job longs (in the first of three such passages; see 16:19; 19:25) for some third party, here a neutral arbiter, who might stand between him and God and work out a fair judgment. But he knows that this is hopeless; again, he loathes his life (vv. 9:32–10:1a).

Job now returns to lamentation. Since he does not know what else to say, he will at least speak his complaint (as in 7:10), "Let me know why . . ." (10:1b-2). Does God get pleasure from afflicting this creature, God's handiwork? Job appeals to God's memory of happier days, namely, when Job was created, and compares God then to a potter, a maker of cheese, and a tailor doing their work with care and skill (vv. 9-12). So why does God pursue Job, hunting him down like a wild animal (v. 16)? As in 3:11 and 7:15, Job once more longs for death. His days are so few; why does God not just leave him alone for a breather (see 7:19) before he goes to the dark land of death, from which there is no return (vv. 18-22)?

11:1-20 Zophar's first speech. Zophar's opening attack on Job makes Bildad's (8:2) seem polite in comparison. Job has indeed been outtalking his companions about two to one, but should the one who talks the most be declared right (v. 2)? Zophar sums up Job's excessive "babbling" in five words in Hebrew! "My doctrine is true; my life is clean." Even though Job has not said this in so many words, it seems a fair inference. In fact, Job has not been trying to communicate doctrine but a sense of his own confusion and pain, something the friends completely fail to hear. You may be missing something, Zophar suggests, namely, the "secrets of God's wisdom," and God knows you are guilty! While rebuking Job for being too sure of himself and not respecting the mystery of wisdom, Zophar is himself quite sure and not aware, apparently, of limits to his own wisdom.

Extended praise of the vastness and immeasurability of God's wisdom follows (vv. 7-12). Zophar shares with his friends their low opinion of human beings as worthless and full of iniquity (v. 11). The proverb in verse 12 is illusive, partly because the Hebrew text is not completely clear. As translated in the New American Bible, it suggests that certain crea-

tures cannot really be changed. Can one make a silk purse out of a sow's ear?

Like the two others (Eliphaz, 5:8; Bildad, 8:5), Zophar gives Job advice on what he should do: get rid of those radical ideas, say your prayers, and shape up (vv. 13-14). If he does, then, in accord with his friends' doctrine of retribution, he will enjoy a prosperous life and will find rest (see 3:13, 17, 26). He will also recover the honor and respect of others, for many will recognize his virtue and come asking for his intercession (v. 19b). This is especially ironic because at the end (42:8-9), the friends *will* have to rely on Job's intercession. The last phrase (v. 20c) makes a final point: it is the wicked who eagerly look forward to death. Job has been doing exactly this (3:11; 10:18-19); just what you would expect from one who is wicked!

12:1–14:22 Job's reply to Zophar. Unfazed by Zophar's accusation of verbosity, Job launches into what is, with the exception of chapters 29–31, his longest speech. Chapter 12 abounds with wisdom terminology and ideas; chapter 13, with legal expressions; and chapter 14, with lamentation.

Taunted by the sarcasm of his friends, Job shows himself able to rise to the occasion (vv. 2-3). "Intelligence" in verse 3 is literally "heart" in Hebrew, the core of the person from which flow thoughts, feelings, and actions. In a shame culture, "what the neighbors say" is very important, and in verses 4-6 Job tells us. His misfortunes have made him a mockery and brought him disgrace.

In 8:8-10 Bildad had appealed to the authority of tradition passed down from the ancients. Here Job parodies this with his own appeal to the dumb animals, all of which know what the friends do not—that misfortune equally comes from God, and it is not always connected with sinful behavior. The proverb in verse 11 makes the point that the traditional wisdom must be tested by experience, just as the mouth tastes food. Job has already said that he finds his friends' advice indigestible (6:6-7). In this light, verse 12 is almost certainly sarcastic.

Eliphaz had earlier (5:10-13) sung a hymn to the God of order and creation. Here Job sings to the God of chaos and uncreation (vv. 13-25). For the people of the Old Testament, the world was all of a piece; nature and human society were closely interconnected (an insight we, with our ecological and social crises, would do well to relearn). God brings on chaos in natural creation (vv. 15, 19-21, 22; the Hebrew phrases echo the flood story of Gen 6-8) and also in human society, where social order (that is, justice) depends on the wise governance of kings, counselors, and judges (vv. 17, 18, 20). Verse 20b supports our reading of verse 12 as sarcastic. Job does not say that all this is haphazard and pointless. God's might and strength go together with wisdom and prudence (vv. 13, 16). The problem is that we cannot figure it out; we grope in the dark and stagger with drunken senselessness (vv. 24-25). Like his friends, Job has heard and seen much; he has had much experience (13:1-2), but he wants more.

Job again wants to take God to court (13:3)! The word translated as "reason with" in verse 3b is the same technical legal term translated as "rebuke" in verses 6 and 10. The sense of verse 4 is that the friends whitewash God with their lies (a theme to recur in vv. 6-10), and their treatment of Job exposes them as quack doctors—not to mention their bedside manner! If they were indeed wise, they would know when to be silent (see Prov 17:28).

In an oral culture like Job's, words were the very fabric of society, and this was nowhere more important than in the most formal situations of religion and law. Thus we find in the Old Testament a great stress on bearing truthful witness (Exod 20:16; Deut 5:20; 19:16-21) and on the necessity of two or three witnesses to establish a charge (Deut 19:15). Job does have three witnesses, but their testimony is false! Do they think that God is served by their falsehoods? Is it for God that they are lying? Or is it perhaps for themselves and for their theology, which brings them such security (vv. 6-8)? Verses 9-11 foreshadow what will happen in 42:7-9.

Job will not be intimidated or silenced by the ashen aphorisms of his friends, but persists in speaking out of the depth of his experience (13:12-13). The expression in verse 14 occurs only here in the Old Testament, but the sense is clearly that Job will speak even at the risk of his life. Job is so sure of his innocence that he says he will argue his case in God's very presence—and survive! This alone will prove him right, because sinners cannot live in God's presence (v. 16).

"Pay careful heed to my speech" (v. 17)—the plural verbs here are addressed to the friends, but also to all of us who hear Job's words. The issue at stake, we recall, is precisely that of Job's speech. In verses 20-27 Job addresses God (something the friends never do!) and realistically prays that if he is to stand a chance with God, there have to be some ground rules: God must promise not to overwhelm Job with divine power ("hand") nor divine "terror," which renders helpless those at whom it is directed (see Exod 23:27; Josh 2:9). Then Job is willing to be either defendant (v. 22a) or plaintiff (v. 22b).

From his almost foolhardy confidence, Job suddenly turns to lamentation. He is caught in a quandary: God is either too far away (v. 24a) or much too close (v. 24b). The Hebrew of verse 24b contains a pun: God is treating Job ('iyyob) as an enemy ('oyeb). This is a source of recurring pain for Job; no one can hurt a person as close friends can. The image in verse 25 is almost ridiculous. The mighty God (v. 21) is relentlessly chasing Job, a mere leaf in the universe. Job has been accused, sentenced, and punished (the shame of the stocks!), but he does not know why. He does not claim to be completely sinless (v. 26), but whatever he may have done, he does not deserve what he is getting.

In chapter 14 Job's lament returns to the dark side of human existence. Two aspects particularly are highlighted:

1) All human life ("Man" in verse 1 is all humanity) is weak and transitory (vv. 1-6). We fade, wear out, disappear like a flower, a shadow, a leather bottle, a garment (13:28 has been moved to follow 14:3). The text and interpretation of verse 4 is obscure; surely a reference to original sin, which some early Church theologians saw here, is most unlikely.

2) There is no hope for life after death (vv. 7-22). Job's remarks on this move through four stages: (a) A tree does have hope. Even though it has been cut down, all one need do is water it and it will sprout again (vv. 7-9). (b) Human life is not like that at all! When we are gone, we are gone, like evaporated water (again, water imagery). Three times it is affirmed (v. 12): no rising, no waking, no being roused. To say something three times in Hebrew (for example, "Holy, holy, holy, Lord God of hosts," Isa 6:3) gives a superla-

tive emphasis. We are dead and that is it—period! (vv. 10-12). (c) Job wishes that things were otherwise. "Oh, wouldn't it be nice if . . ." God would call, and Job, once again in good graces, would respond, whatever misdeeds he may have committed sealed up and forgotten. (d) There is no "if." This is impossible. Reality imposes itself on the dream. Like water (again, water imagery) wearing away stones, so God erodes human hope. The only survival lies in the continuation of the family, in the next generation. And do they know honor or shame? The dead are oblivious of what transpires. The afflicted one is left only with bodily pain and inner distress (vv. 18-22).

And so, on this dim note, the first round of speeches comes to an end. The issues are squarely on the table. For the friends, God's justice is at stake; for Job, the integrity of his experience. Given the choice, the friends side with God, or better, with their theory about God, which, all too easily for "religious people," replaces God. But Job will not give in. He holds to his experience and, perhaps even worse, refuses to keep quiet.

IV. SECOND ROUND OF SPEECHES

Job 15:1–21:34

15:1-35 Eliphaz's second speech. In his first speech (chs. 4–5), Eliphaz was rather gentle and encouraging, but having sat through three speeches of Job, he now changes his tone. If Job were indeed as wise as he claimed (13:1-2), he would not have replied with so much hot air (vv. 2-3). He has, in fact, uttered folly and not wisdom; his words tear down true religion (v. 4; Hebrew, "fear [of God]"; NAB, "piety"). Job is condemned out of his own mouth, tongue, and lips; all the speech organs get into the picture (vv. 5-6). A better translation of verse 5 might be: "Your mouth instructs wickedness, and your tongue chooses craftiness."

Continuing his attack on Job's wisdom, Eliphaz sarcastically asks Job if he is some mythic, primordial sage (see Ezek 28:11-19), begotten in some special way before creation (v. 7). The same image in almost identical words is applied, in Prov 8:25b, to the personified figure of God's wisdom. Or has Job been privy to the council (better than "coun-

sels") of God (v. 8)? This is especially ironic, because we, the readers, know that it was precisely there, in the divine council, that Job's troubles have their root and cause.

Verse 10 perhaps implies two things: that Eliphaz includes himself among the wise, gray-haired elders; and that Job might not be as old as we often depict him. Since he will later beget and raise another family, he might now be in middle age. The godly consolation and gentle speech in verse 11 probably refer back to Eliphaz's first speech; in case Job has forgotten, some of its highlights are repeated here, but in harsher tones. Since not even the members of the heavenly council are completely clean, how much less the abominable, disgusting, sinful creatures we call humans! (vv. 14-16; see 4:17-19).

Appealing, typically, to ancient tradition (vv. 17-18; see 8:8), Eliphaz offers, not as before (5:17-26) a description of the blessings of the righteous, but a harrowing, admonitory account of the fate of the wicked (vv. 17-35). They live in constant inner torment and anxiety (vv. 20-24); impending death lies particularly heavy (vv. 23b-24). Verse 25 surely contains a barbed reference to Job's behavior, and with it the implication that he deserves all that he has received. Grown fat and lazy (v. 27), the wicked cannot survive adversity. Using a series of botanical comparisons, Eliphaz concludes his description, ending with a proverbial comment (see Ps 7:15; Isa 59:4) on the futility of folly (vv. 30-35).

16:1–17:16 Job's second reply to Eliphaz. Job is getting exasperated with the unimaginative advice of his "comforters," who bring weariness (v. 2b) and not the rest he longs for. If they could change places, it would be easy for Job to give them some of the same medicine (see 13:4). In the context verse 5 is ambiguous. It is either sarcastic, or it means that Job would in fact teach them the proper way to bring consolation, with appropriate speech or appropriate silence. But whether Job speaks or keeps silent, it makes no difference; he cannot escape his pain (v. 6).

In typical lamentation language (see, for example, Ps 22:7-9, 13-14, 17, 22) Job speaks of the assaults of his enemies. At times the thought moves back and forth between God and the friends. They are described as traitors (vv. 8, 11), ferocious beasts (vv. 9-10a), bullies (v. 10b), assault-and-battery muggers (v.

12a), an archer (v. 12c-13a), and a fencer who pierces Job's kidneys (not "sides," v. 13bc). Job has reacted with gestures of grief and mourning (see 1:20); they are not expressions of penance. He continues to affirm his innocence; he has not committed deeds of social injustice (a common meaning of "violence"), and his prayer is sincere (vv. 15-17).

Job feels that he is fast approaching death (16:18-17:2). In the Old Testament the blood of an innocent victim was believed to cry out from the ground asking for justice (for example, the blood of Abel in Gen 4:10; see also Ezek 24:8). Job hopes that even after death has closed his lips, his blood will not be silent. Earlier, forsaken by his friends, Job looked for an arbiter to stand between him and God (9:33-35); then he dreamed of God's restoring him after death (14:13). Here, in the midst of his somber reflections, he hopes for a witness, an intercessor on high (16:19). This has been variously interpreted. Is it God? Or Job's prayer? More likely it is some member of the heavenly council who, unlike the Satan, would speak on Job's behalf. He hopes that God may be moved to justice by his weeping. But, as in the two previous situations (9:35-10:1; 14:18-22), Job knows that his dream is hopeless. He is fast on the road to death (16:22-17:2).

The interpretation of 17:3-10 is difficult because the Hebrew text is far from clear. Job seems to ask God to grant someone to offer a pledge for him (v. 3), a practice common in legal and commercial contexts (see Gen 38:17; Deut 24:6-17). Again, there is no one. Job has become a mockery and byword for all; he is held up to shame. If verses 8-9 are accurate, they should probably be read as being sarcastic: "If there were any upright or righteous people, they should be astonished, but since no one is astonished, I guess there are no upright or righteous ones among you."

Forsaken, alone, and mocked, Job returns to thoughts of death (vv. 11-16). The grave is presented under a series of negative images: the land of the dead (vv. 13, 16), darkness (v. 13), corruption and maggots (v. 14), the dust (v. 16). Some of the poignancy of verse 15 is lost in the translation. In the Hebrew, the word "where" is expressed twice in a row with slightly different words: "Where? Where is my hope?" There is none; all go down to death.

18:1-21 Bildad's second speech. With a few words of rebuke, Bildad begins. When will Job be quiet? Let him stop and think a little first; then we can discuss! In 16:9 Job had accused God of angrily tearing him apart. Bildad turns the words against Job (v. 4): "You tear yourself apart in your anger!" and then he adds sarcastically, "because you are upset, you want the whole order of the universe to be rearranged to suit you" (v. 4bc).

The rest of Bildad's speech is an extended depiction of the fate of the wicked, not unlike that of Eliphaz in 15:20-35. Again, a series of images is used. Those who sin forsake the light, so they dwell in darkness (vv. 5-6). Their own counsels and behavior bring retribution with them; they are ensnared in traps of their own devising. Six different hunting terms are used (net, pitfall, trap, snare, noose, toils [a type of net]); their precise meanings are not always clear, as a comparison of translations will show (vv. 7-10). The terrors of Death (the king of terrors), disaster, and disease (the first-born of Death) haunt the wicked at every turn (vv. 11-14).

The references to the tent being destroyed (vv. 14b-15) and to dying childless (vv. 16-19) probably recall Job's afflictions in chapter 1. In the tribal society of Job's time, people had no belief in an afterlife and therefore survived only in descendants who bore their names and preserved their memories. Without these, it would be as if they had never existed. With no children, grandchildren, or survivors, they were surely "banished out of the world" (v. 18b). No worse fate could be imagined.

The people who are appalled and struck with horror at the fate of the wicked (v. 20) are ambiguous. The Hebrew terms, literally "the after-ones/the before-ones," can refer either to time (younger and older ones, as in the New American Bible) or to space (westerners and easterners; directions were taken facing east). The latter is perhaps more likely. This, then, is the fate of the wicked.

19:1-29 Job's second reply to Bildad. Bildad had just asked "When?" Using the same Hebrew word, Job throws it back, "How long?" The "ten times" in verse 3 is to be taken in the same sense as our "I've told you a thousand times," that is, often and repeatedly (see, for example, Gen 31:7, 41; Num 14:22). While unclear textually, verses 4-5 seem to imply something like "Even if I am at fault, that is my business; and you have no right to gloat over me." For the record, Job affirms again that God has dealt with him in a crooked way (v. 6).

As earlier (16:7-14), Job recounts the ways God has mistreated him. When he cries for help, his screams fall on deaf ears (v. 7); he has been stripped of his honor (v. 9; NAB: "glory"). He repeats his charge (16:9), reversed by Bildad (18:4), that God's wrath is turned against him (v. 11a). Although the Hebrew pun is missing, verse 11b expresses the same idea as 13:24: once friends, Job and God now seem to be enemies.

Not only has God forsaken him, but as a result all Job's friends and relatives do the same (vv. 13-22). Not only is he alone, but his shame is so great that his servants ignore his calls, and young children poke fun at him (vv. 15-16, 18). Those whom we love and with whom we have shared intimately can hurt us more than anyone (v. 19). The whole web of relationships that make life both possible and meaningful is cut; Job is as good as dead. While verse 20 has contributed a phrase to our language (escape by the skin of one's teeth), its exact text and meaning are uncertain. The sense must be something like, "I am reduced to such extremities that I am barely alive." In agony, Job calls for some pity from those who should have offered it unasked (v. 20). Verse 22b is better translated, "Are you not satisfied with my flesh?" This is a common ancient idiom referring to calumny. "Aren't you finished," Job asks, "with telling lies about me?" (see 13:7-8).

Close to death and all alone, Job turns, as so often before, to some last hope of vindication (vv. 23-29). First he wishes that his proclamation of innocence be chiseled in stone to speak for him after he is gone. Certainly no other voice has been found in his defense (vv. 23-24). Next (vv. 25-27) Job looks for a different kind of vindication, but what? And when? These are among the most famous—and most difficult—verses in the book. "Vindicator" was an office within the tribal society with the obligation of protecting and defending the weaker members of the family. Perhaps the closest parallel in our experience might be the Mafia Godfather! While the responsibilities of the vindicator could take various forms (see Lev 25:23-24, 47-55; Deut 25:5-10; Ruth 4:1-6), the basic concern was the preservation of the living unity of the family or tribe. Job has just said that all his friends and kin have forsaken him; now he grasps at a straw. He is innocent, and there must be a kin somewhere who will stand up in court ("stand forth") and deliver him.

Who is this vindicator? Some commentators think it is God, like the arbiter (9:33) and the witness (16:19); others, however, see here some third party who can stand with Job against God (who is, in fact, judge, prosecutor, and executioner!). This second opinion is more convincing. And when will the vindication take place? St. Jerome's translation in the Vulgate and its use in Handel's *Messiah* make belief in a resurrection on the last day very explicit. This is surely too much; such a belief goes against the clear position scattered throughout the rest of the book (for example, 14:10-22). Job seems to be clinging to a hope of some last-minute rescue that he will see while still "in the flesh." He will at last see his vindication before God. Such, at least, is his urgent longing (v. 26b). However, given the confused state of the text (apparent also in the ancient translations), any interpretation must remain somewhat tentative.

Job ends with a final warning (and foreshadowing). Those who persist in blaming him and holding him guilty will ultimately have to face judgment themselves (vv. 28-29; see 42:7-9).

20:1-29 Zophar's second speech. Like Eliphaz (15:17-35) and Bildad (18:5-21) before him, Zophar rushes to give his description of the fate of the wicked. Verse 3 is the only instance of one of the friends admitting that anything Job has said has made any impression at all. To answer Job, Zophar relies, in good wisdom style, on both his own reflection (v. 2) and on tradition handed down from of old (v. 4; see Bildad's remarks in 8:8-10).

The wicked ignore God and God's commands and set themselves up in God's place. Almost by definition, then, the wicked are proud and arrogant (v. 6). But any apparent success is short-lived. The wicked perish forever like their own dung (v. 7; NAB: "like the fuel of his fire"). What is more, the actions of the wicked bring with them their own built-in consequences. What seems sweet and delicious in the eating turns to poison in the stomach (vv. 11-16). One of the major consequences of setting oneself up in God's place is that one soon violates the rights of others.

Social injustice follows upon idolatry. The following verses focus on this issue, which will recur later (22:6-9; 29:12-16; 31:16-23). The greed for riches leads one to oppress the poor and the needy (vv. 17-22).

Enjoyment of ill-gotten gain does not last. God, like a mighty warrior, will assail the wicked with a display of cosmic weaponry (vv. 23-28). Both the opening (v. 23) and closing (v. 28) verses of this section contain references to God's wrath, about which there has already been much discussion (16:9; 18:4; 19:11a). If Job is indeed experiencing, as he himself has said, God's wrath, what does he expect? This is the portion of the wicked (v. 29).

21:1-34 Job's second reply to Zophar. This particular speech of Job is a remarkable one; in a real sense, it is a response to the arguments of the friends. It contains many allusions (too numerous to note here) to their previous remarks and thus approaches genuine dialogue or debate. And it is directed entirely to the friends; unlike any other speech of Job's, it contains no soliloquy or prayer to God.

If the friends cannot offer Job their silence (13:5), they can at least pay attention to what he is saying (v. 2). The import of verses 3-5 is this: "My argument is not about (better than "toward") humanity in general; I'm not interested in abstract philosophy. I am a real, concrete individual in pain. Look at me and stop mouthing your platitudes."

A large part of the friends' argument thus far has focused on the respective fates of the wicked (the brunt of the second round of speeches) and the righteous (more in the first round; see 5:15-27; 8:5-7; 11:13-19). Here Job takes this up and rejects it. The wicked do not suffer; as often as not, they thrive and prosper. Wickedness separates one from God, the giver of life, so sinners belong instead to the realm of death. But look at their ripe old age, at the fertility of their families and flocks (vv. 8-11)! This is all evidence of the power of life. And their growing family life is one continuous party (v. 12).

On the one hand, sinners manifest the outward signs of the power of life; on the other, they experience neither the terrors of death (see 15:20; 18:11-14) nor inner torment, but they die a peaceful death (v. 13b). And what is more, they actually thumb their noses at

God! "Who needs you? We have no desire to learn how you want us to live ('your ways,' v. 14). We're doing just fine without you" (vv. 14-15). Does experience tell us that they are wrong? No! God's anger is not their portion (vv. 16-17). Here Job directly refutes Zophar's last words to him (20:28-29).

It was a common belief that the effects of a person's sins flowed out and affected the family and its descendants. This may have its truth, but it is not enough for justice. The one who sins must personally feel the punishment; what happens after death makes no difference (vv. 18-21; see also Jer 31:29-30; Ezek 18:1-4). Job's remarks on death as the great leveler (vv. 23-26; also 3:13-19) resemble those of Qoheleth (for example, 9:2-6).

Job turns on the friends directly. "I know that you think I am guilty. If your experience convinces you that you are right, then you haven't been around very much! Ask any traveler; they can tell you how life really is (vv. 27-29). No, the wicked do not suffer; they prosper and die a peaceful death. That is pretty much the way things are now, have been before, and will be afterward" (v. 33b). The friends' "vain comfort" is "empty wind," "vanity" (a word dear to Qoheleth; see, for example, 1:2 and *passim*); they persist in speaking falsehood (see 13:7-9). So ends the second round of speeches.

V. THIRD ROUND OF SPEECHES

Job 22:1-27:21

Unlike the first two rounds, which proceeded in orderly fashion, the friends speaking in turn and Job responding to each, the third round is considerably confused. Eliphaz speaks, and Job responds; Bildad's speech, five verses long, is surely truncated; Zophar does not speak at all. In addition, part of what Job says seems more appropriate in the mouth of his friends (for example, 26:18-25; 27:13-21). Chapter 28 is generally recognized to be a separate composition. Various scholarly attempts have been made to sort this out and provide a more balanced representation; the New American Bible follows none of these but does signal the problems in Job's speeches with a series of asterisks. Here we will follow the New American Bible text, simply noting that the overall effect of these chapters, starting out normally but degenerating into a chaos, as if everyone were trying to shout at once, might not be an unfitting ending for the "dialogue" about cosmic and moral order.

22:1-30 Eliphaz's third speech. After Job's rebuttal, Eliphaz flies right back with a series of rhetorical questions meant to show how wrong Job's position is. Ironically, as we, the readers, know from the prologue, the answers to verses 2, 3, 4 are "Yes." Eliphaz draws the obvious (for him) conclusion (v. 5).

Eliphaz then accuses Job of a series of serious sins (vv. 6-11) that could easily be committed by the "man of might" and "the privileged" (v. 8) against the poor and the helpless. In the ancient Near East the widow and the orphan were especially helpless because they had no one to defend them at law. Throughout the Old Testament it is the task of those in positions of power to stand with the weak and helpless and to work for the establishment, not the perversion, of justice. The "therefore" in verse 10 is ironic. "Because you have done these things, therefore you are now suffering." Eliphaz's reasoning process is exactly the opposite: "You are now suffering; therefore you must have done these things." Job is also accused of thumbing his nose at God. "God is too far off; God will never see me!" In this he is acting just as the generation swept away by the flood did (see Gen 6-9).

But Eliphaz does not give up on Job. One last time he urges Job to come to terms with God (vv. 21-30). If Job will repent (v. 23; NAB: "return"), he will again enjoy prosperity, peace, and power (v. 28). Apparently Eliphaz cannot conceive of serving God without getting something out of it.

So Eliphaz has said his last. He began (ch. 5) with some sensitivity, deference, and encouragement for Job; he ends making wild, raving accusations for which there is not a shred of evidence. In Eliphaz we see a sad picture of the degeneration of a religious person who has too easily confused his own attempts to understand God with divine revelation itself. It would be naive to consider this only an ancient problem.

23:1-24:25 Job's third reply to Eliphaz. Returning to his former pattern, Job reflects, in soliloquy fashion, on his predicament. God's hand lies so heavily upon him that he longs once again (see 9:13-21; 13:14-27) to take his case to court. These verses (vv. 3-7) abound in technical legal vocabulary. Curiously, here Job does not wish for a mediator (arbiter, witness, or vindicator) but is ready to plead his case in person. He is sure he will be proven innocent.

Things are not so easy, however. God is nowhere to be found (vv. 8-9). Verse 10 is probably better translated, "Indeed, he knows (his) way with me." The problem is that Job does not have a clue. The irony of verse 10b is striking: God is testing Job, and Job does come out vindicated. The next verses (11-14) juxtapose two very important concepts. Job has been completely faithful to God, whose dealings, however, are mysterious. And who knows what other surprises lie ahead (vv. 13-14)? Here we have in focus the pervasive tension between Job's fidelity and God's freedom, which cannot be reduced to the size of our human minds.

It is precisely this tension that underlies Job's confusion and fear (v. 15; the Hebrew word used here is different from that representing "fear of God," religious piety). Job is left in his dark night of the soul. He wonders why God does not have scheduled times for holding court and rendering decisions, presumably scenes such as we saw in 1:6 and 2:1 (24:1).

Picking up the theme of social injustice, Job describes the work of the wicked oppressing the weak and helpless (vv. 2-4), but he then goes on to give us an extended portrait of the plight of these poor as they struggle to survive (vv. 5-12). Again, it would be naive to think that this was only an ancient problem; the scene is repeated daily in our streets. But, inexplicably, God does not interfere; the wicked are not punished nor are the poor rescued (v. 13b). The simple view of justice espoused by the friends simply does not work.

The following unit (vv. 13-17) is a wisdom-like reflection on the two ways, light and darkness, and those who love the darkness. Day and night are symbols for two different ways of life. The murderer, the adulterer, and the thief love the dark to accomplish their evil deeds. For them, the coming of darkness is like morning when they rise to go to work. Their lives thus reverse the natural order of things.

The next few verses are very problematic, the text being both corrupt and obscure. The New American Bible has, in effect, thrown up its hands. Given the situation, not much else can be said. Verse 25 would be an appropriate comment after verse 12.

25:1-6 Bildad's third speech. Bildad begins his final words, not with the customary sarcastic remarks about Job, but with hymnic praise of the creator-God who establishes peace (v. 2b; NAB: "harmony") in heaven. Behind this language lies the familiar myth of cosmic combat in which the warrior-god overcomes Sea, the force of chaos, thus establishing cosmic peace. This heavenly condition is expected to be reflected in our earthly situation as well.

The following verses (vv. 4-6) reprise the oft-repeated anthropology of the friends (see 4:17-21; 11:11; 15:14-16). All human beings are corrupt and filled with iniquity. Job's claim to be innocent is thus impossible; there is no such thing as an innocent human being. If the heavenly bodies are unclean (earlier the other heavenly beings were also called unclean; see 4:18 and 15:15), how much more human beings, who are nothing but maggots and worms.

Some scholars see this very brief speech as merely interrupted by Job's outburst in 26:1-4 but resumed in 26:5-14, where similar creation imagery recurs. This is possible but conjectural. In the text as it stands, the exalted reflections on the human condition are the friends' last recorded words.

26:1–27:21 Job's final reply. The following two chapters are problematic and seem almost to be patched together from fragments. Job begins with a typical taunt of his friends and rebukes them with an abundance of classical wisdom terminology: counsel, wisdom, advice (vv. 2-3). However, by failing to take account of a large block of experience, namely Job's, they have departed from the path of authentic wisdom.

As noted above, the magnificent description of God's creation that follows (vv. 5-14) may be a continuation of Bildad's hymn to the Creator (25:2-6), but as our text now stands, Job, after cutting Bildad off, goes on to finish the hymn for him. As we might anticipate in material of this kind, mythological references abound.

God's power is not limited to the heavenly bodies and the earth, but extends even to the realm of Death, variously called the land of shades, the nether world, and Abaddon (place of destruction) (vv. 5-6). In the ancient mythology, the North was the place where the gods dwelled. As if putting up a tent, God stretches out the North over the primordial chaos (the same Hebrew word as Gen 1:2 used to describe the disorder from which creation, or ordering, began); the earth is then hung over the same primordial "no-thing" (v. 7). It would be anachronistic to see later ideas here, such as creation out of nothing or our view of the world hanging, as it were, in space. The next two verses (vv. 8-9) deal with the clouds, first viewed as cosmic wineskins intended to hold the rain, and then seen as the dark clouds which cover the light of the moon and upon which the storm-god rides out to battle.

God then marks out the horizon of the ocean, which is the place where we see the separation of night and day (v. 10). The cosmic pillars (v. 11) hold up the heavens, that is, the dish-shaped dome (or firmament) that keeps out the "waters above" (see Gen 1:6-8). God's "rebuke" (v. 11) is the storm-god's thunder or war cry, which strikes fear in the heart of God's foes (see Ps 104:7-9). Verses 12-13 name the sea dragon, the mythological figure for chaos: God stirs up Sea (better than NAB, "the sea"), crushes Rahab, and splits open the dragon. And all this is but the outline (Hebrew: "the extremities") of God's ways (v. 14)! In the speeches of Yahweh soon to follow (chs. 38–41), some of the outline will be filled in.

The New American Bible omits the new heading in 27:1, "Job once again took up his discourse." Beginning with a solemn oath, "As God lives," Job goes on to maintain yet again his innocence. It is God who is wronging him; unlike his friends, Job will not serve God with lies and falsehood (v. 4; see 13:7-9). He will not concede anything to his friends' position. That Job maintains "my justice" does not imply that he is or has been completely sinless; rather, his position is correct, that of his friends false (v. 6).

The remaining verses (27:7-21) remind us once more of the fate of the wicked. This was the constant theme of the second round of speeches and was thoroughly refuted by Job in chapter 21. For this reason, these verses have struck scholars as curiously out of place in the mouth of Job. The same scholars have tried to reconstruct from them a lost third speech of Zophar. Be that as it may, the verses are now in the mouth of Job; can we make any sense of the text as it stands?

In ancient Israelite law, one convicted of false witness against an innocent person was subject to the same penalty that the innocent party would have undergone. Job wishes that his enemy (that is, his friends who are bearing false testimony) be as the wicked (v. 7), and then quotes back to them the penalties with which they had previously threatened him (vv. 8-21). The only new element is verse 17, which says that the innocent will possess the riches of the wicked.

VI. POEM ON WISDOM

Job 28:1-28

This chapter stands rather loosely in the book. A general scholarly consensus holds that it was originally an independent composition before being incorporated here. Its present function is to act as a resting place, an interlude, or better, an editorial aside of the narrator. Its theme is set in the refrain found in verses 12 and 20, "Whence can wisdom be obtained, and where is the place of understanding?" The answer is captured in the caption, "The Inaccessibility of Wisdom." The Hebrew text is difficult, and while the rearrangement of verses in the New American Bible is rather extensive, that is what we will follow here.

28:1-6 Wisdom cannot be mined. Beginning rather abruptly, the poem mentions precious metals that are taken from the earth. Humans use their ingenuity, skill, and resourcefulness to find them and mine them: silver, gold, iron, copper, precious stones. The New American Bible has regarded verse 4 as hopeless, and a glance at other translations indicates that it may be right. But in all the search for precious things, where is wisdom to be found? What is the way to understanding (v. 12)?

28:13-18 Nor can it be purchased. That wisdom is more precious than silver and gold is a truism of the wisdom literature (see Prov 3:14-15; 8:10-11, 19; 16:16). Here the same thought is developed as we stroll through the whole literary jewelry store. Ophir (v. 16; see also 22:24) was the source par excellence of

gold (see 1 Kgs 9:26-28; 10:11; 22:48), but its location is not known. The two great sources of human achievement, ingenuity and skill on the one hand, and riches on the other, are of no avail in the search for wisdom and understanding.

28:21-22 Nothing in creation knows the way to it. Not only is human effort of no avail but no help can be found anywhere else in creation. The sharp-eyed birds have seen nary a trace; the proud beasts have not come on it either. Nor do the two great mythic symbols of chaos, Sea-Abyss and Death-Abaddon have a clue. The quest for wisdom would seem to be hopeless. But is it?

28:23-28 God knows. In the fullness of knowledge and creative power, God alone knows the way to wisdom. General creative activity is described first (vv. 3, 9-11). The association of wisdom with creation is found throughout the Old Testament wisdom tradition. Prov 3:18-20 and 8:22-31 are especially good examples. Verses 25-26 narrow the focus to God's control of the thunderstorm, perhaps a foreshadowing of God's speaking to Job from the storm in 38:1. Then it was that God saw, appraised, established, and searched out wisdom. Just as human wisdom is manifested in human behavior, so too God's wisdom is manifested in God's activity.

It might seem at this point that the human quest for wisdom is at a dead end. Such is not the case. God has told us that fear of the Lord and keeping from evil are the beginning of wisdom. In other words, the human quest for wisdom begins with getting our relationship with God in right order; then our quest will not violate the limits of creaturehood. Interestingly, these are precisely two of the four terms used to describe the virtuous Job in 1:1, 8.

Chapter 28 does serve an important editorial role at this point in the book. It looks back over the preceding debate and suggests that the search recorded there has been misguided. The friends certainly have not respected their limits and have claimed too much. On the other hand, the chapter looks forward to the Yahweh speeches and the end of the book. There it is affirmed that wisdom is with God, manifested in creation, but beyond human grasp. The focus shifts to Job's relationship to God and away from his understanding of God's ways.

VII. JOB'S MONOLOGUE: HE RESTS HIS CASE

Job 29:1–31:37

Job is left with little recourse. His pleas for arbitration, for an "out of court" settlement, as it were, have fallen on deaf ears. God cannot be found to receive a subpoena; the witnesses are false witnesses who will lie on the stand. These three chapters (29–31) constitute one extended speech presenting Job's review of his case, his final lament, and a ringing reassertion of innocence. Like chapter 3, it is a public outcry addressed to any or all who will listen.

The discussion up to now has been fairly general. With the exception of 22:6-9, the friends have accused Job vaguely of being a sinner; just as vaguely (see 6:29; 27:6), Job has rejected their accusations. Now Job replies with much more detail and specificity. He begins with a description of his past happy relationship with God (ch. 29), proceeds to a painful lament from his present situation (ch. 30), and ends, looking to his future vindication, with a resounding oath of innocence illustrated by a series of very specific moral behaviors.

29:1-25 "Oh, for the good old days!" This nostalgic poem begins by recalling God's closeness in the past and the blessings that flow therefrom. Blessing is, above all, the power of life, and this was manifested first in fertility (the life-force) of family, flocks, and field (vv. 5-6). It is manifested in other ways as well, and chief among these in the ancient Near Eastern culture was the experience of honor. The rest of the chapter develops this. At the city gate, where people gathered for social, business, and legal matters, Job was an honored sage, elder, and counselor (vv. 7-10, 21-25, moved in the New American Bible to follow verse 10). Others honored Job especially by the way they waited for, responded to, and respected his speech (vv. 21-23). In the context of the whole book, this is particularly ironic.

Job's honorable behavior appears clearly in the way he has treated others. Refuting Eliphaz's groundless accusations (22:6-9), Job has dealt justly with the poor, orphans, widows, the blind and lame, the needy, strangers, and those being victimized by the wicked (vv. 12-17). Job, therefore, had every right to expect that he would experience these blessings into his old age. Verse 18 is uncertain: Job will multiply years either "like the phoenix" (a legendary bird thought to rise anew from its own ashes, hence a symbol of immortality), or, more likely, "like sand (on the seashore)." Verse 20 summarizes: Job knows strength and vitality (v. 20b) as well as "glory" (v. 20a; in Hebrew the root means "to be/have weight," here social weight, honor). Job was, alas, mistaken.

30:1-31 "Now the tables are turned." Now the situation is reversed. Instead of honor, Job is held in shame and disgrace. Above all, and most painfully, he is derided by the dregs of society, who deserve the mean situation in which they live ("saltwort" and "roots of the broom plant" in verse 4 both represent bitter foods that only the most destitute would consider eating). They are not only poor and hungry (Job had protected and fed these), but they are people "without a name" (v. 8), that is, with no claim to reputation or honor. The hands of such as these have snatched away Job's dignity and welfare (v. 15; literally, "salvation," but here the reference is to the outward signs of abundance, comfort, and honor).

Job's lament now turns to God (vv. 20-26). As usual, God is deaf to Job's cries of distress. Not only this, it seems God will consign Job to death and the nether world. When others were in a similar situation, Job stood by and helped them. Now that he is in need, who will stand with him (vv. 24-26)?

Job has spoken of his enemies and of God; now he describes his own situation (vv. 16, 17, 27, 28-31). His inner life is flowing away; his bones ache; his inward parts (v. 17; literally, "his intestines") are in constant turmoil. He is forsaken and alone. All along he has cried out for a friend to stand with him. Pathetically, his only friends now are the jackal and the ostrich, both beasts of the wilderness known for their offensive "speech" (v. 29).

This chapter is in many ways a classical lament. It echoes many characteristic phrases and images, and moves through the threefold relationship of the lamenter to enemies, to God, and to self. A comparative reading of Psalms 22, 88, and 102 in this light might prove helpful here. Psalm 88 in particular could almost be a prayer straight from the mouth of Job himself. But Job does not stop here.

31:1-40 "I swear I am innocent!" In the prologue, Job, deprived of all, had prayed, "The Lord gave, and the Lord has taken away" (1:21). Chapter 29 described what the Lord gave; chapter 30, how the Lord took away. But now Job has somewhat more to say. Twice before (13:13-19; 23:2-7) he had called on God directly to stand in court and answer his charges. In the form of a "negative confession" (known elsewhere in the ancient Near East), he now utters a lengthy oath of innocence. This was an especially serious step to take. As we have seen, in the ancient, oral culture, words were of utmost seriousness, and words of blessing (see, for example, Gen 27:31-38) and cursing were among the most solemn. Here Job avers his innocence using a self-curse form: "If I have done X, then may Y happen to me" (see Ps 7:4-6). If Job is guilty, God should bring the curse to pass; if innocent, the curse will not happen, and Job's name is cleared publicly. This is a move of desperation to force God's hand.

Job first calls on God to weigh him in the scales of justice, that is, with a true balance (v. 6). False scales are frequently condemned in the Old Testament (see Lev 19:36; Prov 11:1; Amos 8:5). The figure of God's judgment as weighing may derive from Egypt, where the heart of the deceased was often pictured being weighed against the feather of Truth. Job then begins his "negative confession": "If you accuse me of X, I plead 'Not Guilty!'" He presents a truly exalted and challenging moral summary, but the exact number of areas mentioned is problematic. The text is at times uncertain; the New American Bible makes three changes: verse 1 precedes verse 9; verse 6 follows verse 4; and verses 38-40 follow verse 8. Thus we end up with nine general areas of moral concern.

1. Falsehood and deceit (vv. 5-8).
2. Exploitation of the land (vv. 38-40). In our day of ecological crises, we need not belabor the need to recover a sense of the seriousness of this concern.
3. Lust and adultery (vv. 1, 9-12). Coveting the wife of another (see Exod 20:17; Deut 5:21) is the subject of frequent warning in the wisdom tradition (Prov 2:16; 5:3-6; 6:27-35; 7:6-23). Here the self-curse punishment dramatically and graphically fits the crime.
4. Rights of servants (vv. 13-15). Slaves were usually considered one's property and did not strictly come under justice. This was not adequate for Job; not only did he treat slaves fairly, but men and women were equal before him. The reason for this was simple: our common humanity—we are all creatures of the one Creator. This idea is a commonplace in wisdom literature (see Prov 14:31; 17:5; 22:2; 29:13).
5. Hardheartedness against the poor and needy (vv. 16-23). Concern for the poor and oppressed runs throughout the Old Testament and has already appeared several times in the Book of Job (22:6-9; 24:2-9; 29:12-17).
6. Idolatry (vv. 24-28). Social injustice is the reverse side of idolatry; the two go together and are often intertwined (see, for example, Jer 7:1-11; Ezek 18:5-9). It is very appropriate that here numbers 5 and 6 come back to back. Verses 24-25 depict the idol of wealth and money; verses 26-28 warn against the surrounding pagan religions, which worshiped the sun and moon and other heavenly bodies.
7. Hatred of enemies (vv. 29-30). Calling down curses on one's enemies is not uncommon in the lament psalms (for example, 69:23-29; 109:1-20), but other parts of the Old Testament urge us to help our enemies (Exod 23:4-5) and to repay evil with good (Prov 20:22; 24:17-18; 25:21-22). Job is in line with this more difficult position, which is concerned not only with outward behavior but with inner attitudes as well.
8. Hospitality (vv. 31-32). In ancient society, without a police force or highway patrol for help and protection, a stranger traveling alone was an easy and inviting target. Hospitality toward strangers was an especially sacred social obligation. Attempts to find reference here to sexual abuses are not convincing.
9. Hypocrisy (vv. 33-34). Again Job focuses on attitudes of inner integrity. We can all, I suspect, appreciate Job's honesty; it is not an easy virtue.

Job's review has covered all the types of relationships that run throughout the webs of our lives: to God, to self, to others (friends, enemies, servants, the poor and needy), to the natural environment itself. All these are covered by the biblical concept of justice; Job is clearly just and cries out to be recognized as such. If his accuser would write out the charges, they would be so obviously false that Job could wear them proudly as a badge of honor for all to see (vv. 35-37). This is his final plea. The Hebrew (v. 35b) says, "Behold my tau." Tau is the final letter of the Hebrew alphabet and, in ancient times, was written like our letter X. Job is saying, in effect, "I sign on the bottom line; here is my X; I have nothing more to say. Now let God answer me!"

VIII. ELIHU'S SPEECHES

Job 32:1–37:24

Job has finished his defense by calling on God to respond. We wait, eagerly anticipating what will happen next. Totally out of the blue, an intruder called Elihu jumps on the stage. Previously unmentioned, he says his piece and disappears into the oblivion from which he came. Scholars discuss whether these speeches were part of the original book and whether they were composed by the same author or added by a later editor. These questions need not detain us as we seek to understand the text before us.

Elihu (the name means "He is my God") is an angry young man who has apparently been following the proceedings closely. Thoroughly dissatisfied with what he has heard, he is bursting to have his say (32:19). He does this in four speeches (32:6–33:33; 34:1-37; 35:1-16; 36:1–37:24), which add little that is new, but he does this with passion, conviction, and long-windedness.

32:6b–33:33 Elihu's first speech. Despite his youth, Elihu will speak. Wisdom does not always or necessarily abide with age; it is a gift of the breath/spirit of God (32:8, 18), and Elihu has as much a right to speak as they who have been unable to answer Job satisfactorily. "We can't do it; let God answer him!" (v. 13). Unlike the friends, Elihu addresses Job by name (33:1, 31). Job need not be afraid; after all, he and Elihu are both creatures of God.

After a long windup (32:6b–33:7), Elihu comes to the point. In his speeches he refers to earlier statements of Job, but the quotations are less *verbatim* and more *ad sensum*. Here (33:9-11) it is recalled that Job has claimed to be innocent, that God is wrongly treating him as an enemy and ignores his cries for help (see 9:20; 10:7; 13:24, 27; 19:11). In this Job is wrong (33:12). God does speak; perhaps Job has missed it. God uses dreams and nightmares on the one hand, and sickness on the other to warn sinners and to get them to return to the path of life (vv. 14-22). Elihu, too, mentions a heavenly mediator, one of the divine court (v. 23) who will help lead the sinner to repentance. Job had longed for such a mediator (16:19-22), but had something else in mind for this mediator to do. The friends had often begun by taunting Job; Elihu here ends in that way.

34:1-37 Elihu's second speech. Elihu now turns his attention directly to the friends, sarcastically called "wise" (v. 1). The ability to adapt proverbs to different situations was a skill of the wise; Elihu quotes a proverb (v. 3) similar to one Job had used in a rather different context (12:11). Again, Job is cited (vv. 5-6), but instead of arguing with him, Elihu mocks him as a blasphemer who wallows in evil company (vv. 7-9). A lengthy defense (vv. 10-29) of the justice and righteousness of God follows. Addressing Job, Elihu rebukes him. "You wouldn't talk to a king or prince that way! And who are they in comparison with God?" (vv. 18-19). God sees all and renders judgment. Those who turn away from God have only themselves to blame (vv. 24, 27). As the friends had done in the first round of speeches, Elihu suggests to Job what he might say to God in repentance (vv. 31-32). The choice is up to Job. The concluding verses (vv. 34-37) are as harsh and cruel (and irrelevant) as anything the friends had said.

35:1-16 Elihu's third speech. Elihu continues to develop the theme of God's transcendence and grandeur. "Look at the skies, the heavens above" (v. 5). Human behavior, for good or ill, affects only other humans; what arrogance to think it somehow affects God (vv. 6-8)! The oppressed (like Job) cry out for deliverance, and God seems not to hear. But God does hear. Perhaps no answer is given because they have been too self-centered and have not sufficiently "trembled before him"

(v. 14). This is a glib answer given all too often and all too casually to protect a pet theory about God.

36:1-37:24 Elihu's fourth speech. The first part of this speech (36:1-21) continues the debate of the previous sections. The fate of the righteous and the wicked is reviewed once again. Suffering can be sent by God to educate and instruct us (v. 15). Verses 16-21 are very corrupt and so are omitted in the New American Bible.

The second part (36:22-37:13) is a hymn in praise of the vastness of the Creator. God's power, wisdom, and knowledge are beyond our ability to understand (v. 26). Elihu focuses on God's gift of rain and draws, as we might expect, on the common Near Eastern language about the storm-god who rides on the dark clouds, gives off a war shout (the voice of God, the thunder; see Psalm 29), and hurls spears (the lightning) to the ground. It is an awesome experience; animals and humans react with fear and wonder.

"Consider, Job, the wondrous works of God" (v. 14). In other parts of the Old Testament, the "wonders" of God refer to the mighty deeds that delivered Israel out of Egypt. In the wisdom tradition, with its more universal creation perspective, God's wonders are the deeds of creation, which all can see and respond to. Elihu hurls a series of questions at Job, to which, of course, Job can only answer "No" (vv. 15-21).

God comes from the North, the mythological home of the gods. We cannot call God to account, however wise we may be. All we can do is "fear" (worship and revere) God, and this is, after all, the beginning of wisdom (28:28).

Elihu is indeed an intruder on the scene, but nonetheless he is a real transition figure. His earlier remarks look back to the speeches of Job and his friends. Some of this is reviewed and attacked for one last time, without much new being added. The latter speeches look ahead, focusing more and more on God and ending with the description of a storm and a series of questions meant to humble Job. Now Yahweh will speak from the storm and with a similar list of questions.

IX. THE YAHWEH SPEECHES

Job 38:1-42:6

The Yahweh of the prologue who has, as Elihu observed (35:13), been hearing and taking notice now speaks, and it is a surprise for all involved. The friends had said, in effect, that it was unnecessary for God to speak— Job's condition could be adequately explained by their theory. They were wrong. Job had called either for a list of charges against him or for a verdict; he gets neither. Yahweh enters the argument as another debater.

Yahweh's replies are given in two speeches (38:1-40:2; 40:6-41:26), to which Job gives brief replies (40:3-5; 42:1-6). None of Job's questions are answered. In fact, Yahweh's remarks are little more than a series of counterquestions. Like a teacher springing a surprise quiz, Yahweh is trying to involve Job in the process of learning and to lead him out (the literal meaning of "educate") of his own small context into the larger world. If the speeches contain no answer *to* Job, do they perhaps contain an answer *for* Job? We will return to this later when we discuss the meaning of the book.

38:1-40:2 Yahweh's first speech. Yahweh speaks out of the storm (v. 1). In the Old Testament, appearances of God are frequently described with storm terminology (see Exod 19:17-20; Ps 18:7-17). In fact, Job had predicted just such an eventuality (9:17). Girding the loins (v. 3) is preparation for a difficult and arduous undertaking (see Exod 12:11; 1 Kgs 18:46). Now it is Yahweh's turn to ask questions and Job's turn to respond. This, too, Job had earlier requested (13:22) but with slightly different expectations.

God interrogates Job about the marvels of creation, which manifest the divine power and wisdom. Does Job understand any of these? Can he do any of these? Job is led back to experience anew the mystery of the cosmos from its beginning. First, the founding of the earth is described as if it were a house being built to architectural specifications. The heavenly council rejoiced; where was Job (vv. 4-7)? Next, God restrained the primordial sea (vv. 8-11). There is no hint of a struggle against a monster, as in the myths. Instead, the sea is born, clothed, and confined to its cosmic playpen with clear parental orders. And what of the morning (vv. 12-15), when dawn colors everything (v. 14) and brings to light the dark deeds of sinners (v. 15)?

Verses 16-18 return to the theme of the primordial chaos, but here sea appears with its destructive partner, death. Does Job's understanding reach that far? Verses 19-20 resume the theme of light, which now appears with its partner, darkness. Does Job know where they dwell? Verse 21 records a touch of divine irony.

Having discussed the primary structures of the cosmos, Yahweh now turns to mysteries within the universe, particularly weather phenomena (vv. 22-30). First come the snow, hail, and wind (vv. 22-24), followed by the rain, which also falls in the wilderness (vv. 26-27). God's concern is larger than Job's humanity-centered preoccupations (vv. 25-28). Finally, what of the ice and hoarfrost? All this manifests God's continuing providence for creation.

For many in the ancient world, human destiny was written in the stars. The heavenly constellations are now cited (vv. 31-33). The reference in verse 32 to "the Mazzaroth" is unclear. Various proposals have been made; it may have something to do with the zodiac. Can Job exercise any control over these? Or can he bring the rain, wrapping himself in a storm cloud (vv. 34-35)? Yahweh has indeed created all with wisdom (see also Prov 3:18-20; 8:22-30).

In the remainder of the speech, attention turns to the animal world (38:39–40:30). Five pairs of wild animals are mentioned: the lion and the raven (38:39-41); the mountain goat and the hind (39:1-4); the wild ass and the wild ox (39:5-12); the ostrich and the war-horse (39:13-25); the hawk and the eagle (39:26-30). Yahweh's knowledge and provident care are highlighted. But perhaps there is more here than meets the eye. This animal parade might not have been chosen at random. Studies in ancient Near Eastern art and iconography have shown that almost all these animals are associated with negative images (demons, wilderness, chaos). They represent a world in opposition to human society. Yahweh is saying not only that these mysterious beasts and their ways are understood but that they are controlled and that this is a boon to human society.

Thus the two parts of Yahweh's first speech answer Job's charge that there is no plan, direction, or providence in the world (Job obscures divine plans, 38:2). First, Yahweh shows who is in charge of the natural cosmos, both in its structure and its regular operation; it will not revert to chaos. Then, as Lord of the threatening wild animals, Yahweh protects human civilization from reverting to the same chaos.

40:1-5 Job's first response. Yahweh pauses to catch a breath and to give Job a chance to respond. In his final speech in chapters 29–31, Job had spoken of his honor (weight) and of how others, in a deferential gesture, had placed their hands over their mouths (29:9). Now Job feels small; he has been "overweighted" by God. His response in verse 4 could be translated literally, "I am a lightweight," and he covers his mouth in respect. Job does not confess any sinfulness. He has, rather, been caught up into the mystery of God and the universe. His stance now is somewhat different from that of his concluding words in chapter 31.

40:6–41:26 Yahweh's second speech. Yahweh renews the challenge for Job to stand up like a warrior and respond (see 38:3). Then, at long last, Yahweh shows that he is aware of Job's challenges (v. 8). Is it really necessary for Job to condemn God in order to affirm his own innocence? Yahweh goes on to ask Job, basically, "Are you as big and strong as I am? If so, let's see you administer justice to the wicked." Job had not in fact claimed or requested superhuman power; his desire to understand had motivated him.

The description of two mighty beasts follows—Behemoth (vv. 15-24) and, at much greater length, Leviathan (40:25–41:26). Scholars have noted resemblances to the hippopotamus and the crocodile, but they are also symbols of primordial chaos, which Yahweh subdues in creating. Thus we probably have a mixing of the zoological and the mythological here. Of both of them Job is asked, "Can you put a rope through their nose? Can you capture them?" (vv. 24-26). They can thrash and strut around, trying to return things to chaos, but they are not in charge. Yahweh is! Yahweh does not demolish them but limits them, gives them some rope. In fact, he looks on them with something like joy and admiration.

Perhaps we can go further. It has been suggested that the two beasts are used by Yahweh not only to rebuke Job but also, and especially, to console him. The two beasts are meant as symbols, even caricatures, of Job himself, who thrashes and struts about saying, "Everything is going back to chaos!" Job does compare himself at birth to Leviathan (3:8) and later to the sea monster (7:12). As Job sat on the dust (2:8), so Leviathan knows no equal "on the dust" (v. 25; NAB: "upon the earth"). By looking at these animals as described by Yahweh, Job may also be instructed and consoled. Not only will God not destroy Job, but, in fact, God actually takes pride and delights in him ("Have you seen my servant Job?" 1:8).

42:1-6 Job's second response. Job's final words recognize God's power and purpose, and admit that these are beyond his ability to understand. The wondrous works (v. 3; 37:14) are too much for him. Previously Job had learned of God from the words of tradition, but now, caught up in his experience of Yahweh, he has a more direct kind of knowledge. Job disowns what he has said and "repents" (v. 6). Has Job finally done what they all (the Satan, his wife, his friends, Elihu) have been trying to get him to do? That is hardly likely. Now, as earlier, God is not served by lies. Job may have overstepped his limits in his search for understanding, but his suffering was not the result of sin. The Hebrew word translated "repent" does not primarily convey a confession of sinfulness or guilty remorse; it means "to change one's mind" or "to be sorry." Even God "repents" (see Gen 6:6). "Dust and ashes" is most likely a reference to Job's new realization of creaturely limitation.

X. EPILOGUE

Job 42:7-17

The book began with a narrative prologue; a narrative epilogue brings the story quickly to an end. Job finds that for which he has so ardently hoped: vindication from God and before the community. The conclusion moves through three stages:

1) Yahweh reprimands Eliphaz and the friends, "You have not spoken rightly of me as Job has done!" (v. 7). This is as ironic as it is important. Job has just said that he had

spoken of things he did not understand and "repented" his words. "I spoke wrongly." The first thing God says is, "No, you did not!" And in case we might gloss over the remark, it is repeated in the next verse. Job's speaking has been vindicated. Now, if the friends are to escape more severe punishment, they must approach Job, once again called God's "servant," and ask for his intercession. This he gives, and God accepts it. The friends are spared.

2) In addition to having his speech vindicated, Job has his property restored (vv. 10-11). He himself had never mentioned or asked for this; the friends had promised him this, but only if he confessed his guilt. Job's friends and relatives come now and offer real comfort.

3) Finally, Yahweh blesses Job (vv. 12-17). As we have seen before, blessing is the power of life in its various manifestations. Now Job's livestock are returned, but double the quantity in chapter 1. He begets seven new sons and three new daughters, who receive names symbolic of their attractiveness: Jemimah (dove), Keziah (precious perfume), Kerenhappuch (mascara jar). Job dies, full of years and surrounded by his children to the third generation.

XI. THE MEANING OF THE BOOK

Now that we have read, studied, and reflected on the Book of Job, we can return to the question we left open in the Introduction: What is the meaning and the message of the book as a whole? We will look at four aspects of the question.

1) **The problem of the suffering of the innocent.** This is surely the first of the recurring themes that catches our eye; it forms, in fact, the substance of the debate between Job and his friends. Suffering, they affirm, is a punishment for sin (see 4:7-9; 8:20; 11:4-6; 22:4-5). When Job rejects this in his own case, they respond, "Don't give us that! All humans, maggots that they are, are sinners!" (14:1-4; 15:14; 25:4-6). Both these positions of the friends deny that there is any such thing as a sufferer who is innocent.

The situation is, however, more complicated, and other answers appear. Suffering is mysterious, and who are we to understand God's ways (11:7-10; 15:8-9; 28; 42:3)? Suffering is God's way of disciplining us and making us better (5:17-18; 36:15). Suffering is allowed by God to test the virtue of the righteous (chs. 1–2). All these answers allow us to hold on to both human innocence and divine justice. Both Job and his friends, in fact, hold strongly to divine justice. For the friends, it is the basis of their pat, traditional explanation; for Job, it is the basis of his crying out for a hearing and of his certainty of being acquitted.

As pervasive as this theme is, though, it is not likely that it is the main point of the book. On the one hand, we, the readers, know the answer to Job's particular case from the beginning: his suffering is probationary. Will Job serve God without getting any reward for it (1:9)? On the other hand, the problem is not really answered within the context of the debate. Even the Yahweh speeches are not much help; they do not add substantially anything that has not already been said (for example, by Elihu, 37:14-24). If the main point of the book lies here, it must be judged pretty much a failure.

2) **The mystery of suffering and relationship with God.** The first approach views suffering as a problem to be argued on the intellectual level. This second aspect takes us deeper. A problem is something "out there"; we can see all the pieces, all its dimensions. The question is, How do we put it together? A mystery, on the other hand, is a situation in which I, as a unique human being, am so immersed that I can never get far enough away to see it "out there." Love is a mystery; so is death. So is suffering. Problems are solved; mysteries are lived, and lived most fully in relationship with others.

For Job, the greatest pain comes from the confusion about his relationship with God. Previously he and God were friends (ch. 29); then that friend seems to become an enemy (13:24). From this perspective the Yahweh speeches do provide an answer, and the answer derives less from *what* is said (the content) and more from the fact *that* something is said. The mere fact of Yahweh's response shows that Yahweh has been present and listening all the time and reaffirms the relationship. Job is thus enabled, despite his continuing darkness about why he has suffered (he never does learn about the heavenly contest), to live through the struggle because he knows that he is not, and has not really been, alone. The book, then, addresses less a problem of theology (though this is, as it were, all over the surface) and more a mystery of faith, of our relationship with God, which is, indeed, its own reward.

From this perspective we can notice a real change in the protagonists. Job at the end is not the same as Job at the beginning. This change has been described as "the humanization of Job." The Job of the prologue may be very virtuous, but he is certainly not a human being like ourselves. He is just unreal. From his first speech in chapter 3, Job is in the depths of human anguish and rises progressively through the debate until, at the end, he stands strongly—perhaps a bit too much so—and throws his oath of innocence at God (chs. 29–31). After the Yahweh speeches, Job admits that now he knows quite a bit more about being "dust and ashes" (42:2-6). Even though the concluding idyllic scene seems to be a return to the prologue setting, it is not. Job has been profoundly changed.

We must also observe—and frequently this is not noted—that the other half of the relationship, God, has changed too. God at the beginning is not the same as God at the end. In the prologue God speaks of Job as a proud parent might. Then the test begins. God is not a disinterested spectator, but God's honor and God's person are at stake as well as Job's. It is not God on one side and Job on the other (as Job thinks), but God-with-Job on the one side, and the Satan, Job's wife, and the friends on the other. Perhaps it would be true to the dynamism of the story to picture God looking down on the debate, anxiously hanging on every word, cheering Job on, wincing at the friends, and more often than not holding back until Job has had his say. Finally, unable to prolong the restraint after holding it in for thirty-four chapters (chs. 3–37), God bursts out like a whirlwind, enters the debate, ostensibly chiding Job's audaciousness, but behind it all a proud parent once again. The test has been passed in glorious fashion. God and Job ("my servant," 1:8; 2:3; 42:7, 8), wiser for the journey, are seen again to be what they always were—friends.

In describing this journey through the Book of Job, some scholars have spoken of Job as a comedy. In the classical sense, a comedy is a story that goes through three acts:

(1) all's well; (2) all's not well; (3) all's well once again. (Think of any—or every—*I Love Lucy* episode you have seen!) In addition, there are recurring moments of humor and irony. Humor is very hard to capture across the great gap of time and culture that separates us from the people of the Bible, but certain moments of irony have been suggested in the commentary. For our canonical Book of Job, this does seem to be a helpful analogy. This dimension of the book—the mystery of suffering and relationship to God—is a rich one that moves us deeply into the concerns and structure of the book, but is there more that can be said to situate this movement more concretely?

3) **"Job has spoken rightly of me."** This powerful and ironic statement of Yahweh (42:7-8), which contradicts in a way the evaluation Job has just offered (42:2-6), points to another dimension of the book and its concerns of suffering, mystery, and relationship. A key point at issue, often noted in this commentary, is precisely: How will Job speak in adversity? Will he flagrantly blaspheme God, as the Satan twice predicted (1:11; 2:5)? Twice he was wrong (1:22; 2:10): "In all this, Job did not sin with his lips" (2:10). The core of the book is, appropriately enough, discourse—speech follows speech follows speech. Job accuses his friends of speaking falsely for God (13:7-9), while he himself refuses to be silent (7:11; 10:1; 13:13; 27:4) until he is finished (31:35, "Here is my tau!"). Balancing off the two challenges of the Satan in the prologue, Yahweh, in the epilogue, affirms two times that "Job, my servant, has spoken rightly of me" (42:7-8).

How is "rightly" to be understood? Grammatically, the word, can be either an adverb ("in the proper way") or a noun ("right things"). Both meanings would seem to be operating in this text. First, Job has spoken in a proper way. He has lamented; he has argued; he has prayed (something the friends never do); he has challenged. All this can be summed up in a phrase: in all his speaking, Job has strenuously maintained the integrity of his experience. What else did he have left to claim as his own? If he abandoned that, he would indeed be bereft of all. Despite pressures to the contrary, he honestly spoke his pain, his confusion, and his doubt, but he never doubted or betrayed his own integrity.

God is not served with lies, no matter how well-intentioned (13:7-9). Job knew instinctively that if any healthy relationship was to be maintained with God, it had to be based on the truth; and Job spoke his truth loud and clear for all to hear. He was not satisfied with the theological explanations of the friends, handed down from "former generations" (8:8). Whatever truth they may have had, they violated the integrity of Job, who will not or cannot let them go unchallenged to the next generation. His cry has echoed to the next generation now for over two and a half millennia.

But, secondly, Job has spoken right things as well. Not bought off by cheap "God-talk" and holding to his own integrity, Job was able to see and affirm the presence of a mystery. "I know the theories as well as you; I also know my own experience. What I do not know is what's going on or how I can explain it!" God and our relationship to God are too deep and too vast to be reduced to or contained in our intellectual propositions. The Yahweh speeches (chs. 38–41) are a strong reminder of that. Furthermore, at the center of the mystery, Job has left room for the freedom of God. The speech of the friends had sold short not only Job but God as well. We see once again how Job and God are basically on one side and suffer the same distortions. It is a perennial danger of overly religious people to get their God too much from the past and thus miss the surprises of the biblical God who calls us forward (not backward!) into newness (see Gen 12:1-3). It was speaking rightly of himself that enabled Job to speak rightly of God. Both of these are profound and courageous acts of faith that lie beyond the reach of the friends and their followers through the ages.

4) **The meaning of friendship.** Closely related to this is our fourth and last dimension of the meaning of the book—the role and function of friendship. Here we are drawn first and obviously to the negative example of "the friends." Moved by genuine sympathy, they gathered and came from afar; when they saw Job, they sat on the ground in grieving (and wise, 13:5) silence. But as soon as Job spoke (ch. 3), his words were so shocking that they had to jump to God's defense. We can legitimately wonder if they were defending God or their own overly tidy construction of God. "A

friend owes kindness to one in despair, though he have forsaken the fear of the Almighty" (6:14). Even in the most extreme conditions, a friend should stand by with loving loyalty. Job bewails his friends' unreliability (6:13-27); they have become simply another pain among many. He begins to hope for and dream of someone who will stand with him and say, "That's all right." First it is an arbiter (9:33); then a mediator (16:19); then a vindicator (19:25); finally, any helping hand will do (30:24). But there is no one. As Job says so pitifully, "Only the jackal is my friend" (30:29). He remains alone and forsaken, or so it seems to him.

This is not the only example of friendship in the book. Job himself represents a positive model. He stands by his children, thinking ahead and offering sacrifices to shield them from harm (1:5). He had been friend repeatedly to the needy and the oppressed (29:12-17) and had wept for the hardships of others (30:24-25). Zophar had told Job, with great irony, as things turned out, that if only he confessed his sin, he would prosper and others would come to him, asking his intercession (11:19b). In the end (42:7-9), the three had to come to Job, seeking his intercession. And, good friend that he was, Job stood by them, interceded for them, and turned away their further punishment.

Job has shown himself a true friend, but does he really have no friend at all in the book? We get caught up so easily in Job's speaking that we sometimes forget what we as readers know and Job does not. Despite appearances, God is Job's friend and has done exactly what the three friends did not do: kept silent and let Job have his say. A study of lamentation in the Bible shows that almost every lament psalm ends, rather unexpectedly, with a sudden turn to praise (for example, Pss 22:23-32; 28:69). Scholars have offered various explanations for this, but from a viewpoint of prayer, the meaning is fairly clear. When we experience brokenness and negativity in our lives, it is only after we face it and speak it in some way, only after we lament, that healing can really begin. We may face this negativity in a positive way (lament suggests that we speak it strongly to God) or in a negative way (denial and repression, which eventually take their toll). A friend should stand by and allow us to lament; this is exactly what God has done for Job. It was only after Job had said, "I am finished!" (31:35) that God would speak in turn. God is and has been on Job's side all along.

There is, finally, one more friend who, in some ways, is most important for us. Because of this friend, the situation for us, the readers, is changed. The Book of Job is a classic because it speaks so eloquently to human experience down through the ages. And we, too, know suffering, doubt, and confusion that push us at times to the breaking point. But we need never find ourselves in Job's position, with only the jackal for our friend (30:29). We do have a friend to stand with us and tell us, "That's all right; speak your pain. Hold on to your integrity with all your might. Respect the mystery and freedom of God. Get it all out, even though it be offensive to the pious ears of so-called orthodoxy. God is not served by lies." This friend is the author of the Book of Job, who is also a model of how we can and should be friends to others who are in need. The voice of this author, speaking in the Book of Job, is now part of our wisdom handed down from "former generations" (8:8). If we yield to the "orthodoxies" of our day and falsify our experience, we will falsify God as well, and God is not served by falsehood (13:6-9). If we betray the integrity of our experience, we may never discover in the depths of a renewed, living relationship that God is indeed with us and has been our friend all along.

WISDOM

John E. Rybolt, C.M.

INTRODUCTION

Title

The title "The Book of the Wisdom of Solomon" tells the reader both the subject of the book and the purported author. This is its most traditional designation. Early Latin texts, on the other hand, often name it simply "The Book of Wisdom," and some early Christian writers referred to it as "Solomon." Due to doubts about its authorship, both ancient and modern writers customarily follow the Latin style.

Author

Solomon never appears in the book as the author; the "I," however, refers clearly to acts of Solomon (see his prayer in chapter 9). Unfortunately, we do not know who the author is who masquerades behind the king's history. Scholars have suggested possible authors, but none of these is accepted today. We can conclude from his words that the writer was a pious Jew, loyal to the law. He had a good education, as can be seen from his large and rich vocabulary, some of which contains his own original terms. He knew poetry and demonstrated acquaintance with Greek philosophy. He may have been a teacher, but he was not strictly a philosopher with a firm system to impart.

Unity and structure

The author has presented his readers with a complex structure, using themes and specific terms to hold the form together. This structure has convinced modern researchers that the work is a unified whole. The possibility remains that portions of the work may have been composed previously, even in Hebrew; if so, these sections (perhaps chapters 1–5) have been greatly retouched. No significant differences in theology, philosophy or vocabulary appear among the various parts. The abrupt ending of the book causes questions as to whether the work is complete as we have it. Despite its abruptness, a good case can be made that it was finished. Granted that the structure is clever and complex, scholars differ on the book's outline and the boundaries of its sections.

Date and place of composition

Questions about the date and the purpose of the book are intertwined; hence a decision on one of these issues affects the outcome of the other. It appears that the book uses the Greek translation of certain biblical passages; this translation was done in the middle of the second century B.C.E. Many scholars believe that the Jewish philosopher Philo of Alexandria, born about 20 B.C.E., knew this book. Conversely, many leading ideas in Philo do not appear in the Book of Wisdom. The New Testament, too, seems to know the Book of Wisdom without quoting it exactly. The result is a date in the middle of the first century, about 50 B.C.E.

All these works, however, share in a larger thought-world, with its vocabulary and themes, and it is difficult to untangle the relationships among them. The place of composition was probably Egypt, judging by the author's intense interest in Egyptian matters. His language reflects the upper-class language of Alexandria in Egypt, the largest center of

Jewish life in that country. An origin in Israel is also possible, since so much Greek thinking and language had infiltrated the land by the first century.

Purpose and audience

If the first century B.C.E. date is correct, then the purpose of the book is to build up the faith of its Jewish readers. Some readers would be pious, and the author encouraged their faith amid the troubles of life. Other readers were probably less convinced of Israel's faith, being captivated by Greek philosophy. For them, the book would support the traditional faith against developments of science and free thinking, reminding them of the nobility of their religion in comparison with that of their pagan neighbors. A few readers had abandoned Judaism in Egypt; the book called them back to God. Finally, some readers must have been Gentiles; the book pointed to the folly of idol worship. In all cases, the audience must have been educated, since the book abounds in figures of speech and subtle constructions accessible only to sophisticated readers.

Background and occasion

As mentioned above, the author had a good education, and he betrays his awareness of Greek lifestyle, art, literature, and philosophy. He either quotes or paraphrases the great writings of the Greeks and uses technical terms. He then weds his Greek education to his Hebrew heritage. He knew the Bible thoroughly and dealt with it as educated rabbis did, following similar lines of thought. A good education in Israel must also have included familiarity with Egypt, Israel's closest great neighbor. The author, at least in his attacks on idol worship, demonstrates this. Scholars have pointed to a possible familiarity with the Book of Qoheleth (Ecclesiastes) and theorized that his work appeared in opposition to Qoheleth. This, too, may have been due to certain common ideas in his period.

Language and style

The Book of Wisdom differs from other wisdom works much as Sirach does, that is, both works avoid simple lists of proverbs and write at some length on their topic. The book

was composed in Greek; no Hebrew text exists, unlike Sirach. The Hebrew flavor of the book comes through in the author's use of Hebrew ideas ("heart" for the seat of thinking rather than "mind," as the Greeks taught) and in the poetic style. For his larger purpose, the author has written an exhortatory discourse, designed to move his audience to do something practical based on the reasons he presents. The traditional methods employed are personifications, the supposed speeches of adversaries and their objections (together with the author's answers), ridicule, and invocation of past heroes, whose names are often omitted.

Teaching

Again, like Ben Sira, the author is less a theologian than a preacher, with a passionate attachment to his subject. As a result, his teachings are often not carried out to logical conclusions, and contradictions occur. He teaches that God is everywhere active, knows everything, and loves all creatures. God also punishes and rewards, though the rewards may not be temporal ones. Evil in the world has its source in the envy of the devil. Wisdom is almost the same as God, since it emanates from God and somehow is responsible for doing God's will in the world. The pursuit of wisdom is the highest accomplishment; to attain wisdom is to be close to, even identified with, God.

God's human creatures have immortal souls; after death the just will be with God and the holy ones. The author does not speak of the resurrection of the body, however. Righteousness is the key to this immortality; humans are free in some way to seek God and to reject evil.

It is noteworthy that the author omits mention of sacrifice or Israel's cult. Yet Israel has a central place in God's historical plan. Moses, for the author, is a prophet but not a lawgiver. No personal Messiah appears, yet Israel's destiny speaks to this phase of their thinking.

Importance and authority

Echoes of the Book of Wisdom abound in certain New Testament books, particularly in John and the epistles of Paul; despite that, no New Testament author quotes the book directly. It seems to have influenced the development of New Testament Christology (and even Trinitarian thinking), particularly through the activity of the spirit of God in the world and the personification of wisdom. Christian readers can easily meditate on the pursuit of wisdom, especially when this is understood as an imitation of and even identification with God. Themes of providence in history and the immortality of the soul readily mesh with New Testament thinking.

The rabbis did not include this book as part of Scripture, probably because it was not written in Hebrew and betrayed an origin outside of Israel. Early Christians used it often, though the majority understood it as a work by someone other than Solomon. These hesitations have placed it at the edges of Old Testament thinking, and it thus forms part of the deuterocanonical (apocryphal) books of the Bible.

COMMENTARY

The Book of Wisdom falls into three main sections: wisdom, the reward of justice (1:1–6:21); praise of wisdom by Solomon (6:22–11:1); the providence of God in the Exodus (11:2–19:22). Not all scholars agree on the precise numbering of the verses in each section, but the outline is generally accepted.

Wisdom, the Reward of Justice (1:1–6:21)

The first section of the Book of Wisdom is traditionally divided into several clear parts: an exhortation to justice (1:1-15), the speech of the wicked (1:16–2:24), counsels from God (3:1–4:19), final judgment (4:20–5:23), a closing exhortation (6:1-12). These sections teach the value of wisdom, explore its meaning and results, and offer contrasts between the wise and the foolish.

1:1-15 Exhortation to justice, the key to life. As the entire Book of Wisdom is an exhortation, the author appropriately commences with a thematic exhortation: love justice, for this leads to wisdom. The passage begins with the advice to love, think, and seek—three ways of saying the same thing: the pursuit of God. The judges of the earth (recalling Ps 2:10) are Solomon's equals. In reality this is a figure of speech, giving an exalted tone to an essay addressed to everyone. The lesson of Wisdom applies universally.

In addition, "justice" is not simply legal rectitude. Rather, the term echoes the constant Hebrew notion of God's order imposed on the universe. As one seeks to know and then to live in accord with God's justice, one begins to imitate in personal activity the very life of God.

A series of reasons (vv. 2-11) follows, upholding the author's original invitation. To "test" God (v. 2) implies a basic lack of faith; the Lord does not come to such a person. "Perverse counsels" (v. 3) implies thoughts or plans that seek to go contrary to the manifest will of God. The following verse (v. 4) includes both body and soul, referring to the whole person rather than teaching a profound distinction between the two. The "debt of sin" does not mean that human bodies are by their nature sinful; all creation is good (see 1:14). The expression simply means that a person can freely come under the sway of sin.

Throughout, the author uses different expressions to refer to the same reality, a practice common in poetry. Ultimately even "wisdom" is another way of speaking of God, just as "spirit" is. Even though the reasons are complex, the thought is fundamental: seek God in simple piety, and God will come to you. Without simplicity a person is crooked, devious, deceitful (v. 5), and God is absent. God knows all (v. 6) and judges all evil. The text of verse 6 mentions three parts of the human make-up: inmost self (literally "kidneys," the seat of emotion and instinct), the heart (the seat of thought), and the tongue, which manifests one's life. The author employs a term from Greek philosophy, "all-embracing" (v. 7), to explain that God, by divine creative power, holds all the world in existence.

The text mentions again the act of divine justice (vv. 8-9) to uphold God's universal power: God who created has imposed divine order on reality. Any breach of that will be punished. Even one's words (v. 9) will reach the Lord. This may recall Mal 3:16, where a great heavenly record book is mentioned. Even God's ear (v. 10) finds a place: the Lord is jealous of the right order of creation.

The next three verses (vv. 11-14) advise against any evil utterances (v. 11), since each one must be accounted for. To lie is to violate God's order by freely giving witness to an alternate, ungodly way of life. This can "slay the soul," that is, result in life apart from God. The author does not teach that the soul is immortal—suffering eternal punishment or enjoying eternal bliss with God. The emphasis is more on a condition of temporal living, in which one lives unjustly, thus giving proof of internal death.

To "court death" (v. 12) is an expression taken from ancient initiation rites, implying entering into a relationship with anti-God forces. God's commitment to life is further emphasized by the surprising assertion that God did not create death (v. 13); its author is the devil (see 2:24). The Lord made creation perfect and filled it with life (v. 14). The domain of the netherworld (literally, "the palace of Hades") had no place on earth, apart from human choice of evil.

Verse 15 closes this initial exhortation with an expression called by some the essence of the book. As God is undying, so God's order for the universe is undying. To follow this order in personal living is to open oneself to being possessed by God.

1:16–2:24 The wicked speak. In this section, which both exemplifies the first section and contrasts with the just in 3:1-9, we have the words of the wicked (2:1-20), followed by the author's own reflections (vv. 21-24). The writer, of course, is not quoting a group of people but symbolizing their attitudes in speech. This was a common method of writing in ancient times. Modern writers would doubtless prefer to cite their sources exactly, in order to avoid the charge of biased writing.

The introductory verse (v. 16) states strongly the basis of human evil—individual choice. The "wicked" here might refer to Adam and Eve as those who dallied with the evil one, but more likely the passage is simply a generic assertion about human wickedness. The relationship with evil is direct, involving both deeds ("hands") and words; it deepens into friendship and even lust (implied in the

Greek for "pined"), and then into long-lasting commitment (the covenant, recalling Isa 28:15). That the wicked deserve to be in the grip of evil is a result of choices, just as wisdom comes to those who seek God (1:2). This manifests the concept of proportion, a predominant feature of the Book of Wisdom.

The wicked speak of the shortness of life (vv. 1-5) in a way not unlike the words of Job (as in 7:1-4). If they are Israelites, the wicked are doubly wrong, since they also overlook the instances in Israel's history where the dead revive (as in the case of Elijah, 1 Kgs 17:17-24). Their approach to human conception is godless: "haphazard" rather than due to loving creation (v. 2). The author echoes here, although not systematically, teachings of contemporary philosophers on the origin and end of life and reason (vv. 2-3). The insubstantial end of life has a further terror, particularly so for Israelites: no memory remains (v. 4). The author did not set out to give his readers a scientific treatise, whether on life and death or on weather; yet his occasional comments on the activities of nature betray the thoughts of an educated observer ("mist pursued by the sun's rays," v. 4). The closing verse (v. 5) balances the opening (v. 1), in good Greek style: brief life, no escape from dying, no return from death.

The outcome of such reflections might lead to pessimism (as in Eccl 2:1-3) or even suicide. Instead, they lead here to wanton behavior (vv. 6-9). Such actions have a certain truth about them, since God's creation is wise and good (see 1:14), and the Old Testament does not advocate austerity or self-denial as a virtue. Pleasure, like all reality, must have its limits. This is something fools do not understand; only the wise know the proper order of creation (see Eccl 3:1-8). The "tokens of rejoicing" (v. 9) recall the heedless littering of modern times; here they are empty containers for wine and perfume, dead flowers, trampled meadows. The most horrifying part of this wanton behavior is the conviction that the wicked must live this way ("our portion . . . our lot"). The wise, by contrast, will see the falsehood of this assertion and will live according to God's plan.

The degeneracy of the wicked takes an evil turn when they wish to silence the voice of wisdom and justice (vv. 10-20). They set out both to oppose the wise (including the elderly, wise with experience) and to violate divine prescriptions of care for the poor and the widow (see Exod 22:21). To join the term "needy" with "wise" is also to subvert Old Testament promises of God's blessings on the just (or wise). For them, the norm is not God's law but their own bullying strength (v. 11).

The author's deft psychological touch is evident in verses 12-16. Here the style of life of the just, involving speaking out against evil, and even their own self-understanding prick their consciences. Like white corpuscles in the bloodstream rushing to attack a foreign body, the wicked fall on the just, whose ways differ so from theirs (v. 15). The expression "child of the Lord" (v. 13, as well as "God is his Father," v. 16, and "Son of God," v. 18) speaks of the close relationship of the just with the Lord, a theme of the Book of Wisdom.

The wicked then plan to test the just (vv. 17-20) to see whether, like Job (Job 1:6-12), the just would persevere in their conviction. It does not appear, however, that the wicked are open to conversion, so blind are they. There is a terrible irony in their words in verse 20: if God truly protects their victim, then they will be punished. The Hebrew term that may underlie "take care of" can also mean "punish."

The author comments on their words in verses 21-24. They erred, not out of stupidity, but because of a fundamental option taken long before (see 1:16). For them, God's order of the universe is inverted: good appears as evil, and evil as good. This is the ultimate foolishness. They have denied the traditional Old Testament affirmation that virtue will be rewarded (v. 22). Even more fundamentally, they did not perceive that humans are the image of God (Gen 1:27). As God is imperishable, so too in some way are God's human creatures. This would have been the lot of everyone had not death come into the world in the murder of Abel by Cain, at the instigation of the Serpent and due to resentment (see Gen 4:3-10). As is evident in many parts of the Book of Wisdom, the author does not clearly separate physical death from spiritual death. The two are functions of the same reality.

3:1–4:19 Counsels of God. This section comprises three parts: suffering (3:1-12), childlessness (3:13–4:6), and early death (4:7-19). Because of the fluidity of the author's language, however, it is difficult to mark these sections off precisely; thus, scholars differ as to their extent.

Typically, theme statements (vv. 1-3) open the discussion. The purpose of the entire section is to shed light on God's designs for the world. Both "souls of the just" and "hand of God" (v. 1) are poetic expressions: the just are in God's care. The "torment" refers more to the earthly sufferings they underwent previously at the hands of the wicked (2:19, for example). Christians customarily read this passage as an exaltation of heavenly bliss for the righteous. The author, however, is less clear than that.

Even though the godless thought the end of the just to be a punishment (vv. 2-3), this would reverse God's design of reward and punishment, and make virtuous living absurd. The peace of the just recalls Isa 57:1-2; this peace is the absence of torment. Nonetheless, the concept of life with God, begun through the gift of wisdom, must have led pious Jews to reflect on the ancient expression "forever," such as "his mercy endures forever" (Ps 118:1). Coupled with this reflection was consideration of the Greek expression "immortality," a term appearing here for the first time in the Bible (v. 4). The just died in the hope of continuing life, marking them off from the foolish, who expected nothing (2:5).

Chastisement of the just (v. 5) is not denied; its briefness is emphasized, a theme that reappears later to explain the punishment of Israel (see 11:9 and 12:2). Suffering, therefore, is purifying, removing what little dross remains. The finished products then are in a condition that makes them ready to be assimilated in some way to God. This same idea continues in verse 6: even gold can be purified, but purification demands a furnace. Sacrificial offerings, too, are good in themselves but acquire a special significance when dedicated and consumed in some way, mainly through fire.

The image of fire continues in the following verse (v. 7). The exact time or occasion of this visitation remains unspecified here. Christians traditionally refer to it as the final judgment, though the concepts in the Book of Wisdom were not so well developed. "Sparks through stubble" would be a common experience for farmers, who burned off the grain stubble yearly, and would be particularly captivating at night. The exact import is unclear, although the figure appears elsewhere (as in Obad 18). The just, though fire-tried, stand out from the stubble of the wicked, dark and lifeless.

Changing the figure, the author advances his thought in verses 8-9. The poetic basis for the theme of judging nations comes from the ancient mythology of Canaan: the holy ones (or gods) had their own peoples, whom they ruled under the headship of a supreme deity. The author adopts this perspective, rewarding the just with life with God on the model of the "holy ones" of myth. They live with God (v. 9a). This assertion is buttressed by a psalm-like couplet, more Hebrew than Greek in style (v. 9b). (This same passage appears in some versions at 4:15; the New American Bible omits 4:15 entirely.)

The fate of the wicked forms the theme of verses 10-12. The thoughts of the wicked have appeared previously (see 1:9 and 2:21). Here the punishment is proportionate, that is, as the wicked forsook God, so God will now forsake them. The text joins neglect of justice with forsaking God. The two are actually parts of the same reality: God is the author of justice, and to forsake the one is to forsake the other. The same remarks can be made concerning abandonment of wisdom and instruction (v. 11a). Both the works of the wicked (v. 11b) and their families (v. 12) are accursed. The tradition of the curse of futility is imposed on the works and the family: neither will turn out well. Common experience shows this often to be the case, especially as a parent's evil involves the children in the ruin to come.

The lesson on childlessness (3:13–4:6) connects easily with the foregoing verses. Just as suffering can appear otherwise than purification for the just, so lack of children can be a blessing. Here the author makes an advance on traditional biblical concepts (see Gen 30:23, for example). The woman of the verse could be either unmarried or married. The fruitfulness required of creation at its beginning (Gen 1:28) is spiritual rather than physical. At the great judgment (see v. 7) this woman's true glory will be apparent.

The author builds on Isa 56:3-5 in his discussion of the eunuch who has remained undefiled, like the woman of verse 13. His reward will be inclusion in Israel (against the decision of Deut 23:2), more likely a reference to a heavenly temple than the earthly one in Jerusalem. Like the landless Levite, the eunuch's reward is God. The author concludes with a proverbial expression (v. 15), advancing a motive for the above: great struggles bear great fruit because their root (wisdom) never fails.

By contrast, children of adulterers (vv. 16-19) are doomed to childlessness. The teaching here is not that childless couples must either be holy or the offspring of adultery; rather, the focus is the contrast between the two kinds of childlessness. Even if the children of adulterers survive into old age, God's curse will follow them (see vv. 11-12). The great judgment will be a day of sorrow, since punishment follows evil (v. 19). Due proportion in punishment is a mark of God's wise creation.

The text concludes, in 4:1-6, with contrasts between the virtuous and the wicked. The opening statement, beginning "Better," seems like the first half of a typical proverbial statement, such as the following: Better is childlessness with virtue, than many children amid sin. "Virtue" is a Greek philosophical term, familiar to the original audience of the Book of Wisdom but employed by the author as a synonym for justice or even wisdom. The author then asserts that the memory or recollection of virtue lasts forever (v. 2), especially since God takes it into account. To be "crowned in triumph" recalls the victory processions of Greek athletic and military celebrations.

The author turns to comparisons between the wicked and trees. This ancient figure has been used of both the virtuous (as in Psalm 1) and the wicked (Ps 37:35-36). In the latter case the success of the wicked is only apparent and lasts only for a time. The issue is significant, since the wicked apparently prosper, contrary to repeated biblical promises. Here the wicked may have numerous children (v. 3), and their branches may flourish (v. 4), but this is only temporary: "for a time" (v. 4) and "untimely" (v. 5). The author uses the same ideas in reference to the apparent punishment of the just— it is temporary (see 3:5). The curse of futility also appears: even though fruit exists, it is useless (v. 5). The conclusion (v. 6) repeats past assertions (3:12, 16), which, to modern minds, seem unjustified. Beyond any theological concepts, the author's experience shows that in ill-run families the children will turn out badly.

The third of the teachings in the section 3:1–4:19 treats of untimely death, a new idea in the Old Testament (4:7-19). "The good die young" is contrary to the biblical teaching that length of days is a sign of divine favor. A more precise examination of events, apart from this theological perspective, shows that at least in some cases the good do die young. A wisdom teacher should explain this apparent contradiction. Isa 57:1-2 seems to offer some background here. The author of the Book of Wisdom chooses quality of life over quantity of years (v. 8) and draws out the implication that grey hairs do not necessarily signify virtue (see Prov 20:29). Traditional wisdom teaches that things aren't always what they seem.

Another motive is given in verses 10-12: the good person was taken away by God from a nearly overpowering world of sin. The language of verse 12 is unusual; the author, in fact, coined a new word, translated as "whirl of desire," not an easy concept to tie down, one that speaks more to the heart than to the mind. The author does not specify where the just are being taken; the supposition is that they shall be with the Lord (as in 3:6).

A question also left unanswered throughout the Book of Wisdom is whether God loves only those who have become perfect or loves all creatures indiscriminately. Is there any love for those who turn from God? Is a change of heart possible for sinners? In 4:13-14a, the answer appears to be that God loves the just once perfected, either quickly, as here, or after a long life.

The ideas of the wicked conclude this section (vv. 14b-19; v. 15 is omitted). Being wicked, they are by definition foolish, and the author underscores their ignorance (vv. 14b, 17). An implication is that the wise can ponder the realities of life and death, free of earlier theological formulations. The condemnation of the just (v. 16) is a moral condemnation or a sting to conscience rather than an act of heavenly judgment. In verse 17 the author again hints at the afterlife without giving exact details: "what the Lord intended . . . made him secure."

A curse of reversal of fortune appears in verse 18, building upon Ps 2:4 and 37:13, in which the laughter is more than delight or surprise. It is an act involving final punishment. The last verse (v. 19) contains recollections of a large number of biblical passages, listed in the New American Bible footnotes. This verse sounds almost homiletic in the vigor of its denunciation by means of well-known citations. The author's intent, therefore, is not to teach when or how this punishment will take place (hell?) but simply to bring the weight of tradition to bear on the fate of the wicked. To be a "mockery among the dead" recalls an underworld existence in which the once proud dead are mocked for their pretensions (see Isa 14:9-11 for a vivid example).

4:20–5:23 The final judgment. The fourth major section of Part One (1:1–6:21) concentrates on the outcomes of both evil and just living, the result of the quest for wisdom. As previously, we have the speech of the wicked (5:3b-13), followed by a description of the just at the time of judgment (5:15-23).

The author has spoken of the great judgment before (see 3:7, 13, for example). The picture in 4:20 has more of the idea of the great account book filled with the record of misdeeds, truly a book worthy of heaven. When and where this takes place is, as before, not specified. The Old Testament concept of retribution is also evident—one's sins carry their own punishment.

The just one (that is, the wise one), said to judge nations (3:8), here is the accuser in the great courtroom (v. 1). God apparently is the judge, although it may also appear that misdeeds return to convict their author, apart from God's direct intervention. The author's psychological interests are apparent in verses 2-3; the shaking and groaning of the wicked remind the reader of Saul's encounter with the shade of Samuel (1 Sam 28:20-21). Part of their anguish comes from an act of perverted wisdom: they finally had their eyes opened to the reality of their lives. The expression "unlooked-for" (v. 2) is typical of wisdom writing, especially showing divine entry into one's life.

The speech of the wicked, similar to the reflections in 2:1-20, brings the reader into the heart of foolishness. Their thoughts were in error (v. 3), their acts were perverted (v. 6), they ignored the Lord (v. 7). The reflections here parallel those of 2:10-20, but now the wicked come to the reward they deserve. The traditional reversals of fortune occur in a somewhat transposed format: the just was accounted foolish by the wicked, but the wicked are the fools in fact. "Sons of God" (v. 5) is an ancient expression for semi-divine beings, even the gods of the heathens, and came to Israel from the Canaanites. The phrase disappeared in earlier Old Testament writing but reappeared, shorn of its mythological overtones, in later Jewish life. The translation "saints" masks the original concept of "holy ones," another expression for "sons of God" in ancient times. Also, this traditional view allowed Israel to grow in its understanding of life after death as life with God, such as the "holy ones" enjoyed.

The wicked then confront their own condition in a great confession of their sins (vv. 6-7). Repentance is no longer possible, mainly because the tenor of their entire life was anti-God. The "light of justice" seems better rendered as "the light which is justice," or, "the light offered by justice." Heretofore the wicked spent themselves in the pursuit of temporary pleasure (2:6-9); now with eyes opened they call their lives "mischief" and "ruin" (v. 7). Verse 8, a cry of remorse on their lips, recalls "What shall it profit . . ." of the Gospels (Matt 16:26).

In the next few verses (vv. 9-12) the writer's poetic imagination outstrips the importance of the thought. He may, in fact, be imitating some of the pompous but sterile rhetoric of the wicked. Comparisons are made with shadows (v. 9), ships (v. 10), birds (v. 11), and arrows (v. 12). The vanity of misspent lives leaves no memory—a curse in Israel's thinking. The observations on ships, etc., probably came from school questions in the author's day: Why can we find no trace of a ship? How do birds fly, and why do their traces disappear, unlike those of other animals? How, too, does an arrow find its way? The wise, of course, know the answers. These are the questions of adult fools. The truth of their condition appears again in verse 13.

The author's own comments parallel the earlier descriptions: the wicked have hopes, but they are as insubstantial as down, foam, smoke, and the recollection of a one-day guest (v. 14).

The rewards for the just conclude the passage (vv. 15-23). The first verse (v. 15) is complex, raising many questions, such as: What does it mean to live forever? Is it to live on this earth or to live apart from the body, associated with the Lord in some way? In succeeding verses the author adopts expressions from Israel's earlier writings to help explain the reward coming to the just (see Isa 62:3; Ps 17:8; and 57:2).

As before, the poetry of verses 17-20 overpowers the simple issues. To describe a hero and military armor, both in real and in poetic terms, is not an unknown biblical method (see Isa 59:16-18 and Eph 6:11-17). This idea has its roots in pre-biblical literature, where ancient heroes wear magical armor to overcome the powers of evil. As with other ancient figures, this one reappeared in the last days of Israel's writing. God's sword, too (v. 20), appears in Isa 49:2 and Ezek 21:8-10.

The heavens were said to fight for Barak and Deborah in Judg 5:20, one of the most ancient and lively pieces of Hebrew poetry. So too here, in verses 21-23a, the author's exuberance strikes the modern reader. God's bow was placed in the clouds (Gen 9:13), but God continued to use it to hurl lightning arrows (v. 21). The hailstones recall the great plague in Exod 9:23-25 and Joshua's victory aided by hail in Josh 10:11. "Sea" and "rivers" (or "streams") are regarded as the same in ancient Hebrew poetry (as in Ps 80:12). All these elements pile up here to give a sense of solemn divine judgment: the Creator alone will punish evildoers. The Hebrew hearer or reader of these words would experience an enhanced sense of God's purpose.

Verse 23b concludes the passage and seems to mean that evil acts will destroy creation as we know it. God will restore it in some way for the just.

6:1-21 Seek wisdom. The first major section of the Book of Wisdom concludes with another exhortation, in many ways closely related to chapter 1. The introduction (vv. 1-4) repeats the address to the powerful on earth (see 1:1). What they are to hear and to understand is explained in verses 3-4 and again in verse 9: their works are subject to God's scrutiny, so they should be performed wisely/justly.

As God gave authority to David and his line of kings in the past, so the author asserts that God is the source of every king's authority. This view repeats the emphasis of Yahweh as Lord of history so prominent in Deutero-Isaiah and later books (see, for example, Isa 44:24–45:25 in reference to God's power over Cyrus of Persia). The author of the Book of Wisdom adopts this theme to apply to those latter-day Israelites enticed by a complete freedom of thought and expression to hold themselves arrogantly independent of God. To "walk according to the will of God" (v. 4) recalls many expressions in Deuteronomy (see 5:33; 8:6).

Divine punishment is described in verses 5-8. The reason for punishment is, as always, sin. Its quality varies according to the responsibilities each one exercises: the lowly have problems enough—hence God's special care for them (another echo of Deuteronomy's call to care for the "alien, the orphan, the widow"—16:11; 24:19). The implication also exists that the mighty are in some way the cause of the misery of the lowly. A further theme (v. 7b) is God's universal providence ("provides for all alike"), recalling Jesus' teaching about the rain (Matt 5:45).

The writer states his purpose again in verses 9-11. Note the connection between wisdom and justice (v. 9): to learn wisdom is to learn how to live justly, or without sin. In the Book of Sirach, the author connects wisdom with the content of the law of the Bible. A similar connection appears here in verse 10. The "ready response" refers to the courtroom scene at the great judgment. The writer concludes with two exhortations, "desire" and "long for." These seem to have little real effect, since simple desire will not make one wise. Rather, desire or longing put into practice through study, observation, and prayer will lead to the gift of God.

As if to back up the exhortation, the author turns to a laudatory description of wisdom (vv. 12-21), thus concluding the entire first section of the Book of Wisdom. Wisdom has several attributes that make the pursuit of her both enjoyable and easy. In the first place, she is easy to see (v. 12). The implication is that, being so, the foolish/wicked should have chosen her. Instead, they willingly looked away and so are blameworthy. Secondly, wisdom will be there when one begins to seek her (vv. 13-14). The implication here too is that the wicked would have had the same opportunity but chose to ignore wisdom sitting at the gate. Verse 15 adds an explanatory comment: prudent planning will include a search for wisdom.

Wisdom's willingness to come to those who seek her is expressed again in verses 16-17a. The picture of wisdom walking the streets on the lookout for others reflects Prov 8. The worthiness of candidates for wisdom is somewhat unclear, both here and elsewhere in the book, in terms of time sequence. Who makes the first approach? Is one worthy even before God bestows wisdom, or does the bestowal of wisdom make one worthy? The same questions bedevil Christian theological reflection on the meaning of grace and election. A further answer appears in the next few verses.

Scholars point to verses 17-20 as a type of Greek logical thinking (the syllogism called "sorites") in which one part of a preceding statement is picked up in the next statement, all of which lead up to a climactic conclusion. The terms here are "discipline," "desire," "love," "keep laws," "incorruptibility." The conclusion is that the desire for wisdom leads, through the steps outlined, to closeness to God. This is understood (v. 20) as possession of a kingdom. As is clear from previous chapters, this kingdom is a symbol for the state of just or wise living, leading ultimately to a reward of life with God.

The final sentence (v. 21) moves from earthly power (itself a symbol of intellectual power and freedom) to the truest power, lasting "forever." This last term, unfortunately, is obscure. It may reflect the blessing called down on kings, "May my lord, King David, live forever" (1 Kgs 1:31). But it may refer at the same time to life forever with God, alluded to in the first part of the Book of Wisdom.

Praise of Wisdom by Solomon (6:22–11:1)

This second part of the Book of Wisdom is devoted entirely to words in praise of wisdom. After describing wisdom and explaining its workings in relation to the just and the unjust, the writer furthers his plan by praising wisdom in the person of Solomon. Part Two is therefore divided into several smaller sections: introduction (6:22-25); Solomon, only a mortal (7:1-6); Solomon's prayer and wisdom came after prayer (7:7-12); prayer for help to speak of wisdom (7:13-22a); nature and qualities of wisdom (7:22b–8:1); Solomon sought wisdom (8:2-8); Solomon sought a counselor (8:9-16); wisdom, a gift of God (8:17-21); Solomon's prayer (9:1-18); activities of wisdom in history (10:1–11:1). Several scholars see the material from 7:1 to 8:21 as seven sections arranged around a central passage on wisdom (7:22b–8:1).

6:22-25 Introduction. Similar in style to the self-revelation of Ben Sira, this passage repeats the author's initial exhortation. The difference from the Book of Sirach is that the figure of Solomon is a literary fiction, while Ben Sira himself speaks as the author. The character of wisdom is laid out in 7:22b–8:1. The expression "consuming jealousy" personifies jealousy as consuming either "Solomon" or, as some translations have it, being consumed itself. Jealousy cannot be associated with wisdom, since the wisdom teacher must not claim selfish possession of wisdom. It must be shared, or it ceases to be wisdom (v. 23). In the next verse (v. 24), the author presents a proverb and then comments on it (v. 25), using it as an exhortation self-evident to the wise.

7:1-6 "Solomon" is only a mortal. This first section opens with a theme statement (v. 1). All kings, despite their pretensions or the exalted rhetoric used of them by others, are human in origin. Even the great David, on whom the promises of God rested (see 2 Sam 7:8-16), never claimed supernatural origins. The author also follows his normal practice of not naming his heroes: "first man" instead of Adam. These normal origins are spelled out in verse 2. The ten-month pregnancy has been explained in various ways; it seems simply to be a commonplace expression. His birth was also normal (v. 3). To "fall upon the earth" may signify a method of birth but may just as easily be a poetic expression. The earth is "kindred" in the sense that all humans share the same experience. The section concludes by stating that every king (that is, everyone) shares humanity, with both birth and death. The author repeats the word "same" from verse 1, providing a traditional bracket around the passage through repetition of a key term.

7:7-12 Wisdom and riches came after prayer. The meaning of "therefore" (v. 7) is that "Solomon," having no special advantage of birth, chose to turn to God in prayer. The text of the prayer is 9:1-18, which itself is modeled on 1 Kgs 3:6-7 (and 2 Chr 1:8-10).

In answer to his prayer, he received "prudence" (another term for wisdom). The sequence of events whereby one is led even to ask for wisdom does not find an exact treatment in this poetic text (as in 6:17-20). Repeating 6:21, "Solomon" rates wisdom (in vv. 8-9). The comparisons of gold/silver with sand/mire (or clay) have a typical Hebrew proverb form. Part of the rewards coming to the real-life Solomon were all the elements he compared with wisdom (v. 11): gold and silver (see 1 Kgs 10:14-17, 27, and other descriptions of the building of the temple, 1 Kgs 6:20-32); health, beauty, and light (his long reign of forty years, 1 Kgs 11:42). Note, too, that the expressions "came to me" and "riches" in verse 11 repeat the same words in verses 7 and 8, bracketing the passage. The king did not realize, as he abandoned earthly desires, that wisdom was also the cause of earthly delights (v. 12). It is clear here that "wisdom" is another expression for "God."

7:13-22a A prayer to speak of wisdom. If this entire second part of the Book of Wisdom can be said to have any inherent suspense, it is surely heightened by another interruption before "Solomon" tells his readers the nature of wisdom. The two opening verses (vv. 13-14) praise wisdom again. Verse 14 also demonstrates a kind of logical progression after the manner of 6:17-20; also here wisdom is seen as something leading to, but not identified with, God.

"Solomon's" first prayer is reported, not quoted, in verses 15-20. The distinction between wisdom and God appears in verse 15b and continues in verses 17-20. God is the source of all the king's knowledge, not exactly wisdom itself. The Greek text is emphatic on this point. The knowledge of "Solomon" begins with prudence and handicrafts (called "wisdom" in Hebrew, as in the case of Hiram, the famous bronze worker in 1 Kgs 7:14, where it is translated "skill"). The other intellectual gifts that "Solomon" enjoys correspond to interests of Hellenistic science. Hebrew thought was enriched by Greek inquiry into elements (v. 17), astronomy (vv. 18-19), zoology and pharmacology (v. 20). The author's interests in human behavior are reflected in several places in the Book of Wisdom, but "thoughts of men" seems out of place between winds and plants.

The conclusion (v. 21) means to refer to

all things, encompassed between "hidden" and "plain" (recall "seen" and "unseen" in the Christian Creed). The term "hidden," in addition, is a repeat from verse 13 ("hide away"). Lastly, in verse 22a the author identifies God, the Creator of all, with wisdom.

7:22b–8:1 Nature and qualities of wisdom. This central passage, around which the sections from 7:1 to 8:21 are built, finally lays out the qualities of wisdom. The author follows Prov 1–9 in personifying wisdom apart from God (see Prov 8:22-31, where wisdom attends creation; also Sir 24). As separate, wisdom even has a spirit (v. 22b).

The qualities are not meant to convey exact descriptions in which each word refers to a distinct reality. Like individual colors in a painting, the descriptions give a final picture of wisdom as holy, all-present, and all-knowing (note that there are twenty-one of these attributes, three times the sacred number seven). Wisdom's separation from God (vv. 25-26) has challenged scholars to find background for the terms "aura," "effusion," "refulgence," "mirror." The result is a picture showing wisdom as identical with God in all but the most subtle senses, somehow distinct, somehow the same. The issue of time sequence appears again in verse 27: Are souls holy before wisdom comes or because wisdom comes? "Souls" refers to the entire human person. "Friends of God" may be a technical term from Greek life. Comparisons in verses 29-30 recall verses 9-10, and they end with a moral comparison: night and wickedness with light and wisdom.

The final verse (8:1) forms a fitting conclusion. Wisdom appears as the order which the wise God put into creation and by which it continues its orderly existence. (Note the many repetitions of the word "all," the universe-wide perspective of Greek philosophy embraced by the writer.)

8:2-8 Solomon sought wisdom. This small section parallels 7:13-22a as a report of the "king's" wishes in prayer. It opens with an introductory theme that recalls the marriage imagery of Hosea and the Song of Solomon. The image emphasizes closeness with wisdom, and is repeated in verse 3: "companionship," a term used of marriage in Greek writing. Wisdom's distinction from God is quite clear in verses 2-4.

In verses 5-8 the author lists motives to acquire wisdom: riches, prudence, justice, learning; these recall the prudence and riches of 7:7-12. The four virtues (v. 7) are the traditional "cardinal virtues," or the main strengths of the human character. These four qualities appear individually elsewhere in the Old Testament, but their mutual association comes from Greek thinking. Wisdom as the source of learning (v. 8) corresponds closely with the knowledge of 7:13-22a. The connection with the historical Solomon is evident in 1 Kgs 5:9-14.

8:9-16 Solomon sought a counselor. These verses parallel 8:7-12 in the "king's" prayer for power. Note the bracketing words "live/living with" in verses 9 and 16. The introductory verse (v. 9) connects with the marriage motif of the previous section. The results (vv. 10-15) recall the glories of Solomon in Israel's past: glory, judgment, respect, awesome power, and even immortality. In this latter case, his immortality parallels everlasting memory (v. 13) rather than life with God on the model of the "sons of God" (see 5:5). The conclusion (v. 16) asserts the absence of pain. Unfortunately this did not match the career of the Solomon of history (see 1 Kgs 11:4-13).

8:17-21 Wisdom a gift from God. This last section matches 7:1-6 in reflecting on "Solomon's" origins and repeats the same advantages enumerated just above: immortality, pleasure, riches, prudence, renown (vv. 17-18). The terms for relationship with wisdom are also varied, but convey the same closeness: kinship, friendship, etc.

Verses 19-20 have occasioned much scholarly debate. It may appear that the author teaches that souls (or personalities) exist before being implanted in bodies. The point is, rather, that the author is speaking poetically, not philosophically. Likewise, "unsullied" does not refer to the absence of original sin but to "Solomon's" noble character and natural endowments.

The concluding verse (v. 21) adds another thought to the issue of time sequence: wisdom comes from God, who bestows it as a response to prayer. Even to pray is a mark of incipient wisdom, called "prudence" here.

9:1-18 Solomon's prayer. The prayer divides into three sections. The first two (vv. 1-6, 7-12) have the same general structure; the third (vv. 13-18) has general reflections.

The first part of the prayer opens, like the prayers of the Book of Sirach, with an address to God, followed by attributes of God (vv. 2-3) as Creator. This creation culminates, in the author's mind, in divine wisdom bestowed on humans, particularly on kings for the sake of a just rule. This hierarchical arrangement, with the king closest to God, is more characteristic of the theology of Judah than of Israel in pre-exilic times. The role of prophet or priest is ambiguous in this design.

In the petition that follows (v. 4), wisdom has a position reminiscent of Prov 8 and Sir 24, but also recalls similar statements in current thinking outside of Israel. It is not clear that withholding wisdom will cause "Solomon's" rejection from among God's children. This petition may refer to the "king's" fear of eventual rejection from the "sons of God," those who live with God (see 5:5).

Motives conclude the first part (vv. 5-6). The reflection on weakness comes from the text of Solomon's prayer in 1 Kgs 3:7. To be perfect (v. 6) doubtless refers to having many natural endowments. This expression may also suggest that condition of the human being which is called "worthiness" elsewhere (see 6:16).

The second part of the prayer (vv. 7-12) has a similar structure: address and attributes (vv. 7-9), petition (v. 10), motives (vv. 11-12). The attributes match the occasions of King Solomon's own life. "King" and "magistrate" are parallel terms, with no difference in meaning here. Likewise "temple" and "altar" (v. 8) refer to the same construction. That the earthly temple is a copy follows from reading 1 Chr 28:11-19. This idea in itself may come from earlier pre-Israelite thinking: when the world was created out of chaos, the victor in the battle between order and chaos built a heavenly temple. All earthly temples were in some way modeled on the heavenly one and represented heavenly order on earth. The idea worked forward in time as well: Christians often refer to the heavenly liturgy, to which we join our voices on earth. Personified wisdom also appears: she is said to be with God (v. 9), present at creation (see v. 4 above). As wisdom was present, she must have a sense of God's laws.

The petition (v. 10) asks that wisdom now be with "Solomon" as she was with God, a very bold statement. Just how wisdom could be God's attendant, the king's attendant, and the attendant of all who seek her is left unanswered here. An answer is found in the qualities listed in 7:22-23: subtle, pervading all spirits. The motives (vv. 11-12) differ from those in the first part (in vv. 5-6): here "Solomon" is closer to his goal and, relying on wisdom's power and glory, will be a wise ruler, and his acts will be deserving of God's blessing (v. 12).

The final section is a set of reflections (vv. 13-18). The answer to the questions in verse 13 is "No one." These questions do not look for information; they are intended to form part of an act of praise (see Jer 9:11 for one among many examples). The author then turns to other motives, one built on the other: the plans of mortals are unsure (v. 14), since they are earthly (v. 15), and even earthly problems are difficult (v. 16). Scholars have avidly discussed whether the author of the Book of Wisdom holds to a duality: the earthly and corruptible body versus the spiritual soul. Such dualism would not be consistent with Old Testament thought, which emphasizes the unity of the human person; yet everyone perceives differences between the lofty thoughts of mind and heart, and bodily passions. The poetry of the verse does not set out to solve this complex theological issue.

Questions appear in verse 17, again expecting the answer "No one" (recalling Isa 40:13). The "holy spirit" is another way of saying "wisdom," but undoubtedly the expression led Christians to reflect on the identity of the Spirit apart from the Father and from Jesus.

When God sent wisdom in times past, Israel's ancestors were saved (v. 18). This verse links "Solomon's" prayer with the chapter to follow, as well as with Part Three of the Book of Wisdom: 11:2–19:22. It is absolutely necessary, in the author's mind, for wisdom to be on earth in order for human beings to live correctly.

10:1–11:1 Wisdom's activities in history. "She" is mentioned numerous times in the emphatic first place in sentences, an indication of the author's wish to concentrate on wisdom. Because of this, the author does not mention by name the heroes of Israel's past, familiar enough to his readers and giving pleasure through recognition.

The seven characters are sometimes listed with their adversaries. First is Adam (vv. 1-2) with Cain (v. 3). It is hard to see what wisdom protected Adam from in the Garden; perhaps the reference is to naming the animals (Gen 2:18-20), an action demanding great wisdom.

Noah, in the author's view, was only the means by which creation was saved through wisdom (v. 4). To credit the Flood to the sin of Cain exaggerated his role, but at least it shows historical connections between the first sin and the depravity of Noah's time. "Frailest wood" is poetic and belies the huge size of the ark (Gen 6:15).

Abraham's connection with wisdom is unclear: which came first—Abraham's goodness or wisdom? No matter, wisdom triumphed even over a father's love (v. 5).

Lot (vv. 6-7) was preserved in the nick of time. The implication is that the wicked were being destroyed because of their sin (as Genesis taught, 19:13). The remnants of the disaster are evident even in the twentieth century: burning bitumen, having floated to the surface of the Dead Sea, and the "Sodom apple," impossible to eat despite its outward appearance. It was not the author's purpose to teach that the soul of Lot's wife was entombed in a pillar of salt; his poetic imagination handled the story loosely (Gen 19:26). General reflections on the end of Sodom and Gomorrah follow (vv. 8-9). Note the reverse time sequence: leave wisdom, then lose knowledge of the right way, and finally become a mockery to all (v. 8). Lot's wisdom is seen probably in his choice of Zoar for his escape (Gen 19:20-22).

Jacob, particularly through his dream of the heavenly stairway at Bethel (Gen 28:12-15), was given the resources to make a new life in Egypt (vv. 10-12). The "kingdom of God" occurs here for the first time in the Old Testament and must refer to God's heavenly dwelling shown to Jacob. Verse 11 recalls Gen 29:1–31:21, the story of Laban. The ambush (v. 12) refers to the struggle at the Jabbok (Gen 32:23-33). The prize for this struggle was long life and a numerous family.

Joseph (vv. 13-15) has an extensive account in Genesis (chs. 38–50), but is here reduced to three verses, intended as a figure on which to meditate. Wisdom in the dungeon (v. 14) revealed the meaning of dreams (Gen 40). Joseph rose to prominence just as he had previously dreamed (Gen 37:5-11), thereby reversing his brother's mockery and cruel treatment.

The designation of Israel as "holy people, blameless race" neglects other data present in the text of Exodus and Numbers: the worship of the golden calf (Exod 32:1-6) and the constant murmuring of Israel (Num 14:2). The theological point of salvation at the Red Sea overshadows other considerations.

Moses (10:16–11:1) receives the lengthiest treatment; the account of the Exodus leads into Part Three of the Book of Wisdom. Wisdom came to Moses (his "soul," following Greek thought; not his heart, as in the Hebrew manner), and the future of Israel was secured (v. 16). The "kings" may refer generically to rulers in Egypt or to the other kings whose lands Israel entered (see Ps 135:9-11). The people, again called holy, passed through the sea ("a wondrous road") and continued through wisdom's guidance. The author has, of course, taken liberties in associating wisdom with the cloud ("shelter") and the pillar of fire. "Red Sea" and "deep waters" are synonyms (v. 18). The picture of what happened to the Egyptian pursuers is unclear in historical texts. Here the homiletic flavor has them sinking to the depths and then floating to the surface (v. 19). In Exod 12:36 Israel despoiled the Egyptians before their departure. Here the Israelites despoil the corpses. The author's intent is not to add a second despoiling but to show the reversal, since formerly the wicked Egyptians despoiled Israel (mainly of children, Exod 1:8-22).

The song of Israel is Exod 15:1-18 (v. 20), in which the formerly speechless (possibly Moses, Exod 4:10-17) and even infants took part (see Ps 8:2, although the psalm does not refer to the Exodus event).

The concluding verse (11:1) could belong just as easily to the opening of the next section. To style Moses a prophet recalls one strand of tradition, coming mainly from the north of Israel, emphasizing divine guidance through prophets rather than through the Davidic kingly family (see Deut 18:15 and Hos 12:14, both northern products). By the time of the Book of Wisdom, this distinction had faded.

The Providence of God
in the Exodus (11:2–19:22)

Part Three of the Book of Wisdom can be divided as follows: introduction (11:2-5); first example: water (11:6-14); second example: animals (11:15-16); digression on God's mercy (11:17-12:22); second example again (12:23-27); digression on false worship (13:1-15:17); second example concluded (15:18-16:15); third example: manna (16:16-29); fourth example: darkness and light (17:1-18:4); fifth example: first-born (18:5-19:21); conclusion (19:22). The general purpose of this third part is to demonstrate, by a series of contrasts, how wisdom preserved the people of Israel in the Exodus. The tone is homiletical, and the author takes liberties in explaining the text of the Book of Exodus.

11:2-5 Introduction. The passage reflects on certain aspects of the Exodus without following the historical sequence. The reader finds Israel in the desert after crossing the Sea (see Exod 17:2-6). These few verses (vv. 2-4) recall Ps 107:4-6, although the psalm does not refer directly to the Exodus. "Sheer rock" and "hard stone" are parallel expressions in Hebrew poetic style. Verse 5 sets the theme for this entire part of the Book of Wisdom: Israel benefited by the very things used to punish its foes. This is a new idea in biblical writing, one that borrows from the ancient concept of reversal of fortune occurring often, even in this book. In addition, these realities show the wise teacher at work, looking deeply into events to see hidden order. What is uncovered is a grand design, worthy of the Creator, who has so ordered creation to benefit the people.

11:6-14 First example: water. The first three verses (vv. 6-8) form one sentence both in the original Greek and in English, something virtually impossible in Hebrew. The intricate design of these verses makes the message, and indeed the entire book, more difficult to perceive. The teaching is that God punished Egypt with impure water (Exod 7:17-24) but blessed Israel with pure water (Exod 17:5-7). The author likewise has compressed the events in time, since "instead of a spring" seems to refer to the wells that the Egyptians had to dig laboriously (Exod 7:24); simultaneously, Israel received water without labor. The idea in verse 7, "as a rebuke," does not appear in Exodus and is the author's own homiletic conclusion.

Israel's punishment (thirst in the desert, Exod 17:1-2), was only temporary, and for a purpose (vv. 9-14a). God's punishment is father-like for Israel, but king-like for Egypt (v. 10). (The brief punishment appeared first in 3:5 and is a continuing theme in the Book of Wisdom.) For Israel the punishment was an education, as they were to learn from their sufferings, the lesson being that their punishment was mild in comparison with Egypt's. The question why Israel, God's chosen people, should be punished at all does not form part of the author's commentary, since he was discussing just the existing texts of Exodus.

Psychological observations appear again in verses 12-13. Scholars differ on the meaning of "twofold grief"; it may refer to the Egyptians' own torments (thirst) and the blessings given to their enemies (water to Israel). That Egypt "recognized the Lord" (v. 13) refers to their understanding that God was with Israel (probably Exod 12:31). Among other passages, Num 14:13 shows some conviction that Egypt knew of the events concerning Israel in the desert. In any event, such a conclusion on the author's part is not foreign to his method of writing.

The writer adds a final comment (v. 14) to add a motive for punishment. Moses, once rejected, now is the object of wonder—again, apparently, by the Egyptians. The reversal of fortune—a blessing for Israel, a curse for Egypt—occurs once more. Moses, the instrument of Egypt's thirst, is the instrument of Israel's relief. The thought is obviously densely packed in a few words.

11:15-16 Second example: animals. These two verses begin a long sequence, which is interrupted twice. The message is clearly in verse 16. The Egyptians were senseless or irrational, since they worshiped animals, themselves dumb or irrational. The harmony seen in their punishment is a call for the wise to see in it the hand of the Creator.

11:17-12:22 Digression on God's mercy. This passage parallels another digression (13:1-15:17) and opens with further remarks on God as Creator (vv. 17-22). The phrase "formless matter" (v. 17) recalls Gen 1:2 ("formless wasteland"), but does not mean to say that any matter pre-dated creation. As Creator, God could have sent bears or lions on the Egyptians, as had happened to others (see 2 Kgs 17:26 for one example). God's power could have formed completely new animals (v. 18), which, like the classical head of Medusa, would have frightened them to death (v. 19). God might have tracked them down for instant punishment (v. 20a). Instead the Creator acted wisely, proceeding in order: "measure, number, weight" (a phrase possibly known among the educated, coming from the philosopher Plato). The motive (v. 21) ends with the type of question typical of words of praise. The comparisons in verse 22 recall Isa 40:15: all is nothing in God's sight, save his chosen people.

Yet, God's mercy extends to all, despite their low condition (11:23–12:1). Here the author again expresses his convictions on divine love and punishment: God's creatures are good. Only their choice of sin keeps them from God, who does not punish immediately (v. 23). This also explains the apparent success of the wicked (as in 4:4-5). Nowhere else in the Old Testament is such complete divine love explained with such vigor, and opens up continuing possibilities for reflection on the meaning of Jesus for Christians.

The final motive (12:1) sounds strange to modern readers. Is the author expressing the view that a divine spark exists in all creation, or at least in all humans? If so, this is not a biblical teaching. Yet, from a Hebrew perspective the spirit of God is creative (Ps 104:30), and God's creatures live by this spirit (Gen 2:7, "breath of life").

Verses 2-11 expose God's mercy in a set of examples, while concentrating on the gradual nature of punishment for sin. This theme occurs in verse 2; the purpose is repentance, not vengeance. Evidently sinners are reminded by the type of punishment they receive, which in some way is in harmony with their sin.

Even the ancient Canaanites (vv. 3-8), proverbially wicked, suffered punishment little by little. The author here seems to be following popular legend more than biblical tradition; the charge of cannibalism is not borne out in the historical books (but see Ezek 16:20). The expression "holy land," so popular now, makes its first appearance in Zech 2:12, also a late composition. The divine harmony of creation is evident also in verse 7: "worthy colony," that is, the land's holiness required a people who were holy (see 6:16 for similar teaching).

Verse 8 repeats the theme of "little by little" (v. 2) in recalling the wasps (hornets, Exod 23:28) of the ancient story—a detail still not well understood. The disclaimer in verse 9 reminds one of 11:20, but despite divine mercy, the Canaanites were so evil as to preclude their repentance (vv. 10-11). The author balances the great evil of Canaan against God's delay in exterminating them.

The digression concludes with reflections on God's unchallenged power (vv. 17-22). The very sensitive issue of why innocent people die is broached in verses 12-13. The answer is that God is both their maker and the one who cares for all. Since God's power is complete, it should not be challenged. This is also the teaching of the Book of Job.

In the case of the wicked who perish, God does not hold a judicial court to weigh arguments as a judge (v. 12). There is only one God, supreme over all; hence, questioning the divine decree of death or suffering is sinful. Note the repeated "unworthy," a sign of the writer's sense of divine proportion or harmony. This extends to justice (v. 16), which the wicked held to be a function of brute force (2:11); for God, creative power establishes justice and right, and this will teach others whose faith is weak (v. 17).

Israel, following the model of the disciple in quest of wisdom, should learn from these events (vv. 19-22). The greatest lesson is to imitate God's justice (v. 22). Israel's closeness to God is symbolized as being God's elect with whom God chose to enter into multiple covenants (v. 21). Earlier Hebrew thinking would have concentrated on one or other ancient covenant (particularly the Sinai and Davidic covenants). By the period of the Book of Wisdom, the majority of Israel's experiences were explained in covenant language (see Sir 45:24 for a covenant with Phinehas), hence a multiplicity of covenants.

12:23-27 The second example again. The author's complex language is evident in these few verses, but the issue remains the same: the Egyptians acted like foolish children. By divine proportion or harmony in creation, they deserved to become ridiculous in turn. The harmony was broken, since they attributed godhood to mere animals, "worthless" beasts.

Their punishment was proportionate ("worthy," v. 26). As a result, Egypt, like Israel, came to see God's hand (see Exod 10:16,

Pharaoh's admission of sin). In the case of the Egyptians, further repentance was ruled out, probably since they were sinful to the core, like the Canaanites (12:4, hated by God, a sentiment shared by Ben Sira, Sir 46:6).

13:1–15:17 Digression on false worship. This lengthy section divides into two parts: 13:1-9, on nature worship, and 13:10–15:17, on idol worship. The author's tone in the first part is remarkably peaceful and understanding, at least up to the final verses. The theme is stated in verse 1 and is repeated in verse 9: God's human creatures should be able to see God's power at work in the world (see Rom 1:18-25). "Him who is" conveniently expresses in Greek philosophical terms a traditional explanation of the divine name Yahweh (Exod 3:14). This name—the God who is—contrasts with the final part of the sentence—the God who acts—completing the description of God.

The writer lists (v. 2), not the base animals of the Egyptians, but the heavenly powers (from Mesopotamian religion, which also influenced the early Greeks). Even the author calls the heavenly lights "governors," but only in the sense of Gen 1:16-18: the sun and moon that "rule." Verses 3-4 repeat the same lesson, one that forms part of wisdom training. Wonder or amazement normally forms the basis for attaining wisdom, since it leads to questions and analysis of experience. This experience should lead one to work "by analogy," that is, by comparisons, to reach the beautiful and powerful Creator (v. 5). Note that the emphasis on beauty is not strictly a Hebrew interest but more Greek.

Just why idolaters turned from God is hard to explain, especially in comparison with Canaanites and Egyptians, being completely corrupt. Worshipers of the heavens sought God avidly (vv. 6-7) but were "distracted." What they saw were the externals of creation rather than the deepest level of meaning, the Creator of these marvels. Those gifted with divine wisdom surely perceived the truth. The author, however, does not explain clearly why these individuals are blameworthy. Did they deliberately turn from God? Were they intellectually lazy?

The second part (13:10–15:17) has three major sections (13:11–14:11; 14:12–15:6; 15:7-13), with a reflection on the Egyptians (15:14-17). Following the usual pattern, a theme statement opens the section (v. 10): far

worse than nature worship is the worship of human artifacts. God made the heavens, but humans made idols—the ultimate foolishness. These idols, unlike the sun and moon ("governors of the world," v. 2) are useless. To show better the foolishness of idolatry, the writer makes fun of the entire process, following the lead of several previous writers (see Jer 10:1-16; Bar 6; Isa 44:9-20).

Carpenters have God-given skill (vv. 11, 13), but they can use it badly. The author heaps scorn on them by showing that they can even use the most useless part of leftover wood (v. 13) to make an idol, full of blemishes. Once secured in its shrine, its maker calls on it—turning the divine order of creation upside down. The most succinct statements are in verses 17-18: "for vigor he invokes the powerless; for life he entreats the dead." This is the ultimate in folly. Idolmakers should rather rejoice in their skill, given by wisdom (14:2), than in a work to no purpose and powerless to save.

In verses 3-11 the author turns to God in prayer and exasperation. The term "providence" appears here for the first time in the Bible (v. 3), even though the concept is clear enough in other expressions, such as "hand of God" (see Josh 4:24 and 1 Kgs 18:46 for examples). Providence is a quality of God, whose creative power does not cease at the moment of creation. The road in the sea recalls the path through the Red Sea (see Ps 77:20) but refers directly to the right way to reach a destination (see Ps 107:28-32). To make one's way through an apparently trackless sea is a work of wisdom, but even Noah ("one without skill," v. 4) could rely on divine guidance.

Other goods of the earth, products of wisdom, would perish if they could not be shipped elsewhere (v. 5); even commerce is a work of wisdom. "Raft" and "frailest wood," referring to 10:4, are terms chosen deliberately to magnify God's power, even though transport ships were doubtless more than simple rafts. Noah, "hope of the universe," came safely to land again, and thus the human race was preserved by wood (v. 6). The author connects the account of the giants (Gen 6:1-4) with the great flood, a possible reading of the Genesis account but not the normal interpretation.

As a result, the author can pronounce

some wood blessed and other wood cursed (vv. 7-8), and likewise some woodworkers blessed and others cursed (vv. 8-10). A further reason for a curse is for having bestowed the name "god" on a non-god. In Israel's thinking, the name stands for the reality, and God's name is incommunicable (see 14:21). To dare to act otherwise is to become worthy of punishment. Finally, even the idols themselves will be "visited," that is, judged and condemned (v. 11; see Jeremiah's thoughts on the destruction of the idols of Egypt in Jer 43:12-13).

The author's teaching on the origin and evils of idol worship (14:12–15:6) is the centerpiece of the entire section and is remarkable for its sensitive analysis (like that in 13:1-9). The theme (vv. 12-14) lays out the evil of idol worship: besides being folly in itself, it leads to other sin (v. 12). The writer does not specify when the sudden end will take place (v. 14).

Two origins for idol worship are proposed, and both are understandable in their context: the missing child (vv. 15-16) or a distant ruler (vv. 17-20). However innocent the original motives, corruption takes over. The royal father contrives rites to honor his dead son, and these assume the force of law; afterward they degenerate into folly, since the incommunicable name of the living God is given to a dead man (v. 15).

In verses 17-20 the king may be the same as the father of verse 15. Whether he is or not, his subjects begin in earnest to honor him through God-given artistic work (vv. 17-18). Human folly takes over and rites develop. The conclusion (v. 21) repeats the author's conviction about the proper order of the universe, now overturned by worshipers of idols ("stocks [wood] and stones").

The resulting evils are explained in verses 22-31. The language in verse 22 is complex. Idol-worshipers made two mistakes: they were in error about God, and they saw nothing wrong in evil rites. They gave the name of God to objects and gave the name of peace to war. The social results of such folly are given in verses 23-26: three evil rites (v. 23), murder and adultery (v. 24), and a welter of other disorders (vv. 25-26). Without the Creator, humans left to themselves tend to sin—traces of the original sin. Once the sense of shame has vanished, any evil is possible. The

rites (v. 23) were practiced at various times, particularly in Israel's past (recall the condemnation of the Canaanites, 12:3-6).

The origin, repeated in verse 27, is idolatry. The results are all folly: "mad with enjoyment" is to lose control of reason; "prophesy lies" is to overturn God's order of truth. Without the true and living God, every kind of evil can take place (v. 29, a key verse in understanding how idol worship leads to wicked living). Punishment will overtake idol-worshipers (vv. 30-31) for both reasons; this is the law of the universe, restated in the final clause: it "ever follows" sin.

A second address to God follows (15:1-6); in it Israel disclaims idol worship. Regrettably these earnest words do not square with some periods of Israel's history; recall the idol worship in the Jerusalem temple (Ezek 8–9). It is true that apart from some superstitious practices characteristic of popular religion, Israel held true to the worship of the one God after the Exile.

Verse 1 is quoted from elsewhere (Ps 86:5, 15, for one example), giving traditional warrant for the author's teaching on forgiveness. The following verse is contradictory both in language and in fact ("if we sin . . . we will not sin"). Israel belongs to God by covenant (12:21). The tone of verse 3 is intellectual: justice and immortality come from the knowledge of God. The doing of justice is lacking here; the omission probably signifies nothing. Idol-making is "fruitless," that is, of no real effect and subject to the curse of futility. Note also the proportion in creation, "worthy of such hopes," that is, idol-makers are wicked and foolish, since they long for wicked and foolish things.

A second satire on idol-makers appears in 15:7-13, similar in many respects to that in 13:11–14:2. The writer holds the potter responsible, since he should have learned something from molding clay—namely, that he too was molded from the earth (Gen 2:7). He should in fact have imitated God in creation, working only for the good. Instead he used his God-given skill wickedly, doing meaningless work, a true mark of folly. He should have known, too, the end of his life, when he returns to dust (vv. 8b-9a). That life is lent to God's creatures is an unusual expression (see v. 16). Reflection on the idea, however, could have led Israel to consider that the spirit is tied to individual humans, and does not lose that connection after death. Hence, even though earthly life is ended, the spirit returns to God for reward or punishment.

In addition to the punishment coming to the potter for his foolishness, he is also blameworthy for greed and for making counterfeits. These latter are either imitations of more expensive work or represent gods that do not even exist (vv. 9-12). Like the carpenter's hopes (14:10), those of the potter are doomed (v. 10). A distinction between soul and spirit (v. 11) should not be easily drawn, since the terms are in a poetic parallel construction, signifying the same thing. Nonetheless, the terms eventually came to signify, along with body/flesh, the parts of human existence (as in Paul, 1 Thess 5:23, for a clear example).

The writer concludes with a set of reflections on the guilt of the Egyptians (vv. 14-17). They are foolish, not wise like Israel (v. 14). The main cause was idol worship, especially since the idols had no life, no power to act. The satirical description of idols basically adapts Ps 115:4-7 and Ps 135:15-18. The last two verses (vv. 16-17) also satirize the idol-maker. Being alive, the maker is infinitely greater than the lifeless object. The last sentence recalls 13:18, contrasting true life with death.

The issue of how idol-worshipers judged their worship remains undiscussed. It is quite likely that they understood the difference between life and death, and used the idol to focus attention and respect on other-worldly ideas.

15:18–16:15 The second example concluded. Resuming the argument left off in 12:27 on the worship of animals, the writer concludes. Mention of the Egyptians resumed in 15:14, though not by name, in the usual fashion. Verses 18-19 are quite harsh in their judgment, beyond even traditional biblical teaching on animals. "Loathsome" animals might include dung beetles (scarabs) and various snakes. The assertion that some of these beasts escaped God's approval is a very surprising affirmation in view of the author's teaching on divine wisdom in creation (especially 1:14). It seems quite likely that the writer's vehemence in denunciation got the better of his theology. Punishment for Egypt resulted in insect plagues (gnats and flies, Exod

9:12-20), loathsome creatures in their own way.

Israel, on the other hand, benefited while Egypt suffered. The "novel dish," quail in the desert, satisfied Israel's hunger; an equally novel occurrence—plagues of frogs, gnats, and flies—failed to satisfy Egypt. Israel may have suffered a little, but this follows the author's theory of retribution seen previously (see 3:5). In verse 4 Egypt, formerly an oppressor, did not itself experience hunger. Tormented by Egypt, Israel now sees how Egypt was tormented in turn. This knowledge was not simple vengeance, but gave the Israelites the opportunity to learn God's goodness toward them.

The author contrasts Egypt and Israel again in verses 5-10. True, Israel was punished (Num 21:4-9) as a result of murmuring; but the punishment was not complete, as it might have been in strict justice. To avoid a charge of idolatry, the author makes it clear that it was God who saved, not the serpent symbol erected by Moses. "Savior of all" (v. 7) must refer, in the Book of Wisdom, to God's power to save rather than actually saving all (v. 7).

In the case of the Egyptians, they suffered both from the knowledge of God's power to save from the serpents (v. 8) and from their plagues (v. 9). "He who delivers from all evil" sounds like a divine title, similar to "savior of all." The standard version does not record the death of the Egyptians due to locusts and flies; possibly the author is taking homiletic liberties, based on Exod 10:17, "deadly pest." Divine proportion affects the punishment coming to the oppressors ("they deserved," v. 9).

A few reflections conclude the section (vv. 11-15). Israel's brief punishment is explained again (v. 11), this time using "forgetfulness," a typically Greek expression. This state is a manifestation of folly, since it keeps persons from seeing and knowing God's hand in their lives.

No particular "word" of God seems intended in verse 12, but probably just a general decree or decision to save. To affirm God's power over both life and death claims universal jurisdiction and denies any supreme evil, an adversary of God. "Lead down . . . lead back" (see Tob 13:2) means to bring death and bring life, but more exactly it refers to bringing back from the gates of death, that is, being near death through illness. In the author's day, however, this ancient thought was used more globally, as seen by the contrast in verse 14 (spirit and soul are synonymous here).

16:16-29 Third example: manna. The examples are meant to show divine protection for Israel, contrasted with proportionate punishment for Egypt. Verses 16-19 deal with Egypt's twofold punishment in hail and fire, and open with the usual thematic sentence. Hail, mixed of course with cold rain, is virtually unknown in Egypt. The wonder of it all for the author is that two opposite forces, water and fire (that is, lightning), existed together in doing God's will, whereas they could not do so naturally (Exod 9:22-26). The explanatory clause beginning "for" in verse 17 stems from Israel's most ancient traditions (as in Judg 5:20).

In the text of Exodus, the plague of hail, which kills the animals, follows other plagues involving animals (Exod 9:1-7). In the present text, however, events are compressed; only some beasts are killed (v. 18) so that others could plague Egypt, which in turn would acknowledge God.

Israel thrived on manna, a food that came down from the heavens, pleasing everyone, even those with differing tastes (v. 20). The author follows the older traditions of Ps 78:25 (and Ps 105:40) regarding manna as food of the heavenly beings. Manna had a moral meaning also as a symbol of divine sweetness—another new idea.

Verses 22-29 examine these events more theoretically. Israel took comfort, as noted often before, in the punishment meted out to Egypt (v. 22). Divine creative power so altered the normal operations of nature that God's will was done. Fire (lightning) continued its work even amid water (snow and ice/hail). The explanatory sentence (v. 24) stands as a universal principle to explain miracles. The purpose of it all was to grow in wisdom: "that your sons . . . might learn" (v. 26). In verse 27 the author has also mixed events into one, seeing the hail of Exod 9 as the hoarfrost of Exod 16:14.

The concluding two verses (vv. 28-29) are somewhat disconnected from the foregoing. Verse 29 is a moralizing comment, adding nothing to the strength of the lesson.

17:1-18:4 Fourth example: darkness and light. Following a brief introductory comment (v. 1), the author writes about the darkness afflicting Egypt (vv. 2-21). This section, too, begins with an introduction which, however, treats night as a moral condition rather than a physical reality (see also 17:21). Israel was not, of course, removed from God's providence; it only seemed so.

Apparitions in the night terrified the Egyptians (vv. 3-6). This concept, elaborated at some length here, does not appear in the accounts of the Book of Exodus. The author has dramatized the relatively tame account of Exod 9:21-23, drawing out implications about ghosts (vv. 3-4), sounds in the night (vv. 4, 9), and sights (vv. 5-6, fires). Psychological torment, as always, is worse than physical ones (vv. 6-9). Magicians (as in Exod 9:11), to whom the terrified Egyptians called in the darkness, could do nothing this time. In the thought typical of the Book of Wisdom, shrewd magicians are themselves turned into objects of mockery by the force they sought to expel (vv. 7-10). "To face the air" is an obscure phrase but may be a psychological comment, namely, that the sorcerers were afraid even of harmless air; the only terrors were in their imagination.

Verses 11-13 comment on the fears that accompany evil. The term "conscience" (v. 11) makes its first appearance here; it will be used extensively in the New Testament. The rest of the comments must draw on abundant experience.

On this psychological basis, the writer then explains events further in verses 14-21. The source of this "night" is unusual: the nether world, where eternal night reigns (as in Job 42:17). Sleep is perhaps a symbol of their condition in the darkness rather than their actual state in this period of three "days" (Exod 10:22-23). It is also called a prison (vv. 16-17), taking in Egyptians everywhere. The seven sounds of their terror (vv. 18-19) are beautifully described, but did not form part of the narration of the Book of Exodus. The exemption of Israel and the rest of the world in verse 20 parallels Exod 10:23b. The closing verse (v. 21) refers to night as symbol, similar to the hope of the wicked (in 16:29).

Comments on light for Israel (18:1-4) conclude the example. The author calls the Israelites "holy ones," a new term (repeated in verse 5) destined to move from a description of heavenly beings (as in 5:5) to temple personnel, and finally to the people and the land (12:3). The text puts Egyptians and Israelites in close proximity, a further cause for terror in the night. Once the plague ceased, the Egyptians begged Israel to go (v. 2). "Instead of this" (v. 3) refers to the darkness over Egypt. The pillar (v. 3) and the cloud (causing a "mild sun") lit the night sky for Israel in the desert (Exod 13:21-22). Proportionate punishment ("deserved to be deprived," v. 4) falls on Egypt in the form of darkness, the comparison calling Israel's slavery darkness (17:2, 21). A completely new idea closes the passage: the law, to be given soon on Sinai, is an imperishable light (as in Ps 119:105).

18:5–19:21 Fifth example: Death of the first-born. This last section speaks first of death for both Egypt (18:5-19) and Israel (18:20-25), and then of the events at the Sea (19:1-21).

Following the author's cast of thought, the Egyptians were to suffer a fate proportionate to the murder of Israel's children (v. 5); also, whereas one child of Israel (Moses) was saved from the Nile, all of Egypt's soldiers perished at the Sea. Their time of punishment was announced to Israel (Exod 11:4) when Israel was to celebrate the first Passover (Exod 12:1-28). This Passover (v. 9) was celebrated by the holy people, sanctified in a particular way at this festival and having experienced the dangers of life in Egypt. The praises of the ancestors are either praises of them or more likely the songs of praise they had sung previously. These may be the Great Hallel ("Praise" in Hebrew), Psalms 113–118, which came to be sung at Passover, and may have been used as such in the author's time.

The wailing of families, both high and low, bereft of their first-born sons (vv. 10-12) contrasts with Israel's songs. The Egyptians should have known what would happen, since Moses predicted the disaster to Pharaoh (Exod 11:4-8). The cause of their disbelief was magic, according to the author, who had little other reason to explain this extraordinary obstinacy. A further reason appears in verse 13: Egypt's sons died, but God's son, Israel, was saved. This is a motive in addition to the more usual one of recompense for the death of Israel's children (v. 5).

The next passage (vv. 14-19) elaborates on the traditional accounts of this most dreadful punishment. In the first place, the author sets the stage carefully: at midnight, in the quiet and darkness, the personified word of God appears. At this coming, the scene changes from peace to mourning, and from darkness to a disturbed mixture of ghostly manifestations. These visions found no place in the text of Exodus, but form part of the writer's psychological tools in making his point. We find that the purpose for these visions is to increase the sting of punishment; also, at the point of their death the first-born moved from ignorance to knowledge of the God of Israel.

1 Chr 21:16, which pictures an angel "standing between earth and heaven," may have provided the impetus for later images of a divine figure of great height, that is, of all-encompassing power, similar to wisdom itself (as 8:24). This figure appears in verse 16 as well as in later Jewish writing.

Israel also suffered thousands of deaths in the wilderness (Num 17:14). The difference, as previously, is that Israel's punishment was brief (v. 20). Aaron the priest put an end to the deaths with his weapon (vv. 21-24). Since God sent the punishment for Israel's sins, it is difficult today to appreciate Aaron's role in mitigating it. His priestly robes (praised in Sir 50 for their beauty) here have a mystical power, symbolizing the beautiful world and the tribes of the chosen people. This destroyer, possibly the same figure as the personified word of verse 15, finally yielded (v. 25).

The events at the Red Sea climax the narrative (19:1-21). Even though the Egyptians suffered the full punishment, they were foolish enough to ignore the clear lesson of God's protection for Israel (v. 1). The Lord knew this beforehand and planned an even greater punishment (vv. 1b-2). Their foolishness reached new heights even in their grief (vv. 3-4), with the result that Israel's deliverance was greater again, and the punishment of the Egyptians even more terrifying (v. 5).

The author in the next few verses (vv. 6-12) shows again how the Creator could refashion creation for the benefit of the people. Verse 6 stands as a theme, and the rest of the section gives examples. The Lord brought dry land out of the sea, as happened in the original creation of the world (Gen 1:9-10). The crossing is painted vividly: a grassy plain filled with people roaming like horses or lambs (vv. 7b-9). As usual, the text of Exodus is less colorful (Exod 14:21-22).

Unlike the forgetful, foolish Egyptians (vv. 3-4), the Israelites knew what was happening and why (vv. 10-12). In contrast to the first creation, the land did not bring forth beneficial living creatures (Gen 1:24) but gnats (Exod 8:17). The quail were new, since they came apparently out of the sea, following Num 11:31.

The author moves to an elaborate comparison between the Egyptians and the inhabitants of Sodom. Egypt suffered due to its foolishness, ignoring warnings and enslaving Israel, originally their guests (v. 13; see Exod 1:8-10). The Sodomites did not receive guests hospitably (v. 13b); the guests in this case were heavenly visitors, "strangers" (v. 15). The punishment was destruction. The Egyptians (v. 16) first received Israel with rejoicing (Gen 45:17-20) but later turned to oppression, and their punishment was even greater than that of Sodom. Both the Egyptians and the people of Sodom were punished with blindness (the darkness in Exod 10:21-23; a blinding light in Gen 19:11).

Reversals in nature, a kind of new creation (see v. 16), conclude the book. Verse 18 states the theme by means of a musical image. The "land creatures" were the animals that accompanied Israel through the Sea (Exod 12:38). The water creatures were the frogs that invaded Egypt (Exod 7:25-29). The fire and water (vv. 20-21) appeared in 16:16-29.

The final verse (v. 22) concludes Part Three (11:2-19:22) but applies to the entire book. Addressed directly to God, it praises God's providential care for the chosen people, with whom God has remained, no matter the occasion. The lesson for the disciple of wisdom is to examine Israel's history intently to perceive God's guidance, and thereby to grow in closeness to wisdom, that is, God.

SIRACH

John E. Rybolt, C.M.

INTRODUCTION

Title

There has never been any question about the title of major biblical books, such as Isaiah, Jeremiah, or the Gospels; but books like Sirach are not as well known, and as a result their titles often vary. This book goes by two names, each having several variations. The first is the Book of Sirach (or the Book of the Wisdom of Sirach); the second is the Latin name Ecclesiasticus, meaning "church [book]." The first takes its name from the author, and the second from the use of it made by the church—possibly because others had doubts about it. This commentary uses the name Ben Sira for the author, and Sirach for the book.

Author

It is unusual for an Old Testament book to bear the name of its author, since the books usually contain the words or deeds of individuals—for example, a book *about* Jonah, not a book *by* Jonah. The foreword calls the author "Jesus"; his more complete name is given in 50:27: "Jesus, son of Eleazar, son of Sirach." Ben ("son of") Sira is the common form of his name.

Even though we know the author's name, we know nothing about him other than what we can deduce from the book. He was a family man, given to study and writing. He taught (51:23), read widely, recommended travel, and doubtless enjoyed a good reputation. His concerns reflect upper-class life, and he probably wrote them down in his later life. He has

an extraordinary interest in matters liturgical, but this does not prove that he was a priest. His grandson, who translated the book from Hebrew into Greek, remains completely unknown.

Date and place of composition

Scholars have determined the time of composition as the first part of the second century B.C.E., about the year 180. The high priest Simon (50:1-21) died about 190; Ben Sira speaks of him as having died recently. The foreword speaks of King Euergetes, whose thirty-eighth year was 132 B.C.E. Working backward from grandson to son to father brings us close to 180 B.C.E. Finally, the book does not reflect the revolutionary troubles that broke out in 168 B.C.E.

It is more difficult to ascertain where the book was written. Jerusalem is thought to have been the place of composition, since it was the main center of culture, education, and religious life. The foreword was composed in Egypt; scholars suspect that Alexandria was the place, and for the same reasons: Jewish culture, education, and religion.

Language

The New American Bible took the bold step of using the surviving portions of Sirach in Hebrew as its fundamental text. For centuries Sirach existed only in Greek, together with some quotations in Jewish writings. As the foreword notes, a Hebrew version existed and was translated into Greek. In the years

1896–1900 archeologists uncovered about two-thirds of a Hebrew version, and since that time fragments of other manuscripts have been added. Unfortunately it is not always clear that today's Hebrew version is original or even older than the normal Greek version. In many cases, however, the Hebrew and the Greek are identical, and in some cases the Hebrew makes better sense. The differing versions have led to a differing enumeration of verses, sometimes a very confusing situation for a modern reader.

Authority

The Book of Sirach forms part of the "deuterocanonical" books, or as they are often called today, the "Apocrypha." This designation means that from earliest times Jewish scholars did not include it among the books of Scripture. They did use the book on occasion in worship and for study, but since it was unlike standard Judaism in many respects, it did not take its place in the list of sacred books (or "canon"). Early Christian lists often omitted it or at least questioned its authority, but the church used it extensively, and continues to do so. The foreword is always included with the book but is not regarded as inspired Scripture.

Background

The author's work grew out of the experience of Israel, with its concerns and styles of writing and thinking. However, Greek thought and life had been making an impact on upper-class Jewish life for some time before Ben Sira wrote. His book even quotes or paraphrases pagan Greek texts, and his style as a scholar at leisure is much more characteristic of the Greeks than of the Jews, whose scholars made their living with daily labor. The author also demonstrates his acquaintance with Egypt's thought world and quotes from its literature.

Style

The book appears to be Ben Sira's collected notes put into poetry and arranged for publication. This makes an outline of the book quite difficult, apart from major sections. The poetry abounds in rich images taken from nature and shows wide variety in types of writing. Ben Sira often uses multiple terms for the same idea. Sirach is a work of wisdom literature. Unlike Job and Ecclesiastes, it does not treat of a single theme. It resembles the first part of Proverbs in style but does not contain single proverbs without commentary. It also resembles the Book of Wisdom in its interest in history and theory.

Teachings

Ben Sira himself did not summarize his teachings, but in a book as long and complex as Sirach, a summary seems needed. For him, God is all, the only God, the almighty Creator who brought order to all facets of life, both natural and moral. God, the source of good, acts justly but also forgives sin. God is also active in history and is bound by covenants to a special relationship with Israel. Ben Sira has a worldwide view of God's activity and sees the law as applicable in some way to everyone. For him, life continues in some way after death; but judgment takes place at death, not afterward.

For Ben Sira, fulfilling the law of Moses is great wisdom. The law prescribes the liturgy, a feature of great interest to Ben Sira. His spirituality might be called liturgical in some fashion. Whether humans are completely free or in some way subject to destiny is unclear. It is clear, however, that virtuous living will be rewarded, and wickedness punished. Ben Sira knows reason and its demands; the ethical content of his work is high. For that reason it is hard to say that Sirach is "revealed" in any way.

Particularly disturbing to many is the author's harsh treatment of women. Since the author accommodated Jewish teachings to Greek rational philosophy and did not have much to say about oral traditions, scholars have called him an early Sadducee. This observation is even clearer when one compares his teachings with those of Jesus in the Gospels, where Jesus appears to follow more closely the methods of the Pharisees.

COMMENTARY

The Introduction to Sirach

Foreword

Only the Book of Sirach comes with a prologue of this type. Other biblical books have introductions (for example, Psalm 1 for the Book of Psalms, and Deut 1:1-2 for the rest of that book), but none of them gives such details on the book's composition and translation. In the case of Sirach, the author of the foreword had to refer to the translation from Hebrew (into Greek), since Hebrew was no longer the generally spoken language of Alexandria in Egypt, where a large Jewish community made its home.

In the first paragraph the translator, whose name we do not know, makes mention of the law, the prophets, and the "later authors." Scholars see this as the earliest reference to the division of the books of the Hebrew Bible into their three traditional parts: the law, the prophets, the writings. The last category was not fully developed in Ben Sira's day. Further, the usual order followed in Christian editions is law (Pentateuch), history, writings, and prophets. Israel, however, understood the books of history as one with the prophets and joined the two, leaving the writings till last.

The one mention of Israel's wisdom should be read in the light of a more general attempt on the part of Jewish authors of the period to defend the quality of their wisdom teaching over against that of their pagan neighbors. This defense grew stronger in the next couple of centuries, since it was important for Jews living outside of Israel to realize how valuable their own traditions were. The translator offers his readers the insight that wisdom is not just a matter of learning alone but of proper living, in accordance with the whole Jewish law. His insistence on this is derived from many places in the Book of Sirach.

In the second paragraph the translator comments on the difficulties of translation, from Hebrew in particular. The common understanding of this passage is that he is referring to Greek translations, yet translations into Aramaic, the spoken language of Jews in Israel, were already known in Israel itself. Eventually a number of Greek translations were brought together in Egypt in a version known as the Septuagint (meaning the

"Seventy," after an old story about seventy scholars in Alexandria producing this version).

In the final paragraph of the foreword, the word "reproduction" refers most likely to other wisdom literature, probably in Greek translation. The publication that the translator mentions involved preparing a master text to be given to copyists for mass production. These copies were then sent to those "living abroad." This expression probably has Israel as its point of reference, since living abroad for a Jew meant living anywhere else than in Israel, not just outside of Egypt.

A person evidently acquires wisdom by reading and reflecting on texts, a method recommended even today. Ben Sira's grandson concludes by repeating his insistence that a change of life (we might call it "conversion") must accompany growth in wisdom.

IN PRAISE OF WISDOM

Solemn Introduction to Wisdom (1:1-29)

These verses summarize the teaching of the sages on wisdom up to the period of Ben Sira and give the author's own developed thought.

1:1-8 The origin and character of wisdom. The book opens with a thematic statement contrasting somewhat with other statements in the book praising the wisdom of Israel, which, to be sure, has its origin in God. The author's use of examples drawn from nature (vv. 2-3) and their application to human experience are characteristic of all wisdom writing—encouraging students to have a contemplative regard for God's creation. Ben Sira pairs wisdom with understanding (v. 5) in Hebrew fashion, intending no difference between them. Elsewhere in the Old Testament wisdom is associated with skill, common sense, or even accumulated human knowledge; but here wisdom is of a higher quality: hidden in God (v. 5), created by God alone (v. 7). As in Prov 8:22, wisdom is not understood as coeternal with the Lord but is created by God. The "friends" of God (v. 8) are likely the people of Israel.

1:9-18 Wisdom is the fear of the Lord. Fear is traditionally understood as reverence, devotion, or awe in the presence of God. To have this quality is a great blessing, compared here to the gladness of a festive banquet (v. 9). It brings blessings, including a long life, to the one who has it (v. 10)—a conservative view uninfluenced by thoughts of eternal life (v. 11).

Ben Sira then discusses fear of the Lord, opening with a traditional statement, copied often (see Job 28:28; Ps 111:10; Prov 1:7, 9:10). Then he goes beyond this with his own expansion. Often in this work the author's sense of predestination is evident, as in verses 12b-13. He does not clearly develop this position, however. He continues with sensory descriptions (drunk with wisdom, v. 14; taste, v. 15; sight and smell of flowers, vv. 16-17). The tree metaphor (v. 18) is traditional in wisdom writing (see Ps 1). "Knowledge and full understanding" are here the results of wisdom, not its synonyms (as in v. 4).

1:19-29 Marks of wisdom. Verses 19-21 seem out of place here, contrasting as they do with the previous verses. In fact, some manuscripts are disturbed here, showing hesitancy even in the tradition. The teaching on patience for a time (vv. 20-21) is developed further in Sirach: a proper time reflects God's order in creation, to be modeled in wise living. Likewise, the connection between wisdom and justice, or right living according to the law, is a major theme in Ben Sira's writing (vv. 22-24).

The negatives of verses 25-29 are counsels against duplicity, in prophetic style. The public humiliation of the unwise (with no hint of the final judgment) is rooted in the conviction that reliance on self rather than on God is the ultimate blasphemy and a reversal of divine creation.

Lessons on Faithfulness and Humility (2:1–4:10)

2:1-18 Duties to God by enduring trials. The first lesson opens traditionally with "My son," words that often mark new sections in Sirach. By "son" the author means "disciple," a student in Ben Sira's lecture hall. The author treats first the theme of preparation for trials, that is, adversity and misfortune. The basis for these trials is not given, but it is probably a test of faith. Then follow lessons (vv. 4-6), a natural experience and its moral application (v. 5). Just as impurities can be removed even from gold, so the just can be purified. One's true value will thereby be seen.

Verses 7-11 set a different tone, since Ben Sira writes in the plural. These sound like psalm verses, recalling Pss 46:1; 71:5; 103:4-5, and others. To emphasize his point, the Sage counsels the study of history, chiefly the Scripture. But his advice is too simple, for it does not account for the apparently meaningless suffering of some biblical heroes such as Josiah. As a result of his own biblical studies, Ben Sira claims that the main motive (v. 11) for being faithful is that God's mercy is consistent (recalling Exod 34:6-7).

Verses 12-18 enumerate the curses (or woes) on those without hope in God. This theme appears only here and in 41:8. Those condemned should have known of God's mercy and forgiveness in history. The blessed (vv. 15-17) stand in contrast. Note that "fear" and "love" occur as parallel terms in verses 15-16; the author intends them to refer to the same state of heart. The final verse recalls 2 Sam 24:14.

3:1-16 Honoring parents. Ben Sira divides his lesson on the honor owed to parents into positive (vv. 1-9) and negative duties (vv. 10-16). In general for Ben Sira, the father serves as the focus, and the mother just as a poetic contrast (see vv. 2, 3, 6, 9, 11, 16). If this is Ben Sira's commentary on the fourth commandment, it is the earliest one we have.

For the positive duties, the text opens with a statement about a parent's right, together with the motive: life—a clear echo of Exod 20:12. The basis for the command is found in the Lord's doing, with its rewards: atonement for sin, children, prayers answered, life, family harmony. The concept of atonement for sin by honoring a parent is a feature new to biblical teaching. Before Ben Sira's day it was taught that atonement is accomplished by sacrifice. Ben Sira also develops the atoning value of alms (3:20; 28:2; 34:26; 35:3). Atonement, however, is not automatic; repentance is also required.

Verse 9 is probably a popular proverb, known from the introductory "for." The contrast here is not between father and mother but between a parent's blessing and curse.

The negative duties (vv. 10-16) begin with a contrast between shame and honor. These lines might also be rephrased as follows: to show honor for a father is honor in a son; but shame for a mother is shame in her children. The interpretive possibilities of such a brief proverb are probably intended. Such pithy statements can be twisted and examined from many points of view. Those of us who read them should extract all the meaning possible from them.

Verses 12-15 do not necessarily refer to Ben Sira's views on family life. He counsels consideration or human kindness for all children. The motive is divine: God will take such kindness (literally "almsgiving") into account. Verse 15 continues the lesson, alluding possibly to a storehouse (or account book?) for good acts. This may sound too mechanical for Christians. Verse 16 is in standard proverbial style, with roots in Exod 21:17.

3:17-28 Lessons on humility. Recall here the upper-class situation of the Sage and his students. Against such a background lessons on humility are dramatic. In verses 17-18 he introduces his lesson with the motive: loved by others, rewarded by God. Verse 19 adds another: an assertion of divine power and condescension to the lowly. Verses 20-24 are negatives. Ben Sira introduces another concept characteristic of his writing, namely, one's lot in life (here, "what is committed to you"). He stands in contrast with Greek thinking, which emphasized freedom of investigation. For Ben Sira, one's lot in life reflects God's created order. Verse 23 is an argument from personal experience, and verse 24 offers an example from nature, designed to provoke reflection about right living.

In verses 25-27 the author contrasts the stubborn (literally, "heavy heart"), with the humble. The assertion of punishment here is fundamental to Ben Sira's thought: each act has its own reward bound up with it. Results follow inevitably.

The section concludes with a general comment (v. 28). Proverbs such as these are wise sayings, usually memorable and sharp, briefly summing up human experience. They were the stock in trade of wisdom teachers. (See also 6:35; 8:8; 13:25; 20:20; 21:15.)

3:29-4:10 Alms. These verses form the last part of the lesson on fidelity and humility and fall into three parts: theme (3:29-30), negative (4:1-6), and then positive recommendations (4:7-10).

The theme here is astonishing: alms can atone for sins. As noted above, this teaching is characteristic of our author. Note that the form is typical: experience (water and fire)

and application (atonement). Nothing is implied, however, as to just how alms atone for sin.

The negatives in the next verses are followed by a final assertion of God's activity (v. 6). One would like to read in these verses a completely charitable approach, that is, to do good simply for its own sake. The lesson here is self-protection: doing good to others will involve a reward, just as not doing good (or doing evil) will lead to punishment. Note also that God is called "his Creator," a commonplace expression for us but a relatively new idea in Old Testament times. This term underscores the oneness of all creatures: God made both the rich and the poor.

The positive recommendations of verses 7-10 change the scene from public life on the streets (implied in verses 1-6) to the assembly, some sort of general gathering that heard cases and gave judgment. Ben Sira presumes here that his students will be in a position to help, given their social status. Verse 7 itself is general and may be a quotation. The results of this charitable activity will be the same as in the previous section—reward from God for oneself. ("Most High" is a title for God used principally in the late Old Testament period.) The motherly tenderness of God is surprising, given the rigidly masculine viewpoint in Sirach.

Pursuit and Marks of Wisdom (4:11–10:5)

4:11-19 Rewards of wisdom. The theme statement in verse 11 is typical: wisdom is a female. (The father of these children is not otherwise specified because of the poetic nature of these teachings.) Various rewards are specified: life, favor, glory (or renown). The connection between wisdom and God ("the Holy One") is very close (v. 14). It has proven difficult in many cases to separate wisdom and God clearly (as in the opening chapters of Proverbs). Such a division is rather the task of theology than of biblical poetry.

Verse 15 ("judges nations") refers to the Gentiles among whom the Jews live. The original Hebrew, however, may mean "judges aright." The difference is due to a possible confusion of terms.

Growth in wisdom comes by trusting her (v. 16). This itself comes through testing by wisdom, possibly by the decision that an official might have to make (reflecting the social status of Ben Sira's students). Small, wise decisions will lead to a conviction that wisdom can be trusted. The secrets of wisdom (v. 18) come only with struggle. To abandon wisdom is an evil, and Ben Sira's treatment of this is normal—a reversal of positions takes place: to abandon wisdom means that wisdom will abandon us, and misery will be our lot. We have only ourselves to blame for this, since that is the way God's creation is ordered.

4:20–6:4 Excess and defect of wisdom. Ben Sira knew public life well enough to realize that balance or proportion is needed in all things, even in humility. His teaching here probably revolves around proportion rather than any specific element. Proportion would be, for example, a feature of well-ordered creation, and an observant or wise creature would seek to imitate it.

Verse 21 is a learned explanation of one word with two meanings. Ben Sira may be citing Hesiod, an ancient Greek author; whether directly or indirectly is not known. This points to the general international character of wisdom teaching.

The issue of proportion is carried through lessons about speech (speaking at the proper time, v. 23) and about being vulnerable (admitting guilt or ignorance, v. 26). The proper proportion (or "truth," v. 28) is ultimately at stake, and God, the guarantor of right order, will uphold it. These lessons about created order contrast to some degree with the sense of right and wrong Christians have traditionally learned from a meditation on the commandments. Ben Sira teaches an alternative form of reflection on God.

One of the defects of wisdom is arrogance (vv. 29-31). These negatives recall the prophetic distinction between words and actions, but the text (particularly verse 30) is obscure. The early church (in the *Didache*) quoted verse 31 as a typically Christian attitude toward life.

The section 5:1-10 treats of self-reliance as a defect of wisdom. The introductory theme (vv. 1-2) is a true religious message, counseling against reliance on two false gods, wealth and power. Although self-reliance can be recognized as a good—and was so by many Greek philosophers—its excess is being considered here.

A series of contrasts follows (vv. 3-7), using prohibitions and assertions proving the point at issue. An exception is verses 5-6, which seem to allude to a psalm. The motive for this prohibition contains another instance of the balance or proportion characteristic of Ben Sira's teaching: God's mercy and anger are both in proportion to the human acts involved.

The conclusion (vv. 8-10) is homiletic in style, which is unusual for Sirach. The summary in verse 10 points to the danger of reliance on apparent power; wealth has no real power in the ultimate issues of life.

The next section, on sincerity in speech (5:11–6:1), marks the first appearance of a common theme in Sirach. The author lays out his general views (vv. 11-16), beginning with a rural proverb and drawing out its implication (vv. 11-12). Since some winds are too strong, the prudent person will choose the proper occasion to winnow or speak. The Epistle of James (1:19) quotes verse 13, although in another setting; verse 15 recalls the lengthy discussion in Jas 3:1-12 on restraining the tongue.

The motives behind the general teaching are shame (v. 17) and disgrace (6:1). In a small and closely knit society, shame would be more evident than in today's large, impersonal cities. Notice that both motives are human conditions rather than eternal punishment for sin. Ben Sira has discussed shame with guilt in 4:21; this passage is an example of that teaching.

A few verses on lust (6:2-4) complete Ben Sira's teaching on excess and defect in wisdom. His principal idea is that the wise person should never be in the grip of anything—in this case lust. The comparison differs in the Greek text, which mentions a bull consuming one's soul; even though the versions differ, the idea is clear enough. Both fire and bull can destroy a strong tree, the traditional picture of the wise (see Ps 1:3).

6:5-17 True friendship. One of the loveliest aspects of Sirach is the author's thoughts on friendship, developed in this book more thoroughly than elsewhere in wisdom literature. His normal caution is evident here and is a good check against multiplying friends; his experience teaches him that one's truest friends are few and far between (v. 6).

In verses 8-13 Ben Sira contrasts false and true friends in a set of assertions and explanations. Inconstant friends (vv. 8-10) are the opposite of wise friends, who are true to their word and selfless. The refrain "be with you" (vv. 8, 10) has deep biblical roots, drawn mainly from the presence of God with the chosen people or with particular heroes as a guarantee of success and blessing. Experience shows that a friend must be present particularly in times of need, even though words or solutions to the problems encountered are not available. A very cautious summary (v. 13) concludes these contrasts coming from a long life and broad experience; scholars have seen here an echo of the words of the Greek author Theognis, possibly known to educated Jews like Ben Sira.

True friends, by contrast, are described and praised (vv. 14-16) in a fashion recalling the virtuous wife of Prov 31:10-31. The concluding motive (v. 17) calls for fear of God (internally), coupled with good behavior (externally).

6:18-37 Attaining wisdom. One of several similar sections, these few verses lay out ways for disciples to grow toward wisdom. In the first place (vv. 18-23), the attainment of wisdom involves toil. Discipline, self-control, and longing are prerequisites for a life of work (v. 18). By contrast, the undisciplined (vv. 21-22) will never attain wisdom. The stone (v. 22) may be a heavy stone cast aside by the fool or perhaps a touchstone used to test genuine metals. The Hebrew text of verse 23 contains a play on words: the same word may mean "discipline" or "bond" or "removed."

Another lesson on the same topic opens solemnly with "my son" (vv. 24-31). This section, on submission, has a schoolroom atmosphere, with emphasis on activities—carry, draw close, search, seek (vv. 26-28). As a result, rest and joy will follow. The purple cord (v. 30) recalls Num 15:38-39 and links the law and wisdom. The burden, therefore, is not that of slaves but of scholars and royalty.

The author closes with a lesson emphasizing the will (vv. 32-33). On this basis he mentions other means (vv. 34-37a), principally the company of the wise and virtuous. The connection of law and wisdom (Torah wisdom) is clearly expressed here in summary (v. 37). The last half-verse parallels 1:1: if a person prepares for wisdom, God will grant it.

7:1–9:16 Advice and counsels. This section forms part of 4:11–10:5, on the pursuit of wisdom, and is further divided into public life (7:1-17), states in life (7:18-36), and relations with others (8:1–9:16).

Ben Sira's advice on public life opens with reversals of fortune (vv. 1-3). These are normally employed in Sirach to show how punishment takes place (evil acts carry with them their own punishment). The wise will want to avoid evil consequences. The verses on leadership (vv. 4-7) carry a double message: do not seek leadership, it leads to evil (v. 7); but if you have native abilities, then it is a good (v. 6). At root here is the conviction that all have their own places given them by God. Favoritism (v. 6) is unjust, since it violates the integrity or proportion to be observed in life's dealings.

In verses 8-10 the message is that each sin is punished; this is the order of the universe. Hence God cannot be bought off (v. 9); rather, true piety consists in both prayers and alms (faith and works, v. 10).

Insensitivity in public life (vv. 11-16) is also a great evil. Ben Sira has offered us a series of prohibitions, with a few reasons or motives, such as verse 13: lying always begets more lying. Verse 15 contrasts with the upper-class ethic seen in other places in Sirach. The author's approach recalls Paul's work as a tentmaker (Acts 18:3), living as a scholar by the work of his hands. The truly humble will have their reward (v. 17) elsewhere than in death, the common lot of all.

The verses on states in life (vv. 18-36) are arranged in groups, beginning with the family (vv. 18-26). Negative and positive recommendations are gathered together here. Noteworthy is the author's treatment of slaves (vv. 20-21): they are human beings, deserving of good treatment and respect. Theirs was generally an economic slavery, not one based on race or origins, nor were slaves regarded generally as a class in society. (For the release of slaves, see Deut 15:12.) Other property receives similar treatment (vv. 22-26): stock, sons, daughters, wife (evidently this is a man's world).

Honor is due parents (vv. 27-28; see 3:1-16) for their gift of life, now returned to them by a dutiful son. Priests likewise are to be honored (vv. 29-31), not for their own worthiness, but for the God whose ministers they are. (The offerings alluded to are not intended to describe precisely the rituals of the temple.) The poor, that is, the neglected and powerless, and even the dead deserve attentive treatment. The results will benefit the wise person, since God has ordered the universe so. The summary (v. 36) may lead to considerations of an afterlife; more likely Ben Sira had in mind the consequences of a good life on one's descendants.

The author's advice on relations with others (8:1–9:16) is divided into lessons on men (8:1-19), women (9:1-9), and friends (9:10-16).

The lessons on men treat first of the rich and powerful (vv. 1-2). History shows that wealth can corrupt (v. 2b). The unruly (vv. 3-4) should be avoided, since they are controlled by their passions and speak unwisely. The comparisons in verses 5-7 demonstrate Ben Sira's psychological sensitivity, a feature encountered several times in the book. The Sage may be speaking of his own experience also in verses 8-9. Training in proverbs (as in 3:28) will stretch one's mental potential to see clearly into reality. Real knowledge, which enables one for princely service, comes from accumulated experience (as in Deut 4:9; 11:19; Pss 44:1; 78:3; Job 8:8; 12:12).

Those to avoid (vv. 10-16) are described in terms of the reversals that come to the unwise disciple: the impious man (v. 11) will turn on you, for example. Financial matters (vv. 12-13) show that power can be abused; the wise should be in command of their own finances. The message of verse 14 recalls that of 7:6, but the perspective differs; Ben Sira offers no advice on handling disputes with judges.

Special advice on handling secrets (vv. 17-19) further demonstrates the author's well-known caution in matters of human relationships and contrasts to some extent with his teaching on trusting one's friends (see 6:5-17).

The experience of a man's world continues in 9:1-9, where Ben Sira, following the custom of other wisdom writers even outside Israel, writes negatively of women (see also 25:13–26:27). To give a woman power over a man (or to allow anything to have this power, such as desire or wealth) is a great evil (v. 2). Consorting with "strange women" likewise involves handing over self-control—in this case, to prostitutes or unmarried women

(vv. 3-5). The same lessons are featured in verses 6-8a: it is the mark of a fool to hand over control to another. The punishment is to "go down in blood to the grave" (v. 9). This expression (see Prov 2:18; 7:27) probably refers to the death penalty inflicted on adulterers (see Lev 20:10).

The verses on the choice of friends (vv. 10-16) add to the discussion of 6:5-17. The negatives (vv. 10-13) are filled with sound advice. Ben Sira counsels patience, implicitly, concerning the inevitable punishment of sinners (v. 11). Verse 13 recalls Matt 10:28: Avoid the one who can kill both body and soul. The snares and net are pictures taken from bird-hunting.

The positives (vv. 14-16) connect wisdom with holiness, and counsel good companions as the great road to growth in wisdom— timely advice in any age.

9:17–10:5 Wisdom in rulers. This is the sixth and concluding section on the pursuit of wisdom, begun in 4:11.

Ben Sira here compares good rulers with evil ones (9:17–10:3) and then speaks of God as the source of wisdom (vv. 4-5). In the first section the skill of artisans is a kind of manual wisdom. The rash speech of verse 18 reminds one that rulers whose speech is rash or uncontrolled are not successful. The order of 10:1 reflects God's own order in the universe. The traditional proverbial style of 10:2 recalls other proverbs: Like mother, like daughter, etc. God's majesty or glory (v. 5) is a theme seen later in the book, and manifests divine choice and protection.

Lessons on Pride, Violence, and Wealth (10:6–15:10)

10:6–11:28 Eight discourses on pride. These are divided thus: 10:6-18; 10:19-26; 10:27–11:1; 11:2-6; 11:7-9; 11:10-13; 11:14-19; 11:20-28. The first, on the sin of pride, deals also with the violence that can accompany pride. Apparently Ben Sira believes that to act freely involves acting violently (v. 6). The motives in verses 7-8 are that both God and the chosen people hate arrogance, and that history shows that dominion has been transferred to other states.

"Dust and ashes" is a traditional expression for lowliness and the human condition; this is reinforced in verse 10. (Some translations speak here of disease that mocks the doctor's skill.) The origins of pride (vv. 12-13a) point to a central idea: withdrawal from God into self mocks the divine order of the universe and is therefore the worst sort of idolatry. The punishments are the traditional reversals (vv. 14-16) in plant imagery. Two statements (vv. 17-18) conclude the lesson, the second being the stronger.

The second lesson (vv. 19-26) contrasts with verses 6-18. Here Ben Sira has collected various comments reminiscent of rote lessons. The saying in verse 19 is complex, with the English translation making sense of the Hebrew and Greek texts: "can be" means that the human state can be honorable or dishonorable; "are" refers to the certainty of the state of those who fear God or not. In verses 20-21 Ben Sira teaches that personal honor, despite one's social state, comes from honoring God. Since the "poor" fear God alone, they have great honor (vv. 22-23).

The third discourse (10:27–11:1) opens with a theme and a typical introduction, "my son." The question-and-answer format (vv. 28-30) is common in wisdom literature, recalling the scholastic origin of much of Ben Sira's writing. He concludes by going against the upper-class ethic evident elsewhere in his work: wisdom is common to all classes (11:1).

The fourth lesson treats of deceptive appearances (11:2-6). Reflection on the popular proverb on the bee should cause a student to realize that, despite appearances, the bee is a beneficial creature. Likewise, appearances in human beings can deceive. The wheel of fortune (see also 20:10) is not a biblical expression but a way of understanding human experience. The upper-class comments here are apt for Ben Sira's students.

The fifth lesson, on imprudent speech, is very brief (vv. 7-9) and presents a common-sense approach, contrary to the "shoot first, ask questions later" method. The author's usual insistence on maintaining one's proper place (v. 9) involves a sense of the ancient (non-biblical) rule called the Golden Mean, "Nothing to excess."

The sixth lesson (vv. 10-13) deals with self-made men. The sentences in verse 10 recall the Golden Mean and show that violating it brings a curse of futility. "Seek and find" here recalls the gospel injunction to seek and find God. A series of comparisons (vv. 11-13) shows that the Lord, not fate, is the source

of one's success, almost passively so. This is not the whole story for the author, since he also encourages one to pursue wisdom actively.

The seventh discourse (vv. 14-19) treats of wealth and death. In the face of the proverbs here, it is difficult to see the role of human freedom. Ben Sira also teaches that God is in some way the source of all, even evil, death, and poverty. Possibly the author is quoting a popular proverb and contrasting it with verses 15-16. The miserliness of a rich man is ultimately foolish, since this man has not reckoned with God's control of all events (this lesson recalls Luke 12:19).

In the eighth and final discourse (vv. 20-28), Ben Sira speaks of wealth and loss. His basic message is: Do your job, that is, stay at the post assigned you in God's plan, a plan with its own time (v. 21). Ben Sira also speaks to the vexing experience of the (apparent) success of the wicked, a problem faced in all wisdom literature. Ben Sira answers by pointing to the judgment (v. 27) to take place at the end of life. Recall that this judgment does not pertain to life after death.

Warnings Against Exploitation (11:29–13:13)

11:29-34 Exploitation by strangers. The caged bird (v. 30) suggests that this innocent bird is to attract wild birds into a trap. The stain resulting from evil does not describe sin (v. 33) but simply the ruin to come. Ben Sira concludes with a reversal of fortune: if you lodge a stranger, you will become a stranger in turn. The gospel teaches a more open-handed hospitality, but Ben Sira's focus differs here.

12:1-7 Exploitation by the recipient of alms. This passage is simply constructed in terms of opposites, the theme (v. 1) being thoughtful and ordered charity as befits the wise. The rewards are stated as opposites: they come from the Lord (v. 2) and not from the wicked (v. 3). Ben Sira's advice consists in asserting motives for behavior (vv. 5-6): reversal of fortune (arms against you) and double evil. The conclusion is very general, not specific to this brief section.

12:8-18 Exploitation by enemies. This lesson is quite elaborate by contrast, particularly with the symbols (vv. 13-17). The theme (v. 8) can better be understood by reversing its order: in prosperity enemies will remain concealed; in adversity we can know our true friends. The author advises not trusting mere appearances, applying the theme in verse 9 and using an example from daily life: a bronze mirror needs constant care and, once pitted with corrosion, cannot be easily polished. The personal comments (v. 12) are surprising here, bringing us clearly into the classroom.

Lessons about snakes and handlers (vv. 13-17) are applied to the same issues, opening with a rhetorical question, the answer being that either no one or only a fool will pity him.

The applications of the lesson (vv. 14-17) echo the teaching of the prophets to keep one's life virtuous both externally and internally. To plunge one into the abyss (v. 16) means to bring one to death. The conclusion (v. 18) parallels the theme statement about true friends and a true face. The actions (nod, clap, hiss) are intended as signs of derision, mentioned elsewhere in the Old Testament, but not in Sirach.

13:1-7 Exploitation by the rich. The opening statement may conclude the previous lesson but can be understood well enough as a part of this one. The form is traditional: a lesson from nature and its application to daily living. The following verse is similar in style but contains a comparison known to the earlier Greek author Aesop; it is possible that his writings formed part of Ben Sira's education.

A series of examples follows (vv. 3-7), pointing out that riches can cause one to let down personal safeguards and become violent, contrary to the stance proper to the wise. The reversal of the moral order (the poor man must ask forgiveness when he should rather be seeking redress) is an enormous evil, since God's designs are subverted, even temporarily. The gesture of shaking the head is, as in 12:18, one of disrespect or cursing.

13:8-13 Exploitation by the powerful. This lesson recalls Prov 25:6-7 as well as Luke 14:8-11. Ben Sira uses a pattern here similar to previous sections: introduction, examples, results, conclusions. His examples (vv. 9-11a) are basically comments of human wisdom and recall even Egyptian thinking known to us from ancient sources. These may not have been Ben Sira's direct source, but these connections at least reflect the international character of wise teachings. The psychologi-cal tone of verses 11b-12 is typical of the author's close observation of human behavior, seen often in his book.

13:14-14:19 Lessons on wealth. Ben Sira is clearly of the upper class, and has had the advantages of broad experience, travel, and other opportunities. This leads him to look at wealth with wise discernment, condemning excesses and approving what is good.

The introductory or thematic statements (13:14-15) in Ben Sira's lesson on equals (vv. 14-19) advise that people should keep to their own station in life. This conservative position comes from his theological conviction that God has given people their lot in life, and to act against this is a mark of folly. The examples (vv. 16-18) are known from other ancient literature. Ben Sira does not counsel class warfare (v. 17) but emphasizes observance of law to avoid the evils inherent in differences of class and outlook. Note the connection he makes between the rich and the proud (v. 19); the two conditions of life are similar.

The three verses here on support for the rich (vv. 20-22) point to the paradoxes of living with differences. Verse 20 is quite pessimistic but may be a common proverb explained and expanded by the two succeeding verses. There is almost a comic tone to the word picture in verse 22.

Ben Sira's teaching on a clear conscience (13:23–14:2) is probably connected to what has preceded, showing some good in wealth. The proverb in verse 23 can, like other proverbs, be taken apart and reassembled to show the inherent paradoxes: wealth is evil by the standard of the just, poverty is good when there is no sin. This method is one of the ways open to wisdom students to delve into the possibilities of proverbs. The final verses (14:1-2), in the form of a beatitude, are only loosely connected to the rest of this section.

The theme of the subsection on the bad use of wealth (14:3-10) basically leads to issues of being generous with self and others, that is, taking one's full place in society (see 39:1-11). The remaining parts of the lesson are examples. Verse 4 recalls Luke 12:16-21, where others inherit piled-up wealth. The old concept of automatic punishment occurs in verse 6: by God's design each evil act carries with it its own punishment. Verses 7-10 are lessons about miserliness. The miser's eye (v. 10) repeats the same expression, translated "opinion" (v. 8). Note the curse of reversal of fortune in verse 9.

In his teaching on the good use of wealth (vv. 11-19), Ben Sira is no Christian ascetic, practicing evangelical poverty. Rather, he acknowledges the wealth and position of his disciples and counsels them on the best way to live in their conditions. First of all, enjoy wealth (v. 11, the theme). The motive, surprisingly, is the approach of death. The "covenant of Hades" (or Sheol, the Hebrew term) is the literal translation of the Hebrew text and refers to the decree of the date of one's death, determined of old by God. The wise will understand that there exists a time for everything. Ben Sira, here as elsewhere, shows his very traditional view of death (v. 16): no joys in any afterlife.

The lesson concludes in traditional ways. The proverb in verse 17 is found in Gen 2:16-17 and elsewhere. The teaching of verse 18, a lesson from nature and its application, is very similar to Homer's text in the *Iliad*. Indeed, Ben Sira may even have borrowed the text, aware of it from his own education. The handiwork that follows (v. 19) refers to one's work, but not to other goods—family, reputation, example. (See also Rev 14:13, where one's goods also follow.)

14:20–15:10 Associating with wisdom. The extended beatitude in 14:20-27 presents a series of verses extolling the pursuit and nearness of virtue, done in a style more Eastern than Western—giving a multiple impression rather than a clearly logical expression. The picture is evidently of a suitor who eventually gains the object of his desire, moving from pursuit (v. 22) to living with (v. 27). The symbols here will be resumed in 51:13-30.

To "meditate" (v. 20) implies not simply quiet prayer but pondering, working through the meanings of teachings, and examining proverbs and human experience in wisdom fashion (see also Psalm 1).

The author's teachings on good and evil men (15:1-10) open with a theme statement (v. 1) that clearly identifies wisdom with the observance of the law (joining 14:20-27 with this section). This identification is quite characteristic of Ben Sira's teaching. Calling wisdom both mother and bride (v. 2) does not convey any opposition but is simply a parallel expression typical of Hebrew poetry. The bread and water (v. 3) simply bespeak the nourishment coming from wisdom: understanding is like bread, and learning like life-giving water. As a result (vv. 4-6), wisdom never fails and gives an eternal reward (literally, "eternal name" or "reputation"). Note that the reward here is not eternal life. "Joy and gladness" recall for some scholars the vocabulary of the Greek Stoic philosophers, with which the author may have been familiar.

By contrast (vv. 7-8), the wicked never attain wisdom. The four terms here—worthless, haughty, impious, liars—are not four categories of sins but are Hebrew parallel expressions. Ben Sira concludes (vv. 9-10) by contrasting the sinner and the wise. Likewise, he identifies the wise with the pious, joining wisdom and true worship. The ability to offer praise is itself a gift from God.

Lessons on Sin and Sorrow (15:11–18:13)

15:11-20 Free will. This important teaching opens with negatives: God is not the source of human sin. This assertion contrasts with others in Sirach about God as the source of both evil and good (see 11:14; 16:26-28). The theme statement (v. 13) sets the tone, both as to the origin of evil and its power to reach the virtuous. Ben Sira's lesson on free will (vv. 14-15) is key for later theological developments. For him free will goes back to the beginning of creation and forms part of human nature. Thus good and evil cannot be forced on us. "Free choice" translates a Hebrew term understood by the rabbis as "inclination," either to good or evil; for the author the term has a neutral meaning (see also 21:11, "impulses").

The text closes with a set of assertions about God's wisdom and power (vv. 18-20). Even though powerful (v. 18), God does not command one to sin, nor does God even give the power to sin (v. 20). That we do have the power to sin is not considered by Ben Sira, nor does he give his readers a complete theology of free will.

16:1-14 Certainty of punishment. Ben Sira opens with examples taken from child-rearing (vv. 1-4). He basically teaches that it is better to have a few (or even no) pious children than many who are sinners. Sinners with many children might say, "Since I have children, I know that God has blessed me." The author denies this implication. In the Hebrew mind, the short life of sinners is their curse; it appears that Ben Sira believes that for some people there is no possibility of conversion. Verse 4, a short summary proverb, reshapes Prov 11:11.

A personal expression such as that in verse 5 is rare for Ben Sira; here it refers to verse 4 (see also 12:12). Also rare is his choice of various examples from the history of Israel (vv. 6-10), unknown in the book except for the historical section beginning in chapter 44. The examples he chooses are more allusions than direct historical commentary: verse 6 on the rebellion of Korah (see Num 16:35); the leaders (v. 7) appear as "giants" in other translations (see Gen 6:4); the Canaanites are the doomed people (v. 9), seemingly denied free will in Ben Sira's mind; and the six hundred thousand are the Israelites who murmured in the desert (see Num 11:21).

Despite his belief that the Canaanites were doomed (v. 9), Ben Sira holds out the possibility of mercy (vv. 11-14). God is completely impartial; the wicked simply refuse to repent (v. 12). Examples (vv. 13-14) conclude the section to prove his point.

16:15-21 Lack of escape. In this third set of reflections, the author follows his normal pattern: introduction, theme, application, conclusion. The "world of spirits," an unusual expression, means the world of living human beings, that is, creatures who live because of the spirit they have. The theme (vv. 16-17) reviews parts of the visible creation: heaven (sky); heaven of heavens (God's realm beyond the sky; see 1 Kgs 8:27); earth (the world as we know it); abyss (the area below the world, including both seas and the abode of the dead). That the mountains shake (v. 17) is typical of the presence of God (see Hab 3:6). For one to say that God does not know about him/her, since God is so great and he/she is so small, is to deny God's omnipotence; this is justly condemned as foolish (vv. 18-20).

16:22–17:12 Divine concern visible in creation. The introduction is in very solemn form, in the first person (vv. 22-23), similar to 39:12-35 and 42:15–43:33. Some scholars see here a major introduction to a much larger section of Sirach, running to 23:27.

The theme (vv. 24-25) is that all creation is ordered and has its place. This shows divine wisdom existing before creation (as in Prov 8:22-31). The examples (vv. 26-28) bring the reader through a catalogue of creation: stars (v. 26), plants (v. 27), animals (v. 28). The animals return to earth eventually (as in Ps 104:29); presumably, for Ben Sira humans have the same end.

A second theme statement (17:1) continues the series in nature, from stars to plants to animals and finally to human beings. This reflects the order of creation as given in Gen 1. "God's own image" (vv. 2-8) is explained in a series of simple explanations. After life we return to the earth (v. 2); there is a hierarchy of power over objects (vv. 3-4); we have the ability to think and the means to do so (v. 5). In verse 6 there is a shift about good and evil: we are given wisdom and can know how to distinguish between good and evil, as in Gen 3:22.

With this wisdom we are shown God's works (v. 7), and the ultimate purpose is praise, the acknowledgment of God's power coming from a contemplation of his works (see Rom 1:20-23, where pagans are condemned for not perceiving God through creation). Ben Sira concludes his review of creation with a reflection on the great gift of the law (vv. 9-11). Through Moses, God revealed his commands to Israel (vv. 10-11). In summary, Ben Sira gives his version of the two great commands of the law (v. 12): Avoid all evil, both toward God and toward fellow creatures.

17:13-19 The certainty of judgment. This small lesson continues the section on sin, judgment, repentance, and God's mercy begun in 15:11. Through his theme Ben Sira enunciates God's knowledge of all people (v. 13), and then follows up with reasons: Israel is the Lord's special portion, and God knows both good and bad actions. Possibly verse 14 is a common saying, since it does not fit the context too well here, but it recalls the apportioning of the nations among the deities (see Deut 32:8 and Dan 10:13 for this ancient theme). Also, Ben Sira rarely mentions Israel, apart from the historical section beginning in chapter 44.

The reward of the good (vv. 17-19) usually happens later; the wicked apparently are often rewarded immediately. Yet God does not act capriciously and has no favorites who are protected from the effects of their sin. For the sinner, however, there is always a way back (v. 19). This final verse may belong with verse

20, but in any case it is a sort of pivot around which the two sections revolve.

17:20–18:13 Sorrow and God's mercy. The theme (v. 20) continues with the exhortation to hate what God hates (that is, sin and unjust living). The dead cannot praise God from their place in the nether world, so praise God now. Ben Sira mentions the nether world, not to give a clear idea of a separate place for the dead, but to say that the individuals are truly dead.

The assurance of forgiveness begins with a psalm of praise in the format characteristic of other psalms. A major theme is God's incomparability (vv. 25-27): God has no peer, and human beings, by comparison, are "dust and ashes" (see Gen 18:27 for Abraham's view of himself).

The psalm continues with an assertion emphasizing the mercy of God, a characteristic of acts of praise. A similar form is the question about comparability: no one or nothing is like God (see 17:25). In the same vein, contrasts with human weakness point up the greatness of God (vv. 6-8). The question "What is man?" (v. 6) recalls Ps 8:5 and Job 7:17; the age of human life contrasts with the figure seventy or eighty of Ps 90:10. The conclusions (vv. 9-13) contain a surprising assertion about the universal mercy of God, mentioned here for the first time in the Old Testament, and contrasting even with a kind of predestination that has appeared previously in Sirach (16:9, for example). Also appearing here for the first time is the teaching that God's mercy is instructive, that is, one can learn of God's love and care through his acts of mercy toward oneself or others.

Counsels About Behavior (18:14–23:27)

18:14-29 Uses of caution. The few verses on charity (vv. 14-17) teach that one's charity should be complete, and exercised without harshness. The lessons (vv. 15-16) come from nature, and the conclusion is in the poetic and elevated style of literary proverbs.

The author then turns to a series of instructions on forethought (vv. 18-29). His practical advice on acting in good time resembles the gospel lesson on the man building a tower (Luke 14:28-30). A specific example of forethought is the question of vows (vv. 22-23; see also Eccl 5:2-6). A theologically important verse (v. 24) deals with the

problem of evil in the world. For Ben Sira, God's face is hidden. This is an uncommon expression in Sirach and means that God allows evil to happen while not causing it. (To show one's face means to act with kindness.)

The formal conclusion (vv. 28-29) is that the wise are to make wisdom known and to praise her. This involves making their own gift of wisdom known, not hiding their light under a bushel (see Mark 4:21 and parallels). The wise will dispense proverbs (as in 8:8) for the benefit of others and the praise of God.

18:30–19:16 Self-control. After a theme verse (v. 30), Ben Sira offers traditional thinking on the punishment coming from lack of self-control in sexual matters: what causes pleasure will eventually cause pain. It is not quite clear how momentary pleasure will bring on poverty, other than through extravagant living (v. 32). Self-control in food and drink is urged; the apparent reason is simply the possible loss of control that would result from immoderate living—not a preferred condition for the wise. (The events in the story of the prodigal son, Luke 15:11-32, parallel the development here.)

Wine and women can also cause one to lose self-control (vv. 1-4). The theme in verse 1b is a type of ancient proverb, parallel to Prov 23:20-21. The text of verses 2-4 in the New American Bible places verse 4 before verse 3 to make a better flow. When one is giddy there is no self-control, and the wise person can no longer be thoughtful. Ben Sira appreciates merriment and enjoyment but wants to maintain control. "Contumacious desire" (v. 3), that is, reckless or stubborn desire, is an expression not used elsewhere in Sirach. From Ben Sira's perspective, desire also destroys in a kind of reversal, since desire for something else will eventually consume the one who desires. "Rottenness and worms" (v. 3) possibly refers to venereal diseases coming from sexual indulgence.

Self-control in speech (vv. 5-11) opens with a proverb and application (v. 5), and continues on to various lessons (vv. 6-8). Although Ben Sira values friendship, he knows where to be cautious (vv. 7-8). The comparisons in verses 10-11 both refer to the need to remove quickly what is lodged within.

All the sentences on rash judgment (vv. 12-16) have the same general thrust: if you do admonish, know that the person may be innocent, or if guilty, may take the admonition in good spirits. The exception is verse 15, which appears to be an extended commentary on the series, like a teacher's comment in class. The reference to law in the concluding summary (v. 16b) probably is meant generically, with no specific command in mind.

Making Right Distinctions (19:17–20:30)

19:17-26 True and false wisdom. The distinctive Torah wisdom of the Book of Sirach appears in the theme (v. 17); this may have been linked with verse 16b just above, on fulfillment of the law. If so, the method of using key words or ideas helps students to progress through the material of the book. There is also a false knowledge (vv. 18-21), and the author makes distinctions between knowledge, prudence, shrewdness, and intelligence in the righteous, and those same apparent qualities in sinners. The difference is that the truly wise also fear (that is, believe and worship) the Lord.

The word picture of one man (vv. 22-24) brings to mind the injunction of Isaiah: ". . . honors me with their lips alone, though their hearts are far from me" (Isa 29:13; also Matt 15:8). Common sense tells what a person truly is interiorly, despite appearance. Fools may be deceived, and they may also try to deceive (vv. 25-26). Compare this also with 13:25, where natural signs can tell what one truly is.

20:1-7 Speech and silence. The lessons (vv. 2-3) include a "better" proverb and a memorable simile on eunuchs. This latter probably came from court life, where eunuchs were kept to guard the women's quarters. The simile amuses in a bawdy way and speaks of one's results being frustrated.

The comparisons on silence point to paradoxes in life. They show modern readers more of Ben Sira's psychological sensitivity, mentioned elsewhere. The lesson of verse 6 echoes a general theme in Sirach about right order and the proper time to act. This mirrors God's order of the universe.

20:8-16 Paradoxes of reality. This third collection of sayings on proper distinctions (begun in 19:17) presents general paradoxes (vv. 8-11) and lessons on the wise and the fool (vv. 12-16).

In general, paradoxes by their very nature point to real life: it isn't everything it seems.

The wise should learn that life is paradoxical at times and should delve below surface appearances. The concept of "wheel of fortune" is not biblical, but something like it comes through here: one day up, down the next (v. 10). This reflects the incompleteness and tentative nature of human life.

The next few verses present a series of contrasts between the wise and the fool. The two verses on the rogue (vv. 13-14) complete the lesson in verse 9 on gifts. The final verses (vv. 15-16) speak of the realization, known from ancient times, that for both good and evil their present lot in life can be reversed. The curse here comes to the generous fool: the recipients of his ill-gotten goods turn on him. (This lesson recalls 18:14-17.)

20:17-30 Proper and improper speech. The introduction (vv. 17-19) mentions the proverb itself, stock in trade of the wise, who also know when to use it; they have a sense of God's order and the right time to act. The basis for the judgment on lies (vv. 23-25) is that lies bring about their own punishment, entrapping liars in further lies. One's standing in the community is ruined thereby. Similarly, in verses 26-30 appropriate speech will help the wise to advance themselves, and prosperity will be their reward. The fact that doing evil results in shame and doing good results in prosperity points to the wise ordering by God of all reality.

21:1-10 Avoid sin. The religious tone here strikes the modern reader strangely, since it is a feature often absent from other wisdom writings. The theological introduction teaches that forgiveness is possible through prayer and reformation of life. Elsewhere Ben Sira mentions sacrifices and good acts as accomplishing the same end. But the lesson here contrasts with his teaching that the foolish (that is, the wicked) seem destined to live and die in their sins.

Ben Sira does not define or describe sin but only compares its effects on the sinner to the destructive effects of sharp and pointed objects (vv. 2-3). His teaching in verses 5-7 links the poor with those denied justice. As immediately above, the author offers no definition of the poor, yet he is conscious of them and their needs (see 4:1-8; 10:21-26; 13:18-22, for example).

In the comparisons of verses 8-10, the implication is always that unjust activities lead to death. "Tow" (v. 9) is an easily flammable fabric used to give shape to a torch and meant to be burned. The "smooth stones" (v. 10) are also pleasant to the just and may tempt them. Yet, note that Ben Sira also teaches that the end of *both* the just and sinners is the nether world without discrimination (see 14:16). The difference in reward lies either in the miserable end of sinners or in the extinction of their memory.

The Wise and the Fool (21:11–22:18)

21:11-18 Contrasts. The teaching of the theme (v. 11) is the "Torah wisdom" typical of the Book of Sirach: wisdom is not just secular skill or diplomacy. The "impulses" may refer to the Hebrew concept of the inborn tendency to good or evil that we all possess. (The Hebrew text of this chapter is unfortunately lacking, so the reference here cannot be precisely stated; yet the concept is known in late Old Testament and rabbinic writings.)

The comparisons (vv. 12-17) seem to be a series of disconnected proverbs, perhaps original to Ben Sira or his students, on the same subject. The concept of teachability appears here (v. 12) and in the next section (v. 18). Note also the automatic process of evil: evil committed comes down upon the evildoer eventually (vv. 27-28).

22:1-18 The lazy and the foolish. A very vivid comparison sets the theme for the discussion of various types of foolish behaviors (vv. 1-2, recalled in v. 13). Typically the author prescribes very rough treatment for daughters (see also 42:9-14 for a more extended but similar discussion). Women in general have value only as they help and support their father or husband. Verse 6 is a general conclusion, applicable to sons and daughters alike.

The difficulty (or impossibility) of teaching a fool forms the theme of verses 7-15 (as in 21:18-21). The obvious lesson of verses 7-8 is to avoid culpable fools; being with them is a waste of time. This approach contrasts strongly with the gospel teaching of love and care for all; even the ignorant deserve help. The basis for Ben Sira's harsh judgment lies in commonsense observation, not in theology. Verses 9-11 should be read together. The sense is not readily clear, but it need not be in order to engage the student in pondering reality.

One conclusion is: Better to be dead than to be a fool.

Verses 14-15 are a riddle, a device rarely used in the Bible but a form of education and entertainment then and now. Here the riddle presents experience in a question form (v. 14) and applies the answers to the lesson. The last sentences (vv. 16-18) are a fitting conclusion and are of the same type: experience (v. 16) and application (v. 17). The comparison is well wrought, like the wall in the proverb. Verse 18 resumes verse 1 as a contrast and concludes verse 17.

22:19-26 Preserving friendship. The friendship here evidently exists between males, but it can be applied equally to females. Ben Sira made several contributions to the literature of friendship (see 6:5-17; 19:12-14; 37:1-6). The opening verses (vv. 19-20) follow the traditional pattern of experience and application; verses 21-22 show that reconciliation is possible. The gospel calls for a higher perfection, beyond mere human forgiveness. In his typical fashion (v. 23) Ben Sira puts forth self-interest as a motive. (Verse 24 seems out of place here.) The final sentences (vv. 25-26) change perspective. Treating friends well summarizes the section.

22:27–23:27 Prayer and teaching on sins of speech and lust. This remarkable section concludes the long series on discretion in behaviors begun in 18:14. The prayers here and elsewhere in the Book of Sirach are unusual, since such passages do not normally appear in wisdom literature; these are very personal and true to life, whereas other wisdom books are generally abstract and impersonal.

The questions in 22:27 and 23:2 come from the traditional language of praise; they expect the answer "God alone." They also imply that personally it is impossible to avoid sin (see also Ps 141:3). There are some echoes of original sin here, in its passions and lack of control. Petitions follow (vv. 1, 4-6), acknowledging a personal relationship with God, not just as an abstraction (the Creator of the universe) but as a personal Deity. Also, Ben Sira appears to be the first writer to address God as "Father." This also contrasts with Old Testament wisdom, which is more about God than addressed to God. (The only other prayer is in Prov 30:7-9.)

The "brazen look" (v. 5) and the lifting up of the eyes are not signs of pride but of lust (as in 26:9, where the woman acts wantonly).

In verses 7-15 we have an extensive instruction on this topic, with the kinds of distinctions students must learn. The theme (v. 8) also shows a sense of punishment for sin as being involved in the act itself. The "Holy Name" (vv. 9-10) is the divine name of God, gradually drawn out of common speech; in Ben Sira's time it was still apparently used by some in oaths.

Verses 11-12 offer similar lessons on the types of words. The motive is simply: it isn't done. The reason is that the wise are also the just, and thus the wise avoid all sins (as in v. 13).

The discussion on sins of lust (vv. 16-27) is impressive, contrasting men with women. The women, true to Ben Sira's form, come out badly. The theme (v. 16) typically compares lust to fire. What is atypical is the numerical form (introduced here for the first time in Sirach). In verses 19-21 Ben Sira deals with punishment. The answer to the question is: "God alone" can see. The one who questions in this way is a fool, and should have known the answer. The "eyes of the Lord" is an unusual figure, but they should be understood as searchlights blazing rather than as receivers of light or windows to the soul.

Women sinners (vv. 22-26) receive greater condemnation than men, since, according to Ben Sira, the first woman broke the law; even her children will suffer. This teaching should be contrasted with that of Jesus in the Gospel according to John, where the adulterous woman is forgiven and her male accusers leave shamefaced (John 8:1-11).

Verse 27 concludes the whole section, perhaps even the first half of the book according to some scholars. Some suggest that Ben Sira originally concluded his work here, emphasizing anew the connection between law and wisdom. One would expect the conclusion "nothing is better than wisdom" rather than "nothing is better than the fear of the Lord."

Attractive and Hateful Things (24:1–36:17)

24:1-31 A treatise on wisdom. After a brief introduction (vv. 1-2), Ben Sira reports an address of wisdom (vv. 3-21) and comments on wisdom and the law (vv. 22-31). Chapter 8 of the Book of Proverbs is a model for this entire section, connected with it in its use of both terms and themes. The introduction (vv. 1-2) opens the discourse speaking about wisdom; and then wisdom herself, in the heavenly council, speaks to her own people, the people of Israel, understood as assembled in Jerusalem.

The main feature of the section is the address of wisdom (vv. 3-21), which speaks of wisdom's origins being rooted in Israel, and offers an elaborate series of comparisons, closing with a summons to partake of wisdom. The origin of wisdom (vv. 3-7) is in God; wisdom is not a being separate in origin from God. The perspective is that wisdom is basically a word or utterance from God. The description of wisdom is poetic and should not be pressed for firm details. After her creation, wisdom scours the universe high (the vault of heaven) and low (the deep abyss), looking for a dwelling. That wisdom is feminine is a natural development from the feminine gender of the Hebrew *hokmah*; but this may also fulfill some need to see a female side to the Deity.

God commands (vv. 8-12) a residence in Israel. The subordination of wisdom to God is quite clear here: wisdom is God's gift to Israel. The comparisons (vv. 13-17) run the range of human senses (touch, sight, taste, smell) and refer to Israel both north (Lebanon) and south (Jericho). The perfumes recall the act of priestly anointing (Exod 30:23-24). Amid all this beauty (vv. 18-21), wisdom calls out, almost as a street vendor would. Verse 20 appears to contradict human experience— those who need to eat should be filled; but the focus here is on the increasing pleasure in partaking of wisdom.

The next section (vv. 22-31) associates wisdom with the law, a most important theme in the Book of Sirach. Verse 22 quotes Deut 33:4, showing that the Torah in particular, but also the rest of Scripture, commanded by God as Israel's inheritance, is true wisdom (see v. 8). Ben Sira is the major figure in Israel to equate law with wisdom and to draw forth its implications. More comparisons follow: of wisdom with rivers—here the seasons change from Pishon (winter) to Tigris (spring) to Jordan (summer) to Gihon (fall). The order of the universe is God's.

In verses 27-31 Ben Sira gives a major first-person account, nearly unique in biblical books (except, possibly, Jeremiah). The symbolism continues the water theme above. Ben

Sira's words are as vast as a sea. His meaning is like the prophecy of old, an interesting connection of wisdom teaching with the prophets. At root, both prophet and wise teacher interpret reality for the people under divine guidance.

25:1-11 Numerical proverbs. The movement in the introductory verse (v. 1) moves concentrically from brethren (probably Israelites) to neighbors (in town) to husband and wife (the family). This section is in the first person, an unusual occurrence. The next verse (v. 2) is not concentric but speaks of the persons who are the opposite of those in verse 1: the proud man disrupts harmony; the dissembler is lying, devious, and disrupts friendship; the lewd man destroys family love. There is also a contrast between being proud and a pauper; this is fundamentally against divine wisdom, since it violates the established order of life. The detail in this one verse demonstrates how these little proverbs could be examined from various viewpoints.

Verses 3-6 expand and explain verse 2; it appears possible that the preceding two verses are traditional, and Ben Sira adds verses 3-6 himself.

The numerical proverbs (vv. 7-10) have the usual form of one number followed by the next greater. Here there are actually ten persons mentioned. This is a mixed group, including both the fortunate (vv. 7b-8a) and the pious (v. 8b). The reference to the unequal animals is an application of Deut 22:10 to married life. There is an important conclusion in the case of the tenth man. Ben Sira places fear of the Lord as greater than wisdom (see v. 11). The teaching somewhat contradicts the praises of the uncreated wisdom of God living in Israel, known elsewhere in the book.

25:12–26:18 Lessons on good and evil women. This section has mixed passages on good and evil, and some scholars prefer to place them together, not separated as the present text shows. Possibly Ben Sira did so, but the oppositions in the passages point up significant contrasts.

In verses 12-25 there is no question that Ben Sira had a very negative view of women. Verses 12-14 offer a series of comparisons, including women as the source of evil for men. In verse 14 there is the typical form of experience (serpent) and application (the spite of women). In the comparisons in verses

15-17, women fare worse. Ben Sira has obviously given close psychological attention to men with family problems.

After an assertion of the greatness of evil in women (v. 18), the author turns to some assorted proverbs (vv. 19-22), probably collected, or at least adapted, by him. In verse 23 we have the first place outside Genesis where sin is ascribed to Eve. Elsewhere the origin of sin was regarded as the result of the cohabitation of evil heavenly beings with human women (Gen 6:1-4). Ben Sira's point of view is picked up by Paul.

The conclusion (vv. 24-25) teaches that a husband is to control his wife and should divorce an evil wife. The expression in Greek for divorce is a very violent one, unknown in other biblical books.

These verses (26:1-4) discuss the good wife in general, but only from the viewpoint of her husband. As in other passages in the book, women are not valued on their own. Numerical proverbs (vv. 5-6) are so framed to show that the jealous wife is worse than the preceding three evils.

Verses 7-12 present some of Ben Sira's most bitter comments. Note that he has no comparable section on evil husbands, though the evils of various classes of men are discussed widely in the book. The "bad wife" and the "drunken wife" are unknown figures elsewhere in the Old Testament. Ben Sira gives advice in verses 10-12 on watching over such a wife. The concluding verse (v. 12) is a surprisingly obscene statement, unique in biblical language (but parallel to the prophetic indictments in Ezek 23, among others).

The good wife appears again in verses 13-18, treated more precisely this time than in verses 1-4. Still, the focus is on the husband. To show the value Ben Sira puts on a smoothly running relationship, he compares a good wife to the temple, a very high blessing indeed; the columns recall the desert tabernacle in Exod 26. (Note that in some manuscripts a passage partly composed of quotations from Proverbs appears here. The exact numbering of the verses and their placement here and elsewhere in Sirach are a cause of confusion to modern readers.)

Sins and Sinners (26:19–28:6)

Verse 19 is a numerical proverb, possibly out of place here but connecting in some way with what follows concerning business dealings.

26:20–27:3 Business dealings. In verse 20 Ben Sira asserts the difficulty of maintaining justice in business transactions. The shopkeeper or merchant is rarely mentioned in the Old Testament; and there is very little in the Bible about fair business dealings, apart from the early prophets, such as Amos, Hosea, and Isaiah. Verses 1-3 continue this brief discussion.

Verses 4-10 constitute a digression of sorts, following up on the suggestion of the last few verses about honest living. These verses speak of testing to find one's real character. An important statement follows (v. 8) on the possibility of attaining justice. Comparisons (vv. 9-10) show the familiar experience-application method of proverbs.

Ben Sira continues with a lesson on sinful speech (vv. 11-15). Here the wise are associated with the pious, a viewpoint typical of Ben Sira. There are problems with the speech of the godless. It comes from a godless and disordered spirit, and is seen from the multiplicity of oaths (that is, offensive cursing). The result is bloodshed. This picture is perhaps taken from a tavern filled with evil men, whose drinking and wild behavior lead to quarrels, bloodshed, and even death.

Secrets and friendship (vv. 16-21) change the scene to relations among friends. Once secrets are betrayed (v. 16), nothing can repair the evil done; the experience of the bird released (v. 19) and the swift desert gazelle is applied here. This section closes with a summary statement (v. 21).

The following section on deceit (vv. 22-29) is nearly a standard model of Ben Sira's method: theme (vv. 22-23)—the deceitful person will ruin you; comparisons (vv. 24-27)—stones, a pit, a snare; conclusion (vv. 28-29). In the last two verses Ben Sira outlines a theory of retribution that undergirds his entire presentation, namely, that evil necessarily brings about its own kind of punishment. God is not the direct source of retribution; rather, the divine order has established the system (shown by the comparisons in verses 24-27).

27:30–28:7 Vengeance. The introductory theme (28:1) should be compared with Lev 19:17-18, which counsels one not to take revenge, basically the same message as Ben Sira's. Verses 1-2 involve a reversal of fortune,

a typical form of divine punishment. Here the vengeful will have vengeance shown them (itself a reversal of the beatitudes of the Gospels). The next three verses (vv. 3-5) illustrate reversals. In verses 6-7 Ben Sira uses a form of education common in the Old Testament: remember! To do so, his students need a history of some sort, either personal or national, to reflect on.

28:8-11 Strife. This is an additional section with the usual plan: theme (avoid strife, v. 8a), motives (vv. 8b-9), applications based on experience (vv. 10-11). This lesson probably illustrates a common teaching method of the period.

28:12-26 Slander and an evil tongue. This section represents a development in Old Testament teaching, one not dealt with elsewhere, at least in such eloquent detail. Verses 12-16 speak of slander, and verses 17-26 of the evil tongue. Both sections open with lessons from nature and include observations on proper and improper speech.

Both life and death come from the mouth; the abuse of its power makes one "double-tongued" (v. 13), an expression occurring only in Sirach and once in Proverbs. In verse 15 virtuous women have been cast out (divorced) on account of slander of a "third tongue" (following the Greek text); thus they are cut off from their children and household.

The perspective is reversed in verses 18-23, turning from the one who slanders to the victims of evil speech. This involves a kind of living death, being cut off from one's own community, a state worse than physical death. As elsewhere in Sirach, there is no reference to eternal life here. The fire (vv. 22-23) is more a symbol of the consuming power of death than the fires of punishment. Verses 24-26 conclude with comparisons of the normal type in Sirach, and verse 26 concludes the entire lesson. The foe here is death rather than any human enemy.

Borrowing and Lending (29:1-28)

29:1-7 Lending. This is another model section beginning with a theme: to lend to a neighbor is to fulfill a precept of the law (as in Deut 15:8). The point of verses 2-3 apparently is not that lending itself is a good but that its purpose is to cement friendships. By working to restore the divine order of a world in which all have what they need to live, one participates in the creative act of God.

This generosity is contrasted (vv. 4-6) with borrowers who cannot or will not repay loans. The scenes are very true to life, as much so in ancient times as today. Repayment with curses is condemned partly because it violates God's order.

29:8-13 Generosity. The rationale for generosity to the poor here is "the precept," which probably does not refer to any single verse in the Bible but gives the sense of many passages (such as Lev 19:9-10). Ben Sira urges spending money rather than hoarding it idly; the only hoard should be almsgiving (v. 12). This thought recalls the gospel (Luke 12:32-34).

29:14-20 Surety. To go surety is to offer financial guarantees to someone involved in business transactions. The focus of these verses shifts from one who goes surety to one who benefits. The lesson urges prudence and caution, an attitude typical of Ben Sira and summarized in verse 20. The sinner (v. 19) is by definition unwise and does not know or admit his limits. As a result he fails. Interestingly, Proverbs counsels against surety (Prov 6:1-5 and elsewhere), but changed conditions in Ben Sira's time make it acceptable but risky.

29:21-28 Frugality. This lesson opens with what may already be a proverbial statement of life's basic needs: water, food, clothing, shelter. The following verses (vv. 22-23) expand on the theme but urge moderation with piety. The homeless form the subject of verses 24-27. Far better to have a poor home than be at another's beck and call, as a person would be who regularly ate at the expense of another and performed menial tasks in partial repayment. The last verse is a conclusion of sorts, but its connection with what preceded it is not too clear.

Causes of Joy and Sorrow (30:1-31:11)

The sections on children (30:1-13), health (30:14-31:2), and wealth (31:3-11) can be gathered under one heading, although they do not all contain the same format or lessons.

30:1-13 Children. Despite the term "children," Ben Sira undoubtedly refers only to sons, in view of his bias against women. Good care of children must involve discipline (vv. 1-3); this will give the father cause to rejoice in later years. A person's immortality is guaranteed in some way by survival in offspring; no indication of an afterlife is given. Verse 6 contrasts with strictures against vengeance in 27:30-28:7. What is intended here is probably a legal method of guaranteeing the rights of the deceased.

The results of spoiling children are discussed in verses 7-11. Principally, the son will be undisciplined, causing grief to himself and to his father. The wise man has attained wisdom partly through self-discipline, and should therefore help his children grow in it.

The passage closes with two commands: Start early and be severe. The motives include bringing disgrace on the father, much as the discussion on wives focused on the husband rather than on the wife.

30:14-31:2 Health. Here Ben Sira offers a "better" proverb and other comparisons. The "better" form may be an answer to the implied question, "What is better than a rich man with a wasted frame?" The author may even have used this method in his school. Note in verse 17 another expression to cover the issue of the afterlife, "an unending sleep," a poetic parallel to "death." Literally it reads "going down forever," a new expression in the Bible.

Verses 18-20 offer an object lesson on the evils of ill health. Ben Sira also ridicules the religious practice of tomb or idol offerings, which he either saw in his travels or more likely saw in the Israel of his day. Deut 26:14 condemned the practice, which was seen as idol worship. The verses from 30:21 to 31:2 are a remarkable passage on mental health, a positive mental attitude. Ben Sira recognized the close connection between worry or depression and physical illness.

The last three verses (30:25-31:2) are a bridge passage, linking cheerfulness at meals with a proper approach to making a living. Note that weight loss is regarded as a curse (31:1), not as the blessing it would mean today. (At this point the texts of several editions vary, due to a probable disruption of pages. The order in the Greek is 30:24; 33:16-36:11; then 30:25-33:15; finally, 36:12 and on.)

31:3-11 Wealth. Verses 3-4 are both on the pessimistic side, recalling the approach of Qoheleth: no rest for either the rich or the poor. Verses 5-7 concentrate on the pursuit of gold and all it stands for. At root, gold takes the place of wisdom, justice, or even

God; to pursue it is to go astray. Experience has shown this (v. 6); the wise profit from such lessons, but fools never learn (v. 7). That the pursuit of gold is a curse is seen from the traditional formula, "reversal of fortune"— that is, if you try to snare gold, it will snare you instead (v. 7b).

Verses 8-11 are happier in tone, congratulating the one fortunate enough to pass the test inflicted by gold (literally, "mammon" in Hebrew, a word used in Matt 6:24 and Luke 16:13). Verse 10b should be extended beyond this instance to a general praise of all those who overcome temptation. Verse 11 recounts traditional blessings—prosperity and a good name.

Temperance and Good Manners (31:12–32:13)

31:12-24 Eating. These verses are among the most colorful in Sirach, and at the same time the most secular. Certainly no biblical revelation is involved here; rather, the collected common sense of experience is all important. Recall that Ben Sira's audience was mainly wealthy young men, for whom banqueting was common; in earlier times, such meals were generally restricted to religious affairs or victories.

Verses 12-15 call for order, moderation, and sensitivity to the host. Verses 16-18 call for the same, the lesson being that this sort of meal is not principally designed for nourishment but for the event as a whole. Besides, moderation has other rewards, such as health and sound sleep (vv. 19-21). The reference to emptying the stomach may point to the recently introduced practice of inducing vomiting (v. 21). In any case, it is not mentioned elsewhere in the Bible. A general recommendation closes this section: moderation above all else.

The final two verses serve as an appendix (vv. 23-24), referring to generosity in giving a banquet. In this area moderation is not to be counseled.

31:25-31 Drinking wine. Here Ben Sira has collected various statements on the proper use of wine, opening with a theme (v. 25) and a comparison (v. 26). He acknowledges the joys of wine as a gift of God (v. 27). As expected, he also counsels moderation. The author continues this theme, counseling proper order—the essentially wise decision, imitat-

ing divine order (v. 28). Misuse of wine violates this order and brings its own recompense (vv. 29-30). Ben Sira concludes with a separate idea on the proper use of words when others are "merry," that is, light-hearted, but not drunk (v. 31).

32:1-13 Proper behavior at banquets. The preceding sections dealt with attending a banquet given by another; Ben Sira here offers wise counsel for one who hosts his own banquet or who acts as a master of ceremonies—a Greek custom in vogue in his day. His advice follows his usual pattern: be modest with guests (vv. 1-2); be moderate in speech and considerate (vv. 3-4). The types of banquets envisioned in chapters 31–32, together with other of Ben Sira's observations, demonstrate his familiarity with upper-class practices and possessions (carnelian, a semi-precious stone, gold, and emeralds, vv. 5-6).

Ben Sira's comments to the young (presumably his students) counsel modesty and brevity in speech and manner. As previously (vv. 5-6), he closes with a comparison (v. 10). The lesson concludes by shifting the focus from host to guest; evidently the banquet is not for self-indulgence but for socializing. Save self-indulgence for home (vv. 11-12).

The final verse is somewhat unexpected, given the secular tone of the last few lessons (vv. 30-32). Some scholars regard them as a conclusion to the entire section beginning with 24:1.

Stability under Law (32:14–33:6)

The tone changes abruptly here as Ben Sira introduces a solemn discourse on disciplined study and wisdom. He proceeds from a consideration of divine providence (32:14-24) and the trials coming to a fool (33:1-3) to preparations for study (33:4-6).

32:14-24 Providence of God. As before, the author begins with his theme, connecting the pursuit of wisdom with the pursuit of God (vv. 14-15). One of the tasks of the wise is to find divine order even in obscurity—basically to interpret confusing reality; this is the import of verse 16, "to draw forth a plan." Sinners/fools are compared with the wise (vv. 15b, 17, 18).

The wise do not act alone; rather, the pursuit of wisdom demands the help of the wise and the discipline they impose (vv. 18-19). Being on guard is the theme of verses 21-23, where the language recalls Deuteronomy (as in 4:9: be on your guard, keep the commandments, keep the law). Verse 24b recalls various psalm passages (for example, Ps 119:31).

33:1-6 The wise and the fool. These verses are a gathering of apparently independent statements that link the verses together through references to the law and wisdom, and the expected comparisons with natural objects: boat, cartwheel, stallion. Verse 3 refers to a "divine oracle," probably an allusion to the practice of Urim and Thummim (1 Sam 14:41-42) or to words of priestly or prophetic benediction.

33:7-15 Moral order of creation. This extremely important section sets out Ben Sira's views on the divine order undergirding all of reality.

The importance of days comes from divine designation of some of them as feast days—an indication of the author's interest in matters liturgical. The illustration shows a balance between ordinary and special days, and also serves the author's usual method of examples followed by applications to daily life. The examples continue (vv. 10-14) with comments about different kinds of persons: even though man (the Greek text has "Adam") was the first human, yet people differ due to God's free choice. Resuming an old theme, Ben Sira shows that each one has his own function or lot in life as part of God's order—a far cry from the contemporary Western concept of the freedom, progress, and change possible to everyone. The author chooses to examine the realities of life, not their possibilities.

A further example/application is given in verse 14—evil/good, death/life, sinners/just—and this is concluded with Ben Sira's general theory of order. Everything works in pairs, as opposites, with a balance between each one. A person should therefore expect both good and bad out of life. The reason why this must be so is God's choice. In Ben Sira's mind, there is nothing one can do about this—human freedom seems nearly ruled out, apart from the choice to sin. Job struggles against this order but finally abandons himself to divine providence.

33:16-18 Author's note. After the all-encompassing theory presented above, Ben Sira speaks in his own name, acknowledging that he has made some progress (v. 17), not for himself but for all, probably his students

(v. 18). This section may have ended the book at one point in its growth.

33:19-22 Duties to property, servants. A solemn introduction (v. 19) opens this section, which first advises a man to be independent or self-sufficient, allowing nothing to have control over him. This freedom is to be the mark of the wise in all aspects of life. Without it, a person's "glory" (v. 23) is diminished, a concept expanded later in the book.

33:25-33 Slaves. A particular example of control is over slaves, which were regarded as human property, much like wives and even children. Two proverbial sentences open the lesson (vv. 25, 27); verse 26 seemed out of place where it was and hence appears after verse 27 in our version. On the other hand, this reality is to be tempered by consideration for the human dignity of the slave (vv. 30-32); this good treatment will even have benefits for the master (v. 33). Ben Sira did not call for the abolition of slaveholding, but at least he made suggestions for the betterment of the condition of slaves.

34:1-17 Grounds for future hope. This section offers two contrasting grounds for hope: dreams (vv. 1-8) offer false grounds, whereas the Lord alone is the true ground (vv. 9-17). This division itself further illustrates the law of opposites (33:7-15).

As usual, a theme statement begins Ben Sira's lesson (v. 1), followed by perhaps a traditional proverb (v. 2). His teaching continues with a series of observations. Verse 4 is in a traditional proverbial question, expecting the answer no. Verse 5 condemns not only reliance on dreams but also their superstitious use in divination and omens. Such use is blameworthy, since it attempts to control the future, which only God can do. The author concludes with the possibility of divine intervention (v. 6), such as happened to Joseph in Egypt (Gen 37:5-10), but cautions that experience shows how wrong reliance on dreams has been (v. 7). His conclusion (v. 8) shows that the written law is the real means of divine revelation, and the wise become so because of their fidelity to this law.

God's providence, on the other hand, offers sure ground for hope (vv. 9-17). Ben Sira's remarks on the advantages of travel for growth in wisdom are not completely apropos here (vv. 9-12) but seem to focus less on travel itself than on its inherent dangers and the consequent need of relying, not on one's own means, but on God. Ben Sira's travels are evident here and there in his book, but remarks on exotic places or practices do not form part of his teaching.

Verses 13-15 extol the happiness of the one who trusts in the Lord. Such a one has courage (v. 13) and never fears (v. 14). The question in verse 15 is unexpected; the answer is clear: the Lord alone. The final two verses are attributes of God, quite reminiscent of certain psalms. Here as elsewhere Ben Sira shows considerable freedom in gathering citations to support his teaching. This was and is a common method in biblical studies, though not recommended, because the shaping context of the words is lost. "Sparkle to the eyes" (v. 17) is an unusual expression but not completely unknown in the Greek Old Testament.

Worship of the Lord (34:18–36:17)

34:18-26 Unacceptable worship. Verse 18 is the theme statement, recalling numerous prophetic oracles (Hos 7:4; 8:13, etc.). The prophets called for worship from the heart, not just with outward forms. Ben Sira, in a very violent and pointed comparison, denounces gifts made at cost to the poor (v. 20). Alms, he continues, are life-giving for those who give them as well as for those who need them (v. 21). To deprive a laborer of wages is murder, apparently to be punished as such (v. 22).

The next three verses contrast senses of "gain" for the virtuous and the wicked. The only gain comes to the virtuous, despite outward or temporary gain (vv. 23-25). In verse 25 the reference is to ritual impurity (Num 19:11). The conclusion (v. 26) is in the same vein and ends with the usual teacher's question, expecting the answer "No one."

35:1-10 Acceptable worship. In these verses Ben Sira unites the concepts of law and worship. The theme verse (v. 1) sets out the argument. "Oblation" and "peace offering" refer to types of Hebrew sacrifices, as do "fine flour" and "sacrifice of praise" in verse 2 and "atonement" in verse 3. The author must have been speaking generically, for this listing of sacrifices does not exhaust the possibilities envisioned elsewhere in the Old Testament, even with the addition of "tithes" in verse 8.

The individual recommendations of verses 4-9 are in general wisdom form and may even be from other sources used by the author. Verse 10 concludes the lesson with the basic motive, given in the "timeless" form of proverbial motives: the Lord repays—an assertion true in the past, present, and future. Here as elsewhere the concept of personal reward for doing good is mentioned—charity for Ben Sira is not simply its own reward.

35:11-24 Divine justice and mercy. The prophetic strain in Sirach continues in this next lesson, begun in verses 11-12 with a theme statement and motive. The motive asserts justice and no favorites for God, possibly because there can be no favorites in a world already ordered by God's justice (that is, God's founding decree, establishing the right).

Against this static position Ben Sira places the compassion of God in the face of human sin and need (v. 13). "Orphan" and "widow" are traditional terms designating the most abandoned and helpless (v. 14). Like the blood of Abel calling for revenge (Gen 4:10) are the tears of widows.

In fact, the prayers of the lowly are heard (vv. 16-18). They pierce the clouds—not just atmospheric clouds but the attendants at God's throne (see Lam 3:44), or perhaps God's chariot (Ps 104:3); at the very least, God dwells far above the visible clouds. Delay in prayer, a perennial theme, does not form part of Ben Sira's teaching, apart from verses 18-23, where the concentration is on what God will do. The worshiper is to realize that it takes time to root out all evils and that God is constantly engaged in this task. Being merciless and proud is a mark of the same individuals for Ben Sira: those who rely on themselves alone are led to violence. God repays like with like but shows mercy to humble people (v. 23). Against whom or in what court God is to defend the people is not spelled out; the expression in verse 23 is traditional.

36:1-17 Prayer for Israel. This section both continues the previous chapter and concludes the section beginning with chapter 24. The prayers in Sirach are a distinctive feature of the book, in contrast particularly with other books of wisdom. It is difficult to be precise about the conditions that led to the composition of this psalm-like prayer. Since many psalms lack specific references, Ben Sira may have followed that style here. Thus this prayer would be applicable to Israel at all times—in the disturbed period of Ben Sira's life or later.

The oneness and universal power of God are strongly expressed in verses 1-4. As the one God, Yahweh exercises power over all the nations. The Israelites, beginning probably in the Babylonian Exile, began to proclaim God's holiness (the Hebrew term implies separation) by practicing holiness themselves; defeat of these enemies in the future will show God's power to Israel (v. 3).

Ben Sira moves from a plea for renewed wonders (v. 5) to more traditional and violent expressions (vv. 6-8). These latter are more marks of the author's depth of feeling than his actual literal curses of enemies. The "time" (v. 7) recalls the sense of order and proper time of Israel's wisdom teachers (as in Eccl 3:1-8).

The specific petitions for Israel look to a restoration of the ancient order. The people's origin in fact goes back to Jacob/Israel. The latter name has the traditional element *el*, meaning "God"; hence Israel is called by God's own name (v. 11). The plea to fill the temple with God's glory (v. 13) recalls the mournful period when the glory of God departed the temple (Ezek 11:23). If the glory returns, the prophets like Ezekiel will be proved true (vv. 14-15).

Ben Sira repeats his plea in conclusion, along with the motive that God is always and forever gracious to Israel (v. 16). If God answers, the result will be greater glory for God, to be acknowledged as eternal God by all the world (v. 17). This verse shows a blossoming interest in Israel's vocation as the prophet of the one God throughout the world, and may have encouraged a missionary outreach of the type that converted Galilee to Judaism shortly before Ben Sira's time.

Making Right Judgments (36:18–42:14)

These chapters comprise a major section dealing with advice on how to judge reality correctly. Social relationships (36:21–39:11) and good and evil things (39:12–42:14) are the two major divisions.

Social Relationships (36:18–39:11)

This division opens with a brief introduction (vv. 18-20) and then continues with the following subsections: choosing a wife (36:21-27), choosing friends (37:1-6), choosing advisors (37:7-15), speech of the wise (37:16-25), temperance (37:26-30), illness and physicians (38:1-15), mourning (38:16-23), craftsmen and the wise (38:14–39:11).

The introductory verses (18-20) are two proverbial statements of different types: experience (v. 18) and its applications (v. 19); and contrasts (v. 20). All deal in some way with the distinctions to follow.

36:21-27 Choosing a wife. This passage opens typically with a theme statement (v. 21) showing again Ben Sira's bias against women. Her good qualities (vv. 22-23) are not valued for themselves but make the husband fortunate. A good wife is a support to her husband and makes a home for him (vv. 24-25). This last observation is underscored with two rhetorical questions; the expected answer is "No one."

37:1-6 Choosing a friend. The lesson on true and false friends opens with a general introductory statement warning against false friends. Some so-called friends become enemies (v. 2). Ben Sira exclaims in lament for such an outcome, the only time this method of writing is employed in the book. (Some scholars see the "companion" of verse 3 as the "evil inclination" mentioned elsewhere in Sirach and rabbinic sources.) After a comparison of false with true (vv. 4-5), the author shifts the focus, summoning the person addressed to care for his friends in return.

37:7-15 Choosing advisors. This lesson parallels the previous one on friends, opening with distinctions between good and bad advisors (v. 7). The next verses recommend caution—a typical wisdom point of view, one characteristic of Ben Sira. The series of recommendations on whom to avoid appears to be traditional advice, perhaps collected in one spot (vv. 10-11). The wise should rely first on the godly (Ben Sira's association of wisdom, law, and piety) and then on their own best instincts (vv. 12-14). "Conscience" (v. 14) is "heart" in Hebrew, the seat not of emotion as with us, but of decision-making. The best advisor of all is God (v. 15), a fitting conclusion to this lesson.

37:16-25 The speech of the wise. Continuing the subject of proper choices, Ben Sira introduces a lesson on the wise and how they speak. The usual introductory statements (vv. 16-18) are of major importance, since Ben Sira places reason (word/thought/mind) at the center of human acts. By contrast, he might have asserted that human beings are under influences from outside (whether good or bad) or inside, such as the "evil influence" cited above, or even that we have no will at all. The emphasis, in fact, is on the tongue, whose baleful influence even over reason is easily understood.

Next comes a set of distinctions on time and counterfeit wisdom (vv. 19-25). Ben Sira teaches that wisdom is a gift for others—a "charism," in the theological language of the New Testament. Verse 23 seems out of place; it is only loosely connected to the preceding verse.

37:26-30 Temperance. In a few verses Ben Sira offers his students lessons about moderation in food and other delights. Discipline, balance (vv. 26-29), and learning from observation of others (v. 30) are all required in the wise.

38:1-15 Illness and physicians. Though perhaps intentionally joined to the previous discussion on food, this lesson has independent status. The author discusses the physician, the source of medical wisdom, and general ways to think about illness.

Ben Sira doubtless had to call his young hearers to respect physicians, whose profession is mentioned rarely in the Old Testament, and then only in the late period. Under the influence of Greek culture, medicine grew in stature, and its practitioners developed from healers to those who would diagnose and treat illness. The physician draws wisdom (that is, skill) from God, and is justly to be esteemed (vv. 1-3).

Medical skill comes from wise use of the gifts of God on earth; the reference to Exod 15:25 is proof enough (vv. 4-5). The physician thus participates in God's own work of establishing (or re-establishing) order (vv. 7-8). Ben Sira counsels a regimen to effect cures: pray quickly (v. 9), repent of evil (v. 10), sacrifice generously (v. 11). Once in the proper disposition, turn to the physician (vv. 12-13). Note that the shift is from sacred to secular, since the source of medical skill is God (vv. 14-15).

38:16-23 Mourning. Ben Sira introduces here a topic almost new to the Old Testament. In earlier times laments for the dead were certainly practiced, but his explanation, cautions, and sensitive psychological tone are distinc-

tive. For Ben Sira, it appears that custom and civility rather than prayer for the dead or even with survivors were uppermost in his mind (vv. 16-17). The period of mourning was generally seven days (Gen 50:10; also Sir 22:12), probably more for close relatives than for friends. Ben Sira advises a brief time and gives a psychological motive (vv. 18-19).

In the rest of this short lesson the author counsels attention to right living and one's own end (vv. 20-22). No hope of afterlife exists for Ben Sira, apart from God's judgment near or at death. Verse 23 summarizes the passage. The term "soul" represents, not our concept of the composite of body and soul, but the Hebrew *nefesh*, a word implying personality or individuality. By the time of Ben Sira, *nefesh* may have begun to acquire a more philosophical sense.

38:24–39:11 Craftsmen and the wise. This section either closes the unit on social relationships (36:21–39:11) or begins a new section, the third added by Ben Sira to his earlier work. If the latter, the author is opening with a general description of his own lifework.

Ben Sira here compares various skilled occupations (vv. 25-34) with that of the scribe (39:1-11). The scribe in question (v. 24) is a legal scholar, not simply a person who knows how to read and write. The farmer (vv. 25-26), engraver (v. 27), blacksmith (v. 28), and potter (vv. 29-30) all have practical wisdom in the sense of skill, with its attention to practical order, balance, and beauty. Their work is important in its own way (vv. 31-32) and a gift of God (v. 34), but the great work of decision-making at the top is in the hands of others (v. 33).

With a rare exclamation, Ben Sira extols the difference between the intellectual work of scholars and the manual labor of the craftsmen (as 38:24). Despite his reverence for the priesthood and the accolades given to other professions, such as physicians, this section (vv. 1-11) places the legal scholar on the highest level. The scribe is a conservator of ancient wisdom, personally wise, knowing the deeper levels of meaning of proverbs (v. 2). As a result, the scribe enjoys a good reputation among the world's great. The sources of wisdom are in experience (travel, v. 5), but most especially in personal holiness—the scribe prays to be emptied of sins, and as a result is filled with divine wisdom (vv. 6-7).

Ben Sira appears to offer his pupils reasons for the difficult pursuit of wisdom in verses 8-11—in this case public renown. Self-interest predominates here: wisdom sought not for its own sake but for an eternal memory. Christians would more likely place their trust in divine providence, rejoicing in the utterance given them and in giving glory to God alone.

Note the repeat of the traditional divisions within the biblical canon: law (v. 1a), prophets (v. 1b), writings (v. 2); this appeared previously in the foreword. Some scholars see a developing interest in oral tradition (v. 2) alongside the written word, though this opinion is hard to sustain.

Good and Evil Things (39:12–42:14)

The author begins a new section here, the second main division of 36:18–42:14 on proper discrimination.

39:12-35 A psalm of praise. The content of this psalm is similar to that of 16:24–17:14, but the form is typical of certain psalms: an invitation to prayer (vv. 13-15), motives (vv. 16-31), conclusion (vv. 32-35). The invitation, addressed to disciples ("children"), employs sense images, a style foreign to traditional psalms (petals of roses, odors of the lily, blossoms, harp music).

A theological assertion gives the basic motive (v. 16): the perfection of God's works and of divine providence. This assertion finds proof in divine acts (creation, v. 17). The truly wise should know how God acts and, like God, find nothing unexpected. The theological picture that Ben Sira paints is simplistic: the good are blessed at the right time by good things, whereas the evil are cursed by things both good and evil. It appears that death-dealing events or objects never afflict the good and that the virtuous never suffer. The lesson learned in Job was not learned by the author.

A subsidiary consideration is the proper time (vv. 29, 34). This ordering of the systems of the universe should be pondered by the wise, for it is at the heart of the revelation of God's orderly justice. This psalm-like section concludes by repeating the opening exhortation to praise, that is, to acknowledge publicly God's goodness. To "bless the name" (v. 35) is a late Hebrew expression meaning to proclaim God as good (as in Pss 96:2; 103:1; 1 Chr 23:13).

40:1-11 Suffering. In these verses Ben Sira expands on the evils coming to the wicked, sketched in 39:28-31. This brief section, like several others, has a simple structure: introduction (v. 1a), examples (vv. 1b-7), applications (vv. 8-11). This simple format models the activity of anyone seeking wisdom: observe the realities in faith and then draw conclusions for right living.

The Sage does not discuss why God should allot anxiety to human life; he only observes its universality. "Sons of men" in Hebrew may be translated as "children of Adam" (v. 1a); this is followed by an ambiguous reference to Eve ("mother of all the living"), based on Gen 3:20. The previous verse in Genesis makes it clear that Mother Earth is intended here.

Ben Sira shows his usual psychological insight in the description he gives of human fears, even internalized into nightmares (vv. 2-5). He also partially answers the complaint that the wicked prosper—as king (v. 3) or even priest (v. 4—the Hebrew refers to the priestly turban); retribution will come to them eventually. They share common human anxieties. Even animals are troubled (v. 8).

The issue of predestination is not far from Ben Sira's discussion here or in 39:25. It appears that the author holds that the evil are simply so, "of earth," with no hope of repentance; the good, too, are virtuous throughout, "from above." In holding this, Ben Sira is close to some strains of Old Testament thinking. Despite that, the possibility of repentance for the wicked, as well as of sin in the just, plays a part in other strains of biblical thinking, in the Old Testament and certainly in the New.

40:12-17 What is enduring and what is passing. The next few verses present mainly some comparisons drawn from nature— the traditional contemplative stance of the wise person. Such a person will learn that the evil will ultimately suffer punishment, and the good will endure. No matter how powerful and intimidating evil seems, God's plan will triumph. The wise should come to learn this. The comparisons in verse 15 recall the gospel parable of the sower (Matt 13:3 and parallels).

40:17b-27 Joys of life. These verses are loosely connected with what precedes. They give us some insight into Ben Sira's classroom. The Sage would present a riddle (following v. 17b): wealth and wages can make life sweet; what is better than either? This would provoke several answers. Those that the author chose here have no inherent similarity among them. They rather demonstrate flashes of insight, emphasizing the unexpected (v. 17) or the ordinary (vv. 21, 22). A particularly brilliant answer is found in verse 24: "charity that rescues," that is, in times of stress having helpers is truly good, but an act of charity that relieves the root causes of the stress is better.

Verses 26b-27 appear to be a type of gloss or commentary on verse 26a. Ben Sira has previously extolled the fear of the Lord; such references characterize the entire book. The "canopy" of verse 27 appears to derive from Isa 4:6 ("his glory will be a shelter"; the Hebrew terms for "shelter" and "canopy" are related).

40:28-30 Begging, an evil in life. A life of beggary is one of the evils of life, though the reason for its position here is unclear. Note the refinement of Ben Sira's psychological insight. Also, he follows in the footsteps of Israel's prophets who counseled that outward appearances (particularly of religion) should match inward realities.

41:1-4 Death. Ben Sira continues to reflect on good and evil, and here addresses death dramatically. Death is bitter for the strong but welcome for the weak. The seeker after wisdom should ponder the one at peace and see not contentment but a shadow cast over him by death. Though bitter, death can be welcome—the wise should see this as well. The wise (vv. 3-4) will know God's decree in Gen 3:19: death comes to all. Life does not exist after death; only Sheol, the abode of the dead, remains (v. 4).

41:5-13 Memorials. The previous discussion leads Ben Sira to consider the only remnants of the good and evil—children and reputation. While it is often true that evil parents can create a situation in which children will develop badly, modern readers have to reject the author's blanket statements. Neither do all wicked parents have evil children, nor do wicked offspring have evil parents. Free will doubtless has a role to play.

The woe in verse 8 occurs only here and in 2:12-14. Ben Sira does not draw out the theological implications of the verse. Is the man sinful because he forsakes the law (an expression of Deuteronomic origin), or is he sinful

by nature and thus turns from the law? The author closes with a summary statement, noteworthy for its use of the Hebrew term *tohu*, "nought" or "nothingness," a rare word, used in Gen 1:2 ("wasteland") to describe the nothingness existing before creation.

A good name (vv. 11-13) by contrast endures, apparently forever. One may also conclude that virtuous children attest to the virtue of their parents.

41:14-42:8 True and false shame. This section continues the series of observations on good and evil things begun in 39:12. The author focuses on shame, having mentioned the subject in 4:21. After his introduction (vv. 14-17), the text lists evil acts for which one should truly be ashamed (vv. 18-24), and then good and lawful acts for which one should never be ashamed (42:1-8).

The schoolroom atmosphere of Ben Sira's day comes through clearly in these verses. The riddles of 40:17-26 called for student answers; so too the objects of shame before certain individuals seem to call for wise responses. Ben Sira has treated of nearly all the subjects previously (9:8 on lust; 18:44 on harsh words), and the topics here require no lofty insight to be understood. The teaching of Jesus in the gospels follows similar paths (for example, Luke 6:34 on lending).

The motive (v. 24) comes as a surprise: human respect. Doubtless Ben Sira had in mind observance of God's law, which would ultimately bring esteem of the highest type.

Other biblical versions based on the Greek text will show significant differences in the text of verses 15-17.

Ben Sira holds out another kind of human respect in 42:1, here influencing toward sin. Human esteem has its value in enforcing public morality, but the company of the wicked can work just the opposite. The person of integrity will do what is right, specified in verses 2-8.

The first series of acts (vv. 3-5a) focuses on business dealings. Sensitivity about honest dealing (v. 4) took on a special refinement in Israel; prophets voiced similar concerns (for example, Hos 12:8).

The second series focuses on managing one's household. Again, the advice comes from experience and common sense. The chastisement of the aged (v. 8) refers to sexual impropriety in the elderly; the good (read "wise") manager will hold them accountable for their acts as long as they form part of the household. As before, the motive is recognition by others as being wise, one of the chief characteristics of which is caution and discretion.

42:9-14 Wickedness of women. In these few verses the author gives his most extensive treatment of daughters (see also 7:24-25 and 22:3b-5). Nowhere else in the Old Testament are one's daughters discussed as a topic by itself. As elsewhere in the book, Ben Sira treats women from a man's bias. Daughters are usually compared unfavorably with sons; they are a burden and a source of anxiety and potential shame. Since daughters could be a source of economic benefit, the wise father would guard them (v. 9). Women, judged to be foolish, could not have sense enough to preserve themselves from sexual entanglements, so it fell to the father to provide all needed safeguards (vv. 10-12).

Ben Sira concludes this difficult section with two proverbs, possibly not original with him. Verse 14 is particularly difficult for modern readers. Many translators read the text as: "Better a man's evil than a woman's goodness."

Praise of the Lord in Nature (42:15–43:35)

For many scholars the section 42:15–50:24 marks the last great division of the Book of Sirach. In the outline followed here, 42:15–43:35 forms the ninth major section of the book. The passage is psalm-like, similar to others (1:1-10; 24:1-22). This poem has three clear divisions: introduction (42:15-25), catalogue of wonders (43:1-27), conclusion (43:15-25).

Ben Sira concludes his book with the hymn in this section and follows with a lengthy praise of Israel's heroes (44:1-50:29). The two together form an elaborate doxology to his collection of wise teachings. As such, the section serves an educational purpose similar to his use of proverbs: observe the realities of life and draw conclusions for wise living.

Verse 15a introduces the hymn, and the following verses (15b-22) speak of the origin of God's works and the impossibility of describing them all—not even the "holy ones" (v. 17) can (an ancient expression for God's

attendants). "Depths" (v. 18) translates the Hebrew term for the region under the visible world; it and the human heart are symbols of impenetrable realities. The Creator alone can understand them. Verses 23-25 add a series of observations on the goodness and order of creation. Ben Sira does not mean to teach that there will never be an end to the world (v. 24).

43:1-27 Catalogue of wonders. This listing treats the sky and sun (vv. 1-5), heavenly phenomena (vv. 6-12), weather (vv. 13-23), and the sea (vv. 24-26).

The Hebrew text is difficult in the first several verses, and translations differ considerably. The language of praise used here is typical of psalms: exclamations (v. 2), questions expecting a negative answer (v. 3), assertions of greatness (v. 5). Ben Sira's poetic view of the sun drawn across the sky by horses is a commonplace idea in the ancient Near East (v. 5).

The value of the moon, besides its beauty, is that it guarantees the observance of festivals on their proper days; for Israel (and even for many in the modern world) both the feast and its fixed day were of equal value. In verse 8 we have an echo of two Hebrew words, *yerah* (moon/month) and *hodesh* (new moon/month). The poetic view of the relationship between stars and bad weather (v. 10) is clear: the stars must protect against bad weather, since when they appear, weather is good; should they "relax their vigils," bad weather results. God's bow (v. 12) is likewise an ancient poetic view of the rainbow (see 9:13).

Similar to Job 38 is Ben Sira's treatment of weather phenomena (vv. 13-23). The storm serves as an instrument of God's wrath: the arrows from his bow are lightning (v. 13; see Ps 29). The ancient Canaanites viewed the storm as a god; by Ben Sira's day, Israel knew that storms received their power from God (v. 15), at God's command (vv. 16-17).

The images of cold (vv. 18-21) contrast strongly with the heat of verse 22—both phenomena are known in Israel. The dew (v. 23) was regarded as a great blessing in a land of scant rainfall (see Deut 33:28; Ps 133:3; Isa 18:4). Israel's awe in face of the sea is evident in verses 24-26. It is noteworthy that the ancient idea of rivalry between the sea with its creatures and God had disappeared by Ben Sira's time. Here God calms the deep;

God alone is the maker of all its exotic inhabitants.

The final verse (v. 27) appears to conclude this catalogue by asserting that God alone is in control of all the great phenomena, using them to carry out the divine will.

43:28-35 Conclusion. Ben Sira concludes by resuming his former theme of the impossibility of knowing God through and through. "He is all in all" does not express any supposed pantheistic notions, as some scholars have held. It seems rather an expression of praise and wonder at the Creator of all (as in verse 35). The piety of our author is evident: his contemplation of the wonders of creation does not lead him to become a scientist, but instead to give praise. The result of this is the gift of wisdom.

Praise of Israel's Ancestors (44:1–50:29)

Just as the previous section both praises God and shows disciples how to grow in wisdom, so this last section praises God for his greatness toward Israel and leads disciples through a sort of gallery of heroes, holding them up for emulation. We do not have a history here in the sense of a connected series of causes and effects. Consequently, Ben Sira felt free to omit details or even to reshape events for his own purposes.

44:1-15 Introduction. "Let us now praise famous men" is the traditional wording of verse 1. The Hebrew is in the singular and focuses on the piety (Hebrew *hesed*) of Israel's ancestors. "Portion" (v. 2) is a traditional expression recalling the early belief that each deity had his/her own people. Israel was the Lord's portion among all others (see 17:14; also Deut 32:9; Jer 10:16). The twelve types of heroes, probably all Israelites, strangely do not include priests. In verse 4 the "spikes" of the wise makers of epigrams refers to the pointed quality of their words (as in Eccl 12:11), which encourage reflection.

Verse 9 seems to be a general comment on the wicked (as in 10:17). Verses 8 and 10 are joined and repeat Ben Sira's views on the long memory and numerous children of the just.

44:16-23 Early patriarchs. This section begins, not with Adam, but with Enoch. Just why Adam is omitted is not clear. The Enoch verse is enclosed in brackets to show its doubtful place; many say it is an expansion of 49:14. That Enoch did not die but was simply taken up became a source of much speculation in late Old Testament times.

Ben Sira's interest in the preservation of Israel through divine providence is clear in the verses that follow: Noah preserved the race (v. 17), Abraham's (v. 21) and Isaac's (v. 22) descendants. In addition to God's plan, the virtue of the patriarchs was rewarded in the usual way, with numerous offspring. Each of them received signs and had an agreement or covenant with God. A close check of the corresponding passages in Genesis will show the freedom Ben Sira employed in shifting events for the sake of his argument. He also quoted Ps 72:8 in verse 21. The references here to sea and river, at least in the mind of the psalmist, were to the great sea surrounding the land. No specific sea or river (the poetic counterpart of sea) should be looked for, even less a divine promise concerning modern boundaries for the state of Israel.

God's hand in Israel's history is seen in the division of the land and its allotment. That this system no longer existed in Ben Sira's day seems of no concern.

45:1-26 Moses, Aaron, Phinehas. Ben Sira begins this section with Moses, not with Joseph, as one might expect. The omission seems to be corrected in 49:15. Moses is here regarded as a worker of wonders, endowed with divine power. After beholding God face to face, Moses hands on the law, the truest wisdom. Elsewhere Ben Sira has made a close identification of wisdom with the law (see 19:17 and 32:14-16). The basis of God's choice of Moses appears to be his natural but God-given endowments (v. 4).

The treatment of Aaron is surprising in its length (vv. 6-22) and in its detailed descriptions. The attention given by Ben Sira to the priesthood, and to the cult in particular, has been taken as proof of his being a priest. True or not, the author's interest seems to be more in the presence of God to Israel, along with Israel's proper response in worship. The Lord deserves the best and most magnificent worship possible.

Ben Sira points to the single priesthood (v. 7), probably with an eye to the pre-exilic struggles between two priestly branches (Aaron and Zadok). The vestments listed in verses 8-13 are not exactly described (Ben Sira confuses the meaning of ephod); rather, the author gives a poetic evocation of their glory.

The mention of colors (vv. 10-11) is quite rare in this book, indeed throughout the Old Testament.

Similarly, the sacrifices listed in verses 14-17 are only loosely described. Following his usual practice, Ben Sira mentions several covenants (vv. 15 and 24-25). These do not conform exactly to the details of other Old Testament books, where relationships between God and Israel or with individuals are called by various names. Ben Sira has subsumed all these into a single system of covenants—an apt theological construction on his part.

A further element of the ensemble is the focus on permanence: Aaron's priesthood (v. 7), use of vestments (v. 13), Aaronic covenant (v. 15). God's commitment to Israel thus becomes a further motive for his praise. The persistence of the liturgy is a symbol of this commitment.

The zeal of Phinehas (Num 25) had become legendary (see, for example, Ps 106:30-31, where his merit is said to endure forever). Ben Sira, true to his previous thinking, equates Phinehas's act with sacrificial atonement (see 3:3). As a grandson of Aaron, ("third of his line," v. 23), he was already in the priestly line. The author restates the outcome of his zeal—a recommitment to the priesthood (see Num 25:12-13). The office of high priest, however, developed only after the Exile.

The final verse appears to be addressed to the priests of Ben Sira's day, though on what occasion is unclear. His message to them comes from his concern to preserve the cult, guaranteed in a way more wondrous than the covenant with David, which at that time was in fact not being realized, since there was no Davidic king.

46:1-20 Joshua, Caleb, Judges, and Samuel. This brief chapter is clearly divided into accounts of Joshua (vv. 1-6), Caleb (vv. 7-10), the judges (vv. 11-12), and Samuel (vv. 13-20). As previously, Ben Sira has shaped and understood the events of Israel's past from his own perspective: God continues the choice of Israel, the glory given to Israel thereby, manifested in the continuing glory of the cult and in the wisdom given to Israel; lessons for contemporary Israel in the piety of her ancient heroes in the face of foreign oppressors.

Joshua appears here as a prophet, a role not given him elsewhere, since he was chiefly a military leader. As a successor of Moses, he would have to be, in Ben Sira's mind, his successor in all ways, including the prophetic office. Moses, in fact, is styled a prophet only in texts coming from the northern kingdom, where the title of prophet was used more widely than in the south (see Hos 12:14; Deut 34:10).

Joshua as commander of Israel's armies is found in verse 2 (the battle at Ai, Josh 8:18-19) and in verses 4-6 (the battle at Gibeon, Josh 10:12-14). "Most High God" (v. 5) is an ancient designation (*El Elyon*) found here in Sirach for the first time and repeated three times in the rest of the book. In these uses Ben Sira may be consciously adopting a more elevated, liturgical style to correspond to his subject matter.

Joshua and Caleb are linked in the next few verses as the only two spared from the desert wanderings (Num 26:65). The "summits of the land" (v. 9) refers to the hills around Hebron in southern Judah, where the Caleb tribe settled.

In the case of the judges, their record of devotion is not entirely stainless. Possibly Ben Sira refers (v. 11) to Gideon and Samson, not exactly models of piety. "May their memory . . ." becomes a traditional rabbinic expression of regard for the deceased. Verse 12 clearly is not a prayer for the judges themselves to rise from the dead (see his wish for prophets in 49:10); this would run counter to all of Ben Sira's thinking. The prayer is for a renewal of their spirit in the author's age. Despite that, may we not see here a dawning hope of resurrection, prominent in other late Old Testament writings?

Ben Sira includes a quiet wordplay on the name Samuel and the term "dedicated," a feature evident only in the Hebrew. Since Samuel was so complex a figure, later authors see him as prophet, the last of the judges, and a priest. These three roles are developed: judge (v. 14), prophet (vv. 15, 20), priest (v. 16). In addition, Samuel exercised some political power (anointing Saul and David as kings, v. 13b).

Ben Sira's reluctance to paint too dark a picture of parts of Israel's past leads him to mention Saul only indirectly (prince, vv. 13, 19; king, v. 20).

47:1-24a Nathan, David, Solomon. In these verses appear Nathan (v. 1), David (vv.

2-11), and Solomon (vv. 12-24a), the latter two having accounts of the same relative length, but both somewhat sanitized.

The inclusion of Nathan as part of the succession of prophets (Moses, Joshua, Samuel) is a contribution made by Ben Sira to our thinking. The account of David's young life is colored by poetry: parallels between lions and kids, bears and lambs. The account of his military prowess is based on 2 Samuel, and his interest in liturgy on 1 Chronicles. The latter work is notorious for its whitewash of David's career, a decision taken by Ben Sira as well.

"The might of his people" (v. 5) is literally "horn of his people," a traditional expression for power, similar to the power exercised by animals through their horns. Notice also the twofold mention of *El Elyon* ("Most High God" vv. 5, 8). The might of the Philistines (v. 7) had been shattered indeed, but the Roman conquerors of Israel adopted their name for occupied Israel, Palestine.

A possible play on Solomon's name ("man of peace") occurs in verse 13. The peace characteristic of his reign allowed him the leisure to pursue the building of the temple (v. 13), wisdom (vv. 14-17), and commerce (v. 18). He shared a name, "beloved of Yah[weh]" (Jedid-iah) with the whole people of Israel (in Jer 11:15).

The dark cloud that began to overshadow Israel's life in the career of Saul (not mentioned by name, but see 46:19-20) and of David (his sins, 47:11) is quite apparent in Solomon's career (vv. 19-21). His sin, at least in Ben Sira's view, consisted in allowing self-control to slip away in favor of control over him by women. The author has already spoken critically against this (see 9:2; 25:12). Despite sin, God's promise remains—an assertion made here clearly (v. 22). Note also the principle useful for interpreting biblical passages: God does not "permit even one of his promises to fail."

Many translations include both Rehoboam, Solomon's son, and Jeroboam, the first king of the independent northern kingdom. Since the latter should not be remembered (v. 23), some translations omit mention of him. "Expansive in folly" is a wordplay on Rehoboam's name.

47:24b-48:16 Elijah and Elisha. The growth of sin, mentioned previously, continues in ominous counterpoint to the accounts of Israel's heroes. The connection of Elijah with fire (vv. 1, 3, 9) is a brilliant poetic accommodation. This prophet's powers over nature (restricting rain, 1 Kgs 17) reinforces his reputation: because of him the sun scorched the earth and broke the staff on which Israel relied—abundant grain (v. 2). He had powers to raise to life (v. 5) or to cause death (v. 6). So God-like in many ways was he that he did not die a human death but was taken up (like Enoch, 44:16). This event became the source of much speculation in Elijah's case too; Mal 3:23 records it. The allusion here to the text of Malachi shows that that book was known to Ben Sira (see the mention of all the twelve prophets in 49:10).

The author includes some small measure of messianic hope in 48:10: "to re-establish the tribes of Jacob." Despite his interest in the continuation of God's promises, he knew from the facts of daily life that the Davidic monarchy had ceased and that the old tribal organization was long out of use.

If Elijah was a wonderworker, his successor Elisha was even more so. Nonetheless, the wonders worked through him had little effect on righteous living in the northern kingdom. As a result, the people of Israel were destroyed. Ben Sira exaggerates for effect the totality of the destruction and scattering; probably only a small percentage of Israel was taken away and resettled in a few specific locations in the Assyrian domains. Judah's territories were also annexed by Assyria, and what was left to the Davidic kings was tiny indeed (v. 15).

48:17-23 Hezekiah and Isaiah. Ben Sira gives his readers another wordplay in verses 17 and 22: the Hebrew for "to strengthen, hold fast" is at the root of the name Hezekiah. For the people of subsequent centuries as well as for Ben Sira, the salvation of Jerusalem from Sennacherib's attack stood as the most striking proof of God's faithfulness to the Davidic kings. Ben Sira modifies the tradition to include the whole people of Jerusalem at prayer, whereas in 2 Kgs 19 it is Hezekiah alone.

Isaiah appears here mainly on account of his deeds, not his prophetic speeches. Modern scholarship attributes to an unnamed prophet or prophets chapters 40–66 of Isaiah. Ben Sira's view is that prophecy involved foretelling the events of the Exile (vv. 24-25). His reference to these chapters demonstrates that they were known under Isaiah's name in Ben Sira's time.

49:1-10 Josiah and the prophets. Ben Sira gives us abundant proof of his regard for Josiah, appealing to smell (incense), taste (honey), and hearing (music). The reason for Josiah's renown is found in his thoroughgoing piety. Note that the author connects himself and his contemporaries with their ancestors: "our betrayals" rather than "their betrayals" (v. 2). He then turns to a traditional restatement of the causes of Judah's destruction (vv. 4-7): the kings—and the people—turned from God's law. As in other places in the book, we find here the implication "they should have known better." As a result, their foolishness (lack of wisdom and foresight) is proved, and the punishment is a foregone conclusion.

Ben Sira includes Jeremiah, even quoting Jer 1:5, 10, and Ezekiel, whose chariot became a feature of later rabbinic speculation. The reference to Job is customary, as in Jas 5:11; both Ben Sira and the apostle James have neglected the anger and impatience of Job in the main chapters of the book in favor of the conclusion, Job 42:7-9.

The "twelve prophets" (v. 10), Hosea through Malachi, are the minor prophets— those whose names are attached to brief prophetic books, which form almost a fourth major book in company with Isaiah, Jeremiah, and Ezekiel. The role of the minor prophets in the sustenance of Israel has been correctly evaluated by Ben Sira. Yet, through all of these accounts Ben Sira does not mention Babylon—nor Assyria, for that matter— nor the Exile.

49:11-13 Postexilic heroes. The three heroes have one verse each. The concept of the signet (v. 11) may refer to the use God would make of Zerubbabel (see Hag 2:23), as one uses a signet ring to formalize a document or offer proof of authenticity. The obscure Jeshua (the Joshua of Hag 1:12) stood with Zerubbabel and continued the priestly line after the return from exile. To Nehemiah is given the credit for building the city's walls again to shelter the temple. Note, too, the repeated use of "our" (v. 13), joining Israel of the past with Ben Sira's contemporaries.

49:14-16 Heroes before the Flood. There are nearly as many theories to explain the inclusion of Enoch (v. 14), Joseph (v. 15), and

Adam and his sons (v. 16) as there are writers on the subject. Whether included deliberately or not, these men close the historical circle begun in 44:1. The splendor or glory so often mentioned in Sirach comes to a fitting climax associated both with Adam as well as the great high priest Simon, whose praise fills the following chapter.

50:1-24 Simon. We do not know of the repairs mentioned in verses 1-2 from other biblical texts, but the historian Josephus confirms them. These are the only acts mentioned for which Simon should receive praise. The next several verses describe in loving detail Simon's appearance in his high priestly vestments and as presiding at temple sacrifice.

The images employed here appeal almost entirely to sight; as such they contrast with 24:13-17, similar in its attention to detail. A close examination of these images will reveal overtones: for example, clouds (v. 6) recall incense; sun on the temple (v. 7), the golden plates that adorned the Jerusalem temple and were brilliant in the sun; the rainbow (v. 7), God's covenant after the Flood; trees of Lebanon (v. 8), which provided material for the temple's construction and for sacrificial wood; olive tree (v. 10), a symbol of eternal life. Above all is the theme of glory, running all through the sections beginning in 42:15.

The liturgy described here was very likely that prescribed for the Day of Atonement. The detail in verse 15 was not fixed exactly in earlier biblical texts; Ben Sira is describing the practice of his day. The mention of the very name of the Lord (v. 20) refers to the custom of reciting the exact name only once yearly on the festival.

Note also the various designations for God: Lord (vv. 13, 20), Most High (vv. 14, 16, 17, 21), Most High God (v. 15), Holy One of Israel (v. 17), Merciful One (v. 19), God (v. 19), God of all (v. 22). These were all familiar to Ben Sira and his contemporaries from their liturgical life.

The little hymn in verses 22-24 is addressed to no one in particular, but seems to arise from Ben Sira's consideration of the liturgy. He recommended the same praise after contemplation of the majesty of nature (see 43:11 for the rainbow). (The popular hymn "Now Thank We All Our God" takes its origin from verse 22.) The actual Hebrew text of verse 24 is a prayer for Simon; the translators of the New American Bible omitted it here, choosing to follow the canonical Greek version.

50:25-26 Fragments. The surprising numerical proverb (see 25:2; 26:5) focuses on the third group of despised peoples, namely, Samaritans. The Edomites on Mount Seir and the Philistines were traditional enemies of Israel but no longer a threat. Particularly galling for Ben Sira must have been the rival Samaritan temple and clergy at Shechem. The woman of Samaria (John 4:19-20) referred to the ancestral rivalry. Their pretension to the true cult must have led Ben Sira to include these verses.

50:27-29 Epilogue. Another surprise is the signature, a feature unknown elsewhere in the Old Testament, though Ben Sira has referred earlier to himself on occasion in the first person. He concludes with a piece of advice to his students, joining together his themes of wisdom, proper living, and divine guidance.

Appendix (51:1-30)

Several Old Testament books have appendix materials, for example 2 Sam 21–24; Isa 36–39; even Lamentations is attached as a sort of appendix to Jeremiah. The purpose of this appendix is unclear, but it may have been intended to preserve (pseudo?) Ben Sira materials still in circulation but not yet a part of Sirach.

The hymn of thanks is a personal composition, referring to events in the life of Ben Sira that are otherwise unknown to us. In any case, the author has mined the treasures of Old Testament prayers to derive a new composition. It follows the traditional form, known from the psalms: introduction addressed to God (v. 1); a narrative offering motives for thanks (vv. 2-6); a prayer for deliverance (vv. 7-11a); God's response (vv. 11b-12). The reference to death and the nether world may simply be a commonplace expression for danger or suffering. Calling the Lord "father" (v. 10) is not original with the New Testament.

The second poem is an acrostic, each succeeding verse beginning with the next letter of the Hebrew alphabet. This acrostic is incomplete; up to half is missing. The author is probably not Ben Sira himself.

The first section speaks of the quest for wisdom (vv. 13-22), often with erotic overtones. The writer began with a search for wisdom, followed the "level path" (of the law, v. 15), and so grew in wisdom—the object of which is the praise of the Lord (v. 22). This approach is consistent with Ben Sira's methods.

In the second section (vv. 23-30) the author turns to his students. The poem has the feel of an advertisement. The "house of instruction" (v. 23) is an expression that appears here for the first time, meaning a school. He urges hard work and promises rewards ("silver and gold," v. 28, which may stand for blessings other than simply material gain).

The Hebrew text ends with "in his own time," an expression consistent with Ben Sira's teaching about the providence of God, who acts according to the wise divine plan.

PSALMS

Richard J. Clifford, S.J.

INTRODUCTION

At the center of every psalm is the presence of Yahweh, the God of Israel, "the Lord" in Jewish and Christian translations. Yahweh is present to the psalmists most often in the temple. Built on Mount Zion in Jerusalem by King Solomon in the tenth century B.C.E. and rebuilt in the late sixth century B.C.E., after the Babylonian Exile, the temple complex was the site of the three great annual festivals: Passover in early spring, Pentecost seven weeks later, and Ingathering (also called the Feast, or Booths) in early fall. In the temple court the people encountered their Lord; they recalled the moment of their creation, the Exodus-Conquest (sometimes depicted in mythic language of victory over the sea) in solemn liturgical remembering.

According to the psalms, the temple was not the only institution through which Yahweh was present to the people. They also encountered God in the king, son of God by adoption, intermediary between God and people, and conduit of divine blessings to the people. Another mode of presence was the divine word to Israel, the law or *torah*. The Christian church sees in Jesus Christ and in the church that embodies him a presence so definitive as to include and fulfill all previous modes of presence.

The 150 psalms express Israel's experience of the Holy One, directly and concretely, with a wide range of feeling. As deep and as true as the psalmists' feelings are, their expression is strongly marked by the ancient Near Eastern tradition of hymnody. Genuine religious feeling, a strong tradition, and literary craft—

these made the psalms. To know them, to share their religious feeling, one must be willing to study the tradition and the craft.

The most concise approach to the tradition and craft of the psalms is that perfected by Hermann Gunkel (1862–1932), professor of Bible at Berlin and later at Halle, in his great commentary (1926) and in his introduction (1933). Gunkel, with a romantic's love of the popular feeling and spontaneity of the psalms, and with a scholar's mastery of the relevant literatures and languages, recognized that the thoughts and emotions of the psalms are expressed in extremely traditional ways, "forms" or "genres," customary ways of speaking in the ancient Near East. Largely on the basis of his observations, scholars divide the psalms into a relatively few genres or forms: *laments* (individual or communal), *thanksgivings* (individual or communal), and *hymns*. A few psalms do not come directly under the above categories; these include royal psalms, songs of Zion, songs of trust, and psalms influenced by wisdom literature themes. These are classed according to their subject matter rather than according to their formal structure.

We sketch below the typical features of the main genres of (A) lament, (B) thanksgiving, and (C) hymn. References to this general treatment will be given throughout the commentary.

A. Psalms of **lament** are characterized by:
—a direct, unadorned cry to Yahweh.
—Complaint. A vivid description of the affliction of the community, such as military

or agricultural distress, or of the individual, such as sickness, unfair legal process, treachery of former friends, or the consequences of sin. Sometimes there is a protestation of innocence; the punishment is undeserved.

—Expression of trust. Despite the crisis, the psalmist maintains a hope, however modest, that God will act. Such a hope is often introduced by "but" or "nevertheless."

—Petition. The psalmist prays for his own or his people's rescue, and often for the enemies' downfall.

—Words of assurance. A word delivered to the psalmist by a priest in the course of the lament. Only rarely is it transmitted with the text of the psalm, for example, Pss 15:5 and 60:6-8. Apparently, it was considered the priest's part, not the petitioner's.

—Statement of praise. A serene statement at the end of the psalm, in striking contrast to the anxiety of what has gone before. The psalmist states the intention to live the word of assurance delivered by the priest *as the word of the Lord.*

Each lament records a drama with three actors: the psalmist, God, and "the wicked." In the complaint the psalmist dramatizes his plight and protests his innocence so as to move God to action: Will you, just God, allow this innocent poor person to be vanquished by the wicked? In community laments the question is: Will you allow your choosing of Israel to be nullified by another power? The words of assurance, the fifth element in the outline above, function like a judicial verdict, affirming that the Lord does not allow evil to triumph ultimately and will vindicate the poor person. In the vow of praise the psalmist promises to live in the hope that God will act.

B. **Thanksgiving psalms** are closely allied to laments; in essence they are the report of rescue from the hands of the wicked. The term "thanksgiving" is somewhat misleading, for in the Bible to "give thanks" does not mean to say "thank you" but to tell publicly of the rescue that has occurred. The audience then recognizes the hand of Yahweh and gives praise. As a result, Yahweh's glory is acknowledged by human beings.

Most such psalms begin with an expression of thanks and then describe the act of rescue: the psalmist was in distress, even near despair, cried to Yahweh for help, and was saved. The psalmist is conscious of the congregation as he delivers his prayerful report, for the world must acknowledge what Yahweh has done.

C. The **hymn** is simple in its structure: a call to worship, often with the addressees named; for example, "Praise the Lord, all you nations," (Ps 117:1). The main section gives the basis for praise and is introduced by "for." The basis for praise is the activity that displays the Lord's majesty on earth.

The Psalter is an anthology of small collections finally edited into five books, perhaps in imitation of the five books of the Pentateuch: Psalms 1–41, 42–72, 73–89, 90–106, and 107–150. It is sometimes called the hymnbook of the second temple of 515 B.C.E.–A.D. 70, an accurate designation as long as we remember that songs of many periods of Israel's history, including the pre-exilic, are represented in the collection, and that non-liturgical considerations may have influenced the later editing.

A striking feature of the later editing of the Psalter is the superscription, like that written at the beginning of Psalm 51: "A psalm of David, when Nathan the prophet came to him after his sin with Bathsheba" (see 1 Sam 12). Such redactional statements make psalms originally at home in the temple liturgy applicable to any individual, since David was the typical Israelite; what happened to him could happen to each of us.

COMMENTARY

BOOK I: PSALMS 1-41

Psalm 1

This poem is classified as a wisdom psalm because it depicts and contrasts dramatically the "two ways," the two fundamental options for human beings. Hebrew rhetoric often views moral life as action, as choosing, and describes it by mentioning typical actions and their consequences. The psalm divides people into two groups: those obedient to the will of the Lord in verses 1-3, and the wickedly disobedient in verses 4-5. Each group will experience the consequences of their activity: life and prosperity for the obedient, ostracism and unrootedness for the wicked. The psalmist is not self-righteous, disdainfully separating people into righteous and sinners; rather, he celebrates the Lord's world, which is experienced as inherently just, rewarding the righteous and punishing the unrighteous. One places oneself in the community of the righteous or of the unrighteous by one's actions. The psalm therefore invites the person of faith to join those who revere and obey the Lord and to avoid those who rebel against the Lord.

Psalm 2

This royal psalm affirms the Israelite king to be regent of the Lord. In four sections of approximately equal length (vv. 1-3, 4-6, 7-9, 10-11), the Lord's sovereignty over the earth, a sovereignty exercised by the Israelite king, is expressed in a series of actions. In verses 1-3 the kings of the world try to throw off the dominion of the Lord and the Lord's anointed: "Let us break their fetters!" Such a wish is laughable (vv. 4-6). There is but one God in the heavens; the "gods" that the nations believe guide their destinies are not powerful before the one God who chose Israel. In verses 7-8 the narrator pronounces, in the legal adoption language of the day, the divine decree that has made the Israelite king the representative on earth of the one true God. In principle, then, this king is the ruler of the whole world and all its other kings (vv. 8-9). In verses 10-11 the unruly kings are warned: Revere the Lord, revere the king!

Psalm 3

In this lament (A—see p. 754) the psalmist is surrounded by enemies who threaten his

life and deny the possibility that the Lord will come to the rescue (vv. 2-3). Against such taunts, the psalmist hopes that the Lord will answer heartfelt prayer, even managing to boast that the Lord will give protection in life's most vulnerable moment—lying down to sleep (vv. 5-7). Verse 8 prays that the Lord, like a warrior, will defang the taunting enemy. Such defeat of the enemy constitutes public vindication of the psalmist. Verse 9 is a peaceful statement of praise uttered after hearing the oracle of salvation promising rescue. The "salvation," or rescue, that the enemies denied will come without fail.

Psalm 4

This lament shows a more vigorous confidence in the Lord's protection of the just than in most instances of the genre; it can be called a song of trust. The psalmist prays to the God whose help was experienced in the past (v. 2). Out of that confidence he lectures the wicked; they, not he, are in danger and should make their peace with the Lord through ritual means. The psalmist's nearness to God enables him to warn those who have distanced themselves to be reconciled (vv. 3-6). That nearness also makes the psalmist a model of the blessings of God (vv. 7-9).

Psalm 5

In this lament (A) the psalmist contrasts the security of the house of the Lord (vv. 8-9 and 12-13) with the danger of the company of the wicked (vv. 5-7 and 10-11). He therefore prays insistently for God to hear him (vv. 2-4). Both worlds—the danger of the wicked and the enjoyment of the righteous—are imagined concretely: verses 8-9 describe admittance to the temple; in verses 12-13 the verbs "be glad," "exult," and "be the joy of" describe the singing and shouting of liturgical procession.

Psalm 6

This lament (A) is one of the Penitential Psalms, a designation that originated in the seventh century A.D. for seven psalms (6, 32, 38, 51, 102, 130, 143), that are especially suitable to express repentance. The psalmist feels burdened with the consequences of his sin—bodily and mental distress (vv. 3, 7-8) and harassment by enemies (vv. 9, 11). The word "sin" in the Bible can denote not only the act of sinning but its consequences as well. Sin brought consequences that had to be borne, consequences such as personal distress and the taunts of enemies. The speaker pleads for forgiveness not only for the past act of sin but also for the consequences of that act. Thus he asks that his bodily self be healed and that his enemies depart. The return of health and the departure of enemies publicly demonstrate divine acceptance. In the last stanza the psalmist shows the effect of hearing the word of assurance—confidence in the Lord's nearness.

Psalm 7

Psalm 7 is a lament (A), specifically the prayer of an accused person who flees to the presence of the Lord in the sanctuary for justice and protection (vv. 2-3). He takes an oath that he is innocent of any crime that would justify his enemies' attack (vv. 4-6). Since in this case he is innocent, having allowed God to scrutinize his inmost heart, the attacks upon him constitute attacks upon the innocent just person. The God of justice must therefore put the enemies down (vv. 7-14). The rout of the enemies by the Lord is at the same time the judicial verdict: the psalmist is declared innocent, and the enemies are declared guilty. The punishment of the wicked comes about by the inherent force of the wicked actions themselves (vv. 15-17). The psalmist dares to put his whole life in God's hands and to rely on God alone for protection against evil and violence.

Psalm 8

The psalm is a hymn (C) in praise of God for having given human beings responsibility and dignity. One should compare Gen 1:1–2:3 and Psalm 104. Verses 4-5 declare that heaven and earth, now arranged in beauty and order, invite praise. The hymnist expresses wonder at the marvelous world crowned by human beings (vv. 6-7). Human beings stand between heaven and earth; the world is made for them.

Psalms 9–10

The two psalms are actually one acrostic poem, that is, each section begins with a successive letter of the twenty-two letter Hebrew alphabet. Like many other acrostic poems, this one appears to be a series of brief, dis-

parate statements given unity by the outer frame of the alphabet. The poem deals with three themes: (1) the rescue of the helpless and poor from their enemies; (2) the Lord's worldwide judgment and rule over the nations; (3) the prosperity of the wicked, which tempts the believer. A clue to the genre may be 9:14-15, where the psalmist offers thanksgiving (B) for being rescued by God. The psalmist, from the experience of personal salvation, points to other instances of divine power.

Psalm 11

Some themes of lament have been made the basis of a song of trust: instead of calling out for rescue from a specific danger, one rests contentedly in the Lord's presence. The psalmist is in danger; friends counsel flight to the hill country, the traditional hideout for people in danger (vv. 1-2). The chaos that, in the Bible, always lurks on the edge of God's creation is closing in on the psalmist; his own innocence appears to offer no help (v. 3). The psalmist chooses not to follow the advice and leave town but to seek the Lord in the temple. He entrusts his plight to the Lord, all-powerful and all-knowing (vv. 4-5). The psalmist's desire for the punishment of the wicked is a desire that God's justice in its totality be done (vv. 6-7).

Psalm 12

In this lament (A) the psalmist is caught in a human jungle, where violent people and liars oppress the just (vv. 2-3). The psalmist prays that the unjust be punished (vv. 4-5), not from a desire for revenge but from a desire to see God's will appear on earth. Verse 6 preserves the words of assurance delivered to the lamenter; usually it is not transmitted with the psalm. Verses 7-9 are statements praising the word of assurance the psalmist is willing to live by.

Psalm 13

In this lament (A) the psalmist prays to be healed lest his death be interpreted by his enemies as divine condemnation. Untimely death and serious sickness could be interpreted as the consequences of sinful conduct. The psalmist is afraid that his enemies will be vindicated. His healing would be a divine verdict in his favor.

Psalm 14

In this lament of the individual (A), duplicated in Psalm 53, the psalmist imagines the world as consisting of two types of people: "the fool" in verses 1-3 and the "just generation" in verses 4-6 (also called "my people" and "the afflicted"). The psalmist complains that the wicked persecute the community of the just (a better translation than "just generation," v. 5), while God watches from heaven. He expresses a firm hope that God will stride forth from the temple, punish the wicked, and uphold the faithful.

Psalm 15

This psalm, like Psalm 24, reflects the ceremony admitting the Israelite to the temple court. The temple was not like a church that one could enter at any time. It was God's house and could be entered only at certain times and under the proper conditions. One had to be admitted by a priest. The visitor had to answer the question of the priest at the gate: "Who may sojourn in 'your tent'?" (a traditional designation for the temple in Jerusalem). The response in verses 2-5 is a list of twelve stipulations, which sum up the covenantal obligations. Without commitment to the covenant, without conversion, one cannot enter the presence of the Lord. The psalm shows that nearness to the Lord is not a matter of external ritual alone; it demands heartfelt commitment as well.

Psalm 16

In this song of trust the psalmist takes refuge in the temple ("for in you I take refuge," v. 1), expressing trust that the Lord, and not the so-called gods of other nations, reigns over the land of Israel. Verses 3-6, despite corruption in verses 3-4, apparently express the psalmist's refusal to honor the local "gods." Only the Lord, who has displaced the Canaanites and their gods by giving the land to Israel, will receive the psalmist's worship (vv. 5-6). Verses 7-11 express how committed the psalmist is to Israel's God, how willing to trust the Lord who has brought the people here.

Psalm 17

This psalm is a lament (A) of one unjustly accused who has taken refuge in the temple to await divine settlement of the case. Verses 1-2 are a prayer for vindication; verses 3-5 are an affirmation of innocence. Verses 6-9 are another prayer, more anxious than the first because of the pressure of the foe in verses 10-12. Verses 13-14 plead that the wicked be broken, and verse 15 is a serene statement of praise. The psalmist seeks a public judgment. He prays for the public punishment of his enemies so that everyone will know that he has been found innocent by the court of last resort, the Lord.

Psalm 18

Psalm 18, duplicated in 2 Sam 22, is a royal thanksgiving (B) for a military victory. The king, in the throes of his suffering, prays in the temple (vv. 5-7), trusting not in his privileges as king but in his loyalty to God (vv. 21-25) and in his membership in God's people (v. 28).

Thanksgivings are in essence reports of divine rescue. The rescue and establishment of the king are told twice, once in mythic language (vv. 5-20) like that used in the narratives of Pss 77:14-21 and 89:10-28, and then in historical language (vv. 36-46). The outline is as follows: (I) hymnic introduction, vv. 2-4; report, vv. 5-20; conclusions regarding why the Lord effected the rescue, vv. 21-25; (II) hymnic introduction (in the second person), vv. 26-35; report, vv. 36-46; proclamation of the Lord's glory to the nations, vv. 47-51.

The king represents Israel, especially to the nations (vv. 44-46, 48, 50); his victory shows to the nations the power of his patron God, Yahweh. The movement of the king from humiliation and suffering (vv. 5-7, 19) to exaltation over the nations (vv. 44-46) makes him a living witness to the Lord's fidelity to the promises made to David and to the Lord's power.

Psalm 19

This unusual poem is a prayer that the law of the Lord, which contains such power to enlighten and enrich the person (vv. 8-11), not be denied to "your servant," the psalmist (vv. 12-15). The serene functioning of the universe expresses the wide scope and precision of the Lord's victory over what once was unbounded sea and primordial darkness, a chaos that had made human society impossible. The picture is the same as that in Psalm 104 and Gen 1.

The "glory of God" that the heavens declare in verse 1 is the power and wisdom that the Lord displays on earth in arranging them. In comparable religious literatures the sun is a judge and lawgiver; hence verses 5b-7 form a transition to the description of the law. The law is the will of the powerful Lord visible to the servants of that Lord; hence the prayer for openness to it (vv. 12-14).

Psalm 20

The psalm is a prayer for the king, who is the representative of the people, before he and his army set out for battle. In the first section (vv. 2-6) the people ask for divine help, and in verses 7-10 they express confidence that such help will be given. A solemn promise of God's help must have been given between the two sections in the liturgy, something like the promise of Pss 12:6 and 21:9-13. The "name" as a surrogate for the Lord occurs frequently in this psalm (vv. 2b, 6b, 8b) and indeed elsewhere in the Psalter (for example, Pss 44:6; 54:8; 118:10-12; 124:8). The idea is that Yahweh dwells in heaven and the name makes Yahweh present on earth. The name is not a magic force but aids those who trust in it alone (vv. 8-9).

Psalm 21

The first part of this prayer for the king is a thanksgiving for benefits given (vv. 2-8), and the second is a promise that the king will triumph over enemies (vv. 9-14). Verse 14 is a brief prayer. The psalm may reflect a temple ceremony that celebrated the Lord's choice of the Davidic king. The king's trust in the Lord (v. 8) and his confident prayer (vv. 3, 5) enable him to receive divine gifts. Vitality and peace are not the only divine gifts visible in the king; through his military prowess the land is kept secure. Hence verses 9-14 portray the warrior-king as helped by the Lord. The heightened language is typical of the Oriental court. When kings ceased in Israel after the sixth century B.C.E., the language came to be used of a future son of David.

Psalm 22

The exceptionally powerful lament (A) freely recasts the lament structure. The complaint is duplicated. The first complaint, verses 2-12, contains two expressions of trust, verses 4-6 and 10-11, with the petition of verse 12 as the climax. The second complaint, verses 13-22, extended by vivid images, climaxes in the petition of verses 20-22. The psalm is unusual in the length of the statement of praise (vv. 23-32), which usually consists of only a verse or two at the end of the lament. The psalmist appears to have had an intense experience of God who saves, and boldly praises God "in the midst of the assembly" (v. 23) for coming to the poor person who hoped for salvation. The psalmist has come to know the Lord in a new way through the divine act and cannot restrain his appreciation and love.

Psalm 23

This, the most beloved psalm in the Psalter, is a song of trust. The Lord is portrayed as a shepherd, a common designation for the god or king in ancient Near Eastern poetry. The title connotes care for the people and, in the case of Israel, leadership in the Exodus-Conquest (compare Pss 78:52-55; 80; Isa 40:11 and Jer 31:10). The psalmist is so confident of the divine shepherd's leadership as to trust even when the path leads through dangerous mountain passes (v. 4a); the shepherd is there (v. 4b). The Exodus-Conquest ended with Israel safe in the Lord's land. That journey is concluded in the psalm with a banquet. The enemies that tried to hinder the journey toward the divine dwelling are shamed as they see God's favor bestowed on the psalmist in the temple.

Psalm 24

Like Psalm 15, this psalm appears to have accompanied the ceremony of admittance to the temple on a solemn occasion (compare v. 3 with Ps 15:1, and vv. 4-6 with Ps 15:2-5). One had to affirm commitment to the covenant in order to appear before the Lord. Verses 1-2 and 7-10 reflect the ceremony. In the first verses the Lord's sovereignty over the created world is celebrated. People of that time imagined that the earth was suspended over vast waters, supported by great pillars. Verses 7-10 describe the procession of the Lord approaching the temple in triumph. Two choirs, singing antiphonally, identify the approaching Lord (perhaps represented by the ark carried by priests). The psalm invites worshipers to commit themselves anew to their Creator-Lord as they join in the triumphant procession.

759

Psalm 25

The psalm is an acrostic poem, each verse beginning with a successive letter of the Hebrew alphabet. Acrostic psalms are often a series of unconnected statements; poetic unity is supplied by the extrinsic device of the successive letters. Despite the looseness, the psalm is a lament (A) containing complaints mixed with pleas to be delivered from enemies (vv. 1-2, 16-22). The psalmist is acutely conscious of having sinned; there is no claim of innocence as in some other psalms. The psalmist's fragility leads to reiterated prayer to be led along the path taken by the friends of God, where one is safe from one's enemies.

Psalm 26

Psalm 26 is often classified as a lament, but the enemies here do not attack, as in laments. Probably the song was sung by the priests who ritually washed before they offered sacrifice. Exod 30:20-21 states: ". . . when they approach the altar in their ministry, to offer an oblation to the Lord, they must wash their hands and feet, lest they die." The psalm was suitable for use by all who sought God's protection as they entered the temple. Verses 1-3, echoed in verses 11-12, remind God of past sincerity while asking for further purification. Verses 4-5, matched in verses 9-10, make a sharp distinction between the wicked and the just; the psalmist prays to be of the company of the righteous. Verses 6-8 are the central panel and the center of the poem. The psalmist expresses the inner meaning of the ritual: joy before the transcendent God who draws near.

Psalm 27

Tradition has handed down the two sections of the psalm, verses 1-6 and verses 7-14, as one psalm, though each part could be understood as complete in itself. The first section is a song of trust, and the second a lament (A). A common theme unites the poem: those who seek the Lord in the temple are protected (see vv. 4-6 and v. 9). Verses 1-3 remind one of another song of trust, Psalm 23, in which the psalmist's conviction of the Lord's protecting presence is intense. Verses 4-6 refer to the temple and the delight and safety to be found there in the midst of a broken and dangerous world. In the liturgy the living, victorious God appears. Verses 7-13

are an anxious prayer that the saving presence not be withheld from the psalmist, who is in danger from enemies. Verse 14 is the statement of praise that customarily ends such psalms.

Psalm 28

In this lament (A) the statement of praise (vv. 6-8), uttered after the priest's words of assurance (not transmitted in this or in most psalms), is exceptionally lengthy and vigorous. The psalmist turns toward the temple, the unshakable center of an otherwise dangerous universe (vv. 1-2). "Those going down into the pit" in verse 1b is a stereotyped expression for those overcome by death and descending to Sheol, the shadowy nether world. Verses 3-5 are a petition that God judge publicly. The psalmist knows that evildoers are heading toward annihilation as a result of their actions; by praying for their destruction he is lining himself up with the just and is thus able to claim God's promised protection of the just. The last verses express the psalmist's acceptance of the word of assurance as effective divine words. The psalmist does not neglect to pray for the people also (v. 9).

Psalm 29

The hymn (C—see p. 755) invites the members of the heavenly court to join in giving glory to Yahweh, the sole God (vv. 1-2). The "glory and strength [rather than praise]" that they give is their recognition that Yahweh alone is king (v. 10), who alone has shaped the world by means of victory. The weapons in that victory are those of the storm-god—thunder ("the voice of the Lord," in verses 3-9), lightning, and wind. With these the Lord has vanquished the forces hostile to civilization and has made them part of the world of men and women. Verse 11 prays that the Lord will impart the power that shaped the universe to the king of Israel and, through that king, to the people. Thus the hymn celebrates the power of the Lord and the sharing of that creative power with the people of God.

Psalm 30

In this thanksgiving (B—see p. 755) praise is given to God for rescue from near fatal illness. Verses 2-4 describe the divine mercy, the snatching of the sick person from the annihilating power of death. As often in thanksgivings, the one rescued is so relieved and delighted that he teaches and exhorts the assembly to trust the saving Lord (vv. 5-6). The assembly learns about the psalmist's inner journey, from his unthinking self-confidence (vv. 7-8a) to his panicky pleas and bargaining when illness struck (vv. 8b-11). Verses 12-13 express the delight of one who has experienced God's favor and forgiveness.

Psalm 31

The psalm is primarily a lament (A), with elements of a thanksgiving (the rescue seems to have already taken place according to verses 8-9 and 20-21) and a song of trust (vv. 4, 6, and 15-16). Moreover, the psalm seems to unfold in two narrative phrases, verses 2-9 and 10-25, probably an instance of the parallelism characteristic of Semitic poetry.

As usual in laments, the affliction is couched in general terms. The psalmist is in danger of being overwhelmed by evil people. In all these pains the psalmist turns to the "faithful God" (v. 6), whose being is described in verses 20-21.

Psalm 32

This thanksgiving (B) is the second of the seven Penitential Psalms of church tradition (see p. 756). The psalmist reports the Lord's rescue: sin once reigned over him, body and soul. Sin here, as often in the Bible, is not only the personal act of rebellion against God but also the consequences of that act—the waning of vitality and frustration.

Burdened with the consequences of personal folly, the psalmist declares everyone blessed who has been forgiven by God (vv. 1-2). Verses 3-4 describe his past refusal to open himself up to the Lord, and verses 5-7, the happy result of letting God be the forgiving God. In verses 8-11 the psalmist becomes a teacher, sharing with the assembly the fruits of personal experience: the wicked (v. 10), who do not open themselves to the forgiving Lord, are unhappy, but those who trust in the merciful God are filled with gladness.

Psalm 33

In this wonderfully complex hymn (C) the just are called to praise God, who made the world by a mere word (vv. 4 and 9). The world is portrayed as three-tiered: the heav-

enly tier and its inhabitants, the cosmic waters that surround the universe, the earthly tier and its inhabitants (vv. 6-9). The words and plans of human beings, in contrast to God's word, effect nothing (vv. 10-11).

Of all the wonders created by the word of the Lord, human beings are special because they are free to plan and to revere the Lord (vv. 8, 10-11). Verses 12-19 sketch how a people and its king are to conduct themselves on the earth God created. Their greatness consists in God's choice of them and God's clear vision into their hearts (vv. 12-15), in their leader's acknowledgment of the Lord (vv. 16-17). The psalmist directs the people to trust in the One who makes the people great (vv. 20-22).

Psalm 34

This thanksgiving (B) is in acrostic form, each line beginning with a successive letter of the Hebrew alphabet. In this psalm one letter is missing and two are in reverse order. The psalmist, fresh from the experience of being saved by the Lord from danger (vv. 5, 7), calls on all the "lowly" (vv. 3b-4) to praise the Lord, who saves the poor who trust. The "lowly" are the defenseless, who have only the Lord to turn to. If the defenseless person prays, the Lord will hear and that person will become powerful (vv. 7-11). In the second part of the poem, the psalmist, taught true wisdom by his suffering, now teaches the assembly (vv. 12-23). Anyone who is wise will, by right conduct, join the company of the righteous and thus enjoy God's favor.

Psalm 35

In this lament (A) a person unjustly accused by former friends takes refuge in the court of last resort, coming before the divine judge (v. 1) and all-seeing witness (v. 22). Verses 1-8 are a prayer for justice, asking that the evildoers be publicly exposed as such by their punishment. Verses 9-10 are a kind of anticipatory thanksgiving, praising God in advance of the rescue. Verses 11-16 extend the complaint of verse 7: friends have done it! Verses 17-21 press for speedy assistance, and verses 22-26, like verses 1-8, pray for the destruction of the psalmist's unjust persecutors. The modern reader, offended perhaps by the vindictive tone of the psalm, should remember that the psalmist asks for *public* redress of a *public* injustice and leaves in God's own hands the carrying out of the work of justice.

Psalm 36

This lament (A) is the prayer of one who feels threatened by "evildoers," people who attack the just (v. 13). The psalmist depicts the wicked in all their arrogance and moral obtuseness (vv. 2-5), and then comes before the just and merciful God, who punishes such evildoers and draws near in tenderness to the beleaguered just (vv. 6-10). Verses 8-10 show the closeness of the saving Lord in the temple service. "The shadow of your wings" refers to the cherubim in the holy of holies. "They have their fill of the prime gifts of your house" reads literally, "they are sated with the fat [of the temple sacrifices]."

Psalm 37

A wise teacher speaks to disciples troubled by the prosperity of the unjust and the hiddenness of God. The psalm is an acrostic; its statements are unified by the extrinsic device of beginning the verses with successive letters of the Hebrew alphabet. In the culture of the time, lore was handed down orally, its authority being based upon the stature and experience of the teacher. Priests, kings, royal officials, and parents were expected to hand on what they had received.

To people troubled by the fact that the unjust victimize the just without being punished, the wise teacher asserts that the disturbing situation is only temporary; the Lord will punish the wicked in the future. In the view of the psalm, people place themselves in the ranks of the unjust by their actions and attitudes. Each path of life, or "way," has its own inherent dynamism—eventual frustration for the wicked, eventual reward for the just. Good things, especially symbolized by the land, lie in the future for the just, a theme with echoes in the New Testament beatitudes. Let the just wait for the Lord!

Psalm 38

In this psalm of lament (A), one of the Penitential Psalms (see p. 756), the psalmist is afflicted with deadly sickness, commonly a sign of divine disfavor. People believed that actions brought consequences of themselves: health, reputation, and prosperity came from good actions; illness, loss of face and poverty

followed from evil actions. The psalmist is gravely ill (vv. 4, 6-9) and recognizes that his own actions are the cause (vv. 4-5, 19) of physical and mental suffering and ostracism. There is no one to turn to for help; only the Lord can destroy the cause-and-effect chain of past folly and present misery.

Psalm 39

A mortally ill person, keenly aware of the imminent end of life, prays this individual lament (A). In verses 2-4 the psalmist resolves to remain silent, lest he speak against the God from whom all things come. The psalmist's strategy of reverent silence and submission before the all-knowing and all-effecting God has not, however, brought the hoped for healing and peace. Verses 5-7, uttered with a keen sense of the fleetingness of life, ask how long the psalmist has to live. Verses 8-10 are in tension with verses 5-7; they are a hopeful prayer for rescue after the acceptance of death. Verse 9 should read "Deliver me from all those who rise up against me," on the basis of the parallel verse. "Those who rise up" are the ones who have concluded that the illness is a punishment from God for sinful behavior and are ostracizing the psalmist. People judge the sick person to be punished by God and are hurling insults.

Verse 10, recalling the resolve of silent submission of verses 2-4, is key. The psalmist, recognizing that God is the author of all, including the mortal illness, can only lay out the whole situation before God: "it was your doing." Verses 11-12 again reveal the tension between acceptance (v. 12) and change (v. 11), as do verses 13-14 by the reference to Israel as guests in the Lord's land who have no claim on the life to be found there yet have hope.

Psalm 40

Verses 2-13 are a thanksgiving (B). A distinct psalm, a lament, comprising verses 14-18 has been appended, probably because it reprises some of the vocabulary of verses 2-13. (Verses 14-18 appear also in Psalm 70 and will be treated there.)

The psalmist describes God's rescue in spatial terms, as the pulling out of someone trapped in a bog onto dry land. Even in adversity he hoped. Verse 4 states that rendering thanks is not simply a gift one makes to the Lord in return for rescue but is itself a gift of God. It makes visible to one's neighbors the divine act of mercy (v. 4b). The next verse associates the individual salvation with the great acts of salvation of Israel's past.

Verses 7-9 have suffered some displacement but the gist is clear: the rescued person was expected to offer sacrifice but declares that God desires obedience instead. The verse recalls the memorable words of Samuel to Saul in 1 Sam 15:22: "Obedience is better than sacrifice, and submission than the fat of rams." The mysterious "Behold I come" in verse 8 may reflect a scene like that of Ps 118:19, "Open to me the gates of justice; I will enter them and give thanks to the Lord." The psalmist, then, would enter the temple precincts to give thanks, not with the sacrifice of animals, but with a new song and a devotion to "your law." The final verses emphasize the unrestrained, open-hearted proclamation that characterizes one who has experienced the saving mercy of God.

Psalm 41

This psalm of thanksgiving (B) recounts God's rescue of a sick individual (vv. 4, 5, and 9). The psalmist begins by declaring blessed, that is, regarded favorably by God, those who behave well toward the poor (v. 2). Other psalms use the same formula for those who have been placed in a right relation to God (Pss 32:1-2; 34:9; 40:5; 65:5), but here the right relation is toward the special friends of the Lord.

The psalmist has apparently become part of that privileged group who have experienced the Lord's protection (vv. 3-4), sometimes called "the poor" in the Bible. The narrative of the rescue, essential to a thanksgiving, is done in this psalm by quoting the psalmist's lament before rescue (vv. 5-11). Verse 5 is the beginning of the prayer, "Once I said . . . ." The misery of the past contrasts with present safety. The quoted prayer shows that the chief pain was not physical but emotional— betrayal by enemies, among whom were friends. They wanted all memory of the sufferer erased (a horrible fate for the Hebrew) because they judged the affliction to be the fruit of sin. By their talk they encouraged the separation of the sufferer from the community of God.

Verse 11, the petition for health to requite the enemies, is disturbing to modern readers;

the point is that the healing itself is an act of judgment through which God decides for the defendant and against the false friends. The judicial tone carries over to verses 12-13: recovery from illness is a mark of favor showing God's love for this individual. The integrity of which the psalmist boasts is his innocence in the present situation, not for the totality of his life. The blessing in verse 14 is not part of the psalm; it marks the end of Book I, the so-called collection of David's psalms.

BOOK II: PSALMS 42–72

Psalms 42–43

The refrain "Why are you so downcast, O my soul," repeated in 42:6, 12, and 43:5, shows that Psalms 42–43 are a single poem; the traditional separation into two psalms is wrong. It is a lament (A) of an individual who lives beyond Israel's borders in the north and who longs to join the community of God worshiping in the temple in Jerusalem. In the Hebrew scriptures Yahweh is the God of all the world but is revealed only in Jerusalem. What distresses the psalmist is the absence of God, the feeling of deep hunger without the ability to satisfy it because of distance from Jerusalem and the hindrance of enemies. Their taunt, "Where is your God?" (vv. 4, 11), intensifies the pain.

Verses 7-8 show that the psalmist is in the north; Mount Mizar is generally thought to be a mountain in the region of Mount Hermon. In verse 9 the psalmist is caught like Jonah (Jonah 2:3-4) in the deep, a metaphor for the place where Yahweh will not be found. In the last of the three stanzas, Ps 43:1-5, the psalmist prays that Yahweh decide against the enemies who say that Yahweh cannot bring the psalmist to Jerusalem.

Psalm 44

Community laments (A) are often built on the contrast between God's gracious creation of Israel through the Exodus-Conquest and the present distress that seems to negate that creation. The Lord expelled the nations in order to give Israel its land (vv. 2-9), but now the nations expel Israel from that land (vv. 10-17), undoing God's work. Verses 2-9 emphasize the divine initiative in the grant of the land. Israel does nothing—everything is done because of God's own gracious will. But the Lord is now silent as the people are despoiled, even though they are not conscious of any sin against the covenant (vv. 18-23). Here the community struggles with being the Lord's special people and witness while the Lord remains silent before their real pain. Keenly aware of the divine favor that gave them the land in the past, they wait for God's return. The last three verses are a spirited prayer for help, showing that the people do not lose hope.

Psalm 45

This poem is perhaps the most specific in the Psalter; it was sung at the king's marriage to a princess of Phoenicia. Retained in the collection when there was no reigning king, it came to be applied to the anointed king who was to come, the Messiah.

The court poet, conscious of the power of his song (vv. 2, 18), sings first of the Lord's choice of the king over others (vv. 3, 8bc) and of his privilege of establishing the Lord's purpose (vv. 4-8). In verse 9 the poet depicts the ceremony in which the bride, in a majestic procession, is led to the king. The princess is to forget the royal house she came from ("your father's house" of verse 11) and be wife to the king, the viceroy of the Lord of all the earth. Verse 17 is addressed to the king; with his new wife the ancient Davidic (and Abrahamic) promise of progeny and power will come true.

Psalm 46

In this song of Zion, Yahweh is hymned for making the holy city a sure refuge to worshipers, who are terrified by the prospect of a collapsing world. There are three stanzas (vv. 2-4, vv. 5-8, vv. 9-12); the last two are ended by the refrain of verses 8 and 12.

God created the world by subduing the disorderly primal forces that made human life impossible, and established Zion as the glorious divine dwelling. Because God is present at the ordered world's center, the psalmist is confident that there will be no unleashing of those once unruly forces (vv. 2-4), especially in the Lord's own space. The city and temple of the Lord are the place where the memory of God's creation victory is most vivid. That creation can be celebrated in the Lord's shrine,

even though the nations, unruly like the primal forces, rage outside (vv. 5-8). The very buildings of the city make visible to the chosen community how powerful the Lord is over all that is chaotic and anti-human. Verse 11 majestically commands all hateful and hurtful powers to submit to the Lord.

Psalm 47

This enthronement psalm celebrates the kingship of Yahweh over all the beings of heaven and earth. The Lord, invisibly enthroned upon the ark is carried in procession into the temple.

The psalm is divided into two parts of equal length, verses 2-6 and 7-10, each beginning with a call to praise. The thought expressed in each stanza is the same: Yahweh is the king, victorious over the powers of heaven and earth (the powers of earth are emphasized in this psalm), and selects Israel as a special people (vv. 5 and 10). The choice of Israel is part of the establishment of the world. Verse 6 probably refers to the trumpet blasts and shouts that accompanied the entry of the ark into the temple, the entry signifying Yahweh's taking possession of the temple as king.

Psalm 48

This psalm praises Zion, the city where Yahweh's world-establishing victory is remembered. The splendid buildings, especially the temple, bespeak Yahweh's power to protect the people from all attack. So suffused with Yahweh's presence is the site of the holy mountain that the psalmist declares the mountain to be higher and more beautiful than any other and to be impregnable to all enemies.

Verses 2-3 praise the mountain where God graciously encounters human beings. The next section, verses 4-9, describes the great deed that proved the Lord's presence on the mountain: the easy defeat of the enemy kings by means of God's storm wind. Verses 10-12 describe the festivities of triumph, resounding far and wide in celebration of the victory that establishes the world. "We ponder" (v. 10) means "we recite" (the stories of Yahweh's victories). The final part, verses 13-15, sees in the solid structures of the temple and city such clear evidence of divine might and loving protection that one need only walk through them to feel secure and loved.

Psalm 49

Though often called a "wisdom psalm" because it contains reflections about the human condition, Psalm 49 is really a confession of trust in God like Ps 27:1-6, except that here there is a more confident tone (note the assurance of vv. 2-5). Also, the enemy is seen in greater profundity—it is death itself.

The opening verses, like Ps 78:1-4, boldly make a new statement about human life before God. In verses 6-10 the psalmist refuses to fear the wealthy who are wicked; their wealth cannot protect them from the ultimate enemy, death. Experience shows that death takes all, the wise (=the righteous) and the wicked. The wealth that once emboldened the wicked to do violence will be scattered. A refrain stating that death levels all closes the first part in verse 13, as it will the second part in verse 21. Verses 14-15 emphasize the theme of the first part: those who live by wealth and violence somehow have death as their shepherd. In contrast, the innocent afflicted person who refuses to fear (v. 6) has as shepherd Yahweh, who will in a mysterious way protect that trusting person from death. The perhaps deliberately enigmatic "by receiving me" recalls God's taking of Enoch in Gen 5:24 (compare 2 Kgs 2:11-12). The Hebrew of verse 16 sounds like and plays on verse 9: a human cannot ransom or save another human but God can save "me," the trusting or persecuted person. In verses 17-21 the psalmist exhorts from the conviction that human beings are not to be feared—they will all die. Only God is the ultimate ransomer.

Psalm 50

Psalm 50 is the record of a ceremony in which the Lord judges the people gathered on Mount Zion. Have they been faithful to the covenant, positively by worshiping and calling upon the Lord alone (as opposed to false gods, vv. 14-15), negatively by avoiding violations of the Ten Commandments (vv. 16-20)? Only a selection of the basic commandments are listed in the psalm. The liturgy reenacts the great encounter of the Lord and Israel at Sinai (Exod 19-24). In liturgical time Mount Zion stands for Mount Sinai as each generation of Israel faces the Lord.

Verses 1-6 describe the manifestation of the Lord on Mount Zion, mediated, in all probability, through trumpet blasts and smoke and fire. In verse 6 the heavens are summoned as witnesses to the people's conduct; heaven and earth (and other cosmic pairs) were often invoked in antiquity as witnesses at the sealing of covenants. Verses 7-15 are divine speech, mediated by the voice of the priest; the Lord does not need the food of animal sacrifice as do the gods of the ancient world (vv. 8-17) but desires the freely given response of the people (vv. 14-15). In verses 16-21 that same divine voice judges the wicked, that is, those who violate the fundamental covenant relationship. Such people are to repent, change. Verses 22-23, despite their vigor, are a positive conclusion to the liturgical encounter: the Lord seeks the free response of the people.

Psalm 51

One of the great laments (A) in the Psalter, this Penitential Psalm (see p. 756) is primarily a plea for the removal of the personal and social distress that sins have caused. The poem is divided into two parts of approximately equal length: verses 3-10 and 11-19, with a coda in vv. 20-21. The two parts are carefully interlocked by repetition of significant words: "blot (wipe) out" in the first verse of each section (vv. 3 and 11); "wash me" in the verse just after the first verse of the first section (v. 4) and just before the last verse (v. 9) of the first section; the repetition of "heart," "God," and "spirit" in verses 12 and 19.

In the first section the psalmist, relying entirely on God's gracious fidelity, prays to be delivered from sin. Verse 10 suggests that the psalmist is sick, and attributes the sickness to sin. Sin is depicted with intense realism, not just a past act against God but its emotional, physical, and social consequences. The psalmist experiences the destructive results of sin (v. 5) and knows that this suffering is self-inflicted and deserved. Before the all-holy God a human being can plead no self-righteousness (v. 7) but can only ask for God's purifying favor (vv. 8-10).

Verse 11 begins the second part by repeating the prayer for forgiveness. Something more profound than the wiping clean of sin is the theme of verses 12-19, namely, a state of nearness to God, a living by the spirit or power of God (vv. 12-13). Such nearness brings joy (v. 14) and enables the forgiven sinner to speak from personal experience to all who are estranged from God (vv. 15-16). That proclamation is the response that God desires, even more than sacrifice in the temple (vv. 17-19). The last two verses make precise the situation: the experience of sin is the exilic absence of God from the temple and its ceremonies.

Psalm 52

Though often classed as a lament, this psalm is unique. The psalmist pronounces judgment upon the wealthy and self-sufficient violent person whose prosperity is a temptation to "the godly," that is, those loyal to God in all things. One can compare Isa 22:15-18, in which the prophet denounces Shebna, a royal official, for his arrogance.

Verses 3-6 resemble a prophetic accusation against the arrogant. The speaker is one of the righteous: in the psalms they often are the victims of "champions of infamy." Lies, violence, and exploitation are their way of life; their prosperity tempts those who believe that God rewards only the righteous. The cry for judgment in verse 7 comes from the troubled heart of a righteous person who believes that the Lord will not allow the godless to triumph. The removal of the godless from the land of the living assures the righteous that the just God is active in their regard; the divine act makes them rejoice (vv. 8-9). Rejoicing over a fallen enemy is distasteful to modern readers, as are the neat categories "the righteous" and "the worker of treachery." The psalmist, however, is not speaking of permanent categories of being but only of the present unfair situation. The psalmist presumably would not deny that a righteous person could join the ranks of the wicked tomorrow, or vice versa.

The last verses are full of confidence. Nearness to God is the ultimate answer to the experience of injustice. Olive trees grow in the sacred precincts of the Dome of the Rock in Jerusalem even today, their fertility testifying to God's presence in the shrine. The last verses thank God for upholding justice; the godly can rejoice in divine protection.

Psalm 53

Psalm 53 is a duplicate of Psalm 14 (see p. 758 for commentary). As in Psalm 14, the psalmist sees two kinds of people: the fool (v. 2) and the just (called "my people" in verse 5).

Psalm 54

The psalm is almost a textbook lament (A). The troubled person, attacked by the wicked, calls upon Yahweh directly for help (vv. 3-5). The psalmist refuses to despair and hopes in God, who is active in human history and is just (vv. 6-7). Verses 8-9 render thanks with a certitude that suggests that a priest has in the meantime spoken a reassuring oracle (not transmitted) and the psalmist has accepted it as the word of the God who has promised protection to the poor.

Psalm 55

The psalmist, betrayed by those who were once intimate friends (vv. 14-15 and 21-22), prays that God punish those oath breakers and thus be recognized as the protector of the wronged. The customary structure of the lament (A) is verified here: the unadorned address to God (v. 2); the prayer for deliverance and punishment of the enemy (vv. 3, 10, 16); the vivid dramatization of the oppressive situation so as to appeal to God's sense of honor (vv. 4-9, 11-15, 21-22). The malice of the personal enemy is seen by the psalmist as an instance of the mysterious residual evil in the world, an evil that is palpable in the streets of the city (vv. 11-12). It frightens and discourages those who trust in the Lord. As in other laments, the psalmist trusts so strongly in the salvation of God that he can exhort others (v. 23) and live calmly in the expectation of salvation (v. 24).

Psalm 56

The lament (A) of a person whose enemies threaten death (v. 14) but cannot ultimately keep him from uttering a prayer of trust is enclosed by a refrain (vv. 4-5 and 11-12). The psalmist is glad to be one of the poor, the 'anawim, who by their vulnerability to the attacks of the powerful and wicked invite the special protection of the just and merciful Lord (vv. 2-3). So sure is the hope of the poor that they need not fear even at the height of danger (vv. 4-5 and 11-12). At the moment of danger, which the psalmist does not minimize (vv. 2-8), they can be certain that God tenderly regards their tears (v. 9). No enemy can stand in the way of their joyous duty to give thanks publicly, by vows and offerings, for the life that God has given back to them.

Psalm 57

A lament (A) in which the victim of hostile actions by enemies (vv. 4, 5, 7) prays that God be a refuge and a protection. The drama of the lament, featuring the victim, the wicked, and God, is here especially vivid. The enemies are lions with teeth like swords to devour the just (v. 5); they dig a trap (v. 7). The psalmist expresses with deep feeling his fragility and his confidence in God's protecting presence. "The shadow of your wings" (v. 2) probably refers to the wings of the cherubim (powerful winged animals) whose wings spread over the ark, the throne of the invisible Lord, in the inner chamber of the temple (see 1 Kgs 6:23-28). The refrain "Be exalted . . . O God," is repeated boldly in verses 6 and 12. The psalmist's confession, "My heart is steadfast, O God" (vv. 8-11), is exceptionally vibrant and joyous. The whole psalm is the record of a sensitive yet exuberantly trustful person.

Psalm 58

In this lament (A) the psalmist expresses great trust in the Lord's power to dethrone all that stands in the way of the divine governance of the world. The first verses condemn "the gods," the demonic forces that were popularly imagined to control human destinies (vv. 2-3), and "the wicked," the human instruments of these forces (vv. 4-6). Verses 7-12 pray that God take away their ability to harm the just (vv. 7-10). Such divine vengeance will make the righteous glad; they will see that their Lord is not indifferent to their suffering and has in fact upheld them.

Psalm 59

A lament (A) in which a person endangered by the lying tongues of those who seek to separate him from his God (vv. 7-8, 13, 15) prays that God will uphold him and punish them, and hence be seen as the just God of Israel. Verses 2-8 alternate prayer (vv. 2-3, 5b-6) and depictions of the wicked rampaging against the innocent psalmist (vv. 4-5a, 7-8). The psalmist vividly expresses confidence in the God who is just and loving (vv. 9-11). The near curse upon the enemies in verses 12-13 is not a crude desire for blood vengeance but a wish that the supremacy of Yahweh, about to break into human history, be recognized as such by all people (v. 14b).

The God who rules the world (vv. 9, 14b) is also the God who rules the psalmist's life (vv. 17-18).

Psalm 60

In this community lament (A) the people dramatize their situation as defeated and deprived of their God-given land. Informing their complaint before God is their conviction that they are "[God's] people," "those who fear [God]," "[God's] loved ones" (plural; vv. 5-7). They claim the protection of their God Yahweh, who is the Lord of all the nations of the earth. Yahweh has permitted their present plight and hence can reverse it.

The prayer of verse 7 is for an oracle of salvation; "answer us" is a special term for the seeking of the divine word of assurance in crises of war (see, for example, 1 Sam 14:37; 28:6, 15). The oracle of verses 8-10 is the divine response to the prayer, spoken by a priest in the temple. The Divine Warrior, through the priest, declares ownership of the land; the invasion of other nations is not permanent and will ultimately be reversed.

The territories mentioned in verses 8-9 were all part of the God-given territory. Whenever any were taken by an enemy, the people could hold God to that ancient oracle of grant. Verse 11 is the community's faith-response: "The land is ours; let's take it!" Verses 12-14 continue the opening lament, but now, in the light of the favorable divine promise, the words are uttered with a new confidence in the Lord and with a sober awareness of the limits of unaided human power.

Psalm 61

This psalmist, using elements of the lament (A) and thanksgiving form (B), prays in a place far distant from God's saving presence ("from the earth's end," v. 3) to be led to the security of God's presence. The language for security with God is traditional: rock, refuge, tower (vv. 3-5); to dwell forever in the Lord's tent (see Pss 15:1; 27:4); beneath the outstretched wings of the cherubim.

In the second half of the poem the psalmist confesses that God has come to the rescue and given "the heritage [the land] of those who fear [God's] name" to the one who trusted (v. 6). The holy land has a king; prayer is offered that the king reflect ade-

PSALM 61

quately the divine vitality (vv. 7-8). The one rescued is happy to sing praises to the name.

Psalm 62

This song of trust takes from the lament a sense of the fragility and danger of life, and from the thanksgiving a serenity arising from the experience of God's power. The serenity appears in the two refrains, verses 2-3 and 6-7, with verse 8 expanding the theme; the anguish is in the angry taunt against the rampaging wicked in verses 4-5. In verses 9-10 the psalmist steps forward as teacher to the community, so vivid has been his experience of God's power. That experience can be Israel's. Verse 12 reveals the astonishing source of the psalmist's contagious trust and inner poise: not the removal of danger but the word of God received as such, which relativizes all other powers.

Psalm 63

Like Psalm 61, this psalm also has elements of a lament (vv. 3-4 and 10-11), of a thanksgiving (vv. 4-6), and of a song of trust (vv. 7-9). The psalmist's situation explains the unusual juxtaposition of diverse genres: the psalmist, beset by liars and enemies (vv. 10, 12b), seeks God (v. 2) in the temple as an asylum in danger (vv. 3 and 8). He may even be spending the night in the sanctuary (vv. 7-8), intending to provoke a dream of reassurance. The one endangered then goes to the place of God's holy presence, the temple, in whose protective power he may be safe and where he can pray that justice be meted out to the wicked.

Psalm 64

This lament (A) is uttered by a person who feels overwhelmed by the malice of the wicked, the enemies of the righteous in the psalms (vv. 2-7). They seek to cut off the individual from the holy people. Hence the prayer to destroy the evildoers' plan is vehement—that God turn against them the very arrows they had aimed against God's friends. The world will then see who is the true ruler of the world (vv. 8-10). Verse 11 is a vow of praise expressing the lively hope that God will bring about a just world.

Psalm 65

There are hymnic elements in this commu-

nity thanksgiving (B), recited, most probably, at the festival when Israel enjoyed the fruits of the land. The festival could have been Pentecost, when wheat was harvested, or the feast of Ingathering of fruits, grapes, and olives in early autumn, when the rains resumed after the summer dry spell (vv. 10-14).

The Lord is given praise for three mercies: for making Zion a place of encounter and reconciliation for the holy people (vv. 2-5); for overcoming the primordial unbounded waters that once covered the earth and prevented human life from appearing (vv. 6-9); and for making those same waters fertilize the earth to bear fruit (vv. 10-14).

Psalm 66

In genre, this liturgical poem resembles a hymn (C) in verses 1-12 and an individual thanksgiving (B) in verses 13-20; it is now a unified liturgy. Verses 1-2 contain an invitatory exhorting the world to acknowledge Israel's God as uniquely powerful. The greatest proof of this power is the way Yahweh broke the sea's power to keep Israel from its land; let the nations revere this just God (vv. 5-7). Israel's history, the story of its humiliation and exaltation (probably the Babylonian Exile and the restoration), witnesses to God's justice and fidelity—justice, because God punished Israel's sins; fidelity, because God did not abandon the people forever (vv. 8-12).

Any member of this sinful yet rescued people may acknowledge the merciful God through appropriate sacrifice (vv. 13-16). As often in thanksgiving, the one who has experienced God's mercy steps forward as teacher; God is ready to be merciful to all who repent (vv. 16-20).

Psalm 67

The psalm reflects a temple liturgy in which the congregation echoes a part of the famous benediction of Aaron (Num 6:24-26). The people affirm the priestly blessing (v. 2), conscious that their God-given prosperity witnesses to the mercy and power of their God (v. 3). The first of two refrains, inviting the nations to acknowledge Yahweh (v. 4), serves as preface to the statement that Yahweh guides the nations; the second refrain (v. 6) serves as preface to the statement that Yahweh makes the earth bountiful.

Psalm 68

About no other psalm are there so many and such radically different interpretations. The text is disturbed. Some scholars believe that the psalm is simply a collection of short fragments. This commentary sees the psalm as reflecting a liturgical ceremony, a procession to the temple; it is like Pss 24; 106:19-29; and 2 Sam 6.

In verses 2-7 the procession begins, the people following the ark of the covenant, the throne upon which Yahweh is invisibly enthroned. The movement of so powerful a Deity frightens any possible foes but gladdens friends. In verses 8-21 the procession of the ark symbolizes the great battle between Yahweh and Yahweh's enemies, Sea or Death. The evil powers were defeated, and a shrine to the victory was prepared (vv. 16-19). The psalmist acknowledges that the victory of Yahweh over the forces of chaos creates a just world in which the righteous will be safe from the attacks of the wicked (vv. 20-24). The procession includes all the tribes of Israel, rejoicing in their unity (vv. 25-28). The psalm ends with a warning to the nations: recognize the one God and honor God's people.

Psalm 69

The psalm is a lament (A), unusual by its length and by the sufferer's keen sense of suffering for the Lord (vv. 8, 11-12). The depiction of suffering is both metaphorical (vv. 2-3; 15-16: the waters characterize chaos before God creates) and realistic (vv. 4, 5, 9, 11-13: exhaustion, alienation from family and community, misunderstanding of religious acts). Especially in the second part of the psalm is there fervent prayer that the enemies be punished (vv. 23-29). God's punishment of the psalmist's enemies is public vindication of the psalmist. As in other laments, the psalmist expresses hope in God and makes a vow of praise at the end (vv. 31-37); the vow recognizes that God is more pleased with praise than with sacrifice. The sufferer fasts and laments, conscious of the need for purification before the all-holy God, who is no longer encountered in the destroyed temple. These gestures are misinterpreted by his enemies, who judge him to be guilty and rightly afflicted by God. The psalmist's situation of suffering for the Lord and his hope of vindi-

cation by an attentive and faithful God applies to all servants of the Lord (vv. 18, 36-37).

Psalm 70

In this lament (A) one of the "afflicted and poor" (v. 6), a group which recognizes that they have no other resource than Yahweh, cries out to be saved from the enemy, "who seek my life" (v. 3). May the group of righteous, to which the psalmist belongs, be upheld with the divine presence that brings joy to the heart (vv. 5-6)!

Psalm 71

This lament (A) is uttered by an old person (v. 9) who seeks asylum in the temple. Persecuted by enemies, who interpret the afflictions of old age as divine judgment (v. 11), the psalmist turns to the God of righteousness whose praise he has sung from his youth. Verses 1-4 are an impassioned cry to God, the immovable rock of refuge. Verses 5-9 express a hope learned from a lifetime of praising God. Verses 10-13 dramatize the menace of the enemies and pray for their downfall. Verses 14-21 develop a prayer for deliverance. The psalmist has sung of God's wonders all these years. Will God allow that voice of praise to grow silent under the attack of enemies? Verses 22-24 are a vow of praise; the psalmist, in the light of the reassuring oracle given by the priest in the temple, will continue the song of praise begun in his youth.

Psalm 72

This royal psalm presents the king as the vicar of Yahweh. He represents to Israel and to the world the justice and peace with which the world was created. The king, however, is a human being who gives only what he has been given; intercession must be made for him. Intercession is the purpose of the psalm.

In verses 1-4, echoed in verses 12-14, the king is the "lengthened arm of Yahweh," exercising divine judgment. Justice here—and generally in the Bible—is not impartial deciding but vigorous upholding of the oppressed party. Verses 12-14 state that the king redeems the life of the poor; he is the agent of Yahweh's rescue of the people. The king embodies not only divine justice but also divinely intended peace and fertility; in verses 5-7 and 16 he embodies health and fertility for the whole land. Yahweh, the sole Deity in heaven and on earth, has a sole vicar, the Israelite king. To that king, therefore, all the nations of the earth come, bringing gifts that acknowledge the just and life-giving divine presence manifest in him (vv. 17-19).

BOOK III: PSALMS 73–89

Psalm 73

This unique probing of the just power of God fits no single genre but comes closest to the thanksgiving psalm (B—see p. 755). The psalmist tells of his rescue from near despair by an experience of God in the temple (vv. 16-20, 21-26).

The opening verse, "How good God is to the upright," is the conclusion. The painful experience behind that faith-inspired affirmation is the matter of the rest of the poem. What scandalized the psalmist was the prosperity of the wicked (vv. 2-14). Israel imagined life as two paths—the path of the wicked that leads to destruction and the path of the righteous that leads to prosperity (see Psalm 1). The prosperity of the wicked makes a mockery of God's governance of the world. To seek a solution to this temptation, the psalmist goes to the temple and there realizes that the end of the wicked shows that God does indeed rule the world with justice (vv. 15-20). Their sudden destruction shows their impermanence.

In the temple the psalmist receives a special sense of God's care: "Yet with you I shall always be" (v. 23). Verse 24, "and in the end you will receive me in glory," has traditionally been understood as a mysterious rescue by God, like the taking up of Enoch in Gen 5:24. The experience of being near God allows the sufferer to affirm God's justice (vv. 1, 27-28).

Psalm 74

This communal lament (A—see p. 754) could appropriately be sung whenever an enemy overran the temple of Yahweh. The destruction of Jerusalem and the temple by the Babylonians in 587 B.C.E. was surely such an occasion. Verses 1-11 directly summon Yahweh to look upon the ruined sanctuary and to remember the very congregation that Yahweh has created (better than "built up") and redeemed (v. 2). Zion and Israel, Yahweh's shrine and people, are inextricably bound to-

gether; an attack on the temple is an attack on the project Yahweh has initiated. "How long?" (v. 10) is a real question; ancients often looked for oracles that would tell them how long a disaster would last.

To persuade Yahweh to act, the community remembers liturgically the deed that established their world. As often in the Bible, creation is portrayed as conflict; first unbounded water is tamed and then unbounded darkness (vv. 13-17). Will the one who led Israel to dwell in Zion (vv. 1-2) allow the enemy to scoff (vv. 18-23)? "Your dove," "the humble," "the afflicted and the poor" (vv. 19-21)—these are the terms the faithful use of themselves; they prefer to wait for their God Yahweh to defend them rather than take matters into their own hands as if there were no promise.

Psalm 75

The psalm is a national thanksgiving (B). There had been threats against the people from their enemies, the people cried out, and God judged for them, that is, upheld them and put down their enemies. Verses 3-4 state that in crises threatening the very existence of the world, God alone determines the time of an intervention. That intervention is an act of judgment, which is not an impartial judicial decree but an act in favor of the wronged party (vv. 5-6). That judgment comes from no other source than Israel's God (vv. 7-9). The cup of the Lord that the enemies must drink is a common biblical metaphor for the unopposed power of the Lord over all nations. The community rejoices in the peace brought by the just God (vv. 10-11).

Psalm 76

Psalm 76 is a song of Zion that glorifies the holy mountain as the place where Yahweh is revealed as the creator by vanquishing forces hostile to human community. Verses 2-4 state that Zion is the place where God is acknowledged as sole God because it is the site of the world-establishing victory. Yahweh is the God of all but is uniquely revealed in Jerusalem/Zion. Verses 5-7 and 8-11 describe the victory of the Lord; at the divine rebuke all enemies lay stunned. The afflicted of the earth in verse 10 are all those who wait for Yahweh to save them from the arrogant ones of the world. The final two verses urge those who recognize that the Lord is present in Zion to hasten there with tokens of homage.

Psalm 77

In this community lament (A), someone speaking for the community ("I") describes the intense anguish of Israel when its Lord does nothing for the people. "Will his kindness utterly cease?" (v. 9) is the root question. Has Yahweh forgotten the loving commitment meant to ensure the people's peaceful existence? The assurance had been given time and again in the past to the patriarchs and to the people at Sinai. Verses 12-21, the second half of the poem, recite the divine deed that brought Israel into existence; it is retold in liturgical context ("remember," "meditate," and "ponder" in verses 12-13 really mean "recite") so as to awaken the community's faith that Yahweh will not let that initiating act become null and void. The "works" of the Lord (v. 13) are the victory over the sea that enabled Israel to cross over to Canaan and live as a community under Moses and Aaron, as God intended. The psalm prays that God will be faithful to this original intent.

Psalm 78

This long retelling of Israel's traditions of the Exodus-Conquest makes important changes in the ancient story, changes that would be immediately perceived by the sensitive Israelite. The speaker promises, in the tripartite introduction (vv. 1-4, 5-7, 8-11, each section ending with "the wonderful deeds of Yahweh" or a similar phrase), to draw a new meaning from the ancient story. That story contains a lesson: the present generation ought not defy the new act of God as did their ancestors.

The rest of the psalm consists of two parallel recitals of approximately the same length; they illuminate each other.

First Recital

Wilderness events, vv. 12-32
  Gracious act, vv. 12-16
  Rebellion, vv. 17-20
  Divine anger and punishment
    (manna and quail), vv. 21-31
  Sequel, vv. 32-39

Second Recital

From Egypt to Canaan, vv. 40-64
  Gracious act, vv. 40-55
  Rebellion, vv. 56-58
  Divine anger and punishment
    (destruction of Shiloh),
    vv. 59-64
  Sequel, vv. 65-72

The first recital arranges the old narrative so that the crossing of the Red Sea and the water in the wilderness constitute one great miracle of water, making all the more inexcusable the consequent rebellion—"Can he also give bread, or provide meat for his people?" (v. 20). In punishment, God does not hesitate to make use of the gracious gift of manna and quail to smite them. In the sequel the people fail to recognize the true significance of what has happened.

The second recital concerns Israel's movement from Egypt (whom Yahweh defeats in seven attacks) to the holy mountain shrine of Shiloh. The people's infidelity again provokes divine wrath and punishment, the destruction of Shiloh (the gracious gift). The sequel is the choice of a successor to the rejected Shiloh—Zion and David. Will Israel now fail to see the significance of the divine pattern of gift, sin, punishment, new gift? Will the people recognize that the southern kingdom of Judah is the heir to the destroyed northern kingdom? God has not left the people without a shrine and shepherd. But they must come to both in faith.

Psalm 79

This communal lament (A) complains to God that the nations have defiled the temple and murdered the holy people, leaving their corpses unburied (vv. 1-4). The situation is apparently that which existed after the destruction of the temple by the Babylonians in 587 B.C.E. The people ask "how long" the withdrawal of divine favor will last (v. 5). They acknowledge that their sins have brought the suffering upon them (vv. 8-9). In their plea for divine intervention, the people complain that nations that do not acknowledge Yahweh as God are running rampant (v. 6); that Yahweh's honor is compromised (vv. 1, 10, 12); that Israel, Yahweh's servants, suffer (vv. 2-4, 11). The last verse is a vow of praise, a statement of faith in the Lord who saves.

Psalm 80

In this communal lament (A) the people, defeated in war, appeal to the Lord of all heavenly powers ("O Lord of hosts," v. 5). By reciting the story of their founding, they appeal to God's honor: Will God allow the nations to ravage the chosen vine that was taken from Egypt and planted in Canaan? The magnificence of the vine once proclaimed God's greatness; its despoliation now insults God's honor. The people's hope is in God, not themselves; they promise repentance so that God will never again turn away (v. 19).

After the opening two verses call upon the shepherd of Israel to intervene, the usual lament elements of plea, recital of history, and complaint are punctuated by the refrains of verses 4, 7, and 20. The Davidic king in verse 18 represents the people; his restoration means favor again for everyone.

Psalm 81

The psalm seems to be a record of a liturgy celebrated at one of the three great festivals—Passover, Pentecost, or Harvest. The community is summoned before God in verses 2-4, the gathering being commanded by the law (vv. 5-6). A speaker then recites to the community the great act of liberation that made Israel into a people: the Exodus from Egypt (vv. 6b-8). In Egypt the people had been unwilling servants of Pharaoh, but at Sinai they became willing servants of Yahweh, freely agreeing to obey the commandments, the first of which is repeated in verses 10-11. The speaker rebukes the people for violating the commandment that makes them God's people (vv. 12-13). But there is still time to obey, to "hear" the great commandment; to obey will bring divine protection and nurture (vv. 14-17). The psalms bring the people before their God, who seeks from them a free and loving response.

Psalm 82

The psalmist paints a vivid picture of the heavenly assembly, where Yahweh declares that no other divine being controls human history. In the ancient Near East, people commonly assumed there were many gods who controlled human destinies. Yahweh accuses these "gods" of injustice, of not upholding the cause of the defenseless (vv. 2-4), and proclaims judgment in earthshaking thunder

(v. 5). Verses 6-7 strip power from such beings. Because Yahweh is now the sole judge (=ruler), the faithful are to direct their pleas for justice to this God alone (v. 8).

Psalm 83

The community laments (A) the attacks of the nations against Zion. Yahweh's shrine on earth is inviolable (Psalms 2, 46, 48, 76). When enemies overrun it, Yahweh's claim to be the sole Deity comes into question.

After the unadorned cry to God in verse 2, the complaint in verses 3-9 portrays all the enemies who have plagued Israel through the ages as conspiring to wipe out Israel's name. The name (vv. 5, 17, 19) is the means by which one is known. Verses 10-13 pray that Yahweh destroy the current crop of enemies as the enemies of old were destroyed. The children of Lot are Moab and Edom (Gen 19:36-38 and Deut 2:9). The victory of Gideon at Midian is told in Judg 6–8; the defeat of Sisera and Jabin, in Judg 4–5; of Oreb and Zeeb, in Judg 7:25; of Zebah and Zalmunna, in Judg 8:21. Verses 14-19 extend the prayer: Yahweh is to storm against the foes so that they will learn that the sanctuary is indeed a secure place for the people.

Psalm 84

How joyfully the Israelite fulfills the obligation of the law to go up to Jerusalem three times a year (Deut 16:1-17) is vividly portrayed in this psalm. All living things are safe from threat in the presence of the Lord (vv. 3-4). The pilgrim forgets the difficulties of the journey (vv. 5-8). The king is the representative of Yahweh, and prayer is offered by him at the feasts (vv. 9-10). The Lord's presence is not just a matter of space; only those who walk uprightly and who trust enjoy the blessings of divine nearness (vv. 11-13).

Psalm 85

In this national lament (A) Israel recalls how their God in the past has forgiven their sins and restored their land and fortunes (vv. 2-4). To Yahweh, their forgiving and restoring God, they pray in their distress: Once more show yourself a healing God (vv. 5-8). The people, because of their sins, do not demand restoration; they wait in faith for God: "I will hear what God proclaims." God's favor is neither automatic nor indiscriminate;

only those among the people who fear the Lord can hope to enjoy salvation (vv. 9-10). The divine answer comes in verses 11-14. God's attributes, "kindness and truth . . . justice and peace," will once again work in the land, making a place fit for God to dwell. The psalm was probably composed during the sixth-century Exile, when Israel was tempted to believe that God had left forever.

Psalm 86

In this individual lament (A), which draws many of its expressions from other psalms, the singer describes himself as "afflicted and poor" (v. 1); "devoted" (v. 2); "your servant" (vv. 2, 4, 16); "rescued from the depths of the nether world" (v. 13); attacked by the haughty (v. 14). These are the self-designations of one who confesses that there is no other protection from life's dangers than the graciously bestowed protection of Yahweh. All the elements of a lament are here—the unadorned cry for help, the complaint, the prayer, the expression of hope. But in this psalm the distress of the psalmist seems less particular; the servant does not seem to be overly frightened by threats, for somehow they bring him closer to the Lord. In that attitude the servants find their identity.

Psalm 87

This poem, unfortunately textually damaged, is a song of Zion, like Psalms 46, 48, 76, and 132. The situation seems to be the Exile or its aftermath, when Zion's citizens were scattered over Babylon and Egypt. To be a citizen of Zion is protection enough for anyone, for it is the city of the only powerful God.

Psalm 88

In few laments (A) is the fear of death so vividly portrayed. A land of darkness and oblivion far below the earth (vv. 4-8), of separation from friends and human society (vv. 9, 19) is the way the psalmist imagines Sheol in the era before there was any thought of resurrection from the dead. Nonetheless, the frightened and afflicted person continues to cry out to the God of life; prayers punctuate the psalm (vv. 2-3, 10, 14). The psalmist's strategy is clever: he reminds God that only the living remember and celebrate the wonderful divine mercies (vv. 11-13). The life that the psalmist seeks is life with God and with one's community. What is terrifying in death is the loss of others.

Psalm 89

The community laments (A) the defeat of the king, who represents Yahweh's mastery of the world and its inhabitants. That mastery was shown by God's creation victory. The defeat of Yahweh's lieutenant on earth, the king, raises the question of whether Yahweh is truly the powerful God. Verses 2-5 hymn the God who made secure in one creative act the heavens and the Davidic dynasty. Like other communal laments, verses 6-38 narrate the original event that brought Israel into existence—in this psalm, the conquest of primordial sea, the making of the earth through orderly pairs of elements, and the leading of the people to the land (vv. 9-19). Part of that world-establishing victory is the installation of the Davidic king, with whom Yahweh shares the fruit of this universal victory in a solemn promise (vv. 20-38). But now in our day, complains the community, our king is not protected; enemies break through at will (vv. 39-52). The community, despite its grief, has faith enough to hold Yahweh to the original promise.

BOOK IV: PSALMS 90–106

Psalm 90

In most community laments (A) Israel recalls the founding event, the divine act that brought them into existence—the Exodus-Conquest, the act of creation. The people's plea is that God not allow the present danger to wipe out the community that has been graciously established. In this psalm the danger is not external, for example a foreign nation, but the evil intent of the people themselves. Humans and God are incommensurate—their life, plans, and power (vv. 3-11). The psalmist remembers the eternity of God; even before the world was made, God was (vv. 1-2). Hence the prayer in verses 12-17 that God teach the people to know themselves before God, to let them experience the special joy of servants, of those who see the power of God and see their own plans affirmed by grace. The poem is not simply a meditation on human frailty; it speaks from the experience of God's just punishment of sin and from confidence in God's forgiveness.

Psalm 91

This song of trust comes from a person who has experienced the asylum of the temple. From that spot, safe under the wings of the Most High (vv. 1-2; see 1 Kgs 6:23-28), the psalmist assures those laboring under the dangers always besetting the just that God will overcome all. Verses 3-13 are a series of promises that the salvation of the Lord, so palpable in the temple, will be available in all areas if one makes the Lord one's refuge. In verses 14-16 the Lord speaks directly to all who maintain their trust in the face of the danger and bitterness of life. Adapted from the promise of salvation in the lament (A), it invites those in danger to the ultimate protection and loving relationship.

Psalm 92

The song is a hymn (C), in that it states how appropriate it is to praise God for the work of just and gracious governance, and a thanksgiving (B), in that it tells how the psalmist was rescued from personal enemies (vv. 10-11). Because of the triumph of the wicked, the psalmist must have been tempted by the kind of doubts about God's justice that are vividly described in Psalms 37, 49, and 73. Profound rejoicing in the just and merciful God mark this psalm. Verse 9, "while you, O Lord, are the Most High forever," is the exact center of the poem. Also, the same Hebrew verb is repeated at the beginning and end (translated "to proclaim" in verse 2 and "declaring" in verse 16).

Verses 2-5 emphasize how beautiful and fitting it is to praise God for showing justice. Verses 6-12 describe the experience of one who has just seen that merciful justice in action. That supremacy can be seen, however, only by those who are themselves just. "How very deep are your thoughts!" (v. 6) means "your intentions are hidden." The person who waits for the Lord, like this psalmist, will experience rescue. The last section (vv. 13-16) describes what life in the presence of the only God consists in. The trees in the great court of the temple symbolize the life offered to those who are just. The security and happiness of the just will declare the Lord's mercy and fidelity.

Preface to Psalms 93, 95-100

These psalms all elaborate the kingship of Yahweh in a similar way. In all of them "Yahweh reigns." In the ancient Near East, polytheistic except for Israel, a god was acclaimed powerful over the other gods because of a specific act of power. The greatest act was creation, bringing the world of men and women into existence. In the Bible creation is frequently the creation of Israel as a people securely dwelling before Yahweh in the sanctuary. This could be expressed either in the language of the Exodus-Conquest or in the language of cosmogony, the overcoming of forces hostile to human community. The latter language was already centuries old when borrowed by Israel. Yahweh proves to be supreme among the gods by conquering the annihilating power of sea (less frequently, the power of primordial night). Yahweh then arranges the elements to support human community and brings the people to dwell securely in the sanctuary, the temple. The temple and its ceremonies figure prominently in these psalms. The jubilant people are admitted into the court, where they acknowledge Yahweh's great victory that has made them God's people. Whether Israel annually celebrated Yahweh's kingship is a matter that is still unsettled.

Psalm 93

(Read the preface to Psalm 93 above.) This hymn (C) celebrates the kingship of Yahweh, who created the world (vv. 1-2) by defeating sea (vv. 3-4). Sea completely covered the land, making human life impossible. Sea in the psalm, as customary elsewhere in the Bible, is endowed with will; it roars in wrath against the power of Yahweh. The decrees of verse 5 are the designs that the Lord imposes upon the newly ordered world, designs also found in Israel's law. Verses 1ab and 5 thus frame the poem; a gloriously garbed Yahweh utters those words that structure the world.

Psalm 94

This lament (A) complains to God that the wicked and the arrogant have the upper hand and that those who are faithful, "the righteous," are their victims. It is more a personal than a national lament (the psalmist speaks of personal distress in verses 16-19), yet there is concern for the people as well (vv. 5-7, 20-21). It is probably placed among the psalms of Yahweh's kingship (Psalms 93 and 95-100) because of its expectation that Yahweh will judge the earth.

Verses 1-2, a cry to Yahweh, contain the striking epithet "God of vengeance." "Vengeance" here means the intent to right an unfair situation by punishing the wicked. "How long" introduces the complaint of verses 3-7: For what length of time must the psalmist suffer the silence of God in the face of rampant injustice against the poor? Verses 8-11 and 12-15 are declarations of faith. The first bravely tells the evildoers that their statement that the Lord does not see (v. 7) is false and that their plans (rather than "thoughts," v. 11a) are doomed; the second assures the persecuted that their sufferings have meaning and are only temporary. In verses 16-19 the psalmist teaches the people from personal experience that the Lord does indeed console, even in the midst of trials like these. The last section (vv. 20-23) boldly affirms, on the basis of God's justice and the psalmist's experience, that the Lord will indeed rectify the present intolerable situation.

Psalm 95

(Read the preface to Psalms 95-100, p. 774). Verses 1-5 and 6-7 are parallel (ten lines in the first section, five in the second). Each invites the people to come to the temple, the sole place where Yahweh's power is manifested in building and ritual. In verses 3-5 Yahweh's supremacy over all powers in the heavens is shown through the easy arrangement of the paired elements that make up the world: the depths of the earth and the mountains, the sea and the land. After the second invitation in verse 6, the second step in creation is mentioned—the creation of Israel as Yahweh's special flock (v. 7). In verses 7c-11 the flock is abruptly confronted: Will they be obedient as befits Yahweh's flock? People had to be admitted in a gate ceremony like those portrayed in Psalms 15 and 24. "Does your behavior really say you are God's people?" they were asked. This psalm ends with such a scrutiny. The question is not simply a convention; Israel's first generation was never admitted to the holy land because of its apostasy. Yahweh's people must live by Yahweh's word.

Psalm 96

(Read the preface to Psalms 95-100, p. 774.) The theme of the sole kingship of Yahweh is again elaborated in this hymn (C), but with a special call to the nations (vv. 7-10)—indeed all creation, animate and inanimate (vv. 11-12)—to join the chorus of welcome. The first section (vv. 1-6) calls for a new song, that is, a song appropriate to the renewal of the earth through creation. The very proclamation of the act of creation, ("his salvation," "his glory," "his wondrous deeds," vv. 2-3), is itself a denial of other gods, for they had nothing to do with the making of the world (vv. 4-5). The temple, the last great deed in Yahweh's creating, embodies divine glory in a special way (v. 6).

The second invitation, that the nations bring their gifts to Yahweh in the temple (vv. 7-10), flows logically from the first section. Verses 1-6 state that Yahweh, by virtue of creation, is supreme over "the gods," the patrons of the nations, and that this work of creation is specially visible in the temple. The final section (vv. 11-13) exhorts nature to greet the Creator-God who comes to judge, that is, to see that the newly created world operates according to the divine intent.

Psalm 97

(Read the preface to Psalms 95-100, p. 774.) This hymn (C) extols the reign of Yahweh, portraying in its two sections the manifestation of that reign to the world at large (vv. 1-7) and then, in a special way, to Zion and its cities (vv. 8-12). The sections are demarcated by the repetition of the verbs "rejoice" and "be glad" in verses 1 and 8 and the polar opposites of worshipers of images and worshipers of Yahweh in verses 7 and 12. In the first section the kingship of Yahweh is manifested dynamically in the weapons of thunder and lightning that overcame all opposition; other so-called gods and their worshipers are shamed. In the second section Zion welcomes its victorious Creator-Lord. The righteous are those who worship aright; they are the ones who are vindicated when their Lord comes in power.

Psalm 98

(Read the preface to Psalms 95-100, p. 774.) In this hymn (C) the community celebrates the victory of Yahweh, which brings joy to the world and establishes Yahweh as judge over all (v. 9). The victory of which verse 2 speaks (the "wondrous deeds" of verse 1 and the "justice" of verse 2) is specific: the conquest of all threats to the peaceful existence of Israel. The threats are depicted in the psalms in various guises—cosmic forces such as sea, nations bent on Israel's destruction, evildoers seemingly triumphant. Yet all are reductively one: those who condemn Yahweh's will for a just universe in which Israel dwells secure. God's judging can only cause exultation to all peoples, for evil forces will be destroyed (vv. 7-9). God's judging is not an impartial settlement of claims but the vigorous upholding of the wrong and oppressed; such protection was promised to Israel of old (v. 3). The hymn is structured by a threefold invitation (vv. 1, 4, and 7).

Psalm 99

(Read the preface to Psalms 95–100, p. 774.) The emphasis in this hymn (C) to the supreme King is upon Zion, the place where that supremacy is visible, and upon Israel, the people who have transmitted God's royal decrees. Yahweh is, to be sure, the sole God of all the world, but Yahweh is revealed in Zion by means of the people Israel. The poem is structured by the threefold statement that God is holy (vv. 3, 5, and 9) and by the twice-repeated command to extol Yahweh (vv. 5 and 9). Verses 6-8 single out Israel as the sole nation in dialogue with Yahweh by mentioning its most famous spokespersons—Moses, Aaron, and Samuel. They heard the authentic word of Yahweh and handed it on. Yahweh's help, given when "he answered them" (vv. 6, 8), is a sure sign of the validity of that word. All nations are to respond to Yahweh, God of the world, by serving this God in Zion of Israel.

Psalm 100

(Read the preface to Psalms 95–100, p. 774.) Though this hymn (C) does not mention kingship explicitly, it presumes the same thought-world as the other psalms of kingship—the invitations to the world to rejoice and to do so in the court of the temple. Much is condensed in this brief poem. The world is to rejoice and to come to the temple because Yahweh is God. It must be assumed that God's supremacy here is manifested

through the same act as in Psalms 93, 95–99: the creation victory over hostile forces, a victory that makes the world and Israel. It is appropriate, then, to enter and give thanks.

Psalm 101

In this royal psalm the Davidic king liturgically affirms his task of overseeing the justice of God in the kingdom. The first verse is the leitmotif: kindness and judgment describe God's gracious choice of the king, and, through the king, of Israel. The king here, as in Psalms 72 and 89, is the agent of God's holiness and justice in the world of men and women. He cleanses his house of evildoers (vv. 3b-5, 7-8), his "house" (vv. 2, 7) meaning his family and palace. He is the model Israelite (vv. 2-3a) and champions all who are faithful by putting them in positions of responsibility (v. 6). The psalm is a vow in the sight of God; before the people the king promises to avoid Oriental despotism and to be the servant of the just God.

Psalm 102

In this lament (A), a Penitential Psalm, the psalmist's experience of bodily and psychic disintegration (vv. 4-12) impels a cry to God (vv. 2-3), whose "fury and wrath" (v. 11) have caused the suffering. The psalmist attributes whatever happens to God; hence the present affliction must be due to God's "fury and wrath."

Psalms of individual lament include a statement of hope in the midst of the complaint. In verses 13-23 the distressed person, standing in the temple, the very place where Yahweh has promised to be present, hopes that help will be given. In verses 17-18 the Lord has built Zion, and so it is a refuge from every danger. Verses 19-23 are the motto of Zion: In this spot the Lord protects the people; and this protective care is revealed in the sight of the whole world. Verses 24-29 restate the original complaint and prayer for salvation (vv. 24-25) and add an act of faith in the God who will always guard the faithful servants. The psalmist, by going to the temple and being one of the Lord's servants, finds security in the midst of suffering.

Psalm 103

In this hymn (C) the speaker praises the God whose graciousness has been shown in all moments of personal life—in actions of forgiveness and protection from life-threatening forces (vv. 1-5). This is the same Lord who ever acts on behalf of the needy, having acted for Israel through the mediation of Moses. Verses 6-18 characterize the God of Israel as just, yet never allowing justice to circumvent a merciful choice. Human sin cannot destroy God's favor (vv. 11-13), nor can frailty and insignificance (when measured against God's eternity). Those who are faithful to the covenant become members of that company with whom God has promised to remain (vv. 17-18). The praise of the Lord is not the task of Israel alone; the beings of the heavenly world are to join in the praise (vv. 19-22).

Psalm 104

This hymn (C) praises God, who with ease and skill has made primordial night and rampaging waters into a world everywhere vibrant with life. The conception of the psalm is the same as Gen 1, where a dark and watery chaos (Gen 1:1-2) receives light on the first day and dry land on the second day. The two forces, night and waters, that had made human community impossible are not annihilated; they are made into an integral part of creation.

In verses 1-4 the speaker acknowledges that the Lord's palace, entourage, and very self by their splendor reflect God's mastery over the heavenly world. In verses 5-18 the divine mastery extends to the waters; the waters that once completely covered the earth flee to their proper place at the divine rebuke (vv. 5-9). Water now is tamed for the service of people, nourishing life in rivers (vv. 10-12) and in rain (vv. 13-15), and even fertilizing the fabled mountain of Lebanon (vv. 16-17). Verses 19-23 show the mastery over darkness; it is now part of the sequence of night and day, necessary and helpful to humans and animals (vv. 19-23). In the face of such wisdom and power, the psalmist exclaims in awe (v. 24). Even the vast sea, the mysterious fringe of the known world, is under God. There, too, God has placed a living being, Leviathan, that it might enjoy life, (vv. 25-26). God's world is not the clock of the Deist philosophers, wound and left to run mechanically; at every moment each creature looks to God for its being. God's spirit, or breath, is

necessary for life, as it is in Gen 2–3 and Ezek 37:1-14 (vv. 27-30).

Control over the elemental forces on earth shows the glory of the Lord, the theme of religious song (vv. 31-34). The only thing that can obscure God's glory is human sin. The psalmist prays that sinners no longer deface the handiwork of the Lord (v. 35).

Psalm 105

This is a hymn (C) to the Lord who has promised the land of Canaan to the people, the Lord who can be sought in all places and at all times, whose word of promise is everywhere effective. In verses 1-6 Israel, descendant of the patriarchs Abraham and Jacob, is invited to praise and seek the Lord's presence. Verses 7-11 identify God as the Lord of the whole world and as the one who remembers the promise of land to the patriarchs. Verses 12-45 retell the mighty deeds of the past that are relevant to the present situation:

vv. 12-15	the ancestors in the land of Canaan
vv. 16-22	Joseph in the land of Egypt
vv. 23-38	Israel in the land of Egypt
vv. 39-45	Israel in the desert on the way to Canaan

In each of the four episodes there are three elements: (1) a servant(s) through whom appears (2) the ancestral word of promise of (3) the land of Canaan. Yahweh has always been faithful to the promise to give Israel the land of Canaan. The psalm seems to be a song of Israel in the sixth-century Exile, when it did not actually possess the land. It invites praise of the Lord who will act to bring the people home.

Psalm 106

This community lament (A) retells incidents from Israel's national story, the Exodus-Conquest, to show that God's mercy has been as evident as God's justice. The speaker's "I" in verses 4-5 includes all Israelites, whose plea for mercy rests completely in the God whose work has never been destroyed by sin.

The opening five verses praise God and God's great deed of fashioning a people. May the speaker and the congregation always be among those whom God favors! Verses 6-12 portray the first of the eight incidents in the psalm in which the people responded to God's gracious act by rebellion. At the Red Sea (Exod 14–15), the Lord saved the people despite their rebellion. The same will to save is depicted in the scenes of divine deed, rebellion, and punishment of verses 13-15 (see Num 11); vv. 16-18 (see Num 16); vv. 19-23 (see Exod 32–34); vv. 24-27 (see Num 13–14); vv. 28-31 (see Num 25:1-15); vv. 32-33 (see Num 20:1-13); vv. 34-39 (see Judg 3:3-6). Verses 40-46 describe the same general rhythm of apostasy, punishment and rescue that characterized Israel during the period of the judges (see Judg 2:6–3:6). Israel's history shows that God has punished justly but has never let destruction be the last word. Therefore, in verses 47-48 the people pray that God bring them back from the just punishment of their exile so that they might again give praise.

BOOK V: PSALMS 107–150

Psalm 107
This hymn (C) invites all Israelites to praise the Lord, who has brought them into being as a single people, redeeming them from every danger, bringing them from the four corners of the earth (vv. 1-3). In verses 4-32 four archetypal divine rescues of perishing people are described: rescue from the sterile desert in verses 4-9, from the bonds of primordial night in vv. 10-16, from mortal illness in verses 17-22, and from the angry sea in verses 23-32. God's power on behalf of the endangered and needy invites them to praise (vv. 8, 15, 21, 31). The number four in ancient Near Eastern literature often suggests totality, as in the phrase "the four corners of the earth"; the four cases, therefore, represent all cases of extreme need.

The same redeeming activity of the Lord is shown in Israel's story in verses 33-41. Yahweh destroyed Sodom and Gomorrah in Gen 18–19, which this psalm sees as a type of the destruction of the wicked inhabitants of Canaan in order to clear the land for Israel (vv. 33-34). The Lord led Israel in the desert, settling them in the land and giving increase to crop and herd (vv. 35-38). Whenever the people are endangered, as in the four cases of verses 4-32, the Lord rescues them (vv. 39-41). Israel thus becomes a showcase of this Lord's power and mercy to the entire world. Verses 42-43 invite all to see that Israel witnesses to

the Lord's graciousness; in the daily life of the people graciousness of the Lord appears.

Psalm 108
This poem is a composite of old pieces. Verses 2-6 are the same as Ps 57:8-12, and verses 7-14 are the same as Ps 60:7-14. Probably it is a prayer for victory. Verses 2-7 are a bold song of confidence and of petition to God for victory. Verses 8-11 are an oracle of salvation, uttered most probably by the priest in the temple during war; they promise that God the Warrior will defend the land. Verses 12-14 take up and develop the petition of verses 6-7.

Psalm 109
This lament (A) is noteworthy for length and vehemence of its prayer against the evildoer (vv. 6-20). The cry to God in verse 1 and the complaint of verses 2-5 and 22-25 are brief in comparison. The psalmist apparently is the victim of a campaign of slander, which could be devastating in a society where reputation and honor are paramount. In the dramatic perspective of the psalm, there are only two types of people: the wicked and their poor victims. The psalmist is one of the poor (vv. 22, 31), one of the friends of God who are enemies of the wicked. The poor person asks vindication not because of personal virtue but because God has promised to be the friend of the poor.

Psalm 110
In this royal psalm, which resembles Psalm 89 and especially Psalm 2, a court singer delivers three oracles concerning the king (vv. 1, 2, 4). They promise, respectively, a place of honor with God, who achieves victory over evil, divine sonship, and priesthood or mediation between God and people. The three oracles are expanded in verses 5-6; the king, as ruler for Yahweh, will exercise divine sovereignty over the whole world. Verse 3 is corrupt; the translation is a guess. The poem is most probably from the coronation of the Davidic king. The last verse about drinking from the brook may refer to a rite at Gihon brook, like that implied in 1 Kgs 1:38-40.

Psalm 111
Like Psalms 9-10, 25, 34, 37, and 112, this poem is acrostic, each verse beginning with

a successive letter of the twenty-two-letter Hebrew alphabet. Verse 1 gives the situation: a temple singer praises the Lord by reciting the Lord's actions in Israel's history. The singer is a teacher as well as a leader in song. Verses 2-10 teach that the Lord is revealed in historical act. In the recital, precept and gracious act are both divine gift; to remember and to obey are simply two modes of responding to God's initiative.

Psalm 112

Like Psalm 111 and other psalms, this poem is acrostic, each line beginning with a successive letter of the Hebrew alphabet. Like Psalm 1, it assures life to the person who remains close to the Lord by willingly obeying the divine will. In the psalm life consists of abundant progeny (v. 2), wealth that enables one to be magnanimous (vv. 3, 5, 9), and virtue that enables one to support other people in the community (v. 4). The words "forever" or "everlasting" occur three times, spaced evenly throughout the poem (vv. 3, 6, 9), showing how rooted and stable is the person near the Lord. The just person is an affront to the wicked, whose life wastes away in envy and frustration (v. 10). The psalm draws upon the tradition of the two ways of life; the ways are starkly set before every person so as to elicit a choice.

Psalm 113

This hymn (C) exhorts the servants or worshipers of the Lord to praise the divine name, that is, the way in which God is presented to the world. The name is especially manifest in the celebrations of the temple (v. 1), but, since God is over all things, praise cannot be confined to a particular time or place (vv. 2-3). Yahweh, Israel's God, acts in the heavens above and on the earth below. The last three verses celebrate Yahweh acting as judge. In the Bible, to judge is not to render an impartial verdict from afar but to right wrongs and relieve the poor.

Psalm 114

This hymn (C), lacking the usual invitation for others to join in, celebrates the Exodus-Conquest, the act by which Israel came into being as a people. In the concentrated perspective of the poem, the people move directly from Egypt to Israel/Judah, the sacred land of Yahweh (vv. 1-2). Sea/Jordan, which stands between the people and their land as an obstacle, is personified. Like a panic-stricken soldier, it flees before the mighty Yahweh, who fights at the head of the people. The earth quakes at the cosmic battle and victory (v. 4). The natural elements are then taunted, as one would taunt a defeated enemy (vv. 5-6). As Yahweh heads the procession of the rescued people into the safety of the holy land, the natural elements are commanded to greet their new master, Yahweh.

Psalm 115

The psalm probably records a liturgy performed by Israel at a time when its misery and small numbers provoked its neighbors to taunt, "Where is your God?" The community answers with a prayer to Yahweh to uphold the divine name (vv. 1-3) and with a counter-taunt that the neighbor's gods are as impotent as the statues that represent them in the splendid rituals (vv. 4-8). Israel has no images of its God, Yahweh; it is itself the image of Yahweh, testifying to God's glory by its actions. Verses 9-11 describe the Israelite community as constituted by its trust in Yahweh, its sole support. And that hope is answered by the blessing in verses 12-18. Blessing means enhancement of life and increase of progeny. Israel is confident that its own blessed existence on earth redounds to God's glory, showing that Yahweh is a living God (vv. 14-16). This psalm and Psalm 135 make use of ideas about Israel as the image of God found in Second Isaiah. The psalms are probably postexilic.

Psalm 116

In this loosely knit thanksgiving (B), the speaker responds to God's rescue of him from the clutches of death (vv. 3-4) and from near despair (vv. 10-11) with vows and sacrifice in the temple (vv. 13-14, 17-19). The chief praise, however, is expressed in the vivid description of the divine mercy and the public proclamation of the Lord's attentiveness to the cry of the poor. Grievous indeed in the Lord's sight is the death of the faithful ones (v. 17). It is the experience of the saving Lord that enables one to say, "I am your servant" (v. 16).

Psalm 117

In this shortest of all hymns (C), the nations are called to acknowledge Yahweh's sovereignty because of God's never-ending fidelity to Israel. Israel's secure existence, owed entirely to Yahweh's grace, is the proof to the world that only Yahweh is God.

Psalm 118

A thanksgiving (B) after a victory, this psalm accompanies a procession into the temple precincts. Solemn entry into the temple by king and people and their partaking of a banquet were ways of celebrating the Exodus-Conquest, when Yahweh led the people from the domain of Pharaoh to Yahweh's own domain. Verses 1-4 call upon the ranks of worshipers to praise the Lord, for the Lord is faithful. In verses 5-18 the speaker tells of the divine mercy shown by Yahweh's rescue of the people from their enemies. The citation of the old poem about the Exodus-Conquest in Exod 15 (v. 14 = Exod 15:2; vv. 15-16 = Exod 15:6; v. 28 = Exod 15:2) suggests that today's victory is an extension of the original victory that made Israel a people.

Verses 19-29 echo the cries of the procession as it enters the great court of the temple. Only the just, those whom God has chosen, may enter; victory today has shown the people that they are chosen and thus may enter. Verse 22 is a proverb; what is insignificant has become great through divine election. The reference may be to the foundation stone of the temple. The psalm orchestrates the people's movement and shouts a hymn to the Lord of victory.

Psalm 119

Psalm 119 is the longest psalm in the Psalter. The 176 verses of the poem are arranged acrostically, according to the order of the Hebrew alphabet; there are twenty-two sections of eight verses. In its great length and in its utilization of many psalmic genres—the blessing, the individual lament, the song of trust, the individual thanksgiving, the hymn—it is unparalleled in the Bible. It is an anthology of poems praising the law. There are eight words for law in the psalm: way, law, decrees, precepts, statutes, commands, ordinances, words. The poem expresses faith in the word of God delivered to the people in various situations, such as the inexperience of youth (vv. 9-16), pain (vv. 25-32), contentment (vv. 97-104), but mostly the situations of ordinary life. The singer stands for us all—people con-

scious of life's limits and wise enough to ask for the illuminating and strengthening hand of the Lord.

Psalm 120

This thanksgiving (B) was sung in the temple by a person who, like the author of Psalms 42-43, sojourned in a foreign land away from Yahweh's presence, the victim of liars and violent people (vv. 5-7). Verse 1 reports the rescue, verse 2 cites the psalmist's prayer in the grim time before salvation, and verses 3-4 cite the psalmist's wish that the wicked be punished by the Lord. Verses 5-7 further recall sentiments from the past. The verbs of verses 5-7 should be in the past tense. The speaker suffered from being among a people that did not observe the Lord's precepts. Violence prevailed. It is not certain whether Meshech, a region in the far north (Gen 10:2), and Kedar, a tribe of the north Arabian desert (Gen 25:13), are meant literally as places where the speaker actually resided as an alien or metaphorically as typical places far distant from the temple.

Psalm 121

This blessing assures those embarking on a dangerous journey of the Lord's protection. It may well be the priest's dismissal of pilgrims who have come to the temple and have experienced, in common with their fellow Israelites, the presence of the Lord in the services. About to return home from Jerusalem, the people look anxiously at the wooded hills; danger lies along those roads. Will the Lord of the temple protect them on their journey (v. 1)? In their moment of anxiety the priest declares that the Lord is not confined to a place or a time (v. 2), that every step is guarded (vv. 3-4); night and day (vv. 5-6) the Lord guards their return and their dwelling (vv. 7-8).

Psalm 122

The song is sung by pilgrims arriving at the gates of Jerusalem in obedience to the command of the Lord to gather in worship three times a year. The singer can scarcely contain his joy as he waits to join the procession into the court: "We will go up to the house of the Lord" (v. 1). The splendor of the city is not simply its great buildings. Jerusalem is the place of encounter. Here the people praise the Lord (v. 4) and hear God's authoritative words to them (v. 5). The very buildings bespeak the power of Yahweh (see Ps 48:13-15). The last four verses turn into prayer. May the grace and peace experienced here transform the people at all times!

Psalm 123

In this communal lament (A) a speaker for a people taunted by its neighbors for its weakness and poverty cries out to God for salvation. The speaker makes a gesture for the whole community, lifting up his eyes to the powerful God who dwells in heaven, a gesture of obedience and of hope (vv. 1-2). Verses 3-4 contain the plea and the motive for divine action: Take pity for we are scorned. The speaker does not cite the righteousness of the people as the motive. The very poverty of the people is motive enough for the Lord to act on behalf of those who have been chosen.

Psalm 124

In this thanksgiving (B) the singer teaches Israel to attribute its very existence to the Lord who rescues it. Israel's enemies are compared to a mythic dragon (vv. 2b-3a; see Jer 51:34) and to the Flood (vv. 3b-5; see Isa 51:9-10). Sometimes the Bible, in order to express the full malice of historical enemies, portrays them with the traits of the primordial enemies of creation. Verses 6-8 praise the saving God directly and with touching simplicity: Israel is a bird freed from the trapper's snare. Israel is ever a freed people—freed originally from the clutches of Pharaoh and now from the clutches of the current enemy.

Psalm 125

The poem is a song of trust that the righteous, those who are faithful to the Lord and delight in God's law, will inherit the land and live safely in Zion. It is a response to postexilic anxieties about whether God would honor the ancient promises of restoration. Will Israel again possess the land? Will Zion be rebuilt? What about promises like Isa 57:13: "The one who takes refuge in me shall inherit the land, and possess my holy mountain"? The answer is that those who trust are like Mount Zion, surrounded by God like the high mountains that surround Jerusalem (vv. 1-2). Verse 3 cites perhaps an ancient promise that the just will not be contaminated by the wicked. Verses 4-5 are a prayer recognizing that the inheritors are righteous by the Lord's grace, not by their virtue. To live on Zion is a gift.

Psalm 126

This communal lament (A) was most probably sung shortly after Israel's return from exile in Babylon. Verses 1-3 express the intense joy of being in the holy city. Mere presence in Zion, however, is not enough; the people must pray for the divine intervention that will give fertility to the land (v. 4). Verses 5-6 are an oracle of promise: the painful labor of sowing will be crowned with life by the Lord who has brought them back.

Psalm 127

The psalm puts together two proverbs (vv. 1-2 and 3-5), both concerned with Yahweh establishing families, in order to affirm that all life is a divine gift. "House" in verse 1 means the family or household. In biblical times a household often consisted of several families under the authority of the oldest married man. The prosperity and protection of this group are not the work of humans; God has chosen to provide for them (v. 2). Verses 3-5 expand the affirmation with a proverb. "Gift" in verse 3 is the word that traditionally describes the holy land; like the land, children are pure gift, evidence of the Lord's favor.

Psalm 128

The poem is a statement of faith that the ever reliable and just God will always bless those who show reverence. "Fear of the Lord" does not mean craven fear or mere obedience to a set of commandments but a way of life (v. 1b) that sets God above all. As Psalm 1 shows, the Bible often dramatizes human life as two ways, the way of the just and the way of the wicked; each person must choose which of the two paths to walk. Verses 2-4 portray the consequences of the way of the Lord: enhanced life in the family. The perspective is that of the adult male, ordinarily the ruler of the household in the biblical world. In verses 5-6 the speaker, possibly a priest on the temple staff, extends the blessing on the household to the whole people of Israel for generations to come.

Psalm 129

The song resembles a thanksgiving (B) in which the speaker narrates a specific rescue by the Lord. Here, however, Israel looks back, not on one rescue, but on a whole series of divine acts since its "youth." Israel's history has been a series of trials, but the Lord has always given freedom, like the freedom of a beast when its harness is removed (v. 4). Israel's oppressors have been the wicked; in oppressing Israel they have opposed Yahweh. Hence the prayer in verses 5-8 is that Yahweh will continue to uphold Israel and cut off the life of the wicked. Like the stray blades of grass on the roof sod that shoot up and die quickly, may the wicked never know the joy of harvest.

Psalm 130

This poem, one of the Penitential Psalms, seems to be an individual lament (A). As in Psalms 12 and 60, the priestly assurance of salvation (vv. 7-8), given in response to the psalmist's plea, is included; ordinarily the assurance is not transmitted in the lament. The petitioner cries out from the depths, the abyss of the underworld. The pain and alienation make the psalmist feel "like those who go down into the pit" (Ps 143:7). Yet even here one can cry out to the God who does not keep books and whose last word is a word of forgiveness (vv. 3-4). Though the trial is severe, the sufferer still hopes (v. 5). Perhaps the psalmist is keeping vigil in the temple during the night and sees help coming with the dawn (v. 6). The priest's answer to the psalmist is that God's steadfast loyalty to the covenant will be available to each Israelite, as it has always been available to Israel.

Psalm 131

This is a song of trust, like Psalms 16, 23, and others, in which the psalmist lays aside all self-sufficiency in order to be completely open before the God who saves. The psalm is a song of the poor, the 'anawim, who renounce power in order to stand more surely under the divine protection. The image of a child, quiet with its mother, unselfconsciously trusting, memorably sums up the inner attitude.

Psalm 132

This psalm accompanied a liturgical cere-

mony in which the Lord, invisibly present on the ark-throne, was carried in procession to the temple. The Israelite king, "son of God" by adoption, played a central role in the rites. The blessings of God include preeminently the king and his dynasty (vv. 11-12). 1 Sam 4:1–7:1 and 2 Sam 6–7 tell the story of the movement of the ark from the town of Kiriath-jearim ("the fields of Jaar," v. 6) to the temple in the time of David (tenth century B.C.E.). The psalmist reminds God of David's fidelity, in particular his care to build a suitable house for his Lord (vv. 1-5). Verses 6-10 record the shouts of the marchers, who begin their procession in Kiriath-jearim, a few miles north of Jerusalem, and end it at the temple. After having taken possession of the temple, the Lord now founds David's "house," the dynasty. If his sons will be loyal vassals like David today, the dynasty will have no end (vv. 11-12). And the place that the Lord has chosen, Zion, will become a place of blessing—abundant life, joy, and security for all those who rely on God present in the temple and in the Davidic king (vv. 13-18).

Psalm 133

Though often termed a "wisdom psalm," Psalm 133 does not teach but declares a particular situation blessed by God. The situation was a common one in ancient Israel whenever the property of the (extended) family, held in trust as Yahweh's gift, became the eldest son's upon the death of the father. The younger brothers' families then came under the headship of the eldest brother. Would peace still reign among family members? The psalm utters a blessing over the fragile family in crisis. Brothers and sisters living in peace are like the refreshing oil poured out in hospitable greeting, like dew watering the crops in the rainless summer. Both metaphors hint at the key role of the oldest brother, the source of blessings to his siblings. In a peaceful house the Lord's blessings unfold.

Psalm 134

In this brief liturgy a priest exhorts the other temple singers to "bless" (that is, acknowledge publicly) the great deeds of the Lord. The clergy are ministers in the sanctuary during a night service (see Isa 30:29). In verse 3 the priest utters a blessing of the Lord in response to the other priests' blessing, a blessing from the Creator enhancing the life already bestowed. Mount Zion is the place where God dwells and where the fruitful encounter between God and creature takes place.

Psalm 135

This hymn (C) begins and ends with an invitation to Israel to praise the Lord (vv. 1-3, 19-20) who has created Israel, an act demonstrating that the Lord is the only God. Only the Lord creates. The song is appropriately sung in the Jerusalem temple, for it is the gathering place for the people the Lord has created.

In the first verses the people are invited to praise the Lord, to tell God's story to the world. That story is summed up in verse 4, the choosing of Israel as a special possession. Verses 5-14 narrate a single event. Creation in verses 5-7 should not be distinguished too sharply from redemption in verses 8-14, since both describe the emergence of an ordered and secure human society. Verses 6-7 allude to Yahweh's easy mastery over chaos by means of the weapons of wind and lightning. The power that mastered chaos in verses 6-7 also destroys the enemies of Israel in verses 8-14. God liberates Israel from Egyptian bondage, defeating Pharaoh and the kings who stand in the way of Israel's entry into Canaan.

Yahweh's defeat of hostile powers means that images representing those powers are worthless; the inertness of the images shows that what they represent is without power. Verses 15-18 also appear in Ps 115:4-8.

Psalm 136

The hymn (C) praises Yahweh, the only powerful God ("the God of gods" in verse 2), who has created the world in which Israel lives. The refrain "for his mercy endures forever" occurs after every line, suggesting that a speaker and chorus sang the psalm antiphonally. "Mercy" is God's fidelity to the oath to Israel, God's *noblesse oblige*. To "give thanks" (vv. 1-3 and 26) is to tell publicly what God has done. Verses 4-25 ought not be divided into deeds of "creation" in verses 4-9 and deeds of "redemption" in verses 10-22, as is commonly done; rather, the actions constitute a single process. God makes the environment for human community by arranging heaven and earth, and makes the community

itself by freeing the people from Pharaoh and giving them their land. Verses 23-25 are intimately related to the previous verses. The Lord who made Israel a people by giving it this land continues to make it a people by ever rescuing it from its foes and giving it the produce of the land.

Psalm 137

This lament (A) was sung by the community in Babylon during the exile of the sixth century. In verses 1-3 Israel is engaged in a liturgical rite of lament. The lyres for joyful song hang unused nearby. The captors' question, "Sing for us the songs of Zion," are like other taunting questions in the Bible, such as "Where now is your God?" How can Israel sing songs of Zion, such as Psalms 46, 48, and 76, which speak of Zion as impregnable and its inhabitants as happy and safe? In verses 4-6 the singer swears never to lose hope in Zion; the Zion songs will ever be sung. Verse 7 wishes annihilation upon Edom, a country to the east of Judah that raided Jerusalem during the Exile. In verses 8-9, appalling to the modern reader, Babylon, the archetypal enemy of God, is to be eradicated; its children, therefore, are to be killed.

Psalm 138

The psalmist gives thanks (B), telling in the temple how Yahweh heard his cry and came to the rescue. Not because of the psalmist's virtues did Yahweh act but because of Yahweh's own merciful fidelity (vv. 1-3). The deed is not simply a private transaction between an individual Israelite and Yahweh; it is great enough to provoke the nations of the world to praise God's grandeur and God's care for the people (vv. 4-6). Rescued, the psalmist trusts that Yahweh will always be there in moments of danger, continuing the earlier protection (vv. 7-8).

Psalm 139

This famous psalm resembles a thanksgiving (B) in that it narrates God's merciful care in the past (vv. 1-18), and an individual lament (A) in that it prays that sinners be punished (vv. 19-24). The drama is simple: the psalmist is keenly aware of the Lord's penetrating gaze (vv. 1-6), of God's guidance in every part of the universe (vv. 7-12), and of God's control over the psalmist's very self

(vv. 13-14). Verses 17-18 are an expression of wonder summing up verses 1-16. There is only one thing that can keep God and psalmist apart—sin. The psalm speaks of sin in verses 19-24.

The Bible frequently imagines the world as divided into two communities—the wicked and the righteous. The psalmist prays to be reckoned in the number of the righteous, that is to be separated from the wicked. He opens his being to God; if there is any evil, let it be cleansed (vv. 23-24).

Psalm 140

In this individual lament (A) the psalmist, beset by liars and attackers (vv. 2-6), makes a statement of trust in God in the temple (vv. 7-8). The psalmist prays that the wicked people's plans fall back upon their own heads (vv. 9-12). Verses 13-14 presumably are the statement of praise that the psalmist utters after receiving an assurance of salvation from the priest (not transmitted in psalms of lament). The psalmist expects the Lord to exercise judgment in a public way by punishing the liars and attackers and by upholding him, one of "the afflicted," "the poor," "the just," "the upright," that is, a member of the group that God has promised to uphold.

Psalm 141

This individual lament (A) is uttered by a person who is aware that only the righteous can properly worship God and who, consequently, is fearful of becoming one of the unrighteous through personal sin. In the perspective of this and other psalms of the "two ways," there are two groups of people: the righteous, pleasing to God, whose works perdure; and the unrighteous, hostile to God, rootless and doomed. The psalmist prays to be among the just, whose prayer is acceptable (vv. 1-2). God must, therefore, guard the person against being drawn into the plots and feasts of the wicked.

Verses 3-5 may be compared to Ps 85:11. The gist: Better to be reproved by the righteous than to be feted by the unrighteous. Verses 6-7 are corrupt; the translation is a guess. In verses 8-10 the psalmist prays to be saved from the corrupting fellowship of the wicked. Only God can admit one to the company of the just.

Psalm 142

The persecuted speaker of this lament (A) feels utterly alone (v. 5), exhausted (v. 7), and may actually be imprisoned (v. 8) prior to undergoing an ordeal to prove guilt or innocence (see Lev 24:12 and Num 15:34). Prison is possibly a metaphor for general distress. In the temple the psalmist lays out the complaint: attacks by the wicked with no one to give protection (vv. 2-5). Nonetheless, the psalmist still hopes that the just God will rectify the unjust situation ("you know my path," v. 4). The opening cry for help is repeated in verse 6, with a more vivid expression of hope and a more vivid complaint and prayer in verses 7-8ab. The last two verses of the poem are the vow of praise the psalmist makes after receiving an assurance from the priest: the Lord always protects the just, among whom is the psalmist.

Psalm 143

In this lament (A), ranked among the church's Penitential Psalms, the psalmist prays to be freed from death-dealing enemies. Verses 1-2 contain a straightforward address to God, made with a keen sense that there is no equality between God and humans; salvation is utterly gracious. Verses 3-4 contain the complaint: the psalmist is the victim of evil people. Verse 5 is much more vivid than most translations suggest; the verbs mean "to recite aloud." The psalmist recites the old stories of God's rescues of the poor from the power of evil, and the recitation encourages him to pray for personal salvation now (vv. 6-9). Mere rescue from the present danger is not enough, however. The psalmist goes on to pray that God's life-giving breath inspire the psalmist's life and give protection from enemies (vv. 10-12).

Psalm 144

The psalm seems to reflect a ceremony at which the king, the leader of Israel's armies, asked God's help in national crises (vv. 1-8). The tone of the poem shifts abruptly in verse 9 from pleading to thanksgiving, and then (verse 11 apart) it shifts again to prayer for the well-being of the people.

Verses 1-4 acknowledge that all the king's military prowess is from the Lord; the king, like any human being, is fragile and undeserving of God's help. May the Divine Warrior fight for Israel with the storm weapons of thunder and lightning (vv. 5-7). Perhaps in response to an oracle assuring divine assistance to Israel (not transmitted), the king vows to praise God for the expected victory. The victory is given in virtue of the divine promise to be with "David, your servant," not because of the king's military skill (vv. 9-11). The psalm concludes with the king, representing the people before God, praying for *shalom*, peace in its fullness.

Psalm 145

The hymn (C) is acrostic, that is, each verse begins with a successive letter of the Hebrew alphabet. The poem, like most acrostics, states several themes without developing them much. In verses 1-3 and 21 the singer invites "all flesh" to bless the name of the Lord. The "works of the Lord," God's activity in the world, make God present and invite the praise of all. According to verses 4-7, unending generations give thanks to the Lord, their thanksgiving climaxing in the confession of verses 8-9. Verses 10-20 urge all to acknowledge and acclaim the kingship of Yahweh, which directs all human activity in justice and love. The kingship of Yahweh will become a major theme of Jewish and Christian literature.

Psalm 146

The singer of this hymn (C) urges the hearers to praise and rely upon the Lord who rules all, and at the same time warns against relying upon mere mortals, no matter how powerful they seem. Verses 1-2 and 10 constitute the invitatory; the psalmist's exhortation to self is a model to all. The psalmist's concept of praising implies reliance upon God alone—hence the exhortation not to rely on human beings in the place of God (vv. 3-4). Israel's happiness is assured if it relies upon its God, "the God of Jacob," who created all things. Part of creation is the governance of the people. God's powerful care makes an environment fit for humans and maintains society in justice and peace (vv. 5-9). God's kingship is expressed in the favor shown to the oppressed and to those who rely upon God's help alone (v. 10).

Psalm 147

The hymn (C) is divided into three sections by separate commands to praise (vv. 1-6,

7-11, and 12-20). In the first section people are to acclaim God, who has built Jerusalem by bringing back the exiles. Verse 4 shows Yahweh's power over the divine beings who were thought to be in the stars, controlling the fate of human beings. Yahweh's control of even them means that nothing can hinder the people's return.

The second section hymns the God who makes the earth bring forth vegetation for animals and humans; from the latter a free and loving response is called for.

The third and climactic section exhorts the holy city to recognize that it has been re-created and that it is the privileged place of divine disclosure. From there Yahweh sends forth the word to Israel alone of all the nations, a word that is as life-giving as water.

Psalm 148

This hymn (C) invites the beings of heaven (vv. 1-6) and of earth (vv. 7-14) to praise the Lord. The singer does not distinguish between inanimate and animate (and rational) nature. Since every being hangs upon the divine decree (a better translation than "duty" in verse 6), it is oriented by that fact toward God (vv. 5-6). The motive for earth's praise in verse 13 is noteworthy: because "his name alone is exalted; his majesty is above earth and heaven." The name is what makes one present to another. Only Yahweh among all the "gods" is truly present on earth, and hence only Yahweh deserves acclaim. Verse 14 is the climax, which may be paraphrased in this way: Of all the peoples on earth, God has chosen Israel ("lift up the horn" = "to strengthen," "to favor") to render special thanks and praise to God.

Psalm 149

The hymn (C) is sung by "the lowly" (v. 4), who have sought asylum from danger in the temple on Zion. The hymn resembles songs of Zion (Psalms 2, 46, 48, 76): Zion is Yahweh's inviolable dwelling, where impious kings are defeated. Verses 1-3 invite Israel, gathered in Zion, to shout joyfully to its Creator. The reason is given in verse 4: the Lord loves Israel and protects "the lowly," those who have made the Lord their refuge. Verses 5-9 describe the equipping of the people who have sought protection. In the power of their Lord they attack and defeat the kings assaulting the holy city. At this critical hour the people are the means whereby the Lord's glory is displayed to the nations.

Psalm 150

A fitting end to the Psalter, this hymn (C) calls upon all in the temple and under the sky, "all flesh," to give due honor to God. A variety of musical instruments underline and unify the human voices. The reason for the praise is scarcely developed amid all the imperatives to sing and play. Verse 2 explains that praise is due because of Yahweh's mastery of nature and history.

SONG OF SONGS, RUTH, LAMENTATIONS, ECCLESIASTES, ESTHER

James A. Fischer, C.M.

INTRODUCTION

This commentary contains an explanation of five books of the Old Testament called Megilloth ("scrolls") by the Jews. They are gathered together for convenience, since the Jews read them on feast days in the synagogue. The tradition, however, is not constant and unanimous, and it is certainly not as old as the books.

The Song of Songs comes first because it was read during Passover. There are passages in the Song that speak of winter being over, so it is appropriate for the spring. The Exodus seems to be suggested by the reference to Pharaoh's steeds (Song 1:9). Most of all, the Song speaks of youth and love, and that is certainly the theme of Passover.

The Book of Ruth was read for the feast of Shavvoth, an early harvest festival, or what Christians call Pentecost. The story of Ruth takes place during the harvest season. There was also an ancient tradition that King David was born on Shavvoth.

The Book of Lamentations was read on the ninth of Ab, which is in July or August. This is the traditional date for the destruction of the temple by the Roman emperor Titus in A.D. 70. It was, therefore, a day of mourning.

The Book of Ecclesiastes was read on Succoth, the most popular of the three major feasts. Succoth was celebrated in the fall as a farmers' festival for gathering in the grape and olive harvests. The theme of aging, either of the year or of people, fits both the festival and the book. Some traditions said that the Song of Songs remembered Solomon in his youth, and Ecclesiastes in his old age, since both books refer to Solomon. However, using Ecclesiastes for synagogue reading is the least consistent part of the tradition and a rather late development. Some groups do not use it at all.

The Book of Esther contains the story that is the basis for the celebration of the feast of Purim, a kind of Jewish Mardi Gras. This tradition began in Persia and only later spread to Western Judaism. It apparently was an attempt to counteract pagan New Year's celebrations.

The Greek translation of the Bible known as the Septuagint, which was completed by at least 100 B.C.E., has a different order for these five books. The Book of Ruth is put right after the Book of Judges. The New American Bible follows the Greek in the order of books.

The curious grouping here offers an opportunity for a word about the kind of commentary given for these books. There is no common theme or approach in the books themselves. Ruth and Esther are stories, but of very different kinds; the Song of Songs is love poetry, and Lamentations is sad poetry; Ecclesiastes is an essay on human life. Since they are all so different, they cannot all be interpreted in the same way. The conclusions to be reached will depend on the method one adopts to interpret them.

If the principal concern is to discover what the original Hebrew text said, then we must study differences that have occurred in copying the manuscripts and alternate ways of understanding the text. This is called *textual* and *grammatical criticism*. The commentary will occasionally refer to such verbal problems. If we want to find out what actually happened, we need *historical criticism* to get at "the facts," as much as possible. There are no serious historical problems in our books. If we want to know how the original units were composed according to standard forms of writing, we need *form-criticism*. This will concern us often. If we want to know how these units were put together to form a book, we use *redaction criticism*. If we ask what role this book plays within the whole body of the canonical Scripture, we need *canonical criticism*. And if we ask how this story or poetry or essay works as literature and how good it is, we need *literary* or *rhetorical criticism*.

Each of these methods can only tell us something about the text; none of them is immediately the key to interpretation. All of them are important, but they do not get at what the ordinary reader of the Bible wants to know, namely, how does it help my faith or spiritual understanding? To make the step to a spiritual meaning for ourselves, we must appropriate the reading into our own experience. This commentary is written largely from the viewpoint of rhetorical criticism, in the hope that that will give us the quickest and closest approach to experience.

SONG OF SONGS

James A. Fischer, C.M.

INTRODUCTION

The problem with the Song of Songs is to find some honest reason why it should be in the Bible. Unlike most other books of the Old Testament, it has nothing to do with the sacred history, the law, the covenant, or the prophets. In fact, it does not even mention God. It seems to be a somewhat disjointed collection of popular love songs. We do not know when it was written or by whom; we do not know for what purpose it was written or for what it was used.

The Jews themselves had misgivings about including this book in their list of sacred writings. At the final determination made by the teachers of Judaism about A.D. 90, much discussion took place. The matter was finally settled when Rabbi Akiba, one of the leaders, was won over to the interpretation of the Song of Songs as reflecting the marriage of Yahweh to the chosen people. It was finally appointed for reading in the synagogue during the feast of Passover. Christians accepted the book as sacred without dispute, but its use in the liturgy was rather restricted. In later times various passages were applied to the Virgin Mary on her feasts.

Literary form

At first reading the Song seems to be a jumble of poetry in which various parties are speaking. Unfortunately, they keep shifting, and whatever plot there may be keeps disappearing. The New American Bible translation helps by identifying in the margin who is speaking. A girl lover (designated *B* for bride) can be identified as expressing her longing; a shepherd and/or king (designated *G* for bridegroom) is also actively involved. These identifications have a long history; they were first noted in Greek manuscripts made about A.D. 400. A vague "we" and some "daughters of Jerusalem" (designated *D*) also appear. Solomon and brothers of the bride complete the cast (these are not designated by any letter in the text). None of this is particularly consistent; as soon as the poetry begins to concentrate on one person or theme, it dissolves and another scene unfolds.

Discerning some structure in these eight chapters is a frustrating quest. Efforts have been made to read the Song as a story, but there is too little plot, except for a general feeling that the lovers are finally united despite the efforts of antagonists such as the brothers and perhaps the king to keep them separate. Since much of the poetry is couched in direct speech, attempts have been made to cast the Song as a drama or a dramatic reading. No agreement has been reached, however, as to how the parts should be played or by whom. More important, we have no evidence that dramatic presentations, whether in the temple or elsewhere, were ever a part of Jewish life.

This leads to a theory that the Song of Songs is simply an unstructured collection. The use of direct speech in love poetry can be illustrated from other ancient cultures, particularly Egyptian. Different parts of the discourse can be classified on the basis of themes and forms. Thus we have titles assigned by scholars, such as: song of admiration, self-description, the tease, song of yearning, description of a love-related experience, descriptive song, boasting song, and so on. The meanings are usually self-evident, and the forms do show some consistency in the elements used to compose them. Unfortunately, they do not shed a great deal of light on how one should interpret the passages. How these poems functioned is still unknown. Were they simply notes written between lovers? Recited? Used at weddings? Some sort of popular music of which we know nothing? All of this eludes us.

The explanation that the Song is simply a collection of about twenty-five love poems or sayings has its own difficulty by way of being too little. There is something of a story line in the Song. A girl loves a shepherd boy. She desires to be with him and sometimes fantasizes about him as a king and herself as a queen. But something keeps them apart. Verbs of coming and going, which are characteristics of storytelling, abound. And there is tension: at the end something—a lattice, a gate, a departure, watchmen—prevents them from the final touch.

This much of a story line clearly exists: there are characters with a definite form, movement, tension, and a resolution. The outline of it is faint and overlaid with a kaleidoscope of love imagery, which keeps intruding. The pictures are mostly from the rustic life of those who live closely with nature. The girl is a dove, sweet-scented, like a lily of the valley, beautiful, adorned with gems, enclosed in a garden. The boy is a gazelle, fleet, gentle as a lily, glitteringly beautiful as ivory or gold. He is neither warrior nor hunter, but perfumed and handsome. King Solomon enters either as competitor or fantasy. The images of him are always of opulence, and he is rejected. The imagery as well as the story line sets up a tension here.

The mood is one of "love conquers all"—but not yet. Love is celebrated in all its physical joy. Lips are made to be kissed and savored like good wine, breasts to be admired, hair to be caressed, the wedding couch to be enjoyed. The invitation is to meet beneath the apple tree where your mother conceived. The mood of love is unrestrained by prudery, but not by prudence.

Do not arouse, do not stir up love,
    before its own time (8:4).

The mood may be destroyed by our own reaction to some of the imagery. Who could love a girl whose nose is like a tower of Lebanon and whose hair is like a flock of goats, or a boy whose hair is like palm fronds? Our own love imagery may appear as odd to others. At any rate, these comparisons do seem to come from a fairly conventional vocabulary of love.

The meaning of the book

Over the centuries both Jews and Christians have tended to give the Song a symbolic meaning and have thus avoided the plain references to physical love and its ecstatic emotions. The marriage of Yahweh to Israel or of Christ to the Church has dominated. Sometimes, as in the Christian liturgy, the girl has become the Virgin Mary. In the writings of the mystics the individual soul has often been the soul's yearning for her lover, Christ.

How this identification is made determines much of the interpretation. If the interpretation is allegorical, then every verse and every detail has a secret meaning in which this equals that. Obviously this has spiritual value; equally, it may become silly if it is carried too far. Some commentators have opted for parable, that is, it is the story line, not the details, that parallels the spiritual meaning in our own lives, either communal or individual. This avoids difficulties and has much to commend it, but since the story line is so tenuous, it leaves much of the text without meaning.

Completely different is the wisdom interpretation. In this view the Song is indeed composed of popular love songs joined only by a whisper of a plot. Human love is good. It need not be justified by esoteric spiritual reasonings. The sages taught that God's order and goodness pervade all; there is no such thing as the secular. The love of boy and girl is one of God's beauties. Even so, it went far beyond emotion. One was aware of a secret, mysterious force, an uncontrollable power that might overwhelm. So we have the only explanation of the refrain which links together the various songs:

Set me as a seal on your heart,
    as a seal on your arm;
For stern as death is love,
    relentless as the nether world is devotion;
    its flames are a blazing fire.

Deep waters cannot quench love,
 nor floods sweep it away.
Were one to offer all he owns to purchase love,
 he would be roundly mocked (8:6-7).

If one adopts this viewpoint, then the Song turns back the corner of the page of human love to reveal a deeper reality. The overall in-terpretation adopted in this commentary is that the Song originated as somewhat isolated love songs, was arranged in the order in which it now stands to give a faint story line, which built up to the climax expressed in the wisdom saying in 8:6: "For stern as death is love."

COMMENTARY

1:1 The title. The title "Song of Songs" is not part of the canonical text but was added later. "Song of Songs" is simply a Hebrew su-perlative: "The best song." "By Solomon" simply says that the tradition associated the Song with Solomon in some way. As it stands, it has a whole gamut of possible mean-ings: Solomon as author, Solomon as inspirer of all song and wisdom, Solomon as king of marriage, etc.

1:2-4 Invitation to a wedding. This first song seems to be an invitation to a wedding. The bride is looking forward to wedding kisses. The invited "we" are presumably the bride's party ("daughters of Jerusalem"); the king is the bridegroom, either in fantasy or as a title in wedding festivities. Some sort of exchange of voices in the song is indicated by the switch of speakers from "me" to "we" and by the marginal notations. This song in-troduces us to the setting of joy and praise for the bride and groom.

1:5-6 Praise of the bride. The second song is a song praising the bride herself. She is a sunburned girl, perhaps in contrast to the city daughters of Jerusalem. Yet she is not a naive country girl, but a coquette, as her brothers had found out. She had not taken care of her own "vineyard" (a biblical stand-in word for one's self), perhaps by dalliance with her lover, so they put her to work taking care of real vineyards.

1:7-8 A duet of love. This duet sings of the search for love. The girl wants to know where her shepherd-lover is so that she will not be annoyed along her way by falling in with other shepherds. His reply implies that she knows well enough where they are ac-customed to meet.

1:9-11 The girl's beauty. Comparing the girl to a horse may seem ungracious to us. This is a special kind of horse, however—one of Pharaoh's chariot steeds. The text seems to suggest sexual appeal as the point of the com-parison. This horse is a mare, and mares were not used in war; in fact, they were kept far from the stallions lest they distract them. The rest of the song describes the attractiveness of the bride. Perhaps it is another way of look-ing back to those shepherds in verse 7, who would have been glad to have had the girl wandering among them.

1:12-17 A wedding duet. This last duet in chapter 1 is an exchange of anticipations about the wedding feast. The girl can only de-scribe the coming delights in terms of per-fumes; then the bride and groom exchange professions of the beauty they see in each other. Oddly, the girl's eyes are said to be like doves. Just what is intended is not clear—perhaps "sparkling" if the dove's iridescence is the point, or "gentle and loving," as some of the ancients believed. The final wish is for the bridal chamber, pictured here as a mag-nificent hall made of cedar and cypress.

2:1-7 A love duet. This unit consists of a duet between the girl and her lover, followed by a description of the arousal of love, and ending with the refrain in verse 7. It seems to be separate from the springtime song which follows and which is less passionate. The re-frain (see also 3:5 and 8:4) always occurs at the climax of the love scenes. The action here proceeds from the introduction of the girl as a lily of the valley (beautiful) and the boy as an apple tree (a symbol of sexual desirability in some way) to the bridal chamber and a de-sire for sexual union, but it ends with an ad-monition not to go too fast.

2:4 "His emblem over me is love" seems to be the obvious reading of the Hebrew text. The "emblem" seems to be some sort of mili-tary insignia. As such, it does not make much sense, and we do not know to what it might refer.

2:5 Raisin cakes were foods considered to be an aid to love, but we know nothing more specific. Cookies in the form or symbol of love goddesses were used in the banqueting of some fertility rites, but the connection with Israelite courting customs is not at all clear.

2:7 The refrain begins solemnly with an adjuration that interrupts the passionate wishes of the girl. The appeal to gazelles and hinds may be to animals that were thought to be amorous, or the phrase in Hebrew may be a stand-in for the similar-sounding "by the Lord of hosts," just as our old-fashioned "Jiminy Crickets" is really a substitute for "Jesus Christ."

"Do not arouse, do not stir up love before its own time" is not exactly what the Hebrew text says. The word "time" is not used in Hebrew; it is only implied in the conjunction "until," that is, "until it is satiated or eager." Whatever the exact sense, it is clear that some brake is being applied to the runaway love-making previously described, since we have a solemn oath and an admonition of some sort. More will be said about this at 8:6.

2:8-17 The springtime song of love. This delightful love song has left its traces in our own literature from "In the spring a young man's fancy" to "The voice of the turtle dove is heard in the land." It is a self-contained song as defined by the theme and the use of "gazelle" at the beginning and end. This is an ancient way of marking off a unit, much as we use paragraphs.

This song begins with a gentle longing, a considerable cooling off of the passionate phrases in the preceding verses. The young girl seems to be confined at home behind a wall, windows, and lattices. Yet she keeps hearing her lover's invitation: winter is over, the time for love is here. She will not go to him, but she can tease him with hints that others may be vying for her favors.

2:9-10 The lover is pictured as coming from afar to visit his beloved. Something keeps them apart, and he can only rush around, gazing through windows, peering through lattices. Why she does not come out to meet him or invite him in is not revealed, but the poem centers on longing that cannot be satisfied. And yet it should be.

2:11-13 All this delightful imagery, including the dove, which is a sure sign of spring, hints at a proper time for love, as 2:7

had hinted and as Qoheleth will later express in his song about a time for everything (see Eccl 3:8).

2:15 "Catch us the foxes" is apparently a line from a well-known song. Its connection is not entirely clear. The girl is the vineyard; foxes are predators, and the intimation is that this girl has a lot of them watching her and needs protection. This is called a tease song.

3:1-11 A wedding dream. Although this chapter can be divided between a song of seeking and finding (vv. 1-5) and a description of a wedding procession (vv. 6-11), the two need to be connected to account for the second half. The poem begins with a dream wish by the girl and ends with a picture of the king on the day of his marriage. That is what the dream is all about, and the wedding procession is a fantasy creation.

We left the girl in chapter 2 still confined to her home. Now in her dream she is wandering the streets of the city looking for her lover. The watchmen cannot tell her where he is, but love can. She finds him and holds him fast, but then the dream is restrained by the refrain and the admonition not to arouse love before its time. This is followed by another dream fantasy of a wedding procession in which her lover is King Solomon coming to his wedding couch in splendor.

3:3 Among the many shifts of scene in the song we have this change from countryside to city. The watchmen, of course, are the police.

3:4 In the preceding song the girl knew where her lover was but could not or would not go out to him. Now she does not know where he is and must look for him. She intends to bring him to her mother's house (v. 4). We do not know why she would not have brought him there before, or what cultic or mythological background there may be for such a statement. Numerous solutions have been offered.

3:5 Whatever the situation implied in verse 4 may be, it is quite clear that the girl wanted to seal her marriage at home. But just before the final act, the refrain is once more introduced to delay the consuming expression of love.

3:6-11 The description given here is certainly of a royal procession connected with a marriage, but it does not fit the facts we know about Solomon. It is part of a dream sequence like the preceding; the girl is dreaming of her lover as King Solomon and fantasizing her wedding day. The physical descriptions given here, the column of smoke, the perfumes, the sixty valiant soldiers, the dangers in the watches of the night, the wood of Lebanon, the columns and roofs and ivory, etc., are all mentioned in connection with something pertinent to kings and gods and weddings in the Old Testament, but never together. We can only assume that this is a product of imagination.

4:1–5:1 A song of longing. Verses 1-7 are a song in praise of the physical beauty of the girl. It is a well-known type of hymn from Hebrew and Arabic styles. Assigning it a name does not help very much to interpret what it means, but it does take away some of the strangeness of the details describing the girl's beauty. This leads to an admiration song (vv. 8-11) that is more symbolic. It begins with an invitation to a celebration, and then speaks of the girl in terms of a garden (v. 12). This is common biblical imagery for one's beloved. The garden is fragrant, fruitful, and full of delights. Then the beloved is called "a fountain sealed." The fountain of flowing water is a symbol of life. What is being spoken of, therefore, is a faithful and fruitful marriage. This part of the song ends with an invitation to the friends of the bridegroom to eat and drink of the wine of love.

4:1 In content all this verse says is that the girl has long hair, but the image is one of richness and constantly changing shades.

4:2 Once again the physical fact is simply praise for the girl's white and regular teeth, which are as extraordinary as ewes having twins.

4:3 The girl has firm and rosy cheeks. The pomegranate is something like an orange, reddish in color.

4:4 We do not know what David's tower was, but that would not help very much anyway. Apparently the picture is of a lady, stately and erect, who is wearing tiers of necklaces, which suggests the battlements, bucklers, and shields of which the poet speaks.

4:5 The picture is one of softness and perfection. The gazelle is the boy, and he is a lotus-eater. This last image conjures up some idea of a drug-like ecstasy. All these physical images are probably foreign to our tastes.

4:8 Lebanon is far to the north. The other

places mentioned—Amana, Senir and Hermon—are also remote, sometimes unknown. The poet intends to create a feeling that a great distance separates the lovers. To complete the image, he mentions the haunt of lions and the leopard's mountains.

Consistently in this song (vv. 9, 10, 12, and 5:1) the girl is described as "my sister, my bride." Considering the broad usage of "sister" in the Bible, this is not surprising. Love's relationship is reinforced by a reference to family ties, whether real or conferred.

4:12 The Hebrew text has a stronger expression: "sealed garden." The reference is to a signet ring that can be used only by the owner. The enclosure is to keep away those who do not have a right to be present.

4:15 The fountain suggests life, as does the following description: "flowing fresh from Lebanon." Prov 5:15-20 has a beautiful use of the same imagery, with a strong emphasis on the husband's obligation to be faithful to his own fountain: "Let your fountain be yours alone."

5:1 The bridegroom has arrived and shares his gladness by inviting his friends to the wedding banquet.

5:2–6:3 A dream sequence. This is the longest continuous passage in the Song, but it is probably a secondary addition. Basically it is a dream sequence in which the girl loses and finds her lover. As in a dream, the action is disjointed and illogical. However, there is motion as the girl hears her lover trying to get in the gate, but then being too late when she finally gets up to admit him. She pursues him through the city at night but cannot find him. The watchmen beat her, and she has to appeal to the daughters of Jerusalem to help her find him. At the end she finds him in her garden. The search sequence is interrupted by a praise song for the boy, which leads up to a final song of yearning and fulfillment.

5:4 From the later reference to a lock (v. 5), it would appear that the boy was reaching through the keyhole to open the door. Ancient keys and locking devices were huge, often made of wood. Apparently by the time the girl had beautified herself ("With my fingers dripping choice myrrh"), he had already gone.

5:7 In this dream the girl is now roaming the streets at night. The watchmen naturally consider her an intruder or a prostitute.

5:8 It is quite unrealistic for the daughters of Jerusalem to appear so suddenly at night, but this is a dream. The dialogue between them is only hinted at. After the girl explains her search, they ask: "What shall we tell him?" As the next section demands, they also ask what he looks like.

5:11 It is probable that "palm fronds" simply means "curled" or "luxuriant."

5:12 Previously the girl's eyes were described as dovelike, but here there is added "beside running waters." Possibly the bridegroom has dark pupils, as suggested by doves, and sparkling irises, as suggested by running water.

5:14 That the lover's arms should be described as gold is understandable; in the next verse his legs are columns of marble. But the word "rods" is strangely inappropriate, although it is an accurate translation.

6:3 The final statement of the girl is that she, and she alone, claims her lover. "Browsing among the lilies" probably has sexual connotations. The refrain that urges restraint is not used at this point, although the adjuration was mentioned in 5:8. As noted at the beginning, this section seems to be a secondary addition.

6:4-12 A description and a meeting. Most of chapter 6 seems to be a song of admiration for the girl, leading first to a rejection of the royal beauties and then a choice of the girl alone, and ending in an enigmatic description of some meeting between the two. As we will see, the chapter ends in an unintelligible statement where we would expect some decisive development in the love affair.

6:4 Tirzah was the capital of the northern kingdom of Israel between 930 and 880 B.C.E. On this basis some commentators have dated the whole Song of Songs. The text is quite clear about the name of the city, but we have no information as to why Tirzah was considered beautiful or how the girl was like it. Oddly enough, the very ancient Greek translation and the Jewish paraphrases read: "You are beautiful and pleasing," but we do not know how they got this wording.

The phrase "as awe-inspiring as bannered troops" recurs in verse 10. It is the only harsh image used of the girl, and one wonders why it is used. If the text is accepted, some reference must be made to the usual mythology of the goddess of love who is also the goddess of war. If the text is emended, it will probably read: "as awe-inspiring as these great sights."

6:8 Previously the girl had fantasized about her lover as though he were King Solomon; here the boy seems to be daydreaming about his girl as a queen whom he would choose in preference to innumerable royal ladies. The "sixty . . . eighty . . . without number" progression is probably an escalating superlative built up from twenty times three, four, and *x*. At any rate, as the next verse says: "One alone is my dove," and she is better than all.

6:11 The last part of this poem is spoken by the boy, who wants to see if the girl is ready to receive him. Clearly, she is the garden. Here the garden is described as a nut garden, specifically a walnut garden. The word occurs only here in the Bible and we have no idea what its significance might be.

6:12 This must be the decisive verse in chapter 6 because chapter 7 will treat a quite different topic. Unfortunately we have no clear idea what the Hebrew text means. English translations differ widely. The New Jewish Version has: "Before I knew it, my desire set me amid the chariots of Ammi-nadib," and the Anchor Bible reads: "Unawares I was set in the chariot with the prince." In effect, we do not know what happened in the walnut garden.

7:1–8:4 A song of yearning and restraint. It might be well to consider this section together, however disparate and disconnected the individual units. Here we begin with a dance that displays the girl's charms (7:1-6); sexual closeness under the image of climbing a palm tree (7:7-11); a yearning for love under the image of springtime awakening (7:12-14); and finally a fervid desire for union, ending in the refrain that counsels the proper moment (8:1-4). The shifts in scene and speakers (sometimes enigmatic, as in 7:10) suggest that these songs were originally independent and so do not fit neatly together. Yet, they are all full of motion, and the action does seem to be going somewhere—hence the importance of the conception of a story line, however faintly hinted at. All this depends, of course, on what one has read consistently into the refrain.

7:1 We really do not know what the term "Shulammite" implies. It may be the feminine form of Solomon (like the name Salome in the New Testament), or it may be derived from a town in Esdraelon noted for its beautiful women, or it may have a hint of "the peaceful one." None of these meanings, however, helps us to understand the significance better. Neither do we know what kind of dance is referred to here. Suggestions have been made of a sword dance, a special dance before a wedding, or a war dance. However out of place the last-mentioned may be, it does have something to do with the description.

7:5 Whether this is a special, well-known tower, or whether Mount Lebanon looks like a tower is unclear. In any event, it probably does not increase our aesthetic response.

7:8 The palm tree is a symbol of richness and fertility. Its figs hang in clusters by the hundreds.

7:10 As indicated in the New American Bible text, the speaker shifts suddenly from the groom to the bride in the middle of the sentence. We suspect that two poems have been run together here, and not very skillfully. The imagery also shifts suddenly from the palm tree to a springtime scene in the country.

7:11 Previously the girl had said: "My lover belongs to me and I to him" (6:3). There is a different emphasis here. She is committed to him and recognizes that he must be drawn to her. The phrase "for me he yearns" is reminiscent of Gen 3:16: "your urge shall be for your husband." These are the only times in the Bible that the expression is used. Something more than physical passion is hinted at.

7:14 Mandrakes are underground tubers related to the potato and reputed to have aphrodisiac powers. This verse again brings out the intensity of physical love.

8:1 Although this is a separate song of yearning, it goes naturally with the preceding. Indeed, there would be no climax to chapter 7 without this. Something still keeps the lovers apart. The girl wishes that her lover were her brother so that she could freely consort with him.

8:4 The poetic climax is reached with the repetition of the refrain just at the moment of most intense feeling. The Hebrew wording of the text is somewhat different here than previously. The appeal to the gazelles and hinds is dropped; after "I adjure you" we have not

a request but a prohibition. In other words, the reading is shorter but stronger.

The New American Bible translation ends the sentence with "Do not arouse, do not stir up love, before its own time." This implies that the time is not yet here. Various other translations and commentators understand that the time has come to reach the conclusion of the longing. Such an interpretation depends upon an understanding of the total Song of Songs as culminating in the fulfillment of love's desires. Then one needs to explain from a literary, aesthetic viewpoint why this happens three times in the Song and yet the poem continues. The more normal and traditional understanding of the refrain would imply that every time love reaches its climax, something hinders the final consummation. What this is will depend upon the interpretation given to the following section.

8:5-14 Finale. The finale of the Song of Songs is a series of disjointed and perhaps fragmentary pieces. It begins with verse 5, which, according to the New American Bible text, is a jerky dialogue between the daughters of Jerusalem and the groom. The bride is coming to meet her lover. As she approaches, he points out the apple tree under which he was conceived. This is followed by what appears to be a completely incongruous reference to love being as stern as death. Then there is some sort of dialogue between the brothers, who do not want their little sister to get married yet, but she is determined to go ahead. It ends with a final song of the bride that she prefers her lover to all of Solomon's wealth and desires only him.

It is agreed by all that verses 6-7 are decisive for the meaning of the Song of Songs. It is also clear on purely poetic grounds that the songs turn much more serious at this point. The playful celebration of falling in love is replaced by serious thoughts of childbearing. The allusion to the apple tree under which one of them was conceived sounds a new note. The love they have been enjoying is recognized as being as relentless as death. Once committed, they cannot escape. The girl's response is a deliberate and free choice of total fidelity. The final choice of her lover instead of Solomon's wealth also sets her future unchangeably. The insight of the Song, therefore, seems to be that however delightful falling in love may be, its flames have an unquenchable power that cannot be extinguished.

8:5 A problem exists here as to who is speaking. The Hebrew text indicates that it was the boy's mother who conceived and that the speaker is the girl. The whole of verse 5 seems to be rather fragmentary. What is decisive for our understanding is that the question of children is introduced for the first time.

8:6 "Stern" is "relentless." That is the common description of death in many passages of the Old Testament. Death is a hunter that cannot be eluded. The parallel line reinforces the idea: "relentless as the nether world is devotion," and this in turn is further strengthened by "its flames are a blazing fire." It is possible to translate the final word as "a flame of God," but that is unusual both as translation and within the context of the Song.

8:7 The metaphor is not of putting out a fire, but of death as a raging torrent that cannot be held back. The picture is used consistently in the Old Testament. The only power stronger than death is love, but the point of the comparison is the enormous strength of both. The final saying here, "Were one to offer all he owns to purchase love, he would be roundly mocked," is not in poetic form and seems to be an inserted wise saying.

8:8 The brothers object that their sister is too young for marriage and childbearing. The following description about building up a wall and protecting a door describes their strategy in military terms. They do not seem to be cruel in their plans but want to overwhelm the girl with gifts. She rejects this by asserting that she is ready for marriage.

8:11 The sudden shift seems to have nothing to do with Solomon as such. The girl is simply saying that even if she were offered the wealth of Solomon, she would still choose her lover. In verse 12 she asserts her own independence: "My vineyard is at my own disposal."

8:13 The conclusion begins with an appeal by the boy to learn what his lover's final choice will be. Her response is, "Be swift, my lover." We have come to a decisive conclusion. However, it will be noted from the remarks above on this last section that the final choice is not of the pleasure of love-making but of the acceptance of love as a power that demands total commitment.

RUTH

James A. Fischer, C.M.

INTRODUCTION

The story

The best way to read the Book of Ruth is simply as a good story. It really is a short story, one of the best that has come down from antiquity. In four brief chapters the author has created unforgettable characters and a plot that involves us in our own solution.

The actions can be briefly described in scenes:

ACT ONE—*Prelude: Naomi the Loser* (1:1-22)

Naomi, a pleasant and capable Jewish girl, follows her husband into the frontier land of Moab during a famine, raises a family, loses her husband and her children, and is forced by another famine to return to Bethlehem. There she curses God for having taken everything from her.

ACT TWO—*The Harvest and the Matchmaking* (2:1-3:18)

In Bethlehem, Naomi sends her daughter-in-law Ruth to glean in the fields. Ruth meets Boaz, a rich bachelor, and is encouraged by Naomi to court him. Ruth and Boaz fall in love.

ACT THREE—*The Marriage Contract Concluded* (4:1-12)

Boaz must first clear up some legal problems connected with a field that Naomi wants to sell. The terms include an obligation to marry Ruth. Boaz settles the matter fairly and openly, and then takes Ruth as his wife.

ACT FOUR—*Conclusion: Naomi the Winner?* (4:13-16)

In due course a child is born to Ruth, but it is hailed by the local women as Naomi's. A curious genealogy (4:17-22) attributes the child to Boaz and traces the succeeding generations to David.

The history of the book

The setting of the story is during the days of the judges (approximately 1200–1050 B.C.E.), probably toward the end. There are no specific references in the text that would enable us to check more exactly the date or the historical accuracy. Although the Hebrew Bible placed Ruth among the Megilloth, the pre-Christian Greek translation known as the Septuagint put it after the Book of Judges. The least we can say is that there was an ancient tradition that the story belonged to the time of the judges. The picture it paints of early Israelite village life conforms to what we know of the era. Things such as the meeting place at the city gate, the words used for weights and measures, the names, the techniques of harvesting, and so on, all fit into our data.

The story was written at a later time. The first words, "Once in the time of the judges," indicate a distance between the writer and the events. In 4:7 the author explains a forgotten custom about handing over a sandal as a way of concluding an agreement. The book concludes with a genealogy that traces the descendants of Boaz down to the time of David (1004–965 B.C.E.). Most likely the story was written sometime shortly after David. Similar forms of storytelling, such as the story of Joseph in Egypt and the story of David, seem to come from about the same time.

The only alternate date of writing proposed is in postexilic times, more specifically in the fifth century B.C.E. Apart from a few late expressions, the argument for postexilic dating depends upon interpreting the book as a protest against the rather harsh marriage laws of Ezra and Nehemiah. However, this is to base the dating upon a very questionable interpretation of the story as story, as we shall see later.

Interpretation

One type of interpretation would center on the details concerning marriage regulations. The point of the story would be that from ancient times pagan girls were legitimately taken as wives, and entered into the stream of Israel's history. The problem with such explanations is that they do depend upon details, especially the concluding genealogy. That may or may not be an addition to the original text. In any case, it is clear that the story was not told simply to explain the genealogy.

Another set of interpretations centers on the example of the virtuous life illustrated by Ruth and Boaz. The word *hesed* (1:8; 2:10; 3:10), variously translated as "kind," "merciful," "loyal," is a key term in the story. Ruth is a gracious girl who sacrifices everything to embrace the God of Israel. Boaz is a magnanimous and kindly kinsman who rescues a family in distress. Concern for the poor is one of the major obligations of the chosen people. Loyalty to God and kinsfolk ranks high. This is undoubtedly an important impression created by the storyteller. Unfortunately, it has little to do with Acts One and Four of the story. Neglecting the beginning and ending of this story is like tearing out the first and last pages of a detective story.

The approach in this commentary is to consider the story first of all simply as story. As a rule of thumb, all storytelling is either hero story, tragedy, or comedy. The hero story leads the principal character through various perils to victory. It has a rather rigid chain of cause and effect. In the Bible there are very few hero stories, and God alone is the hero. If we interpret the Book of Ruth as an exemplar story of virtuous living, we have made it into a hero story. By and large, that neglects the character of Naomi and certainly downplays the role of God, who appears only in oblique references.

If we interpret the story as a protest against overly harsh marriage laws, then the Book of Ruth is a tragedy of sorts. A tragedy is a story that inevitably results in the destruction of the principal character. It is clear that this is not the plot of this story. The only tragedy may have been that the protest went unheard.

Comedy is the most difficult literary style. To be successful, a comedy must link together actions that have a certain fittingness and yet whose conclusion defies rational expectation. Most of the stories of the Bible are comedies in this sense. God's actions cannot be confined to normal human ways of acting. Obviously, we are not talking about comedy as fun or frivolity.

To get at the literary character of the Book of Ruth, we have to reflect on it as we do on other stories. First of all, it is a self-contained story, and we do not need to worry about where it begins and ends. Secondly, we instinctively develop our own pictures of the characters, and these are finely drawn in Ruth.

NAOMI is pictured at the beginning as an earlier Ruth—pious, practical, and loyal. But when she returns to Bethlehem, she changes into an embittered woman who blames God for all her troubles and demands an accounting from God. In the following chapters Naomi is pictured as a scheming woman who manipulates people to accomplish what God would not.

RUTH is a loving and loyal girl. She has a strange mixture of initiative and submissiveness.

BOAZ is pictured in regal dress. He is rich, magnanimous, discreet, and protective. He talks in a rather formal manner. At the end, however, he simply vanishes from the action.

YAHWEH has no speaking part, but the story is always aware of Yahweh's presence.

A good story needs tension or conflict. There is no tension between Ruth and Boaz or between Naomi and Ruth; the tension is between Naomi and God. It begins at the end of the first chapter when Naomi curses God. At the end the scheming woman has achieved her purpose of having an heir who assures her future. And yet the village women sing:

"Blessed is the Lord who has not failed to provide you today with an heir" (4:14). Who won? The comic conclusion leaps from the page, but the author leaves us to handle it ourselves.

COMMENTARY

NAOMI IN MOAB

Ruth 1:1-22

The first chapter sets the scene for the main action of the story. Here the action rushes along in breathless fashion. The famine triggers the migration to Moab. The characters are introduced briefly: Elimelech, Naomi, Mahlon, and Chilion. The husband dies; the two sons are married to Moabite women, Orpah and Ruth. Then the two sons die, and Naomi makes ready to go back to Bethlehem, since she has heard that the famine there has abated. It will be noticed that no adjectives are used; the story is bare-bone fact, but the facts are arranged in dry-eyed fashion to elicit our sympathy.

Then the pace slows to record Naomi's conversations with her daughters-in-law. This is a loving family that Naomi has presided over; the "Go back!" that is wrenched from her (1:8, 11, 12, 15) is mingled with tears. But Naomi is ever a realist, even when she is fantasizing about her own childless future. She accepts her fate as due to the hand of the Lord. Ruth refuses to leave her: "Wherever you go I will go, wherever you lodge I will lodge, your people shall be my people, and your God my God" (1:16). Ruth's dedication is first to Naomi and then to Yahweh.

So the two women go back to Bethlehem, and there in familiar surroundings Naomi's character suddenly changes. "Do not call me Naomi. Call me Mara, for the Almighty has made it very bitter for me" (1:20). The "amiable one" has become the "bitter one." The challenge to Yahweh has been laid down unequivocally and publicly. We are now fully informed as to what the point of the story will be.

1:1 The narrator indicates clearly that this is a story; no interest is shown in citing specifics of time or place that could be tied to historical facts.

1:2 We do not know the exact significance of Ephrathites. The tribe of Ephraim lived far to the north, so the reference cannot be to them. Perhaps it was a clan name for one of the Caleb families of the tribe of Judah. At any rate, they belonged to the village of Bethlehem and, as emerges later (4:3), Naomi owned property there. Naomi belongs and yet she doesn't; she is always one who is different.

Moab is across the Jordan in an area the Israelites had never fully conquered. Sometimes relations with Moab were hostile and sometimes friendly. The story implies that the Judean family had no problems in being allowed to settle on this high and windy land.

1:3-4 The storyteller makes no comment at all about these mixed marriages, which seem to have been forbidden to the Israelites (see Deut 23:3), although this is not entirely clear. At any rate, the story treats the marriages as well as the sojourning in a foreign land as matters of practicality that need no justification.

1:8 The repetition of the advice to return has already been noted in the preliminary comments. The "mother's house" is odd and of uncertain implication. What is clear is that Naomi is always the practical one. Three widows are now the problem; women know best how to handle such matters and to arrange marriages. It is not the time to grieve but to do something.

1:16 The prose of the Book of Ruth has a lilt to it and can easily pass over into poetic form, as this balanced speech certainly does. Later on Boaz will know about Ruth's conversion. We know this passage as a popular song; perhaps it was so originally. It is also somewhat ironic: Naomi's first defeat in arranging things comes from the girl who loves her most.

1:20 Naomi means "lively," "delightful"; Mara means "bitter." These are authentic-sounding names from ancient times. Whatever may be the connection of such names with God, the storyteller is obviously contrasting personal qualities, perhaps nicknames. The admirable girl who had left Bethlehem in her youth has returned as a quite different character. The change in Naomi's character is essential for the story to work.

1:21 Naomi is exaggerating, for they had to go away because there was a famine. She seems to have enjoyed the good life in Moab, and that was an expected result for being a good Israelite. The problem posed is the eternal one: Why did this happen to me? It is presumed that God is in control. Naomi, like Job, blames God when that control seems irrational. The "Almighty" (Shaddai) is a name given to God particularly as judge.

"The Lord has pronounced against me": These are quasi-legal terms taken from a court setting. As in Job, the conflict between Naomi and Yahweh is open and absolute. At the same time, Naomi, as a practical woman, takes it for granted that nothing can be done about the situation.

THE MEETING

Ruth 2:1-23

Chapter 2 is a self-contained scene. It begins with the storyteller's note that Naomi has a kinsman named Boaz. It ends with Naomi recognizing him as the one in whose field Ruth has been gleaning. The description of Boaz befriending Ruth creates vivid pictures of both the girl and the man. Ruth is energetic in setting out to provide for her mother-in-law and in bringing home both provisions and news. She is also portrayed as highly submissive and deferential toward both Naomi and Boaz. Boaz, on the other hand, is more than generous in safeguarding the rights of the poor and the alien, in protecting Ruth and providing for her convenience. He speaks in formalized language, which sets him above Ruth. He is and acts like a prominent man (2:1). It is precisely these qualities that Naomi recognizes at the end (2:20). The point of chapter 2 is to show how Ruth comes under his protection and how Naomi recognizes it as a good thing.

2:1 The kinsman was not just a relative, but someone bound by custom to take the side of those who were in trouble. It was later used to mean "redeemer." Boaz is honoring an obligation as well as being magnanimous.

2:2 The obligation of allowing the poor and the alien to glean was recognized by law (see Lev 19:9; Deut 14:19-22). Ruth is both poor and alien. There is really no need for her to ask permission of Naomi or even Boaz.

2:8 Boaz is rather peremptory about deciding what Ruth shall do. Still and all, there is a pragmatic understanding that however pleased the young men are at having Ruth working in the fields with them, there is some danger that demands the protection of Boaz (2:9).

2:11 Boaz is not only prominent, but well-informed. However, he makes no allusion to being a kinsman. His initial kindness to Ruth is based simply on the report.

2:14 Boaz is here going beyond the demands of the law in allowing Ruth to glean in his fields. He gives instruction to the harvesters to let her get in with them and even to drop some handfuls of grain for her. All this emphasizes his graciousness.

2:19 The story is very realistic about this at-home talk between the two women. Naomi knows that Ruth has been successful, for she has brought home a bag of barley.

2:20 As readers, we already know of the relationship from 2:1. As a story, however, the identification implies more. Naomi sees in it not happenstance but opportunity.

2:22 Naomi's advice is prudent, especially in the Hebrew text, where the language is considerably more explicit than "insulted." Yet, in the light of Naomi's character, there is already a hint of advantages to be gained by staying close to the prominent kinsman.

NAOMI THE MATCHMAKER

Ruth 3:1-18

Chapter 3 is a model of artistic suspense that will lead up to chapter 4. All the actors think that they know where they are going. Naomi has just identified Boaz as their kinsman (2:20). It was not idle chitchat. Naomi knows that the kinsman-redeemer must provide for the widows. But she must draw him closer.

Nothing further happened during the harvest season. Now it is time for winnowing the grain, a happy time when Boaz will be in the right mood. Naomi makes the bold move of sending Ruth out in her best finery for a night meeting. She does not know exactly what will happen, but she realizes that she must push Boaz.

Ruth has her own mind. She does not wait for Boaz to begin the courting but creeps under his blanket. She reminds him that he is her kinsman, not to justify her bold conduct but to inform him that she has ties to him.

Boaz himself has plans. He wants to marry Ruth, but he is a prominent and honorable man. The setting and the wording clearly imply a tension that night: will they or will they not? Boaz knows what Ruth and Naomi do not: he cannot honorably marry Ruth because a closer relative has a prior claim.

And so the night scene ends inconclusively with nothing happening. It is all kept very quiet. But when Ruth tells Naomi what happened, the old lady knows what she must do. At the end of chapter 1 Naomi lost her faith that God would provide; at the end of this scene she tells Ruth to wait. Naomi already knows why Boaz will settle the matter today. She has her own way.

3:1 Ordinarily it was the duty of the menfolk to provide for widows. Already in 1:9 Naomi expressed her concern about providing for her two daughters-in-law. Yet she is not entirely disinterested. Ruth's security is a guarantee for herself.

3:3 "So bathe and anoint yourself; then put on your best attire and go down to the threshing floor." This is a nicely balanced chain of words in Hebrew; it was meant to go together. There were no highly restrictive customs keeping girls away from boys. However, this is pushing events a bit. Boaz himself is later aware (3:14) of what the neighbors will say.

3:4 Without advising deliberate seduction, Naomi is well aware of what might happen when Ruth lies at the feet of Boaz. The Hebrew words have a certain suggestiveness. The tension is deliberate on the part of the storyteller.

3:9 "Spread the corner of your cloak over me": literally, "spread your wing over me." The words are intended to call to mind the protecting wing of Yahweh. Ruth's intentions are more than amorous; the most important thing she wants to remind Boaz of is that by custom he is her protector. But she makes a mistake in thinking that Boaz is her closest kin.

3:12 Obviously Boaz has done his homework. The protector was not just any relative; there was a definite line of priority, although we do not know precisely how it worked. The point of the story is that Boaz does. In spite of his enthusiasm, however, and his promise to resolve the matter tomorrow, Boaz does not know how to bring this about. The storyteller has caught all of his characters at loose ends.

3:18 Naomi seems very confident, but we are not told why. There is a gap in the story here. In 4:3 we are told for the first time that Naomi is putting up a piece of property for sale. At the end of chapter 3 we are simply left wondering: What will happen now? Quite clearly, Naomi has been busy making sure of what will happen.

BOAZ MARRIES RUTH

Ruth 4:1-12

The marriage negotiations are described with considerable haste. We do not know what some of the customs were about, but the general tenor is clear enough. Boaz knows two things that the other characters do not: there is a nearer kinsman, and Naomi is putting up a piece of property for sale.

The kinsman and the elders are conveniently present when Boaz needs them. As a good trader, he holds out the most attractive prospect first. Naomi's field is available, and in fairness he offers the first bid to the kinsman. Only then does he put in the hook—he must also buy Ruth. The redemption of the widow involves her support, Naomi's support, and that of possible children.

At this the nearer relative cedes the right to buy the field. Boaz is obviously waiting in the wings to take over. And so, in a curious ceremony the arrangement is legally closed. The people at the gate witness to the transaction and pronounce a blessing upon Boaz and his house to come.

At this point it looks as though everybody has won. Naomi has provided for Ruth and for herself. In all likelihood she has also preserved her family line. Boaz has his girl and his field. Ruth has the man who has been so kind and faithful to her. But there is more to come.

4:1 The description of the proceedings corresponds to what we know of biblical times, but there are specific difficulties because we do not know enough. Each town had some sort of governing body of elders. A quorum of these members—ten in this case—sufficed for public hearings and decisions. General principles of law drawn from the Mosaic legislation governed the proceedings, but all citizens were not equally informed about legal niceties, nor are we.

Two general laws were involved in this case. Property was to remain in the hands of members of the same tribe or family. If it was lost, the relative-protector had to help get it back. Secondly, if a husband died before he had a son, then a brother-in-law or some other relative was to marry the widow and have a son in the name of the deceased. This is called a "levirate marriage" from the Latin word *levir*, meaning "brother-in-law." In such cases the brother-in-law or near relative recognized his obligation to continue the family line. Implicitly, this was a way of providing social security for the widow. In this case, it is not quite clear why the two widows are involved.

"He called to him by name, 'Come and sit beside me!'" From the beginning Boaz is totally in charge and dominates the whole scene. The closer relative is never named in the story. Perhaps the storyteller did not want to complicate matters by naming another character at this late point.

4:3 The conditions under which women could own land are somewhat obscure, but they certainly could do so. Just how Naomi came to sell the property at this time or how Boaz knew about it is not made clear in the story.

4:4 Boaz is being fair. At the same time, he lets it be known that he wants to buy the land. He takes it for granted that it would be an attractive purchase.

4:5 First the good news, then the bad. The closer relative had an advantage by his prior claim on the property; now he is told that he also has a stronger obligation to take care of the widow. The widow in question should be Naomi, but it seems taken for granted that she

can no longer have children and that Ruth will have to be the bride.

4:6 With so many more mouths to feed and the need to leave an inheritance, the closer relative recognizes that he will be hurting his present family. No criticism is leveled against him in the story. The obligations fell upon the whole relationship, and it is evident that Boaz is willing to assume them.

4:7 We do not know who took off whose sandal, and we have no references elsewhere in the Bible to this curious custom.

4:10 This is the last time that Mahlon is mentioned. Boaz is always called the father, despite the levirate law, which was intended to preserve the name of the first husband.

4:11 Rachel and Leah were the wives of Jacob. In the next verse the blessing is: "May your house become like the house of Perez, whom Tamar bore to Judah." Jacob was the hero of the northern tribes; Judah, of the southern tribes. Both are mentioned apparently in reference to David, who was king of both north and south. Tamar was the widowed daughter-in-law for whom Judah neglected to provide a husband. By disguising herself as a prostitute, she managed to have a son by Judah himself (Gen 38).

THE BIRTH OF OBED

Ruth 4:13-17

The final scene centers on Naomi. It balances the prologue in chapter 1. Naomi had been the faithful wife who had everything taken away from her by Yahweh. It was Yahweh whom Naomi fingered as the villain. Through the rest of the story Naomi tried to take life into her own hands and to make provision for her old age and for the continuance of her family. Apparently she succeeded, although her manipulations did not always come out as she planned. But now she has a rich son-in-law and a successor. Did she win? As Naomi sits there with her grandson in her lap, the village women once more greet her. They had nothing to say when Naomi bitterly denounced Yahweh at the end of chapter 1. Now they sing: "Blessed is the Lord who has not failed to provide you today with an heir!" The storyteller does not spell out what this means. But it is dramatic.

4:13 Everything happens rapidly at the end. Ruth had been barren for the ten years of her marriage to Mahlon, but now she conceives quickly.

4:14 We cannot miss the point that it is Naomi, not Ruth, who is on stage. We do not know what customs may have been involved, but it is clear that this is deliberate as a storytelling technique. We are brought back to chapter 1, where the village women last appeared.

4:15 Ruth's worth is based on two claims: she loves Naomi and she has provided an heir. This may sound rather self-serving, but Naomi's complaint was precisely that Yahweh did not take care of her, although Yahweh has just now taken care of Ruth. The conflict between Yahweh and Naomi has been resolved, but not by Naomi's craftiness.

4:16 No more seems intended than that Naomi has become a good grandmother to the boy. The glad cry "A son is born to Naomi" need not have any legal implications of adoption.

4:17 It is too legalistic to ask why the neighbor women name the boy. The context indicates that they are celebrating this glorious birth and congratulating Naomi by using the boy's name, Obed. Obed is a name to remember. He will be the grandfather of King David.

THE GENEALOGY OF DAVID

Ruth 4:18-22

The story ends with a genealogy: Perez, Hezron, Ram, Amminadab, Nahshon, Salmon, Boaz, Obed, Jesse, David. There is no question that the genealogy is authentic within the traditional way of citing such lists. Despite all that was said in the story about raising up a son for Elimelech or Mahlon, neither is mentioned in the genealogy. Whether the genealogy was an afterthought of the author or a later addition to the text cannot be determined. It fits in well enough with the storyteller's chorus of village women crying "May he become famous in Israel." In that sense it would simply round off the story without being the central point.

On the other hand, it is rather odd that the author should conclude his story of Ruth with a genealogy that does not even mention her. Nor is she mentioned in the corresponding list in 1 Chr 2. Yet the tradition was preserved. Matt 1:5 does mention Ruth. Three women are remembered in Matthew's genealogy: Rahab the harlot, Ruth the Moabitess, and Bathsheba (although she is mentioned only discreetly in connection with Solomon, "whose mother had been the wife of Uriah"). Even in the final genealogy there are surprises.

LAMENTATIONS

James A. Fischer, C.M.

INTRODUCTION

Traditionally the Book of Lamentations has been pictured as the writing of Jeremiah the prophet as he saw the destruction of Jerusalem in 587 B.C.E. This certainly gives visual expression to much of the thought. The prophet was watching the smoke rise from the destroyed city. He heard the wailing of women as they found their dead ones or sought those long lost. Soldiers milled about, driving victims before them and setting fire to the ruins. It was the prophet's city and his people. Often had he preached in it, imploring his compatriots to turn back from folly. Now the terrible word of the Lord had come. It was too much. God had been right, but who could live with such a ruthless God? Prayer to God had been as useless as preaching to the people. God had made a mockery of former glorious promises and deeds.

Such is the literary setting of the five poems (chapters) that comprise the Book of Lamentations. They are incandescent with emotions of desolation, grief, incomprehension, and indignation. Sin has been revealed in its raw evilness. Nothing of nobility survived except a bleeding memory.

The form of the book

Yet the book is a rigidly controlled outpouring. As poetry it is spontaneous, heartfelt, torn from exacerbated feelings and yet elaborately planned and precisely executed. Three of the poems are acrostics, each verse beginning with a succeeding letter of the Hebrew alphabet; the other two are also built on the pattern of twenty-two. Such a numerical pattern gives a feeling of inescapable completion. In each poem a break occurs just slightly before the middle, setting the two parts against each other. The middle poem (chapter 3) is totally different in mood, as we shall see. All five poems must be read to grasp the overall feeling and meaning; that is the aim of the poet.

Some of the poems are written in the rhythm of a funeral dirge. Some verses have the form of taunt songs. The meter is still disputed; reconstructions and explanations based on it do not seem to get us very far.

Out of the controlled literary form comes a theological insight. God can be faced and prayed to in all the divine anger and stony silence. Grief and bitterness can be surmounted to arrive at repentance and acceptance. When history has become unendurable, faith still endures.

The history of the book

The picture given of Jeremiah at the beginning will not stand up to historical analysis. Although he could have composed the lamentations, it appears more probable that they were written over a period of years after him. Perhaps, indeed, many such laments were written for memorial services in the ruined city or elsewhere and our collection represents a selection by an editor. The first and second poems seem to be eyewitness compositions; the rest are clearly from a later time. All are heavily flavored by the expressions and thoughts of the prophet Jeremiah and so have been traditionally associated with him.

Certainly the book as we know it was completed by 538 B.C.E. It is possible, but not provable, that the poems were sung in some liturgical setting. We know that much later they were used in synagogues for the celebration of the ninth day of Ab in late summer to remember the destruction of Jerusalem.

COMMENTARY

JERUSALEM ABANDONED AND DISGRACED

Lam 1:1-22

The first poem (chapter 1) or dirge is an acrostic, that is, a poem whose lines begin with succeeding letters of the Hebrew alphabet. It is divided into two parts. Each begins with a cry:

> How lonely she is now,
>   the once crowded city! (1:1)
>
> Look, O Lord, and see
>   how worthless I have become! (1:11)

The first section describes the utter loneliness of the daughter of Jerusalem, now a widow. It is a funeral dirge over Jerusalem itself. The precise rhythm of the dirge song is used. The widow weeps. Her friends have betrayed her, and she has no peace. There are no more pilgrims coming to her; her priests groan, her foes triumph, her little ones have gone away, her glory is vanished, she has no home, her foes gloat over her. And added to all this, she is aware that it is her own sins that have brought it about. This first section winds down to a piteous plea:

> Astounding is her downfall,
>   with no one to console her.
> Look, O Lord, upon her misery,
>   for the enemy has triumphed! (1:9)

The second section begins with a confession of guilt and yet a plea for others to understand her misery:

> "Come, all you who pass by the way,
>   look and see
> Whether there is any suffering like
>   my suffering,
> which has been dealt me . . ." (1:12).

Images are heaped up: blazing wrath, fire, sins plaited together and tied around her neck, brought to her knees, young men crushed, trodden into the winepress. There is no one to console her: Jerusalem has become a thing unclean. This section also finally emerges into a prayer, but a prayer for vengeance:

> "Let all their evil come before you;
>   deal with them
> As you have dealt with me
>   for all my sins;
> My groans are many,
>   and I am sick at heart" (1:22).

It is a dark mood that has come upon the poet. Loneliness is the most dreaded evil; there is no one, not even God, to offer any consolation. There is no denying that God has been just in punishing; yet God seems to be playing favorites by not punishing the more sinful invader. Repentance comes down to a need for some immediate vindication against the foe: "deal with them as you have dealt with me for all my sins."

1:1 The note of loneliness is struck from the beginning. Jerusalem never had a large population, but during the festival days it was overflowing with Jews from all over Palestine and foreign countries.

The city is "she." Such was the ancient way of referring to cities. Wealth, education, and power flowed from cities. Capital cities were referred to as "queens." In the Bible "daughter of Zion" or "mother Jerusalem" are the ordinary designations. The metaphor gets mixed up here, for although the dirge is for the female whose funeral song is sung, it is the widow who pronounces it over herself.

1:3 The text is not clear. It seems to refer to Judah in exile, but that has not yet happened and the Hebrew text supports the usual picture of pre-exilic Judah as living among the nations as their savior. If so, the pity is that Judah has failed to bring "rest" or peace to the nations.

1:5 As elsewhere in the Old Testament, there are no explanations about the sociological or political forces at work. The Lord is fin-

805

gered from the first as the cause of disaster. So also in verse 12: "the Lord afflicted me."

1:8 Although Jews were not at all squeamish about sex, they did abhor nakedness. There is some dispute about the actual meaning in Hebrew; perhaps the picture does rely on a known punishment for treaty violations, namely, the political leaders were stripped naked so that they should be shamed before their own people. The same punishment also seems to have been used sometimes for prostitutes.

1:10 The Babylonians carried off the sacred vessels of the temple. What hurt the most was not the loss of money but the desecration of such treasures. The Book of Daniel (Dan 5:2) knows of this tradition (see 2 Kgs 25:13-17).

Deut 23:4 has a most severe rule against any Moabite or Ammonite ever being accepted into the community. The tradition persisted with uneven application for centuries. Actually, there do not seem to have been any Moabite or Ammonite soldiers among the Babylonian conquerors. For the poet this is immaterial; the picture is of utter desecration of the sacred.

1:12 The second section begins with an appeal for help against the Lord. Presumably those who pass by the way are uninvolved people who could make an unbiased judgment. The suffering of widowed Jerusalem is not just another normal tragedy of war; it is unprecedented, since it comes directly from the Lord.

1:14 The poet knows that sin is not a bit of dirt to be brushed off. It is "plaited," woven together into an entangling and heavy burden that cannot be shaken off.

1:17 Jacob is another name used generically for all Israel or for parts of it, such as Judah. Once more the lament is against the Lord directly. The physical terrors of war must be borne; the spiritual terrors of God as the enemy are less perceptible but are the cause of real grief.

1:19 The lovers seem to have been nations such as Egypt and Assyria, with which Judah had attempted to make alliances to stave off Babylonia. The verse also suggests a trifling with paganism. Unfaithful Jerusalem is often called a temple prostitute, a woman willing to abandon her husband to consort with the gods.

1:20 The poet knows that Jerusalem has been unfaithful and that she knows it. The pain lies not so much in the external suffering as in the loss of integrity. "My heart recoils within me from my monstrous rebellion." So the problem is posed in its most excruciating form: Jerusalem knows that the Lord is just (see v. 18), but accepting this is just too painful.

1:21 The ungracious ending begins quite openly. The "Day of the Lord" was a familiar theme—a time when God would defeat the nations and usher in God's glorious reign. The prophets had warned that the Day of the Lord was a two-edged sword; it could be directed against the chosen people also. So it had happened. But the Day had not fallen on the oppressors. If there is vengeance here, it is at least based on the belief that the Lord alone could do it. At this point acceptance is very slight; it is inescapable but narrow-minded.

THE LORD'S WRATH AGAINST ZION

Lam 2:1-22

The second poem is a wild outpouring of grief over destroyed Zion, but the wildness is controlled both by the literary artist and by the believer, as is signified by the same use of the alphabetical arrangement. This poem, too, divides into two parts. The problem is first raised:

How the Lord in his wrath
has detested daughter Zion! (2:1)

The Lord has been ruthless in punishing, even self-distrustful, as the poet implies: "unmindful of his footstool." The Lord has dishonored everything in the land: dwellings, fortress Zion, king, princes. Then follows a poetic reverie: "his hand has brought ruin, yet he did not relent" (v. 8). The images heap up into an overwhelming picture of awesome destruction.

Then the poet turns to his own reverie:

Worn out from weeping are my eyes,
within me all is in ferment (2:11).

Like King Jehoiakim, who saw his children slaughtered and then had his own eyes put out, the poet can see and feel the final scenes:

As child and infant faint away
in the open spaces of the town.

They ask their mothers,
  "Where is the cereal?"—in vain,
As they faint away like the wounded
  in the streets of the city,
And breathe their last
  in their mothers' arms (2:11b-12).

There is no recourse but a cry to God, a cry bound to fall on deaf ears. It is unmerciful and unparalleled in history:

Look, O Lord, and consider:
  whom have you ever treated thus?
Must women eat their offspring,
  their well-formed children?
Are priest and prophet slain
  in the sanctuary of the Lord? (2:20)

No hope pervades these dreary thoughts. The day of wrath continues to the end.

The problem is the total disregard of God for mercy. Rather than deny it or cover it over with pious words of promise, the poet flings it in God's face. It is God's own self-interest that is badly served. What will the enemies think of such a God?

2:1 Each of the first eight verses describes the Lord as an enemy; the Lord detests, consumes in anger, blazes up, shoots, scorns, and so on. What is left unspoken is the implicit paradox: it is the Lord's chosen that is detested.

Zion is sacred soil because it is there that the Lord's feet have touched the earth and consecrated it. It is this sacred touch that the Lord now seems to forget.

2:3 The horn as a symbol of strength is a common Old Testament figure; see Ps 75:11 for an example.

2:6 The exact meaning is unclear. Perhaps the reference is to the shelters that were erected in the vineyards during the growing season so that the owner could mount a guard. They could be easily demolished. Israel is God's vineyard; God should have protected it.

2:8 The image is of an architect measuring a building. He knows precisely the size and shape that he wants. So the Lord has decreed destruction of Zion's wall not haphazardly but with precise planning.

2:9 The reference is to the bars that were put up to lock the gates of the city after they were closed.

Among all the calamities, the worst were the losses of spiritual things, such as the instruction in the law given by the priests. Religious education had come to a halt.

2:10 The esteemed elders are sitting on the ground either humiliated or as a sign of mourning. At any rate, the education by the wise has ceased. Usually the daughters of Jerusalem are pictured as dancing; now they are mourning.

2:11 The first part of the poem has concentrated on what God the enemy has done. Now the thought turns back to the personal dismay of daughter Jerusalem (see 1:20 for the same phrasing).

2:12 Nothing more vivid could be added to this picture of starving children. It is just a few words, but it is the detail that says immense amounts. In verse 20 the poet will allude to women eating their offspring. It was one of the terrors of sieges amply attested by the Old Testament and by other ancient Near Eastern texts.

2:14 The Hebrew text is more vivid: "Your prophets saw visions that were mere whitewash." The reality was horrendous and the prophets knew it; they whitewashed it by crying "Peace!" when they knew that there was no peace of the Lord in the land.

2:15 Obviously the passersby are not clapping in approval as we do. Clapping of the hands is a fairly frequent sign of derision in the Old Testament.

2:20 The paradox here is brought near the surface. The enemies of Israel were obviously the sinners and deservedly suffered defeat, famine, pillage, and siege. But nothing like this had ever happened to the chosen ones. It is a reproach to the justice of God that God has punished the chosen people without mercy.

2:22 The poem ends on a note of total disgust and reproach; God doesn't even have manners, and God's feast day is a grisly banquet of death. There is nothing more to be said than "if that is the kind of God you are, we don't want you." It is notable that it is not said. The twenty-two-verse pattern ends precisely before it, and nothing more can be added.

SUFFERINGS OF THE PROPHET AND HIS PEOPLE

Lam 3:1-66

The third poem is completely different. It is not the agonized outpouring of an eyewitness over Jerusalem in its death throes. It is a personal meditation or reverie:

> I am a man who knows affliction
> from the rod of his anger (3:1).

How can such a man live with his God? The problem of affliction is described in rather traditional images having only a vague reference to the destruction of Jerusalem. But in any affliction, mysterious as it may be, the sages can still assert that God is good.

> The favors of the Lord are not exhausted,
> his mercies are not spent;
> They are renewed each morning,
> so great is his faithfulness.
> My portion is the Lord, says my soul;
> therefore I will hope in him (3:22-24).

Affliction is seen to have a medicinal effect:

> Why should any living man complain,
> any mortal, in the face of his sins?
> Let us search and examine our ways
> that we may return to the Lord! (3:39-40)

At this point the meditation turns from the personal "I" to the collective "we." The rest of the poem is a somewhat conventional lament that confesses sin, complains that the enemy is still triumphant, expresses confidence that God will hear, and ends with a prayer for vindication against enemies.

It is a soothing prayer. The imagery is much less violent than in the preceding two poems. The alphabetic form has been used, but now the poem has stretched out from twenty-two to sixty-six verses to heighten the understanding that not only has all been said, but it has been fully said. The poet often reaches back for hallowed phrases traditionally sung in the temple; some ten verses are very close to psalm quotations. Often the vocabulary and style parallel the wisdom writers' techniques, and so give a calming effect. God is viewed as the Creator, the Most High, the Lord from heaven. Despite the harsh note of vindictiveness at the end, the poem carries the gentler spirit of the sages of Israel. God is hidden in these harsh facts of life, but God is still there, and still there as a good God.

Seen against the background of the first two poems, this lengthy meditation begins to investigate a livable solution. It is a mysterious solution, since, as the sages realized, no one can understand God. But if the question is raised of how Israelites can live with their God, as it was in the preceding poems and in the beginning of this one, then the ancient faith in a good God who eventually uses power both to chastise and to vindicate must be added. It does not solve the problem. This poet has managed to quiet the raw emotions of loneliness and incomprehensibility into something more peaceful where the thought that things may not be what they seem to be can begin to emerge.

3:2 The sharp contrasts between light and darkness, life and death, good and evil in this poem are characteristic of the sages' techniques.

3:6 The Jews of this period did not speculate about what happened in the afterlife, although they believed that life continued for them. The experience of death was that a body was placed in a grave and stayed there. As far as anyone could see, such a life was useless. So death was darkness and a nonentity.

3:8 We are so accustomed to saying that God always hears prayer that we ignore our own experience. The Hebrews felt more comfortable admitting that God did not need to hear anything and that their efforts to reach God often seemed to be ignored. Thus verse 44 says: "You wrapped yourself in a cloud which prayer could not pierce."

3:10 For the next six verses the poet pursues the picture that God is the enemy. The Jews had no theories to explain evil in the world. It simply existed, and in some way it was due to God (see vv. 37-38). The experience of life often seemed to make God the enemy.

3:20 Here again the experience of life dominates. We keep mulling over our problems and the broken-record process gets in the way of our ever seeing more in our situation.

3:22 Note the sudden inbreaking of light here. This is a standard feature of the lament psalms and is called a "certainty of a hearing." No lament is complete without it. Here it introduces a new section.

3:24 "My portion is the Lord": Ps 16:5 and 73:26 use the same metaphor. It was the conviction of all that God has given each person a place in life and a work to do. This might become specific, as in the allotting of portions of the land to the various tribes. There was a portion for all, and it was given not haphazardly but because the Lord decreed it.

3:25 "Good is the Lord to one who waits for him": This is part of the faith statement. It is also put in the form of a wisdom admonition. It will be noted that verses 25, 26, and 27 all have the same form: "It is good . . ."

3:29 The metaphor expresses surrender and is probably taken from a scene of political subjugation.

3:31 We are getting into an insight of how evil actually operates in the world. Experience taught that the Lord always came to rescue Israel, although this might take time. The worst thought was that God simply did not care about what went on here on earth. Verses 34 to 36 are a repudiation of that idea. The same occurs in the Book of Job (see Job 35).

3:37 Here we have, not a philosophical explanation of the problem of evil, but a simple statement of observed fact and faith. Good and evil do come; unless one is prepared to say that there is another god of evil, one can only say that both good and evil come from God in some way. What that way may be is subject to endless philosophizing, but the assertion here bears on the fact that there is only one God who controls everything.

3:39 Whatever turns the notion of disaster and sin took, it seemed reasonable to the Jews to concede that all human beings were sinful, and if they were not punished for one thing, they deserved it for another.

3:40 This is another wisdom admonition, and, typically, it makes practical use of the reflections that have preceded it. Suffering has a medicinal value if only we will search for it.

3:48 This is the first reference to the destruction of Jerusalem, and apart from verses 48-51 there is no other allusion to it in this poem.

3:54 Water as a symbol of trouble is common in the Old Testament.

3:65 There is no doubt about the vindictiveness of this prayer. But it should at least be conceded that the poet was thinking in spiritual terms. The worst evil he could wish was a spiritual one—hardness of heart. From that there was no escape, as he himself knew from his own experience.

MISERIES OF THE BESIEGED CITY

Lam 4:1-22

After the reflective mood of the third poem, the fourth chapter can take a more reasonable approach to lament. Past and present jostle for sorrowful consideration at the beginning.

> How tarnished is the gold,
> how changed the noble metal! (4:1)

The glory of Zion past is compared with the present ignominy, the prosperity of yesteryears with the starvation of today. The poet will not flinch from even the worst:

> The hands of the compassionate women
> boiled their own children,
> To serve them as mourners' food
> in the downfall of the daughter of
> my people (4:10).

Then the mood changes to one of honest admission that all this punishment has come upon them because of their sins. Prophets, priests, elders, even the anointed (king) have proven false and have been dispersed. The last hope is gone with the king in prison:

> He in whose shadow we thought
> we could live on among the nations (4:20).

And the simple fact is admitted: the Lord himself has dispersed us (v. 16). There is one last outburst of resentment—this time against Edom, the traditional enemy. However, it is clear that the poet has made progress in elevating his thought. God is the punisher, and yet punishment is justifiable.

4:3 The starving mothers of Jerusalem know that even wild animals can feed their young; they cannot. "The daughter of my people has become as cruel as the ostrich in the desert." There was a widespread belief that ostriches abandoned their eggs after laying them and allowed them to be trampled on.

4:12 The belief was that of the Israelites; we have no evidence that any others held it. Still and all, Jerusalem remained unconquered from the time of David to the Exile, some four hundred years.

4:13 No specific sin is mentioned, and the Hebrew text is somewhat uncertain. However,

Jeremiah himself was unjustly imprisoned and accused of treason by the priests and the prophet Hananiah (see Jer 26). So also Christ refers to a tradition of bloodshed in Jerusalem caused by the officials (see Matt 23:35). It should also be noted that the Old Testament does not distinguish, in using the title "prophet," between false prophets and true ones, as present-day scholars are accustomed to do. Among those called prophets there were many political sycophants and downright liars.

4:20 The reference is to King Zedekiah, who was captured trying to escape from Jerusalem during the last siege (see 2 Kgs 25:3-6). The king is called "our breath of life," a very ancient Canaanite title for a king. There is no reason to suspect irony.

4:21 "Daughter Edom" is, of course, the country across the Jordan. A somewhat vagrant tradition says that Esau, the brother of Jacob, was their progenitor. Actually, they seem to have been a mixed people among whom the Jews mingled and did business. For some reason that is not entirely clear from the Bible, they are usually singled out by the prophets for the fiercest of denunciations.

4:22 This is about the happiest thing said in the Book of Lamentations. In contrast to Edom, whose punishment is in the future, Zion is on the upswing.

THE PROPHET'S LAMENT AND SUPPLICATION

Lam 5:1-22

The last poem must be seen against the backdrop of the preceding chapters. The poems began with an untrammeled lament over the destroyed city and a questioning of how God could do this. The third poem introduced a reflective mood: God is still the good God, and suffering has its curative value. The fourth poem spoke much about a true confession of faith. Now the poet is ready to put this horrendous experience in the light of Israel's historical traditions.

> Remember, O Lord, what has befallen us,
> look, and see our disgrace:
> Our inherited lands have been turned
> over to strangers,
> our homes to foreigners (5:1-2).

The exiles are the foreigners now, worked to death and begging for water. The facts cannot be belied. Sin has worked its havoc according to the ancient law that children are to be punished for the crimes of their parents. So be it.

But there is more to remembering than that. The destruction of Jerusalem is in the past for these exiles. And it was not simply the sins of the parents that had brought it about.

> Woe to us, for we have sinned! (5:16)

Yet Israel's God has always been a king, unchanging in both goodness and power. Such a king cannot forget his own.

> You, O Lord, are enthroned forever;
> your throne stands from age to age.
> Why, then, should you forget us,
> abandon us so long a time?
> Lead us back to you, O Lord, that we
> may be restored:
> give us anew such days as we had
> of old (5:19-21).

On this humbly supplicant note the Lamentations end. The poet has come to the peace of confession and of waiting for God to remember without any bitterness against God who inflicted the punishment and without resentment against the enemy who did it. There is an opening into a new understanding of the tragedy of the destruction of Jerusalem. As if to indicate this by the literary form used, the poet has dropped the acrostic formula and has not employed the funereal meter of lament. The future is open. It is a simple theological statement of hope.

Title: Some Greek manuscripts have a title prefixed to this chapter: "A prayer." So it is. The tone of this chapter is prayerful and calming. Although it has twenty-two verses, this poem is not alphabetical (an acrostic) like the others. It is in the form of a national lament with all the expression of confidence that such a song demands.

5:6 Although the Exodus from Egypt and the events leading up to it were hundreds of years in the past, it continued to be the central experience and measuring stick for most later reflections on the ways of God. The Hebrew text is not as harsh as the translation: "We shook hands with Egypt . . ."

5:7 The idea that the sins of parents are visited on their children is common in the Old

Testament. It is also common sense from a historical perspective. The poet accepts such guilt, or at least such punishment, as just. He also allows space for the guilt of the present generation.

5:8 The Hebrew word is used as a slur on government officials, especially the lower ones, who were often corrupt.

5:11-14 These verses picture a society in which all the norms of accepted social behavior are overturned. Wives and maidens are no longer respected and protected; princes are executed; elders are not honored; young men have no job opportunities; the elders who govern prudently do not even bother to gather at the city gates, and the young do not have fun.

5:18 The more terrible prophetic threats predicted the destruction of Jerusalem and pictured wild animals as the only inhabitants. That Jerusalem as the center of worship, and so of all religion, should be abandoned was unthinkable. The rallying cry for the preservation of Judaism in exile centered on the unquenchable desire to return to the Holy City.

5:19 The enthronement of Yahweh as King was both a theological conviction and a liturgical celebration of great importance in pre-exilic Judaism. Essentially, the statement expressed the faith that God alone ruled all things and would eventually win. It is noteworthy that the Exile brought out some of the strongest expressions of this faith in Old Testament history. It was a time when the Old Testament was largely edited, and the events of the past reinterpreted in dynamic fashion.

5:21 The New American Bible translation catches the right meaning of the words: "help us to repent!" That repentance was still possible is taken for granted. In synagogue reading the Jews repeat this verse after the end of the chapter, so that the whole of Lamentations ends on a hopeful note that God will grant repentance. Thus was the book conceived. It is not a pious book of idealistic sayings that tell us how we ought to be. It is a human as well as a divine document that witnesses to the power of God to save even when we are in the depths of despair and resentment. It is salvation achieved, but at a great price.

ECCLESIASTES

James A. Fischer, C.M.

INTRODUCTION

The Book of Ecclesiastes is the most damnable book in the Bible and yet the most satisfying for those who have learned to live comfortably with doubt. That it is damnable seems clear; it has been denounced many times as cynical, pessimistic, worldly, and downright heretical. That it is in the Bible at all and provides great comfort for those who are willing to face life honestly is also a fact. Ecclesiastes—or to give him the Hebrew name by which he is often known, Qoheleth— destroys most of the accepted clichés on which the superficially pious live.

> Because the sentence against evildoers is not promptly executed, therefore the hearts of men are filled with the desire to commit evil—because the sinner does evil a hundred times and survives (8:11-12).

> Consider the work of God. Who can make straight what he has made crooked? (7:13)

> A good name is better than good ointment,

and then Qoheleth adds:

> and the day of death than the day of birth (7:1). One man out of a thousand have I come upon, but a woman among them all I have not found (7:28).

That may be the unkindest cut of all. On the other hand, Qoheleth's favorite slogan is "Eat, drink and be merry" (Eccl 2:24; 3:13; 5:17; 9:7-10). Somewhere among all this one must begin to wonder what Qoheleth believed in, if anything. And then there is the greater problem that a whole people accepted this as the word of God. The Book of Ecclesiastes is one of the great books of the Bible and of an-

cient times. It is not an easy book to deal with. But neither is life, and that is what Qoheleth ventured to examine.

We do not know much about the author. The name "Ecclesiastes" is a title made up from the Greek word for "church" or "synagogue." It is roughly a translation of the Hebrew "Qoheleth," but neither is a very happy title for somebody who apparently was much more a professor in an academy than a churchman. He must remain forever unknown.

From the contents of the book we can create a somewhat imaginative but largely responsible picture. Qoheleth lived sometime between 300 and 200 B.C.E. The quality of his diction betrays that. Apparently he was a teacher in Jerusalem. We know too little about the educational system of that time, but we can reasonably suspect that Jewish education was a cut above the average in the ancient world, and that there was a well-organized system from the grades to the college level in Jerusalem. Qoheleth appears to have been one of the more honored members of that academic community. He also appears to have been wealthy, and that certainly was not due to his academic pursuits. Apparently he was happily married, at least in his youth. Children do not figure in his admonitions; "son" is always a conventional term for "student."

After many years in the classroom, Qoheleth was compelled by the usual demon of professors to set down his best discoveries in life. Many young men had sat before him and gone out into the world. They came back occasionally to consult their old teacher. They were successful, full of importance, with a formula for "making it." The old man looked at them and wondered if he had overaccomplished his task. They still had not learned, and beneath the veneer of achievement he detected a great doubt and fear. So he asked the question for them: Is it all worthwhile? He himself had been through it. He realized that he first had to impress them with the impossible question so that they would admit their need. Only then could he give them the answer that life is worth living, not just for the sheer joy of living to the hilt, but for the deeper reason that this is what God had appointed them to do when creating them as caretakers on earth. But that took a good deal of explaining.

The book was originally written in Hebrew. The style is excellent, as is also the somewhat free Greek translation that was made very early on. It is hard to determine for whom it was written. It certainly was not written for church reading, whatever that word may mean. It was an essay to be distributed and cherished among students. But somehow it came to be read in synagogues. Today it is read for the feast of Succoth to add a somber note to the ending of the year. This is not entirely compelling; there is really nothing in the book to suggest fall, and some Jews do not read it at all.

How the book got into the Bible is also something of a mystery. The title, "The words of David's son, Qoheleth, king in Jerusalem," is probably a later addition. It gives some justification for including the work in the sacred Scriptures by placing it within the wisdom tradition, which was always connected with Solomon. Especially in later times, when the title was taken more literally, this seems to have been a powerful argument among the rabbis. The last verses of the book (Eccl 12:9-14) were added by an editor, as is clear from the text itself. Someone else, therefore, published the book.

Between publication and acceptance as a sacred book, however, there is a large gap. This book did not have the backing of priests, prophets, synagogue officials, or other authorities. It had to be accepted because of its own excellence and then transformed from being an insightful essay into being a word of God. There were arguments among the Jewish rabbis of a later date as to whether it should be accepted in the list of sacred writings, but when it was accepted, it was accepted without further argument. Perhaps the ascription to "David's son" did carry the day. If so, the book is in the Bible for the wrong reason—which would please Qoheleth no end. The Christians found no problem whatever in embracing it, although it is obviously no inspiring Sermon on the Mount.

Form of the book

Unlike the Books of Ruth or Lamentations, this book has no intricate or tightly controlled form. For purposes of reading, it may be just as well to simply note the following divisions:

First section—1:1-3:15 is a fairly well organized series of reflections on life as a pursuit of objectives that always end up being unsatisfying. It begins with a poignant poem on the inevitability of the constant round of activity in this world and ends with another poem about a time for everything, followed by a reflection that we do not know why this should be.

Middle section—3:16-11:8 seems to be a jumble of occasional remarks on various topics that Qoheleth found particularly enigmatic. Included here are mostly proverbs— sometimes proverbs that stand traditional proverbs on their heads; occasionally a parable; sometimes that refrain about "Eat, drink and be merry"; and, toward the end, a tendency to indulge in poetry.

Final section—11:9-12:8 strikes a different note, as if the author were aware that he might leave his readers with a dissonant sound reverberating in their ears. So he goes back to his job of giving hope to the young. Live life to the full, he advises. Old age comes too quickly. But what are we walking into? The darkness of a deserted village? The grave? That is only for the dust that we are. What of the life-breath? Where does it go?

Editor's footnote—As indicated above, the final verses are from an editor. It is not your conventional dust-jacket blurb. This editor tells us that Qoheleth taught the people proverbs and true sayings with precision. Yet even here he recognizes that "of the making of many books there is no end." So he published another one. Qoheleth would have liked that.

Theological insight

This is obviously a problem book, and the first need is to define the problem. It seems from the middle section of the book that the young Qoheleth had high ideals of justice and honesty in human affairs. He was perhaps a brilliant and competent student, and had access to the inner chambers of government. Despite the "perhaps," it is clear that he was disillusioned. His first thought in the middle section is of the intractability of injustice in the world.

> And still under the sun in the judgment place
> I saw wickedness, and in the seat of justice,
> iniquity (3:16).

The higher one went, the worse it got. The petty graft of tax-collectors and civil servants was nothing compared with that of judges and administrators.

> If you see oppression of the poor, and violation of rights and justice in the realm, do not be shocked by the fact, for the high official has another higher than he watching him and above these are others higher still (5:7).

And there the author leaves it, although he adds somewhat bitterly that people still say: "Yet an advantage for a country in every respect is a king for the arable land" (5:8).

But Qoheleth was no prophet who could go to his death denouncing injustice in the land. He was a party man who succumbed to the wisdom that one cannot fight City Hall. So he could only fold his hands while protesting:

> I have seen all manner of things in my vain days: a just man perishing in his justice, and a wicked one surviving in his wickedness. Be not just to excess, and be not overwise, lest you be ruined (7:15-16).

On the other hand, he never gave up protesting the dishonesty he saw in his society. Much of his concern about justice was simply that politicians will not call a spade a spade. But then he found out that this was true among his academic friends as well. They peddled knowledge as the cure-all. But it was not true, as Qoheleth knew from personal experience.

> When I applied my heart to know wisdom and to observe what is done on earth, I recognized that man is unable to find out all

God's work that is done under the sun, even though neither by day nor by night do his eyes find rest in sleep. However much man toils in searching, he does not find it out; and even if the wise man says that he knows, he is unable to find it out (8:17).

It was simply dishonest to fool people by repeating the popular wisdom that had been handed down without question through the centuries. Good and evil constantly happened, but no one could say exactly why. The law and the prophets were powerless. Although people did not say so explicitly, they expected that virtuous living would be rewarded with prosperity, peace, family, and happiness; on the other hand, the wicked always perished. Qoheleth knew that it was not true. The older wisdom had extolled the values of hard work, moderate pleasure, and the discipline of wisdom. Indeed, this had become almost a stained-glass picture of a sage. Job had railed against it by using the story of the good man who was afflicted in every way and then demanded to know why.

Qoheleth had suffered the opposite fate. He had everything that the traditional wisdom said that a sage should have. And he found it nothing but a vapor, a puff of smoke, the greatest "vanity" of all. So his essay begins with a rather slashing attack on wisdom, pleasure, and toil as means of attaining any understanding that was worthwhile. The truth was that life kept flowing in the same channel no matter what a person did or was. Life and death, war and peace, love and hatred—these things happened, they were not caused. They were all the inevitabilities of time. What was behind them? The central problem is that we admit they have meaning, but we cannot in any way find the meaning.

> I have considered the task which God has appointed for men to be busied about. He has made everything appropriate to its time, and has put the timeless into their hearts, without men's ever discovering, from beginning to end, the work which God has done (3:9-11).

That is the problem. Without a religious code, there is no problem with the craziness of the world. It is only when a person like Qoheleth really believes, that the incomprehensibility of it all becomes unendurable. The best of human resources fail where they must succeed.

Something of balm comes from the recognition that life itself is good. Qoheleth was one of those normally happy persons who could not doubt the glory of sunshine in the morning.

Indeed, for any among the living there is hope; a live dog is better off than a dead lion (9:4).

We are alive and we can enjoy. So Qoheleth has his comforting refrain (2:24-36; 3:12-13; 3:22; 5:17-19; 7:13-14; 8:15; 9:7-10; 11:7-10):

Go, eat your bread with joy and drink your wine with a merry heart, because it is now that God favors your works (9:7).

Anything you can turn your hand to, do with what power you have (9:10).

Life blossoms in doing something; don't just sit there and die. Even in acquiring knowledge Qoheleth knew that there is a difference between the wise person and the fool even when there was no pay-off.

I went on to the consideration of wisdom, madness and folly. And I saw that wisdom has the advantage over folly as much as light has the advantage over darkness. The wise man has eyes in his head, but the fool walks in darkness (2:12-14).

The sheer exuberance of living is some consolation and validation of life. In all of this there is a usually implied but sometimes expressed understanding that everything good is a gift of God. It cannot really be merited; it is simply there, and sometimes there in surprising places, such as among the unjust. But as long as one has one's own measure, that can be borne. So the goodness of God is also a partial reason for accepting life as it is. That God wants to be good to others may be inexplicable, but not unacceptable.

Yet there was a deeper problem. If the sages had the advantage of having eyes in their heads, they ended up in the same grave as the fools. If the just and the unjust both seemed to enjoy life, the grave swallowed them both. If the wise could save a city by wisdom (Eccl 9:13-16; see 2 Sam 20:14-22), they could also be forgotten along with the fools who started the war. The inexplicability could not simply be accepted; it had to be understood.

And so Qoheleth pursued his way toward his own solution. It was not all that much of a solution, for it too leads to the grave. In the last great and haunting bit of poetry in the book, he pictures himself, an old man now, walking slowly through a devastated village. The strong men stand bent; the mourners inside shroud their heads as he passes; the birds stop singing. He finally comes to the village well, which had been the source of life. As he watches, the waiting pitcher topples and breaks, and the pulley falls into the deep pit.

And the dust returns to the earth as it
    once was,
    and the life breath returns to God
        who gave it.
Vanity of vanities, says Qoheleth,
    all things are vanity! (12:7-8)

What happened after that no one knows. But Qoheleth had gotten them as far as he could. The new revelation awaited the Son of God.

COMMENTARY

THE FIRST SECTION

Eccl 1:1–3:15

Chapter 1

1:1 Despite the apparent meaning, the author is not Solomon but Qoheleth. Forging authorship was not a practice among the Jews. Rather, the need was for one to remain unknown while indicating the kind of writing that one intended. Later the author will dress up his own experience as a well-to-do bon-vivant and businessman in terms more suitable for King Solomon. This was accepted practice.

1:2-8 The introductory poem is matched by the concluding one in 3:1-8. Both concern the relentless succession of events, and both are well-known because of their elegant style. The images conjure up the feeling of endless sameness; the balanced phrases are measured to lull us into acceptance. Here one generation succeeds another endlessly; the sun rises and sets each day; the wind keeps blowing, now from one direction and then from another; the rivers keep running down to the sea but never fill it; we keep explaining, but we never really say anything; we keep seeing and hearing, but we never learn what it is all about. The whole enterprise is the greatest puff of vapor imaginable, "vanity," for that is what "vanity of vanities" means.

1:11 The one thing that is thought to have permanence is a family name. People live on in that endless remembering that is so much a part of their religious heritage. Qoheleth denies it.

1:12-18 Qoheleth's first attempt to solve the riddle is by wisdom. Those with wisdom are the observers, sometimes the natural scientists of their day. Qoheleth sees it all and concludes that it is all made up of crooked lines and leads nowhere—"a chase after the wind." All that work for nothing! He can only reach the opposite conclusion that the sages before him reached: "For in much wisdom there is much sorrow" (1:18). Disillusionment, not contentment, is the fruit of learning.

Chapter 2

2:1-12 This section recounts Qoheleth's attempt to find an answer in frantic pleasure. It is not the heady flower-children escapism in which the Greeks were tempted to indulge (see Wis 2:1-9). This is the more substantial Jewish way of displaying power by banquets and sumptuous building projects—in short, becoming a patron of the arts. "Nothing that my eyes desired did I deny them, nor did I deprive myself of any joy, but my heart rejoiced in the fruit of all my toil" (v. 10). But who will keep it all up when he is gone? "For what will the man do who is to come after the king? What men have already done!" (v. 12).

2:12b-17 An aside is inserted here to reflect on the vanity of it all. Qoheleth might just as well be a fool, one who simply spurns the ethics of Jewish righteousness and lives selfishly as though there were no God; such is the meaning of "fool." Even though those with wisdom have eyes in their head, they come to the same end as the fool; all will be forgotten. And so he loathes a life that has no real meaning whatever one does.

2:18-26 Next Qoheleth buries himself in work. From the beginning he knows how vain this is. He knows not whether he will leave it all to a fool or a wise person. Meanwhile he must worry about it, so that "even at night his mind is not at rest" (v. 23). Still and all, working at play is about the best one can do. "There is nothing better for man than to eat and drink and provide himself with good things by his labors" (v. 24). It was not exactly escapism which Qoheleth embraced, but thankfulness. Hard work did not produce results; it did make one aware that everything good came from the hand of God.

Chapter 3

3:1-8 This famous poem, which we have made into a popular song, celebrates the inevitability of life. "There is an appointed time for everything under heaven." It is not a moral judgment of which times are good and which are bad, but the much worse judgment that they are simply inevitable. Birth and death, sowing and harvesting, killing and healing go on no matter what we do. And so it comes down to those alternatives on which we all take sides: a time to love and a time to hate; a time of war and a time of peace. It will not do to say that we opt for love, not hate; or

816

peace, not war. That is immaterial—they simply happen.

3:9-15 So the poem leads to a meditation on what we are all thinking of: Why? Merely working for peace or love does not seem to affect the outcome very much, despite all the glorious stories of how one person changed the world. Somehow God has placed us all here in these intractable situations that keep us busy without ever bringing us closer to a conclusion or even revealing what it is all about. All we know is hustling time that will not let us rest with the good things we want.

Yet the tradition of the sages said that there is an appropriate time for all things. Nothing happens haphazardly or outside its time. But we do not know what or why the appropriate time is.

> He has made everything appropriate to its time, and has put the timeless into their hearts, without men's ever discovering from beginning to end, the work which God has done (v. 11).

This is the crux of the problem. Unfortunately, the Hebrew is not quite clear about the word we translate as "timeless." It is an adverb, and the translation might be: "he has put the love of the world into their hearts." If so, the final problem is that all are earthbound. The final poem (see Eccl 12:7) seems to persuade acceptance of our translation. At any rate, Qoheleth returns to his refrain about eating and drinking. Now, however, his thought goes further than thanks. All things happen because God has done them; that remains, and nothing can be added to it or taken away from it. God alone can put things back in their proper place: "God restores what would otherwise be displaced" (v. 15). The exact meaning is somewhat obscure.

THE MIDDLE SECTION

Eccl 3:16–11:8

As noted above, the middle section has no real order to it. It seems to be a collection of various proverbial sayings and reflections on almost all aspects of Israel's wisdom. Some of them Qoheleth accepts, others he modifies, and many of them he rejects outright and ridicules. However, it is possible to see a concentration on matters of justice and honesty.

Our commentary will simply investigate the sayings that seem more striking or obscure.

3:16-18 Qoheleth begins his collection with a bitter saying about injustice at the highest government levels. He has a traditional confidence that God will eventually judge all, but meanwhile nothing more can be done than to accept that God is testing us.

3:21 Qoheleth is apparently referring to some popular saying that there is a happy future in store for good people. He challenges them to produce the evidence. Both the good and the wicked return to the dust.

Chapter 4

4:4 It was accepted that Jews should be hard-working, not lazy. But Qoheleth doubts the validity of such high-flown reasons as are given. In the end competition, not spiritual motives, prevails.

4:9 Again Qoheleth is citing a popular saying that teamwork is better than working alone. He continues a similar thought in verse 11 that marriage is better than being single. Then he laughs it to scorn by saying that there is nothing more in it than that a team makes more money and that a married partner is a good bed-warmer.

4:13-16 This section of reflections on the political community might be connected with "court wisdom," as it is called, except that the sentiment expressed would never be taught to young persons aspiring to government office. There is no end to the bootlickers at court, but the one whose boots are licked isn't worth remembering. There are a fair number of such reflections on the lifestyle of government officials; perhaps Qoheleth had had some role in this himself.

4:17 This is one of Qoheleth's few references to temple worship. It is respectful of God and scornful of the hypocrisy that Qoheleth observed.

Chapter 5

This chapter begins by continuing the theme of religious practice mentioned above. Then it shifts to a consideration of the folly of riches and ends with the refrain "Eat, drink and be merry."

5:4 The sentiment was traditional; Deut 23:22 and Sir 18:21 both say the same thing. In Qoheleth, however, it has a sharper tone, perhaps a repudiation of those scribes who were mostly interested in finding a way around fulfilling vows.

5:9-11 The vanity of riches is a consistent theme in both the Old and New Testaments. Qoheleth expresses it in pragmatic terms: "Where there are great riches, there are also many to devour them."

Chapter 6

Chapter 6 is mostly a series of reflections on the canker of wealth. Riches beget a desire for riches; even the approach of death does not seem to assuage it. "All man's toil is for his mouth, yet his desire is not fulfilled" (v. 7). Why people should react like this cannot be explained; that is the way God made them, and they might as well desist from arguing with One mightier than themselves. And yet, is that a tolerable explanation? That is Qoheleth's problem, as it was Job's. "Who is there to tell a man what will come after him under the sun?" (v. 12).

6:1 "There is another evil . . .": In effect, it is the same evil with which chapter 4 ended. The rich are never satisfied. If the rich man has a hundred children, he worries about the money that slips out of his grasp and whether he will be buried with suitable pomp. "The child born dead is more fortunate than he" (v. 3).

6:9 Apparently this is a quote from a common proverb. For once Qoheleth agrees.

6:10 ". . . he cannot contend in judgment with one who is stronger than he": The "one" refers to God. No one can demand that God give a reason for what God does. And if God won't, nobody else can.

Chapter 7

Chapter 7 is particularly unorganized. It begins with a litany of proverbs, some of which Qoheleth accepts and some of which he ridicules. Then it turns to considering a mean that is not a Golden Mean but a livable compromise. Toward the end Qoheleth confesses that he is in over his head as a sage and then compounds it by some scathing words about women in general. Apparently Qoheleth found trouble himself observing his admonition to avoid excess.

7:1 "A good name is better than good ointment, and the day of death than the day of birth": This is usually cited as the typical example of Qoheleth's technique. He has taken a proverb that is exceedingly common and turned it on its head by adding a comment that ridicules it. Verses 2, 3, and 4 use a similar approach but are less biting, since they do not trap us but warn us from the beginning that the author's views are unconventional.

7:13 The cliché is that God writes straight with crooked lines. Qoheleth will not suffer clichés. He turns the saying around. Experience has taught him about the crooked things in life and his inability to do much about them. All one can do is accept (see v. 14).

7:16-18 The New American Bible puts these words in quotation marks to indicate the translator's opinion that they are common sayings that Qoheleth knows but repudiates. Qoheleth was no martyr, willing to die uselessly for a justice he could not achieve. Nor did he think that he himself could lead a blameless life. He could not be self-righteous, nor could he be ruthless. Yet life constantly caught him in such dilemmas. His wisdom did not give him a way out. There was some truth in both sayings, but not enough in either. He went back to the traditional saying that the fear of the Lord is the beginning of wisdom. It arrived, but it was only the beginning. So he would counsel simply trying to stand in awe of the great God and letting things take their course. "He who fears God will win through at all events" (v. 18).

7:23 The personal note gives punch to the traditional view that wisdom, like everything else, is a gift, not a reward for work. The wisdom to unravel the enigma that has just been discussed is beyond Qoheleth.

7:26-29 This section on the human race is characteristic of Qoheleth. It is partly tongue-in-cheek and partly serious. It begins with "the woman who is a hunter's trap." The reference is probably to Egypt or some such symbol of paganism that led Israel astray. Escape from her is due solely to God. Yet there is a more personal note to the section. From experience Qoheleth does not have much faith in the men he knows; he accuses them of being unjust and dishonest. He would say even less of women. It may be a social prejudice or a deliberate slur intended to provoke dissent and proof to the contrary. That, too, would be like Qoheleth.

7:29 The Hebrew text is not quite clear, especially as to who is doing the calculating—the men or the women. Most likely Qoheleth means that the whole race has engaged in spoiling the work that God created good. That would be a normal wisdom viewpoint.

Chapter 8

Chapter 8 begins with some conventional sayings taken from the court wisdom, that is, instructions to students on how to act in the service of the king. Loyalty is stressed, especially sticking by the administration when injustices seem to have been done: "while one man tyrannizes over another to his hurt" (v. 9). The wise man knows that there is a proper time and judgment for all things; he does not know when the proper time or judgment is.

The second half (8:10-17) almost seems to deny the wisdom of the above as Qoheleth reflects on the lack of any apparent consistency in retribution. The wicked are not punished, and so society is tempted to lawlessness. However, he clings to his religious belief that reverence toward God finally pays off, but he does not know when. The wicked still prosper, and the wise can simply try to enjoy life as best they can. This reflection continues into the next chapter (9:1-3). The most perplexing thing about life is the apparent lack of any different result between being good or bad: "Among all the things that happen under the sun, this is the worst, that things turn out the same for all" (9:3).

Chapter 9

This section seems to run from 9:4 to 10:2, as the translation indicates. It begins with the sunshine of seeing the joy of living. Here Qoheleth has put his longest statement of the refrain into almost poetic form. Not only can one find satisfaction in good food and drink; fine clothes and perfumes help. Enjoy life with the wife whom you love. Give all you got in everything you do. Then comes the somber note: death is on the way. Life is a game of chance; victory does not go to the best, and we do not know when uncontrollable accidents will wipe out all we are trying to do.

In Eccl 9:13-16 occurs one of the finest uses of parable in the Bible. A parable is not a simplistic story telling us to do in like manner;

it is a thought-provoking story that traps us with simple pictures and then stings. It is conventional to say that wisdom pays off and the wise are respected. Qoheleth says that it does not happen if you are wise but poor. His sage saved a city—and was promptly forgotten. A single fly falling by chance into the ointment can spoil it all.

9:5 "For the living know that they are to die, but the dead no longer know anything." So also in verse 10 Qoheleth concludes that "there will be no work, nor reason, nor knowledge, nor wisdom in the nether world where you are going." Such was the traditional attitude. Israel had been chosen to be God's worshiper on earth. Very little was said to them about the afterlife. In Qoheleth's time the view was beginning to change. A hundred years later there was not only a full-blown belief in a judgment in a world beyond, but also the clearest statement about the doctrine of purgatory, as we call it. But Qoheleth was a theological conservative; he lived on what had been handed down, even when he challenged it.

Chapter 10

Chapter 10 probably runs from 10:3 to 11:2. It is a grab bag of wise sayings from conventional wisdom.

10:2 The right hand is used as a symbol of skill for biblical authors; the left is used to express foolishness.

10:11 Snake charming was (and is) a realistic feat in the Near East. The proverb is cautionary, like the modern proverb that says: "It's no use locking the barn door after the horse has been stolen."

10:19 This is somewhat cynical but observable. Money does seem to "provide" for all our merrymaking.

10:20 We may well think that this is fanciful, but so is the spy system that gets word back to the king of what one says secretly, and that is the meaning of the admonition.

11:1 The meaning of this familiar quotation is to make doubly sure that one has plenty of everything so as not to be caught short.

Chapter 11

Only verses 3 to 6 are considered here. These are prudential remarks on providing abundantly, since we do not know what the future will bring. The rain falls just so much and that is that; the tree falls and stays there. Too much caution gets in the way. We do not know how babies are fashioned, and we do not know what God is doing in the world, so we should work hard and provide doubly. The words are conventional wisdom that Qoheleth does not contradict, but he centers them on the thought that we do not know what God is doing.

THE FINAL SECTION

Eccl 11:9–12:8

The final hymn is to life. This is one of the most hauntingly beautiful poems in all of literature. The impact is achieved by a careful conjuring up of images and balancing of structure.

We can see the sun shining, the clouds gathering, the dawn and the sunset, the birds in the trees, the village well. Yet these images are also carefully balanced against opposites. Light and darkness, the nothingness of death and the life breath jostle one another. The strong stand but they are bent; the mill still grinds, but slowly; the birds sit in the trees, but do not sing; the well is full of water, but no one is around, and as one looks, the rope breaks and the bucket falls into the depths.

So also the addresses to the youth and the aged are contrasted. Qoheleth gives four verses to youth and then multiplies this to eight verses for those his own age. It is this careful structuring of image against image, age against age, that gives an internal rhythm to the thought and produces the right mood.

The thought can then emerge. Qoheleth first addresses the young men before him. He is consistent with his previous teaching: life is good; live it to the full.

> Rejoice, O young man, while you are young,
> and let your heart be glad in the days
> of your youth.
> Follow the ways of your heart,
> the vision of your eyes;
> Yet understand that as regards all this
> God will bring you to judgment (11:9).

"Judgment" sounds a discordant note, and we wish it meant something else. Apparently it does. Qoheleth knew nothing of judgment as the Last Judgment in our sense, nor does he ever mention any examination of merit and punishment. Judgment is revelation. His consistent cry has been that life is inexplicable; good and bad seem so haphazard; success and failure do not belong to us; justice and injustice mix in such strange ways. He has concluded that only God knows, and God is not talking. Yet somehow, sometime, God will reveal it all. Qoheleth does not admonish youth to live a good life lest they be punished, but not to presume to know more about life than they really do, lest they transgress God's secret border.

Yet, youth is fleeting, and Qoheleth stands at the end of the road. He is like an old man wandering into a silenced village. The sun has gone behind the clouds, the menservants stand bent over, the women waiting at the mill are few, the ladies in the house only occasionally peek out of the windows. The doors of houses are closed; the birds do not sing; the old man totters along precariously as though on a precipice, fearing a mugging; the trees blossom but do no more. And as he passes through this silent village, he arrives finally at the well, the center of town. But no one is trading news at the well. As he looks at this source of life—for good water is called living water—he sees the whole apparatus of pulley, bucket, and counterbalance fall into the pit as the rope breaks. Need anything more be said?

> And the dust returns to the earth as it once was,
> and the life breath returns to God who gave it.
> (12:7)

Qoheleth shrieks for some greater knowledge. Faith says that life is safe in the hands of the Life-giver. But how? And why?

12:1 The tradition of the sages was strong on God the Creator. In spite of everything pessimistic that he says, Qoheleth always believes in a good Creator behind the universe. That conviction of goodness is central to wisdom thinking. It is not God the Judge that youth needs to think of, but God the Creator; and then they must strive to be creators themselves.

12:3 The older Jewish rabbis were accustomed to interpret each of these images as referring to some part of the body. Later scholars thought they saw only a smorgasbord of varied images that had no connection with one another. However, the impression and central theme seem to relate to a silent village or estate. These are the usual employees who are now idle.

12:4 A catastrophe of some sort, such as a plague, has idled all these people.

12:5 This is an old man who is being pictured. He totters as though he were on a high place. He also fears the young who roam the streets.

"When the almond tree blooms": This is not clear. One meaning may be that the trees bloom, but do not bear. The caper berry was reputed to restore sexual powers, but even that does not work anymore.

"Because man goes to his lasting home": It is lasting because it is the grave; it is not much of a home. Meanwhile, he can see the mourners already assembling for his funeral.

12:6 Apparently the rope is old and white. The pitcher is the bucket, and the golden ball is some sort of counterbalance.

12:7 "And the dust returns to the earth": The phrase undoubtedly reflects the well-known saying: "Dust thou art and unto dust thou shalt return." On the other hand, the word used for "life breath" is more normally used for a word of God or a spirit from God. It is not the equivalent of our word for "soul."

THE EPILOGUE

Eccl 12:9-14

The epilogue speaks of Qoheleth in the third person, so we presume that it was written by someone else. He is described as holding some sort of official position as a teacher. He was also something of a research scholar, collecting the traditions of the past. Here the editor makes his own comment, perhaps to apologize that Qoheleth's research did not uncover many comforting proverbs. His were like "fixed spikes." Then he seems to presume that many books of this sort have been published, although we know of only a few. One should appreciate authors; they spend much time doing the writing. And, being a much more conventional man himself, he adds the theme-saying of all wisdom writers: "Fear God and keep his commandments." He is not laying down a law; he is expressing the conviction that the only wise way to live is to be in awe of the incomprehensible God who lives behind the appearances of things and to try to be holy as God is holy. One day God will reveal what this is all about.

Because God will bring to judgment every work, with all its hidden qualities, whether good or bad (12:14).

ESTHER

James A. Fischer, C.M.

INTRODUCTION

The Hebrew Book of Esther is a melodrama. When the story was read in the synagogue during the feast of Purim, the men stomped their feet, banged the tables, hissed the villain, and cheered the hero. It was a riotous celebration with much drinking; "too much" was when one could not tell the difference between "Bless Mordecai" and "Curse Haman," said some rabbis. In medieval times Purim became a kind of carnival celebration with dramatizations of the story spinning off from the biblical tale.

The ancient tradition should be respected for its insight. The story was heard as a hero tale in which the Jews triumphed over their enemies by better intrigue. The hero, Mordecai, was cast in the role of the trickster, as Jacob and Joseph before him had been in more discreet ways. The justification for the celebration was simply that the Jews of Persia had been given relief from persecution and had thus been able to care for their poorer neighbors. Such were the reasons given by Queen Esther in her official decree establishing the feast. Some such justification is also given by many modern Jewish scholars. The story itself does not mention God; it has no pious lesson, nor does it raise any disturbing questions in the text. It was just fun to recall one triumphant moment of salvation for one's people.

The acceptance of the Book of Esther has always been a problem of more or less concern in Jewish circles. Esther has not been found among the Qumram documents (which is unusual), and even after its acceptance as

Scripture by the Jewish scholars at Jamnia around A.D. 90, it was still denounced by some rabbis as unworthy of honor as sacred Scripture. Present-day Jewish scholars tend to vindicate the book on the basis that whatever preserves the Jewish community must be part of God's plan. God is not mentioned in the Hebrew text, but Jewish spirituality rests on the conviction that God is present in the most mundane affairs, even when not seen. There is much to be said for this viewpoint.

The Hebrew and the Greek versions

The hero story is the one preserved in Judaism and in most non-Catholic Bibles. The Greek translation, which Catholics use, introduced a more somber note. The moral problem raised by the slaying of so many pagans was addressed by a dream sequence added to the beginning and the end. The pious need was met by interspersing various prayers to God and confessions of guilt.

The history of the Book of Esther

Since the Hebrew story of Esther is so obviously a tale to be enjoyed, there seems to be little reason to delay over questions of historical accuracy. That there was a King Ahasuerus, otherwise known in Persian chronicles as Xerxes I, who ruled from 486 to 465 B.C.E., is indisputable. In many places, the book reflects authentic information about the Persian period. On the other hand, there is nothing known about a Queen Vashti or a

Queen Esther or a Haman or a pogrom against the Jews. Some of this seems unlikely. The most prudent supposition seems to be that some master storyteller welded together several stories that may have arisen from local events and produced a story of intrigue that was credible and exciting without being an attempt to chronicle actual facts.

We do not even know whether the story produced the feast of Purim or whether a pre-existing feast attracted the story to itself. The feast was called Purim ("lots") from the mention of the lots that were cast before the king to determine the date for the extermination of the Jews (3:7). It was celebrated in the spring of the year on the fourteenth and fifteenth of the month of Adar. The story and the feast originated among Persian Jews sometime between 465 and 167 B.C.E. and spread westward to the rest of Judaism.

The story

The Hebrew story (designated in our text by the usual chapter numbers from 1 to 10) tells of how Mordecai, a Jew at the court of King Ahasuerus, revealed a plot to kill the king, but was left unrewarded. The king had to choose a new queen, and Mordecai was able to have his cousin Esther selected. She became the favorite and learned of a plot to destroy all Jews. This was the work of Haman, the prime minister, who personally hated Jews, and Mordecai in particular. One night the king suddenly remembered that Mordecai had saved his life and summoned Haman to tell him how to honor a man to whom the king was indebted. Haman thought that he was the man and heaped up the honors. He planned to execute Mordecai on a huge scaffold in his yard. But then he discovered that Mordecai was to be the honoree. Moreover, Esther revealed to the king that Haman had already issued a decree that all Jews be killed. Haman knew that he was undone and went to plead before Queen Esther and threw himself before her. The king entered the room and thought he was attacking the queen, and ordered him hanged on his own scaffold. Then Esther got another royal decree that the Jews would be allowed to defend themselves. So they did, and that day was proclaimed by both Mordecai and Esther as a great festival day for the Jews.

Such is the Hebrew story. To it the Greek translators added the chapters that are designated in the text by the letters A to F. The first and last chapters are dream sequences reminiscent of a kind of literature called apocalyptic. They have two dragons, a saving river, and a cosmic battle. The other chapters are prayers of confession and petition or official documents. Only one piece of additional narrative is supplied; chapter D tells how God made Esther appear even more beautiful and so averted the king's anger.

The touch is light, but the implications for the story are enormous. In the initial dream Mordecai sees two dragons threatening every nation. In the final explanation of the dream, Mordecai identifies the two dragons as Haman—and himself. The story had raised disturbing moral questions about the Jewish role in the pogrom. The Greek editors had fingered their own people as equal culprits. The dream sequence is a common enough way for an author to add editorial comment, but the apocalyptic technique did elevate the problem to one of the cosmic struggle of good and evil. God enters the story. Mordecai's character gets changed around at the end. He is no longer the trickster but the honest man who must face his own lack of integrity in victory. God alone is the hero; the story has passed from straight fun to irony.

COMMENTARY

INTRODUCTION

Esth A:1-17

A:1 Ahasuerus is very probably Xerxes I (485–464 B.C.E.), known to European history as the villain who attacked Greece. He was, however, an enlightened ruler. Mordecai is unknown to secular history, although we know of a Marduka, an imperial accountant from the capital of Susa under Darius and Xerxes. Mordecai is described as a prominent man, and later on we learn from the Hebrew text that he was a minor official at court.

"Mordecai had a dream . . .": This is a storyteller's technique for indicating that the author already knows what the story means. It is used frequently in the Bible in such narratives as those of Joseph in Egypt, Gideon, and Daniel, and in Matthew's infancy narrative (see v. 11).

A:4 Mordecai's dream includes a cosmic battle, darkness, confusion among all nations, dragons, and a saving river. This is common stock-in-trade for writers of apocalypse (Ezek 47; Dan 12:5-7; Rev 12 have similar elements). All this introduces us to a world in which good and evil fight on a cosmic level.

A:12-16 The plot against the king's life is also narrated in the Hebrew text (2:21-23). However, the Greek editor has combined the apocalyptic dream sequence and a political awareness of some future pay-off to capture the bi-level approach of apocalyptic, which deals with both heaven and earth.

A ROYAL BANQUET

Esth 1:1-22

1:3 No occasion is given for the feast. It will be noted that most of the action in the story takes place during banquets. This motif ties the story together and serves as an appropriate connection with the feast of Purim.

1:10-22 It is difficult to judge whether the author admired Queen Vashti for refusing to perform for the king or whether he agreed with the decree that women should be kept in a proper place. In either case, he is simply telling a story, and he certainly sets up a contrast between the strong-willed Vashti and Queen Esther, who does what she is told to do. Evidently Esther is not so much a heroine as a pawn.

1:19 The royal decree is irrevocable. This odd provision of Persian law is referred to also in the story of Daniel in the lion's den (compare Dan 6:8), but it is not known from any other source.

ESTHER MADE QUEEN

Esth 2:1-23

2:2 The theme of the contest to choose a new queen is fairly common in literature, most notably in the Arabian tale *A Thousand and One Nights.* A historical difficulty exists here, since Esther was a Jewess and the Persian queens were always selected from the seven dominant Persian families. Xerxes' queen was named Amestris. The name Esther seems to be a take-off on the Babylonian name for the goddess Ishtar, but that does not seem to have any significance in the story.

HAMAN'S PLOT AGAINST THE JEWS

Esth 3:1-15

3:1 Haman the Agagite is unknown to history. Obviously he is intended to be a Persian, but his genealogy is traced back to Agag, the king of the Amalekites whom Saul slew (see 1 Sam 15:7ff.). Mordecai's ancestry is traced back to Saul. This looks suspiciously contrived but explains that the antagonism between the two men is irrevocably rooted in the past.

3:6 In the story there is no Persian prejudice against the Jews. This seems to be factual. Mordecai the Jew was accepted as a royal official without comment. The same is also implied in the story of Daniel. As the storyteller had it, the sole cause of hatred for the Jews was the personal animosity of Haman.

HAMAN'S LETTER

Esth B:1-7

This letter was composed by the Greek editor as a propaganda piece, specifying the racial prejudice of the nations against the Jews who lived outside Palestine. It probably reflects Alexandrian social situations more than those of Persia.

ESTHER'S PROBLEM

Esth 4:1-16

Now that Esther has become queen, she begins to use some of her power to protect Mordecai. However, it will be evident to the end of the story that Mordecai is the principal actor throughout, both as a Persian official and as the family advisor of Esther.

4:9 Verses 8-9, which refer to invoking the Lord, are not in the Hebrew text. They have been imported into the English translation from the Greek.

PRAYERS OF MORDECAI AND ESTHER

Esth C:1-30

C:1-11 Mordecai's prayer is a rather traditional lament recalling God's past favors to the Israelites.

C:12-30 Esther's prayer is a traditional complaint against paganism and a confession of righteousness. The Greek interpretation, which makes Esther some sort of savior of her people, describes her far more piously than the incidents of the story warrant.

ESTHER RECEIVED BY THE KING

Esth D:1-16

This is the only Greek addition to the narrative itself. It quite clearly shifts Esther's success from her beauty and cunning to the initiative of God, who makes all things happen rightly.

ESTHER'S PLOT

Esth 5:1-14

5:1-8 The banquet motif is here expanded to introduce an essential tension to the plot. The first banquet is apparently useless except as an invitation to a second banquet. However, this allows time for Haman to act.

5:9-14 Haman thinks that he is to be exceptionally honored by the second banquet.

Full of confidence in his own success, he anticipates his victory by building a mammoth scaffold, fifty cubits high, on which to hang Mordecai. For vanquishing a superior foe no ordinary gibbet would do.

HAMAN'S DOWNFALL

Esth 6:1-14

Haman is now firmly set on the road to tragedy. In the classical understanding of tragedy, the final destruction must necessarily occur because of some essential weakness in a noble character. Haman has been portrayed as a quite successful prime minister. His flaw is his own hatred and pride. Esther is merely the catalyst that sets the tragedy in motion. So in verse 13 the inevitable tragedy is predicted by Haman's wife and friends. Nothing can prevent it from occurring. Later in the story (see 9:1, 24-26) the word *pur*, "lot," will be interpreted as fate.

THE PUNISHMENT OF HAMAN

Esth 7:1-10

7:1-6 Esther's appeal to the king to cancel the pogrom against the Jews is based on his own self-interest. She cites the harm that will be done to the king by the destruction of the Jewish community. That does not seem to convince him. It is only then that she reveals that Haman is behind the plot. Obviously the king has not been paying much attention to business.

7:7-8 The king, who is already angered, re-enters the room and finds Haman on the couch with his wife, pleading his case. He makes the natural conclusion and executes Haman, not for any official policy decision, but for the personal insult.

7:9-10 The theme of reversal is again stressed in the ironic execution of Haman on the grandiose scaffold he himself has erected.

THE DECREE REVERSED

Esth 8:1-17

8:2 The king's signet ring is given to Mordecai, and that virtually makes him prime minister. It is noteworthy that it is Mordecai and not Esther who is given the regal power.

8:3-17 King Ahasuerus once again shows his little interest in the pogrom against the Jews by simply commissioning Esther to write anything she wants. In her letter she instructs all the officials to ignore Haman's letter. According to the previous reference to the laws of the Persians, which cannot be changed, this is impossible, so she adds a separate protocol that allows the Jews to defend themselves on the thirteenth of Adar. She also encourages them to celebrate.

8:11 "To kill, destroy, wipe out, along with their wives and children, every armed group of any nation or province which shall attack them, and to seize their goods as spoil": This bloodthirsty decree is actually required to reverse the earlier edict of Haman, which was put in the same terms (see 3:13).

THE ATTACK

Esth 9:1-32

9:5 The text records that five hundred Persians were killed in Susa, in addition to the ten sons of Haman. More were killed on the second day. In the provinces, the Hebrew text says, seventy-five thousand were killed; the Greek version mentions fifteen thousand. Numbers, especially round numbers, in Old Testament texts are subject to considerable doubt. Since this is a story, the author's intention was simply to say that there was a great victory for the Jews. The decree had authorized the killing of any who attacked the Jews. The numbers are limited to indicate restraint. So also the text in three places (9:10, 15, 16) emphasizes that the Jews took no booty, although they were commissioned to do so.

9:21-22 It is noteworthy that it is Mordecai who writes the first and decisive letter authorizing the feast of Purim. Although the slaughter of the Jews was set for the thirteenth day of Adar, the feast is celebrated on the fourteenth, when the riots took place in the provinces, and on the fifteenth, when the mopping up was completed in Susa. Even with this explanation the chronology of the feast of Purim does not work out exactly. It is to be noted that Mordecai stresses that the feast commemorates the "rest" that was

granted to the Jews on this occasion. Rest is a gift of God. He also specifies that Purim is to be a time of feasting and gladness, with the sending of food to one another and of giving gifts to the poor. The victory concept is considerably played down.

9:24-26 A curious summary of the whole plot is given here. However, it brings in the essential concept of tragedy. In the original story of Saul and Agag (see 1 Sam 15), Saul failed to put Agag the Amalekite to death as God had commanded. That led inevitably to Saul's destruction. The text here mentions Mordecai as the descendant of Saul, and Haman as the descendant of Agag. In this case, it is inevitable that Mordecai should destroy Haman. In our text the word pur, "lot," is taken in its Akkadian sense of "fate." Purim does symbolize the inevitable destruction of God's enemies.

THE DREAM EXPLAINED

Esth F:1-10

F:1 The dream will now explain how God, who was not mentioned in the Hebrew text, nevertheless was working behind the scenes. That there is an order in the world is the general supposition of wisdom literature, and the Greek Book of Esther is certainly related to wisdom.

F:2-6 The identifications are clearly made. The saving river is Esther; the nations are the persecutors of the Jews, who are in turn saved by the Lord. The surprising identification is: "The two dragons are myself and Haman." Dragons are biblical symbols for the enemies of the just. The Hebrew story had developed a series of reversals: Mordecai the oppressed became Mordecai the victor; Haman the Jew-hater was executed on his own gibbet; the day of slaughter became a day of rest for the Jews. The Greek editor simply carried the motif to its final step; Mordecai the hero became Mordecai the villain. His hands were as bloody as Haman's.

F:7 To continue the tragic or saving theme, the author once more has recourse to the doctrine of fate. God arranged two lots—one for the people of God, the second for all other nations. The lot for God's people is the joy and happiness of the feast of Purim (see v. 10). Nothing is said about the nations' lot.

JONAH, TOBIT, JUDITH

Irene Nowell, O.S.B.

INTRODUCTION

It has been said that we use stories to tell ourselves the truths we cannot explain. Biblical authors used many types of literature to convey the word of God. Besides historical accounts, parables, hymns, and love songs, they also used stories, fictional tales crafted to carry truths more profound than a simple recital of everyday facts could bear.

The Books of Jonah, Tobit, and Judith are among the best examples of such fiction in all of biblical narrative. The authors of these three books took essential elements of biblical faith and used all the techniques of their literary skill to weave stories that illustrate the dynamic effectiveness of traditional beliefs in the situation of their audience. They constructed plots that show the workings of God in ordinary human activities and events. They drew characters who, through stubborn resistance and courageous obedience, would be witnesses to the ongoing relationship between God and believers. They used irony and humor to attract their audience and to fix the message in their memory. In short, the authors of these three books were master storytellers. Their message was vital for the audience of their time, and it remains vital for us: the word of God is living, effective, and demanding in every age, including the present one.

The authors of these three little books do not directly answer the questions put to them; rather, they tell stories. To a fifth-century audience bent on separating itself from the rest of the world, one author tells the story of an eighth-century prophet who fled from God's call to bring the good news to the rest of the world (Jonah). To a second-century audience wondering if God is still active in their lives, another author tells the story of a seventh-century family who find God's healing power hidden in their obedience and care for one another (Tobit). To a mid-second-century audience despairing of God's deliverance from horrible persecution, a third author tells the story of God's victory through the hand of a woman (Judith). Each author used the power and beauty of literary skill to bring the word of God to life in the stress and need of the contemporary situation.

The basic truths about God and the people who strive to be faithful to God can be found throughout the Bible. The application of these truths to the specific audience of their own time was the mission and service of the authors of the Books of Jonah, Tobit, and Judith. It is our task to discover what these three books have to tell us about the dynamic presence and insistent demands of God in our own time.

JONAH

Irene Nowell, O.S.B.

INTRODUCTION

The Book of Jonah was written in Palestine around the fifth century B.C.E., when the Jews were still recovering from the Babylonian Exile, a serious threat to their existence. Throughout the ninth and eighth centuries B.C.E., major foreign powers had nibbled away at the territory once controlled by David and Solomon. In 722 B.C.E. Assyria had conquered the northern kingdom of Israel, taken its leading citizens captive, and settled groups of people of other nationalities in northern Palestine. The little kingdom of Judah hung on through another century, survived a change of power in Mesopotamia from Assyria to Babylon, but could not escape indefinitely. In 587 B.C.E. Nebuchadnezzar and the Babylonian army destroyed Jerusalem and led the blinded king and much of the population into exile in Babylon. Fifty years later, in 538 B.C.E., the Persian king Cyrus, having defeated Babylon, issued a decree permitting the Jews to return to Jerusalem and to rebuild the temple there. The struggles between the returning exiles and those who had remained behind, along with grinding poverty and the incessant labor necessary to rebuild a land left desolate and destroyed, provide the background for the Book of Jonah.

The returning Jews were convinced that they had suffered exile because of their infidelity to God. As a result, they developed an attitude of exclusivity and rigorous observance of the law. They avoided anything that might lead them away from God, such as foreign customs or even foreign wives (see Ezra 9:1-3; 10:10-15; Neh 13:23-30). Even the people of the former northern kingdom of Israel, called Samaritans because their capital city had been Samaria, were scorned because they had become a mixed race after the Assyrian invasion (see Ezra 4:1-5).

The author of the Book of Jonah sets his story in opposition to the attitude of exclusivity. In the story, God calls Jonah to prophesy, not to his own people, but to the people of Nineveh, the hated capital of Assyria. Not only must Jonah associate with the idolatrous Gentiles of that city, but he is called to be the instrument through which God's mercy is brought to them. Jonah makes a desperate attempt to flee from God's call. As he complains in chapter 4, he knows what God is like. "I knew," he says to God, "that you are a gracious and merciful God, slow to anger, rich in clemency, loathe to punish" (Jonah 4:2). Jonah knows what effect his message might have. Because he knows that God is merciful, Jonah fears that Nineveh will be converted. Jonah would prefer a god who would destroy Nineveh to one who would forgive it. The author told this story to an audience that desired to avoid other peoples in order to be faithful to God. The story of Jonah presents the shocking truth that "other nations" may also be dear to the heart of God. It is a hard truth, conveyed through a powerful story.

COMMENTARY

CONFRONTATION BETWEEN JONAH AND YAHWEH

Jonah 1:1-16

The Book of Jonah opens with a title announcing the word of the Lord to Jonah, son of Amittai. Jonah, son of Amittai, was the name of an eighth-century prophet who prophesied the restoration of Israel's boundaries by Jeroboam II (see 2 Kgs 14:25). The Book of Jonah, however, was written much later, probably in the fifth century B.C.E. The author wanted to establish his main character as a prophet and so chose the relatively unknown Jonah to fill the role.

The call of Jonah is an exaggerated version of the call-narrative pattern, which consists of the following parts: (1) divine confrontation; (2) introductory words of God; (3) commission of the prophet by God; (4) objection by the prophet; (5) reassurance by God: "I am with you"; (6) promise of a sign. There are some noteworthy correspondences between this pattern and the events in the Book of Jonah. Jonah is confronted by the word of the Lord (1:1) and commissioned to go to Nineveh to preach against it (1:2). Jonah not only objects to this task but flees from it (1:3). The Lord does not simply reassure him but goes after him and brings him back by force (1:4–2:10). Then the call narrative begins again: "The word of the Lord came to Jonah a second time . . ." (3:1).

The city of Nineveh to which God sent Jonah was hated by the Israelites. It was the capital of Assyria, the major power in Mesopotamia in the eighth century. The Assyrians conquered Israel, the northern kingdom, in 722 B.C.E. and took its most powerful citizens into captivity. Israel's hatred of the Assyrians is powerfully described by the prophet Nahum. Jonah is reluctant to go to Nineveh, not so much because he wants to avoid the prophetic call, but because he is unwilling to bring the word of the Lord to such a hated enemy.

The story of Jonah's flight is a masterpiece of irony. According to the narrator, it is Jonah's purpose "to flee away from the Lord" (1:3), so he boards a boat sailing for Tarshish. A storm arises. The sailors pray to their gods to no avail until, by casting lots, they determine that it is Jonah's God who is angry. When the sailors wake Jonah to question him, he tells them, "I worship [fear] the Lord, the God of heaven, who made the sea and the dry land" (1:9). (If he believes this, why does Jonah think that Tarshish is far enough away to escape the Lord?) When the storm begins, the sailors have enough wisdom to pray to their gods while the prophet sleeps. When Jonah tells the sailors that he is running away from God, they are wise enough to be afraid, while the self-proclaimed God-fearer Jonah seems untouched by fear. The word "fear" is repeated in 1:16, after the men have thrown Jonah into the sea. The sailors themselves become God-fearers: "Struck with great fear of the Lord, the men offered sacrifice and made vows to him" (1:16).

Jonah describes Yahweh as the one "who made the sea and the dry land" (1:9). Yahweh controls the sea and its creatures. Yahweh sends the wind to stir up a great storm, stills the storm as soon as Jonah is stopped in his flight by being cast from the ship, and commands a great sea creature to bring Jonah back to his starting point. The sea and the sea monsters are mythological images of creation (see Pss 74:12-14; 89:10-11; 104:25-26; Isa 27:1; Job 40:25). Yahweh created the world by defeating the sea monster, set limits for the sea that it might not pass (Ps 104:9), and made the sea monsters to play in it (Ps 104:26). The image of Yahweh in chapter 1 of Jonah is the image of the all-powerful Creator who commissions the prophet and pursues him until he accepts.

JONAH'S PRAYER

Jonah 2:1-11

Chapter 2 consists of a psalm probably inserted into the narrative from another source. It is set in context by putting the prayer in Jonah's mouth as he rides home in the belly of the docile sea monster.

The prayer belongs to the genre of lament. It is constructed of standard phrases of lamentation and begins and ends in the pattern of laments. The psalmist opens by calling upon God (2:2) and moves immediately to a description of his distress. The end of the prayer is an expression of confidence and thanksgiving to God by the psalmist, who, with unwavering trust, believes in God's salvation.

Many of the phrases in this prayer are common to the psalms; for example:

2:3a—Pss 86:6-7; 120:1;
     compare Pss 34:7; 81:8
2:3b—Pss 18:6-7; 116:3-4
2:4b—Ps 42:8
2:5a—Ps 31:23
2:6a—Pss 18:5; 69:2-3;
     compare Pss 88:17-18; 116:3
2:7b—Pss 16:10; 30:4
2:8a—Ps 42:7
2:8b—Ps 18:7; compare Ps 88:3
2:10a—Pss 50:14; 116:17
2:10b—Pss 22:26; 50:14; 66:13-14;
     116:14, 18; 3:9; 37:39

There seems to be a special correspondence between the lament of Jonah and Psalms 18 and 116.

The psalm lends itself well to Jonah's situation. He is certainly in lamentable straits and needs to turn to Yahweh in confidence. The references to the nether world (vv. 3, 7), however, indicate that the psalm describes general distress. Water, a symbol of primeval chaos, is only one of the images used, but it fits Jonah's situation well. The psalm is well placed, but probably not original to the context.

JONAH IN NINEVEH

Jonah 3:1-10

Chapter 3 begins with Yahweh's second call to Jonah. This time Jonah makes no objection. Jonah surrenders to God's call far more readily than Moses did. Moses objected to Yahweh's call five times before he surrendered (Exod 3:11, 13; 4:1, 10, 13). His last objection is the most poignant: "If you please, Lord, send someone else!" (Exod 4:13). Jonah's compliance with the Lord's second call is only outward, however; his inner feelings will become obvious in chapter 4.

Jonah goes to Nineveh, the ancient city on the left bank of the Tigris River across from modern Mosul. In the nineteenth century, two tells (mounds covering ancient ruins) were

identified as Nineveh. Archeologists found many historical treasures in the ruins, among them relief sculptures from the palaces of Sennacherib, Esarhaddon, and Ashur-bani-pal and an extensive library of Ashur-bani-pal. The city itself was occupied from the fourth millennium B.C.E. to 612 B.C.E., when it fell to the Babylonians and Medes. The inner wall, which encloses a space of less than three square miles, is about seven and one-half miles long. One day's walk would have put Jonah well beyond its center.

The description of Nineveh as an "enormously large city" that required three days simply to go through it, illustrates a key technique in the whole book—exaggeration. "Great" or "large" is one of this author's favorite words; it occurs fourteen times in the book. Nineveh is a "great" city (1:2; 3:2; 3:3; 4:11). Yahweh sends a "great" wind upon the sea, and the tempest that results is "great" (1:4 [twice], 12). The sailors fear with a "great" fear (1:10, 16). After the sailors throw Jonah into the sea, Yahweh sends a "great" fish to swallow him (2:1). The repentance of the people of Nineveh extends from the "great" to the small (3:5), and it is proclaimed throughout Nineveh by decree of the king and his nobles (his "great" ones, 3:7). When God shows mercy toward Nineveh, Jonah's displeasure is "great" (4:1), but his delight in the gourd plant is also "great" (4:6).

The frequent use of the word "great" emphasizes the exaggeration in the content. Everything is larger than life-size. Nineveh is not only great, it is exceedingly great (literally, "great even for God," 3:3). The fast that is proclaimed is worthy of such a great city. It extends from king to beasts and is a total fast even from water (3:7). Jonah's objection to his call is excessive; Yahweh's pursuit of him is equally excessive. In this story there is no moderation.

The numbering of days has a significant balance. Jonah spends three days in the belly of the fish and is then returned to his responsibility to Yahweh. Three days, however, are not enough to bring about a real change of heart in Jonah. The city to which Jonah is sent is reported to be a city so large that it requires a three-day journey to go through it. Yet the city does not need even three days for its repentance; one day is sufficient. Yahweh's mercy, however, does not limit Nineveh to three days. Yahweh allows "forty days," a very large number of days, before the city will be destroyed (3:4).

The message of Jonah proclaims destruction. The response of the Ninevites contains a key word of conversion, "turn." The king proclaims that everyone should "turn" from evil ways; then perhaps Yahweh might "turn" and "repent" of retaliating against Nineveh. Indeed the Ninevites "turn"; indeed Yahweh "repents" (3:8-10). The word "turn" is a key word in the writings of the prophets. It is developed particularly by Jeremiah, and forms the basis of his call to the people. The word "repent" is used primarily of Yahweh in the prophets. If the people "turn," Yahweh "repents" (see Joel 2:12-14). These two words merge into the concept of *metanoia*, or repentance, which, in the New Testament, is demanded of those who would belong to the kingdom of God (see Mark 1:15 and parallels).

RESPONSE TO NINEVEH'S CONVERSION

Jonah 4:1-11

The final chapter contrasts God's merciful response to Nineveh's conversion with Jonah's anger. The chapter is a modified palistrophe (mirror):

A. Jonah's anger (4:1).
    B. Jonah knows God's mercy (4:2).
        C. Double refrain: Let me die (4:3).
            Do you have a right to be angry (4:4)?
            D. God's mercy on Jonah (4:5-8; note "appoints" 3 times).
        C'. Double refrain: Let me die (4:8b).
            Do you have a right to be angry (4:9)?
    B'. God knows Jonah's anger and lack of mercy (4:10).
A'. God's mercy (4:11).

Both the irony and the theology reach a peak in this chapter. First of all, we discover Jonah's reason for fleeing in chapter 1. He dreads the conversion of Nineveh. Because he "knows" that God is "a gracious and merciful God, slow to anger, rich in clemency, loathe to punish (4:2; compare Exod 34:6; Num 14:18-19; Joel 2:14), Jonah fears that he will be a successful prophet and convert the Ninevites. He is angry because he knows that God is not a judge who exacts retribution equal to the crime but rather a merciful God who repents of anger.

God, on the other hand, is merciful because God knows who Jonah is. Instead of punishing Jonah for his flight, for his half-hearted prophesying, for his lack of mercy, God works with Jonah as if he were a child who "cannot distinguish his right hand from his left." God teaches Jonah a lesson. Near his hut God provides a gourd plant that gives Jonah joy and shade. The next day God allows a worm to destroy the plant; this angers Jonah. Then God sends an east wind so hot that Jonah desires death. This is the heart of the chapter and the center of the palistrophe. Divine mercy knows no bounds. God is even merciful to the recalcitrant prophet.

The book ends with a question that challenges the audience of the author's time and all its future readers. God asks: "Should I not, may I not, be merciful even to Nineveh?" Is God free? Or must God act, as Jonah thinks, according to the narrow limitations of human justice?

TOBIT

Irene Nowell, O.S.B.

INTRODUCTION

Not all canonical lists of biblical books include the Book of Tobit. There are seven books which, for various historical reasons, are found in the Roman Catholic canon and not in Jewish or Protestant canons of the Bible. They are: Judith, Tobit, Wisdom, Sirach, Baruch, and 1 and 2 Maccabees, along with additions to the Books of Daniel and Esther. These books are referred to as "deuterocanonical" by Roman Catholics and "apocryphal" by others. They are universally recognized as good books. The primary distinction in modern times is in their use in the liturgy. They are used liturgically by Roman Catholics, but not by Jews or Protestants. They are sometimes found in a separate section in some editions of the Bible.

The Book of Tobit was written around the beginning of the second century B.C.E. Alexander the Great's powerful sweep through the Near East had brought Palestine under his domination in 332 B.C.E. Alexander's death in 323 resulted in a division of his territory, with Syria falling to the Seleucids and Egypt to the Ptolemies. Palestine, a buffer zone between these major powers, was controlled first by the Ptolemies and then, after 198 B.C.E., by the Seleucids. This period was marked by growing Hellenization. Greek customs were adopted, the Greek language became common, and Greek cities were built with gymnasia and hippodromes.

Jewish response to Hellenization was mixed. Zealous Jews resisted every trace of Greek influence, while others found ways to adapt Greek philosophy and language to the service of Judaism. The question of whether to adapt to Greek culture became crucial under the Seleucids, who began to force what had been a rather peaceful progress of Hellenization. The author of Tobit wrote for Jews who were concerned about being faithful to God and who were questioning God's fidelity to them in the midst of this cultural turmoil.

The author uses several old folk tales—the Grateful Dead, the Monster in the Bridal Chamber, and the Story of Ahiqar—as the framework for his story about two ordinary believers, Tobit and Sarah. From the beginning Tobit declares that he has "walked all the days of [his] life on the paths of truth and righteousness" (Tob 1:3). Sarah can say to God, "I have never defiled my own name or my father's name" (Tob 3:15). Each of these faithful people is struck by disaster. Tobit is blinded by bird droppings; Sarah is grieved and humiliated by the sudden deaths of seven successive bridegrooms on the wedding night. The question raised by these crises plagued the faithful Jews under the domination of the Ptolemies and Seleucids: How can we be virtuous if the only result is increasing darkness and disaster?

The author proposes an answer to the question through a story that demonstrates the fidelity of God and the courage of believers. Tobit and Sarah each turn to prayer in their grief. The author informs the readers that their prayer is answered; an angel has been sent to bring them healing. The characters, however, do not know the end of the story, and their continued fidelity bears witness to their courage. Their healing comes about and their fidelity is demonstrated in the midst of the joys and sorrows of family life. The characters trust in a God who is both merciful and just. They in turn act in mercy and justice toward God and one another by rigorous observance of the law, hospitality, almsgiving, and loving respect within the family. Through their fidelity to one another, and specifically through the courage and obedience of Tobit's son Tobiah, who becomes Sarah's husband, both Tobit and Sarah are healed and the power of God's love in their lives is revealed. The story shows that, although God's fidelity may be hidden, human beings are ministers of God's providence, and ordinary human events are the setting for God's faithful care.

COMMENTARY

THE DISTRESS OF TOBIT AND SARAH

Tob 1:1–3:17

1:1-2 Title. The Book of Tobit opens with the common introduction to a historical work: "The book of the words of . . ." In the Septuagint (Greek version) and in English Bibles where it is included, this book is put with the historical works. It cannot, however, be considered a historical work. First of all, there are many historical inaccuracies, which indicate that the author had no intention of producing strict history. The story is set in the reigns of the Assyrian rulers Shalmaneser V (726–722 B.C.E.), Sennacherib (704–681 B.C.E.), and Esarhaddon (680–669 B.C.E.). Sargon II, who should be listed between Shalmaneser and Sennacherib, is missing. It seems that the author of Tobit used 2 Kgs 17:1-6 and 18:9-13 for his list of kings. In that account Sargon is not mentioned. Thus the author of Tobit may have presumed that Sennacherib was the immediate successor of Shalmaneser.

The style of the book also indicates that the author did not intend to produce a historical account. The prayers and monologues could not possibly have been known to a recorder of facts. Parallel events occur simultaneously in such a striking fashion that they indicate an author's manipulation of facts rather than a strict account of happenings. The interests of the book also indicate a period much later than the seventh century B.C.E. in which it is set.

The use of historical information, however, conveys an important theological point in the book. The chronicle of public events, which situates the story in the context of world history, occurs only in the first and last chapters. In the first chapter we find the succession of Assyrian kings—Shalmaneser, Sennacherib, and Esarhaddon. A few notes about Tobit's life indicate what life was like under each of these kings. Under Shalmaneser there was civil order, and exiles like Tobit could hold positions of importance and acquire reasonable sums of money. Under Sennacherib travel was unsafe, and the exiles were persecuted. Restoration of order occurred under Esarhaddon (2:1). There is no mention of public events from the last mention of Esarhaddon in 2:1 until the discussion of the fall of Nineveh to Cyaxares, king of Media, in chapter 14. The fall of Nineveh is mentioned twice in the last chapter. Tobit predicts its fall, and Tobiah rejoices over it.

By setting his story within the context of Assyrian history, the author has made a subtle commentary on the main events of Tobit's life. The Assyrian kings mentioned in chapter 1 are wicked. Shalmaneser takes the Israelites into exile; Sennacherib persecutes them. In chapter 14 Assyria is punished. In contrast, Tobit is righteous all the days of his life, and in chapter 14 he and his family are rewarded. The contrast is subtle but effective.

1:3-22 Tobit's life. After the title (1:1-2) chapter 1 continues with the exposition. Three main sequences are set in motion: (1) Tobit walks in the way of truth and righteousness; (2) Tobit marries Anna; (3) Tobit deposits money in Media. These three sequences open the plot and prepare the way for the questions that will finally be answered in the resolution.

The exposition opens with Tobit speaking in the first person: "I, Tobit, have walked all the days of my life on the paths of truth and righteousness." Three key words in 1:3 are repeated in 14:9 to form an inclusion. The book is a story of "truth," "righteousness," and "almsgiving/mercy." Chapter 1 portrays Tobit's life as an example of truth, righteousness, and almsgiving or charitable works. His righteousness during his youth is illustrated by his fidelity to worship in Jerusalem and his strict keeping of tithes. He follows the rigorous interpretation of tithing common in the second century. It was believed that Num 18:21-24, Deut 14:22-26, and Deut 14:28-29 referred, not to different ways of distributing the one tithe, but to three different tithes. Josephus, a Jewish historian, interprets the texts in this fashion: "In addition to the two tithes which I have already directed you to pay each year, the one for the Levites and the other for the banquets, you should devote a third every third year to the distribution of such things as are lacking to widowed women and orphan children."

Almsgiving is another example of Tobit's fidelity. During Shalmaneser's reign, Tobit reports, he fed the hungry, clothed the naked, and buried the dead (1:16-17). Burying the dead put Tobit in danger of death during the reign of Sennacherib (1:18-20). He flees Nineveh, returning only during the reign of Esarhaddon, when he again begins to invite the poor to dinner and to bury the dead (2:1-7). Tobit's active charity is his most evident characteristic.

In chapter 1 Tobit says that he has been faithful to Jewish law and custom. He has observed the dietary laws of Judaism and has married a woman from his own lineage and family (1:9).

Tobit's marriage to Anna introduces the second sequence of the plot. His marriage is not only an example of his fidelity to Jewish law and custom, but it also introduces two other main characters: Anna, Tobit's wife, and Tobiah, his son. Tobiah becomes the major instrument of God's providence in the rest of the story. Marriage, with its joys and sorrows, is a major theme of the book. The relationships in marriage manifest the working of God.

The third sequence of the plot opens with Tobit's trip to Media to do business for Shalmaneser (1:12-14). On one of his trips, Tobit deposits a large sum of money with a kinsman, Gabael, who lives in Media. The central section of the plot revolves around Tobiah's journey to Media to regain the money. He is guided on his trip by an angel, Raphael, and he becomes the instrument of healing in both families.

Two questions are raised by these three sequences. Tobit is a model of fidelity. What will be his reward? In Media there is money that belongs to Tobit. How will he regain it? The marriage sequence does not raise an immediate question. The solution to the questions from sequences one and three, however, will be found in sequence two.

2:1–3:6 The affliction and prayer of Tobit. We must read chapters 2 and 3 as panels of two different events happening simultaneously. The first scene is set at Tobit's home in Nineveh, the second at Sarah's home in Media. The first scene (2:1-8) opens with Tobit the almsgiver telling Tobiah to find a poor kinsman with whom he can share his Pentecost dinner. Tobiah finds a dead man in the square instead. Tobit immediately buries the dead man, a practice that had previously won for him exile and poverty. The neighbors mock his folly, and the reader wonders what his reward will be for such selfless righteousness.

That night Tobit, weary after the burial, sleeps in the courtyard of his house and is blinded by droppings from birds nesting above him. His reward for righteousness seems to be suffering rather than blessing. The blindness gradually becomes total. Tobit is left dependent on his wife Anna, who goes to work weaving cloth. In an incident that illustrates the tension in the household, Tobit accuses his wife of stealing a goat that was given to her as a bonus. Her retort cuts to the heart of the matter. Since the righteous should be rewarded and Tobit is being punished instead, Anna taunts: "Where are your charitable deeds now? Where are your virtuous acts? See! Your true character is finally showing itself!" (2:14). Tobit is grief-stricken and prays to God for death (3:1-6).

3:7-15 The affliction and prayer of Sarah. Simultaneity is a key technique in this chapter. "On the same day" that Tobit quarrels with Anna and prays for death, Raguel's daughter Sarah is taunted by one of her father's maids and also turns to prayer. Sarah is troubled by a demon who has killed her seven bridegrooms on the wedding night. There is no other near kinsman for her to marry (3:15). She is driven to despair and considers suicide. She reconsiders, however, for love of her father and turns instead to God in prayer. Her prayer is similar to that of Tobit. She, however, gives God a choice: she prays either for death (3:13) or for another solution to her problem (3:15).

Sarah's story picks up the important theme of marriage. She recognizes the significance of marriage and is willing to comply with her father's wishes and the prevailing Jewish custom by marrying a close relative. But the demon, who loves her and wants her for himself, keeps killing off her intended bridegrooms. Her situation has become unbearable.

The two prayers in chapter 3 also demonstrate the importance of prayer in this book. Both a man and a woman turn to prayer in desperate situations. Their prayers are equally significant for the plot. Both pray with phrases familiar from other biblical prayers. Tobit asks to die. He thinks that death is the only solution to his problems. Sarah puts herself completely in God's hands. She illustrates the proper way to pray: she spreads out her hands and turns to face Jerusalem.

3:16-17 The answer to prayer. The conclusion to the chapter emphasizes both the importance of prayer and the technique of simultaneity. The prayers of Tobit and Sarah are heard simultaneously, and God sends the angel Raphael to answer both prayers for help. Raphael's task is to heal both of them. He is to restore Tobit's sight and to free Sarah from the demon. While Raphael is God's messenger to both Tobit and Sarah, the instrument of both healings will be Tobit's son Tobiah. "At that very moment" both Tobit and Sarah return from prayer to their families. Now both lives are linked, both prayers are linked. The reader now knows that both of their prayers will be answered. Only the characters in the story must continue in the darkness of faith. The exposition of the story's plot ends here, but the reader is left with three questions: How will Tobit be healed? How will Sarah be delivered from the demon? How will the lives of these two families continue to be linked?

THE JOURNEY

Tob 4:1–6:18

4:1-21 Preparation for the journey: a father's speech. Chapter 4 belongs to the genre of farewell discourse. In biblical literature this genre has several distinct parts. Some of the parts found in the farewell discourse in the Book of Tobit are: (1) the speaker announces his departure; (2) the speaker recalls the past, either of the people or himself; (3) the speaker exhorts the hearers to keep God's commandments; (4) the speaker exhorts the hearers to unity of spirit; (5) the speaker predicts the future of his children; (6) the speaker wishes peace and joy to his children; (7) the speaker promises his children that God will be with them. Examples of this genre in the Old Testament are the farewell of Jacob (Gen 47:29–49:33); Joshua's farewell (Josh 22–24); David's farewell (1 Chr 28–29); and the whole book of Deuteronomy, which is cast as Moses' farewell discourse. In the Book of Tobit there are three farewell discourses: two of Tobit (4:3-21 and 14:3-11) and one of Raphael (12:6-10).

Tobit instructs Tobiah in the three virtues characteristic of his own life: truth (fidelity), righteousness, and almsgiving. The instruction to almsgiving is the most lengthy. Tobit tells Tobiah to care for Tobit's burial just as his father has cared for the burial of others (4:3; compare 4:17). He instructs Tobiah to pay servants' wages immediately (4:14), to feed the hungry and to clothe the naked (4:16), and to give alms in proportion to what he has (4:7-8, 16). Almsgiving will be for him a protection from death and will be a worthy offering, a worthy worship, to God (4:9-11; compare Sir 35:1-9).

Tobit also instructs Tobiah in the basic theory of retribution: if you are righteous, you will be blessed; if you are evil, you will be cursed (see Deut 28). Even though Tobit's own situation seems to belie the theory—he seems to be cursed even though he has been righteous—he tells Tobiah that doing good works "will bring success" to him and to all who live in righteousness (4:6, 21). Even as he recites the theory, however, Tobit leaves God free to choose how to execute retribution. He tells Tobiah that "if the Lord chooses, he raises a man up; but if he should decide otherwise, he casts him down to the deepest recesses of the nether world" (4:19). Whatever happens comes from God. Tobiah is to trust that God, too, is faithful, righteous, and merciful.

Marriage is the third major subject of Tobit's instruction. In the last centuries of the Old Testament period, the custom had arisen for Jews to marry within close kinship. The Book of Nehemiah reports the harsh requirement that returning exiles who had married non-Jewish women had to put away their foreign wives and marry Jewish wives (Neh 10:31; 13:1-3, 23-30) if they wanted to remain in the Jewish faith. Tobit cites the example of the patriarchs marrying close relatives: Abraham (Gen 20:12), Isaac (Gen 24:3-4), and Jacob (Gen 27:46–28:5). The tradition that Noah married a relative is not found in the Pentateuch but in the Book of Jubilees (4:33). The practice of marriage not only with Jews but within close family ties is probably based on the story of the daughters of Zelophehad (Num 27:5-11; compare Num 36:2-10), who had no brothers to inherit Zelophehad's property. In their case, they were to marry within their clan so that their father's property might remain within the clan. Sarah's situation, since she has no brothers, is the same as that of the daughters of Zelophehad. There is no evidence, however, that for her to marry outside her relationship would be "a capital crime," as Raphael says in 6:13.

The plot is advanced through this section by comments before and after Tobit's speech. The reason given for his farewell discourse is twofold: he has prayed for death and therefore expects it. He remembers the money that he deposited with Gabael and decides to send his son Tobiah to Media to get it (4:1-2). Tobit tells Tobiah about the money and, characteristically, connects it with the theory of retribution: "Do not be discouraged, my child, because of our poverty. You will be a rich man if you fear God, avoid all sin, and do what is right before the Lord your God" (4:21).

5:1–6:1 Preparation for the journey: a guide. Chapter 5 begins immediately with the practical preparations for the journey. Tobiah, although willing to obey his father's wishes, brings up two difficulties: since he does not know Gabael, he will need a sign to give him so that Gabael will give him the money. Also, he does not know the way to Media.

The answer to the first difficulty is simple. Tobit informs his son that when he deposited the money with Gabael, they exchanged signatures on a document written in duplicate. One copy was put with the money. It is implied that Tobit kept the other copy.

Finding a guide to Media occupies the rest of the chapter. Tobit instructs his son to look for a trustworthy man who knows the way. Raphael's immediate appearance answers the question left at the end of chapter 3: How will Raphael function?

The narration of the hiring of Raphael as guide is a masterpiece of irony. With the exception of Raphael, the audience knows more about what is happening than any of the characters involved. As soon as Tobiah finds Raphael, the narrator informs the audience that he is an angel but that Tobiah does not know it (5:4-5). Raphael ("God heals") tells Tobiah that his name is Azariah ("Yahweh is my help"). From this point on, all the characters will call the angel Azariah. The narrator, however, will continue to refer to him as "the angel Raphael," "Raphael," or simply "the angel" (see 5:8, 10, 12, 13, 16; 6:2).

Raphael's disguise makes his conversation with Tobit and Tobiah another element of the irony. When Tobiah asks Raphael who he is, Raphael replies that he is a kinsman who has come to find work (5:5). Indeed he has. He was commissioned in 3:17. When Tobit greets Raphael, the angel replies that there is healing in store for Tobit (5:10). He surrounds his assurance of healing with words that appear in all the healings: "Take courage" (5:10; compare 7:17; 11:11). Tobit ignores the promise of healing and moves on to the business at hand, but the readers know that Raphael's assurance is true.

Tobit, who is careful about his son's associations, quizzes Raphael regarding his identity. He is interested not only in his ability as a guide but also in his tribe and family. After turning the question aside once (5:12), Raphael finally answers: "I am Azariah ['Yahweh is my help'], son of Hananiah ['Yahweh is merciful']." Tobit adds the information that Hananiah is the son of Shemaiah ("Yahweh hears"). It is true that Raphael is there because Yahweh is merciful and Yahweh hears, but not true in the way that Tobit understands it. Raphael's statement inspires Tobit to exclaim, ". . . you are a kinsman, and from a noble and good line!" (5:14). That statement is far truer than Tobit realizes!

The chapter ends with a final twist of irony. Anna, Tobiah's mother, worries in typical motherly fashion. Tobit, equally worried, as we will learn later (see 10:1-3), reassures her by telling her what he has also prayed in blessing over his son: "A good angel will go with him, his journey will be successful, and he will return unharmed" (5:22; compare 5:17).

The relationship between Tobit and Anna and their parental concern for their son are carefully drawn in this chapter. Anna's attention throughout the book is concentrated on her son. The narrator identifies her as "his [Tobiah's] mother." She complains to Tobit: "Why have *you* decided to send *my* child away?" (5:18, emphasis added). After a single mention of "our child" (5:19), she refers to Tobiah as "*my* child" from this point until his return (10:4, 7). Only when she sees him coming down the road does she turn and tell Tobit, "*Your* son is coming" (11:6, emphasis added). In her relationship with Tobit, Anna tends to be sharp-tongued and quick (compare 2:14). In this chapter she turns the conversation to an attack on Tobit, accusing him of preferring money to the life of "her" son (5:19).

Tobit is also devoted to his son, who is the center of his life (see 11:14). He is careful to instruct him in the ways of righteousness (ch. 4). He, too, worries about Tobiah's journey (see 10:1-3). He characteristically puts aside his worry, however, to reassure Anna (5:21-22; compare 10:4-6), who, for the moment, stops weeping (6:1).

6:2-18 The journey. Tobiah's journey is outlined by the few statements that make up the itinerary. On the first night the travelers make camp beside the Tigris River (6:2). "Afterward they traveled on together till they were near Media" (6:7). They enter Media, and finally, in 7:1, they arrive at Ecbatana, which seems to be the goal of their journey. This is a surprise to the reader, who thinks that the two set off for Rages to get Tobit's money from Gabael (see 4:1, 20; 5:3). Raphael's instructions to Tobiah, however, indicate the real goal of the journey: the healing of Sarah and her marriage to Tobiah.

The angel's instructions to Tobiah form most of the material written concerning the journey. They consist of three parts, each one occurring in a different segment of the journey: instruction concerning how to prepare the fish (6:4-6); information about the healing properties of the fish's heart, liver, and gall; and detailed instructions concerning Tobiah's marriage to Sarah and her healing (6:10-18).

The fish represents a common element in romantic quests in folklore. The hero on a romantic quest conquers a dragon or a water monster such as Leviathan. This sea monster then becomes the source of life for the hero and for other characters in the story. Water as a source of both life and death is a common biblical image (see Gen 1:2; 2:5-6, 10-14; Job 38:8-11; 40:25–41:26; Pss 74:13-15; 89:10-11). The fish in the story of Tobit attempts to swallow Tobiah's foot (or to swallow Tobiah in the shorter Greek text!), but when Tobiah follows Raphael's instruction, seizes the fish, and saves its gall, heart, and liver, it becomes a source of healing.

The struggle with the fish occurs on the first night of the journey. Night is a common image for death. The alternation of the words "night" and "day" in the Book of Tobit reveals an important progression in the plot. There is a concentration of references to "night" in the chapters referring to Tobiah's journey and the healing of Sarah. Between 6:2 and 8:18, "night" occurs ten times (6:2, 11, 13 [twice], 14, 16; 7:10, 11 [twice]; 8:9). It occurs only twice more: once in 2:9 when Tobit is afflicted with blindness, and once in 10:7 when Anna weeps all night. "Day," on the other hand, is concentrated toward the beginning and end of the book: fourteen times in the first five chapters (1:2, 3, 16, 18, 21; 3:7, 10; 4:1, 3, 5 [twice], 9; 5:6, 21); eighteen times in chapters 8 through 14 (8:20; 9:4 [twice]; 10:1 [4 times], 7 [twice], 12 [twice], 13; 11:17, 18). The movement of the plot goes from apparent light and life for both Tobit and Sarah, to darkness with Tobit's blindness and Sarah's affliction on her wedding nights, back into light with the return of Tobit's sight and the transformation of Sarah's wedding night into joy. The skillful use of these two words symbolizes the direction of the plot.

Raphael begins to fulfill his commission from 3:17 when he gives instructions regarding the healing of Tobit and Sarah. In the first instruction (6:7-9), Raphael informs Tobiah that the heart and liver of the fish are useful in removing an evil spirit from a man *or a woman*, and the gall is useful in curing blindness *in a man*. The reader, of course, knows that it is a woman who is afflicted by a demon and a man who is blind. Tobiah, instructed by Raphael and supplied with the parts of the fish, will be the means of their healing.

Raphael's detailed instructions concerning Tobiah's marriage to Sarah and her healing point forward and backward in the plot. Raphael reminds Tobiah that he has been instructed by his father to marry someone from his own kindred (6:16; compare 4:12-13). The reader also knows that Tobit himself married a wife from his own lineage (1:9) and that Sarah expects to marry either a relative or no one (3:15). It is not only the reader who knows that marriage to Sarah is a dangerous enterprise. Tobiah also knows that she has had seven husbands who have already dropped dead on the wedding night and that it is a demon who killed them (6:14-15). However, Tobiah also knows from Raphael that burning the heart and liver of the fish can drive off demons. Once the demon is banished, Tobiah is to begin his marriage in the spirit of prayer, and that prayer, joined to his willing obedience to his father and the great love he already feels toward Sarah, will seal the marriage that was determined "before the world existed" (6:18).

THE HEALING OF SARAH AND TOBIT

Tob 7:1–11:18

7:1–8:18 The wedding. When the travelers arrive in Ecbatana, they are immediately greeted by Raguel and introduced to his family. The greetings lead to a discussion of Tobit after Raguel recognizes Tobiah's likeness to him. The dialogue is well structured. Edna, like her counterpart Anna, is a strong woman who emerges as the moving force in the questioning of Tobiah. Two emotions characterize the meeting: joy at seeing Tobit's son and grief over Tobit's blindness.

The narrative moves immediately to a banquet scene that sets the stage for the wedding of Tobiah and Sarah. The scene fits a common pattern for betrothals in the Old Testament, for example, that of Isaac (Gen 24:1-67) and that of Jacob (Gen 29:1-30). The structure of Isaac's betrothal scene is much like that of Tobiah's. The father commands his son to take a journey to find a bride among his own kindred. (This is the obvious motive in Gen 24:3-4; in Tobit the motive is disguised by the matter of the money.) The travelers are given a meal (Gen 24:33; Tob 7:9) but refuse to eat until the betrothal is arranged (Gen 24:33; Tob 7:11). The host yields, recognizing that the marriage has been decided by the Lord (Gen 24:50; Tob 7:11). There are other similarities to the betrothal scene of Jacob. After an opening conversation, which in Tobit is cited directly from Genesis (Gen 29:4-6; Tob 7:3-4), the traveler is greeted warmly when he makes himself known as a relative (Gen 29:12-13; Tob 7:6). The father of the bride is reluctant to agree to the marriage (Gen 29:23-27; Tob 7:10-11). By using the common pattern of the betrothal scenes of the patriarchs, the author of the Book of Tobit is linking the marriage of Tobiah and Sarah to the patriarchal marriages, a connection already made by Tobit (4:12).

The wedding scene reveals much about the characters. Raguel, who is modeled after Abraham, is a man of hospitality. His favorite words are "Eat and drink" (7:10, 11; compare 8:20). He loves his daughter and is reluctant to see her suffer an eighth attempt to marry. Tobiah, who has been in the shadow of Tobit and Raphael until now, emerges in this scene as a man in his own right. When the travelers arrived in Ecbatana, Tobiah instructed Raphael to take him straight to Raguel's house (7:1). In the banquet scene, he refuses to eat until the marriage is determined (7:11). He has taken hold of the instructions given him by Raphael, and he will carry them out.

The wedding itself follows the pattern of a marriage contract found among the fifth century B.C.E. papyri discovered at Elephantine in Egypt. The marriage contract of Mibtahiah reads: "She is my wife and I am her husband from this day for ever" (compare Tob 7:11).

The phrase "Be brave" introduces the healing of Sarah (7:17; compare 5:10; 11:11) as Edna prepares her daughter for her eighth wedding night. When he is led into Sarah's bedroom, Tobiah remembers Raphael's instructions and performs the necessary ritual of burning the fish's heart and liver (8:2). This is the third description of the manner of Sarah's healing (see 6:8, 17-18). Each of the healings is described three times.

Sarah's healing, however, is not accomplished by means of the fish's heart and liver alone. They are only the physical symbols. Raphael pursues the demon after he flees and binds him (8:3). Even more significantly, Tobiah and Sarah turn to prayer, in accord with Raphael's instructions (8:4-9; compare 6:18). Prayer is an important activity throughout the book. At every crucial moment the main characters turn to prayer (see 3:2-6; 3:11-15; 11:14-15; 13:1-18). It is this turning to God in prayer that finally delivers Sarah from the demon Asmodeus.

In his prayer Tobiah links their marriage, not only to the patriarchs, but to creation and Adam and Eve. It is in this spirit of unity with the people of God that Tobiah and Sarah are united in marriage. Sarah joins Tobiah in the "Amen," the only word she speaks in the presence of another human being in the whole book.

Sarah is healed; the marriage is consummated. The irony of the book, however, continues. Raguel has given his daughter in marriage for the eighth time because he has no choice (see 6:13; 7:11), but he is not convinced that the end will be other than tragic. Protecting himself, he has a grave dug so that Tobiah can be buried "without anyone's knowing about it" (8:12). Had Tobiah died, one wonders whether Raphael would simply have gone home alone. Would Anna and Tobit have inquired about their son? Raguel, however, is worried about the neighbors. After the grave has been dug, he asks Edna to send a maid to see if Tobiah is dead. The maid becomes the messenger of the good news: "He is alive!" Raguel immediately turns to prayer and then instructs his servants to fill in the grave before the new day dawns. All signs of death will be wiped away from the new day (8:18).

8:19–10:7 The delay. As soon as day comes, Raguel prepares a feast (compare 7:9). In his great joy he doubles the length of the normal seven-day wedding celebration. He puts Tobiah under oath to stay the full fourteen days and bring joy to Sarah. The resulting delay in Tobiah's journey has two consequences.

First of all, Tobiah, who cannot leave Ecbatana, sends Raphael to Rages for Tobit's money, the original goal of the journey. Raphael is also instructed to bring Gabael back with him to the wedding feast. The journey to Rages and back seems to take very little time. This corresponds to Raphael's statement in 5:6 that Rages is only two days away from Ecbatana. As a matter of fact, it took Alexander's army eleven days of forced march to cover the same distance, approximately three hundred kilometers. We can draw two conclusions from this discrepancy. For one thing, the author is not interested in geographical details, nor is he intending to present a historical account. Also, the aura of speed and haste that seems to surround Raphael is not inconsistent with his angelic character (compare 5:8; 8:3; 11:4).

The second consequence of the delay is the effect on Tobiah's worried parents. Both parents act in typical fashion. Tobit, "day by day, was counting the days," and when the appointed day arrives and Tobiah has not returned, he begins to worry and to imagine all sorts of alternatives. Anna, who was already worried on the day Tobiah left, is convinced that her son is dead. She is not so convinced, however, that she does not go out every day to watch the road by which he will return. Just as he reassured his wife and concealed his own worry at Tobiah's departure (5:21-22), Tobit attempts now to console Anna. This time he is unsuccessful. She refuses to eat, and she weeps all night. She and Tobit are still in the dark, even though the day has dawned in Ecbatana.

10:7–11:18 Vision. The next section picks up the thread of the story after the fourteen-day delay. The scene in which Tobiah and Sarah prepare to leave Ecbatana and return to Nineveh illustrates several of the ideas concerning marriage in the book. First of all, marriage is seen to link families. Raguel instructs Sarah to honor Tobiah's parents, since, as he says, "they are as much your parents as the ones who brought you into the world" (10:12). Both Raguel and Edna refer to Tobiah as their son (10:11, 13). Edna tells Tobiah directly that she is his mother and that Sarah is his sister (10:13; compare Raguel's speech in 8:21). ("Sister" as a term for "beloved" is used throughout the book [7:11-12; 8:21; 10:12]. The same term is used in the Song of Songs [4:9-12; 5:1-2; compare also Prov 7:4].) Joy is an expected outcome of marriage (10:13; compare 8:20). Children are expected and are considered a blessing (10:11, 13; compare 4:12).

After being blessed by both Raguel and Edna, Tobiah begins the journey back to Nineveh in a spirit of prayer (10:14). The journey itself is summarized in one verse (11:1). The arrival, which is masterfully set up in a series of scenes alternating between the travelers and the parents as they approach each other (Raphael and Tobiah, 11:1-4, 7-8; Tobit and Anna, 11:5-6, 9-10), is a character study of all concerned. Raphael is hurrying again (11:3) and functioning in his angelic role as giver of information (11:4, 7-8). Tobiah, obedient to Raphael's instructions, is on his way to be the instrument of healing. Anna is still watching the road for *her* son, who she is sure is dead (compare 10:4-7). When she sees him coming, however, her true love for Tobit emerges. She turns "to *his* father, and exclaims, 'Tobit, *your* son is coming' " (11:6; emphasis added). In response, the blind Tobit gets up and stumbles toward the son whom he cannot see (11:10).

Tobiah begins the process of healing his father with the words that are characteristic of all the healings, "Take courage" (compare 7:17). The description of his actions is the third description of the method by which his father's blindness is to be healed (see 6:9; 11:8). Tobit's first words after vision returns are an exclamation of joy at seeing his son, the light of his eyes (11:14). Then he immediately turns to prayer.

Tobit prays in praise of God, whom he sees both as a source of affliction and as a source of healing (11:15; compare 13:2-5; 1 Sam 2:6; Wis 16:13). He thus declares one of the major theological principles of the book: God is free, and God's actions are beyond human understanding. Tobit, although he believes that God rewards obedience and punishes wickedness (see 1:12-13; 4:6, 21), accepts his blindness as coming from God (see 3:5). Throughout his affliction he never turns away from God and never ceases praying. His prayer as his sight is restored is a striking manifestation of his own extraordinary faith.

The joyful scene concludes with the greeting of Sarah, who has just arrived at the gate of Nineveh. Tobit continues the insistence that marriage has linked the two families. He refers to Sarah as "daughter" four times in his effusive welcoming speech (11:17).

Another seven-day celebration is begun, with Ahiqar (see 1:21-22; 2:10; 14:10) and his nephew Nadab in attendance (11:18). The Story of Ahiqar is one of the major sources of the Book of Tobit. Knowledge of the story is presumed in 11:18. The story probably originated as an Assyrian tale, and was written down in Aramaic around 500 B.C.E. It circulated widely in many languages, and several late versions are still in existence. The outline of the plot concerns a man named Ahiqar, who was a royal official under Sennacherib and Esarhaddon. He adopted his nephew Nadab and trained him to succeed to his royal position. Nadab, however, accused Ahiqar of treason, and Ahiqar was condemned to death. The executioner spared his life and hid him because of a kind deed Ahiqar had done for him earlier. When the king began to wish for Ahiqar back again, the executioner produced him, and Ahiqar was restored to his former honor. Meanwhile, Nadab was imprisoned and died. Thus the story, like that of Tobit, concerns a man who suffers unjustly but who, in the end, is rewarded for his virtue.

DENOUEMENT

Tob 12:1-14:15

12:1-22 The angel. The final chapters of the Book of Tobit reiterate the main themes and conclude the remaining details of the plot. The first detail to be settled is the matter of Raphael's wages. Tobit had assured Tobiah that his guide would be paid well (5:3), and Tobiah repeated the assurance to Raphael (5:7). In Tobit's conversation with Raphael he promised him a bonus as well (5:15-16). The journey has been completed with far more success than either Tobit or his son anticipated. Thus the two decide not only to give Raphael a bonus but to pay him half of the money that was brought back from Gabael (12:1-2). This motif belongs to a folk tale widely known in the Near East and in Eastern Europe called The Grateful Dead. This folk tale is one of the sources for the plot of

Tobit. In the folk tale a dead man, whom the hero has buried at great difficulty to himself, returns to act as a guide for him in his quest for a bride. The grateful dead man saves the hero from the demons that afflict the bride and kill her bridegrooms. As a reward, the hero offers the grateful dead man half of all the treasure he has acquired. At that point, the grateful dead man reveals his identity and disappears.

Raphael, following the model of the grateful dead man, refuses the wages and reveals his identity. This is the occasion for the second farewell discourse of the book (see 4:3-21; 14:3-11). Raphael's speech reiterates the major themes of the book. He exhorts Tobit and Tobiah to pray, to give thanks to God, and to praise God before all the living (12:6-7, 17-20). He also exhorts them to give alms, one of Tobit's characteristic virtues, in which he has also instructed his son (12:8-10; see 1:3, 16-18; 4:7-11, 16-17).

The major content of Raphael's speech is the revelation of his identity: "I am Raphael, one of the seven angels who enter and serve before the Glory of the Lord" (12:15). The developed figure of the angel is a primary contribution of the Book of Tobit to Old Testament theology. Four functions of angels, all of which derive from the identity of angels as messengers (the word *angelos* in Greek means "messenger"), can be seen in the character of Raphael. The angel is guide and protector, instructor, mediator, and tester.

The function of guide and protector is the primary function of the angel in this book. Raphael emerges as a main character only in the scenes that involve the journey (5:1–6:18; 11:1-8) and in the farewell speech (12:6-22). It is in those scenes that the narrator continually reminds us that Raphael is an angel (5:4; 6:2, 4, 7). After the opening scene with Tobiah, the first dialogue in which he participates is the discussion with Tobit concerning his qualifications as guide (5:10-17); his first activity is the journey (6:2–7:1). It is he who travels to Rages to get Tobit's money in order to complete the initial task of the journey (9:1-6). In answer to the initial question, Raphael will function primarily as guide and protector.

Raphael also functions as instructor and conveyor of information. He has two major conversations with Tobiah in which he func-

tions in this role. In 5:5-9 Raphael is a channel of information concerning the trip to Rages and Ecbatana. The second exchange is far more important (6:7-18). He is the conveyor of information concerning the three major events of the plot: the marriage and the two healings. Raphael performs few actions, but he consistently instructs other characters how to act. He tells Tobiah how to gain mastery over the fish (6:4) and how to use its parts for the healings (6:5, 8-9, 16-18; 11:4, 7-8). He instructs him to marry Sarah (6:10-13). In his farewell discourse he instructs Tobit and Tobiah to pray and praise God (12:6-7, 17-20).

Raphael is a mediator of prayer. He comes in answer to prayer (3:16-17). He instructs Tobiah to pray on his wedding night (6:18). In this chapter he exhorts Tobit and Tobiah to pray in thanksgiving (12:6-7, 17-20). He identifies himself as one who presents prayers before the Glory of the Lord (12:12).

Finally, Raphael is a tester. He tells Tobit that he was sent to put him to the test (12:14). There is no indication of what his function in the test is. Does he bring the blindness? Is his hidden identity part of the test? He certainly tests Tobiah's obedience (6:4-5, 11-18). Beyond those implications, we have only Raphael's own statement concerning his function as a tester.

The angel in this book is a messenger. He mediates between God and the believers. The primary agents of God's providence are the human beings. Throughout the book, Tobiah is the instrument of healing. The primary actor is God. It is God who heals, as Raphael's name ("God heals") asserts; it is God who deserves thanks and praise (see 12:17-20).

13:1-18 Praise and thanksgiving. Raphael's exhortation to Tobit and Tobiah in chapter 12 to praise God is followed in chapter 13 by Tobit's song of praise. The prayer falls into two major sections: God's freedom and mercy (vv. 1-8); Jerusalem's distress and glory (vv. 9-18).

The first section is cast in the form of a hymn, with several calls to praise (13:1, 3, 4b, 6cd) alternating with the reasons for praise (13:2, 3b-4, 5-6). It ends with Tobit's presenting himself as an example to his kindred (13:7-8). The message of the first section reflects several themes of Deuteronomy. God is one who both scourges and has mercy (see

Deut 32:39; compare 1 Sam 2:6). Although the people have been scattered, God will again gather them (see Deut 30:1-5). The condition for their restoration is their turning back to God, an idea common to both Deuteronomy and Jeremiah (see Deut 4:29-31; 30:1-10; Jer 3:12, 14, 22; 4:1).

The second section, also a hymn, is addressed to the city of Jerusalem. After an introductory section that links the situation of Jerusalem, scourged and raised up, to the situation of the exiles, scourged and raised up (see 13:2, 5), the poem moves into a modified ring structure. A description of Jerusalem as a bright light drawing all nations (13:11) parallels a description of Jerusalem built of precious metals and jewels (13:16b-18). These descriptions of Jerusalem surround a set of curses and beatitudes:

Cursed are those who harm Jerusalem (13:12).
Happy are those who bless the Lord of the ages in Jerusalem (13:13).
Happy are those who love Jerusalem and rejoice in its prosperity (13:14).
Happy are those who grieve over Jerusalem's distress; they shall rejoice (13:15).
Happy is Tobit if a remnant of his offspring survives to rejoice in Jerusalem (13:16).

The second section is dependent on the imagery of the prophets. The vision of Jerusalem built with precious stones is found in Isa 54:11-12. Jerusalem as the source of great light to which many nations will come is the image of Isa 60:1-14 (see also Mic 4:2; Zech 8:22). Those who love Jerusalem will rejoice (Isa 66:10, 14) while those who do not serve Jerusalem will be destroyed (see Isa 60:12). Tobit believes in the word of the prophets (see 14:4), and the description of Jerusalem in his prayer is dependent on the prophets' vision.

The prayer of Tobit reflects the story of his own life. In his prayer he makes himself an example for his people. He exhorts them to praise God (13:1, 3, 4, 6, 8) as he does (13:7) and to trust God in adversity as well as joy (13:2-3, 5). In the second section he makes the same call to praise (13:10) and to trust God both in sorrow and in joy (13:9). He concludes the prayer with a hymn of joy over Jerusalem's future glory (13:16-18).

Joy is a primary characteristic of Tobit in the last part of the book (see 14:7). The prayer he composes is described as "joyful" (13:1), and "joy" is its constant refrain. Tobit himself rejoices (13:7). He prays that God's tent be rebuilt in Jerusalem with joy (13:10), that all the former captives be made glad (13:10), and all generations give joyful praise in Jerusalem (13:11). He exhorts Jerusalem to rejoice over the children of the righteous (13:13). He declares happy those who love Jerusalem, who rejoice with it, and who grieve over its distress. They shall rejoice in it as they behold its joy forever (13:14). Even the gates of Jerusalem shall sing hymns of gladness (13:18).

Tobit sees his own distress as a model of the distress of Jerusalem during the Exile. Just as God had mercy on him (see 11:15), so God will have mercy on Jerusalem. The return of Tobit's sight parallels Jerusalem's return to glory. Just as he praises God, so Jerusalem shall praise. His prayer makes it clear that the author understands the story of Tobit as a paradigm for the Exile and the restoration of the people.

14:1-15 Farewell. The third and final farewell discourse is found in 14:3-11 (compare 4:3-21; 12:6-10). It is introduced by the information that Tobit was indeed rewarded with the Deuteronomic blessings for righteousness: long life, joy and prosperity, and many descendants (14:1-3; compare Deut 4:1, 40; 5:32-33; 12:7, 12, 18; 30:15-20; 32:46-47).

Just as Tobit had called his son Tobiah to him in order to instruct him after Tobit had prayed for death (4:2-3), once again Tobit calls his son and his seven grandsons to him (14:3). First he tells them to trust the word of the prophets (14:3-4, 8). The prophet Nahum's dire prophecies concerning Nineveh will surely come to pass. In fact, the word of all the prophets shall come to pass in the proper time; therefore, it will be safer for Tobiah and his family to flee Nineveh and to take up residence in Media.

The second prophetic word to be proved true concerns the Exile and the destruction of Jerusalem (14:4-7). Just as the prophets announced the fall of Jerusalem, however, they also announced its restoration. The key word in the first section of this exhortation is "desolate," which is repeated three times. The country of Israel will be "desolate"; the capitals,

Samaria and Jerusalem, will be "desolate"; God's temple will be "desolate." The key word in the second section is "rebuild." They will "rebuild" the temple; they will "rebuild" Jerusalem; within Jerusalem the temple will be "rebuilt"; the temple will be "rebuilt" for all generations to come, just as the prophets said. Finally, as the prophets said, all nations will "turn" and fear God. All true Israelites will remember God and will be gathered in Jerusalem. The land in which they will dwell is the land of promise, promised generations ago to Abraham with a promise that has never been taken back.

Tobit ends his discourse with an exhortation to his descendants to live as he has lived. He walked all the days of his life "on the paths of truth and righteousness" and "performed many charitable works" (1:3). He exhorts his children to "serve God in truth," "to do what is right," and "to give alms" (14:9). As he has remembered God and constantly turned to God in prayer (see 3:2-6; 5:17; 11:14-15; 13:1-18), so his descendants are to do (14:9). As he is instructing them (see also 4:3-21), they are also to instruct their children (14:9). Tobit concludes with the story of Ahiqar, which illustrates the reward for almsgiving, just as his own life illustrates the reward for almsgiving (14:10). His final sentence summarizes the message of the book: Almsgiving gives life; wickedness brings death.

After Tobit's death, Tobiah proves himself a worthy son of his father. As his father had concern for the honorable burial of others, so Tobiah buries his parents and his wife's parents (compare 1:16-20; 2:1-7; 4:3-4, 17). He obediently leaves Nineveh and lives to see his father's faith in the prophets vindicated by Nineveh's destruction (14:15). Like his father, Tobiah is rewarded with prosperity and a long life (14:14).

JUDITH

Irene Nowell, O.S.B.

INTRODUCTION

The Book of Judith was written in the second century, somewhat later than the Book of Tobit. This book was a response to a new crisis that arose to threaten Jewish believers in Palestine. In 175 B.C.E. the Seleucid ruler Antiochus IV Epiphanes came to power in Syria and Palestine. He soon embarked on a policy to force the Jews not only to adopt Greek ways of thinking and worshiping but also to abandon traditional Jewish practices such as circumcision and special dietary laws. Stories of the horrible persecution that ensued can be found in the Books of the Maccabees.

At the height of the persecution (167 B.C.E.) a courageous Jew named Mattathias, forced to offer sacrifice on a pagan altar, killed the king's messenger and fled to the hills with his five sons. Soon other faithful Jews joined Mattathias and his sons and began what came to be known as the Maccabean revolt. (The name "Maccabean" comes from the nickname of Mattathias' son Judas, who was called Maccabee, which probably means "hammer.") The Maccabees reclaimed the temple and rededicated it in 164 B.C.E. After a long period of guerrilla warfare and intrigue, the Jews finally achieved a period of relative independence under Hasmonean rulers who were descendants of Mattathias and his sons.

The Book of Judith was written during the period of the Maccabean revolt. Its setting is in an earlier period, but many details reveal the author's interest in his own time rather than that of the seventh century B.C.E. In the story, an Israelite town is besieged by Holofernes, commander-in-chief of the Assyrian army. The town leaders despair of help from God and declare that if deliverance does not come within five days, they will surrender. A beautiful widow—an observant Jew—upon hearing the decision of the elders, scolds them for their lack of faith. She prays, placing herself in the hands of God. Finally, she prepares her weapon—beauty. Because God works through her beauty, she beheads Holofernes and delivers her people.

The message of the book is that victory comes not from human might but through the power of God. God can deliver the faithful people at whatever time and in whatever way God wishes. Even though the way of deliverance may look like folly from a human point of view, the story of Judith demonstrates that the real fools are those who place their trust in human power and weapons. The whole army of Holofernes is defenseless against God's weapon—the beauty of a faithful woman.

COMMENTARY

THE ASSYRIAN THREAT

Jdt 1:1–3:10

1:1-16 Nebuchadnezzar's war against Arphaxad. The opening chapter of the Book of Judith sets the stage for the conflict that is to follow and presents Nebuchadnezzar, one of the main protagonists. The date and names given in the first verse signal immediately that the intention of the author is not the presentation of historical material since they are not accurate. The story opens in the twelfth year of the reign of Nebuchadnezzar, 593 B.C.E. Nebuchadnezzar is identified as one of the Assyrian kings who ruled in Nineveh. Actually, Nebuchadnezzar reigned as king of the Babylonians from 604 to 562 B.C.E.; his capital was the city of Babylon. Nineveh, the capital of Assyria, was destroyed in 612 B.C.E. by Nabopolassar, the father of Nebuchadnezzar, during the Babylonian rise to power.

Other historical inconsistencies abound throughout the book. In the first chapter, Nebuchadnezzar's enemy is Arphaxad, king of the Medes (1:1). The ruler Arphaxad is unknown. The name is found in Gen 10:22 in the list of descendants of Shem. The city named as his capital, Ecbatana, was fortified around 700 B.C.E. by Deioces. The kingdom of the Medes, founded by Phraortes (675–653 B.C.E.), lasted until 550 B.C.E., when Cyrus, not Nebuchadnezzar, conquered Astyages, not Arphaxad (see 1:13-16).

The geographical information is equally inconsistent. The list of peoples summoned to assist Nebuchadnezzar in his battle against Arphaxad (1:7-10) includes regions moving from Mesopotamia in a counterclockwise fashion to the northwest and down the Mediterranean as far as Egypt. The places mentioned are in the right general area, but many are out of sequence. For example, Anti-Lebanon belongs between Damascus and Lebanon, the plain of Esdraelon between Carmel and Gilead. The cities of Egypt (1:9-10) also seem to be in no particular order.

Nebuchadnezzar, the protagonist in this drama, is, like everything else in the work, painted larger than life. He expects the inhabitants of most of the known world to come to his aid. The peoples of the West, however, are not impressed. They see him as one lone mortal (1:11) and not only refuse to assist in his battle but even turn away his messengers. Nebuchadnezzar's impression of himself is that of a divine being rather than a mortal. At the refusal of the western peoples to assist him, he falls into a violent rage and swears, not by a god but by himself, to destroy all the nations as far as the two seas (the Mediterranean to the Persian Gulf). Before he can begin that terrible expedition, however, he must destroy Arphaxad, king of the Medes. He achieves this victory in the seventeenth year of his reign (588 B.C.E.). The chapter ends with Nebuchadnezzar feasting for 120 days in celebration with his army. The stage is set for the campaign against the West.

2:1-28 The war against the West. The second chapter begins with another date, the eighteenth year of Nebuchadnezzar, the twenty-second day of the first month (Nisan). Both the year and the month are significant. The eighteenth year of Nebuchadnezzar was 587 B.C.E., the year in which his siege of Jerusalem succeeded and he took its citizens captive (see Jer 52:29; but compare Jer 52:12). The twenty-second of Nisan is the day after the Passover celebration ends (see Exod 12:2, 18). The author, by means of one date, is reminding the readers both of Israel's most terrible defeat (587 B.C.E.) and Israel's greatest deliverance by God, the Exodus, which is memorialized in the Passover.

Nebuchadnezzar's divine pretensions are clearer in the second chapter than in the first. He declares his intention of taking revenge on "the whole world" in verse 1. His vengeance will be nothing less than total destruction. The language he uses in summoning Holofernes is language that ordinarily belongs to Yahweh in biblical literature. For example, he begins, "Thus says the great king" (see Exod 4:22; Jer 11:3; Amos 1:3), "the lord of all the earth" (see Josh 3:11; Zech 6:5). Other phrases include: "to the very ends of the earth" (see 1 Sam 2:10; Ps 59:14; Isa 41:5); "what I have spoken I will accomplish by my power" (literally, "my hand will accomplish"; see Deut 32:39; Isa 43:13; compare Isa 10:12-15). He swears with a formula proper to divinity: "as I live" (see Isa 49:18; Jer 22:24; Ezek 5:11). Nebuchadnezzar, the first major character, has set himself up as a god, thereby opposing

Yahweh. In this opposition, the Book of Judith is similar to the Exodus event in which the opponents are Pharaoh, considered to be divine, and Yahweh (see Exod 4:22-23; 15:3-4).

Each of the divine figures is represented in the action by a mortal figure. Nebuchadnezzar is represented by his general in chief, Holofernes; Yahweh is represented by the holy woman Judith. Holofernes is introduced in chapter 2. The name Holofernes is found among the generals of Artaxerxes III Ochos (359–338 B.C.E.). The name Bagoas (see Jdt 12:11) is also found in lists of his retinue. For this reason some scholars have thought that the Book of Judith originated in the fourth century, either with regard to the events it narrates or to the period of its writing.

When Holofernes is summoned by Nebuchadnezzar, he is identified as "general in chief of his forces, second to himself in command" (2:4). From this point on, as soon as Nebuchadnezzar finishes his speech of instruction, Holofernes is in the foreground, and we see Nebuchadnezzar only through him. Nebuchadnezzar's punishment of the West, his challenge to Judea, and his ultimate defeat are acted out in the person of Holofernes. The power of Nebuchadnezzar comes to an end as Bagoas cries out: "A single Hebrew woman has brought disgrace on the house of King Nebuchadnezzar. Here is Holofernes headless on the ground!" (14:18).

Holofernes begins the campaign with an army consisting of 120,000 select troops and 12,000 cavalry (2:15-16). He gathers abundant provisions and much money for the support of his army. He sets out with this regular army and its provisions, along with a huge irregular force, "like locusts or the dust of the earth" to "cover all the western region" (2:19-20). This mammoth war effort will be matched against Bethulia, a tiny Israelite village whose main hero is a woman. The battle is between gods. Each god summons the best in human power in order to defeat the other. Nebuchadnezzar trusts in human force, Yahweh in human virtue.

The geographical notations continue to be confusing. The general direction again seems to be toward the northwest, then sweeping down along the Mediterranean. Bectileth, the camping place reached by the army after a three-day march, is unknown. Upper Cilicia, the next camping place, is, however, at least three hundred miles from Nineveh, an impossible distance for such a short march. Put and Lud are mentioned in Gen 10 (compare Nah 3:9); they are generally understood as African and Semitic peoples. Lud, however, is also identified as a place in Asia Minor (see Isa 66:19), maybe the same as Lydia. In any case, if the two names are taken together, they cannot be taken literally as part of the progress of Holofernes' army. Many of the other locations are unknown, such as Rassis and Japheth. Some identify not places but nomadic tribes, such as the Ishmaelites and the Midianites. Many of the names come from the table of nations in Gen 10, for example, Japheth, Put, and Lud. The effect of the geographical notations is to create a list of peoples long enough and disparate enough to indicate that Nebuchadnezzar, through Holofernes, is well on his way to conquering the whole world. Fear of him has indeed spread to the ends of the earth.

3:1-10 Surrender of the West. Holofernes expects that the result of his sweep through the lands west of Mesopotamia will be the surrender of all peoples to him. Chapter 3 seems to confirm that expectation. The author says that "they," presumably all the peoples listed in the last ten verses of chapter 2, "sent messengers . . . to sue for peace" (3:1), offering total surrender: "Do with us as you will." Wherever Holofernes and his troops arrive, they are welcomed with feasting and dancing.

Holofernes, however, responds to the welcome by devastating the territory and destroying all the shrines to local gods. "He has been commissioned to destroy *all the gods of the earth*, so that every nation might worship Nebuchadnezzar alone, and every people and tribe invoke him as a god" (3:8, emphasis added).

It would seem that Holofernes' victory is complete and that no one stands in the way of Nebuchadnezzar's being declared god of all the earth. At this point Holofernes stops in the plain of Esdraelon to rest and refurbish his army before attacking the Israelites. Now, the territory of Esdraelon is familiar to the biblical reader who knows that this is not the first time that Yahweh has appeared to be defeated here. More than once here the people of God have had defeat turn to victory in the most surprising circumstances. In the time of the judges, when the Israelites were oppressed by the Canaanite king Jabin and his general Sisera, Yahweh won a great victory for his people at the Wadi Kishon in the valley of Esdraelon. Even the stars fought for the people of God (Judg 5:20). The army of Sisera was defeated by the Naphtalite Barak. The final victory, however, belonged to Yahweh, who worked through two women. The prophetess Deborah, judge of Israel, instructed Barak, telling him that God had delivered the enemy into Israel's power (Judg 4:4-7). Jael, wife of the Kenite Heber, killed the enemy general, Sisera, with a tent peg (Judg 4:17-22; 5:24-27). For this victory Jael was declared "blessed among women" (Judg 5:24).

The people of God would also remember that the valley of Esdraelon had received the blood of their own kings. Saul was defeated there and died on Mount Gilboa with his son Jonathan (1 Sam 31). Josiah, "before [whom] there had been no king who turned to the Lord as he did, . . . nor could any after him compare with him" (2 Kgs 23:25), was killed there defending the pass at Megiddo against Pharaoh Neco in 609 B.C.E. (2 Kgs 23:29-30).

It would seem that nothing stands in the way of Holofernes' victory and Nebuchadnezzar's pretensions to divinity. But the army of the enemy rests in the valley of Esdraelon, the valley of defeat and victory, and the people await the action of Yahweh.

SIEGE OF BETHULIA

Jdt 4:1–7:32

4:1-15 Resistance of Israel. Just as all the peoples to the north and west of them feared Holofernes' army, so all the Israelites who lived in Judea were afraid when they heard of Holofernes' exploits. The Israelites' reaction to invasion differs from their neighbors in two respects: the nature of their fear and their response. Their fear is not only for themselves but primarily for Jerusalem and the temple of the Lord (4:2). The temple is the center of their lives and the sign of God's presence among them. They had, the narrator reports, only lately returned to their own land from exile. Only lately had the temple been purified from profanation (4:3). The people fear another profanation of the temple and perhaps even another exile.

The historical inaccuracies are a manifestation of high irony. The profanation of the temple and the deportation of the people to Babylon did indeed take place under Nebuchadnezzar in 587 B.C.E. The exile from which it seems the people have only lately returned was the Babylonian Exile (587-538 B.C.E.). Thus Nebuchadnezzar functions as a symbol for the worst that could possibly happen. With regard to the second century, the author's own time, the most recent profanation of the temple was that which took place under the Seleucid ruler Antiochus IV Epiphanes during the Maccabean war. The temple was restored and purified in December of 164 B.C.E., after the victory of Judas Maccabeus. (The yearly celebration of this rededication forms the basis of the feast of Hanukkah.) Thus the author, by claiming that the people have only lately returned from exile (538 B.C.E.), that the temple has only lately been purified (164 B.C.E.), and that the threat comes from Nebuchadnezzar (587 B.C.E.), has layered three events one on top of the other: the major disaster of the past, the major restoration of the past, and the crisis of his own time. Nebuchadnezzar may have brought the greatest disaster, but even that disaster was turned to victory within forty years. The crisis of the second century, it is implied, will also be reversed.

The second way in which the Israelites differ from their neighbors is in their response to invasion. Their neighbors surrendered and welcomed Holofernes with joy, but the tiny country of Judea prepares to defend its most precious possession, Jerusalem with the temple, against Holofernes' advance. Their preparation takes two forms. First of all, there is material preparation. The Israelites in Judea notify the whole region. The people post guards and store up provisions from the newly gathered harvest. Those living near the Esdraelon valley prepare to hold the mountain passes that give the only access from that region through the Carmel range to the country in the south.

The people's most important preparation for siege, however, is spiritual. They pray and fast, practices that will later become two of the three pillars of Pharisaism. They act like the people of Nineveh in the Book of Jonah. Not only the men, women, and children but even the domestic animals join in penance

(4:9-10; compare Jonah 3:8). Their efforts, like those of the people of Nineveh, are rewarded: "The Lord heard their cry and had regard for their distress" (Jdt 4:13). Thus the narrator informs the reader of the eventual outcome of the story. The people of Judea, however, will face many days of distress before *they* know the answer of the Lord.

A key word in this chapter is "cry." During the oppression in Egypt the people seemed to be doomed. God appeared to be absent and is only mentioned twice between Exod 1:1 and 2:22, and then only with regard to the Egyptian midwives. Yet when the people "cried" out to God, "he heard their groaning and remembered his covenant with Abraham, Isaac and Jacob" (Exod 2:24). Their cry was the beginning of their deliverance. In the Book of Judges this pattern is repeated consistently: (1) Israel abandons Yahweh; (2) Yahweh is angry with them and gives them over to their enemies; (3) they "cry" out to Yahweh, and (4) Yahweh sends a judge to deliver them (see Judg 3:2-11). In Judith, the people "cry" to Yahweh three times in seven verses (4:9, 12, 15), and Yahweh hears their "cry" (4:13).

5:1–6:21 Holofernes' response. Holofernes reacts to Israel's resistance in two ways. He summons the leaders of the lands surrounding Israel, indicating that he has the military power to squeeze the little nation to death. Then he asks two key questions: (1) Who are these people? Why are they different? Why has every other nation of the West surrendered and this tiny country refused? (2) Who is their king? What is their power? In the answers to these questions the reader finds the central message of the book.

Achior, leader of the Ammonites, answers Holofernes' first question, and the dialogue between the two men forms the basis of this section. Achior functions as the reporter for Israel, and the author indicates that through him the truth will be told (5:5). Achior begins by reciting the history of the people of God. He starts with Abraham and continues through the patriarchs, the sojourn in Egypt, the Exodus, and the conquest. He ends with the story of the Exile and the return. His historical survey is reminiscent of Joshua's speech during the covenant renewal that took place at Shechem after Israel had gained a foothold in the land of Canaan (Josh 24; see also Deut 26:5-10; Neh 9:6-31).

The historical recital answers the question "Who are these people?" Achior turns next to the second question: "What is their power?" He repeats the basic principles of the Deuteronomic theory of retribution: If Israel is obedient to God, the people will be blessed; if Israel is disobedient, they will be cursed. This theory finds its clearest expression in Deut 28. It is one of the basic principles illustrated in the Deuteronomic history (Joshua–2 Kings), and in the Book of Judith, Achior incorporates it into his advice to Holofernes. "If these people are at fault, and are sinning against their God, . . . then we shall be able to go up and conquer them. But if they are not a guilty nation, . . . their Lord and God will shield them" (5:20-21). The power of this people comes from their God.

The question Holofernes should ask, according to Achior, is whether or not the people of God are faithful. If they are, then God will fight for them and they cannot be defeated. If they are not, then Holofernes will be able to conquer them. The implication of Achior's speech is unavoidable: Even if Holofernes wins, it will not be because of his own power but because God has sold the Israelites into the hands of their enemies on account of their infidelity (see Judg 3:7-8; 4:1-2). Holofernes has finally met a power stronger than his own.

Holofernes, however, misunderstands the real question. Neither he nor his attendants can envision a power greater than the material power of arms. His advisers tell him that the Israelites are a powerless people, incapable of a strong defense. "Let us therefore attack them; your great army, Lord Holofernes, will swallow them up" (5:23-24). This misunderstanding of true power will prove to be a fatal error for Holofernes.

Holofernes ignores the advice of Achior and follows the advice of those who counsel attack. However, before the attack he makes a three-point response to Achior's recommendations. First of all, he recognizes that Achior's function is that of prophet (6:2), even though he condemns Achior for delivering the message of the God of Israel. Holofernes' analysis of Achior's role is accurate. A prophet is "one who speaks for," one who delivers a message for another. Achior is delivering to Holofernes God's message concerning Israel: If they are faithful, you cannot defeat them. Achior is also delivering God's message concerning Israel to the people of the second century: If you remain faithful, you will not be defeated in this time of distress. Achior the Ammonite functions as a prophet of the God of Israel, a role recognized although repudiated by Holofernes the Assyrian.

Secondly, Holofernes proposes a course of action directly opposed to the advice of Achior. He refuses to accept Achior's message because he does not recognize the God from whom the message comes. He recognizes no god but Nebuchadnezzar (6:2); therefore Holofernes thinks that the God of Israel is powerless to save the people. Holofernes thinks that he himself will be the instrument by which the power of Nebuchadnezzar, "lord of all the earth," will be unleashed. No other god exists to withstand him. The words of Nebuchadnezzar "shall not remain unfulfilled" (6:4). Holofernes, in the name of Nebuchadnezzar, has declared war on Yahweh, God of Israel.

Thirdly, Holofernes condemns Achior to share the fate of the Israelites (6:5-9). He instructs his servants to hand Achior over to the people of Bethulia. Because the Israelites hurl stones down at them, Holofernes' men leave Achior bound at the foot of the mountain below Bethulia. When the Israelites untie him and bring him into the city, Achior again functions in the role of messenger-prophet. All the people gather to hear his report concerning Holofernes' declaration of war, and the Israelites' response is in direct contrast to that of the Assyrians. The Israelites understand the question about the source of their power. They *know* that their only power, their only hope is in God, and they call upon God to witness the arrogance of the enemy and their own lowliness.

7:1-32 Siege of Bethulia. The siege of Bethulia is described by a series of scenes that alternate between the Assyrian army and the Israelites. The two opening scenes are brief. Holofernes initiates a threefold action against the Israelites: to move against Bethulia, to seize the mountain passes, and to engage them in battle (7:1). Holofernes completes the first maneuver immediately, and his army lies spread out before the eyes of the Israelites at the spring that waters their city (7:3). The Israelite response is mixed (7:4-5). They are ter-

rified by the size of the army that opposes them, yet they continue to keep watch and to maintain communication with the surrounding towns by means of fire signals. There is a reference to the use of such fire signals in one of the letters found at Lachish describing the siege of the city in 589 B.C.E.

The two remaining scenes (7:6-18, 19-32) portray the siege in greater detail. Holofernes seals off the approaches to the city and seizes the water sources. Traditional enemies of Israel—the Ammonites, the Edomites, and the leaders of the seacoast—advise him not to attack but to wait. The siege, in midsummer, will soon render the inhabitants of Bethulia helpless from thirst. In one respect, the time of year proves to be an advantage to the Israelites because the harvest has already been gathered (see 4:5); however, they cannot expect any rain until October. Thirst will be the Assyrians' weapon.

The Israelites, meanwhile, begin to suffer the effects of the siege (7:19-32). They suffer thirst. Water is rationed, and people begin to collapse from dehydration and weakness. The physical effects, however, are far less serious than the spiritual ones. The people become disheartened and begin to lose faith—first of all in God. Perhaps God has sold them into the power of the enemy as in the days of the judges (Jdt 7:25; compare Judg 3:8; 4:2; 10:7). They begin to murmur as the Israelites did in the wilderness: It would be better to fall into the hands of the enemy and live than to continue resisting them and die (7:26-27; compare Exod 16:3; Num 14:2-4). They also lose faith in themselves. The Deuteronomic theory of retribution says that suffering comes as a result of sin; therefore, they must be suffering because of their own sins and those of their ancestors (7:28). In either case the only solution is to surrender to the enemy.

Uzziah, whose name means "Yahweh is my strength," exhorts the people to have courage; however, he demands that God act within five days. If not, the people of Yahweh will abandon themselves to the army of Holofernes, and Nebuchadnezzar will declare himself god of all the earth (see 3:8; 6:2-4).

The five days stipulated by Uzziah (7:30), added to the thirty-four days of the siege (7:20), make a total of thirty-nine days. Deliverance will come on the night between the fourth and fifth days of Uzziah's limit (see

12:10). Thus within forty days, the traditional length of affliction (Moses' forty days of fast on Sinai, forty years in the wilderness, forty years of exile, Judith's forty months of mourning [see 8:4]), Yahweh will indeed send help to the people.

JUDITH, INSTRUMENT OF YAHWEH

Jdt 8:1–10:10

8:1-8 Judith, Yahweh's representative. War has been declared between Yahweh and Nebuchadnezzar, God against god. Each divinity has an acting human representative. The reader has been introduced to Holofernes, who functions as the representative of Nebuchadnezzar. In this chapter the reader meets the representative of Yahweh, the widow Judith.

Judith's introduction is one of the most lengthy genealogies in the Old Testament. It extends back sixteen generations. This alone declares the importance of this woman. It also indicates that her name, "Jewess" or "Judahite," is a true indication of her identity. In exilic and postexilic times the ability to trace one's ancestry back to the patriarchs, to know oneself to be a true descendant of Abraham and thus heir of the blessing, was of great importance. The Priestly tradition in the Pentateuch, which developed in the exilic period, lays great stress on genealogies. The people of God, when they regather in the land, need also to rediscover their roots. Judith's genealogy indicates that she is indeed a true Judahite, a true exemplar of her people.

Judith is a model of Jewish observance. She had, according to custom, married within her own tribe and clan (see the commentary on Tob 4:12-13). She lived piously—fasting, wearing widow's weeds and sackcloth, and fearing God. She was beautiful, a clear indication in biblical literature of virtue as well (see Gen 29:17; 39:6; 1 Sam 16:12; Esth 2:7; Dan 1:4-15). She is not only a model for her people because she is a true descendant of the patriarchs; she is also a model for their behavior.

Judith is a widow. Widows are significant in biblical stories. They are, first of all, objects of special concern, especially in Deuteronomy (see Deut 10:18; 14:29; 16:11, 14; 24:17, 19, 20, 21; 26:12-13; 27:19). Care for them is required because God cares for them (Deut 10:17-19; compare 24:18, 22). They are among those people who know that they have no help except in God; therefore, they are under God's special protection.

In addition to their special status as a group, there are several individual widows who have affected the history of the people of God. In the patriarchal narrative, Tamar, widow of Judah's son Er, continues to insist on the right of levirate marriage even after she is left a widow a second time by Judah's second son, Onan. Her determination finally leads her to take matters into her own hands and pose as a prostitute so that her husbands' father might give her a child to raise up in the name of her husbands (Gen 38). Judah himself claims that Tamar is more righteous than he (Gen 38:26). Because of her courage, the line of Judah continues. Twins, Perez and Zerah, were born to Tamar. A second widow who took matters into her own hands married into the line of Perez. Ruth, the Moabite woman who left her homeland to follow her mother-in-law back to Bethlehem, married Boaz, descendant of Perez, in another levirate marriage. A son named Obed was born to Ruth and Boaz. Obed became the father of Jesse, who was the father of David (see Ruth 4:18-22). Thus the genealogy of Israel's greatest king was shaped by the lives of two courageous widows. In the Book of Judith, another courageous widow becomes the instrument by which God delivers the people.

8:9-36 Judith and the elders. When the holy woman Judith hears that the people, in their despair, have challenged the elders' judgment (see 7:23-32), she sends her maid to ask the elders to visit her. She talks to the elders about the two major doubts of the people—their lack of faith in God and their lack of faith in themselves. She concludes her speech with an exhortation to action and a statement of the basic theological principle in question.

The first doubt that Judith treats is the people's lack of faith in God's fidelity to them (see 7:25). She scolds the elders for limiting God to the human understanding of the Deuteronomic theory of retribution. They have allowed themselves to be convinced that if God is just, God must reward all virtue and punish all disobedience according to human understanding of reward and punishment. They can see only the immediate distress;

therefore, if God is just and they are virtuous, God must relieve their thirst within five days. Judith corrects this misunderstanding by declaring the basic principle that God is free, that God's ways are not human ways (8:12-16; compare Isa 55:8-9; Tob 4:19). The proper thing to do is to wait for God's salvation and trust in God's good pleasure (8:17).

The second doubt that Judith treats is the people's lack of faith in their own fidelity to God (see 7:28). They think that if God is just and yet they are suffering, then they must have been unfaithful. They have made the theory of retribution into an equation that is automatic and interchangeable. If disobedience brings suffering, then all suffering must be the result of disobedience. But the relationship between God and the people is personal rather than mathematical. Just as God is free to send blessing when it is undeserved, so also is God free to send suffering for purposes other than punishment. The people must not abandon hope in God. They have reason for hope because they have been faithful. They have not worshiped other gods; they *know* no other god but Yahweh (8:18-20, emphasis added). They have need for hope because if they despair and abandon God, the sanctuary will be profaned, the people will be slaughtered, and the land will be devastated. They will then bear the responsibility for this destruction because they have failed in hope. As a result, they will be enslaved and become the mockery of all (8:21-23).

Having treated the two problems of the people, Judith concludes with an exhortation to action and a restatement of the basic theological principle involved. Her call for action has three parts. The people of Bethulia must set an example because the fate of the land, the temple, and the people depends on them. They must be grateful to God, even in the midst of distress and even on account of their distress, because their affliction is a proof of God's love for them (see Prov 3:12). Finally, they must remember God's dealings with their ancestors so that they will understand God's fidelity and the meaning of their own suffering. The theological principle upon which Judith bases her argument is the freedom of God: God can send blessing even if it is undeserved; God may send suffering, not as punishment but as a test (see Deut 8:2-5, 16; Judg 2:22-23; Tob 12:14; Job 5:17-18).

Uzziah responds to Judith by confirming her wisdom but excusing the weakness of the elders for succumbing to the demands of the people (8:28-31). Even though he recognizes the rightness of Judith's words, he is caught in a dilemma. The elders have sworn an oath that they cannot take back (see Gen 27:33). The two different solutions to the dilemma, proposed by Uzziah and Judith, emphasize the contrast between Uzziah's small hope and Judith's great courage. Rain is the only solution he can imagine to relieve the immediate distress (8:31). Judith, on the other hand, envisions a total liberation to rank with the Exodus, a liberation that "will go down from generation to generation among the descendants" of Israel (8:32).

Judith does not tell Uzziah her plans. Both he and the readers are left in suspense, wondering how God will rescue Israel through her. The readers, however, have an advantage over Uzziah: they have been told by the narrator that God *will* deliver Israel (4:13). What they do not know is how.

9:1-14 Judith prepares for war: prayer. Judith makes two preparations for her war of liberation. The first preparation is prayer. Her prayer is important, first of all, as a model of how to pray. Judith prays during the time when the incense is being offered in the temple in Jerusalem, thus joining her prayer to the official prayer of her people (9:1). Her prayer posture is the classic posture of radical humility—prostration. Her attire is symbolic of penitence—sackcloth and ashes. She prays in traditional fashion, first reminding God of the mighty deeds performed for her ancestors (9:2-4; we may disagree with her evaluation of the slaughter of Shechem by Simeon and Levi), and then calling upon God to exercise divine power in her behalf (9:5-11). She concludes by reminding God of the benefits that will come from aiding her (9:12-14). Her prayer mirrors the exhortation she has given to her people to call upon God in hope (see 8:17).

The content of her prayer illustrates three basic principles of Holy War. The first principle has to do with trust. Those who trust in horses and chariots will be defeated; those who trust in Yahweh will be victorious. It is not possible to trust in both (see Ps 20:8-9). Trust in armaments is the same as trust in another god. It is idolatry (see Mic 5:9-12). The

Assyrians' folly is that they trust in weapons of war, horses, and chariots. They do not know that Yahweh crushes warfare (Jdt 9:7-8; see Exod 15:3; Ps 76:4-7).

The second principle has to do with power. Those who trust in armaments trust in human power, those who trust in Yahweh trust in divine power. A key biblical word for power is "hand." Divine power is exercised for the people by Yahweh's mighty hand (see Exod 3:19-20; 6:1; 13:9). Frequently the power of Yahweh comes through the hand of a chosen instrument such as Moses (see Exod 9:22-23; 10:21-22; 17:11-12), the judges (see Judg 3:15, 21, 28; 6:36-37), or David (see 2 Sam 3:18). Yahweh's chosen instrument is sometimes weak, for example Jael (Judg 4:9, 21; 5:26) or the reduced army of Gideon (Judg 7:2, 7, 14-15). The weapons of Yahweh are not the same as human weapons. Judith, trusting in the power of Yahweh, asks for a strong hand so that by the hand of a woman the pride of the Assyrians might be crushed (9:9-10).

The third basic principle of Holy War has to do with victory. Victory belongs to the lowly and the vulnerable. The lowly, the oppressed, the weak, and the forsaken are not tempted to trust in human power; they have none. They know that they have no hope except in the power of God (Jdt 9:11; compare 1 Sam 2:4; Zeph 2:3).

On the basis of these three principles, Judith makes her plea to God. She does not trust in horses and chariots. She does not trust in human power. She knows that she has no hope except in the power of God; therefore she calls upon Yahweh to win the victory (9:12-14).

10:1-10 Judith prepares for war: beauty. Judith's second preparation for war is the enhancement of her beauty. After bathing, she uses all the human arts available to her to make herself both beautiful and captivating: perfumed ointment, a fancy hairstyle, festive clothing, and jewelry (10:1-4).

Judith understands the goodness of her body. She knows that her physical beauty is good and that it comes from God. She also knows that the power of her beauty comes from within her, from her holiness, from her faithfulness to God. Since both her exterior and interior beauty come from God, her beauty must be devoted to the service of God.

God intends to use her beauty as a weapon to liberate the people. She will wield the weapon to the best of her ability.

The response of others to this second preparation of hers testifies to its effectiveness. The men of her own city are astounded at her beauty (10:7). After she arrives at the enemy camp, the guards of Holofernes gaze at her face in awe because of its wondrous beauty (10:14). The crowd that gathers within the camp at her arrival marvels at her beauty. They say to one another: "Who can despise this people that has such women among them? It is not wise to leave one man of them alive, for if any were to be spared they could beguile the whole world" (10:19).

Judith's preparation is now complete. She gathers provisions (kosher food) and departs with her maid for the enemy camp. Let Holofernes beware!

JUDITH GOES OUT TO WAR

Jdt 10:11–13:20

10:11-19 Judith in the enemy camp. In her words to the elders, Judith advised her people to trust in God and to call upon God to help them (8:17). She has already been an example of calling on God in prayer (9:1-14). Now she demonstrates her trust in God. With great courage, alone except for her maid, she leaves her city at night and walks to the Assyrian camp. She has proclaimed in her prayer that God protects the powerless (9:11). Now she puts that word to the test.

Her trust in God is not misplaced. As soon as she meets the guards of the enemy camp, they are overcome by the weapon of God, her beauty (10:14-17). The same victory is won when she meets the crowd of soldiers within the camp (10:18-19).

Judith's words are a masterpiece of irony. She treads lightly through deceit and guile (a true Israelite, indeed!—see Gen 27:36; 30:25-43; 32:28-29). In her prayer, she had already announced her intention to deceive (9:10, 13). An element of truth is consistently present in what she says but cleverly masked throughout. She tells the guard truthfully that she is a daughter of the Hebrews (10:12). She announces that she is fleeing, which is false, but the reason for her flight seems true to everyone but her: the Israelites are about to be delivered up to the Assyrians as prey (10:12). She announces truthfully that she has come to see Holofernes, and the message that she has for him is indeed trustworthy. Those who will be saved from loss of life, however, are not Holofernes' men but her own people (10:13).

The statements of the soldiers are also high irony. They do not know the implication of their words when they tell Judith that by coming to see Holofernes she has saved her life (10:15). She has indeed saved her life, but Holofernes has lost his. The soldiers unwittingly recognize Judith's power. They proclaim that the power of Israel is in women such as she. Women like Judith, they declare, could beguile the whole world (10:19). They are soon to discover how right they are.

10:20–11:23 Judith meets Holofernes. The encounter between Judith, servant of Yahweh, and Holofernes, servant of Nebuchadnezzar, opens with Holofernes reclining on his bed. The scene of Judith's victory over Holofernes will be that same bed. As soon as Holofernes sees Judith, it is evident that she will be successful against him because her beauty strikes Holofernes with amazement.

Their encounter proceeds with two speeches. Holofernes makes the initial statement. At the beginning and end of it, he exhorts Judith to take courage (compare Tob 5:10; 7:17; 11:11) because he presumes she serves Nebuchadnezzar, the king (Jdt 11:1, 3-4). In actual fact, she has already taken courage because she serves the Lord. Holofernes has missed the key point. Judith is courageous and her life is spared because she is a servant of Yahweh, the true king of all the earth (compare 11:1).

Judith's answer to Holofernes, like her speech in chapter 10, is a cunning mixture of truth and deceit. She weaves her message through three topics: the destiny of Holofernes, the message of Achior and its effect on the Israelites, and the deed that she herself will accomplish. She says to Holofernes that if he follows her advice, "God will do the deed perfectly" with him (11:6). *Her* Lord will not fail in any undertaking (11:6). Holofernes presumes that this means *he* will be victorious. Precisely the opposite interpretation—that Yahweh will be victorious—is also possible. Judith continues to deceive him when she refers to "the power of him who has sent you

to set all creatures aright" (11:7). Holofernes again presumes wrongly that she refers to Nebuchadnezzar.

Judith concludes her treatment of Holofernes' destiny with words of great flattery and turns to the subject of Achior's speech and its effect on the Israelites (11:9-15). Again she begins by telling the truth. She confirms Achior's message that if Israel is guilty (which she knows is not true), then Israel will be punished; then she turns to deceit by reporting the imagined guilt of her people (11:11-15). Her description of their guilt provides a list of the most significant practices of Judaism in the second century: dietary laws, laws regarding first fruits and tithes, laws regarding the sanctuary (see commentary on Tob 1:3-22).

She concludes her speech by declaring her own intentions. It is true, as she says, that God has sent her "to perform with [Holofernes] such deeds that people throughout the world will be astonished on hearing of them" (11:16). She is indeed a God-fearing woman. It is also true that she will set up the judgment seat of Holofernes (11:19), but it is he who will be judged and found worthy of condemnation. She deceives by her report of the truth.

Holofernes and his servants respond to her speech in wonder. Previously they had marveled at her beauty; now they marvel at her wisdom. Holofernes ends the encounter with a speech worthy of Judith. Even though he does not understand the truth, there is truth woven through his words. "God has done well in sending you ahead of your people. . . . You are fair to behold, and your words are well spoken. . . . You shall be renowned throughout the earth" (11:22-23). The battle lines have been drawn.

12:1–13:10 Battle and victory. The conflict between Judith and Holofernes is introduced by the narrator with a series of incidents that demonstrate Judith's piety, even while in the enemy camp (12:1-9). She continues to keep the dietary laws. Holofernes offers her food, but she insists that her mission will be accomplished before her own provisions run out. She continues to depend upon prayer. Every morning before dawn she leaves the camp to beseech God to "direct her way for the triumph of his people" (12:8). She keeps ritual purification. Along with her daily prayer, she bathes in the spring of the camp.

The primary function of these incidents is to demonstrate Judith's piety. They serve two other functions, however. First of all, they further the plot by establishing a regular routine for Judith. When the crucial morning comes, she will need to leave the camp before dawn to avoid being questioned. Her ordinary daily practices provide the means of her escape after Holofernes' death. The second function served by these daily incidents is the creation of suspense. For three days, long enough to establish the routine, Judith bides her time and follows a regular daily schedule. The reader knows that her time is short. On the fifth day Uzziah is bound by oath to surrender the city. The crucial encounter does not come until the last possible day. Trust in Yahweh is pushed to the limit before relief comes.

On the fourth day Holofernes invites Judith to a banquet. The excuse he gives to Bagoas is that Judith will laugh them to scorn if they do not entice her (12:12). Judith's response continues the impression that she is eager to be enticed. She sends the messenger back with the response that the evening's activities will be a joy for her until the day of her death (12:14). As she begins her preparations, however, it soon becomes evident who is enticing whom. She prepares her weapon, her beauty, with care and sallies forth to battle.

The power of her beauty is immediately evident. Holofernes is overcome with desire for her, and because of her charm he drinks a greater quantity of wine than he has ever drunk in a single day in his life. As a result, by the end of the banquet he lies drunk on his bed. The stage is set for the victory. All the other guests have departed. Holofernes and Judith are left alone. Judith is armed; Holofernes is helpless.

Judith begins by turning to God, the source of her power, her hope for victory (13:4-5). She reminds God that she acts for the sake of God's people and God's sanctuary in Jerusalem. She draws Holofernes' own sword, prays for strength, and with all the power that God gives her, she beheads him (13:8). Judith, widow of Israel, servant of Yahweh, has vanquished Holofernes, general in chief of the Assyrian army, servant of Nebuchadnezzar. The Assyrian advance is stopped; the Assyrian victory has been reversed. Nebuchadnezzar, who claimed to be king of all the earth, has been defeated by Yahweh, true Lord of all the earth.

Judith then returns to her normal routine. After she wraps up the head of Holofernes and gives it to her maid, who has been waiting for her, the maid puts the head in the food pouch, and the two go out of the camp together "as they were accustomed to do for prayer" (13:10).

Judith's words throughout this section continue to be ironic. When Holofernes asks her if she has enough food, she replies, "As surely as you, my lord, live, your handmaid will not use up her supplies till the Lord accomplishes by my hand what he has determined" (12:4). As surely as Holofernes lives, this is true. As soon as the Lord accomplishes the victory through her, Holofernes will no longer be alive. There can be no more than five days to wait. When Judith is invited to the banquet, she replies, "Who am I to refuse my lord? Whatever is pleasing to him I will promptly do. This will be a joy for me till the day of my death" (12:14). The misunderstanding turns on the meaning of "my lord." The servant undoubtedly understands her to mean Holofernes; the reader knows that she means Yahweh. Her action will please Yahweh because it will bring about the downfall of Holofernes. It is that action which will be her joy. At the banquet itself, Judith tells Holofernes that she has never enjoyed life as much as on that day. That day will bring victory to her, death to Holofernes.

13:10-20 Liberation proclaimed. Before dawn on the fifth day, Judith announces their liberation to the people of Bethulia. This whole section is built around proclamation and prayer. Judith calls out the news in three statements, each one more specific than the one preceding it. Her statements are answered by two blessings, one by all the people and the second by Uzziah, to which the people answer, "Amen! Amen!"

The parallel structure and the repeated words in Judith's statements and in the responding blessings indicate an underlying poetic base in the original Hebrew. Her first two statements begin with repeated words (vv. 11 and 14; compare Ps 24:7). All three of her statements are rich with parallel structure (vv. 11 and 15). If the blessings by the people and by Uzziah are taken together, they form a threefold beatitude (vv. 17-18). The poetic style is significant. At the moment of victory, both the savior and those saved break forth into praise of God, by whose power they have been victorious. Prose has been sufficient to announce their distress; their deliverance calls for poetic praise of God.

VICTORY

Jdt 14:1–16:25

14:1–15:11 Response to the news of Holofernes' death. After the initial liturgy of rejoicing when Judith proclaims the news of Holofernes' death, several clean-up activities remain to be done. The story of the response to Holofernes' death is set in three scenes: (1) in Bethulia, (2) in the Assyrian camp, and (3) throughout Israel.

In Bethulia, Judith acts as general of the army and leader of the people. She has won the victory by assassinating the enemy's general. What remains is to consolidate the winnings. She gives orders, first of all, to the Jewish men to hang the head of Holofernes on the city wall and then to fake an attack on the Assyrian camp (compare Gideon in Judg 7:16-22). This action will rouse the enemy camp and will bring about the demoralizing discovery of the death of Holofernes.

Secondly, Judith summons Achior the Ammonite, whom Holofernes had sent to share the fate of the Israelites (see 6:10-14). Achior had understood the source of the Israelites' power (see 5:17-21). He had recognized that their victory would be through God alone (5:21). Now, when he sees the head of Holofernes in the hand of one of the Jewish men, he recognizes the manifestation of the power of God. He responds in threefold fashion. Recognizing the presence of God in the victory, he faints (see Gen 32:31; Judg 6:22-23). Recognizing in Judith the instrument of God's power, he falls at her feet in homage and blesses her. Recognizing God's fidelity to the Jews in Judith's account of her visit to the Assyrian camp, he believes in God and joins the house of Israel through faith and circumcision (14:6-10).

Meanwhile, the Assyrian camp responds to the fake attack of the Israelites as Judith had predicted. Observing protocol, the enemy soldiers notify all the proper authorities until the news comes to the tent of Holofernes (14:11-13). Bagoas attempts to rouse Holofernes discreetly, but getting no response, he enters Holofernes' tent, only to find him headless and Judith absent (14:14-17; compare Eglon in Judg 3:24-25). Bagoas proclaims the news to the troops: "A single Hebrew woman has brought disgrace on the house of King Nebuchadnezzar!" The announcement causes complete disarray among the Assyrian troops (14:19–15:3). *"No one* kept ranks any longer" (15:2, emphasis added). Judith's action has completely ruined the army of Nebuchadnezzar.

Throughout Israel messengers arrive to report the good news and to summon the Israelites to pursue the fleeing Assyrians. From Jerusalem in the south to Damascus in the north and Gilead in the east, the Israelites pursue and eradicate the enemy. The victory is complete; the quantity of booty is enormous (15:4-7).

The high priest Joakim and the elders arrive from Jerusalem to recognize the victory officially. They come to "see for themselves the good things that the Lord had done for Israel and to meet and congratulate Judith" (15:8). They officially recognize God, the source of the victory, and Judith, the instrument of God. They sing another hymn of blessing (15:9-10), to which all the people respond "Amen!"

Their hymn points out succinctly what has been evident throughout the story. Judith, "the Judahite," is a type of the whole people. Her fidelity to God is symbolic of the fidelity of the Jewish people as a whole. Her victory, by her own hand, is the victory of the whole people. God is pleased with her, as with the whole people, and God's blessing is called down upon them all forever. The message for the people of the author's time, the second century, is evident. God will win their deliverance from oppression. What they must do, together and individually, is remain faithful. God may choose the weakest hand among them, even that of a woman, to bring about the victory. But even though the whole people is weak, the victory is not impossible for God.

15:12–16:17 Judith's prayer. Judith's prayer of praise and thanksgiving is set within the victory celebration of the whole people (15:11-12; 16:18-20). Before and after the prayer there is a report of the physical results of victory. Before the prayer the Israelites plunder the Assyrian camp and Judith is given the choicest booty, Holofernes' tent and furnishings. After the prayer all the people go to Jerusalem to worship God and to offer holocausts and gifts. Judith offers God all Holofernes' things that she possesses. The booty hardly passed through her hands. No sooner had she received it than she loaded it on wagons to take to Jerusalem (15:11). This is not a war for personal gain; it is a war for the liberation of God's people. After offering their gifts to God in thanksgiving at the temple, Judith and the people remain in Jerusalem to celebrate for three more months.

The material gains from victory are turned back to God. The spiritual results, the people's joy and exultation, are also returned to God in celebration. The celebration begins in Bethulia with a dance by the women in honor of Judith. Then Judith joins the dance as leader. Finally, the men, dressed in their armor, join the procession singing hymns.

The celebration is reminiscent of other victory celebrations in Israel. When Saul and David returned after David's victory over Goliath, a victory in which God acted through a youth with a slingshot who seemed powerless, the women came out to meet them, singing and dancing, with tambourines and joyful songs (1 Sam 18:6-7). The model for every deliverance, however, and for every victory celebration, is the Exodus. After Israel marched through the sea, a victory over the pursuing Egyptians in which Israel was powerless, "the prophetess Miriam took a tambourine in her hand, while all the women went out after her, dancing with tambourines, and she led all Israel in the victory song" (Exod 15:20-21). Judith's victory over Holofernes is a victory to be compared to that of David over Goliath; the deliverance of her people is comparable to the Israelites' deliverance from slavery in Egypt.

The song of Judith is a hymn built according to the basic structure of that genre. The song opens with a call to praise (16:1) and continues with the reasons for praise (16:2-12). There is a new beginning in verse 13, which is followed by additional reasons for praise (16:13b-16) and a concluding remark on the fate of the wicked (16:17).

The theme of the book is stated in verse 2: "The Lord is God; he crushes warfare" (see 9:8). The statement is a quotation from the

Septuagint of Exod 15:3, the victory hymn of Miriam. Judith's song, as well as her victory, is comparable to the corresponding section in the Book of Exodus. After the announcement of a song to the Lord (Jdt 16:1; compare Exod 15:1; Jdt 16:13) and the declaration of Yahweh's power (Jdt 16:2; Exod 15:2-3), each song continues with a description of the powerful enemy and his boasting (Jdt 16:3-4; Exod 15:4-5, 9). In Exodus (15:6, 12), the right hand of the Lord shatters the enemy; in Judith, the Lord confounds the enemy by a woman's hand (16:5). Foreign nations are dismayed at the story (Exod 15:14-16; Jdt 16:10). Each song refers to the power of Yahweh's breath/wind/spirit (Exod 15:8, 10; Jdt 16:14). In the Exodus, the deliverance of the Israelite people by Yahweh when they were utterly helpless is celebrated by a hymn to Yahweh's power. Judith personifies the powerlessness of the people in the face of the Assyrian threat (Jdt 16:5-6, 11-12). The victory that Yahweh accomplishes through her is also celebrated by a hymn to Yahweh's power.

Judith's hymn may also be compared to Deborah's victory song in Judg 5. The situation is similar. In Judg 4 the hero who exhorts the people to have hope is a woman, Deborah; the deliverer who conquers the enemy by cunning is also a woman, Jael. The announcement of a new hymn to be sung to the Lord is found in both (Judg 5:3). The mountains tremble at the power of Yahweh (Judg 5:5; Jdt 16:15). In the midst of each hymn is a song of praise for the woman whose hand Yahweh used to bring deliverance (Judg 5:24-27; Jdt 16:5-9). Each song concludes by contrasting the fate of Yahweh's friends with that of Yahweh's enemies (Judg 5:31; Jdt 16:15b-17). The Book of Judges is built on the premise that Yahweh sends heroes to deliver the people when they cry out for help. The victory of Judith confirms that premise.

The hymn of Judith is called a "new song" (16:1, 13). That phrase is common in the psalms of Yahweh's kingship (see, for example, Psalms 96; 98). Those psalms share a common imagery connected to the autumn feast of Sukkoth (Booths). The references to fire, heat, earthquake, and wind suggest the fall weather pattern of the sirocco (see Pss 97:2-5; 99:1; Jdt 16:14-15, 17; compare also Isa 66:15; Joel 4:15-16). These psalms also describe the great eschatological battle of the nations (see Pss 48:5-8; 98:2; 99:1-3; Joel 4:1-2, 11-12; Isa 66:16, 24; Jdt 16:17). Yahweh has won victory, and will bring the new creation (see Pss 96:11-13; 98:7-9; Isa 66:22-23; Jdt 16:14). The people will rejoice and sing a new song to the name of Yahweh (see Pss 96:1; 98:1; Jdt 16:1, 13). Much of the imagery throughout the Book of Judith reflects the Exodus event and the feast of Passover. The Passover celebration is also suggested by the reference to Nisan (Jdt 2:1). But the siege begins after the end of the harvest (4:5; compare 2:27), a time closer to the feast of Weeks, or Pentecost. The thirty-nine days of siege (7:20, 30) and the thirty days of plundering (15:11) suggest a time for the celebration close to Sukkoth. Judith's victory would then be symbolic of Yahweh's final victory over evil, the preservation of the sanctuary, and the deliverance of the people. Later exegesis, which saw in Judith's beheading of Holofernes a symbolic defeat of the devil, would support this interpretation.

The Vulgate adds a note at the end of the chapter (16:25) concerning the feast day on which Judith's victory is celebrated. There is no such celebration known in the Jewish calendar. In Jewish folklore, however, the story of Judith has been connected with the feast of Hanukkah, the celebration of the purification of the temple at the time of the Maccabees, the time in which the book was written. Thus the Book of Judith has connections to the whole Jewish liturgical year, to Passover, Weeks, Sukkoth, and Hanukkah.

16:21–16:25 Conclusion. The rest of Judith's life is a confirmation of the Deuteronomic theory of retribution. Judith remains faithful beyond the demands of the law, both in life and in death. She honors the memory of her husband Manasseh, although taking a husband would have been acceptable. At her death she frees the maid who shared in her daring exploit and distributes her wealth to her own and her husband's relatives. In reward for her obedience to God in crisis and her fidelity throughout her life, she is prosperous, renowned, and lives to a ripe old age.

The book ends with a statement similar to the ending found in the stories of the judges: During her life and after her death, no one disturbed the Israelites (see Judg 3:11, 30; 5:31; 8:28). This section of the book is clearly reminiscent of Judges. Bagoas' discovery of Holofernes' body is like the discovery of Eglon (see Judg 3:23-25); the Israelites' faked attack is like the action of Gideon (see Judg 7:16-22). Judith herself is modeled in part on Deborah and Jael (Judg 4–5). The message of the Book of Judith is like the pattern of the stories in Judges: (1) the people are in distress; (2) they cry out to Yahweh; (3) Yahweh sends a judge to deliver them; (4) they have peace throughout the lifetime of the judge.

The people of the author's time, who suffered under Seleucid persecution, needed to hear the message of the Book of Judith. The message remains pertinent for us, who face powers of evil beyond our strength. The story of Judith teaches us that the power of God can bring victory even through the most vulnerable. Judith's example exhorts God's people to persevere in hope. Uzziah proclaims: "Blessed are you, Judith, by the Most High God, above all the women on earth . . . . Your deed of hope will never be forgotten by those who tell of the might of God." And all the people answer "Amen! Amen!"

Little Rock Scripture Study

Scripture and Tradition form the foundations of the Catholic faith. To help you learn more about that faith, the Little Rock Scripture Study recommends a group of studies especially designed to introduce you to its biblical roots.

The FOUNDATION group consists of four studies:

The Acts of the Apostles tells the story of the early community of believers, and shows the perennial struggle to build community, live the faith in the world, and spread the Gospel.

A Synoptic Gospel (Matthew, Mark or Luke) leads to an encounter with the person of Jesus and the message he proclaimed. We recommend you choose the Gospel of the current liturgical cycle.

Paul's Captivity Letters introduce one of the Church's most zealous missionaries, St. Paul. The theology that began to develop in the early Christian communities continues to direct and motivate the Church today.

Exodus recounts the story of God's people as they travelled from captivity to the promised land. The key concepts of journey, covenant, and redemption introduced in Exodus are found throughout the Scriptures and have influenced all of Judeo-Christian thinking.

The FOUNDATION group provides the groundwork you need to study other books of the Bible and will make further study easier and more spiritually rewarding. Subsequent studies may be chosen based on the interests and maturity of your group.

Little Rock Scripture Study
for Young Adults

Many Catholics—young adults included—have expressed a need to experience God more deeply and to share that experience with others. Little Rock Scripture Study for Young Adults taps into that desire and provides a method and materials that work effectively with small groups of young people.

The program is designed for use by peer groups of high school and college age. It can be adapted for parish youth groups, as an extra-curricular or supplementary program in schools, within campus ministry, or in neighborhoods and homes. Wherever there is a group of young people who have a desire to share their faith, this program can be an ideal vehicle.

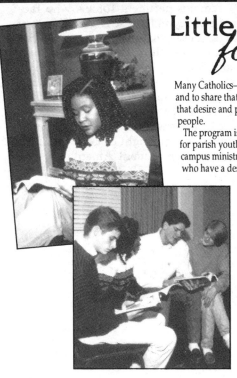

Participants will
- share with other Christians who desire to grow in faith
- grow in their relationship with Jesus
- be motivated and supported to live out their faith more visibly
- develop a habit of daily Bible reading

THE AUTHOR

Father Stephen Binz holds an S.T.B. from the Gregorian University and an S.S.L. from the Pontifical Biblical Institute, Rome. He works as a campus minister and teacher of religion at Mount St. Mary Academy, Little Rock, Arkansas. He serves as a priest in the Diocese of Little Rock as well as an instructor in theology for the diocesan Permanent Diaconate Program. Father Binz is a board member, writer, and lecturer for the Little Rock Scripture Study Program.

WHAT MAKES LITTLE ROCK SCRIPTURE STUDY YOUR BEST CHOICE?

Four essential elements--daily personal study, personal and shared prayer, small-group faith sharing, and a wrap-up lecture--lend balance to the study of Scripture. LRSS also has a five-session Leadership Training component to enable lay parishioners to plan and facilitate the program. Developed as a ministry of the Catholic Diocese of Little Rock, LRSS now has nearly twenty years of success and experience behind it. It has proven itself to be adaptable, affordable, and a spiritually enriching part of parish life.

WHERE DO I BEGIN?

Anyone who is considering starting LRSS in their parish or small group will find the following introductory materials helpful in the decision-making process:

Introductory Packet
The Introductory Packet (1663) provides details on LRSS and contains the following program materials: the Coordinator's Manual, a Study Set and Answer Guide for *Acts of the Apostles*, and the leaflet *Reading the Bible as God's Word*. This Packet is available for only $9.95 plus $3.00 postage and handling.

Informational Video
The Informational Video (7649) explains the program, how and why it works, and what it means to those involved in it. The video concludes with ten minutes of clips from video lectures for three courses. When you order the video, you will be billed $20 plus $3.00 postage and handling. If you return the video in 30 days, the $20 invoice is cancelled (Include your name and address for proper crediting). You pay only the $3.00 postage and handling charge.

MATERIALS FOR THE STUDY

The **Participant's Book** contains the assigned Scripture passages, a brief commentary, questions for study and reflection, and space to write responses.

The **Leader's Guide** explains the program. It includes time lines for planning, responsibilities of the leadership, and other details of the program.

The **Answer Guide** offers guidance in helping the group facilitators prepare for the weekly sessions. It contains suggested responses to some of the study questions.

A Bible is needed by each participant. Suggested translations are the New American Bible, New Jerusalem Bible, Good News Bible (Today's English Version), and the Contemporary English Version.

THE STUDIES

NEW! No Greater Love *(7 weeks)*
NEW! Peter, Fisherman and Shepherd of the Church *(7 weeks)*

The Gospel According to Mark *(10 weeks)*
God's Call to Justice and Peace *(7 weeks)*

AVAILABLE JANUARY 1993
The Way of the Cross, The Way to Life *(7 weeks)*

"It was fun! It was great to be able to get together with others my own age who were interested in developing their relationship with God."

"I read Scripture in another light now. This study has helped me grow closer to God and my classmates."

INTRODUCING THE MOST IMPORTANT BOOK YOU'LL EVER READ!

Little Rock Scripture Study

INTRODUCTION TO THE BIBLE

Now your first step into Scripture study is an easy step!

This exciting course will help the beginner become comfortable with studying the Bible and understanding its themes; for the experienced, it offers information concerning use and interpretation of the Bible. *Introduction to the Bible* combines scholarly expertise with a hands-on approach to open this most important book to all its readers.

A four-week study, *Introduction to the Bible* can be used at any time in the course of your studies and does not require that Little Rock Leadership Training precede its use. It is appropriate for both adults and young adults.

Father Stephen Binz, a frequent contributor to the Little Rock Scripture Study, is the author and lecturer.

LECTURE TOPICS:
* God's Self-Revelation
* Choosing a Bible Today
* Exploring the Bible
* The Church and the Bible
* The Word of God in Human Words
* The Canon of the Bible
* Biblical Scholarship
* How to Read and Study the Bible

WHAT TO ORDER

Order one *Introduction to the Bible* Packet (7676-6, $95.00) containing the basic materials necessary for the course. The Packet includes
* One Leader's Guide
* Eight lectures on two video cassettes
* One Participant's Book

Order one Participant's Book (1673-9, $3.95) for each participant and leader.
Order one Leader's Guide (1674-7, $4.95) for each leader.

To order any of the items on these pages
or for more information, write

Little Rock Scripture Study
The Liturgical Press
P.O. Box 7500, St. John's Abbey
Collegeville, MN 56321-7500

or call toll-free
1-800-858-5434

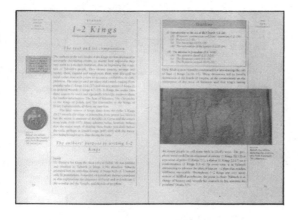

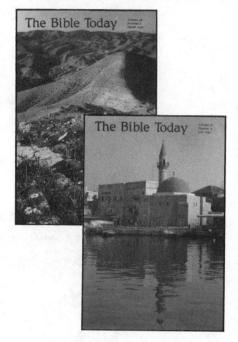